AMERICAN WRITERS

AMERICAN WRITERS

A Collection of Literary Biographies

LEONARD UNGER
Editor in Chief

VOLUME I
Henry Adams to T. S. Eliot

Charles Scribner's Sons, New York

11 13 15 17 19 QD/C 20 18 16 14 12 10

Printed in the United States of America
Library of Congress Catalog Card Number 73-1759
ISBN 0-684-13662-7 (Set)
ISBN 0-684-13673-2 (Vol. I)
ISBN 0-684-13674-0 (Vol. II)
ISBN 0-684-13675-9 (Vol. III)
ISBN 0-684-13676-7 (Vol. IV)

Acknowledgment is gratefully made to those publishers and individuals who have permitted the use of the following materials in copyright.

Introduction
from "Mr. Apollinax," *Collected Poems 1909-1962*, by T. S. Eliot, by permission of Harcourt Brace Jovanovich, Inc. and Faber and Faber Ltd.
from "Sweeney Agonistes," *Collected Poems 1909-1962*, by T. S. Eliot; copyright 1936 Harcourt Brace Jovanovich, Inc.; copyright © 1963, 1964 T. S. Eliot, by permission of Harcourt Brace Jovanovich, Inc. and Faber and Faber Ltd.

"Henry Adams"
from Henry Adams, "Prayer to the Virgin of Chartres," *Letters to a Niece and Prayer to the Virgin of Chartres*, by permission of Houghton Mifflin Company

"James Agee"
from "Draft Lyrics for Candide," *The Collected Poems of James Agee*, ed. Robert Fitzgerald, by permission of Houghton Mifflin Company and Calder and Boyars Ltd.
Part of this essay first appeared, in a different form, in the *Carleton Miscellany* and is used by permission.

"Conrad Aiken"
from *Collected Poems*, copyright 1953 and *Selected Poems*, copyright © 1961, by permission of Oxford University Press

"John Barth"
from John Barth's unpublished lecture "Mystery and Tragedy: The Two Motions of Ritual Heroism," by permission of Mr. Barth

"John Berryman"
from *Short Poems*: *The Dispossessed*, copyright 1948 John Berryman; *His Thoughts Made Pockets & the Plane Buckt*, copyright © 1958 John Berryman; *Formal Elegy*, copyright © 1964 John Berryman; *Berryman's Sonnets*, copyright 1952, © 1967 John Berryman; *Homage to Mistress Bradstreet*, copyright © 1956 John Berryman; *His Toy, His Dream, His Rest*, copyright © 1964, 1965, 1966, 1967, 1968 John Berryman, by permission of Farrar, Straus & Giroux and Faber and Faber Ltd.
from "The Lovers" and "The Imaginary Jew," first published in *The Kenyon Review*, by permission of Mrs. Berryman

"Randolph Bourne"
from letters and manuscripts of Randolph Bourne, by permission of Columbia University Libraries

"Van Wyck Brooks"
material drawn from William Wasserstrom, *The Legacy of Van Wyck Brooks*, copyright © 1971, by permission of Southern Illinois University Press

"James Fenimore Cooper"
material drawn from Robert E. Spiller, Introduction to *Cooper: Representative Selections*, copyright 1936, by permission of the American Book Company

"James Gould Cozzens"
from James Gould Cozzens, *Men and Brethren, Ask Me Tomorrow, The Just and the Unjust, Guard of*

Acknowledgment

The essays which comprise *American Writers* were originally published as the University of Minnesota Pamphlets on American Writers. It was the late William Van O'Connor who conceived of the pamphlet series and who persuaded John Ervin, Jr., Director of the University of Minnesota Press, that it was a good idea. Editors of the pamphlet series during various periods have been William Van O'Connor, Allen Tate, Robert Penn Warren, Richard Foster, George T. Wright, and Leonard Unger. Advisory editors have been Philip Rahv, Karl Shapiro, and Willard Thorp. Jeanne Sinnen has been the publisher's editor for the entire period during which the pamphlets were produced.

Introduction

American Writers. A Collection of Literary Biographies provides information about the lives, careers and works of American writers. The essays contained here are appropriate reading for the widest audience, for students in high school and graduate school, for teachers at all levels, for librarians, for editors and reviewers, for American writers themselves, including scholars and critics, and for the general reader. Specialists may in some instances regard the essays as being of primary interest (or as being controversial!), and high-school students will find them within their reach, if not always entirely within their grasp.

Such claims for the essays comprising these volumes (and other relevant matters) are explained by the story of how and why the essays came to be written. To give first a quick summary of the story, these ninety-seven essays were first published as the University of Minnesota Pamphlets on American Writers. The series of pamphlets, published over the period 1959 to 1972, has become widely known and has been highly and repeatedly praised. Its reputation contributed to the decision to publish the series in a set of volumes which would serve as a convenient and interesting reference work. For this purpose, authors have been invited to review their pamphlets and (wherever appropriate) to revise and bring them (and

their bibliographies) up-to-date. (Throughout this Introduction the authors of the pamphlets are called *authors*, and the subjects of the pamphlets are called *writers*.)

The story of the essays, then, is the story of the pamphlets. When the pamphlet series was first conceived, the purpose was (as defined in a statement to prospective authors) "to provide introductions to the work of significant American writers." The projected pamphlets were also described as follows: "These introductory essays are aimed at people (general readers here and abroad, college students, etc.) who are interested in the writers concerned, but not highly familiar with their work. Each pamphlet contains a brief amount of biographical material and a selected bibliography of the author's books and of books and articles about him, but the heart of the pamphlet is a critical analysis and evaluation of the writer's work, in which the pamphlet author typically uses comment, comparison, interpretation, and discussion." Still another aspect of policy for the series was that an author "feels that the writer he is discussing is sufficiently important to deserve a place in the series, even though he might have some reservations to express about certain aspects of the writer's work." As it turns out, the pamphlets on American writers are aimed by no means exclusively "at people

. . . not highly familiar with their work," although that group of people is well served by the essays—better served, indeed, than it would be by catalogues of hard facts and by summaries and digests of what had already been said about the writers. The hard facts are always provided, but the "heart of the pamphlet" is typically a critical performance where the author interprets as well as introduces, and evaluates as well as interprets, sometimes doing these things separately, and sometimes doing them simultaneously and inseparably.

At this point it is useful to speak more personally. As an editor of the Minnesota pamphlet series, I have read all the essays at least once. I wrote the essay on T. S. Eliot, one of the earliest in the series, so I have had the experience of composing an introduction fitting the spatial limits of a pamphlet and otherwise appropriate to the series. On first confronting this task, I had the benefit of extensive reading in the large body of comment that had been written on Eliot's work, and also of my own previous writing on that subject. Certainly, this preparation served me at all stages of my work on the introductory essay, and to some extent the essay was something put together out of elements that were already in my possession—but only to some extent. One of my purposes was to provide the reader with an overview of Eliot's work that was based on consideration of selected parts of that work, and in pursuing that purpose I was arriving at an overview, a perspective on the development and continuity of Eliot's writing which I had not previously experienced. The introduction, then, may be something truly experienced by the author rather than something merely assembled as a utility for the reader.

This aspect of the essays as overviews is accurately described by the subtitle *Literary Biographies*, for each essay is primarily an ac-

count of the subject's career as a writer. In addition to information about a poem, a story, a novel, and so on, there are appreciations of such individual works and also appreciations of a writer's overall achievement throughout his career, or of the degree and kind of achievement in the case of writers still living and writing. By appreciation is meant, of course, not unqualified praise, but analysis, interpretation and evaluation, which does not exclude indicating limitations—even aspects of fault and failure at points in a career or as elements in a larger pattern of achievement.

One clear effect of the pamphlet series having been adopted as a reference set is the emphasis which this brings to the essays as sources of information and also as critical performances. The ninety-seven essays are, thus, not only a dictionary, but also an anthology of critical performances. This means that the essays may be interesting and useful as examples of criticism—and as varieties of criticism—since it is in the nature of an anthology to provide variety. The variety exists, of course, within a uniformity: the general purpose of the essays, as stated earlier, and the more-or-less standard length. I will not attempt a detailed account of the variety, certainly not a formal (or forced) classification, but it may be interesting to consider some of the aspects of variety. Most obvious is the fact that American writers are themselves a variety, yet there are categories which constitute meaningful similarities and differences. At this point I will emphasize these categories with respect to the subjects of the essays. Henry Wadsworth Longfellow and Emily Dickinson are both New England poets of the nineteenth century, one a man and the other a woman, among other differences. Marianne Moore and Robert Frost are poets of the first half of the twentieth century, one experimental and innovative, the other traditional. Whatever the differences, these are four poets, and the essays about them may be compared as critical discussions of poets and poems—as poetry criticism, just as other essays serve as examples of fiction criticism, drama criticism, and criticism of critics, as in the essays on Van Wyck Brooks and Edmund Wilson.

Such aspects of variety, of similarities and differences, are readily evident from the circumstances (including the work) of the writers themselves. Thomas Wolfe and Richard Wright provide one more example of this kind. They were close contemporaries, born at the start of the twentieth century, both of them natives of the South, both writers of stories and novels which were markedly autobiographical, but one was white and the other was black. Another kind of variety among the essays arises from differences not only among writers but among the authors of the essays and their several approaches and methods in discussing the writers and their work. In this collection there are varying degrees of emphasis on the literary and on the biographical and on the relation between the two. A number of the essays are examples in more or less measure of what we call biographical criticism, relating a writer's work to his personal history, or relating it to fixed and obsessive components of a writer's personality, or doing both of these in some measure. C. Hugh Holman's essay on Thomas Wolfe and Robert Bone's essay on Richard Wright are in large part biographical criticism, as we might expect. So is Charles Shain's essay on F. Scott Fitzgerald. In each case the author is concerned with particulars by which the writer failed or succeeded in transforming personal material into the forms and effects of literary art. Indeed, many of the essays partake of biographical criticism in varying degrees and in varying ways. A number of the essays provide examples (at least in part) of psycho-analytic criticism, where the author finds in a

writer's work themes and symbols which derive from the writer's unconscious, which are deeply personal, obsessive, compulsive. Essays of this kind are Leon Edel's on Henry David Thoreau, Roger Asselineau's on Edgar Allan Poe, Philip Young's on Ernest Hemingway, and Stanley Edgar Hyman's on Nathanael West. These essays differ among themselves in the use made of psychoanalytic ideas and techniques, and none of them is reductive and mechanical— the familiar, sometimes valid, criticism made of psychoanalytic interpretations of literature. If psychoanalytic interpretation is subject to controversy, the fact is that all criticism (and much literature) is a kind of controversy, and there has always been some contention about Thoreau, Poe, Hemingway and West.

Not all critical analysis concerned with themes and symbols in a writer's work is necessarily psychoanalytic or even biographical. My own essay on T. S. Eliot is frequently concerned with themes and symbols, noting how these relate to Eliot's career as a writer and to the continuity of his work, but the emphasis of the essay is not biographical. Sherman Paul, calling Josephine Miles's essay "an original contribution to Emerson scholarship," says that she "demonstrates, by inspecting vocabulary, syntax, tone, theme, and form, the profound unity of Emerson's thought." The essay not infrequently brings Emerson the person into view, but the main focus of the essay is on one and another example of Emerson's writing, and finally on pattern and interrelationship within the body of the writing. Denis Donoghue takes account of Emily Dickinson's personal history and temperament, but in his essay such information is finally assimilated into considerations of language, imagination, sensibility. The information is assimilated into a reader's (Donoghue's) experience of the poems and his abiding awareness of the writer's achievement. It is such abiding awareness of writers and their work which the essays as overviews aim to provide.

It has already been noted that *American Writers* is an anthology of critical essays, but it is like an anthology also with respect to the American writers included, and with respect to the questions which must arise on that subject. Such questions relate finally to the pamphlet series, and they would be questions as to why some writers were omitted. To such questions there would be a variety of answers. An answer that comes most readily is that any anthology, any selection, extends at some points into the realm of the arbitrary. Another answer might be that no American writer was deliberately omitted from the pamphlet series. During most of the period when the pamphlets were being published, it was the view of the editors of the series that there should be pamphlets on all major American writers, and that pamphlets on minor writers would be produced sooner or later, so that when the series was terminated (a decision based on practical and extraliterary circumstances), there were inevitably writers who had not been included. In some instances the omissions represent the critical priorities of the editors, and also the critical priorities of the times. Such writers as William Cullen Bryant, Oliver Wendell Holmes, James Russell Lowell, John Greenleaf Whittier suffered from having been overrated once. Their priority was relatively low with the editors and the times, so they were delayed and finally omitted. But Henry Wadsworth Longfellow is included, thus still benefitting from the popular and critical esteem he once received. Harriet Beecher Stowe and Upton Sinclair have an historical importance, but not a comparable literary merit, so they were passed by. If Edmund Wilson or Kenneth Burke or Norman Mailer or John Updike had volunteered to write a pamphlet on one of these writers, or some other, then that would

have made a difference. In some instances the pamphlets were written by authors who did volunteer. In a few cases, especially of writers still living and even in full career, pamphlets were commissioned but the essays were never produced during the course of the series. Such omissions are regrettable but probably inevitable where such large numbers of authors and writers are involved.

If this collection is an anthology of critical essays on American writers, it is also an anthology of critics. Each author is a kind of specialist in the subject by virtue of having written the essay, but some authors were already well known as scholars and critics with special qualifications for a particular American writer. A few examples are Leon Edel on Henry James, Lawrance Thompson on Robert Frost, Mark Schorer on Sinclair Lewis, and Philip Young on Ernest Hemingway. Besides being distinguished for their work on particular writers, these authors are of course known for a wide authority in the world of literature. Such wide authority belongs to most of the authors. Because they are too many to name here, I will give examples by way of paying tribute to those who are now dead: Richard Chase, F. Cudworth Flint, John Gassner, Frederick J. Hoffman, Stanley Edgar Hyman, William Van O'Connor, Margaret Farrand Thorp and Dorothy Van Ghent. For a few authors the pamphlets were at the time debuts in such publication, or performances at relatively early stages of their careers. A list of contributors gives a brief biographical note about each author.

Although there was no deliberate and detailed plan for the pamphlet series, the ninety-seven writers on whom essays were written are representative in ways that might be expected. About three-fourths of them are writers of the twentieth century, meaning writers whose careers began in or extended well into the twentieth century, as well as those who were born in the century. This ratio hardly needs explaining, or even comment. It is easily in accord with the increase of the American population and with other obvious factors. Well over half of all the writers are primarily writers of prose fiction, and these are mainly novelists. It is a well-known fact that the novel has been the characteristic and prevailing literary form of the modern world. Why this is so remains an engaging question, although a number of reasons are obvious enough. Everyone likes a good story, everyone has an appetite for vicarious experience, everyone is curious about times and places beyond his own. With the steady expansion of literacy and the printed word, the novel has satisfied these interests more widely and more abundantly than ever had the stage or the narrative poem (but for some decades not more than movies and television). It so happens that America and the novel are about the same age, their history going back only two or three centuries, depending on what is meant by one and the other. Certainly American novels—*The Scarlet Letter, Moby Dick, The Adventures of Huckleberry Finn*—are among the classics in that form, and in the twentieth century American novelists (for example, Hemingway and Faulkner) have had international reputations of the broadest range and of the highest order. But this consideration is part of a larger subject: the fact that American literature is acknowledged to be one of the major national literatures of the modern world.

As for the short story, it is even more recent than the novel, especially if it is allowed that it was invented (as the detective story was indeed invented) by Edgar Allan Poe. In any event, American writers have a large share in the history of the short story. The history of the novel involved publication in periodicals, and this is even more emphatically the case with the short story. Compared to the novel, the short story has a more demanding economy and a greater (if also simpler) unity of form and of effect. For some American writers the short story has been the essential form of achievement and reputation. It is their short stories which give Sherwood Anderson, Ring Lardner and Katherine Anne Porter secure places in American literature. Other writers with formidable achievement in the short story have also been eminent novelists, from Henry James to Hemingway, Faulkner and Fitzgerald, from Robert Penn Warren to Flannery O'Connor and John Updike.

If most of the essays are predictably on writers of prose fiction, many other essays are predictably on writers who are primarily poets. Although the novel has been the dominant literary form, certain features of American literature have been more conspicuous in its poetry. Writers' reputations and popularity are inevitably subject to cycles of rise and fall, and such changes have occurred most strikingly among the poets. This is probably related to the fact that there has been a relative decrease in the reading audience of poetry, while the number of readers of prose fiction mounted steadily in the nineteenth and twentieth centuries. But while there was a decline in the popularity of poetry, a sustained and analytical critical awareness of poetry developed. Along with the reaction in the twentieth century against tastes and values of the nineteenth century, an increased critical awareness was at least in part responsible for the fading of reputations like those of Longfellow, Holmes, Bryant and James Russell Lowell. An example of re-evaluation and rediscovery is the admiring attention which Robert Penn Warren has given to the poetry of Whittier and Melville. No critical proposition remains uncontested, yet it has been a critical commonplace for some time that the greatest American poets of the nineteenth century are Emily Dickinson and Walt Whitman.

There is clearly a relationship between this high evaluation of Emily Dickinson and Walt Whitman and the fact that they prefigure the modernism of twentieth-century American literature, especially poetry. Despite conspicuous differences between these two writers, they share some of the features which characterize more recent American poets as modernist. For some early readers their poetry seemed to fall short of being *literature* because it is free of the familiar and well-worn literary conventions. Traditional verse form is almost wholly absent from Whitman and is only minimally present in Dickinson. They produced a quality of contemporaneity, of the modern, by giving expression to a consciousness of their own time and place. Each in his (and her) own way is an emphatic example of the American writer exploring the profound and complex question of identity, and this has meant both personal and national identity. Because American writers were faced with the question of national identity, the question of identity itself (of personal identity) was accentuated and intensified.

"There is a new voice in the old American classics." "Somewhere deep in every American heart lies a rebellion against the old parenthood of Europe." These statements are made in the opening pages of D. H. Lawrence's *Studies in Classic American Literature* (1923). Lawrence claimed that American writers of the nineteenth century were the first full-fledged modernists. At any rate, if American writers spoke with a "new voice," it is because they themselves were new, and that was a fact which operated in their concerns with personal and national identity. Since the beginning of its history, American society has compared itself with Europe and criticized itself on both sides of the question: as being, or trying to be, too much like Europe; or as being not enough like Europe. This debate, which is reflected by all kinds of American writing, seems inevitable. In this respect American society resembles Russian society, for Russia, too, at the other geographical extreme, has had its continuing debate with itself as to how much or how little it participates, or should participate in Western civilization, meaning Europe.

In the United States, in the early decades of the nineteenth century, Ralph Waldo Emerson entered forcefully upon this debate. The defense and celebration of America—especially in its difference from Europe—is a central theme in much of his work. In a fragment of poetry he speaks of his country as

Land without history, land lying all
In the plain daylight of the temperate zone, . . .
Land where—and 'tis in Europe counted a
    reproach—
Where man asks questions for which man was
    made.
A land without nobility, or wigs, or debt,
No castles, no cathedrals, and no kings;
Land of the forest.

Although today there is a huge debt, a pretty big wig industry, and a much smaller forest, the spirit of this statement has lived on for some Americans and in some American writers. Throughout his essays and addresses Emerson celebrates this "plain daylight" of his own country. He finds virtue and value in the near-at-hand, the contemporary and the commonplace, as against the remote, the ancient and the exotic. And he does not hesitate to criticize and to scold Americans when they do not share this view, which is really a defense of America along the lines where it was open to criticism. In his address called "The American Scholar" he deplores greed, materialism and smugness in American life, and he insists that these defects follow from too great a dependence on Europe and the conventions of the past. Toward the end of this address—which Oliver Wendell Holmes called "our intellectual Declaration of Independence"—Emerson said: "We have listened too long to the courtly muses of Europe."

Emerson said this, and Walt Whitman believed it. Emerson had called for a genuine American poet, and Whitman offered himself. "I was simmering, simmering, simmering," he said, "Emerson brought me to a boil." In his Preface to *Leaves of Grass* he said, "The direct trial of him who would be the greatest poet is today." Following Emerson's advice, he celebrated the modern and the commonplace, and in doing this he celebrated, and hence idealized, America and American society. But if Whitman was idealistic and romantic, he was also critical. Years after having celebrated and sung himself and the American scene in unconventional verse, he turned to prose to make serious criticism of business, politics and other aspects of American life as he found it during the unlovely years immediately following the Civil War. Like Emerson before him, he scolded Americans for their own shortcomings, and at the same time, for looking to Europe and to the past, as in this statement from *Democratic Vistas*: "America has yet morally and artistically originated nothing. She seems singularly unaware that the models of persons, books, manners, etc., appropriate for former conditions and for European lands, are but exiles and exotics here."

In spite of all his emphasis on an independent Americanism, Walt Whitman seemed like an exile and an exotic to many of his own countrymen. Not so Mark Twain. He was too fully American himself to feel the need of lecturing others on how American they should be. He directed his satire against Europe, against Europeanizing Americans, and also against provincial and all too genuine Americans. If Whitman simmered and boiled, Mark

Twain was cool. Compared to Twain's masterful use of the American language as a medium of literature, Whitman seems like something imported, or translated from a foreign tongue. Whatever their differences, the two writers do stand together in opposing what they regarded as the worn-out and irrelevant traditions of an old world. But what is even more interesting is their common opposition to the code of polite society, to the genteel tradition, to the standards of respectability. In *Song of Myself* Whitman said that he admires the animals because they are not respectable. In *Huckleberry Finn* an underprivileged boy and a Negro slave, by their honesty and compassion, put to shame the shams and cruelties of civilized society. But we know now that Mark Twain never attacked the claims of respectability in his published writing so clearly and so sharply as he did in his private notebooks. And recent critics tell us that this represents not only a practical concession to society, but a conflict and a compromise within Twain himself.

There is a continuity from Emerson's rejection of the "courtly muses of Europe" to Mark Twain's mockery of middle-class respectability. There is a fairly complex pattern of common elements involved, such as, the hostility to established institutions, the pursuit of the genuine and the honest, and the extension of the democratic principle beyond the frontiers of respectability.

Nathaniel Hawthorne saw the American writer's trial in a different light from Whitman and Twain. In his preface to his novel *The Marble Faun* he spoke of the peculiar difficulties for the American who would write a novel: "No author, without a trial, can conceive of the difficulty of writing a romance about a country where there is no shadow, no antiquity, no mystery, no picturesque and gloomy wrong, nor anything but a commonplace prosperity, in broad and simple daylight, as is happily the case with my dear native land." This is not a serious complaint about American society. In fact, Hawthorne pictures it here as young and healthy and happy as compared to Europe with its shadow and mystery and gloomy wrong. But Hawthorne does complain that America provides a very thin material for the American who would write novels, and perhaps he is tempering his complaint with expressions of apology and affection. But this passage from the preface to *The Marble Faun* is the best—or the worst—that Henry James can find to quote in his life of Hawthorne (1879), when it is his own purpose to complain at length of the disadvantages suffered by the American who would write novels. Henry James's complaint is obviously more a subjective and heart-felt complaint than an objective account of Hawthorne.

His criticism of America and of American society is made from the point of view of the novelist who needs a rich world of material, but in spelling out that point at considerable length, James reveals that his deepest sensibilities, as well as his professional needs, were involved. We hardly dare say this about Henry James without remembering that for such a dedicated artist there can be no separation of professional needs from deepest sensibilities. Hawthorne's America, in James's words, was a "crude and simple society." He saw his own America as not much different. "History, as yet," he said in *Hawthorne*, "has left in the United States but so thin and impalpable a deposit that we very soon touch the hard substratum of nature, and nature herself, in the Western World, has the peculiarity of seeming rather crude and immature. The very air looks new and young; the light of the sun seems fresh and innocent, as if it knew as yet but few of the secrets of the world and none of the weariness of shining; the vegetation has the appearance of not having reached its majority.

A large juvenility is stamped upon the face of things, . . ." But this is not even society.

When it came to speaking in detail about American society, the details were negative— they made a picture of all the things that America was not. "One might enumerate," said James, "the items of high civilization, as it exists in other countries, which are absent from the texture of American life, until it should become a wonder to know what was left." I continue quoting. "No State, in the European sense of the word, and indeed barely a specific national name. No sovereign, no court, no personal loyalty, no aristocracy, no church, no clergy, no army, no diplomatic service, no country gentlemen, no palaces, no castles, nor manors, nor old country-houses, nor parsonages, nor thatched cottages, nor ivied ruins; no cathedrals, nor abbeys, nor little Norman churches; no great Universities nor public schools—no Oxford, nor Eton, nor Harrow; no literature, no novels, no museums, no pictures, no political society, no sporting class. . . ." Then James raises the question of what remains, if all this is left out, and he observes: "the American knows that a good deal remains; what it is that remains—that is his secret, his joke, as one might say. It would be cruel, in this terrible denudation, to deny him the consolation of his natural gift, that 'American humour' of which of late years we have heard so much." Surely Henry James was having his own joke here, and a pretty cruel joke, at that.

If this negative account is somewhat unfair to Hawthorne's America and to his own America, it is still farther from the fact of what America has become in the twentieth century. But in spite of this, we can say of James what we said of Emerson—that the spirit of his statement lives on, even though certain facts have changed. "A large juvenility" has continued to be found not so much in the atmosphere and landscape as among Americans themselves. As for James's own fiction, there is in it very little of the texture of American life or the texture of any other kind of life. I mean that he was not much interested in the density and detail of the external world. It is well known that to the end of his brilliant career he was interested in the encounter of sensibilities, and especially in the encounter between Americans and Europeans. By now it is a familiar observation that James's Americans, as compared to his Europeans, are simple, naive, immature, and so on—but they are also innocent, wholesome, generous, uncorrupted. Although American society was too thin a material for this novelist, he was still writing about Americans in the great novels which close his career. James was preoccupied with the mixture of the good and the bad in the genteel tradition, in middle-class respectability, and Americans seemed to represent this aspect of middle-class respectability most clearly. James was certainly no enemy of respectability, but he was its astute and gentle critic. Let me hasten at this point to connect a couple of strands of thought. While Walt Whitman and Mark Twain looked critically at American middle-class respectability from the point of view of the animal, a Negro slave, an underprivileged boy, Henry James looked at it critically from the point of view of the eminently civilized European.

Henry James brings us back to the twentieth century. He died in 1916. This was one year before T. S. Eliot published his first small book of poems. There is, of course, a large area of similarity between the poet and the novelist, these two Americans who chose to spend most of their lives in England and who chose to become Englishmen. In my essay on Eliot I call attention to a facet of similarity between these two writers: "Eliot, like James, presents a world of genteel society, as it is seen from within, but seen also with critical penetration, with a consciousness that is deliberately and intensely self-consciousness. Both writers, in their ultimate meanings, show a liberation from the genteel standard of decorum, while the style and manner which have familiarly attended the decorum not only remain, but have become more complicated and intense." I suppose that's another way of saying that they criticized middle-class respectability from the point of view of the eminently civilized European. This is certainly what Eliot was doing in a very early poem called "Mr. Apollinax," from which I quote the opening and closing lines:

When Mr. Apollinax visited the United States
His laughter tinkled among the teacups.

. . . .

I heard the beat of centaur's hoofs over the
    hard turf
As his dry and passionate talk devoured the
    afternoon.
"He is a charming man"—"But after all what
    did he mean?"—
"His pointed ears... He must be unbalanced,"—
"There was something he said that I might
    have challenged."
Of dowager Mrs. Phlaccus, and Professor and
    Mrs. Cheetah
I remember a slice of lemon, and a bitten
    macaroon.

The fragments of conversation are the comments on Mr. Apollinax made by Mrs. Phlaccus, Professor and Mrs. Cheetah, and perhaps other Americans. They recognize that he is a charming man, but they also know that he has unsettled and threatened their sense of respectability. The poet associates Mr. Apollinax with centaurs, those splendid creatures of Greek mythology, horse from the neck down and then, so curiously, human from the waist up. The slice of lemon and the bitten macaroon, which the poet associates with the Americans, are transparent enough as symbols of superficiality, of appetites meagre and atrophied, of the posture of respectability.

It is perfectly clear that the Americans who have been having tea with Mr. Apollinax are utterly refined and cultivated, genteel beyond all question, the most solid members of the politest society. Eliot wrote about another kind of American in *Sweeney Agonistes*, the experiment in dramatic verse dialogue first published in 1926. Here the Americans are businessmen visiting in London. The scene is the apartment of some young ladies, to whom they have just been introduced. When they reply in the affirmative to the question, whether they like London, they are then asked why they don't come and live in London, and they answer as follows:

Well, no, Miss—er—you haven't quite got it
(I'm afraid I didn't quite catch your name—
But I'm very pleased to meet you all the same)—
London's a little too gay for us
Yes I'll say a little too gay.

Yes London's a little too gay for us
Don't think I mean anything *coarse*—
But I'm afraid we couldn't stand the pace.

London's a slick place, London's a swell place,
London's a fine place to come on a visit—

These American businessmen are noticeably different from the Americans who have tea with Mr. Apollinax. In presenting these two kinds of Americans, Eliot has treated the subject of middle-class respectability by showing both sides of the coin. The tea-party Americans are so genuinely and utterly respectable that they are sterile, lifeless and vapid. The businessmen are not lifeless—but neither do they evoke the beat of centaurs' hoofs. They

do claim to be respectable. London is a little too gay for them. They don't mean anything *coarse*, but they're afraid they couldn't stand the pace. They embody the deterioration and vulgarization of respectability. If Professor and Mrs. Cheetah are solemnly genteel, these businessmen are cheerfully vulgar. It is significant that Eliot chose to make these vulgarians American. It is also significant that American middle-class respectability can be represented by these opposing extremes.

We have associated Mr. Apollinax and his American friends with the world and the point of view of Henry James. The American businessmen of T. S. Eliot's *Sweeney Agonistes* may be associated with a more recent American novelist. I refer to Sinclair Lewis. The special American accent and the cheerful vulgarity of these businessmen were already familiar voices and types in American literature by the time Eliot was writing his satirical verses, and they had been made familiar by the tremendously successful novels of Sinclair Lewis. Lewis has a special relevance to the subject of the American writer as a critic of American society. For this is what Lewis was, above all else. Since his period of success and popularity—the twenties and early thirties—he has had no reputation as a literary artist or as a teller of interesting stories. He has historical importance because he wrote novels which were effective and provocative criticisms of American society. It was his vivid portrayal of smugness, shallowness, vulgarity, materialism, and so on, in the American middle class which made him for awhile the leading American novelist, and which brought him in 1930 the first Nobel Prize awarded to an American writer.

Main Street (1920) and *Babbitt* (1922), Lewis's first successes and the novels where he discovered his skill as a satirist, portray the cultural bleakness and deadening provinciality of life in the American Middle West. Lewis was not primarily concerned with contrasting America and Europe, but the contrast with Europe is certainly present in his criticism of America. We can see something of this in a speech delivered by George F. Babbitt to a meeting of the Zenith Real Estate Board. "Some time I hope folks will quit handing all the credit to a lot of moth-eaten, mildewed, out-of-date, old, European dumps, and give proper credit to the famous Zenith spirit, that clean fighting determination to win Success that has made the little old Zip City celebrated in every land and clime, wherever condensed milk and paste-board cartons are known! Believe me, the world has fallen too long for these worn-out countries that aren't producing anything but bootblacks and scenery and booze, that haven't got one bathroom per hundred people, and that don't know a loose-leaf ledger from a slip cover; and it's just about time for some Zenithite to get his back up and holler for a show-down!" But if this is the voice of a man who is vulgar, immodest and shallow, it is also the voice of a man who is acutely aware of the criticism that has been levelled against the society with which he identifies himself. The aggressiveness does reveal a sense of inferiority. There was an admission here that the world regarded Europe as superior to America.

Lewis was as deeply immersed in the world of America, both as man and writer, as Mark Twain had ever been. Some of his earliest interpreters had detected a sympathy with the middle class and the Middle West even in Lewis's harshest satirization. This was confirmed by his novel *Dodsworth*, which came in 1929. And his subject was by now a familiar one in American fiction—the American in Europe. The Americans here are a successful American businessman and his wife, Mr. and Mrs. Sam Dodsworth. They are having marital diffi-

culties, and these difficulties make up the familiar formula of Europe versus America. The wife, aspiring to culture and sophistication, criticizes America and all that is American in her husband, by applying what she regards as superior European standards. The husband does not wholly escape Lewis's satire, but it is the wife who receives most of it. In the end Sam Dodsworth divorces this wife and marries another American woman who is better able to appreciate the virtues of his American middle-class character. Mark Schorer, author of the extensive, detailed and penetrating biography of Sinclair Lewis, has said of this novel, "what Sinclair Lewis himself believed in, at the bottom of his blistered heart, was at last clear: a downright self-reliance, a straightforward honesty, a decent modesty, corn on the cob and apple pie." But the larger context of Schorer's study of Lewis and his work shows that Lewis's position was not really as clear and simple as apple pie. His attitude was ambiguous and unresolved. In his attacks on the American middle class there is an element of sympathy, and in his affirmation of it there is an element of criticism. Like other American writers before him, he had mixed feelings and mixed attitudes toward American culture and American society. And like American writers who were to come after him, he exposed and berated what he found dishonest, hypocritical, pretentious, smug and phoney.

The subject of American literature as a criticism of American society could be pursued through a dozen more writers, and even several dozen, including writers of fiction, poetry and plays. I think it is safe to predict that we would find in other writers—even the most recent ones—the same essential patterns (and of course, there would also be patterns that I have not considered). By now it is a commonplace observation that Holden Caulfield, the "hero" of J. D. Salinger's *Catcher in the Rye*, is a modernized and urbanized Huckleberry Finn, an unconventional boy who will not accommodate himself to the conventions of society. The best-known character of the modern American stage, Willie Loman of Arthur Miller's *Death of a Salesman*, is a man whose life becomes a nightmare of frustration because he has so blindly accepted the American dream of success.

Although his image seems to have receded into the landscape of the past, it is still a fact that Ernest Hemingway has been the most famous and most influential American writer of the twentieth century. We don't readily think of Hemingway as being a critic of American society, but we do think of him as being decidedly American. Although he spent so much of his life outside the United States, he never lost his American personality or his American point of view. Much of his writing —in fact, most of his writing—is about actions which take place outside the United States, but with few exceptions, the central characters in these actions are Americans. For this reason Hemingway belongs to that tradition of American writing which tells of the American abroad, and especially of the American in Europe. He belongs to the tradition which compares America with Europe or some other part of the world, and that is a kind of criticism.

Besides being the American abroad, Hemingway's central character, the Hemingway hero, is typically a man who has been wounded, either physically or psychologically or both. In being wounded, the hero is a symbol of Hemingway himself, and also of man's plight in the modern world, and perhaps in any world. This subject of the wounded Hemingway hero has been discussed in great detail by Philip Young. Other critics had already discovered in Hemingway's fiction another kind of character who appears in various but similar forms, such as the professional athlete, the prizefighter, the bullfighter, the professional hunter or fisherman. This character has been called the "code hero," and Young has found a relationship between the code hero and the wounded hero. I will quote some of his remarks on the subject. "Now it is . . . clear that something was needed to bind these wounds, and there is in Hemingway a consistent character who performs that function. The figure is not Hemingway himself in disguise (which to some hard-to-measure extent the Hemingway hero was). Indeed he is to be sharply distinguished from the hero, for he comes to balance the hero's deficiencies. . . . We generally . . . call this man the 'code hero' —this because he represents a code according to which the hero, if he could attain it, would be able to live properly in the world of violence, disorder, and misery to which he has been introduced and which he inhabits. The code hero, then, offers up and exemplifies certain principles of honor, courage, and endurance which in a life of tension and pain make a man a man, as we say, and enable him to conduct himself well in the losing battle that is life. He shows, in the author's famous phrase for it , 'grace under pressure.' " This is a valuable explanation, I think—and I would add only one point.

When Philip Young speaks of what it is that makes "a man a man" he is, properly enough, speaking in Hemingway's own terms. There is a sense in which the prizefighter or the bullfighter or the hunter is a man's man—a full-grown man, as we say. But there is also a sense in which this full-grown man is not a man's man at all, but a boy's man—the man as seen from an immature point of view. This idea brings us to a familiar criticism which has been made of the American character, that it is immature. From this I will jump to the proposition that Hemingway exemplifies this aspect of the American character, its immaturity. Hemingway the writer and his wounded hero had put away childish things, but in their pre-occupation with and admiration for the heroics of the code hero, they had picked them up again. Life is not a game or a sport, after all. It is not that simple. For all his splendid achievement as a stylist and a narrator, it is a very limited view of life which he presents. The immaturity for which America has so often been criticized seems to have entered deeply and seriously into one of its finest writers. This may be put another way. Hemingway is one kind of typically American writer in the respect that he has dramatized over and over again a nostalgia for the simple, the youthful, the past. But the nostalgia itself is not simple—and it may not even be peculiarly American.

Nor is the America-Europe dualism, or dispute, so simple either, although it provides a useful perspective on the course of American literature. It is even useful to acknowledge that the perspective has been altered by the course of history, history at large, but also literary history. America has moved from being on the frontiers of Western culture to being itself a center of world culture. The conditions of American life were never as plain, as simple, as commonplace, as Emerson and Hawthorne and Henry James believed. Now we are aware of this discrepancy. America was always more than could be recognized from any single perspective. And certainly in the twentieth century America has become aware of its great diversity and complexity. It is this sharpening awareness which has given an enlarged status to Walt Whitman's inclusive vision. William Faulkner and other Southern writers have explored and dramatized the special problems and experiences of Southern identity. Richard Wright and other black writers have created literature out of their personal knowledge of

the world of black experience. Saul Bellow and other Jewish writers have portrayed the varieties of Jewish identity and circumstances. These are only the more familiar illustrations of the steadily increasing diversity of American writing. The fact is not only that American literature is a major national literature but that it involves international and extra-national developments. Henry James and T. S. Eliot became British citizens and are claimed as British writers. Vladimir Nabokov, because of his personal history, stands outside of all national boundaries, yet it may be said that he developed from being a Russian writer into being an American writer. Few novels catch the flavor of certain parts of the American scene so genuinely as the once sensational *Lolita*. The same can be said of the more recent fiction (long and short) by Isaac Bashevis Singer. Composing in Yiddish, collaborating with his translators, he defies national identity, and is read more widely in English translation than in the original.

Diversity is a good subject for bringing an Introduction to its end. This anthology includes a body of writers whose diversity is almost inexhaustible. This diversity may otherwise be considered as range and variety, and such consideration calls attention to the versatility of individual writers. It calls attention as well to the continuity of literature, a continuity that is especially well illustrated by American literature throughout its history. Emerson and Thoreau, classics of our prose and of our intellectual history, are also poets. Poe is poet, fiction writer, critic and editor, and so are Allen Tate and Robert Penn Warren. Washington Irving, Walt Whitman, Stephen Crane, Theodore Dreiser and Ernest Hemingway are some of the writers whose earliest writing was as reporters and commentators for newspapers. Travel literature, reportage, autobiography have flourished from Franklin and Irving to

Twain and James to Norman Mailer and Mary McCarthy. Such observations only begin to indicate diversity, range, variety and continuity. Behind these generalizations lie the particular works of American writers, the plays, essays, poems, novels, stories which are analyzed, evaluated, introduced and recalled by the essays of this collection. Whatever differences there may be from essay to essay, the common assumption is that the literature has been read and will be read, and that the experiences of writing and of reading are experiences of living.

—LEONARD UNGER

List of Subjects

VOLUME ONE

HENRY ADAMS   1

JAMES AGEE   25

CONRAD AIKEN   48

EDWARD ALBEE   71

SHERWOOD ANDERSON   97

JOHN BARTH   121

SAUL BELLOW   144

JOHN BERRYMAN   167

AMBROSE BIERCE   190

RANDOLPH BOURNE   214

VAN WYCK BROOKS   239

KENNETH BURKE   264

ERSKINE CALDWELL   288

WILLA CATHER   312

JAMES FENIMORE COOPER   335

JAMES GOULD COZZENS   358

HART CRANE   381

STEPHEN CRANE   405

E. E. CUMMINGS   428

EMILY DICKINSON   451

JOHN DOS PASSOS   474

THEODORE DREISER   497

RICHARD EBERHART   521

JONATHAN EDWARDS   544

T. S. ELIOT   567

VOLUME TWO

RALPH WALDO EMERSON   1

JAMES T. FARRELL   25

WILLIAM FAULKNER   54

F. SCOTT FITZGERALD   77

BENJAMIN FRANKLIN   101

HAROLD FREDERIC   126

ROBERT FROST   150

ELLEN GLASGOW   173

CAROLINE GORDON   196

NATHANIEL HAWTHORNE   223

ERNEST HEMINGWAY   247

WILLIAM DEAN HOWELLS   271

WASHINGTON IRVING   295

HENRY JAMES   319

WILLIAM JAMES   342

RANDALL JARRELL   367

SARAH ORNE JEWETT   391

RING LARDNER   415

SINCLAIR LEWIS 439

JACK LONDON 462

HENRY WADSWORTH
    LONGFELLOW 486

AMY LOWELL 511

ROBERT LOWELL 534

MARY McCARTHY 558

CARSON McCULLERS 585

VOLUME THREE

ARCHIBALD MacLEISH 1

NORMAN MAILER 26

JOHN P. MARQUAND 50

HERMAN MELVILLE 74

H. L. MENCKEN 99

EDNA ST. VINCENT MILLAY 122

ARTHUR MILLER 145

HENRY MILLER 170

MARIANNE MOORE 193

WRIGHT MORRIS 218

VLADIMIR NABOKOV 244

HOWARD NEMEROV 267

REINHOLD NIEBUHR 290

FRANK NORRIS 314

FLANNERY O'CONNOR 337

JOHN O'HARA 361

EUGENE O'NEILL 385

EDGAR ALLAN POE 409

KATHERINE ANNE PORTER 433

EZRA POUND 456

JOHN CROWE RANSOM 480

EDWIN ARLINGTON ROBINSON 503

THEODORE ROETHKE 527

J. D. SALINGER 551

CARL SANDBURG 575

GEORGE SANTAYANA 599

VOLUME FOUR

ISAAC BASHEVIS SINGER 1

GERTRUDE STEIN 25

JOHN STEINBECK 49

WALLACE STEVENS 73

WILLIAM STYRON 97

ALLEN TATE 120

EDWARD TAYLOR 144

HENRY DAVID THOREAU 167

MARK TWAIN 190

JOHN UPDIKE 214

ROBERT PENN WARREN 236

EUDORA WELTY 260

NATHANAEL WEST 285

EDITH WHARTON 308

WALT WHITMAN 331

THORNTON WILDER 355

TENNESSEE WILLIAMS 378

WILLIAM CARLOS WILLIAMS 402

EDMUND WILSON 426

THOMAS WOLFE 450

RICHARD WRIGHT 474

INDEX 499

List of Contributors

Listed below are the contributors to *American Writers*. Each author's name is followed by his institutional affiliation at the time of publication, titles of books written, and titles of essays included in these volumes. The symbol † indicates that an author is deceased.

GAY WILSON ALLEN. Emeritus Professor of English, New York University. Books include *American Prosody*; *The Solitary Singer: A Critical Biography of Walt Whitman*; *William James: A Biography*; *A Reader's Guide to Walt Whitman*; *Herman Melville and His World*. Editor of *A William James Reader* and with Sculley Bradley *The Collected Writings of Walt Whitman*, in process. Carl Sandburg; William James.

ROGER ASSELINEAU. Professor of American Literature, the Sorbonne. Books include *The Literary Reputation of Mark Twain* and *The Evolution of Walt Whitman*. Edgar Allan Poe.

LOUIS AUCHINCLOSS. Lawyer, novelist, and critic. Books include *Reflections of a Jacobite*; *Pioneers and Caretakers: A Study of Nine American Women Novelists*; and many novels, among them, *The Rector of Justin* and *I Come as a Thief*. Henry Adams; Ellen Glasgow; Edith Wharton.

WARNER BERTHOFF. Professor of English, Harvard University. Books include *The Example of Melville*; *The Ferment of Realism: American Literature, 1884-1919*; and *Fictions and Events: Essays in Criticism and Literary History*. Edmund Wilson.

ROBERT BONE. Professor of English, Teachers College, Columbia University. Books include *The Negro Novel in America* and *The Afro-American Short Story*, in progress. Richard Wright.

EDGAR M. BRANCH. Research Professor of English, Miami University, Oxford, Ohio. Author of *The Literary Apprenticeship of Mark Twain* and *Clemens of the "Call."* James T. Farrell.

JOHN MALCOLM BRINNIN. Boston University. Poet, biographer, and critic. Books include *Dylan Thomas in America*; *The Third Rose: Gertrude Stein and Her World*; and *The Selected Poems of John Malcolm Brinnin*. William Carlos Williams.

MERLE E. BROWN. Professor of English, University of Iowa. Author of *Neo-Idealistic Aesthetics* and *Wallace Stevens: The Poem as Act*. Kenneth Burke.

J. A. BRYANT, JR. Professor of English, University of Kentucky. Author of *Hippolyta's View: Some Christian Aspects of Shakespeare's Plays*. Eudora Welty.

JEAN CAZEMAJOU. Professor of American Literature and Civilization, University of Bordeaux. Author of *Stephen Crane, écrivain journaliste*, and contributor to *Stephen Crane, Maggie, The Red Badge of Courage* and *Presse, Radio, Television aux Etats-Unis*. Stephen Crane.

RICHARD CHASE.† Walt Whitman.

RUBY COHN. Professor of Comparative Drama, University of California, Davis. Editor of magazine, *Modern Drama*. Books include *Currents in Contemporary Drama* and *Dialogue in American Drama*. Edward Albee.

LOUIS COXE. Pierce Professor of English, Bowdoin College. Books include *The Second Man and Other Poems*; *The Wilderness and Other Poems*; *The Middle Passage*; *The Sea Faring and Other Poems*; and *Edwin Arlington Robinson: The Life of Poetry*. Edwin Arlington Robinson.

ROBERT GORHAM DAVIS. Professor of English, Columbia University. Author of *Meet the U.S.A.*; *C. P. Snow*; and many short stories. John Dos Passos.

REUEL DENNEY. University of Hawaii, East-West Center. Books ranging from poetry to social criticism, including *The Lonely Crowd*, of which he is co-author. Conrad Aiken.

DENIS DONOGHUE. Professor of Modern English and American Literature, University College, Dublin. Books include *The Third Voice*; *Connoisseurs of Chaos*; *The Ordinary Universe; Jonathan Swift*; and *Yeats*. Emily Dickinson.

LEON EDEL. Books include *The Modern Psychological Novel* and *Henry James*, a biography in five volumes. Henry James; Henry David Thoreau.

F. CUDWORTH FLINT.† Amy Lowell.

RICHARD FOSTER. Professor of English, Macalester College. Author of *The New Romantics* and co-editor of *Modern Criticism: Theory and Practice*. Norman Mailer.

OTTO FRIEDRICH. Editor and critic. Books include *The Poor in Spirit* and *The Loner*. Ring Lardner.

W. M. FROHOCK. Professor of French Literature, Harvard University. Books include *André Malraux and the Tragic Imagination*; *Rimbaud's Poetic Practice*; *The Novel of Violence in America*; and *Style and Temper: Studies in French Fiction*. Theodore Dreiser; Frank Norris.

STANTON GARNER. Professor of English, University of Texas at Arlington. General Editor, definitive edition of works of Harold Frederic. Harold Frederic.

JEAN GARRIGUE.† Marianne Moore.

JOHN GASSNER.† Eugene O'Neill.

WILLIAM M. GIBSON. Professor of English, New York University. Compiler, with George Arms, *Bibliography of William Dean Howells*, and Editor, with Henry Nash Smith, *Mark Twain-Howells Letters*. William Dean Howells.

LAWRENCE GRAVER. Professor of English, Williams College. Author of *Conrad's Short Fiction*. Carson McCullers.

JAMES GRAY. Literary critic, novelist, and historian. Formerly Professor of English, University of Minnesota. Books include novels, criticism, and history. Edna St. Vincent Millay; John Steinbeck.

BERNARD GREBANIER. Professor Emeritus of English, Brooklyn College. Books include *The Heart of Hamlet, The Truth about Shylock,* and *Playwriting.* Thornton Wilder.

EDWARD M. GRIFFIN. Associate Professor of English, University of Minnesota; has been visiting professor at the University of San Francisco and at Stanford University. Jonathan Edwards.

GEORGE HEMPHILL. Professor of English, University of Connecticut. Editor of *Discussions of Poetry: Rhythm and Sound,* and author of *A Mathematical Grammar of English.* Allen Tate.

GRANVILLE HICKS. Author and former weekly contributor to *Saturday Review.* Among recent books, an autobiography, *Part of the Truth.* James Gould Cozzens.

EDWARD L. HIRSH. Professor of English, Boston College. Henry Wadsworth Longfellow.

FREDERICK J. HOFFMAN.† Gertrude Stein.

ROBERT HOGAN. Teacher of English, University of Delaware. Publisher of Proscenium Press and Editor of *The Journal of Irish Literature.* Author of *The Experiments of Sean O'Casey; The Independence of Elmer Rice; Dion Boucicault;* and *After the Irish Renaissance,* among other books, and of two plays *Danaher Talks to McGreevy* and *A Better Place.* Arthur Miller.

C. HUGH HOLMAN. Kenan Professor of English, University of North Carolina at Chapel Hill. Co-founder and co-editor of *Southern*

Literary Journal and author of fourteen books, including *The American Novel Through Henry James; Three Modes of Modern Southern Fiction; A Handbook to Literature;* and *The Contradictions of Southern Literature.* John P. Marquand; Thomas Wolfe.

THEODORE HORNBERGER. Professor of English, University of Pennsylvania. Co-editor of *The Literature of the United States* and author of *Scientific Thought in the American College 1638-1800,* among other books. Benjamin Franklin.

LEON HOWARD. Emeritus Professor of English, University of California, Los Angeles, and Visiting Professor, University of New Mexico. Books include *Herman Melville: A Biography.* Herman Melville; Wright Morris.

STANLEY EDGAR HYMAN.† Flannery O'Connor; Nathanael West.

GERHARD JOSEPH. Professor of English, Herbert Lehman College, City University of New York. Author of *Tennysonian Love: The Strange Diagonal.* John Barth.

JAMES KORGES. Erskine Caldwell.

ERLING LARSEN. Professor of English, Carleton College. Author of *Minnesota Trails: A Sentimental History* and *Something about Some of the Educations of Laird Bell.* James Agee.

LEWIS LEARY. Professor of English, University of North Carolina, Chapel Hill. Books include *Mark Twain's Letters to Mary* and *John Greenleaf Whittier.* Washington Irving; Mark Twain.

FREDERICK P. W. McDOWELL. Professor of English, University of Iowa. Author of *Ellen*

Glasgow and the Ironic Art of Fiction and *Elizabeth Madox Roberts*. Caroline Gordon.

JAY MARTIN. Professor of English and Comparative Literature, University of California, Irvine. Author of *Conrad Aiken: A Life of His Art*; *Harvests of Change: American Literature 1865-1914*; and *Nathanael West: The Art of His Life*. Robert Lowell.

WILLIAM J. MARTZ. Professor of English, Ripon College. Editor of *The Distinctive Voice*, General Editor of The Modern Poets Series, and author of *Shakespeare's Universe of Comedy*. John Berryman.

PETER MEINKE. Professor of Literature, Eckerd College. Author of poems, reviews, and articles which have appeared in such journals as *The New Republic*, *The Antioch Review*, *The New Orleans Review*, *The New York Quarterly*. Howard Nemerov.

JOSEPHINE MILES. Professor of English, University of California, Berkeley. Books include *Poems 1930-60*; *Kinds of Affection*; *Eras and Modes in English Poetry*; *Style and Proportion*. Ralph Waldo Emerson.

JAMES E. MILLER, JR. Professor of English, University of Chicago. Books include *A Critical Guide to Leaves of Grass*; *Start with the Sun: Studies in the Whitman Tradition* (with Bernice Slote and Karl Shapiro); *Walt Whitman*; *Reader's Guide to Herman Melville*; *F. Scott Fitzgerald: His Art and His Technique*; *J. D. Salinger*; *Quests Surd and Absurd: Essays in American Literature*; *Word, Self, Reality: The Rhetoric of Imagination*. Books edited include *Walt Whitman: Complete Poetry and Selected Prose* and *Man in Literature: Comparative World Studies in Translation*. J. D. Salinger.

RALPH J. MILLS, JR. Professor of English, University of Illinois at Chicago Circle. Books include *Contemporary American Poetry*; *Edith Sitwell*; *Creation's Very Self*. Editor of *On the Poet and His Craft: Selected Prose of Theodore Roethke* and *Selected Letters of Theodore Roethke*. Richard Eberhart; Theodore Roethke.

JULIAN MOYNAHAN. Teacher of English, Rutgers University. Author of novels *Sisters and Brothers* and *Pairing Off*, and of a critical study of D. H. Lawrence entitled *The Deed of Life*. Vladimir Nabokov.

WILLIAM VAN O'CONNOR.† William Faulkner; Ezra Pound.

SHERMAN PAUL. M. F. Carpenter Professor of English, University of Iowa. Books include *Emerson's Angle of Vision*; *The Shores of America: Thoreau's Inward Exploration*; *Louis Sullivan: An Architect in American Thought*; *Edmund Wilson*; *The Music of Survival: A Biography of a Poem by William Carlos Williams*; and *Hart's Bridge*. Randolph Bourne.

RICHARD PEARCE. Professor of English, Wheaton College. Author of *Stages of the Clown: Perspectives on Modern Fiction from Dostoyevsky to Beckett*. William Styron.

M. L. ROSENTHAL. Professor of English, New York University. Books written or edited include *Beyond Power: New Poems*; *The New Poets: American and British Poetry since World War II*; and *A Primer of Ezra Pound*. Randall Jarrell.

EARL ROVIT. Teacher of English, City College of New York. Author of *Herald to Chaos: The Novels of Elizabeth Madox Roberts* and *Ernest Hemingway*. Saul Bellow.

CHARLES THOMAS SAMUELS. Teacher of English, Williams College. Author of *A Casebook on Film*; *The Ambiguity of Henry James*; and *Encountering Directors*. John Updike.

MARK SCHORER. Professor of English, University of California, Berkeley. Books of fiction, literary criticism, and biography include *William Blake: The Politics of Vision*; *Sinclair Lewis: An American Life*; *D. H. Lawrence*; and three novels. Sinclair Lewis.

NATHAN A. SCOTT, JR. Shailer Mathews Professor of Theology and Literature, University of Chicago. Books include *The Wild Prayer of Longing: Poetry and the Sacred*; *Negative Capability: Studies in the New Literature and the Religious Situation*; *The Broken Center: Studies in the Theological Horizon of Modern Literature*; and *Samuel Beckett*. Reinhold Niebuhr.

CHARLES E. SHAIN. President of Connecticut College. F. Scott Fitzgerald.

BEN SIEGEL. Professor of English, California State Polytechnic College. Books include *The Puritan Heritage: America's Roots in the Bible* and *Biography Past and Present*. Isaac Bashevis Singer.

GROVER SMITH. Professor of English, Duke University. Author of *T. S. Eliot's Poetry and Plays: A Study in Sources and Meaning* and *Ford Madox Ford*, and editor of *Josiah Royce's Seminar 1913-1914, as Recorded in the Notebooks of Harry T. Costello* and *Letters of Aldous Huxley*. Archibald MacLeish.

MONROE K. SPEARS. Libbie Shearn Moody Professor of English, Rice University and former Editor of *Sewanee Review*. Author of *The Poetry of W. H. Auden: The Disenchanted Island*. Hart Crane.

ROBERT E. SPILLER. Felix E. Schelling Professor of English, University of Pennsylvania. Books written or edited include *Literary History of the United States*; *The Cycle of American Literature*; and *The Third Dimension*. James Fenimore Cooper.

NEWTON P. STALLKNECHT. Professor of Comparative Literature and Criticism, Indiana University. Author, co-author, or editor of books in comparative literature, history of philosophy, and history of literary criticism, including *The Spirit of Western Philosophy* and *Comparative Literature: Method and Perspective*. George Santayana.

DONALD E. STANFORD. Professor of English, Louisiana State University and Editor of *The Southern Review*. Author of two books of poems, *New England Earth* and *The Traveler*, and editor of *Poems of Edward Taylor*. Edward Taylor.

JOHN L. STEWART. Professor of American Literature, University of California, San Diego. Books include *John Crowe Ransom* and *The Burden of Time: The Fugitives and Agrarians*. John Crowe Ransom.

IRVIN STOCK. Professor and Chairman of English Department, University of Massachusetts. Author of *William Hale White (Mark Rutherford): A Critical Study*. Mary McCarthy.

LAWRANCE THOMPSON. Professor of English and American Literature, Princeton University. Books include a major biography of Robert Frost. Robert Frost.

MARGARET FARRAND THORP.† Sarah Orne Jewett.

WILLIAM YORK TINDALL. Professor of English, Columbia University. Books include

Forces in Modern British Literature; *Literary Symbol*; *The Joyce Country*; and *A Reader's Guide to Dylan Thomas*. Wallace Stevens.

EVE TRIEM. Poet. Poems published in *Parade of Doves* and *Poems*, as well as in magazines and anthologies. E. E. Cummings.

LEONARD UNGER. Professor of English, University of Minnesota. Author of *The Man in the Name: Essays on the Experience of Poetry* and editor of *T. S. Eliot: A Selected Critique*. T. S. Eliot.

DOROTHY VAN GHENT.† Willa Cather.

HYATT H. WAGGONER. Professor of American Literature, Brown University. Books include *Hawthorne: A Critical Study*. Nathaniel Hawthorne.

PHILIP WAGNER. Former Editor, *Baltimore Evening Sun*, newspaper columnist, and author of books on wine growing. H. L. Mencken.

CHARLES CHILD WALCUTT. Queens College, City University of New York. Books written or edited include *Man's Changing Mask: Modes and Methods of Characterization in Fiction*. Jack London; John O'Hara.

WILLIAM WASSERSTROM. Professor of English, Syracuse University. Books written or edited include *Heiress of All the Ages*; *The Time of the Dial*; and *Civil Liberties and the Arts*. Van Wyck Brooks.

GERALD WEALES. Teacher of English, University of Pennsylvania. Books include *American Drama since World War II*; *The Jumping-Off Place*; *Clifford Odets, Playwright*; a novel and two children's books. Tennessee Williams.

BROM WEBER. Professor of American Studies and English, University of California, Davis. Books include *An Anthology of American Humor*; *The Complete Poems and Selected Letters and Prose of Hart Crane*; and *Sense and Sensibility in Twentieth-Century Writing*. Sherwood Anderson.

PAUL WEST. Visiting Professor of English, Pennsylvania State University. Author of novels, poetry, and criticism, including *The Modern Novel*. Robert Penn Warren.

RAY B. WEST, JR. Professor of English, San Francisco State College. Katherine Anne Porter.

GEORGE WICKES. Teacher of English and Comparative Literature, University of Oregon. Editor of *Lawrence Durrell and Henry Miller: A Private Correspondence* and *Henry Miller and the Critics*. His latest book is *Americans in Paris*. Henry Miller.

ROBERT A. WIGGINS. Teacher of English, University of California, Davis. Ambrose Bierce.

PHILIP YOUNG. Research Professor of English, Pennsylvania State University. Books include *Ernest Hemingway*; *Ernest Hemingway: A Reconsideration*; and *Three Bags Full: Essays in American Fiction*. Ernest Hemingway.

AMERICAN WRITERS

Henry Adams

1838-1918

ON DECEMBER 6, 1885, fate almost, in Henry Adams' words, "smashed the life" out of him. His wife, Marian Hooper Adams, on that day took a fatal dose of potassium cyanide. Suicide makes a clean sweep of the past and present; worst of all, it repudiates love. Adams was a man of few intimacies. "One friendship in a lifetime is much," he wrote; "two are many; three are hardly possible." Certainly his two were Clarence King, the geologist, and John Hay, the biographer of Lincoln. And there were others like the painter John La Farge with whom he had warm and pleasant associations. But it is doubtful if Adams, who used a sharp wit and a gruff, kindly cynicism as a barrier to and possibly a substitute for the closest human communion, ever revealed his deepest emotions or thoughts to any but Marian. She was quick, even caustic, but blessed with gaiety and an exquisite sensitivity. She adored her husband, and their childlessness was only a further bond. But nothing could pull her out of the black depression into which she sank after her father died.

Until that day of tragedy Henry Adams might have reasonably considered that his life was successful. He had not, to be sure, been President of the United States, like his grandfather, John Quincy Adams, or like his great-grandfather, John Adams, or minister to England, like his father, Charles Francis Adams, but he had been a brilliant and popular teacher of medieval history at Harvard, a successful editor of the *North American Review*, a noted biographer and essayist, and he was in the process of completing his nine-volume history of the Jefferson and Madison administrations which even such a self-deprecator as he must have suspected would one day be a classic. But above all this, far above, he had believed that he and his wife were happy.

Recovering from the first shock, he took a trip to Japan with John La Farge. Then he went back to Washington and worked for three laborious years to finish his history and prepare it for the press. After that, at last, he was free. He had neither child nor job, and his means were ample. In August of 1890 he and La Farge sailed again from San Francisco for a voyage of indefinite duration to the South Seas. His life, at fifty-two, seemed over. Like a worn-out race-horse, he had quit the course and was seeking pasture. "Education had ended in 1871, life was complete in 1890; the rest mattered so little!" And yet that rest was to contain the two great books for which Adams is chiefly remembered today: *Mont-Saint-Michel and Chartres* and *The Education of Henry Adams*.

The Pacific opened up a new dimension of color. La Farge taught Adams to observe the exquisite clearness of the butterfly blue of the sky, laid on between clouds and shading down to a white faintness in the distance where the haze of ocean covered up the turquoise. He made him peer down into the water, framed in the opening of a ship's gangway, and see how the sapphire blue seemed to pour from it. He pointed out the varieties of pink and lilac and purple and rose in the clouds at sunset. Adams never learned to be more than an amateur painter, but his vision was immensely sharpened. For the first time he began to allow the long-repressed aesthete, the author of two anonymous novels, to predominate over the intellectual, the historian.

In Samoa the natives, grave and courteous, greeted the travelers benevolently and made them feel at home. They drank the ceremonial *kawa* and watched the *siva,* a dance performed by girls seated cross-legged, naked to the waist, their dark skins shining with coconut oil, with garlands of green leaves around their heads and loins. The girls chanted as they swayed and stretched out their arms in all directions; they might have come out of the nearby sea. It was a world where instinct was everything.

After Samoa came the disillusionment of Tahiti. Adams described it as a successful cemetery. The atmosphere was one of hopelessness and premature decay. The natives were not the gay, big animal creatures of Samoa; they were still, silent, sad in expression, and fearfully few in number. The population had been decimated by bacteria brought in by Westerners. Rum was the only amusement which civilization and religion had left the people. Tahiti was a halfway house between Hawaii and Samoa. Adams complained that a pervasive half-castitude permeated everything, a sickly whitey-brown or dirty white complexion that suggested weakness and disease.

He was bored, bored as he had never been in the worst wilds of Beacon Street or at the dreariest dinner tables of Belgravia. While waiting for a boat to take them elsewhere, anywhere, he amused himself by returning to his role of historian and interviewing members of the deposed royal family, the Tevas. Next to Mataafa in Samoa, he found the old ex-queen of Tahiti, Hinari, or Grandmother, the most interesting native figure in the Pacific. She showed none of the secrecy of the Samoan chiefs, but took a motherly interest in Adams and La Farge and, sitting on the floor, told them freely all her clan's oldest legends and traditions. Adams was even adopted into the Teva clan and given the hereditary family name of Taura-Atua with the lands, rights, and privileges attached to it—though these consisted of only a few hundred square feet.

But later when he attempted to recapture Hinari's tale in a book which he had privately printed, it was little more than an interesting failure. Tahiti had no history, in the Western sense of the word, until the arrival of the white man. Of the thousands of years that had preceded Captain Cook, when generation had succeeded generation without distinguishable change, there was nothing left but genealogy and legend. The genealogy, which makes up a large part of Adams' book, is boring, and, as for the legend, he admitted himself that he needed the lighter hand of Robert Louis Stevenson, whom he had met in Tahiti.

Yet the *Memoirs of Arii Taimai* (1901) nonetheless marks an important step in Adams' career. He had gone, by 1890, as far as he could go as a historian in the conventional sense. His great work on Jefferson and Madison was history at its most intellectually pure. The author stands aside and lets the documents tell the story, from which a few precious rules may be deduced. In the South Seas he had tried to abandon intellect for the sake of simplicity and instinct. He had sought peace and found ennui. Even the unspoiled natives, in the long run, palled. He had to return, in Papeete, to his profession, but he had to try it with a new twist, for how else could Tahitian history be done? And if the *Memoirs* was a bore, was it altogether his fault? Might it not be in the subject? Suppose he were to happen upon a subject that required not only the imagination of the man who had sat on the floor with the old queen of Tahiti as she intoned the poems of her family tradition, but also the industry of the devoted scholar who had pored through the archives of European foreign offices? Suppose he were to find a subject, in short, that required an artist as well as a historian? A subject like the Gothic age of faith?

To go back to his origin (as he himself so often did), Adams was born in Boston in 1838, in Mount Vernon Street under the shadow of the State House. He always loved to dramatize the irony of the seemingly fortunate circumstances of his birth. According to his claim, he had been less equipped for life in America in the nineteenth century than had he been born a Polish Jew or "a furtive Yacoob and Ysaac still reeking of the Ghetto, snarling a weird Yiddish to the officers of the customs." The notion is not to be taken too seriously. If Adams was aloof from the political and economic competition of his day it was not because he was the grandson of a president and, on his mother's side, of the richest merchant in Boston. It was quite of his own volition. Had he been born obscure the idea would never have occurred to him, as an old and respected seer, that he was a failure.

From earliest childhood he was close to the great. When he refused to go to school, it was old John Quincy Adams himself who took him by the hand and led him there. When he went to church, it was to sleep through the sermons of his uncle, Nathaniel Frothingham. Studying his Latin grammar in a corner of his father's library in Mount Vernon Street he heard Charles Sumner hold forth on the politics of antislavery, and at the age of twelve he was taken to Washington to call on President Zachary Taylor and the leaders of Congress. The pattern of receiving his impressions of current history from the very apex of the political pyramid was to continue for the rest of a long life.

He grew up in a large and happy family of six children, two girls and four boys, with devoted parents who were always close to them. He attended the Dixwell School in Boston and entered Harvard College in 1854. When he graduated, four years later, he was elected class orator. Although he always maintained that he learned nothing at Cambridge, this was part of an affectation that covered every stage of his life. In fact, he seems to have read widely, obtained good grades, and made friends with classmates who were also to make their mark in life. One was Henry Hobson Richardson, the Romanesque architect who later built Adams' house in Washington; another was Oliver Wendell Holmes, Jr., of the Supreme Court. Adams' class oration contained none of the pessimism for which he was afterwards noted, and his Class Book has this entry under his signature: "My immediate object is to become a scholar, and master of more languages than I pretend to know now. Ultimately it is most probable that I shall study and practise law, but where and to what extent is as yet undecided. My wishes are for a quiet literary life, as I believe that to be the happiest and in this country not the least useful." This should rebut those who claim that Adams abandoned public life in later years because he disliked the rough and tumble of competition. At twenty he had already elected to be a writer.

After graduation he spent two years in Europe. His original purpose had been to study German civil law in Berlin, but he found it hopelessly boring and decided to learn only the language. Ultimately his trip turned, more profitably, into a sort of grand tour. In Sicily he had an interview with Garibaldi, and in Rome he sat, like Gibbon, on the top of the steps to Santa Maria di Ara Coeli and mused over the great work of history that that historian had visualized on the same spot. When he returned to Boston, he was still determined to read for the bar, but he was interrupted again—this time by his father's election to Congress and the latter's proposal that he accompany him to Washington as private secretary.

Adams remained his father's secretary for nine years, from 1860 to 1868. It was the nearest he ever came to public office. After a brief time in a capital seething with secession, Charles Francis Adams was sent to London as minister. He occupied this position brilliantly and successfully throughout the Civil War and during the difficult period of the adjustment of war claims that followed. There is little reason to believe that his son felt estranged from his generation—as did his friend Henry James—by not having seen combat. Adams knew that his father, supported by a tiny staff, was fighting a battle against British Confederate sympathies that was quite as vital as any in the field, and his older brother warned him sternly from his army camp that if Henry left his post to enlist he would be derelict in his duty to both family and nation. There was no feeling on anyone's part that the little isolated Union group in London was having an easy time. Adams was perfectly sincere

in his belief that combat, under the circumstances, would have come as a relief.

But whatever the pressures during crises, there must have been periods, in the more leisurely diplomatic life of that era, when there was not enough to do, for Adams in these years traveled all over England and began to write. He gave considerable attention to a piece on John Smith and Pocahontas, ultimately published in the *North American Review*, in which he was able to disprove some of the foundations on which that flimsy legend rested. Why he took this article, then and later, so seriously is hard to see. He seemed to think, a bit naively, that it might upset those British aristocrats who claimed descent from the Indian princess. At any rate, it is only interesting today as his first serious historical work and because it shows his method, developed more skillfully later, of letting the quoted documents tell most of the story.

When the war ended, he continued to write solid, scholarly articles, such as "The Declaration of Paris" and "The Bank of England Restriction," but it was not until his return to live in Washington as a free-lance correspondent that his distinctive style and point of view began to appear. It took anger and disgust to bring this out: the anger and disgust that was felt by thousands of idealistic young men who saw what they had hoped would be the brave new world of an emancipated and now indissoluble union turned over to a gang of ward politicians and economic pirates. Abraham Lincoln was dead, and Jay Gould seemed to reign at the White House.

"The New York Gold Conspiracy," dealing with the attempt of Gould and Fisk to corner the gold market with the aid of President Grant's brother-in-law, is a fine, taut narrative that crackles with the author's contempt for the crooks and dupes of the sordid adventure.

Adams had by now completed his mastery of finance, and his exposition is as clear as it is eloquent: "The Legal Tender Act," about the sorry federal financing of 1862, and "The Session," about the congressional session of 1869–70, are in much the same vein. But the world was not interested in the lucid diagnoses of this brilliant thirty-two-year-old reformer. The world cared about votes and dollars, and Adams lacked the temperament needed to acquire the first and the greed for the second. Besides, he was well enough off, not rich, by the standards of Wall Street, but able to make himself completely comfortable. Adams was always to live rather exquisitely; he was at heart a bit of a sybarite. In his old age this was to make his pretenses of being an anarchist seem an occasionally tiresome parlor joke to younger observers.

In 1870 his life changed again when Charles W. Eliot offered him the post of assistant professor of medieval history at Harvard. Characteristically, Adams told Eliot that he knew nothing about medieval history. Characteristically, Eliot responded by offering to appoint anyone who, in Adams' opinion, knew more. He held the job for seven years, during which he also held the editorship of the *North American Review*. His classes were small and select, and his students were turned loose to forage for themselves in original source material. Adams worked with them, rather than over them. He called the experiment a failure in the *Education*, but his students remembered the course as an inspiring one. One class even wrote and published a book under his direction, *Essays in Anglo-Saxon Law*. One may doubt that Adams, at the time, really believed that this was failure.

At any rate, he gave up both teaching and editing before he was forty. He and his wife, Marian Hooper of Boston, whom he had mar-

ried in 1872, settled in Washington, and he began at last a full-time career as a historian. The next eight years were the happiest of his life. The young Adamses were the center of the brightest, gayest group in the capital. Henry James was to describe them at this period with good-natured sharpness in the guise of the Alfred Bonnycastles in "Pandora." Mrs. Bonnycastle in that tale has a fund of good humor that is apt to come uppermost with the April blossoms; her husband is "not in politics, though politics were much in him." They solve their social problems simply by not knowing any of the people they do not want to know, although here Mr. Bonnycastle sometimes finds his wife a bit too choosy. He remarks toward the end of the season: "Hang it, there's only a month left, let us be vulgar and have some fun—let us invite the President!"

But with all of the fun and the parties Adams was still hard at work. He had acquired the Albert Gallatin papers which he edited in three large volumes, with a fourth for his own biography of Jefferson's secretary of the treasury (1879). As history the life is admirable; as entertainment it is very dry. One doubts if even such a literary magician as Lytton Strachey could have made Gallatin's personality interesting. However high-minded, judicious, industrious, patriotic, conscientious, Gallatin was dull and his correspondence is dull, and dullness permeates his biography. Adams demonstrates all of his subject's best qualities in his own careful, clear rendition of the important facts, and there they remain for students, and for students only.

Just the opposite is true of Adams' biography of John Randolph of Roanoke (1882). Here he is dealing with an absolutely reprehensible man who was the scourge of the House of Representatives for two decades and who ultimately came to symbolize everything that was violent, recalcitrant, and irrational in the point of view of the southern slaveholder. Randolph's importance in history is that he became the prophet around whom the forces of secession could ultimately rally. It is certain that he was alcoholic; it is probable that he was partially insane. No more different character from Gallatin could possibly be conceived, and they face each other a little bit like Milton's God and Milton's Satan, with the balance of interest falling in Satan's favor. Fortunately, the book on Randolph is short, for about halfway through one begins to lose interest. The character is too absurd to hold the stage except as a grisly historical fact, and once that historical fact has been set forth there is little to be gained by summaries of his irrational speeches. The work ultimately fails, like *Gallatin*, because of its subject. It could have only been strengthened if Adams had had the material and the inclination to delve into the psychological reasons for Randolph's behavior. He would have done better to have made it the topic of one of his masterly essays in the *North American Review*. As he said himself, Randolph's biographer had the impossible job of taking a "lunatic monkey" seriously.

Gallatin and Randolph were both to play major roles in the great historical work on which Adams now embarked: *History of the United States of America during the Administrations of Thomas Jefferson and James Madison*. When completed it ran to nine volumes, the last of which was not published until 1891. Before the appearance of Dumas Malone's study of Jefferson's first term, Adams' *History* was considered by many the definitive work on the first years of the American nineteenth century.

The short chapters, the straightforward, vigorous, masculine prose, the geographical and political sweep of the narrative, and the sharp, pungent assessments of motives and failings

conceal the enormous and laborious research in American, French, English, and Spanish state papers that underlay them. Adams was to say in the *Education* that he had published a dozen volumes of American history for no other purpose than to satisfy himself whether, by the severest process of stating, with the least possible comment, such facts as seemed sure, in such order as seemed rigorously consequent, he could fix for a familiar moment a necessary sequence of human movement. He selected his period (1801 to 1817) because it represented a natural semicolon in American history. By the turn of the century the United States had established itself as an independent nation that was bound, one way or another, to survive, and by 1815 that nation had accepted the fact, whether all of its statesmen did so or not, that it was going to survive more or less as other nations survived. It was not, in other words, to be an Arcadia—set apart. The two double terms of Jefferson and Madison represent, therefore, the historical hiatus in which Americans gave up their dream that they were different from other human beings. Adams' central theme is the disillusionment of two presidents who found that their governments were ineluctably controlled by facts and not ideals.

Both presidents were to find themselves in the position of Napoleon in Tolstoi's *War and Peace*, pulling at tassels inside a carriage under the illusion that it was they, rather than the charging horses, who made it go. Adams demonstrates that when history offered Jefferson the chance to purchase Louisiana, he discovered that he could not turn it down—that he did not even want to. So he doubled the size of the union by means of a treaty for which there was no shadow of authority in the Constitution whose strict construction he had so passionately urged. And Madison, in his turn, according to Adams, found himself obliged to build up the armed forces that he had wished to abolish and to engage in warfare which he had believed fatal to liberty. And both he and Jefferson found themselves caught up in the job of enforcing an embargo as despotically as any tyrant abroad.

This conception of Jefferson as an idealist philosopher-president, imbued with the fatuous faith that there were no international difficulties that could not be solved by negotiation, has been subject to the criticism that Adams was prejudiced against the third president, who, after spurning the political ideas of John Adams, ended by adopting them. There may be some truth in this. Why should Adams attack Jefferson for inconsistency, which can be a very great virtue in a statesman, unless he believed that the latter had preempted a credit in history that more properly belonged to his great-grandfather? Then, too, Adams, with the down-to-earth thinking of the scholar who has never been tempted to compromise, may have found it difficult to appreciate the enormous range and flexibility of Jefferson's political mind. Adams admired diplomats and rarely politicians. Jefferson was rarely a diplomat and always a politician. One is reminded at times of Lord Morley's statement that if Adams had ever surveyed himself naked in a mirror, he might have been more tolerant of human deficiencies.

Adams' predilection for diplomacy is the source of the best and weakest parts of the *History*. The more brilliant passages are those that take place outside the United States: in London, Paris, and Madrid; in Santo Domingo and on the high seas. The chapters that deal with Napoleon have a particular fascination, not only because they put the naive, serious-minded American statesman in dramatic contrast with this monster of Old World cynicism and champion of brute force, but because they show Adams, the historian, strug-

gling desperately in his quest for sequence, for cause and effect, against the tide of chaos, against the appalling evidence that a single individual was turning history into whim. Napoleon plays in the *History* just the reverse of the role that he plays in *War and Peace*. It is ironical that Adams, who largely agreed with Tolstoi's concept of political leaders being carried along in the flood of events which they try vainly to control, should take exception to Tolstoi's primary illustration of his theory. Yet so it is. Napoleon seems to strike Adams as the one human being of the period who contains in himself an energy equivalent to a nation's energy and who is thus able to deflect history from its normal course. When one sees the emperor lolling in his hot bath and shouting at his brothers about the Louisiana Purchase, one feels that Adams is here dealing with a different kind of force from that generated by Jefferson, by Burr, by Canning, or even by Andrew Jackson. The mere fact that Napoleon is the only man in nine volumes whom we see in a bathtub underlines his individuality. Eventually, the processes of history would right themselves, and Napoleon's empire would disintegrate, even more quickly than it was put together, but it still remains a phenomenon unique in European history.

One can see why Adams was ultimately disappointed in his sequences. For despite all his labors and all his perceptions, the true cause of the War of 1812 is never made clear. Through several volumes of lucidly described diplomatic negotiations between England and the United States we see the government first of Jefferson and then of Madison submit tamely to every humiliation imposed upon it by a British crown determined not only to keep its former colony a small power but to seize by any means, legal or illegal, its growing trade. Adams pursues skillfully, if at times tediously, the endless negotiations in the seven years preceding the war: in Paris, Washington, and London, over the American embargo, the American Act of Non-Intercourse, the British Orders in Council, and Napoleon's Berlin and Milan decrees. Fixed in the policy of isolation, hallucinated by the vision that the new democracy, left to itself, would develop powerfully and peacefully, Jefferson and his successor are seen deliberately blinding themselves to the fact that neither Canning nor Napoleon will give the slightest consideration to any diplomatic protest that is not backed up by force.

But why then the war? Why did the United States, having suffered every diplomatic rebuff, finally elect to throw away the price of its shameful submission? So far as the reader can make out, the country was hounded unprepared into a war which its administration did not seek by a group of young hotheads in Congress led by Henry Clay and John C. Calhoun. But Adams did not know why: "The war fever of 1811 swept far and wide over the country, but even at its height seemed somewhat intermittent and imaginary. A passion that needed to be nursed for five years before it acquired strength to break into act, could not seem genuine to men who did not share it. A nation which had submitted to robbery and violence in 1805, in 1807, in 1809, could not readily lash itself into rage in 1811 when it had no new grievance to allege; nor could the public feel earnest in maintaining national honor, for every one admitted that the nation had sacrificed its honor, and must fight to regain it. Yet what honor was to be hoped from a war which required continued submission to one robber as the price of resistance to another? President Madison submitted to Napoleon in order to resist England; the New England Federalists preferred submitting to England in order to resist Napoleon; but not one American expected the United States to uphold their national rights against the world."

It is difficult for the reader at this point not to ask why, if a war is going to be created simply by an unreasonable war fever, such an inordinate amount of space has been devoted to the unraveling of the diplomatic skein that is not directly related to it. Of course, it might be answered that the unraveling of the diplomatic skein is part of a historian's task simply because it is there to unravel, but even conceding this, one cannot escape the conclusion that the diplomatic chapters could be summarized without losing much of their importance. One suspects here that Adams, being a pioneer in the British, French, and Spanish archives, fell a little bit in love with material so far virgin to the historian and indulged in overquotation. There is also the fact that, having himself spent eight years as secretary to the United States minister in London, he had a natural fascination in peering under the formal cover of diplomatic interchange to the reality beneath.

Adams believed that a historian should first detach himself and his personal enthusiasms and disapprovals from the field of human events that he has selected to study. He should then develop his own general ideas of causes and effects by observing the mass of phenomena in the selected period. After the formation of such ideas, he should exclude all facts irrelevant to them. In his *History,* his most important general idea is that the energy of the American people ultimately seized control of a chain of events which was initiated by energies in Europe. He attempted to trace this American energy in finance, science, politics, and diplomacy. Individuals were not of primary importance to him, which explains why even Jefferson is never presented in a full portrait and why Madison remains a more shadowy character than any of the British statesmen described. Adams believed that in a democratic nation individuals were important chiefly as types. In the end, his *History*, like most great histories, is a failure, if a splendid one, because we are never brought to a full comprehension of what this all-important energy consists. It seems possible that Adams might have approached its nature more closely had he widened his field of study, had he spent more time observing the commercial society of American cities, the farms of the North and the plantations in the South, and less of the day-to-day negotiations of the Treaty of Ghent.

During the years of heavy work on his *History*, Adams relaxed from one discipline, characteristically, by subjecting himself to another. He wrote and published two novels, *Democracy*, which appeared anonymously in 1880, and *Esther*, which he brought out under the pseudonym of Frances Snow Compton in 1884. The identity of the author was for years a carefully guarded secret. These novels have aroused an interest in our time incommensurate with their merit. They are in the class of Winston Churchill's paintings—of primary interest to the biographer. That is not to say that they are bad. Indeed, competently organized and agreeably written, they cause no squirms of embarrassment even to the most critical reader. But compared to Adams' other work they are pale stuff, and commentators are reduced to the scholar's game of spotting the origins of the *Education* in *Democracy* and that of *Mont-Saint-Michel and Chartres* in *Esther*. Mrs. Lightfoot Lee's disenchantment with her corrupt senator, exposed by Adams' alter ego, John Carrington, reflects the author's own disgust with post-Civil War Washington, and Esther Dudley's rejection of the Episcopal Church contains the seed of Adams' nostalgia for a church that she might not have rejected. Yet neither novel significantly illu-

minates the later works. They remain in the end footnotes for Adams enthusiasts.

Democracy attained considerable popularity in its day as a political *roman à clef*. Certainly, the characters are more subtle than the issues. Mrs. Lightfoot Lee, like a Jamesian heroine, has money and social position and a bright, fresh spirit full of ideas. She has come to Washington in quest of some great and enlightened statesman whose humble and helping consort she may become. Her cousin John Carrington falls in love with her, but he is not at all what she wants. He is a Confederate veteran who has lost all and accepted defeat, but only because he has grimly accepted the verdict of history. Despising the victors, he concentrates on making a lonely living as a lawyer in the conquerors' land, a cynical, trenchant, attractive figure, the only real man in the book, so much like Basil Ransom in Henry James's novel *The Bostonians* (1886) of the same period that one wonders if he and Adams might not have used the same model.

Madeleine Lee wants something much more effervescent than Carrington; he is cold tea to the champagne that she visualizes. At last she thinks that she has found her ideal in Senator Ratcliffe, the colossus of Illinois who is able to gain control of the administration of the new president before the latter has even taken office. It is Carrington's distasteful duty to disillusion Madeleine, and he resolutely goes about putting together the necessary proof that the senator's career has been founded on a bribe. Madeleine, convinced, flees both senator and Washington. That is the whole story.

It is flat. One might have hoped that Madeleine would at least fall in love with the villain—if only to make her decision harder—but her creator, who detested senators, could not allow this. One might also have hoped that the senator would devise an interesting defense to her charge. But he tells Madeleine that the end justifies the means, and his end is nothing but the tired old rhetorical goal used by every contemporary statesman who ever waved the bloody shirt; preservation of the union. Adams might have answered this criticism of his plot by pointing out that he was telling the simple truth. Statesmen like Senator Ratcliffe in the Reconstruction era *did* dominate the scene, and men like Carrington *were* helpless to do more than record their own indignant dissent. Madeleine Lee, in flying off to Europe, has only expressed the despair of her creator at the prospect of Washington. Living a century later in not dissimilar times, should we not appreciate her position? Perhaps. But we are dealing with a novel, and novels must be concerned less with truth than the appearance of it.

Esther Dudley's choice in *Esther* is a good deal harder than Madeleine's for she is very much in love. The story again involves a renunciation, her renunciation of a deeply religious young minister whose faith she finds she cannot share. The novel is full of their arguments and finally bogs down in the reader's inability to see why an agnostic, with a little bit of tact, could not be a perfectly good minister's wife. One is almost surprised, in the end, that the subject has not been more interesting. It cannot be only that we care less about the question of faith today. Our interest in *Anna Karenina* is not diminished by our knowing that today the heroine could have divorced her husband and married Vronski with no loss of social position. No, it is rather that Adams himself has so little sympathy for the Reverend Stephen Hazard. He makes his evangelicism ridiculous, so that one suspects that Esther may be well out of her engagement. If the man of political power in the 1870's and 1880's was a pirate, the man of God was an anachronism. As husbands went, there was not much to choose between them.

Esther would have to wait twenty years and visit Chartres Cathedral, as one of Adams' adopted nieces, before she would encounter a religion that could move the hearts of men. And even then it would only be the memory of one.

There is a distinct similarity between Adams' two heroines and the heroines of Henry James's early and middle periods. Madeleine and Esther each have the impulsiveness, the charm, and the strict integrity of Isabel Archer in *The Portrait of a Lady* (1881). It is probable that this freshness and ebullience, this happy idealism united with a stubborn, at times gooselike, refusal to compromise, was a characteristic of American girls of the period and perhaps of Marian Adams herself. It was what made them ultimately pathetic, at times even tragic. One can find analogies in the American girls of Anthony Trollope's later novels. But certainly with Adams himself, this concept reflects a deep preoccupation. All his life he was more at ease with women than men, and after Marian's death he transferred some of his dependence to Elizabeth Cameron, the beautiful wife of Senator Don Cameron of Pennsylvania. When he wrote Mrs. Cameron that he valued any dozen pages of *Esther* more than the whole of his *History*, he may have been only half serious, but he may also have been expressing an intuitive conviction that the charm of Esther Dudley was precisely what was missing from the historical work.

Esther was Adams' last publication before his wife's suicide, and the years that followed, as we have seen, were occupied with the laborious completion of the *History*. His winters were now spent in the house designed for him by Henry Hobson Richardson on Lafayette Square directly opposite the White House. The adjoining larger mansion, also designed by Richardson, belonged to the John Hays.

Adams had given up going out socially, but he continued to entertain a select number of friends for lunch, or what he called breakfast. In the other seasons he traveled: in the Pacific, in the Caribbean, in Europe, in the Middle East. He had ceased to consider himself a historian. He was simply a student of the universe, an asker of questions, a humble seeker after knowledge who hoped to have a peek into the essential nature of man and matter before he died. This picture of a small, gruff gentleman, poking about the planet and asking questions of every sphinx, is the character, of course, that he himself was to make the subject of *The Education of Henry Adams.*

Among Adams' intimates was Senator Henry Cabot Lodge of Massachusetts, who had been one of his students at Harvard. The friendship at times was a rather prickly one, since Adams tended to distrust senators in general and Lodge in particular, but with Mrs. Lodge, a woman of large sympathy and intellect, the relationship was always good. It was she who invited him on the tour of northern France in the summer of 1895 which first aroused his interest in Norman and Gothic cathedrals. In the Cathedral of Coutances he suddenly saw his ideal image of outward austerity and inward refinement and felt a consequent release from the era in which he had been condemned to live. From this point on he began to play a mental game in which he identified himself with his Norman ancestors.

It did not matter whether these had been peasants or princes. All classes, in the eleventh century, must have felt the same motives. It had been, as Adams saw it, a natural, reasonable, complete century in which to live. Its cathedrals showed neither extravagance nor want of practical sense. He could almost remember the faith that had given his ancestors the energy to build them and the scared bold-ness that had made their towers seem so daring. Within these citadels of faith no doubts existed. There was not a stone in the whole interior of Coutances that did not treat him as if he were its own child. Going back eight hundred years, he mused: "I was simple-minded, somewhat stiff and cold, almost repellent to the warmer natures of the south, and I had lived always where one fought handily and needed to defend one's wives and children; but I was at my best." The fatal mistake had been ever to conquer England and its "dull, beer-swilling people." From 1066 to the Boston of Adams' own childhood, there had been nothing but a long decline in religion, in art, in military taste, until now, in the summer of 1895, the Back Bay descendants of Caen and Coutances had pretty nearly reached bottom.

In Mont-Saint-Michel the party encountered large numbers of tourists. Adams described them petulantly as pigs and the meals that he had to eat as hogpens. He does not seem to have run into many tourists in the other places, and one shudders to think what his reaction would have been had he traveled today. What struck him most in the Mount was that its character was more military than religious. He was fascinated by Senator Lodge's enthusiasm for it. Adams had not anticipated much from his friend as a sightseer. Lodge, he had been afraid, would visit the dreary old capitals of Europe as though he was still twenty and as though Napoleon III was still reigning. Now, however, Lodge returned to the enthusiasm that he had manifested as a student under Adams at Harvard, and lectured the party brilliantly on the construction and fortifications of the monastery.

The climax of the trip came with Chartres. After "thirty-five years of postponed intentions," Adams worshiped at last before the splendor of "the great glass gods." For the first time he encountered something that even his critical mind could regard as perfection. It was an experience that he was never to get over. He divined in the cathedral the intention of twelth-century man to unite all arts and sciences in the service of God. It was an architectural exhibit, a museum of painting, glass staining, wood and stone carving, music (vocal and instrumental), embroidery, jewelry, gem setting, tapestry weaving. It was the greatest single creation of man, to whom it gave a dignity which he was in no other instances entitled to claim. Adams likened himself to a monkey looking through a telescope at the stars.

Chartres was a beautiful gate by which to leave his Norman paradise, but he could hardly bear to leave it. The châteaux of the Loire seemed now as vulgar as Newport. Valois art was a "Jewish kind of gold-bug style" best fitted to express the coarseness and sensuality of Francis I and Henry VIII and their unspeakable Field of the Cloth of Gold. And when Adams returned to Paris, it was even worse. He was sickened by the "dreadful twang of his dear country people" on the Rue de la Paix. But people did not so much matter so long as one had the Gothic cathedrals.

After his trip with the Lodges Adams returned every summer to Paris. He rented an apartment as a base for his excursions and always invited a niece or nieces to visit him. Friends of nieces were also welcome, and "Uncle Henry" became a cult, the adored center of a group of attractive and intelligent young women. He would usually take one or more with him on his motor trips in search of the twelfth and thirteenth centuries. By the summer of 1904 he wrote to John Hay that these expeditions had become a craze and that he had fallen a victim to his Mercedes. He spent the warm months running "madly through the centuries" hunting "windows like hares," covering sixty miles in a morning and ninety in an afternoon. Traveling down a straight French road through the countryside hypnotized him "as a chalk line does a hen." He gathered the fruit of these excursions into the volume which he entitled *Mont-Saint-Michel and Chartres.*

It has always been a difficult book for librarians to classify. Should it be catalogued under travel or history or even fiction? Certainly, it purports to pass in the first category. The narrator claims that he is writing a guidebook for a niece, adoptive or actual, on a long, leisurely summer tourist trip from Brittany to Paris to Chartres. The point of view from which we take the story is the uncle's. He, of course, is Adams himself, a first-class traveler, as selective in his scholarship as he undoubtedly is in his foods and wines, with nothing to interrupt him in a happy season of poking about in Gothic cathedrals. The atmosphere of the golden age of tourism pervades the story. A generation before, and travel was all dusty roads, jolting carriages, and pot-luck inns. A few years later it would be the sharing of treasures with a million seekers and a thousand buses. But just at the turn of the century, with the advent of the automobile, for a brief delectable time, the past belonged to a few happy exquisites, who wrote big illustrated volumes such as Henry James's *Italian Hours* (1909) and Edith Wharton's *A Motor-Flight through France* (1908). The "pigs" whom Adams had seen in Brittany were easily avoided.

The reader of *Mont-Saint-Michel* soon learns that he is in the hands of no ordinary guide. The uncle disclaims any pretensions of being an architect, a historian, or a theologian; he insists on only one virtue, an indispensable one in any honest tourist: he is "seriously interested in putting the feeling back into the dead architecture where it belongs." That he succeeds in this I think no reader will dispute. Whether it is always the appropriate feeling may sometimes be in question. When it is,

Adams is a great historian. When it is not, he is a great romantic.

We start in the eleventh century at Mont-Saint-Michel in Brittany just before the Norman Conquest of England. Adams' architectural plot begins with the Romanesque, the rounded arch, the age of the conquering soldier and militant priest, of the *Chanson de Roland*, an age of simple, serious, silent dignity and tremendous energy. We move through Caen to Paris and at last to Chartres and the year 1200, the time of the Gothic arch and the cult of the Virgin. This Adams sees as the finest and most intense moment of the Christian story. The chapters on the Cathedral of Chartres, on its statuary, its apses, its incomparable glass, are a remarkable lyrical achievement. Adams sees Mary as superior to the Trinity. She is what equity is to law. There is no hope for sinful men in the rigid, logical justice of Christ. He is law, unity, perfection, a closed system. But the Virgin is a woman, loving, capricious, kind, infinitely merciful. She is nature, love, chaos. The cathedral is her palace, and the most beautiful art in history is displayed there to please her. Adams makes us feel at one with the crushed crowd of kneeling twelfth-century worshipers as we lift our eyes after the miracle of the Mass to see, far above the high altar, "high over all the agitation of prayer, the passion of politics, the anguish of suffering, the terrors of sin, only the figure of the Virgin in majesty." But the chapter ends on a dry note. Moving suddenly back to his own day the uncle leaves the Virgin "looking down from a deserted heaven, into an empty church, on a dead faith."

That is the end of the architectural trip, yet the book is only half finished. Adams now traces the influence of the Virgin in literature, in contemporary history, and in theology. He offers translations of some of the versifications of her miracles; he describes the great royal ladies of the period; he conveys the sense of Mary's ambience in the world of court poems and courteous love. The emotion in these chapters begins to approach that of the naive and passionate chroniclers whom he quotes. He sternly warns us that if we do not appreciate the charm of this or that, we may as well give up trying to understand the age. Our guide has become a priest and one of Mary's own. The feeling conveyed is a unique aesthetic effect.

He does not, however, leave us in the days of Mariolatry. The priest now turns professor. In the last chapters he explains how the church was taken away from the Virgin. She was a heretic, in essence, for she denied the authority of God and asserted the greater force of woman. The theologians had to put her back in her place and build a religious philosophy that would stand up to the most unsettling questions of the logicians. In the final chapter on Saint Thomas Aquinas Adams sees him building his theology as men built cathedrals: "Knowing by an enormous experience precisely where the strains were to come, they enlarged their scale to the utmost point of material endurance, lightening the load and distributing the burden until the gutters and gargoyles that seem mere ornament, and the grotesques that seem rude absurdities, all do work either for the arch or for the eye; and every inch of material, up and down, from crypt to vault, from man to God, from the universe to the atom, had its task, giving support where support was needed, or weight where concentration was felt, but always with the condition of showing conspicuously to the eye the great lines which led to unity and the curves which controlled divergence; so that, from the cross on the flèche and the keystone of the vault, down through the ribbed nervures, the columns, the windows, to the foundation of the flying buttresses far beyond the walls one idea controlled every line; and this is as true of Saint Thomas's Church as it is of Amiens Cathedral. The method was the same for both, and the result was an art marked by singular unity, which endured and served its purpose until man changed his attitude toward the universe. . . . Granted a Church, Saint Thomas's Church was the most expressive that man has made, and the great Gothic cathedrals were its most complete expression."

Is it true? Was France like that in the twelfth and thirteenth centuries? It has often been pointed out that Adams' idyllic era of true faith was actually a period of lawless strife and brigandage in which a few ambitious and secular-minded priests raised cathedrals to their own glory. Undoubtedly he oversimplified, exaggerated. His Chartres may be to cathedrals as Moby Dick is to whales. But if the religious spirit that he so brilliantly evokes in his strong sinuous prose did in fact exist, he may, by isolating it from the turmoil in which it was embedded, have come closer to the essence of his era than some more comprehensive historians.

How far Adams has traveled in his experiments with historical method may be measured by contrasting his *Gallatin* with *Mont-Saint-Michel*. The former shows the historian at his most restrained. The documents speak for the author, while in the latter the historian (or guide) propels us despotically by the elbow, allowing us to see only what appeals to his own taste (at times almost his whim), and colors the whole panorama with his violent personal distaste for his own times. But the guide is always entertaining, and the reader, one submits, may know Eleanor of Guienne and Abélard better than, in the earlier works, he knows any member of Jefferson's cabinet.

At this period of Adams' life he was close to political power for the first time. He had always been close enough to observe it, but now he was in a position, if not to exercise it, at least to influence its exercise. John Hay, his most intimate friend, his soul's brother, was Theodore Roosevelt's secretary of state. Might Adams not be a Gray Eminence? He had always maintained that a friend in power was a friend lost, but this cynical observation had to be modified to except the case of Hay, whose gentle, affectionate, and loyal disposition was proof against all strains of high political life. Also, Hay was an ill man who held on to the office which finally killed him only at the promptings of duty. A necessary relaxation was his daily walk with Adams, after which Mrs. Hay would give them tea. If Adams, according to Hay, could "growl and tease" in "hours of ease," he could also be a "ministering angel" in times of anguish. When Hay died, still in office, in the summer of 1905, Adams wrote to his widow: "As for me, it is time to bid good-bye. I am tired. My last hold on the world is lost with him. I can no longer look a month ahead, or be sure of my hand or mind. I have hung on to his activities till now because they were his, but except as his they have no concern for me and I have no more strength for them. . . . He and I began life together. We will stop together."

The exaggeration was characteristic. Adams had another thirteen years to live, and he was already at work on his most famous book. He had planned the *Education* as a companion piece to *Mont-Saint-Michel*. It would present the twentieth century in contrast to the twelfth: the chaos of infinite multiplicity as opposed to Saint Thomas Aquinas' divine order. Adams had been fascinated at the Paris Exposition of 1900 by the Gallery of Machines of the Champ de Mars. This he had visited day after day to watch in entrancement the silent whirring of the great dynamos. He wrote to Hay that they ran as noiselessly and as smoothly as the planets and that he wanted to ask them, with infinite courtesy, where the hell they were going. He saw in them the tremendous, ineluctable force of science in the new century. Surely, it was the very opposite of the warm concept of the overwatching Virgin of Chartres. As his new book came to mind, it may have occurred to him in that very gallery that the narrator who would constitute the most dramatic contrast to the dynamo would be the one who was then watching it: Henry Adams himself.

He may also have been induced to put the book in the form of a memoir (in the third person) by two other factors: first, his dislike of biographies in general, coupled with the fear that he himself might one day be the victim of a hack, and, second, by his enthusiasm for Henry James's life of William Wetmore Story, a complimentary memoir, written at the request of the family, in which the author avoided the embarrassment of facing up to his subject's bad sculpture and poetry by a colorful evocation of his background, including the Boston of his origin. Adams saw much more in this than James had ever intended. He professed to find in the picture of Boston all the ignorance and innocence of a small, closed parochial society that had been blind enough to believe that a Story could sculpt or a Sumner legislate. It gave him the point from which to start his own *Education*.

It is less the story of an education than the story of the purported failure of one. Adams contends that his family background, his schooling, even his experiences in political and diplomatic circles, in no way prepared him for life in the second half of the nineteenth century. When he and his parents returned to the United States from London in 1868, they were as much strangers in their native land, he

claimed, as if they had been Tyrian traders from Gibraltar in the year 1000 B.C. But this, he should in fairness have conceded, was not so much the fault of Harvard or of Boston society, or even of the Adams family, as it was the fault of the raging speed of change in his century. Grant, the new president in 1869, was not, according to Adams, a thinking man, but a simple energy. To achieve worldly success in his era, very little in the way of education was needed. But was worldly success the only kind of success? Because a tycoon had not been educated, was education useless? Adams never convinces us that he would have been willing to scrap the least part of his own maligned education.

Having made his basic point that he was not educated by any of his supposedly educating experiences, Adams proceeds to outline the kind of quasi-education that he received through a series of disillusionments. As a boy he had regarded Senator Charles Sumner as a great statesman and friend; in later years he found him a vain and malicious old peacock. In the early London days he had been convinced that Lord Palmerston was bent on the destruction of the American union and that Gladstone favored the North; later he discovered that just the opposite was true. Friends turned out to be enemies; enemies, friends. Even in the world of art there was no certainty. No expert could tell him whether or not the supposed Raphael sketch that he had bought in London was genuine.

Adams tells the story of each disillusionment entertainingly enough, but in the illusionless world in which we live, we may find his surprise a bit naive. It does not seem to us in the least astonishing that a statesman should say one thing, intend another, and desire a third. Self-interest is so taken for granted that we require our most eminent citizens to sell their stocks before serving in the president's cabinet, and, as for art, we should simply shrug in amusement if it turned out that the roof of the Sistine Chapel had been painted by Boldini.

Finally, in the *Education*, the "uneducated" author, on the threshold of old age, amalgamates his own laws of the sequence of human events with those of the physical sciences to deduce a "dynamic theory" of history that is not taken seriously by either scientists or historians today.

If, then, Adams' claim that he was never educated is simply a paradox for the sake of argument, if his disillusionments strike us as naive, and if his dynamic theory is without validity, wherein lies the greatness of the book? It lies, I submit, in the extraordinarily vivid sense conveyed to the reader of history being formed under his eyes, in the crystallization of the twentieth century out of the simple substance of the eighteenth. I know of no other autobiography (as I shall impenitently insist on calling it) which conveys anything like the same effect. And in no other of his writings does Adams more luminously demonstrate what Henry James called "his rich and ingenious mind, his great resources of contemplation, resignation, speculation."

The first chapter introduces us immediately to the philosophic distinction between unity and multiplicity on which the whole work rests. The ordered world of the Federalist era is exemplified by the Adamses and their spare, dignified house in Quincy with its Stuart portraits, family Bibles, and silver mugs, its mementos of Bunker Hill and air of republican simplicity. Surely, this is unity which must have emanated from a single substance, which must radiate a supreme being's will. And the opulent, plush, crowded world of the Brookses in Boston, on the distaff side, with all its tassels and bric-a-brac, its State Street commercialism,

must be multiplicity. Is it not town against country, the mad many against the wholesome one? But Adams can spin this wheel so it stops where he wants, and he can make us see each world in terms of the other even at the expense of contradicting himself: "The double exterior nature gave life its relative values. Winter and summer, cold and heat, town and country, force and freedom, marked two modes of life and thought, balanced like lobes of the brain. Town was winter confinement, school, rule, discipline; straight, gloomy streets, piled with six feet of snow in the middle; frosts that made the snow sing under wheels or runners; thaws when the streets became dangerous to cross; society of uncles, aunts, and cousins who expected children to behave themselves, and who were not always gratified; above all else, winter represented the desire to escape and go free. Town was restraint, law, unity. Country, only seven miles away, was liberty, diversity, outlawry, the endless delight of mere sense impressions given by nature for nothing, and breathed by boys without knowing it."

Now follows the unforgettable picture of John Quincy Adams taking his grandson to school. Adams, at six, on a visit to Quincy, had refused to go, and his mother, embarrassed to exercise discipline in her father-in-law's house, was giving in to him when suddenly the door to the ex-president's library opened, and the old man came slowly down the stairs. "Putting on his hat, he took the boy's hand without a word and walked with him, paralyzed by awe, up the road to the town." Not till they had traversed almost a mile on the hot morning did the grandfather release his hand. But Adams did not resent this treatment. "With a certain maturity of mind, the child must have recognized that the President, though a tool of tyranny, had done his disreputable work with a certain intelligence. He had shown no temper, no irritation, no personal feeling, and had made no display of force. Above all, he had held his tongue. During their long walk he had said nothing; he had uttered no syllable of revolting cant about the duty of obedience and the wickedness of resistance to law; he had shown no concern in the matter; hardly even a consciousness of the boy's existence. Probably his mind at that moment was actually troubling itself little about his grandson's iniquities, and much about the iniquities of President Polk, but the boy could scarcely at that age feel the whole satisfaction of thinking that President Polk was to be the vicarious victim of his own sins, and he gave his grandfather credit for intelligent silence. For this forbearance he felt instinctive respect. He admitted force as a form of right; he admitted even temper, under protest; but the seeds of a moral education would at that moment have fallen on the stoniest soil in Quincy, which is, as every one knows, the stoniest glacial and tidal drift known in any Puritan land."

This quotation gives the flavor of the book. We travel through the nineteenth century with a guide who is a good deal less detached than he claims, who is almost at times romantic, almost at times passionate. It is a unique fusion of history and memoir. We see the century growing more diverse and chaotic until it becomes terrifying, but always in the foreground, shrugging, gesticulating, chuckling, at times scolding, is the neat, bustling figure of our impatient but illuminating observer. He can stretch his imagination to any limit, but not his tolerance or his personality. He ends where he began, an aristocrat, a gentleman, a bit of a voyeur. The fixed referent of Henry Adams holds the book together even more than the constant pairing off of unity with multiplicity. At times it almost seems as if Adams himself, cool, rational, skeptical, were the one, and observed mankind, moving at a giddy rate of acceleration toward nothingness, the many.

Only in the very end, when the observer disappears into the theorist and the memoir into a theory, does multiplicity at last prevail. One's trouble in reading the *Education* is that as one moves from unity to multiplicity, the story inevitably loses its character and vividness. Most of the memorable passages are from the earlier chapters.

One remembers particularly, after the walk with the grandfather, the desperate snow fight on the Common between the Latin School and the Boston roughs and blackguards, the charm, ignorance, and mindlessness of the handsome Virginians at Harvard, Adams in London exulting over the long-awaited, tragically belated, first victories of the Union armies: "Life never could know more than a single such climax. In that form, education reached its limits. As the first great blows began to fall, one curled up in bed in the silence of night, to listen with incredulous hope. As the huge masses struck, one after another, with the precision of machinery, the opposing mass, the world shivered. Such development of power was unknown. The magnificent resistance and the return shocks heightened the suspense. During the July days Londoners were stupid with unbelief. They were learning from the Yankees how to fight."

Nothing is more notorious about the *Education* than the fact that Marian Adams is never mentioned in it and that the years of her marriage to the author are eliminated. There has been much speculation concerning the reason. An obvious one is that her loss was so terrible that he could not speak or write about her. But this seems inconsistent with his continued lively interest in attractive women and his long romantic friendship with Senator Don Cameron's beautiful wife, Elizabeth. Perhaps he simply could not bear to contemplate the attitude toward their marriage which Marian's suicide appeared to imply. The nearest he comes to speaking of her is when he discusses the statue which Augustus Saint-Gaudens made for him in Rock Creek Cemetery. This, of course, is the famous brooding figure of indeterminate sex which was placed over the inscriptionless grave of Marian Adams and under which Adams himself now lies. Its significance has been much debated, though more in Adams' time than in ours, for enigmatic art was more of a novelty then, but "the peace of God which passeth all understanding" is probably as good an explanation as any.

Adams used to sit by the statue in springtime and listen with acid amusement to the comments of visitors. In a famous and characteristic passage he gave vent to his distaste for the world of his time: "He supposed its meaning to be the one commonplace about it—the oldest idea known to human thought. He knew that if he asked an Asiatic its meaning, not a man, woman, or child from Cairo to Kamtchatka would have needed more than a glance to reply. From the Egyptian Sphinx to the Kamakura Daibuts; from Prometheus to Christ; from Michael Angelo to Shelley, art had wrought on this eternal figure almost as though it had nothing else to say. The interest of the figure was not in its meaning, but in the response of the observer. As Adams sat there, numbers of people came, for the figure seemed to have become a tourist fashion, and all wanted to know its meaning. Most took it for a portrait-statue, and the remnant were vacant-minded in the absence of a personal guide. None felt what would have been a nursery-instinct to a Hindu baby or a Japanese jinricksha-runner. The only exceptions were the clergy, who taught a lesson even deeper. One after another brought companions there, and, apparently fascinated by their own reflection, broke out passionately against the expression they felt in the figure of despair, of atheism, of denial. Like the others, the priest saw only what he brought. Like all the great artists, St. Gaudens held up the mirror and no more. The American layman had lost sight of ideals; the American priest had lost sight of faith. Both were more American than the old, half-witted soldiers who denounced the wasting, on a mere grave, of money which should have been given for drink."

The "education" of Henry Adams might be defined as his own belated conviction that science, for all its achievements, had not resolved the basic mystery of the one and the many, the eternal question of whether the universe is a divine unity or a composite of more than one ultimate substance, a super-sensuous choas that no single theory can encompass. The only thing of which the author of *Mont-Saint-Michel* and the *Education* could feel absolutely sure was that in the twelfth century man had believed in such a unity and that in the twentieth his less fortunate descendant did not. All Adams could now see in the dark and dangerous era that lay ahead was the seemingly unintelligible interplay of forces.

After finishing the *Education* he devoted himself entirely to trying to make that interplay intelligible. He hoped that it might still be possible to derive some rule from these forces by which he could make a projection of the future. Defining force as anything that helps to do work, and identifying man and nature as forces, he was able to turn history, or social evolution, into a gravitational field in which man and nature constantly acted on and modified each other. The declining force of the church in the past few centuries, for example, gave place to the force of a secular society energized by gunpowder and the compass. In the twentieth century man had to reconcile himself to the loss of the concept of unity and follow the movements of the new forces of nature discovered by experiment. This following would open a new phase in history, the phase of the acceleration of mechanical forces. Adams, spending his mornings at his desk playing with magnets, became obsessed with the vision of human society approaching the ultimate forces with a dizzily accelerating speed, like a comet shooting to the sun.

His writings of this period, "The Rule of Phase Applied to History" (1908) and *A Letter to American Teachers of History* (1910), contain postulations of human life and psychical activity more or less corresponding to the physical phases of solids, liquids, and gases. He finally worked out a mathematical formula based on the law of squares by which he predicted a change of phase (following the human phases of "instinct" and "religion") in 1917 and a breakdown in human thought four years later. All of this is beyond the scope of this essay, but in the opinion of many commentators Adams went hopelessly astray in applying the laws of physics to human events so that his theorizing amounts to little more than brilliant and imaginative fantasy.

It was a waste, unhappily, of valuable energy. Adams' obsession with the mystery of the universe deflected him from the true path on which Mrs. Lodge had set him when they toured the Gothic cathedrals of northern France. Who today would give up *Mont-Saint-Michel* for "Rule of Phase"? With old age he gave in more and more to the nervous habit of questioning everything which had so irritated his friend Justice Oliver Wendell Holmes. The latter wrote this description of him to Lewis Einstein, eight years after Adams' death: "He was very keen and a thinker, but seems to me to have allowed himself to be satisfied too easily that there was no instruction for him in the branches in which he dabbled. When I would step in at his house on the way back from Court and found him playing the old Cardinal, he would spend his energy in pointing out that everything was dust and ashes. Of course one did not yield to the disenchantment, but it required so much counter energy in a man tired with his day's work that I didn't call often. And yet meet him casually on the street and often he was a delightful creation."

Mont-Saint-Michel and the *Education* were both printed privately (in 1904 and 1907 respectively) in large, handsome blue-covered editions, one of a hundred and fifty and the other of forty copies, and distributed to friends and a few libraries. Adams did not think the public at large would be interested; he probably thought it was not intellectually ready. He refused to allow an eager young publisher, Ferris Greenslet, from Houghton Mifflin, to tempt him with a contract for the *Education*, but he finally allowed the same firm to bring out an edition of *Mont-Saint-Michel*, which appeared, with an introduction by Ralph Adams Cram, in 1913. One wonders if he would have been altogether pleased had he foreseen the enormous popularity that both books would enjoy in the next half century. Would he have been gratified to find himself a "best seller" in an age whose intellectual taste he despised?

I believe that Adams always misconceived his principal talent. He wanted the recognition of scientists for his theories in a field where he was not equipped to make any serious contribution. The picture of Adams, the descendant of presidents, a kind of early American "Everyman," a survival from the Civil War in the day of the automobile, traveling from one end of the globe to the other in quest of the absolute, pausing before Buddhas and dynamos, has so caught the imagination of the academic community that his biography, which he wrote as well as lived, has become, so to speak, one of his works, and his most fantastic speculations the subjects of serious theses. Yet to me his primary contributions to our literature were aesthetic. He is far closer to Whitman and Melville than to Bancroft or Prescott, and he is not at all close to Einstein.

In history he went as far as could be gone on the basic presumption, later repudiated by himself, that the study of trade, diplomacy, and politics can be made to reveal the sequence of human events. No historian has unraveled with more illuminating clarity the exchange of thought in chancelleries, the effects of embargoes, and the influences of electorates on legislators and administrators. If Adams historical writing leans to the austere, it is because he was determined not to be sidetracked by the quaint, the picturesque, the sensational, or the merely entertaining. Although he denied this from time to time, as when he wrote his publishers that he had given the public a "full dose" of Andrew Jackson because of its "undue interest" in that soldier and statesman, his denial is not convincing, for nobody could think that the portrait of Jackson in the *History* is more than a minimal sketch.

Adams gave up writing American history because he did not believe, after long consideration of what he had done, that he had made any really significant contribution to the long quest for cause and effect. Yet, when he turned from the austerity of historical writing to the looser and more copious field of the novel, he discovered that he did not have the kind of imagination that operated much more easily without limitations of fact. The historian is only too evident in *Democracy* and *Esther*. Both tales are confined to the bare bones of their situations. There is almost no detail of background, and the characters are analyzed only insofar as necessary for us to understand their plotted actions. As in seventeenth-century French fiction, we are confined to essentials. Adams may have considered that in de-

picting his senator as a monster he was allowing himself a riot of indulgence, but Ratcliffe is given the smallest possible crime to justify his classification as villain.

It is interesting in this respect to contrast his mind with that of Henry James, a lifelong friend whose fiction Adams consistently admired. No two minds could have been more different. As Leon Edel has pointed out, Adams always sought a generalization while James sought to particularize. Adams wanted to know the law of the universe, while James was studying the effect of Paris on a single American soul. Yet each man appreciated the other. Adams loved the subtlety of James's characterizations, and James admired the sweep of Adams' reaching. James, however, would not have approved of Adams' experimentation with the novel form. To him the art of fiction was only for the totally dedicated. We know that he read *Democracy* and said of it that, despite the coarseness of its satire, it was so good that it was a pity it was not better, but he did not know that Adams had written it.

Adams did not find the medium of expression best adapted to his talents until he left the world behind and went to the Pacific with John La Farge. In Tahiti he expored the reconciliation of instinct with logic in his history of the island. There was no even seeming sequence of events to be derived from economics or diplomacy. He had to find it in legends and customs inextricably tied up with the emotions which, as a historian in the older sense, he had tried to eliminate from the field of observed phenomena. The experiment was not a success, but it was a rehearsal of what he was next to do when he came to the Gothic cathedrals of France. "Putting the feeling back" in the stones of Chartres was his goal there, and he attained it. He then proceeded to expand this goal, in the *Education*, to putting the feeling back into his own life and into the contemporary history of the United States and wrote one of the monuments of American literature.

It is not to denigrate the earlier work of Adams to say that *Mont-Saint-Michel* and the *Education* represent the finest flowering of his mind. The biographies and the *History* are not only valuable in themselves; they were indispensable preliminaries. But one may regret that Adams did not more fully recognize his own major phase. He was always determined to be valued for something other than his best.

The great bulk of his correspondence, filling three volumes, shows this. Some of the letters, particularly those from the Pacific, are as brilliant and evocative as John La Farge's water colors of the same subject. But through the ones that deal with social and political life the shrill, constantly repeated strain of dramatic and rhetorical pessimism becomes a great bore. One wonders why Adams thought that it would divert his correspondents. And then, too, he seems to take a perverse pleasure in *not* giving descriptions of people and events that one knows he could describe incomparably. Perhaps it was because all his friends knew the same people and events, but to the modern reader it is like reading Saint-Simon with the characterizations removed. If Adams had only had a correspondent on the moon to whom he had had to give an impression of our planet, a niece in space, he might have been the greatest letter writer in American literature.

His last book, *The Life of George Cabot Lodge*, was published in 1911. It was a memoir that he had written about the senator's son, "Bay," a poet who had died prematurely two years before. The memoir had been written at the request of Senator Lodge and given to him to publish or not as he pleased. It is a tactful and charming piece in which the narrative is largely used to string together quotations from the young man's letters. This is not because

Adams was embarrassed by a task that he could not well refuse. He enormously liked Bay Lodge and evidently admired his poetry. But he was by nature too reticent for this kind of eulogy. Perhaps it was just as well. The letters reveal a young man whose talent must have been more in his flaming good looks and enthusiasm than in any originality of imagination or poetic aptitude. Bay Lodge's idealism and aspiration seem to have charmed the aging Adams. They went to the theater together in Paris and discussed ideas for Lodge's plays. They formed together a fanciful political party called the Conservative Christian Anarchists. Lodge was a rebel against Boston society, but he expressed his rebellion largely by appearance, in the manner of some youths today. He wore a huge black hat and a gold watch around his neck and let his hair grow long. At least he was going to *look* like an artist. Perhaps he fascinated Adams because he was so exactly his opposite. Adams always dressed and acted the conservative, but his black frock covered the heart of a poet.

In 1912 Adams reserved passage from New York to Europe on what would have been the second voyage of the *Titanic*. This brought the disaster of her maiden trip very close to him, and he was much affected. No doubt it seemed even more a symbol to him than it did to others of the disastrous acceleration of science of our century. A week later, he was stricken with a slight stroke. Despite his conviction that he would not survive, he recovered full use of his mind and body, but it became necessary for him to have somebody to supervise the details of his housekeeping, and Aileen Tone, a beautiful young woman who was the friend of two of his nieces, undertook the job. She became his secretary, companion, and adopted niece, and remained with him until his death six years later. As a member of the Schola Cantorum she had learned piano arrangements for old

French songs which she used to sing to Adams and his friends. He found in their atonalities a possibility of recapturing the music of the twelfth-century poems that he so loved. In his letters to Miss Tone, during her brief visits away to look after her mother, he made constant references to medieval France, addressing her as "Comtesse Soeur" (as Richard I had addressed his sister) and describing himself as "Robin," the shepherd in a chante-fable. As the end approached, he lived more and more in his chosen century.

The last year was darkened by bad war news. It seemed the long anticipated Götterdämmerung. Adams continued, however, to read, to study, to write letters and see friends. Miss Tone took him for daily drives, read to him, and helped, as he put it, to keep him alive. The end came in the winter of 1918.

His family discovered the manuscript of a curious and beautiful poem in Adams' wallet. It was entitled "Prayer to the Virgin of Chartres" and was published with some of his correspondence in *Letters to a Niece* in 1920. Because of the depth of its mystical feeling, some of Adams' friends, particularly Mrs. Winthrop Chanler, to whom he had shown the poem in his lifetime, thought that he might have been turning toward Roman Catholicism. But if there is religious feeling in the "Prayer," it is heresy even by the most liberal standards of the Church today. The poem very neatly synthesizes Adams' philosophy.

He sees himself as appearing before his "Gracious Lady" to ask her aid, as simple and humble as his counterpart of seven hundred years before, in the year 1200. He identifies himself with Mary's worshipers throughout medieval history; he has prayed before her portal with Abélard and sung the "Ave Maris Stella" with Saint Bernard of Clairvaux. However, for all his devotion, he recognizes that

Mary has always been helpless to help him, even back in the days of her greatness when Chartres was built:

For centuries I brought you all my cares,
    And vexed you with the murmurs of a child;
You heard the tedious burden of my prayers;
    You could not grant them, but at least you
        smiled.

Because Mary is impotent in the affairs of men, Adams, or Everyman, the "English scholar with a Norman name," abandons her to seek the Father, as Christ himself did, when he went about his Father's business. In this there may be a reference to Saint Thomas Aquinas restoring the Trinity to the center of creation and dethroning the Virgin. In looking for the Father Adams only loses the Mother. The Church of Saint Thomas, without the love and laughter of Mary, without the illogic of her abounding grace, is a sterile combination of cold virtue and damnation.

Adams now visualies himself as crossing the Atlantic to the New World with a greedy band of Europeans, intent on the plunder of America. He has turned his back not only on the Virgin, the Mother, but on God the Father, too. In the secular society that man is now creating, there is no room for a deity. If man is to revere anything, it must be himself alone, even if that self is mortal without a soul to survive its body.

And now we are the Father, with our brood,
    Ruling the Infinite, not Three but One;
We made our world and saw that it was good;
    Ourselves we worship, and we have no Son.

But this independence is illusory. Man discovers that there is still a god to worship, not a just god, like the Father, or a loving and merciful one, like the Virgin, but one that is only force, primal force. The meter changes, and the "Prayer to the Virgin" is interrupted by the "Prayer to the Dynamo," the last of the strange orisons that humanity has "wailed."

Whether the primal force is matter or mind, the only thing man knows about it is that it is blind and cannot respond to prayer. Man and force, lords of space, may both be approaching some end or limit at a terrifying rate of acceleration. It remains only for man to wrest the secret from the atom, but here Adams, with a prescience that is more alarming in the 1970's than it may have been in 1920, sees the hollowest of victories. The victor over the atom will have little on which to congratulate himself.

Seize, then, the Atom! rack his joints!
   Tear out of him his secret spring!
Grind him to nothing!—though he points
To us, and his life-blood anoints
   Me—the dead Atom-King!

The poem now reverts to the form of the prayer to the Virgin. Adams, or Everyman, has come again to seek the help of the helpless Mary. He has no further faith in science and has fled modern man who needs the force of solar systems for his grim play. The latter, too, will find the hopelessness that Adams has found. There is nothing left but the Virgin and the barren consolation that she has to offer.

Does he mean the Virgin or his idea of the Virgin? It seems to me that he means a fusion of the last two. Adams seems to be clinging to a faith in his own concept of a historical conception that has no current validity and that must have been only an illusion in the twelfth century. For the Virgin was helpless even then. She did not exist. She was an idea, no more, but such a magnificent idea that she could and can console men who *know* that she was and is only an idea, that, indeed she is now only the memory of one.

In the end he prays to the Virgin to give him her sight, her knowledge, and her feeling. She must have the strength to help him, he argues, because she has had the strength to endure the failure of the very concept of God. It is on this note of ultimate pessimism that the great pessimist leaves us:

Help me to feel! not with my insect sense,—
   With yours that felt all life alive in you;
Infinite heart beating at your expense;
   Infinite passion breathing the breath you
      drew!

Help me to bear! Not my own baby load,
   But yours; who bore the failure of the light,
The strength, the knowledge and the thought
   of God,—
   The futile folly of the Infinite!

Selected Bibliography

WORKS OF HENRY ADAMS

BIOGRAPHIES
The Life of Albert Gallatin. Philadelphia: Lippincott, 1879.
John Randolph. Boston: Houghton Mifflin, 1882.
The Life of George Cabot Lodge. Boston: Houghton Mifflin, 1911.

HISTORY
History of the United States of America during the Administrations of Thomas Jefferson and James Madison. 9 vols. New York: Scribners, 1889–91.
Historical Essays. New York: Scribners, 1891. (Containing "Captain John Smith," "The Bank of England Restriction," "The Declaration of Paris," "The Legal Tender Act," "The New York Gold Conspiracy," "The Session.")
Memoirs of Arii Taimai of Tahiti. Paris: Privately printed, 1901.

Mont-Saint-Michel and Chartres. Boston: Houghton Mifflin, 1913.

The Degradation of the Democratic Dogma. New York: Macmillan, 1919. (Containing "The Rule of Phase Applied to History," *A Letter to American Teachers of History.*)

AUTOBIOGRAPHY

The Education of Henry Adams. Boston: Houghton Mifflin, 1918.

NOVELS

Democracy: An American Novel. (Anonymous.) Leisure Hour Series No. 112. New York: Henry Holt, 1880.

Esther: A Novel. (Pseudonym, Frances Snow Compton.) American Novel Series No. 3. New York: Henry Holt, 1884.

VERSE

Letters to a Niece and Prayer to the Virgin of Chartres. Boston: Houghton Mifflin, 1920.

BOOKS EDITED

Essays in Anglo-Saxon Law. Boston: Little, Brown, 1876.

The Writings of Albert Gallatin. 3 vols. Philadelphia: Lippincott, 1879.

LETTERS

Letters of Henry Adams 1858–1891, edited by Worthington C. Ford. Boston: Houghton Mifflin, 1930.

Letters of Henry Adams 1892–1918, edited by Worthington C. Ford. Boston: Houghton Mifflin, 1938.

Henry Adams and His Friends, edited (with a biographical introduction) by Harold Dean Cater. Boston: Houghton Mifflin, 1947.

CRITICAL AND
BIOGRAPHICAL STUDIES

Adams, James Truslow. *Henry Adams.* New York: Albert and Charles Boni, 1933.

Blackmur, Richard P. "The Novels of Henry Adams," *Sewanee Review,* 51:281-304 (Spring 1943).

Brooks, Van Wyck. *The Confident Years 1885–1915.* New York: Dutton, 1952.

Chanler, Mrs. Winthrop. *Roman Spring.* Boston: Little, Brown, 1936.

Jordy, William H. *Henry Adams, Scientific Historian.* New Haven, Conn.: Yale University Press, 1952.

Levenson, J. C. *The Mind and Art of Henry Adams.* Boston: Houghton Mifflin, 1957.

Samuels, Ernest. *The Young Henry Adams.* Cambridge, Mass.: Harvard University Press, 1948.

————. *Henry Adams: The Middle Years.* Cambridge, Mass.: Harvard University Press, 1958.

————. *Henry Adams: The Major Phase.* Cambridge, Mass.: Harvard University Press, 1964.

Stevenson, Elizabeth. *Henry Adams.* New York: Macmillan, 1955.

—LOUIS AUCHINCLOSS

James Agee

1909-1955

On May 16, 1955, while riding in a taxi-cab on his way to a doctor's office, James Agee died of a heart attack. Two days later, the *New York Times* ran his obituary. With the photograph that appeared next to the headline, the whole took up about three-fourths of a column. It included a brief summary of Agee's career as poet, critic, novelist, reporter, and writer of movie scripts. It mentioned three books: *Permit Me Voyage,* the volume of youthful verse; *Let Us Now Praise Famous Men,* the account of a sojourn among the tenant farmers of Alabama; *The Morning Watch,* a short novel about life at an Episcopal school in the South. It quoted excerpts from one review of each of these books. Those concerning the poetry and the novel were kind. That concerning *Let Us Now Praise Famous Men* described the book as "arrogant, mannered, precious, gross." About two weeks later, in its issue dated May 30, *Time* printed an obituary in its "Milestones" section. It was six lines long.

With no other evidence than these obituaries, one would assume that Agee had achieved no great literary fame. Of course, he died as a comparatively young man and his output had been small. Further, many of his years had been spent in near anonymity as a reporter and editor for *Fortune* and as a critic for *Time.* Still, his signed output, his "own work" as he frequently called it, had been widely reviewed, and Agee had friends and admirers who were certain they could recognize his hand in whatever he wrote however anonymously.

It is true, though, that Agee's greatest fame came posthumously. It began to grow when he was awarded the Pulitzer Prize in 1957 for his novel *A Death in the Family.* It increased during the next three years as his movie reviews were gathered and published in a celebration of the intellectuals' new interest in what they now called "film." In 1960 *Let Us Now Praise Famous Men* was reprinted. Since then, three volumes of Agee's work have been published: one containing his collected poetry, another his collected shorter prose, and a third the letters he wrote to his teacher and friend Father James Harold Flye. The letters, frank and intimate, cast invaluable light on the life and the nature of the man who wrote them. They are certainly among Agee's most important writings.

James Rufus Agee was born on November 27, 1909, in Knoxville, Tennessee. His father, Hugh James Agee, died in 1916. In 1919 his mother took for the summer a cottage near the campus of Saint Andrew's, a grade and high school directed by members of the Order of the Holy Cross, a monastic order of the Episcopal Church. Mrs. Agee eventually decided to stay at Saint Andrew's (which was near enough to Knoxville for frequent visits) so that her children, James Rufus and his sister Emma, might attend the school. Among the teachers was Father Flye. Agee was to find his major literary themes in the death of his father, in the life of the Knoxville family, in the intellectual concerns that he shared with Father Flye, and in the social and religious attitudes of the Saint Andrew's community.

The correspondence with Father Flye started when Agee entered Phillips Exeter Academy shortly before his sixteenth birthday. In October of 1925 he wrote that his literary life had begun. "I have written stuff for the *Monthly*, and I am to get a story and 2 or 3 poems in this month. This will get me into the Lantern Club, I hope. That is one of the big things to be in here. It runs the *Monthly*, and is a literary club." In 1927 he was elected editor of the *Monthly* and president of the Lantern Club. From Exeter he went to Harvard, where he became president of the *Advocate*.

In his letters he gave a running account of his very wide reading, and he was usually careful to steer a middle course in his criticisms. *Elmer Gantry* was "disappointing, although excellent in spots." *Manhattan Transfer* was "an unalleviatedly filthy book . . . [but] full of lovely descriptions." And not only did he read, but he met and corresponded with various established writers. S. Foster Damon even read one of Agee's poems and said "he thought [it] was good"; he gave Agee the names of others to whom he might show his work. Among them was Robert Frost, who "said even better things" about it than had Damon. At Harvard, Agee came under the influence of I. A. Richards, "altogether the most important thing in

that spring [of 1931]." Richards "thinks my poetry good—maybe more than good."

Such judgments on his work no doubt reinforced Agee's wavering determination to become a writer, and he clearly needed whatever moral support he could get. Letters from his years at school and college show him torn and uncertain, enduring periods of sterility caused by failures in attempts obviously too ambitious, wanting above all to become a writer but not knowing what he wanted to write, neglecting his schoolwork in order to write and then deciding he would never be more than a minor poet. At times he was "conscious of a gradual spiritual and ethical atrophy," but in his junior year at Harvard he experienced "the most extraordinary and grand 3 months" of his life, working on the *Advocate* and busy with "courses, reading, my own writing, tutorial reading. . . . Everything going *continuously* at top speed—mind, body and nerves; and with an intensity I've never known before."

Nor was he to escape these changes in mood during his later life. After graduating from Harvard and going to work on *Fortune* he "felt like suicide for weeks . . . and not just fooling with the idea, but feeling seriously on the edge of it." That was August 14, 1932. By August 18, however, he was "a lot better" and working hard.

The publication of his first book did not solve his problems. He wrote to Father Flye: "I am in most possible kinds of pain, mental and spiritual that is. In this pain the book and its contents are a relatively small item, only noticeable in the general unpleasantness because they are tangible. The rest of the trouble is even more inexpressable, and a lot more harm, but revolves chiefly around the simple-sounding problem of how to become what I wish I could when I can't. That, however, is fierce and complicated enough to keep me balancing over suicide as you might lean out over the edge of a high building, as far as you could and keep from falling but with no special or constant desire not to fall." The solution, "the wise answer . . . would be that there is only one coordinator and guide, and that he is come at through self-negation. But: that can mean nothing to me until or unless I learn for myself. . . . There is much to enjoy and more to be glad for than I deserve, and I know it, but they are mostly, by my own difficulty, out of my reach."

Permit Me Voyage was published in 1934, a little more than two years after Agee's graduation from Harvard. The poems in the book vary in quality, perhaps inevitably: the earliest poem was written while Agee was still at Exeter and the latest were composed in the year of publication. The earliest, "Ann Garner," is a longish narrative poem that derives in manner and matter from the work of Robert Frost. The latest show that Agee had worked with increasing interest in and skill in using traditional Elizabethan and Jacobean forms. Nothing in the volume would then or now be considered "modern" or revolutionary. And the entire collection shows a bent toward literature, its sources being in literature rather than in current affairs or in Agee's daily life as journalist and observer.

This is not to say that the poetry is neither personal nor expressive. Indeed, it is very personal. But it voices personality in an abstract and lofty way, in sustained flights high above the mundane. And some of the poems in their lushness of language and in their mannered rhetoric anticipate some of the more tortured parts of *Let Us Now Praise Famous Men*. The abstracted tone rises from the nature of the subject common to the greater number of the poems, a very deep concern for matters of religion and the spiritual life. Robert Fitzgerald, who edited *The Collected Poems of*

James Agee, writes in his introduction that *Permit Me Voyage* evidences a "preparation of spirit."

The "Dedication" of *Permit Me Voyage* appears not at the beginning of the volume but after an opening section composed of "lyrics" and "songs." It is eight pages long, written in a King James kind of prose, and its tone shifts from one of solemn dedication to one of diatribe and finally of prayer. Agee dedicates the book, the poetry, and by implication the poet himself "in much humility to God in the highest in the trust that he despises nothing." He proceeds as if he were trying to list all the influences upon his life, and he succeeds in pointing to what were to be his continuing major literary interests. He dedicates the book to Christ and Van Gogh and Charles Spencer Chaplin, to his "brave father," James Agee, and to "those unremembered who have died in no glory of peace," to "my land and the squatters upon it," and to "Leopold Bloom, and in his mildheartedness to all mankind." He dedicates the book even to those who cause war and who profit from it but he takes pleasure in calling down punishment upon them. May their "loins thaw with a shrieking pain . . . to the sweet entertainment of all men of good will." And he ends with a prayer that God will "make the eyes of our hearts, and the voice of our hearts in speech, honest and lovely within the fences of our nature, and a little clear."

Although Agee never put together for publication another volume of verse, he was to continue writing poetry. *The Collected Poems* makes a volume of 179 pages. Among the poems is "John Carter," a long Byronic satire which the poet worked on for at least four years but never completed. The collection also contains poems that show Agee's abiding assumption that poetry (and prose, for that matter) is essentially music—"Theme with Variations," for example. A number of poems are on religious subjects and one of them combines religion with Agee's Tennessee origins—"Lines Suggested by a Tennessee Song" tells in a mountain-ballad manner of the Annunciation of the Virgin and of the birth of Her Son. Others show a growing concern about "politics and economics"—"Two Songs on the Economy of Abundance," "Period Pieces from the Mid-Thirties," and so forth. And the volume concludes with "Draft Lyrics for *Candide,*" written in 1954. This *Candide* was a comic operetta, with book by Lillian Hellman and score by Leonard Bernstein, for which Agee was called upon to write some lyrics (none of them finally used). In a sequence entitled "Love Poet" the last stanzas read:

> See how Love takes
> Man's true measure:
>
> Man's true hope begins:
> Head to hold us:
> Heart to bring us:
> One, in Love's sane hand.

Agee submitted these lyrics with a note that mentions the "preachiness problem" they raise. He concludes: "To preach seems valid and obligatory."

In his short stories, too, Agee frequently preached. Or, if he did not preach, he tried to put into the stories messages, more or less hidden, about religious and philosophic problems. He did not write many short stories, however. Most of them appeared very early. One of the earliest, printed in the *Advocate* of December 1929, when Agee was a sophomore at Harvard, is called "A Walk before Mass." It is not an easy story, being in part perhaps deliberately murky and obscure. It begins with a Hemingway trick—"He awoke at a little after four, and knew it was upon him again." The next two sentences point to the later Agee addiction to photographic pre-

cision: "It was scarcely daylight, and rain was dropping out of a bare sky. He watched blades of water delicately overlap and riffle down the pane." And a sentence near the end prefigures the later overblown rhetoric: "For a few seconds he stood motionless, arms above his head, flayed eyes fixed on the water."

The story is a trifle melodramatic. We soon learn that the "it" of the first sentence is the man's awareness of his inability to "bear" living with his wife. The only thing that keeps him from bolting is a young son, and we learn that at least once before the man had wished the son "had never been born . . . or were out of the way." On this rainy morning the man tries to pray. "O God, deliver my wife out of her iniquity. . . . Blessed is the fruit of thy womb, Jesus." He gets out of bed and goes to little Jerome, asks him to dress, tells him that they "must go for a walk." Together they go down to the bank of the river, to the place where the man first had wished the death of the boy. He wants to confess this to the boy and then go with him to Confession and Mass. But when he begins to speak, "My dear, my beloved son," he catches the boy up and hurls him into the water. It is then that we see the man's "flayed eyes fixed on the water."

The story presents difficulties. We know that the wife's name is Mary, but we are in some doubt about the nature of her "iniquity." We know that the son's initial is J and we assume that his death will free the man from his bondage to his wife. But remorse *may* hinder him. And we are in the final sentence presented with a number of symbolic difficulties when the man clenches his fists and strikes himself on the temple so hard that he has to lean against an elm.

Trees and temples, indeed. But we do wrong to jest about what is clearly a very serious youthful work and one dealing with problems Agee was to wrestle with all during his life.

If we simplistically reduce the theme of the story to a vague generality—man's fear and awe and wonder in the face of the apparent gratuitousness and the inevitability of death and its effect upon the living—we can argue that the theme of this early story is the same as that of the last one, "A Mother's Tale," and of *A Death in the Family*.

Of these works, "A Mother's Tale" comes closest to failure. It is marked not by the vagueness of "A Walk before Mass" but by a great piling up of very specific detail about a matter that in lesser hands than Agee's could have been utterly incredible and verged upon silliness. The tale is not about a mother but one told by a mother who is a cow. Most of what we learn in the story we learn through the mother's words, addressed to the young calves around her. Agee in the role of omniscient narrator enters the story only briefly at the beginning and the end.

When the story opens, one calf had run up the hill to the cow. " 'Mama!' he cried out, all out of breath. 'What *is* it! What are they *doing*! Where are they *going*!' " The author describes what has caused this curiosity, "an immense drove of cattle" being moved across the plains, dogs yelping at them, men on horseback shouting, but only "tinily audible above a low and awesome sound which seemed to come not from the multitude of hooves but from the center of the world." Then, in answering the further questions of the young, the mother explains that the herd is going "away." The young are interested. "Where are they going?" The mother says she is not sure. The young keep pressing her until she finally admits, "There was one who came back. . . . Or so they say." The young "gathered a little more closely around her, for now she spoke very quietly," and we realize that we are in the midst of a small bovine epic. " 'It was my great-grandmother who told me,' she said.

'She was told it by *her* great-grandmother, who claimed she saw it with her own eyes, though of course I can't vouch for that.' " And the mother launches into her long story of the one who had returned and "told it all in a rush, they say, the last things first and every which way, but as it was finally sorted out and gotten into order by those who heard it and those they told it to, this is more or less what happened."

She describes the crowded cattle cars, the sudden jerks as the train advances and stops again for the loading of another car, the fright among the cattle, the "sudden and terrible scream" of the locomotive, the great speed when the train finally departs, the terror when the train goes around curves, the many stops at which the cattle hope for food and water but are given none, the great noise on the sidings as the cattle train waits for another train to pass. She tells "with a certain pleased vindictiveness" about the meeting with a train "as full of human beings as the car he was in was full of our kind."

From this point the story insists upon that analogy to human experience and even develops an analogy to man's making of myths and religious systems. When the cattle are finally released from the train they are moved to wonder by the beauty of the white fences in the stockyards and to fear by the smells that come from the slaughterhouse. They debate their situation, some thinking that the whole experience is a bad dream and others arguing that after their suffering and pain it is only right they should have earned their way into this new bliss, for they are now eating and drinking well and are among their own kind.

The hero, however, almost forgets this tribal unity or identity when he is being driven up the increasingly narrow corridors leading into the slaughterhouse. He takes pride in being a "creature separate and different from any other" and assumes he is going to some even greater reward when suddenly he looks up and sees on a bridge above him The Man With The Hammer. The hero emerges from unconsciousness hanging by the tendons of his heels while knives slice between his skin and his flesh. With a super-bull effort he tears himself loose from the hooks, charges past the knife-wielding men, breaks out of the slaughterhouse, and starts back to the West.

After an agonizing journey he reaches the ranch and calls the cattle together. He is a terrifying sight; his hooves buckle under him, the mark of the hammer is deep in his forehead, his skin flaps loose to expose his muscles. But when he begins to tell his fellows about Man's ultimate purpose many of them doubt his word and wonder whether anyone in his right mind would suffer so for others, and to still their doubts he permits them to touch and to examine his wounds. Then, as he continues to talk, men come among the cattle and shoot him. The mother says that she doubts the shooting will ever be understood; argument still persists whether it was done to end his suffering or to silence his message.

Now, as at the beginning of the story, we have a long series of questions and answers, mostly having to do with the message The One Who Came Back had brought. At first the mother says that he "*must* have been out of his mind," but finally she divulges what he is reported to have said. "*Each one is himself . . . Not of the herd. . . . Obey nobody. . . . Break down the fences. . . . For if even a few do not hear me, or disbelieve me, we are all betrayed. . . . Let those who can, kill Man. Let those who cannot, avoid him. . . . So long as Man holds dominion over us . . . bear no young.*" And the mother says that far out on the range still live some "very old ones, who have never been taken" and who come together "to talk and just to think . . . about the heroism and

the terror of two sublime Beings, The One Who Came Back, and The Man With the Hammer."

The mother then tries to disarm this legend by saying it is only something "to frighten children with." But in the last few sentences of the story we learn that she has failed to frighten the young one who dreams of the day he shall "charge . . . The Man With The Hammer" and "put Him and His Hammer out of the way forever," and we learn too that she has failed to make the story clear to the youngest, who whispers the question "What's a train?"

The essential Agee ambiguities are here. The mother is right to tell the story, and right to say that it is only a story. The One Who Came Back is right in his heroism and defiance, and The Man With The Hammer is right in his ultimate and final judgment. It is proper to rail and struggle against fate, but fate cannot be avoided. One might even make a parallel here between Oedipus and The One Who Came Back To Be Shot: to try to avoid one's fate is sin. The Man With The Hammer will not be gainsaid.

And here also is what at least one critic has taken to be an essential part of the Agee style, the use of the narrator's eye as a camera that pans back and forth and booms in and out. Such a technique was perhaps inevitable. "A Mother's Tale" was written about the same time as was a television script on the life of Abraham Lincoln, when Agee was nearing the end of a distinguished career as a critic of the movies and a writer of scripts, and two years after he had written in an essay on the work of John Huston that the movie was "the greatest art medium of [the] century." Agee was, in fact, more involved and for a longer time in the movies than in any other form of art. While in his first job at *Fortune* he produced his earliest scripts. During much of the time between 1941 and 1948 he was *Time*'s movie critic, and from 1942 to 1948 he wrote his famous column about the movies for the *Nation.*

Perhaps the first record of this interest in the movies dates from 1930 when Agee wrote for the Harvard *Advocate* a review of *God's Man: A Novel in Wood Cuts* by Lynd Ward, a book that he says "could certainly never have existed, but for the movies." The review is blandly undergraduate in tone. Without argument or evidence it makes easy distinctions between good directors and conventional artists. It labels Murnau's *Sunrise* "one of the best movies ever made." And it argues that although *God's Man* is a "ham narrative" it is "ideally suited to the author's chosen medium," apparently meaning that the artist and his medium are more important than what the artist says, that personality and manner are more important than message.

In Agee's more mature criticism this easy personalism obtrudes from time to time. He was always to put his close attention upon the film under examination, but he was rarely to view it in the light of any formal theory or standard. In his first piece for the *Nation* Agee described himself as an amateur who was "deeply interested in moving pictures, considerably experienced from childhood on in watching them and thinking and talking about them, and totally, or almost totally, without experience or even much second-hand knowledge of how they are made." And he said that "it would be a question entirely of the maturity of my judgment, and not in the least of my professional or amateur standing, whether I were right or wrong" about the pictures he would review.

This "amateur subjectivism" makes him a difficult man to pin down. He often took refuge in adjectives like "false" and "wooden" and "real." And he sometimes came close to fall-

ing into what later became the "camp" trap. About the film version of *To Have and Have Not,* for instance, he wrote that it showed "a kidding appreciation of honky-tonk," was "specious," but that he had a "weakness" for this kind of thing. He could, on the other hand, wax fairly eloquent about these campy things. "The best of [the picture] had for me at least a little of the nostalgia of highballs that taste like rotten mahogany, defective mechanical pianos at implacable fortissimo, or gents-rooms strangled with the fragrance of mentholated raspberries." "Mainly subjective" of course this is, as he was to admit openly in an essay on D. W. Griffith.

Although he was aware of his subjectivism, and perhaps because he was so aware, he wrote many reviews filled with what might be called either hedges and evasions or honest attempts to be unbiased and objective. A picture condemned for being "boyscoutish in its social attitudes" would be praised for having attitudes, condemned for having photography that "goes velvety" but praised for having photography that "earnestly" strives for a "real, not a false, attitude." Perhaps his most readable criticism, therefore, is almost purely descriptive. He explains John Huston's direction by describing the picture or the scene. And one of the high points in his famous nostalgic essay "Comedy's Greatest Era" is a long description of the way in which Buster Keaton and the girl pursue and finally find each other in *The Navigator*; to read it is almost as much fun as to watch the movie.

During his career as critic, Agee saw the Great Depression give way to the New Deal, and World War II followed by the era of Senator Joseph McCarthy. Events shaped the movies of the time, and Agee spoke out both about the movies and about the events. He did not dodge political issues. He doubted that "the politicians of [any] camp" could "supply me, the world in general, or even their closest associates, with the truth. . . . I am immobilized . . . by my conviction that a primary capacity for telling or discovering the truth is possible, today, to few human beings in few types of occupation or allegiance." In the face of these doubts, it may have been naive for Agee to argue that certain films of certain kinds would be instrumental in bringing truth to the people of the United States. Even when he knew that many of the movies produced were either outright propaganda or rank escapism, he continued to express the hope that truthful films would be produced, that they would explain the way things actually were. During the war he saw the United States as suffering "a unique and constantly intensifying schizophrenia. . . . Those Americans who are doing the fighting are doing it in parts of the world which seem irrelevant to them. . . . This chasm widens and deepens daily between our fighting and civilian populations. . . . Their experience of war is unprecedented in immediacy and unanimity. Ours . . . is essentially specialized, lonely, bitter, and sterile; our great majority will emerge from war almost as if it had never taken place." He pleaded therefore that the documentary films from the fighting fronts be released. To his readers he said, "I can only urge you to write your Congressman, if he can read."

But his sense of involvement with his fellow men later led him to almost the opposite view. In 1945 he wrote that he was "beginning to believe that, for all that may be said in favor of our seeing these terrible records of war, we have no business seeing this sort of experience except through our presence and participation. . . . Pornography is invariably degrading to anyone who looks at or reads it. If at an incurable distance from participation, hopelessly incapable of reactions adequate to the event, we watch men killing each other, we may be quite as profoundly degrading ourselves and, in the process, betraying and separating ourselves the farther from those we are trying to identify ourselves with."

Obviously, Agee was during these years developing a deep awareness of social and economic and moral problems. He was so moved by the moral implications of Chaplin's *Monsieur Verdoux* that he devoted three of his *Nation* columns to the picture. In part because Chaplin dealt with a man who murdered women in order to support his crippled wife and his son, *Verdoux* was not generously received by those who thought they knew what Chaplin *should* have done. But Agee wrote that Chaplin's theme was "the greatest and the most appropriate to its time that he has yet undertaken"—"the bare problem of surviving at all in such a world as this. . . . [Verdoux] has made the assumption that most people make, today—one of the chief assumptions on which modern civilization rests. That is, that in order to preserve intact in such a world as this those aspects of the personality which are best and dearest to one, it is necessary to exercise all that is worst in one. . . . When the worst and the best in the personality are . . . segregated, and the worst is . . . utilized in the best, it is inevitably the good which is exploited; the evil, which thinks of itself as faithful slave, is treacherous master; and evil, being active and knowledgeable, grows; and good, rendered motionless and denied knowledge, withers."

That was written in 1947, in June. By December even colder winds were blowing, with Hollywood writers and others being cited for contempt by Congress and even being fired by their employers. "I believe that a democracy which cannot contain all its enemies, of whatever kind or virulence, is finished as a democracy. . . . It seems to me that the mere conception of a vigorous and genuine democracy . . .

depends on a capacity for faith in human beings so strong that on its basis one can dare to assume that goodness and intelligence will generally prevail over stupidity and evil. This is, I would presume, the bravest and noblest faith of which men . . . are capable; but I cannot see that this faith is any longer available. . . . It seems to me that virtually nobody, any more, chooses even to try to honor and trust even himself, or even his best potentialities. Failing that, it is of course impossible to deal honorably or trustworthily with others; and we have harrowing evidence of what a peculiarly infernal mechanism democracy inevitably becomes when it is manipulated by and for people who no longer understand its meaning and purpose."

By 1950 Agee had begun to "preach" and to argue about the camera in moral terms also. In his essay on John Huston he deplored Huston's having become a "camera" man. The camera "should not impose on the story." True, this might be read as a purely aesthetic argument, but what we have seen of the development of Agee's thought indicates that it is more. His argument, of course, was not that the camera should be static or undirected. In fact his very first script, as did his last, contained directions for the camera so precise and so explicit that a director, in shooting the script, could if he desired be simply a taker of direction.

Agee's earliest script, "Notes for a Moving Picture: The House," is not a standard script but rather the description, almost frame by frame, of a completed picture. It anticipates the "modern" film in many ways. It calls for the use of color and black and white in the same frame. It echoes Dada with neon signs that "spell out not real sign-words but semi-intelligible or international names and nouns for suspense and disaster." Its characters appear out of nowhere and sometimes disappear "ten feet in front of the camera." One of them is distinguished by a "swinging penis nose." One woman wears a corsage in the form of an "exhausted phallus" that two pages later turns into the head of a Pekinese dog and finally goes to sleep.

"The House" deals symbolically with the rise of Hitlerism and with a decadent family whose selfishness and egocentricity might be inferred to be among the causes or results of fascism. It ends with the destruction of that family's big house in a great storm of wind and rain, when a group of "very poor children" comes upon the scene and one of the girls finds "a film of drowned lace curtain" and a boy picks up a derby. In the closing shot "only the bride in the curtain, the groom in the derby, remain," apparently heirs to a ruined and devastated civilization.

Agee makes certain that we know just what the camera is doing. "For as long as three minutes the camera is absolutely stationary: then, first with flickerlike flashes and later with a more jabbing and steady rhythm, the basic position-one shot is crosslanced (not in double exposure) with swift intimate detail of childish feet grinding faces of Negroes, Jews; a heel twisting out the lenses of horn-rimmed spectacles; a little hand grabbing at an open book and ripping out leaves (blood springs after); hands (childish) belaboring drums, cymbals." At one point the camera "settles gently to rest in the dark front hallway before an ornate hatrack and looks at itself close and hard in the mirror, beginning very softly to purr (the reduced dry sound of its motor); swings back to center of hall, beneath center of stairwell, and delicately takes flight" to resume its normal function, the observer seeing again not the camera but what the camera sees.

"The House" was never filmed. Nor was Agee's second script, "Man's Fate—A Film Treatment of the Malraux Novel," which was also a described picture rather than a formal shooting script. In this manner too and never filmed was a later satire, "Dedication Day," first published in 1946. Of all the scripts, only "The House" and "Dedication Day" were original compositions. The rest were based on novels, *The African Queen* and *The Night of the Hunter,* on Stephen Crane short stories, "The Bride Comes to Yellow Sky" and "The Blue Hotel," and on the journal of Paul Gauguin, *Noa Noa.*

In all of them, however, Agee paid careful attention to the camera's precisely defined function. But no matter how carefully he outlined the process of filming, he wanted the result to look not like a movie but like reality. (He frequently called for the use of orthochromatic film, for grainy film, for the look of the newsreel.) In the scripts one may see the aesthetic and philosophic dilemma that arose on the one hand from Agee's doubts about the validity or importance of art and on the other hand from his feeling that the artist is better and more important than the ordinary man.

For example, to "Man's Fate" he appended a set of "Notes" in which he explained what he hoped would happen when the director came to manage the chorus of offstage voices called for in the script. "The problem would be to find the right voices—entirely untrained, un-'cultivated' and above all unhistrionic. . . ." He wrote similarly that "various head-groupings, faces, etc., would not be 'composed' and romantic but literalness intensified to become formal out of its own substance." It is as if art were inferior to actuality, and the artist incapable of achieving anything as beautiful as the material he uses. The "untrained" is raised to the level of Keats's "unheard."

In one of the last things he ever wrote, however, the script for *Noa Noa,* he spoke up for the artist, apparently having decided that even though art might be at its best when it looked the least like art it still had to be made by the artist. In writing this script he was himself the most self-conscious of artists. To a portrayal of the funeral of the Maori king he devoted four pages showing brilliant virtuosity and laid out note by note and frame by frame a scripting in which medium shots and long shots and cuts are synchronized with the beating of the drums, sometimes calling for eight shots to a beat and working up to "a series of fluttering shots . . . so similar in frame that, at this fluttering speed, they form a composite."

The central character is Paul Gauguin, standing alone, fighting against civilization and the government, overcoming disease and pain, struggling to his artistic apotheosis despite drug addiction and even blindness. The script opens and closes with scenes in which the artist, if not quite equated with, is at least compared with Jesus Christ. And at one point in the story, one of Gauguin's Tahitian friends says to him, "You give men everything, beyond their just staying alive. You make them know that it is a great wonder to be alive; a great joy; a mystery and fear; an honor." The man who gives man "everything" is the absolutely revolutionary antiestablishment artist, who gives even though he is destroyed by those to whom he gave, and abandoned by his friends.

W. M. Frohock, writing about Agee and "the question of wasted talent," seems to agree with the doctrine of art's sacredness, but he thinks that Agee did not live by the doctrine. "The truth is that with all the different possibilities open, [Agee] did not want to choose one and put the rest aside." This Frohock blames on America, which "invites talent to disperse." He argues that Agee was deficient as an artist (or less significant than he might have been) because he did not make the kind of choice that Paul Gauguin made.

Evidence exists that Agee himself sometimes

feared he had not made the proper choices. It is even possible that he punished himself for his nonmessianic behavior. John Huston says that Agee "held his body in very slight regard altogether, feeding it with whatever was at hand, allowing it to go sleep when there was nothing else for it to do, begrudging it anything beneficial such as medicine when he was sick. On the other hand, he was a chain smoker and a bottle-a-night man. . . . His body destruction was implicit in his make-up."

David Cornel DeJong tells of an evening with Agee. This was in the 1930's, when De-Jong's "income from writing amounted to all of two thousand dollars a year" and when Agee was preparing to go to Alabama on the *Fortune* assignment that resulted eventually in *Let Us Now Praise Famous Men*. It was "an evening of . . . smoke. . . . Somewhere along the way I got a pretty clear idea about the definite figures, money figures, Agee and Evans were to receive from their labors for *Fortune* . . . a sum roughly seven times greater than I was earning annually. The great rue of being made to perpetrate what they were perpetrating eluded me. The envy of others present didn't. After I left and had already reached the street, Jim Agee opened a window and shouted down to me: 'DeJong, don't you dare sell your soul and guts. You have them for free, keep them so.' All things are relative and it isn't even fair to take this Agee text out of context. But wasn't he actually asking me to hold on to my free soul and guts because if I didn't I might be inducing him and others like him to become more mournful? No, I wasn't romantic enough, and I badly lacked a sense of gainful social consciousness. I was such an integral part of it I couldn't afford to step outside of it and look down upon it with anger and remorse."

Some bitterness is evident here and some anger. But clearly DeJong saw a difference between his way of living—by writing when he could write and by publishing when he could publish and in the intervals of financial or creative dryness taking manual-labor jobs—and the Agee way of living and writing. The great Agee difficulty, what DeJong calls rue, lay perhaps in Agee's attempts to use the establishment, or at least to work inside it, while coming to an increasingly acute awareness of its great failings and its essential ungodliness.

Agee described his years on the staff of *Fortune* from two viewpoints. As a student he had written that "nothing gives me more delight than getting hold of . . . a question that I've really read up on and 'writing myself dry' on it." While at *Fortune* it was still true that "no other earthly thing is as important . . . as learning how to write." But at the same time he was living through "three years of exposure to foulness through *Fortune* and the general News" that were to lead him into "cynicism" and almost into communism. As for communism, "there are things about it I despise. But there are things all through the world that look to me bad, and there are many things in that set of ideas which look to me good."

He wrote for *Fortune* articles about the Mohawk Carpet Mills and about TVA. The editor-in-chief "was much impressed" by the TVA article and proposed that Agee learn more about "the business ropes." Agee replied that he would "work as hard and as much as possible." The big thing was to learn to write—about anything. But he was, alas, learning in a world that was coming apart at the seams. The article on the carpet mills was followed in the same issue of the magazine by an article on "Germany's Reichswehr." And Agee wrote a series of captions for a set of Bourke-White photographs from the dust bowl of middle America. He also wrote an article on modern furniture and one on "The U.S. Commercial Orchid," of which he wrote to Father

Flye that "people's reactions to [the flower] have been and are so vile that I hate its very guts along with theirs."

In November of 1935 Agee had saved enough money to get away from *Fortune* for a time. He spent almost six months in Anna Maria, Florida, during which time he was to write, among other things, a remarkable letter to Father Flye. He had learned that "things have to be believed with the body or in other words soul, not just perceived of the mind." He had learned that "I care mainly about just 2 things. . . . They would be (1) getting as near truth and whole truth as is humanly possible . . . and (2) setting this (near-) truth out in the clearest and cleanest possible terms." Standing between him and these ends was "a pretty strong undertone of cold fear or despair." This is the letter that contains the description of his "cynicism" and also the argument about communism.

In June of 1936 Agee was back in New York. *Fortune* assigned him to go to Alabama with the photographer Walker Evans "to do a story on: A sharecropper family (daily & yearly life): and also a study of Farm Economics in the South (impossible for me): and also on the several efforts to help the situation: i.e. Govt. and state work; theories & wishes of Southern liberals. . . ." This assignment he called the "best break I ever had on *Fortune.*" And he felt a "terrific personal responsibility" toward the story, but he had "considerable doubts" of his ability to "bring it off" and "considerable more of *Fortune's* ultimate willingness to use it as it seems (in theory) to me."

Agee moved with Evans into the South, planning on "a month's work," but actually staying for eight weeks. In September he wrote to Father Flye from New York that the trip had been "very hard," but still "one of the best things I've ever had happen to me." At the time of writing this, Agee was at work on putting his material into shape for *Fortune,* but he was finding it very difficult and was afraid that in trying to fit what he had into the *Fortune* formula he was losing his "ability to make it right in my own way." In the end, *Fortune,* under a new editor, decided not to use the material at all.

It was five years before the Alabama story found its way into print. When it appeared, as *Let Us Now Praise Famous Men, Time's* reviewer called it "a distinguished failure." The book is both a piece of reportage and an agonizing self-examination by a Puritan who both despised and was "sized" by Puritanism, a mystic divided against himself and still struggling with problems that had first occupied him in boyhood, who could not believe in psychoanalysis "enough to subject myself to it," and who trusted only "a feeling of God, and love, and in part myself." The book demands, as few other books do, a reading in the light of the writer's own life. Agee, for instance, in October of 1937, made application a second time for a Guggenheim Fellowship, listing almost fifty projects to which he said he would like to devote his energies. Among the projects was something he called "An Alabama Record," which was to be "as exhaustive a reproduction and analysis of personal experience, including the phases and problems of memory and recall and revisitation and the problems of writing and of communication, as I am capable of, with constant bearing on two points: to tell everything possible as accurately as possible: and to invent nothing. It involves as total a suspicion of 'creative' and 'artistic' as of 'reportorial' attitudes and methods, and it is likely therefore to involve the development of some more or less new forms of writing and of observation. . . . One part of the work, in many senses the crucial part, would be a strict comparison of the photographs and the prose as relative liars and relative reproducers of the same matters." The application was rejected, perhaps because its scope and variety and brilliance made the Guggenheim authorities think of a fireworks factory ablaze on a dark and windy night, and perhaps because Agee's obvious desire to see and to report everything led him to describe his "anti-Communist manifesto" first in terms of an "assumption and statement . . . of belief in ideas and basic procedures of Communism" before he moved on to the "anti" part that was to deal with "misconceptions, corruptions, misuses," and all the rest.

Agee was able, however, to obtain a small advance from a publisher. He retired to Frenchtown, New Jersey, to work on what was then called *Three Tenant Families*. It was difficult both financially and spiritually. He could not write as well or as quickly as he wanted. He was troubled by what he called "a form of inverted snobbery . . . an innate and automatic respect and humility toward all who are very poor and toward all the unassuming and non-pompous who are old," and he saw the book as a "piece of spiritual burglary." When it finally appeared in 1941 and Father Flye had written to him about it, Agee responded, "What you write of the book needless to say is good to hear to the point of shaming me—for it is a sinful book at least in all degrees of 'falling short of the mark' and I think in more corrupt ways as well."

The corruption was not quite of a piece with the *Fortune* "foulness." *Fortune*, of course, during the years of Agee's association, had been staffed by men at least some of whom did not believe that business was America's primary business. Because of the biases of these men, and the terror of the times, *Fortune* ran stories about strikers and men on relief alongside articles about "Mr. Rockefeller's $14,000,000 Idyl" at Williamsburg. A "Success Story" bore the subtitle "The Life and Circum-

stances of Mr. Gerald Corkum—Paint Sprayer in the Plymouth Motor Plant [or] How to Own Your Own Home on $1,200 a Year, Which You Are Not Sure of Making." Even families on relief were dealt with in these terms; Steve Hatalla was considered significant by *Fortune* because, although he had "lost his job four years ago" his family of six had lived since then "on $50 a month, or $100 per year per person."

Some of this was "foulness," but the "corruption" was something deeper. In *Let Us Now Praise Famous Men,* Agee explained. In one of the early pages of his book Agee writes: "It seems to me curious, not to say obscene and thoroughly terrifying, that it could occur to an association of human beings drawn together . . . for profit . . . to pry intimately into the lives of an undefended and appallingly damaged group of human beings . . . for the purpose of parading the nakedness, disadvantage and humiliation of these lives before another group of human beings, in the name of science, of 'honest journalism' . . . of humanity, of social fearlessness, for money, and for a reputation for crusading and for unbias . . . and that these people could be capable of meditating this prospect without the slightest doubt of their qualification to do an 'honest' piece of work. . . . It seems curious, further, that the assignment of this work should have fallen to persons having so extremely different a form of respect for the subject, and responsibility toward it, that from the first and inevitably they counted their employers . . . among their most dangerous enemies."

Although that paragraph is aimed primarily at *Fortune*, its editors and owners—part of the Luce empire—a reading of the first section of his book soon shows that Agee was thinking of *Fortune* as a symptom or symbol of a deeper corruption, a more serious problem. His deepest doubts concerned the function of any writer, whether or not he worked for *Fortune,* and the possibility that unhuman feelings of superiority can arise in any man calling himself "writer" or even "reporter." In this book we see Agee worrying about a division in his own soul, a division more tragic than any of the standard accepted divisions between rich and poor, scab and striker.

Of course, large parts of the book show that when Agee and Evans found their assigned tenant farmers they went about their journalistic job with dispatch and precision. In typical Luce-man fashion they catalogued the contents of the rooms in the farmhouses, of the drawers in the chests. They described carefully the clothing of their subjects even to the manner in which overalls wrinkle. They moved furniture in order to get pictures that would effectively show what the tenant family house was like; the bed that is described as "directly opposite this partition door" and standing with "its foot . . . just short of the kitchen door" was moved crossways for an angle shot. Perhaps this proves that the use of photographs and matching texts is practically impossible. For instance, in another section of the report, oilcloth on a kitchen table is described as "worn thin and through at the corners and along the edges of the table and along the ridged edges of boards in the table surface, and in one or two places, where elbows have rested a great deal . . . rubbed through in a wide hole"; the photograph makes the oilcloth look shiny and nearly unworn, only wrinkled a little here and there, with a small hole where it creases at the table's edge.

This part of the job, the prying and the semblance of "unbias," gave Agee the deepest pain and forced him into the gravest self-examination. And his account of this self-examination and his description of his pain make this book something entirely apart from the usual reporter-photographer collaboration in

a piece of journalism. At one point he describes how he catalogues the contents of a house while the occupants are away and then, when he hears them returning, "the innocence of their motions in the rear of the hall," he writes: "I am seated on the front porch with a pencil and an open notebook, and I get up and go toward them. In some bewilderment, they yet love me, and I, how dearly, them; and trust me, despite hurt and mystery, deep beyond making of such a word as trust. It is not going to be easy to look into their eyes."

That he loves them, that he sees great beauty in them and in their lives, leads him to see that these houses "approximate, or at times by chance achieve, an extraordinary 'beauty' " and that "the beauty of a house, inextricably shaped as it is in an economic and human abomination, is at least as important a part of the fact as the abomination itself: but that one is qualified to insist on this only in proportion as one faces . . . the brunt of the meanings, against human beings, of the abomination itself." To write of "economic abomination" would of course offend *Fortune*'s editors, but to Agee this possible offense was of less consequence than his own falling into the "sin" of "feeling in the least apologetic for perceiving the beauty of the houses." He understood the economic causes, was struggling to find his way beyond them, or through them, to the human souls that were afflicted and injured by those causes. He was seeking humanity in inhumanity.

In trying to avoid the sin of feeling apologetic, Agee devotes long pages to an argument about the " 'chance' beauty of 'irrelevances' " and about the intellectual justification for his deep feeling that "the partition wall of the Gudgers' front bedroom *IS* importantly, among other things, a great tragic poem." This leads him of course to something he does not like to admit, that journalism because it exists is as "true" as the wall. Therefore he argues beyond this, that even though "journalism is true in the sense that everything is true," it must be despised for "its own complacent delusion, and its enormous power to poison the public with the same delusion, that it is telling the truth even of what it tells of," and he argues then by analogy that literary "naturalism" is ineffective and sinful unless the writer brings it "level in value at least to music and poetry" and makes certain that his "representation of 'reality' does not sag into, or become one with, naturalism."

This argument is not easy to follow, but we have no doubt that it arises from a love for the people he is writing about. He sees himself as belonging to a world they do not know, a world bent on destroying them. When a group of singers performs for him he is "sick in the knowledge they felt they were here at our demand." When he comes upon a young Negro couple on the road and realizes he has frightened them, he feels that "the least I could have done was to throw myself flat on my face and embrace and kiss their feet." And when he stops himself, describing feelings that recall the early letters about suicide, it is "exactly and as scarcely as you snatch yourself from jumping from a sheer height." He feels "humble, and respectful" and is "careful that I should not so much as set my foot in this clay in a cheapness of attitude, and full of knowledge, I have no right, here, I have no real right, much as I want it, and could never earn it, and should I write of it, must defend it against my kind."

This leads to "the most intense . . . nearly insane . . . frustrations." At times he feels that to show his love for these people he would have to share their lives and experience their sufferings. He wants himself, actually, to be punished. At one time he wishes, in a dirty lunchroom, that the "three hard-built, crazy-eyed boys of eighteen," who looked at him "with immediate and inevitable enmity," would "for their sake and mine" start a fight. At another he has an urgent desire to expose himself, as he feels in his work he is exposing others, and from a bug-ridden bed in a tenant farmer's house he walks out naked into the night. "The instant I was out under the sky, I felt much stronger than before, lawless and lustful to be naked, and at the same time weak. I watched the house and felt like a special sort of burglar; but still more I felt as if I trod water in a sea whose floor was drooped unthinkably deep beneath me, and I was unsafely far from the wall of the ship." Then he goes back to the bugs that they may eat of him. "I don't exactly know why anyone should be 'happy' under these circumstances, but . . . I was: outside the vermin, my senses were taking in nothing but a deep-night unmeditatable consciousness of a world which was newly touched and beautiful to me." And at still another time he watches preparations for breakfast in the Ricketts house. The beauty of the people and of their lives puts him in a sacramental mood and he recalls how as "a child in the innocence of faith" he had got "out of bed . . . to serve at the altar at earliest lonely Mass."

Such an experience is the foundation for *The Morning Watch*, a short novel first published in 1951, ten years after *Let Us Now Praise Famous Men*. The story is simple. It tells of one night in the life of the twelve-year-old Richard whose father had died sometime before and who is now attending an Episcopal school because his mother thinks he needs "to be among other boys." Richard had determined to stay awake during the entire night before Good Friday. But he had fallen asleep and is awakened by a teacher-priest at a quarter of four in the morning to stand his watch before the altar. He performs his religious duties for the first watch and decides to remain in the chapel for a second watch, despite his having been told to come right back to bed. After the second watch, aware that they will be punished anyway, Richard and two of the other boys go swimming in a nearby river and afterward return to the school.

The story is divided into three parts—the awakening, the watches, and the trip to the river and back. The story might be said also to have three major themes: that of the religious struggle in the heart of young Richard; that of his feeling excluded and lonely; that of the growth during the night of his own self-awareness. In the very first paragraph we learn that Richard is disappointed with his religious life, that he has been unable to dedicate himself in the way he thinks he ought. The social theme is also stated early. As the priest comes around to awaken the boys we learn about the discipline in the school and we see a good deal of horseplay like the throwing of shoes and hear a good amount of down-to-earth Tennessee profanity and obscenity. Despite the horseplay, Richard has a feeling "something like the feeling . . . he now seldom and faintly recalled, during the morning just after he learned of his father's death." In the second part of the story, the religious and the social again are intertwined. When Richard arrives at the chapel he finds there two older boys who, "alone among the boys now at the School, might have a Vocation." Their job is to trim and change candles and to "remove and replace the withering flowers" on the altar. Richard feels apart from these boys and also from "the great athlete Willard Rivenburg" who is with them but openly irreligious and who "never even crossed himself at a hard time in a game." Richard understands that he has failed; he is not a religious and he is not the athlete whose stance and carriage he has imitated "whenever he had done anything physically creditable." And he knows that his desire not to fail may very well be motivated only by pride.

During the course of the two watches he follows in his mind the events of Good Friday and imagines that he might crucify himself and then rebuke all of the people, his mother, his friends, his teachers, who would ask him to bring himself down from the cross. But the result is only an increased awareness of his pride, and, at the end, a sense of frustration. Despite his attempts to torture himself, to assume awkward and painful positions so that his knees and back and arms ache, he whispers to himself, "My cup runneth over," and realizes that "what he saw in his mind's eye was a dry chalice, an empty grail." Ambiguously, "*It is finished*, his soul whispered."

In the third section we see Richard asserting himself and starting down toward the river with the boys surprisingly following him. Again, even though he has apparently achieved one of his ambitions, he thinks that his pride in his success should be condemned. Once in the river, the same self-doubts arise. Richard dives to the bottom and tries to hold himself there. He thinks to himself, "Good. That's fine. *For Thee!*" But then the doubts come again. "*No right! Get out!*" At the surface he consoles himself by thinking "*Anyhow I tried*, meaning at once that he had tried to stay down too long as an act of devotion and that he had tried to save himself from the deadliest of sins." He is a resurrected being. "I could have died, he realized almost casually. *Here I am!* his enchanted body sang." One might argue that "Here I am" is a victory of pride over religious subjection. But one suspects that Agee's sympathy is with Richard and that in the endless struggle between pride and submissiveness, between spirit and flesh, we have a sympathetic account of the struggle through which Agee obviously went during his own life.

The Morning Watch is written in a language that is rich to the point of being almost cloying. Still, the musical complexity in the book is of great importance in the development of the story. We are given, for instance, upon Richard's first entering the chapel, a very long description of the decorations on the altar. Crowds of spring flowers "fainting in vases and jars of metal and glass and clay and in drinking glasses and mason jars and in small and large tin cans," together with the burning candles, make "all one wall of dizzying dazzle." Later, the altar boys come in to put out the "shrunken candles" and to remove from among the flowers those that are dying. Petals fall. Smoke lies upon the air. And when the boy opens the door to bear away the wasted candles, "upon the fragrance of fire and wax . . . there stole the purity of water from a spring." In counterpoint to this long description is one equally long that comes after the boys have left the chapel and started for the river. Going into the woods is to Richard like "leaving a hot morning and stepping into a springhouse." He sees "each separate blossom" of dogwood. He observes the colors of all the tree trunks and the "forms and varieties of bark." The coming of spring is heralded by "mild clouds of blossom" in the "stunned woods." Clearly this is related to Richard's coming out of the river after having plumbed the dark depths and looked upon death. In further counterpoint is Richard's thinking about the death of Christ. After coming out of the river, resurrected, Richard happens upon a snake that has "just struggled out of his old skin" and is full of "cold pride in his new magnificence." He draws his friends' attention to the snake, and one of the boys begins to throw the snake about, flipping him with a long stick. When another boy prepares to kill the snake with a stone, Richard arrests his arm only to realize that he has committed another sin against the society of which he wants to be a part. In expiation he kills the snake, not knowing whether it is poisonous, by hammering it with a stone, "putting his bare hand within range of that clever head." He

understands that in his recklessness and brutality he has lost the "contempt" of his friends and could "belong among them if he wanted to." Still, he is not sure that he wants to. He rejects the privilege of carrying the snake back to the school as a sign of his bravery. He reflects upon the fact that the snake will not die before nightfall even though its head is smashed flat. Then, as his friend carries the snake back up the forest path, Richard thinks again of Christ's lingering death—"so hard and so long. It won't be over till sundown." But Richard is "neither surprised nor particularly troubled" when, a few moments later, the boys decide that the snake had best be thrown into the hogpen, where it is gobbled down while "its two portions still tingled in the muck."

The major and third theme of the story grows out of the first two. Out of Richard's grapplings with his spiritual problems and out of his anguished attempts to become a part of a society for which he has only small respect (only he and one other boy in the school like to read, for instance) he comes to realize he can take satisfaction even in alienation and exile. This theme is symbolized first during the walk into the woods when he stops to see the shell of a locust with its "hard claws . . . so clenched into the bark that it was only with great care and gentleness that he was able to detach the shell without destroying it." He does remove it, and after examining it very carefully, "with veneration" places it again "in its grip against the rigid bark." Doing this, "he tried to imagine gripping hard enough that he broke his back wide open and pulled himself out of each leg and arm and finger and toe so cleanly and completely that the exact shape would be left intact." He falls behind the other boys and has to hurry to catch up with them and to prepare himself for the rite of diving into the river. Then, on the way back, the snake killed and rejected, he hurries to the tree where he had left the locust shell and removes it "gently" and puts it into his shirt pocket. In the closing paragraphs of the story we see him at first not troubled about the fate of the snake, then full of "horror and pity" because the snake is still alive, and finally understanding that by now the snake was "beyond really feeling anything." This reminds him of his mother's saying that his father at the time of his death had been so "terribly hurt" that God took him "up to Heaven to be with Him." Richard walks back to the school, "his left hand sustaining, in exquisite protectiveness, the bodiless shell which rested against his heart." In the course of his morning watch Richard has learned a great deal, not necessarily about eternal truths but certainly about himself.

An intense desire to know himself marked Agee's work in the three great pieces of sustained prose that lie at the heart of his achievement. In *Let Us Now Praise Famous Men* Agee describes the process by which he came to a new and deep understanding of himself and his world. In *The Morning Watch* he looked back at himself as at the age of twelve he had come to an earlier appreciation of his own identity and importance. In *A Death in the Family* he looks even farther back and exposes the roots from which that twelve-year-old character had grown. And of the three works perhaps the frankest and most revealing is *A Death in the Family*. The young boy who is the central character in this novel is named Rufus, Agee's middle name, which was the name he used almost exclusively in signing the letters to Father Flye.

Frohock writes that shortly "before he died Agee told a friend that he needed two months to finish *A Death in the Family*." When the book appeared in 1957, it contained a publisher's note which explained that "the only editorial problem involved the placing of sev-

eral scenes outside the time span of the basic story. It was finally decided to print these in italics and to put them after Parts I and II." This, the publisher explained, "obviated the necessity of the editors having to compose any transitional material. The short section *Knoxville: Summer of 1915*, which served as a sort of prologue, has been added. It was not a part of the manuscript which Agee left, but the editors would certainly have urged him to include it in the final draft." Whoever they were, the editors produced a very sophisticated and complex work that runs in two streams, the one italicized and the other not, detailing two times of growth in the young Rufus.

The interweaving of these two streams of narrative is accomplished without the use of "modern" psychological tricks. Agee assumes the position of the narrator who understands and explains both of the stories. The tone is set in the very first sentence: "We are talking now of summer evenings in Knoxville, Tennessee in the time that I lived there so successfully disguised to myself as a child." The careful removal of this disguise is the theme of the novel and subsequently of *The Morning Watch* and *Let Us Now Praise Famous Men*. The three books can be read either in the order of Agee's learning about himself, or in the order of their narrative chronology, as an account of the growth of the young Rufus.

This opening Knoxville section establishes the theme and sets the tone. It is a description of an evening of lawn sprinkling and family communion, a description by a mature and intelligent man who is trying to reconstruct his feelings as a small boy. The sophistication of the man's mind can be seen in his remarks about the noises of the locusts. This "is habitual to summer nights, and is of the great order of noises, like the noises of the sea and of the blood her precocious grandchild, which you realize you are hearing only when you catch yourself listening." But more important than physical things, than the observed life of family and neighbors, is the prayer that these matters cause to arise in the mind of the boy after he has been put to bed: "May God bless my people," all those who "quietly treat me, as one familiar and well-beloved" but who "will not, oh, will not, not now, not ever; but will not ever tell me who I am."

Rufus begins to learn something about this in the first non-italicized pages of the novel itself. Rufus' father, Jay Follett, proposes taking the boy to see a Charlie Chaplin movie, and when the mother objects that Chaplin is "nasty" and "vulgar" the father laughs and Rufus feels that the laughter "enclosed him with his father." Jay and Rufus go to the movie, walk home through the dark, stopping twice on the way, first for the father to have two drinks at a saloon, and then on a quiet hillside. During the course of these simple goings on we learn that Rufus is confused by the apparent differences between his mother and his father, that the father has overcome a strong addiction to liquor, and that although the boy feels "enclosed" with his father he still cannot understand him entirely. In the saloon the father lifts Rufus and rests him on the bar and tells all the laughing men that the boy is very bright. This makes Rufus uncomfortable. He has been told many times that "bragging" is a bad thing. and he feels "the anguish of shame" because "you don't brag about smartness if your son is brave."

The story from this point is very simple. The telephone rings in the night and Jay answers it. His brother Ralph is calling to tell him that their father has had a stroke. Although Ralph is not very lucid, Jay decides, from a simple sense of duty and devotion and responsibility, that he will have to drive out into the hills to the family's old home. Returning the next night, having learned that his father is not at death's door, Jay drives fast along the mountain roads. He is anxious to be home by the time he had said he would. A cotter pin wears loose in the steering mechanism of his car, the car goes into the ditch, and Jay is killed instantly by a brain concussion when his chin strikes the steering wheel. The only visible mark of death is a small cut on the chin and a small bruise on the lower lip. The rest of the story tells how Mary, the wife and mother, learns about Jay's death, tells of the arrangements for the funeral and of the funeral itself, and ends a few hours after the burial.

The sub-narrative in the italicized section is equally simple in outline. Rufus wakes up frightened in the night and calls for his father who comes and sings him to sleep. "I hear my father; I need never fear." Rufus' mother has at other times sung to him also. "I hear my mother; I shall never be lonely, or want for love." Rufus learns about the textures of his parents' clothes, about how their cheeks feel, and about how they smell. He discovers after a time of being "aflame with curiosity" that his mother is pregnant. And he is introduced to the problem of race when he asks the majestic black Victoria about her color and says that she smells good. He endures the teasing of his schoolmates who play upon his innocence and trust and who laugh at him after he sings for them as they have asked him to and who tell him that he must be a nigger because he has a nigger's name. With all his family he goes back into the hills to make a call upon his grandfather's grandmother who is over a hundred years old and who recognizes no one but whose "paper mouth" he kisses when ordered and then when "her deep little eyes giggled for joy" he kisses again "with sudden love." And the last part of this sub-narrative is the story of how Rufus goes, again with many members of the family, on a summer trip by train into the Great Smokies. One night at supper when

Rufus asks for more cheese "Uncle" Ted, a family friend, says, "Whistle to it and it'll jump off the table into your lap." This precipitates what comes very close to being a family quarrel. Rufus' mother rebukes Ted who retreats by saying it was just a joke and that the boy ought to "learn common sense." Mary is not satisfied and continues to argue that Rufus has "*plenty* of common sense. He's a very bright child *indeed*, if you must know. But he's been brought up to *trust* older people when they tell him something." This of course reminds the reader of the argument that Rufus had with himself earlier about being smart and being brave. The episode ends with Mary still angry and with Jay frowning at her and trying to keep her quiet. This sub-narrative deals in small with the large problem that Rufus faces during the course of the main story about his father's death and burial.

As the sub-narrative weaves in and out of and gives a kind of psychological basis for the main narrative, so within the main narrative do we also have a kind of double vision. Much of what we learn we get through the eyes and the mind of Rufus, but we also learn much that Rufus did not think or see. Large chunks of the story are given us by the humane and intelligent narrator who dwells with loving attention upon the relation of Jay and his wife. While Rufus is asleep and after the telephone call comes to break forever the peace of this little family, he describes with great affection how Mary insists upon making breakfast for Jay before he departs, how Jay warms a glass of milk to help Mary go back to sleep after he leaves. He takes almost two pages to describe the noises the automobile makes as it is cranked and starts and moves away down the street, and ends with a kind of E. E. Cummings construction. And finally he tells us how Mary returns to her bed and finds the glass of milk now only tepid, drinks it without pleas-

ure, sees that Jay had drawn the covers up over the bed again but is unaware that he had done it in order to keep the bed warm, for now of course the warmth had all departed.

Rufus and his younger sister are asleep again the next night, when the family gathers after the news has come that Jay is dead. Rufus doesn't hear a long conversation about funeral arrangements, he doesn't hear the family's almost hysterical laughter at a small unintentional joke. And the children are not permitted to attend the funeral itself. But a friend in whose charge they are does permit them to watch the movement of the funeral procession away from the house. Neither does Rufus learn except indirectly about the large conflicts and differences that are described in the main narrative. But the narrator lets the reader see that Mary's father had at first opposed her marriage to Jay, that Mary is devoutly and devotedly religious while her brother and her father are agnostic or nearly atheistic. He also lets us see this difference of opinion against the background of what is really a kind of antagonism between Jay and Mary. The small argument about Charlie Chaplin that opens the novel is paralleled by later small arguments about how much sexual information, for instance, should be given to Rufus. Nor does Rufus understand, except as he had begun to acquire a glimmering understanding in the sub-narrative, the essential split between Mary's and Jay's backgrounds. Mary is intellectual and obviously has some education; she is religious almost to the point of hysterical mysticism; she is quite certain that she knows and can speak to Jay's wandering spirit on the night of his death. Jay, on the other hand, is earthy, has solved that problem of liquor, has at least some liking for the bawdy. He has the manners and habits of the man from the hills and he opposes them to the attitudes of his more urbane wife and her family. Still, and

JAMES AGEE / 45

perhaps this too marks him as the man from the hills, he has an absolute and undeviating respect for and allegiance to each and every one of his wife's prejudices.

These differences are suggested in the first chapter about the movie and the walk home, but are made most clear during Jay's drive out into the hills: Jay loves the darkness and the thought of being out in the town at this early morning hour, and he feels very close to the country people who are sleeping in the marketplace awaiting the dawn and a chance to sell their produce. And they are given their most objective correlative when Jay wakes the ferry man, enjoys the feel of the ferry and of the great force in the river, and on the opposite bank meets a hill man and his wife with their mule who have been waiting for the ferry and who will be late for market and so lose their chance for sales. This hill couple is described in great detail and in love, as are their mule and the straining and heaving that accompanies the movement of the wagon down the bank onto the ferry. On the other hand, it is clear that not everything in the hills is good. Jay's brother Ralph is a weakling and a drunkard, and we are given a very long description of the way *he* reacts to his father's illness and to Jay's death and of his own final awareness that he is the "baby," useless, undependable, being thus exposed as the antithesis of Jay and, for that matter, of Mary.

Agee describes these people and these conflicts with unvarying sympathy and with the kind of human acceptance that led him earlier in *Let Us Now Praise Famous Men* to suggest that rather than writing a book he ought to be offering to his audience the actual objects, the food and the excrement, that were parts of the lives of his three tenant families. And it is toward this kind of understanding that Rufus gropes through the main part of *A Death in the Family*. When Mary tells the children

about the possibility of their grandfather's death, the conversation turns to the problem of good and evil, and in response to the children's questions she says, "We just have to be sure that God knows best. . . . *God— doesn't—believe—in—the—easy—way.* . . . God wants us to *come* to Him, to *find* Him, the best we can." Rufus, of course, is baffled by this. Nor does he comprehend why he should not be permitted to go to school the day after his father's death, why he should not be allowed to go into the streets to tell the passersby that his father is dead. He is puzzled when the priest, come to conduct the funeral service, scolds him and his sister for staring at him. But he feels the presence of death when he rubs his finger around the inside of his father's ashtray and tastes the blackness. And at the end he is confused and hurt by his conversation, after the funeral, with his uncle Andrew.

Andrew takes Rufus for a walk in order to explain what had happened at the burial. Andrew finally says, "If anything makes me believe in God . . . Or life after death . . . It'll be what happened this afternoon." And he explains how as the coffin began to lower into the ground "a perfectly magnificent butterfly" settled on it, "just barely making his wings breathe, like a heart." Then, as the coffin reached the bottom of the grave, the sun came out and the butterfly flew "straight up into the sky, so high I couldn't even see him any more." Rufus is moved by this. "He could see it very clearly, because his uncle saw it so clearly when he told about it." But he also sees very clearly that Andrew is angry because the priest insisted upon being called *Father* Jackson and even more angry because Father Jackson had been unable to read the complete burial service. "They call themselves Christians. Bury a man who's a hundred times the man *he'll* ever be, in his stinking, swishing black petticoats, and a hundred times as good a man too, and 'No, there are certain requests and recommendations I cannot make Almighty God for the repose of this soul, for he never stuck his head under a holy-water tap.' "

Rufus is troubled; Andrew, who had a moment before been speaking with great love, is now speaking with hate. He decides that Andrew hates Mary, but he is also sure that he doesn't *really* hate her. He remembers "how many ways [Andrew] had shown how fond he was of" his mother and his family, and he wishes he could ask his uncle, "Why do you hate Mama?" But he doesn't. And the walk, which completes the pattern begun when Jay and Rufus had walked from the movies, continues. "His uncle did not speak except to say, after a few minutes, 'It's time to go home,' and all the way home they walked in silence."

Whether this novel is considered the capstone of the career or a description of the first steps in a long-continuing search for certainty, it is one of the most important things that Agee wrote. It has been compared on the one hand to the work of the young James Joyce and on the other it has been pointed to as proof that Agee should have devoted himself exclusively to what he always called "his own work" rather than skittering about and fooling with things like the movies and criticism. But, whatever our opinion on this matter might be, it seems clear that Agee did during his life what he wanted to do. As early as 1931 he wrote to Father Flye about his good friends the Saunderses, a family that had befriended him and had a large influence upon his development. Agee wrote, "Inevitably barring one's own family, they're the most beautiful and most happy to know and watch, I'd ever seen. ... Mr. Saunders is something like my grandfather, with the bitterness and unhappiness removed, but with the same calm, beauty and

fortitude. I don't know how brilliant a man he might have been, if he'd grimly fought out one of his talents (music most likely, or painting): at any rate, he evidently decided, when he was quite young, not to try it: rather, to work calmly and hard, but with no egoism, on *all* the things he cared most about—and he's resolved his life into the most complete and genuine happiness." Such, one hopes, was the life of James Agee. He was married three times and had four children. His friends and his letters have described how he struggled against and enjoyed liquor and tobacco, how he neglected to have his teeth repaired, how he wore old suits, how he abused his body rather than took care of it, and how during the last years of his life he suffered many severe and painful heart attacks. And the work produced during this life proves that he must have achieved some "genuine happiness."

When Father Flye arrived at the Agee house after Agee's death he found on the mantle in the living room a letter addressed but never mailed. Among other things it contained a long argument about cruelty to animals and, perhaps related to that, a scheme for a movie about elephants. Agee had closed the letter by writing, "Almost nobody I've described it to likes this idea, except me. It has its weaknesses, but I like it. I hope you do."

Selected Bibliography

WORKS OF
JAMES AGEE

BOOKS
Permit Me Voyage. New Haven, Conn.: Yale University Press, 1934.
Let Us Now Praise Famous Men (with Walker Evans). Boston: Houghton Mifflin, 1941. (Re-

printed, with an essay and additional photographs by Walker Evans, in 1960.)

The Morning Watch. Boston: Houghton Mifflin, 1951.

A Death in the Family. New York: McDowell, Obolensky, 1957.

Agee on Film: Reviews and Comments. New York: McDowell, Obolensky, 1958.

Agee on Film: Five Film Scripts. New York: McDowell, Obolensky, 1960.

Letters of James Agee to Father Flye. New York: Braziller, 1962.

The Collected Poems of James Agee, edited and with an Introduction by Robert Fitzgerald. Boston: Houghton Mifflin, 1968.

The Collected Short Prose of James Agee, edited and with a Memoir by Robert Fitzgerald. Boston: Houghton Mifflin, 1968.

SHORT PROSE

"Sheep and Shuttleworths," *Fortune,* 7:43 (January 1933).

"T.V.A.," *Fortune,* 11:93 (May 1935).

"Europe: Autumn Story," *Time,* 61:24 (October 15, 1945).

"Religion and the Intellectuals," *Partisan Review,* 17:106 (February 1950).

"A Word or Two about the Author," *Esquire,* 60:149 (December 1969).

"Essay," in *A Way of Seeing,* by Helen Levitt. New York: Viking, 1965.

"A Walk before Mass," *Harvard Advocate Centennial Anthology,* edited by Jonathan D. Culler. Cambridge, Mass.: Schenkman, 1966.

"The Silver Sheet," *Harvard Advocate Centennial Anthology,* edited by Jonathan D. Culler. Cambridge, Mass.: Schenkman, 1966.

CRITICAL AND BIOGRAPHICAL STUDIES

Barker, George. "Three Tenant Families," *Nation,* 153:282 (September 27, 1941).

Bluestone, George. *Novels into Film.* Baltimore: Johns Hopkins, 1957.

Breit, Harvey. "Cotton Tenantry," *New Republic,* 105:348 (September 15, 1941).

Croce, Arlene. "Hollywood the Monolith," *Commonweal,* 69:430 (January 23, 1959).

DeJong, David Cornel. "Money and Rue," *Carleton Miscellany,* 6:50 (Winter 1965).

Deutsch, Babette. "The Poet as Social Philosopher," *Survey Graphic,* 24:134 (March 1935).

Evans, Walker. "James Agee in 1936," *Atlantic Monthly,* 206:74 (July 1960). (Reprinted in 1960 edition of *Let Us Now Praise Famous Men*).

Fitzgerald, Robert. Introduction to *The Collected Poems of James Agee.* Boston: Houghton Mifflin, 1968.

————. "A Memoir," in *The Collected Short Prose of James Agee.* Boston: Houghton Mifflin, 1968.

Frohock, W. M. *The Novel of Violence in America.* Dallas: Southern Methodist University Press, 1950.

Gregory, Horace. Review of *Permit Me Voyage, Poetry,* 46:48 (April 1935).

Grossman, James. "Mr. Agee and the *New Yorker,*" *Partisan Review,* 12:112 (Winter 1945).

Holder, Allen. "Encounter in Alabama," *Virginia Quarterly Review,* 42:189 (Spring 1966).

Huston, John. Introduction to *Agee on Film: Five Film Scripts.* New York: McDowell, Obolensky, 1960.

Kazin, Alfred. *On Native Grounds.* New York: Reynal and Hitchcock, 1942.

Larsen, Erling. "Let Us Now Praise Ourselves," *Carleton Miscellany,* 2:86 (Winter 1961).

Macdonald, Dwight. *Against the American Grain.* New York: Random House, 1962.

Ohlin, Peter H. *Agee.* New York: Ivan Obolensky, 1965.

Phelps, Robert. "James Agee," in *The Letters of James Agee to Father Flye.* New York: Braziller, 1962.

Thompson, Ralph. Review of *Let Us Now Praise Famous Men, New York Times,* August 19, 1941, p. 19.

Updike, John. "No Use Talking," *New Republic,* 147:23 (August 13, 1962).

—ERLING LARSEN

Conrad Aiken

1889-1973

*E*ARLY in his work Conrad Aiken wrote:

> There are houses hanging above the stars
> And stars hung under a sea.

These suave, unsettling lines from *Senlin: A Biography* (1918) suggest in miniature much of what was to follow. The world of these verses is no other than the round world on which we live. Man's visual logic, if he tries to extend it very far, is turned upside down by the gravitational logic of the globe. "Can the same be true of all of man's mental life?" Aiken seems to be asking. In that event our thoughts and feelings are subject to fields of force in which fall is flight and flight is fall and high and low are interchangeable. Aiken's work in both verse and prose is concerned with just such circularities and reversibilities, and his success with them is the success of all his best writing.

In the late 1940's the American critic Lionel Trilling, in a troubled appraisal of his favored "liberal imagination," remarked that "the sense of largeness, of cogency, of the transcendance which largeness and cogency can give, the sense of being reached in our secret and primitive minds—this we virtually never get from the writers of the liberal democratic tradition at the present time." There are, however, grounds for considering the best of Ai-

ken's work as having provided some of what Trilling said he could not usually find. That work has now extended over more than half a century and has encompassed haunting poetry, prophetic criticism, varied fiction, and journalism. He has been justly called, by Allen Tate, "one of the few genuine men of letters left."

Conrad Aiken was the first (1889) of three sons born to New England-bred William and Anna Aiken. His surname points to the Scotch blood he shares with his thematic and stylistic ancestor Poe. His birthplace, Savannah, Georgia, was the city in which his Harvard-trained father practiced medicine, and the family lived on one of those pleasant squares whose back alleys provided a playground for boys of the neighborhood, both black and white. When Aiken went to Harvard in the fall of 1907 he joined without being at first aware of it one of the most influential groups of writers and intellectuals in the twentieth century. The classes of 1910-15 matriculated, among others later famous, T. S. Eliot, John Reed, Walter Lippmann, E. E. Cummings, and Robert Benchley.

Since his graduation Aiken has pursued one of the most distinguished careers in his literary generation, capturing and holding from the time of his earliest publications to the present an audience in both England and the United States. Along with this there has been a broad and genial exchange with many of his most luminous contemporaries. Outspoken and often unfashionable in his public statements on literary affairs and reputations, and sometimes waspishly bantering in his conversation on such matters, Aiken has nevertheless been blessed with a gift for friendship with his artistic peers. The public record of this is characterized by cooperation without hint of coterie machinations and controversy unmarked by tones of rancor. The mutual regard of Allen Tate and Conrad Aiken, for example, is some sort of monument to the transcendence by affection of deep differences in temperament and virtually diametrical perceptions of art and politics. Working to please himself, sometimes in New York, sometimes in Sussex or on Cape Cod, more recently in Georgia as well, Aiken has earned most of his living solely by writing and has memorialized his experiences in a remarkable autobiographical work of human and artistic self-analysis, *Ushant: An Essay* (1952).

Ushant, of which more must be said later, touches upon major aspects of Aiken's life and art: the unstinting dedication to poetry; the interest in psychoanalytic doctrine and "musical" form; the self-reversing attachments to the United States and England; the conscious continuance of a family tradition of liberalism and humanism; and the overcoming of tragedy in his early life. The third-person protagonist of *Ushant,* "D.," a reference to the character Demarest in the novel *Blue Voyage,* is a persona of Aiken himself, and if there is such a thing as an interior-monologue autobiography of a literary man, perhaps *Ushant* is it. Indirectly candid in factual reference, it provides a Proustian regress toward the tragedy of Aiken's eleventh year (when both his parents died by the hand of the father, and he,

"finding them dead, found himself possessed of them forever"). A high point is the scene in which the New England grandmother who has taken an interest in the orphaned D. gradually and tactfully brings his suicide father into the conversation, thus restoring the father to a place of conscious respect—and turns over the writings of the tragic man to the child so that the child can reach for identification with what was best in the father's life and work. Since it is these more profoundly personal aspects of *Ushant* that will monopolize our attention later on in this essay, it is necessary to notice here that the work has an important public interest as a chapter in modern literary history. Providing an informal commentary on literary men Aiken has known, it presents them in half disguises: Ezra Pound, for example, is "Rabbi Ben Ezra"; Eliot, the "Tsetse."

The global generality of the fragment quoted above from one of Aiken's earliest reputation-making poems might hint even to a reader who has not yet read *Senlin* that he gives himself freely to rhapsodizing forms. The play with incongruities, especially in the complex concreteness with which the poet evokes a relativized viewpoint, seems to be a prevision of lines by Dylan Thomas:

And I am dumb to tell a weather's wind
How time has ticked a heaven around the
    stars . . .

Consider the masterly larger unit of verse containing the lines quoted at the opening of this essay:

It is morning, Senlin says, and in the morning
When the light drips through the shutters like
    the dew,
I arise, I face the sunrise,
And do the things my fathers learned to do.

Stars in the purple dusk above the rooftops
Pale in a saffron mist and seem to die,
And I myself on a swiftly tilting planet
Stand before a glass and tie my tie.

Vine leaves tap my window,
Dew-drops sing to the garden stones,
The robin chirps in the chinaberry tree
Repeating three clear tones.

It is morning. I stand by the mirror
And tie my tie once more.
While waves far off in a pale rose twilight
Crash on a coral shore.
I stand by a mirror and comb my hair:
How small and white my face!—
The green earth tilts through a sphere of air
And bathes in a flame of space.

There are houses hanging above the stars
And stars hung under a sea.
And a sun far off in a shell of silence
Dapples my walls for me.

(It should be noted that Aiken has sometimes made changes in his poems before reprinting them in selected or collected editions. The quotations included here are taken from the latest editions, for the most part from *Collected Poems* of 1953.)

Surely the young Aiken richly let himself go in *The Jig of Forslin* (1916), *The Charnel Rose* (1918), *Senlin: A Biography* (1918), and the other pieces—*The House of Dust* (1920) and *The Pilgrimage of Festus* (1923)—that make up *The Divine Pilgrim*, the long sequence of "symphonies" published between 1916 and 1925, when he was in his late twenties and early thirties. The literary influences are unconcealed. Swinburne's tone had already been present in *Nocturne of Remembered Spring* (1917): "After long days of dust we lie and listen / To the silverly woven harmonies of rain . . ." *The Divine Pilgrim* shows Aiken as the rapt reader of others who had preceded

him. Poe: "For seven days my quill I dipt / To wreathe my filigrees of script . . ." Browning: "Here's my knife—between my fingers I press it, / And into the panic heart . . . / Do you still hear the music? Do you still see me?" Wilde: "Death, among violins and paper roses . . ." As R. P. Blackmur says, Aiken's readiness to continue to call upon the conventional poetic vocabulary that he relied upon in this early work has remained with him all his life. At the same time the inventive advances he achieved in these pieces constitute some of his strongest claims to attention. *Forslin,* says Allen Tate, is the first poem in the English language in which a symphonic texture is employed to develop a philosophical theme. In this blend of the lyric and the narrative the lyric predominates and is centered on the feeling and thought of a single character.

These poems, besides showing how closely Aiken along with other *littérateurs* of his generation at Harvard studied Arthur Symons' *The Symbolist Movement in Literature* (1899), tell us much about what kind of an artist Aiken wished to be. A first clue is his interest in drawing upon music for suggestions about the forms of poems, an interest centered upon the capacity of music for presenting simultaneously several different levels of sound and meaning. This perhaps Wagnerian preoccupation with a thematic plurality of voices is directly connected, in turn, with Aiken's leading intuition of human character and circumstance. Influenced by the early psychoanalytic movement, Aiken sees man as a creature existing in both awareness and unawareness. The voices from the unawareness deserve to be rendered. But how? Aiken's solution is one that has now become conventional but was not always so. He makes these voices carry a symbolic content in which traditional and psychoanalytic motifs are blended. The manner is also what the composer might call "chromatic" and "impressionistic." It is worth noticing that although Aiken himself has made not a few references to the French Symbolists, he attached himself to them far less programmatically than some other American poets of his generation and his own style is that of impressionism—impressionism strongly tinged with that still older school that the French called Parnassian. Such predilections led him to produce poems whose strength lies in their brilliant and fulsome rendering of typical human temperaments. Let us consider his own analysis of his method.

In *Poetry Magazine,* in 1919, Aiken remarked that the arrangement of the four parts of *The Jig of Forslin* was such that part IV gains, in its position, a certain effect it could gain at no other position in the sequence. Each emotional tone in the poem is employed like a musical tonality. "Not content to present emotions or things or sensations for their own sakes . . . this method takes only the most delicately evocative aspects of them, makes of them a keyboard, and plays upon them a music of which the chief characteristic is its elusiveness, its fleetingness, and its richness in the shimmering overtones of hint and suggestion." This idea of impressionistic musicality in poetry follows suggestions popularized by, among others, a writer who was a noticeable influence upon Aiken and his generation, Walter Pater. In his essay on "The School of Giorgione" Pater lent his elegant pen to the notion that any art (painting, for example) could learn from another art (music, for example, or literature) employing another sensuous medium and (somewhat contradictorily) that "all art constantly aspires to the condition of music."

Aiken himself sometimes used the word "chorus" in connection with his method. A character in the early poems is conceived as generating a wide-range band of voices from various levels and temporal sectors of the psyche; and the themes carried by these voices are elaborated in a sequence of variations somewhat in the way the composer undertakes the expansion and development of themes in a symphony or, perhaps more properly, a tone poem. While it is certainly true that Aiken's poems do have parts in which the mingled voices of many selves of the principal character seem to vocalize together in the same lines at the same time, the word "chorus" is not entirely satisfactory. The reason is that the various aspects of a character also are frequently rendered in a manner quite different from that of the chorus: it is a regular occurrence for them to appear in separate successive solos. The method is operatic or oratoric rather than choral, and might as well be called so.

Although Aiken referred to a "chorus" in the sense of its use as a musical rather than a dramaturgical device, there is a sense in which he could just as properly have emphasized the latter meaning. A trait of the chorus in an early Greek play was that it took a standpoint distinct from that of both the protagonist and the audience, serving as a narrative and meditative "we" disjoined from both. One of the expository advantages of this was that the chorus could be made to share information and feelings with the audience that were not made available to the protagonists, thereby generating one type of dramatic irony. There is a sense in which the voices emanating from the unawareness of the agent in a poem by Aiken serve similar purposes. The principal resemblance lies in the fact that these voices make available to the reader a certain knowledge of the agent not possessed by the agent himself. This involves the use of the now-familiar literary device best known as "interior monologue." Aiken early employed it in his poems to obtain a contrast between a character's conscious and unconscious motivations, thus effecting what we might term "psychoanalytic irony." It is not clear that Aiken himself was entirely aware of what he had hold of here. His comments on his own work do not fully identify the originality of a form he had discovered partly as a result of his interest in psychology.

Senlin is crucial to our analysis so far. A dreamlike poem, like a dream, represents the same relatively simple thing over and over again, whatever the disguises and semi-disclosures. What does *Senlin* represent and render? A poem influenced by Eliot's "The Love Song of J. Alfred Prufrock," it is concerned with a raw young man forced by his age and his character into a state of intense self-consciousness. On one level he is expressing and struggling with self-pity and a sense of isolation. On another he is expressing and struggling with solipsism. On both levels he is confronted with the problem of the relativity of perceptions and judgments. One of the results and signs of Senlin's crisis is the confusion between the stages of his life. While still not aged, he acts old, thus missing his youth. This habit of acting while young and raw as if he were older and more jaded is both the cause and the effect of his incomplete identity. A particular form taken by this crisis is the fear that he may be hurt by women or that this expectation will itself eventuate in his hurting them. When all sections of the poem are taken into account the basic statement of *Senlin* is this:

A young man keeps walking and climbing, with a feeling that he has been abandoned by the goal that is at the end of the road and the powers that are at the top of the stairs. He is returned incessantly to a situation in which he digs up a young woman.

This can be condensed:

A young man digs up a young woman.

This sentence states the whole dramatic meaning of *Senlin*: the ascent to the transcending other of a fatherly greater maleness, greater age, and wisdom is unsuccessful or at least difficult. Attempts to ascend to this are always accompanied or followed by rediscoveries of the dead traces of the non-male in the self. Senlin is too much like a woman to be a woman's lover. Yet the non-male in Senlin is not alive and active; it is, in every sense except recollection of it, dead.

When Aiken, in the early and middle 1920s, directed much of his attention toward fiction he marked, one might say, not only the beginning of a new kind of productivity but the end of a stage of the old. If Aiken had never collected more of his poems than those represented in the dozen or so that culminated in *Senlin,* he would have been assured of a place in twentieth-century American writing. In the period from the early twenties to 1940, however, Aiken completed not only new poems in new forms but also all of his novels, most of his short stories, and a fair share of his prose and criticism. The move into fiction had its adventurous elements, as we shall see when we examine the work itself, but it may also have had its elements of necessity. Aiken was the father of three children by his first marriage (1912) and he remarried twice after that, once in 1930 and again in 1937. His own small patrimony was probably not adequate for these financial responsibilities and what he could earn by his pen was therefore crucial to him. Although Aiken never became a big seller in fiction, his success in the field was not, to his gratification, solely an artistic one. Its artistic merits, however, along with its developmental place in his lifework, invite our attention now.

Few fictional works by a modern poet are as well known as Aiken's "Silent Snow, Secret Snow." A tapping into the stream of consciousness of a boy who appears to be relapsing into isolation and death wish, it is one of the best of the short stories in which Aiken has demonstrated his skill. Admiring Chekhov, James, and Andreyev, Aiken has worked mostly in the twentieth-century form of psychological fiction that we associate with Edouard Dujardin, Joyce, Dorothy Richardson, and Virginia Woolf. We should take special notice of Aiken's ability to repossess from the writers of fiction some of the tools they borrowed so readily from poets. The question of the relation between the poetry and the prose of Aiken might seem to be satisfied by referring to the blend of the symbolic and the psychological that we find in both. This reminiscence of the ambidextrous Poe is reinforced not by any interest of Aiken's in shrewd plotting but by his general attraction to the macabre and by the pleasure he sometimes takes in poetic texture as a resource of prose. Yet while most of Aiken's short stories offer complexity of character rather than plot, they are not eventless. They ground themselves in those slowly gathering expectations that create suspense, provide the basis for dramatic reversal in the condition of the characters, and qualify the pieces as stories rather than portraits. The same is true of his novels.

Blue Voyage, earliest of his five novels, appeared in 1927. Returning to his ship's bunk each night, William Demarest re-creates not only the events of the day and his expectations of the day to follow but also his deeper past. Does he possess a true identity—or rather, will the interactions of the voyage reveal one to him? This question is seen as pivoting on his chase of Cynthia, the girl of his past who has turned up as a passenger of the very ship on which he has sought to reach her in Europe. Aiken establishes a nice contrast between the sophistication ascribed to Demarest by his co-passengers and the abdominal Jell-O that is Demarest's other self, though he is probably dilatory in exploiting the comic possibilities in his portrait of a shipboard prig. As Demarest (which could be read as the Latin-like *de mare*

est, "from the sea he is") comes toward the end of his voyage, having lost Cynthia even before the voyage began, we have been treated to episodes vitalized by an action whose course has described a circle.

Great Circle (1933) employs a massive flashback to explore two events separated in time by a generation. The later event is the protagonist's stealthy discovery of his wife's infidelity; the earlier is his parallel loss of childhood innocence when he is the witness of a tragic affair between his mother and his uncle. A sort of Harvard Square *Hamlet, Great Circle* is not so much a novel as a morality play in print, vexed by problems of viewpoint, tone, and central action. The binary pattern, in which each of the crises, past and present, is at once more important and less important than the other, is true enough to the temporal relativism of the twentieth century. But Aiken's symbolic loadings, such as the hero's loss of one eye—emblem perhaps of his Oedipal situation—seem arbitrary and distracting. The best section of the book is one in which the hero's Harvard classmate, who has alcoholically graduated into the status of a completely self-understanding and clairvoyant bum, provides an amateur psychoanalysis of the hero in exchange for an evening of drinks.

King Coffin (1935) is a descendant of Hogg, Poe, Stevenson, and Dostoevski and a predecessor of Camus's *The Stranger.* Jasper Ammen, the hero, has become obsessed with his observations of a stranger, Mr. Jones. Jones is unaware that Ammen has not only voyeuristically selected him for study but also elected him as the future victim of a gratuitous homicide. Told in roughly chronological sequence from a viewpoint somewhere "just back of" third-person protagonist Ammen, it shows us how Ammen's plan to commit the Raskolnikovian murder of the stranger, Jones, is reversed by the mournful birth of a stillborn baby to Mrs.

Jones and its seemingly perfunctory burial. The death of the baby, by linking Jones with the banality of human life in general, disqualifies Jones as the pure and single stranger-victim of the crime. After the infant's burial, Ammen's desire to kill Jones evaporates, leaving Ammen himself as the only possible victim for the supreme jape in "Nietzschean" aggression that he has been cryptically telling his friends about.

In view of this construction, it might be thought that Aiken would foreshadow without revealing the unexpected appearance in Jones's life of a baby; but both the reader and Jasper Ammen become too early aware that a baby is to be born to the Joneses and this works against the force of the denouement. The convergence apparently intended between the simpler plot (Ammen's exposure of his vague plans to his confidants; his challenge to them to reveal those plans; and their alerting of his father) and the more complex plot (the transformation of Jones into a family- and life-connected person who cannot be defined as a pure ritual victim) does not fully work. Yet there are passages of remarkable success in the book. The experiments of Ammen with the air paths of the smoke of his cigarette signal to us, perhaps before Ammen himself knows it, that he is verging toward suicide by self-asphyxiation. Equally moving are the sections in which Aiken renders the succession of psychosomatic calms and storms through which Ammen passes on his way to final self-isolation and self-destruction.

These productions, along with *A Heart for the Gods of Mexico* (1939), with its quest motif, and the Cape Cod comedy *Conversation* (1940), with its portraiture of children, show that Aiken is the many-gifted literary man who turns with fascination, confidence, and professional energy toward current forms of fic-

tion, and they demonstrate that he can work with them quite as well as many practitioners and better than most. (His one attempt to write a play, *Mr. Arcularis,* by turning a short story into a script, was not, however, a success.) He offers us no large-scale "Conrad Aiken World" of narrative prose but rather a winding "Post Road" through eastern American urban and suburban social scenes, passing through self-conscious counties connected with those of C. Brockden Brown in the past, Robert Coates among his contemporaries, and John Updike in the present. It is quite understandable that Aiken was one of the very first (in 1927, in a review in the *New York Post*) to recognize and raise significant questions about the genius of Faulkner.

Discussion of Aiken's fiction leads us naturally in the direction of his other major experiment in prose narrative, *Ushant.* Readers of this work meet in it the two principal masks of the artist-hero D. created by Aiken. The first is seeking the gratification he thinks he will be content with. The second is a gloomier bemoaning of the loss of the gratification or its excessive price. The title itself indicates not only this polarity but others as well. Ushant is a dragon-shaped rock on the French side of the English Channel's opening into the Atlantic. Its associations include both departure and landfall, the idea of a westward limit to inquiry but also the notion of a taking-off place from Europe. This title was plainly offered in the expectation that it would be received as a Joycean transliteration of "You shan't" and as a metaphor both for the Ten Commandments and the superego. The work strives to render, by the expansion of a single state of the consciousness of D. (a moment in a streamer bunk, late in his life), the totality of D.'s struggle with the world and himself. The forward movement in time is left to be reconstructed by the reader from nonchronological recollections concerning three conscious goals of the writer's life: literary excellence, women's favors, and self-understanding.

This anthology of formative scenes in D.'s life is rendered with less clinical self-analysis than one might have tolerated and this has the advantage of leaving it up to the reader to complete the connections where he himself thinks they make sense. There is a chilling moment when D.'s mother comes to tuck him in as a child of seven or eight and asks him if, when he grows up, he will "protect her." This scene may point forward to D.'s family tragedy—and more than that; it may even foreshadow the episodes in the life of D. when his pursuit of women can be interpreted as a response to exorbitant demands made upon him as a child. A burden of comic complaint running through the book is that the searcher for art and love cannot attain both.

How are the disclosures of *Ushant* to be taken? If psychology is wrong or irrelevant about such lives as Aiken's or if Aiken is wrong or irrelevant about how it applies to them, the retrospection of *Ushant* produces not an autobiography but, as Jay Martin suggests, an art work half revealing and half veiling the life of an author—D.—*Ushant*'s author. On the other hand, if psychology is right and relevant about such lives as Aiken's and if Aiken is right and relevant about how it applies to them, the work has a kind of biographical weight over and beyond the artfulness of its portraiture. It seems appropriate here to assume that Aiken himself understood that *Ushant*'s readers would be pulled in the direction of both interpretations. Therefore, even if the reader inclines toward enjoying *Ushant* more as a literary artifact than as a biographical record he is compelled to have considered

the latter dimension as a built-in aspect of the former. *Ushant,* it is clear, obliges us to take a much closer look at Aiken's relation to psychological teachings.

Aiken's first acquaintance with psychoanalytic thought was made while he was still an undergraduate at Harvard, around 1909, just about the time when Freud delivered to Americans his now-famous lectures at Clark University. From almost the beginning Aiken was regarded as an accomplished hanger-on of the movement, especially in the conversational games of "Latent Motive" and "Dream Analysis" as they were then practiced by devotees upon each other. As a consequence of Freud's admiration for Aiken's novel *Great Circle,* there was an opportunity for Aiken to be himself analyzed by Freud in Europe, with a friend offering the necessary financial aid. Aiken decided not to undertake the experiment. Years later, in *Ushant,* he wondered whether this might not have been a mistake. More or less characteristically, he could not make up his mind about the foregoing opportunity. There is no doubt, however, that the fifth *Divine Pilgrim* "symphony," *The Pilgrimage of Festus,* has qualities that permit us to view Aiken as philosophical expositor as well as artistic exploiter of psychoanalytic views.

Aiken describes *Festus* as a study in "epistemology," and so it is. According to Freud, the cognitions of man are reshaped and distorted, as in a warped lens, by wishes that are the father to the thought. Festus, the hero, who is a kind of Faustus as well as a *Festung* (or fortress) and *festive,* is seen constructing a world out of his own "projections." Extending this theme to its limit, Aiken portrays Festus as a "paranoid" giving free rein in his fantasy and his actions to a sadistic vein. The whole poem is an exploration of the idea that knowledge is obtained when a Subject fully imposes itself upon an Object—the perception that Freud expressed by arguing that a surgeon's therapeutic violation of the body can be considered as the sublimation of an impulse originally cruel. Knowledge begins in hurting as well as wishing and willing and searching; and we had better recognize that systems of knowledge, being systematic, are also sadistic. As a remapping of the Faust legend, *Festus* implies the recognition of and recoil from the fact that scientific experiment sometimes is driven to contaminate its own object of research even to the point where, as in biology, it kills its specimens and thus denatures the nature it aims to study. Moreover Festus himself is, in effect, his own victim.

On the basis of what has been said so far, what can be suggested about the role of psychological theories in Aiken's life and in Aiken's work? To begin, some generalizations on the biography whose tragedy and triumph were sketched above:

First, Aiken's life story is quite unlike that of many of his artistic contemporaries who were also interested in Freud. The aberrations that in their families may have lain under the surface were in Aiken's family the conditions for a tragedy that was acted out to its end. Aiken, we can imagine, was drawn toward a general psychiatric interest in his own past more forcefully than most of his artistic contemporaries.

Second, his general psychiatric interest in his own past was stimulated by his knowledge of certain factors in his background, namely hereditary and organic ones, which happen to be, by definition, precisely the sort from which Freud withdrew his interest in the course of developing his nonsomatic theory of mental disorder. We are told in *Ushant,* for example, that Aiken's mother and father were cousins, and there are remarks in the work suggesting that Aiken was aware that he may have inherited a strain of petit mal, the milder form of epileptic seizure.

Third, Aiken's active response to the threatening disorders of the period of his latency had probably already brought him to a certain state of mental health before he ever heard of Freud.

Fourth, the "Oedipal conflict" in Aiken's life was presumably left uncompleted in Freud's terms because of his father's self-removal from the family scene while Aiken was between eleven and twelve. The same act that deprived the child of the conflict also deprived him of his mother, the conflict's prize.

It is Aiken himself, in *Ushant,* who provides the data of these four speculations. In this situation it would be irresponsible for us to follow certain valuable self-denying ordinances of modern criticism. What is required is precisely what these ordinances forbid: the pursuit of clinical themes in the work and the linkage of these themes with the makeup of the writer. Given the four biographical conditions of Aiken's relationship to psychological doctrines, it can be suggested that one would not expect to find in Aiken's work a fully developed concern with Freud's Oedipus theme. Nor do we. It also follows that a generally psychiatric, as opposed to specifically psychoanalytic, concern for his own past would be at work in Aiken. The psychoanalytic interest would arise only when he had to consider the consequences for his own identity of having been deprived of the Oedipal conflict. This is noticeable also. Although there are hints of the Oedipal theme in *Senlin* (II, 8), it is broached more overtly in *Blue Voyage,* when Aiken's hero relocates his girl Cynthia only to learn that she is already engaged to be married. Read "mother" for "Cynthia" and the Oedipal rivalry theme is complete. It also turns up in *Mr. Arcularis,* in which an uncle is substituted for a father as the mother's lover. It appears somewhat the same form in *Great Circle.* In all these references, the weight of the Oedipal theme is not heavy and the emphasis is almost entirely on the jealous search for possession of the mother, hardly at all on the direct struggle with the father. Although *King Coffin* portrays an open enmity between father and son, it is offered chiefly as one of the explanatory conditions of subsequent events and is not much dwelt upon in itself. The poems, the prose, and *Ushant* all suggest that this weighting reflects Aiken's own life and preoccupations. Even D.'s discovery later in his life that he had been taking his rebelling grandfather as a model can be interpreted as a conventional and mild critique of D.'s father.

This does not exhaust, however, the relationships joining Aiken's biography, his psychologizing, and his work. In a section of *Ushant,* D. recalls a picture drawn of him in early infancy by his father. Retrospection tells him that in this portrait his father showed an infant possessing godlike self-assurance. The passage implies that the picture dramatizes the father's recoil before the potential power of his first child, a male. After such infantile omnipotence, what innocence? D.'s comment is simple, brilliant, and touched by Mark Twain: "That child's father and mother were already as good as dead"—a bodily ironic apology for being born. Here Aiken seems to acknowledge both as doctrine and as indirect biography the idea that the son of a father who has killed himself may sometimes feel the event as the materialization of his own wish. It is not odd therefore that the themes and situations developed by Aiken in his early work involve fantasies of horrid actions, nightmares capable of serving to rationalize a guilt already felt. One fantasy after another is tested in order to see which one fits best a preestablished mood of guilt. *The Charnel Rose* explores survivals of the "infantile polymorphous perverse";

Forslin, the autistic stages of mentality; *Senlin,* the homosexual identification of self; *Festus,* "paranoid" sadism. Later, in *Punch* (1921), Aiken explored another face of sadism.

Since our major interest here is directed not toward Aiken's life but toward his writing, the foregoing speculations can be useful to us chiefly because they suggest how Aiken's psychologizing influenced his self-definition as an artist. The identification of five characteristics seems in order here. First of all, his intellectual appeal to psychological doctrine as a clue to the meaning in life. Second, his concern with substitutes or "surrogates" in human experience—Aiken early wrote of himself as having an interest in "the process of vicarious experience by which civilized man enriches his life and maintains emotional balance." Third, his employment of a "musical" method in verse composition, a method which emphasizes the associative stream of imagery both in the minds of the characters represented and in the compositional habits of the writer. Fourth, his exploration of themes of ego, identity, and the "defense mechanisms." Fifth, his use of phallic symbolism in a manner suggesting that the reader can be expected to possess a knowledge of that code. The doctrinal details of these concerns dominated Aiken less and less as he matured.

Despite these conjectures pressed upon our attention by the masquerade of *Ushant,* it will occur to many readers of Aiken that even if his life experiences had been different, his art might have demonstrated the same concerns; and that, for readers who know nothing or who could not care less about his life, the poems present themselves not as fragmented history but as the make-believe of art. It follows that they make a claim to be concerned with the destiny of all men rather than one man alone and that this exploration of the general as opposed to the particular involves an examination of the evils that all men encounter and a search for sources of value that all men can share. In effect, this involves a research into the depths of universal guilt, conscience, and indeed the sense of human solidarity. Aiken's approach to these matters deserves greater clarification than it has as yet received.

Lest what needs to be said about this seem to make Aiken a rhetorician rather than a poet it would be well to look for a moment at how well Aiken defended the claims of art in his criticism as well as in his poetry. For the intellectual background of Aiken's beliefs about the relation between life and art presents itself quite clearly in his criticism, not because it is programmatic but because, despite its range, it is consistent and coherent in its drive. Aiken undertook considerable reviewing, much of it at the behest of Marianne Moore for the *Dial,* and his criticism has the vitality of taste-in-the-making. It is rather to its credit that his is not the sort of criticism that labors first of all to pre-establish a position of defense for the writer's own poetry. Nor does it rework ground already covered by others. One could summarize its strength by noticing Aiken's early perception of grandiose confusions in Pound. To get an idea of Aiken's range and perception as a critic one has to turn only to *Scepticisms* (1919), in which he writes freely and incisively about himself as well as his contemporaries. Or one may take advantage of Rufus Blanshard's service to Aiken's reputation by examining his *A Reviewer's ABC*, a 1958 publication which reprints most of the pieces on which Aiken is willing to rest his critical reputation. As displayed in the *ABC,* the ranginess and independence of this work calls up Hazlitt and Baudelaire; and what may most distinguish it is the magnanimity by which it rises above the professional animus and often intrusive pedantry that burden much of the criticism in English that has appeared in the twentieth century. A most perceptive and helpful commentary on Aiken's development as a critic is provided by Jay Martin. According to Martin, Aiken's early attitude toward literature leaned toward that of Tolstoi in *What Is Art?* The stress was placed upon the moral effects of the artist upon his audience. Later, Martin tells us, Aiken gradually articulated quite a different position, one that gave rather more attention to the artist as autonomous explorer of reality. Perhaps it would be fair to say of this process that Aiken has given up Tolstoi in order to replace him with Croce. Yet even though Aiken's criticism leans closer and closer to a Crocean core as it proceeds, it does not forsake all sense of the instruction that is found in art, and may even, like his poetry, constitute more of a teaching than Aiken has been prepared to admit.

We should keep in mind these aspects of Aiken's attitude toward the poetic art as we try to come closer to an understanding of how Aiken involved himself in poetry as a channel of total feeling and thinking. In the "symphonies" Aiken undertook to study the engulfing vice or virtue of a human temperament from the point of view of new scientific doctrines about such matters. While the background of this can be seen extending from Aristotle and Theophrastus to Ben Jonson and La Bruyère, the particular intellectual source of Aiken's "symphonies" is the interest in characterology handed forward by such men as Wilhelm Dilthey from early nineteenth-century philosophies to Freud, Spranger, Scheler, Jung, Fromm, and Erikson. This line of thought is concerned quite as much with "identity" as with "personality" and it includes a consideration of ethical problems. Since Aiken is true to this tradition—the moral worth of a character such as that of Senlin is studied in the poem in the light of his perilous preoccupation with himself—it is hard to understand the habit of minimizing the moralist in Aiken. But it appears that there are two reasons for this judgment, one involving a development in philosophy and one involving Aiken's manner of constructing the moral orientation of his characters.

The first, or philosophical, consideration is that we have witnessed a narrowing of the province of ethics in Great Britain and the United States since the turn of the century. This is seen in the tendency of ethics to pursue "normative" as contrasted with "descriptive" inquiry. For philosophers following such men as Bradley and McTaggart and for critics such as Eliot and Winters, a system of ethics appears to be validated largely by showing that it is entailed by the nature of an ultimate reality. But this can only be an article of faith rather than philosophy, since no system of ethics can be validated merely by this warrant. Besides, there are those who hold that descriptive as well as deductive inquiry is required in ethics; and Aiken is one of these. The source of ethics that others seek in an intuition of duty to a metaphysical realm Aiken seeks in an intuition of human purposes in the realm of nature; and his poems constitute a teaching in this ancient tradition of moral judgment—a tradition which is as evident to us in Epicurus and Lucretius as it is in Freud. And if we pursue this line of investigation more fully we shall see why Aiken employs a particular and significant method for developing the moral orientation of his characters.

David Bakan, in one of the chapters of his work in progress on modern psychology, has called attention to the power of dynamic psychology as a system of metaphor. He suggests that thought is renewed from time to time by revolutions in its systems of metaphor and that not the least of Freud's contributions was of just this sort. This is one of the principal ways in which Aiken understood psychoanalysis

and it is a way that is not yet grasped by many who claim to understand Freud. Along similar lines John Chynoweth Burnham, in one of the chapters in his study of the intellectual climate in which modern psychiatry arose, notes that Edwin B. Holt of Harvard, in *The Freudian Wish and Its Place in Ethics,* as early as 1915 saw Freud as translator into modern terms of the idea that knowledge, including knowledge of self, is a virtue. Aiken read this book when it first appeared. Scattered throughout Aiken's work, including *Osiris Jones* (1931) and *Preludes for Memnon* (1931), appear systematic comments along this line. Aiken's Freudian belief in the determination of all mental life by all of its past did not make him a psychological determinist in the sense that Hardy was an environmental determinist and Dreiser a naturalistic determinist. Rather it encouraged him to develop the voluntarism and relativism of his minister grandfather's dissenting brand of the Unitarian view.

As a consequence Aiken moved from the very beginning toward views of human nature that stand in contrast to comparable concerns in many of his artistic contemporaries. For them the center of interest is the family as the source of an oppressive cultural superego and they seek a new compact with the guilt they believe has been forced upon them by their upbringing. Aiken on the other hand is concerned with the development of ego in situations in which the outside world must be substituted for the family. From the outset, therefore, he is led in the direction of an interest in character disorders rather than the neurotic or the psychotic. The questions he asks himself are more like those asked by a psychoanalyst such as Harry Stack Sullivan, with his sensitivity to social aspects of personality, than like those of earlier and more "classical" masters of the field. By accident and insight Aiken anticipated the interest in "identity" as contrasted with the interest in "personality" that appeared in fullest form in the American school of Freudian revisionists. Aiken's relationships to dynamic psychology are therefore about as different as they can be from the picture of them provided by some critics of Aiken's work such as Peterson, Martin, and Hoffman and even by some opaque remarks in Aiken himself. "The cosmic ironist" in Aiken pivots not so much upon a struggle of personality for a place in an impersonal cosmos as upon the struggle of the human being, over and beyond being possessed of a "personality," to arrive at an identity.

Consider the persistence of this theme in the eloquent late poem "The Crystal":

At seven, in the ancient farmhouse,
cocktails sparkle on the tray, the careful answer
succeeds the casual question, a reasoned dishevelment
rufflling quietly the day's or the hour's issue.
Our names, those we were born with,
or those we were not born with, since all are born nameless,
become the material, or the figment, if we wish,
of which to weave, and then unweave, ourselves.
Our lives, those we inherited, of which
none can claim ownership in fee simple, but only
a tenant's lease, of unpredictable duration,
rented houses from which have already departed perhaps
those others, our other selves, the children . . .

It is important to notice that whereas Frost's Social Darwinism and Eliot's anthropology and Pound's culture-history have all dated, Aiken's psychology anticipate a half century ago a major viewpoint in psychology today.

We do not dismiss writers for the obsolescence of the intellectual fashions that once nourished them any more than we praise them for their anticipation of scientific world views. On the other hand we can praise them for the coherence with which a unified view of man is dramatized in, and dramatizes, their work. On this score Aiken displays an intelligent consistency that makes some contemporaries of his, for example Pound, sound incoherent and others, for example Stevens, seem bloodless. Thus, in analyzing how Aiken's view of man led him to undertake certain crucial experiments in form we dare not fail to evaluate what he says about man and for man—all the more so because Aiken has avoided the role of guru accepted for themselves by some of his best-known contemporaries.

With this observation, however, we are brought close to a crucial question not only for Aiken but for others in his generation. It is ordinarily expressed in the following terms: does the twentieth-century poet inherit a set of beliefs that make the triumphs and the failures of men significant? A set of beliefs that, because they are general beliefs about human action, assist the artist to portray human actions as possessing a sharp contour, against a clear-cut ground? The question develops some of its importance out of the observation that even poets such as Eliot or Claudel who have attached themselves to the authoritative belief system of traditional Catholicism have not been able to present in verse or in drama anything so artistically clear-cut as the doctrine itself claims to be in dogmatic terms. It develops further importance out of the observation that an artist who, like Brecht, has attached himself to the doctrinaire prophecies of Marx has not been more convincing than the traditionalists as a dramatizer of man's good and evil. Aiken did not escape such difficulties by his attachment to a psychological liberalism that, if anything, supplies even less dramatizable contrast in human affairs. Even if it be true that classical Freudianism "rescues" for us some of what we still possess of the dramatic and the tragic, Aiken has not chosen that line of psychoanalytic thought. He has chosen rather an outlook that deemphasizes contrast between absolute good and absolute evil, and disqualifies traditional hard-line distinctions between passion and action. The more experienced, anguished, and pessimistic version of this viewpoint, with its simultaneous rejection of Greek beliefs in fate, Christian assurance of salvation, and revolutionary expectations of a new social order, is probably to be found in such a Continental writer as Camus. Aiken's version of it, like that of most Americans who espouse it, is not so pessimistic as the European and contains as a major element its radical rejection of two leading American intellectual traditions of the nineteenth century: the earlier Scottish realism, with its inadequate account of the human emotions, and the later Kantianism, with its glowing assurances that the universal law outside of man was reflected in, and reflected, the moral law within him.

Such a world view multiplies the difficulties of the literary artist in his attempt to objectify and dramatize the moral orientation of the characters he is representing. One reason, suggested and developed by the philosopher Maurice Mandelbaum in *The Phenomenology of Moral Experience,* is that in making judgments of the moral worth of fictional characters as well as real people we make a distinction between two situations. One occurs when we make a judgment of an agent's "actional" traits; in this situation we can pass a judgment upon the action without second thoughts about the motive. The other appears when, in passing a judgment upon his action, we dare not dismiss the agent as lacking this or that moral attribute without inquiring into his motives and

thus into the history of his relationship to the action. Aiken, in the "symphonies" and in *Punch,* invites us to judge his characters almost entirely in the latter terms and hardly at all in the former. Each character, that is, is like a delinquent standing before a liberal-minded judge: nothing that he has thought or done is to be judged independently of the temperament or disposition he evinces and represents. Aiken, whose true interest is in character and identity rather than personality and ego, achieves by this approach a singular power in the rendering of certain character types. The price of the method is shown, however, by the difficulties Aiken experienced in going from the portrait-poem and lyric to the narrative poem.

Aiken's biggest experiments with the narrative poem came toward the beginning and after the end of his novel-writing years, in *John Deth* (1930) and *The Kid* (1947).

John Deth follows its subtitle, *A Metaphysical Legend,* in being too complex. Inspired in part by the names on an English tombstone and in part by Aiken's Jungian advertence to the idea of mankind's collective dreaming, it draws on medieval myth. Aiken's own commentary on the genesis and the aim of the poem multiplies the difficulties of the piece. Yet it can be read with great enjoyment, as Jay Martin reads it, as a derivation from the dance of death allegories, with a dreamlike persuasiveness and a certain narrative get-up-and-go.

The Kid is Aiken's contribution to the "lyric-epic" tradition that began in the United States with Whitman, was continued by Crane and Williams, and is also represented in sequences of the later Stevens. In this poem William Blackstone (inexplicable man who was willing to be Boston's first settler) is seen transmogrified into a sequence of American heroes in search of an inner frontier that is related to but not identical with the physical and national frontier to the westward. The poem owes as much to Owen Wister and Theodore Roosevelt as it does to Hart Crane and William Carlos Williams. *The Kid* contains wonderfully sustained passages, concludes with less than the obsessive brilliance of Crane's *The Bridge* or the pawky mythography of Williams' *Paterson*. The truth is that few poems of Aiken's force us to construct their protagonists so fully that we see and hear them ever after. His poems are not intended in this way any more than Ovid's or Spenser's poems are. The most persistently narrative efforts in Aiken's poetic work are aimed at representing an adventurous and problematic pursuit as it is undertaken by an allegorized temperament.

Aiken's definitely mixed accomplishments with narration and dramatization in verse pivot, as has been said, upon the difficulties inherent in moving from a poetic form that achieves a lyrical rendering of a character type whose actions and whose thoughts constantly flow into each other to a poetic form in which a character—since he exists among other characters—must be objectified clearly as someone who actually exists in the viewpoint of those other characters. A better understanding of how this familiar challenge presented itself to Aiken is obtained by examining more closely than we have so far the methods of composition that he employed in the early groundbreaking "symphonies." It can be shown that these methods were largely as successful as they were ingenious—but that they also entrenched habits that exerted a limiting influence upon Aiken's later experiments in narrative.

In those important early long poems that Aiken called "symphonies" the unit next largest to the whole is a section headed by a subtitle (or in some cases by a Roman numeral)

that deals pretty much with one emotional tone or one emotional episode. This unit is perhaps the "movement" of the "symphony." The next smaller unit of composition is a group of traditional stanzas separated from their surroundings by an Arabic numeral, or by a space, from similar units before and after it. This unit, in turn, is composed of subsections fairly tightly unified by rhythm and by coterminous grammatical units. These subsections, written generally in lines of end-stopped character, are frequently enough made up of lines in couple, triple, or quadruple formation; each succeeding line undertakes to develop by repetition or variation a theme stated in the opening line. Here are examples of the part-Imagist, part-biblical manner:

Things mused upon are, in the mind, like
music,
They flow, they have a rhythm, they close and
open,
And sweetly return upon themselves in rhyme.
                              The Jig of Forslin, i, 7

Rain slowly falls in the bitter garden;
It rains: the streets grow dark.
The leaves make a sorrowful sound in the
hidden garden;
It rains, and the streets grow cold.
                              The Charnel Rose, ii, 2

This crucial smaller unit of Aiken's prosodic and poetic organization which I have called the "subsection" seems to me to be the fundamental building block of most of Aiken's poetry. As it is seen in the early work, it possesses an expressive unity reinforced not only by anaphora and other types of repetition but also by its formation around a unified cluster of sensuous impressions. Within this basic unit Aiken increasingly learned to build up such variations upon imagery that certain other features of its construction pass unnoticed. Of all the figurative devices that Aiken employs, one of his favorites is the substitution of a sign associated with one sense for a sign associated with another sense: synesthesia. Made both famous and fashionable by Baudelaire's sonnet "Correspondences," this device has been exploited by Aiken in ways that are particularly his own. Emphasizing the mutual substitution of the auditory and the visual, he also likes to play the natural and the artificial off against each other. Thus, when he makes reference under the auditory component to a natural sound such as the sound of rain, he likes to make reference under the visual component to something artificial; when he makes reference under the auditory component to an artificial sound, such as the note of a trumpet, he likes to make reference under the visual component to something as natural as the shape of a flower. This is why, for example, the interchange of the visual and the auditory in the opening movement of the title poem from *And in the Hanging Gardens* (1933) speaks for him so typically:

And in the hanging gardens there is rain
From midnight until one, striking the leaves
And bells of flowers, and stroking boles of
     planes,
And drawing slow arpeggios over pools,
And stretching strings of sound from eaves to
     ferns.

Now the more we read early Aiken the more we notice the single-cast construction of his subsections. But what do single-cast, coupled- and tripled-line structures have to do, even in freely unrhymed fashion, with poems of the kind that Aiken said he wished to write? Is the unconscious so tidy? Would not the movements of the psyche with which Aiken claims to deal render themselves more persuasively in line and sentence arrangements less sweetly formal than this? The dependence on end-

stopped clusters of lines in the subsections of the "symphonies" introduces a prosodic formality that forfeits some of the gains made by abandoning formal stanza patterns. Such early critics of Aiken as Blackmur and Winters, it is to be guessed, felt not only an over-smooth, redundant, and even cloying tone in some of Aiken but also this related problem in the prosody of the "symphonies." We can safely say, in any event, that this method and texture is even less adaptable to the requirements of narrative verse than it is to those of the symphonic poem. The reason is that although it may facilitate the force of single-character portraiture by repetition, variation, and expansion, it does not contribute to narrative what narrative needs: the deft introduction to the reader of distinguishable characters and the rapid rendering of events linked to each other in time and in causality.

Clearly a question of language in general, as well as the question of the figurative and prosodic modalities in smaller basic parts of Aiken's poetry, presents itself to us here. It is probably fair to say that during the years of Aiken's greatest poetic productivity a general debate was proceeding on questions of poetic diction. To a large extent the issues were lexical rather than, as they tend to be today, structural. That is to say, the poetic practitioner or critic examining, say, a poem by Robert Frost paid somewhat more attention to the general choice of usage, idiom, and word than to the ways by which Frost deployed the underlying intonational patterns that reinforce the sense of English in order to place his emphasis precisely where he wanted it to be in the line or verse-paragraph. Most discussion of Aiken's "texture" focuses its attention therefore on such lexical questions as his unmodish pleasure in adjectives and his willing dependence upon verbal constructions which had first been made expressive and then stereotyped by the progress of Romantic literary experiment. The point is not an unreasonable one even though it probably has been overemployed as a critique of Aiken's style. Since such observations have been a staple of Aiken's criticism for a long time, it is necessary here only to acknowledge them and to suggest that other dimensions of Aiken's language are equally worthy of study: his sentence, for example.

The sentence in which Aiken achieves his cadence is the familiar informal declarative run-on sentence of American speech, made rather more formal in most respects than speech itself—Aiken is as free with the artful and unvernacular flourish ("This is the shape of the leaf and this of the flower") as any poet of his time. Generally, it is his habit to use a fairly loose sentence, adding clause upon clause in an unperiodic structure that follows the pulse of association as waves follow each other to a shore. The grammatical antecedents sometimes grow vague, and a natural accompaniment of this sentence is a good deal of anaphora and echolalia, as if the propulsion of feeling could be renewed from point to point only by associative returns to climaxes previously passed:

It is morning, Senlin says, and in the morning
When the light drips through the shutters like
    the dew,
I arise, I face the sunrise,
And do the things my fathers learned to do.

Little in the sentence structure of Aiken achieves a tension between what is carried in a principal clause and what is carried in a subordinate clause. The compound-complex organization, with its emphasis upon the compound, simply takes the form of refined rumination as it reaches the level of speech, adapting itself readily to the compulsive repetition that Aiken emphasizes in his rendering of the movement of human feelings. Anticlimax in this mode of composition is related to the employment of underconnected independent clauses that prevails in Hemingway ("He swung the axe and the chicken was dead") and Eliot ("Six o'clock. / The burnt-out ends of smoky days").

The language Aiken worked out for himself is the result of imitation, intuition, and trial and error. Successful though it is, it is far from being the sophisticated product of a "structural-linguistic" talent such as we find in Cummings and Thomas, remaining by and large at the conventional and lexical level characteristic of American linguistic thinking before, say, Leonard Bloomfield. It is a mistake to take Aiken's own somewhat ponderous comments on the "problem of language" as evidence for a keen philosophical or technically informed sense of the matter. They add little to our understanding and critical attention to them adds even less. The main thing to notice is Aiken's William Jamesian determination to let the thought think itself—and to stand by the consequences of the experiment. In his more ventriloquistic constructions the reader does not always know who is speaking or from what situation or from what context. The separation of the author and the fictional agent and the separation of the situation from the agent's sense of it has little of the clarity with which these matters are represented in, for example, Frost. Nor are they necessarily intended to. The purpose of Aiken's style as well as of his total construction is to evoke mood and character and not to dramatize. It pictures, and it expatiates upon what has been pictured; and it represents what a character dreamed or wished or hoped as being on somewhat the same level as what he did or had done to him.

It was a tincture of cosmic purple among other things that was responsible for some of the bad reviews Aiken received in the 1920's—and even later, when it had become more frequent to speak of him as being overdetached from social values. It appears that points were sometimes missed about the earlier poems. It will help us to understand this if we go back for a moment to the famous earlier "Discordants" (*Turns and Movies*, 1916):

Music I heard with you was more than music,
And bread I broke with you was more than
  bread;
Now that I am without you, all is desolate;
All that was once so beautiful is dead.

The effect of "Discordants" arises partly from a trochaic foot in which the sharpest stresses combined with the highest pitches are placed toward the end of each line, to be reinforced there by the terminal junctures. It also depends upon alliterations and consonances attached to these strong-stressed and high-pitched syllables; and upon the placement toward the line end of most of the consonantal collisions heard in the poem, almost all of them bringing together smoothly a voiced consonant (a consonant requiring the voice box to vibrate, such as "b" contrasted with "p") with another of the same kind. The smoothness of the piece suggested to some that this was about the best that Aiken could do with English prosody—and that perhaps he had "done" too much.

But surely this was grudging praise, and Aiken after 1930 forced a gradual reversal of such judgments by the meditative poems of *Preludes for Memnon, Time in the Rock,* and *Brownstone Eclogues.* In these poems he pursued the verbal refinement of all that he had learned before—and much that was new. This movement away from the quasi-dramatic or narrative is reinforced and enriched by Aiken's gradual discovery of freer variations, and part of the excitement of the *Preludes* is our par-

ticipation in Aiken's finding of new rhythms. The Wagnerian brass line of the earlier poems is transposed for woodwinds; and although the lines are still heavily end-stopped, the freedom and variation seem both effortless and endless as if from a self-renewing source:

Watch long enough, and you will see the leaf
Fall from the bough. Without a sound it falls:
And soundless meets the grass . . . And so you
  have
A bare bough, and a dead leaf in dead grass.
                    Preludes for Memnon, XIX

Consider also this section:

Two coffees in the Español, the last
Bright drops of golden Barsac in a goblet,
Fig paste and candied nuts . . . Hardy is dead,
And James and Conrad dead, and Shakspere
  dead,
And old Moore ripens for an obscene grave,
And Yeats for an arid one; and I, and you—
What winding sheet for us, what boards and
  bricks,
What mummeries, candles, prayers, and pious
  frauds?
You shall be lapped in Syrian scarlet, woman,
And wear your pearls, and your bright
  bracelets, too,
Your agate ring, and round your neck shall
  hang
Your dark blue lapis with its specks of gold.
And I, beside you—ah! but will that be?
For there are dark streams in this dark world,
  lady,
Gulf Streams and Arctic currents of the soul;
And I may be, before our consummation
Beds us together, cheek by jowl, in earth,
Swept to another shore, where my white bones
Will lie unhonored, or defiled by gulls.
                    Preludes for Memnon, II

It should be evident by this point that Aiken speaks in terms of a creed, liberalism, which has been on the defensive among the most inquiring poetic minds of the past two generations. He has written, to be sure, in terms of not classical political economic liberalism but rather the social-psychological liberalism which since the 1880s has rejected that earlier laissez-faire liberalism almost as much as it rejects absolutism. The coherence of creed and art in Aiken is rather more noticeable than it is in many of his contemporaries. Yet Aiken's own vaguenesses as well as the development of psychological doctrine in his own lifetime are probably responsible for some of the oversimplified views of the Freudianism that was a formative element in his art, liberalism, and relativism. It has not yet been said clearly enough that the classical Oedipus complex plays a minor part in his work; that his early interest in the ego and identity as over against the theory of complexes distinguishes his work utterly from the Freudian rhetoric of Robinson Jeffers and Eugene O'Neill; that, despite his interest in characterology, his poems have rarely received the "Freudian reading" that they deserve; that for better or worse (some think better), his Freud approaches the Freud of the "revisionists"; and that despite his reputation as a poet of chaos his work embodies a total, consistent, and normative view of man.

The orientation is visible in the earliest accomplished work. Certain common tones in Pound's "Hugh Selwyn Mauberley" (1915), Aiken's *The Jig of Forslin* (1916), and Eliot's "The Love Song of J. Alfred Prufrock" (1917) remind us of what these writers shared with each other. The central figure of each is a self-involved man out of tune with his warring time and not getting any younger. He is sketched by a method that recalls Browning's dramatic soliloquy while at the same time it deliberately disarranges this form toward impressionistic vagueness and Symbolist mystery. *Forslin,* because it includes a version of the Salome story in its middle passages, invites special attention to that theme. Mallarmé's poem *Hérodiade,* followed by a short tale by Flaubert, a prose poem of Huysmans, a novel by Sudermann, an opera by Strauss, paintings by Moreau, and a verse play by Oscar Wilde, all show a preoccupation with the theme at the century's turn. Developing the vampire figure of Romantic writing, this motif became a flaming fashion during a time when the feminist movement was acquiring respectability and effectiveness and it touches on the discomfiture of the male in a period when he was continuing to lose his traditional dominance. Appearing almost simultaneously in "Prufrock" and *Forslin,* the theme helps us to understand the differences in the effects of the two poems.

In both poems an analogy is suggested between the absence of masculine initiative in love and the absence of the ability to experience, feel, and create. In Eliot's version we see the male dismissed or even victimized by the female and his own attitude toward her; and the whole relationship is passionately embalmed from an ironic and comic point of view. In Aiken's version we see the female told off by the male in a series of fantasies in which the male counter-anticipates the power of the female; and the whole relationship is rehearsed from a more or less melodramatic and pathetic point of view. Just as there is something like a European *tedium vitae* in the attitude taken by Eliot toward the battle of the sexes, there is something "contrary" and American about Aiken's choice of the other attitude. Not apart from these perspectives, the reader of today is likely to feel that Eliot, by going in the direction of ironic and comic treatment, attained somewhat greater control over his material than Aiken but also that he played it more or less safe by taking the myth at its inherited value.

Given these strategic choices that Aiken

made when young, the important thing is that the poetic gifts he brought to them attained a richer and more controlled form when he was older. Consider this poem, "Doctors' Row" (in the *Brownstone Eclogues* of 1942):

Snow falls on the cars in Doctors' Row and
    hoods the headlights;
snow piles on the brownstone steps, the
    basement deadlights;
fills up the letters and names and brass degrees
on the bright brass plates, and the bright brass
    holes for keys.

Snow hides, as if on purpose, the rows of bells
which open the doors to separate cells and
    hells:
to the waiting-rooms, where the famous
    prepare for headlines,
and humbler citizens for their humbler
    deadlines.

And in and out, and out and in, they go,
the lamentable devotees of Doctors' Row;
silent and circumspect—indeed, liturgical;
their cries and prayers prescribed, their
    penance surgical.

No one complains—no one presumes to
    shriek—
the walls are very thick, and the voices weak.
Or the cries are whisked away in noiseless
    cabs,
while nurse, in the alley, empties a pail of
    swabs.

Miserable street! — through which your
    sweetheart hurries,
lowers her chin, as the snow-cloud stings and
    flurries;
thinks of the flower-stall, by the church, where
    you
wait like a clock, for two, for half-past two;

thinks of the roses banked on the steps in snow,
of god in heaven, and the world above, below;

widens her vision beyond the storm, her sight
the infinite rings of an immense delight;

all to be lived and loved—O glorious All!
Eastward or westward, Plato's turning wall;
the sky's blue streets swept clean of silent birds
for an audience of gods, and superwords.

Explorations of Aiken led by Blackmur and Tate and later by Schwartz, Blanshard, Martin, and Hoffman have laid the foundations for a fuller view of his work. Aiken is the poetic, less carapaced, side of the American mentality of his generation that represents itself on the more intellectualized and discursive side in the confident criticism of Edmund Wilson. As artist and as man, he displays an affection for the very world that he attacks for being too distinct a giver of pain, too uncertain a giver of pleasure, and too monstrous to be grasped by a divided consciousness. His perception of suffering is not Christian, or Nietzschean, or tragic, or skeptical, or withdrawing. It is liberal, ironic, humane, conscious of the discontents that civilization itself imposes and therefore relativistic and partly hopeful. It is probably inconsistent for those who emphasize in Aiken a sympathy for the Freudian formula of the "pathology of everyday life" to see him as a poet of clear-cut pessimism about personality or culture. There is to be found in Aiken as well as in Freud the belief that "Where id was, there shall ego be"—enough of a commitment to a rationalistic hope to leave major aspects of Freud's thought and Aiken's poetry this side of tragedy. Of all the themes that Aiken inherits from Freud, he emphasizes the one that is "non-tragic" in the inherited sense of the word, but painful enough in its human meaning: the quietest life, devoid of tragic incident or suffering, is already the victim of the internalized aggression that, in the form of conscience, punishes gratuitously the psyche that it inhabits.

This almost Baudelairian theme of the "heroism of everyday life" was well realized in "Tetélestai," written in 1917, when Aiken was twenty-eight. The title, drawn from the last words of Jesus in John 19:30 ("When Jesus therefore had received the vinegar, he said, It is finished; and he bowed his head, and gave up the ghost"), has the meaning, in John, of fulfillment as well as conclusion. An elegy for the obscure heroes of everyday life, this poem of Aiken's calls up a line like that of Marlowe to decorate the theme that Gray's *Elegy* is remembered for and Whitman himself would have understood:

How shall we praise the magnificence of the
    dead,
The great man humbled, the haughty brought
    to dust?
Is there a horn we should not blow as proudly
For the meanest of us all, who creeps his days,
Guarding his heart from blows, to die
    obscurely?
I am no king, have laid no kingdoms waste,
Taken no princes captive, led no triumphs
Of weeping women through long walls of
    trumpets . . .

Close to forty years later the humanism and the relativism were still there, finding a sparer and pithier form in part IX of the title poem of *A Letter from Li Po* (1955):

The winds of doctrine blow both ways at once.
The wetted finger feels the wind each way,
presaging plums from north, and snow from
    south.
The dust-wind whistles from the eastern sea
to dry the nectarine and parch the mouth.
The west wind from the desert wreathes the
    rain
too late to fill our wells, but soon enough,
the four-day rain that bears the leaves away.
Song with the wind will change, but is still song
and pierces to the rightness in the wrong

or makes the wrong a rightness, a delight.
Where are the eager guests that yesterday
thronged at the gate? Like leaves, they could
    not stay,
the winds of doctrine blew their minds away,
and we shall have no loving-cup tonight.
No loving-cup: for not ourselves are here
to entertain us in that outer year,
where, so they say, we see the Greater Earth.
The winds of doctrine blow our minds away,
and we are absent till another birth.

There can be little doubt that Aiken's independence of the neoclassicism brought in by such men as Hulme and Eliot and his equal independence of the automatic Marxisms of the 1930's were costly to his vogue. Nor did the New Criticism find his work congenial to explication, an activity that could have made it more well known than it has been to university students of recent decades. One result, quite apart from the matter of his fame in general, is that much remains to be understood about the interaction of Aiken and his time. It is not merely that he has still to receive due credit for the concerned, cosmopolitan, and equable attitudes he displayed toward the nightmare issues and events of social politics in the last fifty years. It is also that his art, with its manifold sources in American rebellion and European sophistication, is worthy of even fuller exploration than it has received.

The anonymous writer of the lead article in the London *Times Literary Supplement* of April 19, 1963, credited Aiken with being original in advance of his time and the possessor of a cosmic sense that outsoars Eliot and Pound. The writer continued: "Increasingly poetry has become a way of writing, not a way of thinking. Yet not to like Aiken (or Shelley, of course) is a confession of not being capable of thinking in poetic terms; that is to say with the whole consciousness."

Aiken has created a fluent and colorful picturization of man learning to enjoy and realize himself. The process is conceived of as a response to a universal challenge, first in the sense that the ancestral gods are against enjoyment and ultimately in the sense that enjoyment leads to a need to transcend itself. The poetic art in which he embodies this view of life is Indian in its luxuriance, repetition, and decoration. It stands over against the sparer poetic line that has won much of the lip service as well as some of the practice of the more influential poets since Hulme and Pound made their voices felt half a century ago. The energetic profusion of Aiken has a masculine bouquet that allies him more closely with Yeats and Tate than with most of his contemporaries. Aiken, as they say, has written lines below his own best level and was thoughtful enough in his *Selected Poems* of 1961 to anthologize himself at his best. His lifelong performance in a luxuriant style is not only one of the strongest testaments to the power of his youthful insights but also the preserver of a tradition whose vitality, we should be glad to say, he has helped to pass on.

Selected Bibliography

WORKS OF CONRAD AIKEN

POETRY

Earth Triumphant and Other Tales in Verse. New York: Macmillan, 1914.

Turns and Movies and Other Tales in Verse. Boston: Houghton Mifflin; London: Constable, 1916.

The Jig of Forslin: A Symphony. Boston: Four Seas, 1916; London: Secker, 1921.

Nocturne of Remembered Spring and Other Poems. London: Secker, 1916; Boston: Four Seas, 1917.

The Charnel Rose; Senlin: A Biography; and Other Poems. Boston: Four Seas, 1918.

The House of Dust: A Symphony. Boston: Four Seas, 1920.

Punch: The Immortal Liar, Documents in His History. New York: Knopf; London: Secker, 1921.

Priapus and the Pool. Cambridge, Mass.: Dunster House, Harvard University, 1922.

The Pilgrimage of Festus. New York: Knopf, 1923; London: Secker, 1924.

Priapus and the Pool and Other Poems. New York: Boni and Liveright, 1925.

Prelude. New York: Random House, 1929.

Selected Poems. New York: Scribners, 1929.

Gehenna. New York: Random House, 1930.

John Deth: A Metaphysical Legend, and Other Poems. New York: Scribners, 1930.

The Coming Forth by Day of Osiris Jones. New York: Scribners, 1931.

Preludes for Memnon. New York: Scribners, 1931.

And in the Hanging Gardens. Baltimore: Garamond, 1933.

Landscape West of Eden. London: Dent, 1934; New York: Scribners, 1935.

Time in the Rock; Preludes to Definition. New York: Scribners, 1936.

And in the Human Heart. New York: Duell, Sloan, and Pearce, 1940.

Brownstone Eclogues and Other Poems. New York: Duell, Sloan, and Pearce, 1942.

The Soldier: A Poem. Norfolk, Conn.: New Directions, 1944.

The Kid. New York: Duell, Sloan, and Pearce, 1947.

Skylight One: Fifteen Poems. New York: Oxford University Press, 1949.

The Divine Pilgrim. Athens: University of Georgia Press, 1949.

Collected Poems. New York: Oxford University Press, 1953.

A Letter from Li Po and Other Poems. New York: Oxford University Press, 1955.

Sheepfold Hill: Fifteen Poems. New York: Sagamore Press, 1958.

Selected Poems. New York: Oxford University Press, 1961.

The Morning Song of Lord Zero. New York: Oxford University Press, 1963.

NOVELS

Blue Voyage. New York: Scribners; London: Howe, 1927.

Great Circle. New York: Scribners; London: Wishart, 1933.

King Coffin. New York: Scribners; London: Dent, 1935.

A Heart for the Gods of Mexico. London: Secker, 1939.

Conversation: or, Pilgrim's Progress. New York: Duell, Sloan, and Pearce, 1940.

SHORT STORIES

Bring! Bring! and Other Stories. New York: Boni and Liveright; London: Secker, 1925.

Costumes by Eros. New York: Scribners, 1928; London: Cape, 1929.

Among the Lost People. New York: Scribners, 1934.

The Short Stories of Conrad Aiken. New York: Duell, Sloan, and Pearce, 1950.

Collected Short Stories. Cleveland, Ohio: World, 1960.

PLAY

Mr. Arcularis. Cambridge, Mass.: Harvard University Press, 1957.

CRITICISM AND OTHER PROSE

Scepticisms: Notes on Contemporary Poetry. New York: Knopf, 1919.

Foreword to *Two Wessex Tales,* by Thomas Hardy. Boston: Four Seas, 1919.

Introduction to *Selected Poems of Emily Dickinson.* London: Cape, 1924.

Ushant: An Essay. New York and Boston: Duell, Sloan, and Pearce–Little, Brown, 1952.

A Reviewer's ABC: Collected Criticism, edited by Rufus A. Blanshard. New York: Meridian, 1958. (Reprinted as *Collected Criticism.* New York: Oxford University Press, 1968).

BIBLIOGRAPHIES

Stallman, R. W. "Annotated Checklist on Conrad Aiken: A Critical Study," in *Wake 11,* edited by Seymour Lawrence. New York: Wake Editions, 1952.

Tate, Allen. *Sixty American Poets 1896-1944.* Washington, D.C.: Library of Congress, 1945.

CRITICAL STUDIES

Hoffman, Frederick J. *Conrad Aiken.* New York: Twayne, 1962.

Lawrence, Seymour, ed. Conrad Aiken Number, *Wake 11.* New York: Wake Editions, 1952.

Lerner, Arthur. *Psychoanalytically Oriented Criticism of Three American Poets: Poe, Whitman, and Aiken.* Rutherford, N.J.: Fairleigh Dickinson University Press, 1970.

Martin, Jay. *Conrad Aiken, A Life of His Art.* Princeton, N.J.: Princeton University Press, 1962.

Peterson, Houston. *The Melody of Chaos.* New York and Toronto: Longmans, Green, 1931.

ARTICLES AND REVIEWS

"Answer to the Sphinx," *Times Literary Supplement* (London), April 19, 1963, pp. 257-58.

Beach, Joseph Warren. "Conrad Aiken and T. S. Eliot: Echoes and Overtones," *PMLA,* 69:753-62 (1954).

Benedetti, Anna. "Sinfonie in Versi," *Nuova Antologia,* 204:202-06 (January 16, 1920).

Blackmur, Richard P. "Mr. Aiken's Second Wind," *New Republic,* 89:335 (January 13, 1937).

Kunitz, Stanley. "The Poetry of Conrad Aiken," *Nation,* 133:393-94 (October 14, 1931).

Moore, Marianne. "If a Man Die," *Hound and Horn,* 5:313-20 (January-March 1932).

Schwartz, Delmore. "Merry Go Round of Opinion," *New Republic,* 108:292-93 (March 1, 1943).

Tate, Allen. "The Author of *John Deth,*" *New Republic,* 68:265-66 (July 22, 1931).

———. "Conrad Aiken's Poetry," *Nation,* 122:38-39 (January 13, 1926).

Van Doren, Mark. "Effects in Verse," *Nation,* 112:86-87 (January 19, 1921).

Winters, Yvor. Review of *Selected Poems, Hound and Horn,* 3:454-61 (April-June 1930).

—REUEL DENNEY

Edward Albee

1928-

ABANDONED soon after his birth on March 12, 1928, Edward Albee was adopted when he was two weeks old. His foster parents, Reed and Frances Albee, were, respectively, the millionaire owner of a chain of theaters and a former mannequin who was twenty-three years younger than her husband. They brought Edward up in the lap of luxuries he appreciated only sparely. He was a problem child at various expensive boarding schools, where he early began to write fiction and poetry. Years of disaccord with his foster parents were truncated by his departure from home at the age of twenty. For almost a decade afterwards he led a hand-to-mouth existence in Greenwich Village, working fitfully as office boy, salesman, and Western Union messenger. Continuing to write, he sought the advice of two authors—W. H. Auden, who suggested that he turn to pornographic verse, and Thornton Wilder, who suggested that he turn to plays. Albee wrote his first play, *The Zoo Story,* "as a sort of thirtieth birthday present to myself." The play was rejected by American producers but was performed at the Schiller-Theater Werkstatt in West Berlin; Albee attended, though he understood no German. Five years later, *Who's Afraid of Virginia Woolf?* catapulted Albee from avant-garde attention to public notoriety.

When *The Zoo Story* was first produced in America in January 1960, it shared the stage of Greenwich Village's Provincetown Playhouse with *Krapp's Last Tape* by Samuel Beckett, and since that time Albee has been intermittently linked with European dramatists of the Absurd. He himself has admitted: "My exposure to Beckett and to late O'Neill was probably important right at the time I gave up poetry and the novel." In a widely reprinted essay, "Which Theatre Is the Absurd One?" (1962), Albee himself distinguishes between Realistic theater and that of the Absurd: "The Theatre of the Absurd . . . facing as it does man's condition as it is, is the Realistic theatre of our time; and . . . the supposed Realistic theatre . . . pander[ing] to the public need for self-congratulation and reassurance and present[ing] a false picture of ourselves to ourselves, is . . . really and truly The Theatre of the Absurd."

Like European Absurdists, Albee has tried to dramatize the reality of man's condition, but whereas Beckett, Genet, Ionesco, and Pinter present that reality in all its alogical absurdity, Albee has been preoccupied with illusions that screen man from reality. For the Europeans, absurdity or non-sense *is* metaphysical reality; for Albee, the world "makes no sense because the moral, religious, political and social structures man has erected to 'illusion' himself have collapsed." In Albee's drama, however, illusion is still present, and the action often dramatizes the process of collapse, so that we, the audience, arrive at a recognition of the reality behind illusion. Often, death helps dispel illusion, and often, obliquity helps reveal reality.

The Zoo Story already announces the suggestive indirection of subsequent works. Significantly, the method of indirection is explained by an Outsider who has suffered at the hands of the Establishment. Early in *The Zoo Story,* Jerry, the near-tramp informs Peter, the conformist: "I took the subway down to the Village so I could walk all the way up Fifth Avenue to the zoo. It's one of those things a person has to do; sometimes a person has to go a very long distance out of his way to come back a short distance correctly." The only purpose of Jerry's long walk is to accommodate his methodology. Jerry could have gone to New York City's Central Park Zoo by the cross-town bus, but, deliberately indirect, he chose the circuitous route. On Fifth Avenue, a street of many sights, Jerry apparently noticed nothing, though he has remarkable powers of observation. That luxury-laden avenue is simply the "distance out of his way to come back a short distance correctly" to the zoo. Through Jerry's explanation, indirection and animality enter Albee's play. Jerry couples these two themes to introduce his dog story, the verbal climax of the play: "THE STORY OF JERRY AND THE DOG! . . . What I am going to tell you has something to do with how sometimes it's necessary to go a long distance out of the way in order to come back a short distance correctly." By the time we hear the dog story, we are familiar with Jerry's "out of the way" dialogue, and we should be ready to see in the dog story an analogue for the zoo story.

In *The Zoo Story* non-conformist confronts conformist on a park bench; in the dog story man confronts animal in a dark hallway. Peter replaces the dog, friend-enemy to Jerry. Jerry views Peter as he does the dog—with sadness and suspicion; Jerry forces Peter to defend his premises as the dog defends *his* premises; Jerry hopes for understanding from the dog ("I hoped that the dog would . . . understand") and from Peter ("I don't know what I was thinking about; of course you don't understand"); as the dog bit Jerry, Peter stabs Jerry.

However, the dog's hostility to Jerry *begins* the dog story whereas Peter's hostility to Jerry *ends* the zoo story. The dog's hostility is at the surface of his animality, but Peter's hostility is calculatedly aroused by Jerry after he tells the dog story. Jerry went to the zoo to study "the way people exist with animals, and the way animals exist with each other, and with people too." But after he meets Peter, Jerry changes from student to teacher: "I have learned that neither kindness nor cruelty by themselves, independent of each other, creates any effect beyond themselves; and I have learned that the two combined, together, at the same time, are the teaching emotion." Jerry proceeds to combine the two in his education of Peter, with cruelty more apparent.

So vicious is Jerry's verbal attack that Peter screams when Jerry opens his knife: "YOU'RE GOING TO KILL ME!" But Jerry's intention is more subtle; combining cruelty with some of the previously announced kindness, "Jerry tosses the knife at Peter's feet"; he urges Peter to pick it up, and then punch-baits him into using the knife. Since Peter is a defensive animal only, not an attacker, Jerry "impales *himself* on the knife" (my italics). Though Jerry cries like a "fatally wounded animal," he dies like a man—talking. In dying, Jerry comes to partial self-recognition through his stream of associations: "Could I have planned all this? No . . . no, I couldn't have. But I think I did."

His final broken phrases imitate the disjunctive quality of his behavior.

Jerry's fragmented life and speech contrast with Peter's coherence and order. Peter's effort to light his pipe triggers Jerry's first pedagogic taunt: "Well, boy; *you're* not going to get lung cancer, are you?" With this thrust, Jerry exposes Peter's caution and upon this thrust death floats into the lazy Sunday air. It hovers over Jerry's account of his parents and aunt, over the dog story, and it culminates in Jerry's impalement. Only in dying does Jerry shift from cruel to kinder words, reassuring Peter: "You're not really a vegetable; it's all right, you're an animal. You're an animal, too." The "too" is significant; there are seals, birds, and lions at the zoo; there are parakeets and cats in Peter's apartment. In his dog story Jerry says he mixed *rat* poison with the hamburger bought as "a bite for . . . pussy-*cat*" (my italics) so as to kill the landlady's *dog*. Since animals are ubiquitous and virtually interchangeable, Albee's *Zoo Story* generalizes that men are animals; beneath the illusion of civilization, they may use words and knives instead of fangs and claws, but they still can kill.

Beyond this, however, *The Zoo Story* suggests another meaning in man's search for God. Albee himself has pointed out the influence upon *The Zoo Story* of *Suddenly Last Summer* by Tennessee Williams, Albee's play, like that of Williams, contains a search for God climaxed by violence. Like the Old Testament Jeremiah, whose cruel prophecies were a warning kindness to his people, Jerry may have educated Peter in his relation to God. Like his namesake, Jerry lapses into prophetic language: "And it came to pass that . . ." "So be it!" Before the dog story, Jerry exclaims, "For God's sake." After poisoning the dog, Jerry promises its owner that he will pray for it though he does not "understand how to pray." At the end of the dog story, Jerry re-cites a list of those with whom he sought communication—a list that begins with animals and ends with God, anagram of dog. In his cruel-kind deviling of Peter, Jerry calls on Jesus, and Peter replies with a "God damn" and a "Great God," almost in the same breath.

This undercurrent of divine suggestion is climaxed by the final words of the play. Toward the beginning Peter reacted to Jerry's unconventional life story with "Oh, my; oh, my." And Jerry sneered, "Oh, your what?" Only after the impalement is Jerry's question answered—by Peter's whispered repetitions: "Oh my God, oh my God, oh my God," and these are the only words Peter speaks while Jerry dies, thanking Peter in biblical phrases: "I came unto you . . . and you have comforted me." After Jerry's revelation of Peter's animal nature, and Peter's subsequent departure according to Jerry's instructions, "OH MY GOD!" is heard offstage as a *howl*—the final proof of Peter's animality, but also of his humanity, since he howls to his God. Jerry, who tells animal stories, closes the play by echoing Peter's "Oh my God" in the difficult combination demanded by Albee's stage direction, "scornful mimicry and supplication." That tonal combination is Jerry's last lesson in the pedagogy of cruel kindness; much of his scornful wit has been mimetic, and yet the wit itself is an inverted plea for love and understanding; the very word *undesrtand* echoes through the play.

Because life is lonely and death inevitable, Jerry seeks to master them in a single deed of ambiguous suicide-murder; he stages his own death, and by that staging, he punctures Peter's illusion of civilization, converting Peter into his apostle who will carry the message of man's caged animality—the zoo story. Jerry's death brings us to dramatic definition of humanity—bounded by animal drives but reaching toward the divine. Though this definition is at least as old as Pascal, Albee invests it with contemporary significance through his highly contemporary idiom—an idiom manipulated in tense theatrical rhythms.

So forceful is the indirection in Albee's first drama that even amateurs compel attention in performance. In *The American Dream,* on the other hand, the caricature of contemporary America often depends, in production, on elaborate set and props. In *The American Dream* Mommy and Daddy spout the clichés of middle-class America, and the implication is that such clichés lead to a kind of death for Grandma, who represents the vigorous old frontier spirit. Grandma resembles Jerry in her independence, but age has made her crafty, and she has learned to roll with the punches. In both *The American Dream* and *The Sandbox* it is Mommy who delivers the punches, and yet she does not literally kill Grandma.

Of the relationship between these two plays, Albee has written: "For *The Sandbox,* I extracted several of the characters from *The American Dream* and placed them in a situation different than, but related to, their predicament in the longer play." *The Sandbox* is named for the grave of Grandma, the first-generation American, and *The American Dream* is named for the third-generation American, a grave in himself; in both plays, murderous intention is lodged in the middle generation, especially Mommy. In *The Sandbox* Mommy and Daddy deposit Grandma in a child's sandbox. Half-buried, Grandma finds that she can no longer move, and she accepts her summons by the handsome Young Man, an Angel of Death.

In *The American Dream* Ionesco is a strong influence on Albee. Like *The Bald Soprano,* *The American Dream* thrives on social inanities. Like Ionesco, Albee reduces events to stage entrances and exits. As in *The Bald Soprano,* a recognition scene is based on circum-

stantial evidence; such proof reunites a husband and wife in the Ionesco play; in the Albee play such proof reunites Mrs. Barker with the American family for whom she barked. Albee also uses such Ionesco techniques as proliferation of objects (Grandma's boxes), pointless anecdotes (mainly Mommy's), meaningless nuances (beige, wheat, and cream), cliché refrains (I don't mind if I do; How fascinating, enthralling, spellbinding, gripping, or engrossing).

Within this stuffy apartment of Ionesco motifs, Albee places a family in the American grain, with its areas for senior citizens, and its focus on money. When Mommy was eight years old, she told Grandma that she was "going to mahwy a wich old man." Sterile, Mommy and Daddy have purchased a baby from the Bye-Bye Adoption Service, which puns on Buy-Buy. In *The Sandbox* Mommy and Daddy carry Grandma to *death,* but in *The American Dream* Mommy makes Grandma's *life* impossible. She informs a feebly protesting Daddy that he wants to put Grandma in a nursing home, and she threatens Grandma with a man in a van who will cart her away. Mommy treats Grandma like a naughty child; she discusses Grandma's toilet habits, warns her that she will take away her TV set, worries about her vocabulary: "I don't know where she gets the words; on the television, maybe."

And Grandma, who is treated like a child, tells the story of the family child to Mrs. Barker. Since "the bumble of joy" had eyes only for Daddy, Mommy gouged its eyes out; since it called Mommy a dirty name, they cut its tongue out. And because "it began to develop an interest in its-you-know-what," they castrated it and cut its hands off at the wrists. Our acquaintance with Mommy has prepared us for Grandma's account of Bringing Up Bumble. But more painful than the physical mutilations are the verbal ailments, containing

Mommy's cruel American platitudes: "it didn't have a head on its shoulders, it had no guts, it was spineless, its feet were made of clay." This is Mommy's more insidious castration, nagging the child into a diminutive Daddy, who is "all ears," but who has no guts since he has "tubes now, where he used to have tracts." In *The American Dream* "Like father, like son." Daddy "just want[s] to get everything over with," and his bumble-son does "get everything over with" by dying before Mommy can complete her murder of him.

In *The American Dream* it is an offstage bumble that predicts Grandma's death, as an offstage rumble announces Grandma's death in *The Sandbox*. Like the bumble, Grandma escapes Mommy's murderous malice by a kind of suicide. As Jerry turns Peter's reluctant threat into the reality of his own death, Grandma turns Mommy's repeated threats into the reality of her disappearance from the family.

When a handsome Young Man arrives, Grandma is alone onstage, and she recognizes in him the American Dream shaped by Mommy. He shares only appearance and initials with the Angel of Death in *The Sandbox*, but he has the same meaning. The American Dream is an Angel of Death who is linked both to the mutilated bumble and to Grandma. In a confessional monologue the Young Man tells Grandma of a twin "torn apart" from him, so that it seemed his heart was "wrenched from [his] body," draining him of feeling. As his twin brother was mutilated physically, the American Dream is mutilated emotionally.

When Mrs. Barker intrudes upon this confrontation of the numb young modern man with the vigorous old frontier spirit, Grandma introduces him as the man in the van, Mommy's bogeyman. Asking him to carry her boxes, Grandma follows the Young Man out. Boxes and sandbox are coffin and grave; the American Dream leads but to the grave, and

Grandma, accepting her fate, goes out in style—escorted by a handsome swain whose gallantry substitutes for feeling.

Though minatory Mommy later admits that "There is no van man. We . . . we made him up," she readily accepts the American Dream as a replacement for Grandma. Thus, the "comedy" ends happily, though Grandma is dead to Mommy: "Five glasses? Why five? There are only four of us." In spite of Mommy's malice—expressed in the clichés of contemporary America—Grandma and bumble manage to die their own kind of death. As in *The Zoo Story*, murderous invective leads indirectly to death, each victim staging his own stylized death.

The slackness of *The American Dream* contrasts with the tightness of *The Zoo Story*. In the earlier play indirection is both theme and technique, exploding into the death that reveals man's attachments to the animal and the divine. In *The American Dream* Albee borrows from Ionesco the techniques of proliferation and disjunction, using them as middle-class modes. Unlike Ionesco, however, Albee stops short of the savage anarchy of farce, and he dilutes his satire with a sympathetic Grandma and an ambiguous American Dream. In spite of her pithy frontier comments and her asides on "old people," Grandma does not oppose Mommy openly. And since the Young Man is first caricatured, then sentimentalized, the play sags when he speaks and preens. He will "do almost anything for money," and he tries to sell us the sad story of his life. Apparently ignorant of the mutilations to his twin brother, he describes his parallel loss of sensation that has resulted in his inability to love. His abstract statement of losses is much duller than Grandma's pungent summary of the mutilation of his twin. In spite of the Young Man's warning that his tale "may not be true," the mutual sympathy of Grandma and the American Dream is incongruously maudlin in this play that Grandma herself labels a "comedy." The Young Man claims to accept the syntax around him, but he is remarkably deaf to the tone of a satiric comedy that borders on farce. Albee makes an effort to restore that tone by bringing back Mommy and Daddy with their mindless clichés, and the play ends with Grandma's aside: "Everybody's got what he wants . . . or everybody's got what he thinks he wants." The American family accepts its illusion of sex and success.

In *The Death of Bessie Smith* Albee avoids sentimentality by keeping the sympathetic titular protagonist offstage. The play is based on a newspaper account of the death of the Negro blues singer; its documentary origin is unique in Albee's works. But his Bessie Smith is a presence rather than a character. The most sustained character, in contrast, is a voluble young Nurse who lashes out against her invalid Father, her Intern suitor, and her Negro Orderly. Lacking Jerry's self-proclaimed kindness and Mommy's hypocritical conformity, the dialogue of the Nurse is unrelievedly vicious, and yet she is not responsible for the death of Bessie Smith.

In the eight scenes of the play Albee attempts to counterpoint two story threads—the trip north of blues-singer Bessie Smith and the Nurse's sadistic control of a southern hospital. However, the Nurse story overshadows that of Bessie Smith, who is known only through the dialogue of her chauffeur-companion, Jack. The sympathetic Negroes have names—Jack, Bernie, Bessie Smith—whereas the white world is typecast—Nurse, Father, Intern, light-skinned Orderly, Second Nurse. The Nurse is the only coherent character in the play, and she coheres through her verbalization of scorn and conformity.

About halway through the play Jack's car, with Bessie Smith as passenger, crashes off-stage, while onstage the Nurse carries on a bored telephone conversation with a Second Nurse at another hospital. It is this Second Nurse who is indirectly responsible for the death of Bessie Smith, but we do not learn that until the end of the play.

In the two longest of the eight scenes (sixth and last) the cynical, reactionary Nurse and her liberal Intern suitor engage in a thrust-and-parry dialogue. At his rare dialectical best, the Intern is able to be as cruel as the Nurse. Though ideologically opposed to her, he desires her—a desire inflamed by her taunts. When his sneer about her chastity evokes her threat to "fix" him, he stares at her admiringly: "You impress me. No matter what else, I've got to admit that." But she also arouses his sadism: "I just had a lovely thought . . . that maybe sometime when you are sitting there at your desk opening mail with that stiletto you use for a letter opener, you might slip and tear open your arm . . . then you could come running into the emergency . . . and I could be there when you came running in, blood coming out of you like water out of a faucet . . . and I could take ahold of your arm . . . and just hold it . . . just hold it . . . and watch it flow . . . just hold on to you and watch your blood flow. . . ."

The death of Bessie Smith occurs between the last two scenes of the play. In the brief seventh scene the Second Nurse refuses hospital admission to Bessie Smith, injured in the automobile accident: "I DON'T CARE WHO YOU GOT OUT THERE, NIGGER. YOU COOL YOUR HEELS!" Similarly, when Jack brings Bessie Smith to the central hospital, the First Nurse refuses admission to the singer. As the Intern and Orderly go out to examine Bessie Smith in the car, Jack tells the Nurse about the accident, and she recalls the Intern's wish that he might watch while her blood came out "like water from a faucet." But it is Jack who had watched the ebb of the lifeblood of Bessie Smith. When the Intern and Orderly re-enter, "their uniforms are bloodied." They report the death of Bessie Smith.

In *The Death of Bessie Smith* nurses do not tend the sick; they sit at hospital admissions desks, refusing care to the injured. The First Nurse says she is sick of things, and Albee implies that Bessie Smith dies of such sickness. The Nurse speaks of her letter opener in the Intern's ribs, of a noose around his neck, but it is Bessie Smith who dies. The Nurse likes Negro blues, but she will not lift a finger to save a Negro blues singer; rather she mocks dead Bessie Smith, singing until the Intern slaps her. Albee indicts the whole South for the murder of Bessie Smith; nevertheless, the singer's story remains fragmentary, and we are left with a more vivid impression of the verbal duel of Nurse and Intern—gratuitous skirmishing in this loosely constructed morally earnest play.

The Intern exhibits more spirit than Peter in *The Zoo Story* or Daddy in *The American Dream*. In his thrust-and-parry exchange with the Nurse we can almost hear George and Martha of *Who's Afraid of Virgina Woolf?* In that play, as in Albee's shorter plays, murderous dialogue leads obliquely to murder. As the shadow of death lay over the sun-drenched afternoon of *The Zoo Story*, death lies like a sediment in Martha's gin, Nick's bourbon, Honey's brandy, and mainly George's "bergin." Though George claims that "musical beds is the faculty sport" in New Carthage, the sport that commands our attention is verbal fencing in the most adroit dialogue ever heard on the American stage.

Popular taste has often cloaked unpopular themes, and Albee has used the popular taste for punch lines to expose an anatomy of love. Although there are four characters, the play's three acts focus on the relationship of George

and Martha, who express their love in a lyricism of witty malice. Act I, "Fun and Games," rises toward a dissonant duet: Martha chants about George's failures as he tries to drown her voice in the party refrain, "Who's afraid of Virginia Woolf?" Toward the end of the Act III "exorcism" George and Martha reach "a hint of communion." Two of the three acts thus close on views of the togetherness of George and Martha, and during the three acts each is visibly tormented by the extended absence of the other. However malicious they sound, they *need* one another—a need that may be called love.

George and Martha have cemented their marriage with the fiction of their child. Outwardly conformist, they privately nourish their love upon this lie. Yet George's play-long preoccupation with death hints that such lies must be killed before they kill. George and Martha's distinctive love-duet is played against a background of death. In Act I George tells Martha "murderously" how much he is looking forward to their guests. Once Nick and Honey are on the scene, George shoots Martha with a toy gun, and then remarks that he might really kill her some day. In Act II Nick and George exchange unprovoked confessions; Nick reveals intimacies about his wife and her father, but George's anecodotes play upon death. He tells of a fifteen-year-old boy who accidentally shot his mother; then, when the boy was being taught to drive by his father, he swerved to avoid a porcupine; he crashed into a tree and killed his father. Later in Act II Martha summarizes George's novel about a boy who accidentally kills both his parents. Martha's father had forbidden George to publish the novel, and George had protested, "No, Sir, this isn't a novel at all . . . this is the truth . . . this really happened . . . to ME!" George reacts to Martha's narration with a threat to kill her, and he grabs her by the throat. Athletic Nick, who resembles the American Dream both in physique and in lack of feeling, tears George from Martha, and she accuses her husband softly, "Murderer. Mur . . . der . . . er." But George's murder kills only illusion.

While Nick and Martha disappear upstairs, drunken Honey voices her fear of having children, and George needles her: "How you do it? Hunh? How do you make your secret little murders stud-boy doesn't know about, hunh?" With Honey's unknowing help, George proceeds to plan the "secret little murder" of his child of fantasy. George and Martha declare "total war," and George vows "to play this one to the death." But death takes only their fantasy son, who, by George's account, swerves his car to avoid a porcupine, and crashes into a tree. George's imaginary child and his perhaps imaginary father die in precisely the same way.

Though George tries to throttle Martha, and she leaps at him when he kills their child, the only stage murder is verbal. Such murder is oblique, and George leads up to it obliquely, with his "flagellation." The idiom that has nurtured their love serves also to kill the illusion at its heart.

Their interdependence has been fed on a rhetoric of taunts. At the play's opening Martha evokes Bette Davis, the film star of acid wit. George acknowledges that Martha is a "devil with language," and she calls him "Phrasemaker." Though Martha may have downed George with boxing gloves, he outpoints her in linguistic tennis. And (to force the image) their imaginary child is the ball in this private game that keeps their love limber, preventing it from softening into academic mediocrity.

The sado-masochistic marriage of George and Martha is sustained through their verbal dexterity and their imaginary child. Far from

a *deus ex machina*, the child is mentioned before the arrival of Nick and Honey; George warns Martha not to "start in on the bit about the kid." By that time they have been sparring in their recurrent pattern, Martha beating George with his lack of professional success and George cutting at Martha's age, drinking, and promiscuity.

Guests heighten the pitch of the George-Martha exchange, as the couple moves into gamesmanship. Though George has cautioned Martha not to mention their child, he is tantalizingly evasive when Nick asks whether they have any children. While Martha "is changing," George learns that she has told Honey about their son, and that is the change that sets this evening off from similar evenings in the life of George and Martha. Once revealed, their son must die.

But George perceives this only slowly, and Martha never does. When Martha returns, changed, the verbal match continues with Nick as goad. And again it is Honey who introduces the subject of the son. After trying to retreat, Martha uses the child in Strindbergian fashion—as a weapon against her husband, taunting him with not being the father of the child. Unlike Strindberg's males, however, George is not vulnerable to this thrust about their "bean bag."

Act II, "Walpurgisnacht," introduces some variation in the verbal fencing: George and Nick toward the beginning, Martha and Nick in the middle, and George and Honey at the end; but the bedrock remains George versus Martha. They have a momentary fling in French, and like the tramps in *Waiting for Godot* George invents insults: "Book dropper! Child mentioner!" The insults point to the two lies of George's own life—the fictional murder which is the expression of the end of childhood, and the fictional murder to come, which may be the expression of the end of marriage.

George charges Martha with "slashing away at everything in sight, scarring up half the world." Each insists that the other is sick. In the prelude to their declaration of "total war," each assaults the other's dominant fantasy:

MARTHA: . . . before I'm through with you you'll wish you'd died in that automobile, you bastard.

GEORGE: *(Emphasizing with his forefinger)* And you'll wish you'd never mentioned our son!

Each predicts the other's wish to renounce lies, to embrace truth, but predictions are only obliquely fulfilled.

In the destruction of illusion, which may lead to truth, "snap" becomes a stage metaphor—sound, word, and gesture. Martha snaps her fingers at George and plays variations on the theme of snapping; she rhymes snap with crap, then uses snap as a synonym for the cipher she claims George has become. In Act III when George announces the death of their son, he pays her in kind. Entering from the garden with a bunch of snapdragons, George begins the game he calls "Bringing Up Baby": "Flores; flores para los muertos. Flores." Soon he throws snapdragons—*his* flowers for the dead—at Martha, one at a time, stem first, spear-like, phallic, as he echoes her "snaps" at him. St. George slew the dragon; Albee's George slays with snapdragons.

Before throwing snapdragons, however, George starts a story about a Mediterranean trip, a graduation present from his parents. "Was this after you killed them?" asks Nick. *"George and Martha swing around and look at him."* Then George replies ambiguously, "Truth or illusion. Who knows the difference, eh, toots?" And Martha charges, "You were never in the Mediterranean . . . truth or illusion . . . either way." It is when Martha tells George that he cannot distinguish between truth and illusion that he pelts her with snapdragons. Then Martha repeats the dichotomy: "Truth or illusion, George. Doesn't it matter to you . . . at all?" This time George doesn't bother to throw anything as he answers her, "SNAP!" And with relish, he sets the scene for the snapping of their common illusion from which truth *may* arise.

In his triumphant enactment of the murder, George snaps his fingers for Nick to join the final game, and he snaps his fingers for Honey to support his outrageous claim that he ate the death telegram. Death rites are played against this background of snaps, choreographed as a dance of death. The death scene and its aftermath contain the most perfectly cadenced dialogue of the drama. George's attack on Martha's illusion is so theatrically punitive that his redemptive intention is questionable.

George and Martha fire a salvo of mutual sexual accusation. Before breaking the news of the son's death, George joins Martha in a discordant duet, as at the end of Act I. Martha recites another litany of George's failures while George recites the Requiem Mass. As Martha slowly wilts like the scattered snapdragons, George repeats the best-known phrases: "Requiescat in pace . . . Requiem aeternam dona eis, Domine." Suddenly, Nick reveals his illumination about their child, asking, "You couldn't have . . . any?" And George replies, "*We* couldn't"—a sentence that Martha echoes with Albee's scenic direction: *"A hint of communion in this."* It is the broadest hint we have. After the departure of Nick and Honey, the dialogue narrows down to monosyllables until George hums the title refrain, and Martha admits that *she* is afraid of Virginia Woolf— a woman afflicted with a madness that drove her to suicide.

Martha's fear is understandable. Whatever will they do, now that their bean bag is dead, their illusion exorcised? Since Albee once planned to give the Act III title, "The Exorcism," to the entire play, we know the importance he attaches to it. To exorcise is to drive out evil spirits, and in New Carthage the evil spirits are the illusion of progeny—Honey's "hot air" pregnancy and Martha's imaginary son. These are comparable illusions, but they differ in causes and effects. Honey seems to have forced Nick into a marriage which "cured" her of the illusion of pregnancy. During marriage her "delicacy" is the apparent reason that they have no children. Without truth or illusion, they live in a vacuum of surface amenities, a mishmash of syrupy Honey and trivial Nicks. But when Martha indulges in an idealized biography of her son (before George kills him), Honey announces abruptly, "I want a child." She repeats this wish just before Martha shifts from the son as ideal biography to the son as weapon against George. Though Honey's conversion is sudden (and scarcely credible), it seems to be sustained.

For George and Martha, the exorcism is less certain, less complete, and more involving. The marriage of Nick and Honey kills their illusion, but the illusion of George and Martha is born in wedlock, perhaps because they could have no real children, and Martha "had wanted a child." Martha's recitation indicates that the conception of the child—intellectual rather than biological—may have originated as a game, but the lying game expressed their need. Since we never see George and Martha alone at their game, we do not know whether it is played soft or hard, though it probably varies between Martha's penchant for sentimentality and George's probing thrusts. Until this *Walpurgisnacht* when magic runs rampant, the couple seems to have kept private both tender and taunting use of the son.

Uninteresting in themselves, Nick and Honey function as foils and parallels of George and Martha: the syllabic similarity of the names, the parallel fantasies of the women, the opposing professions of the men, and the cross-couples advancing the plot. Without Nick, Martha's adultery would not have driven George to murder their son; without Honey, George could not have accomplished the murder.

Albee's repetitions of "True or False" and "Truth versus Illusion" emphasize truth, but it is problematical whether truth will succeed, and Albee deliberately leaves it problematical, refusing Martha the easy conversion of Honey. Unless the Act III title, "The Exorcism," is ironic, however, George and Martha rebuild their marriage on the base of truth, though their gifts seem more destructive than constructive. The lasting impression of the play is not of exorcising but of exercising the wits of George and Martha.

In *Who's Afraid of Virginia Woolf?* Albee reaches a pinnacle of mastery of American colloquial idiom. Since colloquialism is usually associated with realism, the play has been viewed as realistic psychology. But credible motivation drives psychological drama, and Albee's motivation is designedly flimsy: Why does George stay up to entertain Martha's guests? Why, for that matter, does she invite them? And why do Honey and Nick allow themselves to be "gotten"? The play coheres magnetically only if we accept the *Walpurgisnacht* as a *donnée;* these four people are together to dramatize more than themselves.

George describes his novel: "Well, it's an allegory, really—probably—but it can be read as straight, cozy prose. . . ." No one has called Albee's prose "cozy," but it too has been read and heard as "straight" realism, sometimes of "crooked" sexuality. Like George's novel, however, Albee's drama is "an allegory, really—probably."

Albee sets *"Who's Afraid of Virginia Woolf?* in a fictional New Carthage. Carthage, which means "New City," was founded in the ninth century B.C. by a semilegendary, deceitful Dido, and it was razed to the ground by real Romans in 146 A.D. By the fifth century it had again become a power, which St. Augustine in his *Confessions* called "a cauldron of unholy loves." Albee uses the historical conjunction of sex and power as spice for the American stew he simmers in this cauldron. He himself suggested: "George and Martha may represent the Washingtons and the play may be all about the decline of the West."

Albee's unholy lovers are George and Martha, whose names evoke America's first and childless White House couple. As the legendary George Washington could not tell a lie, Albee's George murders in the name of Truth. George describes his fictional son as "Our own little all-American something-or-other." Albee suggests that illusion is an American weakness, and American drama has been much concerned with illusion. But Albee's America is representative of contemporary Western civilization.

An early stage direction indicates Albee's inclusive intent: George *"With a handsweep tak[es] in not only the room, the house, but the whole countryside."* He characterizes the region as "Illyria . . . Penguin Island . . . Gomorrah. . . ." Realm of fantasy, realm of social satire, realm of sin—George's condemnatory geography seems to be that of Albee as well, with an academic foursome representing the decline of the fabulous, sinful West. Within the West, a humanistic George opposes a mechanized Nick; George can see the handwriting on the wall, and it is the penmanship of Oswald Spengler, whose book George flings at the chimes that become a death knell. On one broad level, then, *Who's Afraid of Virginia Woolf?* is in the American dramatic tra-

dition of Attack-the-Illusion: O'Neill's *The Iceman Cometh,* Williams' *The Glass Menagerie,* and Miller's *Death of a Salesman.*

Albee also reaches out beyond America into a metaphysical examination of the nature of love, which may be a metaphor for Western civilization. Concealing eschatology beneath surface psychology, however, Albee's play is limited by its camouflage. George's vitriolic idiom overshadows his anemic humanist yearnings; his views of history are simplistic—the construct-a-civilization speech; his views of biology are simple-minded—the mechanical Nick-maker. George wants to defend Western civilization against its sex-oriented, success-oriented assailants ("I will not give up Berlin") but his defense of life and love is too closely centered in his scrotum. Better at attack than defense, George is more effective *against* illusory dragons than *for* bastions of civilization.

Since that civilization is classico-Christian in tradition, Albee unobtrusively sprinkles the play with classical and Christian resonances: Martha's opening expletive is "Jesus," and both men swear Christian oaths; the imaginary child is associated with the sun and golden fleece; the offstage fathers of Martha and Honey are seen as god-figures. But these hints remain peripheral in *Who's Afraid of Virginia Woolf?* The focus on human love leaves little room for the divine.

Tiny Alice, in contrast, interweaves human and divine love (and hatred) so that the strands are virtually inseparable. In an interview Albee claimed that *Tiny Alice* is a mystery play in two senses of the word: "That is, it's both a metaphysical mystery and, at the same time, a conventional 'Dial M for Murder'-type mystery." But the one murder in *Tiny Alice*—the Lawyer's shooting of Julian—takes place before our eyes, bereft of detective-story mystery. Instead, the mystery of what is happening onstage dissolves into the larger mystery of what happens in the realm of ultimate reality. Governing both is a conception of mystery as that which is hidden from human understanding. With *Tiny Alice* Albee's ambition grows as large as that of O'Neill, who claimed to be "interested only in the relation between man and God."

Albee's protagonist is Brother Julian, who claims to be "dedicated to the reality of things, rather than the appearance," but who has to be violently shocked—mortally wounded—before he recognizes reality, and even then he tries to rearrange it into familiar appearance. Using the disjunctive technique of Absurdism and the terminology of Christianity, Albee drapes a veil of unknowing over a mystery of wide relevance. Thus, the play is nowhere in place and time, though the flavor is vaguely contemporary and American. The three stage settings are fantastic, and Miss Alice's millions are counted in no currency. Time moves with the imprecision of a dream, and yet it is, as the Lawyer claims, "the great revealer." Except for pointed references to Julian's "six blank years," Albee obscures the *passing* of time; the Lawyer says that Miss Alice's grant is a hundred million a year for twenty years, and after Julian is shot, the Lawyer offers the Cardinal "two billion, kid, twenty years of grace for no work at all." The play may thus have lasted twenty years between the twelve "tick's" in the Lawyer's opening gibberish and Julian's dying question, "IS IT NIGHT . . . OR DAY? . . . Or does it matter?"

Of the five characters, two have names, two are named by their function, and one—Butler—bears the name of his function. Albee has denied the suggestion that Alice stands for Truth and Julian for Apostasy, but he cannot expunge such associations for us. Named or unnamed, however, all characters are locked into their functions: Brother Julian into serv-ice to his God, the Cardinal into service to his church, and the castle trio into service to their deity, knowable only as the mouse in the model. Servants of Tiny Alice, they appear to master the rest of the world. Like the trio in Sartre's *No Exit,* they are bound in an eternal love-hate triangle, but *their* mission is to deliver victims to Tiny Alice, at once a reduced truth and a small obscene aperture into an aspect of being. (Tiny Alice is homosexual slang for a tight anus.)

Julian, a lay brother, is Albee's Christian hero in this modern mystery play. John Gielgud, creator of the role, commented, "The wonderful relief that I had about this part was that I was *supposed* to keep wondering what it was all about." So pervasive is Julian's bewilderment that some critics have suggested the entire play takes place in Julian's mind. But Albee is working on a larger stage. As in medieval mystery plays, we are involved in the conflict within a tempted soul, but we are aware too of our world in which that conflict resonates. Rather than Virtue versus Vice, Albee's Julian is torn between Truth and Illusion, between a desire for the real and his irrepressible imagination.

Though Julian is at the center of the play, Albee delays introducing him. Instead, he begins the drama with personifications of power, à la Jean Genet: Cardinal and Lawyer, sacred and profane, church and state, buddies and enemies, with a long past behind them. We first see Julian at the castle, in conversation with the Butler, whose symbolic function is central—a stewardship based on his serving of wine, Christian metaphor for blood. The Butler also offers Julian water, tea, coffee, before port and champagne—sweet and effervescent forms of wine—and, appropriately, the Butler tries to sweeten the ineluctable claims of Tiny Alice upon Julian. The Butler guides Julian through the wine cellar of the castle, and he pours champagne at Julian's wedding, which is his last supper.

Albee mocks his own dialogue in *Tiny Alice*: Julian comments on the Butler's name, Butler, "You would be in for some rather tiresome exchanges," and the Butler retorts, "None more than this." The Butler describes the Lawyer's imagery, "This is an endless metaphor." Though Albee continues to build his dialogue with monologue and insulting exchange, he uses them somewhat differently in *Tiny Alice*: the verbal skirmishing often ends in a draw, and the monologues sound painfully explicit but are buried in the central mystery, which is unknowable.

As in earlier Albee plays, thrust-and-parry dialogue leads obliquely to murder. The master verbal fencer of *Tiny Alice,* the Lawyer, shoots Julian, but Miss Alice is the principal agent of his undoing, and she, as the Lawyer remarks, was "never one with words." Rather, she acts through surprises: the old hag turns into a lovely woman; unprompted, she confesses to Julian her carnal relations with the Butler and the Lawyer; abruptly, she inquires into Julian's sex life; before marrying and abandoning Julian, she alternates a mysterious prayer with an address to "someone in the model." She cradles the wounded Julian, making *"something of a Pietà."* At the end she is cruel and kind; her last words are "Oh, my poor Julian." Yet she leaves him.

Miss Alice's seduction of Julian is accomplished through deeds rather than words, but Julian himself translates the erotic into a highly verbal mysticism. He defends his loquacity to Miss Alice, "Articulate men often carry set paragraphs." In each of the play's three acts Julian indulges in a rhapsodic monologue that does not sound like a set paragraph, since the rhythms are jagged. The cumulative effect is apocalyptic, but Julian's apocalypse is sexually rooted, *lay* brother that he is (Albee's

pun). In Act I Julian describes a perhaps hallucinatory sexual experience with a woman who occasionally hallucinated as the Blessed Virgin. Not only does Julian speak of ejaculation; he speaks *in* ejaculations. Julian's mistress with an illusory pregnancy recalls the illusion-ridden women of *Virginia Woolf;* as the imaginary child of that play is an evil spirit to be exorcised, the imaginary pregnancy of the hallucinating woman of *Tiny Alice* proves to be a fatal cancer. And even as Julian confesses to Miss Alice what he believes to be his struggle for the real, she tempts him with her own desirability—very beautiful and very rich.

In Julian's Act II monologue about martyrdom he shifts his identity—a child, both lion and gladiator, then saint and the hallucinating self of the Act I monologue. While Julian describes this eroto-mystical, multi-personal martyrdom. Miss Alice shifts her attitude, first urging Julian to marry her, then spurring him to sacrifice himself to Alice, whom she invokes in the third person.

In Act III Julian, who left the asylum because he was persuaded that hallucination was inevitable and even desirable, embarks on his final hallucination which ends in his real death. Abandoned and dying, Julian recollects (or imagines) a wound of his childhood, as Miss Alice in her prayer recollected (or imagined) being hurt in *her* childhood. Alternately a child and the hallucinating woman who called for help, Julian is forced to face himself in death—the prototypical existential confrontation. With phrases of the Thirteenth Psalm, Julian very slowly and desperately dissolves Miss Alice into Tiny Alice into the Christian God. Unable to accept "the ceremony of Alice," Julian recoils from the hermetic, dust-free vacuum of Tiny Alice, from the unblinking eyes of the phrenological head ("Ah God! Is that the humor? THE ABSTRACT? . . . REAL?

THE REST? . . . FALSE?"). Unable to laugh at such absurd humor, Julian reverts to Christian illusion, to ready-made images that protect him from the reality of abstraction, which is death. Though buried in mystery, death is omnipresent in *Tiny Alice*.

Julian calls on deity in the words of Christ on the cross: "ALICE? MY GOD, WHY HAST THOU FORSAKEN ME?" As a "great presence" engulfs him, panting and stamping, Julian takes the crucifixion position, injecting his God into Alice, "God, Alice . . . I accept thy will." Albee's play opens on Genet's *Balcony*, and it closes on the blackness of Ionesco's dying king; both Julian and Bérenger go down fighting against predatory death, but they both go down—into the void. On a throne, or crucified, or whimpering in bed, Everyman is food for Tiny Alice, who devours in mystery.

Julian's three experiences pivot on his confusion between illusion and reality; the sexual experience may have been a hallucination; the experience of martyrdom has haunted Julian's imagination, and he dies in an evocation of Christ the martyr, who may be his last illusion. Rhythms of ecstatic agony and the image of blood link the three experiences, or the three descriptions of experience, which may become experience *through* description.

Between his three monologues as within them, Julian's speech is fragmentary, interrogative, recapitulatory. In contrast to the sinewy syntax of the Lawyer, Julian's sentence fragments are heavy with gerunds, adjectives, efforts at definition through synonyms. As Jerry's indirection mirrored the theme of *The Zoo Story*, Julian's phrasal fragmentation—skillfully arresting in the theater—mirrors the theme of *Tiny Alice,* and that fragmentation functions partly as synecdoche.

"In my Father's house are many mansions," said Christ (John 14:2), and in the mansion of Tiny Alice are many rooms; true to his heredity and calling, Brother Julian praises library, chapel, and wine cellar—all with religious associations. Alone in the library after his wedding, he recalls the childhood loneliness of an attic closet. But all rooms belong to Tiny Alice, and space does not contain them. When the fire in the model announces a fire in the chapel, Julian asks Miss Alice, "Why, why did it happen that way—in both dimensions?" After his wedding, Julian likens the disappearance of people to "an hour elaps[ing] or a . . . dimension." And shortly before shooting Julian, the Lawyer remarks to his buddy-enemy, the Cardinal: "We have come quite a . . . dimension, have we not?" In *Tiny Alice* dimensions are deliberately diffused and confused; one does not move, as in the Great Chain of Being, from an animal dimension, to a human, to angelic, to divine. Rather, all dimensions are interactive, and point to the whole metaphysical mystery in its private parts.

Those parts are sexual, but Albee also suggests them through insistence on birds and children—vulnerable both. Bird imagery embraces everyone: the play opens with a nonsense address to birds; the Cardinal has cardinals in his stone and iron garden; the Butler speaks of swallows "screeping"; the Lawyer's poem has the grace of a walking crow; Miss Alice is first visible in a *wing* chair, and she later envelops Julian in the "great wing" of her robe; Julian is variously a "bird of pray," a drab fledgling," and a "little bird, pecking away in the library," summarizing his piety, innocence, and sexual vulnerability. At times, too, the characters act like children, or they summon recollections of childhood. Julian is often and explicitly called "little," and in his dying soliloquy he becomes a little boy calling for his cookie. All these lines suggest the helplessness of birds and children in the world of Tiny Alice, who is mouselike, monstrous, and feline.

Like imagery and fragmentation, Albee's language in *Tiny Alice* is highly complex. Familiar is the stinging salaciousness of the opening scene between Cardinal and Lawyer. This functions symbolically since the Cardinal-church is the son of a whore, and the Lawyer-state eats offal and carrion. The titillation of these disclosures is counterpointed against the formality of the syntax—first-person plurals, avoidance of contractions, emphasis on prepositional nuance, and self-conscious wordplay (the eye of an odor). Only rarely does the Lawyer slip into a vigorous Americanism: "Oh, come on, Your Eminence." "You'll grovel, Buddy. . . . As automatically and naturally as people slobber on that ring of yours." "Everyone diddled everyone else." "We picked up our skirts and lunged for it! ɪɪɪɪɪ! Me! Me! Gimme!"

The Lawyer, who evokes Satan for the Cardinal, is the chief instrument of Albee's mutilating dialogue. Not only does he thrust at the Cardinal; he sneers endearments to the Butler, and he woos Miss Alice as "clinically" as he fondles her. At his first meeting with Julian he belittles the Cardinal and humiliates Julian. After shooting Julian, the Lawyer directs the death scene, with no pity for the dying martyr. The Butler characterizes the Lawyer: "You're a cruel person, straight through; it's not cover; you're hard and cold, saved by dedication; just that." And yet, both the Cardinal and the Butler call the Lawyer "good," for he *is* good in his dedication to Tiny Alice, and his virulent wit sparks through the play's dark mystery.

In *Virginia Woolf* George's wit lashes out to "Get the Guests," but his cruelties zero in on Martha, whose illusion he murders. Despite the four characters in that play, the sustained duel is between George and Martha. In *Tiny Alice* the Lawyer lashes out indiscriminately, though he claims never to have shot anyone before Julian. The deed of murder is his, but the responsibility is shared by the other three; murder is "an accident"—"What does it matter . . . one man . . . in the face of so much"—for the dedicated agents of Tiny Alice.

On Julian's wedding day, which becomes his death day, the Lawyer sneeringly dubs him Frank Fearnought. Frightened that he may be married to Tiny Alice, Frank Fearnought threatens to return to his asylum; it is then that the Lawyer shoots Julian. The surrogates are evidently charged with wedding Julian to the castle in which Tiny Alice dwells, the castle which *is* Tiny Alice. Married by the Lawyer's shot rather than the Cardinal's ceremony, Julian slowly proceeds to pattern his passion on that of Christ.

Earlier, Julian used clichés of ecstasy for a business deal: "That God has seen fit to let me be His instrument in this undertaking." Dying, Julian flings the same word at the Lawyer, as a last insult: "Instrument." Albee's play has developed the Lawyer as the instrument of Absurd reality, which is Tiny Alice. Julian, on the other hand, is first and last the instrument of his own imagination. He is both Everyman and the victim of the "awful humor" of Tiny Alice, precisely because he claims to reject illusion for reality. *That* is his illusion, with which he commits himself to an asylum. And rather than accept the reality of Tiny Alice, he is ready to commit himself again but is prevented by the Lawyer's fatal shot. The cynical lucid Lawyer has already foretold the pattern of Julian's final behavior, mixing the formal and the colloquial in the same speech: "face the inevitable and call it what you have always wanted. How to come out on top, going under."

Because he bends his imagination to embrace the inevitable, Julian achieves the difficult martyrdom he seeks. Onstage the long dying scene borders on the ridiculous, as Julian's initial resistance to the inevitable is ridiculous. But, "going under," he summons the herioc illusion of his culture; not a "Gingerbread God with the raisin eyes," but a human god crucified for man. Julian dies in imitation of Christ, deaf to Tiny monstrous Alice, who comes thumping and panting to devour him. The curtain falls on blackness, Alice, truth, reality, after Julian has been crucified in his illusion. Our lasting impression is that of a hero—vulnerable, loquacious, willfully blind, but nevertheless heroic in the intensity of his imagination.

Even puzzled audiences have been involved in Julian's plight, which the Butler describes: "Is walking on the edge of an abyss, but is balancing." Albee's next play, *A Delicate Balance,* is named for that perilous equilibrium. Like *Virginia Woolf,* the play presents a realistic surface; as in *Virginia Woolf,* a love relationship in one couple is explored through the impact of another couple. There is enough talking and drinking to convey the impression of a muted, diluted *Virginia Woolf.* And yet *A Delicate Balance,* like *Tiny Alice,* is death-obsessed symbolism.

Each of the six characters of *A Delicate Balance* "is walking on the edge of an abyss, but is balancing"; a middle-aged marriage is balancing too, until a makeshift home in a "well-appointed suburban house" is threatened by both family and friends. In Friday night Act I, terror-driven friends seek refuge in the family home; in Saturday night Act II, the master of the house, Tobias, assures his friends of their welcome, but his daughter Julia reacts hysterically to their presence. In Sunday morning Act III, the friends know that they are not welcome, know that they would not have welcomed, and they leave. The delicate balance of the home is preserved.

The play begins and ends, however, on a different delicate balance—that of the mind of Agnes, mistress of the house, wife of Tobias, mother of Julia, sister of Claire. In convoluted Jamesian sentences she opens and closes the play with doubts about her sanity; at the beginning she also extends these doubts to an indefinite "you"—"that each of you wonders if each of *you* might not . . ." As we meet the other members of the family, we can understand the wonder: Claire the chronic drunk, Julia the chronic divorcée, and Tobias who heads the house. Though Agnes starts and finishes the play on her doubts about sanity, each of the acts dramatizes the precarious stability of the other members of the family: first Claire, then Julia, and finally Tobias. In each case the balance is preserved, a little more delicate, perhaps, for being threatened.

Each member of the family contributes to the atmosphere of emptiness, but no one exists in a vacuum; they are bound by love. In Claire's words to Tobias, "You love Agnes and Agnes loves Julia and Julia loves me and I love you . . . Yes, to the depths of our self-pity and our greed. What else but love?" Claire's definition may be brushed by modern psychology, but Albee's plays are never reducible to psychology. If Agnes is responsible for Claire's continuous drinking and Julia's four marriages, she is also concerned "to keep in shape." Blaming the others for their faults, she describes such blame as the "souring side of love" in this drama about the limits of love.

Agnes early characterizes the family to Tobias: "your steady wife, your alcoholic sister-in-law and occasional visits . . . from our melancholy Julia." But her description is only a first approximation; her own steadiness is severely strained, Claire insists that she is not "a alcoholic," and Julia is more hysterical than melancholy. By Act III a harassed Tobias, having suffered his Passion, offers a contrasting description of the same family: "And you'll all sit down and watch me carefully; smoke your pipes and stir the cauldron; watch." He thus groups wife, daughter, sister-in-law as three witches, or the three Fates "who make all the decisions, really rule the game . . ." and who preside over the term of life, until death cuts it off.

As in other Albee plays, death lurks in the dialogue of *A Delicate Balance*, but death is not actualized in this drama; violence is confined to a single slap, a glass of orange juice poured on the rug, and an ineffectual threat with a gun. In words, however, Claire urges Tobias to shoot them all, first Agnes, then Julia, and herself last. Agnes suggests that Claire kill herself, and Claire in turn asks Agnes, "Why don't you die?" It is this sisterly exchange between Claire and Agnes that inspires Tobias to his digressive monologue, his cat story. Because his cat inexplicably stopped liking him, Tobias first slapped her and then had her killed. Out of the depths of his self-pity and greed, he had her killed.

Like Jerry's dog story, Tobias' cat story (suggested by director Alan Schneider) is an analogue for the whole play of which it is part. As Tobias kills the cat, he will effectively kill his friends, Harry and Edna, when he denies them a home. As Claire and Agnes approve his conduct toward the cat, Claire and Julia will approve his conduct toward Harry and Edna. The death of the cat maintains Tobias' delicate emotional balance in spite of his bad conscience, and the departure of Harry and Edna will maintain Tobias' delicate family balance in spite of his bad conscience.

The threat of death is almost personified by Harry and Edna. Julia tries to aim her father's gun at the visitors, and Agnes calls their terror a plague. In demanding that Tobias make a decision with respect to Harry and Edna, Agnes reminds him of the intimate details of their sexual life after the death of their son, Teddy. By the end of the play, Harry and Edna, conscious of their own mortality, decide to leave, taking their plague with them.

A Delicate Balance is itself in most delicate balance between the cruel kindness of its surface and dark depths below, between a dead child and a new dawn, between ways of living and ways of loving. Albee has posed his equilibrium discreetly without the symbolic histrionics of *Tiny Alice,* without the coruscating dialogue of *Virginia Woolf.* At the most general level, the arrival of Harry and Edna raises the question of the limits of love; Tobias to Harry: "I find my liking you has limits . . . BUT THOSE ARE MY LIMITS! NOT YOURS!" And Edna to the other women: "the only skin you've ever known . . . is your own." Harry and Edna reveal the terror beneath bland surfaces. Before their arrival, Agnes thanks Tobias for a life without mountains or chasms, "a rolling, pleasant land." But the plague can arrive in rolling, pleasant lands, and it is carried by one's best friends.

In Harry and Edna, Albee creates prismatic symbols, for they are at once Tobias and Agnes and their friend-enemies. Described in the players' list as "very much like Agnes and Tobias," Edna and Harry live in the same suburb and belong to the same club. They are godparents to Julia, as Agnes and Tobias are her parents. When Harry serves drinks, Agnes remarks that he is "being Tobias." When Edna scolds Julia, Albee's scenic direction indicates that she "become[s] Agnes." Just before leaving, Edna speaks in the convoluted formal sentences of Agnes.

Otherwise, however, Harry and Edna do not sound like Tobias and Agnes, and they did not look like them in the original production supervised by Albee. Edna weeps whereas Agnes rarely cries; Edna shows desire whereas Agnes conceals it. As clearsighted Claire (Albee's pun) points out to Tobias, all he shares with Harry is the memory of a summer infidelity with the same girl (who may be Claire). Tobias denies being frightened, while fright ambushes Harry and Edna. Harry admits honestly what Tobias conceals clumsily: "I wouldn't take them in." At the last, when her best friends leave, Agnes lapses into a rare cliché: "Don't be strangers," and Edna replies, "Oh, good Lord, how could we be? Our lives are . . . the same." Rather than being *like* Agnes and Tobias, Edna and Harry are *the same as* Agnes and Tobias—minus a family.

Terror drives Harry and Edna from their house because a couple is inadequate bulwark against emptiness; they are free of the blood ties which protect one from the loneliness of self and the encroachment of living death. Harry and Edna come onstage after a family conversation about the bonds of love; their terror has no cause: "WE WERE FRIGHTENED . . . AND THERE WAS NOTHING." They were frightened *because* there was nothing.

In dramatizing·the failure of love, Albee is ascetically sparing of his dazzling dialogue and subtle imagery. Though he does not quite indulge in the fallacy of imitative form, he implies that a drama with emptiness at its center must echo in hollowness. Each time two characters start a verbal thrust-and-parry, the spark is damped. Each of the characters apologizes at least once, snuffing out verbal fireworks. Damped, too, are the few threads of imagery—the household, childhood, helping, and sinking.

Sparing his imagery, Albee plays upon the verb *want* to sustain the delicate balance. Its double meaning, wish and lack, were already suggested in *Tiny Alice*, and Albee exploits this ambiguity in *A Delicate Balance*. Claire wishes Agnes to die but doesn't know whether she want it. Hysterical, Julia shifts from "they [Harry and Edna] want" to "I WANT . . . WHAT IS MINE!!" Agnes asks Harry and Edna pointedly, "What do you *really* . . . *want*? And some

minutes later, Edna replies, playing on the same verb: "if all at once we . . . NEED . . . we come where we are wanted, where we know we are expected, not only where we want." Harry insistently questions Tobias: "Do you *want* us here?" And in Tobias' final aria, he shifts from: "I WANT YOU HERE!" to "I DON'T WANT YOU HERE! I DON'T LOVE YOU! BUT BY GOD . . . YOU STAY!!" Love is lack and love is wish in *A Delicate Balance*, and Albee suggests that the human condition is to be bounded by want—lack and wish.

Each of the sisters uses her own rhythm to state the play's theme:

AGNES: There *is* a balance to be maintained, after all, though the rest of you teeter, uncaring, *assuming* you're on level ground . . . by divine right, I gather, though that is hardly so. . . .

CLAIRE: We can't have changes—throws the balance off.

The death of their son, Teddy, has thrown off the balance in the home of Tobias and Agnes, who teetered in a household that gradually took on the new balance of a home. Rather than upset the balance, Claire and Harry both lie to Agnes about the infidelity of Tobias. Rather than upset the balance, the family members play out their identity patterns, with only momentary shifts: Agnes poses as Julia's father, Tobias imitates Julia's hysteria, Claire plays a Tobias who explains to a judge the murder of his family, Julia spouts the opinions of her most recent husband, and Claire may be the nameless upended girl whom Tobias and Harry seduced one "dry and oh, so wet July." Edna speaks of and for them all when she summarizes her recognition of the delicacy of all balance, which is life: "It's sad to come to the end of it, isn't it, nearly the end; so much more of it gone by . . . than left, and still not know—still not have learned

. . . the boundaries, what we may not do . . . not ask, for fear of looking in a mirror."

In generalizing the predicament of his characters into the human condition, Albee relies on biblical associations of "house," as on associations of the names of the two couples, and of the three days between Good Friday and Easter Sunday, when Christ suffered his Passion. Harry, whom clear-sighted Claire calls "old Harry," is a nickname of the devil, whereas Agnes is the lamb of God. The two couples, who are identical, range from angelic expressions of love to diabolic noncommitment. The other two names, Tobias and Edna, figure in the Book of Tobit; by angelic intervention Tobias was able to marry Sara, though her first seven bridegrooms died before possessing her; the mother of Sara was Edna. Albee's parallels with the Book of Tobit are obscure; nevertheless, the Book of Tobit is concerned, like *A Delicate Balance*, with ties of blood and with the burial of the dead. Albee's Tobias is occasionally called Toby or Tobe, and like his biblical eponym, he is faced with the problem of Being, assaulted by death.

In Albee's "two inter-related plays," *Box* and *Quotations from Chairman Mao Tse-tung*, he again explores being threatened by death. Like Proust, Albee finds that art alone conserves traces of being, and he conveys this by a unique dramatic form. Nothing happens onstage. The plays deny passing time, and the set abstracts specific place.

Box presents us with the titular box that takes up *"almost all of a small stage opening."* While we look at the box, in a constant bright light, we hear the disembodied voice of a woman, which *"should seem to be coming from nearby the spectator."* In the second of the two inter-related plays, *Quotations from Mao Tse-tung* (about eight times the length of *Box*), an ocean liner appears within the outline of the box. Aboard are four visible char-

acters—Mao Tse-tung and an Old Woman who addresses the audience directly, a Long-Winded Lady in a deck chair who *"uses as a sounding board"* a silent clergyman in his deck chair. The three monologues are soon punctuated by phrases from the disembodied voice of *Box*. In a final *Reprise* about half the *Box* monologue is heard while we watch the four silhouettes of *Mao*—now silent. Throughout both plays we see a box, that three-dimensional building-block in space. The four characters, as Liliane Kerjan suggests, sail upon a sea of infinite time: the past of the Old Woman, the present of the Long-Winded Lady, the future of Chairman Mao, and the eternity of the silent clergyman.

Though the voice of *Box* does not emanate from the stage box, it uses that figure as a springboard. Albee has already used boxes in *The Sandbox* and *The American Dream*, where they were associated with Grandma, who is close to death. And coffin associations spring readily to mind in *Box*. But the voice of *Box* moves quickly beyond the visible, to the possibility of a rocking chair in the box, to generalizations about crafts, and on to art. Through a lyric threnody of loss, the voice suggests that art is powerless to prevent catastrophe— "seven hundred million babies dead"—and that the very practice of art is a kind of corruption in times of disaster. But only art can give us "the memory of what we have not known," can introduce us to experiences we cannot otherwise know, as sea sounds can frighten the landlocked. In a world where "nothing belongs" art strives for order.

Mao opens the second of the inter-related plays with a fable from Chapter XXI of the Red Book, which glorifies the Chinese masses. Mao then moves on to Communist theory and tactics, growing more and more aggressive in language, though *"his tone is always reasonable"* and his purpose always pedagogic. Many of his quotations are drawn from Chapter VI of the "little red book," "Imperialism and All Reactionaries are Paper Tigers." In that chapter the arch-imperialist is the United States, so Mao's final words damn America: "People of the world, unite and defeat the U.S. aggressors and all their running dogs." Mao's patiently positive attitude culminates in an injunction to widespread killing.

The Old Woman *"might nod in agreement with Mao now and again,"* perhaps because she is poor, perhaps because she feels oppressed. We cannot know the reason, since her words, like those of Mao, are restricted to quotation—from Will Carleton's "Over the Hill to the Poor-House." The persona of that poem whines her way through rejection by each of her six children, and she closes on an accusation disguised as prayer: "And God'll judge between us; but I will al'ays pray/That you shall never suffer the half I do today."

Mao has delivered a formulaic diatribe, the Old Woman a formulaic lament, but the Long-Winded Lady is wholly personal. She starts with an onomatopoeic splash, imagining the reaction of "theoretical . . . onwatchers." Associationally, she continues to a childhood memory of breaking her thumb, then a more recent recollection of a taxi going wild. As she enters with a plate of crullers on the last bloody scene, the Long-Winded Lady comments on the utter inadequacy of any response to disaster. More and more, the theme of death begins to link her disparate associations: uncle, sister, and husband speak of death in her monologue, and her husband was aware of the perpetual process of dying before he was attacked by the cancer that killed him. Though his dying is now over, "his *death* stays." And it is with that death that the Long-Winded Lady lives, having no communion with her daughter, and no relationship with anyone else.

Finally, toward the end of the play, the Long-Winded Lady describes the opening splash in detail. It is *her* splash, but she describes it without a single "I." She fell off an ocean liner (like the one on which we see her) *splash* into the ocean. Ironically and improbably, however, she did not sink but was rescued. After congratulations came questions: Could anyone have pushed her? Did she throw herself off? Try to kill herself? The Long-Winded Lady closes her monologue and the *Mao* part of Albee's play with a half-laughing denial: "Good heavens, no; *I* have nothing to die for." It is a brilliant twist of the cliché: "I have nothing to live for." We live—most of us—by natural momentum, but voluntary death demands a dedication beyond the power of the Long-Winded Lady—or of most of us in the long wind of our lives.

As the disembodied woman's voice opens the "inter-related plays," so it closes them in a "reprise." But between *Box* and *Reprise*, Albee expunges catastrophe from the Voice's monologue, having suggested disaster in each of the three separate monologues of *Mao*. *Reprise* retains the *Box* images of music, birds, order, and an art that hurts. Though the Voice is matter-of-fact, even *"schoolmarmish,"* it is lyrical in the hint that emotion alone invests events with meaning, and yet the emotion evoked by art cannot act upon events. Pain can merely be contained by the order of art—"Box."

From Chekhov on, we have been familiar with characters who talk past each other, rather than engaging one another in dialogue. But in *Mao* each of the characters is unaffected by the other's speech; we cannot even tell whether they hear it. And the speeches are linked not by plot but by the theme of death. Stylistically, they differ, but they all use repetition. Mao emphasizes single words or ideas by reiteration.

The Old Woman does not recite Carleton's poem straight through, but chooses certain lines or stanzas to linger over and dwell upon. Occasional phrases of the Long-Winded Lady recur—above all, "dying." After the initial performance of *Box*, all the words of the disembodied voice are repetitions, and the final *Reprise* is what it means—a repetition. The *Reprise* joins end to beginning of Albee's play in a kind of musical parallel for a box, but since music moves in time, repetition becomes thematic through the strains of the dialogue.

Because the Long-Winded Lady alone has a personal, a *dramatic* monologue, she is at the center of Albee's play. Seeking the counsel of a silent clergyman, she is implicitly threatened by the two other figures on this ship of fools within the box of art—the ruthless system of Mao and the maudlin poverty of the Old Woman. Long-winded, unrooted, the Lady is a middle-aged, middle-class Miss America, that dying outpost of Western civilization. But unlike George, Julian, or Tobias, who also represent the Western tradition in Albee's plays, the Long-Winded Lady utters no words of optimism or heroism. Harrowed by death, she offers the stuff of her life through the words of Albee's art. In these "inter-related plays" Albee has used the symbol of a box as both coffin and work of art. Living experience is coffined by the artifact of art, but, paradoxically, such coffining is the only way to preserve the experience. *Box-Mao-Box* is Albee's Cubist play, not only in form but in content. Like Cubist collage, *Box-Mao-Box* is *about* the art it is.

All Over returns to more traditional imitation of an action. As in *The Intruder* by Maeterlinck (who is mentioned in Albee's play) or *Waiting for Godot* by Beckett, the action is waiting. A family waits at the deathbed of its head. Seven people wait for a man to die.

"Waiting for death" might summarize these plays, as it might summarize the human condition. In *All Over* Albee moves death to the dead center of his drama. As the play's Nurse phrases it: "Death, yes; well, it gets us where we live, doesn't it?"

In the sequence of Albee's work, *All Over* seems to follow *A Delicate Balance* after the interlude of *Box-Mao-Box*. Both *A Delicate Balance* and *All Over* focus on a family at a point of crisis—Husband, Wife, Sister, Daughter in *A Delicate Balance;* Wife, Son, Daughter, and, almost family, Best Friend and Mistress in *All Over*. Both plays are set in a single large tastefully furnished room which seems to mute loud or vulgar sounds. The very language is muted in both plays, where short exchanges are punctuated by digressive monologues of recollection. Though *All Over* accommodates several monologues, the density of recollection is thin. One has the impression that the characters of *All Over* have spent their lives waiting for life, as they are now waiting for death. And that impression is reinforced by the paucity of physical action onstage. Behind a hospital screen backstage, a man is invisibly dying, but onstage the few exits and entrances become events: The Daughter slams out of the room three times, The Son leaves twice, and The Best Friend once. Doctor and Nurse occasionally disappear behind the screen of the dying man. Just before the Act I curtain The Daughter allows two Photographers and a Reporter to enter the stage room, but The Wife and Mistress drive them out.

The action of the play is rhythmed by a few signs of tension: near the beginning of the play The Wife and The Daughter exchange slaps. Toward the middle The Doctor announces that the dying man has skipped three heartbeats. Near the end The Nurse emerges from behind the hospital screen with bloody uniform (a vivid scarlet and white that recalls the death of Bessie Smith in Albee's second play). Physically, the action of *All Over* is nearly all over, lying in individual and collective reactions to the process of dying.

All the family is onstage almost all the time. Their type names darken the emphasis upon the central situation, and their type names darken the fact that the characters depend on the dying man for their definition of identity. In waiting for death, the seven characters connive at a kind of murder, as we all do when we outlive those we love.

Unusual in the family grouping is the inclusion of The Mistress, who says explicitly that she is always the Outsider at time of ritual. In this group, however, only The Daughter registers hostility toward her, whereas The Wife accepts her with something like friendship. Albee suggests the repetitive nature of the Wife-Mistress sharing of the life of a man. The Newspaper people· "have their families . . . their wives, their mistresses." The Nurse was long ago The Mistress in another triangle, where the dying man bears the only name we hear in the play—Dr. Dey, which puns on day, a metaphor for man's life. During that brief period a man lives both privately and publicly; he lives through a series of particular intimacies and a sequence of recognized rituals, and he is faithful in his fashion to both aspects of living. Onstage The Wife and The Mistress are aware of the intermittent primacy of the other. Only in a brief scene before the end does The Wife accuse The Mistress while the two are alone onstage.

Albee's use of type names and static situation caused reviewers to condemn *All Over* as "abstract," but Albee is experientially concrete in his depiction of reactions to dying. In the face of death, one becomes one's relationship to the dying person, and yet, in the last hours of what is ambiguously still called life, one registers that relationship through trivia, tensions, or an occasional sick joke—"Is it flame or worm?" Dutifully, one may try to summon memories, to discard stray thought, but the wayward mind will not be reined. A point of grammar may loom large; not "Is he dead?" but "Has he . . . *died?*"

Practical problems may recall us to the immediacy of death, as, in *All Over*, distaste for hospitals pits The Wife and The Mistress against The Daughter and The Nurse. Disposal of the body leads to brief battle between The Wife, who wants traditional burial, and The Mistress, who wants cremation. Though both try to re-create the man they both love, each can lean only on a pair of memories. The Wife recalls his traveling halfway round the world to his son's sickbed. When the children were grown, however, he asked incredulously whether he had really made them. The Mistress recalls that he didn't know about the affair between The Wife and The Best Friend because she ensured that he didn't. And she recalls that he missed his family at Christmas. The Son, The Daughter, and The Best Friend voice no memories, but The Son breaks down upon seeing the dying man's toilet articles— in their usual place in the bathroom. Here too, Albee is true to experience, for things often dominate a death-scene. Like the unnamed characters, unseen things reach out to generalize their meaning.

Generalization is not the abstraction for which Albee has been faulted. His characters are no more abstract than those of *Pilgrim's Progress*, who go through a comparable Valley of the Shadow of Death. Muffled hostility individualizes them: The Wife vs. The Daughter, The Wife vs. The Son, The Best Friend vs. The Son, and at the last The Wife vs. The Mistress. For us the characters take on varying density to the degree that they reveal an individual past. That of the family members is paper thin, but The Mistress has had three other loves in her life, and The Best Friend has had an insane wife whose emotional hold on him is still stronger than that of The Wife, with whom he has had an affair.

Because The Mistress and The Best Friend can recall a past, they can imagine a future of adjustment to the absence of the dying man. But the three members of the family will go their separate ways into a kind of dissolution. The Daughter's slamming of the door, The Son's sobbing, and The Wife's finally incantatory repetitions of "Because I'm unhappy" achieve emotional summits for this family that has lived in its shadow of death. For them, as for the new corpse, it will soon be "all over."

The play's title is heard in its last line—The Doctor's announcement of the death for which they have all been waiting. The two colorless words are a pun. Throughout the play the dying man has been "all over" in two senses—ubiquitous and dead. In spite of their poverty of recollection, the characters have lived largely through their relationship to the invisible man behind the screen. He has been "all over" them, and at the end it is "all over" for them.

A few minutes before the play ends, The Wife realizes: "All we've done . . . is think about ourselves." That is all most of us do in the face of death, and it is what we have heard this family do in the face of its particular death. We have heard it through Albee's deliberately stiff and stylized language, which Harold Clurman has aptly called "frozen fire."

Several reviewers have compared Albee's language to that of Henry James or Ivy Compton-Burnett, and such comparison is apposite for the bravura speeches of The Wife, The Mistress, or The Best Friend. But like the dog story in *The Zoo Story* or the cat story in *A Delicate Balance*, such pieces are rare, and the bulk of the dialogue consists of brief cool phrases, meaning more than they seem to say. The title is the most obvious example of this, but the opening quibble about grammar poses the problem of human nothingness: non-being should not use the verb "to be."

Deliberately muted, Albee's language can characterize or comment with extreme economy. In Act II of *All Over*, under the cover of extreme fatigue, characters repeat words of Act I, but with cumulative meaning. The Daughter's repetitions of "Stop it" contrast with The Mistress's repetitions of "Ah well!" The Daughter is the only character who never says "I'm sorry" (though she wants to waken her mother to tell her that), and she alone is empty of the grief that the others feel to different degrees. That The Wife repeats "I'm sorry" most often implies that her grief is deepest, though she manages her stiff upper lip until almost the end.

In a comparably telling way, Albee deploys the phrase "All right." The Daughter uses it to cut short her mother's account of all that is *wrong* in her life. Sporadically, several characters ask whether one or the other is "all right." It is used absently when a character has not been paying attention. At a climactic moment, when The Nurse enters from behind the screen, she quiets the group with: "It's all right," though the evidence of wrongness—a hemorrhage—is splotched on her uniform.

In their reflective monologues the characters sound similar, but this is Albee's way of underlining the similarity of human reaction to death—morassed in selfishness. In spite of such self-centeredness—almost too explicitly recognized in the play itself—there has been cross-talk, and words have communicated briefly, sharing an experience of death. And who but Albee could have written these lines about a dying man in our scientific age: "A city seen from the air? The rail lines and the roads? Or, an octopus: the body of the beast, the tentacles, electrical controls, recorders, modulators, breath and heart and brain waves, and the tubes?, in either arm and in the nostrils. Where had he gone? In all that . . . equipment. I thought for a moment *he* was keeping *it* . . . functioning. Tubes and wires."

Happy endings are not for Albee; nor does he strain, like Eugene O'Neill and Arthur Miller, for tragedy. Rather, Albee shares with Absurdist writers, in his words, "an absorption-in-art of certain existentialist and post-existentialist philosophical concepts having to do, in the main, with man's attempts to make sense for himself out of his senseless position in a world which makes no sense—which makes no sense because the moral, religious, political and social structures man has erected to 'illusion' himself have collapsed." In successive plays Albee has dramatized man's several attempts to make sense *of* himself and *for* himself.

Albee has been moving away from political and social structures toward moral and religious illusion. Thus, the greedy, conformist American family of *The American Dream* differs markedly from the greedy, love-bound family of *A Delicate Balance*, as apocalyptic Jerry of *The Zoo Story* differs markedly from apocalyptic Julian of *Tiny Alice*. Common to several of Albee's plays is the existentialist view of an Outsider who suffers at the hands of the Establishment—social, moral, or religious—which announces itself in "peachy-keen" clichés that indict those who mouth them—Peter, Mommy, the Nurse, Nick. Albee has moved from this American anti-American idiom into the metaphysical suggestiveness of *Tiny Alice, A Delicate Balance, Box,* and *All Over.* His language accommodates both colloquialism and convolution, both excruciating specificity and relentless generality.

The shadow of death darkens all Albee's plays, but witty dialogue sparks through his first few plays. Transitional, *Virginia Woolf* touches on the fear in human love without illusion. *Tiny Alice* probes the heroism of human illusion about the divine. *A Delicate Balance* returns to a shrunken earth; the house appointed for all living is shaken by the living dead, but accident and brinkmanship salvage the equilibrium. *Box* theatricalizes art and the inadequacy of art in the face of death. *All Over* presents a waiting for death, omnipresent and ineluctable.

Like the Absurdists whom he defends, Albee is anguished because men die and they cannot make themselves happy with illusion. He absorbs this condition into art by counterpointing interrogation and repetition, familiar phrase and diversified resonance, repartee and monologue, minute gesture and cosmic sweep, comic wit and a sense of tragedy. The Albee-gory is that distinctive allegorical drama in which ideas are so skillfully blended into people that we do not know how to divorce them or how to care about one without the other.

Selected Bibliography

WORKS OF EDWARD ALBEE

PLAYS

The Zoo Story. New York: Coward-McCann, 1959.

The Death of Bessie Smith. New York: Coward-McCann, 1959.

The Sandbox. New York: Coward-McCann, 1959.

Fam and Yam. New York: Coward-McCann, 1960.

The American Dream. New York: Coward-McCann, 1960.

Bartleby. 1961. (Unpublished libretto adaptation of Herman Melville's short story.)

Who's Afraid of Virginia Woolf? New York: Atheneum, 1963.

The Ballad of the Sad Café. New York: Atheneum, 1963. (Adaptation of Carson McCullers' novel.)

Tiny Alice. New York: Atheneum, 1965.

Malcolm. New York: Atheneum, 1965. (Adaptation of James Purdy's novel.)

A Delicate Balance. New York: Atheneum, 1966.

Everything in the Garden. New York: Atheneum, 1967. (Adaptation of Giles Cooper's play.)

Box and *Quotations from Chairman Mao Tsetung.* New York: Atheneum, 1969.

All Over. New York: Atheneum, 1971.

ESSAYS

"Which Theatre Is the Absurd One?" *New York Times Magazine,* February 25, 1962, pp. 30-31. (Reprinted in *American Playwrights on Drama,* edited by Horst Frenz. New York: Hill and Wang, 1965. Pp. 168-74).

"Introduction" to *Three Plays,* by Noel Coward. New York: Doubleday, 1965.

"Apartheid in the Theater," *New York Times,* July 30, 1967, II, pp. 1, 6.

"Albee Says 'No, Thanks'—to John Simon," *New York Times,* September 10, 1967, II, pp. 1, 8.

"The Future Belongs to Youth," *New York Times,* November 26, 1967, II, pp. 1, 7.

CRITICAL STUDIES

Ballew, Leighton M. "Who's Afraid of *Tiny Alice?*" *Georgia Review,* 20:292-99 (Fall 1966).

Baxandall, Lee. "The Theatre of Edward Albee," *Tulane Drama Review,* 9:19-40 (Summer 1965).

Bigsby, C. W. E. "Edward Albee," in *Confrontation and Commitment.* London: MacGibbon and Kee, 1967. Pp. 71-92.

Brustein, Robert. *Seasons of Discontent.* New York: Simon and Schuster, 1965. Pp. 26-29, 46-49, 145-48, 155-58.

Chester, Alfred. "Edward Albee: Red Herrings and White Whales," *Commentary,* 35:296-301 (April 1963).

Coleman, D. C. "Fun and Games: Two Pictures of Heartbreak House," *Drama Survey,* 5:223-36 (Winter 1966-67).

Debusscher, Gilbert. *Edward Albee: Tradition and Renewal.* Brussels: American Studies Center, 1967.

Downer, Alan S., ed. "An Interview with Edward Albee," in *The American Theater.* Washington: USIS, 1967. Pp. 123-36.

Dukore, Bernard F. "A Warp in Albee's *Woolf,*" *Southern Speech Journal,* 30:261-68 (Spring 1965).

————. "Tiny Albee," *Drama Survey,* 5:60-66 (Spring 1966).

Esslin, Martin. *The Theatre of the Absurd.* New York: Doubleday, 1961. Pp. 225-26.

Flanagan, William. "Edward Albee," in *Writers at Work.* New York: Viking, 1967. Pp. 321-46.

Flasch, Mrs. Harold A. "Games People Play in *"Who's Afraid of Virginia Woolf?"* *Modern Drama,* 10:280-88 (December 1967).

Goodman, Henry. "The New Dramatists: Edward Albee," *Drama Survey,* 2:72-79 (June 1962).

Gould, Jean. "Edward Albee and the Current Scene," in *Modern American Playwrights.* New York: Apollo Editions, 1966. Pp. 273-86.

Gussow, Mel. "Albee: Odd Man In on Broadway," *Newsweek,* 61:49-52 (February 4, 1963).

Hamilton, Kenneth. "Mr. Albee's Dream," *Queen's Quarterly,* 70:393-99 (Autumn 1963).

Hankiss, Elemér. "Who's Afraid of Edward Albee?" *New Hungarian Quarterly,* 5:168-74 (Autumn, 1964).

Harris, Wendell V. "Morality, Absurdity, and Albee," *Southwest Review,* 49:249-56 (Summer 1964).

Hilfer, Anthony Channell. "George and Martha: Sad, Sad, Sad," in *Seven Contemporary Authors,* edited by T. B. Whitbread. Austin: University of Texas Press, 1966. Pp. 119-40.

Knepler, Henry. "Conflict of Traditions in Edward Albee," *Modern Drama,* 10:274-79 (December 1967).

Kostelanetz, Richard. "Edward Albee," in *On Contemporary Literature.* New York: Avon Books, 1964. Pp. 225-31.

Lewis, Allan. "The Fun and Games of Edward Albee," in *American Plays and Playwrights of the Contemporary Theatre.* New York: Crown, 1965. Pp. 81-98.

Lyons, Charles R. "Two Projections of the Isolation of the Human Soul: Brecht's *Im Dickicht der Staedte* and Albee's *The Zoo Story*," *Drama Survey,* 4:121-38 (Summer 1965).

McDonald, Daniel. "Truth and Illusion in *Who's Afraid of Virginia Woolf?*" *Renascence,* 17:63-69 (Winter 1964).

Markus, Thomas B. *"Tiny Alice* and Tragic Catharsis," *Educational Theatre Journal,* 17:225-33 (October 1965).

Miller, Jordan Y. "Myth and the American Dream: O'Neill to Albee," *Modern Drama,* 7:190-98 (September 1964).

Nelson, Gerald. "Edward Albee and His Well-Made Plays," *Tri-Quarterly,* 5:182-88 (n.d.).

Oberg, Arthur K. "Edward Albee: His Language and Imagination," *Prairie Schooner,* 40:139-46 (Summer 1966).

Phillips, Elizabeth C. "Albee and the Theatre of the Absurd," *Tennessee Studies in Literature,* 10:73-80 (1965).

Plotinsky, Melvin L. "The Transformations of Understanding: Edward Albee in the Theatre of the Irresolute," *Drama Survey,* 4:220-32 (Winter 1965).

Roy, Emil. *"Who's Afraid of Virginia Woolf?* and the Tradition," *Bucknell Review,* 13:27-36 (March 1965).

Rule, Margaret W. "An Edward Albee Bibliography," *Twentieth Century Literature,* 14:35-44 (April 1968).

Samuels, Charles Thomas. "The Theatre of Edward Albee," *Massachusetts Review,* 6:187-201 (Autumn-Winter 1964-65).

Schechner, Richard. "Who's Afraid of Edward Albee?" *Tulane Drama Review,* 7:7-10 (Spring 1963).

Schneider, Alan. "Why So Afraid?" *Tulane Drama Review,* 7:10-13 (Spring 1963).

Valgemae, Mardi. "Albee's Great God Alice," *Modern Drama,* 10:267-73 (December 1967).

Way, Brian. "Albee and the Absurd," in *American Theatre.* London: Edward Arnold, 1966. Pp. 188-207.

Witherington, Paul. "Language of Movement in Albee's *The Death of Bessie Smith*," *Twentieth Century Literature,* 13:84-88 (July 1967).

Wolfe, Peter. "The Social Theatre of Edward Albee," *Prairie Schooner,* 39:248-62 (Fall 1965).

Zimbardo, Rose A. "Symbolism and Naturalism in Edward Albee's *The Zoo Story*," *Twentieth Century Literature,* 8:10-17 (April 1962).

—*RUBY COHN*

Sherwood Anderson

1876-1941

*L*IFE, not death, is the great adventure." So reads the inscription engraved on Sherwood Anderson's tombstone in southwestern Virginia in accordance with a request he made not long before his death at sixty-four in 1941. At first glance, the buoyancy of the epitaph seems strangely at variance with the facts of his career. For a few triumphant years after the publication of *Winesburg, Ohio* (1919), Anderson was acclaimed a major figure of modern literature. He was regarded with Theodore Dreiser as a liberator of American letters from the debilitating effects of the genteel tradition. Then, in the mid-1920's, repudiated by critics, abandoned by his early discoverers, parodied by his protégés, he slipped from the foreground, even though his writing continued to influence diverse writers such as Ernest Hemingway, Hart Crane, Erskine Caldwell, Katherine Anne Porter, Henry Miller, William Faulkner, Nathanael West, and James T. Farrell.

Anderson thought humbly of himself at the end as merely a minor artist who had contributed only a minor classic—*Winesburg, Ohio*—to American culture. Still, it was his dedication as an artist that enabled him to sustain his faith in the adventure of life—and fully examined, his career truly justifies his epitaph. It was with grace and justice that Faulkner,

responding to an inquiry from a *Paris Review* interviewer in 1956, declared of Anderson's stature: "He was the father of my generation of American writers and the tradition of American writing which our successors will carry on. He has never received his proper evaluation."

The major theme of Anderson's writing is the tradegy of death in life: modern man, lacking personal identity and with his senses anesthetized, has become a spiritless husk unfitted for love of man and community. This perennial theme is common enough in our time, though it was relatively dormant in the late 1910's when Anderson first enunciated it. It became his leitmotiv when, in 1912, at the age of thirty-six, he suffered a nervous breakdown and rejected his past. Thereafter he viewed this event as a symbolic rebirth which had purified him of false values and freed him from the confines of deadening institutions.

The pattern is classic in Western culture. It has recurred often in American life since Puritan times, with special frequency in the nineteenth century after the rise of transcendentalism. But in the 1920's it was somewhat anachronistic for a man to present himself dramatically, not only as artist but also as human being, in the messianic role of someone who had achieved a second birth and now had come forth to utter prophetic truths. Nor did Anderson's lower-class origins in Ohio, his vaunted and obvious lack of education, his emphasis upon the American and the common, his bohemian dress and manners, his concern with lust and love, and his charismatic religious overtones make him more palatable either to the intellectual or to the average man.

The reasons for suspicion are understandable. It followed upon a perversion of the idealism and romanticism of Emerson, Thoreau, and Whitman by nineteenth-century disciples who, regardless of their original motives, too often degenerated into cultists and opportunists. Emerson and Whitman are not responsible for followers who took advantage of the masters' paradoxical universality and founded quasi-religious movements such as New Thought, which misused idealistic concepts to justify materialism. Nor should the masters be blamed for the phenomenon of an Elbert Hubbard, who had publicized his idealistic escape from business in the 1890's in order to pursue a life of pure art, plain living, and high thinking, then proceeded to befoul American culture with a shamelessly commercial literature, handicraft, art, and thought until he sank with the *Lusitania* in 1915. Yet many had been fooled by the Emersonian-Whitmanian pose of Hubbard, with the result that Anderson— who, like Hubbard, came from the Midwest, sported an arty costume, and had also worked in business and advertising—was regarded with some wariness even while his writing was being praised.

In private life, letters, and autobiographical publications, Anderson tenaciously mixed art and life until he became a fictional character for himself and his times. Many supposedly objective details in *A Story Teller's Story* (1924), *Tar* (1926), and the posthumous *Memoirs* (1942) were products of "fancy," a term he used interchangeably with "imagina-tion." He preferred these imaginative constructions to "facts" which he believed concealed "the essence of things." The angry corrections of relatives and friends did not alter his belief that a man's vision of himself and his world contained more meaningful truth than did a birth certificate or an identification card. There was no real ground for embarrassment. In the opening pages of his autobiographical works, readers were forewarned at once about Anderson's method. There is something playful and ingenuous in such typical fictions as his Italian grandmother and his southern father; they happened to be profoundly true in revealing the surprise and shock of a passionate "Ohio Pagan" who couldn't otherwise explain the incongruity of having been spawned in an American Midwest dominated by what he regarded as the chilly values of its "Puritan" New England settlers.

Sherwood Anderson was born on September 13, 1876, in Camden, Ohio. He was the third child of Irwin M. Anderson, who made and sold leather harness, and Emma Smith Anderson. The Anderson family had moved about from town to town in Ohio before Sherwood's birth. A few years after that event, Irwin Anderson's small business failed and the Anderson family resumed its travels. Not until 1884 was a permanent home established, this time in Clyde, a small farm town.

The strain of economic difficulties and wandering seems to have affected the father, who began to drink heavily and was so often unemployed that the family's needs frequently were satisfied only by the children's earnings and the strenuous efforts of their mother. Irwin Anderson as father and fictional character was to be an obsessive and ambivalently treated concern of Sherwood's thought and art. He and the other children would feel that Emma Anderson's death in 1895 might have been caused by her husband's neglect and frivolity. But Irwin was nevertheless lovable, in many respects admirable. His misfortunes had not soured his temper, and he joyfully gave rein to his aptitudes for music, theater, and literature. If a parade or vaudeville performance had to be arranged, Irwin Anderson was the man for the job; he acted; he blew the cornet in a local band; he entranced his friends and children with skillfully told tales. Such a role could excite admiration and respect; there were penalties too—family hardships and the probability that town and family alike would consider one a quixotic clown and fool. It was not until Sherwood Anderson was in his mid-forties that he highly valued what he had earlier feared, namely, his similarity to his father.

Young Sherwood's willingness to take on odd jobs earned him money and the nickname of "Jobby." He worked as a farmhand in the surrounding country; in Clyde as grocery delivery boy, laborer in a newly established bicycle factory, and newsboy, and in various menial capacities in a livery stable and a racehorse stable, where he mingled happily with drivers, jockeys, grooms, and trainers. Though an average student, his various jobs and interests made it difficult for him to attend school regularly; he finally quit high school before graduation.

Anderson's life in Clyde ended when he left in 1896 for Chicago, where his brother Karl had gone earlier. For the next two years, Anderson was a manual laborer in a cold-storage warehouse. With the outbreak of the Spanish-American War, he volunteered for army service in Cuba. His regiment arrived there in January 1899, almost four months after hostilities had ceased. Though he never underwent the combat experience which other American novelists such as Hemingway, John Dos Passos, Thomas Boyd, and Faulkner were to in-corporate into their fiction, Anderson had an opportunity to become aware of the problems faced by the individual in a mass society requiring conformity to a single mode of conduct. That Anderson knew how to adjust himself may be gauged from his attainment of a corporal's rank. It was probably this slight success which encouraged a belief—embodied most fully in an early novel, *Marching Men* (1917)—that a man as individual was ineffectual until, absorbed into a faceless mass led by a charismatic leader, he contributed his will and body to an invincible social entity.

At loose ends in 1900 after his army service, Sherwood again followed his brother, this time to Springfield, Ohio, where the latter was employed as an artist by the Crowell Publishing Company, which issued mass-circulation magazines. Aware of his need for more education, Anderson in September enrolled at Wittenberg Academy, a preparatory school, where he earned eleven grades of A and three of B for his proficiency in Latin, German, geometry, English, and physics. He was twenty-four years old at the time, but he did not feel it demeaning to pay for his food and lodging by working as a "chore boy" in the boardinghouse where he, Karl, and various editors, artists, advertising men, and teachers resided.

These men and women were the most culturally advanced Anderson had met as yet. Their interests in art and literature, as well as business, uncovered new, if limited, worlds of action and thought for him. But as it happens it was in the field of business that the Springfield group ultimately did most for him. Through the intercession of the advertising manager of Crowell, Anderson was appointed to the Chicago advertising office of the firm as a copywriter. He was among the first and not the last of modern American writers whose imagination and expression have been affected by such experience.

Anderson initially took to advertising with gusto and a belief in the efficacy of the products he touted and the means used to sell them. Businessmen whom he met in his later role as advertising salesman liked him because of his "charm, interest, and sympathy," his physical attractiveness and lively spirit. His mental alertness and sensitivity to the language of the average mind made him an irresistible copywriter. One of his associates related that Anderson "bragged to the office girls that he could get them good husbands by mail-order letters."

The most revealing expression of his attitudes is to be found in the inspirational articles and sketches he contributed to *Agricultural Advertising*, his firm's house organ, during 1903 and 1904. Written in a clumsy, banal style, these pieces on the whole echo the platitudes of popular American business philosophy, uncritically expounding the virtues of industry, acquisition, aggressive competition, optimism, success, and service, while chiding those who prated reform morality and ignored the ethical values and practices of the businessman. Though Anderson in later years would denounce success and extol failure, he never became an enthusiast of social reform except sporadically during the 1930's. He regarded social liberals and revolutionists as opportunists who concealed their search for power under showers of misleading "talk." During the 1930's, when most of those who had championed his work were involved in leftist activities, his unwillingness to commit himself fully to radical programs led to sharp criticism or neglect of his last writings.

Whatever confidence and success advertising brought Anderson—and it also enabled him in 1904 to marry Cornelia Lane, the daughter of a wealthy Ohio wholesaler of footwear—the afflatus of sales promotion did not continue to satisfy him. His rising sense of frustration was fanned by the genteel achievements of his wife, who had been graduated from Western Reserve University, possessed the traditional knowledge of literature and the arts which he lacked, and had even studied in Europe. In a conversation of the mid-1900's with a Chicago advertising associate before departing on a business trip. Anderson said that he had decided to choose between becoming "a millionaire or an artist." He explained that, "if only a man will put the making of money above all other things in life," wealth could be attained. The role of an artist was more difficult, "but if it is in a fellow, he can do it. I don't know what I shall do—paint, sculpt, maybe write. But I think I will come back determined on an artistic career."

The transition from copy writing to literature as art, which Anderson was to make, seemed easy and natural to him because in both language is manipulated to give an illusion of meaningful reality. His view was implicit in an advertising man's comment on a verbally gifted railroad man in one of Anderson's *Agricultural Advertising* sketches: "He knows how to use words and that's why I think he'd make an advertising man. How to use words, and say, Mr. Cowman, that's what advertising is, just using words; just picking them out like that fellow picked out his swear words and then dropping them down in just the right place so they seem to mean something. I don't want you to be making fun of that brakeman. . . . He's a word man, that brakeman is, and words are the greatest things ever invented."

Anderson's reverent attitude toward language was a wholesome sign of his promise as a writer. In the 1900's, it was useful to him because of his limited vocabulary and his unfamiliarity with the range of rhetorical devices to be found in literature. But his emphasis upon "words" as self-sufficient entities, and his lack of concern with their meaning, foreshadowed his later obsessive preoccupation with them. As he struggled unsuccessfully with the expression of ideas and emotional nuances in his first two novels, he came to believe that his failure resulted from the faulty character of his words rather than from the absence of that profound imaginative experience which willy-nilly finds vivid expression even in a limited language. "There is a story.—I cannot tell it.—I have no words," he would write in 1921.

This was to an extent only an element of the guileless and natural literary personality Anderson fashioned as a self-portrait. It came properly indeed from one whose advertising experience had shown him that words could be used without responsible interest in their human meaning and was determined not to repeat his errors. On the one hand then, Anderson's love and fear of the word stimulated great stylistic purity; on the other hand, this ambivalence also led on occasion to a "basic mistrust of language itself" and to the artistically destructive belief that "reality remains ultimately inexpressible" to which Anderson alluded in the epigraph of *A New Testament* (1927): "They talked and their lips said audible words but the voices of their inner selves went on uninterrupted."

Anderson continued to nourish hopes of an artistic career while adjusting himself to the responsibilities of a bourgeois husband who had fathered three children. Leaving Chicago in 1906, he returned to northern Ohio. During the next six years, he managed a mail-order business in Cleveland and later two paint manufacturing firms. In dress, country club membership, church attendance, and all other externals, Anderson conformed to the standards of respectable convention. But first secretly, in the night-time privacy of an attic at home, and later openly, in his office and elsewhere, Anderson began to write with such industry and devotion that friends and business acquain-

tances could not help becoming aware of his double existence. He centered more and more energy in his writing as an estrangement from his wife deepened in intensity and as financial difficulties made it likely that his business was going to fail.

On November 27, 1912, Anderson left his office in Elyria, Ohio, suddenly and was not heard from again until he turned up in Cleveland on December 1, disheveled and in a state of shock. In the Cleveland hospital to which he was taken, examining physicians diagnosed his condition as a mental collapse. Although he recovered quickly, the event was a turning point. He severed connections with his manufacturing business and, in order to support himself and his family, returned to his old Chicago advertising job in February 1913, bringing with him the manuscripts of *Windy McPherson's Son*, *Marching Men*, and other works.

Anderson's version of his departure from Elyria, presented in an article entitled "When I Left Business for Literature" (*Century*, August 1924) and incorporated in *A Story Teller's Story*, became a classic anecdote in the 1920's and 1930's. For Anderson and some younger writers, it symbolized the heroism of rebellion against the materialistic values of a business-dominated culture. Predictably, however, not all of his version was accurate. As he viewed the event in 1924 and later in the *Memoirs*, he ignored his psychic breakdown and slighted his precarious financial state, thus giving the impression that his flight had resulted from a wholly conscious decision to repudiate wealth and embrace art. To this extent, his story was misleading. But he also stated the essential truth and it was unimpeachable: after much struggle, he had committed himself to a disinterested life of art and thereafter had flaunted his disbelief in the moral integrity and social value of the advertising copy he continued to write so brilliantly until 1922.

Anderson's first two novels are apprentice efforts. He was never proud of these books, even when they were published. Later, in the *Memoirs*, he called them imitative and "immature." It is regrettable that Anderson permitted them to be published without extensive improvement, for in 1915, before their appearance, he was already writing the first brilliant tales of *Winesburg, Ohio* and undoubtedly was aware of the weaknesses of the novels. At this time, as later in his career, Anderson made the mistake of publishing work which did not reflect his achieved talent and thus gave rise to mistaken impressions of his progress and promise.

Although Anderson later said that he had tricked the reader with a happy ending, *Windy McPherson's Son* (1916) has a tragic or at least an ambivalent ending. Sam McPherson's search for meaning in life concludes in a chaos of emptiness and negation. The dominant tone is one of darkness and frustration, steadily increasing in intensity. Young Sam—eager to acquire wealth—flees to Chicago from his Iowa village and becomes a robber baron. He is diverted from his unsatisfying material quest after meeting a perfect woman who convinces him that he will achieve fulfillment by creating perfect children with her. This eugenic goal is abandoned after she proves incapable of giving birth. Sam returns to business and finance, attaining vast power but no more satisfaction than before. He rules faceless men and cannot discover his own face. The social reform faddishly taken up by his frustrated wife does not attract him. In all action, idealistic or selfish, theories are discarded and the urge for power nakedly revealed as motive force. Sam flees Chicago in desperation.

Dressed in the costume of a Whitmanian rough, Sam McPherson wanders about as vagabond and workman "to seek Truth, to seek God" among the common people. He finds labor confused and its leaders power-hungry. Love is missing. Dissipation and vice have destroyed the moral character of the people. Sam cannot find God in man or society, thus repeating a boyhood experience when he had read the Bible and discovered that "Christ's simple message" of love and community had been rejected by the Iowa villagers. Wearied by "thinking" and searching, Sam loses faith in hope.

The resurgent theme of fertility rouses Sam briefly. He brings three neglected children home to his lonely wife, who has found solace, ironically, in the writing of Emersonian "articles about life and conduct." Upon Sam's return, she derides them as "pettiness." Both hope that, with the aid of the children, they may be able to realize their earlier unifying aim of nurturing perfect beings for the future. But the concluding paragraph of the novel is far from hopeful. The last lines are unmistakably despairing: "A shudder ran through his body and he had the impulse to run away into the darkness, to begin again, seeking, seeking. Instead he turned and going through the door, walked across the lighted room to sit again with Sue at his own table and to try to force himself back into the ranks of life." Nothing in the novel promises that Sam will be able to remain in the light.

Anderson's later weakness as a novelist is evident in his inability to make Sam McPherson see, feel, and evaluate his experience with concrete details and expanding complexity. Sam yearns to break loose from the sterilizing confines of existence but his spirit is subdued by a numbing sameness that renders him unfit for observation and participation. Had Anderson created suspense by involving Sam in a more detailed inner drama of conflicting emotion and idea or a more detailed outer drama of disturbing social interaction, the tragic conclusion would have embodied a persuasive force. As it is, Sam's impotent isolation ultimately tends to become more pathetic than deeply tragic.

The limited dimension of Sam is paralleled in most of the other characters, who remain undeveloped sentimental stereotypes. Some of these recur with haunting regularity in Anderson's later work: the kind, maternal schoolteacher who talks about books and art; the loved and hated braggart father; the exhausted, sacrificial mother who dies too soon; the wife who doesn't understand her husband or give herself to love; the promiscuous woman who cheapens physical passion.

The strengths of *Windy McPherson's Son* reside primarily in the first eight chapters dealing with Sam's village life before his quest for money and power in Chicago. This section of the book might almost be a discarded draft of *Winesburg, Ohio*. Many sentences are packed with the hum of feeling and have a Biblical cadence; "tears" express a specific emotional reaction and are not just plashed for dubious sentimental effect; imagery and diction generally are free from cliché and stereotype. Three characters anticipate the figures of *Winesburg, Ohio* in their expressiveness, the depth of their passion and insight, and the incongruity between their powers and their limited achievement.

John Telfer is an articulate and vivid man whose failure as painter has led him to a richer role: artist of living. His talk of Whitman, love, purpose, and ideals almost sways Sam from devotion to money; it is Telfer who emphasizes the difference between corn as a symbol of materialism and corn as a symbol of the *élan vital*: "I see the long corn rows with the men and the horses half hidden, hot and breathless, and I think of a vast river of life. I catch a breath of the flame that was in the mind of the man who said, 'The land is flowing with milk and honey.'" But Telfer cannot affect Sam's future any more than Sam's emotionally profound father, Windy McPherson, or the "savage and primitive" Mike McCarthy. The latter delights in fertilizing village wives whose miserly husbands have forsworn "carnal love," and the children it produces, in favor of saving money. Like Telfer, both have virtues worth emulating. Yet each is ultimately defeated, Windy by his hollow pretensions and Mike by the uncontrollable passion which leads to his murdering a resentful cuckold.

Anderson's second published novel, *Marching Men* (1917), although structurally flawed, is noteworthy for its stylistic fluency and its fusion of ideas and dramatic action. This is not surprising, for Anderson was by no means a literary *naïf* in the mid-1910's as he and others have suggested. In Chicago after 1912 he had come to know such literary figures as Floyd Dell, Carl Sandburg, Margaret Anderson, and Ben Hecht; Anderson also contributed to the *Little Review*, along with *Poetry* the most important American "little magazine" of the 1910's. There are references to Poe, Browning, Carlyle, Keats, Balzac, Whitman, and Mark Twain in *Windy McPherson's Son*, as well as allusions to unspecified French, Russian, and other European writers; in a 1923 letter, Anderson asserted that he had read Turgenev about 1911 and Tolstoi and Dostoevski afterward. Shakespeare and Dante are mentioned in *Marching Men*. According to Anderson's *Memoirs*, he was already familiar with the novels of Bennett, Wells, Hardy, and Moore. His brother Karl had introduced him to Gertrude Stein's experimental *Tender Buttons* (1914) soon after its appearance; he had read her *Three Lives* (1909) earlier.

Marching Men is a social novel. In it Anderson examined the destructive impact of industrialism in a Pennsylvania coal-mining town upon a sensitive boy and traced the harmful effect of his warped personality upon society. Ironically nicknamed "Beaut" because of his gawkiness and physical ugliness, Norman McGregor's lyrical response to nature and his affectionate spirit are brutally crushed. Beaut McGregor grows to hate man and society. In Chicago he finds opportunity, as lawyer and charismatic leader, to obtain revenge for his youthful sufferings. Viewing urban, industrial man as a dehumanized shell, he accelerates the dehumanization by organizing the masses into battalions which, subjected to strict discipline, march in military fashion. His intelligence and emotional mystique bring him the devotion of many men who are glad to surrender the last remnants of individuality. McGregor thus becomes the master of a terrifying collective force whose power can be exerted against society. The collective mass, rejecting the false premises of a democracy that is disorderly, will create a new order, a new mind. "When you have marched until you are one giant body then will happen a miracle," McGregor tells his followers. "A brain will grow in the giant you have made."

Had Anderson been able to stop the novel at that point, he would have written a meaningful indictment of American life and a warning of its self-destructiveness. Supporting the indictment are many valid social criticisms, some in the form of Anderson's authorial comments and others in passages of description and narration. His ideas on the shoddy ugliness of goods, homes, cities, and living patterns, on the inequitable character of law, on the avid quest for sensation, and on other problems of the day were pertinent for the early twentieth century and are still relevant in many respects. Anderson was echoing earlier protests by Melville, Thoreau, and Whitman; he was in tune with such perceptive contemporaries as Thorstein Veblen, Frank Lloyd Wright, and William James.

But though Anderson could objectively summon up the root causes for McGregor's Nietzschean nihilism, clearly portrayed as a negative philosophy, he paradoxically shared McGregor's faith in blind action. The novel struggles unsuccessfully to maintain equilibrium between Anderson's constructive critical temper and his unabashed impulse for collective physical violence and social destruction. As if to mark his inability to resolve the novel's chaotic lack of focus, Anderson dropped McGregor from his narrative before its close. The final chapter completes the book's disintegration. A foreshadowing of *Many Marriages* (1923), the conclusion whips up a mélange of sex and philosophy in portraying the success of a Chicago industrialist's effort to persuade his daughter that he is more desirable than McGregor, whom she has loved but to whom she has been afraid to give herself.

The idea and form of *Marching Men* were confused. But Anderson's style had progressed beyond the clumsy rawness of most of his earlier novel, had moved closer to the prose poetry of *Winesburg, Ohio*. His growing mastery of imaginative detail is visible in young McGregor's shocked perception that the coaltown minister is laughing callously at a cruel story about the boy: "The Reverend Minot Weeks also laughed. He thrust four fingers of each hand into the pockets of his trousers, letting the extended thumbs lie along the swelling waist line. From the front the thumbs looked like two tiny boats on the horizon of a troubled sea. They bobbed and jumped about on the rolling shaking paunch, appearing and disappearing as laughter shook him."

The urban scene evokes cold, sharp disgust: "The people of Chicago go home from their work at evening—drifting they go in droves, hurrying along. It is a startling thing to look closely at them. The people have bad mouths. Their mouths are slack and the jaws do not hang right. The mouths are like the shoes they wear. The shoes have become run down at the corners from too much pounding on the hard pavements and the mouths have become crooked from too much weariness of soul. . . . It is evening and the people of Chicago go home from work. Clatter, clatter, clatter, go the heels on the hard pavements, jaws wag, the wind blows and dirt drifts and sifts through the masses of the people. Every one has dirty ears. The stench in the street cars is horrible. The antiquated bridges over the rivers are packed with people. The suburban trains going away south and west are cheaply constructed and dangerous. A people calling itself great and living in a city also called great go to their houses a mere disorderly mass of humans cheaply equipped. Everything is cheap. When the people get home to their houses they sit on cheap chairs before cheap tables and eat cheap food. They have given their lives for cheap things."

In opposition to that nightmare horror, Anderson chanted the promise of nature in prophetic Biblical cadences: "And back of Chicago lie the long corn fields that are not disorderly. There is hope in the corn. Spring comes and the corn is green. It shoots up out of the black land and stands up in orderly rows. The corn grows and thinks of nothing but growth. Fruition comes to the corn and it is cut down and disappears. Barns are filled to bursting with the yellow fruit of the corn. And Chicago has forgotten the lesson of the corn. All men have forgotten. It has never been told to the young men who come out of the corn fields to live in the city."

The invigorating effect of Gertrude Stein's experimentation with language in *Tender Buttons* is evident in *Marching Men*. Her theory is virtually summed up by Anderson in the novel: "It is a terrible thing to speculate on how man has been defeated by his ability to say words. The brown bear in the forest has no such power and the lack of it has enabled

him to retain a kind of nobility of bearing sadly lacking in us. On and on through life we go, socialists, dreamers, makers of laws, sellers of goods and believers in suffrage for women and we continuously say words, worn-out words, crooked words, words without power or pregnancy in them."

For Anderson, Miss Stein always remained a "writer's writer," a literary pioneer, not a writer for the general reader. He recognized that her abandonment of conventional syntax, punctuation, and spelling was therapeutic for the American writer because it made him conscious of the deadness of conventional language and rhythm, of a literature based on literary custom rather than on objects, associations, functions, and speech freshly articulated. In 1914 such a revivification of style was needed. Gertrude Stein was a pioneer in the undertaking, soon to be joined by Anderson, Pound, Eliot, Joyce, the Dadaists, Cummings, Hemingway, and Faulkner. The poetic repetition and variation of words and phrases, the uncluttered images of objects, the varying musical beat and swing of sentences and paragraphs, noticeable in the passages quoted above from *Marching Men*, were stylistic techniques Anderson learned from her and passed along to Hemingway and Faulkner.

In the late fall of 1915, Anderson began to write the tales that make up *Winesburg, Ohio*. The majority were executed before the middle of 1916. A controlling plan apparently guided him, for the tales were composed in almost the sequence they occupy in the book. (An exception must be made for the four-part "Godliness," which Anderson salvaged from an unfinished novel of 1917.) The tales' unusual quality was recognized almost at once by "little magazine" editors in rebellion against the values dominating American letters and culture. Floyd Dell, Anderson's Chicago friend who helped arrange publication of *Windy McPherson's Son* and was an editor of *Masses*, printed three tales in 1916 beginning with "The Book of the Grotesque." Waldo Frank, editor with James Oppenheim and Van Wyck Brooks of *Seven Arts,* published four tales in 1916 and 1917. Two tales appeared in 1916 and 1918 respectively in the *Little Review.* Anderson had gained an audience that was small but appreciative of his lyrical prose.

William Phillips' study of the Winesburg manuscripts shows that Anderson wrote his first drafts with spontaneity and speed, and then polished with considerable care. The manuscript of "Hands," the second tale written, bears "almost two hundred instances in which earlier words and phrases are deleted, changed, or added to, to provide the readings of the final published version of the story." The revisions, ninety per cent of which were made after the initial writing, added to the size of the draft; they amplified the tale's subtlety by increasing its suggestive elements and symbolic content. The style was molded into greater informality by the addition of colloquial words and repetitive rhythms, and by the deletion of words that were "overworked or awkwardly used."

Much in the tales had prior existence in Clyde, Ohio, and Anderson's earlier life, thus justifying the subtitle: "A Group of Tales of Ohio Small Town Life." But the book, written in retrospect in Chicago, also reflects and illuminates urban American life. Winesburg as a microcosm is ultimately more than a national phenomenon; its proportions are universal, like the whale ship in Melville's *Moby Dick* and Faulkner's mythical Yoknapatawpha County.

The structure of *Winesburg, Ohio* was suggested by Edgar Lee Masters' *Spoon River Anthology,* an elegiac series of character sketches in poetry. The influence of Turgenev's *A Sportsman's Sketches,* in which a sympathetic but unsentimental narrator permits Russian character types to reveal themselves, is also evident. There are as well precedents for the book in nineteenth-century American literature, most notably the local-color collection of tales centered in a single geographical place, the obsessed monomaniacs of Hawthorne's fiction, and the mordant temper of E. W. Howe's *The Story of a Country Town.* The uniqueness of Anderson's book consists of the unusual quality of the precise, ironic voice offering delicate accounts of grotesque human creatures.

A partial key to the elegiac form and tone of the tales is embodied in the book's theory of the grotesque. At some distant time in the past, man had created and believed many satisfying, contradictory truths, "each truth . . . a composite of a great many vague thoughts." Then the healthy wholeness of a multiplicity of truths was lost; man picked out one particular truth, based his life upon it, and became a grotesque, his exclusive truth "a falsehood." The theory, like Hawthorne's statement in *The House of the Seven Gables* that in "an odd and incomprehensible world . . . a man's bewilderment is the measure of his wisdom," epitomizes the philosophy of uncertainty that dominated Anderson's thought and art: the "meaning of life" could not be defined by an absolute truth which limited man's possibilities, for the universe was open rather than closed. "Seeds," a tale first published in 1918, rounds out Anderson's theory by asserting that a confused woman who has mistaken selfish lust for selfless love "is a grotesque, but then all the people in the world are grotesques. We all need to be loved. What would cure her would cure the rest of us also. The disease she had is, you see, universal. We all want to be loved and the world has no plan for creating our lovers."

Everything in *Winesburg, Ohio* sets forth Anderson's vision of the grotesquerie of modern life, though in surrealistic rather than realistic fashion. The characters are deluded and solipsistic; they misunderstand themselves and others; they speak jerkily, explosively, mumblingly, or are inarticulate; their bodies are deformed or subject to muscular twitches, sometimes remain rigid while parts such as hands or feet move about independently. Frustrated, distorted, violent or passive, aggressive or self-destructive, the citizens of Winesburg are the living dead, victims of limited, life-denying truths and guilty for having chosen them.

The grotesques strive to tell their life stories to George Willard, young newspaper reporter. Their recitals are disjointed; their encounters with Willard episodic and inconclusive; his understanding of them incomplete. The tales are static episodes, empty of discovery and change. George Willard is on the whole a passive participant, himself a victim like the others, incapable of distinguishing between love and lust until the conclusion of the book, at which time he leaves Winesburg for a future that is dubious.

Anderson's subtle literary voice enriched the static nightmare of grotesquerie by infusing it with the dynamism of irony. The self-depreciating narrator struggles to be free of the limitations imposed upon him as a Winesburg grotesque. "And yet that is but crudely stated," he confesses humbly and typically in "Hands." "It needs the poet there." But it was as a truly great prose poet that Anderson took up the dormant literary tradition of mock oral narration, briefly revivified by Mark Twain, and transformed it afresh into a vibrant literary medium.

The book's narrator lacks the godlike knowledge and consequent arrogance of an omniscient author. Only to the extent that he artfully presents other grotesques, implying that he has attained an objective distance from them, will he transcend his grotesque configuration and justify his difficult effort to assume the role of artist rather than remaining a Winesburg zombie. The narrator, therefore, abjures sentimentality and pity as much as possible; his tenderness and sympathy are restrained and balanced with an astringent objectivity frequently brutal in contrast to the sufferings of his characters. The narrator's distance from his characters is established by reticence concerning physical details and by the use of a minimal amount of speech and scenic confrontation: the entangling possibilities of physical and dramatic immediacy are thus avoided. However, the narrator cannot help becoming subjectively involved. He observes, feels, digresses, analyzes, and generalizes. Yet he is often wrong, shortsighted, naive. He has become a major character in the tales who, like the symbolic objects liberally strewn about the pages of *Winesburg, Ohio*, must be metamorphosed into full meaning by the imaginatively stirred reader.

At the last, the narrator's stance of simple, artless sincerity revealing all is but a guise for artistic purpose and effect: all is actually given only as hint, clue, suggestion, implication, ambivalence, indirection. The covert truths proffered by Anderson never become didactic absolutes imposed by the narrator but remain implicit and open-ended. Each reader of the tales will grasp only as much of their essence as his individual insight is capable of apprehending.

Winesburg, Ohio is the first modern American expression of the wasteland theme later adumbrated in T. S. Eliot's *The Waste Land* (1922), F. Scott Fitzgerald's *The Great Gatsby* (1925), Hemingway's *The Sun Also Rises* (1926), John Steinbeck's *To a God Unknown* (1933), and Nathanael West's *Miss Lonelyhearts* (1933), the latter, like Hemingway's novel, greatly indebted to Anderson's model. Unlike most of the writers who followed, Anderson attempted to fructify his wasteland, which symbolized the world of provinciality, gentility, and business he had rejected spiritually in his flight from Elyria to Chicago in 1913.

Winesburg, Ohio had delineated the arid context of Anderson's first life. Having given it aesthetic form, he believed it imperative to create—again in art—the context of his new life. The aim had been formulated with yearning simplicity by George Willard, like the new Anderson an artistic creation: "In every little thing there must be order, in the place where men work, in their clothes, in their thoughts. I myself must be orderly. I must learn that law. I must get myself into touch with something orderly and big that swings through the night like a star. In my little way I must begin to learn something, to give and swing and work with life, with the law."

The difficulties Anderson faced were great, particularly since he was still working on the Winesburg tales during 1916 and 1917, when he began his quest for new definitions, and the mood of Winesburg pervaded him. There was nothing in Winesburg as he had portrayed it, with the exception of nature, to which he could return; the ties which bound men in community had withered; love had degenerated into conflict, sexual repression, and disappointing lust; familial relations mirrored the larger social emptiness; the traditional reliances of religious orthodoxy and ritual modes of cultural behavior were nonexistent. He had cast aside the illusions of business and the ugliness of the city. In every respect, then, he was free and unattached, young in situation and possibility, ready to make the world live up to its fruitful potentialities and become a habitable place for human beings.

In actuality, of course, the matter was not so simple. Anderson was in his early forties, exuberant but also physically and mentally weary. As he later granted in his *Memoirs,* the Winesburg vision of his Ohio town had been harshly biased and he had too hastily rejected its few worthy attributes. It is apparent from the revelations in the early novels and letters of this period that he had been psychically maimed by the experiences of his first forty years. Nor, regardless of how much will he exerted, could he easily slough off the worldliness of his mind, or easily assume the role of newborn infant or virginal adolescent after the mature triumph of his repudiation of business and familial ties, after the even greater triumph of having transformed himself into an accomplished artistic creator. The record of Anderson's Progress as a new Adam is inevitably a compilation of noble effort, heroic attainment, and pathetic failure. As it must have been for one who, as he wrote in the poetic epigraph of "From Chicago" (*Seven Arts,* May 1917), was a "man child, in America, in the west, in the great valley of the Mississippi . . . a confused child in a confused world."

Henceforth, Anderson's art and life were inseparable. Instead of remaining hidden behind his work like James Joyce, Anderson made the problem of self-understanding the focus of his best work. He found it as necessary to write about himself as an artist as to work at his art: "While he is still young and pregnant with life it behooves the artist who would stand unashamed among men to make his contribution to the attempt to extend the province of his art. And as his struggle as an artist is and must be inseparably bound up with his struggle as a man, the attempt may fairly be said to fall under the head of an effort to extend the possibilities of human life." So opens "From Chicago," but it concludes humbly on a foreboding note so strong that Anderson self-consciously omitted the section when reprinting the piece in *Sherwood Anderson's Notebook* (1926): "I am looking forward to the coming of the new artist who will give us

. . . the beautiful and stirring story of the spirit that failed, just as the artist himself shall fail and who, like the Christ, on that dramatic night in the garden, must come at last to the facing of truth and know that he must always fail, that, even in keeping alive the memory of his struggle, all men shall fail." This tempering of egoism with limitation helped save Anderson from becoming, except briefly in the 1920's, a tiresome brayer of virtuous Selfhood in the manner of some of his less gifted imitators.

Mid-American Chants (1918), a collection of free-verse poems in the Whitmanian manner which Anderson began writing early in 1917, illustrates one phase of his attempt to fill his void. The poems are generally inept. Only a few manage coherently to unite their fragmentary rhapsodic ejaculations with the kind of sustained emotional energy, intellectual content, and symbolic structure present in Whitman's best poems. Anderson wanted to recreate the religious spirit and mythology of pagan Indian culture in the Ohio Valley before the culture's destruction by New England's pioneers. But he was insufficiently familiar with the details to do more than refer vaguely to the culture. On the other hand, when he did achieve a fragile identification, he blurred it with an alien prophetic exhortation and imagery derived from the Old Testament and Carl Sandburg. Not until Hart Crane wrote "The Dance" (*The Bridge*, 1930) were the primitive fertility rhythms of sacrifice, harvest, and rebirth celebrated in modern American poetry with the Dionysian richness Anderson sought to express.

Anderson was surprised that the editors of *Seven Arts*—one of whom, James Oppenheim, even wrote Whitmanesque poetry—frowned upon the poems later collected in *Mid-American Chants*. The apocalyptic spirit of the magazine, which found hope for an American Renaissance in "self-expression without regard to current magazine standards" and eulogized Anderson in the first issue as an emergent Whitman, had diverted him from the disciplined temper governing the Winesburg stories. It had encouraged him to assume the role of ebullient national bard and to find in the seeds, roots, stalks, and husks of corn— the recurrent symbol of the chants—a means of ordering his chaos. However, the excesses which *Seven Arts* encouraged as one product of its doctrines were actually abhorrent to men like Frank and Brooks. Their most fervent aim was to awaken an idealistic national art rather than to discard traditional standards of literary taste and accomplishment. Anderson's friendship with these men and his respect for their judgment declined in the heat of argument, though he maintained his intimacy with them for some years thereafter.

"An Apology for Crudity" (*Dial,* November 8, 1917) was a manifesto of his independent literary position which sniped at the formalism of his *Seven Arts* critics and others who had ridiculed several poems that had appeared in *Poetry* (September 1917). Significant literature, he asserted, could only come after a writer's immersion in the life of his times. Since "crudity and ugliness" were prime characteristics of American industrial society, modern literature must be affected by it. He rejected, consequently, the "intellectuality" and subtlety" of Henry James and William Dean Howells as ends in themselves, though he granted that both men were "American masters in prose." He linked himself to the tradition of Walt Whitman, Mark Twain, and Theodore Dreiser, who had not ignored the common.

But Anderson did not espouse realism. Vaguely he set forth the ideal of "subjective writing" as an alternative, the writer serving as an imaginative distiller of persons and experience. Later, in "A Note on Realism" (*New York Evening Post Literary Review*, October 25, 1924), he phrased his conception more concretely: "The life of the imagination will always remain separated from the life of reality. It feeds upon the life of reality, but it is not that life—cannot be. . . . Upon the fact in nature the imagination must constantly feed in order that the imaginative life remain significant. . . . The life of reality is confused, disorderly, almost always without apparent purpose, whereas in the artist's imaginative life there is purpose. There is determination to give the tale, the song, the painting Form— to make it true and real to the theme, not to life. Often the better the job is done the greater the confusion." Essentially, then, form and style were organic discoveries of imaginative creation, not pre-existent molds chosen in advance of the literary adventure.

Despite Anderson's impatience with the conventional novel and his recurrent effort to discover a "looser" form, his next major work failed to demonstrate any "experimental" characteristics. *Poor White* (1920) delineated the decline of the "pastoral golden age" in his Midwest during the 1880's and 1890's, the years of his childhood and adolescence. The book is crammed with information, for Anderson tried to anchor it in the facts of cultural, social, and economic history. Furthermore, he enveloped life in the Ohio town of Bidwell— which also appears in other post-Winesburg fiction—with a quiet charm derived from stable community relations, proximity to nature, intellectual curiosity and discussion, old houses, and streets shaded with old overhanging trees. Much of the vision is valid, but Anderson's nostalgia led him to idealize the town and its region until they became as exaggeratedly beautiful as Winesburg earlier had been exaggeratedly ugly. Yet this excessively rosy portrait of Bidwell was also aesthetically

sound, for it enabled Anderson to dramatize the emotional and social significance of its degeneration into Winesburg.

The corrupting agent in the agrarian paradise was industrialism, which had elevated materialism and turned men into mechanical monsters. Hugh McVey, a Huckleberry Finntype from the Mississippi River town of Mudcat Landing, Missouri, symbolically embodies the process. With unsparing realism, young McVey is shown to be a shiftless and lazy "poor white," redeemed, however, by his tendency to daydream and transcend himself pantheistically in sky, earth, and water.

Orphaned, McVey lives with a family which indoctrinates him with the virtues of industry and profit. Gradually he becomes wholly mathematical in mind and mechanical in spirit, channeling his imagination into the invention of labor-saving agricultural machinery. The machines bring him financial success even though, ironically, they turn out to be unworkable and thus symbolically fraudulent. They involve the town in a fever of speculation, disrupting all patterns of behavior, all relations. The novel contains many vivid episodes of the degenerative transformation of characters into tormented grotesques when they are suddenly deprived of the self-fulfilling creative tasks of old. In all of Bidwell, the only creatures who remain virile and sentient are horses. McVey is also a grotesque, unable to consummate his marriage because of psychic impotence, roused finally from his dehumanization by the beautiful appearance of some brightly colored stones he has found. At the end, after a symbolic attack upon McVey by a maddened handicraftsman, Hugh's patient wife—a "new woman" given to thinking rather than feeling —is roused to maternal womanliness by his reversion to adolescent helplessness. The novel grinds to a confusing halt as Hugh, stirred by "the disease of thinking," is told by "his woman" of the forthcoming arrival of "a man child." This news is greeted mockingly by "a great whistling and screaming" from Bidwell's factories.

The style of *Poor White* is effectively elegiac and muted as befits the portrait of an unrecoverable past. It is also generally free of the grammatical errors and poor punctuation that had marred *Winesburg, Ohio* slightly and to a greater extent the earlier novels. *Poor White* was the high point of Anderson's novelistic career. However, it represented a mere refinement of the structure and materials of *Windy McPherson's Son* and *Marching Men* rather than a significant advance. All three novels are essentially accounts of the distortion of a man in youth, his subsequent involvement in a maturity of social fraud and emotional impoverishment, his attempt to attain self-fulfillment in escape and love with an unsatisfactory woman who symbolizes reason and convention rather than emotion and revolt, and the uncertainty of the man's future at the conclusion.

Undoubtedly these novels served Anderson as self-analysis. But the requirements of their objective form kept him from venturing deeply into a personal probing that would have brought him profoundly into himself and encouraged analytical subtlety and particularized detail. The novels come perilously close to being true-confession literature in which the apparent openness of the writing hardly conceals the complacent obduracy with which the author reiterates rather than explores the troubles from which he supposedly has escaped.

Anderson's next novel, *Many Marriages* (1923), exemplifies the impasse to which such writing could lead; with its publication—it was initially printed serially in the *Dial*—came the first strong reaction against Anderson by the newer generation of American writers.

Abandoning the chronological time sequence of the early novels, *Many Marriages* focused upon an extended moment of escape. This was given a past by means of flashbacks that vividly re-create the inhibition of feminine passion. But Anderson did little to set forth the positive hopeful quality of his masculine protagonist's passion beyond having him posture nakedly in presumably ritualistic fashion before a statue of the Virgin Mary. This ritual is neither primitive nor Catholic, for Anderson failed to provide any meaning for his key symbol, which he had picked up in *The Education of Henry Adams*. The result was a stasis, the temper of the Winesburg tales, that violated the thematic meaning of *Many Marriages* and revealed a disturbing lack of literary self-consciousness. What should have been a short story had been turned into a faulty novel.

Anderson published three more novels: *Dark Laughter* (1925), *Beyond Desire* (1932), and *Kit Brandon* (1936). All of them, like his preceding novels, have extraordinary scenes and passages whose high quality has been overlooked. These last novels also show that he endeavored to cope with the problems of extended narrative fiction in different ways; his solutions, however, were generally unsatisfactory, whether it was the attempt to portray the stream of consciousness in *Dark Laughter* or the device of having a central character relate her life story in an extended monologue in *Kit Brandon*.

Anderson's letters and writings from the mid-1910's until shortly before his death reveal that the objective novel, particularly the social novel, had interested him deeply only before the composition of the Winesburg tales. During the late 1910's, before the publication of *Poor White,* he began and abandoned several novels. After 1925, the pattern was repeated. His impulse was for expression in short forms: the poem, prose poem, and lyrical short story. But he was compelled, particularly since he had begun his career as a novelist, to continue writing novels. As late as 1933, for example, the publishing house of Scribners invited him to become one of its authors with the stipulation, according to Anderson, that the first of his books "must be either a novel or a continuous narrative."

It was not merely the pressure of publishers, as well as readers and critics, which pushed Anderson toward the novel against his natural inclination to work in shorter forms. Anderson shared the erroneous cultural belief that a novel is qualitatively as well as quantitatively more valuable than a short work. Had he been a younger man in the late 1910's and early 1920's, it is possible that he might have been able to develop the lyrical novel, a delicate form that would have best utilized his talents as it did those of Virginia Woolf, his admirer. But he had insufficient time in which to work slowly and perfect his art in every form. By 1919, at the age of forty-three, he was exhausted with the difficulty of earning his living as an advertising man and writing in his spare time. Not until 1922 did he finally leave the advertising business, convinced by the size of his earnings from books and magazines that he would be able to survive as a professional writer.

As it turned out, he was unprepared to work at the pace required of a professional writer whose contractual obligations force him to produce publishable materials on a regular basis. He wished to experiment, to work as the impulse to create arose, to make discoveries as any other young writer who still has his future ahead of him: Anderson believed that his life had begun in 1916 with the publication of his first book. Yet as a professional writer in the 1920's he allowed himself to publish whatever he wrote, regardless of whether or not he was proud of it. Thus he ironically was seduced by the same dream of success that he had repudiated in business.

Nevertheless, the bulk of Anderson's important creation is far greater than most critics and readers appear to have realized. His significant contribution to American literature begins with *Winesburg, Ohio* and includes many pieces of prose and poetry published in books and magazines from 1916 to 1941. To that body of work should be added the successful chapters and sections from generally unsatisfactory books, as well as the luminous autobiographical sketches compiled in the posthumous *Memoirs*.

One reason Anderson's writing has not received full recognition, apart from the disappointment aroused by his novels, is the uneven character of his books. Anderson's eagerness to publish, encouraged by editors and publishers, is partially responsible. For example, the two books which crystallized his fame as a short fiction writer in the early 1920's—*The Triumph of the Egg* (1921) and *Horses and Men* (1923)—are mixtures of quality and dross. In both books he included pages salvaged from discarded novels which were on the whole below the level of his current work. "Unlighted Lamps" and "The Door of the Trap" (*The Triumph of the Egg*) are sections of novels begun before 1913. "A Chicago Hamlet" (*Horses and Men*) is a portion of a 1918 novel; "An Ohio Pagan" and "Unused" in the same collection are parts of unpublished novels begun in 1920. A little more than half of *Horses and Men* thus belies the subtitle's description of the contents as "tales." Anderson's last collection of short fiction, *Death in the Woods* (1933), is similarly uneven. It should be noted, however, that the novel fragments frequently contain some of Anderson's most evocative writing. The pantheistic embrace of nature in "An Ohio Pagan," for example, has rarely been equaled in American literature.

Another reason for the relative neglect of Anderson's total accomplishment is the special nature of his talent. He wrote in an age which believed it could master the disorder of existence with patterns of order derived from myths and ideologies of the past or else with descriptions of objects and behavior that possessed the irreducible precision of scientific writing. Because Anderson did not adopt either one of these solutions, his reputation was severely damaged during the 1920's. A reassessment is now in order, for his alleged weaknesses ironically have become strengths which link him with some of the most vigorous currents in contemporary literature. Anderson's vision and method reappear triumphantly in recent American literature in the writing of Carson McCullers, Bernard Malamud, Flannery O'Connor, Tennessee Williams, Edward Albee, Saul Bellow, and John Hawkes. Anderson's pioneering conglomeration of the picaresque, the antiheroic, the grotesque, the passionate, and the rebellious is no longer puzzling nor is it a sign of irresponsible "mindlessness."

One of the most interesting discoveries to be made is that sentimentality is not one of the chief characteristics of Anderson's writing. When dealing with characters whose suffering and confusion he delineated at excessive length, failing to complicate and particularize their uniqueness or impart visible moral and intellectual significance to their predicaments, he did become pathetic and sentimental. Illustrations of his failure to claim the complex response of a reader are *Many Marriages* and "Out of Nowhere into Nothing."

But Anderson's critical temper conflicted strongly with his tendency toward acceptance and complacency. He could become exceptionally sharp, often brutal, in combating the impulse of quiescence. The lively battle he carried on elicited an amused, ironic attitude toward himself and his world. He often wrote satirically ("The Egg," 1920, and "The Triumph of a Modern, or, Send for the Lawyer," 1923) and often comically ("I'm a Fool," 1922, "There She Is—She Is Taking Her Bath," 1923, and "His Chest of Drawers," 1939). To have separated satire and comedy is misleading, however, for Anderson at his most humorous gives us that rare blend known as the tragicomic. When he achieved it, as in "The Egg," it rested in a delicate suspension of irony that looked back to the narrative voice of *Winesburg, Ohio*. Despite lapses into what Faulkner in 1925 described as an "elephantine kind of humor about himself," Anderson's vision remained deeply, incongruously tragicomic. Despite the dark years through which he passed in the late 1920's, this vision reemerged in his last decade of life, typically in his insistence in *Plays: Winesburg and Others* (1937) that the dramatized version of "The Triumph of the Egg" must be carefully directed in order to maintain a balance between comedy and tragedy; to play it either for "laughter" or "tears" alone would destroy the play.

Essentially Anderson was a lyric writer. Having accepted middle-class thought uncritically at first, then having rebelled against it, he feared that any other system of thought would be equally delusive, would limit and frustrate him, especially since reason tended to become abstract and to ignore the heart. "Feeling instinctively the uncertainty of life, the difficulty of arriving at truth," he resolved to remain "humble in the face of the great mystery" (" 'Unused,' " 1923). He might have been describing his own work when he wrote in *A Story Teller's Story*: "Dim pathways do sometimes open before the eyes of the man who has not killed the possibilities of beauty in himself by being too sure."

Anderson could be irritatingly blunt in stating his position, sneering at "slickness," "smartness," and glibness in all fields including literary criticism; thus he inevitably aroused charges of "mindlessness," "immaturity," and "distrust of ideas." Though he winced under the blows of increasingly harsh criticism, he unhesitatingly rejected ready-made truths of past and present. He turned his gaze inwards, searching for tentative explanations of mystery in the texture of his own emotional and social experience. His writings articulate the development of his perceptions of self in relation to the world, of the difficulties encountered on the way.

Anderson never abandoned the vision of himself as a poet despite the unfavorable reception of *Mid-American Chants*, as late as 1930 writing an extraordinary prose poem in "Machine Song" (*Perhaps Women*, 1931). From 1919 to 1927 he assiduously wrote prose poems which appeared in magazines and *The Triumph of the Egg* and were collected in *A New Testament* (1927). He regarded this work at the outset as "a purely insane, experimental thing . . . an attempt to express, largely by indirection, the purely fanciful side of a man's life, the odds and ends of thought, the little pockets of thoughts and emotions that are so seldom touched." The poems on the whole are inchoate, too vague and incoherent to communicate more than faint hints of subconscious existence. But they were valuable exercises nonetheless. When Anderson turned to prose during this period, he passed beyond the mere undisciplined expression of self and made skillful use of poetic techniques which he never forgot.

As in *Winesburg, Ohio*, the varying percep-

tions of a poetically conceived narrator animate and unify most of Anderson's best stories, quite a few of which are products of the 1930's. For the sake of convenient reference, I cite only those stories that are easily accessible in one of Anderson's three collections and *The Sherwood Anderson Reader* (1947), though any comprehensive view of his work must also take into account many of his fine uncollected stories still available only in magazines: *The Triumph of the Egg*: "I Want to Know Why," "Seeds," "The Other Woman," "The Egg," and "Brothers"; *Horses and Men*: "I'm a Fool," "The Triumph of a Modern, or, Send for the Lawyer," "The Man Who Became a Woman," "Milk Bottles," "The Man's Story"; *Death in the Woods*: "Death in the Woods," "There She Is—She Is Taking Her Bath," "In a Strange Town," "A Sentimental Journey"; *The Sherwood Anderson Reader*: "The Corn-Planting," "A Walk in the Moonlight," "The Yellow Gown," and "His Chest of Drawers." The first-person narrator sometimes merely introduces the monologue of another character, as in "The Other Woman" or "His Chest of Drawers." Only a few of Anderson's stories related from a third-person point of view possess high quality: "Senility" and "The New Englander" (*The Triumph of the Egg*), "Another Wife" and "Brother Death" (*Death in the Woods*), "Daughters" and "Not Sixteen" (*The Sherwood Anderson Reader*).

The uncertain, groping narrator of an Anderson story employs an art of suggestion to articulate his search for pattern and meaning in human existence. His experiences are fragmentary, incoherent, inexplicable. The chronological sequence of time may be interrupted and reversed by memories, inadvertent thoughts, gusts of emotion, and frustrated attempts at comprehension. Objects and people are haphazardly perceived, grotesquely distorted. Absurdly helpless, the narrator may succumb to impotence, give vent to explosive stirrings in his subconscious, flee the envelope of his body in mystical anguish or ecstasy, obsessedly focus upon trivialities such as a bent finger, find momentary relief in the muscular health and grace of animals.

Since the story is an articulation of the narrator's experience, its movement is repetitive and circular; it is not rounded off with a meaningful conclusion, for that would violate the narrator's integrity, his stance of wonder and search. Anderson's rejection of conventional plot and climax was aesthetically appropriate. So was his frequent representation of physical detail as incomplete image and generalized noun, his emphasis upon the musical sound of language before it becomes sense in order that he might portray the transformation of undifferentiated sensation and emotion into intelligible form.

The welter of sensuous and emotional perceptions is integrated—despite the powerful centrifugal impulse—by various unifying elements. The narrator maintains a consistent tone of voice. Whether youth or adult, light or serious, comic or satiric, critical or suppliant, he is also visibly interested and compassionate, anxious to discern the reality behind appearance. Moments in the story—episodes, sensations, repetitions—suddenly blaze up to give intense thematic illuminations. Objects, gestures, and events are encrusted with symbolic meaning. These symbols recur and invest the narrator's perceptions with deepened or new significance. Often these symbols are transformed into archetypal patterns of elemental human experience, such as sacrifice, initiation, and rebirth; Anderson's corn seed, for example, is a fertility symbol, its planting a ceremonial drama of death and resurrection.

Many of Anderson's stories, like his novels, are autobiographical either wholly ("In a Strange Town") or partially ("I Want to Know Why"). Presentation of a story from the first-person point of view encouraged an autobiographical concern. On the other hand, as a writer of autobiography, a form that fascinated him because of his vision of himself as "the American Man . . . a kind of composite essence of it all," he tended to fictionalize the details of his biography. This fusion of fact and fiction produced some of Anderson's finest lyrical prose. For example, "Death in the Woods," regarded as one of Anderson's best stories even by unfavorable critics, appeared as a third-person narrative (Chapter XII) in his autobiographical novel *Tar* (1926). In the same year, it also appeared as a story in the *American Mercury;* the name "Tar" had been replaced by "I" and third-person pronouns and other details revised to clarify the narrator's personal relations and experiences. "A Meeting South," the subtle account of Anderson's intimacy with Faulkner in New Orleans, conceals Faulkner under a pseudonym and was probably read as fiction in the *Dial* (April 1925). It reappeared the next year as an autobiographical sketch in *Sherwood Anderson's Notebook* and finally was identified as a story in *Death in the Woods.* Anderson's autobiographical writings, which compose much of his total work, must be taken into account before any definitive conclusions about his literary significance can be ventured.

A starting point might well be Chapters X and XI of *Tar,* portrayals of horse racing as brilliantly colored and airy as Raoul Dufy's watercolors of French tracks, written in a supple vernacular that captures motion and youth with clear-eyed verve. Another excellent piece is "The Nationalist" (*Puzzled America,* 1935), a satirical dialogue with "the rat king of the South" who wants Congress to abolish the law protecting snowy egrets from shooting by feather-hunters. " 'It isn't the money I am thinking about,' he said. There was a grave injustice being done. 'These egrets,' he said again, 'are not American birds. They are foreign birds and they come up here only to eat our American fish.' " Two sketches, "White Spot" (1939) and "Morning Roll Call" (1940), both published posthumously in *The Sherwood Anderson Reader,* are brilliant examples of his ability to express himself during his last years with the vibrancy that had been a basis for his distinction during the early 1920's.

"White Spot" and "Morning Roll Call" had been intended for *Sherwood Anderson's Memoirs,* a work left unfinished when he died on March 8, 1941, in the Panama Canal Zone while on an unofficial goodwill tour to South America. According to James Schevill, the book was faultily edited by Paul Rosenfeld. Such sketches as "White Spot" and "Morning Roll Call" were omitted; a few random magazine pieces more than a decade old were included despite their incongruous misrepresentation of the style and aim of the autobiographical sketches Anderson wrote during the late 1930's and which constitute most of the volume. Unfinished though the book is, however, it represents a fitting culmination of his career. All of his earlier concern with self-revelation and stylistic nuance bore fruition in charming, lyrical pages that leave one in awe at the resiliency of the human spirit as it copes with the mysteries of being in art.

The vivacity and insight of Anderson's memoirs are remarkable in view of the severe decline of his reputation in the mid-1920's and the lengthy emotional depression that affected him thereafter. To those critics who did not read his works attentively or at all after 1925, when *Dark Laughter* appeared, and to those who know Anderson's writing only on the basis of *Winesburg, Ohio* and two over-anthologized stories—"I'm a Fool" and "I Want

to Know Why"—the vibrancy of the memoirs will be truly inexplicable.

Perhaps Anderson should not have expected his work early or late to be wholly or widely appreciated. From the very beginning his literary reputation was shaky. Newspaper and magazine reviewers of his early books regularly oscillated between praise and blame, often mixing both.

Since Anderson was an avant-garde writer, however, a "little magazine" phenomenon, he was at first more enthusiastically received by young writers and critics interested in an American literature that was original, complex, unsentimental, and bold in dealing with taboo subjects such as sex. Thus young Hart Crane in 1921 wrote an encomium of Anderson's "paragraphs and pages from which arises a lyricism, deliberate and light, as a curl of milk-weed seeds drawn toward the sun. . . . He is without sentimentality; and he makes no pretense of offering solutions. He has humanity and simplicity that is quite baffling in depth and suggestiveness. . . ."

But before long even the recognition of the avant-garde was qualified or withdrawn. It generally began to misjudge and overlook Anderson's method and to conclude mistakenly that he was an elderly, provincial American realist because he wrote about the Midwest and praised Dreiser for his human sympathy and his frankness in the treatment of sex. Anderson's persistent criticisms of Dreiser's style as clumsy and of Sinclair Lewis' style as superficial were ignored. The epitome of ultimate avant-garde response to Anderson is best seen in the pages of the *Dial,* which published him frequently, printed laudatory statements, and early in 1922 bestowed upon him the first *Dial* award for distinguished service to American letters, then in the next few years directly and allusively in reviews and other forms of comment gradually formulated a negative attitude toward him.

Anderson's rejection by the avant-garde deepened a sense of estrangement from vital currents of modern literature that had begun earlier when his first prominent supporters— Frank, Brooks, Paul Rosenfeld—kept finding fault with his theories and writings. In such works as *A Story Teller's Story* (1924), *The Modern Writer* (1925), and *Sherwood Anderson's Notebook* (1926), he hopefully sought to define and justify his credo. He was not helped in this task by his antipathy to "talk" about literature and ideas or by his aversion to systematic exposition. Much of what he said had the nub of good sense but it was insufficiently clarified, overcast with a playfulness inappropriate for the occasion, and gave the impression of being narcissistic self-praise of an aesthetic phenomenon superior to traditional morality and critical judgment. Self-consciously ironic and derisive references to the "modern" began to appear in his fiction and articles. An attempt to demonstrate superior "modernity" in *Dark Laughter* was a fiasco: its style, supposedly an emulation of that in James Joyce's *Ulysses*, revealed a misunderstanding of the stream-of-consciousness technique; its rendition of expatriate American experience in Europe was ludicrously uninformed and unperceptive.

The strongest blows against Anderson's prestige and well-being came from young writers whom he had befriended. Hemingway, in whom Anderson had discovered "extraordinary talent" in 1921 and whose *In Our Time* (1925) had been published as a result of Anderson's efforts, parodied Anderson in *The Torrents of Spring* (1926). Faulkner, whose *Soldiers' Pay* (1926) had also been published following Anderson's efforts, less publicly but just as sharply ridiculed Anderson in the fore-

word to *Sherwood Anderson & Other Famous Creoles* (1926), a book published in a limited edition in New Orleans.

For the rest of his life, from the mid-1920's on, Anderson engaged in a quest for rediscovery of the talent which seemed to have atrophied. F. Scott Fitzgerald had written: "To this day reviewers solemnly speak of him [Anderson] as an inarticulate, fumbling man, bursting with ideas—when, on the contrary, he is the possessor of a brilliant and almost inimitable prose style, and scarcely any ideas at all." Anderson perceived, with utter rightness, that there is no style without form, no form without content, that ideas are no more important than the evocative enunciation of experience. He had traveled much during his early years as an advertising man and now he resumed his travels. His second marriage had ended in divorce in 1924, two years after he left the advertising business; his third marriage broke down in 1929. Restlessly he went about the country, observing men and women, listening, attempting to regain the equilibrium of mind, emotion, and voice that had earlier produced his particular artistic vision. The idea that a permanent home might provide stability attracted him. In 1926 he built a house in the mountains of southwestern Virginia; for several years beginning in 1927 he edited two newspapers in the nearby town of Marion, Virginia. Meanwhile he continued to write stories and articles, to struggle desperately with new novels. He was often stricken with black, destructive moods, on one occasion even threw the manuscript of an unpublished novel out of a hotel window, but persisted in his search for orientation. In 1930 he fell in love with his future fourth wife; their marriage was successful. Slowly he regained his self-confidence, his talent, and his sense of humor. These are embodied in writings which swell the enduring corpus of his work beyond that already produced by 1926, writings in which he returned to the common people and locales he had earlier portrayed with similar irony, pity, and understanding.

The ultimate test of a writer's permanence is the power of his words to rekindle generations other than his own. If that be granted, then Sherwood Anderson's stature as a major American writer seems established for decades to come. The "proper evaluation" for which Faulkner called in 1953 has been in progress ever since, and during the 1960's, with special impetus and great critical intelligence devoted to Anderson's rare talent. His works have been widely reprinted in translation abroad and new editions and collections continue to appear in the United States. With characteristic humility, Anderson himself had said in 1921 "that after all the only thing the present generation of men in America could expect to do is to make with their bodies and spirits a kind of fertilizing element in our soil." The issue of final grandeur and subsequent fame was a matter he left to others. Anderson's legacy has been wonderfully fruitful.

Selected Bibliography

WORKS OF SHERWOOD ANDERSON

NOVELS AND COLLECTIONS OF SHORT STORIES

Windy McPherson's Son. New York: John Lane, 1916. (Revised edition, New York: B. W. Huebsch, 1922.)

Marching Men. New York: John Lane, 1917.

Winesburg, Ohio: A Group of Tales of Ohio Small Town Life. New York: B. W. Huebsch, 1919.

Poor White. New York: B. W. Huebsch, 1920.

The Triumph of the Egg: A Book of Impressions from American Life in Tales and Poems. New York: B. W. Huebsch, 1921.

Horses and Men: Tales, Long and Short, from Our American Life. New York: B. W. Huebsch, 1923.

Many Marriages. New York: B. W. Huebsch, 1923.

Dark Laughter. New York: Boni and Liveright, 1925.

Beyond Desire. New York: Liveright, 1932.

Death in the Woods and Other Stories. New York: Liveright, 1933.

Kit Brandon: A Portrait. New York: Scribners, 1936.

POETRY AND PLAYS

Mid-American Chants. New York: John Lane, 1918.

A New Testament. New York: Boni and Liveright, 1927.

Plays: Winesburg and Others. New York: Scribners, 1937.

AUTOBIOGRAPHY AND OTHER PROSE

A Story Teller's Story: The Tale of an American Writer's Journey through His Own Imaginative World and through the World of Facts . . . New York: B. W. Huebsch, 1924.

The Modern Writer. San Francisco: Lantern Press, 1925.

Sherwood Anderson's Notebook. New York: Boni and Liveright, 1926.

Tar: A Midwest Childhood. New York: Boni and Liveright, 1926.

Hello Towns! New York: Liveright, 1929.

The American County Fair. New York: Random House, 1930.

Perhaps Women. New York: Liveright, 1931.

No Swank. Philadelphia: Centaur Press, 1934.

Puzzled America. New York: Scribners, 1935.

A Writer's Conception of Realism. Olivet, Mich.: Olivet College, 1939.

Home Town. New York: Alliance, 1940.

Sherwood Anderson's Memoirs. New York: Harcourt, Brace, 1942.

The Sherwood Anderson Reader, edited with an Introduction by Paul Rosenfeld, Boston: Houghton Mifflin, 1947.

The Portable Sherwood Anderson, edited by

Horace Gregory. New York: Viking, 1949. (Revised edition, 1971.)

Letters of Sherwood Anderson, edited with an Introduction by Howard Mumford Jones in association with Walter B. Rideout. Boston: Little, Brown, 1953.

Return to Winesburg: Selections from Four Years of Writing for a Country Newspaper, edited by Ray Lewis White. Chapel Hill: University of North Carolina Press, 1967.

The Buck Fever Papers, edited by Welford D. Taylor. Charlottesville: University of Virginia Press, 1971.

BIBLIOGRAPHIES

Sheehy, Eugene P., and Kenneth A. Lohf. *Sherwood Anderson: A Bibliography.* Los Gatos, Calif.: Talisman Press, 1960.

Rideout, Walter B. "Sherwood Anderson," *Fifteen Modern American Authors,* edited by Jackson R. Bryer. Durham, N.C.: Duke University Press, 1969.

Tanselle, G. Thomas. "Additional Reviews of Sherwood Anderson's Work," *Papers of the Bibliographical Society of America,* 56:358–65 (1962).

White, Ray Lewis. *Checklist of Sherwood Anderson.* Columbus, Ohio: Merrill, 1969.

————. "A Checklist of Sherwood Anderson Studies, 1959–1969," *Newberry Library Bulletin,* 6:288–302 (1971).

CRITICAL AND BIOGRAPHICAL STUDIES

Adams, Richard P. "The Apprenticeship of William Faulkner," *Tulane Studies in English,* 12:113–56 (1962).

Anderson, David D. "Sherwood Anderson after 20 Years," *Midwest Quarterly,* 119–32 (1962).

————. *Sherwood Anderson: An Introduction and Interpretation.* New York: Holt, Rinehart and Winston, 1967.

Asselineau, Roger, ed. *Configuration critique de Sherwood Anderson, la revue des lettres moderne,* Nos. 78–80 (1963).

Beach, Joseph Warren. *The Outlook for American Prose.* Chicago: University of Chicago Press, 1926.

Bishop, John Peale. "The Distrust of Ideas" [1921], in *The Collected Essays of John Peale Bishop.* New York: Scribners, 1948.

Burbank, Rex. *Sherwood Anderson.* New York: Twayne, 1964.

Chase, Cleveland B. *Sherwood Anderson.* New York: McBride, 1927.

Crane, Hart. "Sherwood Anderson," *Double-Dealer,* 2:42–45 (1921).

Dahlberg, Edward. *Alms for Oblivion.* Minneapolis: University of Minnesota Press, 1964.

Duffey, Bernard. *The Chicago Renaissance in American Letters.* Lansing: Michigan State College Press, 1954.

Faulkner, William. "Sherwood Anderson: An Appreciation," *Atlantic Monthly,* 191:27–29 (1953).

Fenton, Charles A. *The Apprenticeship of Ernest Hemingway.* New York: Farrar, Straus, 1954.

Fitzgerald, F. Scott. "How to Waste Material: A Note on My Generation," *Bookman,* 63:262–65 (1926).

Frank, Waldo. "Emerging Greatness," *Seven Arts,* 1:73–78 (1916).

Geismar, Maxwell. *The Last of the Provincials.* Boston: Houghton Mifflin, 1943.

Gregory, Alyse. "Sherwood Anderson," *Dial,* 75:243–46 (1923).

Herbst, Josephine. "Ubiquitous Critics and the Author," *Newberry Library Bulletin,* 5:1–13 (1958).

"Homage to Sherwood Anderson," *Story,* Vol. 19 (September–October 1941). (Contributions by James Boyd, Van Wyck Brooks, Theodore Dreiser, Waldo Frank, Julius W. Friend, Lewis Galantière, Harry Hansen, Henry Miller, Paul Rosenfeld, William Saroyan, Gertrude Stein, Thomas Wolfe, and others.)

Howe, Irving. *Sherwood Anderson.* New York: Sloane, 1951.

Phillips, William L. "How Sherwood Anderson Wrote *Winesburg, Ohio,*" *American Literature,* 23:7–30 (1951).

Rosenfeld, Paul. "Sherwood Anderson," *Dial,* 72:29–42 (1922).

Schevill, James. *Sherwood Anderson: His Life and Work.* Denver: University of Denver Press, 1951.

"Sherwood Anderson Number," *Shenandoah,* Vol. 13 (Spring 1962). (Articles by James K.

Feibleman, Frederick J. Hoffman, Jon S. Lawry, Walter B. Rideout, and Cratis D. Williams.)

"Sherwood Anderson Memorial Number," *Newberry Library Bulletin,* Second Series, No. 2 (December 1948). (Articles by George H. Daugherty, Waldo Frank, Norman Holmes Pearson, and Roger Sergel.)

"Special Sherwood Anderson Number," *Newberry Library Bulletin,* Vol. 6 (July 1971). (Articles by John H. Ferres, Walter B. Rideout, David D. Anderson, Welford D. Taylor, and an annotated checklist of an anniversary exhibit by Richard Colles Johnson.)

Sutton, William A. Four articles on Anderson's life from 1884 to 1896 and 1899 to 1907, in *Northwest Ohio Quarterly,* 19:99–114 (1947), 20:20–36 (1948), 22:39–44 (1950), 22:120–57 (1950).

————. *The Road to Winesburg: A Mosaic of the Imaginative Life of Sherwood Anderson.* New York: Scarecrow Press, 1972.

Trilling, Lionel. *The Liberal Imagination.* New York: Viking, 1950.

Walcutt, Charles C. *American Literary Naturalism, A Divided Stream.* Minneapolis: University of Minnesota Press, 1956.

Warren, Robert Penn. "Hawthorne, Anderson and Frost," *New Republic,* 54:399–401 (1928).

Weber, Brom. "Anderson and 'The Essence of Things,' " *Sewanee Review,* 59:678–92 (1951).

White, Ray Lewis, ed. *The Achievement of Sherwood Anderson: Essays in Criticism.* Chapel Hill: University of North Carolina Press, 1966. (Selections by Waldo Frank, Francis Hackett, Rex Burbank, Bernard Duffey, William L. Phillips, M.A., Irving Howe, Edwin Fussell, Joseph Wood Krutch, Walter B. Rideout, James Schevill, Charles Child Walcutt, Frederick J. Hoffman, William Faulkner, Lionel Trilling, Malcolm Cowley, and David D. Anderson.)

Wright, Austin McGiffert. *The American Short Story in the Twenties.* Chicago: University of Chicago Press, 1961.

—BROM WEBER

John Barth

1930-

THE biographical surface of John Barth's life appears to be all but seamlessly academic. Born in Cambridge, Maryland, in 1930, he attended public schools, graduating from Cambridge High. After a brief stay at the Juilliard School of Music, he entered Johns Hopkins, from which he graduated with a B.A. in 1951 and an M.A. in 1952. He immediately began teaching at Pennsylvania State University in 1953, moved on to the State University of Buffalo in 1965, and then on to Boston University in 1972. At all three schools he has served as writer in residence and professor of English. Barth's published fiction, therefore, has developed without exception within the sheltering and/or confining umbra of the American school. To be sure, the tiresomely repeated question of whether the academic groves have been a blessing or a curse for the American writer is—certainly in Barth's mind —beside the point. As he has noted in an interview, excellent art has always come from all sorts of backgrounds: "any kind of life at all . . . can be shown to have produced work that you admire." The university atmosphere and the profession of writer-teacher just happen to be conditions of his work, inherently neither better nor worse than conceivable alternatives.

Still, an interim account of Barth's devel-opment may as well document the truism that his continuing immersion in a self-consciously intellectual world has crucially determined his direction as a writer. While his novels are not conventionally "academic," the educational experience either as theme or all-encompassing metaphor is central to each of them. They look back vaguely to the *Bildungsroman,* for in them, as the very title of Barth's second work would suggest, Western man has come to the end of the philosophical road first explored in this eighteenth- and nineteenth-century genre. And the complex response of a tutee to his tutor or psycho-spiritual adviser is a primary confrontation in several works. This abiding interest in the metabolism of human learning finds its terminus, thus far, in the novel-long pun of *Giles Goat-Boy* (1966) wherein the hero's life in the universe is allegorized as a movement through the cosmic University.

In their local effects as well the novels allude to their seminal idea of education—and frequently education in its institutional forms. Jake Horner and Joe Morgan of *The End of the Road* (1958; rev. ed., 1967) are compared partially in the light of their respective progress through the Johns Hopkins Graduate School. The protagonist of *The Floating Opera* (1956; rev. ed., 1967), Todd Andrews, glances back at his own Johns Hopkins education with a momentary verve that sharply contrasts with his habitual torpor. A phlegmatic soul rarely given to enthusiasm for anything, he can throw off a tribute to "the men, the professors, the fine independent minds of Johns Hopkins" and their disinterested search for wisdom. For better or worse, Barth is the kind of novelist that one might expect to come out of the Johns Hopkins graduate program, with its rigorous scholarly standards and history of ideas orientation. Certainly, while he somewhat disingenuously denies any philosophical competence ("I don't know anything about philosophy. I've never studied it, much less learned it"), the character conflicts of his novels are grounded less in temperamental differences than in philosophical debates of a rather abstruse sort. Sexual encounters between men and women occur frequently enough, but there is usually something tentative and halfhearted about the participation in them by semi-impotent or virginal protagonists. Barth's real narrative passion is reserved for voracious clashes of mind. His heroes, as Todd Andrews says of himself, tend "to attribute to abstract ideas a life-or-death significance," while his women are hollow, accommodating disciples in whom the men deposit the seed of not so much a sexual passion as a philosophical obsession. The struggle of intellectually well-entrenched male opponents who are inverted "doubles" of each other and whose ideas meet upon the essentially empty and undefended battlefield of a woman is most fully elaborated in *End of the Road,* but this paradigm serves either as the structural base or as the architectural ornament of Barth's other novels.

Such skirmishes of mind are rather firmly grounded, at least at first, in regional verisimilitude. For Barth is in his early work an accurate comic observer of Dorchester County, Maryland, and his books abound in local circumstance, character, and mores. *Floating Opera, End of the Road,* "Landscape: The Eastern Shore" (1960), and the "Ambrose" stories of *Lost in the Funhouse* (1968) are filled with the details of Maryland law and legal maneuvering, with the dry, hard texture of Maryland beaten biscuit, with evocations of Ocean City boardwalk and Baltimore social life. Barth's intimate knowledge of Maryland history, at any rate of the devious intrigues of the Chesapeake tidewater country in the seventeenth century, emerges with a hyperbolic exhaustiveness in *The Sot-Weed Factor* (1960; rev. ed., 1967). But the regional and historical verisimilitude of the first three novels merely supplies a base—and an increasingly mock one—for moral allegory and mythic flight. As Barth's interest in the ancient archetypes of his early "seekers" became more sharply focused, he began in his later work to trace the pattern of the hero's education into selfhood ("that hero business") with an increasingly experimental and self-reductive playfulness. In *Giles* the pretense of social and historical, if not entirely psychological, realism is altogether eschewed, as Barth follows the mythic configurations of the Western hero with a purposeful directness and artificiality.

This flight from realism to parodic fable turns out to be a flight from time to timelessness. The credible contemporary reality of *Floating Opera* and *End of the Road* gives way in *Sot-Weed Factor* to a seventeenth-century setting, a burlesque upon the Maryland past which employs the historian's questionable "facts" in the service of the novelist's quasi-historical, universal fable. And while the goat-boy's *Heldensleben* plays itself out against the background of crudely disguised Cold War politics, the political allegory is so patently subordinate to its pan-historical archetype (as is the life of the goat-boy) that the University of *Giles* with its multiple historical and cultural cross-references encompasses all times.

The irreversible quality of Barth's drift from time-bound realism to timeless fable is encapsulated in his comments, during an interview, on experiments in the novel by the French: ". . . the *nouveau roman* isn't just my cup of tea. They're all fighting Balzac, as I understand it, and I guess some of *us* are mad at Flaubert instead, in a friendly way. From what I know of Robbe-Grillet and his pals, their aesthetic is finally a more up-to-date kind of psychological realism: a higher fi to human consciousness and unconsciousness. Well, that's nice. A different way to come to terms with the discrepancy between art and the Real Thing is to *affirm* the artificial element in art (you can't get rid of it anyhow), and make the artifice part of your point instead of working for higher and higher fi with a lot of literary woofers and tweeters. That would be my way. Scheherazade's my *avant-gardiste*."

Like Scheherazade's tales, the thematic stuff of Barth's preposterous fictions does not undergo enormous change from work to work. His heroes try to find a philosophical justification for life, search for values and a basis for action in a relativistic cosmos, concern themselves with the possibilities of philosophical freedom and with the question of whether character and external reality are stable or floating phenomena. His novels, in other words, abound in many of the conceptual chestnuts of a post-Frazerian, Freudian, Wittgensteinian, Jungian, Sartrian world, and they usually parody the formulations of such classical modernists. What distinguishes Barth's habitual tone is a sophisticated, self-mocking awareness of how late in the game he has come to such "inquiries" (Todd Andrews' word) and how burned out the techniques of social and psychological realism are for handling them. Understanding that "God wasn't too bad a novelist, except he was a Realist," Barth has progressively committed himself to dreaming up "fictional" (in Jorge Luis Borges' sense of the word) alternatives to the cosmos, to reinventing the whole history of the world (in *Giles,* the world's sacred computer tape) with a coherence that the Real Thing lacks.

The Floating Opera, the first novel of a remarkably finished craftsman (or as the early Barth might prefer, boatwright), seemed to many of its early reviewers a comedy of manners with an "existential" keel. Securely tied to its Chesapeake Bay moorings, it ripples forth the widening circles of Barth country—Cambridge and the Choptank River, Dorchester County, the Eastern Shore of Maryland with its social and intellectual hub in Baltimore. The breezy accent, the eccentric but well-mannered intelligence, and the border-South financial security of the novel's protagonist bespeak a social ambience reminiscent of the Maryland that F. Scott Fitzgerald occasionally evoked in his work and of a cosmopolitan South that has more recently been Walker Percy's preserve. Todd tells his tale in the first person—of Barth's novels, only *Sot-Weed Factor* does not employ this habitual perspective which allows for progressively deepening experimentation with the sounds of the human, quasi-authorial voice.

The narrative's temporal dislocations are the accomplished tour de force of an author who wishes to involve his audience as demandingly as possible in the protagonist's self-discoveries, but Barth handles such a staple device of the modern novel with a virtuosity that suggests complete mastery of the convention. What was technically revolutionary in Conrad or Faulkner, so this first novel implies, is the veriest commonplace of the contemporary writer. Todd at age 54 tells the story in 1954 from which perspective he zigzags up to, through, and away from a watershed day of his life in 1937 His tongue-in-cheek excuse for the rudderless vessel his narrative resembles— a mélange of foreshadowings, anecdotal digressions, retrospective glances—is that he is something of a novice and bungler at storytelling. But we soon recognize the validity of his insistence that his method, while unsystematic, is justified by his intention.

For one thing the refracted structure is the ideal foundation for the phantasmagoric trope upon which the novel is erected. Todd enjoys spiking the reader's symbolic imagination by himself explicating heavy-handed symbols everywhere—his name (almost *Tod,* almost "death"), his ridiculous "weak heart" (clubbed fingers persistently remind him of his subacute bacteriological endocarditis, a condition that has made him live the better part of his life with the knowledge he is apt to fall down dead at any moment), and, most elaborately, "Adam's Original and Unparalleled 'Ocean-Going' Floating Opera." A tidewater country showboat with a realistic enough anchorage in the plot and in Barth's memories of his youth, the Floating Opera becomes in Todd's mind the apt correlative for his tale. In a fireworks display of his metaphorical talents he builds the fancy of such a boat drifting up and down the river with a play going on continuously. As the viewers sit upon the banks snatching at pieces of the plot and dialogue and relying for the best on their imagination or on that of their more attentive neighbors, the boat moves back and forth before their single limited perspective. Since that is how much of life works, that's how Todd's vagrant narrative, a "philosophical minstrel show," will work as well. Todd's Floating Opera within Barth's *Floating Opera* achieves a further permutation in Todd's unsuccessful attempts at literal boat-building, and the replicating device is Barth's earliest handling of the *regressus in infinitum*

—the refracting funhouse mirror, authorial echo chamber metaphor for existence that will become more pronounced in his later work.

Perspective, then, in life as in art is all-important in its distortion of event, and the 1954 perspective of a 54-year-old child of his century randomly blurs a profound division in Todd. His narrative focuses upon the day when he "changed his mind," when after having decided to commit suicide he decides, after a botched effort, not to. But the resonant phrase refers more importantly to a radical alteration of personality. For there are "two" Todds: the pre-1937 one, who if "almost dead" is also half-alive, sexually active, and apparently master of his life, gives way to a post-1937 Todd rendered moribund by a philosophical nihilism and sexually undone. The absolute force of this change is indicated by its dating. In the novel's 1956 edition Todd mentions repeatedly that the "change of mind" occurred on "either the 23rd or the 24th" of June 1937. The reason for this pointed vacillation becomes apparent only in the 1967 edition, where the correction to "either the 21st or the 22nd" clarifies Todd's abrupt declension from one house of the zodiac (Gemini, which ends on June 21) to another (Cancer, which begins on June 22).

The pre-1937 Todd was not precisely a robust innocent: he had passed through several stages, given himself over to several tepid commitments, and engaged in his share of "halfhearted" affairs. The first significant event in Todd's life occurs at seventeen when during his earliest clumsy attempts at lovemaking he happens to look into a full-length mirror and explodes into laughter at the absurdity of human copulation. The first of many optical epiphanies in Barth's work, that laugh partially unmans Todd, for he can never thereafter take liaisons with complete seriousness. True, he does carry on an extended affair between

1932 and 1937 with Jane Mack, one that has been engineered primarily by her husband for any number of quaint motives. But though a child is born who may or may not be Todd's, he keeps a discreet emotional distance between himself and both Macks. The recognition of his and mankind's animality is embellished by a World War I experience of the single "purest and strongest emotion" of his life, a moment of unadulterated, sphincter-opening terror when during a lull in battle he discovers himself to be "a shocked, drooling animal in a mudhole." This insight receives its existential cast when a German soldier in whom he induces a terror akin to his own leaps into his mudhole. After befriending the soldier in some hours of delirious intimacy, Todd bayonets him in an act as arbitrarily gratuitous as the initial embrace. And finally there is the inexplicable suicide of his father that becomes the subject of a systematic, lifelong *Inquiry*. Reflecting Todd's awareness that any single act is endlessly mysterious, that if it is not "free" (causation, with Hume, being merely an inference), then its motives are tortuously complicated, this "search for the father" becomes the instrument of Todd's attempted comprehension of the son.

Such a tissue of experiences has made for a passionless and stunted, but nevertheless comfortable, life up to 1937. Having drifted into law, as much as anything to please his lawyer father, Todd is by his own admission and as his narrative illustrates "perhaps the best lawyer on the Eastern Shore" precisely because of his detachment and his hypersensitivity to life's contingent nature. Aware of the whimsicality of choice behind the illusion of conscious intention, he takes an expert, disinterested pleasure in the law's labyrinthine and prescribed arbitrariness. He has some aged cronies in the Dorset Hotel where he lives, some friends in Cambridge proper, and his mistress of five years' standing. What bursts

his unenthusiastic metaphysical ease on the night of the 20th is Jane Mack's chance remark concerning the ugliness of his clubbed hands in an otherwise admirable body. The remark triggers a sudden overwhelming nausea at the realization that his whole life has been governed by the brute, animal fact of his heart. His despair at the certainty that *"there is no way to master the fact with which I live"* makes him decide upon the "stance to end all stances," suicide.

The inescapable presence of those ugly fingers, Whitehead's sheer "withness of the body," suddenly releases a pent-up self-loathing and hatred of the too too sullied flesh of this world that, beneath Todd's congenial voice, is virtually Manichaean in its intensity. Barth's sexual and excremental humor, which in *Sot-Weed Factor* will approach the savage playfulness of a Swift, has precisely such a gnostic base. To be sure, the artificial constructs of Todd's mind conceal much of this. He makes a good deal of the "philosophical grounds" for his suicide: the discovery that his successive intellectual positions—those of rake, saint, and finally cynic—have been so many masks he has accidentally exchanged for one another and the syllogistic conclusion of the *Inquiry* that nothing, not even life itself, has any intrinsic "value." But Todd's—and Barth's—rudimentary, derivative ideas merely paper over what is most powerful in the book—the comically controlled revulsion against man, the riotously copulating Caliban, the drooling animal with twisted fingers in his mudhole.

The all-inclusiveness of Todd's naysaying determines the form of his suicide attempt— the blowing up of the Floating Opera during a performance at which seven hundred townspeople including the Macks, his possible daughter, and most of the novel's other characters are present. (In the 1956 edition Barth's publisher insisted as a condition of publication that he tone down such monstrous callousness by having Todd attempt only single suicide.) The performance itself is a climactic extravaganza. A vaudeville-paced, disjunctive, surrealistic mime of Todd's own mental peregrinations, it begins with a recitation of Hamlet's "To be or not to be" soliloquy and ends with a GREAT STEAMBOAT EXPLOSION (the Armageddon point of which is entirely clear only in the "original" 1967 conclusion). When for some accidental reason or other the real explosion does not come off, Todd refuses to try again. Why bother? If there's no final reason for living, there is no reason for dying either—*nothing* finally makes any difference. Such a retreat into the clouds of ersatz abstraction represents, it seems to me, a final failure of nerve before the "fact with which we live," for the blasé nihilism of the 54-year-old Todd seems no less of a mask than the earlier ones he has discarded. And this ultimate flinching is of course Barth's as much as Todd's (the later Barth comes to make a virtue of the necessity that his characters are funhouse mirror images of an author-protagonist), for we are meant to take with complete seriousness the terms of Todd's intellectual journey.

A lugubrious concentration upon Todd, however, does a limited justice to the novel. It ignores the fascinating minor characters and the various tales within a tale which enliven his journey—Mister Haecker's parallel struggle with the Hamlet question; Harrison Mack Senior's seventeen wills and the pickle jars filled with his excrement that become the focus of one of Todd's typical, meticulousy described cases; Todd's arbitrary gift of the $5000 his father had left him to Colonel Morton, the town's richest man, and Morton's frenzied attempts to come to terms with the puzzling gift. Todd's Floating Opera—like all of Barth's works, whatever their weakness—is indeed "fraught with curiosities, melodrama, spectacle, instruction, and entertainment." But the very furiousness of invention and Todd's casual unwillingness to order the narrative swirl create a solipsistic effect. None of the characters as creations have the immediacy of the narrator's isolated voice—they are primarily part of the lonely spectacle we are asked to view from the shore; their distancing suggests movement toward an autistic cul-de-sac by a speaker too torpid to shun that oblivion.

Still, the end of Todd's intellectual road has not quite been reached by novel's end. The "happy ending" (words included in the title for the final chapter of the 1956, but not the 1967 edition) is Todd's upbeat realization that if values are only relative, there are relative values by which one can live and such phlegmatic souls as he can manage quite comfortably in such moral twilight. The originally intended ending that Barth restored in the second edition is somewhat less sanguine. There Todd puts whatever consolation he can find into the form of an offhanded question rather than a delighted assertion: "I considered too whether, in the real absence of absolutes, values less than absolute mightn't be regarded as in no way inferior and even be lived by. But that's another inquiry, and another story."

The End of the Road, written in the last three months of 1955 after *The Floating Opera* had been written in the first three months of the year, is precisely that inquiry, that story. Structurally the tightest and technically the least flamboyant of Barth's works, this last leg of Barth's serious-minded youthful journey ("I thought I had invented nihilism in 1953") focuses in relatively chronological, uncharacteristically undigressive fashion upon a *ménage à trois* agreed to by the husband, a situation that had been only one of the many whizbang "curiosities" of *Floating Opera*. Whereas Todd Andrews had been a spectator to a floating reality that refused to accentuate any single dramatic antagonist, *End of the Road* transforms the "chameleon-like," lightweight Harrison Mack of the earlier work into Joe Morgan, a fanatical ideologue whose philosophical wrestling match with Jacob Horner (a refurbished Todd) ends disastrously. Instead of a sequential single life (blurred slightly by a rambling, temporal dislocation) wherein Todd Andrews is "split," as it were, by his change of mind, we witness a dialectical clash between conflicting value systems embodied in two characters.

Jake Horner, the modern rationalizer in his corner, provides a generic name for Hamlet's disease to which Todd had succumbed—*cosmopsis,* the cosmic view of things which makes for emotional hollowness and intellectual hypertrophy. The earlier novel has described Todd's evolution into the condition; this presents us with the tendency toward cosmopsis as a given of Horner's temperament. Jake is on the one hand inclined to "weatherlessness," feelings of utter nonexistence when the certainty of an essential "I" completely disappears; on the other he is agonizingly self-conscious and can usually observe himself thinking, can spot the limits of every intellectual way station he inhabits and therefore shifts from one contradictory position to another with purposeless fluidity. The price of this modern intelligence is the physical immobility into which he periodically falls. During one such bout in the Baltimore railroad station he is taken in tow by a Negro doctor—part quack, prophet, psychoanalyst ("Father Divine, Sister Kenny, and Bernarr MacFadden combined")—a vaguely threatening figure who materializes from the same numinous cosmos out of which Jacob R. Adam brought his Floating Opera to its solid moorings at Cambridge. With his preternatural understanding of Jake's disease the Doctor proceeds to put

him through a series of baroque, increasingly sophisticated therapies to teach him how to choose. One such ploy, the teaching of prescriptive (*not* descriptive, the Doctor insists) grammar with its codified rigidity, becomes the extension of Todd's legal career; the conscious manipulation of "masks" that the Doctor advises at a later stage in the treatment transforms into a cure—a "Mythotherapy" remarkably like Baron de Clappique's "Mythomania" in André Malraux's *Man's Fate*—what had in *Floating Opera* been the disease itself.

If Jake's inability to choose echoes Todd's awareness that in a world devoid of absolutes nothing has intrinsic value, the Joe Morgan whom he meets during a job interview at Wicomico State Teachers College answers affirmatively the question introduced in the last paragraph of *Floating Opera* of whether man can arbitrarily set up some less than absolute value and live by it. Where Jake wanders tolerantly among equally random commitments, Joe insists that man can create his own essence by transforming a single relative value into the "subjective equivalent of an absolute." The two characters are drawn to each other precisely because their complementary minds, each initially impressive in its own erratic way, branch off from the same acceptance of modern relativism. But, having deified intellectual clarity and order, Joe lives his credo that "a man can act coherently; he can act in ways that he can explain, if he wants to." While Horner's lassitude provides him with no good reason to complete his M.A. at Johns Hopkins, a robust, vital Morgan plugs steadily away at an "odd, brilliant" thesis on the saving roles of innocence and energy in American history.

Indeed, there is a hint of an international theme in the thoroughgoing opposition of the two characters. The ancient heritage of Jake's suffering is suggested by the bust of Laocoön he carries with him from rented room to rented room, a figure whose unfocused grimace of abstract, noncommittal anguish is the archetype of Horner's own sense of a meaninglessness that is ageless. During periods of paralysis Jake's eyes take on the blank gaze that the German archaeologist Winckelmann attributed to the classical gods: he rocks in his chair "sightless, gazing on eternity, fixed on ultimacy, and when that is the case there is no reason to do anything." In contrast, Joe's buoyancy and puritanical perfectionism (a scoutmaster, he is completely aware of but impervious to the ridicule this may occasion) are peculiarly American, as he himself bouncily insists: " 'What the hell, Jake, the more sophisticated your ethics get, the stronger you have to be to stay afloat. And when you say good-by to objective values, you really have to flex your muscles and keep your eyes open, because you're on your own. It takes *energy*: not just personal energy, but cultural energy, or you're lost. Energy's what makes the difference between American pragmatism and French existentialism—where the hell else but in America could you have a cheerful nihilism, for God's sake?' "

The third character of the triangle, Rennie Morgan, becomes the crucible within which Joe attempts to prove his ethical system. Initially attracted by her surface self-sufficiency, Joe has married Rennie because he will not have to make allowances for her as a woman. Once he has finished training this apparently independent, but actually hollow disciple, he will be able to meet her as a tough-minded Galatea whose intellect he can take seriously. When Jake enters the lives of the Morgans, Joe recognizes how "diabolically" opposed Jake really is to everything he—and presumably Rennie—believes in and he intentionally throws Rennie and Jake together as an ethical experiment. For reasons as complex as his ac-

commodating character, Jake agrees to the role of tempting devil and proceeds to chip away at Rennie's vulnerable belief in her "God's" coherence and solidity of personality.

The key blow is struck one evening when Jake challenges Rennie to spy on Joe through a living-room blind. There she sees her pillar of rationalism in his scoutmaster's uniform—grimacing, saluting, and curtseying before a mirror; making animal sounds; and then while sitting at the table where he does reading for his dissertation, simultaneously picking his nose and masturbating. The horns that Jake puts to Joe's head a few nights later seem inevitable after such a revelation, though the actual bedding down with Rennie, as Jake describes it, is initiated by neither and just "happens." When Rennie in a paroxysm of guilt and self-recrimination tells Joe what she has done, he adheres to the strait of reason with a tenacity that becomes more and more monstrous. The relentless testing that Rennie undergoes as Joe makes her return again and again to Jake's apartment in order to face up squarely to the "cause" for the betrayal transforms her into a modern-day Grisilde sacrificed upon the altar of reason rather than upon that of some medieval virtue. The obsessive talk, the microscopic probing, the scurry from one earnest conversation to another among the three characters become grotesquely comic, as Joe and Rennie pursue their analytic search and Jake insists upon the mystery of any human action wherein so many unconscious elements are involved.

It is precisely here that the novel reveals a serious weakness. Structurally, it leads up to and away from the scene at the window, although the characters all seem to mistake the adulterous act as the one that requires dissection. Jake's narration of this act goes to painful lengths to avoid any suggestion of causality, but one can easily see the "reason" why Rennie is so susceptible to a betrayal of her husband. What she learns at the window—the certainty that Joe's fierce rationalism is, if only in an unguarded moment, a mask for the Barthian fact that he like anyone else is "part chimpanzee"—weakens her belief in his authenticity. If the Morgans seek a rationale for Rennie's lapse, there it is, clear as day. Since we have but a distanced view of their introspection through what they report to a first-person narrator, we cannot be certain that the crucial nature of the window episode never occurred to them. But nothing that the Morgans say to Jake or report to him of their conversation suggests an admission to each other that Rennie's lesson at the window, not the act of adultery, ought to be the true focus of their inquiry. During a talk with Jake in which Joe does for once consider his share in the blame, he contemplates only the possibility that "for some perverse reason or other I engineered the whole affair." Joe *never* alludes to the window scene; Rennie does at one point admit to Jake that the sight at the window "started everything," but one suspects that despite the days of tortured analysis this is not an emphasis she would have insisted upon to a "God" she feared.

Such a psychic lacuna certainly takes away from the putative "brillance" of Joe Morgan, which, of course, is suspect for other reasons; more importantly, Jake's inability to spot this suppression undermines the continuing implication of his subtlety of mind. Nor does he ever explore with requisite profundity the perversity of *his* motives for initiating Rennie into a knowledge of human complexity that night at the window. What he hides from himself is murky. It may be the homosexuality that Stanley Edgar Hyman sees as a preoccupation of all the novels; it may be that same disgust with the human body that unmanned Todd—certainly the mythotherapeutic games Jake

plays with Peggy Rankin, a sexually starved, forty-year-old pickup, are a tawdry enough byplay to the central action, and he describes with fascinated loathing the abortion of Rennie, who, pregnant with either Jake's or Joe's child, suffocates upon her own vomit at the novel's brutal conclusion. But despite much lip service to "human irrationality," etc., he responds with unconvincing reservations to Joe's hypothesis of a purely philosophical antagonism. The ultimate limitation of insight is once again Barth's, who suffers with his characters from a tendency to simplify an emotionally intricate, fully human confrontation into an intellectual scheme.

That a flaw in psychological structure is so glaring—one would never remark similar lapses in either *Sot-Weed Factor* or *Giles*—indicates the extent to which this novel, like *Floating Opera*, relies upon the assumptions of realism, conventions pointed up comically at the window scene and horrifyingly in the naturalistic amplitude of Rennie's abortion. But the lapse is not fatal to the novel's considerable power because the patina of realism covers with redeeming imperfection its fabular essence. Once we accept the premise of a Jake physically paralyzed by an abstract response to the world and of a Joe "who will see, face up to, and unhesitatingly act upon the extremest limits of his ideas," the larger-than-life hostility of such ideologues will inevitably lead beyond realism into philosophical fantasy. The novel's "ideas"—in part because they are embodied in such grotesques as Jake and Joe, in part because they are not as profoundly impressive as the 25-year-old Barth felt them to be—are most appropriately conveyed through parody and burlesque, a fact that may account for *Sot-Weed Factor*'s change of mode. Barth recognized something like this when in looking back upon his early novels he remarked that "I had thought I was writing about values and it turned out I was writing about innocence." That the world-weary Todd Andrews and Jake Horner are just as much naifs as Joe Morgan the novels only imperfectly convey. The stark philosophical conclusion implied in the title of the second novel therefore seems, in the light of Barth's subsequent development, sophomorically nihilistic.

Both Jake and Joe are "responsible" (a notion continually bandied about) for Rennie's disaster. Joe's mad egoism forces his wife to her death for the sake of an abstract value, while Jake resembles his Laocoön whose limbs are bound by the serpents Knowledge and Imagination that, "grown great in the fullness of time, no longer tempt but annihilate." Cursed with an excessively fertile imagination, he can never commit himself to anything or anyone. As a price for performing the abortion Jake's sinister Doctor has insisted that Jake accompany him, presumably for good, to the new location of his Remobilization Farm in Pennsylvania (a private joke, no doubt, concerning Penn State). He has in desperation agreed to the price with no intention of paying, but once Rennie is dead Jake recognizes his inability to play the same role long enough as a kind of ethical leprosy that can only destroy his friends. His decision to go to the terminal (the novel's last word) to keep his bargain after all indicates a final retreat from life.

The *No Exit* conclusiveness of *End of the Road* is slightly misleading in that Barth's next novel, *The Sot-Weed Factor*, carries forward motifs introduced in the antiphonal early works. But this third variation on the theme of innocence—Barth's as well as that of his characters—struck its initial readers as a radical departure. Not only was it in a surprisingly new mode, it also widened Barth's range spatially and temporally. Where the first two novels were parochially constrained within their twentieth-century Maryland locale, the historically reverberating, transoceanic *Sot-Weed Factor* charts the life of its hero, Ebenezer Cooke, in and around London, glances at his American birth, follows his enforced trip across the Atlantic to claim his father's Maryland estate and his wanderings after gulling himself out of it. *Floating Opera*, while implying the social density of its Eastern Shore microcosm, made do with a small cast of characters, and *End of the Road* was downright claustrophobic. The structural and characterological tightness, especially of the latter work, was the formal correlative for a confinement of minds in wandering mazes lost. In *Sot-Weed Factor* Barth loosens his form, conceivably in the hope that temporal and spatial amplitude will permit his characters to burst their psychological and philosophical prisons.

What Barth perhaps means in the passage quoted earlier by being "mad at Flaubert . . . in a friendly way" is that he had come to feel the necessity for moving away from a tradition that *End of the Road* in part exemplifies—the novel as ordered, organic artifact where every *mot juste* creates its calibrated impact. The jeweled perfection of Jane Austen, Flaubert, and Joyce's *Dubliners* notwithstanding, for the later Barth the grounds of highest value in fiction are expansive grandeur, the wastefully panoramic sweep, a self-confident and even self-indulgent completeness. Both *Sot-Weed Factor* and *Giles* seek to recapture the boisterousness, the grandiose scale of Cervantes and Rabelais and the exuberant innocence of the English eighteenth-century novel. Todd Andrews had apologized that his Floating Opera was to be a baggy monster; in fact the pretense of random garrulousness conceals a carefully patterned narrative mosaic with a rigorously controlled point of view. Still, from Todd's intention to use a free form we can recognize the early appeal of the loose, open-ended structure for Barth (his desire to write a book with a plot "fancier than *Tom Jones*"), and *Sot-Weed Factor* is even more of a Floating Opera than the actual novel of that name. Its 756 pages in the 1967 hard-cover edition (trimmed from 806 in the 1960 edition) bulge with incident and character—it's a rambling, Gargantuan affair studded with absurd coincidences, with London tavern and bookseller scenes, with thinky exchanges embedded in excremental humor that throw into an ironic shade the "serious" encounters of Jake Horner and Joe Morgan; the book is asprawl with comic servants and Oxford dons, with poets and pirates and prostitutes, with Maryland tobacco growers and renegade Indians, with slaves and opium peddlers. Such furiousness of invention swirls out of the backwater intrigues of Maryland history, already complicated enough in the *Archives of Maryland*, but further muddied by Barth for thematic purposes: the labyrinthine obscurity, and ultimately the complete impenetrability, of seventeenth-century plot and counterplot conveys the difficulty of knowing the moral status of anything or anyone in the great world. The many rhetorical changes of pace reinforce Ebenezer's (and the reader's) epistemological quandary, for the novel ventriloquizes from one set piece to another—from fluent passages of Hudibrastic poetry to the Jacobean prose of John Smith's *Secret Historie*, from compressed disquisitions on historiography to interpolated short stories à la *Tom Jones*, from a fabliau with the same structure as Chaucer's *Reeve's Tale* to a six-page, bilingual cursing match in which a French and an English whore surely exhaust the metaphorical labels for their calling (a mock testimony to Barth's dazzlingly offhanded learning).

The "flabbergasting plot" in its veering precipitousness carries forward the trope of the road to suggest that, whatever the final disablement of Todd Andrews and Jake Horner, the

fabular abilities of their creator are far from their terminal (though Barth seems to be hypersensitive to the possibilities of imaginative aridity). By widening and making more florid the terms of Todd's inquiry, Barth frames the philosophically naive "big" questions this time within the interstices of the historical novel, a maneuver that creates a variety of echo effects. The return to the burlesque mode of Sterne and Fielding allows for the unfettered expansiveness of the novel's youthful period; but onto that wide canvas Barth thrusts characters who, in the dialects of the late seventeenth century, are beset with ailments that *Floating Opera* and *End of the Road* tended (Laocoön notwithstanding) to define as primarily modern. The resulting comic suspension between two historical periods provides a breezily detached perspective upon the agonies of both, at the same time that it implies the venerable age of Barth's road.

Ebenezer Cooke, the gawky, taciturn young man who haunts London taverns in search of a vocation and, familiarly enough, an "identity," is not quite the youthful naif of the picaresque tradition. The recipient of an unusually comprehensive education from his gifted tutor, Henry Burlingame, Eben arbitrarily admires whomever he meets—"expert falconers, scholars, masons, chimneysweeps, prostitutes, admirals, catpurses, sailmakers, barmaids, apothecaries and cannoneers alike." "Dizzy with the beauty of the possible" he throws up his hands at the task of choosing—whether notebook, a position on gambling, or a career. He is still a virgin at 28 because of a highly developed sense of mask, because he has never been single-minded enough to adopt a particular style of lovemaking. This habitual paralysis resolves itself in part when, as an undiscriminating admirer of *l'amour courtois*, scholastic metaphysics, and Neoplatonic idealism, he apotheosizes a London whore, Joan Toast, into a goddess of love. In such a transformation Barth rearranges the philosophical determinants that had been "split" between Jake and Joe in the previous novel: Eben's cosmopsis, once he deifies Joan, gives way to a polar exuberance in defense of his "essence" that reminds one of nothing so much as Joe's fanatical rationalism. The overblown mock-epic gusts of language with which Eben defends his virginity against this tart who rather enjoys her work typify his capacity to rhapsodize the most ungainly jetsam into something rare and beautiful: " 'Was't for gold that silver-footed Thetis shared the bed of Peleus, Achilles' sire? Think thee Venus and Anchises did their amorous work on consideration of five guineas? Nay, sweet Joan, a man seeks not in the market for the favors of a goddess!' "

Once he has discovered his calling as lover of Joan, Eben is led quite naturally to its twin, the vocation of the poet who will sing the praises of his sullied Beatrice. When his father, informed of his unproductive London life, orders him to cross the ocean to the family tobacco estate at Cooke's Point, Maryland, Eben includes within his apotheosis the jewel of the New World, Maryland itself. His overblown *Marylandiad*-to-be, as he describes it during an interview with Charles Calvert, Third Lord Baltimore (actually Henry Burlingame in one of his disguises), will be " 'an epic to out-epic epics: the history of the princely house of Charles Calvert, Lord Baltimore and Lord Proprietary of the Province of Maryland, relating the heroic founding of that province! The courage and perseverance of her settlers in battling barb'rous nature and fearsome savage to wrest a territory from the wild and transform it to an earthly paradise! The majesty and enlightenment of her proprietors, who like kingly gardeners fostered the tender seeds of civilization in their rude soil, and so husbanded and cultivated them as to bring to fruit a Maryland beauteous beyond description; verdant, fertile, prosperous, and cultured; peopled with brave men and virtuous women, healthy, handsome, and refined: a Maryland, in short, splendid in her past, majestic in her present, and glorious in her future, the brightest jewel in the fair crown of England, owned and ruled to the benefit of both by a family second to none in the recorded history of the universal world—the whole done into heroic couplets, printed on linen, bound in calf, stamped in gold . . . and dedicated to Your Lordship!' "

The actuality of "beshitten Maryland" throws such lofty expectation into grotesque relief. Eben's chastity and poetic elevation are sorely tried by the intricate plots and all-pervasive scurviness of his voyage and misadventures in the New World. The history of Maryland is world history in small, "a string of plots, cabals, murthers, and machinations," a vortex of conspiracy within the larger whirlpool of late seventeenth-century colonial politics. From such actual historical personages as the several Lord Baltimores, Henry More, Isaac Newton, William Claiborne, and John Coode down to the lowliest besotted tobacco planter, all is bleared with comic sludge and smeared with excremental humor. For every imposing historical reputation there is a scurrilous "secret historie": the novel, for example, follows the sexual adventures of John Smith, whose scatalogical career emerges from his journal entries scattered throughout the novel. All this is rendered with a circumstantial, enthusiastic mock realism. The tale's sheer length and the convolutions of plot and large cast of fools and knaves give the impression of heaviness—of the weight, the ubiquitousness, but also the attractiveness of the great world's power of corruption.

Inevitably, the gradual furnace of that

world burns away Eben's illusions. His tobacco estate is an opium den and brothel; Joan Toast's beauty, after she follows Eben to America, is irretrievably blasted by opium and syphilis; and *The Marylandiad* becomes not the panegyric that Eben had originally intended but *The Sot-Weed Factor*, a Hudibrastic satire filled with bitter misanthropy. Nevertheless, Eben retains the accouterments of his twin calling of epic poet and virgin long after experience has stripped him of belief, for he will not disavow his cardinal philosophical principle that there is a solidity to human character, an essence that no amount of disillusionment can alter.

Eben's opponent in this ancient debate about the one and the many is the "cosmophilist" Henry Burlingame, his friend and tutor, who moves among the many professions of his life with gusto and a sure mastery. If Eben's continuing presence in the novel implies the stability of personality, Burlingame's discontinuous appearance as he threads his way among various disguises seriously challenges Eben's precarious sense of selfhood. Burlingame's America is itself an epistemological wilderness in which Eben wanders because of identities bestowed upon him by a traditional philosophical idealism and by his personal past—a father who insists that he take over the Maryland tobacco plantation. Conversely, Burlingame, an orphan who does not know his father, floats with consummate skill through a new world that is his proper metaphysical home. America's appeal for Burlingame is that it makes possible the shifting choice of identity: " 'There is a freedom there that's both a blessing and a curse. 'Tis more than just political and religious liberty—they come and go from one year to the next. 'Tis philosophic liberty I speak of, that comes from want of history. It makes every man an orphan like myself, that freedom, and can as well demora-

lize as elevate.' " Burlingame does not find the New World the Hell or Purgatorio that Eben comes to know, but "just a piece o' the great world like England—with the difference, haply, that the soil is vast and new where the sot-weed hath not drained it. What's more, the reins and checks are few and weak; good plants and weeds alike grow tall." Burlingame pits such a capacity for pragmatic acceptance against Eben's "mystic ontological value," and the novel's many debates about the nature of history, of civilization, of man's position in the cosmos, of the appropriate life style for this poor forked animal sitting upon "a blind rock careening through space . . . rushing headlong to the grave" develop out of the dialectical confrontation of Eben's "innocence" and Burlingame's "experience."

The Sot-Weed Factor also explores more fully and consciously than the earlier novels the connection between identity and sexual knowledge. Eben's single-minded devotion to Joan Toast is now a cause, now an effect of his search for selfhood. But Barth interjects a post-Freudian motive into what Stendhal would have called such "crystallizations": Burlingame at one point suggests that it is Eben's sister, Anna, that Eben really loves. The idealization of Joan Toast projects a passion for his sister upon an acceptable woman, and his insistence upon chastity makes it possible for him to avoid a carnal commitment to any woman other than his sister. The perverse element in Eben's innocence finds its mirror reversal in Burlingame's perverse doctrine of experience. Burlingame is anxious to take on sexually all comers—women, men, and, in one of the novel's more hilarious chapters, pigs. It is with typical tongue-in-cheek hyperbole that he proclaims his catholic sexual tastes to Eben: " 'I love the world, sir, and so make love to it! I have sown my seed in men and women, in a dozen sorts of beasts, in the barky boles of trees and the honeyed wombs of flowers; I have dallied on the black breast of the earth, and clipped her fast; I have wooed the waves of the sea, impregnated the four winds, and flung my passion skywards to the stars!' "

The *ménage à trois* of the first two novels receives a further turn of the screw from this juxtaposition of Eben's virginity and Burlingame's pan-sexualism. The incestuous bond between Eben and Anna is complicated by Burlingame's love of them both or, more accurately, of their twinhood (he defends that love to Eben by means of a learned historical survey of geminology). Barth here makes explicit what had been a subterranean motif of his earlier work—the degree to which the *ménage à trois* offers the novelist an opportunity to explore the competing homosexual and heterosexual impulses in man. The multiple sexual confusions do more or less straighten themselves out by novel's end in a traditional enough way: Eben, who comes fully to realize the destructive effects of his platonizing on himself and on others, does marry and bed the opium-addicted, syphilitic Joan Toast; and Burlingame's promiscuity, an extension of his belief in a New World philosophical freedom, is revealed to cover a sexual impotence that he cannot cure until his "search for the father" is successful. Only when he can come to a conventional awareness of a limited self does he get his beloved Anna with child. To be sure, this symmetrical comedic straightening out of lovers is blurred in the novel's final chapter by Joan Toast's death in childbirth and Burlingame's disappearance for good among the Indians, whereupon the twins are plagued by their old suspicions of incestuous feelings as together they bring up Anna's child. But by and large the mask of the eighteenth-century picaresque mode which looks back to the ancient patterns of New Comedy (in both of which the possibility of incest operated as a stock comic obstacle) serves to dilute any "serious" conclusion.

As *Sot-Weed Factor* and the *Giles* to follow suggest, a degree of emotional flatness is the price that the parodist agrees to pay for his knowledgeable artificiality and mannered thoroughness. Whether in his depletion of the picaresque mode, in his erudite catalogues of ideas, or in his name-calling contest between the prostitutes, Barth tries to convey the impression that sheer exhaustiveness for its own sake contributes to a meaningful comic order. The longer and more contrived the shaggy-dog fiction, the better. But because of Barth's intellectual passion for following a literary genre, a philosophical assumption, or a linguistic pattern to the absolute end of its road, his characters frequently do not have much emotional depth, since he sends up hurrahs for "the literal skin of things." He delights in composing what he has called Smollett's *Roderick Random*—"a novel of nonsignificant surfaces." Aware of the ancient resonances of his hero's experience, Barth can wittily and with considerable rhetorical gusto explore the meaning of the archetype. But insisting upon a mock-epic distance, Barth only rarely enters, and lets his reader enter, fully into his character's suffering and loss. For the most part he writes "novels which imitate the form of the Novel, by an author who imitates the role of Author."

Of course, as he has noted, this sense of being at several removes from reality is nothing new for the novel—"it's about where the genre began, with *Quixote* imitating *Amadis of Gaul*, Cervantes pretending to be the Cid Hamete Benengeli (and Alonzo Quijano pretending to be Don Quixote), or Fielding parodying Richardson." Eben's defense of his virginity which echoes that of Joseph Andrews which in turn parodies that of Pamela, etc., creates the *regressus in infinitum* effect that

Barth admires in the fiction of Nabokov and Borges, the literary funhouse in which the reader is invited to amuse himself. But Barth's characters, interesting as they are, cannot possess the achieved sense of clearly observed humanity, the degree of characterological "originality," that one feels in the great characters of realistic fiction or even in the parodic characters of the early novel. For the further the regression from the pre-existing archetype, the more surely a character becomes a learned and witty commentary upon the archetype, a pale fire indeed. Like Nabokov and Borges, then, Barth tries in his most recent work to make a virtue of the necessity of parody and self-parody: to create original works of art out of the certainty that at this late date in the history of Western narrative, it is impossible to write original narratives.

Though Ebenezer Cooke and Henry Burlingame obviously combine to echo the traditional hero of Western literature in manifold ways, Barth was apparently not aware of *Sot-Weed Factor*'s comprehensively paradigmatic design until he happened, after its publication, to read Lord Raglan's *The Hero*. Raglan's work establishes the pattern of mythic heroism by abstracting from the lives of the world's culture heroes a list of twenty-two characteristics and then "grading" representative heroes according to the number of characteristics they possess. Barth was struck by the fact that Cooke and Burlingame taken together (as they might be) do almost as well by Raglan's standards as Oedipus (who fulfills twenty-one of the twenty-two prerequisites—"there's always one smart guy in the class who messes up the curve"). Out of a subsequent absorption in modern mythographers and comparative religionists—Otto Rank, Joseph Campbell, Jung, Frazer, Freud (whatever came to hand)—Barth apparently set out in his next novel to

create a parable of mythic heroism with a controlled relentlessness and an exactitude that went beyond the accidental typicality of *Sot-Weed Factor*. If the implied moral allegory of Eben's pilgrimage through life is frequently swamped by the rich detail of Maryland history, *Giles* accentuates its allegory with deliberate artifice, annotating the meaning of each step that its hero takes in his cyclical adventure from mysterious birth, through rites of passage, to his momentary illumination at the womb of things, through the mature period of lawgiving to his civilization, and toward an extraordinary sacrificial death.

The formal educational experience that had at times been peripheral and muted in earlier novels becomes the radical trope of *Giles*, a *Bildungsroman ad absurdum*. After some Nabokov-like publisher's disclaimers describing the editorial vicissitudes of this highly controversial manuscript and a "cover letter" to the editors and publishers by "J. B." describing how the text came into his hands, the fable proper assumes the form of the Revised New Syllabus, a sacred computer tape chronicle of the life and teachings of George Giles, the Grand Tutor of New Tammany College, as spoken by George himself, prepared by the West Campus Automatic Computer (WESCAC) from several texts fed into it by George's son and disciple, and given to the public in its present form by Barth, a recent convert to Gilesianism. (Such a playful refraction of the author's vision into written, spoken, and mechanical "voices" from several problematical sources—Barth's latest statement of man's epistemological dilemma—will receive its most technical elaboration in *Lost in the Funhouse*.) Rescued from the tapelift of WESCAC after a mysterious birth, the narrator is reared as Billy Bocksfuss, the Ag-Hill Goat-Boy, by Max Spielman, an outcast professor with a fondness for the company of goats. The naive goat-boy gradually discovers that he is more human being than goat, and, journeying forth from his caprine Eden after having killed a brother goat, he bids farewell to his "hornless goathood" and strikes out, "a horned human student," for Commencement Gate. But his progress across the Great Mall is no ordinary one, for he takes upon himself the profession of the hero who will in his time save all of studentdom. The form of his quest will be the entrance into the belly of WESCAC to change its AIM (Automatic Implementation Mechanism), which threatens to destroy the entire student body. And as George learns, he is peculiarly suited to this task in that he is himself GILES (the Grand Tutorial Ideal, Laboratory Specimen), son of WESCAC and a human mother.

The novel thus becomes a hybrid of genres: part sacred book, animal fable, science-fiction fantasy, political allegory, educational satire, epic, and what not else, the work has so exasperated some reviewers that they have been unable to see in it more than an ingeniously prolonged put-on that self-indulgently stitches together the shreds and patches of Barth's learning. As it insinuates with wild incongruity the jargon of computer technology into the combined structures of contemporary politics and ancient myth, the reader is engulfed, as Richard Poirier has protested, "with the wastes of time, with cultural shards and rubbish."

But what is most striking about Barth's alternative to the real world is the ultimate seriousness of the gigantic hoax, the *lacrimae rerum* that the comic audaciousness only partly conceals. Furthermore, whether hoax or not, the encyclopedic range and vastly complex order of this reinvention of the world are mightily impressive. Giles Goat-Boy—the very name in its amalgamation of the mechanical, animal, and strictly human aspects of man's destiny encapsulates the novel's illustration of

Spielman's Law, that ontogeny recapitulates cosmogeny. "My day, my year, my life, and the history of West Campus," the hero learns, "are wheels within wheels,.." As George advances toward his moment of illumination, rewinding the very tape of time, his ritual return to WESCAC's belly becomes a compendium of human history, ancient and contemporary. Heroes and Grand Tutors of the ages—Christ, Buddha, Moses, Socrates, Oedipus, Aeneas, Dante—illuminate or baffle George with the examples of their earlier journeys. George must at the same time define his local quest against the backdrop of recent political events, for it takes place during the Quiet Riot between East and West Campus just after Campus Riot II. The goat-boy has thinly veiled versions of Eisenhower, John and Jacqueline Kennedy, and Khrushchev to contend with while he tries as part of his initial assignment to resolve the boundary dispute between East and West Campus. The humorous richness of such characters usually arises from a clash between their allegorical significances and certain bizarre, usually sexual, personal quirks.

To isolate a figure whose make-up indicates Barth's method, Max Spielman is driven by psychosexual cravings that are the animal foundations for the "higher" political and philosophical meanings of his character—Barth will insist upon a like ontological continuum for every one of his characters. Because he is a professor of Mathematical Psycho-Proctology interested in getting to the bottom of things— his masterwork is *The Riddle of the Sphincters*—he is content to spend his time among goats where he can fully indulge his interest in nether regions. The "father of WESCAC" who has taught the compter how to EAT all of studentdom, he has been exiled to the Ag-Hill goat farm during the wizard hunts of the Quiet Riot; in the vaudeville-stage German accent with which he utters his ambivalent profundities (" 'Der goats is humaner than der men, und der men is goatisher than der goats' ") he refers vaguely to J. Robert Oppenheimer, just as his arch-opponent, Dr. Eblis Eierkopf, has some momentary connections with Edward Teller. At his most archetypal Spielman becomes the Eternally Suffering and Wandering Jew, as well as the "helper" who prepares the hero for the return to the *Axis Mundi* of his birth so that he may acquire the wisdom to carry history forward.

In the past and at its most successful allegory has made such centrifugation of character as seamless as possible, and readers have legitimately been disturbed by failures of integration and serious inconsistencies of denotation. The primary way in which Barth parodies the traditional techniques of allegory is to jump with tonal and thematic abandon among the various referents of his allegory in the recognition that "you don't have to explain a myth at all these days. . . . what you do is to look for correspondences, merely, between it and other things, and correspondences of course may be manifold, coexistent, and equally 'legitimate,' though of unequal interest and heuristic value." The "meaning" of any character is the integrated totality of his roles (a Burlingame thesis), just as the meaning of Giles' tale of heroism is the sum of its correspondences. Whatever the quality of *Giles,* its size is thus as necessary as the size of such other literary cosmologies as *Paradise Lost* and the *Divine Comedy.* Its ritual motions are as comprehensively allusive, and the characters who move into the goat-boy's purview as loaded with historical, philosophical, and sociological significance, as the synthesizing imagination of a mock-cosmologist can manage. Anastasia, the innocently promiscuous eternal woman with whom George finds his moment of illumination within WESCAC; Pete Greene, the prototypical American (Huck Finn, Will Rogers, George Babbitt

rolled in one), and his castrating wife, Sally Anne; Maurice Stoker, the diabolical Dean o' Flunks and controller of the West Campus Power Station, who is related to and cynically corrupts many of the novel's more respectable characters—such figures keep shifting their ethical and emotional shape as correspondence is piled upon correspondence in West Campus' spectral landscape.

Still, most of the characters are relatively easy for the goat-boy to understand since the meanings they simultaneously or sequentially embody tend to have a common ideological center. The true Burlingame of the novel, a configuration of elliptical poses who continually defies the goat-boy's attempts at comprehension, is Harold Bray. A false Grand Tutor, a mocking anti-Giles, Bray now anticipates, now shadows the tragic pattern of George's pilgrimage. Against a Western conception of tragedy, he flaunts a malign transcendental mystery; against George's serious vocation as Grand Tutor, he pits a talent for metaphysical mockery as he shifts from pose to pose; against George's hard-won integrity, he brays forth his magical proliferation into the many.

This familiar question of whether unity or multiplicity is the primary tendency of existence poses itself anew as the theme of optical difficulty. George is provided with *the* exemplary model for his own journey toward self-knowledge during a theatrical performance: *Taliped Decanus,* a forty-seven-page, scene-by-scene recasting of *Oedipus Rex* in contemporary doggerel, which describes the fall of the Dean of Cadmus College, "who'll go to any lengths for answers" and who blinds himself when he discovers his ancient crime. The novel's other optical sideshows that spin off from this root burlesque (Pete Greene, for instance, accidentally puts out his eye in a funhouse) and the different mirrors and lenses pressed upon George as phenomenological aids all point to the difficulty of "seeing," of knowing whether the essential cognitive act in judging one's fellow beings and the great world is discrimination or synthesis.

Thus the key to asserting control over WESCAC is the understanding of the assignment to "Pass All Fail All," the cryptic circular message which WESCAC had imprinted upon George's Pre-Natal Aptitude Test card and which is repeated at the time of his matriculation. As George performs his initial labors he discovers and systematically applies the principle of analysis, distinguishing "Tick from Tock, East Campus from West Campus, Grand Tutor from goat, appearance from reality" and, climactically, Passage from Failure. When such sharpening of definition produces the worst kind of chaos, George commits himself to its opposite, a union of contraries, which is no more of an answer. Finally in a transcendence of categories by which an awareness of body and soul, male and female, passing and failing is triumphantly obliterated, the goat-boy and Anastasia sexually joined to one another make their way through WESCAC's belly satisfied to "feel a way through the contradictions" of this life, to accept on ecstatic faith "the seamless University" that "knew aught of . . . distinctions." From the sexual loathing of Todd Andrews and Jake Horner through Ebenezer's reluctant intercourse with this world as syphilitic whore, Barth moves to the goat-boy's lyrical sexual embrace of the cosmos, even if it be a cosmos of Barth's making.

And yet the goat-boy's blinding insight is at best a momentary affirmation. In the Revised New Syllabus' posttape (possibly spurious, of course) George toward the end of his life views with plangent weariness the steady distortion of his gospel, and the Grand Tutor's momentary triumph is placed within the larger context of the tragic hero's inevitable loss. All of his way stations have merely been preparation for an ultimate futility: "the pans remain balanced for better and worse. . . . Nay, rather, for worse, always for worse. Late or soon, we lose. Sudden or slow, we lose. The bank exacts its charge for each redistribution of our funds. There is an entropy to time, a tax on change: four nickels for two dimes, but always less silver; our books stay reconciled, but who in modern terms can tell heads from tails?"

Such slang-drenched lyricism never quite loses its undercurrent of self-mockery; the novel's many flashes of wit and genius as well as its longueurs are grounded in a self-reductive circumspection. But by journey's end the parodic mode has become a melancholy instrument indeed. The final effect of *Giles* is precisely one of controlled hovering—among intellectual oppositions, mythic correspondences, and literary attitudes. It is undoubtedly infuriating in its obsessive insistence upon filling in every nook of its closed system while admitting in a self-deprecation Dante or Milton would never have imagined that the vast metaphor is something of a joke. The fit audience willing to sit through to the end of the cosmic joke has apparently been small. But for the reader who can admire the hit-and-miss audacity of the system, who can shrug off the heavy-handed and follow with delight the witty play of correspondence, and who will imaginatively enter into the spirit of the goat-boy's deepening vision, the impression of facile ingenuity gradually gives way to one of moving earnestness. As for the quality of that vision, the critical response to *Giles* merely illustrates the truism that in all but the very greatest novels of ideas one reader's imaginative profundity is another's puerile shallowness and irresponsible navel-gazing. On the whole, the life-and-death game seems well worth the candle.

While alluding sympathetically, in an essay on Borges, to a putative remark of Saul

Bellow's that to be technically up to date is the least important attribute of a writer, Barth adds that this least important attribute may nevertheless be essential. The writer must, he feels, pay attention to the innovations of the best of his contemporaries—he singles out Beckett, Nabokov, and Borges for himself— for he can and does learn from them even when he does not directly imitate. Barth's most recent book, *Lost in the Funhouse*, provides ample evidence that, aside from all questions of aesthetic success, he is one of the two or three most aware, most technically experimental writers of acknowledged power at work in America today.

This collection of short pieces, most of which were published separately from 1963 to 1968, complicates his urge to blur received discriminations among genre by attacking the traditional expectation of fiction as the printed word. Of the fourteen fictions only a few are designed expressly for print, others are meant for live voice—either authorial or nonauthorial—or tape, still others for various combinations of those media. "Title," as Barth describes the most versatile of the lot, "makes somewhat separate but equally valid senses, in several media: print, monophonic recorded authorial voice, stereophonic ditto in dialogue with itself, live authorial voice, live ditto in dialogue with monophonic ditto aforementioned, and live ditto interlocutory with stereophonic et cetera, my own preference." (A recent *Esquire* piece, "Help," actually provides a musical score to show how such verbal counterpointing will look on the printed page.) As Giles compressed within himself the continuum of the race from primitive animal to autonomous computer, so Barth is working in these latest intermediary experiments toward a recapitulation of fictional expression from oral through printed to electronic means.

The earliest written pieces take the print medium for granted while the later ones become more and more experimentally intermediary. And just as Barth's novels move from Maryland-based verisimilitude through historical fable to mythic allegory, so do these stories follow a like pattern. Several of the early, frankly autobiographical "Ambrose" stories set on the Eastern Shore detail with a conventional realism a young boy's search for a name and an identity. "Ambrose His Mark" recounts the biazarre incident which led to the "naming" of the child and the resultant strangeness with which his ego thereafter contemplated its sign. In "Water-Message" this same child's voyeuristic initiation into sexuality is incomprehensible until he experiences a "greater vision, vague and splendrous," in the form of a bottle at the seashore with an all but empty piece of paper in it, a messenger from the universe that sends him an intimation of its meaning. His macroscopic insight is matched in the story's final lines with a new microscopic precision as well, for he notices that "those shiny bits in the paper's texture were splinters of wood pulp. Often as he'd seen them in the leaves of cheap tablets, he had not thitherto embraced that fact." The optical strangeness of Ambrose receives its climactic treatment in the volume's title story, "Lost in the Funhouse," which describes a family outing to Ocean City, his adolescent erotic fantasies about a young neighbor along on the trip, and the deterioration of a coherent sense of self while wandering through the funhouse mirror room in which he unaccountably finds himself. The funhouse becomes the excruciatingly self-conscious symbol for the many distorted perspectives from which he views his troubled psyche, a barely disguised reflection of the authorial narrator's own disintegrating self. The fictional technique verbally duplicates the endless replication of images in a funhouse mirror, meandering with an artful lack of control between the point of view of Ambrose in various guises and a self-chastising narrator lost within his own story. As the narrator interrupts his tale with literary and linguistic exegesis of the most obsessive sort, we have instead of the tight structure of the first two Ambrose stories a monstrous plot that "doesn't rise by meaningful steps but winds upon itself, digresses, retreats, hesitates, sighs, collapses, expires." And as Ambrose accepts his lifelong entrapment within a labyrinth of his mind's making, he merges with the amazed narrator to provide a rationale for the entire volume: "He wishes he had never entered the funhouse. But he has. Then he wishes he were dead. But he's not. Therefore he will construct funhouses for others and be their secret operator—though he would rather be among the lovers for whom funhouses are designed."

Some of the chambers in Barth's funhouse are merely that—self-contained inventions into which the author has stumbled as if by mistake, metaphorical playground for his habitual themes. In "Petition" Body and Soul are conceived of as fueding Siamese twins, with Soul having to put up with gross indignities because his belly is fastened to the small of Body's back. In a marvelous echo of Barth's earlier love triangles, both twins—the anterior profanely, the posterior sacredly—are in love with the same pretty contortionist and the three earn their living by an act billed as The Eternal Triangle. (The funhouse is, after all, a place of amusement, no matter how desperate the wanderer.) The bizarre psychomachy takes the form of a petition addressed by Soul to a Siamese potentate visiting White Plains, New York, asking that he arrange the surgical separation of the mismatched brothers. In words recalling the epistemological vacillations of the novels, the eloquent brother concludes his plea with a Barthian *cri de coeur*: "To be one: paradise! To be two: bliss! But to be both and neither is unspeakable."

These fabular concoctions transcend the time and space of the Ambrose stories and exist entirely within a chosen metaphor whose ambivalent implications a speaker, entrapped within its aesthetic context, explores. "Night-Sea Journey" transforms the Barthian "road" into a conceivably endless and purposeless swim by a speaker who gradually reveals himself to be a philosophically sophisticated sperm toward a shore (the ovum?—at any rate, a goal eventually postulated as "She"), the doubtful union of swimmer and shore overseen by a Maker who is just as problematic. The influence of Borges seems especially clear in the brevity and attenuation of these fictions. Although they seem informed by the same creative principle of metaphorical elaboration as *Giles,* they lack its purposeful exhaustiveness. In each of the chambers within the larger funhouse, a single voice momentarily struggles with its metaphor to be replaced a few pages or a tape later by another voice. The most puzzled voices of all are those of the author himself in "Autobiography," "Title," and "Life-Story" trying to get a story told, a plot going—all unsuccessfully and with a maximum of fierce self-loathing ("Another story about a writer writing a story! Another regressus in infinitum! Who doesn't prefer art that at least overtly imitates something other than its own processes?").

What emerges powerfully from this wildly reverberating volume is a sure sense of voice, of the modulated resonances that these echo chambers take from one another. The optical confusions uniting the Ambrose stories and focused most explicitly in the funhouse mirror trope give way in Barth's recent, most experimental fiction to aural distortion as the proper trope for man's metaphysical puzzlement. And Barth has always had a better ear than eye—his work is relatively bare in landscape and visual detail, but he has the ventriloquist's gift of parodying voices, especially lyrical voices, out of the literary past. The two most interesting pieces in the volume, "Echo" and "Menelaiad," demonstrate clearly the aural direction in which Barth is moving.

If narrative originality is impossible for the modern artist, if he accepts his fate as parodic translator and annotator of pre-existing archetypes, what can still be original is the unique source of the voice, the authorial instrument that shapes the retelling. "Echo," a monologue describing Narcissus' attempt to escape Echo by seeking advice from Tiresias in the prophet's cave, accomplishes the complete amalgamation of the first- and third-person point of view. Narcissus seems to be the speaker, telling his familiar tale in the third person to Tiresias as antidote to self-love: "One does well," the story opens, "to speak in the third person, the seer advises, in the manner of Theban Tiresias. A cure for self-absorption is saturation: telling the story over as though it were another's until like a much-repeated word it loses sense." As Narcissus explores this perspective, lapsing at one point into the first person within the first person, we are led to suspect that the speaker may be either Tiresias or Echo, in which case the identity of the interlocutor is just as doubtful. While the narrative line is relatively clear because of the myth's familiarity, it becomes impossible for everyone involved to distinguish teller from listener and, ultimately, narrative from narrator. For the point of the myth is precisely the "autognostic verge" on which all three of the characters interchangeably live (with the author and reader).

Barth's op fictions thus explore visual and aural distinctions to dramatize an endlessly refracting and reverberating reality. But this insight is a dangerous one for the artist, who finds it increasingly difficult to maintain any aesthetic distance from his creations. Human character, including his own, becomes for him

a series of Chinese boxes, each one containing a different version of itself in an infinite aural regression. The epitome of this entrapment within a fabular *regressus in infinitum* is also the volume's longest fiction, "Menelaiad." In this slangy, wisecracking redaction of Book IV of the *Odyssey* Menelaus attempts to wrest from Proteus on the beach at Pharos the gift of immortality, the secret of Helen's love after her return from Troy. Menelaus must hold fast to the slippery god as he shifts identity from beast to beast, object to object, person to person. The difficulty of the task is formally caught as Menelaus peels away the layers of voices that constitute his tangled point of view. At the very center of his "ravelled fabrication" the reader is at a seventh remove from the outer voice (" ' " " ' " ' " in print) as Menelaus imagines his own voice telling Telemachus and Peisistratus of imagining Helen hearing Proteus hearing Eiodethea (Proteus' daughter) hearing Menelaus (critic within critic!) describing the fall of Troy and the repossession of Helen. Only by exhausting the guises that reality can take may he fable back to the single identity from which he began, that single voice which "yarns on through everything to itself"; only at the end of his rhetorical tether can he accept "Proteus's terrifying last disguise, Beauty's spouse's odd Elysium: the absurd, unending possibility" that Helen has always loved him and only him.

Such mind-boggling acrobatics as Menelaus' attempt to "hold on" to something—a beloved, a god, an audience—intimate a desperation which must in some sense be autobiographical. Authorial experiments like "Life-Story," after all, enclose such painfully playful admissions as the fact that "while he did not draw his characters and situations directly from life nor permit his author-protagonist to do so, any moderately attentive reader of his oeuvre, his what, could infer for example that its author feared for example schizophrenia, impotence creative and sexual, suicide—in short living and dying." More important than any personal difficulties is Barth's awareness that he is working within an "apocalyptic ambience" to create a "literature of exhausted possibility" at a time when the novel, if not the printed word altogether, is in its last stages of depletion. It is then the conjunction of a personal and a literary ultimacy, both passionately felt, that accounts for the baroque style and the increasingly involuted experiments of *Lost in the Funhouse*. To be sure, one occasionally feels in this work as in earlier ones that the advertised awareness of literary ultimacy acts as too self-indulgent a mask, as too uncontrolled a rationalization for the author's psychic dislocations.

But those reviewers who have read the volume as a dead end from which no forward progress is possible have perhaps underestimated the resourcefulness of the fabulist's endgame. Scheherazade, Barth's *avant-gardiste,* must unfortunately court the disaster of silence. (Barth has remarked of two authors relevant to his own situation that Borges is blind and Beckett is approaching virtual muteness.) Her perilous balance between fantasy and reality is not a chosen condition but one forced upon her by the need to confront her odd situation intelligently. And that is a meaningful way for her to confront her "times" as well, although the indirection of fable will always strike some readers as an evasion of the Real World. As one contemplates the cheerful ingenuity of her stratagems to avoid the creative impotence that will mean her death, one realizes that her sentence while a source of terror gradually becomes the necessary and even the conventional goad for her fables. A thousand and one fictions would, no doubt, be a decent output for any lifetime.

Selected Bibliography

WORKS OF JOHN BARTH

"Lilith and the Lion," *Hopkins Review*, 4:49–53 (Fall 1950).

The Floating Opera. New York: Appleton-Century-Crofts, 1956; revised edition, New York: Doubleday, 1967.

The End of the Road. New York: Doubleday, 1958; revised edition, 1967.

"Landscape: The Eastern Shore," *Kenyon Review*, 22:104–10 (Winter 1960).

The Sot-Weed Factor. New York: Doubleday, 1960; revised edition, 1967.

"My Two Muses," *Johns Hopkins Magazine*, 12:9–13 (April 1961).

Afterword to *The Adventures of Roderick Random*, by Thomas Smollett. New York: New American Library, 1964.

"Mystery and Tragedy: The Two Motions of Ritual Heroism," unpublished lecture given at State University of New York at Geneseo, December 10, 1964.

Giles Goat-Boy. New York: Doubleday, 1966.

"The Literature of Exhaustion," *Atlantic Monthly,* 220:29–34 (August 1967). (Reprinted in *The American Novel since World War II*, edited by Marcus Klein. New York: Fawcett Publications, 1969. Pp. 267–79.)

Lost in the Funhouse. New York: Doubleday, 1968.

"Help," *Esquire*, 77:108–09 (September 1969).

"Dunyazadiad," *Esquire*, 77:136–42, 158–68 (June 1972).

BIBLIOGRAPHY

Bryer, Jackson R. "Two Bibliographies" (Barth and John Hawkes), *Critique*, 6:86–89 (Fall 1963).

CRITICAL STUDIES

Bluestone, George. "John Wain and John Barth: The Angry and the Accurate," *Massachusetts Review,* 1:582–89 (May 1960).

Bradbury, John M. "Absurd Insurrection: The

Barth-Percy Affair," *South Atlantic Quarterly,* 68:319–29 (Summer 1969).

Diser, Philip E. "The Historical Ebenezer Cooke," *Critique,* 10:48–59 (1968).

Enck, John. "John Barth: An Interview," *Wisconsin Studies in Contemporary Literature,* 6:3–14 (Winter–Spring 1965).

Fiedler, Leslie A. "John Barth: An Eccentric Genius," *New Leader,* 44:22–24 (February 13, 1961).

————. *The Return of the Vanishing American.* New York: Stein and Day, 1968.

Garis, Robert. "Whatever Happened to John Barth?" *Commentary,* 42:89–95 (October 1966).

Holder, Alan. " 'What Marvelous Plot . . . Was Afoot?' History in Barth's *The Sot-Weed Factor,*" *American Quarterly,* 20:596–604 (Fall 1968).

Hyman, Stanley Edgar. "John Barth's First Novel," *New Leader,* 48:20–21 (April 12, 1965).

Kennard, Jean E. "John Barth: Imitations of Imitations," *Mosaic,* 3:116–31 (Number 2, 1970).

Kerner, David. "Psychodrama in Eden," *Chicago Review,* 13:59–67 (Winter–Spring 1959).

Kiely, Benedict. "Ripeness Was Not All: John Barth's *Giles Goat-Boy,*" *Hollins Critic,* 3:1–12 (1966).

Knapp, Edgar H. "Found in the Barthhouse: Novelist as Savior," *Modern Fiction Studies,* 14:446–51 (Winter 1968–69).

Majdiak, Daniel. "Barth and the Representation of Life," *Criticism,* 13:51–67 (1970).

Miller, Russell H. *"The Sot-Weed Factor*: A Contemporary Mock-Epic," *Critique,* 8:88–100 (Winter 1965–66).

Noland, Richard W. "John Barth and the Novel of Comic Nihilism," *Wisconsin Studies in Contemporary Literature,* 7:239–57 (Autumn 1966).

Olderman, Raymond M. *Beyond the Wasteland: The American Novel in the 1960's.* New Haven, Conn.: Yale University Press, 1972.

Poirier, Richard. "The Politics of Self-Parody," *Partisan Review,* 35:339–53 (Summer 1968).

Rovit, Earl. "The Novel as Parody: John Barth," *Critique,* 6:77–85 (Fall 1963).

Samuels, Charles T. "John Barth: A Buoyant Denial of Relevance," *Commonweal,* 85:80–82 (October 21, 1966).

Schickel, Richard. *"The Floating Opera,"* *Critique,* 6:53–67 (Fall 1963).

Scholes, Robert. "Disciple of Scheherazade," *New York Times Book Review,* May 8, 1966, pp. 5, 22.

————. *The Fabulators.* New York: Oxford University Press, 1967

Smith, Herbert. "Barth's Endless Road," *Critique,* 6:68–76 (Fall 1963).

Stubbs, John C. "John Barth as Novelist of Ideas: The Themes of Value and Identity," *Critique,* 8:101–16 (Winter 1965).

Tanner, Tony. "The Hoax That Joke Built," *Partisan Review,* 34:102–09 (Winter 1967).

————. "No Exit," *Partisan Review,* 36:293–99 (Number 2, 1969).

Tilton, John. *"Giles Goat-Boy*: An Interpretation," *Bucknell Review,* 18:93–119 (Number 1, 1970).

Trachtenberg, Alan. "Barth and Hawkes: Two Fabulists," *Critique,* 6:4–18 (Fall 1963).

—GERHARD JOSEPH

Saul Bellow

1915-

*P*ROBABLY the most significant American novelist to come to maturity in the 1950–60's has been Saul Bellow. Given critical acclaim early in his career for the beautifully wrought constructions of *Dangling Man* (1944) and *The Victim* (1947), he won national popularity with *The Adventures of Augie March* in 1953. The succeeding publications of *Seize the Day* (1956), *Henderson the Rain King* (1959), and the best sellers *Herzog* (1964) and *Mr. Sammler's Planet* (1970) widened the extent of this popularity, while stabilizing his reputation as a novelist of ranking stature. The first of the American Jewish writers to capture a large reading audience without departing from an American Jewish idiom, Bellow has been instrumental in preparing a way for other writers like Bernard Malamud, I. B. Singer, and Philip Roth. But his achievement has been impressive enough in its own right; he has developed a marvelously supple style of grotesque realism modulated by an ever-present sense of irony. However, the very success of his fictions may have drawn attention away from the intense moral seriousness of his concerns. In my attempt to expose the underlying substance of his work as a whole, I may appear at times to be denigrating his success. Nothing could be further from the truth. Bellow's achievement, it seems to me,

is so impressive and so relevant to our contemporary needs that only the most rigorous analysis and evaluation can suggest its prime importance or point to what I believe to be its most enduring qualities. And that his work possesses such qualities is what I shall try to demonstrate.

"Nobody truly occupies a station in life any more. There are mostly people who feel that they occupy the place that belongs to another by rights. There are displaced persons everywhere." These happen to be the words of Bellow's displaced millionaire, Eugene Henderson, but they could have been spoken by almost any of Bellow's characters, or, for that matter, by Bellow himself. As a pronouncement, of course, such a statement is hardly susceptible to proof, but it seems to me undeniable that Henderson's observation is one valid way of expressing a generally accepted "truth" of our time. Our current history has been a constant succession of massive dislocations in the scheme of our traditional social patterns; our incessant complaint is a nagging sense of anxious insecurity. And whether approached from a sociological or a psychological viewpoint, the problems raised by displaced persons and displaced personalities have become ever more common and ever more pressing. To put it largely, we might say that the events of the last fifty years have laid upon man an enormous lopsided burden of incomparable freedom without the balancing accompaniment of meaningful choices. The average citizen has been liberated from the daily siege of brutal physical labor; an abundance of the traditional luxuries has been lavished upon him; and yet he finds himself dangling in the midst of his new comforts without possessing a reason or a title for his occupancy. And thus, ironically enough, his new freedoms have increased the pressure of his responsibilities without adding a whit to his meager holdings of power or control. Under the weight of what can become an enervating sense of displacement, there develops a regular rhythm of steady frustration, spasmodically interrupted by sudden bursts of violence which are almost always vastly disproportionate to their activating causes. In this situation, neither rational analysis nor indignant censure seems particularly pertinent because the stresses themselves are almost wholly irrational. It is the rooted feeling of displacement that appears to be the immutable mark of our age and not the historical events that stand in antecedence to it.

I suppose that every serious artist of the mid-century has directly or indirectly addressed himself to this central problem, bringing to it his own strategies of interpretation and nomenclature. The catchwords have multiplied: the age of anxiety; the affluent society; the death of God; the discontinuity of tradition; the loss of self; the anti-hero; victims and rebels; picaresque saints and clowns of the absurd; radical innocence and unpardonable guilt; reactions of alienation and accommodation. Bellow's special position on this matter has been his unwavering conviction that man's fate and his opportunities for nobility are essentially no different today from what they were two thousand years ago; and his achievement as a writer of fiction has been his patient capacity to deal with this central theme of displacement without being lured into the fashionable hysterics of either apocalyptic rhetoric or nostalgia. His own constant concern has been a single-minded attention toward defining what is viably *human* in modern life—what is creatively and morally possible for the displaced person that modern man feels himself to be. As his theater critic, Schlossberg, declaims in *The Victim*: "It's bad to be less than human and it's bad to be more than human. . . . Good acting is what is exactly human. And if you say I am a tough critic, you mean I have a high opinion of what is human. This is my whole idea. More than human, can you have any use for life? Less than human, you don't either."

Like Schlossberg, Bellow has a high opinion of what is "human." ("What is it, now, this great instrument? Played wrong, why does it suffer so? Right, how can it achieve so much, reaching even God?") But to isolate the problem is not the same as discovering solutions. The search for the "exactly human" is a direct plunge into the dark heart of our contemporary mysteries. After all, it may be that only the desire and the need to know are themselves human. "Who can be the earnest huntsman of himself when he knows he is in turn a quarry? asks Joseph of *Dangling Man*. Or, as Asa Leventhal differently poses the problem in *The Victim*: "The peculiar thing struck him that everything else in nature was bounded; trees, dogs, and ants didn't grow beyond a certain size. 'But we,' he thought, 'we go in all directions without any limit.'" The total reach of Bellow's work—seven novels, several plays, a handful of short stories and essays—constitutes his attempt to define habitable limits for contemporary man, within which he can rest secure and still seize hold of the day with a partial power and the responsibility for his employment of that power.

Men have traditionally been aware of their human limitations through the confining strictures of religion, society, or some sanctioned belief in an order, independent of man, discoverable in nature and natural processes. When these strictures are working properly, men may not be necessarily happy, but at least they have no difficulty in recognizing the exquisite balance between their obligations and their liberties. But such an almost spontaneous awareness is not possible for a man of Bellow's temperament and background. Born in Lachine, Quebec, in 1915, the youngest of four children—his parents had emigrated from Russia two years earlier—Bellow was raised in the Rachel Market section of Montreal. After the family moved to Chicago in 1924, he was educated in the public schools and attended the University of Chicago, taking his degree from Northwestern University in 1937 with honors in anthropology and sociology. In terms of family and childhood background, Bellow's is a specimen case of multiple dislocation—from the *shtetl* life of East Europe to Montreal to Chicago. In his early youth he received an orthodox religious education, but he emerged from the American university system with the preparatory training of a social scientist. The recurrent accent of his growing up would seem to be one of unremitting change, discontinuity, fluidity. The traditional sanctions of Jewish *shtetl* orthodoxy may have lingered artificially in the old Montreal ghetto, but they rapidly dissolved in the secularism and relative prosperity of Chicago in the 1920's and 1930's.

Here it is interesting to note the ambiguous roles that religion and family play in Bellow's works. There is a persistent, usually muted, religious referent in all his fictions, but Joseph, the dangling, waiting-to-be-drafted hero of

Bellow's first novel, is probably a fair spokesman for his author's rejection of any active adherence to a religious faith: "I did not want to catch at any contrivance in panic," Joseph says. "In my eyes, that was a great crime. . . . Out of my own strength it was necessary for me to return the verdict for reason, in its partial inadequacy, and against the advantages of its surrender." Twenty years later, Herzog reluctantly confesses: "Evidently I continue to believe in God. Though never admitting it." But this belief in God, common to all Bellow's protagonists, is merely an additional burden for them to carry. It increases their suffering of shame or guilt, without being in itself an alleviation of that suffering or a source of moral strength. Their belief in God may be slightly more than a mere religious sentimentality, but it is certainly a good deal less than a fundamental mode of defining what is legitimately human. Ritual has become incontrovertibly dissevered from daily behavior and the Bellow hero is driven to justify his own life—to press his actions into his own idiosyncratic rites of worship, since the traditional laws bear little relevance to his present needs. ("Herzog had been overcome by the need to explain, to have it out, to justify, to put in perspective, to clarify, to make amends.")

The persistent presence of "family" is likewise an ambiguous factor in Bellow's fictional world. Typically, his protagonists are products of fairly sizable families; frequently, one parent is dead or institutionalized. In their maturity the protagonists tend to live apart from their brothers and sisters, to marry one or more times, and to sire children on all their wives. But what is more to the point is that they are "family-minded" people. Reluctantly accepting the obligations of marriage and fatherhood, they worry about their children, they make sporadic efforts to understand and improve their relationships with their wives, they search the faces of their nephews and nieces for family likenesses, and they are subject to sudden overwhelming seizures of love for those who are connected to them by ties of kinship. And yet, in a perverse way, they manage to evade attachment to even their most intimate relatives and friends. The introspective point of view from which their fictions are usually narrated, as well as the arbitrary circumstances of plot, succeeds in isolating the protagonists as though they were genuine solitaries. Joseph spends the bulk of his days alone while his wife, Iva, works at the Chicago Public Library. Leventhal's wife is away helping her widowed mother move to Charleston when Kirby Allbee assaults the tenuous security of his life pattern. Augie March wanders through the terrain of his adventures in a thoroughly subjective and ultimately casual connection to the landscape. Tommy Wilhelm (*Seize the Day*) is legally separated from his wife and children. Henderson goes off to Africa by himself and Herzog ruminates on the past in his bachelor apartment in New York and in the peace and quiet of his abandoned house in Ludeyville. The "family" comes into actual existence only when the protagonist desires contact or aid; otherwise, except for the subplots in *The Victim* (in many ways, Bellow's most uncharacteristic novel) and in *Mr. Sammler's Planet*, family obligations exert no real demands on the protagonist. The family can be ignored or treated as a stable marginal presence unless the protagonist wills it to be otherwise.

And still the sense of family is one of the most urgent possessions in the life of the Bellow hero. Joseph recalls his early youth in St. Dominique Street in Montreal with such vividness as to conclude that it was "the only place where I was ever allowed to encounter reality." In a similar confessional mood, Moses Herzog discovers that his "heart was attached with great power" to the Napoleon Street of his boyhood: "Here was a wider range of human feelings than he had ever again been able to find." Nor are these the offhand comments of a nostalgia sentimentalized in tranquillity. The Montreal reminiscences in *Herzog* and the opening seven chapters of *The Adventures of Augie March* (the description of Augie's Chicago childhood and his relationships with Grandma Lausch, the Coblins, and the Einhorns) attain a density of texture and poignancy of emotion that are unequaled elsewhere in Bellow's writing. Similarly, and probably for the same reasons, the father-son confrontation in *Seize the Day* and the grotesque battle of "the brothers" (Leventhal and Allbee) in *The Victim* are the most cogent dramatic conflicts that Bellow has as yet managed to project.

In other words, the idea of family has much the same force in Bellow's work as does religion. It intrudes itself on the present as an ironically *un*usable past. It compels the memory of a way of life in which personality seemed not to be fragmented and isolated; in which men were integral parts of a congenial whole, able to share their griefs and joys spontaneously and directly, instead of carrying them onerously on their own shoulders. But more than a memory, it is also an unattainable standard of moral obligations. The "placed" child is father to the displaced man and the child holds the man accountable. A man must be *ehrlich*; he must be a *Mensch*. "Choose dignity," says Schlossberg. "Nobody knows enough to turn it down." Bellow's heroes yearn after dignity, but as soon as they catch themselves groping to achieve it, they are quick to mock their own attempts as comically futile. As Irving Malin has pointed out, there is a startling preponderance of *weight* and *deformity* imagery in all of Bellow's stories. His protagonists seem always to be laboring under immense loads and pressures from which they receive only momentary release. Here is Tommy Wilhelm, for example, in a fairly representative posture: "The spirit, the peculiar burden of his existence lay upon him like an accretion, a load, a hump. In any moment of quiet, when sheer fatigue prevented him from struggling, he was apt to feel this mysterious weight, this growth . . . of nameless things which it was the business of his life to carry about. That must be what a man was for." It is possible that this weight is precisely the measure of that amount of life which the Bellow hero is doomed to bear because the supporting structures of family and religion are no longer available to him. He has no option except to submit to the implacable judgments of his lost family and religious traditions, even though his radical displacement has made these standards impossible for him to live up to. He is alone and fragmented because there is no whole place for him. He cannot will his mind to cease posing impossible questions and each reiterated question riddles the temporary security of his life. And still he carries in his solitude a desperate need to realize the assurances of love which only participation in a communal life can provide. It is small wonder, then, that his spirit buckles and agonizes under such burdens.

It is in this sense, I suppose, that the Bellow hero can be justly termed a *schlemiel* type. If he is a victimized figure, he is a victim of his own moral sense of right and wrong—his own accepted obligation to evaluate himself by standards that will inevitably find him lacking. And it is for this reason that all Bellow's heroes are, like Joseph, "apprentices in suffering and humiliation." In what other way could they respond to their findings of spiritual deficiency without giving the lie to the possibilities of moral behavior? And not for them the "stiff-upper-lip" stoicism of American Protestantism. Bellow's heroes suffer intensely and rehearse their agonies at operatic volume for all to hear. "I am to suffering what Gary is to smoke," says Henderson. "One of the world's biggest operations." But it would be a serious mistake to confuse this characteristic reaction of the Bellow hero with one of passive lamentation or self-pitying surrender. Even in his partly sincere and partly mock self-revilings, he is determined to believe that "human" means "accountable in spite of many weaknesses—at the last moment, tough enough to hold." And in final effect, none of Bellow's heroes actually resigns himself to his suffering. Painfully they climb again and again out of "the craters of the spirit," ridiculing their defeats with a merciless irony, resolved to be prepared with a stronger defense against the next assault that is sure to come.

Perhaps this aspect of Bellow's work has been the least appreciated by contemporary critics. Some have interpreted his thematic preoccupation with the sufferer as a device of compromise, a "making do," or accommodation—an argument which implies that Bellow is gratuitously surrendering the heroic ideal of a fully instinctual life to the expediency of flabby survival within the status quo. But this, it seems to me, is precisely to miss the moral point and to misread Bellow's deliberate irony. Trained in anthropology, Bellow is quite willing to regard the species *man* as merely one of the evolutionary products of nature and natural processes. But Bellow is determined to insist on the qualitative difference between *man* and the other sentient species that nature has produced. He may occasionally invest animals with "human" characteristics; and he is always careful to show that although his protagonists may loudly protest their innate "docility or ingenuous good will," brute animality resides deeply and subtly in their basic natures. The difference between the human animal and the brute, for Bellow, is a matter of essential kind rather than degree. As Augie March discovers, only "mere creatures look with their original eyes." For man is that creature who also creates himself. He has never owned "original eyes." His vision is filtered through the lenses of history and self-awareness. And it is because men do not possess "original eyes" that both the generous vision of love and the blindness of malice are fundamental human attributes which must be accounted for. It is not surprising, therefore, that those readers who find Bellow's heroes contemptibly self-conscious and alienated from nature are also the ones who must deny the efficacy of laughter as an anodyne for human misery.

The role of nature in Bellow's fictional world is thus far less significant than that of either religion or family. It has a prominence and a grandeur, to be sure, but it exists at a distance from the main struggles with which Bellow is concerned. His protagonists are urban-bred and urban-oriented. Their native habitat is the modern metropolis—cities of elevated trains, overheated apartments, traffic, universities and museums, slums and suburbs, city parks and anonymous cafeterias, the subway rumbling underfoot and the smog polluting the upper air. In the city the Bellow hero is almost at home; he can take the city for granted because he knows its ways—its bus routes, its expressway exits, the correct tip for the cabdriver, the right response to the newspaper vendor. And he knows as well the sudden absurd beauties which are a gratuitous by-product of its thriving ugliness. But he is at least equally responsive to the traditional attractions of nature also. He has an unusual competence in the names and habits of fish, birds, animals, and even insect life. Not only is he a devotee of zoos and aquariums, but he is a rapt student of trees and flowers, a follower of the seasonal changes in the foliage and the mysterious portents of weather. In fact

there are moments in Bellow's fiction which come very near to a wholehearted acceptance of some variety of nature mysticism. One remembers Leventhal discovering that "everything, everything without exception, took place as if within a single soul or person." But such instants of ecstatic revelation are, I think, ultimately incidental in Bellow's fictional world. His heroes feel a great sensuous joy in nature, but nature fails to become for them a dictionary or a bible of life. Nature remains always *outside*—a spectacle—for the Bellow protagonist; his unique individuality never becomes merged into its larger mystical embrace. As Herzog regretfully concludes, "I am a prisoner of perception, a compulsory witness." And the most intense and appreciative witness can never completely participate in what he is witnessing. He would have to possess "original eyes" in order to do that. Thus, for Bellow, nature remains an inexhaustible source of delight without becoming a dwelling place for the human spirit. It offers sensation, but not "truth"; endless mute instruction, but no sureties for the soul's search.

That Bellow has deliberately constructed his heroes along these lines is clear not only from his fictions, but also from his direct personal statements. In a review in 1951, he chides the American Jewish author for his reluctance to exploit the fullest depth of his cultural situation: "He [the Jewish writer] cannot easily accept the historical accident of being a Jew in America that is nonetheless among the first facts of his life. But this accident—the strangeness of discontinuity and of a constant immense change—happens to all and is the general condition. The narrowly confined and perfect unit of a man, if we could find him now, would prove to be outside all that is significant in our modern lives, lives characterized by the new, provisional, changing, dangerous, universal." And elsewhere he remarks,

"It is obvious that modern comedy has to do with the disintegrating outline of the worthy and humane Self, the bourgeois hero of an earlier age." Bellow's significance, it seems to me, is partly a consequence of his arrogant assumption that the historical accident which has formed his own special view of character can be universalized into an image of modern man. It is too early to judge Bellow's long-range success in this effort, but his warm reception, as well as his being given three National Book Awards, suggests that his arrogance may be amply justified.

Thus, the creation of a recognizable character type, the Bellow hero, is Bellow's major accomplishment. The faces and individual circumstances of this hero have varied from fiction to fiction. He has been rich and poor, well- and ill-educated; he has grown from youth to middle and old age, gone to war, multiplied his wives and mistresses, narrowed and extended his field of operations with the world. But when we compare the personae of his earliest published sketches in 1941 ("Two Morning Monologues") with his latest, we realize that the alterations in the hero are surprisingly superficial. He postures to a Dostoevskian rhythm in *Dangling Man*; he is clumsy and vulnerable in *The Victim* and *Seize the Day*; as Augie March, he affects the freewheeling manner of an unlikely reincarnation of Huck Finn; in the character of Moses Herzog, he absorbs all his previous roles in a comical apotheosis of despair; and in Artur Sammler, he walks a thin detached line above all his incarnations. The variations among the individual protagonists seem largely to be due to the expedients of their different dramatic settings. Any one of them could collapse into a paroxysm of welcome tears over a stranger's funeral bier. Any one of them could fulminate with the righteous rage of a Jeremiah and be capable of no greater violence than the spank-

ing of a fifteen-year-old niece. And any one of them could find himself knotted in impotent frustration, praying desperately: "For all the time I have wasted I am very sorry. Let me out of this clutch and into a different life. For I am all balled up. Have mercy." The Bellow hero is a composite of them all, a blend of Leopold Bloom and Stephen Dedalus, a cogent blur of modern man as comic sufferer. He is Jewish, an avid undisciplined reader with an erratic memory for assorted trivia and passages of moral exhortation, a city dweller oscillating between seizures of inarticulate yearning ("I want!") and "narcotic dullness." In a strange way he is the introspective inversion of the Hemingway hero, his most immediate Chicago predecessor. Like him, he is fearfully alone and afraid; like him, he struggles incessantly to achieve dignity and to impose a moral dimension upon life. But unlike him, he is cursed or blessed with a pervasive sense of irony; he is mistrustful of action, skeptical of heroics, painfully aware of the limitations of reason as only an intellectual can be, but unwilling, at the same time, to surrender himself to the dangerous passions of unreason.

Given such a concept of character, and given as well a desire to render this character into fictional form, Bellow has had serious technical difficulties in finding an adequate structure for his novels. His preoccupation with a single introspective consciousness has placed heavy limitations on the range and variety of his fictional world. And while these limitations recur throughout his work, they are most nakedly apparent in his first novel, *Dangling Man*, which is almost entirely the novel of Joseph's brooding. The awkward device of the journal form and the egotistical inward focus of Joseph's temperament inexorably determine the claustrophobically closed world of that novel. Nothing can enter this world save what Joseph chooses to allow, and since Joseph is not only a sedentary man, but also one who is not a particularly interested observer of anything that is outside himself, the resulting fictional world will be doubly closed. And this is precisely what happens. Joseph's wife, his father, his in-laws, his circle of friends, his mistress, his brother's family—in effect, the whole outside world of draft boards, winter, and a war raging around the globe—appear at the peripheries of his brooding vision in sudden surreal flashes of distorted life. And the effect of suffocation is further intensified because the novel lacks any real dramatic conflict except for the highly abstracted struggle that Joseph undergoes in the recesses of his own tortured spirit. In a way that might have been fatal to Bellow's art, *Dangling Man* is almost as much a brooding exposition on the ambiguities of directionless freedom as it is a novel at all.

But already there are evidences here of the brilliant techniques which Bellow will develop to enlarge and illuminate this obsessively closed world. From the beginning of his career, Bellow has been attracted by the disconnected gesture of the grotesque, the uninvestigated contortions of reality which constantly impinge, as it were, on the edges of our vision when we are concentrating primarily upon ourselves. A character like Mr. Vanaker, who leaves the bathroom door ajar when he goes to the toilet, who steals Joseph's socks and Iva's perfume, who throws bottles out of his window, will become one of Bellow's favorite strategies for stretching and lightening his restricted world. Mr. Vanaker is the first in a long line of grotesques, static representatives of the silent lives that exist on the margins of the Bellow hero's self-involvement. In that same novel, Joseph's father-in-law, Mr. Almstadt, is a similar conception. In the novels that follow, these dramatically and thematically unnecessary characters recur and proliferate, coming

tantalizingly close to the central protagonist without ever touching him. One thinks of Elena's mother in *The Victim*; of Augie's feeble-minded brother, George, of the Coblins and Padilla; of Mr. Perls and Mr. Rappaport in *Seize the Day*; of Lucas Asphalter and his monkey, of Nachman outside the cheese shop; of Eisen and the Gruner family in *Mr. Sammler's Planet*; of the taxi drivers and cigar vendors and innumerable insignificant encounters which the Bellow hero has in the course of his brooding days. Occasionally the disconnected grotesque may assume a more full-bodied substance in those rare instances when he enters vitally into the protagonist's life. Kirby Allbee, Dr. Adler, and perhaps Valentine Gersbach are examples of those whom the hero is forced to confront full face, from whom he cannot avert his eyes or his life, and who consequently take on real dramatic power because of this engagement. But, in general, the grotesque-as-actor is an exception in Bellow's fictional world. So powerfully and self-centeredly does the consciousness of the hero dominate and define the field of his contemplation that drama remains almost stifled in a succession of frantically mute gestures of grotesquerie which exist merely for their own sake, or to give the hero an opportunity for reminiscence or speculation.

Bellow's other device for creating an illusion of space is the introduction of the grotesque as spellbinding, marathon talker. All his life Bellow has been fascinated by authoritative orators of all varieties—by eloquent cranks, hucksters, confidence men, and city-park haranguers. He has experimented with the form of the monologue in an effort to capture the power of the obsessive speaker ("A Sermon by Doctor Pep"); he has interviewed the notorious "Yellow Kid" Weil, a man whose talent with words had earned him eight million dishonest dollars; and his attempt at a full-

152 / AMERICAN WRITERS

length play, *The Last Analysis*, is largely an extended speech in two acts by his ex-burlesque and TV ham comedian—turned sham Freudian—Philip Bummidge. Given the concept of a static protagonist, it becomes a natural fictional device for Bellow to surround this protagonist with gargantuan, hobbyhorse-riding theoreticians, with self-convinced "Reality-Instructors," as Herzog comes to define them. Beginning with Schlossberg in *The Victim*, such talkers appear again and again as one of Bellow's consistent resources for interrupting the closed concentration of his hero's endless broodings. Grandma Lausch, Einhorn, Mintouchian, Bateshaw—these are the speech-makers whom Augie describes as "those persons who persistently arise before me with life counsels and illumination throughout my earthly pilgrimage." The brilliant pseudo-Socrates, Dr. Tamkin, in *Seize the Day*; King Dahfu in *Henderson the Rain King;* Sandor Himmelstein and Simkin in *Herzog*; Govinda Lal in *Mr. Sammler's Planet*: their grotesque voices swell in volume or fall into inveigling whispers; they harangue, cajole, exhort, excoriate throughout Bellow's fictions. And, as in Dickens, these voices become compellingly alive on the printed page. For Bellow has the rare power of presenting characters who can talk themselves into life, and the best of his talkers achieve a magical reality beyond the echoes of their voices.

However—and this is a strangely paradoxical quirk in Bellow's fiction—they talk to deaf ears. Only in *The Victim* and *Seize the Day* does a genuine dialogue occur. The Bellow hero is a patient, willing, but heedless listener. He has "opposition" in him. The voices enchant him, but he learns nothing from what he hears. With Bellow's predilection for the first-person narrative focus and the "autobiographical tale," we would expect the curve of his hero's adventures to be cast in the form of the *Bildungsroman* or "educational romance." That is, we would expect the hero to advance from some kind of innocence to experience, from a position of ignorance to one of knowledge. And we would suppose that the chorus of instructional voices must exert some influence on his progress toward his own acquisition of values. But this does not happen. In the first place, with the exception of Schlossberg's, the voices are patently unacceptable to the protagonist's temperament. They are either too Machiavellian or too crankishly eccentric for the hero to take them seriously. And in the second place, the hero never learns anything from his experiences anyway. To be sure, he goes through all the external forms of the educative experience, but he ends up in pretty much the same state as he began, just a little bit older perhaps and a little bit more weary. In an irony that may be even more bitter than Bellow had intended, the Bellow hero's fate *is* his character, and his character is his doom. His basic commitment to an ideal of amorphous possibility is so tenacious as to make both growth and acquired truth impossible.

A closer look at *The Adventures of Augie March* may make this more evident. The novel brings Augie from early boyhood to his postwar maturity as a black marketeer in Europe. Along the way, he has outgrown his family, the Depression, and Chicago; he has passed through his adventures with Thea and Caligula, survived war and shipwreck, temporized with several varieties of utopian dreams, and concluded his tale by describing himself winsomely as a "sort of Columbus of those near-at-hand." All his eloquent, self-assured instructors have been left behind, defined—and, therefore, finite—in the various formulas with which they have tried to struggle to an understanding with life. Grandma Lausch, Simon, Einhorn, Thea, Mintouchian—each has succeeded in creating a personality for himself, each has attempted to impose that personality on life, and each has been discarded by Augie as a kind of heroic failure. Augie alone refuses to formularize his existence. He has been everywhere and suffered everything; but he has learned no more than he knew already when he used to go to the Harrison Street dispensary for free eyeglasses. He has experienced grief, loss, and betrayal. He has grieved and betrayed others. He has listened to all the voices and he has himself speculated on life's deeper meanings. But in no real sense has he impressed a form on his experiences; in no real way has he shaped his life under the positive imprint of his character. For Augie is a strangely passive hero—and is this not true also of Moses Herzog, and even Henderson? People and life happen to Augie. He is readily responsive to women, but all his amorous liaisons are female-initiated. And, similarly, it is the "adoptional" quality that men sense in him and it is they who seek him out. In the long run, his "adventures" are little more than his blandly following the momentum of someone else's desires. And each episode comes to an end when the external initiator disappears from the scene to be replaced by his succesor. Augie's novel could have been legitimately concluded two hundred pages earlier, or, for that matter, it could have been continued almost indefinitely. Invention, not necessity, prescribed the duration of the form. And this is because the Bellow hero incarnates a curiously static immobility at the very center of his existence—a kind of metaphysical inertia which is firmly rooted in introspective despair.

But the first point to be noted here is that while Bellow has retained the traditional narrative structure for rendering a hero's growth from innocence to experience, he has cunningly discarded as irrelevant the substance of the dialectical terms. Augie comes very close to the pith of the problem when he says, "You couldn't get the admission out of me that a situation couldn't be helped and was inescapably bad, but I was eternally looking for a way out, and what was up for question was whether I was a man of hope or foolishness." To be a "man of hope" when hope is unyoked to any faith or purpose save the involuntary buoyancy of the spirit is, I should think, to be a man of foolishness. Or if one is merely *pretending* the hope, it is to be a clown of despair. Bellow's realization that "innocence" and "experience" are outmoded terms—superfluous baggage left over from "the disintegrating outline of the worthy and humane Self"—is perhaps his most radical and subversive perception, but it deprives him of any dialectical resonance in his employment of the mythic structure of the quest. For the seminal image in all Bellow's fiction is not the image of a man seeking, but that of a man brooding in the midst of his solitude: of Joseph arguing wearily with the Spirit of Alternatives; of Herzog writing mental letters to the quick and the dead; of "Bummy" Bummidge conducting a psychoanalytical session with himself in which he plays the roles of both analyst and analysand. Only in *The Victim* and *Seize the Day* does the all-smothering act of brooding separate itself into genuinely interactive hostilities, and in both these fictions, Bellow can let his dramas work themselves out in the open without the deceptive disguise of a fruitless identity-quest or an account of a fabulous journey through the lion-haunted regions of the underconsciousness.

Perhaps there is no literary structure capable of making an effective drama of unpassionate, self-conscious brooding. Drama requires some vital collision between antagonistic powers, and a meandering discussion with the Spirit of Alternatives is simply too rational and wearily ironic to excite dramatic interest or suspense. Hence, Bellow's selection of the journal form for *Dangling Man* would seem to be the one best fitted to his personal eclectic preoccupations as a displaced and brooding intellectual. The journal convention requires and expects no tidy plot-design, nor any intrusive characters save the all-pervading personality of the journal writer himself. Its structure is almost completely a random one, subservient only to the mechanical movement of chronological time, punctuated by the arbitrary datings of its individual diary entries. It allows for the inclusion of barely relevant anecdotes, scenes briefly observed and biasedly rendered, reminiscences, fragmentary musings and theorizings, realistic and surrealistic effusions of attitude and opinion, expository arguments, hymns of lyrical invocation—indeed, it is open to whatever the writer is minded to inscribe in clear or murky mood. And the very haphazard quality of its form releases the writer from any obligation to deal with ultimate matters—with problems of destiny and eternity. That is, if the artist can be regarded in some sense as God-like in his creation of a structurally whole world, the journal writer is more a partaker in, than a creator of, a universe. He is free to pick and choose, start and stop abruptly; he is free to exploit the bits and pieces of his own personality without having to fix the place of man in the unshifting scheme of eternal values. And further, among its more obvious and practical functions, the journal may be the literary form in which a desperately lonely man can make his last-ditch effort to explode the constriction of his solitude and evade his imprisoning consciousness by attempting to communicate with another—even if that *other* is only himself.

At any rate, Bellow's choice of the journal form seems to have been responsive to some deep-seated urgency which has persisted throughout his writing career. In *The Adventures of Augie March,* and in *Henderson the Rain King,* he takes the traditional variant step away from the straight journal form to the autobiographical tale narrated in retrospect. Structurally, this merely means that the final diary notation of the journal is placed at the beginning rather than at the end, which gives the illusion of the form circling back on itself. The arbitrary dated entries are avoided, and there is a far greater narrative freedom in the treatment and compression of time sequences. So Augie declares the license of his idiosyncrasies at the beginning of his tale: "I am an American, Chicago born . . . and go at things as I have taught myself, free-style, and will make the record in my own way. . . ." And Henderson begins his tale by informing the reader that "the world which I thought so mighty an oppressor has removed its wrath from me. But if I am to make sense to you people and explain why I went to Africa I must face up to the facts." In *Herzog,* Bellow improvises brilliantly on the total resources of the journal form, carrying it, one would suppose, about as far as it can go. He succeeds in suggesting a duplicitously wide range of levels for his one brooding focus of narration; he reshuffles time sequences expertly, shifts Herzog's point of view from first- to third-person, employs the device of the fragmentary "mental" letters as a masterly bridge between solipsism and communication, and casts an ambience of irony over his entire construction. But if we are to understand properly what Bellow has accomplished, we must see that the silence which rests at the end of these three novels is the identical silence out of which the novels began. (*Herzog* concludes with the phrases "Nothing. Not a single word.") And in between these two silences, nothing has happened. The hero has been artfully displayed in a scintillating illusion of motion as a personality constitutionally invulnerable to change. For Augie was every bit as much a "Columbus of those near-at-hand" in his early Chicago days as he finds himself to be in the snow of Normandy. We know that the "wrath" of the world is only temporarily lifted from Henderson, who was born to be oppressed by it. And Moses Herzog ends as he began—a sentimentalist with a rigid heart, an adamant solitary who believes in the salvation of brotherhood.

To explain this without seeming to do disservice to Bellow's real achievements is difficult, because the weight of the analysis must necessarily appear more censorious than his successes deserve. But in this connection it is useful to examine the conclusions of Bellow's novels. No other elements of his work have been subject to more confusion and critical disapproval. Is Joseph's final abandonment of freedom and acceptance of regimentation to be read as a capitulation of the spirit or as an ironic defiance? What does the final meeting in the theater between Allbee and Leventhal *mean?* Is Tommy Wilhelm weeping for himself or for mankind? What is the purpose of the coda in *The Adventures of Augie March* —the scene where Jacqueline confesses her secret dream of Mexico and Augie laughs? What are we to make of the bearish Henderson galloping over the Newfoundland snows with his lion cub and the Persian boy? And should we see Herzog's final "peace" as the product of complete nervous exhaustion or as an attainment of harmony with the universe? The interpretative confusion is endless and I do not propose to offer a judicious settlement. But the habit of ambiguous conclusions suggests a radical deficiency in Bellow's capacity to bring his structures to an inevitable termination. In each of the finales, an implication is built into the plot action that the hero is at the point of surrendering, in some decisive way, his overweening and world-denying self-concern; the protagonist is frozen in a gesture

of readiness to embrace mankind. However, the dynamics of his character make such an embrace patently impossible. It is not enough to say—as all Bellow's heroes do resolutely say—that "I really believe that brotherhood is what makes a man human. If I owe God a human life, this is where I fall down. 'Man liveth not by Self alone but in his brother's face. . . .' " Correctly they diagnose the cause and fatal consequences of their isolation from their fellows; but only for the theoretician or the paralyzed dreamer is an accurate diagnosis sufficient in itself The Bellow hero—in this case, Herzog—continues: "The real and essential question is one of our employment by other human beings and their employment by us. Without this true employment you never dread death, you cultivate it. And consciousness, when it doesn't clearly understand what to live for, what to die for, can only abuse and ridicule itself."

Is this not explicitly the root problem of Bellow's fictional themes? His heroes are not, in the end, mere theoreticians of life's ironic cul-de-sacs; what they are best qualified to do is to recognize themselves as diagnosticians who suffer from their own acuity of vision and find no solution except to abuse and ridicule themselves. And what brings the Bellow hero to despair is the knowledge that with his temperament as a self-conscious intellectual and what Bellow has called "the mind's comical struggle for survival in an environment of Ideas," self-directed ridicule and abuse are the only options open to him. Or perhaps the despair is inherent in such a temperament and the self-ridicule is its principal means of expression. The Bellow hero is so keenly aware of the unceasing polarity of moods and human urgencies that his foreknowledge keeps him from either pursuing intensity with a full ardor or accepting without protest life's plateaus of quietude. Herzog despises the world's "potato love" and yearns after something finer and more dangerous, knowing at the same time that "intensity is what the feeble humanity of us can't take for long." Leventhal perceives within himself the dual desires to move and to be at rest, to risk everything and sacrifice nothing: "Everybody wanted to be what he was to the limit. . . . There was something in people against sleep and dullness, together with the caution that led to sleep and dullness. Both were there. . . ." From this viewpoint, Schlossberg's definition of "human-ness" can be interpreted as exactly that exquisite compromise between vegetable ("less than human") and ecstatic ("more than human") existence. But why should this cause the hero to despair? Because, under the honorific rationale of humanity, love, and moral dignity, this balanced compromise runs the inevitable hazard of exalting glandular dullness, acquiescence, and torpor as worthy life-goals.

This, as I take it, is the real force of Kirby Allbee's ranting criticism of Leventhal and the Jews in general: ". . . you people take care of yourselves before everything. You keep your spirit under lock and key. That's the way you're brought up. You make it your business assistant, and it's safe and tame and never leads you toward anything risky. Nothing dangerous and nothing glorious. Nothing ever tempts you to dissolve yourself. What for? What's in it? No percentage." In Bellow's other novels the same charge is more obliquely repeated in the accusation which the hero unfailingly directs at himself that he belongs "to a class of people secretly convinced that they had an arrangement with fate; in return for docility or ingenuous good will they were to be shielded from the worst brutalities of life." And the fact that the "arrangement with fate" is specious and ineffectual in no way deflects the bite of the accusation. Moses Herzog copies out the words of his daughter's favorite

nursery rhyme ("I love little pussy, her coat is so warm . . .") as a motto to revile himself with. And even Joseph catches himself up with the mocking revelation that he had "believed in his own mildness, believed in it piously." In their studied concern to be "exactly human" while avoiding "the worst brutalities" of human existence, Bellow's heroes cling to a pernicious closure of selfhood that tends to extinguish their most fundamental passions under the ashes of a bland passivity. And in full cognizance of what they have done to themselves, of what monstrous sin they have committed against God and mankind, they despair.

Several times Bellow has portrayed these fearful "brutalities" that exact such a heavy price for self-defense. They are imaged for Asa Leventhal in terms of his brief experience as a clerk in a lower-Broadway hotel for transients. His abiding fear is that he might fall in "with that part of humanity . . . that did not get away with it—the lost, the outcast, the overcome, the effaced, the ruined." These vague abstractions are more concretely rendered in a sordid street fight which Leventhal observes from his apartment-house window: "The scene on the corner remained with him . . . and he returned to it every now and then with the feeling that he really did not know what went on about him, what strange things, savage things. They hung near him all the time in trembling drops, invisible, usually, or seen from a distance. But that did not mean that there was always to be a distance, or that sooner or later one or two of the drops might not fall on him." Kirby Albee's disruptive invasion of his privacy is such a "drop." And its naked menace to Leventhal is terrifying and direct, not because it makes a victim of him—he has had an abundance of that experience!—but because it exposes him to himself as a passive victimizer. It closes the distance between the savage realities of the outside and the perilously taut artifices he has constructed to keep the world away from his timorous spirit. Similarly, such episodes as Mimi Villars' abortion or Stella's seedy intrigues with Oliver and Cumberland represent for Augie March the seamy life that rages beyond his fingertips—a savage order of life that his cool neutrality successfully ignores. A better illustration is the murder trial which Herzog witnesses as a courtroom visitor and which he is unable to watch without becoming physically sickened. The awful spectacle of calloused degradation (the defendant has killed her three-year-old son because he was a toilet-training problem and he cried a good deal) forces Herzog to realize that the power to act with passion bears within it the possibilities of such monstrous behavior as to make the term "human" equivalent to a cosmic insult. Better to dangle in brooding, self-centered passivity—to be guilty only to oneself—than to take the chance that opening a breach between oneself and the outside will automatically result in a fresh breeze of sweetness and light.

Thus the Bellow hero is entangled in an inextricable skein of vacillation and dread. The barriers which he erects to ward off the crudity and abandon of the external world can become as much a stultifying prison as a means of self-protection. To dangle uncommitted or to fall into the abyss—these seem to be his sole alternatives. And caught in that dilemma, deeply aware of the awesome dimensions of that abyss (the fate of the six million East European Jews is never very far from his mind as an example of what men can do with deliberation and self-righteousness), he can adequately express his anguish and outrage only in the accents of self-mockery and self-abuse. And thus, it seems to me, Bellow's curiously incomplete fictional structures reflect accurately the basic indecisiveness of his moral

position. Viewed in a harsh light, his final scenes may seem confused and contradictory—mere devices to terminate the fictional posturings of a brooding consciousness which lacks the moral energy to uphold a fully responsible position. But from a more sympathetic point of view they may be fruitfully ambiguous in that they leave his meanings honestly suspended between action and stasis, between commitment and withdrawal.

Of course there are those temperaments and philosophies for which sex may serve as at least a partial breakthrough from closed solipsistic brooding. Henry Miller, for example, is as much addicted to the form of the introspective journal as is Bellow. And the Bellow hero has doggedly explored the possibility of self-expansion through sexual union—but with generally negative results. The twice-married and multi-mistressed Herzog seems to sum up Bellow's conclusions on the matter when he says, "To look for fulfillment in another, in interpersonal relationships, was a feminine game. And the man who shops from woman to woman, though his heart ache with idealism, with the desire for pure love, has entered the female realm." This is an interesting statement, not only in its oddly ascetic insistence that "woman-shopping" be conducted on the idealistic level of "pure" love rather than "impure" sex, but in its implicit denial of the principles of brotherhood that we have earlier seen to be at the very heart of Bellow's philosophic perspective. It is a strange paradox that the Bellow hero should consciously reject fulfillment in "interpersonal relationships" even as he quotes with melancholy pleasure the dictum that "Man liveth not by Self alone but in his brother's face." In part there would seem to be a religious inheritance of female degradation that may be related to the traditional prayer that orthodox Jews recite every morning, offering thanks to the Almighty that they were born men and not women. At any rate, if the central problem of the Bellow hero is his ambivalent self-centeredness, then we must surely examine the role of the women with whom he shares his life. Moses Herzog, remembering the scene when his father returned to the Napoleon Street flat, his clothes torn and his face bleeding, thinks back on the giant figures of his earliest childhood and laments "Whom did I ever love as I loved them?" And in terms of our previous discussion, we can more clearly understand that the powerful emphasis of "family life" as the fundamental erotic influence on the Bellow hero will make all the later intrusions into his mature unfamilied life rootless and partial and lacking that greater adhesion which his idealism so desperately requires. If we recognize this, we should not be surprised to discover that Bellow's gallery of female characters tends to be composed of almost identical stereotypes, differing somewhat in ethnic background, erotic inventiveness, and the capacity for bitchiness; in other respects they will be similar, one to the other, whether they happen to bear the temporary title of wife or mistress.

Iva, Mary, Stella, Margaret, Frances, Lily, Daisy—it is impossible to keep the various wives separate and distinct. They are just *there* on those infrequent occasions when they appear in the novels. Unreal voices on the telephone, signatures on letters, additional elements of the prison furniture which surrounds the hero, exerting no significant stimulus on his behavior, and representing no real means by which he can escape himself. Nor are the mistresses any easier to distinguish from one another. Kitty, Sophie Geratis, Olive, Wanda, Zinka, Sono, Ramona—perhaps their names have a more romantic ring than those of the wives. They are all more or less acessible to the hero's uses in terms of the same function; and while they are sincerely enjoyed and appreciated for their physical talents, they are clearly unrealized on any deeper level of engagement. But there are two exceptional women in Bellow's fiction; two distinct occasions when the hero is caught up in a love affair that goes beneath the superficialities of nuptial boredom or amorous release. These are the cases of Thea Fenchel in *The Adventures of Augie March* and Madeleine Pontritter in *Herzog*. These are both special encounters in Bellow's fiction; these are the only women who force the Bellow hero to rise to a qualitatively different kind of challenge than that of mere bedfellowship. And, inevitably, he fails both challenges.

Augie's surreal affair with Thea, which sweeps him away from labor-organization work in Chicago to an extended sojourn in the wilds of Mexico, entangling him in an exotic whirl where money is kept in the refrigerator and eagles are trained to hunt prehistoric lizards, can be easily misinterpreted. Nor, I think, is it entirely the reader's fault. Bellow goes out of his way to invest Thea with details of grotesque eccentricity, partly to conceal the nakedness of the demands which she makes on Augie. She wants simply to break out of her own prison of loneliness. She asks of Augie that he merge his life with hers in order that together they might create a world inside and secure from the demeaning outside world. This is most evidently seen when she rejects his plea for a second chance: ". . . I thought if I could get through to one other person I could get through to more. . . . Well, I believed it must be you who could do this for me. And you could. I was so happy to find you. I thought you knew all about what you could do and you were so lucky and so special. . . . I'm sorry you're here now. You're not special. You're like everybody else. You get tired easily." And although Thea's odd preoccupation with eagles and snakes may tend to make the reader discount her as a real woman, she must still be credited with an unqualified determination to follow a life of pure intensity. It is on this level that Augie fails her; he lacks the stamina to remain with her on the rarefield heights of an all-inclusive love. Afterwards, he himself wonders: ". . . was it true, as she said, that love would appear strange to me no matter what form it took, even if there were no eagles and snakes?" An affirmative answer to this question is implicit in all Bellow's fiction. Love *is* strange to the Bellow hero because it demands exactly that rejection of caution which Kirby Allbee propounded to Leventhal; it requires that the lover submit to the temptation to dissolve himself, to risk his primal security for something "dangerous" and "glorious." Perhaps because he has the least to lose, Augie comes closest of Bellow's heroes to success in such an all-consuming love; but he does tire easily ("My real fault was that I couldn't stay with my purest feelings") and he offers himself the dubious consolation that he who would pursue "an independent fate" must necessarily do without love.

The precise nature of Madeleine Pontritter's challenge to Herzog is more difficult to assess in this context because she is rarely presented full face in a direct dramatic situation. What we know of her must be gathered from the distorted fragments of Herzog's bitter recollections and from the pervasive pain which his memories engender in him. The actual outlines of her personality are concealed by the elliptical effects of the novel's narrative technique, and, then, further blurred by the assemblage of grotesque details which Bellow heaps upon her. Her frenetic family background, her impresario father, her theatrical conversion to Catholicism, the tomes of Slavic mysticism which she piles under the bed, the sense of absolute premeditation and treachery with which she conducts the affair with Valentine Gersbach, her cold manipulation of the credulous Dr. Edvig—this overweighted accumulation of melodramatic matter and manner makes the reader suspicious of Herzog's capacity for distinguishing between an actual Madeleine and a Madeleine that he needs to portray to his own consciousness. What does seem to emerge with great reluctance from his reminiscences is the possibility that Mady offers the same kind of challenge to Herzog that Thea did to Augie. "Compared with her he felt static, without temperament," Herzog confesses at one point. Elsewhere he remarks that "Everyone close to Madeleine, everyone drawn into the drama of her life became exceptional, deeply gifted, brilliant. It had happened also to him." And in another place he says sarcastically that "The satisfaction she took in herself was positively plural—imperial." Superficially, it may very well be that Madeleine's overwhelming egotism is a sufficient explanation of her character, but if this is all she is, Herzog's anguish and fury at her infidelity and his loss seem surely disproportionate and misplaced. The domineering monstrosity whom Herzog consistently invokes in his memories—a Madeleine assembling herself for early Mass with the machined deliberation of an astronaut preparing for a launch; a Madeleine charming Professor Shapiro with herring, liver paste, a gaily adorned rear-end, and passionate talk of Tikhon Zadonsky and the younger Soloviëv; a Madeleine who expresses "a total will that he [Herzog] should die. . . . a vote for his nonexistence"—such a Madeleine could not have brought Herzog to the sterile depths of nervous exhaustion which the novel scrapes upon. It is as though there were something vitally important left out of Herzog's description of his life with Madeleine —a mosaic piece, as it were, without which the total portrait remains seriously incomplete

—compelling, perhaps, in its shocking grotesquerie, but finally unconvincing.

In other words, even though Herzog describes himself as being always under "the flavor of subjugation" to his second wife, the reader misses a scene which might display the two of them, equally loved and loving—and, hence, having equally something to lose. Whether the lack of such a scene is due to the repressive action of Herzog's instincts for survival or Bellow's failure as a novelist, such a scene might have redressed the balance in Madeleine's portraiture, making her less operatic in her ruthlessness and explaining more fully why Herzog suffers her rejection so intensely. This might then indicate that his deeper remorse is connected to the same realization of failure in himself that Augie should have felt, but did not feel. And it might have suggested that whatever love Madeleine did offer to Herzog was too "strange" and too costly for him to accept. That, for a second time, the challenge of a vivid self-effacing love was proffered to the Bellow hero, and for a second time his frozen psyche could not thaw itself sufficiently to accept. Nachman and his Laura drift away on the streets of Paris and Brooklyn, a shabby modern Paolo and Francesca, and Herzog counterpoints their destruction with a covert chronicle of his own unqualified defeat. For himself, such destruction is more than he can afford. In the end, love is a challenge which he deflects by translating it into the harmless world of metaphysical abstractions; he elects instead the pleasant performance of affectionate sex which he can control at a safe remove from the "distant garden where curious objects grow, and there, in a lovely dusk of green, the heart of Moses E. Herzog hangs like a peach."

Thus the Bellow hero returns ever to the prison of himself, uncommitted to religion, to society, to family, or to love, jeering impotently at himself for his bitter knowledge "that people can be free now but the freedom doesn't have any content." Once, in *Dangling Man,* he considers a narrow path of escape, the adolescent artist's classic rationalization for withdrawal and studied alienation. "The real world is the world of art and thought," writes a friend to Joseph. "There is only one worthwhile sort of work, that of the imagination." It would have been relatively simple for Bellow to have embraced the fashionable aesthetic standard of existence, bestowing upon his brooding intellectual heroes a measure of transcendent salvation from the rainbow shapes of order and harmony which it was within the power of their imaginations to create. But he has been too honest in his moral intransigency—too loyal, perhaps, to his early religious training—to have seized this facile egress from despair. As the comically conceived careers of Joseph, Henderson, Herzog, and Philip Bummidge teach us, "Humanity lives mainly from perverted ideas." To have accepted the primacy of a "world of art and thought" would have belied the deeper truth that man is a "throb-hearted character," a "strange organization" that will eventually die, a "most peculiar animal" that sometimes is filled with "an idiot joy" to which it must spontaneously exclaim, "Thou movest me." The Bellow hero has too much integrity of the flesh to try to escape himself in systems of thought or fancy that would deny his integral position in the sentient world. He has learned that his moods are subservient to the tidal undulations of his own blood, and over these he has no control. He knows that, in the end, his "balance comes from instability," and that such small intense joys as he may be blessed with when the spirit's sleep is burst will be inevitably followed by the shades of ever-returning despair. And for him there can be no permanent release from that despair—not in the exciting spume of theory or the framing of gaudy metaphors; not in a nostalgic clutching at a way of life that is forever lost; not in a rancid disgust at the mediocre quality of life that is at least available to him.

But such a summation of Bellow's fictional world makes too bleak a picture to do justice to the splendor of his achievement. For while I believe that I have been accurate in sketching the essential structure of that world, I have neglected to take into account the mollifying and humanizing effects of the humor which is so basic a part of Bellow's craft and life style. One recalls Philip Bummidge's proclamation of identity in *The Last Analysis*—a proclamation which is surely Bellow's as well: ". . . I formed my own method. I learned to obtain self-knowledge by doing what I best knew how to do, acting out the main events of my life, dragging repressed material into the open by sheer force of drama. I'm not solely a man but also a man who is an artist, and an artist whose sphere is comedy." From his earliest work to the present, Bellow's natural sphere has been comedy, and if it is true that his most significant recurrent theme has been despair, it is also true that this despair has been projected prismatically through a consistently comical lens. Walking across the fields of Normandy with his housekeeper, Jacqueline, Augie thinks of her dream of Mexico and bursts into laughter. "That's the *animal ridens* in me, the laughing creature, forever rising up," he thinks. "What's so laughable, that a Jacqueline, for instance, as hard used as that by rough forces, will still refuse to lead a disappointed life? Or is the laugh at nature—including eternity—that it thinks it can win over us and the power of hope? Nah, nah! I think. It never will. But that probably is the joke, on one or the other, and laughing is an enigma that includes both." This laugh has always been present in Bellow's fiction as a double- or triple-voiced response to the mortal enigma of consciousness. The Bellow hero who mocks himself without mercy is, at the same time, mocked by the pittance of life which Bellow gives him to live. And yet the brute impersonality of life itself is also mocked; mind can always extract its human superiority over mindlessness—even when mindlessness assumes proportions that are as large as eternity. Humor is an enormously complex and problematical affair in modern literature, and one particularly protean and evasive in the work of a moral ironist like Bellow; here we can but point to some of its isolated effects without hoping to do more than suggest the larger ambience it may include.

Traditional satire and parody have not usually interested Bellow, nor has he been especially successful in their uses. The attempts, for example, to satirize a specific social group or idea—the Servatius party in *Dangling Man,* the Magnus family in *The Adventures of Augie March,* the Freudian hijinks of *The Last Analysis*, or the wilder inanities of hipsterism and radical revolt in *Mr. Sammler's Planet*—are, on the whole, rather labored and unconvincing efforts. Writers like Philip Roth and Bruce Jay Friedman have followed Bellow's lead and been far more effective with such satirical material. And similarly, although there is a sprinkling of parody in Bellow's work—most notably in *Henderson the Rain King*—this comic strategy is also clearly tangential to his central interests and talents. Bellow's dominant strength as a humorist has been his powerful sense of the grotesque and his accomplished capacity to communicate that sense to his reader. In *Dangling Man* Joseph remarks that "there is an element of the comic or fantastic in everyone," and Bellow, agreeing so completely with Joseph's perception that he sees Joseph himself as "fantastic," writes under the full ironic force of that conviction. That is, not only does the Bellow hero view the world in terms of the grotesque, but he is himself viewed in the same way. Bellow's art holds a deliberately warped mirror up to life and it is the task of the reader to focus the moral proportions as best he can. There are, of course, severe limitations in such an artistic perspective. As we have noted, this vision tends to freeze all action into a virtual paralysis, while it puts an inflated premium on passivity. It tends inevitably to shift values like love, faith, and truth from the turbulent immediacy of the real world into the placid realm of abstractions. And since it offers us the authority of the grotesque measured by the grotesque, it runs the danger of evading objective judgment almost entirely. But it does succeed in establishing a perverse buffer against the onslaught of despair, and such a defense is its major function.

It accepts despair as a basic reality of human life—perhaps the ultimate reality—but it deflects its enervating power through the agency of laughter, transforming despair into something that becomes the pragmatic equivalent of hope. At one point in *Seize the Day*, Dr. Adler chides Tommy Wilhelm for his sloppy, unheroic attitude toward life: " 'You make too much of your problems,' said the doctor. 'They ought not to be turned into a career. Concentrate on real troubles—fatal sickness, accidents.' " There is no question but that Dr. Adler is clinically correct in his diagnosis. His is the measured judgment of the real world, but Tommy and Bellow are humanly wiser than he. They are aware that the doctor's "truths" are irrelevant; that men's human lives are not lived in the real world; that terminal

sicknesses and accidents are not the real problems at all. These will, in due course of time, arrive, and they will dispense finality to man, but only a fool would expend his energies on fatalities that are impervious to the energetic action of the mind. What obsesses Tommy and all Bellow's heroes is the quality of the lives they are given to live—the porous quotidian texture which is squeezed between the accidents of birth and the fatal sicknesses which end in death. Submerging themselves in this texture, Bellow's heroes are in a constant froth of self-examination, checking the daily temperature of their happiness, measuring the degrees of deficiency in their self-fulfillments. This is the relentless focus of their brooding concerns. This is where they are most human and this is where they are most humorously treated by Bellow's art.

Indeed one might suggest that Bellow's humor rises to its most excruciating pitch when the despair bites closest to the bone. The opening forty pages of *Henderson the Rain King*, for example, voice an almost uninterrupted shriek of pain and outrage, and they are also among the most humorous pages that Bellow has written. Eugene Henderson, that grotesque amalgam of Holden Caulfield and Papa Hemingway, is purporting to explain why he has decided to go to Africa. Rich, and in vigorous health, Henderson has the material freedom to do what he will with his life; yet all he can effect with his millions and his magnificent incoherent ideals is to raise pigs on his ancestral Connecticut estate, take violin lessons in order to serenade his dead parents, shoot at cats under the table, and suffer the increasing stridency of the voice that bursts compulsively from his pent-up heart, "I want! I want!" Nor can one discount Henderson because he is eccentric and askew. His torment persuades us otherwise. He may be grotesque, but his sufferings are real and significant. As Joseph, an earlier prisoner of the same pinioning freedom, concluded many years before, ". . . reality . . . is actually very dangerous, very treacherous. It should not be trusted." Or, as Joseph explains more directly, "To be pushed upon oneself entirely put the very facts of simple existence in doubt." And the massive drift of twentieth-century life has pushed the Bellow hero upon himself entirely. The dissolution of the centripetal religious family-unit, the economic emancipation of the worker, and the creation of a mass affluent society have succeeded in isolating the individual imagination from both the sources and the goals of all belief. The Bellow hero is too honest to pretend that his situation is other than a displaced one. He is too desperate in his psychic needs to be able to accept the bland compromises that everyone around him seems to accept. But he is finally, at bottom, too human to be able to regard himself all that seriously. Too human, beause he is always aware that his is just one tiny life in an infinite multitude of lives and deaths. And so he suffers his real pains and mocks his torment with a single cry that is at once laughter and agony inseparably mingled.

The fact that Bellow has managed to view this plight of modern man as pathetic rather than tragic—probably because he also is too human to take himself all that seriously—is what has given him his characteristic comic methodology. For we must not forget his dictum that modern comedy has to do with "the disintegrating outline of the worthy and humane Self, the bourgeois hero of an earlier age." The Bellow hero is a specimen case of that worthy Self in the process of breakdown —a consciously quixotic blunderer who is designed to evoke his own and our laughter in his frantic efforts to avoid or absorb his own pain. And the special kind of humor which

makes this transaction of energies possible is exposed and released in Bellow's style. This, I believe, is the point where Bellow differs most significantly from the contemporary "black" humorists and nihilistic practitioners of "the absurd." While their works tend to extract a dark humor from the very senselessness of the inhuman condition, concentrating on the stark outrageousness of their fictional situations for their comic effects, Bellow's concern is directed toward the articulated human response to that condition—the verbal phrases and kinetic metaphors with which suffering man escalates implacable defeats into comic impasses which are, at least, barely tolerable. For, with the contemporary hostility against language and logic—against words as a mechanism of submission and compromise—Bellow has nothing to do. For him, man becomes human because he uses words. And, more than that, *style* is the final resort for the victim— his means of transcendence out of slavishness into a kind of comic heroism. This, of course, does not mean that Bellow is advancing a rhetoric which besmears reality—which gives the grandiloquent lie to life. Rather, it is an employment of language to define more accurately the crosscurrents which roil the spirit between a will to live and an awareness of death. For Bellow, neither demonic rhetoric nor silence can define the human condition correctly. Rhetoric invites dishonesty and silence cuts both below and above the level of the human. Bellow's notion of man is far too dependent on the miracle of rationality—on man's internal dialogue with himself—for him to be hostile to words. And hence, it is in his style that the complexities of his humor and his moral concern with the human unite and most persuasively develop.

And his prose style is a formidable instrument for his purposes. Eclectic, vital, raucous, it is unusually flexible in its different capacities. It delights in making grandiose catalogues—in chronicling the inventory of smells, tastes, and colors in a New York City delicatessen, or the three-dimensional turbulence of a modern city-scape, or the intellectual history of mankind gleaned erratically from the stacks of libraries and museums. This style of open-ended aggrandizement is one of Bellow's major devices for imparting a sensuous texture to his fictional world. But on the other hand, his style is equally adept at capsuling a welter of impressions into one firmly seized image in which the grotesque detail becomes comically, shockingly, irrefutably fixed in the prose: "Her lips come together like the seams of a badly sewn baseball." "And my face . . . is no common face, but like an unfinished church." Further, the tempo of Bellow's prose is susceptible to a large range of modulation. It can move at the "larky" pace of Augie's rambunctious recitation; it can lumber with the sullen clumsiness of Leventhal; or it can explode like firecrackers with the zany mock-hysteria of Henderson. It is comfortable with the logical rigors of formal exposition and, as I have already noted, it can be an acute mimic of the speech tones of the crank and the huckster. Perhaps it tends to become artificial and stilted in straight dramatic dialogue, and sometimes a little embarrassing in those lyrical flights where sentimentality escapes the realistic grip of the comic spirit; however, these awkwardnesses are relatively infrequent because Bellow's introspective focus tends to avoid both dramatic dialogue and untempered lyricism.

But whatever demands Bellow assigns to his style, that style is almost always under the controlling influence of a dominant oral tradition —that of spoken or argued Yiddish. The echo of a discernible human voice is deeply residual even in the most abstract of his prose passages; and that voice carries the ironic, chiding melody of the speech of the ghetto. In fact, it is entirely possible that the "voice" came first in Bellow's development as an artist—prior to his conscious shaping of thought or ideal. It is a voice which in its very rhythms mocks both speaker and the spoken, which has mastered a way of expressing lamentation and joy simultaneously, which loves to argue and analyze, which is balanced in a stance of aggressive defense at all times, which has a poised control over the affectionate insult, the cosmic curse, and the rare release of blessing. Bellow's prose and the life style which his fictions have figured forth are, in a sense, an expansion and extension of that brooding voice—a rich fusion of sophisticated erudition and earthiness which brings the full current of man's coursing blood into the world of mind and spirit, and which is careful to retain the sensual as the root metaphor of all experience. It is Bellow's style, thus, which subsumes and encompasses the direction and shape of his achievement as a writer. Rational, honest, ironic, cognizant of human limitations but struggling not to be cowed by them, it gropes and grapples and learns to accept itself as a deliberate comic thrust against life. It is, at the end, its own justification, but one severely fought for, and one which holds its victories as cheap because it knows well the heavy price it has had to pay for them. It is in his style that one can see Bellow's weaknesses as a writer—the narrowness of his scope, the solipsistic closure, the forfeits which his imagination has had to surrender to irony, and to the realism of mortal flesh. But his style is triumphantly a record of his remarkable strengths as well—his success in establishing and making viable an image of the human in the face of the dual tides of mechanism and brute animality that threaten to obliterate the very concept of humanity in their sweep. And it is here, I believe, that his finest achievement will be read and reckoned.

Selected Bibliography

WORKS OF
SAUL BELLOW

NOVELS

Dangling Man. New York: Vanguard, 1944.
The Victim. New York: Vanguard, 1947.
The Adventures of Augie March. New York: Viking Press, 1953.
Seize the Day. New York: Viking Press, 1956.
Henderson the Rain King. New York: Viking Press, 1959.
Herzog. New York: Viking Press, 1964.
Mr. Sammler's Planet. New York: Viking Press, 1970.

PLAY

The Last Analysis. New York: Viking Press, 1965.

SHORT STORIES

"Two Morning Monologues," *Partisan Review,* 8:230–36 (May–June 1941).
"The Mexican General," *Partisan Review,* 9:178–94 (May–June 1942).
"Dora," *Harper's Bazaar,* 83:118–88 (November 1949).
"Sermon by Doctor Pep," *Partisan Review,* 16:455–62 (May–June 1949).
"Trip to Galena," *Partisan Review,* 17:779–94 (November–December 1950).
"Looking for Mr. Green," *Commentary,* 11:251–61 (March 1951). (Collected in *Seize the Day.*)
"By the Rock Wall," *Harper's Bazaar,* 85:135–205 (April 1951).
"Address by Gooley MacDowell to the Hasbeens Club of Chicago," *Hudson Review,* 4:222–27 (Summer 1951).
"A Father-to-be," *New Yorker,* 30:26–30 (February 5, 1955). (Collected in *Seize the Day.*)
"The Gonzaga Manuscripts," *discovery, IV,* edited by Vance Bourjaily. New York: Pocket Books, 1956. (Collected in *Seize the Day.*)
"Leaving the Yellow House," *Esquire,* 49:112–26 (January 1958).
Mosby's Memoirs. New York: Viking Press, 1969.

ARTICLES

"How I Wrote Augie March's Story," *New York Times Book Review,* January 31, 1954, p. 3.
"The Writer and the Audience," *Perspectives U.S.A.,* 9:99–102 (Autumn 1954).
"Isaac Rosenfeld," *Partisan Review,* 23:565–67 (Fall 1956).
"A Talk with the Yellow Kid," *Reporter,* 15:41–44 (September 6, 1956).
"Distractions of a Fiction Writer," *New World Writing,* 12:229–43 (New York: New American Library, 1957).
"Deep Readers of the World, Beware!" *New York Times Book Review,* February 15, 1959, p. 1.
"Some Notes on Recent American Fiction," *Encounter,* 21:22–29 (November 1963).
"The Writer as Moralist," *Atlantic Monthly,* 211:58–62 (March 1963).

CRITICAL AND
BIOGRAPHICAL STUDIES

Alter, Robert, *After the Tradition.* New York: Dutton, 1969.
Axthelm, Peter M. *The Modern Confessional Novel.* New Haven, Conn.: Yale University Press, 1967.
Baumbach, Jonathan. *The Landscape of Nightmare.* New York: New York University Press, 1965.
Clayton, John J. *Saul Bellow: In Defense of Man.* Bloomington: Indiana University Press, 1967.
Detweiler, Robert. *Saul Bellow.* Grand Rapids, Mich.: William B. Eerdmans, 1967.
Donoghue, Denis. "Commitment and the Dangling Man," *Studies: An Irish Quarterly Review* (1964), pp. 174–87.
Dutton, Robert R. *Saul Bellow.* New York: Twayne, 1971.
Eisinger, Chester E. *Fiction of the Forties.* Chicago: University of Chicago Press, 1963.
Enck, John. "Saul Bellow: An Interview," *Wisconsin Studies in Contemporary Literature,* 6:156–60 (1965).
Fiedler, Leslie. *Love and Death in the American Novel.* Cleveland: World, 1962.
Galloway, David D. *The Absurd Hero in American Fiction.* Austin: University of Texas Press, 1966.

Gross, Theodore. *The Heroic Ideal in American Literature*. New York: The Free Press, 1971.

Guttmann, Allen. *The Jewish Writer in America*. New York: Oxford University Press, 1971.

Harper, Gordon Lloyd. "Saul Bellow: An Interview," *Paris Review*, 36:49–73 (Winter 1965).

Harper, Howard M., Jr. *Desperate Faith*. Chapel Hill: University of North Carolina Press, 1967.

Hassan, Ihab. *Radical Innocence*. Princeton, N.J.: Princeton University Press, 1961.

Kazin, Alfred. *Contemporaries*. Boston: Little, Brown, 1962.

Klein, Marcus. *After Alienation*. Cleveland: World, 1964.

Ludwig, Jack. *Recent American Novelists*. Minneapolis: University of Minnesota Press, 1962.

Malin, Irving, ed. *Saul Bellow and the Critics*. New York: New York University Press, 1967.

———. *Saul Bellow's Fiction*. Carbondale: Southern Illinois University Press, 1969.

Opdahl, Keith Michael. *Saul Bellow: An Introduction*. University Park: Pennsylvania State University Press, 1967.

Podhoretz, Norman. *Doings and Undoings*. New York: Farrar, Straus, 1964.

Poirier, Richard. "Bellow to Herzog," *Partisan Review,* 32:264–71 (1965).

Sokoloff, B. A. *Saul Bellow: A Comprehensive Bibliography*. Folcroft, Pa.: Folcroft, 1972.

Tanner, Tony. *City of Words*. New York: Harper & Row, 1971.

———. *Saul Bellow*. Edinburgh: Oliver & Boyd, 1965.

Weinberg, Helen. *The New Novel in America*. Ithaca, N.Y.: Cornell University Press, 1970.

Wisse, Ruth R. *The Schlemiel as Modern Hero*. Chicago: University of Chicago Press, 1971.

—*EARL ROVIT*

John Berryman

1914-1972

DESPITE career-long unevenness in the quality of his work, John Berryman has become a major American poet, has achieved a permanency that places him in a group with Theodore Roethke and Randall Jarrell. Berryman, it seems to me, has taken on the whole modern world and has come to poetic terms with it. At the same time he has taken on himself, and has come to poetic terms with that too. He has seen the wreck of the modern world (or, better, the modern world insofar as it is a wreck) and the wreck of his personal self in that world. He is not a pessimist but has, rather, what we would have to call a tragic view of human life—with good reason for holding it. Yet, not surprisingly, the tragic view finds its complement in a comic view, his wild and so often devastatingly effective sense of humor. He is preeminently a poet of suffering and laughter.

To understand his achievement it is necessary to look first at the life of the man, for his poetry will emerge as strongly autobiographical, and the intensity of his personal suffering must be understood. He was born October 25, 1914, in McAlester, Oklahoma, and grew up in Anadarko, Oklahoma, a town of 3000. His father was the town banker, his mother was a schoolteacher, and he had a younger brother. His upbringing was strict Roman Catholic,

which was the faith of both his parents, and, though in his last years he attended mass only occasionally, he remained a Catholic in spirit, religiously questing. Until he was ten he spent summers on a farm, throughout the year fished and hunted, and was from the beginning a bright boy in school rather than a young rebel. When he was ten the family moved to Tampa, Florida, where his mother and father had severe marital difficulties. His father, fearing that his wife was about to leave him, repeatedly threatened to drown himself and John with him. Lack of money was not the problem; in fact, young John had an allowance of $25 a week, all of which he spent on his stamp collection. His relationship with each of his parents was, moreover, close. His father, a captain in the National Guard, even took the boy with him occasionally when he went on maneuvers to Fort Sill, Oklahoma, as well as on hunting and fishing trips. But when John was twelve he suffered an ultimate trauma—his father shot himself right outside his son's window. The father was buried in Oklahoma, but the son never returned to his grave.

After the death of the father, the family settled in New York. John's mother then married a Wall Street banker named John Angus McAlpin Berryman, who formally adopted John and his younger brother. (John's father's name had been John Allyn Smith.) His mother and stepfather were divorced after ten years of marriage, but whatever the strains of their relationship the children were not adversely affected, and Berryman was good to his adopted children. John was sent to South Kent School in Connecticut, which his mother chose for him. South Kent was, in John's later words, "very muscular," that is, devoted to athletics, and very high-church Episcopalian. Though he came to feel friendly toward it later, at the time John hated South Kent with heart and soul. He was much bullied there, had many fights—usually with stand-off results—began to have literary ambitions, and rebelled because he was an intellectual and the school, as he saw it, was not sympathetic to intellectuals. At South Kent the boys were beaten regularly with a paddle, upon the command "Assume the angle." But the experience of the school was partly redeemed for John by two masters, one in English and one in history, who were sympathetic to him personally.

Following four years at South Kent, he attended Columbia, from which he took his B.A. in 1936. The teacher who inspired him was Mark Van Doren, all of whose courses he took. His development as a writer probably begins at about the age of nineteen under the close personal influence of Van Doren, whose book of poems *A Winter Diary* he reviewed, and then Van Doren got him going on other poets. He flowered at Columbia despite dismissal for half a year for flunking one of Van Doren's courses because he read only seventeen of forty-two assigned books. He returned to make A's and be elected to Phi Beta Kappa.

Following graduation from Columbia, a traveling fellowship took him to Cambridge, England, for two years. There he wrote poetry all the time and was known as a poet though he was not actually publishing at the time. He took a B.A. from Clare College in 1938 and

returned to New York, where he became a close personal friend of Delmore Schwartz, then poetry editor of *Partisan Review,* a friendship renewed when both were teaching at Harvard, Berryman from 1940 to 1943 and Schwartz from 1940 to 1947. Berryman's long teaching career had begun at Wayne State in 1939. He taught at Princeton intermittently from 1943 to 1949, held a fellowship there in 1950–51, and received a Guggenheim Fellowship in 1952–53. He had been rejected for service in World War II on medical grounds. His eyesight was poor and he had recurrent serious nervous difficulties.

He married for the first time in 1942. The marriage lasted eleven years. One of the love affairs he had during this time became the basis of his *Sonnets.* It was this affair that brought him to the point of suicide, with thoughts of killing both himself and his mistress because she flatly refused to leave her husband and marry him. His wife, who was ignorant of the affair, persuaded him to undergo psychoanalysis, and he stayed under analysis from 1947 to 1953. The analysis relieved his suicidal depression and led him to renounce the affair; thereafter he still saw his analyst occasionally. At the time of his separation from his wife in 1953—his heavy drinking and the tensions accompanying the writing of *Homage to Mistress Bradstreet* acting as causes—both were hoping for reconciliation.

In 1955 he moved to the University of Minnesota, where he remained, and became a professor of humanities. He remarried in 1956, had a son by this marriage, and was divorced in 1959. Again heavy drinking and disorderly behavior acted as causes, as well as the tensions accompanying his writing, this time, of the Dream Songs. He married once more in 1961. He and his third wife, Kate, who was twenty-five years younger than he, had two daughters, Martha and Sara. Like her husband, Mrs. Berryman was also a Catholic living outside the Church because of their marriage. In his last years John Berryman was evangelistically opposed to adultery. On Friday, January 7, 1972, he jumped to his death from a bridge over the Mississippi River, landing on the west bank about 100 feet below.

Formal honors for his poetry have been awarded to Berryman throughout his career. These include the Shelley Memorial Award in 1949, the Harriet Monroe Poetry Prize in 1957, the Pulitzer Prize for poetry in 1965, the Bollingen Prize in 1968, and the National Book Award for poetry in 1969.

Throughout his career—and underlying the unevenness in the quality of his work—Berryman was beset by the problem of style. It is as if he wrestled with artistic agonies at the same time as with personal ones, or that the former were perhaps a deep reflection of the latter. Although it is safe to say that he arrived at widespread and qualitatively certain recognition with his 1968 volume, *His Toy, His Dream, His Rest,* his earlier reviewers show great consistency in recognizing the problem of style. Going back to 1948 and Berryman's first important collection of poems, we find Dudley Fitts writing that it is "somehow without the excitement that attends the transformation of a craft into a completely realized art," and Randall Jarrell saying, "Doing things in a style all its own sometimes seems the primary object of the poem, and its subject gets a rather spasmodic treatment." Stanley Kunitz, with language strongly in mind, called *Homage to Mistress Bradstreet* a failure "worth more than most successes." John Ciardi wondered whether the same poem was "a thing literary and made," and John Holmes thought that it would "fascinate the intellectuals." Louise Bogan responded to *77 Dream Songs* with the incisive phrase "this desperate artificiality." Even Berryman's biography of

Stephen Crane revealed the problem of style. As Morgan Blum acutely observed, Berryman's trouble in the biography "apparently resides in an inability to reduce his insights to reasoned discourse." One could as easily say that in the biography Berryman so insisted on style, on being his own man, that he paid a price for it. Blum's summary judgment, "Flawed and distinguished," has the force of an epithet summarizing a central reaction to Berryman. But implicit in the reaction is the fact that there is only one Berryman, the Berryman of tension, agony, and struggle.

The biography of Crane, which appeared in 1950, is almost a tour de force. It is as if nothing but tension, agony, and struggle could have produced it. The closer one looks at its organization, the more one realizes the truth of Morgan Blum's comment. Despite the fact that it must be granted in advance that the art of writing biography is extraordinarily challenging—in my own opinion the most difficult of all literary writing—there is hardly an excuse to be found for the diffuseness it displays. Even when Berryman comes to a climactic chapter on the all-important subject of Crane's art, he seems unable to pull his materials together, despite the fact that in a cumulative way, as the reader by that time knows, he has the basic resources to do it. What makes matters even more frustrating for the reader is that Berryman's purpose is clearly to make an intelligent and balanced attempt at a fair evaluation of Crane. He obviously wants to do what the academically oriented critic normally does do. He is also too honest to make excuses. Although he remarks with casualness in his preface that it is a "psychological biography," he does not use that fact as a device to mitigate his own responsibility as a critic to make judgments when judgments are called for. And yet he persistently falls short of doing what he is telling himself that he must do.

The biography of Crane represents, then, Berryman's inability to reduce his insights to reasoned discourse or, to give the matter another emphasis, a values choice of passion over reason. Trite as it sounds, the poet in him wins out. His style is vigorous and vivid, and his eloquence is the kind found in only the very finest biographies. His eye for detail, his sensitivity to the selection of detail, is acute. One of the best parts of the book, for example, is in his description of Crane's childhood, as when he describes the young Stephen's contact with the color red or the boy's terror when his hands brush a handle of his father's coffin. In broad terms Berryman communicates sympathy for his subject by means that are often poetic. He leaves the reader with a vivid picture of Crane, a man who had teeth among the worst those who knew him had ever seen, an artist dead at twenty-eight of tuberculosis. It should be emphasized, however, that the biography is a far cry from being merely a poetic outpouring. Some of its vigor of thought, which relates ultimately to a poetic talent of forceful expression and projection of a speaker's character, is similar to that distinguishing the best academic writing. Berryman wisely sees, for example, that our own period of literature has developed toward increasing absorption in style, and he emphatically sees Crane as a great stylist, particularly as an impressionist, mentioning, as one of Crane's friends recorded it, Crane's assertion that impressionism was truth. Berryman also sees Crane as a writer of will, and comes to the very sensible conclusion that the world emerging from some of Crane's early sketches was one of "perfect aloneness." Sympathy and insight give the biography a unity that counters its diffuseness. There is a pattern here, I would suggest, than anticipates Berryman's experi-

ence with "The Dream Songs," but by that time he is all poet and whatever his organizational problems with the poem, he is also far beyond the possibility of any flirtation with a tour de force.

Berryman's poetic output divides into what might conveniently and after the familiar pattern be called the early Berryman and the later Berryman. The early Berryman, whose work began appearing in such journals as *Southern Review, Kenyon Review, Partisan Review, Nation,* and *New Republic* in the late 1930's, publishes twenty poems in 1940 in the New Directions book *Five Young American Poets* and a pamphlet called *Poems* in 1942. Then in 1948 he publishes the important *The Dispossessed,* which collects, often in revised form, many previously published poems. He also writes a sonnet sequence in the 1940's but this is not published until 1967. The later Berryman publishes *Homage to Mistress Bradstreet* in 1956, *77 Dream Songs* in 1964, *His Toy, His Dream, His Rest,* which completes the poem "The Dream Songs," in 1968, *Love and Fame* in 1970, and the posthumous *Delusions, etc.* in 1972. The 1958 *His Thought Made Pockets & the Plane Buckt* is a group of thirteen poems which may be regarded as an extension of *The Dispossessed,* and the 1967 *Short Poems* merely brings together *The Dispossessed, His Thought Made Pockets,* and a rather ineffectual poem called "Formal Elegy" written in 1963 on the occasion of the death of President John F. Kennedy.

So much for orientation to the poet's life and output. The immediate basis for the division between early Berryman and later Berryman is a striking contrast in style. Indeed, *Homage to Mistress Bradstreet* is rightly regarded as a breakthrough for Berryman, though the early Berryman obviously meshes with the later Berryman and the later Berryman does not hold, as it were, to the style of his breakthrough. Always conspicuously conscious of his identity as a poet, he provides us in Sonnet 47 with the perfect epigraph for his contrasting styles when he refers to "Crumpling a syntax at a sudden need." The early Berryman tends not to crumple his syntax but to write "normal," or we could say "traditional," verse sentences such as these:

Images are the mind's life, and they change.
"A POINT OF AGE"

We must travel in the direction of our fear.
"A POINT OF AGE"

An ultimate shaking grief fixes the boy
As he stands rigid, trembling, staring down
All his young days into the harbour where
His ball went.
"THE BALL POEM"

I hope you will be happier where you go
Than you or we were here, and learn to know
What satisfactions there are.
"FAREWELL TO MILES"

How could you be so happy, now some
thousand years
disheveled, puffs of dust?
"NOTE TO WANG WEI"

But in *Homage* a crumpling of syntax is typical and will be recognized as an element of the stream-of-consciousness or shift-of-association technique so common in the twentieth century—and also harking back to Gerard Manley Hopkins' sprung rhythm—that it too must be called "normal":

So squeezed, wince you I scream?   (19.1)

Pioneering is not feeling well,
not Indians, beasts.   (23.2–3)

This technique is, of course, larger than the crumpling of the syntax of a single sentence; since it is basically a device to dramatize the condition of the mind the crumpling in *Homage* is also a movement, often abrupt or rapid, from sentence to sentence, from thought to thought, or emotion to emotion. Quantitatively speaking, there are numerous normal verse sentences in *Homage*, but the steady effect of the poem is one of associational shift. Consider now a few examples of crumpled syntax from the Dream Songs:

Maybe but even if I see my son
forever never, get back on the take,
free, black & forty-one.
NUMBER 40

The course his mind his body steer, poor
Pussy-cat,
in weakness & disorder, will see him down
whiskers & tail.
NUMBER 49, "BLIND"

Henry—wonder! all,
when most he—under the sun.
NUMBER 52, "SILENT SONG"

But it must be said that this syntax, conspicuous as it is, does *not* dominate the Dream Songs, which are replete with normal English verse sentences. At the same time the first 77 Dream Songs do, like *Homage*, have a steady shift-of-association effect. Their crumpled language tends to be an untraditional drunken lurching consonant with the central character, Henry, and the psychic or dream world which he inhabits. To simplify a complicated matter we may say for the moment that the later Berryman writes in a style, or styles, directed toward dramatic immediacy. The early Berryman writes in a style that is ultimately dramatic but he tends to be a "speaker" of individual poems who does not become a developed character such as, for example, Frost's mythic New England Yankee or, in identity closer to the real-life poet, the Roethke who journeys to the interior in

"North American Sequence." We could easily imagine the later Berryman—Mistress Bradstreet and Henry—on a stage in some kind of performance, but not the early Berryman. Clearly the early Berryman was searching for a poetic identity which could only be found by an experiment in style.

Style, however, can be a false light to follow. The pre-eminent question to ask about the early Berryman is, I think, whether or not he creates a substantial number of poems that establish not so much a style as the fact of his talent and particularly that talent as it identifies itself in terms of essential subject and theme. The question is, What does the Berryman of *The Dispossessed* care about? Though he is an individual speaker of poems rather than a developed character, is there nevertheless a certain unity to his early work, does the speaker of his poems take on a singleness of character? And to suggest the answers to these questions is naturally to anticipate his later development.

The most essential thing to say about the Berryman of *The Dispossessed* is that he offers a subjective response to the objective reality of the modern world. His early poems typically do not encounter objective reality in terms of an elaboration of the facts of that reality. He thus forgoes what we might call pure or external subject interest in favor of a focus on the individual as the individual responds to his world. It is most decidedly not an egocentric emphasis, but rather a steady and a dynamic relationship between the individual, the sensitive individual, and the world to which he *must* respond. The speaker of his early poems is typically anxious to generalize about humanity from a variety of specific experiences, but to proceed from a specific experience is not the same as to detail the specifics. The persistent concern is broad, and distinctly in the humanistic tradition. It would be fair to

say that the basic character of the speaker in *The Dispossessed* is that of a sensitive and rather desperate humanist—we think too of the man who has abandoned his Catholic faith. What he cares about, broadly speaking, is our common humanity and its survival in the face of terrible threats. He cares about caring. His poetic attempt, his subject, is *how it feels* to be in a certain kind of world.

The pivot point of the world he finds himself in is World War II, the beginning of which he regards as a dark time for mankind, and as reason for feeling hatred and bitterness. It is a dark time because he finds fascism so evil and committed to destroy precious individual freedom. He sees the state as a monster of oppression, "At Dachau rubber blows forbid" ("Letter to His Brother")—this written in 1938. Or consider the terror and bitterness in these sensitive lines:

The time is coming near
When none shall have books or music, none
  his dear,
And only a fool will speak aloud his mind.
"THE MOON AND THE NIGHT AND THE MEN"

He looks out and sees "tortured continents" ("Boston Common") and becomes inwardly tortured by what he sees. His reaction to the world of the 1930's and 1940's is to take its burdens upon himself—much as Robert Lowell was shortly to do—and, as a result, to enter into the abyss of himself, which, as Yeats remarked, may show as reckless a courage as those we honor who die on the field of battle.

The early Berryman as a speaker of poems interests us, then, as a sensitive individual meditating upon and absorbing the shocks of a grim time. His perspective is broad in the sense that besides the state he sees other threats to human freedom: materialism, for example, as he calls out, "Great-grandfather, attest my hopeless need/Amongst the chromium luxury of the age" ("A Point of Age"). In a poem called "World-Telegram" he even catalogues the ordinary events of the day, and masks his horror with this reportorial matter-of-factness:

> An Indian girl in Lima, not yet six,
> Has been delivered by Caesarian.
> A boy. They let the correspondent in:
> Shy, uncommunicative, still quite pale,
> A holy picture by her, a blue ribbon.

At the end of the same poem he speaks in desperate understatement to dramatize the condition of civilization as he sees it: "If it were possible to take these things/Quite seriously, I believe they might/Curry disorder in the strongest brain." To take upon oneself the horrors of such a world as the *World-Telegram* reports is clearly to go mad. Berryman knows that we are saved, if we can be saved, by the strength of rational awareness and perhaps a final necessary refusal to accept burdens which are beyond our capacity as individuals to endure.

The Berryman of *The Dispossessed* also emerges in the poignant terms of more personal experience, as, for example, this reference to the loss of his father: "The inexhaustible ability of a man/Loved once, long lost, still to prevent my peace" ("World's Fair"). Or the reader can look at the fine poem "Farewell to Miles" on the simple subject of saying goodbye and the "ultimate loss" which that involves. But it must be said that the pessimism, the despair, and the bitterness which characterize the early Berryman are balanced by hope and such affirmation as these lines from "Letter to His Brother": "May love, or its image in work,/Bring you the brazen luck to sleep with dark/And so to get responsible delight." And he affirms especially the life of nature, "natural life springing in May," with a healthy sense of man's mortality, "Those

walks so shortly to be over" ("The Statue"). Or the reader may wish to look at another fine early poem, "Canto Amor," which tells us "Love is multiform" and sings to the end of joy.

It is clear that the early Berryman creates a substantial number of poems that establish the fact of his talent as it identifies itself in terms of essential subject and theme, or in terms of the singleness—the sheer interestingness—of the character of his speaker. What, then, qualifies praise of *The Dispossessed*? The answer to this is probably as obvious as it could be. Vagueness, obscurity, a failure to project a clear dramatic situation, characterize a number of the poems in the volume. We hear, too, often, a flat academic voice, given to a kind of punchless abstraction:

Cold he knows he comes, once to the dark,
All that waste of cold, leaving all cold
Behind him hearts, forgotten when he's tolled,
His books are split and sold, the pencil mark
He made erased, his wife
Gone brave & quick to her new life.

"SURVIVING LOVE"

Even the grammar—"leaving all cold/Behind him hearts"—fails. Or we encounter a dreadful triteness, as in these opening lines: "The summer cloud in summer blue/Capricious from the wind will run" ("Cloud and Flame"), suggesting a verse exercise, an unauthentic voice. It is worth noting that any poet who lets himself become so sloppy in his craft is sure to irritate his critics, especially if it is obvious that he is intelligent and should know better.

But what is really intriguing about *The Dispossessed* is not so much its obvious weakness as a phenomenon involving the relationship between what Dudley Fitts calls *craft* and *art* and Randall Jarrell calls *subject* and *style*. I refer to poems that are very appealing in their rhythms—and generally speaking expert in their craft—but nevertheless do not finally work as poems, or fulfill the treatment of subject. "Winter Landscape," for example, transcribes skillfully from the Brueghel painting "Hunters in the Snow" but does not realize a meaningful theme about it or, as Berryman intended, about something else. Or consider the following from the title poem, "The Dispossessed":

That which a captain and a weaponeer
one day and one more day did, we did, *ach*
we did not, *They* did . . cam slid, the great lock

lodged, and no soul of us all was near was
    near,—
an evil sky (where the umbrella bloomed)
twirled its mustaches, hissed, the ingenue
    fumed,

poor virgin, and no hero rides. . . .

Not even notes or a rationalization of context can rescue lines like these from their lack of exact, or exactly suggestive, imaginative coherence. It is relatively easy to dismiss egregious verse, but here we are frustrated by a sense of talent going to waste. What is not so apparent, though perhaps hardly hidden, is that the early Berryman is seeking to find himself as a poet. His bent, I think, is toward impressionism, but in *The Dispossessed* he does not readily shape impressions into the final imaginative world we call the poem. "Winter Landcape," the first poem in the chronologically arranged volume, and the title poem, the last, are different aspects of the same problem. The general movement of the book, in terms of style, is toward a loosening of form, a syntax crumpling that distinctly anticipates *Homage to Mistress Bradstreet*. This movement is particularly apparent in sections IV and V. The temptation, at first, is to see Berryman's development as linear from traditional to modern, but this would be exactly to miss

the point. His basic problem as a young poet is not so much stylistic development, important as that is, but rather discovering *how* or *to what* style is best applied. His bent toward impressionism was to become the impressionism of the mind of *Homage* and the Dream Songs. This, I believe, is the basic reason why *Homage* and the Dream Songs do not look imitative, though there is obviously nothing startling in the twentieth century about their technique. Both have their roots in the active soil of the early Berryman's struggle for poetic identity.

That struggle produced a good number of successful poems, some mellifluous misses, and a forgivable amount of weak verse. It was also a period in which Berryman produced two short stories which relate importantly— partly because they *are* short stories—to his early development. The first, and his first, "The Lovers," appears in the Winter 1945 *Kenyon Review* and is reprinted in *The Best American Short Stories 1946*. "The Lovers," which recalls Joyce's "Araby," tells of the discovery that adolescent first love cannot last. Like "Araby" it is told from the point of view of the mature man looking back over his past experience, but it is not a powerful story, chiefly because it is more expository than dramatic. It does, however, contain this comment from the narrator which implies strong awareness of personal development: "Purity of feeling, selflessness of feeling, is the achievement of maturity. . . ." Viewed as an aspect of the struggle of the early Berryman, this statement both defines his basic problem as an artist and points to his later achievement. His second story, "The Imaginary Jew," also appeared in *Kenyon Review* (Autumn 1945) and won first prize in the *Kenyon Review*–Doubleday Doran story contest. Although superior to "The Lovers," it is a cross between a fairly good short story and a beautiful essay. The speaker is a man who has gone through the harrowing experience in the late 1930's of being mistaken for a Jew. The story ends: "In the days following, as my resentment died, I saw that I had not been a victim altogether unjustly. My persecutors were right: I was a Jew. The imaginary Jew I was as real as the imaginary Jew hunted down, on other nights and days, in a real Jew. Every murderer strikes the mirror, the lash of the torturer falls on the mirror and cuts the real image, and the real and the imaginary blood flow down together." Berryman did not go on to become a short-story writer, though he has written other stories yet unpublished. Poetic language and firm subject matter, such as may be seen in "The Imaginary Jew," were not enough to make him a wholly successful short-story writer. He needed to escape from his own intellect, his academic intelligence, in order to achieve selflessness of feeling, or the power of the truly dramatic. Mistress Bradstreet and Dream Song Henry were to become his challenge to selflessness.

Our descriptive definition of the early Berryman completes itself as we examine *Berryman's Sonnets* (1967). Except for their number, 115, they could easily be construed as a section, perhaps a later section, of *The Dispossessed*. They give us a greater sense of dealing with an objective as well as a subjective reality than is characteristic of *The Dispossessed*, probably for the obvious reason that behind them lies the story of a love affair, illicit, between "the poet" and a Danish-American blonde named Lise, but their subject, paralleling *The Dispossessed*, is preeminently *how it feels* to love, which is to say, how it feels to respond to a personal situation as opposed to more general world conditions. The singleness of situation of the sonnets and the fact that the speaker is talking directly to his lady love doubtless helps to give them a somewhat greater dramatic immediacy than the poems

of *The Dispossessed*, but they fall far short of creating a speaker who is also a developed character in a developed situation, in what we would recognize as a good plot. Nevertheless, as with the speaker of the poems in *The Dispossessed*, the speaker of the sonnets does take on a singleness of character and further suggests a certain unity in Berryman's early work.

The sonnets—apparently written over a period of several months in 1946—are a sequence of emotions hinged on the ecstasy and the pain of a particular love. The speaker's epithet for himself is "The adulter and bizarre of thirty-two" (105), but the sonnets hardly make us feel much about his guilt. What they do make us feel is his energy, his humor, and his exuberance. He coins an appropriate epigraph for the affair as "knock-down-and-drag-out love" (97). But this is, of course, rhetoric for an old ideal, elsewhere simply stated, "without you I/Am not myself" (94), "you are me" (27), or love's goal is "To become ourselves" (45). Though somewhat repetitious in theme, the sonnets are appealing in their sheer erotic exultation, their reveling in sex—breasts, blonde hair, soul kisses, biting and kissing, even an orgasm compared to a rumbling subway train. But the speaker, fortunately, never takes himself too seriously and can see their quarrels as funny, as when his lady breaks her knuckle in smashing objects. He has a quick wit: "In the end I race by cocky as a comb" (52), ". . The *mots* fly, and the flies mope on the food" (53). He speaks to his lady with tender and somewhat formulaic but delightful irony: "You, Lise, *contrite*, I never thought to see" (18), or laughs wryly, laughs inside: "My glass I lift at six o'clock, my darling,/As you plotted . . Chinese couples shift in bed" (13), a reference, of course, to the renowned particulars of Oriental lovemaking. He loves to kid his lady about her drinking, and to kid himself—"we four/Locked, crocked together" (33). What the sonnets best accomplish is finally to sing assuredly of joy: "What I love of you/*Inter alia* tingles like a whole good day" (86). The spirit of E. E. Cummings is here.

As with *The Dispossessed* there is an unevenness in the quality of the sonnets as poems. The following, for example, is conventional to the point of being banal: "I feel the summer draining me,/I lean back breathless in an agony/Of charming loss I suffer without moan,/Without my love, or with my love alone" (59). As is rhyming like this: "I grope/ A little in the wind after a hope/For sun before she wakes . . all might be well" (68). But the amount of this kind of writing over the span of the sonnets is relatively small. More difficult to assess is the difference between the sonnets that really work as poems and those that, though they may have outstanding qualities or lines, do not. In any case, style as the primary object of the poem does not characterize the sonnets, for they always have subject and are, moreover, seldom "difficult" in the sense that the poem "The Dispossessed" is difficult. But their technique often shows signs of strain, or tends to be nonfunctional, and thus they have a certain link to Berryman's preoccupation with style, his straining for effect at the price of poem quality. Berryman's typical devices in the sonnets are ellipsis and variations of normal sentence structure. He often omits connectives, such as prepositions, relative pronouns, and conjunctions, and secures an elliptical effect by an omission of punctuation, an omission which when it works creates a functional ambiguity of syntax. His variation of normal sentence structure takes such form as wide separation of a verb from its direct object, sudden interruptions and shifts from one sentence pattern to another, and inversion both for rhythmic effect and

to aid in speeding the movement of the speaker's thoughts. The net intent of such technique, healthily, is better dramatization, and there is, of course, an obvious anticipation of what he is to do some years later. But the questions, as always, is not what technique is used—including devices and conventions as traditional as his Petrarchan rhyme scheme or as modern as rapid shift of association—but whether or not a chosen technique works.

A contrast will serve us well in evaluating Berryman's achievement as a sonneteer. Consider the opening octave of Sonnet 71:

Our Sunday morning when dawn-priests were
    applying
Wafer and wine to the human wound, we laid
Ourselves to cure ourselves down: I'm afraid
Our vestments wanted, but Francis' friends
    were crying
In the nave of pines, sun-satisfied, and flying
Subtle as angels about the barricade
Boughs made over us, deep in a bed half made
Needle-soft, half the sea of our simultaneous
    dying.

Although at first glance this might look fluid and controlled, the opening metaphor is both strained and vague. It functions to set the time of the lovers' action as simultaneous to a communion service, with an obvious ironic contrast between the sacred and the profane, the familiar Donnean paradox that profane love may be sacred. But what precisely is a "dawn-priest"? If merely a priest who gives communion at dawn, then the speaker is forcing us to make an association that offers no more than short literal mileage. Why are the priests "applying" wafer and wine? The word is ill chosen. Why "the human wound"? Such a phrase tells us nothing about the communicants and has a gravity suggesting that the speaker is a prig. Is the tongue, moreover, in some meaningful

JOHN BERRYMAN / 177

sense suggestive of "wound"? Why even bother to say "human" wound? With such a start there is little hope for the poem, but craft gets worse. The device of separating the adverb "down" from its verb "laid" helps the rhythm of the line at the price of creating a dull academicism. By line 3 we are, moreover, scarcely ready to believe that the lovers really have anything wrong with them that needs to be cured. If sin, original or recent, the premise is just too much to accept. In line 4 the reference to "Our vestments" merely belabors a contrast already made. By the time we come to the periphrasis "Francis' friends" for "birds" we suspect—perhaps with a groan—that the speaker is not only a bore but also a sentimentalist, especially if the birds are "crying" tears as well as just crying out, and it is useless to argue that since the birds are "sun-satisfied" the context excludes the suggestion of crying tears since the context is established too late for such exclusion. The phrase "Subtle as angels" is meaningless as description of how the birds are flying, nor is it, even if accepted in some metaphysical way, a phrase to which the speaker has established his right. And then, why does the speaker describe the boughs about which the birds are flying as a "barricade"? The description is arbitrary rather than in relation to the feeling of the presence of some enemy, real or imagined. Finally, the metaphor of the bed, half "Needle-soft" and half "sea," fails, for the two halves do not relate to suggest the total quality of the lovers' experience. Even the final phrase, "simultaneous dying," dying used in the Elizabethan sense of orgasm—with now a groan from English teachers—is too much. Since these are lovers, dare we not assume their simultaneity? At the end of the octave we feel nothing about either the sacred or the profane, and the sestet, which includes such miserable phrases as

"Shivering with delight" and "Careless with sleepy love," is more of the same.

Here by contrast is a Berryman sonnet (9) that works:

Great citadels whereon the gold sun falls
Miss you O Lise sequestered to the West
Which wears you Mayday lily at its breast,
Part and not part, proper to balls and brawls,
Plains, cities, or the yellow shore, not false
Anywhere, free, native and Danishest
Profane and elegant flower,—whom suggest
Frail and not frail, blond rocks and madrigals.

Once in the car (cave of our radical love)
Your darker hair I saw than golden hair
Above your thighs whiter than white-gold hair,
And where the dashboard lit faintly your least
Enlarged scene, O the midnight bloomed . .
    the East
Less gorgeous, wearing you like a long white
    glove!

The general reason why this sonnet works is that the character of the speaker is interesting, not boring, not sentimental, not priggish, but instead honest, tender, sensuous, erotic, realistic, acutely aware, and wittily self-ironic. But there is a touch of circularity in this argument, since the character works because the craft succeeds, and the craft works because the character is well conceived—such paradox is poetry's way. The first line of Sonnet 9 is fatuously conventional and toneless, but the poet immediately establishes a personal tone that frames the impersonality in an ironic way. By line 3 he is calling his love a "Mayday lily," which ordinarily might be fatuously conventional but here has sincerity because it is touched with irony. Lovers, we feel, ought to have a sense of humor, especially about sex, because ironic self-awareness is part of love's delight. In a similar way, the bawdy pun on "balls" in line

4 falls within the frame of the speaker's irony. He earns the right to call his love a "Profane and elegant flower," a phrase which also refers back ironically to the epithet "Mayday lily." By the end of the octave we feel something about the sacred and the profane, something about delight. The sestet becomes its vivid, erotic, profane, and yet humorously sacred example. "O the midnight bloomed."

Such a fine poem as Sonnet 9 represents Berryman's achievement as a sonneteer. Many others of the 115 could be named. As a sample, I would suggest these: 12, 13, 32, 33, 37, 53, 67, 75, 104, and 115. The unevenness in the quality of *Berryman's Sonnets* seems to me patent, though opinion on individual sonnets will naturally vary. What is important is the high quality of those that succeed, which leads us to conclude that a good number of high-quality poems from *The Dispossessed* combine with a good number of high-quality poems from *Berryman's Sonnets* to establish the fact of Berryman's talent, and particularly that talent as it identifies itself in terms of *how it feels* to respond to his world. Such talent is always rare and makes us hope that it will flower into new achievement. It is, however, a talent that is distinguished only in the narrow sense of basic ability. It is a talent that typically carries a poet to a plateau of challenge. The early Berryman, at the not surprising age of approximately forty, had to make a new turn or fall back with the talented nondescript. Turn he did, and with his turn came 456 lines, 57 eight-line stanzas, called *Homage to Mistress Bradstreet.*

Homage is a poem that requires definition. It is basically an interior monologue narrative, with Anne Bradstreet revealing the story of her life in the early colonies. Born Anne Dudley in England in 1612, she married Simon Bradstreet at sixteen, crossed the Atlantic in the *Arbella* in 1630, had the first of her eight children in 1633, became the first woman in America to devote herself to writing poetry, and died in 1672 (her husband became colonial governor of Massachusetts in 1679). But *Homage*, though it functions to tell a story, is primarily concerned with a sensibility, with *how it feels* to be a sensitive individual in a certain kind of world. It is the voice of Anne that we hear, for example in a moment of peace following the delivery of her first child: "Blossomed Sarah, and I/blossom" (21.7–8). Her voice is, however, a voice that we hear only in relationship to the voice of the poet, for the poem opens with the poet rather than Anne as speaker. He imagines her in her grave:

The Governor your husband lived so long
moved you not, restless, waiting for him? Still,
you were a patient woman.—
I seem to see you pause here still:
Sylvester, Quarles, in moments odd you pored
before a fire at, bright eyes on the Lord,
all the children still.
'Simon . .' Simon will listen while you read a
     Song.

Because of the tenderness of the speaker toward his subject, *Homage* immediately defines itself as a poem of personal caring, and the poet takes on the character of the caring self. To this—implying, as it does, that human relation is the ultimate reality—all else, it seems to me, is eventually subordinated. As a poem of personal caring, with consequent emphasis on personal identity, *Homage* also immediately defines itself as a poem distinctly and appealingly modern in subject and in theme. But the personal identity is the *combined* identity of the poet and Anne, the union, if you will, of past and present. Although the voice of the poet opens the poem and thus provides a framing point of view for what follows, the two voices blend, modulate from one to the other, and, though often distinct, are finally one voice, a voice of passion and caring, which is the final identity sought, and an emblem of our common humanity.

This identity—emerging from a technique appropriately called fluid characterization—has to be set forth in terms that seem faithful to the complexity of human experience. To the dramatic immediacy of voice must be added substance, detail. In this respect the first stanza is particularly instructive, and reveals the later Berryman's extraordinary mastery of economy of means—sonnets were good practice. In one stanza is established (1) the character of the poet, his tenderness, his caring, his distinctive tone, (2) the character of Anne, wife, mother, intensely religious person, and would-be poet, and (3) a sense of relationship between them. In fact, it is not going too far to say that the sexual love of the sonnets is transmuted into the poet's caring for Anne, as in the simple and direct "Lie stark,/thy eyes look to me mild" (2.8–3.1), or in the question "How do we/linger, diminished in our lovers' air" (3.4–5). Or as in this explicit expression of the caring theme: "We are on each other's hands/who care" (2.7–8). Moreover, this caring later becomes a love dialogue directly between the poet and Anne, which is to say, a symbolic marriage or consummation of identity. The first stanza introduces the identity of poet as the specific link between the two. In the accurate words of the notes on the poem, Sylvester and Quarles were "her favourite poets; unfortunately." Despite her prolific output, Anne was not much of a poet at all, a fact of which Berryman makes us acutely aware. She is "mistress neither of fiery nor velvet verse" (12.8); her poems are "bald/abstract didactic rime" (12.5–6), and are "proportioned" and "spiritless" (42.6). Through her Berryman seems to be expressing by implication his own fear of not succeeding

as a poet. What it means to be a poet is obviously an important theme of the poem, not, however, in the contemporary mode of self-conscious artiness but rather as an aspect and epitome of what it means to be a person.

Neither the first stanza nor the other examples thus far cited suggest that the language of *Homage* presents us with a problem, but it does. In general terms the problem is, How is the poem to be read? More specifically, the reader encounters a good deal of speech that is stylized or mannered. This is not in itself a fault. On the contrary, it is an acceptable device and even, for both Anne and the poet, an acceptable premise of character. The problem is rather one of degree.

Ciardi refers, for example, to Berryman's eccentricities in *Homage* and observes as chief among them "a constant queer inversion of normal word order." "Can be hope a cloak?" (40.8) asks Anne, and the reader rightly asks why this is not simply, "Can hope be a cloak?" One could argue from the negative and say that the latter, with its lightly accented rapid syllables between two long o's, sounds like doggerel and thus has to be avoided. But when poetry modifies actual speech for the sake of rhythm or meter, it usually manages to retain the quality of speech, as Frost does so beguilingly when his New England Yankee speaks an iambic pentameter that no New England Yankee ever spoke, or as Hopkins does when, to quote Kunitz, "however radical his deflections from the linguistic norm," he "keeps mindful of the natural flow and rhythm of speech, which serves him as his contrapuntal ground." So the question is whether or not the inversion "Can be hope a cloak?" has some relation to a quality of speech or thought that is Anne's. It would, I think, be merely a formal rationalization to say that she is a would-be poet, or even a bad poet, and thus reflects that fact in her mannered speech. But I do not think it merely a formal rationalization to relate this inversion to the meditative quality of her mind. If the short sentence is read very slowly, the inversion functions to heighten its questioning power, whereas this is not true in the doggerel-like noninverted version. My example, to be sure, is rather extreme, and if *Homage* were permeated with such extremes I suspect it would be a freak or at least would break down as a poem. But the following inversions, by contrast, are more representative of this aspect of the language of the poem and even out of context reveal a "contrapuntal ground":

> Out of maize & air
> your body's made, and moves. I summon, see,
> from the centuries it.   (3.1–3)

> Winter than summer worse   (9.1)

> The shawl I pinned
> flaps like a shooting soul
> might in such weather Heaven send (11.2–4)

> Brood I do on myself naked.   (27.4)

> so shorn ought such caresses to us be (30.5)

> Once
> less I was anxious when more passioned to
>   upset
> the mansion & the garden & beauty of God.
>   (49.7–8, 50.1)

The reader's response to such lines depends desperately on how they are read. *Homage* becomes a poem that demands to be read aloud; it requires, moreover, a willingness not only to be in but to participate in a reflective or a meditative mood, to join the perceiving spirit. Whenever it seems not to be reading smoothly, the reader may find that all that is necessary is a change of pace, or a pause (sometimes a short pause, sometimes a very long one), or an accent for emphasis. There is, of course, a limit to how much of this kind of demand a poem may make on us, for a poem must draw us into an imaginative world, not shut us out. The reader's response is finally dependent upon his orientation to a paradox. Every poem stands lifeless on the page until the reader gives it life by interpreting it, and yet every poem stands on the page only with the life that it inherently contains. In *Homage* Berryman has extended the typical twentieth-century shift-of-association device to a stylizing or mannering of speech, the intent of which is to create a new dynamics of language. As Kunitz remarks, "the peculiar energy of language compels attention." In compelling attention the language also succeeds in compelling our sympathetic involvement in character, and all that that implies. In *Homage* Berryman modifies natural rhythms of speech to suggest, which is to say to dramatize, the dynamics of human thought and emotion. In doing so he often sacrifices some but far from all of the quality of natural speech, leading critics to use such terms as "peculiar" and "queer." To this I can only say that today's "peculiar" and "queer" may become tomorrow's standard, though *Homage* is the kind of poem that may require the reader to become an amateur actor to know its rewards.

Critics have tended, I think, to make too much of the language of *Homage* and as a consequence to ignore its structure, which combines with its language and characterization to give it hard dramatic impact. Berryman takes just four stanzas to establish the character of the poet as the caring self, ending with quietly powerful lines that declare the feeling of universal brotherhood poised with an awareness of our mortality (4.2–8). We then hear the voice of Anne, who describes the ocean crossing and early hardships in the New World with cinematographic immediacy—sleet, scurvy, vermin, wigwams, a tidal river, acorns, brackish water. The controlling sensibility is that of a pioneer spirit, as shown in this religious affirmation discreetly couched in lyrical understatement: "Strangers & pilgrims fare we here,/declaring we seek a City" (8.4–5). The word *city* is charged with Biblical echo, "holy city," "city of God," "they of the city shall flourish like grass" (Psalms, 72:16), "Glorious things are spoken of thee, O city" (Psalms, 87:3), "he shall build my city" (Isaiah 45:13). Specifically the reference seems to be to Hebrews 11:13–16: "These all died in faith, not having received the promises but having seen them afar off, and were persuaded of *them,* and embraced *them,* and confessed that they were strangers and pilgrims on the earth. For they that say such things declare plainly that they seek a country. . . . But now they desire a better *country,* that is, an heavenly: wherefore God is not ashamed to be called their God: for he hath prepared for them a city." This is echoed in Anne's own meditation 53: "We must, therefore, be here as strangers and pilgrims, that we may plainly declare that we seek a city above and wait all the days of our appointed time till our change shall come." At this point we should note that in *Homage* Anne speaks from a point of view that both is and is not the poet's point of view. It is not the poet's point of view in the sense that he is specifically a Christian believer. It is his point of view in the sense that his humanistic fervor is a religious phenomenon. The "city" which the poet seeks is, we feel, a heart's union, an existential consciousness of the human reality as it suggests a divine reality; it is a spiritual meaning in life urgently lived as human relationship. Such a comparison and contrast, uniting and yet separating past and present, is integral to the dramatic impact of the poem. This is another aspect of fluid characterization functioning to dramatize the dynamics of human thought and emotion.

At 12:5 the voice of Anne is interrupted by the voice of the poet, and their dialogue continues until 39.4. But the focus continues to be on Anne's description of her experiences and feelings. The distinctive characteristic of that description is that it unites soaring religious and metaphysical concerns with the raw reality of the pioneer experience. Although Anne's final concern as a Puritan woman of the seventeenth century may be for a divine reality, she is also—though the terms are not hers—an existential consciousness in the act of searching for meaning in life. Religion, for her, is not a pat answer to anything. At fourteen she was carnal, and knew it. She states flatly, "Women have gone mad/at twenty-one" (15.7–8). "O love, O love" (18.6), she exclaims, and that love is multifarious in its quality, carnal, erotic, marital (one flesh and one spirit), motherly, religious, universal, what Goethe called eternal womanly. Her consciousness is epitomized now in a long passage on the birth of her first child. It is a time of mixed emotion, of horror combined with joy, of pain and shame, until "it passes the wretched trap whelming and I am me/drencht & powerful, I did it with my body" (20.8, 21.1). Identity: "I am me." Anne—as any psychiatrist would say—is healthily not alienated from her own body. The childbirth becomes her symbol for what it means to be human, the ultimate symbol of the caring self; also, of the continuity of past and present, and of a sense of our mortality and immortality. Everything that she is or could be seems beautifully summarized in a single line: "Mountainous, woman not breaks and will bend" (21.5).

The childbirth passage marks the end of the first third of the poem. The second third is the remainder of the love dialogue between the poet and Anne, with dialogue as dialogue receiving more emphasis and becoming quite explicit. Kunitz—in a reaction parallel to that of Jarrell commenting on an early Berryman poem called "At Chinese Checkers"—feels that it "tends to collapse into bathos somewhat reminiscent of Crashaw's extravagant compounding of religion and sex." He finds that Berryman lapses into the incongruous when the poet interrupts Anne's flights with, for example, such lines as "I miss you, Anne" (25.3), or "I have earned the right to be alone with you" (27.6). Berryman himself says that the latter line belongs to Anne, and we should also notice that it completes a couplet: "A fading world I dust, with fingers new./—I have earned the right to be alone with you." The general point, however, still has to be reckoned with. Kunitz cites, for example, Anne in reply to the poet: "I know./I *want* to take you for my lover" (32.4–5). But this, it seems to me, is to read out of context. Out of context in two senses; first, the immediate, for Anne, as is typical with her, is in a moment of self-recognition: "I am a sobersides; I know./I *want* to take you for my lover." I think too that a long reflective pause, a dramatic turning to the poet, at the end of the first line charges the lines with a quality that is anything but bathos. Secondly, the larger context should not be ignored. When Anne, whom, following the childbirth passage, we know as a woman, not a girl, speaks of such desire, it is not a cliché of romantic youth but an earned truth. What is true, of course, is that such lines as "I *want* to take you for my lover" could be out of a soap opera. In addition to context, the question is one of proportion. A powerful context has to be created; if every other line is a cliché, it never will be. Berryman's use of such lines seems to me distinctly sparing. They fall, I think, well within the framework of the poem's fidelity to the complexity of human experience, a fidelity which, of course, a soap opera never wants to have and never can have.

The dialogue following the childbirth pas-sage functions to unite the poem's two caring selves, a marriage, symbolizing the fact that life finds its meaning in terms of human relationship. This is naturally a complement to rather than a denial of Anne's concern with obedience to the will of God. The last third of the poem is the voice of Anne except for the final three stanzas, in which the poet says his farewell. Anne continues her story, but the tones of passion, appropriately, subside. Her spirit in these last stanzas is essentially one of reconciliation. "I lie, & endure, & wonder" (51.3). We have the sense of reflecting on a whole life and all that it has meant and could mean. When the poet says farewell, we, I think, say it too. "I must pretend to leave you" (56.1). The experience of the poem has, finally, been the experience of love:

>   still
> Love has no body and presides the sun,
> and elfs from silence melody. I run.
> Hover, utter, still
> a sourcing   whom my lost candle like the
>   firefly loves.
>
>   (57.4–8)

And so with *Homage to Mistress Bradstreet* the early Berryman becomes the later Berryman. The move is made, at approximately the age of forty, from talent to talent best applied. With *Homage* Berryman achieves poetic maturity and becomes a poet of the first rank. The process harkens back to, of all places, his short stories. *Homage,* after all, is a modern narrative, and Berryman has the narrative bent. In his short stories, moreover, he uses poetic language, and in *Homage* he is language's daring master. In *Homage* he combines in narrative form the vivid detail of American history with the sensibility of the present. But in the short stories he does not live up to his own excellent dictum: "Purity of feeling, selflessness of feeling, is the achievement of maturity," for in the short stories he remains an academic personage. But in *Homage* he achieves purity and selflessness of feeling, he creates the caring self, paradoxically retaining his academic intelligence while yet losing it. In *Homage* he is not expository, but dramatic. And in *Homage* he combines the best elements of his early self. His language is original and his musicality, his sound, is not less than marvelous. He has depth of feeling, passion, and humane concern, combined, all, in an authentic voice, or voices, with a fidelity to the complexity of human experience that only really mature poets can show. In *Homage* he is, moreover, not really "difficult," as he is in a number of his early poems, though *Homage* requires a certain careful attention if the reader is to feel its power. In American poetry following World War II, only two long poems emerge as great. Roethke's "North American Sequence" is one, and *Homage* is the other. Allen Ginsberg's "Howl" would be a third except for the fact that it is based on a false premise, that the poet, as he says in the first line of the poem, saw the best minds of his generation destroyed by madness, whereas in fact no best minds in any sense are then forthcoming, despite the poet's elaborate and passionate effort to describe them. But from premise to dramatic power Berryman in *Homage* and Roethke in "North American Sequence" are true. With *Homage* Berryman is indelible on the American scene.

The inevitable question of what was to follow *Homage* was answered eight years later by the Pulitzer Prize-winning *77 Dream Songs,* the first installment, Parts I, II, and III, of the very long poem called "The Dream Songs," and four years after that by *His Toy, His Dream, His Rest,* the second and final install-ment, Parts IV–VII. The total number of Dream Songs, each one eighteen lines long, is 385, thus making a poem of 6930 lines, or nearly twice the length of *Hamlet*. The arithmetic alone prompts the question, Does it all hang together? Is it finally a poem in the ideal sense of a final imaginative coherence? Does it have a single dramatic impact similar to that of *Homage*? The answer is flatly no. In plain terms, it lacks plot, either traditional or associative. In fact from an artistic point of view the Dream Songs parallel the sonnets. It is altogether appropriate that they are collected and numbered as a single poem, for as a sequence they are distinctly homogeneous, but this is not the same as to say that they have an organic structure (plot in its ultimate sense). What distinguishes them from the sonnets, however, is the range and quality of their imaginative power. They are even in their maturity, their purity and selflessness of feeling, in some ways an achievement beyond *Homage,* which is no light compliment. But they are not a poem that takes the logical step beyond *Homage,* the creation of a new masterpiece with *Homage*'s exciting singleness of effect and yet in every way deeper and richer.

By what standard, then, are we to judge Berryman? If we compare "The Dream Songs" as poetic structure to *Hamlet*—that is, to any impressively long and tightly knit poetic work recognized as great—"The Dream Songs" comes off a poor second. We may ask whether or not Berryman's flaws fall reasonably within the framework of a distinguished achievement. For "The Dream Songs" the answer would, I believe, be yes, not merely because many of them are brilliantly successful as individual poems but, more important, because there is a cumulative impact, a wholeness that is distinctly short of a fully realized organic structure and yet participates in some of the final effect that organic structure is known to yield. I would say that Berryman made a serious mistake in not culling the Dream Songs more carefully, in not ruthlessly discarding those that are inferior. But even if this were done, we would end by talking about cumulative impact as opposed to organic structure.

Not that such a matter as judging a poem as long and complex as this will be settled in a day, for critics may well be puzzling over it for years to come. But even Berryman himself attests to the crucial nature of the problem of its structure: ". . . so to begin Book VII/ or to design, out of its hotspur materials,/its ultimate structure/whereon will critics browse at large . . ." (293). But this is, I think, essentially Berryman the academic man—and a very good one at that—assuring himself of success merely by recognizing the existence of the problem. His assertion about structure doubtless relates to his terrible unrest over the possibility that he might not succeed wholly, in final terms, as a poet. In a word, he hungers for fame, "his terrible cry/not to forget his name" (266). This all too human hunger relates, in turn, to the depths of his own personal insecurities, as might be suggested, for example, by his repeated references to mere sexual conquests, which imply great insecurity and immaturity of personality, not that he does not recognize, simultaneously, the grief of it all and seek, as always, a mature understanding of it. Put another way, there is a strong element of defensiveness in his personality, but since this is coupled with piercing honesty he emerges as a poet who delves into life and takes us with him rather than yielding to what the critic would come to judge as tired formulas.

At the heart of the Dream Songs is the character of Henry, who, according to Berryman, "refers to himself as 'I,' 'he,' and 'you,' so that the various parts of his identity are fluid. They slide, and the reader is made to guess who is talking to whom." In a somewhat defensive note to *His Toy, His Dream, His Rest* he adds that the poem "is essentially about an imaginary character (not the poet, not me) named Henry, a white American in early middle age sometimes in blackface, who has suffered an irreversible loss. . . ." This raises the important question of how imaginary is Henry and how much the real-life John Berryman he is. This in turn raises another question, which is that of the relationship between *77 Dream Songs* and *His Toy, His Dream, His Rest*. The answer to this latter question, in general terms, is that "The Dream Songs" becomes increasingly autobiographical. But its more specific terms involve an aspect of technique, a description of which is necessary to an understanding of the relationship between imaginary Henry and the real-life poet.

In technique *77 Dream Songs* is clearly an extension or variant of *Homage,* with a movement, however, from a relatively ordered consciousness, Anne's, to a relatively disordered (dream) consciousness, Henry's. But we immediately confront the problem of the relationship between Henry's life as reality and his life as dream. It is a problem that prompts recall of Jarrell's comment, "Doing things in a style all its own sometimes seems the primary object of the poem, and its subject gets a rather spasmodic treatment." *77 Dream Songs* certainly shows us a style (mainly Henry's way of speaking) all its own and, like the sonnets, has a clear subject, Henry's, or more broadly the modern world. Nevertheless, these Dream Songs not only are difficult but remain difficult in spite of the reader's sympathetic acceptance of their dramatic situation, of their intent, and of their technique, whereas *Homage* by contrast does not remain difficult for long. What, then, is the best way to define the problem of these Dream Songs remaining difficult? Frederick Seidel calls it withdrawing "into abstraction" and "disguised personal allusion," but it is, I think, more than both of these things. It is essentially what Edmund Wilson was talking about when he made this comment in *Axel's Castle* on Symbolism: ". . . what the symbols of Symbolism really were, were metaphors detached from their subjects—for one cannot, beyond a certain point, in poetry, merely enjoy color and sound for their own sake: one has to guess what the images are being applied to." In *77 Dream Songs* Berryman persistently takes the risk of detaching metaphor, broadly construed, from subject. That he is talking about psychic reality does not change this fact. The strange thing is that any poem in the volume may seem to have the quality of simultaneously being a metaphor detached from its subject and yet realizing its subject, giving it a treatment that could not be called spasmodic. If, on the whole, the first 77 Dream Songs emerged as metaphors detached from their subjects they would be incomprehensible and fail as poems. If, on the whole, they emerged as metaphors that fully realized their subjects (and as a structure created a world) they would probably constitute the first installment of the finest long poem in the twentieth century. Instead they tend to exist in a perilous balance which puts an extraordinary demand on the reader and holds both frustration and reward.

But the Dream Songs of *His Toy, His Dream, His Rest*, as if in acknowledgment of this problem and in a desire to do something about it, tend to drop the extraordinary demand and move in the opposite direction, often becoming such flat and explicit statement that a child, or at least a young adult, could hardly

mistake their meaning, their clarity as metaphor in a broad sense. Style, in other words, is distinctly no longer the primary object of the poem. Louise Bogan could never use the phrase "this desperate artificiality" in reference to *His Toy, His Dream, His Rest* as she did with *77 Dream Songs*. What this all means in simple terms is that "The Dream Songs" grows increasingly and plainly autobiographical, though aspects of the earlier technique do persist. We become, that is, increasingly aware that Henry is indeed John Berryman struggling with his own life, with the whole problem, human, spiritual, call it what you will, of his own identity. We become increasingly aware that Henry is an imaginary character simply in the sense of serving as an alter ego, a device whereby the poet may look at himself, talk about himself, talk to himself, and be a multifarious personality. But, just as with the early Berryman, it is not an egocentric emphasis but rather a question of "how I feel" (120) in the sense of how a sensitive individual feels in response to his own psyche and to the world he inhabits. Henry is John Berryman saying, Here I am as a man, as the particular implies the universal. In this he succeeds. Henry is interesting. He has sheer interestingness, which is, of course, not to say that every Dream Song succeeds by this standard. That the poetic technique of "The Dream Songs" tends to shift from *77 Dream Songs* to *His Toy, His Dream, His Rest* is, it seems to me, a weakness, and this is true despite the flexibility gained by the device of fluid characterization. For a shift in technique must be functional, must be, in fact, part of the organic character of the poem as a structure. Henry, in sum, is a brilliant but insufficient unifying device. The question of how imaginary he is, and of how much the real-life John Berryman he is, is important only insofar as the poem creates a nonfunctional tension between the two. Who would object if Henry were wholly imaginary and one were hardly able to see or to care about a reference to the real-life John Berryman in the poem? Who would object if Berryman deliberately wrote an autobiographical and perhaps even a confessional poem? What we care about is only that the poem exists beautifully as a poem, and yet in the final analysis the device *is* the poem, and so it is unsettling to lose our sense of the fictional Henry in favor of the quasi-fictional Berryman.

In *77 Dream Songs* Henry is essentially a picaresque hero in the ironic mode, a comic type who begins as a stereotype from vaudeville and ends as distinct in his humanity and suffering. He is described as "a human American man" (13), "free, black & forty-one" (40), a man whose basic problem is clearly to bear the slings and arrows of outrageous fortune, particularly the outrageous fortune of being black in white America, though fluid characterization does enable us to accept Berryman's later statement that Henry is white, which is to say, for dramatic purposes, a white man who imagines how it feels to be black. Henry is described, often in an ironic context, by such words as *bewildered, horrible, desolate, bitter, industrious, affable, subtle, somber, savage*, and *seedy*. Or in a somewhat more extended way: "hopeless inextricable lust, Henry's fate" (6), "with his plights & gripes/ as bad as achilles" (14), and "savage and thoughtful/surviving Henry" (75). The words used to describe him in *His Toy, His Dream, His Rest* are quite consistent with those found in *77 Dream Songs*: *disordered, obsessed, stricken, sad, wilful, sympathetic, lively, miserable, impenetrable, mortal, joyous, perishable, anarchic, apoplectic*, and *edgy*. But in *77 Dream Songs*, although we have a visual, a concrete sense of what he is, he is not detailed

in the sense that Mistress Bradstreet is detailed. When we finish *Homage* we can recall the facts of a biography, but when we finish *77 Dream Songs* we can recall only the existence of a man. The Henry of *77 Dream Songs* is a character in a mode perhaps best described as impressionistic or mildly surrealistic. The Henry of *His Toy, His Dream, His Rest* is in the realistic mode. Although there is certainly a strain of the picaresque hero in the later Henry, Henry *as* picaresque hero gives way to the quasi-fictional John Berryman. There is a great deal of consistency in this, but significant inconsistency too.

The complexity of the problem of responding to "The Dream Songs" as a whole poem inheres, finally, in the relationship between the conception of the character of Henry and the degree of success of the individual Dream Song. It will be instructive to select a fairly representative Dream Song from *77 Dream Songs* for commentary, and then to put it next to a fairly representative autobiographical passage from *His Toy, His Dream, His Rest*. Here is Dream Song 76, "Henry's Confession":

Nothin very bad happen to me lately.
How you explain that?—I explain that, Mr.
    Bones,
terms o' your bafflin odd sobriety.
Sober as man can get, no girls, no telephones,
what could happen bad to Mr. Bones?
—*If* life is a handkerchief sandwich,

in a modesty of death I join my father
who dared so long agone leave me.
A bullet on a concrete stoop
close by a smothering southern sea
spreadeagled on an island, by my knee.
—You is from hunger, Mr. Bones,

I offers you this handkerchief, now set
your left foot by my right foot,

shoulder to shoulder, all that jazz,
arm in arm, by the beautiful sea,
hum a little, Mr. Bones.
—I saw nobody coming, so I went instead.

For purposes of analysis we can disregard the fact that the character of Henry has been previously defined and ask how this poem handles the key problem of characterization. It opens with Negro dialect, the voice of Henry, who is speaking with Mr. Bones, a friend, a vaudeville stereotype, an alter ego, a mere name suggesting death. Both characters are comic, with the comedy springing from Henry's premise that he normally expects something very bad to happen to him every day. We are at once in the world of the vaudeville skit. It is a charming and disarming world, and in its way a fit place to discuss the nature of man. But at the end of the first stanza the voice of Henry—and the vaudeville skit—is dropped, and the poet's voice enters. The handkerchief sandwich motif at the end of the first stanza continues the vaudeville joke but some of the tone of the joke is abandoned. There is nothing particularly funny in the second stanza about the death of a father or a bullet on a stoop, especially if it is read as a reference to the suicide of Berryman's father. But at the end of the second stanza we return to the voice of Henry, though the poet is also speaking the line, "You is from hunger, Mr. Bones." In the first line of the third stanza we return to the voice of Henry in his conversation with Mr. Bones, but the voice that follows seems to be more that of the poet than that of Henry, and the vaudeville humor is but slightly sustained. But if the poem is to realize its subject, which I take to be man's mortality or his isolation in the universe, then the handkerchief and the sea must become unifying symbols, must take us into the subject. This they do not do in a complete way. A fuller situation for the handkerchief offering is needed, and the relationship between the popular song phrase "by the beautiful sea" and "a smothering southern sea" is not at all clear—metaphor is detached from its subject. Part of the problem is that the reference to "a smothering southern sea" (with *bullet, stoop, island,* and *knee*) is itself vague. The referent of lines 9–11 is too personal to the speaker to have universal meaning. The "smothering southern sea" happens to be the Gulf of Mexico, but knowledge of this fact does not improve the poem as a poem. And yet the poem as a whole does have singleness of effect. ". . . hum a little, Mr. Bones" becomes Henry's sprightly understatement, right from a vaudeville skit, of self-persuasion and universal affirmation, not to mention the suggestion of darker agony as we hear the line as the poet's voice, or one could say a non-vaudevillian Henry. And the last line seems particularly effective as a summary of the human condition that the poem has been defining: "I saw nobody coming, so I went instead."

Consider now these lines from Dream Song 143 on the subject of the father's suicide:

He was going to swim out, with me, forevers,
and a swimmer strong he was in the phosphor-
            escent Gulf,
but he decided on lead.

That mad drive wiped out my childhood.

It might aid our appreciation of these lines to recall the biographical fact that Berryman's father had threatened to drown himself and John with him, but the lines stand well as they are. What is being said is perfectly plain, and this plainness, this direct treatment of subject, is typical of *His Toy, His Dream, His Rest.* There are poems in *77 Dream Songs* that also treat subject directly—such as the rather conventional and quite unsuccessful 18, "A Strut for Roethke," the perfectly successful 35, "MLA," and the moving 37–39, "Three around the Old Gentleman," honoring Robert Frost—but these are more the exception than the rule.

What we have in *His Toy, His Dream, His Rest,* then, is the mature Berryman grappling in a straightforward way with the meaning of his life. One is prompted to recall the dictum of F. Scott Fitzgerald that if you begin with an individual you create a type, but if you begin with a type you create nothing. Berryman sees himself as a dying man, "in love with life/which has produced this wreck" (283). With a discreet sense of mortality he affirms his individual dignity and worth: "If the dream was small/it was my dream also, Henry's" (132). The life he looks back on is one full of wives and rages, though with typical humor he comments, "The lust-quest seems in this case to be over" (163). Though often angry and protesting, he celebrates many things, a democratic society, the sheer mystery of love, the birth of his daughter, the success of his third marriage, autumn, which seems so much to be an American season and "comes to us as a prize/to rouse us toward our fate" (385), his old friends, particularly, and elegiacally, Delmore Schwartz, the poet's ideal of perfection, "to craft better" (279), anything and everything which out of suffering he can emerge to affirm.

Taken as a whole the Dream Songs are a panoramic meditation on life and death. The title of the second volume sums them up best of all. His toy is life as a game we play (and the stakes are not less than everything), his dream is life in its psychic aspects and the poet's goal of fame, and his rest is an infinite sense of man's mortality and immortality, and finally death itself. He proclaims the value of life as a thing lived: "No, I want rest here, neither below nor above" (256), and we believe him when in Dream Song 83 he writes, "I know immense/troubles & wonders to their secret curse."

Selected Bibliography

WORKS OF JOHN BERRYMAN

POETRY
Twenty poems in *Five Young American Poets.* Norfolk, Conn.: New Directions, 1940.
Poems. Norfolk, Conn.: New Directions, 1942.
The Dispossessed. New York: William Sloane Associates, 1948.
Homage to Mistress Bradstreet. New York: Farrar, Straus and Cudahy, 1956.
His Thought Made Pockets & the Plane Buckt. Pawlet, Vt.: C. Fredericks, 1958.
77 Dream Songs. New York: Farrar, Straus and Giroux, 1964.
Berryman's Sonnets. New York: Farrar, Straus and Giroux, 1967.
Short Poems. New York: Farrar, Straus and Giroux, 1967.
His Toy, His Dream, His Rest. New York: Farrar, Straus and Giroux, 1968.
Love and Fame. New York: Farrar, Straus and Giroux, 1970.
Delusions, etc. New York: Farrar, Straus and Giroux, 1972.

PROSE
"The Imaginary Jew," *Kenyon Review,* 7:529–39 (Autumn 1945).
"The Lovers," *Kenyon Review,* 7:1-11 (Winter 1945). (Reprinted in *The Best American Short Stories 1946,* edited by Martha Foley. Boston: Houghton Mifflin, 1946.)
"Young Poets Dead," *Sewanee Review,* 55:504-14 (July-September 1947).
"The Poetry of Ezra Pound," *Partisan Review,* 16:377-94 (April 1949).
Stephen Crane. New York: William Sloane Asso-

ciates, 1950. (Reprinted in 1962 as a Meridian paperback with an additional preface.)

"Shakespeare at Thirty," *Hudson Review,* 6:175-203 (Summer 1953).

"The Long Way to MacDiarmid," *Poetry,* 88:52-61 (April 1956).

"Spender: The Poet as Critic," *New Republic,* 148:19-20 (June 29, 1963).

"Despondency and Madness" (on Robert Lowell's "Skunk Hour"), in *The Contemporary Poet as Artist and Critic,* edited by Anthony Ostroff. Boston: Little, Brown, 1964. Pp. 99-106.

"One Answer to a Question," *Shenandoah,* 17:67-76 (Autumn 1965).

REVIEWS AND CRITICAL STUDIES

Blum, Morgan. "Berryman as Biographer, Stephen Crane as Poet," *Poetry,* 78:298-307 (August 1951).

Bogan, Louise. "Verse," *New Yorker,* 40:242-43 (November 7, 1964).

Brinnin, John Malcolm. Review of *77 Dream Songs, New York Times Book Review,* August 23, 1964, p. 5.

Carruth, Hayden. "Love, Art and Money," *Nation,* 211:437-38 (November 2, 1970).

Ciardi, John. "The Researched Mistress," *Saturday Review,* 40:36-37 (March 23, 1957).

Connelly, Kenneth. "Henry Pussycat, He Come Home Good," *Yale Review,* 58:419-27 (Spring 1969).

Cott, Jonathan. "Theodore Roethke and John Berryman: Two Dream Poets," in *On Contemporary Literature,* edited by Richard Kostelanetz. New York: Avon Books, 1964. Pp. 520-31.

Eberhart, Richard. "Song of the Nerves," *Poetry,* 73:43-45 (October 1948).

Evans, Arthur, and Catherine Evans. "Pieter Bruegel and John Berryman: Two Winter Landscapes," *Texas Studies in Literature and Language,* 5:310-18 (Autumn 1963).

Fitts, Dudley. Review of *The Dispossessed, New York Times Book Review,* June 20, 1948, p. 4.

Holmes, John. Review of *Homage to Mistress Bradstreet, New York Times Book Review,* September 30, 1956, p. 18.

Howard, Jane. "Whiskey and Ink, Whiskey and Ink," *Life,* 63:67-76 (July 21, 1967).

Jarrell, Randall. Review of *The Dispossessed, Nation,* 167:80-81 (July 17, 1948).

Kessler, Jascha. "The Caged Sybil," *Saturday Review,* 51:34-35 (December 14, 1968).

Kunitz, Stanley. "No Middle Flight," *Poetry,* 90:244-49 (July 1957).

Meredith, William. "Henry Tasting All the Secret Bits of Life: Berryman's 'Dream Songs,' " *Wisconsin Studies in Contemporary Literature,* 6:27-33 (Winter–Spring 1965).

Rosenthal, M. L. "The Couch and Poetic Insight," *Reporter,* 32:53-54 (March 25, 1965).

————. *The New Poets: American and British Poetry since World War II.* New York: Oxford University Press, 1967. Pp. 118-30.

Seidel, Frederick. "Berryman's Dream Songs," *Poetry,* 105:257-59 (January 1965).

Shapiro, Karl. "Major Poets of the Ex-English Language," *Washington Post Book World,* January 26, 1969, p. 4.

—WILLIAM J. MARTZ

Ambrose Bierce

1842-1914?

MANY know him, but no one knows very much about him. This might have been said of Ambrose Bierce in his own time, and it can be said with as much justice today. Bierce remains an enigmatic figure; most of what has been recorded about the man mingles fact and legend. Very little has been written about his work, though his stories are frequently carried in anthologies. Most critical judgment has dealt in easy generalities that fit only a handful of his stories and perpetuate the hasty opinions formulated by his usually hostile fellow journalists.

The legends that circulated in his lifetime, abetted by his own reticence, add up to a portrait of a satyr organizing midnight graveyard revels, a misanthrope pessimistically at odds with all mankind, a bitter adversary of social progress, a demanding friend and a deadly enemy. In his writing, the legend would have it, he added his own sardonic flavor to the Gothic brew he inherited from Edgar Allan Poe.

The legends and myths persist, and in them there is a portion of truth. He was a writer of his time, sharing similar formative experiences with such a figure as Mark Twain. But he set himself stubbornly against the literary currents of local color and realism. He remained out-side the mainstream of American letters and cultivated an eccentric taste for the bizarre. His reputation after his death seemed about to be submerged by the rising tide of naturalism in fiction. Literary developments since then have taken such a turn, however, that Bierce now seems a prophetic writer. Many of the techniques developed by Bierce anticipate those employed by such writers as Conrad Aiken, Ernest Hemingway, Nathanael West, and William Faulkner, to name only the major ones. Even more contemporary writers like Flannery O'Connor, Robert Penn Warren, and Carson McCullers reflect similarities that bring Bierce closer to the mainstream of American letters than was thought in his own time. We must assign him a minor role in literary history, but that role grows larger as the tradition of the grotesque develops in the twentieth century. It is now possible to see Bierce as a writer who has had some influence upon the course of American literature.

Ambrose Gwinett Bierce was born June 24, 1842, in Meigs County, Ohio, the tenth child of Marcus and Laura Bierce. Four years later the family moved to Walnut Creek Settlement, three miles south of Warsaw, Indiana, where Ambrose grew up. One is tempted to say that he passed an uneventful childhood within an undistinguished family, very much like their neighbors on that rural frontier. But no childhood is really uneventful. And no one can quite call a family ordinary that gave each of thirteen children a name beginning with the letter "A."

The Western Reserve was an outpost of puritanism, and Bierce's parents were piously given to much Bible reading and attendance revivals. The shade of Calvin had been brought from New England and hovered over the household. It was undoubtedly this heritage Bierce recalled in one of his satiric parodies:

> My country, 'tis of thee,
> Sweet land of felony,
>   Of thee I sing—
> Land where my father fried
> Young witches and applied
> Whips to the Quaker's hide
>   And made him spring.

The father, Marcus Aurelius Bierce, was a shadowy, retiring figure who preferred books to plowing. His chief claim to local fame seems to have been owning the largest library thereabouts. To earn this distinction, only a modest collection was needed. He appears to have had considerable native intelligence and rather cultivated tastes, but lacked the ambition and application to do more than scrape a poor living from eighty acres. It was Laura, the mother, who, with a Bible in one hand and a switch in the other, ruled the household.

An uncle, General Lucius Verus Bierce, a year or two younger than Marcus, was the family hero. The two brothers had gone from Connecticut to Ohio together as young men. Marcus Aurelius went equipped with a somber disposition and soon acquired hostages to fortune in the form of a bride and the beginning of a large family. Lucius went equipped with a flamboyant personality and a fifth of a quarter of a dollar in the "cut" money of the day. Marcus dragged his expanding brood from farm to farm, each a little less prosperous than the last. Lucius promoted his way through Ohio University, studied law, and became the leading citizen and mayor of Akron. When Ambrose was growing up in Indiana the family from time to time appealed to Uncle Lucius for help; it was he who staked the seventeen-year-old boy to a year at the Kentucky Military Institute to "straighten him out."

Ambrose left home when he was fifteen. From then on he returned only to visit. His first removal was three miles to the town of Warsaw, where he roomed and boarded with the editor of a newly established paper, the *Northern Indianan*. Ambrose remained there as a printer's devil for two years. Legend has it that he left in an argument over an unjust accusation of theft. Whatever the circumstances, the family was concerned enough to accept Uncle Lucius' solution, a term at military school. The discipline and training gave Ambrose an advantage in his later army career. At the end of this schooling he went to Elkhart and worked for a year in a combination store and café, waiting on table, clerking, and sweeping floors. During this period he seems first to have shown a little sociability—by courting a young lady named Bernie Wright. When the Civil War broke out, he was among the first to enlist as private in the Ninth Regiment, Indiana Volunteers.

Bierce rarely discussed his early years in Indiana, and when he did he shuddered in remembering the grinding poverty, squalor, insularity, and ignorance. He apparently had no affection for any members of his family except Albert, his next older brother, who followed him to California. Bierce's attitude toward the scenes of his early years seems best summed up in lines he eventually wrote in the

Wasp as a Bierce-bucolic parody of "The Old Oaken Bucket":

With what anguish of mind I remember my
    childhood,
    Recalled in the light of a knowledge since
        gained;
The malarious farm, the wet, fungus grown
    wildwood,
    The chills then contracted that since have
        remained.
The scum-covered duck pond, the pigstye close
    by it,
    The ditch where the sour-smelling house
        drainage fell,
The damp, shaded dwelling, the foul barnyard
    nigh it . . .

Apart from a little formal schooling, Bierce's education proceeded from an early taste for reading first acquired in his father's library. The habit remained with him all his life. Equally important was his experience as a printer. The printshop and the country newspaper were the Yale and Harvard of many a nineteenth-century writer. Like William Dean Howells and Samuel Clemens, Bierce developed his love of words, accurately and effectively used, while setting type. And undoubtedly this early experience led to his long career as a journalist.

Bierce was precocious in his rebellion against the oppressive intellectual atmosphere of the community. Biographers with a Freudian bias might speculate upon the extent to which boyhood hostilities were acted out in the writer's numerous stories involving patricide and matricide. Such speculation is fruitless; we do not have enough reliable evidence to support a detailed psychological portrait. For example, Bierce supposedly told his publisher Walter Neale that his first real love affair, though not his first "passage at arms," was at the age of fifteen. This would have been during his apprentice years in Warsaw. His clandestine affair was with "a woman of broad culture . . . well past seventy . . . still physically attractive, even at her great age." The relationship lasted for some time and with her he frequently talked about literature and the arts. One hardly knows how to evaluate such testimony. Bierce was not a liar and discreetly managed his conquests, but we have no corroboration of this alleged confidence. At any rate, this "evidence" is typical of the bits that make up the Bierce legend.

The Civil War opened another chapter important in Bierce's early experiences. He was proud of his service in the Union Army, though he seems not to have chosen sides on the basis of issues or principle. He served with distinction and was profoundly impressed by what he saw, for the theme of war runs throughout his life and writing up to his death in 1914 (?) during the revolution in Mexico.

His first enlistment ended after a brief summer of campaigning in West Virgina. The Ninth returned to muster out and reorganize. Bierce, who had just passed his nineteenth birthday, re-enlisted and became a sergeant. By the time his unit returned to action that winter, he was sergeant-major. His outfit was assigned to General W. B. Hazen's brigade. He wrote home admiringly about his commander, a regular army officer with a testy, caloric temper. Hazen was a fearless and brilliant tactical leader, constantly at odds with higher authority. Upon this commander's conduct Bierce doubtless modeled much of his own. In the winter of 1862–63 he received a battlefield commission, and soon afterwards he became a first lieutenant, assigned to Hazen's staff as acting topographic officer.

He followed Hazen through Shiloh, Chickamauga, and the siege of Chattanooga; at Kennesaw Mountain he was wounded in the head. Several times he was cited for bravery. In the course of three years he had one furlough, during which he became engaged to Bernie Wright. His letters addressed her as "Fatima" and were signed "Brady." Curiously he wrote just as often, and in terms just as affectionate, to her sister. When he came home on leave after being wounded, his engagement was broken. He felt that he had been jilted; apparently Miss Bernie had been cool for some time and was tired of his jealous demands. Returning to duty, he was assigned to the staff of General Sam Beatty. Within a few months he applied for a discharge, which he received in January 1865.

He immediately signed on as a federal agency aide to track down the confiscated Confederate cotton that kept disappearing. His duties, though primarily in Alabama, sometimes took him to New Orleans and once even Panama. The job was occasionally dangerous; more than one colleague was beaten, and now and then one lost his life. A Yankee was not regarded as a welcome ambassador in the deep South, especially when his mission was taking cotton away from its "rightful owners." Bierce tells about this part of his life in "Down in Alabam'." The period came to a close when he was offered a chance to accompany General Hazen on a mapping and inspecting expedition through the Far West.

In the early summer of 1866 Bierce joined the expedition at Omaha after applying for a commission as captain. He described the trip later in his essay "Across the Plains." The group moved on from Nebraska to Montana through hostile Indian territory. At Fort Smith they received orders to return by way of Salt Lake City, San Francisco, and Panama. Hazen, interpreting the orders freely in his usual fashion, did not take the most direct route, but continued with his own plans. Bierce called him "my commander and my friend, my master in the art of war." He characterized the

general in one sentence: "He was aggressive, arrogant, tyrannical, honorable, truthful, courageous—a skillful soldier, a faithful friend and one of the most exasperating of men." He might have applied the description to himself. Like Hazen, the mature Bierce also had a vibrant personality that attracted a hero-worshiping crowd of young admirers.

When the expedition finally reached San Francisco, Bierce found there his commission from the War Department. To his disappointment it was for second lieutenant. He immediately resigned and abandoned any further hope of a military career, though he later accepted the brevet rank of major. Deciding to remain in San Francisco, he became a watchman at the United States Mint. He was twenty-four when he arrived, and San Francisco remained the center of his career for most of his life thereafter, although he lived very little in the city itself.

Bierce soon revived his early literary ambitions and began contributing poems and essays to the local papers. In 1868 he joined the staff of the *News-Letter* and within a few months became the editor and wrote a column, the "Town Crier." Mark Twain had left San Francisco for the East only a few months before Bierce's arrival, but the rest of the literary bohemian crowd remained, and Bierce soon took his place as a worthy bibber and yarn swapper. Chief among them was Bret Harte, but there were also Ina Coolbrith, Joaquin Miller, James Bowman, Charles Warren Stoddard, and Prentice Mulford.

Bierce's mentor, whom he replaced as editor on the paper, was James T. Watkins. Bierce was an apt pupil and quickly learned the newspaper business, but more important he looked up to Watkins as "my master in variety of knowledge, definition of thought and charm of style . . . among Americans incomparable and supreme." He wrote this tribute years later, but it seems to have been an accurate reflection of the young Bierce's admiration for the older man. Watkins recognized a fellow cynic and took Bierce under his wing, introducing him to Swift, Voltaire, Thackeray, and Poe. It is not an exaggeration to say that Bierce's views on literature were substantially taken over from Watkins' own prejudices.

Bierce continued to contribute poems, essays, and stories to various publications like the *Californian* and the new *Overland*. But chiefly he was making a name for himself locally in the rough-and-tumble personal journalism characteristic of the West. Within a couple of years he had earned the title of wickedest man in San Francisco. Bierce was ready to take on any person he suspected of sham, hypocrisy, or deceit. By his standards this included most public figures, and many of them felt the sting of his satire. This freewheeling style of journalism had obvious origins in the frontier brand of tall-tale humor. Here, for example, is an item from his "Town Crier" column for September 25, 1869: "The Oaklanders report that they were favored with an earthquake last Monday. It was only a young one that got lost in the foothills last October. Messrs. Rhodes and Stewart happened to be out there hunting quail and writing poetry, and seeing it lying round laid hold of its tail, and got into a row for the possession of it. . . ."

The column was made up of short pieces. The following excerpts strike a good average, showing how he began each of the paragraph items:

Charles De Young, of the *Chronicle,* is "a liar, a scoundrel and, perhaps"—indeed quite probably—"a coward."

The Nicholson pavement is still being laid down upon divers of our streets. Will some one kindly inform us what private arrangement the supervisors have with the company? Twenty-eight cents per superficial foot leaves a handsome profit, and it is useless to attempt to convince us that it all goes to the contractors. . . .

An Episcopal clergyman in New York is endeavoring to prove that there are no essential points of difference between the Catholic and Protestant churches. Nor is there; except in the trifling matter of doctrine.

"The best bond is a man's unsullied reputation."—*Call.* [Yes, but how the deuce can he have one in a city that boasts six daily newspapers, averaging three columns of local matter each? The thing is impossible.]

The Great Incohonee is the title of one of the chiefs of the Order of Red Men. As *in* is a negative prefix, in what kind of a fix is this individual?

Bierce's targets for satire, sarcasm, and invective ranged over the personality and habits of journalists, officials, ministers, and all figures in public life. His subjects most often were religion, politics, and public immorality. This mixture was a popular one, and, although he might tread upon various toes, his column was avidly read, even by those whom he abused.

Bierce's personal and work habits were somewhat unorthodox even for the bohemian crowd he ran with. Recurrent bouts of asthma throughout his life convinced him that he could not sleep at normal hours. Even after convivial early-evening dinners and sprees he would begin writing at midnight and would go to bed about six in the morning. His usual residence was outside the city in a warmer, drier climate. At various times during his California days he lived in San Rafael, St. Helena, Angwin, Auburn, Oakland, Sunol, Berkeley, and Los Gatos. In San Rafael he met Mollie Day and surprised his companions by marrying her in December 1871.

Mollie was the attractive only daughter of a prosperous Forty-Niner. Her domineering mother had higher ambitions for her than marriage to a poor journalist with a wicked reputation, but Mollie for once prevailed. Father Day was rarely at home. From the gold mine he was currently supervising he sent his blessing and the gift of a honeymoon trip to Europe. Here was an opportunity for Bierce to make a name for himself beyond the limits of San Francisco. Mark Twain and Bret Harte only a year or two earlier had become enormously popular in the East. Harte and Joaquin Miller were now the idols of London. So he set off to England to make his literary fortune.

But Bierce was not like Twain, Harte, and Miller in being shrewdly able to capitalize upon the far western vogue. He coveted the polish of literary respectability. With aristocratic tastes he scorned appeal to a mass audience and insisted upon his own standards as opposed to local color, dialect, and realism. He regarded himself as a satirist in the classical tradition. Nonetheless, at the behest of his London editors he tried his hand at the breezy humor popularly associated with Far West.

Having parked the pregnant Mollie in Bristol, he spent most of his time in London, where he began writing for Tom Hood's *Fun* and for *Figaro*, employing the pseudonym Dod Grile. Biographers have puzzled over this nom de plume. It is probably just a coinage. Dod was a popular euphemism, usually an expletive, for God, and Grile is a portmanteau word made by telescoping *grin* and *smile*. The combination would have satisfied Bierce's cynical sense of humor.

He spent three years in London and as Dod Grile published his first three books there: *The Fiend's Delight* (1872), *Nuggets and Dust* (1872), and *Cobwebs from an Empty Skull* (1874). They were collections of newspaper items from his "Town Crier" column, grim bits

of fiction, and some sketches he had produced for *Fun* and *Figaro*. The books are interesting because they are so thoroughly Biercean. They cannot be regarded as apprentice work; seldom thereafter did he rise notably above the level of writing contained in them. The sharply satirical pieces treat man's universal folly, and the fiction announces the subjects that interested him—for example, a child eaten by a dog, a minister having his skull bashed in. His Fleet Street companions were soon calling him Bitter Bierce.

Although he roistered with other journalists, he cared most for the younger Tom Hood, the man he admired and saw frequently at his home. As he wrote a few years later, they "commonly passed the entire night in a room upstairs, sipping grog, pulling at our pipes, and talking on all manner of things." Hood was one of the few famous men with whom Bierce ever felt comfortable. More often than not he shied away from an older or more illustrious name. In London he met the friendly and approachable Mark Twain, with whom he had much in common. Twain had hired Charles Warren Stoddard as secretary for his English lecture tour, and Bierce once joined them for dinner at the Whitefriars Club. He stiffly held back, however, from developing a friendship with one whose reputation overshadowed his own, and such reserve was always characteristic of him.

Bierce seemed content to remain an expatriate, and only his domestic life finally pulled him back to San Francisco. Two sons, Day and Leigh, had been born in England. The family was usually established at Bath or some other comfortable place while Bierce himself spent most of his time in London. Mother Day lived with them awhile, and when she returned to California, Mollie and the boys soon followed for a visit. Safely back in San Francisco, she wrote her husband that she was expecting another child in three months. There was little for Bierce to do but pack up and join his family.

Back on the West Coast he again went to work at the Mint while awaiting a chance to resume his career in journalism. The opportunity came through Frank Pixley, a wealthy man with political experience. A disciple of Leland Stanford, he was devoted to the Republican party and disturbed by the social and political unrest attending the depression of 1875–76. Especially was he concerned about the "rabble-rousing" Irish Catholics and their objection to cheap Chinese labor. In March 1877 Pixley established the *Argonaut,* a weekly paper, to express his editorial views. As co-editor he chose Fred Somers, and they both invited Bierce to join them as a circulation-boosting columnist. Bierce became associate editor and wrote "The Prattler," a column much like his earlier "Town Crier." In it he commented upon the latest murders, battled against feminism, bludgeoned clergymen, roasted amateur writers, lampooned actresses, ridiculed suffragettes, denounced public officials, and generally delighted his readers.

Bierce enjoyed his work. As editor he could pass judgment upon the writing of others. Among occasional contributors he attracted were such local celebrities as Ina Coolbrith, T. A. Harcourt, and Charles Warren Stoddard. He did nothing to discourage his blossoming reputation as an authority on literature and most other subjects. As a traveler, an author with London connections, he was a rather large fish in the San Francisco pond, a position he admitted he found more attractive than that of a minnow in the national ocean.

If things became dull he could always stir up a little excitement, like the time he pulled an elaborate hoax with T. A. Harcourt. Together they wrote a book—*The Dance of Death*—and published it under the pseudonym "William Herman." In this cynically inspired performance the authors, ostensibly denouncing the waltz as lascivious, dwelt in detail upon the lewd nature of the dance in titillating terms. With great glee Bierce watched clergymen squabbling among themselves over whether the book was deeply moral or shameless. He took a hand by denouncing it in his column as "a criminal assault upon public modesty, an indecent exposure of the author's mind." The sales boomed locally to almost twenty thousand copies in less than a year.

Bierce took a leave from journalism to try his hand at business, without success. He returned to his true calling by becoming editor of the *Wasp,* a weekly paper with Republican but anti-railroad sympathies. He revived his "Prattler" column and in the first one began including items under the title "The Devil's Dictionary." These continued fairly regularly and were eventually published as a book in 1906. These definitions offered him a congenial outlet. Some of them were wittily cynical epigrams.

PREJUDICE, *n.* A vagrant opinion without visible means of support.

TRUTHFUL, *adj.* Dumb and illiterate.

YANKEE, *n.* In Europe, an American. In the Northern States of our Union, a New Englander. In the Southern States the word is unknown. (See DAMYANK.)

POSITIVE, *adj.* Mistaken at the top of one's voice.

REVERENCE, *n.* The spiritual attitude of a man to a god and a dog to a man.

GRAVE, *n.* A place in which the dead are laid to await the coming of the medical student.

HAND, *n.* A singular instrument worn at the end of the human arm and commonly thrust into somebody's pocket.

HAPPINESS, *n.* An agreeable sensation arising from contemplating the misery of another.

CONSUL, *n.* In American politics, a person who having failed to secure an office from the people is given one by the Administration on condition that he leave the country.

ALONE, *adj.* In bad company.

More of the definitions are longer—little homilies illustrated by examples, often in the form of verses (by Bierce) attributed to such authors as Jamrach Holobom, Phila Orm, Ambat Delaso, Orrin Goof, Joram Tate, and Judibras.

HISTORY, *n.* An account mostly false, of events mostly unimportant, which are brought about by rulers mostly knaves, and soldiers mostly fools.

Of Roman history, great Niebuhr's shown
'Tis nine-tenths lying. Faith, I wish 'twere known,
Ere we accept great Niebuhr as a guide,
Wherein he blundered and how much he lied.
—*Salder Bupp*

INK, *n.* A villainous compound of tanno-gallate of iron, gum-arabic and water, chiefly used to facilitate the infection of idiocy and promote intellectual crime. The properties of ink are peculiar and contradictory: it may be used to make reputations and unmake them; to blacken them and to make them white; but it is most generally and acceptably employed as a mortar to bind together the stones in an edifice of fame, and as a whitewash to conceal afterward the rascal quality of the material. There are men called journalists who have established ink baths which some persons pay money to get into, others to get out of. Not infrequently it occurs that a person who has paid to get in pays twice as much to get out.

In form the entries in *The Devil's Dictionary* reflect a common variety of humorous satire employed in nineteenth-century journalism.

From the same sources Mark Twain later drew inspiration for "Pudd'nhead Wilson's Calendar." An added similarity between these performances is their pessimistic tone. Twain's entry beginning the second chapter of *Pudd'nhead Wilson* would have been right at home in Bierce's dictionary: "Adam was but human—this explains it all. He did not want the apple for the apple's sake, he wanted it only because it was forbidden. The mistake was in not forbidding the serpent; then he would have eaten the serpent." Bierce's definitions are, if anything, more consistently pessimistic in their view of human nature, more sardonic and savagely satirical. They surpass Wilson's aphorisms in their mordant display of wit. The difference, of course, is that Twain's were a decoration for a more important work, while Bierce's were an end in themselves. Definitions from Bierce are still quoted, or more often circulate without reference to their source. It is not a book to be read at a sitting. Rather, it is a reference work to be consulted at cynical hours, when one at first will have his mood confirmed and then gradually lightened as he contemplates opinions more jaundiced than his own.

Bierce continued on the *Wasp* until 1886. Gradually he gave up his editorial duties and confined his attention to the column. He rarely showed up at the office, but managed his column from wherever he was staying. For a time the family was in Oakland; Bierce lived awhile in Auburn on the western slope of the Sierras. Then he moved the family to St. Helena in the Napa Valley. He himself stayed seven miles away up on Howell Mountain at Angwin and visited his household on weekends. Young poets and writers sought him out for advice. Afternoons he spent bicycling or hunting for arrowheads. When he stopped working for the *Wasp*, he took a small apartment in Oakland.

It was here that the young William Randolph Hearst found him and invited him to join the San Francisco *Examiner*. Although Bierce never approved of this employer, he began what was to prove a twenty-year association. Many a time during that period he resigned, but his paychecks continued, and he always returned to his duties. In fairness he claimed that Hearst allowed him a free hand: "I persuaded myself that I could do more good by addressing those who had greatest need of me —the millions of readers to whom Mr. Hearst was a misleading light."

On the *Examiner* Bierce assumed an autocratic role as the dean of West Coast critics. His column belabored his usual targets; occasionally a whole installment might be devoted to an essay on one subject. (He also contributed fiction to the paper, for which he was paid separately.) A favorite topic was literature; Bierce as a sort of literary dictator freely made pronouncements flavored by his salty prejudices, but sometimes acute and perceptive. In distinguishing between wit and humor, for example, he wrote: "In a matter of this kind it is easier to illustrate than to define. Humor (which is not inconsistent with pathos, so nearly allied are laughter and tears) is Charles Dickens; wit is Alexander Pope. Humor is Dogberry; wit is Mercutio. . . . nearly all Americans are humorous; if any are born witty, heaven help them to emigrate! You shall not meet an American and talk with him two minutes but he will say something humorous; in ten days he will say nothing witty; and if he did, your own, O most witty of all possible readers, would be the only ear that would give it recognition. Humor is tolerant, tender; its ridicule caresses. Wit stabs, begs pardon—and turns the weapon in the wound. Humor is a sweet wine, wit a dry; we know which is preferred by the connoisseur."

Frequently religion was the subject: 'The missionary is one who goes about throwing open the shutters of other men's bosoms in order to project upon the blank walls a shadow of himself." Politics was a never-ending source of amusement: " 'Party lines' are as terribly confused as the parallels of latitude and longitude after a twisting earthquake, or those aimless lines representing the competing railroad on a map published by a company operating 'the only direct route.' " Women, particularly the emancipated sort, were discussed: "The frosty truth is that except in the home the influence of women is not elevating, but debasing. When they stoop to uplift men who need uplifting, they are themselves pulled down, and that is all that is acomplished."

Of all topics, the one most calculated to arouse his ire was the rascality of men in public life, not only officials but also magnates like Huntington and Stanford. He referred to the latter often as £eland $tanford or Stealand Landford. The railroads especially were a target: "The worst railroads on the Pacific Coast are those operated by the Southern Pacific Company. The worst railroad operated by the Southern Pacific Company is the Central Pacific. It owes the government more millions of dollars than Leland Stanford has vanities, it will pay fewer cents than Collis P. Huntington has virtues."

It would not be accurate to say that Bierce's splenetic and bilious attacks in print were produced by jaundiced views, themselves the result of personal misfortunes. Bierce's troubles were largely of his own making. Far from being a satisfactory husband, he was just an occasional boarder in his own home. As a father he seemed indulgent, but not attentive. A friend told of the little daughter rushing in to tell Bierce in front of starchy visitors that her brother Leigh had exclaimed, "Damn God!" Bierce calmly told the little girl to go back and correct the boy—"I've told him a thousand times never to say *damn God* when he means *God damn!*"

His marriage disintegrated not long after he started working for the *Examiner*. The exact circumstances are obscure, but the final rupture came during the winter of 1888, when he moved away to Sunol. He did not see his wife again except at their elder son's funeral a half year later. Day had run away at fifteen and begun working in Red Bluff on a newspaper. About a year after leaving home he became involved with a sixteen-year-old girl in Chico. Eventually, in a jealous fit, he killed a rival suitor and committed suicide.

Bierce plunged himself into his work and various literary enterprises. Although he moved from place to place near San Francisco Bay, seeking a climate more hospitable for his asthma, he attracted a large following. About him gathered a circle of would-be writers and admiring young women, who came to visit and stayed to be instructed. The decade from 1890 to 1900 was the high point of his career.

As a teacher he was opinionated and dogmatic. He set himself deliberately against the current of realism and "local color" in fiction. As far as he was concerned, literary principles had been discovered and fixed for centuries. The best writers were those who worked within the established forms. Only the charlatans sought to substitute novelty and innovation for talent. His literary taste was that of an eighteenth-century Londoner. Among writers who expressed varying degrees of indebtedness to him were a number of Californians, invariably much younger. The single exception at a later period was H. L. Mencken, whom he came to know after moving permanently to Washington, D.C. Some of the names are still familiar: George Sterling, Edwin Markham, Emma Dawson, W. C. Morrow, Adolphe Danziger, G. H. Scheffauer, and Gertrude Atherton. There were also Blanche Partington, Walter

Blackburn Harte, Carroll Carrington, C. W. Doyle, Flora Shearer, Nellie Vore, Margaret Schenk, Alice Rix, Eva Crawford, Mabel Wood, Agnes and Margaret MacKenzie, Kitty and Julie Miles, and a host of others, chiefly young women with little talent to whom Bierce was invariably indulgent and kind in exchange for their flattering attention.

A brief essay of 1889, "To Train a Writer," summarizes the general advice he gave his disciples. "I have," he says, "had some small experience in teaching English composition, and some of my pupils are good enough to permit me to be rather proud of them." He goes on to affirm that if given five years to train a writer he would not permit him to write, except to take notes, for the first two years. This time would be spent in study. "If I caught him reading a newly published book, save by way of penance, it would go hard with him. Of our modern education he should have enough to read the ancients. . . . But chiefly this fortunate youth with the brilliant future should learn to take comprehensive views, hold large convictions and make wide generalizations. . . . And it would be needful that he know and have an ever present consciousness that this is a world of fools and rogues, blind with superstition, tormented with envy, consumed with vanity, selfish, false, cruel, cursed with illusions— frothing mad! . . . He must be a sinner and in turn a saint, a hero, a wretch." This is enough to indicate that Bierce would mold his pupils after his own image of himself. When they were no longer docile, he banished them. Eventually he alienated almost every one of them, especially the more talented.

During this decade he published the books that established his permanent reputation. The first was *The Monk and the Hangman's Daughter*. Adolphe Danziger had translated from the German a story, "Der Moench von Berchtesgaden," by Richard Voss. Danziger proposed that Bierce polish and edit the story as a collaborator. It appeared in the *Examiner* in September 1891 and a year later it came out in book form. One can easily see why Bierce found it congenial: it is a psychological study of an aberrant mind torn between sex and religious ecstasy, and it ends in murder and madness.

Bierce and Danziger later squabbled over the authorship of this story, each minimizing the other's contribution. The truth is that neither had a very strong claim; their version is practically a translation. Bierce did not read German and relied entirely upon Danziger's crude rendering; he can be credited with no more than the polished English, for the plot, characterization, and incidents all belong to Voss, the original author.

Bierce's first collection of short stories is another matter. *Tales of Soldiers and Civilians* was published in 1891. The English edition, which followed shortly after, appeared under the title *In the Midst of Life*. The book, containing nineteen stories, was divided almost evenly into two sections labeled "Soldiers" and "Civilians." The English edition differs in omitting four of the stories and adding nine. Later editions have mostly followed the English table of contents. The reviews were generally favorable, some even enthusiastic. But the thin-skinned Bierce was annoyed when any critic made comparisons with Edgar Allan Poe or emphasized the dispassionate tone.

For having been composed over a period of years, the stories show a remarkable degree of uniformity in tone, theme, and structure. The curious student who tries to find some significant change between early and later work will be disappointed. Apart from technical skill there is little to distinguish Bierce's fiction of 1871, when he first contributed "The Haunted Valley" to the *Overland*, and that of 1908, when he sent his last stories to *Cosmopolitan*.

The only valid generalization concerning such a change is perhaps that he modified the humor. Some early stories, like "Curried Cow," show a kinship with the boisterous tall tale; but uniformly the late work is pessimistic, its humor sardonic and cynical.

In the Midst of Life contains his best-known stories, and as a group they are most representative of his art. Among the war narratives perhaps the most widely known is "An Occurrence at Owl Creek Bridge." It begins in simple, matter-of-fact prose: "A man stood upon a railroad bridge in northern Alabama, looking down into the swift water twenty feet below. The man's hands were behind his back, the wrists bound with a cord. A rope closely encircled his neck." The preparations for the execution are described in detail, the entire scene emerging with clarity and vividness to the moment the sergeant steps off the plank that tilts to plunge the man down. The objective description extends to include some insight into the man's consciousness: awareness of the watch ticking; final desperate thoughts of escape. Then in a brief flashback we see Peyton Farquhar before his plantation house, talking to a gray-clad soldier. By inference we discover the reason for his execution. After the flashback the story resumes: "As Peyton Farquhar fell straight downward through the bridge he lost consciousness and was as one already dead. From this state he was awakened —ages later, it seemed to him—by the pain of a sharp pressure upon his throat, followed by a sense of suffocation." The rope had broken, and the story then becomes the suspenseful narration of the man's desperate attempts to free himself in the water, to evade the bullets of his pursuers, and finally to struggle through the tangled forest back to his home. There is considerable detail, involving the reader in the conflict. Finally as the man drags himself to his doorstep where his wife awaits, "a blinding white light blazes all about him with a sound like the shock of a cannon—then all is darkness and silence! Peyton Farquhar was dead; his body, with a broken neck, swung gently from side to side beneath the timbers of the Owl Creek Bridge."

The reader is shocked by this revelation. He may even feel cheated that the desperate struggle, the pursuit, the yearning toward home and family were only fantasy, the feverish imaginings of a man the instant before death. The detailed description must be revaluated not as objective reality, but as the vividness of a psychological state—the truth that the mind makes its own reality. But the reader is not cheated—not as by the surprise endings of O. Henry or Frank R. Stockton. Withholding the information here is not trickery, but a logical, calculated end to shock the reader with the realization that he has been witnessing a life-and-death struggle of some poignancy; death is the real cheat in dangling the lure of escape up to the final moment when we discover that there is no escape. This conclusion, although bitter, even cynical, logically extends the ironic theme.

This withholding of information until the end is Bierce's characteristic way of intensifying the horrific impact. In "Chickamauga" we see the device operating again. That story opens with a six-year-old boy wandering away into the forest, armed with a wooden sword and playing at war. The introductory paragraphs assume ironic overtones, for they invest the boy with a symbolic value as the racial inheritor of a long military tradition. His father, a poor planter, has been a soldier: "In the peaceful life of a planter the warrior-fire survived; once kindled, it is never extinguished. The man loved military books and pictures and the boy had understood enough to make himself a wooden sword. . . ." The childish martial play is in ironic harmony with the romantic conception of war. In contrast Bierce shows the harsh reality. The boy wanders lost and falls asleep exhausted, hidden among some rocks. The tide of battle washes over him and recedes while he sleeps. He awakens to a surrealistic, dreamlike scene, the wounded crawling toward the creek away from where they have fallen. The boy, after playing among them, leads the silent mutilated company in a horribly grotesque march to his home. The place is burning, however, and he finds his mother's body with its brains oozing from a shell hole in the temple. "The child moved his little hands, making wild, uncertain gestures. He uttered a series of inarticulate cries—something between the chattering of an ape and the gobbling of a turkey—a startling, soulless, unholy sound, the language of a devil. The child was a deaf mute. Then he stood motionless, with quivering lips, looking down upon the wreck." The chaotic horror of war descends upon the reader with this final revelation. Again it is not trickery, but a means of heightening the effect. We might have expected the boy to awaken from the nightmare, but instead we discover that the nightmare is real.

The child-symbol standing alone amid such desolation goes far beyond a tug at the heart. The reader is numbed; he not only understands the earlier grotesque episode, but perceives man's helplessness in the catastrophe that is war. One cannot easily forget the tortured men moving as in a trance away from horror, the more terrible because all is silent. The only comparable scene perhaps is the wounded-soldier episode in Stephen Crane's *The Red Badge of Courage*.

Not all of Bierce's war stories are so successful; the long arm of coincidence may intrude. "One of the Missing" is a case in point. A brave scout preceding his unit is trapped underneath some fallen timbers so that his cocked rifle points at his forehead. Again the body of the story deals at length with unusual circumstances and with psychological reactions. The soldier's courage disintegrates until, at the climax, he deliberately pulls the trigger. Though the rifle had already been discharged, without his knowledge, in the accident, he dies instantly of fright. In the denouement we learn that what seemed an eternity to him has been only minutes. A short time later the advancing line of his companions passes his body without recognition. The lieutenant, observing the drawn features, laconically estimates the corpse to be a week old. So far the irony is effective. But when we learn that this lieutenant is the dead man's brother, the coincidence seems gratuitous—a flaw in an otherwise powerful narrative.

Coincidence, however, can be for Bierce the very heart and theme of a story. In "The Affair at Coulter's Notch" Captain Coulter, commander of an artillery company, is ordered to take an exposed position and fire upon the rear guard of the enemy emplaced near a plantation house. After a hellish artillery duel, the enemy retreats. The climax comes when the enemy positions have been occupied and the house is taken over as headquarters. That evening the brigade commander discovers a bedraggled, powder-marked figure in the cellar mourning over the corpses of a woman and child. Readers familiar with the Biercean touch will not be surprised that it turns out to be Captain Coulter. These are his house and his wife and daughter. What appears to be a ghoulish coincidence has a rational explanation of sorts. Enough hints and clues have been planted to show that the commanding general deliberately put Captain Coulter to an appalling test of loyalty and duty. We are left to speculate upon the general's motives.

No similar explanation, however, renders probable the coincidence underlying "A Horseman in the Sky." A young Federal soldier on outpost is forced to shoot a horse with its rider to prevent the man from reporting the nearness of Federal troops. We learn at the end that the young soldier had recognized the rider as his own father. Improbable though we may find such happenings, they are a common convention of Civil War stories; in both fact and fiction, there are many variations on the theme of relative opposing relative. For a generation to whom the war was a recent experience, the device was not merely interesting and curious. The convention embodied a tragic theme—that the Civil War had involved, both figuratively and literally, brother against brother. In "The Mocking-Bird" Bierce used the same device again, this time concerning twins.

The remaining stories of the Soldier group, if not so successful as these, help us to understand Bierce's opinion of war. Some dwell upon the variety of horrors, like "The Coup de Grâce," in which dead and wounded soldiers are fed upon by wild swine. Others add suicide to the normal carnage of battle. Not all, however, dwell upon war's most gruesome aspects. "George Thurston" deals with a curious form of pride and courage. Indeed two stories—"A Son of the Gods" and "Killed at Resaca"—present examples of bravery, the former in admiring tones. In two stories women play critical roles. They do not appear significantly as characters; they are foils to the superior men whom they betray. This unflattering view of women is characteristic of Bierce. In "Killed at Resaca" a giddy young woman in a heedless letter goads her fiancé to rash displays of courage until he meets his death by a bullet; in truth, as the narrator concludes, "He was bitten by a snake." In "An Affair of Outposts" a brave man is driven to war by his wife's infidelity. There he meets his death—ironically, in rescuing his wife's betrayer.

The "Civilians" section of *In the Midst of Life* is less compelling than "Soldiers." The stories do not naturally form a group; they lack the unifying motif that holds the first half together. There is a wide variety of subjects and settings, and even the style shifts from story to story. This lack of unity is overemphasized by the fact that in subsequent editions two of the original stories were omitted, and four added which had first appeared in the volume *Can Such Things Be?*

Only one (later dropped in most editions) is a ghost story—"The Middle Toe of the Right Foot." Set in the Southwest, it tells of a man who has murdered his wife and children; years later he revisits his former home, now a haunted house. There he meets his death by fright; the only ghostly evidence remaining is the footprint of his murdered wife, who had lost the middle toe of the right foot. "Haïta, the Shepherd," the other story that was dropped in the English edition, is an allegorical fable built upon the elusiveness of a beautiful girl, who personifies Happiness.

The remaining stories are more representative of Bierce. "A Watcher by the Dead" recounts a bizarre wager made by several San Francisco doctors that one of them could not sit alone all night in a room with a body. "The Man and the Snake," also set in San Francisco, concerns the horrible attraction of a reptile's eyes. The climax reveals a psychological study in autosuggestion. "A Holy Terror" has a mining camp setting and describes a graveyard scene, again with a man dying of terror. "A Lady from Redhorse," also western, is unusual for Bierce in that it employs an epistolary form and ends happily. It might easily have graced the pages of a women's magazine. Its ominous tone, suggesting imminent terror, is Biercean enough, but not the surprise conclusion with a cheerful ending.

Some of the stories are not without a grim kind of humor. "The Suitable Surroundings" is built upon the notion that a story must be read in the right setting in order to make its full emotional impact. To demonstrate the point, an author of ghost stories persuades a friend to read a manuscript of his in a haunted house. Of course, this being a Bierce story, the man is found next day dead of terror. The story concludes with the report of the author being led away in a straitjacket; according to the final sentence, "Most of our esteemed contemporary's other writers are still at large."

Many of Bierce's narratives deal with death by violent means, and in this respect he invites comparison with certain other authors of his day. Violent death seems to have been common on the American frontier. Bret Harte saw in it a picturesque part of the "local color"; Mark Twain saw it as a subject for humor. Ambrose Bierce saw it for what it was. Curiously, the literary historians have classed Harte and Twain as realists and have accepted Bierce's own classification of himself as a romantic.

It is not easy to pin a label on his fiction. His contemporaries compared him most often to Poe. Bierce resented the comparison, not because he disliked Poe but because he was irritated by the narrow critical view that gave Poe a priority right to the supernatural. Speaking of one critic he said, "If he had lived in Poe's time how he would have sneered at that writer's attempts to emulate Walpole! And had he been a contemporary of Walpole that ambitious person would have incurred a stinging rap on the head for aspiring to displace the immortal Gormley Hobb."

Bierce's stories, though many are bloodcurdling and deal with the supernatural, often have a rational explanation and display psychological insight. He is a master of the *outré*. What interests him is not the ordinary, but the unusual, and this is part of his conscious opposition to the school of realism, headed by William Dean Howells, that objected to any breach of probability. "Fiction has nothing to say to probability; the capable writer gives it not a moment's attention, except to make what is related *seem* probable in the reading—*seem* true. Suppose he relates the impossible; what then? Why, he has but passed over the line into the realm of romance, the kingdom of Scott, Defoe, Hawthorne, Beckford and the authors of the *Arabian Nights*—the land of the poets, the home of all that is good and lasting in the literature of the imagination." The *outré*, the unusual, is not enough to define Bierce's subject in fiction. The story must have a cynical ironic twist. The old man turned away from the Home for the Aged must be the philanthropist who, in his palmier days, founded the place.

The year after his success with *Tales of Soldiers and Civilians* Bierce published his first volume of poems, *Black Beetles in Amber* (1892), a collection of verse from his newspaper columns. Apparently he had the notion that in a modest (for Bierce) way he was doing to some of his own contemporaries what Alexander Pope had done to his in *The Dunciad*. He would embalm a few beetle reputations in the satirical amber of his verse.

What! you a Senator?—you, Mike de Young?
Still reeking of the gutter whence you
    sprung? . . .

Dr. Jewell speaks of Balaam
And his vices, to assail 'em.
Ancient enmities how cruel!—
Balaam cudgeled once a Jewell.

Beneath his coat of dirt great Neilson loves
    To hide the avenging rope.
He handles all he touches without gloves,
    Excepting soap.

Many of the poems are more ambitious in form and length. With much wit and some skill Bierce flays various hides and hangs shredded reputations up to public view—all undoubtedly great fun but not great poetry. His targets were too small for his weapon. The invective and wit are leveled against men now forgotten, and few of his barbs were directed at universal human follies.

Can Such Things Be? appeared in 1893. Its twenty-five stories continue the vein struck in the "Civilian" section of the earlier book. For *The Collected Works* and later editions of this volume about half of the original were dropped and other stories added, to make a total of forty-two. Those dropped were subsequently included in new editions of *In the Midst of Life* and other volumes of *The Collected Works*. Later editions of *Can Such Things Be?* therefore have greater unity in supernatural tone. Five of the original stories were in the vein of his London days—humorous satire in the manner of the western tall tale. One might profitably compare them to similar performances by other writers making use of the same tradition. "The Famous Gilson Bequest" recalls the subject and the pessimistic tone of Mark Twain's *The Man That Corrupted Hadleyburg*. Gilson, having been run out of a number of mining camps, finally is hanged as a horse thief. His will names his chief persecutor—the town's leading citizen— as his heir, provided he clears Gilson's name of the ugly rumors surrounding it. The heir does so in the period stipulated. At the end of the story he is left penniless and broken, but clings to his faith in the name of Gilson, which so much effort and bribery have whitewashed.

"Jupiter Doke, Brigadier General" tells satirically how a backwoods politician bumbles his way successfully as a general in the Civil War. The grotesque climax, with hundreds of mules trampling into the attacking rebels, reminds one of William Faulkner's turning to this native tradition in *The Hamlet, The Un-vanquished*, and *The Town*. And the narrative style in "The Major's Tale" reminds one of James Whitcomb Riley, whose favorite device was to keep a long-winded narrator sublimely unaware of larding the story with irrelevancies, repetitions, and false starts. "My Favorite Murder," however, reminds us of no one except Bierce in his handling of the tall tale. The story opens with this sentence: "Having murdered my mother under circumstances of singular atrocity, I was arrested and put upon my trial, which lasted seven years." With great glee and many satirical digs at frontier justice, Bierce then recounts the chief defense argument— that the judge is wrong in thinking this the most horrible murder. The killing of the defendant's uncle surpassed that of the mother. The story concludes thus: "Altogether, I cannot help thinking that in point of artistic atrocity my murder of Uncle William has seldom been excelled."

The remaining stories in the first edition of *Can Such Things Be?* and those added later are more uniform in their serious treatment of the supernatural. Some are masterly examples of an eerie, macabre art. "The Death of Halpin Frayser" is such a one: apart from the evident skill and effectiveness in its telling, it is an interesting pre-Freudian study of an Oedipal theme.

Halpin Frayser suddenly awakens with the words "Catherine Larue" upon his lips. This name is strange to him. He has been sleeping in the open on the ground after becoming lost while hunting. Rather than stumble around in the dark, he has lain down to await daylight. He goes back to sleep and dreams of walking in a forest splattered with blood. A sense of oppression overwhelms him; a hideous laugh accompanies his dream, fading into a vision of his mother dressed for her grave.

Frayser has been unnaturally close to his mother. Business took him to the West Coast, where he was shanghaied and kept away for six years. Upon returning to California, he tried to get in touch with his mother back in Tennessee. Meanwhile, however, she had come to California looking for him. After an unsuccessful search, she remarried, but her husband in a maniacal fit soon murdered her.

Two detectives discover Frayser's body the day after his hunting trip. They have been searching for the madman reported in the vicinity, perhaps returning to grave of his murdered wife. Catherine Larue, of course, was Frayser's mother's new name. Inadvertently in the dark he chose her grave for his resting place; and the madman, mistaking the armed man for a detective, murdered him there.

Out of such an improbable plot hinging upon coincidence Bierce creates a gloomy mood and sustains the tone. With convincing details he makes the events "seem reality." He does not seek, however, to convince his readers that such goings-on are true. Rather, the ghost story is a symbolic projection of the psychological states—horror, terror, fear—that his characters present. In *The Devil's Dictionary* Bierce defines *ghost* as "the outward and visible sign of an inward fear." He saw fear as a powerful motivating force; the mind creates and projects a hell more real and horrible than the visible world can produce. Indeed the horrors projected in the visible world may be regarded as the product of group endeavor. Only many minds acting in accord, for example, could create the horror that is war. In the cynic's view the boundaries separating the real from the unreal, sanity from illusion, are hard to fix. The cynic need not stand on his head to right the world. He need only cock his head at a slight angle to see appearance and reality quickly shifting places. The chilling conclusion is that this world is the logical product of human minds irrationally motivated. The nineteenth-century pessimistic cynic saw with the clarity of common sense what the twentieth-century Existentialist philosopher only confirms in more recondite terms.

"A Jug of Sirup" is a good example of mass hysteria at work, for what other rational explanation can account for a group's seeing a ghost? With elaborate circumstantial detail Bierce establishes the orderly habits characterizing the storekeeper Silas Deemer; nothing but death could disturb this man's regular attendance in the store. One evening Alvan Creede, a banker, returns home and is greeted by his wife at the door. When Alvan turns to pick up a jug of sirup he is carrying, it is gone. Yet he put it down only while getting out his keys, and it has not been out of his sight since he purchased it from Deemer a short time earlier. Then he suddenly realizes that Deemer has been dead for weeks. The story spreads that Alvan has seen Deemer's ghost, and the next evening a curious crowd gathers at the deserted store, where they see Silas Deemer moving about in a dim light. As they go inside all is dark, and they mill about in terror. The next day the store looks like a recent battlefield; the account book is open at a page dated the day of Deemer's death—there is no record of a sale to Creede.

Two other Bierce narratives deserve some mention as examples of his somber art: "Moxan's Master" and "The Damned Thing." The former tells of one who created a robot that learns to think. The climax occurs when the monster murders its creator. The second concerns a man meeting a violent death at the hands of some invisible being. Both stories are good examples of Bierce's technical excellence. Carefully and skillfully he builds a convincing set of realistic circumstances and establishes an appropriate mood before introducing the element of unreality upon which the plot hinges. Often there is a rational explanation;

but even if there is not, one is moved to accept the psychological account.

The 1890's saw Bierce at his zenith as journalist-critic. Although his chief interest was in literature, he held decided views on a variety of timely topics. In his column he occasionally announced political and economic opinions paradoxically at odds with his criticism of socialists for their bomb-throwing and their mushy idealism; for example, he proposed to abolish private ownership of land, stop importing cheap labor, curb the control of property by the dead, require the state to provide work in hard times, limit fortunes by taxation, and abolish wage competition. Not even the New Deal at a later time dared to adopt more than a few such measures advocated by Bierce in his *Examiner* column for March 11, 1894.

As a result of such unorthodox literary, economic, social, political, and religious views Bierce was himself frequently a target. Arthur McEwen, writing in his *Letter* on May 25, 1895, drew blood; he stated that Bierce had not satisfactorily followed through on the promise shown in the first volume of stories. The article touched on a number of sore spots: "In outliving his wit he is rapidly becoming a mere blackguard. His highest aim now . . . is to insult . . . in an ingenious phrase . . . his vanity is large and sore. Touch that, and he . . . becomes savage and mean . . . he is a pretender. He affects in print an independence which he does not enjoy. His matter is subject to editorial supervision. . . . He is matchless in his petty trade of village critic and scold, and his book, 'Tales of Soldiers and Civilians,' is capital. . . . But the possibilities of Mr. Bierce are all there . . . what is left is a millionaire's literary lackey, whose soul is cankered with disappointment at his own emptiness, and whose narrow mind is ulcerated with envy of writers who are out of livery."

Most of the charges hurt because there was

some truth in them. Bierce was vain and dictatorial. He was envious that fame passed him over for other writers with less talent. He did like apple-polishing from his young admirers. He probably recognized that he had not properly exercised his talents. Most such charges he met with silence, but he justly resented being called a millionaire's lackey. As a working journalist, he was subject to editorial supervision, which he acepted so long as it was reasonable. Whenever he felt that his copy was blue-penciled excessively, he blew his top and resigned. Hearst, when appealed to, usually supported the temperamental columnist. Although Bierce disapproved of much about his boss, often he testified that Hearst had the good newspaper sense to pick good men and leave them alone. The few times Bierce was asked to take a special assignment, he did so because he found it congenial—not because he was a lackey.

In 1896 such an assignment carried him to Washington, D.C. The *Examiner* had waged an unrelenting campaign against the Southern Pacific Railroad. In the winter of 1895–96 Congress debated a funding bill that would cancel the western railroads' indebtedness to the government for past land grants, subsidies, and loans. Collis P. Huntington was in Washington lobbying for the bill. With his usual blunt methods and checkbook, he seemed to have lined up the railroad bloc in Congress and to have supplemented its power with liberal vote buying; San Franciscans feared he was well on his way to another steal. Hearst asked Bierce if he would go to Washington and lead the newspaper attack through the *Examiner* and the *Journal*, the new Hearst acquisition in New York. Bierce left immediately, in January 1896, and in Washington directed a staff of reporters. Almost daily dispatches and editorials went to the *Journal* and *Examiner*. When an aroused public interest

threatened to kill the bill, Huntington attempted to bribe Bierce. The latter replied in print that his price was seventy-five million dollars paid over to the treasurer of the United States. Ultimately a long-range bond repayment plan was substituted by the bill's sponsors, which could not be acted upon until the next session of Congress. Thus Huntington was defeated, and Bierce returned home something of a hero.

For a period of three years he maintained his position as the dean of West Coast literature. He continued writing for Hearst and revived his "Prattler" column. He managed a voluminous correspondence and manuscript-reading service for his growing circle of admirers and followers. There were signs, however, of some disciples falling away. George Sterling remained faithful, but Edwin Markham incurred the master's wrath by managing to get "The Man with the Hoe" published in the *Examiner*—without Bierce's sponsorship —and acclaimed as the product of a new genius. Bierce was annoyed on several counts. Having long encouraged Markham, he resented his "discovery" by someone else. Moreover, Markham had been consorting with a bad lot of what Bierce regarded as radicals and labor types. Finding the poem especially repugnant, Bierce leveled his critical guns against it and exiled its author from the master's favor.

Still rigidly set against the tide of realism flowing in American fiction, Bierce wrote in one of his columns, "I had thought there could be only two worse writers than Stephen Crane, namely, two Stephen Cranes." *The Red Badge of Courage* had just been received with critical and popular acclaim that far overshadowed the reception accorded Bierce's Civil War stories only four years earlier. Envy apart, Bierce also disliked the work because it was a novel, and a realistic one at that. Gertrude

Atherton accused him of rationalizing, since writing a novel was beyond his powers.

By the end of the decade he must have realized that he had passed the peak of his career. Rather than watch the slow decline of his prestige in California, he decided to return to the East; he was still employed by Hearst, however, and still writing for the *Journal* and *Examiner*. Arriving in Washington in January 1900, he worked at first as a political reporter, observing Congress and filing regular dispatches. But at fifty-eight he was too old a dog not soon to revert to his accustomed pace, producing a weekly column of commentary, this time called "The Passing Show." More temperate and less entertaining than his earlier columns, it was a weekly stint of sensible remarks, usually on politics and economics. To a friend he confided that he had given up literature for journalism.

His remaining son, Leigh, a New York reporter, died suddenly of pneumonia; and his own health troubled him during these years in Washington. When sufficiently recovered, he continued his column and made ocasional forays to New York to sample the night life. In 1903 George Sterling, still a devoted admirer and pupil, decided to publish a volume of Bierce's poetry. *Shapes of Clay* was a bulky collection of newspaper gleanings. Sterling singled out several for praise, but his critical judgment was blinded by affection. When rattling his rapier wit or consigning someone to hell in an epitaph, Bierce could hold his own in *vers de société*. But in a "poetic" mood, well, he was at least regular in his meter. As he put it, "I am not a poet, but an abuser." He was sometimes a good critic.

Whatever judgment he had was laid aside for friendship, however, when he published Sterling's poem "A Wine of Wizardry," in *Cosmopolitan*. Bierce had transferred to writing a monthly column for that magazine after

Hearst took it over in 1905. In a fresh outburst of creative energy he had contributed a number of stories besides. Using his editorial privilege in the issue for September 1907, he accompanied the poem with a critical essay proclaiming Sterling "a very great poet—incomparably the greatest . . . on this side of the Atlantic." Of the poem he said, "It has all the imagination of 'Comus' and all the fancy of 'The Faerie Queen.' " Bierce's taste in poetry was as faulty at times as it was romantic always. The storm of objection released by this praise roused the old firehorse in him to do critical battle, and while knocking heads about he momentarily achieved some of the national fame that had so consistently eluded him.

The Devil's Dictionary entries finally found a publisher, though the American edition changed the name to *The Cynic's Word Book*. But the best publishing news was the offer by Walter Neale to bring out a *Collected Works,* edited by Bierce, in ten or twelve volumes. Bierce was enthusiastic. With pastepot and scissors ready he plunged into the trunkloads of old newspapers, magazines, and clippings in his apartment. Soon he was reading the first proofs.

In 1909 a volume of his essays, *The Shadow on the Dial,* was published in San Francisco. The reviews were uniformly critical of his inconsistencies, lack of information, and journalistic haste. The book was a grab bag collection of assaults on government, socialism, women's rights, and labor unions. They betrayed their hastily written origins; as one reviewer said, "These wrathful passages seem to have no natural glow—only the steam heat of journalism."

Later in the year the first two volumes of the *Works* came out. The second was *In the Midst of Life,* the fifth edition in Bierce's lifetime, and it suited the book reviewers. The first volume contained a number of satirical pieces in the manner of Swift and a group of autobiographical essays. Three satires—"Ashes of the Beacon," "For the Ahkoond," and "John Smith, Liberator"—all look back in archaeological fashion upon a quaint race which had inhabited this land around 1900. They are still readable, if not particularly valuable. "The Land beyond the Blow" was more ambitious, being patterned upon *Gulliver's Travels.* The opening reminds one of Mark Twain's Boss recovering consciousness at the beginning of *A Connecticut Yankee,* although Bierce's performance suffers by the comparison. The narrator's adventures are fairly interesting, and the prose has an eighteenth-century flavor. But Bierce remains too close to his source. One misses Jonathan Swift's more biting satire and more effective prose.

The autobiographical essays, however, show Bierce at his stylistic best when deeply engaged by his subject; they are based upon personal experience, chiefly in the Civil War. The prose is clear, simple, straightforward, and effective. The narrative portions make absorbing reading and compare favorably with Mark Twain's prose in *Life on the Mississippi,* without the colloquial character, but with the same stylistic ease and grace of the born raconteur. One is moved to speculate upon what Bierce might have accomplished had he not fenced himself in with his literary prejudices. But then he would not have been Bierce, for these eccentricities go far toward defining his personality and character.

The enthusiasm of Bierce for the *Collected Works* began to flag with the third volume, *Can Such Things Be?* Editing and proofreading became drudgery. In 1910 the labor of editing was relieved by a visit to California, where he enjoyed fellowship with his brother Albert and a few old friends. Through Sterling he met Jack London, but the two did not hit

it off, being possibly too much alike. Back in Washington by the close of 1910, he saw volumes four and five out, *Shapes of Clay* and *Black Beetles in Amber.* Both were much padded with more verses piled on the original collections, and both encountered a hostile press. The best satirical verses of these two bulky volumes at most might have made a slim book.

The sixth volume contained *The Monk and the Hangman's Daughter* and a collection of "Fantastic Fables." The latter are very short homilies, uniformly pessimistic and cynical. Volume seven reprinted *The Devil's Dictionary* under Bierce's preferred title. All of the extant word entries are collected here, with such additions as the following: "RUM, *n.* Generically, fiery liquors that produce madness in total abstainers. SAINT, *n.* A dead sinner revised and edited." Volume eight was called *Negligible Tales.* The title is appropriate; here are stories that could not be squeezed into the second and third volumes.

Numbers nine and ten are collected essays. *Tangential Views* represents Bierce the social critic. As a dissenter he expressed his views on a variety of topics—socialism, politics, economics, religion, horses, and women. *The Opinionator,* aptly titled, contains literary criticism —his jaundiced opinions about the state of contemporary letters, tempered with nostalgic reflections upon the past, a vague period combining the glories of romantic fancy and neoclassical technique. The eleventh volume reprinted the journalistic gleanings of *The Shadow on the Dial,* and the twelfth and final volume, *In Motley,* mixed together everything left that could not logically find a place in the other eleven volumes. Half the contents are Little Johnny fables, and the rest are labeled "Miscellaneous."

Before the last volume came off the press in 1912, Bierce had already made his plans for leaving Washington, although he did not finally get off until late in 1913. All his effects he tied and labeled in neat bundles and deposited with various persons, chiefly his daughter Helen and Carrie Christiansen, a longtime friend and his secretary during his last years. With the *Collected Works* finished he would labor no more. He bade good-bye to H. L. Mencken, drinking companion and fellow cynic. His letters to a number of friends mentioned plans for observing the revolution in Mexico and then taking passage to Europe.

On his way to Texas he made a sentimental tour of the country he had seen during the Civil War. Having left Washington early in October, he stopped off at Chattanooga to visit Chickamauga, then journeyed on to Murfreesboro, Franklin, Nashville, Shiloh, and finally —before the end of the month—New Orleans. Reporters looked him up there at his hotel and reported his intentions of going to Mexico to see the fighting. On he went to Fort Sam Houston, Laredo, and El Paso. Late in November, after crossing the border into Juarez, he received credentials as an observer attached to Pancho Villa's army. On December 26, 1913, the seventy-one-year-old traveler posted a letter in Chihuahua telling about his first witness of battle and his acceptance by the revolutionary forces. This was the last word ever received from Ambrose Bierce. It seems certain that the old soldier did not die peacefully in bed.

During the years that followed many obituaries appeared. Every inquiry and investigation turned up nothing but rumors about Bierce's end, but provided the occasion for another set of obituaries. The old cynic would have enjoyed the spectacle. Living memory of the man has faded, leaving in print a half-dozen books and numerous articles of reminiscences by those who knew him. They are a mass of factual contradictions about his character and his personal life. Added up, they show how reticent he was about his private

affairs and how he refrained from contradicting the legend that grew up in his lifetime.

Of his literary reputation three facts may be noted. First, several of his stories have found their way into anthologies and seem destined to stay. Second, many of his entries in *The Devil's Dictionary* have a steady, if anonymous, circulation. Third, perhaps because of the ready availability of his books (few living writers have been so honored with collected works), a small but faithful number of readers continues to discover and to value Bierce.

In recent years he has had scant critical attention. The literary historians usually dismiss him with a few generalities about his bohemian character, his pessimism, his indebtedness to Poe, and the merits of a few Civil War stories. Even significant minor status seems begrudged to any writer who does not work in a major contemporary genre—the novel, drama, or lyric poetry—particularly to one outside the mainstream of literature. But Ambrose Bierce legitimately may claim our notice for his relation to several themes and techniques; this may go far toward explaining the persistent appeal of his otherwise flawed career and performance.

William Dean Howells—Miss Nancy Howells, as Bierce dubbed him—called the "smiling aspects" of American life the more typical and therefore more appropriate for a realistic literature that deals in probabilities. In fairness we cannot easily dismiss a point of view that has had such wide acceptance. Most literary historians and critics have found the dominant temper of American letters in the past essentially optimistic and rational. There is a firm, albeit at times naive, commitment to the motion of progress—the idea that man's best nature will prevail, conditions will improve, and the more abundant life result "if we will all just understand one another and pull together." Our literature, they say, inevitably has, allowing for minority dissent, in the main reflected this cheerful, forward-looking character.

There is, however, a dark side to American literature. A strong and persistent current runs through the work of our best writers that denies the "smiling aspects" of our experience. In recent years critics have begun to point this out. Their views are in harmony with the turn that our literature seems to have taken in the years following World War II. Bierce set himself obstinately against the tide of realism associated with Howells and his followers—a tide which was dominant well into the third decade of the twentieth century and is still the moving force of most best sellers. But serious fiction in the forties and fifties has exhibited certain changes that make Bierce seem less remote. For one thing, the realistic works that survive strike us now as fundamentally symbolic. For another, the literature of the grotesque and absurd appears increasingly significant. Both characteristics bring Bierce closer to a tradition of importance in our literature.

From the very beginning there was a dark side to New England culture. The Calvinistic doctrine of man's depravity and the uncertainty of election led to an inordinate preoccupation with the state of one's soul, turning one's gaze inward upon the writhing and twisting bestiality of one's psyche. Even when he looked outward the Puritan regarded what he saw as an arena featuring contending diabolic and Providential phenomena. The facts of everyday experience became the symbols of supernatural forces. Early American writing presents a strong thematic current dealing with sinners in the hands of an angry God.

Our Puritan heritage provided the setting, but other influences operated to modify and shape this tradition. Charles Brockden Brown imported some of the trappings of the English Gothic novel. German *Sturm und Drang* impressed a number of our writers traveling abroad. The exaggeration of European naturalism, especially Zola's, played a part. And, of course, such Russian writers as Dostoevski and Chekhov exerted a powerful attraction. And there were other influences as well—all of them contributing in some way to modifying the subterranean character of a part of our literature.

A hint may be found in the later novels of James Fenimore Cooper and in the work of William Gilmore Simms. There is no doubt of the tradition's operating in Washington Irving's tales and sketches. It emerges full-blown in Hawthorne, Melville, and Poe. It is partially pushed aside by the flood of realism in the latter part of the nineteenth century, but it crops up nonetheless in the later Twain and Henry James. Bierce, Lafcadio Hearn, and Fitzjames O'Brien were other voices. Although naturalism ran strong into the twentieth century, we find it often hospitable to the tradition we are discussing in the works of Stephen Crane, Frank Norris, and Sherwood Anderson. These dark qualities are important in such other figures as Conrad Aiken and Nathanael West. Ernest Hemingway and William Faulkner have important roots in the tradition. In addition we can add such names as Robert Penn Warren, Erskine Caldwell, Flannery O'Connor, Carson McCullers, Nelson Algren, Tennessee Williams, and Paul Bowles. The list could be extended; it is enough, however, to suggest that the tradition has increased in importance, and is a significant part of the American experience.

Precise definition is difficult because like any vital tradition this one changes as it develops. Certain characteristics, however, are associated in varying degrees with the fiction identified with it. There is a marked concern for abnormal or heightened psychological states. Characters frequently deviate widely in the direction of grotesque, twisted, or alienated personalities. Often physical appearance will symbolize the inner state. The events depicted are disposed toward the unusual rather than the ordinary, particularly the perverse, the violent, and the shocking. Similarly there is a disposition toward fear, terror, horror, insecurity, and the failure of love. There is a tendency to see problems within the individual soul, psyche, or unconscious rather than in terms of outward circumstances—society and institutions, for example.

Ambrose Bierce is squarely within this tradition. In his best work he has given us a number of powerful symbolic studies firmly grounded upon psychological insights into bizarre incidents and characters. The theme of war in its grotesque and horrible aspects, so intimately associated with Bierce, seems not so much his private property as it once did. Certain scenes in *The Red Badge of Courage* and *A Farewell to Arms,* for example, remind us of Bierce. And a number of post-World War II novels have incidents recalling *In the Midst of Life.*

His satire, too, finds an echo in H. L. Mencken and Sinclair Lewis. (His Juvenalian voice has been neglected because satire in America has been principally Horatian—more gentle, urbane, and humorous.) He still speaks to a discriminating audience, in ambiguous and ironic tones, to an age that increasingly values conscious ambiguity of metaphor.

The chief flaws in his work seem to proceed from a limited range of emotional experience. Bierce never matured emotionally. Much of his iconoclasm has the fervor of adolescence; he could not see the many-sidedness of human behavior. Much of the violence in his work seems as much an extension of his personal and journalistic aggression as it does a result of direct observation of life. His personal aloofness, even in his closest relationships, is reflected upon his work. There is not sufficient sympathy in his stories to allow any all-out attachment; the characters, especially the women, are two-dimensional. The great compression and economy so characteristic of his stories keep the reader from becoming involved; we are left detached and remote. Though this situation sometimes reinforces the ironic treatment, more often it prevents a full realization of the story's possibilities. Bierce's satire, despite the allure of its surface wit and force, suffers from the same cause. Much of it is trivial, and even the best seems to lack a substratum of human sympathy; he never earned by his compassion the privilege of harshly indicting his fellow man.

Despite his faults—perhaps partly because of them—Bierce makes us aware of a distinctive voice; if not one of the best in our literary chorus, it is nontheless an interesting one, important to an understanding of a significant part of our literature.

Selected Bibliography

WORKS OF
AMBROSE BIERCE

Nuggets and Dust, by Dod Grile. London: Chatto and Windus, 1872.
The Fiend's Delight, by Dod Grile. London: Hotten, 1872.
Cobwebs from an Empty Skull. London: Rutledge and Sons, 1874.
The Dance of Death, by William Herman. San Francisco: Henry Keller, 1877.
Tales of Soldiers and Civilians. San Francisco: E. L. G. Steele, 1891. (Reprinted under the title *In the Midst of Life.* New York: G. P. Putnam's Sons, 1898.)
The Monk and the Hangman's Daughter. Chicago: F. J. Schulte 1893 [1892].
Black Beetles in Amber. San Francisco: Western Authors, 1892.

Can Such Things Be? New York: Cassell, 1893.
Fantastic Fables. New York: G. P. Putnam's Sons, 1899.
Shapes of Clay. San Francisco: W. E. Wood, 1903.
The Cynic's Word Book. New York: Doubleday, Page, 1906. (Reprinted under the title *The Devil's Dictionary* as Vol. 7 of *The Collected Works.*)
The Shadow on the Dial. San Francisco: A. M. Robertson, 1909.
Write It Right. New York and Washington: Neale, 1909.
The Collected Works. 12 vols. New York and Washington: Neale, 1909–12.
The Letters of Ambrose Bierce. San Francisco: Book Club of California, 1922.
Battle Sketches. New York: Walter V. McKee, 1930.

CRITICAL AND BIOGRAPHICAL STUDIES

Boynton, Percy H. *More Contemporary Americans.* Chicago: University of Chicago Press, 1927.

Brooks, Van Wyck. *Emerson and Others.* New York: Dutton, 1927.
Fadiman, Clifton. Introduction to *The Collected Writings of Ambrose Bierce.* New York: Citadel, 1946.
Fatout, Paul. *Ambrose Bierce, the Devil's Lexicographer.* Norman: University of Oklahoma Press, 1951.
Grattan, C. Hartley. *Bitter Bierce.* New York: Doubleday, Doran, 1929.
Grenander, M. E. *Ambrose Bierce.* New York: Twayne, 1971.
McWilliams, Carey. *Ambrose Bierce.* New York: A. C. Boni, 1929.
Mencken, H. L. "Mr. Mencken Presents: Ambrose Bierce," *New York World,* March 1, 1925.
O'Connor, Richard. *Ambrose Bierce: A Biography.* Boston: Little, Brown, 1967.
Sterling, George. Introduction to *In the Midst of Life.* New York: Modern Library, 1927.
Wilson, Edmund. *Patriotic Gore.* New York: Oxford University Press, 1962.

—ROBERT A. WIGGINS

Randolph Bourne

1886-1918

THE BRIEF career of Randolph Bourne began in 1911 when he published in the *Atlantic Monthly* a rejoinder to one of those perennial animadversions on the younger generation. In its February issue the magazine had featured "A Letter to the Rising Generation" by Cornelia Comer, a frequent contributor. Adopting a Roman sternness and a sarcastic religious voice, she censured the young men of good families for abandoning the ways of their fathers. She knew that new conditions would not produce the sort of men the old conditions had, that the rising generation had been "conceived in uncertainty [and] brought forth in misgiving"; to be "nobly militant" would be difficult for a generation victimized by educational experiments and the eroding belief and authority of the elders. Yet everything about these young men annoyed her: their "agnostic-and-water" religious viewpoint, their Whitmanian notion of Personality and Shavian delight in the liberation of the natural will, and especially their experimental approach to ethics and advocacy of socialism, which she indicted as justifications of irresponsibility. The younger generation, she believed, lacked force and fortitude, was "soft," was deformed by "mental rickets and curvature of the soul."

Mrs. Comer's annoyance indicates the extent to which communication between fathers and sons had broken down. She accurately observes the postures of these "Whitmanshaws" but considers them "cheap"; she will not have them enjoy without a large outlay of pain. She says that "the final right of each generation to its own code [of manners] depends upon the inner significance of those manners," but she does not search—to the limit of an elder's sympathy and power—for that significance. This, to be sure, only the new generation itself can fully express, thereby declaring itself and adding its increment to human history. Meanwhile, failing to understand that she is disturbed by the role of youth—by the fact that change, as Erik Erikson says, is "the business of youth and . . . challenge the essence of its business"—she prophesies: "It may easily happen that the next twenty years will prove the most interesting in the history of civilization. Armageddon is always at hand in some fashion. Nice lads with the blood of the founders of our nation in your veins, pecking away at the current literature of socialism, taking out of it imperfectly understood apologies for your temperaments and calling it philosophy—where will you be if a Great Day should really dawn?"

In replying to Mrs. Comer, Randolph Bourne had one of the few advantages in the confrontation of generations: he understood her generation more fully than she understood his. Her viewpoint and tone were as familiar to him as Bloomfield, New Jersey, the old respectable middle-class town in which he was born (in 1886) and raised and which, all his life, bitterly attracted him. He confessed to a correspondent, whose small-town plight was similar to his, that he owed most of his political, social, and psychological education to Bloomfield, that "its Church, its social classes, prejudices, conservatism, moral codes, personalities—all furnish the background against which I throw all my experience, and in terms of which I still see life and suppose always shall." In his master's thesis he studied the effects of suburbanization on the social life of the town, explaining that the process was slower there than in nearby Glen Ridge and Montclair because the "Calvinistic religion was bred in the bone of the town, and it [would] take much urban sophistication to get rid of it." And, perhaps to find a purchase for himself and others after the war, he began an autobiographical novel of which only the chapter on his sixth year in Bloomfield was published—a chapter with which the monthly *Dial* was launched.

In everything except money, Randolph Silliman Bourne belonged to the "comfortable classes" for whom and to whom Mrs. Comer spoke. The quarrel between them was a family matter, an affair almost entire of the middle class. He was, in fact, one of the "nice lads" of worthy native ancestry and good family whom she threatened with class displacement and the rough discipline of "life." He, however, was already intimate with both. His birth, as he said, had been "terribly messy"; inept forceps delivery had left his face scarred and misshapen. Then, in his fourth year, he had been ill with spinal tuberculosis, had been stunted and bent, "cruelly blasted," he once complained, "by the powers that brought him

into the world." (According to his passport, he was five feet tall, had brown hair and a medium complexioned long face with blue eyes, a large nose, straight mouth, and receding chin. A close college friend reported that it was not his deformed back, which he learned to hide with a black cape and by carefully seating himself, but his malformed ear—"a rudimentary appendage"—that repelled people, and that Bourne himself disliked his "sloping chin.") He also knew a disability more common in his generation of writers: the failure of the father, itself a sign of the crumbling edifice of Victorian middle-class values. His father, Charles Rogers Bourne, had failed in business and had consented to leave home when his brother-in-law made this the condition of his support of Sarah Barrett Bourne and her four children. A cruel banishment! A martyrdom, Van Wyck Brooks might have said, to the "acquisitive life," and one that would have impressed the boy with the inexorable Calvinism of the household and with the belief, for which he said he "suffered tortures," that failure was always the result of moral weakness. Genteel impoverishment and dependence is perhaps the worst affliction of the respectable—to have to live constantly, as Bourne remembered, under the "awful glowering family eye of rich guarding relatives," who also, as far as he was concerned, remained "dumb and uninterested." An aunt and grandmother were warm sustaining presences, but his mother's unhappiness, a proper disposition in such circumstances, established the ground tone of what he called his "doleful home."

Perhaps the absence of his father confirmed the gentility of his upbringing. Like Miro, the fictive hero of "The History of a Literary Radical," he found in his environment little genuine cultural nourishment but much cultural devoutness. In his home, as in many more, the classics, in Eliot's exact description, "Upon the glazen shelves kept watch"; only the metropolitan newspaper opened to him a portal to the world, and to it he attributed his real education. He was a well-behaved boy whose success as a student had been due, he admitted, to "my moral rather than my intellectual sense." Indeed, in the few pages of the diary he began in his fourteenth year, he reveals himself to be the phenomenon he later thought appalling, the "good" child. Here he records the eager steps of a culture-famished, priggish youth intent on success and social acceptance: he and his sister have joined the church ("Mamma wants us to very much"); he has begun to excel in school ("Wonder of wonders! I got 100 in a Greek exercise that I did tother day. I have never gotten it before"); he has been elected class president, though "not very popular in the school and very little known"; he has begun to collect stamps and well-printed and -bound books—Lowell's and Whittier's poems, *Ivanhoe* and *The Vicar of Wakefield*—and to record his literary opinions ("I have just finished reading 'Eben Holden.' It beats 'David Harum' by a good deal. . . . The love story is about the prettiest and sweetest I have ever read"); and he has discovered that babies are "cute," has sent his finest valentine to a girl named Grace Wade, has gone to a "very dainty and lovely" luncheon, and has been taken by his Aunt Fan to *Lohengrin*.

The career of respectability begun here might have continued had Bourne been able to enter college on graduating from high school in 1903. But his uncle was unwilling to provide this privilege, and he was turned out to work, learning, as he said in "A Philosophy of Handicap," that "the bitterest struggles of the handicapped man come when he tackles the business world." He worked for six years: in an office, as an accompanist and music teacher (he was a competent pianist), and as a "factory hand" perforating music rolls for player pianos, an indelible experience of the piecework system that he described in "What Is Exploitation?" Desperate to escape such lower depths, he finally practiced the "dodging of pressures" he preached to those similarly trapped: "I solved my difficulties only by evading them, by throwing overboard some of my responsibility [he was the eldest child]." At the age of twenty-three, he entered Columbia University on a scholarship to discover, gratefully, that "college furnishes an ideal environment where the things at which a handicapped man . . . can succeed really count."

In 1909, Columbia was already a great metropolitan university and headquarters of modern thought. In many departments, its professors belonged to the vanguard: Franz Boas, in anthropology; John Dewey, in philosophy, psychology, and education; Charles Beard, in political science; James Harvey Robinson, in history—to mention only those most frequently considered in the history of American revolt against formalism. There, Bourne was befriended by his teachers, especially by his "great hero-teacher" Frederick P. Keppel, who helped him financially, and was surrounded by bright, sympathetic young men many of whom shared with him the editing of the *Columbia Monthly*. There, he declared, he found a spiritual home. The congenial intellectual world and the fresh atmosphere of ideas represented for him the valuable "college education" that then, as now, was overwhelmed by "college life." "What we all want the college to be"—he later wrote in "What Is College For?"—"is a life where for youth of all social classes the expressions of genius, the modern interpretations of society, and the scientific spirit, may become imaginatively real." Having quickly abandoned fusty literary studies for the "intellectual arena" of the social sciences, he got what he said a student should: "a fused and assimilated sense of the world he lives in, in its length and breadth, its historical perspective and social setting." Columbia, he told a prospective student, had revolutionized his life.

When he wrote this to Prudence Winterrowd of Shelbyville, Indiana, he was thinking mostly of the thwartings he had known in Bloomfield and the heady release Columbia had provided him. But it had revolutionized his thought and, in a more modest way, his action. He had a certain notoriety because he protested such things as the exploitation by the university of its scrub women and page boys. If not a big man on campus, he was an older, notable one: a socialist, an editor of the highbrow literary magazine that in his time had repudiated *fin de siècle* symbolism for critical realism. On the magazine he had served a valuable apprenticeship, had found his vocation; and after his appearance in the *Atlantic Monthly,* he had the glamour that invests the undergraduate who arrives in the real world ahead of the rest.

Bourne's praise of Columbia was not extravagant because, with his inability to set himself in motion, he owed much of his achievement to its stimulus. In the struggle to get a foothold, he explained in "The Experimental Life," "the difference is in the fortune of the foothold, and not in our private creation of any mystical force of will." Columbia was a fortunate foothold, which he did not readily give up; it had awakened his capacity, produced activity and success. Dean Frederick Woodbridge, for example, had suggested that he reply to Mrs. Comer and had forwarded his essay to Ellery Sedgwick, the editor of the *Atlantic Monthly,* who served Bourne, for as long as he permitted, as literary counselor. Bourne acknowledged that the magazine was his "good angel" and "coddled" him. Sedgwick prompted several essays—some of Bourne's most significant essays and a large proportion of his best work were printed by him—and Sedgwick made the magazine another foothold. With his help, Houghton Mifflin Company published Bourne's first book, *Youth and Life* (1913), a collection of *Atlantic* and *Columbia Monthly* essays, and so he established himself. Columbia postponed the crisis of vocation and prepared him for it by enabling him to spend a year in Europe; and when this crisis was again at hand, Sedgwick and Charles Beard secured a place for him on Herbert Croly's new liberal weekly, the *New Republic.*

To the psychological and intellectual weather of these exciting turbulent years, *Youth and Life* is excellent testimony—"thoroughly and almost uncannily autobiographical," Bourne ruefully admitted. Walter F. Greenman, a Unitarian minister in Milwaukee, one of the many educated people (social workers, ministers, teachers, and idealistic housewives) the book inspired, believed it to be "the truest interpretation of Youth to itself" that he knew. It made him feel "as if my beloved Emerson had had a reincarnation in the 20th Century," and he told Bourne that it was "the most innocent looking sweetest stick of dynamite anybody ever chewed." In these essays, which include the reply to Mrs. Comer, is the full statement of the case for the younger against the older generation. The reviewer in the *Columbia Monthly* praised them highly as a declaration but complained that the essay form had eliminated the poetry of youth. Yet no other book of this time expresses so well, even while making youth an ideology to which to be loyal, the precarious condition and the virtues of this season of life. For all of its faults, deriving mainly from reliance on the rhetoric of uplift—a rhetoric, however, that in conjunction with candor and fresh ideas effectively expresses the new idealism—it is an irreplaceable book of this generation, like the war essays of Bourne's *Untimely Papers,* and belongs with his best work.

The title itself brilliantly states the issues, which, because of Bourne's fidelity to experience, address every younger generation as well as his own: the confrontation of youth, a new generation, with "life"; the resources of life, which youth bears; and the responsibilities it has for its replenishment. At the very moment in Western history when Ortega announced that the theme of our time was the restoration of life to its proper relation with culture, Bourne called the young men and women of his generation to life and showed them an open and daring stance toward the world, one flexible yet resilient, that would enable them to master and enjoy the "experimental life." Using these essays as a form of self-therapy— they are continuous with this remarkable correspondence—he investigated his identity crisis, one of more than usual significance because profound historical changes contributed to it. In doing this, he either anticipated or confirmed the advanced thought of men like Ortega, Erikson, and Paul Goodman, for he recognized the concept of the generation and its historical, social, and psychological components. He knew what it meant to grow up absurd and how much absurdity was due to an older generation; he knew that life had stages, each with its necessary virtue, and that in the cycle of generations youth, having the regenerative function, was especially important; and he knew that for psychological and social reasons the conflict of generations was as inevitable as it was necessary, yet sometimes irreconcilable, because beneath the rebellion over child-rearing and education, philosophies and values, was the stark fact of power—that the older generation, as he said, wished "to rule not only their own but all the generations."

The first three essays specifically treat these themes, although the remaining essays, by way of exploring the thoughts and solutions of youth, consider them too. The general case gives way to particular applications, and the book concludes with the most intimately personal essay, "A Philosophy of Handicap," which had stirred the readers of the *Atlantic* and Sedgwick had insisted Bourne reprint— an essay that now certified the book by giving it a signature and fastened to the younger generation the virtue of unassuming courage.

As Bourne describes it, youth is a condition, the result of a profound psychological crisis and coming-of-age when one is "suddenly born into a confusion of ideas and appeals and traditions" and enters a "new spiritual world." Whether or not this crisis is fruitful depends on awareness and spiritual force, on finding release for oneself not in "passion" but in "enthusiasm." For the way of passion is not "adventurous"; it is the way of "traditional" youth, who, like most of those friends of Bourne's youth in Bloomfield whose social life excluded him, pass easily through the crisis by avoiding it, by following pleasure and settling for as well as into established routines. To seek security at the expense of consciousness is to forfeit youth, and Bourne does not speak for these young people but for those radical ones, like his Columbia friends, who have not been cautious and have exposed themselves "to the full fury of the spiritual elements." These adventurous youth discover the precious gift of life and become the responsive ones who, if they continue to seek and search, alter the sensibility of the age. Only the young, Bourne says, "are actually contemporaneous; they interpret what they see freshly and without prejudice; their vision is always the truest, and their interpretation always the justest." Not burdened with stock moralities, they follow the open road of experience, always susceptible to the new, eager for experiment, ready to let ideas get them. Their enthusiasm is for fresh ideals to which to give their loyalty, and nothing angers them more than the spiritual torpor and "damaged ideals" that, in this account, define old age.

The attack on the elders is directed to this condition. As in *Walden,* so here: "Age is no better, hardly so well, qualified for an instructor as youth," Thoreau says, "for it has not profited so much as it has lost." What it has lost, essentially, is the spontaneity of being— "the soul's emphasis," in Emerson's wonderful phrase—that sustains the virtue of each season of life and impels one's moral growth. Age has lost the very condition of youth, which Bourne believes to be the epitome of life. It has forsaken the "battle-ground of the moral life" to which childhood familiarization with the world opens and all subsequent stages of life, to be worthy, must contribute support. Just as toward children the duty of elders is to refrain from imposing moralities and, by permitting natural growth into the world, to prepare them for the vital morality of self-mastery, so toward youth the duties of middle and old age, respectively, are to "conserve the values of youth" by living up to them and then, in relinquishing power, wisely to understand "the truth and efficacy of youth's ideal vision."

The aim of this gospel of youth is "to reinstate ideals and personality at the heart of the world." Tested by this gospel, the older generation has failed. The older accuses the younger generation of being soft when, in fact, it is palpitant, for the virtue of all its virtues, the passion for justice, has been kindled by the kind of world the elders have given it. To them Bourne attributes the cardinal fact about the younger generation: that it has had to bring itself up and, accordingly, has learned to judge by its own standards. The education provided it has not fitted the needs of its freer social life and wider awareness of the world.

The formulas of the elders have not been helpful, and their models of success have not been attractive. It finds distasteful the routine, chicanery, and predation of the business world to which they would guide it, regrets the lack of individual social responsibility in the increasingly corporate economy, and is hampered by the high cost of professional education. In every way the elders refuse it confirmation, deny it by evading with "nerveless negations" the issues raised by its "positive faith" in social reform. And so, at the pitch of his indictment, Bourne says, "the stupidities and cruelties of their management of the world fill youth with an intolerant rage."

What is hardest to understand about another generation is the very thing Bourne tried to explain in the body of his book: its way of being in the world. He begins, in "The Life of Irony," by defining its point of view, the "comic juxtaposition" it has adopted in order to revivify the world. Irony, to be sure, is deadly accurate and reveals the absurdity of many things; it has a negative power and, as Bourne's friends complained of his use of it, is often accompanied by "malicious delight." Yet for Bourne it was much more than a hostile critical weapon: it was a social mode of being, his way of embracing the world and finding in it a field of vital intelligence. He speaks of irony as the "science of comparative experience," as "a sweeter, more flexible and human principle of life, adequate, without the buttress of supernatural belief, to nourish and fortify the spirit." It is the foe of both "predestined formulas" and spiritual apathy, unfixing things, restoring fluidity, and, at the same time, bringing "a vivid and intense feeling of aliveness." It admits to experience the "noisier and vivider elements" that the New Humanists wished to exclude, and is therefore "rich" and "democratic." Like Whitman's mode of acceptance, irony requires that one take another's position and contact the world. It is an "active way of doing and being" that confronts one with his own firsthand experience, occasions "surprise," and brings with it (in one of Bourne's favorite words) the "glow" of life.

Of greatest significance in this redefinition of irony is the fact that it weaves itself "out of the flux of experience rather than out of eternal values." But of greatest moment to Bourne is the fact that the experience he has in mind is social and that what he needs most to nourish it are friends. This relish for friendship is not merely the reflection of the life he was living at Columbia; it is also an affirmation of temperamental need. To the deprivation of everything else, he says, he is invulnerable; and Clara Barrus, a friend of John Burroughs and student of Whitman, when she read the essay on friendship was moved to send him Whitman's poem, "I saw in Louisiana a Live-Oak Growing." Bourne used his friends, as Emerson did, to discover aspects of himself, but he did not demand of them, as the Transcendentalists did, a running together of souls. He asked much, but on a lower plane: the excitement that generates thought; not binding spiritual relations so much as lively intellectual occasions. His conception of friendship was social where their conception was personal; he was the least of solitaries, a thoroughly social being, and the sociality he required of friendship he required also of the great community. His personal need for friendship inspired his correspondence and, after the camaraderie of Columbia, his search for another rewarding form of social life. But it also inspired, as a similar need had in Whitman, the vision of a pluralistic fraternal society that fired his generation.

Bourne's feeling for the possibilities of an intensely individual yet socialized life generated the gaiety of spirit that, in spite of his awareness of the world of fright, characterizes

his book. He is familiar with the despair of naturalism, but he knows that the adventure as well as the precariousness and peril of life is grounded in this condition. To alleviate the sickness of scientific materialism, he proposes a new idealism, scientific in method but mystical in scope, such as he found in Whitman, Maeterlinck, and William James—an idealism whose newness he suggests when he writes that youth "must think of everything in terms of life; yes, even death in terms of life." In addition, he limits responsibility to social rather than metaphysical evil, to those evils that human "interests" and "ideals" can remedy, and, by explaining the appeal of the "social movement," defends the radicalism of the younger generation while rousing in it his own desire to "ride fast and shout for joy."

In behalf of his generation, Bourne presents an objective that enlists loyalty, that satisfies the claims of both social action and religious sentiment; and, implementing it, he offers a new conception of success and strategy for achieving it. He treats success in "The Experimental Life" and finds its touchstone in the readiness of spirit that contributes also to the adventurous life of irony. "I love people of quick, roving intelligence, who carry their learning lightly, and use it as weapons to fight with, as handles to grasp new ideas with, and as fuel to warm them into a sympathy with all sorts and conditions of men"—this remark (and self-portrayal) in a letter describes the achievement of a way of being, the transformation of personality that for Bourne constitutes success. He detests the doggedness and prudence of planning one's life, for life is not plan and cannot be taken frontally. One must go roundabout, must consult his "interests" (the solicitations of the world) and stand "poised for opportunity." Life is not a battle, as the elders believe, but an experiment. "Life is not a rich province to conquer by our will, or to wring enjoyment out of with our appetites, nor is it a market where we pay our money . . . and receive the goods we desire," Bourne says, repudiating the notions of the older generation as well as those of the still younger generation of Fitzgerald and Hemingway. "It is rather [as Thoreau demonstrated] a great tract of spiritual soil, which we can cultivate or misuse."

Bourne upholds the intrinsic success of self-culture. He believes as firmly as any Transcendentalist in the primary duty of living one's own life—like Thoreau, he hugs himself. The unpardonable sin is "treason to one's self," the easy self-betrayal of letting outer forces arrest the development of one's inner nature. He says that "convention is the real enemy of youth" and advises them to dodge the pressures that "warp and . . . harden the personality and its own free choices and bents." Of these pressures, the most formidable and intolerable is the family, for intimacy compounds its force. In a letter to Prudence Winterrowd encouraging her to leave home, Bourne writes bitterly of the spiritual cannibalism of parents who demand that their children sacrifice their lives for them. He tells her that he wants "independent, self-reliant, progressive generations, not eating each other's hearts out, but complementing each other and assuming a spiritual division of labor."

Now Bourne does not incite youth to rebellion for light and transient reasons. He is aware of their obsession with sex, but mentions it only to set them the task of taming it; his advice is to neglect rather than repress this desire. (He himself was disturbed by desire because he felt debarred from its fulfillment and was still Puritan enough, as "The Major Chord" indicates, to divide the claims of soul and body and imagine them in the conventional terms of light and dark lady. In this unpublished dialogue, the cool, luminous light

lady stands for the pleasures of mind and spirit —for the kind of intellectual relations Bourne actually has with women. The dark lady, warm and naked, represents the body, "the surge and passion of life," and the imperious injunction to live in the body: "You must live, my poet,/ And the body only lives." The poet admits his sexual hunger, but does not take the dark lady. Instead he confronts the light lady, who he notes resembles the dark lady, with his desire and compels her to be both body and soul and to yield a safer passion: "Not the smoky fires of passion," "Not the voluptuous fumes . . ." Certainly what Bourne told a confidante, Alyse Gregory, was true: that the struggle with unrealized desire hampered him, yet colored "all his appreciations," motivated "his love of personality," and filled his life "with a sort of smouldering beauty." (And considered along with all Bourne said in support of desires of other kinds, his solution to the problem of sexual desire confirms Dorothy Teall's statement that the sexual revolution of their generation was more a matter of "refreshment of emotion . . . than a revolution in morals.") Bourne does not treat this problem, except by sympathetic indirection in sketches like "Sophronsiba." The liberation he preaches is neither sexual nor an end in itself but a means to a new "spiritual livelihood." Youth, he says, "must see their freedom as simply the setting free of forces within themselves for a cleaner, sincerer life, and for radical work in society." He asks youth to find socially productive vocations, to contribute to reform *in their vocations*—by following journalism or art, medicine or engineering, not the law, ministry, or business. They must pursue their self-culture in society and stake the fulfillments of self on social reconstruction. He announces these ends in "For Radicals," his directive to the American Scholar, and calls the "idealistic youth of today" to the work of reform that Emerson had spoken of as "the conversion of the world."

The Reverend Walter Greenman wondered how long Bourne would go on using the antithesis of youth and age, and told him to guard against the assault of age and the drying-up of literary material by finding a "new cleavage." The advice was needless. *Youth and Life* was not quite the "charmingly immature book" Norman Foerster, a New Humanist professor, thought it, for youth and age, as Bourne used them, were exactly what Van Wyck Brooks meant by opposed catchwords that correspond to genuine convictions and real issues. Bourne may have approached these issues youthfully, but they were issues of profundity and scope and, followed out, disclosed an abyss in American culture.

Two years before the publication of *Youth and Life,* Santayana had spoken of America, in "The Genteel Tradition in American Philosophy," as "a country with two mentalities, one a survival of the beliefs and standards of the fathers, the other an expression of the instincts, practice, and discoveries of the younger generations." These mentalities were represented, in Stuart Sherman's adaptation of Emerson's phrases, by the Party of Culture and the Party of Nature; and the battle between them, long in preparation, was the bitterest in our cultural history because the insurgent modernists were at last strong enough to attack the entire nineteenth-century orthodox inheritance. Since Emerson's time, the Party of Nature had returned to society; the "nature" in its title was merely a New Humanist slur word designating its arch foe, naturalism. This party was in fact Emerson's Party of Hope, inspired anew by the possibilities of social reform. Radical in its theories of education, socialistic in politics, cosmopolitan and urban, this party exuberantly embraced contemporary America. The Party of Culture, on the other hand, was what Emerson had called the Party of the Past, renamed in tribute to Matthew Arnold, and rightly, because it looked to "culture" to maintain its traditional social and religious values. It was predominantly eastern, Anglo-Saxon, professional; it spoke for the good families of native stock, for the established and wealthy. To these parties Bourne fixed the distinctions of youth and age, for in the battle between them he saw "the struggle of the old to conserve, of the new to adapt"—that "overlapping of the generations, with their stains and traces of the past" that, instead of evolution, accounted for social change.

Ortega has said that a generation is not a succession but an argument. The truth of this observation is especially evident at those times when assumptions are exposed by loss of conviction and points of view alter radically. The Transcendentalists had engaged in such an argument about the nature of human experience and creativity and the ends of American life—an unfinished argument resumed in Bourne's time. He put the issue when he said that his generation wanted "a new orientation of the spirit that shall be modern." And Walter Lippmann, another spokesman for this generation, put it in another way when he wrote in *Drift and Mastery* (1914), a book Bourne greatly admired: "The sanctity of property, the patriarchal family, hereditary caste, the dogma of sin, obedience to authority,—the rock of ages, in brief, has been blasted for us. Those who are young today are born into a world in which the foundations of the older order survive only as habits or by default." Industrialization has changed precipitately the ways of economic and social life, and since the 1880's thinkers—a whole literature—had been assailing the modes of thought supporting the old order. Its guardians, however, seemed neither prepared nor willing to meet the challenge of "experience"—to fulfill new needs and, in Lippmann's phrase, restore the "moral texture of democracy."

The enemies of those who at every stage of our history have responded to the moral imperatives of democracy have been cowardice and complacency, the moral deficiencies Bourne attributed to the older generation. Here, it was most vulnerable because of its assumption of virtue, and Bourne, often with devastating lightness, continued to attack it. He drew its several portraits—caricatures, perhaps, when compared with his tender sketches of the young—in "One of Our Conquerors," "The Professor," and "The Architect."

The conqueror, barely disguised, was Columbia's president, Nicholas Murray Butler, one of the "sleek and successful elders" who was "against everything new, everything untried, everything untested." With his ideal of service and gospel of success, his Anglo-Saxon prejudices, absolute idealism in philosophy, and Republican political rectitude, he was the representative public man of the older generation, an intellectual Horatio Alger, the Captain of Learning who, in the *Columbia Monthly,* had told the undergraduates, "Don't Knock! Boost!"

The professor, drawn appropriately with delicate irony, was John Erskine, also of Columbia. This professor of English had acquired from Henry Van Dyke and Charles Eliot Norton the "ideals of the scholar and gentleman" and protected the "chalice of the past." Himself free from "philosophic or sociologic taint," he deprecated (as Bourne personally knew) "the fanaticism of college men who lose their sense of proportion on social questions."

The architect, an American whom Bourne had met in Italy, shared the professor's gentility and cultural colonialism, for he was an exponent of the Gothic style and a devotee of art for art's sake. Both belonged with the Arnoldians treated in "The Cult of the Best" and "Our Cultural Humility"—those, Bourne said, who believed that "to be cultured . . . mean[s] to like masterpieces" and whose reverential, moralistic attitude toward art closed their eyes to the "vital." Of their company—indeed, with Irving Babbitt, one of their spokesmen—was Paul Elmer More, whose *Aristocracy and Justice* prompted one of Bourne's sharpest replies to the older generation. More, he claimed, not only completely misunderstood modernism and was out of touch with "the driving and creative thought of the day"—was derelict as an intellectual—but was an intellectual partisan of plutocracy, a defender of class exploitation, a judgment More never lived down.

The common want in all of these members of the older generation was the social conscience, which, Bourne said, was "the most characteristic spiritual sign of our age." His generation, he believed, had shifted its spiritual center from the personal to the social. It sought social rather than individual salvation—did not, as he trenchantly explained the religious motives of the older generation, accumulate personal virtue by morally exploiting others and condone social evil as a foil for individual goodness. The older generation believed "in getting all the luxury of the virtue of goodness, while conserving all the advantages of being in a vicious society." Its ideals were selfish and did not appeal to the young who, Bourne said, had begun to "feel social injustice as [their] fathers felt personal sin" and had been converted to a belief in "the possibilities of a regenerated social order."

Youth could no longer be contained in a world "all hardened and definite," by "tight little categories," as he said of More. For More's ethics of repression was the ethics of a "parsimonious" world and had no place in a new world of "surplus value, economic and spiritual." The young had responded to the appeal of a more abundant life, and their response was complete—economic, spiritual, aesthetic. Like More, however, the elders were as insensitive to aesthetic as to moral experience. They did not see that the vision of the social movement was very much an aesthetic one, and their deficiency of social conscience was compounded by "genuine anesthesia," an inability to respond to the petitionings of life and deliver themselves, as Bourne claimed he had, "over to the present."

Bourne's generation had been able to do this because it had acquired from the pragmatists a "new philosophical vista," as Santayana said of the thought of William James, one "radically empirical and radically romantic." Ralph Barton Perry, in *Present Philosophical Tendencies,* an excellent review of contemporary systems that the bright young men of the *Columbia Monthly* considered elementary, treated pragmatism as an especially significant sign of the spirit of the age. Negatively, he wrote, pragmatism represented a "reaction against absolutism, long enthroned in academic and other orthodox circles"; positively, it represented the " 'biological' imagination," the conception of an exigent naturalistic environment from which, in the need for adaptation, knowledge and religion themselves arise as "modes of life." Pragmatism, however, was not a philosophy of renunciation or despair, but an enabling melioristic philosophy of collective human effort: "It teaches that the spiritual life is in the making at the point of contact between man and . . . nature" and that knowledge is instrumental, a power that, guided by desire and hope, may "conquer nature and subdue the insurrection of evil." Santayana said that this philosophy

was "a thousand times more idealistic than academic idealism" and observed that it was the "philosophy of those who as yet had had little experience"; Perry concluded that it was the philosophy of "impetuous youth, of protestanism, of democracy, of secular progress— that blend of naïveté, vigor, and adventurous courage which proposes to possess the future, despite the present and the past." Such, in any case, was the philosophy which, Santayana announced, had "broken the spell of the genteel tradition, and enticed faith in a new direction."

Bourne had discovered pragmatism at Columbia, where, he told Prudence Winterrowd, "we are all instrumentalists." To her, in fervent letters explaining this "most inspiring modern outlook on life and reality," he also related the story of his conversion. He had moved from Calvinism ("I began in the same way as you") to Unitarianism ("mild and healing") to rank materialism ("I . . . took great delight in lacerating a rather tender and green young man whose delight was in Emerson and Plato, whom I despised"). Then, in 1911, in a course with Professor Woodbridge, the "virus of the Bergson-James-Schiller-instrumental-pragmatism" got into his blood; and now, two years later, he preached James as a prophet. In view of his later relationship with Dewey—his discipleship and apostasy—it is interesting to note in these letters Bourne's failure to mention Dewey and, in other letters, his low opinion of Dewey's courses. He was not fired by Dewey; James was his man because he had what Bourne missed in Positivism—"the verve, the color, the music of life." He told Miss Winterrowd that James kept alive for him "a world where amazing regenerations of the vital and spiritual forces of man take place . . . [a world at once] so incorrigibly alive and so incorrigibly mystical." James's world was one of "fluid, interpenetrating, creative things," and Bourne described its appeal when, in a letter to Brooks, he distinguished between mere intellectualism and the "warm area of pragmatic life."

Pragmatism satisfied both the old, now bereft, religious sentiment and the new clamorous scientific spirit. It mediated the extremes of idealism and naturalism. It provided scope for faith and action—and for faith in action. Grounding everything in experience and toward everything proposing an experimental attitude, it upheld the prerogatives of personality at the same time as it encouraged social reform. Itself a product of the biological imagination—a life philosophy—it stimulated the sociological imagination and the faith in salvation by intelligence that were then characteristic of liberal thought. It inspired men to master social drift in the way that the votary Lippmann suggested, by substituting "purpose for tradition," by deliberately depising means for achieving chosen social ends. And to those who adopted its method, it also imparted a democratic vision—it laid, as Bourne said of the new social sciences, "an inexpugnable basis for the highest and noblest aspirations of the time."

How fortunate for Bourne that, finding at home no work for himself equal to these aspirations, he was able to nourish his social imagination elsewhere. Having been awarded a Gilder Fellowship, a handsome patent for sociological investigation, he embarked on July 5, 1913, on the *Rochambeau* for a year's stay in Europe. There he did not follow a course of intensive study so much as a course of extensive travel; he allowed himself a true *Wanderjahr*, rushing over the Continent during the first summer, settling in England and France for most of the autumn and winter, and resuming in the late spring the travels that

ended, on the eve of war, with a midnight escape from Berlin to Sweden.

"Impressions of Europe, 1913–1914," the report he reluctantly wrote to satisfy the terms of his grant, is the summary account of this year, the year in Bourne's life, however, for which his correspondence, diary, and articles provide the fullest record. In contrast with the amplitude and immediacy of these materials, the "Impressions" seem thin and belated. Bourne had by this time told his story too often, and he now chose to tell it differently (for which it is valuable), from the perspective of war and in the light of "the toddlings of an innocent child about the edge of a volcano's crater." "Impressions," in any case, was the right word because he was honest enough to claim no more for his researches and, in a genuine sense, had been another Irvingesque saunterer. He called his travel articles to the Bloomfield *Citizen* "Impressions of a European Tour" and told a friend that he liked "to go sauntering about the streets, looking at all sorts of charming and obscure scenes." He enjoyed the picturesque, as on his journey from Paris to Italy, appreciated the formal achievements of European culture, and knew how to extract the flavors of experience. But he also knew how to grasp a city as a living form by searching out the close textures of its actual social life. He knew that culture was not only the artifacts to which Baedekers were guides, but a process, a present way of life, with which he must make contact. His vision was seldom indolent and, whether sauntering or rushing about, he saw sharply with the eye of a social psychologist.

For Bourne this year abroad was especially formative. He considered it a good test of the experimental life and admitted that at times he was not up to its demands. He missed most his close little world of friends, and to some extent the degree of his success in finding similar groups colored his judgments of England and France. His need and tenacity—and his range of response—are evident in his voluminous correspondence. To Arthur Macmahon and Carl Zigrosser, former roommates at Columbia, he wrote, respectively, of political events and art; to Henry Elsasser, reputedly the most brilliant of his Columbia friends, he sent his profounder speculations; and to Alyse Gregory, whom he had met shortly before his departure, he wrote about socialism and suffragettism—and about himself, for during this period of his life, she was the woman in whom he had chosen to confide.

One of the books that he read with appreciation at the beginning of his travels and soon felt confirmed his European experience was James's *The American*. For Europe immediately forced him to measure his personal resources and those of America, and offered the occasion of a slight, which, one suspects, was more damaging to Bourne than he let on because he never "literized" it as he usually did his experiences. He had been rudely turned out of the country house of S. M. Bligh, a Welsh psychologist to whom he particularly looked for sponsorship in intellectual circles. The smart set he met there did not, it seems, delight in his kind of irony. "My prophetic strain would come out," Bourne wrote Elsasser, "and my Socialism appeared as wild and hair-raising, if not actually mad, in that society of tough British and class-prejudice." His values were turned upside down: "Ideals of militarism, imperialism, moneymaking, conservation of old English snobberies and prejudices, all swept before me in an indescribably voluble and brilliant flood, and I was left, as you may surmise, stranded like a very young Hosea or Amos at the court of some wicked worldly king." To another correspondent he confessed that he had had "a hell of a time emotionally"

—he had indeed been shocked and wounded, and nothing he later experienced in England mollified him. He made his way eventually, meeting the Webbs and Wells, listening to Shaw and Chesterton, studying garden cities, visiting at Oxford, attending the meetings of suffragettes at Knightsbridge. But England made him feel "just about ready to renounce the whole of Anglo-Saxon civilization." The only live thing, he told Carl Zigrosser, had been the suffrage movement. Otherwise, he found "the whole country . . . old and weary, as if the demands of the twentieth century were proving entirely too much for its powers, and it was waiting half-cynically and apathetically for some great cataclysm." By contrast, he exclaimed in a letter to Alyse Gregory, "How my crude, naive, genial America glows!"

Although Bourne had reason to feed his grudge on England, his attitude was characteristic of the younger generation, which discovered in England and France the cultural representatives of the battle it was waging at home. What better example of the Victorianism it had rejected in the Genteel Tradition than old Anglo-Saxondom itself, with its "fatuous cheerfulness" and "incorrigible intellectual frivolity" and "permanent derangement of intellect from emotion"? What better example than France of its youthful modernism—of its delight in quick intelligence, its ardent fraternal sentiment, its responsiveness to social issues and capacity for social change, its pleasure in the taste and color and movement of life? When Bourne turned from London to Paris in December, he entered, he said, "a new world, where the values and issues of life got reinstated for me into something of their proper relative emphasis." To this world the reading of Rousseau's *Confessions* had been his introduction, for it had, he wrote Alyse Gregory, "cleared up for me a whole new democratic morality, and put the last touch upon the old English way of looking at the world, in which I was brought up." It had opened to him the culture of France, which, within less than a month, he felt had completed the "transvaluation of values begun ten years ago when my Calvinism began to crack."

Kept from much about him by his poor command of French, Bourne, nevertheless, established a more satisfactory life in Paris than he had in London. He settled near the Sorbonne, whose greatness he contrasted to "poor little Oxford." The intellectual orientation was agreeably sociological and psychological, and he read sociology in the Bibliothèque Ste. Geneviève and attended the lectures of Bouglé, Delacroix, and Durkheim. He associated with students who were as representative of Young France as he was of Young America (at this time, Youth was an international movement) and he was invited to speak to them about their ideals, the philosophy of William James, and the poetry of Whitman, who had influenced Jules Romains, the author of *La Vie unanime*. Although he had complained at first of the lack of feminine society and in desperation took tea with a silly married American woman—his description of her in a letter to Alyse Gregory is choice—he eventually found a French girl with whom he enjoyed an "intellectual flirtation," the girl of "Mon Ami," his most radiant portrait of youth. The campaign for parliamentary election aroused his political sympathies where the weary Liberal politics of London had not, and, if what and how much he wrote is any measure, the culture of France stimulated him more profoundly than that of any other country.

After France, he did not settle long anywhere because the pace of his travels increased and European life itself was unsettled. In Italy the political activity was as coruscating as the

light, as clamorous as the marketplace. Bourne attended most to the mind of Young Italy through which, it seemed to him, "Nietzsche was raging": to the students demonstrating for Italia Irredenta, to the futurists in art, to the signs of modernism that, he believed, promised for Italy a "new renaissance of the twentieth century." He witnessed in Rome the violent three-day general strike of June—his taste of revolution—and was pleased with the solidarity of the radical classes; and he observed election night in Venice, which, he noted in his report, perhaps with mischievous intent, confirmed "the economic interpretation of politics." Working northward, he returned for the Bern Exposition to Switzerland, his land of delight, "a country . . . that knew how to use its resources for large social ends!" And then he went to Germany, where he studied enthusiastically its planned towns and housing schemes, its new architecture and decorative arts—the evidence of an efficient municipal science that was curiously "undemocratic in political form, yet ultrademocratic in policy and spirit"—but was troubled by the people, by their "thickness and sentimentality and . . . lack of critical sense." There his travel plans were altered and much that he hoped for came to an end. On July 31, he arrived in Berlin, where he experienced the hysteria and outbreak of the war under whose shadow he was to live for the remainder of his life.

The most important result of Bourne's travels was a clearer awareness of the nature and diversity of culture. This was the very thing he emphasized in his report as a corrective to the American tendency (especially dangerous in time of war) to consider the picturesque aspects rather than the fundamental emotional and intellectual differences of foreign countries. "My most striking impression," he said, "was [of] the extraordinary toughness and homogeneity of the cultural fabric in the different countries. . . . Each country was a distinct unit, the parts of which . . . interpreted each other, styles and attitudes, literature, architecture, and social organization."

The three essays that he published in the *Atlantic Monthly* during the summer and fall of his homecoming probe this theme. "An Hour in Chartres" is an essay on cultural style —on "the way things hang together, so that they seem the very emanation of a sort of vast over-spreading communal taste." "Maurice Barrès and the Youth of France" considers the cultural foundations of nationalism and the role of youth in its preservation and advancement. In this essay, Bourne expresses admiration for what Brooks, in *Letters and Leadership*, would call "the collective spiritual life." He knows the evils of nationalism, yet seeks the "intimate cultural fabric" so lacking in America; and he offers a conception of nationalism, emotionally powerful but still somewhat vague, that enhances the quality of life by satisfying social and mystical needs. Although he understands the origins in French military defeat of Barrès' idea and recognizes its essential traditionalism, he finds it overwhelmingly attractive: ". . . the nourishing influences of a rich common culture in which our individualities are steeped, and which each generation carries on freely, consciously, gladly the traits of the race's genius,—this is a gospel to which one could give one's self with wistfulness and love!" Here, for Bourne—and youth—national culture has become an object of loyalty.

Finally, in "Our Cultural Humility," he applies the idea to America, where the very appreciation of European culture (Arnold's "the best") keeps us from engaging in the vital process of our own culture and from producing indigenous art. He asks us, therefore, to foster a national culture of our own: "This cultural chauvinism is the most harmless of patriotisms;

indeed it is absolutely necessary for a true life of civilization." We have already, as he himself had been learning, an indigenous tradition of great artists; he mentions here and in letters Emerson, Thoreau, Whitman, William James, Henry James, Edward MacDowell, and Augustus Saint-Gaudens. (Brooks, whose *America's Coming-of-Age* would be more influential in forming this generation's sense of the past, mentions favorably only Whitman.) Now all we need do, he advises, is "turn our eyes upon our own art for a time, shut ourselves in with our own genius, and cultivate with an intense and partial pride what we have already achieved."

The substance of this culture is conveyed best in another essay of this time, "A Sociological Poet," where Bourne speaks of Unanimism as Whitman "industrialized" and "sociologized." He advocates the larger collective life of "democratic camaraderie," the replacement of the old individualistic life by a new "mass-life" to be lived in the city; and he carefully distinguishes the emergent group feeling he desires from the herd instinct, which fear rather than the warm social conscience feeds. Bourne considers the metropolis to be the "human" milieu and maintains that "the highest reality of the world is not Nature or the Ego, but the Beloved Community"; and he believes, as he wrote later in "American Use for German Ideals," that the pragmatism of James and Dewey and the social philosophy of Josiah Royce strengthen the possibility of such a democratic socialized life.

Bourne derived the functions of this culture from his experience in France and its form from his study of the civic art of Germany. Whenever he defends German ideals or culture, as in the essay cited above and in "A Glance at German 'Kultur,'" he has in mind the civic art that he once told Carl Zigrosser was "the king of the arts, because of its completely social nature." He placed Hampstead Garden Suburb above any planned town in Germany, but he placed Germany above all other nations, "in the very vanguard of socialized civilization." In this respect, Germany epitomized the twentieth century, which explained, Bourne thought, American hostility toward her: she challenged our attitudes and social habits, and, in repudiating her organization and collectivism, we were repudiating the "modest collectivism" of our own progressive movement. Wherever he went in America—to the Midwest, for example, whose urban chaos he described in "Our Unplanned Cities"—he appreciated anew the achievement of Germany: "I love with a passionate love the ideals of social welfare, community sense, civic art, and applied science upon which it is founding itself. . . . I detest . . . the shabby and sordid aspect of American civilization—its frowsy towns, its unkempt countryside, its waste of life and resources. . . ."

Fed by subsequent experience and urged by the intense pressures of wartime, the lessons of the European year took form in Bourne's most important essay on American culture. "Trans-National America" (1916), which the admirably tolerant Sedgwick accepted for the *Atlantic*, was at once Bourne's most incisive analysis of the failure of the older generation and his clearest, most challenging directive to the younger generation. It presents his vision of the kind of culture to which America should aspire and the redeeming role such a culture would enable America to play in the debacle of European nationalisms; and when set up as an alternative to participation in the war ("the war—or American promise" of Bourne's "A War Diary"), this vision of culture provided the test of pragmatic sociology. Bourne's vision anticipated the program of *The Seven Arts*, the magazine that Robert Frost said died "a-Bourning," and first disclosed the landscape described in books such as Waldo Frank's *Our America*.

This deeply personal vision has collective sources. In *The Promise of American Life*, Herbert Croly had spoken of "an over-national idea" and had cited Crèvecoeur's account of the melting process that made the American a new man. To this notion of Americanization, Israel Zangwill's play *The Melting-Pot* had given currency and approval; but Horace Kallen, whom Bourne knew, had repudiated it and proposed instead a "federation of nationalities," or "cultural pluralism," as he subsequently called it. During these years, cosmopolitanism, associated with the city and its immigrant populations, was a cultural stance toward America as well as Europe. H. W. L. Dana, a teacher at Columbia whose dismissal during the war Bourne protested, wrote him, in 1914, that Columbia was "more than national," more than "Anglo-Saxon"; and writing from Europe to Edward Murray (a friend described in "Fergus") Bourne had observed that "the good things in the American temperament and institutions are not English . . . but are the fruit of our far superior cosmopolitanism." As a child, he had been offended by the unattractive Polish girls who worked in the kitchens of Bloomfield; but now he appreciated immigrant life, the Italian settlement, for example, at Emerald Lake (similar to the Guinea Hill district of William Carlos Williams' nearby city) which, he said, injected "sudden vitality into our Puritan town."

"Trans-National America" faced directly the problem of immigration and the making of Americans that had become a conspicuously serious issue of our culture when the show of loyalties provoked by the war revealed our cultural diversity. Sedgwick disapproved of the essay—he called it "radical and unpatriotic" when informing Bourne of the many commendations it received—and insisted that America was "a country created by English instinct and dedicated to the Anglo-Saxon ideal." One recalls another editor of the *Atlantic*, another "hereditary American" (the phrase is Van Wyck Brooks's) who warned us to guard the gates; and Brooks put their fears very well when, in *America's Coming-of-Age*, he retold the story of Rip Van Winkle, the story of an innocent old America that hears in its sleep, not Henry Hudson's men, but "the movement of peoples ["Jews, Lithuanians, Magyars and German socialists"], the thunder of alien wants." Bourne, speaking, he said, as an Anglo-Saxon, threatened the Anglo-Saxon hegemony by announcing that "America shall be what the immigrant will have a hand in making it, and not what a ruling class . . . decides that America shall be made," by questioning the efficacy of Americanization and redefining the meaning of Americanism.

Bourne's most damaging charge is twofold: that the Anglo-Saxon has not transformed the "colony into a real nation, with a tenacious, richly woven fabric of native culture" and that its theory of Americanization is destructive of this very possibility. For Americanization has not produced socialized men but insipid mass-men, "half-breeds," he says, who have been deprived of their native cultures and given instead "the American culture of the cheap newspaper, the 'movies,' the popular song, the ubiquitous automobile." In this way, Americanization contributes to the wreckage rather than creation of culture.

"Just so surely as we tend to disintegrate these nuclei [various immigrant cultures] of nationalistic culture do we tend to create hordes of men and women without a spiritual country, cultural outlaws, without taste, without standards but those of the mob. We sentence them to live on the most rudimentary planes of American life. The influences at the center of the nuclei are centripetal. They make for the intelligence and the social values which mean an enhancement of life. And just because the foreign-born retains this expressiveness is he likely to be a better citizen of the American community. The influences at the fringe, however, are centrifugal, anarchical. They make for detached fragments of peoples. Those who came to find liberty achieve only license. They become the flotsam and jetsam of American life, the downward undertow of our civilization with its leering cheapness and falseness of taste and spiritual outlook, the absence of mind and sincere feeling which we see in our slovenly towns . . . and in the vacuous faces of the crowds on the city street. This is the cultural wreckage of our time . . . America has as yet no impelling integrating force. It makes too easily for this detritus of cultures."

This eloquent passage arises from the deepest tensions of Bourne's social imagination: "I must be interpreting everything," he once said, "in relation to some Utopian ideal, or some vision of perfection." It suggests some of the values he hoped to restore by means of "an enterprise of integration." The new peoples were "threads of living and potent cultures, blindly striving to weave themselves into a novel international nation." Having at their disposal the very agencies that had transformed Bourne and enabled his vision, they might, with its help and practical civic measures of the kind he outlined in "A Moral Equivalent for Military Service," someday achieve it.

"Trans-National America" was not published in the *New Republic* because its editors, as Sedgwick recognized, never gave Bourne space enough to work out his ideas and because, from the start, as Bourne complained, they never gave him any say in policy. When he returned from Europe, the *New Republic* was being organized and staffed; it was the forum he had been seeking, and it gave him a place at $1000 a year. These wages, he felt, were minimal; he was, so he told Alyse Gregory, "a very insignificant retainer." Though he attended the weekly luncheons of the editors, he found his relations with them uncomfortable and remained outside their circle. Sedgwick had warned him of the dangers of magazines—that most are not "loyal to ideas" and are "treacherous to taste" and that radical ones often "set their sails to other breezes." Of Croly and crew, he said: ". . . they are the solemnest procession that ever marched. . . . They can celebrate a Puritan Thanksgiving, but whether they will make the Fourth of July hum, remains to be seen" When Bourne expressed disappointment at Croly's reluctance to "go in instanter for smashing and quarreling," Sedgwick counseled him to give the magazine time to develop a soul. He did, maintaining a connection with the *New Republic* until his death, but he was dismayed.

On coming home, he had tried to re-establish his Columbia life. For a time he lived with Carl Zigrosser at the Phipps model tenements on East 31st Street and socialized—and fell in love—with Barnard girls. But eventually his center shifted. The *New Republic* set the boundaries of his intellectual world: the Public Library, the Russell Sage Foundation, and Greenwich Village. And there he began to meet other people, Elizabeth Shepley Sergeant, for example, who introduced him, in the summer of 1915, to the elite New England summer colony at Dublin, New Hampshire. ("Housekeeping for Men," a light essay, describes the cabin life that was sustained by dinners and evenings with worthies like Amy Lowell and the Abbott Thayers, the latter of special importance to Bourne because through them he met Scofield Thayer who tried to promote his interests on the *Dial*.) He also met

Elsie Clews Parsons, a vigorous, intelligent anthropologist and sociologist, who offered him a haven at Lenox, Massachusetts. His typically full social life is recorded in a datebook for 1916, where one now finds the names of Agnes de Lima, a social worker, and Esther Cornell, an actress, the one the guardian spirit of his life and legacy, the other, her friend, the beautiful girl who would have married him and with whom, at last, he entered a mature emotional life. With them, and Frances Anderson, he shared a house at Caldwell, New Jersey, the summer of 1916. Agnes de Lima recalls that "it was a delicious setting for R., the center of attention with three devoted and high spirited girl companions paying him obeisance"; and she conveys the quality of devotion that still enshrines Bourne's reputation when she writes that "we all adored him of course, fascinated, stimulated, enormously fired by his brilliant intellect, his thrilling range of interests, his unique flair for personal relationships." (One is grateful for Edward Dahlberg's not so foolish surmise, that Bourne was "a sensual gypsy Leporello with [to?] women." All remember his piano-playing—music, he once approvingly noted in a book review, was an emotional equivalent for otherwise unexperienced raptures.) Of male friendships he said very little, but one sees, in his relationships with Paul Rosenfeld and Van Wyck Brooks, that they were strong and good, founded on the conviction of a common intellectual enterprise.

For the *New Republic* Bourne wrote almost one hundred pieces, nearly half of them reviews, the remainder articles, portraits, and editorials. Occasionally he was permitted to write about war issues, but he had been recruited to write about other matters, and most of his work was confined to education and a small but significant amount to city planning. Many of his essays on education were reprinted in *The Gary Schools* (1916), a study of the work-study-and-play schools that William Wirt, a disciple of Dewey, had organized in the new steel town and was proposing for New York City, and in *Education and Living* (1917), a general collection held together by Bourne's insistence that the long process of education be a living now, not a postponement of life. These books contributed to Bourne's reputation as (to cite one reviewer) "the most brilliant educational critic of the younger generation," but neither has the solidity of achievement that makes reputations permanent. In the first, he was encumbered by the publisher's demands that he write for teachers and superintendents and subdue his enthusiasm for Wirt; in the second, repetition drains away the force some of the essays have singly. These books, however, represent the mastery of a field. They develop the primary themes of *Youth and Life* and bridge Bourne's personal and social concern for human fulfillment. And in them one begins to appreciate the extent to which Bourne has become a publicist of the kind he admired in J. A. Hobson—a man with "immense stores of knowledge, poise of mind, and yet radical philosophy and gifts of journalistic expression."

In retrospect, Agnes de Lima depreciated these books, remarking, however, that Bourne was finely perceptive about the needs of children, a truth confirmed by "Ernest: or Parent for a Day," a charming *Atlantic* essay that readers may find sufficiently representative of this strand of his thought. Yet there is value (and pleasure) in reading more: the realization of the alliance of educational with modern thought, of the place of education in democratic society as an essential and democratic process, as a revivifier of its faith and instrument of its reform. *Democracy and Education* —such was the title of Dewey's challenging book of 1916, when education had become an urgent domestic issue and no other social enterprise seemed to partisans like Bourne so hopeful, rational, and democratic. "To decide what kind of a school we want," he said, "is almost to decide what kind of society we want" —a disclosure of faith that may explain the presence among his unpublished papers of an essay (of 1918) extolling the efforts of the British to prepare for social reconstruction by initiating educational reforms during the war.

Much of Bourne's work before and after America entered the war was educational, either about education or in the interest of overcoming what, in 1915, he called our "mental unpreparedness." War had been the means, he explained, of shocking even his up-to-date generation into an awareness of a world where war happens, and it had given the intellectuals the task of replacing the "old immutable idealism," no longer credible, with a "new experimental idealism." "We should make the time," he told them, "one of education." Instead of military preparedness, our need, he said, was "to learn how to live rather than die; to be teachers and creators, not engines of destruction." Before war was declared, he had worked for peace, the essential condition of democratic reform; for the American Association for International Conciliation he edited a symposium of peace proposals and programs, *Towards an Enduring Peace* (1916). And he had been a leader of the Committee for Democratic Control, which tried to halt the descent to war by publishing in the newspapers (and the *New Republic*!) antiwar advertisements and appeals for popular referendums. With war declared —"the effective and decisive work" that the editors of the *New Republic* claimed had been accomplished "by a class which must be . . . described as the 'intellectuals' "—Bourne took on the role for which he is most often remembered: he became the critic of the war strategy and, especially, of the intellectuals who had broken faith with pragmatism and had closed out the promise of American life by eagerly joining "the greased slide toward war."

It is fashionable now to admire Bourne's unyielding spirit and intellectual rectitude but to pity him for assuming that the drift of things is susceptible to human mastery. When depressed by the penalties of lonely opposition, he also indulged himself in deterministic views (see "Old Tyrannies"). Yet however much in a metaphysical sense drift may be a true account of things, it is not a true account of the diplomacy that led to war. Here events seemed to have their own way but were actually chosen and, as Bourne maintained (see especially his comments on the presidency in "The State"), other choices might have prevailed. The question seldom raised by those who, curiously, speak up for intellectuals but impugn their force is the one with which Bourne in effect challenged the boastful intellectuals of the *New Republic*: had the intellectuals taken Bourne's position, would the outcome have been otherwise? By assuming that it would, one grants Bourne the condition of justly understanding him.

The wayward course of the war strategy and the policy of the *New Republic*, which Bourne cogently analyzed in five essays published in 1917 in *The Seven Arts* (collected in *Untimely Papers*, 1919), is now of less interest than his assessment of pragmatism and inquiry into the motives and roles of intellectuals. War taught Bourne that pragmatism was not so much a philosophy for fair weather as one requiring for its survival an open world of alternatives. Where choice is impossible, pragmatism ceases to exist, for intelligence ceases to have a function; in "total" or "absolute" situations like war, it is without leverage. This was the point Bourne directed specifically to John Dewey, whom he had once petitioned in an essay of praise to become an intellectual leader in "the

arena of the concrete," and who, since 1916, had done so by becoming the philosopher-statesman of the *New Republic* and *The Seven Arts* (until July 1917, when Bourne and Brooks replaced him) and of the *Dial*.

To read Dewey's essays is an uncomfortable experience, wholly justifying Bourne's judgment that the philosophy of Dewey "breaks down . . . when it is used to grind out interpretation for the present crisis." Dewey speciously justified the use of force and was concerned more with winning intellectual assent to participation than clarifying the values for American national life that he claimed would come of it. Once committed to war, he wished only to get the job done in a "business like way." He insisted that "an end is something which concerns results rather than aspirations," and considered pacifists, including Bourne, "passivists," victims of "moral innocency" and "futility." Yet aspirations were the issue. For Dewey, father of a noble conception of America and leader of the educational work to be done, had himself chosen war, had turned from his own best vision and had become, as Bourne, feeling betrayed, said, a fatuous instrumentalist who believed naively that he was controlling the "line of inevitables" war brings. "It may be pragmatism to be satisfied with things that work," Bourne wrote in an unpublished essay, "but it is a very shallow one." Pragmatism was always for him a philosophy in which ends count, and he remained true to it by demanding alternative courses of action and by keeping in view the "American promise"—and nowhere so demonstrably as in these *timely* papers, where, in the exercise of intellectual responsibility, he mastered his materials, argument, and tone in writing of unusual incandescence.

As Dwight Macdonald recognized (in *Politics*, his personal attempt to propose courses during another war), Bourne had "continued along the way [the pragmatists] had all been following until the war began." They, however, took the path Bourne describes in "The War and the Intellectuals." Feeling that to be out of the war was "at first to be disreputable and finally almost obscene," they assumed "the leadership for war of those very classes whom the American democracy has been immemorially fighting." Joyfully they accepted this leadership and willingly abandoned criticism for propaganda, "the sewage of the war spirit." Neutrality had put the intellectuals under the strain of thinking; it was easier to act; and action brought relief from indecision. So the thinkers, with their "colonial" (Anglo-Saxon) sympathies and their eagerness to be responsible for the world, with their "emotional capital" idle for want of domestic spending but ready for investment in Europe, "dance[d] with reality." And this reversion to "primitive" ways, though understandable, was not only costly beyond measure ("the whole era has been spiritually wasted") and supremely ironic (for how can war and democracy be coupled?) but especially shameful because it led the intellectuals to repudiate everything that becomes the intellectual and to impugn the work of the few who were peace-minded. Included in their company, moreover, were those younger intellectuals of a different kind whom the elder pragmatists had trained: those "experts in the new science of administration" hailed by Lippmann in *Drift and Mastery*, whom Bourne now found "vague as to what kind of society they want, or what kind of society America needs, but . . . equipped with all the administrative attitudes and talents necessary to attain it."

Bourne himself accepted the role of the "excommunicated," of an "irreconcilable." He tried to make his apathy toward the war "take the form of a heightened energy and enthusiasm for the education, the art, the interpretation that make for life in the midst of the world of death." But the role, which he defined in such therapeutic essays as "Below the Battle" and "The Artist in Wartime" (unpublished), was a very hard one, requiring, as Croly long before had warned the intellectuals, "sharp weapons, intense personal devotion, and a positive indifference to consequences." In a sense, Bourne was a war casualty, unwounded, he bravely said, by "all the shafts of panic, patriotism, and national honor," yet deeply dispirited. He suffered—more, according to Elsie Clews Parsons, from the renegation of the intellectuals than from personal exclusion —and he was hurt by the bitterness that he predicted would grow and "spread out like a stain over the younger American generation." He frequently expressed the wish to escape to the "great good place" and, as if desperately fighting to attain it, struck out, in the book reviews to which he was limited in his last year, at those who seemed to stand in his way: he quarreled with Dewey over a disciple's book; discredited Sedgwick's judgment by slashing at Paul Shorey's strident defense of the New Humanism; turned on Dean Keppel, who was currently working for the War Department, by gratuitously pointing out that "his mind is liberal and yet it serves reaction"; and needlessly punished Brander Matthews in order to express his misgivings over wartime Columbia.

Yet what is impressive in Bourne's career, finally, is the attempt to master disillusionment and despair by recovering the very history of his generation, by learning the lessons it had to teach and plotting the course it might take. Bourne never shirked the responsibility of thought and began the "anxious speculation" that he told Brooks "should normally follow the destruction of so many hopes." The most ambitious project of this kind was the long unfinished essay, "The State," in which he vented the "scorn for institutions" that had once combined "with a belief in their reform." This essay, overrated by those who consider it an especially prescient political treatise, has the frantic quality of one whom events have forced back on himself—its companion work was the unfinished autobiographical novel. Bourne did not write it because the state, as legend claims, coerced him, but because he needed to understand the social behavior of the time: why, for example, an apathetic nation goes to war and centralization of power contributes not to the creation of social wealth (as Croly had once said it would) but to its spoliation in war. The essay exhibits a sharp analytical power but also a conspiratorial mentality: Bourne makes the Anglo-Saxons the betrayers of democracy throughout American history and explains the failure to reform in his "ephemeral" time by ascribing it to an evil power which he thinks simply awaited the war to make itself known. The cynicism of the essay is protective and, like its bitterness, was accepted too uncritically by the next generation. Bourne appeared to put too high the odds against idealism, ruling out the very agency that he still believed to be necessary and efficacious.

"Bourne was keenly conscious of lost values," Elsie Clews Parsons wrote, "but he was resourceful in compensations." And by way of exemplification, she noted the suspect but important strategy of his essay: "In his essay on the State he had begun to battle for distinctions between State, Nation, and Country, in which the State became the conceptual scapegoat for the sins of patriotism, leaving Nation and Country immaculate and worthy of devotion."

Bourne's goal had not altered, only the way. War taught him what any crisis may teach a reformer: that society is not as plastic as the ideas in our minds, that freedom runs into limitation, that wholesale social reconstruction must submit to the slower processes of education. It did not destroy his faith in political action, although it made him distrustful of the "cult of politics" and increased his appreciation of the social uses of personal expression —of the resources "malcontents" might find in art and criticism. His own essays in criticism such as "The Art of Theodore Dreiser" and "The Immanence of Dostoevsky" reveal a maturing critical sense and represent the kind of criticism he defined in "Traps for the Unwary" and in the closing pages of "The History of a Literary Radical." As he had pointed out earlier in a review of H. L. Mencken, Puritanism was no longer a significant cultural issue; criticism had work to do more important than moralizing. For the real enemy of art was the widening, responsive, but still genteel public that wanted "the new without the unsettling."

A "new criticism," accordingly, was needed to rectify "the uncritical hospitality of current taste" and to give the artists, who promised, he believed, "a rich and vibrant literary era," an "intelligent, pertinent, absolutely contemporaneous criticism, which shall be both severe and encouraging"—the latter to be obtained only when "the artist himself has turned critic and set to work to discover and interpret in others the motives and values and efforts he feels in himself." This criticism, Bourne explained to Harriet Monroe, editor of *Poetry*, was not aesthetic in the sense of being merely appreciative or of providing "esoteric enjoyment" (what she called "pink-tea adulation"), nor did it treat art wholly in terms of itself or move "hazily in a mist of values and interpretations." He insisted that it also be social criticism—that it take into account "ideas and social movements and the peculiar intellectual and spiritual color of the time." To have conceived of these requisites of criticism and of a "new classicism" demanding "power with restraint, vitality with harmony, a fusion of intellect and feeling, and a keen sense of the artistic conscience" is evidence of Bourne's unfailing sensitivity to the directon of his culture and, although the critic he seeks had need of the strengths of an Eliot, Pound, and Edmund Wilson, evidence of his awareness that the work he set himself should be less prophetic (not like that undertaken by Brooks and Waldo Frank) and nearer to his developing capacities.

In an autobiographical essay, "The History of a Literary Radical," he called himself a literary radical chiefly to distinguish the intellectual type of his generation from that of the older generation. The literary radical possesses an imagination at once aesthetic and sociological. He wishes to nurture his art in society and to use it to reform and enhance social life. His most common difficulty is the adjustment of aesthetic and social allegiances. In his own case, Bourne told Elizabeth Shepley Sergeant, "the reformer got such a terrific start in my youth over the artist that I'm afraid the latter is handicapped for life." But he knew, as he said with respect to his friend John Burroughs, that the "eternally right way and attitude of the intellectual life" is to look at the world with "the eye of the artist" and to employ one's science to "illumine . . . artistic insight"; and this he always tried to do by being radical in another sense: by going back to the root of perception. For all of his science, Bourne remained an essayist who addressed the world in the first person and in his writing attempted to reproduce the atmosphere of discussion that he valued so much, and whose style, as Alvin Johnson noted, possessed "warmth with light [and] logical straightforwardness combined with charm and sympathy." He had, to borrow a phrase from Santayana's applicable discussion of romantics and transcendentalists, "a first-hand mind." Autobiography was the mode he cherished, the staple thread of all his work, his way of being true to himself and his circumstances and of bearing witness, which makes his true inheritors not so much those who took over his topics as those who discovered for themselves the necessity and resources of an autobiographical method. The autobiographical novel upon which Bourne was working at the time of his death is not of interest as a novel but as an example of what, at the beginning of his career, he said was needed: "true autobiographies, told in terms of the adventure that life is."

Bourne began "An Autobiographic Chapter" by telling how, when he was six, his family had moved from a house on a back street to another house offering a life more spacious: "And his expanding life leaped to meet the wide world." This characteristic fronting of the world with "its new excitements and pleasures" was, he wrote, "like a rescue, like getting air when one is smothering." This image was perhaps more premonitory than he knew when, in the last dismal months of his life, he used it to describe the sense of relief he had felt on the occasion of his first rescue; for on December 22, 1918, in his thirty-second year, with the war over and new prospects before him, he succumbed to influenza.

The legends about Bourne that almost immediately arose created the impression of martyrdom that his example of intellectual courage neither sustains nor needs, and hindered a just appreciation of his work. He deserves the prominent place he has acquired in the history of his generation and, because his actual literary achievement was small, a modest place in the literary tradition that in his time he was one of the few to value. At the end of "The History of a Literary Radical," he speaks of "a certain eternal human tradition of abounding vitality and moral freedom" that may be found in such American writers as Thoreau,

Whitman, and Mark Twain. This is the tradition he served.

Selected Bibliography

PRINCIPAL WORKS OF RANDOLPH BOURNE

BOOKS
Youth and Life. Boston: Houghton Mifflin, 1913.
The Gary Schools. Boston: Houghton Mifflin, 1916.
Towards an Enduring Peace, edited by R. S. Bourne. New York: American Association for International Conciliation, 1916.
Education and Living. New York: Century, 1917.
Untimely Papers, edited by James Oppenheim. New York: B. W. Huebsch, 1919.
The History of a Literary Radical and Other Essays, edited by Van Wyck Brooks. New York: B. W. Huebsch, 1920.
The History of a Literary Radical and Other Papers, edited by Van Wyck Brooks. New York: S. A. Russell, 1956. (A slightly different collection.)

ARTICLES
Bourne wrote chiefly for the *Columbia Monthly* (January 1910–November 1913), the *Atlantic Monthly* (May 1911–June 1917), the *New Republic* (November 7, 1914–September 28, 1918), the *Dial* (December 28, 1916–December 18, 1918), *The Seven Arts* (April 1917–October 1917). Consult Schlissel and Moreau for detailed citations.

LETTERS AND DIARY
"Some Pre-War Letters (1912–1914)," *Twice a Year*, 2:79–102 (Spring–Summer 1939).
"Letters (1913–1914)," *Twice a Year*, 5–6:79–88 (Fall–Winter 1940, Spring–Summer 1941).
"Diary for 1901," *Twice a Year*, 5–6:89–98 (Fall–Winter 1940, Spring–Summer 1941).
"Letters (1913–1916)," *Twice a Year*, 7:76–90 (Fall–Winter 1941).

The World of Randolph Bourne, edited by Lillian Schlissel. New York: Dutton, 1965. Pp. 293–326.

BIBLIOGRAPHIES
Filler, Louis. *Randolph Bourne.* Washington, D.C.: American Council on Public Affairs, 1943.
Moreau, John Adam. *Randolph Bourne: Legend and Reality.* Washington, D.C.: Public Affairs Press, 1966. Pp. 210–27.
Schlissel, Lillian, ed. *The World of Randolph Bourne.* New York: Dutton, 1965. Pp. 327–33.

CRITICAL AND TESTIMONIAL STUDIES
Brooks, Van Wyck. "Randolph Bourne," in *Emerson and Others.* New York: Dutton, 1927.
————. "Randolph Bourne," in *Fenollosa and His Circle.* New York: Dutton, 1962.
Dahlberg, Edward. "Randolph Bourne: In the Saddle of Rosinante," *Can These Bones Live.* Revised edition. New York: New Directions, 1960. (First edition, 1941.)
————. "Randolph Bourne," in *Alms for Oblivion.* Minneapolis: University of Minnesota Press, 1964.
Filler, Louis. *Randolph Bourne.* Washington, D.C.: American Council on Public Affairs, 1943.
Lasch, Christopher. "Randolph Bourne and the Experimental Life," in *The New Radicalism in America (1889–1963): The Intellectual as a Social Type.* New York: Knopf, 1965.
Lerner, Max. "Randolph Bourne and Two Generations," *Twice a Year*, 5–6: 54–78 (Fall–Winter 1940, Spring–Summer 1941). (Reprinted in *Ideas for the Ice Age.* New York: Viking Press, 1941.)
Madison, Charles. "Randolph Bourne: The History of a Literary Radical," in *Critics and Crusaders: A Century of American Protest.* New York: Henry Holt, 1947.
Moreau, John Adam. *Randolph Bourne: Legend and Reality.* Washington, D.C.: Public Affairs Press, 1966.

Resek, Carl. "Introduction" to *War and the Intellectuals: Essays by Randolph S. Bourne, 1915–1919*. New York, Evanston, and London: Harper and Row, 1964.

Rosenfeld, Paul. "Randolph Bourne," *Dial*, 75:545–60 (December 1923). (Reprinted in *Port of New York*. New York: Harcourt, Brace, 1924; Urbana: University of Illinois Press, 1961.)

Schlissel, Lillian. "Introduction" to *The World of Randolph Bourne*. New York: Dutton, 1965.

—SHERMAN PAUL

Van Wyck Brooks

1886-1963

THE displacement of Van Wyck Brooks from the center to the farthest margins of literary influence today is surely a stunning shift of taste. In 1920 Brooks was regarded as the undisputed heir of the great tradition in American thought—the radical, reformist, prophetic, "organic" tradition which adopted Emerson as its source of inspiration, took "The American Scholar" as its point of departure, and envisioned as its point of terminus a civilization in which the creative spirit, in all its social and imaginative forms, might flourish. To this old enterprise Brooks had brought intransigent zeal and incomparable flair—a genius for clarifying thought, said his comrade-at-arms on *The Seven Arts*, James Oppenheim. Today, Brooks's sovereign role in the transmission of this classic American tradition, his *oeuvre* of inquiry into its bearing on modern letters in America, is either ignored or disdained.

"The most interesting American books," Richard Poirier observes in his presumably definitive study of this tradition, *A World Elsewhere* (1968), "are an image of the creation of America itself, of the effort, in the words of Emerson's Orphic poet, to 'Build therefore your own world.'" For reasons of ignorance or disdain, I guess, Poirier excludes Brooks from his study—even though Brooks had ac-

quired, a half-century ago, an international fame and following as the leading spokesman for Emerson's idea, as a most compelling opponent of those younger writers who decided that American genius could flourish only outside the United States. At first he shared their view. But eventually he came to think that America, by virtue of its history and ideology, was not only itself the very emblem of the creative life but was, too, the best place on earth to locate the republic of letters. And he composed a series of books which monumentalized Emerson's Orphic vision. Suddenly, when his art had achieved certain marvels of transformation, he lost voice, heart, taste, courage for the task. Somehow he lost the thread of his own passion and found himself in an abyss of his own devising. A really major figure in the seedtime of modern thought, he became a minor figure in the time of efflorescence—victim of the very forces he had discerned, named, and condemned. Although he turned out to be a critic of divided mind, a man whose life was broken in half, in one respect his career was all of a piece: from first to last he sought to transform America from an industrial jungle into a place fit for the realization of Emerson's Romantic dream.

There was no sign of faltering will in those early books, published between 1908 and

1925, which introduced a prodigy endowed with audacity of learning, fluency of speech, an apparent assurance of mind, and a cosmopolitan experience unmatched in American criticism of that day. Born in Plainfield, New Jersey, in 1886, educated there and in Europe where his family had spent a year in 1898, Brooks had entered Harvard in 1904. Completing work for his degree a year early, in 1907, he had gone on a second European journey, to England, where for eighteen months he had lived as a free-lance journalist and where he had written and published *The Wine of the Puritans* in 1908. He came back to New York that year and remained until 1911 when he went to California. There he married Eleanor Kenyon Stimson, whom he had known as a friend of childhood and youth and whose own life, both before and after Wellesley, had been spent going back and forth from Europe: "we were both in love with Europe and always had been."

Returning to England in 1913 with his new family—a son had been born in 1912—Brooks published the work written during his California years, *The Malady of the Ideal*. This and *The Wine of the Puritans* make a pair quite as the next pair, *John Addington Symonds: A Biographical Study* (1914) and *The World of H. G. Wells* (1914), were conceived and composed in concert. The four, taken together, provide initial statements of those ideas, passionately held, which were to shape Brooks's critique of and program for America in the celebrated essays *America's Coming-of-Age* (1915) and *Letters and Leadership* (1918), and the psychological studies *The Ordeal of Mark Twain* (1920) and *The Pilgrimage of Henry James* (1925). In these eight interconnected pieces of work, representing two decades of resolute and concentrated Brooks focused his whole energy He sought to penetrate the

conditions which devastate and to disclose the environments which nurture the springs of art in Europe and the United States.

I speak of these intricate things as if there is no problem in reducing a thousand pages of intense prose—and hundreds of pages of criticism of Brooks's prose—to a simple formula. But the very resourcefulness of Brooks's mind and the opulence of comment on Brooks's books have obscured certain obvious matters about which it is, at this late stage of judgment, no great task to be forthright. Indeed, a certain likeness from book to book has always been fairly plain. Stanley Edgar Hyman, for example, describing Brooks's distinction between the actual "wine" of the Puritans and the "aroma" of wine, recognized in this play of metaphor an embryonic version of those distinctions between highbrow and lowbrow on which Brooks was to build the myth of America's coming of age. If you read backwards from lowbrow you discover Brooks maintaining that it was the Puritans' taste for the material life of the New World which led in later centuries to a sheer and bald commercialism: "wine." Read backwards from highbrow and you find Brooks arguing that it was the Puritans' simultaneous joy in the "aroma of the wine, the emphasis on the ideal, which became transcendentalism." The essential questions raised in *The Wine of the Puritans*, then, introduced a perplexity which was ever to vex Brooks, a man who retained all his life the habit of formulating modern questions in an archaic language. If art is defined as the Soul's perception of the Ideal, how can art enrich a society which was itself created out of a breach between Soul and Body, between Ideal and Real? Could America be made into a place where the life of thought and the life of action might be reconciled?

These were the lofty problems, invariably cast into pairs of metaphor, which led Brooks in *The Malady of the Ideal* to contrast the temper of German thought with the French. The French temperament, fixed firmly in the real world and engaged by the problems of social order, he called *rhetorical*. In contrast, the German mind, concerned with "truth, good, and beauty," the realm of the Ideal, was *poetical* in its drift. The true poet, rooted in the Real, fixed his attention unwaveringly on the Ideal and became therefore a great source of reconciliation, a visionary of order on earth. A rhetorician, however, was committed to the study of exterior consistency alone. "He takes his point of departure from an idea which in its primitive form is a sincere expression of himself. The next day looking deeper he perhaps discovers a new idea that cuts away the ground from under his former idea. But he is a practical man—he . . . therefore forces a consistency between the two ideas." As the circle of his thought arcs farther and farther away from that first, genuine perception, finally "he achieves a logical consistency; his work has a compact, finished quality. But where is truth?" Illustrating the practical effects of his theory, Brooks referred to Senancour and Maurice de Guérin, and arrived at last at Amiel, "true child of Geneva," in whom French and German influence came to a standoff, a sterile, immobilizing "fatal mixture of the blood." Neither German enough, "foolhardy" enough, to trust in intuition, nor French enough, rhetorical enough, to rely on disciplined rationalism, Amiel sat "like a spider in a kind of cosmic web spun from his own body, unable to find himself because he could not lose himself."

Before long, as we shall see, Brooks himself was to arrive at the condition in which *The Malady of the Ideal* leaves Amiel. Ironically, too, his next books, on Symonds and Wells, mark the emergence of Brooks the rhetorician, the practical critic whose work was compact and self-contained and consistent but—said his critics—Where was truth?

A disappointing book to read in 1914, the study of Symonds is an especially rewarding book to read now. For Brooks was only superficially preoccupied with his ostensible subject and was deeply engaged inquiring into his essential subject—himself. In its tiniest detail and in the sweep of its theme, the biography of Symonds is a clairvoyant essay in self-appraisal and self-revelation. Taking up the subject of his *Malady*, applying its theoretical system to English letters, Brooks presents Symonds as a victim of neuroticism so acute as to render him blind to the distinctions between "mundane and visionary values," between Real and Ideal. Symonds to his credit possessed a visionary mind; to his discredit, so Brooks believed, he was incapable of bearing the cost of vision and he turned instead to rhetoric, to the study of the humdrum. In order to support this reading, Brooks adopted a strategy which led him away from the ordinary pursuits of literary criticism and plunged him into the first of his exercises in the psychology of failure, the sociology of despair. Whatever else must be said, it cannot be gainsaid that this was pioneer work of a most taxing kind. And what has hitherto been left unsaid about Brooks is that his pioneering studies in literary psychology were informed by his reading a single source, Bernard Hart's *The Psychology of Insanity*. This famous handbook was first published in England in 1912, shortly before Brooks's third European and second English sojourn in 1913. As he later told Robert Spiller—who repeated the anecdote to me—Hart's little book represented all that he knew of psychoanalysis. Whether or not he read Freud or Jung too, whom he mentions in print now and then, is uncertain. But there is no mention of Hart's work in Brooks's writing—a strange omission in the light of his remark to Spiller.

The Psychology of Insanity is a historic work. It is the first essay, both technical and lucid, which incorporates Freud's views on the general subject. This book, Hart wrote, "does not really occupy any definite place in the direct line of Freudian history, but is at once narrower and wider in its aim." It is narrower in that it deals with certain selected aspects of Freud's thought (Hart adopted the unconscious and the concept of repression but rejected Freud's views on sex) and it is wider "in that it attempts to bring those aspects into relation with lines of advance followed by other investigators." In its own right a remarkably sage and balanced essay, it is typical of its period, too, in its tone of wonder and certainty—wonder that some classic riddles of the psyche had been solved at last, certainty that some tentative propositions would turn out dogmatic truth.

In Hart's habit of discovering simple trauma behind complicated events, Brooks found sanction to support his own custom of searching out a "causal complex" which would simply explain everything. As applied to Symonds, this habit led Brooks to ascribe neurotic failure to a state of war between reason and action, passion and thought. Symonds' thought could not satisfy appetites generated by Symonds' passions; nor could Symonds, for reasons of health and "conscience," translate thought into action: "it was this complex [which] remained with him to the last" and ended ultimately in breakdown. Upon recovery, he discovered Whitman and through Whitman acquired "a lusty contempt for purely intellectual processes." Symonds struck a bad bargain with his instincts, Brooks said, and in consequence was transformed into a "congested poet" and *vulgariseur*, a maker of scholarly books which struggled to do what "only poetry can do" and are therefore best described

as "high fantasy," not high accomplishment in humane letters.

Reading this comment on Symonds, anyone with even the skimpiest knowledge of Brooks's career must recognize in the pattern Brooks ascribes to Symonds' life the very pattern which best describes Brooks's life—including the rediscovery of Whitman. If I seem to be forcing a consistency where there is resemblance alone, Brooks's peroration dispels all doubt. The portrait of Symonds, chronology altered but otherwise changed only to include metaphoric rather than literal detail, could stand as a self-portrait: "Neurotic from birth, suppressed and misdirected in education, turned by early environment and by natural affinity into certain intellectual and spiritual channels, pressed into speculation by dogmatic surroundings and aesthetic study, his naturally febrile constitution shattered by over-stimulation, by wanting vitality denied robust creation, by disease made a wanderer, by disease and wandering together aroused to an unending, fretful activity—the inner history of Symonds could be detailed and charted scientifically."

After completing this book and publishing it in 1913–14, along with *The Malady of the Ideal* and *The World of H. G. Wells*, Brooks left England once again for New York. This time, however, the decision to return signified at last an end to wandering, an end to the disease of indecision which had plagued him since his departure from Harvard. Brooks's wanderings during this period of his life are not just of documentary interest. Nor do these represent mere sprightliness of curiosity on the part of a provincial bright young man. It is a rather more radical thing. For it was during these half-dozen years of inquiry into and contrast of certain American and European styles of life that Brooks cast about for reasons why he should remain at home or return abroad to live in determined rather than tentative exile. In these early works he sought to resolve a disquietude more pressing than troubled Amiel or Symonds. It is useful, therefore, to present a detailed chart of the inner history of Brooks's mind at the moment when he achieved his greatest fame and widest influence.

A "wanderer, the child of some nation yet unborn, smitten with an inappeasable nostalgia for the Beloved Community on the far side of socialism, he carried with him the intoxicating air of that community, the mysterious aroma of its works and ways." These are Brooks's words, written in eulogy to his beloved friend Randolph Bourne. But again biography and autobiography fuse: the sketch of Bourne is also a work of self-portraiture which intimates the state of Brooks's mind in the period beginning in 1914. Completing the book on Wells, whom he called a man of "planetary imagination," an "artist of society," Brooks convinced himself that America was ripe for rebirth on the far side of socialism. Smitten with an inappeasable nostalgia for utopia, he convinced himself, too, that a socialist America would be the place in which the life of the mind (the realm of the Ideal) and the life of action (the Real) might be brought to equilibrium. America, he said, was H. G. Wells "writ large."

Brooks at mid-decade was by no means a man of composed mind but was instead a man of divided will: the chief obsession of his divided mind was Europe. This obsession he shared, strangely, with the man he most despised, T. S. Eliot. To say that Brooks despised Eliot is no exaggeration. Although his published comment is restrained, his private comment, particularly in the later days of fascism, exihibits a barely controlled revulsion. The "Elioteers" are almost as bad as the Germans,

he blurted in a letter (November 1941), to Bliss Perry. Brooks was peculiarly fierce not just because he despised Eliot's ideas but because, deep down, he shared Eliot's taste for the well-upholstered life of a European man of letters.

In Brooks's instance and Eliot's, in Pound's and Conrad Aiken's, John Gould Fletcher's and H. D.'s—that first wave of expatriate American writers—the dream of literature was inextricable from the dream of Europe. In the world Brooks knew as a child, that well-heeled and well-placed society of the eastern seaboard, Henry Adams' world, "a voyage to Europe was the panacea for every known illness and discontent." Unlike his compatriots who had few second thoughts about cloaking themselves in the "iridescent fabric" of Europe, Brooks was deeply torn. The causes of conflict lay in the special circumstances of his early life, that family which was at once in harmony and in conflict with the Harvard cult of Europe, incarnate in Santayana. Why am I abroad, he had forced himself to think in 1908, when I believe in living at home? Part of the answer was by no means complicated—though it did involve some complications within his family. He was determined to escape Plainfield, New Jersey, and to avoid the "sadness and wreckage" which diminished the lives of his father and brother. In that town where Brooks's neighbors were the "quiet solid men of money," he had never been at home. Nor had his brother, Ames, who had solved the problem of displacement by placing himself as far as possible from Plainfield. "He walked in front of the early commuters' train one morning at the Plainfield station." Nor indeed had Brooks's father—a man of business, doomed to invalidism, yearning for Europe—ever been at home in that suburb of Wall Street. "Had my father's practical failure in life over-affected my own mind, as his European associations had affected it also, so that perhaps his inability to adjust himself to existence at home had started my own European-American conflict?"

Although Brooks's thought tends often to lunge toward the pat answer, he did come to adulthood within a family in which Europe was represented as the solution for everything. But if his family proved anything it proved that Europe solved nothing. Eventually, believing that "deracination meant ruin," Brooks found himself impaled: "the American writer could neither stay *nor* go,—he had only two alternatives, the frying-pan and the fire." And Brooks made a self-conscious and brave choice: "the question was therefore how to change the whole texture of life at home so that writers and artists might develop there." All tremulous with misgiving he took on the truly formidable task, as Sherman Paul has observed, of making America Europe. Or, said in the terminology Brooks had devised, he would bring Ideal and Real, visionary imagination of the Germanic kind and cogency of systematic thought of the rationalist French sort, into a new and radically American balance. Returning to this country at a time of "Arctic loneliness for American writers," perhaps he would escape the wreckage his own family suffered.

This decision, a thing of high drama, was less momentous for American literature than the acolyte of art could have imagined and far more portentous for his inner life than he could have foreseen. Embracing a flimsy but plausible notion—deracination meant ruin—he returned to America almost in Puritanic renunciation of his deepest want. As is well known but ill understood, the scheme worked from 1914 when it was completed until 1925 when it and Brooks himself collapsed. In virtual casebook display of what Freud called the return of the repressed, Brooks in breakdown was haunted by the apparition of Henry James,

by nightmares in which James "turned great luminous menacing eyes upon me." It was the figure of James that turned the screw of nightmare in the late twenties. But many years earlier, in childhood, it had been not James but a Hindu who appeared in the "earliest dream I remember," a "dream of flight." On the lawn a Hindu suddenly appeared, dressed in a suit of many colors, and chased the child Van Wyck with a knife. Just as he approached, running, "I soared into the air and floated away, free, aloft and safe. On other occasions, the fiend was not an Oriental, he was merely a nondescript minatory figure that pursued me, and I was not even anxious when I saw him approaching, for I knew I possessed the power to float away." That power—flight—deserted Brooks during the years of crisis when his intricately conceived scheme to evade wreckage was itself wrecked. And that figure, neither Oriental nor nondescript but now a most elegant avatar of deracination, of ruin, terrified Brooks with the minatory lesson: he who would evade himself is lost.

If this seems too fanciful a proposition, consider the trope to which Brooks resorted in all moments of crisis throughout his life, the image of seafaring, of journeying through troubled waters. It appears first in a pamphlet, *The Soul* (1910). "An Essay toward a Point of View," it is composed of some forty gnomic, Emersonian paragraphs on the transcendent subject Art. The genius of poetry, that "ancient companion of the human soul," is its capacity to console: "in literature, I seemed to see a refuge." Safe harbor, too, literature, for a man to whom in fantasy human existence appeared as a "vast ocean which contained all things known and unknown . . . without a bottom." The lives of men, "like so many ships," were "sailing, tacking, drifting across the ocean. Some sailed swiftly . . . as if they steered for a distant shore: but this ocean had no shore." Now and then a pilot would drop a line into that bottomless sea and as it struck he "would take his bearings from this depth, supposing it to be the bottom. But this bottom was in reality, though he did not know it, only the wreckage of other ships floating near the surface." Then with a startling reversal of intent in what was conceived as a fantasy of consolation, Brooks says, "I will be this ocean: and if I have to be a ship I will be only a raft for the first wave to capsize and sink." That is to say, he would settle for nothing less than absolute literary triumph but he feared cataclysmic defeat.

Given this expectation of disaster, it is understandable that similar thoughts and images should have tortured him during that "time in the middle twenties when my own bubble burst . . . What had I been doing? I had only ploughed the sea." The wretchedness of those years is understated in Brooks's published reminiscence but the letters, especially certain exchanges between Mrs. Brooks and Lewis Mumford, record a state of sheerest horror all round. I must refer again to this unhappy matter, for it is a storehouse of images which connect Brooks's writings with the lower depths of Brooks's mind Thoroughly "bedevilled," Brooks in print was later to say, he had seen himself as a "capsized ship with the passengers drowned underneath and the keel in the air. I could no longer sleep."

For five years he was unable to rest or work. Before then, from 1915 to 1925, he had achieved renown as the most metaphysical mind, the most urbane and eloquent voice, the most poised and coherent theorist of diverse movements in literary nationalism which flourished in the day of Resurgence. First with a group of pacifist, Wilsonian radicals on *The Seven Arts*—Bourne, Waldo Frank, Oppenheim, Paul Rosenfeld—and later as literary editor of Albert Jay Nock's paper, *The Free-*

man, he acquired unparalleled authority among American intellectuals committed to one or another program of literary reform. Beginning in 1915 with *America's Coming-of-Age*, he contrived to sail a brave course across the "Sargasso Sea" of American literary and social history, that "prodigious welter of unconscious life, swept by ground-swells of half-conscious emotion . . . an unchecked, uncharted, unorganized vitality like that of the first chaos." Then came *Letters and Leadership* in 1918, the noted essay introducing Bourne's posthumous *History of a Literary Radical* in 1920, and the last of these studies, "The Literary Life of America," which was published in Harold Stearns's symposium *Civilization in the United States* in 1922 and which prepared the way for the appearance of his climactic work, the book on Mark Twain. At mid-decade, barely forty, he had acquired national eminence as the leading spokesman for the Beloved Community, remorseless in his attack on a society which subverted the creative life in favor of the acquisitive life. Unlike H. L. Mencken, who chose the easy target of official Philistine culture, Brooks assailed his colleagues for having assisted at their own sacrifice. Jolted by and thankful for this shock of recognition, they had presented him with the Dial Award (for service to American letters) and offered him the editorship of that distinguished magazine. In print his many admirers expressed their gratitude for his labors in their behalf.

Brooks's fame represented a matchless moment of coalescence between the man and the epoch. His enterprise coincided with a general attack on the outrages of capitalism, with a rising labor movement, with an emerging Socialist party. Brooks, a socialist-pacifist who shared Woodrow Wilson's sense of mission, hoped to inspire, to exhort the American people to fulfill its destiny by presenting to the international community of nations a model of disinterested service to mankind. Simultaneously, he himself presented to the nation at large and to a special circle of rebel-intellectuals in small, a bill of particulars listing the reasons why Americans would be hard pressed to realize Wilson's program. Conflict within the national consciousness thus ran parallel to a polarity of will within Brooks's own consciousness.

As he wrote those works which, as Mary Colum said, helped to create "the conditions in which the artist can work and flourish as a free spirit," he discovered in classic American letters "two main currents running side by side but rarely mingling." In America "human nature itself exists on two irreconcilable planes"; its poetry, deprived of organic life, is therefore denied the right to fulfill its true office. In contrast to Europe, where art is the source of rapture and where artists mediate between the material and the spiritual life of man, Americans prefer the state of rupture. Two kinds of public, "the cultivated public and the business public," pursue divergent tastes which perpetually widen the gulf that separates them. The highbrow public exists on the plane of "stark intellectuality" and the lowbrow public exists on the plane of "stark business," of flag-waving and money-grabbing. Under these conditions poetry cannot harness thought and action, cannot transform the great American experiment "into a disinterested adventure." Brooks, having come this distance by way of his customary route—the language of dualism—ended his essay *Letters and Leadership* with his characteristic imagery. "So becalmed as we are on a rolling sea, flapping and fluttering, hesitating and veering about, oppressed with a faint nausea, is it strange that we have turned mutinous?"

In *Three Essays on America* (1934), he would seek to prepare the way for a guild of artists, men of "exalted soul" who would fuse the life of poetry with the life of action so that America, unified at last, would realize its old dream of utopia. But before this program of salvation could be properly carried forward, its theory wanted testing. And Brooks conceived a trilogy of books on classic American writers, Mark Twain and Henry James and Whitman, which would exhibit the full effects of all those patterns of disjunction—of wine and the aroma of wine, of French temper and German, of rhetoric and poetry, of Real and Ideal, of lowbrow and highbrow—he had traced during more than a decade's study. The books on Mark Twain and James would exhibit the consequences of lowbrow debasement and highbrow attenuation of spirit in American literature. And a final book would present Whitman as the very model of a perfect poet, a very Antaeus of a man who, "for the first time, gave us the sense of something organic in American life." Brooks substituted Emerson for Whitman, so the story goes, when he learned of Whitman's homosexuality. On hearing this at lunch with Malcolm Cowley in the Harvard Club he left the table immediately.

However that may be, the revised project was greeted by members of his circle as the proper work of a man whose learning and eloquence were more than equal to the labor of representing what was then called the Young Generation in its debate with received opinion. And indeed by 1925 Brooks had discredited a whole tribe of university scholars who conducted literary affairs according to laws of taste which excluded the new criticism, the new poetry, the new painting—the new age. Reading Stuart Pratt Sherman on Mark Twain, Bourne told Brooks in a letter (March 1917), "made me chortle with joy at the thought of how much you are going to show him when you get started. You simply have no competition." Sherman "hasn't an idea in the world that Mark Twain was anything more than a hearty, healthy vulgarian . . . But you will change all that when you get started." Stuart Sherman, Irving Babbitt, Paul Elmer More— these were the men whom Edmund Wilson listed high among those Brooks cast out of authority.

The book with which he most outraged that older generation was *The Ordeal of Mark Twain*. Despite the fury this work roused among ritual cultists of Clemens, the *Ordeal* remains a compelling book. Securely placed among specialist studies of Mark Twain, it has an even more imposing place among bench-mark books in another kind of literature. For all its humorlessness, its ax-grinding and thesis-mongering, the *Ordeal* bore some marvelous first fruits of inquiry into the connections between neurosis and art, unconscious motive and literary act. And particularly as it raised some radical questions about the discontents of civilization in the United States, questions which its chief critic Bernard De Voto failed to discredit, has it earned its fame and proved its worth.

Mark Twain was no frontiersman of American jollity, Brooks argued, but was deep down afflicted by a "malady of the soul, a malady common to many Americans." His "unconscious desire was to be an artist; but this implied an assertion of individuality that was a sin in the eyes of his mother and a shame in the eyes of society." In fact the "mere assertion of individuality" was a menace to the integrity of "the herd," incarnate in that mother who "wanted him to be a businessman." This "eternal dilemma of every American writer" Mark Twain solved by choosing the mode of comedy even though he felt that as a humorist he was "selling rather than fulfilling his soul." His "original unconscious motive" for surrendering his creative life had been an oath, taken at his father's deathbed, to succeed in

business in order to please his mother, Jane Clemens. This first surrender had been followed by another, to his wife, Olivia, who imposed on her "shorn Samson" the prissy rules, sterile tastes, and vacant intelligence of the genteel tradition. Until then surrender had been half- not wholehearted. But when he married Olivia his life took permanent shape. Mark Twain, as his somnambulism indicates, became a "dual personality."

Somnambulism, gloom, obsession with double identity—these represent the effects of a "repressed creative instinct" which it is "death to hide." Repressed, Mark Twain's "wish to be an artist" was supplanted by another less agreeable but inexpungible want: to win public approval and acquire great wealth by conforming to public opinion. The impulse to conform clashed with the impulse to resist. This struggle, which implicated two competing wishes or "groups of wishes," undermined the genius of a man in whom "the poet, the artist, the individual" barely managed to survive. Because the poet lived on in cap and bells, the man managed to maintain a small measure of self-respect, to acquire high accolade and vast fortune, and preserve balance enough to outlast the despair which almost overcame him in the end. "I disseminate my true views," Mark Twain said in 1900, "by means of a series of apparently humorous and mendacious stories." The remark is given in Justin Kaplan's biography, *Mr. Clemens and Mark Twain* (1966), and Mr. Kaplan adds that at this time in Mark Twain's life "fiction, dreams, and lies had become confused, and he could not tell them apart. They were all 'frankly and hysterically insane.'" Mr. Kaplan's is a fine book, incidentally, which dispenses both with Freud, and, unneccessarily, with Brooks—even as it takes up, amplifies, modifies the thread of Brooks's thought. What was hastily argued in 1920 is pursued at leisurely pace in 1966: *Mr. Clemens and Mark Twain* ends with the old man at the instant before his final coma talking about "Jekyll and Hyde and dual personality."

On publication, *The Ordeal of Mark Twain* split its readers into two camps which engaged in guerrilla warfare until Bernard De Voto in 1932, the year Brooks published a revised edition, offered in rebuttal *Mark Twain's America*. Accusing Brooks of having initiated a "fatally easy method of interpreting history," De Voto condemned him for incompetence in psychoanalysis, for "shifting offhand from Freud to Adler to Jung as each of them served his purpose" and (I refer to Stanley Edgar Hyman's view of the affair) for "contradictions, distortions, misrepresentations, and unwarranted assumptions on page after page." Following De Voto nearly two generations of critics have taken up the debate. And in consequence today neither Brooks's wholesale derogation of Mark Twain's genius nor De Voto's wholesale condemnation of Brooks's thesis is quite acceptable.

Brooks's 1932 revision of the *Ordeal*, itself a product of his own years of desperation, represents a retreat from some hard-won positions. Far more ground was given up than is accounted for in a simple arithmetic of words changed or phrases dropped. This particular matter, comparison of texts, has been amply studied and I shall not reproduce details. It is true, however, that the ground he conceded was easily surrendered, and its loss did not appease those of his critics who admired the shape of his thought, as Gamaliel Bradford said in a letter (June 1923), but were distressed by the way he had used Mark Twain as a mannequin to hang a garment on. Brooks's tendency was to falsify—just a trifle maybe, Bradford agreed, but a trifle all the same. Brooks responded with an apology and a

promise: he was very keenly aware of his evil tendency to impose a thesis on an individual. He agreed that the *Mark Twain* suffered from this, but promised that the *Henry James* would not, even if he had to spend two more years on the book.

The Pilgrimage of Henry James was to be an exercise in many kinds of self-discipline but it would confirm, not correct, iniquity. Brooks wrote both books in barely muted stridency of distaste for America, in an unrecognized and unwelcome ecstasy of longing for Europe. But the *Ordeal* was irretrievable for another, plainer reason: Brooks had lifted its skeleton from Hart's book on insanity. He was therefore flatly unable to accomplish the sort of radical revision which friendly critics would have admired. And since he chose not to identify Hart as his source of psychological learning, he left his critics to make out, with good guess and bad, the origins and ends of his thought. "Like the Freudians," Alfred Kazin remarked, "Brooks was writing to a thesis; but it was not a Freudian thesis." Nor was it an idiosyncratic pastiche, as other critics complained. It was Hart's composite portrait of the life of the psyche, Hart's synthesis of four schools of psychological thought—Freud's, Janet's, Adler's, Jung's—which Brooks adapted to his study of Mark Twain's psychic life. And it could not be jettisoned.

I have already remarked on Hart's contribution to Brooks's understanding of psycholgy. But this does inadequate justice to the tightness of connection which binds *The Ordeal of Mark Twain* to *The Psychology of Insanity*. Here is one of those rare and fortuitous instances in the history of ideas when direct and presiding influence, one work on another, is incontrovertible. Reading Hart today, you can recapture a measure of the excitement Brooks must have felt as he found in this handbook the key which unlocked the riddle of Mark Twain's life, of the creative life in America. In Hart's two chapters on "Repression" and "Manifestations of Repressed Complexes," he learned all the Freudian theory he needed in order to understand the principle of unconscious conflict. And in Hart's chapter on Janet, on "Dissociation," Brooks was given a ready-made system and language which accounted for some hitherto unaccountable traits of Mark Twain's character. The conception of dissociation enables us to represent the mental state of those patients, Hart said, whose delusions are impervious to facts. "They pursue their courses in logic-tight compartments, as it were, separated by barriers through which no connecting thought or reasoning is permitted to pass." One main form of dissociation was somnambulism; another was the commonly known one of "double personality." Illustrating the origins of somnambulism, Hart used an example offered by Janet: Irène, a young woman whose mother's death had been peculiarly painful, developed "an abnormal mental condition" whose symptoms resembled "those exhibited by the ordinary sleepwalker." Irène would live through the deathbed scene again and again, her whole mind absorbed in the phantasy . . . oblivious of what was actually taking place around her."

What a thrill of recognition Brooks must have felt as he sorted out Hart's ideas, then reshaped Hart's pattern to match the design of Mark Twain's life and art. Retelling Albert Bigelow Paine's version of the deathbed oath —to which Brooks clung even though Paine's account, relying as it did solely on Mark Twain's recollections, was an undependable report of what Mark Twain chose to remember or misremember—Brooks let out the stops. "That night—it was after the funeral—his tendency to somnambulism manifested itself."

It is "perfectly evident what happened to Mark Twain at this moment: he became, and his immediate manifestation of somnambulism is the proof of it, a dual personality." Now that psychology has made us "familiar with the 'water-tight compartment,'" we realize that Mark Twain was the "chronic victim of a mode of life that placed him bodily and morally in one situation after another where, in order to survive he had to violate the law of his own spirit." Having submitted to his mother's will, he assumed the character and attitudes of a "money-making, wire-pulling Philistine," a "dissociated self" which was permanently at odds with his "true individuality."

In explanation of the reasons for Mark Twain's submission, Brooks relied on Hart's paraphrase of ideas drawn from another prestigious work of the time, W. Trotter's *The Instincts of the Herd in Peace and War*. Trotter demonstrates the existence of a fourth instinct, Hart said, "of fundamental importance in the psychology of gregarious animals," a herd instinct which "ensures that the behaviour of the individual shall be in harmony with that of the community as a whole. Owing to its action each individual tends to accept without question the beliefs which are current in his class, and to carry out with unthinking obedience the rules of conduct upon which the herd has set its sanction." In "these struggles between the primary instincts and the beliefs and codes enforced by the operation of the herd instinct, we have a fertile field for mental conflict." What Trotter called herd Freud called horde. But Hart preferred Trotter to Freud on this subject, and Brooks followed Hart. Repression of Mark Twain's creative instinct was accompanied by the rise "to the highest degree" of his "acquisitive instinct, the race instinct." His individuality sacrifices itself, "loses itself in the herd," and in the end becomes the supreme victim of that epoch in American history, the pioneer, when "one was required not merely to forgo one's individual tastes and beliefs and ideas but positively cry up the beliefs and tastes of the herd."

Obviously Brook's thesis was neither Freudian nor a pastiche of Freud and anyone else. *The Psychology of Insanity* provided a system of ideas on individual and social behavior which Brooks absorbed, paraphrased, and exploited in his programmatic study of both Mark Twain and Henry James. It was a matter of lock, stock, and barrel. To have tampered with this system would have been to dismember Hart's thought. Revising the *Ordeal*, Brooks could correct a howler or two, tone down or play up: pure cosmetics.

Revision of that book was his last sustained essay in the psychology of literature. A few years earlier, attempting to carry on with his projected three-book series of standard American authors, he had applied the techniques of psychology to the biography of Henry James —a work which he looked upon as a Purgatorio, following the Inferno of Mark Twain and preceding the Paradiso of Whitman: strange fruit of the Harvard cult of Dante. In *The Pilgrimage of Henry James*, he had incorporated other aims as well. He had intended to examine the validity of James's view that the artist cannot thrive in the American air— an intention which he took very seriously indeed. For in this way, as he described the project to Bradford, he would rescue James from the Jacobites and show that James spoke the sober truth about the "immense fascination of England (applied to himself, that is, and in consequence of certain weaknesses in his own nature)."

In order to rescue James, Brooks was compelled to show that the great man, confronting frying-pan and fire, had deliberately chosen the frying-pan, Europe. The choice had been a bad one but James's judgment of the fire's heat had been accurate indeed. For James was "the first novelist in the distinctively American line of our day: the first to challenge the herd-instinct." Unlike Brooks, who immersed himself in the primitive American community, who fought it out with the "herd"—James fled. Flying, he "lost the basis of a novelist's life." He laid down a siege of London, won the war, lost himself. English society cut him "in two" and the public Henry James emerged, a "vast arachnid of art, pouncing upon the tiny air-blown particle and wrapping it round and round." Like Amiel, James spun large circles around the tiniest molecules of nuance. This was the James adored by the Jacobites, the Old Pretender whose play of style, a "mind working in the void," represented the ruin of art. Tracing ruin to James's deracination, Brooks concluded that a writer without a country of his own must sink in "the dividing sea."

Mark Twain the infernal lowbrow and James the expurgated highbrow were victims of a civilization which it was Brooks's holy mission to reform. This was all the truth he cared about, his Dantesque vision of America. Perhaps, too, the study of James was intended to serve as a lesson in self-admonition at the very moment in the twenties when the fascination of Europe was irresistible to nearly all Americans. Having denied himself that refuge, Brooks had chosen literature as his safe harbor. But suddenly, shortly after he published this book, his ship capsized. And during the next five years as Eleanor Brooks and Lewis Mumford consulted physicians, enlisted friends, desperate for an effective way to restore Brooks to himself, he went from asylum to asylum in search of extinction, haunted by Henry James.

Until this time of crisis he had said marvelous things about the nature of conflict within the social and literary imagination. Out of his divided mind had come a new and stirring—though hyperbolic—account of polarity in the national experience. He had invented an ingenious vocabulary of antithesis, had analyzed diverse forms of dualism in England, on the Continent, and in America where, at last, he addressed to the Young Generation a full-fledged psychology, sociology, and philosophy of literary reform. A guild of evangels, these men and women would create a poetics of the body politic which would harness art and action.

Out of duality, singleness; out of diversity, unity; out of unity, wholeness; out of organic wholeness, order; out of order, utopia—this sequence of ideas served as the theme of Brooks's rhetoric until 1925. One fixed idea suffused the lot. Drawn from German and English Romanticism, it proclaimed that the creative life, the life of art, the artist's stubborn instinct for self-realization—"self-effectuation," Brooks said—must inspire individual beings to resist the herd. In this way the artist in America, Emerson's Orphic poet incarnate, would furnish all mankind with an exemplary figure of obstinate honor and untrammeled will.

Brooks's timing could not have been worse. He arrived at this stage of thought at the moment least auspicious for its exaltation. War had killed *The Seven Arts*; strain of will and gloom of spirit along with influenza had killed Randolph Bourne. And it was at this grim time of general disillusion that Brooks, completing his allegory, found himself at a loss. Unable to visualize that heaven which his prohpecy had forecast, he was left with rhetoric alone. In 1925, when anybody in his right mind could see that an artist could really thrive virtually anywhere outside the United States, Brooks found himself utterly unable to contend that Emerson had prospered in an American atmos-

phere. Having proved that an artist is doomed if he stays here and damned if he leaves, having arbitrarily decided, for consistency's sake, that Emerson, not Whitman, would embody the triumph of American genius—having shifted from Whitman, whom he adored, to Emerson, whom he had earlier half-reviled as dried manna of Concord—Brooks reached exactly that state of impasse he had observed in Symonds' life. First cul-de-sac, then breakdown. Having negotiated the Inferno and scaled Purgatorio, he found himself stalled at the gates of Paradise.

In the state of emotional collapse which followed we can discern some strange but telling conjunctions between Brooks's Dantesque allegory of the American soul, its progress from damnation to salvation, and Brooks's despair. In breakdown, his whole terror was fixed on the certainty of reprobation. Speaking with one of his closest friends, the scientist-adventurer-writer Hans Zinsser, whom Lewis Mumford brought East from California to consult and advise, Brooks tried to convince Zinsser that he, Brooks, was doomed to die of starvation in jail. In that panic time of guilt and self-accusation, he foresaw one sure end: punishment in hell. Much later, in autobiography, he was able to turn terror into a figure of speech, "Season in Hell," but in the late twenties he had no taste for conceit. What had begun as a term of rhetoric had become infernally real.

A man who accuses himself of crimes he does not commit must surely be convinced he is condemned for some reason. When we remember that Brooks, a man of Puritanic conscience—"a conscience that was like a cancer," as he said in another connection—was terrorized by the apparition of Henry James, we cannot be far wrong if we guess that Brooks feared retribution induced by his "evil tendency" to falsify, to impose a thesis. And no advice could redeem regret or could assuage guilt or diminish the sense of evil. Mary Colum, for example, later told Brooks that in 1927 in Paris she had spoken with Janet— the theorist of dissociation—and Janet had said that Brooks's cure hinged on an end of meditation, of inquiry into the laws of his own inner being and into the inner nature of all other general laws of whatever kind. But he could scarcely disown overnight two decades of forensic, of meditation on the laws governing the creative life in Europe and America. Then, too, William A. White, another distinguished psychiatrist, gave contradictory advice. He told Mrs. Brooks that her husband should be encouraged to round out his work, should be urged to complete the book on Emerson. Indeed, apart from Janet, everyone was convinced that Brooks would be miraculously restored to health if only he could finish that third volume. If the Emerson succeeds, Mrs. Brooks wrote to Mumford, he will be cured. Only Brooks himself was unconvinced.

The problem he alone understood and could not resolve—whatever his physicians, wife, friends said—was not simply how to get on with Emerson but how in heaven's name could he speak of salvation when he felt himself cast out, condemned, disgraced. That this feeling was unreasonable is hardly worth saying: the strongest complaint that anyone could register against his work was that it was tendentious or, as Gorham Munson in 1925 maintained, that his kind of social and "genetic" criticism too often substituted moral fervor for formal analysis. But what drove him to distraction was loss of faith in his power of vision. The condition of life in America, he decided, was sheer hell from which there was no escape—neither in the classic American and paternal solution, flight to Europe, nor in immersion in private fancy. The only thing he could do was wait for

the descent of that Hindu's knife, fit punishment for a faithless man.

External evidence in support of these speculations is scanty, but internal evidence is plentiful. For when *The Life of Emerson* (1932) did finally appear, it expressed no reassertion of faith, but rather displayed Mrs. Brooks's, Mumford's, and the publisher's, Dutton's, faith in the healing power of love. This triumverate sought to do for Brooks what he was incapable of doing for himself, raise him from the slough of despond. Mumford's role is especially notable in that he performed a variety of literary tasks with exactly the kind of fidelity he brought to bear on multitudinous works of friendship during these hard years. For it was he who undertook to arrange for treatment by Jung, who assured Mrs. Brooks that money would not be permitted to interfere with therapy. Advising her that, contrary to Brooks's belief, the book was finished—that the final chapter summarizing Emerson's philosophy, could not be tacked on because it was incompatible with Brooks's intention to re-create the quality of Emerson's life by relying on Emerson's own words—Mumford worked to persuade everyone concerned with Brooks's affairs to go ahead with the book. "Believing that a financial lift would help Brooks's condition, and might make him willing to publish the work," Mumford says in a letter (September 6, 1968) intended to set right some statements I had made in print, "Maxwell Perkins and I approached Carl Van Doren and got him to accept it for the Literary Guild, without its having been offered to them by Dutton. (John Macrae, up to then, had been so irritated by having his offerings turned down by the two book clubs that he had vowed never to submit another manuscript to them: so we had, somehow, to break down both Brooks's resistance and Macrae's.) Van Doren, on his own responsibility, gallantly accepted the book; and after that, Brooks's acquiescence—and Macrae's too—was easy to achieve."

It is this book, momentous for its value in helping to restore Brooks's health, his first to have a wide popular sale, which both pleased and disconcerted its admirers. "Your pictures of Emerson are perfect in the way of expressions," Santayana wrote Brooks; "but just how much is quoted, and how much is your own?" *The Life of Emerson*, Stanley Hyman said, flatly, harshly, "marked the end of his serious work." Whether or not this book marked the end of Brooks's important work, it was the first of many books which exploited a style of work that marks the breach in Brooks's career. "Instead of thundering like a prophet," Cowley said in 1961—an essay which Mumford says that Brooks especially liked—"he became a scholar quoting unobtrusively from Emerson's writings and weaving together the quotations into an idyllic tapestry." Cowley is accurate indeed, and generous. But I suspect that Brooks adopted this method of composition in order to vanish from his book quite as, upon recovering from malaise, he banished from his mind any notion of completing his allegory.

"May I say one further word about the method I have pursued," he was to comment in *The Writer in America* (1953). Answering Santayana's question, responding to those critics who treated the five volumes of literary history as "a sort of irresponsible frolic or brainless joyride," Brooks described his method as that of a novelist whose every character, scene, and phrase were "founded on fact." But a more important word on method he left unsaid, its attribution to H. G. Wells, whose habit of composition in 1914 he had cited and approved. "I make my beliefs as I want them," Wells wrote. "I make them thus and not thus" as an artist "makes a picture . . .

That does not mean I make them wantonly and regardless of fact." From Wells, Brooks learned to make brush strokes of the intuitive imagination which, he hoped, would lift the writing of history to the lofty realm of visionary art.

Beginning in the early thirties, Brooks engaged in a herculean labor of inquiry into the folklore and mythology of the creative spirit in all spheres of the American imagination from its origins until the present day. He described this project as a search for a usable past and his phrase stuck. Indeed, it is today no longer recognized as Brooks's phrase at all and seems to represent a peculiarly American attitude toward history itself, as is shown in recent volumes of historiography by Daniel Boorstin, *An American Primer*, and by Henry Steele Commager and Allan Nevins, *America: The Story of a Free People*. Strikingly, too, the kind of censure registered against these books is identical to that registered against Brooks's *The Flowering of New England* on its appearance in 1936. In accord with the doctrine of a usable past, "American history has invariably been written from Columbus to yesterday without the slightest change of pace or tone," we read in the *New Statesman* (June 2, 1967). The problem with this doctrine is that it contains within itself the idea of "the disposable past." Whatever does not fit goes to the scrapheap. It has "no place in your 1968 Model Past."

Reading *The Flowering of New England* and *New England: Indian Summer* (1940), the first two volumes in *Makers and Finders*, René Wellek in 1942 mourned the disappearance of the old trenchancy of Brooks's mind, its replacement with a "belletristic skill of patching together quotations, drawing little miniatures, retelling anecdotes and describing costumes and faces." Still harsher criticism was uniform among a wide group of academic intellectuals which had been roused by Brooks's first books. "All my reading of American literature has been done during the era of Van Wyck Brooks and Parrington," F. O. Matthiessen said, but Brooks's new method of composition robs history of its clash and struggle and so dilutes the character of leading persons that it becomes hard to tell one man from another. However severe, these critics struggled to be just to the man who had revitalized their study of American themes. But even as they admired the very considerable merits of scholarship exhibited in these volumes, they condemned him for initiating that attitude toward history which today has apparently become stock-in-trade among our historians of a usable past. Brooks's nineteenth-century New England, F. W. Dupee remarked, "purged of conflict and contradiction," is presented as an "idyll of single-hearted effort." What was found unfit for this "fairy-tale" was disposed of.

The heart of the matter, as others have perceived, involves the interplay of proportion and distortion in Brooks's art. Although all writers must find external forms for internal states, must make their way through a labyrinth of motives, only a few are able to achieve an immersion in and conversion of but not subversion by their deepest wants. Brooks's myth-making embodied his inner life in vastly larger measure than it represented the exterior world, but until 1925 he contrived to transform the urgencies of private need into a prescription for society as a whole. Discovering in personal perplexity the key to a national dilemma, he defined some central confusions in American life and found for himself a short-lived relief from neurosis. In the early thirties, however, he wrote history with his eye on that cold black draughty void out of which he had so lately emerged. Our minds are darkest Africas, he told Granville Hicks in 1936, and he

was at that moment exploring his own jungle trying to discover what he believed. Or, as he was to say in his sketch of Helen Keller, "She might have taken as her motto Theodore Roethke's line, 'I learn by going where I have to go.'"

Roethke's line could serve as his motto, surely, but could not justify the results of his explorations. Brooks himself maintained, in the books to which we turn now, those written during the last three decades of his life, that his early work had undervalued the American experience and that his later work merely restored balanced judgment to American studies. This position he staked out in the five volumes of history, the sketches of John Sloan (1955), Helen Keller (1956), and William Dean Howells (1959), the acount of American expatriates in Italy, *Dream of Arcadia* (1958), as well as in the imposing array of works in self-explanation and self-justification: *Opinions of Oliver Allston* (1941), *The Writer in America* (1953), *From a Writer's Notebook* (1958), the three volumes of autobiography published intermittently from 1954 to 1961.

Makers and Finders, the chief ornament of Brooks's second career, is both a splendid achievement and a pernicious work. "Our greatest sustained work of literary scholarship," Malcolm Cowley has said, it has also been responsible for that view of the past which claims that authentic American literature avoids extremes, is neither highbrow nor lowbrow, but draws its inspiration from a will to resolve antithesis, banish contradiction. This view leads to the celebration of a style of literary culture, middlebrow, in which contrarieties are denied. It is a view, too, which bolsters an ideal of social order, in the style of President Johnson, where in the name of consensus radical conflict is ignored or suppressed. Above all it is a view which rests not on the history of ideas but on an illusion, a fable. And fables, as Descartes said in the *Discourse on Method,* "make one imagine many events possible which in reality are not so, and even the most accurate of histories, if they do not exactly misrepresent or exaggerate the value of things in order to tender them more worthy of being read, at least omit in them all the circumstances which are barest and least notable." Those persons who hope to regulate their conduct by examples derived from such a source are "liable to fall into the extravagances of the knights-errant of Romance, and form projects beyond their power of performance."

Makers and Finders memorializes Brooks's decision to transform himself into a knight-errant of this order. Determined to avoid Mark Twain's situation or James's fate, he divorced himself from the immediate concerns of his day and turned his curiosity on the practices of earlier centuries. He expatriated himself not to England but to Old New England, that golden land where no base circumstance undermined the conduct of life.

The key to Brooks's failure as a historian is contained in a remark addressed to Cowley (October 1939): "For there is an American grain, and I wish to live with it, and I will not live against it knowingly." Adopting William Carlos Williams' phrase, he decided that this figure of speech, taken literally, would enable him to discover exactly what was "organic" in the American past. Whatever else must be said of this doctrine it can be seriously faulted as an example of what the medievalist Johan Huizinga called historical anthropomorphism and defined as "the tendency to attribute to an abstract notion behavior and attitudes implying human consciousness." This tendency, Huizinga noted, leads all too smoothly to another, to a reliance on the resources of figurative speech—metaphor, personification, allegory. Whenever "historical presentation is fraught with passion, whether political, social,

religious," figurative language shades into myth and dispatches all hope of science. And if "beneath the metaphors the claim somehow remains that the figure of speech is still to be taken philosophically and scientifically," then indeed is anthropomorphism a subversive act of the mind.

Although Huizinga in this essay ("Historical Conceptualization," 1934) doubtless intended these reflections to bear on the problem of writing history in that day of ideology, fascist and communist, his thought illumines the problem of Brooks's ideology, too, the ideology of the American grain. Brooks, who was himself alert to the dangers of his position, wrote into the *Opinions of Oliver Allston* a crucial chapter, "A Philosophical Interlude," designed to circumvent judgments of this kind. As figures of authority he chose a heterodox group of system-makers—Croce, Thoreau, William James, Spengler—and drew from each what it suited him to have. Croce it was who led him to understand that America was "idealistic in its grain and essence" and that "the American mind was saturated with a sense of 'that which has to be,'—again in Croce's words, as opposed to 'that which is.'" If this view was considered unscientific, as Brooks anticipated his critics saying, so much the worse for science which is after all a discipline of thought not a guarantor of wisdom. Besides, he could make no "headway with abstract thinking, and, feeling that life was short, he abandoned himself to his tastes. To justify himself again, he copied out a passage from Thoreau's Journals (Vol. V): 'It is essential that a man confine himself to pursuits . . . which lie next to and conduce to his life, which do not go against the grain, either of his will or his imagination. . . . Dwell as near as possible to the channel in which your life flows.'"

Thoreau's view is unexceptionable. But nothing he said could justify Brooks's conviction that a peculiar socialismus of art and politics was apple pie but that "the communist mind runs counter to the American grain." This assertion occurs in the chapter on socialism in *Oliver Allston* where Brooks commended Williams for his fine phrase, then repeated the sentence from his letter to Cowley, and propelled himself headlong into the task of devising a whole new vocabulary of terms generated by the talismanic word, grain, itself. Thus reified, endowed with independent and objective life, the word conferred on Brooks's criticism the authority of pure American speech.

Expanding its range to include an infinitude of reference, he went to the language of psychotherapy for his formula of praise and blame. Having introduced Hart's language into the study of Mark Twain's life, he now concentrated his fire on the "Elioteers." To be always in reaction was "juvenile or adolescent" —were not, therefore, Eliot and Pound and Joyce infantile, sick, immature? "Were they not really unequal to life," these nay-sayers? Had not these very influential men of letters "lost a sense of the distinction between primary literature and coterie literature—was it not time to make this distinction clear?" Like primary instinct, "primary literature somehow follows the biological grain," he said, defining the exact "centre of his thought." Primary literature "favours what psychologists call the 'life-drive.'" The only value of coterie literature was its shock value which, like "insulin treatment for schizophrenia," restores the mind to its primitive state, a state of readiness for the fresh start. This treatment, coterie literature, is hardly necessary in America where the primary virtues of courage, justice, mercy, honor, and love represent the "tap-root" of art and "the sum of literary wisdom." To live in harmony with the American grain, in short, was to ally oneself with the forces of eros and

set oneself in resolute opposition to the forces of thanatos, to the vanguard, coterie-writers, "children sucking their thumbs," who incarnate "the 'death-drive' more than the 'life-drive.'"

His opinions helped to confirm an opposition to modern literature in that new audience which read *The Flowering of New England* and *New England: Indian Summer* and presented Van Wyck Brooks with its highest awards. No longer addressing himself to the Young Generation of literary men, Brooks became a hero of middle-aged middlebrow culture—became, as the *Partisan Review* said, a pilgrim to Philistia. All too comfortably, his former colleagues felt, Brooks slipped into the role of spokesman for a public to which modernist literary forms were impenetrable. All too easily, many former allies thought, he assumed the role of laureate of American chauvinism. Mary Colum, whose essay in 1924 had described Brooks as a pathfinder, a contributor of transforming ideas, spoke for nearly all his former colleagues when she told him in a letter two decades later that nothing he wrote about modern art showed that he knew what he was talking about.

There was in truth nothing in modern writing that Brooks cared anything for. What he did care about was to flush and dispel once and for all the issue of expatriation. He confessed that in his youth he had been "morbid" about this matter, that he had been "drawn to Europe over-much," that "many years had passed before he had learned to love his country," before he had realized that "he must cling to America to preserve his personality from disintegration"—and these extraordinary confessions explain the reasons for the conversion of Van Wyck Brooks and signify which motives underlay his fable. Along with the first two, the remaining three books in the series—*The World of Washington Irving*

(1944), *The Times of Melville and Whitman* (1947), *The Confident Years* (1952)—result of nearly twenty years of independent research, supported only now and then by a grant-in-aid, form a national archives of forgotten documents, misplaced books, lost lives. Reading everything he could find lest anything of the least interest be neglected, Brooks restored to general view enormous numbers of hitherto ghostly figures. And if it were possible to set aside the fable, to take these five books as a movable feast of the American imagination, *Makers and Finders* would represent an absolute triumph of humane learning. If Brooks had had no larger aim than to revive a sort of racial memory among American readers and writers, there would be universal agreement to Cowley's view: these books caused "a revolutionary change in our judgment of the American past" and a "radical change in our vision of the future."

But it is impossible to set aside either the idealogy of the American grain or the allegory of a usable past. How, for example, can we square Brooks's remark in a letter of 1933—"I wish we could have in America the guild-life that writers have in England"—with the remark, made exactly two decades later in the essay "Makers and Finders" (*The Writer in America*) in which Brooks set down his final thoughts on his study of American history: "It seemed to me that . . . our writers formed a guild, that they had even worked for a common end." Presumably it was twenty years' research into the usable past which had led him to a major discovery. A reader making his way through the five volumes, however, is nonplused trying to retrace the ground of Brooks's discoveries, trying to learn where Brooks had located this guild-life of American writers. Apart from a modest measure of support for this notion as applied to Boston during its heyday, the whole drift of evidence con-

tradicts Brooks's point. Here are some examples taken nearly at random from *The Times of Melville and Whitman*: For nineteen years in New York, Melville was "all but forgotten as a man of letters." And Whitman—"to the end of his life the great magazines excluded him." After the first "flurry of interest on the part of Emerson and the dead Thoreau, he had for years only a handful of readers." Undoubtedly Whitman was "warped" by this treatment, Brooks says. Mark Twain, too, was warped by his conviction that American writers were merely "manacled servants of the public" —as if Walt Whitman "had never existed or Emerson or the free Thoreau or Cooper." Again, speaking of the main patterns of literary life in the seventies and eighties, when a few writers fled America, Brooks quotes Charles Godfrey Leland, whom in an earlier volume he had treated as a man with deep intellectual and emotional ties to his native Philadelphia: "I have nothing to keep me here. There is nothing to engage my ambitions."

Despite contentions made after the fact, Brooks was unable to prove that nineteenth-century American writers had indeed formed a guild. And in time he substituted another theme, the replacement of rural life with urban life. "More and more, as the eighties advanced and the cities grew larger and larger, the old life of the farm receded in the national mind." It was to this theme that Brooks committed himself without reserve. Deciding that the "immemorial rural life" had formed "the American point of view," he wove arabesques of history which were intended to show how a once "homogeneous people, living close to the soil, intensely religious, unconscious, unexpressed in art and letters, with a strong sense of home and fatherland" was uprooted and dispersed.

Determined at any cost to display the consistency of these ideas, Brooks engaged in exactly the kind of struggle he had recognized in Symonds, that "congested poet" who, upon recovery from breakdown, had assumed the "fretful activity" of a *vulgariseur* and had set down with great labor large works of scholarship which tried to do what "only poetry can do." I do not know, in 1934 he told M. A. De Wolfe Howe, "how to use my thousands of notes," but it was increasingly clear to him that he could not "think in the expository form." As he proceeded from book to book his vision clarified itself: he would re-create the dream of paradise. And there his fancy fled in order to preserve his mind against disintegration, against any relapse of despair. No matter how far he ranged, this aim remained constant. Facts could not dislodge it though certain non-facts could be introduced to support it—the posthumous papers of Constance Rourke, for example (which he edited), or the phenomenal fact of Helen Keller's life.

Perhaps the most succinct way to crystallize the meaning of Brooks's double career is to note that the first half of his life was spent in demonstrating the ulcerous effects of America on the human spirit and that the second half was spent in an effort to prove that *America*, in its root meaning, signified the very spirit of health. Thus in 1956, publishing his sketch of Helen Keller, he sought to do justice to the biography of this marvelous woman and simultaneously to sanctify, by way of this inspirational tale, the whole design of his natural history of the American spirit. Was ever the physical life of man or woman more radically disfigured than Miss Keller's? Was ever the contour and lineament of moral health given more vivid configuration? She was "one of the world's wonders"—like Niagara Falls! He thought of Miss Keller when he read in Arthur Koestler's *The Age of Longing* that American women were too busy playing bridge to be cut

out for the part of martyrs and saints. (Gladys Billings, Brooks's second wife—he had remarried in 1946, following Eleanor Brooks's death—was one of Henry Adams' "nieces," a figure out of Henry James.) Clearly Koestler had missed the point of America, had not got the point of James's *The Portrait of a Lady*, of Isabel Archer whom Miss Keller resembled in her "fixed determination to regard the world as a place of brightness, of free expansion, of irresistible action." Brooks repeated James's words in order to contend that Miss Keller's decision—"life was worth living only if one moved in the realm of light"—must be taken both as a personal victory and an American conquest, a triumph of private will and of national buoyancy, vitality. Didact to the end, he was convinced that the spirit's health was confirmed by those powers of "affirmative vision" inherent within the unconscious American "collective literary mind" which, as revealed in *Makers and Finders*, enables us to revere, promote, maintain, renew our "dream of Utopia."

Two years before his death in 1963, admitting that he was known mainly as the author of *America's Coming-of-Age* and *The Ordeal of Mark Twain*, he confessed that his chief hope for some kind of relative permanence was in his historical series. We are tempted to ratify this hope. But when we draw together the main lines of belief on which his claims rest—when we realize that one way to take these five volumes, according to Morton and Lucia White's *The Intellectual versus the City* (1962), is as "the most striking example of anti-urbanism" in contemporary popular thought—we cherish the brilliance but mourn the uses to which it has been put.

At the point of origin in American civilization, we can now say in paraphrase of his final position on this whole matter, a primary literature develops out of one of the two primary instincts of the unconscious, the life-drive. Serving as the source of high-mindedness in politics, it brought American national experience to fruition, united high art and heroic action, joined the cities and the plains during a century of national life. Then, in manifestation of cyclic laws governing all organisms, in conjunction with the decline of rural life, the death-drive acquired authority. And it in turn generated that coterie literature which accompanied the rise of great urban centers. Made of greed, fruit of thanatos, these deracinated modern cities brought catastrophe to birth out of the world's body. The last pages of the final volume, *The Confident Years* (1952), present recent American history as a battleground between the forces of urban and the forces of rural life, a vision of apocalypse in which the "life-affirmers" engage in a battle of the books with the "life deniers." Wherever one "looked, in literature or in life, one found the two contrasting types," fighting it out as Brooks fought it out in unceasing battle with Eliot and the Elioteers. "So deeply engrained in the American mind" is life-affirmation, however, that the outcome was never in serious question. Because life-affirmation expresses the ineradicable will of the American spirit, it must eventually bring into being a new primary literature which will save the world from destroying itself.

Is it fair to say of all this, as he himself said of Symonds' achievement, that it was mere "high fantasy"? Had he composed book after book in praise of roots in order to devise for himself an utterly fanciful sanctuary? Is the figure of speech which he chose to describe Amiel and James an apt figure of self-description too: did he surround himself, spider-like, in a shelter spun from his own body? Had he labored to transform the ideas of expatriation and escape and flight into so sticky and labyrinthine a version of the American pastoral myth that only the most determined and powerful of Hindus could have found him out?

None of these is a fair question and all propose answers which are probably less true than false but are just true enough to record the fact that Brooks's unconscious life played a more intrusive and persuasive role in deciding the course of his career than was good for Brooks or for the history of ideas in our time. No essay in the psychology of motive, however, can deprive Brooks of his role as a leader of the new radicalism in American letters. And I am at a loss to understand why Christopher Lasch's good book on this subject, *The New Radicalism in America* (1965), takes up Bourne but utterly disregards Brooks. This lapse is the more startling in that Mr. Lasch's account of the radical tradition, very little modified, might stand as a virtual biography of Brooks's mind. At the outset, in 1900, reformers sought to see society from the ground up "or at least from the inside out," Mr. Lasch says. Eventually this new class of intellectuals came to distrust the intellect, "to forsake the role of criticism and to identify themselves with what they imagined to be the laws of historical necessity and the working out of the popular will." Of this movement and process Brooks is indisputably the prime example.

Before he renounced the role of a radical critic, he imposed his stamp on two generations of reformist literary men, on Mumford, Waldo Frank, Matthew Josephson, Granville Hicks, Newton Arvin—above all on F. O. Matthiessen, whose *American Renaissance* undertook to augment the Brooksian study of myth with the techniques of formal, textual analysis. In this way, Matthiessen believed, American criticism might achieve the repossession of "all the resources of the hidden past in a timeless and heroic present." As Matthiessen took up the subject where Brooks left off, so too others carried forward certain main themes of Brooks's thought which today receive cachet of the most flattering kind in that these are no longer recorded as Brooks's ideas at all but seem to express perennial wisdom. Reading a series of axioms on American literature in *The Times Literary Supplement* (July 20, 1967), we realize that the writer is unaware that he has reproduced a configuration of ideas which goes back fifty years to those first books in which Brooks examined our "impulse toward literary cosmopolitanism" and explored the "springs and sources of art and the right environment for its creation." It is this impulse "which has been of enormous importance in shaping the character of modern literature. Indeed it has been of the greatest importance for western literature generally, since the very idea of modernism seems to have its roots in this cosmopolitan, expatriate spirit." This matter of expatriation and cosmopolitanism has been of presiding importance in modern writing not because some leading American writers have been expatriates but because Brooks, obsessed by the problems of rootedness and deracination, their effect on the creative life in Europe and America, undertook to disclose the genesis of literature and discover the right environment for its creation.

This vast realm was once his private preserve. At the point when he turned his mind toward other problems, his friends tried to recall him to himself. "Do not, we beg you," Edmund Wilson addressed him in 1924, "lose too much the sense of that wonder," that excitement of the artist "enchanted by the spectacle of life." It was both good advice and bad. And in any event it came too late. For Brooks was already disabled by some critical side effects of a state of mind which the English writer Tony Tanner in *The Reign of Wonder* (1965) has found to be enlivening and debilitating in classic American literature. Mr. Tanner talks round Brooks but frames the general issue in ways which correlate his life with the lives of those great men of the nineteenth century, Emerson and Whitman and Mark Twain, who loom so large in Brooks's imagination. Like them, he was "too suspicious of analytical intellect, too disinclined to develop a complex reaction to society, too much given to extreme reactions, too hungry for metaphysics" to avoid what Brooks himself had recognized as an American malady, the malady of the Idea.

Surely it is time to install Brooks among his predecessors and peers, those American romantics who have traditionally yearned to experience and to portray the "wholeness of the universe." It is time, too, to save him from entombment in the American Academy of Arts and Letters and from enshrinement as Bishop of Bridgewater, Connecticut. For if it is just the effigy of a former oracle that is preserved, then the legend of Van Wyck Brooks will in the end turn out to be simply routine and we too will have assisted at this waste of history. But because no man ever wanted less for himself, as Bernard Smith remarked thirty years ago, and more for his fellow men, the time has come to restore Brooks to the highest place among the most eminent of twentieth-century literary intellectuals in America, those celebrants of conscience in whom the idea of America served both as a cause of malady and as a genesis of motive. "My 90th birthday was a surprising occasion. Friends wanted to celebrate it," said W. E. B. DuBois, but were hard put in 1958 to find sponsors. Among the few who appeared at the dedication of William Zorach's bust of DuBois in the New York Public Library, "Van Wyck Brooks took part."

Convinced though I am of Brooks's honor I cannot end my essay on so pious a note. Its tone is wrong. For Brooks is no legendary hero of American writing who must be once more restored to fashion, nor is he a clay idol, who must be finally cast out. And if it is true that he was in very large degree a selfless servant of his cause, it is also true that his ideas very often served to screen, from himself and his public, deep-seated and very personal passions: he adopted the cause of messianism in order to save himself from disintegration. For it required a lifetime's labor to establish and maintain a truce between the thrust and counterthrust of his ambition and temper. An expatriate, he decided that submission to an American fate was the price of peace. A pacifist, he broke with his friends in order to support the First World War. A socialist who believed in "a socialized world and a socialized country," he sentimentalized the American farmer. An antitotalitarian who in 1939 refused to support the League of American Writers because it did not oppose Stalin's dictatorship as staunchly as it opposed Hitler's, he would have welcomed the sight of Eliot behind barbed wire. As a pacifist, socialist, utopist, therefore, he somehow evaded the final consequences of his belief. And as a critic of literature, he invented a complicated metaphysics with which he hoped to justify his inability, a sheerly emotional incapacity to anchor his thought in the firm and convincing ground of textual analysis and debate. Thereby he lost the favor of those to whom he owed his fame—of James Sibley Watson, Jr., for example, publisher of the *Dial*: "Brooks says that Margaret Fuller was a more significant critic than Poe because she was 'less interested in the technical aspect of literature and more in its spirit.' The distinction is suspicious; the word 'spirit' more so. And Brooks has gone Margaret Fuller one better by criticizing modern literature without naming work and author. It is all spirit for him." Watson, whose pseu-

donym was W. C. Blum, backed W. C. Williams' version of the American grain, not Van Wyck Brooks's.

But in Margaret Fuller and the transcendentalists, in Van Wyck Brooks and his school of evangels, we discover a peculiarly national style to which Continental or English intellectuals—René Wellek, Tony Tanner—are immeasurably more sympathetic than Americans are. And it is their judgment, drawn in this final instance from the *Times Literary Supplement* (November 9, 1967), with which I end this essay on the most ingenious, persistent, influential contributor to the prophetic tradition in contemporary American life and thought.

"But among the few genuine types that America has contributed to the repertoire of feeling that of . . . the lofty or ribald annunciator of values—moral, national, cosmic—does stand out. We find it at precisely those places in which the diverse strains of the American tone, the puritanical and the lyric-prophetic, the homely and the crass, crystallize. It helps define Emerson and H. L. Mencken, Will Rogers and Thoreau. It is as crucial to the high flights of Walt Whitman as to the lapses of Mark Twain . . . it animates the public intimacies and histrionic clairvoyance of Paul Goodman and Norman Mailer. Watcher at the gate . . . vatic bard or television humorist—there is a distinctive brand of American writers and 'talkers' who carry on the tradition of the frontier publicist travelling the wide land with . . . shreds of apocalypse and nostrums for spirit and bowels.

Mr. Lewis Mumford is very much of that tribe."

So he is—the last Orphic voice of the twenties generation, as Brooks was in his time the first.

Selected Bibliography

WORKS OF VAN WYCK BROOKS

The Wine of the Puritans: A Study of Present-Day America. London: Sisley's, 1908.

The Malady of the Ideal: Obermann, Maurice de Guérin, and Amiel. London: A. C. Fifield, 1913.

John Addington Symonds: A Biographical Study. London: Mitchell Kennerley, 1914.

The World of H. G. Wells. London: Mitchell Kennerley, 1914.

America's Coming-of-Age. New York: B. W. Huebsch, 1915.

Letters and Leadership. New York: B. W. Huebsch, 1918.

The Ordeal of Mark Twain. New York: Dutton, 1920.

History of a Literary Radical: Essays by Randolph Bourne, edited by Van Wyck Brooks. New York: B. W. Huebsch, 1920.

The Pilgrimage of Henry James. New York: Dutton, 1925.

The American Caravan, edited by Van Wyck Brooks, Alfred Kreymborg, Lewis Mumford, and Paul Ronsefeld. New York: Macauley, 1927.

Emerson and Others. New York: Dutton, 1927.

Sketches in Criticism. New York: Dutton, 1932.

The Life of Emerson. New York: Dutton, 1932.

The Journal of Gamaliel Bradford, 1883–1932, edited by Van Wyck Brooks. New York: Houghton, Mifflin, 1933.

Three Essays on America. New York: Dutton, 1934.

The Flowering of New England, 1815–1865. New York: Dutton, 1936.

New England: Indian Summer, 1865–1915. New York: Dutton, 1940.

Opinions of Oliver Allston. New York: Dutton, 1941.

Roots of American Culture and Other Essays by Constance Rourke, edited by Van Wyck Brooks. New York: Harcourt, Brace, 1942.

The World of Washington Irving. New York: Dutton, 1944.

The Times of Melville and Whitman. New York: Dutton, 1947.

A Chilmark Miscellany. New York: Dutton, 1948.

The Confident Years, 1885–1915. New York: Dutton, 1952.

The Writer in America. New York: Dutton, 1953.

Scenes and Portraits: Memories of Childhood and Youth. New York: Dutton, 1954.

John Sloan: A Painter's Life. New York: Dutton, 1955.

Helen Keller: Sketch for a Portrait. New York: Dutton, 1956.

Days of the Phoenix: The Nineteen-Twenties I Remember. New York: Dutton, 1957.

Dream of Arcadia: American Writers and Artists in Italy, 1760–1915. New York: Dutton, 1958.

From a Writer's Notebook. New York: Dutton, 1958.

Howells: His Life and World. New York: Dutton, 1959.

From the Shadow of the Mountain: My Post-Meridian Years. New York: Dutton, 1961.

Fenollosa and His Circle, with Other Essays in Biography. New York: Dutton, 1962.

Writers at Work: The Paris Review Interviews, Second Series, introduction by Van Wyck Brooks. New York: Viking, 1963.

CRITICAL AND TESTIMONIAL STUDIES

Angoff, Charles. "Van Wyck Brooks and Our Critical Tradition," *Literary Review,* 7:27–35 (Autumn 1963).

Brooks, Gladys. *If Strangers Meet.* New York: Harcourt, Brace, and World, 1967.

Cargill, Oscar. "The Ordeal of Van Wyck Brooks," *College English,* 8:55–61 (November 1946).

Collins, Seward. "Criticism in America: The Origins of a Myth," *Bookman,* 71:241–56, 353–64 (June 1930).

Colum, Mary. "An American Critic: Van Wyck Brooks," *Dial,* 76:33–40 (January 1924).

Cowley, Malcolm. "Van Wyck Brooks: A Career

in Retrospect," *Saturday Review*, 46:17–18, 38 (May 25, 1963).

Dupee, F. W. "The Americanism of Van Wyck Brooks," in *The Partisan Reader*, edited by William Phillips and Philip Rahv. New York: Dial Press, 1946.

Foerster, Norman. "The Literary Prophets," *Bookman*, 72:35–44 (September 1930).

Glicksberg, Charles I. "Van Wyck Brooks," *Sewanee Review*, 43:175–86 (April–June 1935).

Hyman, Stanley Edgar. "Van Wyck Brooks and Biographical Criticism," in *The Armed Vision*. New York: Knopf, 1948.

Jones, Howard M. "The Pilgrimage of Van Wyck Brooks," *Virginia Quarterly Review*, 8:439–42 (July 1932).

Kenton, Edna. "Henry James and Mr. Van Wyck Brooks," *Bookman*, 12:153–57 (October 1925).

Kohler, Dayton. "Van Wyck Brooks: Traditionally American," *College English*, 2:629–39 (April 1941).

Leary, Lewis. "Standing with Reluctant Feet," in *A Casebook on Mark Twain's Wound*. New York: Crowell, 1962.

Leavis, F. R. "The Americanness of American Literature," in *Anna Karenina and Other Essays*. New York: Pantheon Books, 1967.

Maynard, Theodore. "Van Wyck Brooks," *Catholic World*, 140:412–21 (January 1935).

Morrison, Claudia C. "Van Wyck Brooks's Analysis of Mark Twain," in *Freud and the Critics*. Chapel Hill: University of North Carolina Press, 1968.

Munson, Gorham B. "Van Wyck Brooks: His Sphere and His Encroachments," *Dial*, 78:28–42 (January 1925).

Rosenfeld, Paul. "Van Wyck Brooks," in *Port of New York*. New York: Harcourt, Brace, 1924; Urbana: University of Illinois Press, 1961.

Ruland, Richard. *The Rediscovery of American Literature*. Cambridge, Mass.: Harvard University Press, 1967.

Smith, Bernard. "Van Wyck Brooks," in *After the Genteel Tradition*, edited by Malcolm Cowley. New York: Norton, 1937; Carbondale: Southern Illinois University Press, 1964.

Turner, Susan J. *A History of the Freeman*. New York: Columbia University Press, 1963.

Wade, John D. "The Flowering of New England," *Southern Review*, 2:807–14 (Fall 1937).

Wellek, René. "Van Wyck Brooks and a National Literature," *American Prefaces*, 7:292–306 (Summer 1942).

Wescott, Glenway. "Van Wyck Brooks," *New York Times Book Review*, December 13, 1964, p. 2.

Wilson, Edmund. "Imaginary Conversations: Mr. F. Scott Fitzgerald and Mr. Van Wyck Brooks," *New Republic*, 38:249–54 (April 30, ·1924). (Reprinted in *The Shores of Light*. New York: Farrar, Straus, and Young, 1952.)

—WILLIAM WASSERSTROM

Kenneth Burke

1897-

DURING a career of writing beginning in the early 1920's, Kenneth Burke has worked in so many forms and on so many subjects that he may deserve to be acclaimed as the universal man of modern, mass democracy. He has written poems, short stories, a novella, a novel, essays of literary criticism, reviews of all kinds of books, and a chronicle of musical events; he has addressed audiences of all sorts, not only students and professors of literature, but also psychologists, sociologists, theologians, and even the radicals of the Communist-inspired American Writers' Congress; and he has ranged, in his writing, over a variety of subjects appropriate to audiences of such diverse composition. Such breadth of activity might well have left both his followers and his critics far behind him, silent in awe. Instead, Burke's writing has provoked outspoken responses, both in praise and in blame. Indeed, Kenneth Burke is probably the most controversial literary figure of the past fifty years in America. He is said to have the finest speculative mind of our time; he is adjudged an irresponsible sophist. Leaving a lecture by Burke, one may hear "A superb system!" from one side and "Sheer chaos!" from the other. From a single, exasperated idolater of Burke, one hears him decried as "mad" and lauded as a "genius," even in one and the same sentence.

Burke's spirit is capacious enough to evoke and, perhaps, deserve such diversity of response; but the intensity of the response, both as idolatry and as antagonism, is surprising. Burke believes, above all else, in ingratiation, and his manner is indeed ingratiating. Yet one recalls that the anti-hero of his novel, John Neal, said that "one sneers by the modifying of a snarl; one smiles by the modifying of a sneer." Burke's own ingratiating ways may stem from an essential combativeness.

In any case, the intensity of the commentaries on Burke has not promoted a judicious understanding of his work. To organize one's praise, as Stanley Edgar Hyman has done, around Burke's claim that "the main ideal of criticism, as I conceive it, is to use all that there is to use" is like praising a genius for his weaknesses. For the common criticism of the literati is that they know just enough to make use of everything, but so little as to ensure that they invariably misuse it. To praise Burke as a system-builder, as William Rueckert does, is more reasonable, but if one takes "system-building" in its ordinary sense and looks for its presence in Burke's work, he will be disappointed. In comparison with the great system-builders, Aristotle, Aquinas, Hegel, Croce, and Cassirer, there is little of the system-builder in Kenneth Burke. His structures are like Croce's description of the structure of *The Divine Comedy*: an arbitrary framework around which Dante weaves the garlands that are his true love. If one sees justice in Francis Fergusson's complaint that Burke is overly rationalistic, he must also agree with Sidney Hook that Burke often connects his ideas by random association.

Burke's critics, indeed, come closer to what he is truly doing than do his disciples. They err only in condemning what he is doing on the ground that he is not doing something else, the thing they happen to value most highly. Both Austin Warren and John Crowe Ransom have chastised Burke for his sophistry, for his slippery use of language to confound all conviction and straight thinking. Tracing his progress in the thirties, Warren says that Burke began by undermining dogmatists by means of organized doubt, but then went so far as to doubt his doubt and to sympathize even with the dogmatists. For Warren this "sceptic's progress" is headed toward total collapse, and he urges Burke to recover a faith in reason. Burke is, in truth, a sophist, but not in the sense used by Warren and Ransom. The sophist they are thinking of has been observed, criticized, and superseded by Socrates, whereas Burke is a sophist who has considered the rational criticism of sophistry and would go even beyond that criticism.

If there is a title peculiarly fitting to Burke in all his work, it is one dear to Burke himself, the title of rhetorician. Burke is a rhetorician in a double sense: whatever he considers, he considers it rhetorically as an instance of rhetoric. Rhetoric, as I am thinking of it, is the use of words to evoke a specific emotion or state of mind. Whatever Burke studies, this is what he finds it to be, whether it is open propaganda, the Constitution of the United States, psychoanalysis, philosophy, or even pure poetry. Dialectics itself he defines as a kind of rhetoric; it is "all enterprises that cure us by means of words." Pure poetry differs from other forms of rhetoric only in the sense that the state of mind it evokes is an end in itself, whereas ordinary rhetoric evokes a state of mind which is to lead to practical consequences.

The objective of Burke's own rhetoric is a consistent one: to evoke a state of oneness among men. If he can convince us that we are all rhetoricians, that we are all using words combatively for our own purposes, he will have purified our warlike natures by evoking in us a feeling of our final oneness. We are all, he would say, fighting to overcome an original divisiveness which we inherit with the neurological structure of our bodies. Once convinced of this, once convinced that we are all trying to swallow up and possess the souls of all by means of our symbols, would we not become more tolerant of each other and accept that detached view of ourselves which characterizes the Neo-Stoicism to which Burke himself subscribes? We would continue to fight with words, but, once aware that it is man's fate and delight always to fight with words, would we not, with this sense of our ultimate oneness, fight a little less viciously, with at least a modicum of good humor, with a touch of that sense of the comic which is Burke's measure of the stature of man, that laughing animal? In any case, this is Burke's objective, and to it he will sacrifice all else. This, I think, explains his persistent neglect of the differences that separate the subjects he treats and his emphasis upon that which unites them. It explains, too, why Burke so often arouses the flames of contention in his readers. After all, here is a man trying to swallow up all our souls, trying to possess them, by convincing us that we are all dedicated to using words for the purpose of swallowing each other up. Can anyone endure such engulfment, an ultimate identification which slights and belittles the distinctive aspects of his own use of words? Can we permit the man with the biggest maw of all to have his way? Such feelings explain why this man of peace, or, rather, this man who fights to purify war, stirs up such impure controversies wherever he goes.

The impressiveness of Burke's general objective is enhanced by the fact that his writing is always occasional. He has a keen sense for the peculiar form of divisiveness which he would employ his strategies to overcome. If there is any single situation which he consistently works against, it is that division separating specialists from the masses. The 1920's in America, when the direction of Burke's career was being set, were dominated by this particular division. The country was a melting pot of the masses; and their melted-down life seemed a dreary routine dominated by a technological culture. In consequence, many men of the mind sought to dissociate themselves from this routine by cultivating their specialized talents.

In his recollections of the twenties, in *Days of the Phoenix*, Van Wyck Brooks laments the shift, which he felt to be going on everywhere, from an elevating form of literature, of importance to all human beings, to a highly specialized literature which merely renders subjects, as an end in itself. Joel Spingarn's "The American Critic" (in the 1931 edition of his *Creative Criticism*) is just the sort of thing Brooks opposes. Spingarn pleads for the repudiation of scientific techniques in criticism, usable even by the vulgar, and for a return to that richly spiritual, traditional form of literary studies

then flourishing in Italy. Against such aristocratic divisiveness, men of serious mind sought to bridge the widening gap between the precious and the common. *The Waste Land* itself, often read as Eliot's act of snobbish withdrawal, instead presents a world of spiritual poverty which, even in its deadliness, is seen as a condition appropriate for spiritual rebirth. The sophisticated poet, who scorns the meaningless routine of mass culture, at the same time senses in it a need to die in order to be reborn, a need very like his own. Hart Crane's *The Bridge* is a poetic effort to redeem a technically adept but directionless society by means of a poetic vision which would unite the poetic seer even with the "wop washerwoman" who rides home with him on the subway. A little later, Wallace Stevens will strive, in his "The Man with the Blue Guitar," to unite the masses of men, those "mechanical beetles never quite warm," with the exceptional poet, again by means of poetic insight. And John Dewey, in his *Art as Experience*, will attempt to prove, philosophically, that the most common forms of experience and the most exquisite and intricate form of aesthetic experience are ultimately the same.

With a similar purpose, Burke's most persistent rhetorical strategies are used to overcome this divisiveness. He claims that in his time the language of poetry, of feeling, and the language of science, of information, have been separated. Poetry, he feels, is the language of pieties, of shared beliefs and conventions. The language of science, in contrast, is a methodology of doubt; it has not only been separated from the communal language of feeling but has undermined it so that most men live without a sense of social purpose. To withdraw from such an arid culture, to live a rich, isolated, aesthetic life, this is anathema to Burke as to Van Wyck Brooks, Crane, Stevens, and Dewey. In contrast to most of the New Critics, Burke would accept the science and technology of his environment and would strive to redeem it with a poetic rhetoric. That, indeed, is what is going on in most of his books. They are full of technological jargon and thus tend to offend the purists in style, the antiscientific literary critics. At the same time, the scientific jargon is being used in a most unscientific way; it is being used as part of a poetic rhetoric. As a result, it must offend the rigorous scientist as much as it offends the literary specialist. Though both are offended, Burke's real purpose is to ingratiate and unify them all. The trouble, it would seem, is that Burke's unifications are verbal and rhetorical, whereas the divisions are deeper and involve whole men, each with his own distinctive sense of the world and his place within it.

The basic problem in Burke's writing may be seen most easily in the ambiguous nature of his tolerance. Without a doubt, he is an extraordinarily tolerant man. But tolerance takes different forms. It may be what I should call dialectical, the tolerance of one who is concerned with differences among men, of one who strives to understand another person in all his individuality and to imagine that person's mode of thought and action as it is in itself, and then, and only then, to discover, even with all these differences, a fundamental unity between that person and others. Such tolerance involves endless struggle to harmonize the rich diversity among men and their underlying unity. On the other hand, there is a form of tolerance which is characteristically American and which is of a rhetorical nature. It involves the acceptance of others by means of an indifference to, or neglect of, their differences, of all the opaquenesses and knobby protrusions that make it difficult to swallow their souls into one's own. Such tolerance ignores

individuality, at best attends to specific attributes, and, for the most part, concentrates upon generic sameness. Rhetorical tolerance lends itself to blurring all in a common grayness, a oneness achieved at the expense of that individuality which, finally, makes life worth living. Now Burke's tolerance tends fatally toward the second, the rhetorical kind. At times he resists the tendency, but most of the time he does not. In fact, his tolerance itself is often technological; he sends the human subjects he considers down a mass-production line with no more sense of their differences than one has between two cars of the same make. He achieves a sense of unity, but it is unearned because the very distinctions which make the unity difficult to achieve are being ignored. Thus, in his efforts to poeticize, to unify in feeling, the dominantly technological mode of our culture, he often succumbs to that which he would master.

Having said this, one must add that dialectical tolerance is extremely difficult and may inevitably be limited to small groups of people. How many other persons can the man of most astute thought and sensitive discrimination understand with sympathy? Not, one expects, very many. Burke, of course, is trying to comprehend everything, to be tolerant of all, even of those aloof, aristocratic New Critics. Such a comprehensive enterprise, such an enormous wish on his part, puts genuine, dialectical tolerance out of the question, except for the few occasions on which he writes of close friends. And, to be sure, the rhetorical nature of Burke's tolerance encourages in him a forbidding manner of thought, abstractive and classificatory. Even so, Burke's thought deserves close attention and analysis. No matter how much one emphasizes the sanctity of the individual person, even if one believes that the community itself depends, finally, on the constructive efforts of individual persons, he must recognize that he lives in a mass culture, a non-community. To follow Burke's efforts to encompass this nonpersonal non-community is a rewarding curative for the pain of living in it.

Austin Warren quotes Burke as saying that he abandoned his studies, as a college student at Columbia, "because he feared that he was acquiring a taste for study, research, scholarship, when what he inmostly desired was to learn to write and to write." Burke's passion "to learn to write and to write" is a last characteristic of his work to be considered before we turn to his individual writings. He is not merely a rhetorician, but a rhetorician who writes rather than speaks. For an academic dialectician, faced daily with a need to listen attentively and to gear his speech to that which he has heard, Burke's passion for writing is most disturbing. For Burke writes as though he has not been listening attentively. An attentive listener learns to hear words as part of an integrated action; he develops a capacity to capture the driving passion and the underlying idea of another and to bridge that speech with his own rephrasing of it, in words that combine the otherness of what is heard with his own sense of things. The translation essential to all intelligent hearing is never a mere substitution of a language of one's own for what is heard. It is rather a bridging, an act of transcending, which contains and perpetuates the voice of the other along with one's own. This gives a traditional coloring to the writing of such a listener. He does not simply lacerate what he hears in order to have his own say; he learns from that which he would pass beyond and carries much of it along with him, so that whatever novelty he achieves springs out of the tradition he carries with him. Further, learning to hear others is coincident with learning to hear oneself. Thus, the dialectician writes in such a way as to suggest that he is listening to

himself and evaluating what he says as he says it; his writing seems composed by two personae, one expressive, the other attentive. Finally, as a result of these qualities, it is usually quite simple to determine the precise nature of the audience to whom the dialectician speaks. He has a sense of the critical response of those whom he addresses, and, indeed, he incorporates into his own writing many of the qualities of those for whom he writes. Ordinarily, in fact, his writing is anti-rhetorical. He is not trying to evoke a response from passive listeners who must remain outside his speech. Rather he encourages them to take an active part in it. He has no hidden weapons, no strategies to catch others unawares. All is open, because the very movement of thought is what he would share, with maximum freedom.

Burke does not write as though he belongs to a dialectical community of this sort. He does not seem to hear those about whom he writes. His subjects themselves are treated as so many pieces of writing which one can abstract from and rearrange according to one's own needs. His translations leave what he is presumably translating far behind, so that, by and large, in reading him one feels no need to read also that about which he writes. In fact, usually, if one knows the subject, his knowledge is an impediment. This characteristic makes Burke's work seem quite untraditional; his translations do not provide a bridge between what he would explain and himself; all such bridges are burned, as he writes and writes, without listening. It is this quality which makes Burke appear to be an autodidact. All of us must, finally, teach ourselves; but, even as educated by ourselves, we would tend to carry along a polyphony of other voices, of other personae, from whom we have learned and whose thoughts we have modified. Burke's work, in contrast, is single-voiced; as complex as it is, it is monotonal. Nor does Burke listen very carefully to himself. One has no sense in his work of the constant revision that accompanies dialectical writing. His contradictions, themselves, are never troublesome, because there is never an overarching, attentive persona to be troubled by the need to connect what is being said with what has been said. Finally, as one reads Burke, he is caught up again and again by the question: To whom could he possibly be writing? For his audience is never included actively in his writing; it is never specified with precision. It is, one supposes, everybody and nobody: everybody as a mass willing to forget their distinctions; nobody in the sense that no one, of serious mind, is willing to forget either his own individuality or that of others, since only because of such individuality does life have the purpose and richness that give it value. In a world of nonpersonal, noncommunal masses, however, Burke's manner is most appropriate. If he can evoke a sense of oneness without listening to others or to himself and without addressing anyone in particular, then he may have achieved a worthwhile objective in the world as it really is, in the given world, in the world we are all part of, rather than in that precious world made with thought and passion by men who have an underlying, intellectual, communal purpose.

The three principles which allow for a certain brevity even in the treatment of so prolific a writer as Burke are these: there is more sameness than development in his career; his books are not themselves significant units of thought; and he thinks, always, in patterns of associational reverie. It is inaccurate to say that Burke began by writing poetry, then developed a theory of poetry, and finally, turned his theory of poetry into a philosophy of life. He has always written verse, as his *Collected Poems* indicates. The novella "The Anaesthetic Revelation of Herone Liddell," published in

1957, shows no falling off in quality from the short stories of *The White Oxen*, published in 1924. His theory of poetry was already fixed in the mid-twenties, in the essay "Psychology and Form." Even in the twenties, much that he said about poetry was also implicit in his general comments on life, as evidenced by his reviews for the *Dial*. His ultimate purpose as a writer was not, one must grant, clearly articulated until the mid-thirties, but its seeds are present in his earlier work.

Although his career as a whole is integral, his books are not. Each has its arbitrary framework and an emotional coloring of its own, but what he actually and vitally does within any one book might, with almost equal appropriateness, have appeared in another. What he is actually and vitally doing, wherever one looks, is to bring the most diverse subjects together by means of associational reverie or what he himself calls "qualitative form." His books are full of elaborate afterthoughts, in footnotes and appendixes. But the books themselves are series of afterthoughts. Hobbesian fancy, in contradistinction to judgment, is invariably his mode. He seeks out likenesses and scorns differences. He writes by metaphor and analogy, identifying the most diverse of things. The diversity of the things identified is rarely specified; the reader must provide his own conventional sense of the differences involved. The identifications themselves, through the element emphasized, are never presented with intellectual precision; they are rather an emotion of oneness, an evoked surprise that the things one thought of as basically different may be felt to be the same. If the reader hesitates, if he analyzes a claimed identification, if he criticizes the thought instead of the rhetorical effectiveness, he will forfeit the delight which is Burke's aim and waste his own astuteness. There is little point to a sentence-by-sentence or association-by-association criticism of Burke's thought. He is rarely right or wrong; most of his statements are conspicuously too general to be called in question. From many perspectives, his words are flawed, but they work for his purpose, they evoke the delighted sense of oneness in the reader who gives himself up, passively and uncritically, to their movement. It is academic and perverse to ask more of Burke, just because one asks something else of himself. The rhetoric is extraordinary, and, if its effectiveness has dwindled in recent years, one wonders if it is not because too many of his critics have asked him to be other than he is or because his disciples have praised him for something he is not.

Burke was born in 1897, in Pittsburgh, went to Ohio State and Columbia for his academic training, and began his career as a serious writer around 1920. The essential qualities of this career may be glimpsed as early as 1932, by which time Burke's first collection of essays, *Counter-Statement*, and his novel, *Towards a Better Life*, had been published. The basic mode of his thought, connecting the diverse as identical, is foreshadowed in his enthusiastic review of Spengler's *The Decline of the West* for the *Dial* in 1926. What he likes in Spengler is his bringing together of various aspects of the most diverse cultures with a clash of identity, as in the phrase "puritan Arabs." What he dislikes is Spengler's notion that a critic in the winter of one culture cannot truly communicate with the spring of either his own culture or that of another. Differences matter for Burke mainly as the material for another ringing identification. In *Counter-Statement* he shows a similar enthusiasm for Rémy de Gourmont's notion of the dissociation of ideas. Gourmont believed that divorce is the law of the intellect. Given two conventionally linked ideas, he analyzed them to show that they were held together by noth-

ing essential. This method, like Spengler's, Burke felt to have an important future, especially in criticism. Its future, in Burke's writing, is a simple reversal. Surrounded by divisiveness, by specialists locked in the prisons of their own pursuits, he was to take ideas conventionally dissociated and clash them together as one. Indeed, in a later commentary on Gourmont, he claims that, though Gourmont said he was merely divorcing paired ideas, he was surreptitiously marrying other ideas at the very same time. This, of course, is what one expects of Burke: to show that even opposites, even Gourmont and Kenneth Burke, are really the same.

Burke's theory of poetry was quite fully developed in his "Psychology and Form," which was first published in 1925 in the *Dial* and then included in *Counter-Statement*. Poetry, needless to say, is rhetoric. Poetic form is eloquence and eloquence is psychology, that is, the arousal of emotion. This point, which is extended in other essays in *Counter-Statement*, entails that the poet, who is wide awake, selects a mood or emotion and then decides on certain technical devices by which he evokes the emotion in his audience. To be effective he must know the appetites and emotions of his audience, for his success depends on their being ripe for the evocation of his chosen emotion. He is the isolated magician and manipulates and hypnotizes the audience by his devices, by ringing the bells of their responses, by "saying the right thing," given their emotional makeup. The audience itself is utterly passive; it is his job to make them dream. The psychology of the audience, not of the hero of the work, is what gives it poetic form. One goes to poetry to be aroused, not to acquire information. This distinction between informative and evocative works is not characteristic of Burke. Later he will insist that even works dedicated to knowledge, works of a scientific cast, are basically rhetorical, are means of establishing an identification, say, among members of a school. Nonetheless, even in the early essay, the emphasis is on identification. Shakespeare himself is seen to be a manipulator, one who played the various stops of his audience. The porter scene in *Macbeth* is not in itself important. At that point in the play Shakespeare needed "grotesque buffoonery" to follow a scene of "grotesque seriousness." The skin, the shell, the individual texture of the scene does not concern Burke. He views the scene as simply one of any number of ways in which Shakespeare could do the essential, that is, evoke a particular emotion which he was interested in at that point because he knew it was what the audience needed. A happy bonus of this claim about Shakespeare is that he is seen as doing exactly the same thing Burke himself does in the short stories of *The White Oxen*. Those stories, at least those that work, like "Mrs. Maecenas," are calculatingly composed for their effect upon the reader.

Even the practical criticism of this period is full of anticipations of his later work. His concern for the individualizing traits of a work is subordinated to a general emotion or state of mind which he feels to be its true form. Thus, in a fine essay on Gide and Mann, having suggested that they work in opposite ways, he then surprises and delights us with the claim that they are in truth doing the same thing: "Irony, novelty, experimentalism, vacillation, the cult of conflict—are not these men trying to make us at home in indecision, are they not trying to humanize the state of doubt?" As Burke praises Gide and Mann for their efforts to shake us loose from our own rhetorical postures and to make us doubt our ultimate rightness, one recognizes that he is praising them for what will become central to his own career: the belief that a person ought to be detached from the heat of his own efforts and merged, with all, in a basic state of doubt and indecision.

If any work might represent not a paper death and rebirth of Burke the writer but a genuine transformation, it is his novel. It is, no doubt, written mainly for its effects, being a series of letters in which the only character, John Neal, is given the chance to take on the postures of lamentation, rejoicing, beseechment, admonition, moralizing, and invective. There is no plot, action, character, or scene in the usual sense of those words. The language is pure artifice, inflexible and unrelated to the events only vaguely glimpsed through the fog of its *rondeur*. There is no drama in the novel, unless it is the rhetorical drama between author and audience. All these characteristics are typical of Burke, early, middle, and late.

As Austin Warren points out, however, Burke seems more sympathetic toward his orator Neal than his preface would indicate. In fact, Neal seems to be that part of Burke's character which he would abandon as he moves toward a better life. Neal is enclosed in his own language. He records conversations with the woman he loves, and he writes directly at times to the man who wins her love. But those others are not living characters with feelings and voices of their own. Toward the end, in fact, Neal talks to others who are only projections of himself and who reply to him in his own voice. He has lost all sense of an outer world and is utterly locked within himself. Even so, he continues to write with the same well-rounded, periodic sentences and to dissect things as keenly as before. The verbalizer and analyst lives on, as Warren noted, after the man has died. Should one not infer, then, from Neal's despairing wish that he might have lived twice, and "smiled the second time," that Burke does live twice, once as the eloquent, serious, self-absorbed writer, and thereafter as a comedian? In *Counter-Statement* self-absorbed writers like Flaubert, Pater, and Gourmont find more favor with Burke than ever again. Has he not broken through his monadistic narcissism in preparation for a new interest in society, history, and the outer world? Does he not, after this novel, exhibit a humor and detachment which free him to take others as seriously as he takes himself? As a man he no doubt has always had these qualities. On rare occasions, when the subject is a close friend, he has them even in his writing. By and large, however, his writing does not exhibit them, at any period. He may range over the whole universe of thought, but is always locked in a style that bars entrance to all others, though bits and pieces of others filter through when they are serviceable. A certain solitariness, overwhelming in Neal's letters, colors almost all Burke's writing and gives it a poignancy not to be found in less serious and more facile writers of encyclopedic scope. Thus, though Burke himself, at a later time, looked back upon the novel as a *rite de passage*, it is not, in my opinion, any such emancipation. Neal, one grants, does not laugh very heartily at himself, while the later Burke is full of laughter. But even Neal is doing quite a lot of bitter laughing at others, as he exposes their pretenses. Further, at one point he explains that he is not interested in individual character, but in motives, and that "motives may be common to very different people." That is a clear and simple explanation of why so little individual character appears in any of Burke's writing. *A Grammar of Motives, A Rhetoric of Motives*, motives are always Burke's concern, and he thinks of them as common, as shared by people of the most diverse character.

If there is any change in Burke's career at this time, it is something like the reverse of the change undergone by Shakespeare's Richard II. Until deposed, Richard views the whole of England as though it were moved and moti-

vated by his own whims and imaginings. After the deposition, when in prison, he recognizes that the world of his imaginings is a prison and that those outside this prison do not move according to his tune. Through 1932, Burke is aware that his world is not the world, that his interests are special and exclusive and that much experience goes on outside their range. Thereafter, though his purpose and mode of thought remain much the same, he finds that he can range everywhere by means of them and he writes as if nothing human is alien to the range of his mind.

That this actually does happen, and how it happens, may be discerned in a speech Burke gave to the American Writers' Congress in 1935. "Revolutionary Symbolism in America" is a subtle argument to the effect that the Communists should change their basic symbol from the *Worker* to the *People*. In the process of developing this point, Burke explains his conception of "the complete propagandist," and this conception is a key to all his later writings. He says that "the complete propagandist" should show interest in as many fields as he can and ally his attitudes with everything that is broadest and fullest in the world of his time. "Much explicit propaganda must be done, but that is mainly the work of the pamphleteer and political organizer. In the purely imaginative field, the writer's best contribution to the revolutionary cause is *implicit*. If he shows a keen interest in every manifestation of our cultural development, and at the same time gives a clear indication as to where his sympathies lie, this seems to me the most effective long-pull contribution to propaganda he can make. For he thus indirectly links his cause with the kinds of intellectual and emotional engrossment that are generally admired. He speaks in behalf of his cause . . . by the sorts of things he associates with it." Being wrathful and full of condemnation, Burke continues, may be justified, but the complete propagandist's "specific job as a propagandist requires him primarily to wheedle or cajole, to practice the arts of ingratiation. As a propagandizer, it is not his work to convince the convinced, but to plead with the unconvinced, which requires him to use *their* vocabulary, *their* values, *their* symbols, insofar as this is possible."

The similarity between this advice and Burke's own practice hereafter is too obvious to need emphasis. He would win his way by the sorts of things he associates with, and he associates himself with everything that has prestige in his culture—philosophies of history, the New Criticism, Freudianism, anthropology, sociology, psychology, linguistics, and theology, among other things. Further, he uses the words, values, and symbols of these fields always for an ulterior, rhetorical purpose. This may sound, indeed may be, insidious. I am not, however, suggesting that Burke's own purpose is identical with that of the Communist party or that of any other specific revolutionary movement. He is, to be sure, opposed to a competitive society and in favor of a cooperative one; but he works for this without demanding, at least most of the time, a fundamental upheaval in our economic or political structure. The important point is that by this time Burke is quite aware that he is always doing the same thing, whether he is writing of poetry, politics, philosophy, or religion. Unlike universal men of traditional cultures, like Benedetto Croce, for example, Burke does not try to write of history as a historian, logic as a logician, politics as a political scientist, language as a linguist, poetry as a literary critic, and religion as a theologian. He takes them all in his rhetorical stride, easing his way further by treating them all as forms of rhetoric themselves.

A consideration of the modes of thought and writing in his major books from 1935 on

will support and explain these claims; afterwards, it should be possible to treat, with some economy, Burke's elaborate ideas about literary criticism and his multifarious essays in practical criticism. His three books published between 1935 and 1941 are consistent developments of his loosely framed program for the complete propagandist. The basic method, during this period, is denominated "perspective by incongruity." Burke himself describes this as verbal "atom cracking." "A word by custom in one category is wrenched loose and applied to another." Though this sounds more like dissociation than identification, its actual effect is to blur differences and accentuate oneness. For example, Burke affirms that Rockefeller's economic empire and Milton's epic are both "a symbolic replica" of the man's personal character. "In both cases the men 'socialized' their specific patterns of interest by the manipulation of objective materials in a way whereby the internal and the external were . . . fused." A dour critic might reply: yes, and both Rockefeller and Milton had two legs and both had eyes but could not see. But why bother to entertain oneself when Burke is so entertaining? High finance, he will tell us, is a most spiritual aspect of life. Why? It is very abstract, and so are angels. Sputter one may, but it is a jovial notion that Wallace Stevens was doing identical things as insurance executive and as poet. It is a momentary, but heartwarming joke. No one, least of all Burke, denies all the differences. He simply ignores them.

Another road into the heart of the manner of these books is Burke's modification of I. A. Richards' concept of poetry as pseudo-statement. Richards' notion is that statements are scientific and refer to external objects, whereas pseudo-statements are evocative of attitudes. This idea is undoubtedly the source of Burke's earlier distinction between informative and evocative literature. In this later period he expands the notion of pseudo-statements, with delightful abandon, much further than Richards intended. First, he rips it off the page: "A man can extract courage from a poem by reading that he is captain of his soul; he can reënforce this same statement mimetically by walking down the street as vigorously as though he were the captain of his soul." Poetry and life, then, are identical as rhetoric? Nay, more. Science itself is the same thing. "Yet, what is any hypothesis, erected upon a set of brute facts, but a rationalization?" Indeed, "any explanation is an attempt at socialization, and socialization is a strategy; hence, in science as in introspection, the assigning of motives is a matter of appeal." Burke will qualify these marvelous identifications by distinguishing "I am a bird" as pseudo-statement from "I am an aviator" as statement. But then he will turn about and insist that both are truly statements, because both come to terms with recalcitrant material, that of the first verbal, that of the second physical. Furthermore, though he does insist that attempts to be ingratiating may be more or less accurate, he admits that the only basis for distinguishing the more from the less accurate would be the view of "an infinite, omniscient mind," and needless to say, that is out of our reach. Thus, even though one might debunk Richards' *Principles* by calling it a mass of pseudo-statements, he would need to add that it might as accurately be called pure statement. If reason is, finally, rationalization, it is just as accurate to say that rationalization is reason. All depends on the interests of the speaker. Burke is not a debunker, for what he lowers with one phrase, he raises with the next. He is a leveler. That is the basis of his appeal.

A limit to the sweep of these identifications might seem to be reached with Burke's distinction between the poet and the critic, at least in

Permanence and Change (1935) and *Attitudes toward History* (1937). Burke claims that poetry is pious; that a poet can work hypnotically only in a homogeneous society, in which he may use agreed-upon labels to say the right thing and ring the bells of his audience's responses. From the Renaissance through 1900, during what Burke calls the era of da Vinci, all was called in doubt, impiously, by the endless questioning of all values. Obviously, one does not "hypnotize a man by raising a problem." This, then, was the era of criticism. The scientist treats the universe not as *being created*, but as *having been created*, and then analyzes and classifies it; so the literary critic analyzes the magic of Aeschylus and the religion of Sophocles by reducing them to a poetics, a class system of genres and rhetorical devices. Looking back on such epochal distinctions, Burke says that he was being too much a historicist during the thirties. Even during this early period, however, Burke did not rest content with the distinction between a period of poetry and a period of criticism. He will poetize his own criticism so that it is fundamentally identical with poetry. His perspectives by incongruity, indeed, carry him even further, for in the process of poetically criticizing criticism he identifies even the criticism criticized with both plain poetry and critical poetry. For example (and this is not, in the rhetorical world we are considering, a digression), Burke poetizes the practice of psychoanalysis in the following manner. A pious patient (a poet) approaches the analyst for help. The analyst cures him by impiously and rationally misnaming his distress. The cure Burke calls, with his impious piety, a secular conversion. Though Burke is criticizing psychoanalysis, he is not debunking it. It is the casting out of devils by *misnaming* them, and that is exactly what Burke says he himself is doing by means of his perspectives by incongruity. The rational effort to cure a pious man is a piously impious act. By misnaming psychoanalysis as a means for secular conversion, Burke is himself curing it of its aloof specialness. His impious piety is devoted to redeeming the piously impious curers of the pious. One may laugh at all this—and be cured, as Burke would wish.

For a moment one might have thought that Burke, like Matthew Arnold before him, had decided that he could not write poetry because he lived in a heterogeneous society riddled by doubt, and thus must turn to criticism. It soon becomes apparent, however, that Burke's criticism is just another form of poetry. Burke discovers that even his heterogeneous society is dominated by a piety, by a response of doubt, by a doubt of everything, even of the sanctity of lay conversions by psychoanalysis. With here a clang, there a clang, Burke proceeds to reduce and identify specialty after specialty and profession after profession until his reader experiences the cathartic rejuvenation of that delightful state of oneness detached from any and all specialties. Doubt itself becomes a kind of faith; skepticism becomes mysticism; science and criticism and analysis become poetic ecstasy. To top all else, Burke adds that statistics, as an attempt to extract a generalization common to all situations, also has a mystical cast to it.

Burke has his own name for the position he is advocating during this period. He calls it a "dialectical biologism," a new school merging naturalism, idealism, and dialectical materialism, all leading to a "somewhat Spinozistic conception of substance." What could be more comforting, for one and all? Nothing is omitted.

Before 1941 or so Burke's identifications are quite rowdy, as my last reference indicates. He brings together the most complex things with blithe abandon and our amusement is

shocking. One arrives at his identification of poetry and criticism disruptively, only after puzzling out seeming contradictions like that between poetry as pious and metaphor as impious. In *The Philosophy of Literary Form* (1941), even though the identifications with which the work abounds are as unusual and striking as ever, they are affirmed almost as if beyond question, as if it would be unmannerly to be surprised by them. The astounding identification of poetry and criticism is here affirmed parenthetically, as the obvious sort of thing any decent reader must grant his author. One's situation and his motive, his motive and his burden of guilt, the burden and the unburdening, even the situation and the strategy to encompass it, all these are identified casually, so that one hardly sees them slip by. The machine for identifying the diverse almost seems to run by itself, as though Burke no longer simply enjoys its outrageousness, but has even come to believe in it.

Since 1941 Burke has published four major works. *A Grammar of Motives* (1945), *A Rhetoric of Motives* (1950), *The Rhetoric of Religion* (1961), and *Language as Symbolic Action* (1966). Because these books exhibit a more learned, even a more scientific, façade than his previous ones, it is important to keep in mind that for Burke science itself is but a form of rhetoric. Of the scientist he says: "One acts; in the course of acting, one organizes the opposition to one's act (or, in the course of asserting, one causes a multitude of counter-assertions to come running from all directions, like outlaws in the antique woods converging upon the place where a horn had sounded); and insofar as one can encompass such opposition, seeing the situation in terms of it, one has dialectically arrived thus roundabout at knowledge." This master of outlaws, the scientist, even when at work in his laboratory, is just another version of the "complete propagandist." In these later books the opposition which Burke would encompass is indeed formidable. What is the magic with which he would tame these speaking beasts, these philosophers, men of action, poets, and even New Critics? Tasso's Rinaldo exorcised the wicked spirits from the "antica selva" only after climbing the Mount of Olives and receiving an influx of divine grace. The influx of ingratiation which assist Burke in his new trial and conquest is implicit in what becomes his favorite phrase, "in terms of." That obnoxious cliché has genuine meaning in Burke's later works. What it implies, simply and consistently, is that whatever he considers, even if it is the most arduous philosophical argument, is viewed as no other than a set of words, a terminology.

This strategy is a very keen one, especially as used in *A Grammar of Motives*: to reduce all philosophy to the manipulation of terms. Burke accomplishes this reduction by means of his own terminology, a pentad made of the words "scene," "act," "agent," "agency," and "purpose." He reduces all philosophy to five species, and each species is placed under the sign of one of his terms: materialism under scene, idealism under agent, mysticism under purpose, realism under act, and pragmatism under agency. All philosophies are the same in the sense that, though each features only one of the five terms, all try to account for the other four terms in the rhetorical jiggling of their nomenclatures. Burke uses his terms in a purely rhetorical way, although he calls his pentad dramatistic. He does not attempt to define and delimit the meanings of his terms, but uses them as having whatever traditional meanings dictionaries record for them, varying his use of those meanings according to his occasion and interest. Although he refers to the relationships among the five terms as "ratios,"

he never analyzes these ratios, but considers them rather vaguely as forms of "overlapping." Further, although he admits that each type of philosophy tends to account for other terms besides its featured one, Burke's interest is to claim that realism, under the sign of "act," accounts for all five terms more effectively than the other types do. Thus, in his consideration of two forms of realism, that of Aquinas and that of Marx, he shows how they can account for all five terms. There is no question of arguing for his preference; he simply devotes more space to the expansiveness of what he prefers than to that of the others.

The differences among the types of philosophy are spurious, so that, if a reader attends to them, he will become entangled in fruitless quarreling with Burke. The quarreling will be fruitless because it mistakes appearance for reality. The reality of *A Grammar of Motives* is the marvelously facile technique with which Burke reduces all philosophical thought to the sameness of terminological manipulation. No introductory textbook of philosophy has ever reduced its subject matter to a series of formulas half so effectively as Burke does in this book.

Arduous conceptual thought and the juggling of terms, in truth, have little in common. A serious philosopher works out his thought as an action quite distinct from the act of giving that thought a verbal shape. The act of thought is fundamentally nonrhetorical, is only minimally a verbal presentation. While he is thinking, a philosopher no doubt will, some more and some less, use notations, various forms of shorthand, to record the movement of his thought. Only thereafter will he strive to formulate his thought in words. Even this second act, however, is not primarily rhetorical. Its purpose is to assist others in their efforts to understand the original movement of thought which logically and, usually, even chronologically precedes the philosopher's verbal articulation. It is these distinctions, within the labor of philosophy itself and between it and other forms of labor, like poetry and rhetoric, which Burke studiously ignores. It is by means of this cunning ignorance that Burke is able to sweep across the centuries of philosophy with minimal thought himself and with maximal rhetorical efficacy.

Philosophers use even common words in special ways. If a philosopher would succeed in sharing his thoughts, the very act of his mind, with his readers, he must define his words scrupulously so that they cannot be taken in their conventional designations. The very last thing he can do, even if he is a common-language philosopher, is simply give himself up to the words he uses, and allow all their ambiguous, and often contradictory, meanings to function equally. Burke, however, does exactly that, giving himself up to his key words with abandon; further, he insists that the philosophers he uses for illustration must and actually do give themselves up to their words in the same fashion. As a result, if *A Grammar of Motives* were read as serious philosophy, it would no doubt provoke a riot (as it almost does, even in the review of that most gracious philosopher, Abraham Kaplan). Read properly, the book should not provoke a riot, but should be a riotous experience, occurring under the sign of comedy. A few examples of what is going on should suffice. When Hobbes uses the word "action" in a precisely defined way, he is doing exactly what his job requires of him. Burke says, however, that Hobbes's usage is improper. Hobbes is a materialist; he reduces human action to motion; thus he cannot use the word "action" at all without contradicting his philosophy. Why not? The argument is absurd unless one recognizes that for

Burke all writers, even the philosopher, are merely functions of their words, and their words are full of all the meanings that they have acquired over the centuries.

In another passage, which might be mistaken for philosophical thought, Burke discusses the Kantian (never Kant's) universal, "the object." He says, "the surprising thing . . . is that you can't distinguish it from *no object at all.*" "I realized this when . . . the attempt to represent the appearance of an object in general, in order to show how it was related eventually to an unseen thing-in-itself, led to the embarrassing discovery that such an object in general would be as impossible to represent as would the unseen thing-in-itself that by definition lies beyond the realm of sense relationships." Did Kant think "the object" could be represented? That is beside the point. Not the thought of Kant, but Burkean association is the intended source of our entertainment. Burke's delight is in being able to say that Kantian terms are "all about nothing." He then proceeds: "If, then, you would talk profoundly and intelligently about the conditions of the possibility of the knowledge of nothing, what *do* you have that you can talk about? You have the knower." Can that have been the movement of Kant's thought? Even Burke could not claim that, or even that it is the movement of any thought at all, since he has already pointed out that the Kantian agent, the knower, has been universalized and thus is as much "nothing" as the "object" is. The "object" and the "knower" are equally as available or unavailable for "talk about nothing." Does this confusion rob Burke's book of its value? Not at all. His purpose here is not thought, but placement. He is placing Kant, as idealist, under the sign of the "agent" and has accomplished his purpose. What he is doing is consistently like this: he brings together, as identical, idealism, technology, applied science, knowledge, the problem of knowledge, the epistemological problem, and a psychologistic emphasis, all falling "under the head of agent." A chain of identifications like this defies analysis, but is a fanciful delight.

The philosophy of *A Grammar of Motives*, if it can be said to have one, is not at all a philosophy of action; it is rather a curious kind of pan-verbalism which may be summed up in this climactic assertion: "The great departures in human thought can be eventually reduced to a moment where the thinker treats as *op*posite, key terms formerly considered *ap*posite, or *v.v.*" That Burke's preference for "action" in the discussion of that most common element of human experience, motives as he conceives of them, is of a verbalistic nature is unmistakably clear. He affirms himself that his preference for "act" over the other terms of his pentad is, at bottom, a preference for verbs over nouns. Verbs are preferable because they are most abstract, because it is harder to represent or visualize a verb like "running" or "putting" than a noun like "tree" or "bush." The more abstract a word is, the more it lends itself to summing things up; and, of course, Burke's very concern for motives is primarily a concern for summing things up, for "lumping the lot."

The *bête noire* of *A Grammar of Motives* is all philosophy placed under the sign of agency, all pragmatism and especially the operationalism of P. W. Bridgman. Burke opposes this kind of philosophy because it tends to impose "one doctrine of motives," a doctrine of agency or means, "upon a world composed of many different motivational situations." This is a form of fanaticism, fanaticism itself being one of the two alternatives which Burke recognizes to his own efforts. The other alternative he calls dissipation: "By dissipation I mean the isolationist tendency to surrender, as one finds the issues of world adjustment so complex that he turns to the satisfactions nearest at hand." Even here, the stated alternatives collapse under the force of Burke's zest for identification. To reduce all human experience to a matter of terms, especially to reduce philosophy to mere terms, to terms which are so clearly only its means, its instruments, its agency, is surely a form of technological fanaticism of the first order. It is also a form of isolationist dissipation, as the passage on Kant, discussed above, manifests. To reduce Kant's thought to a set of terms is palpably, for a writer of Burke's dedication, to turn "to the satisfactions nearest at hand." Burkean pan-verbalism is not in opposition to his conception of operationalism, but identical with it.

One of the major mergers going on in both the *Grammar* and the *Rhetoric* is the merger of classification and dialectics. These forms of thought are strictly incompatible, as both R. G. Collingwood and A. J. M. Milne have amply demonstrated. Classification does not attend to individuals as such, but only to particular attributes which they exhibit and which it abstracts from them. All the books on this shelf have the attribute of being bound in paper; they belong to the abstract universal of paperbound books. The individual books are what is real, but they function, in a classificatory system, only as what exhibits the particular instances of a universal, being paperbound. Further, the specific forms of a generic attribute are mutually exclusive. Each of the books on these shelves is either paperbound or clothbound; it cannot be both. Finally, the higher the level of classificatory abstraction, the larger the class which possesses an attribute, the less determinate that attribute will be. The bigger an abstraction, the less it reveals about any individual thing. The primary concern of dialectics, in contrast, is to synthesize the universal and the individual in what is called a concrete universal. Dialectics is not abstractive; it works toward the individualization of a normative universal like rational activity or rhetorical activity. It attempts to show that an individual action, in all the richness of its individuality, is a realization of a universal form. Furthermore, unlike the species of a genus, the subforms within a universal form of activity are not mutually exclusive in dialectical thought. Ethical activity, for instance, is more than utilitarian or self-expressive activity, but it includes those inferior activities within itself as subforms essential to its own nature.

Now the common form of Burke's thought is classificatory. He begins, not with individuals, but with particular attributes, and works his way upward. But he merges this, almost at once, with a blurring and fusing of attributes which, in a classificatory system, would rightly be mutually exclusive. Thus, he arrives at the pinnacle of a ladder of thought with a universal which is invariably abstract (like his word "act"). The sharply distinguished attributes characteristic of a classificatory pyramid and the purity and cleanness both of its master abstractions and the hierarchies subsumed beneath them have been dissolved by Burke's pseudo-dialectics into a muddled conglomeration of free-floating attributes that slide in and out of each other, after the manner of random association. Such equivocal merging would ruin both classifier and dialectician. But it works with brilliant efficacy, especially in *A Rhetoric of Motives*, as Burke merges everything he touches into his major terms of Identification, Hierarchy, and Mystery. Indeed, Burke is at his best and purest in the *Rhetoric*, sweeping together, in swirl after swirl, the most diverse writers conceivable. Of all his books, this is no doubt the most vigorous and brilliant. In confusions of massive proportions, he brings together the pair Bentham-Richards and the pair Cicero-Longinus, and Marx and Carlyle, Mannheim and Plato, Castiglione and La Rochefoucauld, and the crime mysteries of Hollywood with a society of specialists serving one another. When he arrives, near the end, at his hymn to Pure Persuasion, to beseechment for itself alone, as pure, abstract form, one feels, as never before, the almost charismatic power of his ingratiating triumph over clarity of thought and diversity of action.

In *The Rhetoric of Religion*, in contrast, the fires of his genius burn low. Herone Liddell, transparent mask for Burke himself in his novella of 1957, has a hernia operation which provokes much troubled talk about a castration complex. A sense of sterility pervades the writing of *The Rhetoric of Religion*. In a long analysis of Augustine's *Confessions*, Burke reduces the passionate imagining and remembering and speculating of that beautifully whole man to the driest form of crafty rhetoric, the very thing Augustine most despised, after his conversion. Of course, Burke's deep purpose here is to identify the crafty rhetoric of the pagan and the candid passion of the convert and to show that they are, at bottom, the same. Words that bulge with feeling and words moved coldly as mere counters cannot be distinguished at this level of technical analysis. One may write as though castrated and sterile, but it is really the same as writing with passionate exuberance.

The purpose of Burke's analysis of the first three chapters of *Genesis*, in the same book, is to show that they are merely a narrative version of principles of order. The original sin, for example, is merely a narrative version of the principle of guilt. Burke is, to be sure, working with an important idea, the truth that temporal succession, that narrative development both in myth and history, is as much the construct of the human mind as logical thought is. This truth, however, does not lead to an identification of logical development and temporal development any more readily than if logic was man-made but history objectively present, there simply to be observed. But Burke drives the identification home, this time for the salutary purpose of helping theologians, with a penchant for de-mythologizing the Bible on their own, to feel themselves to be utterly at one with the most abstract and rational of thinkers.

Aristotle gives this example of a sophistical enthymeme: women with child are pale; this woman is pale; therefore this woman is with child. One might delight himself by reducing all Burke's writing to variations on this sophistical device. The essence of being a writer is the use of words; philosophers use words; therefore philosophy is essentially the use of words. The use of words involves ingratiation; poets use words; therefore the essence of poetry is ingratiation. Words are the signs of things; things often point to, evoke in us, words; therefore things are the signs of words. But as one toys with Burke's means, he should not lose sight of their end, which is the purifying of war, the evocation of an emotion of oneness, of all with all, in a state of pious doubt, of detachment from the causes in which men most fervently believe. If the end of Burke's Neo-Stoicism is a good, then his means are surely not the worst that might be used. Pacification may also be achieved by means of our great bombs. Burke's enthymemes are preferable, even if less efficient. Whether Burke's end, however, is the ultimate good for which one would sacrifice all else is another question.

No perspective upon poetry and criticism could be further from that of the New Critics than Burke's is. However, because Burke, as the complete propagandist, uses the values, vocabulary, and symbols most fashionable in his age, the surface of his writing sparkles with terms linking him to critics like Cleanth Brooks and R. P. Blackmur. Contributory to the confusion caused by this ingratiating device is the fact that Burke earnestly strives to be at one with even those who differ most from him. Thus, even though what matters most for Burke differs markedly from the central concerns of the New Critics, it must be recognized that an emphasis different from mine, an emphasis, say, on the surface of Burke's language, could lead to conclusions the opposite of those I propose.

For Burke, poetry is invariably a form of rhetoric. Because everything is rhetoric, this means that there is nothing special about poetry. It also means, in line with the enthymemic tendency of Burke's thought, that if poetry is rhetoric, then rhetoric is poetry. For the New Critics, no distinction is more important than that between poetry and rhetoric. Poetry is disinterested; its language is polysignificant; poetic form is individual and unique, never specific or generic; the driving force of a poem is always embodied in the poem itself as a basic feeling or shaping attitude; the poem is organic, composed of words that are interactive rather than acting upon a passive audience; and the audience of a poem are active partners who do not merely suffer the experience of the poem, but re-create that experience with an effort similar to the creative act of the poet. Rhetoric, in contrast, is interested; the rhetorician has a purpose, a principle, a state of mind, with which he begins; his piece of writing is a strategy for evoking this principle or mood or state in his audience; the writing itself is a set of devices used to achieve this end, so that its words are outer-directed rather than internally interactive; the audience is there to be worked upon, it is exposed to receive whatever the rhetorician would inject into it. As a consequence of this distinction, when a New Critic criticizes poetry, he attends to the poem above all else; as for the poet, he is important mainly as the shaping, active spirit within the poem. Although the critic is willing to consider biographical, social, and political aspects of the poet's life, since they may enter into the action of the poem, he invariably treats them as subordinate to, as transformed by, the shaping action of the poem. If the New Critic descends to analyze a piece of rhetorical writing, as he only rarely does, he treats it as a set of devices the value of which is extrinsic, in the purpose of the writer and in the effect desired. Rhetorical form he treats as generic rather than individual; given a purpose, a desired effect, the rhetorician is viewed as using one type of form, one set of devices, rather than another. Individual elements are incidental and could be replaced, without loss of value, just so long as the substitutes belong to the same type and thus would work for the same effect.

Burke does not share this distinction between poetry and rhetoric. More important, though he does not share it, neither does he oppose it; that is, he simply ignores the distinction, never arguing against it and merely assuming its nonexistence. As early, for example, as *The Philosophy of Literary Form*, he says that poetry is basically a strategy to encompass a situation. If a New Critic were to use these terms, he would argue that in poetry all strategies and situations are internal to the poetic action and that this action itself cannot be treated as a strategy to come to terms with some specific situation outside the poem. Rhetorical strategies, in contrast, are, precisely, means and devices to come to terms with an outer situation which can be analyzed and understood only if one studies not the rhetoric alone, but also its historical context. When referring to poetry, Burke blurs the distinction between outer and inner situation and seems unaware of any difference between strategies within a poem and the over-all work

as either a strategy or a poetic action. Indeed, he never shows interest in any work as an individual, poetic whole. He may connect a strategy in a poem to something situational either within the poem or outside the poem. Or he may treat a strategy within a poem as though it were the strategy of the whole poem and then connect it with some outer situation.

Because the New Critical conception of poetry accentuates the individual form of a poem, the New Critics, like Croce, give little attention to genres, and they refuse to set up a critical methodology which can be used on any and all poems. The form of a poem determines the method of criticism appropriate to it; since each genuine poem has it own form, it calls for a criticism that is distinctively linked to it and it alone. Having no interest in individual form, Burke elaborates a critical methodology, with the tracing of clusters of words and images and the listing of the elements in a work according to such generalizations as "what goes with what," "what versus what," and "from what to what." He does this, he says, so that he "will not be called idiosyncratic or intuitive." His reason, however, is less servile and more serious than that. He is always concerned with reducing the work to a motive. His lists assist him in breaking down the realized poetic action so that he can move off to some psychological archetype, some general motive. This motive, Burke feels, is often of a physical nature, some uneasiness concerning urination or defecation or sexual orgasm. The poet writes in order to socialize his uneasiness, to make it respectable by evoking the same uneasiness in his audience. Or the motive may be to make the audience delight in technique itself, to satisfy them by rousing an expectation and then fulfilling it. (This is what Burke means by "Pure Poetry.") Or the poet's motive may be of a political nature, to wheedle the audience into accepting the status quo or to harangue them into working for a revolution. Or, indeed, all these motives may be working at once. Whatever the motive, in any case, as Burke sees it the poem is doing something for author and audience. Because the poem is always a means, the critic is bent upon reducing it, whether to an author's anxiety over his drug addiction or to the types of devices of which the elements of the poem are merely instances or to some specific effect to be realized in an audience.

Although this theory seems consistent and consistently at odds with the New Criticism, in *Language as Symbolic Action* Burke becomes quite explicit about the fact that he has never recognized any real difference between the New Critics and himself. His desire for identification, as always, is a deeper consistency than that of any particular theory he may espouse. As his essay "Formalist Criticism: Its Principles and Limits" shows, Burke knows that Brooks, Blackmur, and Wellek recognize no such identification; but he thrives on trying to convince the unconvinced. His strategy is to adopt the terms central to the criticism of Cleanth Brooks, terms like Form, Unity, and Internal Consistency, but to ignore the ideas that lie behind Brooks's use of the terms. He ignores the fact that for Brooks these terms are both descriptive and normative; and the fact that Brooks's notion of Form is individual, not generic as it is for him; and the fact that for Brooks Form is a synthesis of form (as used by rhetorical critics of the past and by Burke) and content; and the fact that Brooks conceives of poetic unity, not as some abstract principle, as simply one of many ingredients in a work, but as a unique sense of existence that unfolds in the evolvement of the poem and that synthesizes all its parts, from the slightest details to its most general traits, into a unique totality. The terms, but not the meanings, of the New Critics are what he adopts.

Such strategic ignorance permits Burke to use the terms in his own way, just as if he were using them as Brooks uses them. All internal criticism, he claims, is poetics, is the study of various devices used in a poem. Form, as he uses it, is a matter of audience expectancy: it may be progressive, repetitive, or conventional. Internal consistency is unrelated to the individual totality of a poem; it is but one principle at work in any poem and may exist side by side with perversions and deviations from it. Unity itself is just one more principle or device in a poem; and an inferior work may "be better unified than a superior one, simply because it did not encounter such great problems of control." Each of these terms is emptied of its poetic meaning and reduced to its meaning as a rhetorical device. Burke's next strategic move is to claim that it is not enough to attend merely to the poetics of a poem, that one ought to consider its personal and social aspects too. Of course, the New Critics do attend to those aspects of a poem, but because their conception of poetic form is integrative and individual, they attend to them as internal to the poem. Since for Burke form and unity are abstract devices, he must go outside them, outside formalism and poetics, in order to find anything personal or social that has relevance to the poem. Because of this and because he has reduced poetic formalism to rhetorical formalism, he can now say that the New Critics would be unduly narrow if they neglected all but matters of form. Since, furthermore, the New Critics do not limit themselves to formal matters, if such matters are defined rhetorically, but also consider personal and social elements, though always as working within the poem, Burke can then say, with what must be keen pleasure, that the New Critics are not at all the formalists they claim to be. They attend to matters extrinsic to form, just as Burke does. That they do not go sifting about the private diaries or intimate letters of a poet, as Burke does, to find things of personal importance, but find them working effectively within the poem, is another distinction which Burke studiously ignores. He concludes, in a state of mock bepuzzlement: since the New Critics practice both extrinsic and intrinsic criticism, just as Burke himself does, how can they criticize and condemn his procedures?

The subjects of the best of Burke's practical criticism which is consistent with his idea that all writing is rhetorical are, reasonably enough, of an overtly rhetorical nature. Emerson, Nietzsche, Marx, and Veblen, among others whom Burke considers, form strategies to encompass actual, historical situations. There is no need to fancy some hidden motive or to imagine a nonexistent audience in order to make the claim that writing such as theirs is truly rhetorical. The relations between situation and strategy, in their writings, are clear, close, and significant. Burke's essay on the Constitution of the United States, as the "representative anecdote" of the *Grammar*, is an impressive analysis of the difficulties which arise when the historical situation to which the Constitution is being applied differs from that which it was originally framed to counter. "War, Response, and Contradiction," the finest essay in *The Philosophy of Literary Form*, is a study of an argument between Archibald MacLeish and Malcolm Cowley concerning the kind of book which ought to be written, in the 1930's, about World War I. He agrees with Cowley that it is less important to tell things as they were than to tell things in such a way as to help prevent the outbreak of another war. But he opposes Cowley in agreeing

with MacLeish that to write of World War I as it was, as a human war with its horrible aspects, is more effective propaganda than to write of it as though it were an unmitigated horror story. The value of the essay is limited by the fact that what appears to be Burke's subtlest thinking is all to be found in MacLeish's own essay, though in a less emphatic form. Nonetheless, Burke's rhetorical balancing of the mediocre arguments of his friend, Malcolm Cowley, and the brilliant arguments of MacLeish is a masterpiece of delicacy.

When Burke's subject matter is genuine poetry, his practice is less effective, so long as he remains faithful to his general theory and methodology. Much of this criticism is typological, the subsumption of a poem under some class term. "It is a beauteous evening, calm and free," for example, is described in the *Grammar* as featuring the ratio between scene (the evening) and agent (Dear Child! dear Girl!). To make his point, Burke ignores the speaking voice of Wordsworth himself, the poetic action which is an intricate linking of the poet's ecstatic response to evening and his awareness that the "dear Girl" appears untouched by the scene. A similar blindness vitiates his effort to subsume "Composed upon Westminster Bridge" under the lyrical genre, in contrast to the dramatic. Burke is so concerned to show that, as a lyric, the sonnet is static, is lacking in all action, that he ignores the dramatic action of the lines themselves, the subtle development of the poet's thoughts and feelings as he observes London in the early morning light.

Burke's best-known criticism—where the influence of Freud is most obvious—is the reduction of poems to some burden of guilt. In *The Philosophy of Literary Form*, he strives so to exhibit the clusters in Coleridge's poetry linking Sara, his wife, with a marriage problem, and that, in turn, with Coleridge's political interests in Pantisocracy, and that, again, with snakes and the poet's drug addiction, that he wholly misses the hilarious poetic movement of "The Eolian Harp." In that poem, Coleridge sits, on an evening, with his wife and expatiates on the cosmic oneness suggested by what they can see in the surrounding scene. At the end of the poem, in response to a rebuke from Sara, Coleridge shamefacedly apologizes for his exuberance. For Burke, this is simply the raising of the marriage problem, whereupon he goes sailing off into other skies; whereas, in the poem itself, it is the delightful realization that the poet's philosophizing about cosmic oneness was in truth a rather scholarly and involuted form of making love to the woman beside him. Sara sees through the subterfuge, Coleridge confesses to her insight, though again in a most abstract form, and the poem concludes on a playfully pious note of solemnity. Burke's most famous essay, his analysis of the "Ode on a Grecian Urn," which is to be found in both *A Grammar of Motives* and *Perspectives by Incongruity*, is weakened by a similar distractedness on Burke's part. He is so occupied with the idea that the poem is a symbolic action, a symbol of the alternating chill and fever of Keats's sickness, and with the various shifts from scene to act, and with some big identifications, like that between the theme of the second stanza and the Wagnerian *Liebestod* and Shakespeare's *The Phoenix and the Turtle* and a letter from Keats to Fanny Brawne, that he is insensitive to the style and movement of the poem itself. Throughout the poem Keats is bringing together his response to the beauty of the urn and his questioning of the significance of its beauty in relation to the actual world. Burke guts the questioning by calling it merely rhetorical; as a result, he cannot make contextual sense of Keats's identification of truth and beauty. He says that making contextual sense of a poem is just a

game. He must be doing more serious things, like reducing "Beauty is Truth" to "Poetry is Science," or, as he later does, like transposing some letters and changing others, in a Joycean manner, so that the phrase becomes "Body is Turd."

The trouble with scatological reduction, an instrument more and more frequently used in Burke's later criticism, is that our language for secret and shameful aspects of bodily experience, at least those parts of that language which Burke draws upon, is extremely crude and undeveloped. Using such language has a momentary shock value, but this is canceled out by the fact that it reduces the delicacy and intricacy and subtlety of a poem to its crudest possible analogues.

Another major area of Burke's criticism is his treatment of Shakespearean drama as social and political persuasion. This criticism depends largely upon Burke's fanciful and unhistorical notions about the nature of Shakespeare's audience. His analysis of *Julius Caesar*, in "Antony on Behalf of the Play," hinges on his identification of the audience of the play with the Roman mob inside the play. When Antony persuades the mob to be loyal to him as the "Caesar principle," he is really persuading the audience to be loyal to Queen Elizabeth. In the scene before Antony's speech, Shakespeare makes it clear to his audience, but not to the mob, that Antony is irreconcilably opposed to Brutus and the other assassins. As a result, the audience could not be passively swayed by Antony's rhetoric as the Roman mob is. Burke, however, has too much faith in rhetoric and too little in Shakespeare's audience to be affected by this complication.

In a more elaborate analysis, of *Othello* (published in *Perspectives by Incongruity*), Burke's treatment of Othello and Iago as two halves of one motive and of all the characters as rhetorical topics, as means used to advance the rhetorical act of persuasion that is the play, depends upon a neglect of the central value of individual, human character for Shakespeare and, so far as we can tell, for his audience. The weakest of his Shakespearean studies, that of *Antony and Cleopatra* (in *Language as Symbolic Action*) is based upon the phrase "The Ostentation of our love" as "an excellent formula for the sweeping poetic devices whereby, in this play, the naked physiology of sex is so grandly adorned." The movement of the play, for Burke, is this: the audience is deceived by the showiness of Antony and Cleopatra; at the end, when Cleopatra dies as a common woman, the audience is undeceived and recognizes that the ostentation was a sham. In fact, Cleopatra is both common and great from the beginning to the end of the play. Burke gets at his point, of affirming that the greatness of her love is a mere semblance for the raw bodiliness of sex, only by adopting the cold, brutal stance of Octavius Caesar and by viewing the whole play from that point of view. Nowhere else is he led so far astray by his belief in Shakespeare as a cold manipulator.

Burke's weakest essays of criticism are those in which he is mainly compiling lists. These essays, the one on Whitman and the one on Joyce's "The Dead," to name only two, are merely preparatory; in them we move "in and about the workshop." Burke is apt to intersperse asides like "Where are we now?" as though he really does not know, and he may conclude by saying, "Frankly, I don't know what all this adds up to." Their quality is summed up by Burke's claim, in the essay on "The Dead," that a critic can never discuss the quality of a work and that all must go to the story itself for that.

Burke's finest criticism is to be found in three essays in which he abandons his rhetorical schemes, and even the idea that what he is reading is rhetoric, and strives to capture the peculiar aesthetic quality of the poems he discusses. These are essays on the poetry of his friends Marianne Moore, Theodore Roethke, and William Carlos Williams. Even in these essays, in which Burke seeks out the tentativeness and contractility of Miss Moore's poetry and explores the *tactus eruditus* of Williams and vegetal radicalism of Roethke, the basic mode of thought is associational revery. But the subjects of his revery are objects of love, not objects to be dismembered and swallowed; they are objects the beauty of which he would exhibit as it is in itself, not objects to be distorted for hortatory purposes. Of the essays on Roethke and Williams, he says: "my memory of voice and manner is imperious in ways that I have not been able to indicate." He has, nonetheless, indicated enough of their voice and manner, and of that of Marianne Moore, to reveal the fundamental weakness, by contrast, of his other criticism. Of these three writers, whom he knew as persons, he has virtually nothing to say concerning secret burdens of guilt or scatological underpinnings. There is too much respect for their actuality to permit any such destructive maneuvers.

Although these essays are uncharacteristic of Burke, they do exhibit a talent which is characteristic of most of his writing—that is, his marvelous facility with language and that freedom with which he puts words together in the most unconventional and undisciplined ways. At last, in these essays, he finds a purpose worthy of his agile talent. Given objects of genuine love, Burke was prepared, as few critics have been, to do justice to those objects. Not his verbal techniques, but the absence of an ultimately significant purpose is the limitation in so much of his writing. Once guided by such a purpose, once gripped by the living manner and voice of a poet, qualities which are present in all great poetry but which Burke could hear only when he knew the makers of the poetry in person, he could articulate his love of poetry with rare insight and precision and delicacy. Three choice essays, for all that mountain of labor? It would be enough. But, of course, there is much more. Though it may be of lesser value, being rhetorical rather than poetic, it is of immense importance for a mass culture, as possibly the finest effort of our time to make unified sense of the multifarious world as it is, as it is given to us to endure.

Selected Bibliography

WORKS OF KENNETH BURKE

BOOKS

The White Oxen & Other Stories. New York: Boni, 1924; Berkeley: University of California Press, 1968 (paper).

Counter-Statement. New York: Harcourt, Brace, 1931; Los Altos, Calif.: Hermes, 1953; Berkeley; University of California Press, 1968 (paper).

Towards a Better Life. New York: Harcourt, Brace, 1932; Berkeley: University of California Press, 1966.

Permanence and Change, New York: New Republic, 1935; Los Altos, Calif.: Hermes, 1954; Indianapolis: Bobbs-Merrill, 1965 (paper).

Attitudes toward History. New York: New Republic, 1937; Los Altos, Calif.: Hermes, 1959; Boston: Beacon Press, 1961 (paper).

The Philosophy of Literary Form. Baton Rouge: Louisiana State University Press, 1941, 1967; New York: Random House, 1957 (paper).

A Grammar of Motives. New York: Prentice-Hall, 1945.

A Rhetoric of Motives. New York: Prentice-Hall, 1950.

Book of Moments: Poems, 1915–1954. Los Altos, Calif.: Hermes, 1955.

The Rhetoric of Religion. Boston: Beacon Press, 1961.

A Grammar of Motives and A Rhetoric of Motives. Cleveland: World, 1962 (paper).

Perspectives by Incongruity, edited by Stanley Edgar Hyman. Bloomington: Indiana University Press, 1964 (paper).

Terms for Order, edited by Stanley Edgar Hyman. Bloomington: Indiana University Press, 1964 (paper).

Language as Symbolic Action. Berkeley: University of California Press, 1966.

Collected Poems: 1915–1967. Berkeley: University of California Press, 1968.

UNCOLLECTED WORKS

"Revolutionary Symbolism in America," in *American Writers' Congress,* edited by Henry Hart. London: Martin Lawrence, 1935.

"The Relation between Literature & Science," in *The Writer in a Changing World,* edited by Henry Hart. New York: Equinox Cooperative Press, 1937.

"Policy Made Person: Whitman's Verse & Prose —Salient Traits," in *Leaves of Grass: One Hundred Years After,* edited by M. Hindus. Stanford: Stanford University Press, 1955.

"Rhetoric—Old & New," in *New Rhetorics,* edited by M. Steinmann, Jr. New York: Scribners, 1967.

"On Stress, Its Seeking," in *Why Man Takes Chances,* edited by S. Z. Klausner. Garden City, N.Y.: Doubleday, 1968.

"As I Was Saying," *Michigan Quarterly Review,* 11:9–27 (Winter 1972).

CRITICAL STUDIES

Bewley, Marius. "Kenneth Burke as Literary Critic," in *The Complex Fate.* London: Chatto and Windus, 1952.

Fergusson, Francis. "Kenneth Burke's *Grammar of Motives,*" in *The Human Image in Dramatic Literature.* Garden City, N.Y.: Doubleday, 1957.

Holland, Laura Virginia. *Counterpoint: Kenneth*

Burke and Aristotle's Theories of Rhetoric. New York: Philosophical Library, 1959.

Hook, Sidney. "The Technique of Mystification," *Partisan Review,* 4:57–62 (December 1937).

Hyman, Stanley Edgar. "Kenneth Burke and the Criticism of Symbolic Action," in *The Armed Vision.* New York: Knopf, 1948.

Kaplan, Abraham. "A Review of *A Grammar of Motives,*" *Journal of Aesthetics and Art Criticism,* 5:233–34 (March 1947).

Knox, George. *Critical Moments: Kenneth Burke's Categories and Critiques.* Seattle: University of Washington Press, 1957.

Lansner, Kermit. "Burke, Burke, the Lurk," *Kenyon Review,* 13:324–35 (Spring 1951).

Parkes, Henry B. "Kenneth Burke," in *The Pragmatic Test.* San Francisco: Colt Press, 1941.

Ransom, John Crowe. "An Address to Kenneth Burke," *Kenyon Review,* 4:219–37 (Spring 1942).

Rosenfeld, Isaac. "Dry Watershed," *Kenyon Review,* 8:310–17 (Spring 1946).

Rueckert, William H. "Burke's Verbal Drama," *Nation,* 194:150 (February 17, 1962).

————. *Kenneth Burke and the Drama of Human Relations.* Minneapolis: University of Minnesota Press, 1963.

————, ed. *Critical Responses to Kenneth Burke, 1924–1966.* Minneapolis: University of Minnesota Press, 1969. (Contains 67 reviews and essays.)

Warren, Austin. "Kenneth Burke: His Mind and Art," *Sewanee Review,* 41:225–36, 344–64 (April–June, July–September 1933).

————. "The Sceptic's Progress," *American Review,* 6:193–213 (December 1935).

Wellek, René. "Kenneth Burke and Literary Criticism," *Sewanee Reveiw,* 79:171–88 (Spring 1971).

Williams, William Carlos. "Kenneth Burke," in *Selected Essays.* New York: Random House, 1954.

—MERLE E. BROWN

Erskine Caldwell

1903-

Like most best-selling authors, Erskine Caldwell tends to be patronized or ignored by academic critics and serious readers. Many know of *Tobacco Road* and *God's Little Acre*, but tend to dismiss them as merely popular or salacious novels. Few seem to know the full range of the man's work: his text-picture documentaries, such as the remarkable *North of the Danube*; his charming books for children; his neglected *Georgia Boy*, a book that stands with Faulkner's last work as one of the finest novels of boyhood in American literature; and his short stories, some of which rank with the best of our time. A brief study cannot fully redress the indiscriminate neglect of readers and critics (nobody will argue that all Caldwell's works are valuable, or that all need to be considered at length); but I will indicate briefly the achievement of Erskine Caldwell, in an attempt not only to do justice to the writer, but to prevent if possible another disgrace in American letters: the sort of disgrace we visited on Melville, forgotten for years; the sort of disgrace we seem to be visiting on Phelps Putnam, Delmore Schwartz, and other good poets now almost entirely out of print, as well as on Glenway Wescott (who remembers that first novel, so highly praised by Ford Madox Ford?).

The specter of Faulkner, the ways we patronized and misunderstood his work until it was honored abroad and claimed by us all, is sobering, especially when one recalls his famous list of the best contemporary writers: Wolfe, Faulkner, Dos Passos, Caldwell, Hemingway. The list infuriates admirers of Hemingway, their man being last; critics of Faulkner worry that their man should be second; and others are annoyed by the absence of Fitzgerald, Steinbeck, Farrell, and so on. In all this disputation, however, hardly anybody elects to notice that Caldwell's name is there or to wonder about the body of writing Faulkner admired.

Younger readers dismiss him as a writer of the *old* pornography, for how tame, demure, almost tidy seem the passages that were read aloud in courts as evidence of Caldwell's obscenity, back when he was America's most banned writer. Younger critics seem unwilling to read Caldwell with care. For example, John Bradbury, in his 1963 volume, *Renaissance in the South*, says of Caldwell: "Furthermore, Caldwell's flat style, his insensitivity to subtleties of fictional presentation, allow him no means to redeem the crude vulgarities he delights in recording." One might take Bradbury's evaluation seriously if Edwin Granberry,

Kathleen Crawford, Patti Hill, and Edyth Latham did not get fuller treatment than Caldwell.

The "flat style" Bradbury dislikes is called by others "plain style." When a writer of a complex, involuted, rich, moving, powerful prose, like Faulkner's, goes out of his way to praise a lean spare, direct, plain style, like Caldwell's, we do well to pay attention. In *Faulkner at Nagano*, Faulkner answered a vague question about Caldwell: "For plain, simple style, it's first rate. There was a thought or a certain moving power and quality in his first book, *Tobacco Road*, but after that, it gradually grew towards trash, I thought. But in the first book there was a very moving power . . . human and moving, even though I never did quite accept them as actual people." *Tobacco Road* was not Caldwell's first book, and Faulkner leaves unexamined the serious problem of accepting literary creations "as actual people." But he did try to point out the central fictional accomplishment of Caldwell, as at the University of Virginia where he said that "The first books, *God's Little Acre* and the short stories, that's enough for any man, he should be content with that, but knowing writers, I know he's not, just as I'm not content with mine."

Few people are satisfied with the work they do in a lifetime; the greater the attempt, the greater the dissatisfaction. Yet, obviously, though a man may never be wholly content, he need not be wholly discontent. That much of Caldwell's work "grew towards trash" does not alter the fact that Caldwell has produced an important body of work in both fiction and nonfiction.

Erskine Preston Caldwell was born on December 17, 1903, in the small settlement of White Oak, Coweta County, Georgia. His father, a well-known Presbyterian minister,

was moved frequently from congregation to congregation, partly because of his liberal views which irritated Georgia crackers, and partly because of his talents in settling problems within congregations. This early travel afforded young Caldwell with observation of people and places, of motive and action, of countryside and human nature. His mother, thought by some to look too youthful to be a preacher's wife, tutored him at home, though he later received formal education at Erskine College in South Carolina, at the University of Pennsylvania, and at the University of Virginia. He left the University of Virginia without taking a degree and began working as a newspaper writer. In 1925 he married Helen Lannegan, with whom he had three children. He left Georgia in 1926 to settle in Maine and to begin seriously to write prose fiction. His jobs over the years have been diverse: cotton picker, stagehand, seaman, cabdriver, professional football player, bodyguard, cook and waiter, book reviewer, lecturer, editor, motion-picture script writer in Hollywood (1933–34, 1938, 1942–43), and foreign correspondent, in addition to his work as writer of novels and short stories.

Caldwell's early stories came to the attention of Max Perkins, the great editor at Scribners who brought along the talents of Wolfe, Hemingway, and Fitzgerald. Perkins, like other editors to whom Caldwell submitted manuscripts, rejected many stories; but unlike the other editors he saw reason to encourage Caldwell to keep writing. Finally he accepted some of Caldwell's stories set in northern New England for publication in *Scribner's Magazine*. Gradually, Caldwell's work, under the encouragement of Perkins, began to be published in many magazines and journals and to be included in the annual anthologies such as O'Brien's *The Best Short Stories* and the

O. Henry Memorial Award Prize Stories. Scribners published his first two important books, the collection of short stories *American Earth* and the novel *Tobacco Road*. The relationship between Caldwell and Perkins was strained by an argument about the manuscript of Caldwell's next novel, set in Maine, and Caldwell left Scribners for Viking Press. He finally came to agree with objections to the novel, and instead of pressing for its publication he wrote *God's Little Acre*, his masterpiece. His first collection of essays on social problems appeared in 1935. In the same year he was introduced to the celebrated photographer Margaret Bourke-White with whom he did the famous *You Have Seen Their Faces*.

In 1938 he lectured at the New School for Social Research before leaving the United States to be, in 1938–39, a newspaper correspondent in Mexico, Spain, and Czechoslovakia. While in Czechoslovakia he collected material for *North of the Danube*, a book which again combined the prose of Erskine Caldwell and the photographs of Margaret Bourke-White, who became Caldwell's second wife early in 1939. Caldwell traveled in China, Mongolia, and Turkestan in 1940. In the next year he happened to be in Russia when Hitler invaded and was thus one of the few American correspondents to report that phase of World War II firsthand. On his return to the United States he began to edit the *American Folkways* series of regional books (1941–55). In 1942 he married his third wife, June Johnson, having one son with her. His present wife, Virginia Fletcher, whom he married in 1957, did the line drawings which illustrate *Around about America*, one of his more recent books of travel and observation.

Caldwell is a novelist of "the old school" in that he does not earn a living by reporting on political conventions for a magazine or review, does not teach "creative writing" at a university, does not have a separate income from a medical practice or a position in a bank or insurance company. Nor is he one of those "writers in residence" at a university who reside a lot but publish less and less. Erskine Caldwell is a professional novelist, who also produces works of personal observation.

Caldwell's autobiography, *Call It Experience: The Years of Learning How to Write* (1951), begins in backwoods obscurity and hardship, but when it ends with Caldwell the best-selling novelist in publishing history autographing pocketbook editions of his works in drugstores, the shape of the story is the classical shape of the world's great autobiographies. A good autobiography is, contrary to what the general public may think, not just the story a man tells about his life; autobiographies are, when well written, stories of transformation or conversion, from St. Augustine whose confessions begin in cosmopolitan vice and end in a triumph over that vice and a coming to Christian virtue, to André Gide's *If It Die . . .* which ends abruptly after his successful conversion from conventional bourgeois son to cosmopolitan homosexual. Caldwell's autobiography of his public life as a writer is a book about recognition, about the transition from the poor boy from the provinces to the wealthy man whose determination and talent enabled him to transcend humble beginnings. It is a classic American life, the very embodiment of one version of the American Dream. Yet he has successfully avoided the danger of autobiographical writing: alienation of the reader. St. Augustine had to lead up to and away from that episode in the orchard with great care so as not to appear self-righteous; Gide had to exercise subtle control over his material and his readers' responses to prevent immediate revulsion from his story of how he found happiness with his boyfriends; Caldwell had to guard against his readers' admiration for success, admiration which is also touched with envy. Caldwell keeps the narration swift, freighting it with a large portion of verifiable fact and of anecdotes which are lively and not self-centered. Indeed the straightforward report of his many tribulations with ignorant but powerful censors, whether at the level of small-town librarian or of state board, is not self-pitying. It is calm in tone and even good-humored.

Call It Experience has raised a difficulty for some readers, however, in that Caldwell himself says that in the early novels he wanted "to write about Southern life as I knew it." Such remarks lead some readers to assume the novels to be journalistic reporting, or factual social studies, or naive realism. One recalls the same sort of confusion that resulted when Faulkner remarked in an interview: "I write about the people around Oxford." Literary tourists flocked to Oxford to see how many characters they could identify. But writers tend to give these simple, even misleading assertions, so that we must, as D. H. Lawrence insisted, trust the work rather than the writer's statements about it.

To undersand Caldwell fully and thus to illuminate his best books as well as to prevent oversimplification, one needs to know the early *The Sacrilege of Alan Kent*. The book is made of three sections, each separately published: "Tracing Life with a Finger" (1929), "Inspiration for Greatness" (1930), "Hours before Eternity" (1931)—titles significantly different from those of the other short novels published during the same years: *The Bastard* (1929) and *Poor Fool* (1930). Kenneth Burke in his remarkable chapter on Caldwell in *The Philosophy of Literary Form* calls this early work a "sport," in that it is so different from other works by Caldwell. The book is closer to a series or a collection of Joycean "epiphanies" than to a novel or collection of three

stories. The numbered paragraphs, some as short as a sentence, are about what is remembered and about the tricks of memory as the central character recalls moments made sharp by intense feeling, whether of pain or joy. The moments are not idyllic; the tone is often downright grim: life is a sacrilege, we live in pain and hurt.

One section (II:8) sounds like the beginning of a film by Ingmar Bergman: "I lived for a while in a room with two girls. Neither of them could speak English nor understand it, and I never knew what they were talking about." That rich scene is left in this epiphanal form, as in Hemingway's figure of a short story as an iceberg, only a small amount actually showing. In Caldwell's notations most of each story is left unstated. Occasionally sections sound like the "deep images" of Robert Bly, James Wright, and other members of the "Sixties" group, as in II:11: "Once the sun was so hot a bird came down and walked beside me in my shadow." At the end of Part II, the narrator returns to his hometown, but the place is inhabited by strangers except for a girl whose "breast was bursting like a blossom in the warm sunshine."

Part III follows the central character through a winter journey and various odd jobs, including a carnival in which Caldwell, with a great imaginative stroke, has the fortuneteller go crazy. Repeatedly the images lie in one's mind and are suddenly transformed—as in the scene in which the central character sees a girl so beautiful that the sight of her beauty scars his eyes (III:8). One recalls a later work, James Dickey's remarkable poem on faces seen once only. The section contains a good deal of fine ribald humor which foreshadows later plot devices. In III:17 an employer keeps Negro girls for his satisfaction, until one girl defeats him: "The man brought another Negro girl to the house but she had greased her body with lard and he could not hold her." That is the essence, the reader being left to add the usual details of a great tall story in the manner of Twain or Faulkner—the Negro girl lowering herself to the status of greased pig to maintain her higher conception of herself. But that is part of the submerged iceberg, part of the unspoken available.

The book is strange, at times brilliant. Caldwell would not again use this method, except in passages of description in the novels and in pointed details in the essays, as when in an essay in *Some American People* he places an action in perspective by syntactical means: the scene is North Dakota, the time is August 1934, the action is "The Last Roundup" in which the federal government in two days cleared the Badlands of ten thousand head of cattle, shipping them to pastures not destroyed by drouth: "The last great roundup is over, the bones of the culls that fell by the wayside have been picked clean, and the painted canyons of the Badlands are unchanged." *The Sacrilege of Alan Kent* is one of the books we must look to if we are to understand Caldwell's full range and his place in contemporary literature.

His first novel, *The Bastard* (he says he did not select the title), is as weak as some of the more recent novels; yet it is important: it suggests later themes and techniques that give such rich comic effect and insight to his best fictions. *The Bastard* is a novel about chance and control, rendered in various ways: the chance of a man's birth and the ways he may control his life despite his birth; games of chance like craps and of control like pool; chance meetings with women and carefully planned seductions; the chance of falling in love and the willed rapes and murders. The absence of characterization reinforces the theme of chance; but that absence also dam-

ages the book. Not a good novel, it contains fine touches: when Sheriff Jim betrays his steady at the whorehouse by getting married to an out-of-town girl, that girl infects him, his son, his boarder, and the neighboring men with syphilis. The disease is the blight descended on the community when its ruler breaks the code. In another fine, though less mythic, scene a naked and drunk woman leads a mule to the courthouse demanding the animal's arrest "for insufficient rape." These scenes are, however, the high points in the story of the bastard, Gene, violent, lusty, immoral, criminal. He marries, fathers a deformed child, commits infanticide, and wanders away, dispossessed, alienated, alone: the very image of modern man in more recent fiction. He has some of the vain self-consciousness exemplified by Meursault in Camus's *The Stranger* and some of the pompous egotism of Sergius in Mailer's *The Deer Park*. But Caldwell's book is slight, more important, perhaps, for its place in the development of the clichés of alienation in modern fiction than for its literary art.

Poor Fool is a story of fighters and fixed fights. Things just happen, as people just drop dead in the novels of E. M. Forster, and as accident and coincidence are often crucial in the fiction of Thomas Hardy. Yet in this story of chance, love, and death, fights are fixed. The point of the story is that the fights, a metaphor for competition in a "free" enterprise system, are fixed by Mr. Big and that Mr. Little is a "poor fool" for trying to fight the system and bring Mr. Big to justice. Incidental episodes are again the best parts of the book, although the novel shows some of the structural strength that will characterize Caldwell's later work (even an admittedly bad book, like *The Last Night of Summer*, 1963, is almost classical in the purity and force of its structure), and although the themes here tentatively examined will later give power and force to better novels.

Next to these early fictions, probably the least well known works by Caldwell, and thus the most neglected, are the books he did with Margaret Bourke-White. The neglect is unfortunate since although the neglected early fictions are interesting mainly as forecasts of things to come, these text-picture books are some of the finest examples of that genre. The tradition of the text-picture book goes back, in America, at least as far as Jacob A. Riis who published in 1890 *How the Other Half Lives*. The Caldwell and Bourke-White books belong to a five-year spurt of talent in this genre. Their first, *You Have Seen Their Faces*, was published in 1937. Then in 1938 Archibald MacLeish published *Land of the Free— U.S.A.* which is, as he says, "the opposite of a book of poems illustrated by photographs. It is a book of photographs illustrated by a poem." Dorothy Lange and Paul Taylor published *An American Exodus* in 1939, the same year that Caldwell and Bourke-White published what may be the masterpiece of their collaboration, *North of the Danube*. The astonishing year for the genre was 1941 when Caldwell and Bourke-White published their superb *Say! Is This the U.S.A.?* and James Agee and Walker Evans published their celebrated *Let Us Now Praise Famous Men*. The Agee-Evans book has been reissued; unfortunately the rest remain out of print. Successful text-picture books are rare, depending as they do on the accidental harmony of two workers in different media, like the rare conjunction of composer and librettist which leads to grand opera.

In pictorial art, commentary is superfluous; yet iconographic content may be located and may be pointed by commentary. The collaboration of Caldwell and Bourke-White resulted in a group of books in which prose and photograph are in harmony and have a single object, the captions and essays focusing our reading of the pictures, the pictures illuminating what we see in the prose. Both picture and text depict image or situation in moral terms, the moral being in image or situation, with only muted editorial diction in most of the prose and only discreet editorial lighting in the photographs.

In *You Have Seen Their Faces* a Negro boy and his hound stand framed in a doorway, the interior walls of the shack papered with pages from magazines. The "white" advertisements comment ironically on the poverty of the place and its furnishings, and of the lives lived there. One notices the framing doorway, the side lighting from a hidden source in the room beyond, the control of shadow, and more. Yet if we look at this moving composition only as an arrangement of light and shade, we miss the point. Caldwell's caption (and the essay that goes with this section of photographs) helps focus our eyes: "Blackie ain't good for nothing, he's just an old hound dog." The captions do not turn the photographs into anecdotes or literary imitations; but they help achieve a full response to the photograph, as the photographs help achieve a full response to the essays. A caption such as "Bringing the white-boss's fine cotton along" seems banal enough; but its simplicity keeps it from competing with the photograph, and its meaning prevents us from seeing the great photograph as just a study in vanishing points and sky, which it also is. We are led by the prose to those small figures in the field, to a sense of human misery in the midst of visual beauty.

An eloquent photograph of an old man's face in Arkansas: "I used to be a peddler until peddling petered out." A grim-faced woman with a child: "Snuff is an almighty help when your teeth ache." And a lined, leathery face: "I've done the best I knew all my life, but it didn't amount to much in the end." As compared with the remarks of "Existentialists," usually well-fed men in comfortable jobs teaching well-fed students, the "existential" dimension of these text-picture books is staggering: the determined, often even fierce animal urge toward life, even under the most humiliating circumstances, mocks Camus's celebrated remark in *The Myth of Sisyphus* that suicide is the only serious philosophical problem left us. (Some "Existentialists" forget that Sisyphus led a vile, mean, cruel life and got no worse than he deserved.) The withered-limbed, starved-minded, puff-bellied, illiterate bastards —redneck, nigger, poor white—in this book live, perhaps incapable of a sophisticated notion like suicide; for suicide seems a luxury these American peasants could not afford.

The essays in the book argue for a government commission to investigate and propose remedies for the moribund agricultural system in the South. Southerners were outraged by the book, Donald Davidson attacking it in his famous essay-review in the *Southern Review* by saying that the South could never cure its wrongs if people kept drawing attention to those wrongs, especially southerners: "What is the matter with any Southerner who turns state's evidence under circumstances like these?" What seemed wrong Davidson indicated by saying that "as a student of farm tenancy in the South Mr. Caldwell would make a splendid Curator of a Soviet Park of Recreation and Culture." Given the slowness of progressive action in the South, such a commission might have been able to accomplish something by 1968 when Senator Robert Kennedy found illiteracy and actual starvation in Mississippi—conditions that, once revealed, shocked a nation.

You Have Seen Their Faces was an extension of Caldwell's famous essay on tenant farmers, later reprinted in *Some American People*, and of his lectures at the New School. His argument for correction of social and economic evils went unheeded. Indeed things have not changed much for the impoverished tenant farmers; except that, as T.R.B. in the *New Republic* for June 8, 1968, remarks, the absentee landlords now find it profitable to forbid tenants in Alabama the use of land on which they once raised corn and vegetables for their own consumption. Landlords can make money on those garden plots by leaving them unplanted and collecting a subsidy from the government for adding that land to the "soil bank." In the year when the Hawaiian Sugar Company got $1,353,000 for not planting crops, babies were born dead in Mississippi because pregnant women could not afford even minimal diets. Unfortunately, in 1937 Caldwell's prose effected only the rage of Donald Davidson, rather than remedies.

One of the best of the text-picture books composed by Caldwell and Bourke-White, the one Caldwell is fondest of, is *North of the Danube*. Images of camera and language record and report on Czechoslovakia, its edges ceded to Germany and Hungary. It was a place of great scenic beauty; a place of towns, such as Uzhorod, where cars were rare, bicycles were ridden by Ruthenians, Czechs, and Germans, while Jews and gypsies walked; a place in which the sun shone, crops grew, and one generation followed another in a social structure that had changed little in five hundred years. Caldwell treats all this tenderly but without sentimentality.

In the last of the Caldwell and Bourke-White text-picture books on an American theme, *Say! Is This the U.S.A.?* the prose is so clean, almost coldly dispassionate, that one at times almost forgets to notice the reportorial point of view, the implied judgment; just as one at times tends to overlook the moving content of Margaret Bourke-White's photographs, they are so stunningly composed and lighted. This book contains almost no overt editorializing, and does not argue a case as *You Have Seen Their Faces* did. Both text and photographs are starkly objective, but the opinions of writer and photographer are implicit in what they elected to report.

The movement of the book is rich and varied, from commonplace jobs and filling-station sociology to "land-cruising" whores and rich boys out for a thrill; from a wry report on why cattle raisers keep one goat around their horses and cows to a sympathetic view of the problems of a schoolteacher instructing children in an "Americanization" class; from a man trying to scrape up a dollar so his wife and kids can go to the picture show to a manufacturer of electrical equipment in Illinois who argues that war in Europe must be kept going for the sake of America's industrial growth; from good country folk in Soso, Mississippi, to a batch of titillated ladies in Cedar Rapids, Iowa, each fancying herself the prototype of Carl Van Vechten's now almost unread but once notorious *The Tattooed Countess*. Caldwell's range of tone and effect is impressive. He gets the tone of a street-corner evangelist, a pompous lieutenant colonel in the cavalry, a B-girl trying to get a job, a Rotary Club luncheon, and the majestic peevishness of a secretary trying to locate her boss by telephone. The book is neither a broad and balanced historical account of the United States in 1941 nor a penetrating sociological treatise; rather it gives a sense of a nation's movement, the live sense of place and person rendered in prose and photograph, unadorned, clean, and effective.

The essays in another early book, *Some American People* (1935), also afford entry into

Caldwell's world, a sense of the range of his literary art, and a direct presentation of the moral views which inform his novels. The section "Detroit" is a fierce and bitter account of old Henry Ford's empire, that automobile industry being, to Caldwell, "one of the clearest examples of industrial slavery." Then from the abuses of industry the book moves in its final section to "Southern Tenant Farmers" who are "living under decivilized conditions." As "straight" economic and sociological analysis these two essays may be damaged by Caldwell's outrage at inhumanity; but the essays are all the more valuable for that outrage. They are in the central tradition of polemic, and like all great polemics they survive the special circumstances of their creation. Things now have changed in Detroit, but the essay is still witty and moving, still a brilliant document illuminating both one aspect of a period in American history and one aspect of man's use of man. And the essay is still valid, as "A Modest Proposal" is still valid though Ireland is free from absentee English landlords.

As with some of Hemingway's journalism, some of Caldwell's reports could stand as short fiction. An anecdote in the "Cross-Country" section titled "Grandpa in the Bathtub" is a satisfying whole in itself, reminding one of more recent works of fiction and of the theater of Ionesco. The anecdotal report concerns an old man who hoards rainwater until he has ten gallons: "I've never seen so much water since '96." He moves all his furniture into the bathroom in a show of the affluence of poverty, and as though it were his last act in life, he bathes, joyously.

The book contains many scenes of people who because of the vitality of their despair would survive bleak days and hungry nights. In the "Prefatory Note" for the Decennial Edition of *Tobacco Road*, Caldwell writes of people he saw as a boy wandering around the

South: "They believed in cotton. They believed in it as some men believe in God." At the end of the note he sums up the history and the theme: "First, tobacco, and then cotton; they both had come and gone. But the people, and their faith, remained." This is the stark survival of the unfittest in an economic system like that which made the plot of Gogol's *Dead Souls* possible. These people have the stubborn dignity of "surplus miners" who would be all right, one man in *Some American People* suggests, if they "could find something else to do, if they had unemployment insurance to live on, if they removed to South America, or if they committed suicide." They are "wound-up, finished, done," but they survive with a fierce animal will that underlies the desolate characters in Caldwell's great stories, and gives his characters their dignity and vitality.

A later book of nonfiction, *In Search of Bisco* (1965), uses the search for a boyhood friend to structure a report on travel and people. Its superficial structure is a collection of nonfiction short stories; but the book also has a thematic structure. Time, law, and race recur, like motifs in music, the interaction of the three being the book's major theme.

Time is sometimes almost Proustian: Caldwell is literally trying to find (or find out about) Bisco, his Negro boyhood playmate; but in the search for that past friendship, he finds the realities of the present, and he has intuitions about the future. Time is for some speakers in the book history; or time is what works on law; or time is what we try to get through, without too much trouble. For some, the passing of time is traced in the gradual lightening of the Geechee Negroes' color; and we are reminded of the past, of the beginnings of this history of racial strife, by the still shiny coal-black of the Gullah Negroes, a darkness maintained by economic causes. So, in the complex narrative, the very colors of skins come to symbolize the delicate interaction of economics, race, time, and law.

The first chapter sets up certain themes in three scenes, for Caldwell is, in his reporting as in his novels, a great scenic artist. He recalls three Negro boys: Bisco, from whom he was separated when he got too old to sleep in Bisco's bed in the Negro shack; Sonny, lynched for alleged relations with a promiscuous white girl; Roy, sentenced to two years on the chain gang for supposedly stealing an iron washpot too heavy for a man to lift. The white community, to preserve its code, (a) separated friends, and (b) lynched one Negro and imprisoned another by extralegal means. These early sections prepare for later reports on the civil rights movement in which the Negro community, to gain its rights, (a) makes friends, or tries to ("You can't make anybody be your friend by pulling a knife or pointing a gun at him"), and (b) when necessary uses extralegal devices to achieve ends. The southern whites ignored laws to work injustice; southern Negroes took to ignoring laws to work a justice denied them. Active violence of rednecks was met by passive nonviolence of Negroes. And in this struggle of race and law, time is on one side.

These books of report and record are for the most part effective; but the propaganda of Caldwell's wartime books is difficult to judge. The text-picture collaboration of Caldwell and Bourke-White, *Russia at War* (1942), is a valuable record bringing together photography and reporting they did during the war, much of it for *Life*. The commentary is often predictable propaganda about Russia, our wartime friend, but often anecdote and incident blood the propaganda. Caldwell was also Moscow correspondent for the CBS radio network and the newspapers *PM* and *Daily Mail*. From his dispatches and a diary he made two other books published in 1942, *Moscow under Fire* and *All-Out on the Road to Smolensk*. Both record, in that lean and unobtrusive style, sights and sounds of Moscow, the small incidents which most accurately reveal the tension and calm of a great city under attack. Other scenes are a "natural" for Caldwell, like absurd images of fifty-ton tanks ramming head-on, ammunition having been exhausted. The machines of destruction are turned helplessly on their backs, like monstrous turtles. The other book of 1942 is a disappointing novel, *All Night Long: A Novel of Guerrilla Warfare in Russia*. The plotting is tight though episodic, but the characterization is perfunctory, being divided between Russian hero and German swine. On the other hand, the set speeches are effective pieces of rhetoric within the conventions of propagandistic fiction—a set of conventions as yet insufficiently studied, and in many ways as arbitrary and as strict as the conventions of courtly love poems.

Caldwell's talent seems to falter in the longer forms when he leaves a southern setting, as in the war novel and in *A Lamp for Nightfall* (1952), a novel set in Maine and dealing with old ways threatened by outlanders. Some of the short stories, like the celebrated "Country Full of Swedes," succeed in northern settings; but his major fictional accomplishment lies in what Caldwell refers to several times in *Call It Experience* as "a cyclorama of Southern life." This "cyclorama" is unlike Faulkner's mythical county; and if we try to understand Caldwell's cyclorama in terms of Faulkner's county we will end by misunderstanding both men. Faulkner composed a sort of history, the novels linked in various ways to give an incredibly rich fabric of lives and events. It is, nobody doubts, one of the highest moments in Western literature. Caldwell was not after that sort of complex historical fabric, but after scenes and actions that embodied themes and types in the present.

His "cyclorama" consists of ten volumes: *Tobacco Road, God's Little Acre, Journeyman, Trouble in July, Tragic Ground, A House in the Uplands, The Sure Hand of God, This Very Earth, A Place Called Estherville,* and *Episode in Palmetto*.

Tobacco Road (1932) did not become a best seller (indeed sales barely covered Caldwell's advance) until after its dramatization by Jack Kirkland, a play which almost closed after two weeks but managed to survive to become so popular that for years it held the record of longest consecutive run on Broadway. *Tobacco Road* is about tenacity in the spirits of men and women deserted by God and man. The book is not about tobacco or Georgia, about sexology or sociology, but is instead a work of literary art about the animal tug toward life that sustains men even in times of deprivation. The grandmother is one of the central symbolic figures in the book, hovering in the background, lighting a fire in the stove in that great primitive faith that a fire will bring the god, and that a god will provide where men fail.

Life's major vital signs are eating and sexual intercourse, the two motives wittily, grossly, and magnificently rendered in the famous opening section of *Tobacco Road*: Lov with his bag of turnips which are the object of Jeeter's desire, Ellie May wanting Lov's body, Lov being had on all counts as Negroes stop in the road to watch the high-life of the poor whites. This mockery of desire in two of its forms (eating and intercoursing) begins a series of mockeries, such as the mockery of that old-time religion as it is embodied in its modern apostle, Sister Bessie; the mockery of that old-time plantation system, now degenerated into tenant farming, embodied in the absentee landlord "Captain" John; the mockery of the clean-cut wholesome boy who plays ball and is interested in cars, embodied in the simple-minded Dude who almost knocks the house down by chunking his ball against it and who becomes the child groom of Sister Bessie just to get a car to wreck; the mockery of hospitality in the splendidly funny and sad hotel scene in the city where hospitality becomes lust as Sister Bessie is shifted from room to room, to the delight of all.

The book is also a study in relationships and desertions. Man in this symbolic landscape is frustrated in his relationship to the soil because fertility has deserted the land. The sterile relationship of man to land is paralleled in the sterile marriage relationship of Lov and Pearl, in the stupid lust of Sister Bessie for Dude, in the failure of the whole family to speak to the old grandmother—that is, to have a right relationship with the past. The grandmother is a choric figure of silence, commenting by her presence rather than by any words. The currently popular discussions of "failure of communication" as a theme in modern literature have themselves failed to consider the poignance of the theme in *Tobacco Road*, which is almost a novel of silence: no letters come from absent children because there is no rural delivery on the tobacco road; for years Ada did not speak to her husband, and in the course of the novel Pearl will not speak to hers; Jeeter speaks in monologues, usually not addressed precisely to anybody. Once when Jeeter tried to command Dude to quit knocking the house down with his baseball, his injunction goes unheeded. These peasants are the very opposite of the vessels of goodness and wisdom envisioned by Wordsworth and Tolstoi.

In *Tobacco Road* as in *God's Little Acre* the house itself, symbol of family and permanence, is in danger. In the later novel, the house is in danger of sliding into one of Ty Ty Walden's holes, the symbol of his lust for gold literally undermining the symbol of family. In the earlier novel, the house is in danger from the aimless play of the younger generation, and at the end of the novel is victim of a southern tradition, that of burning off the weeds and saplings each spring. The aimless destruction of this traditional fire, erroneously said to kill boll weevils, in the turning of a wind destroys the now aimless lives of Jeeter and Ada. The fire destroys the house but cannot purge the land of accumulated sin and degradation, burning, burning in *this* wasteland.

Yet there is something grand about thieving, lazy, immoral, stupid old Jeeter; and the physical deformities of the harelip girl and the woman without a nose are symbolic deformities. Indeed one suspects that literary historians will gradually see Caldwell in relationship with Flannery O'Connor as a writer whose characters were often deformed not for the purposes of sensational fiction or sales but for purposes which allow the writer to explore, whether under the tragic mode or the comic mode, spiritual conditions. When Jeeter says of God that "Him and me has always been fair and square with each other," and that "I don't know nothing else to do, except wait for Him to take notice," *Tobacco Road* takes its place in a body of modern literature which includes both Samuel Beckett's *Waiting for Godot* and Simone Weil's *Waiting for God.*

God's Little Acre (1933), despite its reputation as comic pornography, is no more an "exposé" of southern mentality or habits than the typist-at-teatime section of *The Waste Land* is about unfair employment practices in London. It is a novel of rich sexuality, sexuality being, in this symbolic landscape, as grim and spectral as the Hollywood landscape of Nathanael West's *The Day of the Locust,* the impressive life-sign. Yet just as the farm produces neither cotton nor gold (except for the crops raised by the Negro sharecroppers on their part of the land), so no woman in the novel is pregnant, despite all the sexuality. Darling Jill is blunt about not wanting to marry until she is "a few months gone." No marriage is in sight, though, despite the complaint of her rotund suitor that she has been "fooling with a lot of men." Pluto Swint's complaint gets a characteristic reply from Ty Ty Walden, the proud father: "I'm tickled to death to hear that. Darling Jill is the baby of the family, and she's coming along at last." Few responses have been so disarming and possessive of such high wit since Lady Bracknell confessed herself glad to hear that Ernest smoked. Ty Ty is a great believer in men and women doing what God made them to do—a Georgia cracker's sort of argument from design. He remarks that Darling Jill is "just made that way. It don't hurt her none, not so that you will notice it, anyway." At the end of the novel Darling Jill will marry the great fat man, even though she is not pregnant. After all, that they should marry seems part of God's plan, being acted out on God's little acre; and if things go wrong, brother killing brother, that must be part of God's plan too. This impossible paradox is one of the central themes of the novel, often most powerfully rendered in sexual terms, as when Pluto says: "It's a pity God can't make a woman like Darling Jill and then leave off before He goes too far. That's what He did to her. He didn't know when He had made enough of a good thing."

It might be read as an exemplum on the natural goodness and natural depravity of man; or, especially those sections set in the mill town, as a document on labor relations at a particular time in American history; or as a broad rural comedy parodying in the manner of recent "black comedy" the notion that farmers live close to the soil, uncorrupted by the devious ways of society and civilization, and so are the salt of the earth, the backbone

of American life; but *God's Little Acre* can be read more meaningfully as a novel about dream and reality, power and impotence, the force of life and the force of death. The characters are studies of how single-mindedness of purpose or desire shapes people and compels them to behave in certain ways as economic, sexual, political, or theological agents. Ty Ty Walden, for instance, in his habitual insistence on being "scientific" in his obsessive digging for gold is as "hobby-horsical" as any character in *Tristram Shandy*. Each character in *God's Little Acre* is identified by and with his driving motive. Ty Ty Walden and his son-in-law, Will Thompson, the central male characters, each has a dream and each wrecks his life and the lives of others with that dream, comically and selfishly in the case of Ty Ty, tragically and altruistically in the case of Will. The two characters are possessed by a yearning to find in deadness and dust (the sliding red dust of Ty Ty's holes or the yellow dust of the mill town into which abused workers spit) the sources of power, of value, of some other kind of life; and part of the darkness of Caldwell's vision of life, bitterly rendered in comic terms, is that these yearnings are defeated as they are acted out either in the withered pastoralism of Ty Ty's farm or in the dehumanized urbanity of mill town or big city.

The dreams of the characters are obsessive and the actions extravagant; yet the literary effect is of order and inevitability. The relation of destiny and personality in the working out of the plot is more complex than previous critics have conceded, just as the range of characters is more complex. The novel has been pigeonholed as a product of some sort of deterministic naturalism or pornographic local color; but clearly it is not that. Rosamond's acceptance of the death of her husband, Will, as inevitable is an expression of the fatalism that haunts the book; yet his death will come at the hands of either the husband of one of the women he elects to seduce or the company police he elects to defy, so that fate is the working out of man's will. The relationship of Moira, Tyche, Hubris, and Hamartia has been the central theme in Western literature, and is no less the theme of *God's Little Acre*, though here presented mainly in Christian terms of God's plan and divine will in relation to the flawed nature of fallen man. Toward the end of the book, after the ruined land has been polluted by blood (Numbers, 35:33), Ty Ty expresses a peasant's version of man's tragic position on the Great Chain of Being: "There was a mean trick played on us somewhere. God put us in the bodies of animals and tried to make us act like people. That was the beginning of trouble."

The characters have often been dismissed by critics as ignorant, lecherous, exotic, and so on; but the novel is structured on a series of contrasts arising from distinctions in characterization. The three brothers Walden, for instance, illustrate different types of son; and the son most often ignored in reductive critiques of the novel is Shaw, the quiet and kindly bachelor. He is silent when taunted by his father, not because he is stupid but because he is understanding. He is the only male in the novel who respects the taboo on incest. He is the one who sees that the Negro sharecroppers are fed, who remembers what he learned in school about the difference between placer mining and lode mining, and who at the end of the book must report to the sheriff that his brother Buck has killed his brother Jim Leslie. Though he is a shadowy character, his presence helps undercut the notion that Caldwell's world is populated exclusively by dumb lechers.

The structure and tone of the novel have also been ignored. The action of the book begins in a slow slide of reddish dust and clay over Ty Ty's feet, and rises to a classic double climax of plot and subplot. This action takes place in a symmetrical seven-part structure, distinguishable by changes in setting: farm, mill town, farm, Augusta, farm, mill town, farm. The chapters about the action in Augusta are at the center of the plot and contain the turning point, after which the tone of the book begins to change. Repetition, for instance, is one of the common devices in comedy, and Caldwell uses it to achieve some of his finest comic effects. But gradually repetition of phrases or tags, like Pluto's "and that's a fact," cease to be funny. Rosamond's repetition of "yes" and "yes, I know" is fatalistic and pathetic. Toward the end of the book, repetition reaches lyric intensity in the work chant of the Negroes, and tragic intensity in the insistent threats and commands of Buck and Jim Leslie during their final encounter, when repetition becomes an index of inflexibility of attitude and motive. Early in the novel Pluto's blinding of a lizard with tobacco juice is echoed in an almost archetypal scene in which Darling Jill blinds Pluto with a handful of suds for having greedily stared on her nakedness as she bathed; but late in the novel, repetitions and echoes become ritualistic, as when the corpses of both Will and Jim Leslie are mourned over by the same three women. One begins to lose some of the condescending assurance a reader normally has in the presence of comic types, and to become aware of the bitter quality in Caldwell's humor. For example, Ty Ty's constant shifting of God's little acre, the portion set aside for God, is one of the mechanical repetitions that becomes funnier on each occasion. Yet at the end of the novel, after Buck, Cain-like, kills his brother and flees over the new ground, Ty Ty realizes that he forgot to shift the acre, and that the murder took place on God's portion. The son who died and the son who fled are the old man's tithe; and the novel ends with one last shift of the acre, as Ty Ty sends it after his fleeing son, so that he will be eternally on God's little acre.

Caldwell's concentration on sex and economics has led to misunderstanding, readers criticizing him as they critize Alberto Moravia for not presenting "higher" aspects of man. Moravia is quoted in Del Buono's book on him as saying: "My concentration on the sexual act, which is one of the most primitive and unalterable motives in our relation to reality, is due precisely to this urgency; and the same may be said of my consideration of the economic factor, which is also primitive and unalterable, in that it is founded on the instinct of self-preservation that man has in common with animals." The astonishing effect of many of Caldwell's novels results from his merging of violence and humor, theology and economics, diet and sex. We have no precise critical terminology to describe exactly that effect.

The dietary and sexual themes are, of course, related. I am not suggesting reduction of characters to the menus in the novels ("What these men had to eat and drink/Is what we say and what we think" is true; but the formula is, as John Crowe Ransom well knew, wittily reductionist), yet recent evidence of starvation and dietary deficiencies in Mississippi seems to indicate another reason for the lethargy and stupidity of some of Caldwell's characters. An inadequately nourished brain does not develop; deprivations in diet lead to deprivations of mind. The caloric dimension of ethics is a theme in these novels, as it is in some plays of Brecht. American audiences perhaps best know the theme in the statement in *Three-Penny Opera*: first give us bread, then morals. The standard meal in *God's Little Acre*, besides the inevitable chicory for breakfast and an occasional watermelon, is grits and sweet potatoes, with once

in a while a piece of ham and maybe some biscuits with sorghum. In the novels of Caldwell's later period the scene moves to the city where people seem better fed, so that food becomes a point of wit instead of need. In *Gretta* (1955) the couple on a honeymoon is in a dilemma about whether to eat or copulate; and in another scene a man "explains" to Gretta how to overcome loneliness, the image being culinary: " 'You take two slices of bread—one's you and one's me—and then you put something in between—that's company. See how easy the whole thing works out?' He leaned against her and smiled." In *Close to Home* (1962) a good deal of the humor hinges on a man's love for his freedom as that love is tested against the greater love for cold sweet-potato pie for breakfast. Eating becomes part of the comic presentation of ethical problems.

A good deal has been made of the special values of the family as the unit of society, as the element most likely to give stability to a social order, and so on. One of the most celebrated fictional embodiments of this attitude is Ma Joad in John Steinbeck's *The Grapes of Wrath*. Caldwell's Ty Ty Walden in *God's Little Acre* also values family, though Caldwell and the characters in his novels tend not to be as somber about it as either Steinbeck or the Agrarians. Ty Ty tries to keep his family together, arguing that his younger son ought to stay away from the corruptions of the city: "There ain't no sense in a man going rutting every day in the whole year. . . . He ought to be satisfied just to sit at home and look at the girls in the house." Later Ty Ty and Will both excuse even incest itself with the homely wisdom: "It's all in the family, ain't it?" The decadent family in *A House in the Uplands* (1946) sinks to sterility and disintegration, since disintegration of family is also a good, though the simplistic arguments in behalf of family and "tradition" would not admit it.

Likewise in *This Very Earth* (1948) the old grandfather is like Steinbeck's Ma Joad until toward the end of the novel. Then he has a superior intuition: instead of trying by any means to hold the family together, he helps the family splinter; since each member had different aims and goals, trying to hold the family together was to impose a willful and womanishly possessive wish on a variety of people. This realization comes too late, as the realization of Oedipus, for instance, comes too late; thus the old man is frustrated in his insight, and dies suddenly at the sight of murder in his house, Noble Hair's murder of his wife. The old verities (the farm, coon hunting, family) do not serve.

In *God's Little Acre* the richly comic presentation of family activity on the farm is contrasted with the unproductive struck mill town and with the brutality of the big city. The family goes to Augusta to try to get money from the son, Jim Leslie, who denies his father and who is married to a barren and diseased woman, though she is "rich as a manure pile." The emotional poverty of the city folks is set off against the richness of feeling of the impoverished country folk, free from the economic meanness of making good marriages or of charging for sex, like the Augusta whores who try to take Ty Ty. This contrast, so important in the thematic development of *God's Little Acre*, may be indicated in another way by comparing two scenes, one from this novel and one from the later *Gretta*. In her confession scene, Gretta tells her husband about her compulsions to seduce men and to perform a ritual preliminary to copulation: sitting on the floor to remove voluptuously her stockings, asking the man for money, and then kissing the man's genitals: "I can't help it. It's like being thirsty and wanting a drink of water—it's like being hungry and craving something to eat." Gretta's homage to the phallus is com-

pulsive and selfish, whereas Ty Ty Walden's appreciation for female beauty and the great generative principle is quite different. He praises his daughter-in-law Griselda's "rising beauties" and says that "the first time I saw you . . . I felt like getting right down there and then and licking something. That's a rare feeling to come over a man, and when I have it, it does me proud to talk about it for you to hear." Whereas Gretta's kiss is a sign of homage, like the adoration implicit in those monumental stone phalluses on Delos or the adoration women of Pompeii gave statues of men with erections, that kiss is put in the context of Gretta's degradation, and so is itself degraded. Ty Ty at no time touches Griselda, his adoration being ironically "pure." He praises perfection of female flesh and acknowledges great admiration: "That's the way, and it's God's own truth as He would tell it Himself if He could talk like the rest of us."

God is not absent from *Gretta* but He tends to be the object of supplication, as in Gretta's prayer: "Please, God, let it be that way—forever. . . . Please, God, please!" In *Tobacco Road* and *God's Little Acre* there is not this longing and supplication, but rather an admission of God's omnipotence and an acceptance of what He has deemed fit to give His creatures. This point is, it seems to me, overlooked by Chester Eisinger when in *Fiction of the Forties* he complains that *The Sure Hand of God* (1947) "suggests by its title the operation of divine providence, but the determining forces in this novel are social and biological." The overlooked point is that God works, if at all, through the biology and society of His creatures.

Journeyman (1935) has been taken as a sensational novel attempting to expose certain religious exoticisms in the South. Though the book seems slight, its wit and irony make it a charming and effective fiction. The action occupies six days constituting a fragmented Holy Week. As in fashionable metaphysical poetry the man of religious feeling finds imagery and ecstasy in sexual happenings, so in *Journeyman* the man of sexual feeling finds imagery and ecstasy in religious happenings. The book opens on Wednesday with the arrival of Preacher Semon Dye, a name playing yet again on the sexual pun "die." He arrives not like God in a whirlwind but in a car that backfires, emitting black odious smoke that drifts onto the porch and into the house. The satanic sign is obvious, though wholly realistic in origin. Clay Horey, the farmer being visited, is outraged: "Damn the man who'd do that right in the front yard!" Semon Dye does not bring spiritual renewal to the grim lives of Clay and the other inhabitants of Rocky Comfort; but he does bring renewal of vital life-signs. Indeed his approach to souls is wonderfully physical. He gooses men ("Good God Almighty!" Clay shouts when Semon gooses him) and strokes the buttocks of women, explaining that "it's just like stroking the wildness out of a colt. You can't do a thing with them until you stroke them some."

Semon arrives on Wednesday to have supper with Clay and to "have" a fetching Negro girl. He plans a revival meeting, to be held in the schoolhouse since the Rocky Comfort church had long since been turned into a guano shed, perhaps reminding us that Christ himself was born in a stable. Semon inverts the acts of the New Testament. Instead of driving moneychangers from the temple, he is expert in getting money; instead of a chaste relationship with Mary Magdalene, he offers to pimp for one of Clay's wives. (Clay has had five wives, taking another when one wanders away, being a bit taken aback when one wife returns unexpectedly: "It makes me feel sort of foolish to be sitting in the house with two of my wives. And, on top of that, it might be against the law, or something.") Indeed Semon manages to get Clay to pay a dollar to lie with his own fourth wife, then gets him to bet his fifth wife in a crap game which Semon wins. Semon is a shrewd man who also happens to be a man of God—a "lay" preacher, as he says. He does not deliver from temptation but brings it; nor give daily bread but takes it; nor forgive debts but makes his host his debtor.

Friday night is occupied with a grandiose bed scene as Semon, having won Dene in the crap game, learns of her disgrace. She has loved and slept with a Negro man. This powerful sin requires a powerful rite of purification which Semon administers with the most trusty instrument of his ministry: "'I love the Lord!' she screamed in the dark room."

The entombment on Saturday (Semon having "died" in Rocky Comfort) is suggested when Semon and Clay find Tom, the "spirit" man (maker of the finest "Georgia dew"), at his favorite place: in a cowshed, sitting on a stool, looking out a crack in the wall. There is nothing but woods to see, but somehow looking at nothing through a crack in the wall is better than looking at nothing. Tom says: "I come down here and sit and look, and I don't see nothing you can't see better from the outside, but that don't make a bit of difference. . . . I don't know what it is, and it might not be nothing at all when you figure it out. But it's not the knowing about it, anyway— it's just the sitting there and looking through it that sort of makes me feel like heaven can't be so doggone far away." This is the rustic southern notion of "beyond" that Robert Frost expressed in a rustic northern poem, "Neither Out Far Nor In Deep." The trinity of hillbillies huddle in the dark of the shed, looking out the crack in turns, getting drunk on "dew." Tom sums up their response: "That's the God-damnedest little slit in the whole world. . . . I can't keep from looking to save my soul." And indeed he cannot.

After this grand scene comes the long Sunday revival service, ending in an autoerotic orgy as Semon Dye helps the congregation do what is indicated in these sects by the phrase "come through." (*You Have Seen Their Faces* contains some photographs of people "coming through.") The whole congregation is possessed by the Holy Spirit which leads the people to speak in tongues (glossolalia) and to writhe in mystical surrender to a jerking rapture. On this Sunday of this inverted Holy Week, everybody comes to life, the women in violent agitation and the men "prancing up and down like unruly stallions." Nor is anybody much surprised that Semon Dye is not to be found in Rocky Comfort on Monday. These people need no angel to tell them "He is not here."

The conclusion is abrupt and apt. The novel is funny and delightful, being one of three remarkable books Caldwell published in 1935: *Journeyman*, the essays in *Some American People*, and a fine collection of stories in *Kneel to the Rising Sun*. The only other year in Caldwell's career that would be quite so rich was 1940, when he wrote one of the most important of the text-picture books, *Say! Is This the U.S.A.?*, and published both a major collection of short stories, *Jackpot*, and his next novel, *Trouble in July*.

Chapter Six of *Trouble in July* contains an incredible comic scene. By an almost Elizabethan ruse, a bed-trick is brought off when the outraged wife jabbers after discovering her husband, the sheriff, locked in a jail cell with a colored girl, as at the same time serious lynchers talk serious business. The mixtures of dialogue, the absurdity of the situation, the fierce intensity of one set of characters played up by the hopeless bumbling of another set, combine to make the scene grandly funny and grandly terrifying. All the while the mulatto girl sits in the cell, silent and observing, like a conscience.

The story focuses on the incompetent sheriff and on his desire to do the will of the white people rather than to impose the will of the law on them. The plotting is tight and the study of the vagaries of human desires (legal and economic as well as sexual) is often penetrating. But some of the best things in the novel are the presentations of interior states of the characters by means of description of natural detail. When the sheriff returns, the restoration of order in their relationship is signaled by the odor of cooking food, even before he sees his wife. Later in *Claudelle Inglish* (1958) an adultery is accompanied by the odor of cut clover, odor being used to give a sense of both distance and presence, since the betrayed husband in the field cuts the clover. When, in *Trouble in July*, the girl who falsely accused the Negro boy of raping her is rejected by her white suitor, who calls her "nothing but a cotton-field slut," she realizes that she has made a mistake—not because she told a lie and got a Negro lynched, but because as a dishonored woman she is no longer fit to be a white man's wife: "The sun was going down, looking as though it had suddenly grown tired after the long day. Towards the east the country was beginning to look cool and peaceful. There was a small dark cloud drifting towards the sun on the horizon. In a few moments the cloud began turning crimson and gold as the sun's rays struck it. For an instant the whole western sky looked as if the world were on fire; then the sun sank out of sight, leaving the cloud dark and lifeless. The air moved a little, for the first time that day, and the branches on the trees swayed, rustling the dark green leaves." The girl "grasped her arms full of weeds and bushes. She had to have something to hold onto." Later, the almost ritual stoning to death of the girl beneath the hanging corpse of the Negro boy, is presented distantly, as the sheriff sees stones in the air and hears sounds: "A piercing scream filled the woods. A roar of angry voices followed. A bluejay fluttered recklessly through the branches of a tree overhead and, screeching shrilly, disappeared." The sheriff "walked to the bank of the branch and stood looking at the water swirling under a fallen log."

Almost wholly neglected in discussions of Caldwell's work, since it does not fit the stereotypes of violence or sexuality into which his novels are usually placed, is what may be his finest book, *Georgia Boy* (1943), which stands with Wright Morris' *My Uncle Dudley* and with Faulkner's *The Reivers* as one of the most delightful and satisfying evocations of a past time in which man and boy had a relationship of joyful innocence and uncomplicated freedom. Caldwell's book is invention rather than recollection, for the "my old man" of *Georgia Boy* is not at all like the Reverend Ira Sylvester Caldwell whose life and relationship with his son are tenderly and lovingly evoked in another of Caldwell's best books, *Deep South: Memory and Observation* (1968). This recent book of nonfiction adds substantially to the rather austere accounts of the Reverend Mr. Caldwell in such works as *The Centennial History of the Associated Reformed Presbyterian Church* (Charleston, 1905), and adds to that information previously available Erskine Caldwell's sense of the vitality of life and the moral tone which informs his best novels. *Deep South* is important in its own right but it is also important because it makes clearer the power of his inventiveness and imagination, as demonstrated in *Georgia Boy*.

Georgia Boy is an episodic novel, almost a collection of very closely related short stories,

in which a complicated adult relationship is presented through the first-person narration of a twelve-year-old boy. The book is dominated by four characters: the boy, William Stroup, who narrates the story and who is himself dominated by his mother although he is wholly devoted to his father; the mother, Martha, who is steady and sane, taking in washing to support herself and her son, trying to inculcate in the boy the middle-class virtues of niceness, hard work, and social acceptance; the father, Morris, who is eccentric, inventive, free, a lusty sporting man who comes up against the restrictive world of women so often that he is led finally to speculate that "the good Lord ought never put more than one woman in the world at a time"; and the Negro help, Handsome Brown, who is the boy's friend and the helpless pawn in the competitions of Martha and Morris, and of man and nature. Handsome Brown stands for all the fall guys in the world, having to go up onto the roof to get some goats down, having to return some boots bought with money Pa Stroup got in one of his harebrain schemes, having to go up into a sycamore tree to chase out the shirttail woodpeckers which subsequently mistake him for part of the tree and act accordingly. He is *that* "close to nature." He is docile and dumb, as one kind of Negro tends to be in the southern landscape of Caldwell's novels; but the reader is led to accept him as the boy narrator does, or as Huck accepts Nigger Jim.

One strain running through many of Caldwell's best stories, though perhaps not part of his conscious intention, is a sort of reply to Thoreau, especially to Thoreau's preoccupation expressed in the chapter from *Walden* titled "Where I Lived, and What I Lived For": "Simplify, simplify, simplify." The characters in Caldwell's stories have often simplified their lives, and they live close to nature. Indeed in *God's Little Acre* Ty Ty Walden, whose name obviously suggests the Sage of Walden Pond, does exactly what Thoreau advised: "if one advances confidently in the direction of his dreams, and endeavors to live the life which he has imagined, he will meet with a success unexpected in common hours." Ty Ty Walden, Will Thompson, and Jim Leslie Walden, each "advances confidently in the direction of his dreams" and each is destroyed by the realities of life. The two best novels Caldwell has written, *God's Little Acre* and *Georgia Boy*, are both radical criticisms of the American Dream of ingenuity, self-reliance, rugged individualism, and the virtues of determination and doggedness. In *Georgia Boy* the narrator innocently admires the ingenuity of his old man who, once he has a political appointment, makes success his goal. Of course the political appointment happens to be as dogcatcher and of course the boy's old man succeeds in catching lots of dogs by offering them meat and getting them to follow him; but success is success, and after all the officer was only doing his duty. When the boy's old man decides to become a financial success by baling wastepaper and selling it, he is wholly devoted to his work, baling not only old newspapers and such, but even his wife's recipes, her dress patterns, Sunday school hymnals, and finally her love letters. Whether he is collecting scrap metal, ringing the church bell, or tickling the local grass widow with a feather, the boy's old man is single-minded; and the boy's report is always admiring and enthusiastic, which leads to some grandly absurd reports, as in his blandly factual report of the time his ma caught his old man in the woodshed with a visiting gypsy queen: " 'Shut up!' Ma said. 'Where are your clothes?' " The success of the episodes as humor rests on just this enthusiastic report of things the boy does not understand. The pacing of the episodes, the blending of comic pathos and broad humor, and the sug-

gesting of serious themes through naive report are all the result of flawless handling of the point of view. The whole book culminates in one of the funniest and saddest episodes, as Ma has her way with the old man's fighting cock, College Boy. The episode is called "My Old Man Hasn't Been the Same Since" and it is one of the finest tales in modern American writing.

After *Georgia Boy* Caldwell began the second group in the series of novels with southern settings. *Tragic Ground* (1944) is about hill people moved to town to work in a munitions plant in World War II. As the title indicates, the very ground is tragic, the ground of a wartime white ghetto called "Poor Boy." As one character remarks, "the finest folks in the world would get mean and bad if they had to live in a place like this." The book contains some of Caldwell's good ribald humor, but the tone is predominantly grim. A social worker functions as a sort of *deus ex machina*, but is a futile one; for as soon as some families are moved out of the ghetto, others arrive, characters who can say about themselves, "I was born poor and I'll die poor and I won't be nothing but poor in between." Such characters may seem unreal to affluent readers; but they are related to the realities of poverty many Americans began to become aware of only when they read Michael Harrington's *The Other America*. It is this other America which is, in Caldwell's novels, the tragic ground. *A House in the Uplands* (1946) has the powerful theme of the decline of a once prominent family, symbolized by the physical decay of the house and set off by the rise of a new breed of men who believe in law and order. But despite some aphoristic dialogue and some brilliant descriptive touches, the novel remains a poor treatment of a great theme. Most of the novels in the second part of the "cyclorama" (those after *Trouble in July*) tend to treat important themes but also tend to sensational plotting and trite characterization.

Typical is the last novel in the series, *Episode in Palmetto* (1950), a comic melodrama with didactic intent showing how the intrusion of a sexually attractive and frank young woman, a schoolteacher, brings to the surface and to a climax the latent violence in a small town. The plot, tightly constructed to take place in a single week, centers on the uses the town makes of sex, from the random lusts of unhappy husbands to the power plays of jealous and ambitious wives who use sex and gossip as weapons. The novel shows these motives, so important to the adult life of the town, developing in the schoolroom, where a girl falls in love with the young teacher and when repulsed attempts to destroy the teacher; and where a boy falls in love with the teacher, but because he cannot learn the rules of deviousness and hypocrisy—the rules which make seduction and adultery possible in the adult world—he destroys himself. The procession of suitors and the profusion of jealousies lead to an attempted murder and to suicide, resulting in a good deal of "schooling" as each character learns some kind of lesson—even the young teacher, whose cruel self-discovery is that she enjoys promiscuous sexuality. The comic and brutal scenes are played by characters like the Reverend John Boykin Couchmanly; Pearline Gough, the rejected schoolgirl; Em Gee Sheddwood, the farmer who needs a wife to care for his children; Cato Pharr, the mail carrier; Milo Clawson, the principal who reprimands the teacher for wearing a tight yellow sweater, but who is anxious to speak to her in private; and Jack Cash, the one-pump filling-station attendant who each year courts the new schoolteacher, but who this year flees in a torment of nervous agitation when the teacher mischievously offers to sleep with him. Unfortunately the wit and broad humor, as well as the social

comment on small-town life, are mixed with a good deal of superficial psychological comment and superficial motivation.

Race relations have become one of the central themes in Caldwell's more recent novels. The earlier treatments had been unsuccessful, as in *A Place Called Estherville* (1949), or had been brief and ironic, as in Jeeter Lester's remark in *Tobacco Road* that "Niggers will get killed. Looks like there ain't no way to stop it," or Clay's remark in *Journeyman* that he "don't mind seeing a dead darky once in a while." Such remarks depend for their effect on the separation of the character speaking them and the author, as in that famous exchange in Chapter XXXII of *Huckleberry Finn*, when Huck explains to Aunt Sally what happened: " 'We blowed out a cylinder-head.' 'God gracious! anybody hurt?' 'No'm. Killed a nigger.' 'Well, it's lucky; because sometimes people do get hurt.' "

In one of the recent good novels, *Close to Home* (1962), a reader is aware of the grotesquery of Native Hunnicutt's marriage to a fat woman fifteen years his senior, Maebelle Bowers, and of his spending his wedding night hunting possums. But this deliciously comic beginning is set off against the tender and loving devotion of Native's relationship with the Negro girl Josene. Likewise, the grotesque murder of the Negro boy Harvey (he is castrated and made to strangle to death on his own testes) is set off by the quiet dignity and justice of Josene's interview with her white father, a successful lawyer and director of the bank. The complex texture of the novel results from Caldwell's blending of humor and melodrama, his modulation of tone and speech rhythm, and his supporting of didactic intent with dramatic incident.

In a more recent novel, *Summertime Island* (1968), he has written a didactic romance narrated by a boy of sixteen who comes of age one summer at a fishing camp on an island in the Mississippi River. The story, slighter and simpler in texture than Caldwell's other recent novels, is another telling of the timeless story of a boy's coming knowledge in a symbolic setting. The "set speeches" of the adults in this novel have irritated some readers. They are long and didactic but they are in character. Certainly one mark of the relationship of generations is that older men tend to monopolize any "dialogue" they pretend to have with sixteen-year-old boys. *Summertime Island* is unsatisfying not because of "set speeches" but because of Caldwell's failure to utilize the point of view. First-person narratives are, of course, of different kinds. In *Georgia Boy* the narrator is a boy who naively reports the scene; but in *Summertime Island* the narrator is a man remembering when he was a boy ("I was almost sixteen years old then") at some time vaguely in the past (women's skirts were almost to their ankles, fire trucks had solid rubber tires, and the town had gravel paths instead of paved sidewalks). The difficulty is that the narrator, once he begins telling the story, must pretend to recall lectures and long speeches and to report them as though he were a boy again. The reader must suppose, if he can, that the now mature narrator can tell the story without seeing that his uncle is a drearily pious bore, or without seeing that his incestuous aunt is little more than an incredible wish fulfillment. Had Caldwell let the mature narrator come to terms with the full implications of what he reports about the past, the novel might have been one of his finest.

Perhaps the best of his novels since *Georgia Boy, Miss Mamma Aimee* (1967), is about the live past and the dead present. Tradition and family history are rich and alive, but the land is being sold off to support a moribund remnant of past glories. Times are changing, for the family, for race relations, for traditional values. The novel is structured on a complex series of reversals, even the final revelation of mother-hate which balances mother-love. As Aimee awaits the arrival of the horny preacher, Raley Purdy, a taxi brings Connie, her "baby girl" who is now a prostitute. Frustrated expectation, an ancient comic device, is here used with great symbolic effect. Miss Mamma Aimee Mangrum is the victim of contradictions implicit in her names, and she is the focus of the reversals: once her name was good for any amount of credit, but now she must try to give a bad check to the gas-station attendant, Gene Infinger, who refuses it. The preacher's manly looks attract women, but he blushes at flattery, and when he sees a girl naked he worries about what "if Billy Graham saw me now." The girl asks, "who's Billy Graham," to which he replies, "I can't talk about Billy Graham when you're stark naked —he wouldn't want me to." After which she strips him and goes to work. This is only one of the reversals: on the wedding night of Russ, Mamma Aimee's brother-in-law, and Katie, *he* had dropped blood on the marriage-bed; Negroes talk back; the preacher wants to make love with a prostitute. The novel brings together some of Caldwell's most effective themes and situations: inactive children, grotesque love, economic problems, religious dilemmas. The novel contains characters as grotesque as any in recent "gothic" fiction; yet the whole is again grandly rendered in the comic mode, as though in his full maturity Caldwell had returned to his major themes with renewed vigor.

Miss Mamma Aimee is a fine return to Caldwell's major themes and methods, as *Georgia Boy* was a brilliant recoup after the war novel. If we discount the two early novels (*The Bastard* and *Poor Fool*) Caldwell's career may be said to begin in 1931 with the publication of the collection of stories titled *American Earth*.

The next decade contains his best work, including *Tobacco Road, God's Little Acre, Journeyman,* and *Trouble in July,* as well as the book of essays *Some American People* and the text-picture books *You Have Seen Their Faces, North of the Danube,* and *Say! Is This the U.S.A.?* After the war, he seemed to have difficulty in getting back into his fictional world and in creating wholly satisfying books. *Georgia Boy* in 1943 and *Complete Stories* ten years later, in 1953, are the exceptions. Otherwise the later novels vary in effectiveness and quality, the most frequent fault being trite characterization and insufficient motivation. The books do contain wit and humor; they are written still in the plain style; and they have the power to make one keep turning the pages. Caldwell's technique developed during this long period, as he began to introduce parenthetical comments in italics, sometimes monologues of characters, sometimes comments from outside the story entirely. Though the novels are not wholly successful, the texture became denser. The parentheses are like those of Virginia Woolf in *To the Lighthouse,* which suggest an author not omniscient, suggest that the characters have lives of their own about which the author has only hints and guesses. Caldwell's parentheses suggest that the author is reporter of objective reality, and the report is submitted to other commentators who come at the action or character from different points of view, thus reinforcing the sense of the solidity and reality of action and character. His experimentation with this technique reaches its most successful point in the more recent books, such as the novel *Miss Mamma Aimee* and the biographical *Deep South.*

Caldwell, now in such disrepute among academic critics, will one day be "discovered," and his reputation will rest on a few books. Although he is one of the American masters of the short story, many of his stories are much of a kind and many others are trivial. Yet one could make a collection of twenty-five of Caldwell's stories which would reveal his talent and which would be a minor classic of American literature, standing in relation to the giant works of our literature much as a selection of de Maupassant's stories stands in relation to French fiction. Although every reader will quarrel with a selection from a large body of short fiction, any selection would need to include such classics as "Country Full of Swedes," "Kneel to the Rising Sun," "The People *v.* Abe Lathan, Colored," "Candy-Man Beechum," and "After-Image." Some of the stories are chillingly terrifying and seem closer to more recent visions of terror and absurdity than to the times in which they were first published. "The Growing Season," for instance, is a story in a remarkably contemporary manner. A farmer, beaten down first by rain and then by sun, gets his shotgun, and in a moment of violent frustration and rage at the ways of nature and of man, he slaughters Fiddler. Even a respected and perceptive scholar-critic like Joseph Warren Beach said that "the negro Jesse . . . cannot bear to witness the suffering of his donkey; he shoots the animal and goes on sharpening the blade of his hoe." Yet clearly that is not what happens in the story. Fiddler is not a donkey, a mule, or an old hound-dog. The vision in "The Growing Season" is as ironic, as black, as any in contemporary fiction. Yet the range of attitude and emotion in Caldwell's stories is wide. "An Evening in Nuevo Leon" is absurd comedy, "The Day the Presidential Candidate Came to Ciudad Tamaulipas" is brilliant political satire, "We Are Looking at You, Agnes" is a subtle psychological sketch, and other stories are richly comic, like "An Autumn Courtship," "Meddlesome Jack," and "The Negro in the Well." To this dozen I would add "Daughter," "Hamrick's Polar

Bear," "Horse Thief," "Man and Woman," "Maud Island," "A Swell-looking Girl," "Return to Lavinia," "A Woman in the House," "Yellow Girl," and "Wild Flowers."

Tobacco Road, Journeyman, and *Miss Mamma Aimee* are all good novels, though I think later readers will find his most satisfying to be *God's Little Acre* and *Georgia Boy*; and those two novels are sufficiently different in theme, attitude, and technique to give some idea of Caldwell's range. *North of the Danube* and *Say! Is This the U.S.A.?* may be too expensive to keep in print, so that a selected volume of essays will form part of the standard works of the "discovered" Caldwell: the essay on Detroit, some of the essays from the text-picture books, and some chapters from the travel books. One might add parts of the loving and dutiful son's recollections of his father in *Deep South*. The book is technically a biography but is actually about a man's travels through the interior landscape of memory, together with reports of his travels in the present and of what men today are saying. Such a selection from the large and uneven body of Caldwell's writing will make clear the strength of his best work in fiction and nonfiction, and will reveal what is now obscured by the very bulk of his output: his is a solid achievement that supports the assertion that he is one of the important writers of our time.

Selected Bibliography

WORKS OF ERSKINE CALDWELL

NOVELS
The Bastard. New York: Heron Press, 1929.
Poor Fool. New York: Rariora Press, 1930.
Tobacco Road. New York: Scribners, 1932.
God's Little Acre. New York: Viking Press, 1933.
Journeyman. New York: Viking Press, 1935.
The Sacrilege of Alan Kent. Portland, Me.: Falmouth Book House, 1936.
Trouble in July. New York: Duell, Sloan and Pearce, 1940.
All Night Long. New York: Duell, Sloan and Pearce, 1942.
Georgia Boy. New York: Duell, Sloan and Pearce, 1943.
Tragic Ground. New York: Duell, Sloan and Pearce, 1944.
A House in the Uplands. New York: Duell, Sloan and Pearce, 1946.
The Sure Hand of God. New York: Duell, Sloan and Pearce, 1947.
This Very Earth. New York: Duell, Sloan and Pearce, 1948.
A Place Called Estherville. New York: Duell, Sloan and Pearce, 1949.
Episode in Palmetto. New York: Duell, Sloan and Pearce, 1950.
A Lamp for Nightfall. New York: Duell, Sloan and Pearce, 1952.
Love and Money. New York: Duell, Sloan and Pearce, 1954.
Gretta. Boston: Little, Brown, 1955.
Claudelle Inglish. Boston: Little, Brown, 1958.
Jenny by Nature. New York: Farrar, Straus and Cudahy, 1961.
Close to Home. New York: Farrar, Straus and Cudahy, 1962.
The Last Night of Summer. New York: Farrar, Straus, 1963.
Miss Mamma Aimee. New York: New American Library, 1967.
Summertime Island. New York and Cleveland: World, 1968.
The Weather Shelter. New York: New American Library, 1969.

COLLECTIONS OF STORIES
American Earth. New York: Scribners, 1931.
We Are the Living. New York: Viking Press, 1933.
Kneel to the Rising Sun. New York: Viking Press, 1935.
Southways. New York: Viking Press, 1938.

Jackpot. New York: Duell, Sloan and Pearce, 1940.

The Courting of Susie Brown. New York: Duell, Sloan and Pearce, 1952.

Complete Stories. Boston: Little, Brown, 1953.

Gulf Coast Stories. Boston: Little, Brown, 1956.

Certain Women. Boston: Little, Brown, 1957.

When You Think of Me. Boston: Little, Brown, 1959.

NONFICTION

Tenant Farmers. New York: Phalanx Press, 1935.

Some American People. New York: McBride, 1935.

Moscow under Fire. London: Hutchinson, 1942.

All-Out on the Road to Smolensk. New York: Duell, Sloan and Pearce, 1942.

Call It Experience. New York: Duell, Sloan and Pearce, 1951.

Around about America. New York: Farrar, Straus, 1964.

In Search of Bisco. New York: Farrar, Straus and Giroux, 1965.

In the Shadow of the Steeple. London: Heinemann, 1967.

Writing in America. New York: Phaedra, 1967.

Deep South. New York: Weybright and Talley, 1968.

PICTURE-TEXTS WITH MARGARET BOURKE-WHITE

You Have Seen Their Faces. New York: Modern Age Books and Viking Press, 1937.

North of the Danube. New York: Viking Press, 1939.

Say! Is This the U.S.A.? New York: Duell, Sloan and Pearce, 1941.

Russia at War. London and New York: Hutchinson, 1942.

CRITICAL STUDIES

Beach, Joseph Warren. "Erskine Caldwell: The Comic Catharsis," in *American Fiction: 1920–1940*. New York: Macmillan, 1941.

Burke, Kenneth. "Caldwell: Maker of Grotesques," in *The Philosophy of Literary Form*. 2nd ed. Baton Rouge: Louisiana State University Press, 1967.

Cantwell, Robert. Introduction to *The Humorous Side of Erskine Caldwell*. New York: Duell, Sloan and Pearce, 1951.

Collins, Carvel. "Erskine Caldwell at Work," *Atlantic*, 202:21–27 (July 1958).

————. Introduction to *Erskine Caldwell's Men and Women*. Boston: Little, Brown, 1961.

Frohock, W. M. "Erskine Caldwell: Sentimental Gentleman from Georgia," *Southwest Review*, 31:351–59 (1946).

Gossett, Louise Y. *Violence in Recent Southern Fiction*. Durham, N.C.: Duke University Press, 1965.

Hazel, Robert. "Notes on Erskine Caldwell," in *Southern Renascence,* edited by Louis D. Rubin, Jr., and Robert D. Jacobs. Baltimore: Johns Hopkins University Press, 1953.

McIlwaine, Shields. *The Southern Poor-White from Lubberland to Tobacco Road*. Norman: University of Oklahoma Press, 1939.

MacLachlan, John. "Folk and Culture in the Novels of Erskine Caldwell," *Southern Folklore Quarterly,* 9:93–101 (January 1945).

—JAMES KORGES

Willa Cather

1873-1947

I<small>T</small> IS customary to speak of Willa Cather as an "elegist" of the American pioneer tradition. "Elegy" suggests celebration and lament for a lost and irrecoverable past; but the boldest and most beautiful of Willa Cather's fictions are characterized by a sense of the past not as an irrecoverable quality of events, wasted in history, but as persistent human truth repossessed—salvaged, redeemed—by virtue of memory and art.

Her art is a singular one. The prose style is suave, candid, transparent, a style shaped and sophisticated in the great European tradition; her teachers were Homer and Virgil, Tolstoi and Flaubert. But the creative vision that is peculiarly hers is deeply primitive, psychologically archaic in an exact sense. In that primitivism was her great strength, for it allowed the back door of her mind to keep open, as it were, to the rumor and movement of ancestral powers and instinctive agencies.

Closely related to this gift was her sensitivity to the land, its textures, horizons, weathers. "Whenever I crossed the Missouri River coming in to Nebraska," she said, "the very smell of the soil tore me to pieces. . . . I almost decided to settle down on a quarter section of land and let my writing go." Elizabeth Sergeant, her friend and a discerning critic of her work, wrote, "I saw that her intimacy with nature lay at the very root . . . of her power to work at all." She had been brought to Nebraska, from Virginia, when she was nine. This was in 1883, when Nebraska was still frontier territory, almost bare of human landmarks; the settlers lived in sod houses, scarcely distinguishable from the earth, or in caves in the clay bluffs; roads were faint wagon trails in a sea of red grass. The removal from an old, lush, settled country to a virtual wilderness was undoubtedly the determinative event of Willa Cather's life; occurring when the child was entering puberty and most sensitive to change, the uprooting from the green valley of her grandparents' home in Virginia, and the casting out upon a limitless wild prairie, opened her sensibility to primordial images and relationships that were to be the most powerful forces in her art.

After a year of homesteading, Charles Cather moved his family into the little town of Red Cloud, where he opened an office dealing in farm loans and mortgages. They lived in a house much like that of the Kronborgs in *The Song of the Lark*, with seven children crowded in a narrow boxcar arrangement of rooms and a leaky attic where the older ones slept. Willa started going to school here; on the farm, her grandmother had begun teaching her Greek and Latin, and she continued these studies now with an old man who kept a general store down the street. Years later her friend Edith Lewis wrote of that Nebraska girlhood, which she too had known: "I remember how lost in the prairies Red Cloud seemed to me, going back to that country after a number of years; as if the hot wind that so much of the time blew over it went on and left it behind, isolated, forgotten by the rest of the world. . . . And I felt again that forlornness, that terrible restlessness that comes over young people born in small towns in the middle of the continent." That aridity and drabness formed another decisive pattern in the girl's emotional nature, a traumatic one that reappears in the stories and novels as a desperate impulse of "escape" from a surrounding and voracious mediocrity. Her own resistances took the form of rebellion against conventionality; she cut her hair short like a boy's, wore boy's clothes, created scandal by setting up a laboratory for zoological experiments, hung around listening to the conversation of the older men of the town.

Her "escape" was slow, uneven, costing years of drudgery. From 1891 to 1895, a period of crop failures and financial depression, she attended the state university at Lincoln, meeting many of her expenses by writing for the Sunday issue of the *State Journal*; at a dollar a column, by writing a tremendous number of columns she was able to scrape through. For the next decade, from her twenty-third to her thirty-third year, she worked at various jobs in Pittsburgh: for five years as a newspaperwoman, at first on the *Home Monthly*, a suffocatingly parochial "family magazine," then on the *Daily Leader*, where she read copy, edited telegraphic news, and wrote dramatic criticism; and five years as a teacher of Eng-

lish and Latin in the Pittsburgh high schools. In 1903 she published a book of poems, *April Twilights*, slight pieces of imitative cadence; and in 1905 her first book of stories, *The Troll Garden*, was published by S. S. McClure—who immediately offered her a post in New York on his then brilliant magazine. Her work on *McClure's Magazine* was highly successful —she rapidly became managing editor—and exhausting; probably the most valuable experience during this period was her brief friendship with the writer Sarah Orne Jewett (Miss Jewett died within the year), whose sensitive criticism seems to have reoriented her writing, away from "literary" models and toward the material and the voice which were genuinely her own. In 1912, the year of the publication of her first novel, *Alexander's Bridge*, she resigned from *McClure's*, and from that time on was able to live the quiet and dedicated life of her craft.

Miss Cather said frequently that the only part of her life which made a lasting impression on her imagination and emotion was what happened before she was twenty. No doubt the remark overcondenses and oversimplifies, but one finds an impressive truth in it when one looks at those early years in the light of her mature work. There was the deprived adolescence in the sterile little midwestern town; there were the traumatic tensions leading to "escape." She was never able to free herself from this negative theme, and under its warping tendency she was led frequently to substitute strained personal emotion and belief for creative intuition. But another, far more subtle, essentially mysterious theme was also an effect of that adolescent deprivation: this was the theme of a "self" at once more generic and more individual than the self allowed to live by the constrictions of American adulthood. It is as if the aridities of her girlhood, and the drudgery that followed, had left her with a haunting sense of a "self" that had been effaced and that tormented her for realization. She was to search for it in elusive ways all her life, and sometimes, in her greatest novels, when she left off searching for it she found it.

Connected with that search was a quest for "ancestors." One thinks of that great faceless prairie, stretching empty to the jumping-off places of the earth, where the nine-year-old child was thrust to find its identity. Where were the beginnings? Where the human continuities, the supporting and enfolding "past," the streets, the houses, the doors, the images of care and contact? Even trees were so rare, and had such a hard fight to grow, that one visited them anxiously as if they were persons. One felt instinctively, in that shoreless emptiness, a special charisma in the secretive animals—snakes and badgers—that warned one to be friendly with them; one might need their help. When Willa Cather first visited the ancient cliff-dweller ruins of Arizona, in 1912, she experienced a shock of recognition as intense, troubling, and exalting as that felt by Keats when he first saw the Elgin marbles. Here, in these desolate little cities, "mountain built with peaceful citadel," were the places of the ancestors, their streets and doorways, their hanging gardens of cactus, their inner chambers, the signs of their care and contact in traces of the potter's thumb on shards of clay vessels. She was to write of them again and again, and make many pack trips back to that country. Like the theme of the lost self, this too was a theme of recovery: to recover the ancestors, to redeem them from their forgotten places, to make them speak. A great loneliness—the American loneliness—invests these themes: and something else, the need of a form of integration between the self and the human past, in order that life may be affirmed

and celebrated. She was to achieve that celebratory form most fully in the two late great novels, *Death Comes for the Archbishop* and *Shadows on the Rock.*

She started late. Her first book of fiction, the seven stories collected in *The Troll Garden*, was published when she was thirty-two; *Alexander's Bridge*, her first novel, when she was thirty-nine; and *O Pioneers!*, the first of her pastoral novels, where the essential nature of her gift began to realize itself, when she was forty. But behind this late start were the years of discipline in which she had been learning how to handle what she knew, and learning what it was that she knew. A number of the stories in *The Troll Garden* are no more than finger exercises in technique and gropings for subject—in a somewhat tenuous Jamesian vein which she was soon to turn away from. But the *novella*-length tale "Paul's Case" is an accomplished piece of workmanship showing her long discipleship to Flaubert. It is done with his scrupulosity of detail and something of his shaping, tragic poetry.

Paul is a Pittsburgh high school boy, dandyish, anathema to his teachers because they feel his contempt for them, amounting to physical aversion. He comes to their aggrieved and rancorous sitting on his expulsion from school with a "scandalous red carnation" in his buttonhole. His life with his fellow students is one of lies: he tells them about his acquaintance with soloists in visiting opera companies, suppers with them, sending them flowers; when these lies lose effect, desperately he bids his classmates good-bye, saying he is going to travel to Naples, Venice, Egypt. Paul has no channeled talents; he suggests no particular capabilities at all; he is merely an amorphously longing teen-ager, "different" from others in the exclusiveness of his devotion to glamour in the teeth of the brutal body of fate. His existence is a continuous fracture of spirit, between his home in a lower-middle-class slum on Cordelia Street ("the cold bathroom with the grimy zinc tub, the cracked mirror, the dripping spiggots") and the theater, where he has an actor friend whom he visits behind the scenes, Carnegie Hall where he ushers, and the street outside the Schenley Hotel where he watches at night, in a debauch of envy and longing, the goings and comings of the theatrical crowd.

One has constantly in the back of one's mind the image of Flaubert's Emma Bovary, for Paul, too, is a creature of *les sens*, isolated in the terrifying hebetude of his environment. And like Emma's, his fate comes running to him with his own features, but more eagerly and swiftly than hers; with his adolescent prescience, he prepares his fate like a diva. His father and the school principal having taken away his "bone" (forbidden him entrance to his aesthetic haunts) and put him to work as a bank messenger, he quietly absconds with a thousand dollars to New York. Once there, he buys with "endless reconsidering and great care" a frock coat and dress clothes, visits hatters and a shoe house, Tiffany's for silver and a new scarf pin. He takes a suite at the Waldorf, sends for flowers and champagne, and in his new silk underwear and red robe contemplates his glittering white bathroom. "The nerve-stuff of all sensations was whirling about him like the snow flakes. He burnt like a faggot in a tempest."

He is run down almost immediately. In the newspapers he sees how they are closing in on him (with promises from his father of total forgiveness), and "all the world had become Cordelia Street." Despite a poisonous champagne hangover, he does not flinch from the logic of his dilemma: he takes a cab to the ferry, and in Newark drives out of town to the Pennsylvania tracks. In his coat are some drooping red carnations, and before lying down on the track, "Paul took one of the blossoms carefully from his coat and scooped a little hole in the snow, where he covered it up."

"Paul's Case" is a brilliant adolescent analogue of the "cases" of Faust and Quixote. He has the Faustian hunger for magical experience transcending the despised soil of his animal milieu; he has Quixote's fanatic heroism in facing to the death, with his poor brave sword of pasteboard and forgery, the assaults of the swinish herd whose appetite is for violation. But most of all—because of his modern and reduced mimetic range—he has Emma Bovary's ineffably romantic sensuality, lusting like a saint for ecstasies that can be embodied only in vulgar artifice—until projected, inevitably, upon death. Within the formal sectors of Willa Cather's fiction, Paul is her earliest model of the young, artistically or merely sensitively gifted person in western America, whose inchoate aspiration is offered no imago by the environment, and no direction in which to develop except a blindly accidental one. The ironic detachment of the story gives it the purity and polish of a small classic.

Two of the shorter pieces in *The Troll Garden*, "A Wagner Matinee" and "The Sculptor's Funeral," take firm grip on the fatality of deprivation, which was an inherent part of Miss Cather's native Nebraska material. "A Wagner Matinee" is a bleakly effective *récit*, holding in concentration the terrible spiritual toll taken by frontier life, especially upon women. An old aunt of the narrator, grizzled and deformed, comes to visit her nephew in New York; she had been a music teacher at the Boston Conservatory, and marriage had taken her to a Nebraska homestead fifty miles from a railroad, to live at first in a dugout in a hillside. He takes her to a concert. At the *Tannhäuser* overture, she clutches his coat sleeve. "Then it was I first realized that for her this broke a silence of thirty years; the inconceivable silence of the plains. . . . There came to me an overwhelming sense of the waste and wear we are so powerless to combat; and I saw again the tall, naked house on the prairie, black and grim as a wooden fortress; the black pond where I had learned to swim, its margin pitted with sun-dried cattle tracks; the rain gullied clay banks about the naked house, the four dwarf ash seedlings where the dishcloths were always hung to dry before the kitchen door."

"The Sculptor's Funeral" suffers from a somewhat ponderous use of the Jamesian-Balzacian reflector, but its observation of the working of the frontier curse, the habit of deprivation—horrifyingly at home in the Protestant mentality—is ferocious. The dead master-sculptor is taken home to Kansas to be buried. There, over the corpse, the observer sees the mother, the voracious mother with "teeth that could tear," frenzied in her sterility, and all the "raw, biting ugliness" that had been the portion of the artist in youth. He understands now the real tragedy of the man's life—not dissipation, as the town-folk say, but "a blow which had fallen earlier and cut deeper . . . a shame not his, and yet so inescapably his, to hide in his heart from his very boyhood." A drunken lawyer makes the final accusing tirade, against the town's suspicion and hatred of excellence, by which the most promising of its children have been harried to exile, degradation, or suicide. One remembers that, about a hundred years earlier, Stendhal's Julien Sorel had, in the shadow of the guillotine, made a similar accusation of his provincial fathers.

The story "The Garden Lodge" is composed on the motif of the lost instinctive self that has been compromised or frozen into a ghost by the complicated successes of American adulthood. The story's protagonist is a sophisticated woman who patronizes the arts in her suburban home. Her own childhood background had been a slummy, bohemian one, her father an indigent violinist, her mother acquiescent to his futile idealism, the unpaid bills, the mess. She has rejected all that, aiming to make her life a soberly rational and emotionally economic success. After entertaining as house guest a distinguished pianist, whose music had charmed her, she is haunted by "an imploring little girlish ghost that followed her about, wringing its hands and entreating for an hour of life." During a storm, she spends a night in the studio, fingering the piano and at last falling to sleep on the floor, disturbed in dream by that lost and violated child. "There was a moment between world and world, when neither asleep nor awake, she felt her dream grow thin, melting away from her, felt the warmth under her heart growing cold. Something seemed to slip from the clinging hold of her arms, and she groaned protestingly through her parted lips, following it a little way with fluttering hands. . . . The horror was that it had not come from without, but from within. The dream was no blind chance; it was the expression of something she had kept so close a prisoner that she had never seen it herself; it was the wail from the donjon deeps when the watch slept."

Alexander's Bridge (1912) is a distinguished first novel, but Miss Cather almost immediately repudiated it as "literary"—which had become a bad word for her—with a just recognition of what was contrived in its framework and stylish in its situation. Bartley Alexander is a famous engineer of bridges, married to a Bostonian heiress, leading in the "dead calm" of his middle age a gracious life that he loves, but nervously squirming under the constraints of his success—positions on boards of civic enterprise and committees of public welfare, the obligations of his wife's fortune. On his business trips to Europe he occasionally seeks, or tells himself he is seeking, the affectionately gay inconsequence of a mistress of his student years, Hilda Burgoyne, who has now become a distinguished actress. But he is intuitive enough to know that it is not really Hilda whom he seeks, but a more shadowy companion, "some one vastly dearer to him than she had ever been—his own young self," a youth who waits for him at the places he used to meet Hilda, links his arm in his, walks with him. He projects this entity upon Hilda and entoils her in its charm, which he makes her think is her own. With this acquiescence, the ghostly companion grows younger and more vigorous and importunate: "He remembered how, when he was a little boy and his father called him in the morning, he used to leap from his bed into the full consciousness of himself. That consciousness was Life itself. Whatever took its place, action, the power of concentrated thought, were only functions of a mechanism useful to society; things that could be bought in the market. There was only one thing that had an absolute value for each individual, and it was just that original impulse, that internal heat, that feeling of one's self in one's own breast." Even when he is most conscious of the satisfactions of his home, his friends, the wife whom he loves, the "thing" breaks loose out of an unknowable darkness, "sullen and powerful," thrilling him with a sense of quickened life and stimulating danger. He sacrifices Hilda to it, and finally is sacrificed to it himself—by the story's contrivance, he is drowned from one of his own bridges, because of a collapse in its faulty structure.

The finger-pointing symbolism (Alexander fell because of a flaw in his character, like the flaw in the bridge) is trite and specious, falsifying the troubled perception which is the story's strength and truth. Alexander's situation is that of the woman in "The Garden Lodge," except that the blocked, imprisoned self approached her only in a dream, attenuated to a child's shape, and she was able when she awoke to force it back into the "donjon deeps" forever; while Alexander's demonic visitor had broken past the watches of the ego and could not be exorcised, although there was no way to establish it, licitly, within the cultural pattern that had trapped his habits.

It would be possible to sketch a kind of allegory of motives between this situation and what happened to Willa Cather when she wrote her next book, *O Pioneers!* (1913). For with *O Pioneers!* the natural forces of her gift —the unknown, unpredictable "self"—suddenly broke through her carefully trained literary habits. If there is a literary precursor, it is Thomas Hardy, but only in the sense that, like Hardy, she had found her subject in her own tribal country, in its ancient geological recalcitrance and its tragic face of blessing. Here she herself was the pioneer, of whom it might be said, as she says of Alexandra, the Swedish farm girl who is the heroine of the book: "For the first time, perhaps, since that land emerged from the waters of geologic ages, a human face was set toward it with love and yearning." But she brought to this discovery a voice that held and used its earlier disciplines, melodically and resonantly.

She scarcely knew what to do with the material, for the way it had put itself together, as a two-part pastoral, seemed to have no formal rationale, and the longer part—the story of Alexandra—had no backbone of structure at all, was as fluid and featureless as the high, oceanic grassland where Alexandra made her farm: the author could only mourn over the "foolish endeavor" she had somehow got on her hands. Ten years later, when she understood better that dark logic which Keats called

"Negative Capability," she wrote of her experience with *O Pioneers!*: "When a writer begins to work with his own material, he realizes that, no matter what his literary excursions may have been, he has been working with it from the beginning—by living it. With this material he is another writer. He has less and less power of choice about the moulding of it. It seems to be there of itself, already moulded. . . . In working with this material he finds that he need have little to do with literary devices; he comes to depend more and more on something else—the thing by which our feet find the road home on a dark night, accounting of themselves for roots and stones which we had never noticed by day."

Alexandra Bergson's parents had come from Sweden to take up land in Nebraska, and their death leaves her, in her early twenties, the head of a family of three brothers. The patch of land, won by homestead rights, is the only survival relationship they have. It is the high, dry, prairie country of the Divide, between two rivers, the coarse, incalculable, primitively resistant ground of an action so ancient in character it might have taken place in neolithic times and in that other austere land between two rivers. "The record of the plow was . . . like the feeble scratches on stone left by prehistoric races, so indeterminate that they may, after all, be only the markings of glaciers, and not a record of human strivings." In winter "it is like an iron country . . . One could easily believe that in that dead landscape the germs of life and fruitfulness were extinct forever." Alexandra faces the exigence of that destiny in the almost unconscious spirit of a person driven by uranian and chthonic gods, and makes her heroic peace with them. "Her personal life, her own realization of herself, was almost a subconscious existence; like an underground river that came to the surface only here and there,

at intervals months apart, and then sank again to flow on under her own fields."

She has a recurrent dream, usually on Sunday mornings when she is able to lie abed late—a dream as archaic as the whole action of her story. The subject of the dream is an authentic god straight out of the unconscious, one of those vegetation and weather gods by whose urgencies she is compelled and whose energies sustain her. "Sometimes, as she lay thus luxuriously idle, her eyes closed, she used to have illusion of being lifted up bodily and carried lightly by some one very strong. It was a man, certainly, who carried her, but he was like no man she knew; he was much larger and stronger and swifter, and he carried her as easily as if she were a sheaf of wheat. She never saw him, but, with eyes closed, she could feel that he was yellow like the sunlight, and there was the smell of ripe cornfields about him. She could feel him approach, bend over her and lift her, and then she could feel herself being carried swiftly off across the fields. . . . As she grew older, this fancy more often came to her when she was tired than when she was fresh and strong. . . . Then, just before she went to sleep, she had the old sensation of being lifted and carried by a strong being who took from her all her bodily weariness." Like Adonis, Attis, and Tammuz, this Eros of the corn and sunlight is a life principle, extending infinitely beyond the human subject, but appearing in the beneficent image of a guardian god to the subject strong enough and obedient enough to attend it.

In a sense, that divine being is the unconscious itself, assuming the image of a strength greater than the personal. Because of the primitive authenticity of the image, it seems right to see reflected here, also, something of the instinctive process by which the book came to be written, as well as those others of Willa Cather's works whose structure obeys laws more obscure and fundamental than literary precepts or even than her own ideas of her purposes: it is the "something else—the thing by which our feet find the road home on a dark night"—a power like that which carried Alexandra in her dream, "larger and stronger and swifter" than conscious intent. The two parts of the Nebraska pastoral—Alexandra's part and that called "The White Mulberry Tree"—are wrought into one form by an instinct as sure as the cycle of seasons, a cycle which itself seems to be the natural commanding form of the novel. The story of Alexandra engages the whole work in the rhythms of the land, powerful tidal urgencies of weather and seasons and their erosions of human life, while the episode of "The White Mulberry Tree"—the love story of Alexandra's young brother Emil and the Bohemian girl Marie Shabata–flashes across those deeper rhythms like a swift springtime, lyrical, brilliant, painful. The episode is saturated with light, bronze and gold on the wide warm fields of grain that smell like baking bread, and gold and green under the leaves of the orchard where Emil and Marie meet their sudden doom, murdered as they lie in first embrace; so that the light ripening the land seems the one great reality, and the blood of the two young lives poured dark into the earth a sacrifice to it.

The Song of the Lark (1915) is a ponderously bulky novel that suffers from autobiographic compulsion. Ostensibly it is modeled on the career of the Swedish opera singer Olive Fremstad. However, Willa Cather's friend Elizabeth Sergeant wrote that she "was deeply—by her own account—identified with her character [Thea Kronborg], who had many of her traits and had undergone many of her own experiences." The setting is changed to Moonstone, Colorado, a small town in the desert west of Denver. Thea, a gifted child in a suffocatingly crowded and brutally inept family, takes her first music lessons from a pathetic, drunken old German; for proper lessons in Chicago she is financed by a brakeman on the Denver train, who is in love with her and who is shortly killed in an accident; from Chicago she goes on to supreme success in New York, where her promoter is a wealthy young dandy, also in love with her. The end of Thea's story explores both the splendors and penalties of success, the bleak asceticism which the artist pays for the presumptions of his gift. The naturalistic, circumstantial form to which the subject lent itself carried its usual vulnerability to "thesis" writing, a weakness inherent also in Miss Cather's attraction to the subject of the artist's struggle. The result is invented plot situations, sagging proportions, made-up dialogue, and a prose that often goes lax. In her preface to a later edition, she wrote that the book should have ended before the successful phase of Thea's career: "What I cared about, and still care about, was the girl's escape; the play of blind chance, the way in which commonplace occurrences fell together to liberate her from commonness." But this too is a thesis, indicating the way in which traumatic personal memory—of her own "escape"—turned into obsessive idea.

"Life began for me," she said, "when I ceased to admire and began to remember." But there is more than one kind of remembering. There is personal memory bound up with the chronology of one's own life and with ego-tensions and resistances. There is what Proust called "bodily memory," which, because it is physical and sensory, may be at once personal and more than personal, for the impulses of the senses register common qualities of experience, timeless as sun and earth, breath and flesh. And there is what the Greeks call *anamnesis,* memory of "important" things, matters whose significance is part of one's heritage—a kind of *com*memoration since it involves other and profounder memories than one's own, buried perhaps as deep as instinct and aroused mysteriously as instinct. There is still a great deal in *The Song of the Lark* that is of the older orders of memory, more broadly based than that of the ego, more essential and more original—in that sense of the word which implies "origins." Toward the end of *O Pioneers!* when Alexandra is almost broken by young Emil's death, she goes to his grave in the night during a storm, and is found there in the morning, drenched, icy, and nearly unconscious, by Crazy Ivar, an old man who lives in a claybank like a coyote and who can talk with animals and heal them. He and Alexandra have always understood each other. She tells him: "After you once get cold clear through, the feeling of the rain on you is sweet. . . . It carries you back into the dark, before you were born; you can't see things, but they come to you, somehow, and you know them and aren't afraid of them. Maybe it's like that with the dead. If they feel anything at all, it's the old things, before they were born. . . ." In *The Song of the Lark,* Thea, an adolescent only beginning to break through the ugliness and mediocrity surrounding her, hears in a symphony a voice immensely ancient and yet sounding within herself: "a soul new and yet old, that had dreamed something despairing, something glorious, in the dark before it was born; a soul obsessed by what it did not know, under the cloud of a past it could not recall."

Thea tries to hold that "soul" under her cloak, as if it were a child or another self that must be protected in tenderness and darkness lest it be snatched from her before it could grow: "There was some power abroad in the world bent upon taking away from her that feeling with which she had come out of the concert hall. Everything seemed to sweep down on her to tear it out from under her cape. If one had that,

the world became one's enemy; people, buildings, wagons, cars, rushed at one to crush it under, to make one let go of it." Like Alexandra's, Thea Kronborg's nature had been formed close to the land, and toughened and simplified in that matrix. She is able to harbor the instinctive self, with its ancient gifts like those a child receives in fairy tales from dwarfs and witches constrained to bless him, because she recognizes both its transcendence and the personal disciplines needed to redeem it from "the cloud of a past it could not recall," to give it feature, to bring it to birth by her own labor.

The voice heard in the symphony is associated with the western desert of her childhood. The desert had moved mysteriously with apparitions older than history, mirages of silver lakes where one saw reflected the images of cattle magnified to a preposterous height and looking like mammoths, "prehistoric beasts standing solitary in the waters that for many thousands of years actually washed over that desert: the mirage itself may be the ghost of that long-vanished sea." Farther south were the ruined dwellings of "the Ancient People." Here, in miniature cities honeycombed into clefts of the canyons, were human features of a past extending "back into the dark," a racial history speaking of immemorial experience with a voice of silence: steep trails worn deep into the rock by the Ancient People's generations carrying water up the canyon wall to their hanging gardens, signs of their mysteries, their food, their fire. "Food, fire, water, and something else—even here, in this crack in the world, so far back in the night of the past! Down here at the beginning, that painful thing was already stirring; the seed of sorrow, and of much delight. . . . A vanished race; but along the trails, in the stream, under the spreading cactus, there still glittered in the sun the bits of their frail clay vessels, fragments of their desire." The discovery of the cliff dwellings is for Thea Kronborg—as it was for her author—a materialized revelation of something unknown and yet remembered, something ancestral and legendary yet recognizable as an image responding from within the self, an *anamnesis* borne directly to the senses by external forms. Her own gift as a singer seems to her the same impulse that made those forms, given to her in order to salvage their meaning.

In Miss Cather's next book, *My Ántonia* (1918), there occurs a majestic, mysterious image that suggests, in another way, the timeless aspect of the subject matter which seems most naturally her own. Jim Burden (the narrator of the story) and some "hired girls" from the little Nebraska town of Black Hawk have spent a lazy afternoon by the river, ending with a picnic supper. "Presently we saw a curious thing: There were no clouds, the sun was going down in a limpid, gold-washed sky. Just as the lower edge of the red disk rested on the high fields against the horizon, a great black figure suddenly appeared on the face of the sun. We sprang to our feet, straining our eyes toward it. In a moment we realized what it was. On some upland farm, a plough had been left standing in the field. The sun was sinking just behind it. Magnified across the distance by the horizontal light, it stood out against the sun, was exactly contained within the circle of the disk; the handles, the tongue, the share—black against the molten red. There it was, heroic in size, a picture writing on the sun. Even while we whispered about it, our vision disappeared; the ball dropped and dropped until the red tip went beneath the earth. The fields below us were dark, the sky was growing pale, and that forgotten plough had sunk back to its own littleness somewhere on the prairie." The image could have been carved, as a sacred life-symbol, on the stones of a lost temple of Yucatan, or in

a tomb of the Valley of Kings. The plow itself, forgotten on the upland farm, could have been left there by some farmer of Chaldea.

The story is as much Jim Burden's as it is Ántonia's. The two children share the initiatory experiences of the wild land to which their parents have brought them. Jim's family, like Willa Cather's, are from Virginia; Ántonia Shimerda's family are Bohemians who have come to take up homestead rights in the new country. Jim's family live in a house, Ántonia's in a cave in a claybank, the children sleeping in holes tunneled into the gumbo mud. Around them is "nothing but land: not a country at all, but the material out of which countries are made." It is like the sea, featureless and barren, but running with obscure, unaccountable movement as of the rushing of theromorphic gods: "I felt that the grass was the country, as the water is the sea. The red of the grass made all the great prairie the colour . . . of certain seaweeds when they are first washed up. And there was so much motion in it; the whole country seemed, somehow, to be running . . . as if the shaggy grass were a sort of loose hide, and underneath it herds of wild buffalo were galloping, galloping. . . ." The ends of the earth are very near. "The light air about me told me that the world ended here": one had only to walk straight on through the red grass to the edge of the world where there would be only sun and sky left.

Out of homely American detail are composed certain friezelike entablatures that have the character of ancient ritual and sculpture. There is the suicide and funeral of Mr. Shimerda, Ántonia's father, a gifted musician who could, finally, not bear the animal life to which the first generation of pioneers was subjected. For his suicide he dressed himself fastidiously in the fine clothes of the concert hall, went out to the cow barn, and shot himself. It was dead winter, and his corpse had got frozen to the ground before it was discovered. It was left there safely till the day of the funeral, when the hired men from the Burden farm "went ahead on horseback to cut the body loose from the pool of blood in which it was frozen fast to the ground." The Shimerdas were Roman Catholic, an anomaly in that predominantly Protestant neighborhood of farmers, and as a suicide he could not be buried in Catholic ground, so his grave was made at a crossroads in the age-old superstition clinging to the suicide. But no roads ever crossed over his grave. "The road from the north curved a little to east just there, and the road from the west swung out a little to the south; so that the grave, with its tall red grass that was never mowed, was like a little island." And Jim Burden says, "I loved the dim superstition, the propitiatory intent, that had put the grave there; and still more I loved the spirit that could not carry out the sentence—the error from the surveyed lines, the clemency of the soft earth roads along which the home-coming wagons rattled after sunset."

There are the hired men on the farm, Jake and Otto, who, with the "sag of their tired shoulders against the whitewashed wall," form a mute memorial as dignified and tender in outline as a Greek stele—nomadic figures who bear with them the ancient pathos of mysterious coming and mysterious departure, "without warning . . . on the westbound train one morning, in their Sunday clothes, with their oilcloth valises—and I never saw them again." And there are the hired girls, girls who like Ántonia came from the farming community to take domestic work in the town of Black Hawk; robust, exuberant, and held in contempt by the townspeople, these girls appear like a sunlit band of caryatids, or like the succession of peasant girls who loved generously and suffered tragically in old ballads, or like the gay interlinked chain of girls in Proust's

A l'ombre des jeunes filles en fleurs. "When I closed my eyes," Jim Burden says, "I could hear them all laughing—the Danish laundry girls and the three Bohemian Marys. . . . It came over me, as it had never done before, the relation between girls like those and the poetry of Virgil. If there were no girls like them in the world, there would be no poetry. I understood that clearly, for the first time."

Jim Burden, who goes away to the city and returns to the Nebraska farmland only after long intervals, is able to register that Chekhovian "suffering of change" which enters Willa Cather's work during this period. On his last return both he and Ántonia are middle-aged, Jim a weary intellectual nomad, Ántonia married to a Bohemian farmer with a brood of children about her, gay in her orchards and her kitchen. With scarcely a tooth in her head, save for some broken brown snags, she is still able to leave "images in the mind that did not fade—that grew stronger with time . . . She lent herself to immemorial human attitudes which we recognize by instinct as universal and true." The suffering of change, the sense of irreparable loss in time, is one polarity of the work; the other polarity is the timelessness of those images associated with Ántonia, with the grave of the suicide at the crossroads, with the mute fortitude of the hired men and the pastoral poetry of the hired girls, and most of all with the earth itself, carrying in mysterious stroke, like the plow hieroglyphed on the sun, signs of an original and ultimate relationship between man and cosmos.

In 1920 Miss Cather collected a number of her earlier short pieces under the title *Youth and the Bright Medusa*; four of them were reprinted from *The Troll Garden*, and the others, which had appeared in *McClure's Magazine*, have merely the quality of competence. She spent four years writing the next novel, *One of Ours* (1922), and it is the least attractive of her books. One would like to see it quietly buried without remark; but the reasons for its dreariness are instructive. The form of the book is the naturalistic, circumstantial form of *The Song of the Lark*, with the same temptation to "thesis," but with grayer circumstances and an almost insufferably relaxed style. The story is the fictionized account of a young cousin of hers who was killed at Cantigny in 1918. Claude Wheeler is a Nebraska farm boy, of somewhat finer fiber than others, painfully thwarted in sensibility because of the meagerness of his education and the bleakness of his small-town environment: there ought, he feels, to be "something splendid" about life. His dull miseries are followed until escape comes through the war; in a strange and disturbing justification of army life and war, Claude finds in France the aesthetic order of which he had dreamed in ignorance, and dies heroically without disillusionment. Miss Cather received the Pulitzer Prize for this novel, and it seemed to justify her own feeling about the book; Elizabeth Sergeant says, "She liked this prize and never ceased to say, in print and out of print, that Claude was her favorite of all her heroes." And Miss Sergeant adds astutely, "Was it because he was almost a piece of herself, left behind in Red Cloud?"

In an interview with a reporter, she gave the most wrongheaded of reasons for her feeling that *One of Ours* was an achievement: she said, "I came to know that boy better than I know myself. I have cut out all picture-making because that boy does not see pictures. It was hard to cease to do the thing that I do best, but we all have to pay a price for everything we accomplish and because I was willing to pay so much to write about this boy I felt that I had a right to do so." Her willingness to write in a dull manner because the boy's life was dull, her rationalization of the

dullness as a personal sacrifice to her intimate knowledge of her subject—for the cousin who became Claude Wheeler was, after all, as she said, "her own flesh and blood"—these are embarrassing comments on the pitfalls of a temperament that would never wholly know itself; they are the negative aspect of an endowment that remained in large degree unconscious. The ethic of human fidelity runs all through her life as through her work; she never confused the importance of her writing with the importance of even the most obscure human relationships; and it is the same characteristic of fidelity that led her to the mistake of *One of Ours*: "that boy" should not die unknown, the significance of his life should not go unrecorded. But the fidelities of flesh and blood are not the fidelities of art.

A Lost Lady (1923) is a short novel constructed on an altogether different principle, that of the "novel *démeublé*" (to use her own term), and novel disburdened of the lumber of circumstantial detail and stripped to functional episodes. The book has been widely praised as a "small masterpiece." Undoubtedly it owes its appeal to the chief character, Marian Forrester, but the magical quality of that portrait is assured by a fastidious economy of narrative means. Mrs. Forrester appears largely as reflected through the sensibility of young Niel Herbert, in a series of sharply focused vignettes that catch her brilliance and also the disturbing shadow of something illicit in her nature that troubles the bright illusion in the boy's mind. She is first seen as the slender, light-footed lady who runs down from the kitchen of the big house on the hill, to bring hot, freshly baked bread to some small boys who are hunting in the Forrester woods. The charming, gratuitous gesture is typical of her relationship with life, for she has the gift of giving; and the small boys, in their mute and clumsy way, thrill with adoration, as do Captain Forrester's famous and important guests who stop over in the little town of Sweet Water, Nebraska, mainly because of the spell cast by Marian Forrester—the spell of a nameless creature-grace, a secret ardor of the senses: "she had always the power of suggesting things much lovelier than herself, as the perfume of a single flower may call up the whole sweetness of spring"; her eyes, "when they laughed for a moment into one's own, seemed to promise a wild delight that he has not found in life." Her gift is a reckless one, dependent on spendthrift opportunities, and her opportunities are circumscribed. On a winter day, one of the boys from the village, crouched behind a log in the woods, sees Mrs. Forrester and Frank Ellinger, a frequent guest from Denver, get out of their sleigh and go off among the trees, carrying fur robes; it is a long time before they return, and they have forgotten to get the pine boughs which had been their excuse for coming. Ellinger goes back to get the boughs, while Mrs. Forrester waits in the sleigh, close to the hidden boy: "When the strokes of the hatchet rang out from the ravine, he could see her eyelids flutter . . . soft shivers went through her body." When Captain Forrester is impoverished by a bank failure, and soon afterwards suffers a stroke, her opportunities are much narrower, for fewer guests stop off at the big house in Sweet Water; then he dies, and her isolation becomes frantic. One day by accident Niel Herbert catches sight of her through an open door, standing at the kitchen table in an old wrapper, rolling out dough (she is still the maker and giver of bread), and behind her, with his hands on her breasts, is Ivy Peters, an underbred and brutal young man of the town (if he were a character in a Faulkner novel, his name would have been Snopes), who has been buying up the Forrester land. In vignettes such as these, one sees the fatality of Marian For-

rester's nature and the slow corrosion overtaking it. Or is it only the corruption of an image in Niel Herbert's mind? He cannot understand her when she says, "I feel such a power to live in me, Niel." And he cannot forgive her because "she preferred life on any terms."

The brilliant, ambiguous portrait to some extent conceals or outweighs a weakness in the book's conception. *A Lost Lady* has consistently been read as a study in degeneration, not only of a character but more especially of a set of values associated with the pioneer generation of Captain Forrester; and evidently Willa Cather thought of the book this way too, for she uses the reflective intelligence of Niel Herbert to appraise and condemn the loss of values. When this happens, the prose immediately becomes cliché, the thought specious, diffuse, and sentimental: "The Old West had been settled by dreamers, great-hearted adventurers who were unpractical to the point of magnificence; a courteous brotherhood, strong in attack but weak in defence, who could conquer but could not hold. Now all the vast territory they had won was to be at the mercy of men like Ivy Peters, who had never dared anything, never risked anything. They would drink up the mirage, dispel the morning freshness, root out the great brooding spirit of freedom, the generous, easy life of the great land-holders. The space, the colour, the princely carelessness of the pioneer they would destroy and cut up into profitable bits, as the match factory splinters the primeval forest." One has only to compare a passage such as this with almost any passage from the great pastorals to feel here the hollow echoes of a prose beating out a thesis and—whether the sentiment itself be true or not—sounding false. Willa Cather's art is an art of the sensuous and concrete, a high art of feeling; the spirit of the "idea" is always deadly to it.

Through Niel Herbert one feels that "suffering of change" that one feels through Jim Burden in *My Ántonia*, and this is truthful and real— but it is something very different from the idea of the decline of the West that comes dangerously near to spoiling the book.

In *The Professor's House* (1925) two major themes reappear and converge: the theme of the disbarred creative energy of the natural self and the theme of recovery of the "ancestors." The book is constructed like a triptych. The first panel describes Professor St. Peter's family—the complicated relationships that now, in his middle age, he realizes are wholly negative, a formidable system of checks on the power to live. The center panel, "Tom Outland's Story," is curiously dissociated in time and quality from the rest: it tells of the discovery of the cliff-dweller ruins, many years earlier, by one of St. Peter's students (later killed in the war), and of the few months of one intense summer when the boy had lived alone on the Blue Mesa in kinship with the lost Ancient People. The third panel is the professor's private adventure: he comes very near death in the crisis of rediscovery of his earlier self, and not unwillingly; for nothing much can be made of the rough and immature shape in which the forgotten self appears— there is no room for it in the busy, negative circumstances of St. Peter's maturity.

His two married daughters loathe each other, the two sons-in-law are at swords' points, his wife (who had been deeply jealous of Tom Outland's relationship with St. Peter) carries on a curiously sinister flirtation with a son-in-law. In this desiccated atmosphere of impotent emotions, glossed by handsome social clatter, the professor maintains integrity only by reticence and courtesy, often envying Euripides' withdrawal in his old age to a cave by the sea, away from women.

The family goes abroad for the summer, and the professor, left alone in the house, begins work on Tom Outland's notes and diary, to prepare them for publication. Criticism of *The Professor's House* has usually dealt with the bold intrusion of the Tom Outland material into the middle of the novel as a "technical mistake." However, it is only with this middle section that the prose rises out of sophisticated competence and begins to move with that warmth and sensuousness that are characteristic of Willa Cather's writing when it comes from the deeper sources of her feeling.

Young Tom Outland, herding cattle to make a stake for college, had been hunting for steers that had run wild in the canyons of the Blue Mesa, when he came on the cliff-dweller ruins. "I wish I could tell you what I saw there," he writes, "just *as* I saw it, on that first morning, through a veil of lightly falling snow. Far up above me, a thousand feet or so, set in a great cavern in the face of the cliff, I saw a little city of stone, asleep. It was as still as sculpture —and something like that . . . pale little houses of stone nestling close to one another, perched on top of each other, with flat roofs, narrow windows, straight walls, and in the middle of the group, a round tower. . . . A fringe of cedars grew along the edge of the cavern, like a garden. They were the only living things. Such silence and stillness and repose—immortal repose. That village sat looking down into the canyon with the calmness of eternity." It was not only the discovery of the ancient people that gave that summer its intensity in Tom Outland's life; living alone on the high mesa, he experienced the freshness of a land that seemed emerged from creation. "And the air, my God, what air!—Soft, tingling, gold, hot with an edge of chill on it, full of the smell of piñons—it was like breathing the sun, breathing the colour of the sky. . . . Up there alone, a close neighbour to the sun, I seemed to get the solar energy in some direct way. And at night, when I watched it drop down behind the edge of the plain below me, I used to feel that I couldn't have borne another hour of that consuming light, that I was full to the brim, and needed dark and sleep."

This sense of organic involvement in the tidal rhythms of the earth, this baptismal freshness of all origins, become related, in the professor's mind, with the creative period of his own youth. He had expected, in fantasy, Tom Outland's ghost to come back again through the garden door to visit with him, "as he had so often done in dreams." But another boy comes, "the boy the Professor had long ago left behind him in Kansas," the original, unregenerate St. Peter. He yields to this "twin," as he calls him, entire possession, as if yielding to an illicit and slightly alarming addiction; and in the arms of his obsession forgets to turn off an old and defective gas heater. He is rescued from asphyxiation by the ancient housekeeper, Augusta, coming to dust the attic where he works. The person of Augusta is beautifully considered: "Augusta was like the taste of bitter herbs; she was the bloomless side of life that he had always run away from,—yet when he had to face it, he found that it wasn't altogether repugnant. . . . She talked about death as she spoke of a hard winter or a rainy March, or any of the sadnesses of nature." She functions, in this delicate and profound psychic drama, as the "mother," older than all knowledge, bitter and at last saving; with her help, in the attic full of old dressmaker's dummies, St. Peter is able to relinquish the young "twin" whose subtle face had suddenly become that of death.

On its fine surfaces, the book confronts the dereliction of middle age with the high, poetic promise of youth, and its dramatic concern is the psychological crisis of renunciation (Willa Cather wrote in Robert Frost's copy that the story was about "letting go with the heart"). True, evidently, as that reading is, there is something wrong under these surfaces. The theme of the lapsed self remains not much beyond the point where it had stood in *Alexander's Bridge*; like Bartley Alexander, trapped in the complicated arrangements he has made for living, St. Peter is able to recover the natural self only as a projection—first upon the youthful ghost of Tom Outland, and then upon the time-bound and uncouth figure of his own boyhood. As with Alexander, the falsification exacts its penalty. But if, by renunciation, the professor escapes death, it is not exactly "life" that he returns to, but the intricate corruption, the emotional and spiritual dearth of his ordinary existence. And despite the youthful exaltation of discovery in "Tom Outland's Story," there is a pervading "deathiness" here also: the immortal repose of the "little city of stone, asleep . . . still as sculpture" is the repose of death.

And, little town, thy streets for evermore
 Will silent be; and not a soul to tell
  Why thou art desolate, can e'er return.

The psychological problems suggested by the two recovery themes are of very great subtlety and difficulty; and in Willa Cather's insistent, unsatisfied returns to them, one recognizes the "problem-solving" function that the artist's work serves for himself—the experimental, hypothetical character of each piece of work as it attempts another provisional answer or resolution. Though the two themes converge in *The Professor's House* (that is, simply by being juxtaposed, with their relationship left to inference), they are not yet congruent; nor are they yet able to deal with their materials as of the substance of life; the ancestors are dead, and the self has only enough life in it to assent to its own death. Willa Cather was fifty-two now, about the same age as the professor, and her energies seem to be concentrated more and more deliberately on these themes. It was not until *Death Comes for the Archbishop*, two years later, that the places of the ancestors became populated with the living, in the experience of a self to whom nothing was lost or outgrown, that could comprehend all its states of consciousness as things within reach of the hand.

Meanwhile she wrote *My Mortal Enemy* (1926). It is a curious little book, artistically very attractive, a "novel *démeublé*" like *A Lost Lady*; that it concerns a malicious—though magnetic—character does not altogether account for the slight feeling of puzzled dissatisfaction with which one turns from it. Myra Henshawe is Irish, and this is perhaps the salient fact about her, one which the author understands very well (her own people were Scotch-Irish). She is seen first in her worldly sumptuousness and glamour, as an adept hostess in New York of the early part of the century, warm, mobile, intense, superb in her effects—the impression is drawn with Tolstoian deftness. Behind her, subtly increasing her glamour, is the whispered story of her girlhood elopement with a young German "freethinker," and her disinheritance by the wealthy, picturesque Irish uncle who had brought her up as an orphan. Signs of malevolence in her charm appear obliquely—the unaccountable Irish malevolence turned against those she loves. After years, Myra is seen again under reduced and somewhat seedy circumstances, living in a run-down apartment-hotel on the West Coast, old and ill, tended with devotion by her engagingly civilized husband, who has always the courtesy to be polite to the devils that run her; she still has the grace of innate magnificence, is still superb in her effects—on her dying bed, she murmurs to the loved husband watching over her, "Why must I die like this, alone with my mortal enemy?"

The malignant sentence is not the last of her stagery. The uncle who had brought her up and disinherited her (he gave his wealth to a convent) had had a proud funeral. He did not go to the Church but the Church came to him; bishop and clergy met the coffin and "bore it up to the high altar on a river of colour and incense and organ-tone." Myra makes her own spectacular arrangements; sensing death, she gathers up her blankets in the night, takes a taxi to a bare headland on the Pacific where an old twisted cedar leans from the sea, and dies there at dawn. She had imagined that death at dawn: "That is always such a forgiving time. When that first cold, bright streak comes over the water, it's as if all our sins were pardoned; as if the sky leaned over the earth and kissed it and gave it absolution."

Aside from the essential interest of the character, the significance of the book lies in its structural movement toward the metamorphosis occurring in middle age, the invasion of ancestry into personality (a phenomenon with which Proust too was concerned—as in Swann's aging into the Jewish patriarchal type, and in Saint-Loup's increasing resemblance to the medieval Guermantes image). As Myra Henshawe ages, she is invaded more and more by the ungovernable powers of inheritance, which she identifies with her uncle. "We were very proud of each other," she says, "and if he'd lived till now, I'd go back to him and ask his pardon. . . . Yes, and because as we grow old we become more and more the stuff our forbears put into us, I can feel his savagery strengthen in me. We think we are so individual and so misunderstood when we are young; but the nature our strain of blood carries is inside there, waiting, like our skeleton." Myra dies overwhelmed by the ancestors—that strange Irish agglomerate of the dark primitive with what is most magical in Christianity and with what is most censorious, turning to the revenge of those magic snakes which St. Patrick drove out of Ireland to lodge in the souls of his converts. The themes of the ancestors and the instinctive self come together here in one person, in a barbaric pattern of destructiveness. But the book leaves one with the unsatisfied sense of something unseated and unreferred, something belonging to a larger context than Myra Henshawe's Irishness, something whose resolution here is perhaps too facile, a kind of ethnic cliché.

After a short prologue, *Death Comes for the Archbishop* (1927) starts in the manner of a legend's "once upon a time": "One afternoon in the autumn of 1851 a solitary horseman, followed by a pack-mule, was pushing through an arid stretch of country somewhere in central New Mexico." The conduct of the book is legendary—with that quality of the most enduring legends that endure because they represent primal human experience, the excesses and elaborative accretions rubbed off by long handling, so that what remains is the rounded core, hand-smoothed to a satiny luster; while the people in the book, the "strong people of the old deep days of life," not only have each their legends but have become their own legends. The prose has the bland, voiced quality of oral telling—not apparently an accident, for Elizabeth Sergeant records that each day, after writing, Willa Cather went alone to a stony place in the woods and read her work aloud to test its sounds and rhythms.

Most of the episodes evoke the virtue of place, textures of earth and weather that are the basis of all sense of reality, and the relationships of human generations silently handing down their wisdom of place. Hence a sacramental character invests not only the experiences of the archbishop, Jean Latour, because of his religious mission, but also the land itself and the habits of the people living there. On that journey in 1851, after traveling three

days thirsty in a desert of brick-colored sand hills, the young bishop comes upon a cruciform juniper tree and kneels there to pray to the Mother for water for his animals and himself; and shortly thereafter he comes upon a place called Hidden Water, where a spring has for unknown ages fed human settlement, and recognizes here something familiar from his own anciently settled country, Auvergne: "This spot had been a refuge for humanity long before these Mexicans had come upon it. It was older than history, like those wellheads in his own country where the Roman settlers had set up the image of a river goddess, and later the Christian priests had planted a cross." Across the "life-giving stream" a boy leads a flock of goats to pasture, the angoras leaping the stream in arrows of dazzling whiteness in the sunlight; the people beat out their grain on an earthen threshing floor and winnow it in the wind "like the Children of Israel." One is in the presence of a way of life like that suggested in the twenty-third Psalm: "He maketh me to lie down in green pastures: he leadeth me beside the still waters. He restoreth my soul."

In Nebraska, the early homesteaders had experienced the emptiness of that wild land as a curse taken into their nerves to be passed on to their children as congenital deprivation (one remembers the gaunt house and the cattle-tracked clay bluffs, the dishcloths hung out to dry and the turkeys picking up refuse about the kitchen door), a curse accommodated by the Protestant taboo on the instinctual. The evocation in this book of the more remote American "ancestors," the southwestern Indians, redresses the balance of instinct, particularly in relation to the land. Moving through the desert with Eusabio, his Navajo guide, the archbishop comes to recognize the vital relationship between land and people: "Travelling with Eusabio was like travelling with the landscape made human." As the white man's way was assertion of himself against the land, "it was the Indian's way to pass through a country without disturbing anything; to pass and leave no trace, like fish through the water, or birds through the air. It was the Indian manner to vanish into the landscape, not to stand out against it. The Hopi villages that were set upon rock mesas, were made to look like the rocks on which they sat, were imperceptible at a distance. The Navajo hogans, among the sand and willows were made of sand and willows." Two Zuñi runners pass them, saluting by gestures of the open palm but not stopping: "They coursed over the sand with the fleetness of young antelope, their bodies disappearing and reappearing among the sand dunes, like the shadows that eagles cast in their strong, unhurried flight."

In the Nebraska of Willa Cather's generation, human landmarks were scarce and the landmarks that were raised were like the town of Red Cloud where she grew up, hesitant and ugly and traditionless, perpetuating an obstinate sterility. The pueblos where Jean Latour goes on his pilgrimages have Homeric names and associations: "Santo Domingo, breeder of horses; Isleta, whitened with gypsum; Laguna, of wide pastures; and finally, cloud-set Acoma." The people of the pueblo of Taos appear on their houses a little before sunset, and it is as if American life were seen in a new dimension, new but very old, connected perhaps with the source-lands of civilization in the Middle East, perhaps with Arabia: there were "two large communal houses, shaped like pyramids, gold-coloured in the afternoon light, with the purple mountain lying just behind them. Gold-coloured men in white burnouses came out on the stairlike flights of roofs, and stood still as statues, apparently watching the changing light on the mountain. There was a religious silence over

the place; no sound at all but the bleating of goats coming home through clouds of golden dust."

As the Ancient People of the continent are brought alive again in their pueblos—the streets of the ancestors in the heart no more desolate—the land too, and the air, tell of creation and an original relationship. At the rock of Acoma, steep and scaled by an old path trodden over thousands of years by water-carriers, the archbishop is overtaken by sudden storm, and stops at the top of the mesa to look out over the great plain glittering with rain sheets, the distant mountains bright in sunlight, and "thought that the first Creation morning might have looked like this, when the dry land was first drawn up out of the deep." The aging bishop, tired by journeying and tempted by thoughts of his homeland in France, chooses to die in exile in New Mexico because of the light, dry, aromatic air that had become habitual to the lungs and spiritually necessary, an air that "one could breathe . . . only on the bright edges of the world, on the great grass plains or the sage-brush desert," blowing in through the windows "with the fragrance of hot sun and sage-brush and sweet clover; a wind that made one's body feel light and one's heart cry 'To-day, to-day,' like a child's."

There is no problem of the natural self here, for the self has been living all its potentialities, embodied in an individual and unique mission, in conversation with inheritance and with the heritable. Dying, the archbishop "sat in the middle of his own consciousness; none of his former states of mind were lost or outgrown. They were all within reach of his hand, and all comprehensible." His last conscious image is one of his youth, of the *diligence* for Paris rumbling down a mountain gorge, to take him on his first step toward the new world; but this image is very different from the demons of youth that possessed Bartley Alexander and Professor St. Peter, insidiously negating the developed personality: the image here is that of a young traveler, setting out again in peril and devotion.

Between this book and *Shadows on the Rock* (1931), Willa Cather's father died, a death from which she suffered severe shock, and she had tended her mother through a long paralytic illness; from the personal point of view, there can be no question of the immediate emotional provenience of the central relationship in *Shadows on the Rock*, that between father and child (Euclide Auclair, apothecary of Quebec, and his small daughter Cécile)—the essential image of human continuity. But the "child" had appeared frequently before, as a psychological symbol, in Willa Cather's writings—the "divine child" of myth and of dreams, making its clamor at the limen of consciousness, requiring entrance. Now the child, the initial and potential self, is the main character.

Again the story starts in the manner of a legend's "once upon a time": "One afternoon late in October of the year 1697, Euclide Auclair, the philosopher apothecary of Quebec, stood on the top of Cap Diamant gazing down the broad, empty river far beneath him." That haunted gaze down the river, where the last ships for France have disappeared before winter isolates the Rock, is a continuous minor motif in the book; for these people are in exile —as, indeed, all the people of Willa Cather's great pastorals are in exile, thrust forth on a wild new earth, cut off from the continuities of the past. But this rock of Quebec—like the desert pueblos of New Mexico—has gathered its own legends out of the raw and dangerous wilderness, and for the child Cécile these impregnate all the steep streets, "ancestors" alive in her love and will and tangible as the air

she breathes. As the autumn fog drifts brown from the river, vapors changing density and color to amethyst and red lavender, "It was like walking in a dream. One could not see the people one passed, or the river, or one's own house. Not even the winter snows gave one such a feeling of being cut off from everything and living in a world of twilight and miracles. . . . On such solemn days [All Souls' Day, particularly solemn in Quebec because it is the day of the ancestors of these exiles] all the stories of the rock came to life for Cécile; the shades of the early martyrs and great missionaries drew close about her. All the miracles that had happened there . . . came out of the fog; every spire, every ledge and pinnacle, took on the splendour of legend."

But the sense of the past—of those continuities which are most saving and fruitful—is not confined to "shadows" on the rock: surrounded by wilderness and constantly called upon for responses to primitive situations, the living characters of the book move in simple, agelessly human patterns of figures in legend. Old Bishop Laval goes to the church to ring the bell for five o'clock Mass: "In winter the old man usually carried a little basin as well as his lantern. It was his custom to take the bowl of holy water from the font in the evening, carry it into his kitchen, and put it on the back of the stove, where enough warmth would linger through the night to keep it from freezing." The child Cécile does not always waken at the first bell, ringing in the coldest hour of the night, "but when she did, she felt a peculiar sense of security, as if there must be powerful protection for Kebec in such steadfastness, and the new day, which was yet darkness, was beginning as it should. The punctual bell and the stern old Bishop who rang it began an orderly procession of activities and held life together on the rock, though the winds lashed it and the billows of snow drove over it."

There is another child in the book, little Jacques, whose mother is the town prostitute, and in this doubling of the symbol, the "child" appears redemptorally and sacramentally. The old bishop has come on a winter night from the house of a sick woman; no one else is abroad in that cruel cold. He turns his lantern on the stone steps of the episcopal residence (occupied by the young, graceful, splendid, and presumptuous bishop who has replaced him), and finds there a child crouching, crying and almost frozen. He takes him home to his small poor rooms in the Seminary, makes a fire in the fireplace to heat water for a bath, and warms milk on the hearth with a little cognac. "One strange thing Jacques could remember afterwards. He was sitting on the edge of a narrow bed, wrapped in a blanket, in the light of a blazing fire. He had just been washed in warm water; the basin was still on the floor. Beside it knelt a very large old man with big eyes and a great drooping nose and a little black cap on his head, and he was rubbing Jacques's feet and legs very softly with a towel. . . . What he remembered particularly was that this old man, after he had dried him like this, bent down and took his foot in his hand and kissed it; first the one foot, then the other." The bishop is told by his servant that the child is the son of the woman called La Grenouille, and the old man nods thoughtfully, "Ah! That, too, may have a meaning." He sits through the night with his swollen legs on a stool, covered in his cloak and sunk in meditation—he has given the child his bed. "This was not an accident, he felt. Why had he found, on the steps of that costly episcopal residence built in scorn of him and his devotion to poverty, a male child, half-clad and crying in the merciless cold? Why had this reminder of his

Infant Saviour been just there, under that house which he never passed without bitterness?"

Before she died in 1947, at the age of seventy-three, Willa Cather published four more books, a book of tales, a book of essays, and two novels; and after her death another book of stories appeared and another book of essays. We are told that from 1932 on, she showed signs of deep fatigue. The prose of the two last novels shows weariness. *Lucy Gayheart* (1935) is another semiautobiographical account of the gifted young person growing up in a little midwestern town; despite its relaxed style, it contains certain moments and insights of great sensitivity. *Sapphira and the Slave Girl* (1940) is Willa Cather's personal quest for her Virginia ancestors—she went back to her early home there to find the materials for the book —but the impulse was perhaps too self-conscious, and the novel has little interest beyond the historical. The stories in *The Old Beauty and Others* (1948) seem only the somewhat querulous writing of old age.

But the three stories in *Obscure Destinies* (1932) are the finest short pieces she ever wrote. "Neighbour Rosicky," a story set in Nebraska, is about an old Bohemian farmer who dies of heart trouble. There is in this tale that primitive religious or magical sense of relationship with the earth that one finds in Willa Cather's great pastoral novels. Old Rosicky, sent home by the town doctor with a warning, stops by the graveyard where a light fall of snow is settling on the red grass: "It was a nice graveyard, Rosicky reflected. . . . A man could lie down in the long grass and see the complete arch of the sky over him, hear the wagons go by; in summer the mowing-machine rattled right up to the wire fence. And it was so near home. Over there across the cornstalks his own roof and windmill looked so good to him that he promised himself to mind the Doctor and take care of himself. . . . He wasn't anxious to leave [that place]. And it was a comfort to think that he would never have to go farther than the edge of his own hayfield." The drama of the story is in old Rosicky's relationship with a daughter-in-law, a young girl from town who resents the isolation of farm life and is snobbish in her shabby town-glamour. She is alone with him when he has a severe heart attack, and she holds his hand, a hand not like that of other farmers, but gypsy-like, "nimble and lively and sure, in the way that animals are. . . . It seemed to her that she had never learned so much about life from anything as from old Rosicky's hand. It brought her to herself; it communicated some direct and untranslatable message."

These stories in *Obscure Destinies* face the child with the old and ancestral, gathering up in gentle concreteness the themes of a lifetime. "Old Mrs. Harris" principally concerns a grandmother brought to the Midwest from Virginia, and used as a willing slave by her daughter Victoria. The "immemorial image" here is of the servant girl, Mandy, washing old Mrs. Harris' feet—a conversion of the image in *Shadows on the Rock*, of the old man washing the child's feet. "That had to be done in the kitchen; Victoria didn't like anybody slopping about. Mrs. Harris put an old checked shawl around her shoulders and followed Mandy. Beside the kitchen stove Mandy had a little wooden tub full of warm water. She knelt down and untied Mrs. Harris's garter strings and took off her flat cloth slippers and stockings. 'Oh, Miz' Harris, your feet an' legs is swelled turrible tonight!' 'I expect they air, Mandy. They feel like it.' 'Pore soul!' murmured Mandy. . . . The kitchen was quiet and full of shadow, with only the light from an old

lantern. Neither spoke. Mrs. Harris dozed from comfort, and Mandy herself was half asleep as she performed one of the oldest rites of compassion."

In the story "Two Friends" the central image is of a child—the child Willa Cather must have been—listening to two elderly men talking in moonlight on the street of a country town. There was "a row of frail wooden buildings, due to be pulled down any day; tilted, crazy, with outside stairs going up to rickety second-storey porches that sagged in the middle. . . . These abandoned buildings, an eyesore by day, melted together into a curious pile in the moonlight, became an immaterial structure of velvet-white and glossy blackness. . . . The road, just in front of the sidewalk where I sat and played jacks, would be ankle-deep in dust, and seemed to drink up the moonlight like folds of velvet. It drank up sound, too; muffled the wagon-wheels and hoof-beats; lay soft and meek like the last residuum of material things,—the soft bottom resting-place. Nothing in the world, not snow mountains or blue seas, is so beautiful in moonlight as the soft dry summer roads in a farming country, roads where the white dust falls back from the slow wagon-wheel." The two men talking seem more than themselves because of their long shadows cast by moonlight, persons representing cosmic relationships like those calculated by Pythagoras: "When they used to sit in their old places on the sidewalk, two black figures with patches of shadow below, they seemed like two bodies held steady by some law of balance, an unconscious relation like that between the earth and the moon." When the two friends quarrel and abandon each other, it is to the young girl as if a truth had been senselessly wasted.

Willa Cather's stature as a novelist and storyteller will probably always withstand those obscurations which happen to a major writer almost with the regularity of the displacement of one generation by another; for her best work reaches into human truths immeasurably older than the historical American past from which she drew her factual materials, truths that provide the essential forms of experience and that therefore cannot become "past" truths, either obsolescent or elegiac—although they are of the primitive kind that may affront our self-ignorance and stir our resistances. For the same reason, the dense world of the five senses which she creates in her best novels and stories is one that cannot be interpreted by an abstraction (a "world-view" of some kind); her work rests on an intuitive or instinctive wisdom, conveying "a direct and untranslatable message" like old Rosicky's gypsy hand, or like the image of the black plow picture-written on the molten sun. What she did was very difficult, for she had to give up conventional literary methods, in which she was accomplished, and go blindly into herself for essential truth. Yet it was through that giving up and blindness that she was able to speak in a way that often reveals to the reader something extraordinarily valuable that seems to have been in his mind always.

Selected Bibliography

WORKS OF
WILLA CATHER

The Troll Garden. New York: McClure, Phillips, 1905.

Alexander's Bridge. Boston: Houghton Mifflin, 1912.

O Pioneers! Boston: Houghton Mifflin, 1913.

The Song of the Lark. Boston: Houghton Mifflin, 1915.

My Ántonia. Boston: Houghton Mifflin, 1918.

Youth and the Bright Medusa. New York: Knopf, 1920.

One of Ours. New York: Knopf, 1922.

A Lost Lady. New York: Knopf, 1923.

The Professor's House. New York: Knopf, 1925.

My Mortal Enemy. New York: Knopf, 1926.

Death Comes for the Archbishop. New York: Knopf, 1927.

Shadows on the Rock. New York: Knopf, 1931.

Obscure Destinies. New York: Knopf, 1932.

Lucy Gayheart. New York: Knopf, 1935.

Not under Forty. New York: Knopf, 1936.

Sapphira and the Slave Girl. New York: Knopf, 1940.

The Old Beauty and Others. New York: Knopf, 1948.

Willa Cather on Writing. New York: Knopf, 1949.

Willa Cather's Collected Short Fiction, 1892–1912. Introduction by Mildred R. Bennett. Lincoln: University of Nebraska Press, 1965.

The Kingdom of Art: Willa Cather's First Principles and Critical Statements, edited by Bernice Slote. Lincoln: University of Nebraska Press, 1966.

The World and the Parish: Articles and Reviews, 1893–1902, edited by William M. Curtin. Lincoln: University of Nebraska Press, 1970.

CRITICAL AND
BIOGRAPHICAL STUDIES

Bennett, Mildred R. *The World of Willa Cather.* Lincoln: University of Nebraska Press, 1961.

Brown, E. K., and Leon Edel. *Willa Cather: A Critical Biography.* New York: Knopf, 1953.

Daiches, David. *Willa Cather: A Critical Introduction.* New York: Collier, 1962.

Geismar, Maxwell. *The Last of the Provincials: The American Novel, 1915–1925.* Boston: Houghton Mifflin, 1947.

Kazin, Alfred. "Elegy and Satire: Willa Cather and Ellen Glasgow," in *On Native Grounds.* New York: Harcourt, Brace, 1942.

Lewis, Edith. *Willa Cather Living.* New York: Knopf, 1953.

Randall, John H. *The Landscape and the Looking Glass: Willa Cather's Search for Value.* Boston: Houghton Mifflin, 1960.

Schroeter, James, ed. *Willa Cather and Her Critics.* Ithaca, N.Y.: Cornell University Press, 1967.

Sergeant, Elizabeth Shepley. *Willa Cather: A Memoir.* Philadelphia: Lippincott, 1953.

Trilling, Lionel. "Willa Cather," in *After the Genteel Tradition: American Writers since 1910,* edited by Malcolm Cowley. New York: Norton, 1937.

—*DOROTHY VAN GHENT*

James Fenimore Cooper

1789-1851

*I*F ANYTHING from the pen of the writer of these romances is at all to outlive himself, it is, unquestionably, the series of *The Leather-Stocking Tales*," wrote James Fenimore Cooper in 1850 when he first brought the five stories together to make a single tale of the life of his wilderness scout.

He was right in his belief that something far more than he had planned—a folk epic of the settlement of America—had emerged of itself from his efforts and that these novels would outlive him. He also guessed unhappily that, with a few exceptions like *The Spy* and *The Pilot*, the rest of his novels, collected into the handsome set of the Mohawk Edition, and his critical and historical prose would be largely forgotten. Memorialized by children in their games of Indians, hunters, and trappers, and acknowledged by adults as the creator of the American wilderness myth—more real than reality—this writer of stiff and wordy romantic prose was for many years little read. Then, in the general awakening of curiosity about our national culture that took place in the 1920's and 1930's, Cooper came into his own. He was, it would appear, the first American man of letters to take the whole of American experience as the private preserve of his ranging imagination and his critical mind.

There is no doubt that, as a man of thought and feeling, more than any other writer of his generation, Cooper understood the time and place in which he lived and gave them voice and meaning. It is he who stands at the portal of American literature, rather than Freneau or Brown, Irving or Bryant, and who is recognized at home and abroad as the first and one of the greatest of American writers of fiction.

How, then, should the serious reader or scholar go about the task of breaking down the barrier that stands between him and this serious writer, the first truly professional American man of letters? How can he become acquainted with this towering figure of his own literary past?

The modern critic would probably answer: "Lay aside your prejudices, read all the text, analyze carefully the meaning and the structure of at least a part of it, and make up your mind." This is good advice, but the literary historian would approach the problem from a different angle with different results. He would suggest that the reader should try to reconstruct as best he can the point of view of the writer and the circumstances of the writing and, with an understanding of the meaning of the work in its own context, he should read and evaluate it both as art and as historical document. From the days of his first biographer, T. R. Lounsbury, down to the near present the best Cooper criticism has been historical, but there have also been critics like D. H. Lawrence, Marius Bewley, and Donald A. Ringe who have attempted a more nearly intrinsic and impressionistic criticism, with mixed results. Of them Ringe—and perhaps because he first establishes and then maintains a basically historical perspective—provides the best balanced if not the most exciting evaluation. There is still much research to be done on Cooper, particularly in the problem of his literary sources, and much careful analytical criticism is needed, especially for the relatively forgotten novels and some of the critical prose, but the essential fact that Cooper is an organic artist for whom the subject is more important than the form, rather than a consciously technical artist like Henry James, will always make the substance and process of his work far more interesting and important than its structure and texture.

Up to the age of thirty, Cooper was a reader, not a writer, of fiction. Suddenly then, he developed the conviction that as an American he had something to say which desperately needed saying and which could only be said effectively through the art of the novel. He spent the rest of his life—thirty years—in a passionate and persistent effort to get that something said. Egged on by success and stung by failure, he never fully gave up his relentless crusade, even though he suffered periods of deep discouragement, and he produced an average of a novel a year, plus a dozen or more works of history and criticism, up to the eve of his death. Translated and appreciated abroad, he was criticized and condemned at home, while his fame increased all over the world and his ideas and his art created a chapter in the intellectual and imaginative history of the American people. Insatiably returning to the attack after each partial failure, he never wearied of experiment or lost his faith in the validity of his efforts. Rough hewn as it was, his total work stands today as a massive monument to his vision and his courage. Perhaps no one of his novels can successfully weather the close examination that a masterpiece demands, but his total work is unquestionably the achievement of a vivid and powerful imagination.

With Cooper's first half-dozen novels American literature came into its own. By 1829, they had been republished in England and were translated into French and German. Several had also found translators in Italy, Sweden, Denmark, and probably other European countries. A critic in the London *Athenaeum* in that year linked Cooper with Irving and Channing as the only American writers who were generally known abroad. At home, *The Spy* was appearing in its seventh edition, *The Pioneers* in its sixth.

At first Cooper did not believe in himself as a literary man, and he was not so considered by others. Samuel Knapp, the first historian of our literature, does not mention him, and he stated his own primary purpose in a letter of 1831: "[My country's] mental independence is my object, and if I can go down to the grave with the reflection that I have done a little towards it, I shall have the consolation of knowing that I have not been useless in my generation."

Moral rather than aesthetic purpose motivated his work as it did his character. Always a man in whom impulse stimulated mind, he absorbed the thought currents of his day and of his inheritance with eager enthusiasm, and he spoke for his cause with the energetic dogmatism of American youth. Whether or not we attribute this moral enthusiasm to his Quaker ancestry as Henry Canby suggested, or to other conventional causes, we can find at least one source for it in the blind optimism and vital energy which are natural products of frontier conditions and unfolding civilizations. He lived at a time when American culture had sent down its first firm roots into the new soil, but what fruits it might bear were still uncertain. It was Cooper's task to profit by the autonomy which political independence had brought and to enlarge the spirit of that independence to include the sense of security which only self-knowledge can produce. Never a man of the frontier himself in spirit or in fact, he was a product of the frontier conditions which became the material of his novels. Literature for him was merely the expression of opinions and imagination in accord with actual conditions. "It is high time," he wrote in 1837, "not only for the respectability, but for the *safety* of the American people, that they should promulgate a set of principles that are more in harmony with their facts." This was the basic motive for his writing. The forms that writing took were largely accidental. Fortuitous circumstances determined his choice of themes for *Precaution*, *The Spy*, *The Pioneers*, and *The Pilot*, the novels which in turn determined the material for most of his later work: American society, American history, the American backwoods, and the sea. He fell into the forms of the domestic novel of manners and the romantic tale of adventure because they were easy and familiar to him, not because he cared deeply about their requirements and uses. The literary principles which he gradually evolved from his experience were not narrowly aesthetic, nor were his social and religious principles the results of imposed or formulated doctrine.

A codified analysis of his position would therefore be fruitless. Rather we must follow him through the stages of his development as a moving, growing, vital, and expressive force in the evolution of American culture through a period of stumbling self-discovery.

Born in 1789, Cooper published nothing until 1820. In the early years, his character and his dominant ideas were molded by his inheritance, by the influence of his father, William Cooper, his home, and his father's friends, and by the post-pioneer conditions in central New York State, as well as by the more highly cultivated society of New York City and the settlements along the lower Hudson and the Sound.

All that Cooper himself has to say about this first and unliterary period was written in later years and is strongly colored by his developed personality and doctrines. Much light is thrown upon it, however, by his father's record and rules of his own experience, *A Guide in the Wilderness*, and by the prefaces and memoirs of his daughter Susan, as well as by what we know of the circumstances of his childhood and youth from other sources.

It is well to keep always in mind the fact that he was not himself a pioneer even though he wrote so extensively of the pioneers and of life on the frontier. His childhood was formal, in a closely knit home and community life, and his own moves were always toward the east and its culture rather than toward the western fringe of civilization. His father, although a pioneer of the homesteading generation, was a Federalist in politics and had many of the attributes of the aristocrat in his social thinking. The Cooper family life was shaped on the patriarchal model. His mother devoted herself to her home and her children who, in their turn, grew up with a strong feeling for family loyalty and integrity and attachment to place.

Compared to the Dutch patroons and the English patentees of northern New York, however, William Cooper's theories of property rights, suffrage, equality, and other "American principles" were liberal and democratic. "The mirror of partisan perfection as a Federal squire," Dixon Ryan Fox has called him, and he appeared to his son as a democratic gentleman, privileged because of his business sagacity and control of his fellows. Cooperstown was named after him, developed by his theories, and shaped around his personality. The "Mansion House," later replaced by Otsego Hall, a large structure at the foot of Lake Otsego, was Cooper's boyhood home, the embodiment of his father's integrity and power. All about this industrious squirearchy were the neobaronial tracts of the Dutch patroons who rented their land to tenant farmers, and beyond them was the unsettled and wooded wilderness; while sixty miles to the east was the town of Albany, capital of an agrarian aristocracy. The picture is vividly painted in *The Pioneers.* "There existed," explained Cabot Lodge, "in New York an upper class, stronger and better defined than in any northern province . . . and closely allied to the ruling class in Virginia." The Cooper home was in accord with this tradition.

When Cooper and his brothers were sent to Yale and Princeton for the education which their father lacked, they went, therefore, with an assurance that they would be permitted, both by him and by the society of which they were a part, to use their intellectual powers to build on the material foundations of family stability which their father had laid. To Cooper, there was nothing inconsistent with democracy in this assumption that wealth permits privilege, as his later attitude toward his own children demonstrates. Furthermore, when he married into one of the Tory families of New York, he adopted and carried on its traditions. He may, therefore, be considered in these early years as an aristocrat in the social sense, as a man who accepted an unequal society and his own place of priority in it.

His experiences at Yale and in the Navy, where he served from 1808 to 1811, were, of course, important to Cooper's development, but they did little to alter his basic attitudes. His marriage, on the other hand, was a profoundly significant influence. Susan Augusta De Lancey was the granddaughter of James De Lancey, chief justice and governor of New York, and leader of the Loyalists in that state during the Revolution. The De Lanceys lost their power with their land when the Loyalist cause was defeated, but Mrs. Cooper inherited a share of the Heathcote family holdings at Mamaroneck on the Sound through descent from James De Lancey's wife, Anne Heathcote. Cooper was married at Heathcote Hall and built his new home, Angevine Farm, a few miles inland. This background is reflected in the social novels, particularly those of the later years, which present us with perhaps the best picture we have of life as Susan De Lancey must have known it, modified by the ideals of William Cooper and seen through the prism of Jeffersonian democracy.

When Cooper began to write novels, he was already established in his own privileged place in a stable society. As yet he took no deep interest in social or political causes. He looked about him with an observant rather than a philosophical eye, and he believed in his country and in the principles of its Constitution because he had nothing to complain of in his own lot. Always a lover of books, he loved life more, and he drew his conclusions mainly from the facts about him and from the opinions of such friends and relatives as Judge William Jay, Governor De Witt Clinton, and Bishop William Heathcote De Lancey. He worshiped at an Episcopal church, joined the local agricultural society and the state militia, built a house on a hill overlooking his land and the distant sea, and brought up his family in all the proprieties and accomplishments of the day. Like the Squire of Bracebridge Hall, he steeped himself in local tradition and history, and he had a lively interest in the characters of the people around him.

In the novels written during the decade 1820–30—ten in all—his attitude is primarily that of the observer rather than that of the critic. In his first, *Precaution*, the moralizer is dominant. It is significant, in the light of his later work, that Sir Edward Moseley "was descended from one of the most respectable of the creations of his order by James, and had inherited, with many of the virtues of his ancestor, an estate which placed him among the greatest landed proprietors of the country," and that his wife was "a woman of many valuable and no obnoxious qualities, civil and attentive by habit to all around her, and perfectly disinterested in her attachments to her own family." We are to meet these types again and again in the novels. The life at Moseley Hall and in the Rectory was presumably English, even though Cooper had never, up to this time, left his native shore. The details were gleaned from his reading, but the social pattern was far from alien to the comparatively crude approximations of aristocracy which he had experienced on the fringe of the wilderness.

He had written the novel, according to a family story told by his daughter, in answer to the challenge of his wife when he had complained of an English novel he had been reading aloud to her: " 'Why don't you write a better one yourself?' " and there is some question as to how seriously he took the task he had set himself. It was rather the challenge of his own failure that spurred him on. The choice of material was wrong; he should write about what he knew about. Both the writing and the printing were careless; he should do well anything that he thought worth doing at all. Accepting full blame for the failure, he would try again, and the world of imagination opened before him.

The ten early novels were experimental in more ways than one although Cooper seems to have sensed from the start the main objectives and the principal ways of reaching them that were to guide him throughout his career. Each of these novels represents a new start and each has in the background one or more models to provide semblance of literary form. From his reading he was familiar with the historical romance of Scott and the domestic novel of manners of Jane Austen and others. Later he turned to Balzac, Dana, Smollett, and other novelists, as well as to biography and travel narratives, for hints on how to organize his material, but what he had to say was always vigorously his own and he contributed more than he borrowed in every case. When he took the neutral ground around New York City for the scene of his Revolutionary War novel, *The Spy*, he probably had Scott's border country in mind, and it was the poor seamanship of *The Pirate* that, according to his own account, inspired *The Pilot*. His use of a single cycle of the seasons in the life of a country house in *The Pioneers* resembles Irving's in *Bracebridge Hall*, and he did genuine research on his historical sources for the New England backgrounds of *Lionel Lincoln* and *The Wept of Wish-ton-Wish*, and on his vision of the open West for *The Prairie*.

Donald Ringe has suggested that it was probably the aesthetic requirements of the associationist psychology of Cooper's day rather than a narrow nationalism that led him and other early American poets, novelists, and painters to turn to familiar materials and themes in order to arouse a suitable train of associations in the reader's mind and thus convey to him a fundamental truth. If so, the turn from English to American material and from the themes of love and marriage to those of rebellion and war in *The Spy* was instinctive rather than planned, for Cooper was never a deliberate and careful artist. It would seem that his first experiment in the art of fiction, by its very failure, taught him that he had something to say about the world he knew and that the English domestic novel of manners was not the form in which it could effectively be said. A tightly constructed society is essential to success in this mode and the primary fact of the American experience was the creation of an open and fluent society in which habits, manners, and ultimate morality were threatened with disintegration. The task of the American writer was therefore more than merely the finding of the most suitable literary form; it was that of probing the effects of democratic theory on inherited and transplanted values. Cooper was not himself aware for a long time of the full implications of his own challenge and it took many experiments to make the issue clear to him and to others; but, long before Hawthorne or Melville, or even Poe, he became deeply conscious of the spiritual and cultural ambiguities of life in the New World. His use of native materials drawn from the primitive wilderness of America's recent past and the sea of her present absorbing interest provided the substance, and the developing themes of these first novels set the issues and the patterns, for the best American literature of the following years. It was necessary to twist and wrench English literary modes to make them fit American materials, but it was also necessary to face the fact that the moral structure of English society was in process of becoming, first flexible, and then disintegrated, in the natural and open environment of the new continent. Often as literature in the past had revealed the tragic issue in human destiny, man seems not to have learned his lesson: he was again pitting his will against fate as though it had never been done before.

This revelation was of course only dimly glimpsed in *The Spy*. The turns to American history for his materials and to the historical romance of Scott for his model were drastic enough experiments, and they brought success. With this novel, American fiction was fairly launched. Whatever its inadequacies as art, it released the pent-up energies of its author into a form of expression which set his problem clearly and gave him the range and the instruments to deal with it effectively. He chose the neutral ground around the British-held New York City for his setting and for his central character a man who, by masking his identity, freed himself from the normal laws and manners of formal society. The role of Harvey Birch, together with his humble origin, frees him from the rigid social structure which remains as background in the two armies and offsets his violations of their limitations and requirements; and the looser technique of the historical romance provides an opportunity for fast action and vivid description, both of which were to prove important gifts of the author. The ambiguities of life in America had found, in a combination of the romance and the novel of manners, a sufficiently flexible mode for their fictional expression and, in Cooper, an inventive and courageous writer who was ready to commit himself to the task. The long road ahead was open.

In *The Pioneers*, Cooper faced his problem even more directly and wrote the semiautobiographical story that every serious novelist must get out of his system before he knows what he has to say or how to say it. Turning to the scenes of his boyhood for his setting and to his father for his central character, he raised again the question of how democracy can create in a wilderness a society stable enough to preserve the values essential to civilized and moral living. Here was a small though primitive community that was attempting to carve out of the frontier an integrated way of life. With a setting sufficiently contained to lend itself to the technique of the novel of manners, the theme demanded the scope and freedom of the historical romance. A laudatory review of Catherine Maria Sedgwick's *A New-England Tale*, tentatively identified as Cooper's by James Beard, in *The Literary and Scientific Repository,* suggests his principal source, and the pattern of the seasons and the milieu of a country squirearchy suggest Irving's *Bracebridge Hall*, which he also reviewed in the same journal. But the spirit of the novel is anything but domestic. With the introduction of such characters as Billy Kirby the woodsman and the versatile if somewhat meteoric Dickon Jones, the native quality of the village life takes over; and with the introduction of Cooper's master character Leather-Stocking, he discovers for the first time the romantic possibilities of the wilderness forest, lake, and stream, even though Natty Bumppo is here realistically presented as a dogged old man of seventy, toughened in both skin and convictions by his long years in the open. His idealization was a slow process which culminated only in *The Deerslayer* two decades later.

We come to *The Pioneers* then with the realization that Cooper intended it as a work of art and that he knew instinctively what he was doing even though more interested in the subject than in the form of his experiment. Its power and its purpose strike home, however, only after the patient acceptance of long and unrealistic dialogues which the author confesses are his means of presenting ideas and actions, of a plot which is full of coincidences and stupidities, and of characters who are either idealized or burlesqued beyond credibility. But when such weaknesses are recognized and forgotten, a vivid picture of the American past comes to life in the imagination. Characters step from the pages by their responses to nature in both her savage and her contemplative moods, and scenes of grandeur and terror unfold in unhampered romantic description. Setting—character—theme: the steady hand of an inexperienced but controlled and directed literary imagination is evident at every point.

The thematic structure of the novel comes to a focus in the conflict between Judge Temple and Leather-Stocking on the issue of killing a deer out of season. Their friendship breaks down because the Judge's belief in the social control of individual "rights" has no common ground with Natty's reliance on the laws of the forest and of God as moral absolutes. These two idealized prototypes of real characters, both of whom Cooper fully understands and admires, admire each other but are critically irreconcilable. The Judge symbolizes the value system of civilized society; Natty that of the single solitary natural man. When Natty loses the battle and turns his eyes to the western prairie, the Judge is left with the realization that there are still more profound and complex ambiguities than even the settlement of this issue cannot solve. Novelist rather than dogmatist, Cooper leaves the problem unresolved to follow Natty later into the setting sun and the open prairie.

Meanwhile, however, romance took over and a younger and further idealized Leather-Stocking leads his four civilized friends through an Indian-infested forest in *The Last of the Mohicans.* For sheer vitality, suspense, action, natural description, and story interest, this is perhaps the most successful, and certainly the most popular, of Cooper's romances. All the conflicts of individual and social values of the other novels are here again, but they are so buried in the requirements of the story that they do not intrude, even though, on second thought, one realizes that in his Indian Chingachgook and in his wilderness scout Cooper has now defined his two types of primitive conduct, the noble and stoic savage and the Christian man of nature, and has given them an epic dimension as part of the American myth upon which Mark Twain and others could draw. Natty came to grips with civilization in his clash with Judge Temple; here he turns the other way and confronts the primitive absolute.

In the third chapter of *The Last of the Mohicans,* these two meet on the banks of a small but rapid stream. Each presents to the other the chief point in his philosophy of life, and they find in each other a deep and primitive sympathy, although the issue of their debate—whether or not the white man has a right to the new lands—is not resolved. Racial traditions contain all the philosophy of the Indian. He believes only what Nature and his fathers have told him: "The land we had taken like warriors, we kept like men." But to the trapper, "everything depends on what scale you look at things." Because he rejects the sophistication of his people, can shoot to the mark, and can respect honesty and courage in his fellows of whatever color, he feels himself on a par with the red man. The right of the intruders to the land depends on their superiority as men, their justice, and their humanity. The scale which Bumppo supplies to enlarge that of the Indian comes from the Bible as interpreted in Protestant tradition. Under Christian influence, the red warrior forsakes his inhuman ways, his brutality, and his ignorance to rely upon justice and charity. Cooper's primitivism is thus in no sense pagan; it is a complete acceptance of Protestant ethical tradition qualified by a rejection rather than by a reform of the social sophistications and corruptions which had resulted in three centuries of evolution in that tradition. Cooper's argument has, therefore, little relationship to that of the "noble savage"; his values are Christian rather than pagan. When in a romantic vein, he assigns ideal primitive traits to the savages; when in a critical vein, he calls for their culti-

vation in civilized society. But he still believed that the problem of differing value systems could and should be dealt with on the level of human reason and justice; it was not until much later that disillusionment made him transfer it to the wisdom of God.

The third novel in the Leather-Stocking series, *The Prairie*, picks up Natty's life where Cooper left it at the end of *The Pioneers.* Unable to reconcile his moral integrity as an individual with the restraints of the civil law, the trapper has now followed through his decision to move farther west. Cooper himself had never seen the prairie and he was now writing from Europe, but the perspective of distance, buttressed by research and imagination, merely sharpened the themes of his story of the quest for moral integrity, this time offset by another of Cooper's symbolic types, the shrewd and unscrupulous squatter Ishmael Bush. Again the question is asked: Is moral integrity, based on a firm faith in Divine wisdom, sufficient to protect human values from the selfish despoiler of nature that is in every man, without the support of civil law and a structured society? The trapper's death supplies a negative answer as well as a moment of high tragedy.

During this early period, Cooper also wrote two historical novels of New England, *Lionel Lincoln* and *The Wept of Wish-ton-Wish,* which, in spite of careful research and important themes, lacked their author's sympathy and therefore never took fire as did the forest romances. But in the first three sea romances, as in the Leather-Stocking series, he discovered an American myth and from it developed a wholly new kind of fiction which he taught to a generation of followers. Even though *The Pilot, The Red Rover,* and *The Water-Witch* are as experimentally and romantically interesting as the tales of land adventure, to discuss them here in the same detail would be repetitious. Ringe prefers *The Pilot* as a more daring break with convention and a better vehicle for Cooper's ideas; Thomas Philbrick, whose work on this aspect of Cooper's art is thorough, has chosen *The Red Rover* for fuller analysis as a better-told story and a more satisfactory representative of the genre. Both agree that Cooper's heavy hand with allegory makes *The Water-Witch* the least acceptable of the group, even though it also reflects an important element in the growth of Cooper's restless imagination.

The inspiration for these three tales of the sea runs closely parallel to that of the three romances of the woods. Launched on his project by a more or less accidental challenge, Cooper discovered, once he was deep in the work of imaginative re-creation, that he had more to say than conventional modes of fiction writing would allow. The theme of maritime nationalism was in some respects even more compelling than that of western expansion, for by 1823, the infant Republic had survived its first major test of strength and was an acknowledged rival of the expanding British sea power. Furthermore, the theme of personal integrity and freedom from civil restraints was more effectively expressed in Cooper's freelance ships and captains than in his Indians and woodsmen, even though Long Tom Coffin is a less convincing seagoing Leather-Stocking and the pirate and smuggler of the later tales assert their rights and live their own lives in their own ways and to their own cost. If the plots of these stories lean even more than do those of the wilderness tales on the mechanics of conventional romance, their settings and characters have more freedom for the development of dominant themes, and it is herein that Cooper's originality finds its opportunity. As Marcel Clavel long ago pointed out and as Philbrick has more recently emphasized, Cooper's break with Smollett and Scott and

his anticipation of Melville and Conrad was accomplished singlehanded, with only a slight assist from Byron. So fully was he seized by the power and freedom of the sea that, in his descriptive passages, the setting comes fully to life, taking over from the dwarfed humans and becoming itself the hero of the narrative. This was Cooper's invention and it gives his sea tales a unique place in the history of fiction; but the absence of a Leather-Stocking to hold them together makes them, even so, of less importance than the wilderness tales in the total evaluation of his work.

The last four of the tales of this first experimental decade were written after Cooper had taken up residence abroad, but they show little or no influence of the impact that European life was having on his feelings and his thoughts. With the *Notions of the Americans: Picked up by a Travelling Bachelor* in 1828 he had initiated a decade in which he turned his main attention from American to European and comparative political and social problems and from fiction to critical and historical prose. The instigating motive for this book was patriotism, as in the case of his earlier efforts to delineate the American scene and character. It is Cooper's first direct statement of his social philosophy, and, instead of expounding his position theoretically as he did later in *The American Democrat*, he attempts, not without critical reservations, to prove that America is a living embodiment of his beliefs.

The immediate provocation of the *Notions* was the increasing flood of books on America by English travelers. "It is with feelings of deep regret that I observe the literary animosity daily growing up between England and America," wrote the mild-tempered Washington Irving in 1819, and by 1828 some forty-odd pretentious works of travel in America by English authors had already appeared. American replies were taking two forms, direct rebuttal and mock travel. To the latter class Cooper's *Notions* belongs, with Royall Tyler's *Yankey in London*, Charles J. Ingersoll's *Inchiquin, the Jesuit's Letters*, and J. K. Paulding's *Sketch of Old England, by a New-England Man* and *John Bull in America; or, The New Munchausen.*

Notions is the most temperate, the best informed, and the best written of the group. Cooper looked upon this book as the most important of his writings up to that time and devoted the summer of 1827 to its composition. He had wished to memorialize in some way the triumphal visit of Lafayette to America in 1824, but the appearance of the general in the resulting fictionalization of his travels was only incidental to the itinerary of the "Travelling Bachelor." In February 1828, Cooper took the unfinished manuscript with him from Paris to London and personally supervised its printing, returning immediately upon its completion late in May.

"The American who gets the good word of England," he wrote later, "is sure of having that of his own country, and he who is abused by England will be certain of being abused at home." The American character and American manners had reached a low ebb in the English mind, and the American mind in its turn was habitually deferential to English opinion. Cooper addressed his *Notions* to both peoples, hoping that a fair and sympathetic picture of America might influence the English and indirectly raise the level of self-respect in America itself. It was an ambitious undertaking, certain of failure in immediate effect, although undoubtedly of ultimate influence. The semifictional formula represented the book as having been written by a foreign gentleman who was guided in his travels and in his observations by a New York counterpart. His readers on both sides of the water misunderstood his in-

tentions and were irritated rather than soothed by the parts which they understood. He offended both the English sense of superiority and the American spirit of independence. The book had a small sale in comparison with his novels.

Cooper was careful of his facts and studied reliable sources in preparation for writing the book. He was one of the best-informed men of his time on social conditions in his own New York State, and he tended to generalize for the nation from the particular locale which he knew. Although this prejudice somewhat detracts from his reliability, a more serious bias was his deliberate intention to present things in their most favorable light. The book may be accepted, however, not only for the value of its opinions, but also for its understanding of actual social conditions.

The presumed author is an enlightened European, a man of sound learning and aristocratic taste, but broad in his sympathies, a character familiar in various guises throughout Cooper's novels and easily to be identified with his own ideal conception of himself. He is here a member of a club of such gentlemen of various nations, bachelors all, who devote their time to travel in various parts of the world to learn what they can of man in his social being as expressed in the ideals and manners of civilized peoples.

Cooper adopted in this work for the first time the epistolary form so common in eighteenth-century English novels and to be used by him again only in the travel books. He did so, he says in his Preface, because "a close and detailed statistical work on the United States of America, could not keep its place as authority for five years." Rather he prefers to emphasize "the principles of the government and the general state of society," which are not so readily subject to change.

During the months—one might almost say

years—of preparation for the *Notions* he had been gradually clarifying his ideas about America. The discrepancies between her principles, as he defined them, and her practices had not yet become apparent to him, but his experience with European society would provide him with an admirable background for judgment. As his mind developed, he came to identify conventional ethics and even etiquette with political theory and he wove them all into a social and moral philosophy which he preached in novel after novel and tract after tract without pause. The integration of his morality and his historical sense took place during his European years when he observed the antithetical political ideals in open conflict. The code which he had at first applied successfully only to individuals he gradually learned to apply to society as a whole.

The *Notions* appeared before he had been in Europe long enough to come into close or varied contact with the life about him. So far he had been concerned almost wholly with the two purposes which had taken him from home: the education of his daughters and young son and the business arrangements for translating and publishing which he hoped would secure his financial independence as a writer. But France and England were in these years testing political liberalism as a means of avoiding the extremes of revolution and the old order. France had tried reaction in the restoration of the Bourbons Louis XVIII and Charles X, and England was on the eve of the overthrow of her Tory government. When Cooper arrived both countries were still at the right; during his residence both swung to a hypothetical middle ground with the July Revolution of 1830 in France and the passage of the Reform Bill of 1832 in England. Cooper took part in the discussion which preceded these changes, and sharpened his political wits. In the main, he was in sympathy with

the turn of events, but he was intensely critical of compromise.

The longer he remained in Europe the firmer his friendship with Lafayette became and the more definitely the latter molded his opinions. Lafayette was, for a brief moment in July of 1830, the deciding political voice in the affairs of France. It was he who made the gesture of the award of the throne to Louis Philippe, of the collateral Orleans dynasty, instead of to the legitimate and reactionary Bourbon who would have become Henry V. But after Louis became king, he proved to be more reactionary than Lafayette expected, and the latter found himself the leader of the Opposition to the *juste milieu* in the Chamber of Deputies. His American friend shared with him the feeling of disgust with government measures which were labeled as liberal but which seemed to the Opposition to be reactionary in the extreme. It was this stand which drew Cooper into the finance controversy in the Chamber of Deputies in 1831–32 and into active aid of the cause of Polish freedom during the same years. In both instances, he felt that he was defending the theory and practice of the United States government against, in the first, a direct criticism of the cost of democratic government, and in the second, a tyranny in another country from which the Constitution protected American institutions.

It was this political background which apparently suggested the general themes of his next three novels. What could be more natural for him than to turn the white light of American liberalism on dark corners of the past in which the darker aspects of the present would find analogy? "I had in view," he writes of *The Bravo*, "to exhibit the action of a narrow and exclusive system, by a simple and natural exposure of its influence on *the* familiar interests of life." The result was the trio of European novels, *The Bravo, The*

Heidenmauer, and *The Headsman*, all of which were written and published during the latter days of his residence abroad. The scenes were laid in Italy, Switzerland, and the valley of the Rhine, where he had seen for himself surviving monuments of the Middle Ages in the forms of palaces, castles, and monasteries. Contrasting the liberal governments and societies of the Swiss cantons and the Italian free cities with their respective pasts, he drew his own moral in favor of the ideals of democracy, quite a different one from that of his Scottish rival in romance.

A Letter to His Countrymen was Cooper's first publication after his return to America on November 5, 1833. It reveals his dismay at conditions of society and politics as he found them, as well as his irritation at the personal criticism which was already being directed toward him by the press. It marks in many ways the principal turning point in his career. His disillusionment is extreme in contrast to his mood five years earlier when he wrote the *Notions*, but for the first time he attempts to reduce his political theories to a generalized statement in other than a fictionalized form.

The primary motive for the tract was its author's desire to defend his personal reputation against the attacks of reviewers. Edward Sherman Gould had contributed to the *New York American* on June 7, 1832, a review of *The Bravo*, in which he not only criticized the social implications in the novel, but expressed the opinion that Cooper had written himself out and was now merely producing romances for the financial return they might bring. The review was sent to Cooper, who answered it in a violent mood in the *Albany Daily Advertiser* for April 2, 1833. His resentment was justified, but its expression was tactless and its form irritating. The *New York Courier and Enquirer* and other American journals took up the quarrel. Finally, Cooper decided to re-

view the whole case in a pamphlet. *A Letter to His Countrymen* announced his retirement as a novelist, and for six years he held to his resolution, devoting his attention mainly to critical prose and social satire.

These years produced five volumes of travel, published under the titles of *Gleanings in Europe* and *Sketches of Switzerland*, and *The American Democrat*. In the order of the journeys they describe rather than that of publication, the travel books are *France; England; Switzerland*, Part I; *Italy; Switzerland*, Part II (Paris, Switzerland, and the Rhine Valley). They are ostensibly made up of letters to friends named in the first two, anonymous in the others; but they actually consist of short topical discussions, of loose unity, presumably based on notes taken during Cooper's residence abroad but later so drastically expanded and amended that no passages from the books can be taken as the record of his opinions at the time of his observations. Cooper's first plan was to write a volume on Europe which might serve as a companion to the *Notions*. "The fragments of travels that are here laid before the reader," he states in the Preface to *Sketches of Switzerland*, Part I, "are parts of a much more extensive work, that it was, originally, the intention of the writer to publish." That work was never written; instead, the travel letters followed each other in haphazard order.

Cooper's main purpose throughout the series is that stated in *A Letter to His Countrymen*: the examination of European institutions and manners, in order to reveal the differences between them and the American which make direct imitation most dangerous to the new country. The works themselves are mere narratives of travel interspersed with comments pointing to this danger. Although the principles which he discusses are themselves political, Cooper's interest in them rests almost wholly in their social applications. His criticism of European society, including the English, reduces itself to a simple formula: European liberal political ideals had advanced far beyond contemporary manners, but the manners themselves had the advantages as well as the liabilities of tradition and were therefore stable enough for the development of culture. In America, the reverse was the case. Whereas European customs must, thought Cooper, eventually be modified to conform to the new ideas, in America well-formulated principles were not yet understood by the mass of the nation and there was no native tradition on which to build. His two attacks, on the disrupting principles threatening an established society in Europe and on the tardiness of America in recognizing her principles and in applying them to her facts, spring from the same source. It became his obvious duty, he felt, to attempt a logical formulation of ideal social standards for America in terms of what he believed to be basic American principles. What had been implicit in his early novels became explicit in his "primer," *The American Democrat*, in 1838.

The American Democrat is Cooper's most direct and comprehensive formulation of his social and political—and therefore by inference his moral—creed. In it, he defines his matured theory of the American democratic principle, and applies his definition to a variety of American institutions, both in themselves and in comparison with those of Europe. It is presented in the form of an elementary text, but it rests on no authority other than the opinions of the writer. The central principle is the belief in liberty for the individual within a society in which common rights are adequately protected by constitutional checks and balances. The republican form of government, as illustrated in the American system and compared with the monarchical and aris-

tocratic forms of European countries, is analyzed and related to limited ideals of liberty and equality; then the following institutions are discussed: the press, suffrage, slavery, party, and formal religion. Although Cooper was at this time still a member of the Democratic party and was under attack by the Whigs as its spokesman, this book is a vigorous exposé of the egalitarian tendencies of both the Jacksonian Democrats and the Whigs and a warning to countrymen against the threats of materialism and corruption from the rising new economic and political power groups. His book was an effort to recapture and to formulate for a new age what he believed to be the ideals and forms of the original order of American society and government.

On the other critical prose of the period, the *History of the Navy of the United States of America* alone demands mention here. Cooper was definitely a "big Navy" man, and his history was undertaken in the interest of this cause. He believed that America's sense of a national being would not be appreciated either at home or abroad until she could build on the foundation of her scattered naval triumphs a strong and regular naval force. As a historian, however, he was no respecter of persons; he told his story as the facts seemed to him to require. Several controversies were the result of his honesty and helped to cloud his later years at the same time that they reawakened his interest in the sea as a source of material for fiction, supplying him with many new story ideas. His later *Lives of Distinguished American Naval Officers* was both a summing up of his ideas on these controversies and a further use of naval materials. He now singled out the most important actors in the drama and retold their stories.

During this period of critical prose, Cooper wrote only three novels, all of them fictional treatments of his newly formulated doctrines.

The first was *The Monikins*, a satirical allegory in which he stressed the contrasting civilizations of two hemispheres. In some respects it anticipates Melville's *Mardi*, in others it harks back to *Gulliver's Travels*. Again the fictional veil is thin. Monkeys or men, these Monikins are Americans, Englishmen, Frenchmen. European civilization fails, he explains, because of caste, corruptions, and unsusceptibility to social change; American because of party, vulgarity, and money-madness. But as yet his criticism of his own countrymen is mild compared to that of the Europeans; at heart he still finds America at least theoretically sound.

The other two novels of these years are really one, *Homeward Bound* and *Home as Found*, the one a romance of the sea, the latter a portrait of Cooperstown very different from that presented in *The Pioneers*. With a long sheet of foolscap in front of him and his pen in hand, he sat down to tell a story in which he planned to record the observations of an American gentleman (himself) on his return with his family from a long residence abroad. The crudities of American society and the purity of American ideals which had been so violated were to have been the substance of the tale. But he made the mistake of opening with a scene on shipboard as the party set sail from England, and a typical romance of a chase, escape, and adventure had to be worked out of his system before the real business of the day could be undertaken in a sequel. It was the second novel, not the first, that he had planned to write, as it was always into social criticism that he was to throw his most deliberate creative effort—whether admitted or implied—from this time forward.

The result was as disastrous to his popularity as had been *The Bravo*. In order to present the case for an American aristocracy of worth, he drew upon the familiar material of his own native town once more, but this time the central character, Edward Effingham, was inescapably a fictionalized portrait of himself. *Home as Found*, in the history of American fiction, is not a bad novel and it marks an advance toward the kind of social fiction that culminated in the work of Sinclair Lewis in that it shows progress in Cooper's ability to build a story with social purpose around a domestic theme; but the realism was too literal for comfort. Neither was the situation helped by Cooper's treatment of the sensitive Three Mile Point controversy in which he was currently involved. In justifying Effingham for asserting his own property rights, as he had himself on Lake Otsego, in defiance of his neighbors, the villagers, Cooper put himself in a very unfavorable light and drew the wrath of the Whig press even more viciously down on his head, as Dorothy Waples has shown.

The close of the period 1838–40 finds Cooper the author of extensive treatises on the national character of America, England, and certain other European countries, a man with a definite social and political creed and a firm base on moral conviction. The novel had for some time ceased to be his central interest; his mission in life seemed rather the reform of the American mind by the rediscovery of national traditions and the battling with what seemed to him the forces of disintegration in the political and social structure of his country. The result was an involvement in controversies on all sides and an expenditure of prodigious effort in libel trials against the Whig press for what he felt to be misrepresentations. Most of these brought him little more than personal vindication on specific points, and all of them have been so thoroughly expounded elsewhere that they do not need to be discussed in detail here. That he was right on most issues does not seem to have mattered; his popularity shrank to a fraction of its former strength, and with it his income. He never regained the popularity which he lost by formulating his theories and applying them to his art and to the civilization of which he was a part.

With his return to Leather-Stocking in 1840, Cooper became once more primarily a novelist and produced what many critics have acclaimed as his masterworks, *The Pathfinder* and *The Deerslayer*, in the midst of the distress and confusion of the libel suits and in the wake of the popular failure of the Effingham duo. It is obvious that he had decided to try once again to express his view of life in fictional form although there is no second *Letter to His Countrymen* to announce his change of intention. His firm handling of theme, setting, character, and action in these two new episodes in the life of his wilderness hero is, however, sufficient evidence that he had lost none of his old zest and skill and that he had grown both as an artist and as a man of feeling. Recapturing his delight in nature, he brings Natty to life against the background of the country north of Cooperstown on the shores of Lake Ontario where, as a midshipman, the young Cooper had spent the winter of 1808. As sheer romance, the love story of Natty Bumppo and the old game of woodland hide-and-seek with hostile Indians combine to make as good a tale as anything Cooper ever did, and the thoughtless reader might well miss the social and moral themes which give it plot and purpose. Cooper's point in *Home as Found* that happiness depends upon taking one's natural place in the society of one's fellows according to one's native gifts, and that democracy can survive as a social structure only if it is based on an aristocracy of worth, is here unobtrusively but fully illustrated in Mabel Dunham's preference for Jasper Western, her masculine "opposite number," among her suitors, and again and again in such issues as the salt-water sailor Cap's failure in a fresh-water crisis.

Without losing his sense of reality, Leather-Stocking, now renamed "Pathfinder," rises to a new level of idealization and, in a story which uses again much of the old plot of *The Last of the Mohicans*, achieves a serenity and firmness of conviction which reflects Cooper's own emotional and intellectual maturity. There only remained for him to re-create the youth of his hero in the last of the series, *The Deerslayer*, and to give his readers at the same time the beginning of his saga and the fulfillment of its meaning; for Natty as Deerslayer has now become a symbol of the human values toward which Cooper had been reaching, and his story the most "poetic" of the Leather-Stocking tales, in which romance and moral import combine to create what many critics hold to be Cooper at his best.

Once in the saddle again, Cooper's revived narrative power seemed inexhaustible. In the decade remaining to him, 1841–51, he produced sixteen full-length novels, as well as a number of lesser pieces. In most of them his imaginative command of his materials shows little or no decline even though, as his social and political convictions become more and more transformed into moral and religious principles, they also tend to become more reactionary and dogmatic. When, however, his romantic joy of life and his narrative gift are in the ascendant, as they are in these later Leather-Stocking tales and in the sea tales of the same period, his convictions blend with the themes and action of the stories and give them firm structure and forward movement; when ideas take over the center of interest, as they do in many of the other later novels, the result is an inner aesthetic conflict between art and didacticism, and didacticism usually wins.

In *The Two Admirals* and *The Wing-and-Wing*, Cooper revived his interest in the romance of the sea as he had in that of the forest and achieved something of the serenity and mature mastery of *The Pathfinder* and *The Deerslayer* with the materials of *The Pilot* and the other sea romances. Returning to some of his earlier themes, situations, and characters, he gives them a firmer and altogether more satisfactory treatment. The time of both novels is the middle and late eighteenth century, the scene the Mediterranean, and the historical background the maritime rivalry between Britain and France, a theme derived from but only distantly related to the conflict between these two powers during the Indian and Revolutionary wars which had provided the drama for the earlier sea romances. Now, with the research he had done for his naval history as foundation, he could make even fleet maneuvers romantic, and with the injection of a love story and other elements of the old romantic formula in *The Wing-and-Wing*, he fully recaptured the spell of the sea and succeeded in bringing this second of his major modes to a new artistic maturity.

If these four novels—two of the forest and two of the sea—may be taken as the maximum realization of all the best elements of Cooper's art in their most satisfactory balance, that balance proved to be as precarious in his later years as it had been in the earlier. Beginning with *Wyandotté* in 1843, Cooper entered a new experimental phase of his career, a phase of moral and religious didacticism which had been specifically indicated in his earlier career only by the Puritan novel *The Wept of Wish-ton-Wish* in 1829, but had been present as an undercurrent in all his work.

The novels of this final phase may be divided into two classes: those in which the problems of society are paramount and those in which the solutions of formal religion take over the center of interest. Such a division is, of course, arbitrary, but because the line of thought in this essay has been based on the theory that Cooper's primary concern was always with the conflict between individual integrity and social structure and with the moral versus the anarchic kinds of freedom on both sides of this equation, emphasis in the discussion of these later novels will be on those in which his mature socio-moral rather than his strictly religious thought is uppermost.

Between 1844 and 1846 Cooper published his five novels dealing with his now matured theory of social structure and, in many ways, achieved in them the fullest realization of his ambition to write a novel of manners in the technique of the romance, but only at a sacrifice of his early flamboyancy to a growing sober realism and a sense of the mutability of human destiny. His approach was historical, but he no longer thought of American history as merely a romantic past. He turned to the early days of settlement and to the war for independence in order to uncover the roots of contemporary society. He had settled his family in the scenes of his boyhood, repaired the old house, and established himself as prototype of the patrician order. In *Home as Found* he had described the condition of society which he had found at Templeton (Cooperstown) by dividing its development into three stages: the first, that of settlement in which "the gentleman, even while he may maintain his character and station, maintains them with that species of good-fellowship and familiarity, that marks the intercourse between the officer and the soldier in an arduous campaign"; the second, in which "we see the struggles for place, the heart-burnings and jealousies of contending families, and the influence of mere money"; the third, in which "men and things come within the control of more general and regular laws." Cooperstown, in William Cooper's day, was in the first stage; his son found it in the second and hoped to move it into the third. To illustrate this process, he took typical landed families of the early days and attempted to tell their histories through several generations.

Afloat and Ashore, with its sequel, is the story of Miles Wallingford, a member of a family that had held Clawbonny, a modest estate on the Hudson, since 1707. Miles succeeded to the property in 1794 at the age of twelve. The "afloat" part of the tale, a good half, is a typical romance of the sea in Cooper's best manner, but modified by the influence of Dana's *Two Years before the Mast,* where the action is determined, as it had been in Cooper's version of the narrative of his old sailor friend Ned Myers the year before, more by the biography of its hero than by contrived situations of suspense. But the "ashore" part of the story strikes a new note. Without the asperity of *Home as Found,* it is a more probing study of ideals, manners, and morals of a type of New York landowner. The plot concerns the courtship of Miles and Lucy Hardinge, member of a neighboring family with somewhat more aristocratic pretensions than those of the Wallingfords. It is not hard to read into this romance, with its idyllic passages and its difficulties and misunderstandings, the social and personal factors which must have operated in the Cooper-De Lancey romance of 1811; and Miles, with his blunt honesty and forthrightness, his recognition of social differences without snobbery or false humility, his love of the sea, and his love for Lucy, is a fair if fictionalized portrait of the youthful Cooper as seen by the elderly. Some of Cooper's most idyllic passages are to be found in these two undeservedly neglected domestic novels of American manners, and his two principals are among his most fully and sympathetically created

characters. The sea passages also reflect a new realism, with a loss of the trappings but not of the zest of romance. And, most important of all if measured in terms of the intentions and hopes of the author, Cooper has at last presented a full-length and unhurried study of his theories of the individual in democratic society.

The Littlepage novels, *Satanstoe, The Chainbearer,* and *The Redskins,* were suggested by the "Anti-Rent War" of 1839–46, but they are a logical consequence of *Afloat and Ashore,* and attempt to follow a family like that of the Wallingfords in detail through four generations, using the techniques of biography and realism rather than a reliance upon plot and action. The Anti-Rent War was a local issue, largely forgotten now by the historians, but important to Cooper because it struck at the heart of democracy. The Van Rensselaer patroonship on the Hudson at Albany, dating from 1637 and still in the hands of the same family, was the scene of the disturbances. Most of its tenants had leases in perpetuity, and the annual rent for a hundred acres varied from ten to fourteen bushels of wheat, plus, for farms of over 160 acres, four fat hens and one day's labor with horse and wagon. In addition, a sale of the lease required that a quarter of the sum received be paid to the patroon. At the death of Stephen Van Rensselaer in 1839, unpaid rents had accumulated to large amounts in many cases and the terms of his will required their payment. The tenants, restless for many years under so un-American a land system, used this demand as a reason for general protest. Writs were served and a local war between sheriffs' deputies and farmers resulted. Troops were called out and offenders punished when the tenants, disguised as Indians, resisted; and it was not until 1846 that the Anti-Renters gained their principal points and the patroon system came to an end.

Cooper held no particular brief for the patroon system as such and the differences between it and the more liberal land theories of his father had come to mean less to him than they did in the early days. The real point at issue was the inviolability of private property, however held or administered. The Anti-Renters defied their contracts established in law, and if they were allowed to do so without restraint, the rights of property owners of all kinds would be threatened. Hence the foundations of his theory of democracy were being undermined, further evidence that the new America had lost sight of its principles and was drifting rapidly toward mediocrity and social disintegration. The only way to point out the error was to follow the stages of development of society from the days of settlement to the present, thereby securing the established order by reference to tradition. This he attempted in the Littlepage trilogy, his most detailed fictional treatment of his matured social views and the best picture of life in early New York that has come down to us from this time.

"It is easy to foresee that this country is destined to undergo great and rapid changes," writes Cooper in the person of Cornelius Littlepage, born May 3, 1737, at Satanstoe (Mamaroneck), Westchester County, New York, and subject of His Majesty, King George II. "Without a stage, in a national point of view at least, with scarcely such a thing as a book of memoirs that relates to a life passed within our own limits, and totally without light literature, to give us simulated pictures of our manners and the opinions of the day, I see scarcely a mode by which the next generation can preserve any memorials of the distinctive usages and thoughts of this." Of combined English and Dutch heritage, and of a family that owned land, Corny is representative of the modest aristocracy of the time. Through him,

Cooper depicts the experiences and discusses the thoughts and feelings of the cultured class in colonial New York. Courage in adversity, chivalric manliness in love, kindliness toward servants, and Christian faith and charity are the chief components of his character. The text of the story is expressed by Mr. Bulstrode in the form of advice to Corny: "There are two sorts of great worlds: the great vulgar world, which includes all but the very best in taste, principles, and manners, whether it be in a capital or in a country; and the great *respectable* world, which, infinitely less numerous, contains the judicious, the instructed, the intelligent and on some questions, the good. Now the first form fashion; whereas the last produce something far better and more enduring than fashion." Throughout his life, Corny acts as a member of this privileged class in a society which freely recognized its right to rule.

In *The Chainbearer,* his son Mordaunt carries on the tradition through a period in which this right is challenged by shifting social conditions. "It must not be forgotten," he warns, "that land was a drug in the State of New York in the year 1784, as it is today on the Miami, Ohio, Mississippi, and other inland streams. The proprietors thought but little of their possessions as the means of present support, but rather maintained their settlements than their settlements maintained them; looking forward to another age, and to their posterity, for the rewards of all their trouble and investments." Thus a moral bond was established between landlord and tenant, which reached beyond their own generation. Tenants who did not respect the rights of their landlords had no rights in return. The story deals with the difficulties of holding land through this period of transition, in the face of depleted values and the inroads of squatters from New England, the latter factor providing most of the narrative interest. As a whole, the novel is less satisfactory than its predecessor, although the character of the old Chainbearer himself is one of Cooper's most successful creations.

A generation is skipped in *The Redskins* and the narrative brought down to the current issue in the person of Hugh Roger Littlepage, thereby becoming more topical and dogmatic instead of entering the third stage when men and things are theoretically supposed to "come within the control of more general and regular laws." As long as the author's social purpose could be used mainly to provide motivation and structure, the story could serve its dual role of narrative art plus instruction. Cooper had apparently learned how to master this formula when he had the advantage of historical perspective on his material; but as soon as he attempted contemporary or nearly contemporary realism, his detachment increasingly gave way to his doctrinaire intentions.

The later novels reflect this tendency to shift from social inquiry to dogmatism as he became increasingly disillusioned with his early hopes for a solution of human problems by human means and, through increasing emphasis on moral absolutes, was drawn rapidly, as Howard Mumford Jones and other recent critics have stressed, into religious commitment. With the Littlepage series his identification with his own past was complete; his social philosophy had become a rationalization of his own personality and family traditions and his efforts to stem the current tide of equalitarianism and vulgarity had apparently been fruitless. With the growing feeling in his later years that the world was against him, the consolation of the religious faith with which he was early associated grew upon him. From Mamaroneck he had driven his family on Sundays to Rye in order to attend the Episcopal church. A quarter of a century later, the faith of that church came back to him with a renewed vitality, and, in July of the year of his death, he was confirmed by his brother-in-law Bishop De Lancey.

It would be a mistake to find in this action any material change of heart. He had concluded *The American Democrat* many years before with a note on religion, in which he said: "As reason and revelation both tell us that this state of being is but a preparation for another of a still higher and more spiritual order, all the interests of life are of comparatively little importance, when put in the balance against the future." As little concerned with sects as with political parties, he had refrained from joining any particular church. The Episcopal church had not been finally established in Cooperstown until 1811, the year of his marriage and settlement far away in Westchester County, and he had been brought up under the influence of a variety of more or less itinerant clergymen. Throughout his writing career he had preferred to preach Protestant ethics in a social context rather than the theological doctrine of any sect. But when the society about him seemed by its actions to deny his social principles, he was forced back upon a theoretical code of ethics as such, and from there the step to a formal theological structure was a short one. Throughout its history, the Church of England had been closely associated with the manner of life of the landed gentry and its American counterpart had not departed far from its predominant attitudes. In it, Cooper found a hospitable refuge for his social views not to be discovered in the secular patterns of American life in 1850. Furthermore, his wife's family, with its Tory traditions, was strongly Anglican, and there was a well-established Protestant Episcopal church in Cooperstown when the Cooper family returned from its European adventures. James Fenimore Cooper, his wife, and his children are buried in Christ Church churchyard, Cooperstown.

This tendency to shift from a social to a theological basis for ethics is apparent in most of the later novels whether they deal with the frontier once more as in *The Oak Openings,* with the sea as in *The Sea Lions* and *Jack Tier,* or with a social problem as in his last novel, *The Ways of the Hour.* But it is in *The Crater,* a capsule allegory of the rise and fall of democratic society, that Cooper reaches his fullest statement of faith in the inexorable will of a Trinitarian God. This is the complete story of a colony founded on a volcanic reef. Mark, its hero, summarizes at the end both the plot and its meaning: "He would thus recall his shipwreck and desolate condition when suffered first to reach the rocks; the manner in which he was the instrument of causing vegetation to spring up in the barren places; the earthquake, and the upheaving of the islands from out of the waters; the arrival of his wife and other friends; the commencement and progress of the colony; its blessings, so long as it pursued the right, and its curses, when it began to pursue the wrong." This was the point at which Mark's rule of benevolent dictatorship of worth was undermined by an ignorant minority's use of the democratic processes. In despair, he recalls his departure, "leaving it still a settlement surrounded with a sort of earthly paradise, and his return, to find all buried beneath the ocean. Of such is the world and its much-coveted advantages. For a time our efforts seem to create, and to adorn, and to perfect, until we forget our origin and destination, substituting self for that divine Hand which alone can unite the elements of worlds as they float in gases, equally from His mysterious laboratory, and scatter them again into thin air when the works of His hand cease

to find favor in His view." Mark's reverie is at once a capitulation of the story, an allegorical interpretation of the history and destiny of both the American people and mankind in general, and a final profession of religious fatalism. Far better than *The Monikins* as social satire, *The Crater* is the novel which, if not his best, is the allegorical statement of the position to which Cooper's complex mind and art had throughout been leading: he had since about 1828 been growing more disillusioned with humanity and its ability to solve moral problems by reason alone. The themes of the ambiguity of right and wrong, the incapacity of man to live up to his ideals, and the vanishing line between reality and illusion, which began to appear in his novels after his return to fiction in 1838 and to dominate them after 1848, were rather the by-products of his own experiences with the press and public than a positive religious awakening. The moral values he had always stressed must be sought in the next world if they cannot be realized in this.

At the same time, English and American fashions in fiction were undergoing radical changes which have only recently been related at all carefully to the changes and experiments in Cooper's development. Scott died in 1832 and *Oliver Twist* and *Twice-Told Tales* both appeared in 1837; by 1848, Thackeray was publishing *Vanity Fair* and Melville his pseudo-travelogues in the South Seas; Cooper's last novel and *Moby Dick* were nearly contemporaneous. We know that Cooper was a wide if not a careful reader, that he knew something of French and German as well as American and English literatures, that he favored fiction, travel narratives, biography, and history and that he was sufficiently anxious about keeping his readership to alter his techniques and forms, if not his convictions, in order to meet changing current tastes. In turning from time to time to realism, the problem novel, and social allegory and satire, he was obviously experimenting with current literary fashions and techniques, at the same time that his mind and feelings were moving from a simple nationalism to deeper social purpose and then to moral conviction.

Wyandotté in 1843 was the first novel to reflect the full force of his disillusionment and surrender to ambiguities. Here for the first time bad Indians are not all bad, good Indians all good, and virtue always rewarded. A hard-bitten realism had pushed aside the idealizations that had sustained his novels through *The Deerslayer* and *The Wing-and-Wing,* a change that was not all loss. One of Cooper's least pleasant novels, it helped to prepare the way for a more realistic treatment of American society and its problems in *Afloat and Ashore* and the Littlepage series and, after the bitterly ironic *Jack Tier* (in many ways, a deliberate reversal of *The Red Rover*), for the symbolism of *The Crater, The Oak Openings,* and *The Sea Lions,* novels that raise the problems which were to provide the substance and the meaning of Hawthorne's and Melville's major works but with which Cooper's techniques and comprehension were inadequate to deal effectively. Experimental right up to the end, Cooper's career during the thirty years 1820–50 was the history of American fiction. He had reached the tragic issue of human destiny, but he lacked the literary means to deal fully and finally with it; he left that task to others.

Cooper's achievement goes far beyond romance but stops short of either realism or symbolism; his best work is in the idiom of the literary principles and fashions which were dominant in his own day. His political liberalism came to a focus during his European residence at the midpoint of his career. On his return, he began to do deliberately what he had been doing all along in stumbling and intuitive fashion, to develop an American novel of manners which was to serve as a commentary as well as a record. To provide this extra dimension of interpretation he applied his romantic theory of the imagination, the raising of literal fact to the level of idealized and generalized truth. That truth then became the ethical absolute which guided the construction of each successive novel and unified them all. The novels which appeared in the period 1840–45, from *The Pathfinder* to *Satanstoe,* vary among themselves but share his achievement of a working balance between the real and the ideal in his art. Perhaps, in the final reckoning, Cooper will be best remembered, not only for the Leather-Stocking tales as he prophesied, but for his pioneering in the realistic novel of social purpose which has become, through the later work of Howells, Norris, Dreiser, and Lewis, the dominant mode of the American novel since his time.

Selected Bibliography

WORKS OF JAMES FENIMORE COOPER

NOVELS
Precaution. New York: Goodrich, 1820.
The Spy. New York: Wiley and Halstead, 1821.
The Pioneers. New York: Charles Wiley, 1823.
Tales for Fifteen. New York: C. Wiley, 1823.
The Pilot. New York: Charles Wiley, 1824.
Lionel Lincoln. New York: Charles Wiley, 1825.
The Last of the Mohicans. Philadelphia: Carey and Lea, 1826.
The Prairie. London: Henry Colburn; Philadelphia: Carey, Lea, and Carey, 1827.
The Red Rover. Paris: Hector Bossange, 1827; Philadelphia: Carey, Lea, and Carey, 1828.

The Wept of Wish-ton-Wish. London: Henry Colburn; Philadelphia: Carey, Lea, and Carey, 1829.

The Water-Witch. Dresden: Walther; Philadelphia: Carey and Lea, 1830.

The Bravo. London: Colburn and Bentley; Philadelphia: Carey and Lea, 1831.

The Heidenmauer. London: Colburn and Bentley; Philadelphia: Carey and Lea, 1832.

The Headsman. London: Bentley; Philadelphia: Carey, Lea, and Blanchard, 1833.

The Monikins. London: Bentley; Philadelphia: Carey, Lea, and Blanchard, 1833.

Homeward Bound. London: Bentley; Philadelphia: Carey, Lea, and Blanchard, 1838.

Home as Found. Philadelphia: Lea and Blanchard, 1838.

The Pathfinder. London: Bentley; Philadelphia: Lea and Blanchard, 1840.

Mercedes of Castile. Philadelphia: Lea and Blanchard, 1840.

The Deerslayer. Philadelphia: Lea and Blanchard, 1841.

The Two Admirals. London: Bentley; Philadelphia: Lea and Blanchard, 1842.

The Wing-and-Wing. London: Bentley; Philadelphia: Lea and Blanchard, 1842.

Wyandotté. London: Bentley; Philadelphia: Lea and Blanchard, 1843.

Afloat and Ashore. London: Bentley; Philadelphia: The author, 1844.

Afloat and Ashore. 2nd ser. (later retitled *Miles Wallingford*). London: Bentley; New York: Burgess, Stringer, 1844.

Satanstoe. London: Bentley; New York: Burgess, Stringer, 1845.

The Chainbearer. London: Bentley; New York: Burgess, Stringer, 1845.

The Redskins. London: Bentley; New York: Burgess, Stringer, 1846.

The Crater. London: Bentley; New York: Burgess, Stringer, 1847.

Jack Tier. London: Bentley; New York: Burgess, Stringer, 1848.

The Oak Openings. London: Bentley; New York: Burgess, Stringer, 1848.

The Sea Lions. London: Bentley; New York: Stringer and Townsend, 1849.

The Ways of the Hour. London: Bentley; New York: G. P. Putnam, 1850.

CRITICAL PROSE AND HISTORY

Notions of the Americans: Picked up by a Travelling Bachelor. London: Henry Colburn; Philadelphia: Carey, Lea, and Carey, 1828.

A Letter to His Countrymen. New York: John Wiley, 1834.

Sketches of Switzerland, Parts I and II. London: Bentley; Philadelphia: Carey, Lea, and Blanchard, 1836.

Gleanings in Europe. London: Bentley; Philadelphia: Carey, Lea, and Blanchard, 1837 (*France*), 1837 (*England*), 1838 (*Italy*).

The American Democrat. Cooperstown, N.Y.: H. and E. Phinney, 1838.

The Chronicles of Cooperstown. Cooperstown, N.Y.: H. and E. Phinney, 1838.

History of the Navy of the United States of America. Philadelphia: Lea and Blanchard, 1839.

Ned Myers. London: Bentley; Philadelphia: Lea and Blanchard, 1843.

Lives of Distinguished American Naval Officers. Philadelphia: Carey and Hart, 1846.

COLLECTED EDITIONS

Cooper's Novels. Illustrated from drawings by F. O. C. Darley. 32 vols. New York: W. A. Townsend, 1858–61.

J. Fenimore Cooper's Works. Household Edition, with introductions by Susan Fenimore Cooper. 32 vols. New York and Cambridge, Mass.: Hurd and Houghton, 1876–84.

The Works of James Fenimore Cooper. Mohawk Edition. 33 vols. New York: G. P. Putnam's Sons, 1895–96.

LETTERS AND JOURNALS

Correspondence of James Fenimore Cooper, edited by James Fenimore Cooper. 2 vols. New Haven, Conn.: Yale University Press, 1922.

The Letters and Journals of James Fenimore Cooper, edited by James F. Beard. 6 vols. Cambridge, Mass.: Harvard University Press, 1960–68.

BIBLIOGRAPHIES

Beard, James F. "James Fenimore Cooper," in *Fifteen American Authors before 1900,* edited by Robert A. Rees and Earl N. Harbert. Madison: University of Wisconsin Press, 1971.

Spiller, Robert E., and Philip C. Blackburn. *A Descriptive Bibliography of the Writings of James Fenimore Cooper.* New York: Bowker, 1934.

Spiller, Robert E., and others, eds. *Literary History of the United States,* Vol. II: *Bibliography.* 3rd ed. New York: Macmillan, 1963.

BIOGRAPHIES

Boynton, Henry W. *James Fenimore Cooper.* New York: Appleton-Century, 1931.

Grossman, James. *James Fenimore Cooper.* New York: Sloan, 1949.

Lounsbury, Thomas R. *James Fenimore Cooper.* Boston: Houghton Mifflin, 1882.

Spiller, Robert E. *Fenimore Cooper: Critic of His Times.* New York: Minton, Balch, 1931.

CRITICAL STUDIES

Bewley, Marius. *The Eccentric Design.* New York: Columbia University Press, 1959.

Clavel, Marcel. *Fenimore Cooper: Sa vie et son oeuvre: La jeunesse (1789–1826).* Aix-en-Provence, France: E. Fourcine, 1938.

Cunningham, Mary E., ed. *James Fenimore Cooper: A Reappraisal.* With an introduction by Howard Mumford Jones. Cooperstown, N.Y.: New York State Historical Association, 1954. (Cooper centenary papers.)

House, Kay S. *Cooper's Americans.* Columbus: Ohio State University Press, 1966.

Lawrence, D. H. *Studies in Classic American Literature.* New York: Thomas Seltzer, 1923. Pp. 50–92.

Parrington, V. L. *Main Currents in American Thought.* New York: Harcourt, Brace, 1927. Vol. II, pp. 222–37.

Pearce, Roy H. "The Leatherstocking Tales Reexamined," *South Atlantic Quarterly,* 46:524–36 (October 1947).

Philbrick, Thomas. *James Fenimore Cooper and the Development of American Sea Fiction.* Cambridge, Mass.: Harvard University Press, 1961.

Ringe, Donald A. *James Fenimore Cooper.* New York: Twayne, 1961.

Smith, Henry Nash. *Virgin Land.* New York: Knopf, 1957.

Walker, Warren S. *James Fenimore Cooper.* New York: Barnes and Noble, 1962.

Waples, Dorothy. *The Whig Myth of James Fenimore Cooper.* New Haven, Conn.: Yale University Press, 1938.

—ROBERT E. SPILLER

James Gould Cozzens
1903-1978

WHEN his first novel, *Confusion*, was published in 1924, James Gould Cozzens was in his twenty-first year and was a sophomore at Harvard College. At the time the Boston newspapers suggested that here was Harvard's reply to *This Side of Paradise* by Princeton's F. Scott Fitzgerald and *The Beginning of Wisdom* by Yale's Stephen Vincent Benét. The novel, however, was not autobiographical in the sense that the other novels were. If its theme was education, it was the education not of a young man rather like the author but that of an exotic young woman with a noble French father and a brilliant British mother. This young woman, Cerise D'Atrée, is at first educated by wise friends of her father and by extensive travels through Europe. After the outbreak of World War I she is taken to New York and exposed to a variety of upper-class American institutions. One of her mentors wonders whether Cerise's sensibility hasn't been so highly developed as to unfit her for life in the modern world, and Cozzens seems to be saying that it has.

Cozzens, born in Chicago on August 19, 1903, grew up on Staten Island, spent six years at the Kent School in Connecticut, and entered Harvard in 1922. While he was still in preparatory school he wrote an article that was published in the *Atlantic Monthly*, and he wrote *Confusion* during his freshman year in college. If he was not so sophisticated as he tried to appear, he was more sophisticated than the majority of college freshmen, and he was already developing an attitude toward life that distinguished him from his contemporaries. He was not concerned with the revolt of youth, of which both Fitzgerald and Benét were exponents, and it is probable that he would have referred to their books, as he later referred to the works of even more distinguished contemporaries, as "kid stuff." In his own immature way he was already a conservative. It would take some time, however, and many books for him to clarify his views and create a style that was appropriate to what he was trying to say. We shall have to proceed novel by novel in order to understand how the author of *Confusion* became the author of *By Love Possessed*.

The publication of *Confusion*, Cozzens has said, went to his head, and he took a year's leave of absence to write another book. This was *Michael Scarlett* (1925), a novel of Elizabethan England, which opens with an adventure at the time of the Spanish Armada. Subsequently Michael attends Cambridge University, where he meets Christopher Marlowe and Thomas Nashe, and later, in London, he enjoys the companionship not only of Marlowe and Nashe but also of Ben Jonson, John

Donne, and William Shakespeare. He is himself a poet of some merit, but he has plenty of time for duels, brawls, and love affairs. Like most of the university wits, he dies an early and violent death.

Although the novel is less serious in intention than *Confusion,* and often descends to romantic claptrap, it seems to grow out of an affectionate feeling for the Elizabethan period and the writers who graced it. Moreover, in the character of Michael, Cozzens made some attempt to portray an ideal aristocrat—a man of letters but also a man of action and a romantic lover. The style is self-conscious and sometimes pretentious, but it does avoid the pseudo-antique language of Maurice Hewlett and other romantic novelists who could have influenced Cozzens. Bad in itself, the book is impressive as a kind of schoolboy exercise.

Instead of returning to college after the completion of *Michael Scarlett,* Cozzens spent a year in Cuba, tutoring the children of American engineers, and out of this experience came his next two novels. *Cock Pit* (1928) is frankly melodramatic and full of violence. The hero is Lancy Micks, chief field engineer for a large sugar company, a man quick with his fists or with a gun, a he-man through and through. His life is threatened in the course of an intra-company feud, and of course he acquits himself valiantly.

The central position in the novel, however, is occupied not by Lancy but by his daughter, Ruth, who is much like him. As a younger girl, she was hot-tempered and uncontrollable: she "had once, in unreasonable fury, horsewhipped a stable boy." Now, after a few years of education in the United States, she has acquired some discipline, but she is still independent, unconventional, and ruthless. (She does not hesitate to have her father's would-be assassin tortured until he reveals his secrets.) Several men find her attractive, but, though she likes male attention, she is in love with no one and perhaps unlikely to be. A wise old man thinks of her as "a clear head working easily among muddled ones."

The style seems less fastidious than that of the earlier books. For one thing, Cozzens goes to great length to avoid "he said": "exploded Lancy Micks," "soothed Mr. Britton," "boomed Mr. Fletcher," "pronounced Mr. Gilbert," "inquired Lancy Micks gently," "urged Mr. Arnold," pleaded Mr. Nortz," "advised Lancy Micks," "snapped Arnold." The dialogue often seems lacking in verisimilitude, and the long conversation that Ruth has at the end with Don Miguel, the big boss, is preposterous.

The second novel about Cuba, *The Son of Perdition* (1929), marks the end of Cozzens' apprenticeship. More firmly written than any of its predecessors, it is also better constructed. All of the characters are believable, and none gets out of hand as Ruth Micks does in *Cock Pit.*

There are two stories, one concerning a group of Cubans, the other a group of Americans. Both themes are introduced in the first four chapters. Pepe Rijo, called Mono Pasmado, "a surprised monkey," is alcalde of Dosfuegos, a town completely under the control of the United Sugar Company. When we meet him, Pepe seems to be demented, his spasm having been brought on by the death of a fellow townsman named Osmundo Monaga, and by the appearance of an American vagabond, Oliver Findley, who Pepe thinks is the devil.

Cozzens drops back to show the events that led up to Pepe's panic, telling first about the Monaga family: Vidal, a proud old fisherman with the virtues of the peasant class; his son, Osmundo, a skillful builder of boats; Osmundo's sister and mistress, Nida. In the end, roused to fury, Osmundo tells his father about the relationship that exists between brother and sister.

The second theme concerns Oliver Findley, well bred and well educated, an alcoholic, a tramp, a sponger, a thief, and a cynic. He meets Joel Stellow, who is dictator over the realm of the United Sugar Company and who decides to help Findley get out of Cuba, believing that he is certain to damage the reputation of all Americans. Findley behaves so badly that Stellow has to take more drastic action. Findley meets Nida, with predictable results, and it is this incident that leads to Osmundo's revelation and his consequent death at the hands of his father.

Stellow is the kind of man Cozzens admires —cool, competent, as indifferent to conventional morality as he needs to be but no more so. An old friend, Dr. Palacios, feels that Stellow has "the strong impersonality and intelligent ruthlessness of which all great men are made." Ultimately, however, Stellow is defeated by the proud integrity of Vidal Monaga and by the inviolable independence of Oliver Findley.

Findley, so far as Pepe and the other natives are concerned, is a feeble sort of fiend, but in Stellow's world he is truly a devil because he cannot be controlled and used. "Wherever you go there'll be trouble," Stellow tells Findley, "and it's not going to be here." By completely rejecting Stellow's values, Findley remains invulnerable. Speaking of the beating his men have given Findley, Stellow says, "You must get a lot out of it to keep on doing it." Findley replies, "I don't 'must' anything. . . . That's one thing I get out of it, Mr. Stellow."

Cozzens does not try to deal with his materials at any great depth. He treats the theme of incest almost casually, and Vidal is allowed to be offhand in describing the horrible manner in which he murdered his son. Findley, for the most part, is an amusing character rather than a demonic one. But Cozzens does certain things well. With only a few details he gives the reader a sense of the power of United Sugar. His characters, including such comparatively minor ones as Dr. Palacios and Fray Alejandro, are endowed with a substantial degree of life, and in the many conflicts that make up the story the opponents are evenly matched. Whatever else may be true, the movement of the narrative is strong and fast.

Cozzens had still to make any strong impression on either the critics or the reading public, but with *S.S. San Pedro* (1931) he reached both, for the short novel was chosen by the Book-of-the-Month Club and was much talked about. It is the earliest book that, in recent years, he has chosen to include in his list of publications. The novel is based on the sinking of the *S.S. Vestris* on November 12, 1928, with the loss of 110 lives. Felix Riesenberg, writing in the *Nation* a fortnight later, called the captain of the *Vestris* "a study of criminal indecision," and continued, "Timidity of almost heroic proportions must have gripped him."

Captain Clendening of the *San Pedro,* who corresponds to Captain Carey of the *Vestris,* is Cozzens' central figure. Cozzens is concerned with the ship, with its officers, to some extent with its crew, and almost not at all with its 172 passengers. Even about the officers we know little except with reference to their performance of their duties. Unlike Thornton Wilder's success of a few years earlier, *The Bridge of San Luis Rey,* which had examined the lives of several victims of a disaster with a view to showing what had gone before, Cozzens focuses firmly on the present.

The novel opens with the kind of succinct statement of precise facts for which Cozzens was to become famous: the tonnage of the *San Pedro,* its destination, its cargo, the number of passengers. After a brief glance at the process of loading the ship, we follow Anthony Bradell, the senior second officer, to the captain's cabin. From the first, emphasis is on Captain Clendening's air of weariness and ill health. He has with him a Doctor Percival, whom he asks Bradell to take around the ship. This gives Cozzens further opportunity to make us acquainted with the ship, but we soon realize that the doctor, who is forbidding in appearance and asks ominous questions, is an intimation of the disaster that lies ahead.

With the ship under way, we see certain officers at their work, particularly Mr. Bradell, whose duties force upon him a reluctant mingling with the passengers. As the night passes, indications multiply that all is not well with the ship. With relentless precision Cozzens describes the coming of the storm and the measures taken to resist it. By the next day Bradell is "extraordinarily tired." "In this state," Cozzens writes in a Conradian passage, "the ocean became almost personified; a purposeful and malicious agent driving its heavy assaults to the unexpected and unguarded points." As the crisis intensifies, it becomes clearer and clearer that the captain is incapable of dealing with it. Bradell does his best, which is not good enough. Clendening fatally delays the order to abandon ship, and when it sinks, he goes down with it. Bradell is presumably saved through the devotion of the quartermaster, a Brazilian of mixed blood, but we know nothing of most of the others on board. Bradell, who has been hit by a boom, recovers consciousness in time to witness the sinking of the ship.

Several early reviewers of the book found it difficult to believe that Cozzens had never been at sea except as a passenger. His willingness to make whatever effort might be necessary to acquire knowledge relevant to his literary aim was to remain one of his distinguishing qualities. If the book is overwhelmingly convincing, it is because the author makes us believe in the omniscience that many novelists assume but fail to validate.

With the air of omniscience goes a kind of objectivity that chills the emotions of the reader, so that one is not greatly disturbed by the calamity. And yet Cozzens exerts himself to make Clendening a sympathetic person. According to the article by Felix Riesenberg, Captain Carey of the *Vestris* was worrying about the profits of the owners, but Cozzens' captain is old and ill and unlucky and much concerned with death. At the outset he wonders "how many more voyages he would be good for, and what would be left then but death, so slow, so horribly swift." As the gale strikes the ship, he says to Bradell, "You don't like going out, boy. Sort of cold. Sort of lonely. Well, we all got to do it." When the ship is foundering, and he is "quietly aware of death like a man beside him," he shrinks from his doom but then a kind of numbness enables him to meet death in the manner prescribed for his profession. Not a heroic character, he is touchingly human.

The only disturbing element in the book is the role played by Doctor Percival. At the beginning, as I have said, we are made to see him as a man of ill omen. Later one of the passengers, the flirtatious Marilee, asks Bradell if the "old gentleman in black" is still aboard. When he tells her that the doctor went ashore, she says, "That's fine. . . . I thought I saw him tonight. He gave me the willies. I'm not fooling you, Bradell. I darn near marched ashore. I'll bet I'll see him in my dreams. You don't suppose he was dead, do you?" And at the end, lying stunned in a lifeboat, Bradell has a vision of a man "in a shabby black overcoat"—"the fleshless face was steady and close, brooding on them." One has to ask whether a symbol such as this is justified in a book that is otherwise so solidly realistic.

With *S.S. San Pedro*, Cozzens was on his way, and it seemed likely that he would travel far, but his readers were not prepared for the stride he took in *The Last Adam* (1933). This is a novel about life in a small town, called New Winton, in Connecticut, but it is not an attack on the small town in the manner of Sinclair Lewis' *Main Street*, which had been published thirteen years earlier. As Cozzens knows and shows, there are skeletons in many New Winton closets, but he takes them as much for granted as the gossip in the post office or the confusion at a town meeting. Although this is one of the best novels about small-town life ever written, the small town is not its principal subject. New Winton is simply the background for a drama of some force, but Cozzens likes to make his background solid, and by this time he knew how to achieve solidity by the economic use of observed facts.

Our introduction to New Winton is by way of a telephone operator named May Tupping. May, it should be pointed out, is not a mere expository convenience but a person whose reflections contribute to the richness of the novel. She is useful, however, and Cozzens skillfully uses her to introduce most of the important characters and to point to certain critical issues. Soon we begin to feel that we know the town. Cozzens' adroit analysis of the class structure might well have been admired by J. P. Marquand. Cozzens knows what is the most important aspect of social distinctions in a small town: "Since no one, by his behavior, gave the faintest sign of considering himself inferior to any one else, these were subtleties you had to recognize by long acquaintance."

But if New Winton is brought to life for us, what really engages our attention is a country doctor, appropriately named Bull. Because Cozzens later wrote a novel about a lawyer and another about a clergyman, critics sometimes said of him that he was making a study of the professions. But *The Last Adam* is not a novel about a doctor in the sense that *Arrowsmith* is. Because his hero happened to be a doctor, Cozzens characteristically acquired enough information about medicine to ensure the accuracy of detail on which he prides himself, but Bull is not and is not meant to be a representative physician, as Cozzens makes clear by contrasting him with the young, up-to-date, fashionable Doctor Verney.

Bull is a maverick, in medicine as in all other ways. He is sensual, malicious, defiant, an unsubduable egoist. No rebel in the ordinary sense, anything but a political radical, he is constitutionally opposed to people in power and to all people who think they are better than other people. He is happily a thorn in the flesh of the Bannings, the town's richest and most pretentious family. Highly vulnerable because of his unprofessional behavior and his defiance of the local sexual mores, he defends himself by striking at his enemies by any means available, and his enemies are numerous. Whatever he does, he does with his whole being, whether he is catching rattlesnakes, making love, cursing out the town fathers, or trying to cope with a typhoid epidemic.

There are other characters of some interest. Herbert Banning is the exact opposite of Bull, a man so reasonable that he is incapable of action. Bullied by his wife, unable to deal with his spoiled, irrational children, he can only meditate upon the reasons for his impotence, but he is not without his admirable qualities. Between Bull and Banning stands Henry Harris, who is no more given to acting on impulse than Herbert Banning but who knows exactly how to act in his own interests and who has become not only well-to-do but also a political force. Cozzens writes of him: "As well as a native, half-knavish wit, his was that careful mean shrewdness by which alone a man can climb, not too visibly soiled, through the sewer-like lower labyrinth of American politics." In the end his wit saves Doctor Bull, not because he loves Bull but because he detests Mrs. Banning.

But of course Bull dominates the book. Janet Cardmaker, his mistress for many years, sums him up: "There was an immortality about him, she thought; her regard fixed and critical. Something unkillable. Something here when the first men walked erect; here now. The last man would twitch with it when the earth expired. A good greedy vitality, surely the very vitality of the world and the flesh, it survived all blunders and injuries, all attacks and misfortunes, never quite fed full. She shook her head a little, the smile half derisive in contemptuous affection. Her lips parted enough to say: 'The old bastard!' "

Unlike other of Cozzens' books, this novel has a good deal of humor—the boisterous humor of Bull, the wisecracking of Henry Harris, the comedy of a school pageant. But what really sets the novel apart is the role played by Doctor Bull. There are plenty of mavericks in Cozzens' work, but usually they come to bad ends, and often they are contrasted with the men of reason who are his heroes. Although Cozzens does justice to the reasonable Herbert Banning, his sympathy—surprisingly, it now seems—is with Doctor Bull.

The year after *The Last Adam,* Cozzens published his least characteristic novel, *Castaway* (1934). The novel, as the epigraph makes clear, is about a modern Robinson Crusoe. A man, never called anything but Mr. Lecky, in flight but we do not know from what, finds himself in the basement of a large department store. Why the store is empty and why it remains empty for the several days covered by the story we are not told either directly or through the thought processes of Mr. Lecky; Cozzens simply asks us to accept the situation as given.

Mr. Lecky's first concern is to protect himself against mysterious and perhaps imaginary enemies, and Cozzens follows in careful detail his search for weapons of defense. As Mr. Lecky goes on to look for shelter and food, we realize how inept he is. He is the modern unself-reliant man; unlike Crusoe, who made so much of little, he has great difficulty in making little out of much. The effectiveness of the early chapters depends on the precision with which Cozzens imagines and portrays the castaway's struggles. Climbing seven flights of stairs becomes an ordeal comparable to the pioneers' crossing of the Rockies.

Eventually there is a Man Friday, footprints and all, but Mr. Lecky, in terror, kills him. As his physical needs are taken care of, the castaway's psychological problems multiply. He is at times lonely, bored, irrationally frightened, reverting to the terrors of childhood. His mind rapidly deteriorates, finally reaching such a state of confusion that the end of the book is difficult to interpret.

On the surface, as has been said, the novel is a portrayal of the helplessness of modern man, dependent on machines that he does not know how to manage. It may also be a parable of the Depression, of a society perishing in the midst of abundance. More fundamentally, however, it is a study of poverty of mental rather than physical resources. Stanley Edgar Hyman has compared the book with Kafka's works, and has said, "It is in the tradition of the American supernatural story, the moral allegories of Hawthorne and Henry James." Cozzens had written nothing like it before and has written nothing like it since.

In *Men and Brethren* (1936), instead of repeating or carrying further the experiment he had attempted in *Castaway,* Cozzens returned to the method he had employed in *The Last Adam*—a realism based on the highly selective use of specific details. It is more accurate to call *Men and Brethren* a novel about a clergyman than it is to describe *The Last Adam* as a novel about a doctor. That is, his being a clergyman is the most important thing about Ernest Cudlipp, whereas the most important thing about Doctor Bull is his rebellious vitality. On the other hand, *Men and Brethren* is a novel about a minister, not, in the fashion of *Elmer Gantry*, a novel about the ministry.

The action in *The Last Adam* takes place in exactly four weeks; the action in *Men and Brethren* takes place in less than two days. They are two crowded days in the life of the Reverend Ernest Cudlipp, vicar of Saint Ambrose's, an Episcopal chapel in a poverty-stricken section of New York City. Let me enumerate the activities in which Cudlipp is involved: (1) He has dinner with an old and rather too affectionate friend, who has quarreled with her husband. (2) He arrives at the apartment of a young woman just in time to prevent her from committing suicide and arranges for her to have an abortion. (3) Back at the vicarage, he talks with his superior, who forbids him to allow a rabbi to speak in the chapel, and with a young assistant who is simultaneously flirting with Communism and Buchmanism. (4) A parishioner, an alcoholic in desperate condition, comes to his office, and he secures help for her. (5) A classmate calls Cudlipp to say that he has broken with the High Church order to which he has been devoted. Cudlipp invites him to spend the night but refuses to talk with him. (6) The next morning he does talk with the man, who is in disgrace because of the discovery of his homosexuality, and gives him sound but unappreciated advice. (7) He secures a Roman Catholic priest for a woman of the neighborhood who is dying. (8) He has to deal with the problems of an irresponsible young poet whom he has tried to befriend. (9) He learns that the woman alcoholic has drowned, probably by intention. (10) He quarrels with the homosexual, who strikes him and calls him a hypocrite. (11) He reads a dull sermon written by his goodhearted but stupid curate. (12) He comforts the woman who has had an abortion.

Cozzens is almost alone among his contemporaries in having written sympathetically about a clergyman. Cudlipp is unconventional enough to worry his superiors, but essentially he is, like Cozzens himself, a conservative. At one time, Cudlipp admits, he was "passionately, priggishly, broad-minded and liberal," but he has got over that. He has had much experience, he tells one of the persons he is trying to help, with "cheap people." "As far as I'm given grace to," he explains, "I try to love them, since in God's sight they are precious. I do what I can for them. It isn't much, because there is usually little to work on. . . . Many of them seem to be simply bad stock, bad blood—just what those things really are doesn't matter. . . . The matter is practical, not theoretical. They have no chance because they are no good. Why they are no good is another matter, not relevant at this point."

For Cudlipp, as for many of Cozzens' heroes, common sense is a major virtue. His argumentative assistant, speaking of a man who has just been jailed, says, "He's the natural product of a society in which property is the source of privilege—until we change that, we won't get anywhere." Ernest replies: "Until we get somewhere, how will we change that? . . . Your friends downtown aren't getting anywhere, Wilber. They're sentimentalists. They don't believe in the doctrine of original sin. Realists are the only people who get things done. A realist does the best he can with things as they are. Don't waste your time trying to change things so you can do something. Do something, do your Christian duty, and in time you may hope things will change." Thinking about the young man, Cudlipp reflects:

"As far as his intention enabled him to be, he was perfect in the first-named fruit of the spirit. What more could you ask of any man? You could ask better sense!"

One cannot very well write about a clergyman without raising theological questions. Of his own religious views Cozzens has said only that he was brought up an Episcopalian. One gets the impression that he is a skeptic but, like Arthur Winner's father in *By Love Possessed*, would think it bad taste to make much of his skepticism. At any rate Ernest Cudlipp is a forthright Christian, and Cozzens appears to respect his orthodoxy. Reflecting on the popularity of Karl Barth's books in the seminaries, Cudlipp decides that "the really valuable thing Doctor Barth did seem to offer was a conception of religious truth which allowed modern-minded young priests like Wilber to recover that sustaining, snobbish ease of mental superiority, loved long since, but, fifty or sixty years ago lost to the clergy for a while. In these well-cut, stylish new clothes, God could be introduced to any company without embarrassment." At the end, talking to the woman who has had an abortion, Cudlipp speaks of his decision to enter the ministry. It had been arrived at by a kind of accident: "In short, the Church gave me an opening." Distressed, she asks if that was all. Smiling, he asks, "Isn't it enough? . . . It seems to me to be. It's the best way to tell it. It can be understood by people who are satisfied with chance as a sufficient cause. To those who have faith in the miraculous and believe that there is a purpose in the world, it is just as purposeful and miraculous as the conversion of St. Paul."

There is another problem that Cozzens has to face and does face: Cudlipp's chastity. Cozzens knows that many readers, under Freudian influence, will suspect that the vicar is at least latently homosexual, and he does not deny this possibility. He speaks of Cudlipp's de-

pendence on his mother, alludes to a rumor that he was "unduly interested in young men," and mentions, though in a tentative way, his "psychological aversion to women." But, since Cudlipp is not overtly homosexual and is chaste, Cozzens is not concerned with what may be going on in his subconscious.

To Cozzens, Cudlipp is simply a man doing a job and, all things considered, doing it well. In this respect he foreshadows the Cozzens heroes to come—Abner Coates, Colonel Ross, and Arthur Winner. He is not quite so stolid as they, but he would like to be.

Before he went on to Coates and the others, Cozzens had in *Ask Me Tomorrow* (1940) another kind of hero to deal with, a very different sort of person and of special interest because he seems to bear some rather intimate resemblance to Cozzens himself. This is Francis Ellery, who, at twenty-three, has written a couple of novels and is living abroad. (Cozzens spent the year 1926–27 in Europe.) Whether or not the novel is in any strict sense autobiographical, we can assume that in it, as in nothing else he has written, Cozzens has made direct use of personal experiences.

So much being true, it is interesting to note that Cozzens did not try to make Ellery an attractive character. When we are introduced to the young man, he is leaving Florence, where he has been living with his mother, to take a job as tutor in Montreux. His mother asks him to look out for a girl named Faith Robertson, who will be on the train. "I wish you could be pleasanter to people, darling," she says. "I think she was rather taken with you the other day." He replies, "I wasn't much taken with her," and goes on, "These musicians! They're all simply insufferable. Like actresses. There's always something wrong with a person who performs in public." Soon after his encounter with Faith, he says, "I think Milan's one of the most boring cities in the world," and since she disagrees, saying, "I always think it's one's own fault if one's bored," they get off to a bad start. She remarks on his touchiness, and says, "Why can't you be natural? . . . Why do you bother to try to cut a figure?" He shows off, making many literary allusions, and she threatens to leave the car when he talks coarsely and scornfully of women. Later they get on better, partly because she knows a girl in Paris, Lorna, in whom he is interested, and he takes her to dinner in Milan. Ellery gets a little tight, and, as Cozzens delicately puts it, "physical urgency flooded his body in a vast impatience, recommending to his mind the idea or image of Miss Robertson's female body." But the urgency is not strong enough to overcome both her reluctance and his. When they separate, she says, "Tomorrow we'd both be sorry. It isn't worth it." He manages to say, in his "lofty manner," "The reflexes have reasons that the heart knows not of," but he realizes that she is right.

The boy Ellery is to tutor is twelve-year-old Walter Cunningham, lamed by infantile paralysis and a victim of asthma. Mrs. Cunningham is rich, well educated, beautifully mannered, and relentlessly domineering. Ellery foresees difficulties, but he likes Walter reasonably well, and Walter likes him. Moreover, Mrs. Cunningham can be kind as well as bossy.

Cozzens makes no effort to conceal or mitigate Ellery's prejudices. When Ellery quarrels with a hotel proprietor, his anger swells "to a blaze of contempt for the whole monkey house of Europe and Europe's mostly undersized, jabbering, mostly not quite clean inhabitants. In this view, all was lumped together, a year's accumulation of passing annoyances and small disgusts—the shoddy posturing bombast of the new Italy . . . La Belle France with its savage avarice and all-pervasive smell of urine; the belching, blockheaded Germans—why should anyone have any patience with any of them?" In a kind of survey of the European scene, Ellery comes to Russia: "Where, for instance, was Trotzky tonight? Francis tried to think of him, too; of the tailor's body like a dwarf in its Cossack's greatcoat, of the hope and fear, the love and hate, behind the screwed-up Jewish comedian's face, brooding (in ever deadlier personal peril as, his great services forgotten, enemies in his party worked to pull him down) on the havocs and ecstasies of the Soviet apocalypse—the Byzantine treachery, the torture chambers, the spies in the wall, the concealed revolvers, the monster parades, the waving red flags, the broken furniture and the frozen plumbing. Like scenes from Gulliver's Travels, all day and all night a double column serried past the mummy of Lenin; and in the factories the moron mechanics sang as they ruined the new machines; and in the fields the peasants like Nebuchadnezzar ate grass; and in crowded halls a thousand commissars shouted speeches; and in a thousand frowzy committee rooms the illiterate architects of the future scratched for lice and made mistakes in arithmetic as they tinkered with their millennium."

The Cunninghams move to the south of France, where Ellery again sees Lorna, but he has little chance to continue the courtship begun in Paris. Through a series of unfortunate incidents, he displeases Mrs. Cunningham, and there is a major crisis when Walter has an almost fatal attack of asthma.

Ellery has grown increasingly impatient with Lorna because he has had no opportunity to talk with her privately, and just before Walter's seizure they have a quarrel, in which, as he immediately realizes, he behaves badly. "It was not by any means the first time that, angry or resentful, he had, for little reason and that not good, said what it was stupid to say and done what it was foolish to do." There is a reconciliation after Walter's crisis, and Ellery asks Lorna to marry him. His words and his manner are not calculated to sweep a young woman off her feet, and Lorna understandably hesitates. Finally, after observing that it's been a hell of a day, she says, "Ask me tomorrow—I mean, if you still want to." But we know and she must know that, once he has had a chance to think calmly about the practical objections to a marriage, he will not repeat his proposal. His well-stocked mind brings consolation from Michael Drayton: "Since there's no help, come let us kiss and part." But they don't even kiss.

Before this, meditating on his degree of responsibility for Walter's condition, Ellery lets "his disgusted mind [wander] its ugly and futile way. He thought of the doctor, whose manner with Walter, whose sympathy and intelligence, had been so different from what Francis wildly expected; and yet (how mean and petty to think of it; how impossible not to notice it) the collar, or neckband, or whatever it was, of the shirt worn under his tunic could be seen inside the uniform collar, and it was greasy with dirt. Recoiling in disgust from human beings, you had to recoil, in another disgust, from your own recoiling; and so it went; and after years of distaste, with little done and nothing not somehow spoiled, you could look forward to the appropriate rewarding of patience or effort. You would be old— like Mr. McKellar, with everything going, so that wit began to labor, elegances grew grotesque or sinister, zest for life creaked at the joints—nearly a joke. And then, perhaps, you could hope to grow into an outright joke, like the Admiral at Grindelwald, with everyone secretly laughing; and then (far past a joke,

a horror) you might enjoy the longevity of that old man, what was his name, his mother's acquaintance. . . ."

These are dark thoughts for a man in his middle twenties, and they are not the expression of a passing mood. It is no wonder that Ellery, just a few minutes later, makes his proposal to Lorna less than romantic. Ellery is not romantic, and even "physical urgency" does not carry him far. At the end of the novel he is again in favor with Mrs. Cunningham, and is running away from Lorna. What will happen to him we do not know; perhaps he will write some good books, and probably he will marry, but not out of passion.

As I have said, Cozzens does not try to make Ellery likable, and Ellery does not even like himself. Cozzens may have been reacting against the glamorous expatriates that figured in the novels of Hemingway and Fitzgerald; this, he may have said to himself, is what life was really like for one American writer in the twenties. Insofar as the novel is autobiographical, it suggests that even at the beginning of his career Cozzens was very different from the writers who have made the decade famous. It also suggests that he was unsparing in self-analysis, that he sought to conceal his faults neither from himself nor from others.

In *The Just and the Unjust* (1942) Cozzens returned to life in a small town, but this time the town was located in eastern Pennsylvania. The hero is a young lawyer, Abner Coates, who has been assistant district attorney for the past four years but has just been given his first opportunity to take part in a murder case. Cozzens describes the courtroom and its occupants, emphasizing how many dull hours there are in a trial, even a murder trial. He then states the facts of the case: four men, none of them a native of Childerstown, kidnaped a dealer in narcotics and killed him;

the leader of the quartet died accidentally while trying to escape from police who in fact were not looking for him; a second man has turned state's evidence; the other two are on trial.

As he had taken the trouble to learn about medicine before he wrote *The Last Adam* and about theology before he wrote *Men and Brethren*, so Cozzens made a careful study of trial law before he wrote *The Just and the Unjust*, and the extent to which he mastered the subject has amazed many lawyers. The legal details may fascinate or may bore the layman, according to his temperament, but he can be sure they are right. Furthermore, Cozzens is not being correct just because he likes to be correct, though obviously he does; it is in terms of these legal details that the novel's essential conflicts are worked out.

Although Cozzens has told us a good deal about the character of Childerstown in his description of the people in the courtroom, he goes further in his account of a barge party that takes place in the evening of the day on which the trial proper has begun. The party is being given by the Calumet Club, of which Cozzens says: "Of the four thousand odd inhabitants of Childerstown, about a hundred belonged to the Calumet Club. About thirty-eight hundred had not the least desire to belong, and if they thought about it at all, laughed not merely at the pretentious sound of calling the dances coming-out parties, but at the idea itself, with the suggestion that the course of nature waited on formal Calumet Club recognition. That left a few people who did have a desire to belong, but had not been asked. Since they considered themselves plenty good enough in all basic or important qualifications they spoke bitterly of those hoity-toity snobs. Calumet Club members thought the accusation of snobbishness absurd. Qualifications for membership were ordinary respectability and education, and some interest in the avowed objects of the club. You did not have to have money, and your grandfather did not have to have been a member. It was not their fault that most of the members were in fact children or grandchildren of former members. It was not their fault that respectability and education so often went with an adequate income. If people with means but no grandparents were congenial they were invited to join; if people with grandparents suddenly lost their means they would certainly not be invited to resign. Since giving parties was now the club's principal activity, it would be silly to have members who didn't fit it. That was all there was to it."

Accompanying Abner on the excursion is the girl he may marry, Bonnie Drummond, whom he has been taking to parties for a long time. At this point Bonnie is rather dissatisfied with Abner, and small wonder, for he is as deficient in ardor as Francis Ellery. Later on his invalid father, Judge Coates, says to Abner: "It's a good thing to be steady and level-headed; but the defect of the virtue can make you seem a little remote, or apathetic. Phlegmatic, maybe. Women don't like it." Obviously Bonnie doesn't like it, but she has been putting up with it for several years.

The party also introduces the reader to Jesse Gearhart, the local Republican boss, whom Abner distrusts as he tends to distrust all politicians. When Jesse asks him if he would like to run for district attorney, Abner is immediately uneasy, feeling that he will have to do errands for Gearhart and his friends. After worrying the point for some time, he takes his doubts to his father. Judge Coates says, "If you want to get away from them [the politicians], you'll have to get away from human society. There wouldn't be any society without them. It's attempted every now and then. Some so-called reform movement made up of people who aren't politicians sometimes wins an election. Either they learn how to be politicians pretty quick, or they don't last." Martin Bunting, Abner's boss and the man he may succeed, tells him, "Standing off and saying you don't like the way things are run is kid stuff."

Meanwhile the trial goes on, not without its surprising developments, and, as usual in Cozzens' novels, there are several secondary themes, all having some relation to the law. In particular there is the matter of a schoolteacher who has persuaded some of his students to pose for him naked. When the editor of the local newspaper tries to use the scandal as an excuse for getting rid of the school principal, Abner's sense of fair play is offended, and he is happy to find that Jesse Gearhart is on the same side. The murder trial ends with a partial disappointment for Abner but he does resolve the problem of Bonnie and the problem of his political future.

As he had long since learned to do, Cozzens shaped the novel with precision and economy. Although the time occupied is only three days, the minor themes as well as the major ones are fully stated, developed, and brought to climax. The tone is lower pitched than in any of the earlier books, perhaps because Cozzens wanted to avoid the sensationalism so often found in fictional accounts of trials. Abner is a quiet, sensible man, almost but not quite bland, and it is not easy to get excited about him, but Cozzens does make him credible.

More explicitly than anything Cozzens had previously written, *The Just and the Unjust* defends the status quo. Abner has none of the rebelliousness to be found in Doctor Bull and, in different forms, in Ernest Cudlipp and even Francis Ellery. Yet he is not an unthinking conformist, as is shown by his distrust of Jesse Gearhart and of politicians in general. He is

a man of conscience who acquires wisdom and learns to be more realistic without becoming an opportunist. He is not unaware of his shortcomings, but recognizes that they are associated with his virtues: "Though a sense of humor was generally spoken of with approval, and a man was pitied for lacking one, Abner supposed that he must lack one himself. When he saw a sense of humor in action, it always seemed to Abner a lucky thing, since somebody had to do the work of an unappreciative world, that a certain number of people could be relied on to lack it."

Although one should not hold Cozzens responsible for the opinions of his characters, it is important to note that all the more admirable characters in *The Just and the Unjust* are conservatives. Abner himself, reflecting on the men he is prosecuting, thinks: "Criminals might be victims of circumstance in the sense that few of them ever had a fair chance; but it was a mistake to forget that the only 'fair chance' they ever wanted was a chance for easy money." Again: "The rank and file [of criminals] could count on little but drudgery and economic insecurity; and for the same reason that most men in lawful pursuits could count on little else. They had no natural abilities, and lacked the will and intelligence to develop any." Martin Bunting, after telling Abner that all reformers are self-seeking crackpots, speaks of Communists. Cozzens continues: "In Cambridge Abner had seen a few people who said they were Communists. Naturally they had not bothered to explain their ideas to Abner. If they had, he would not have known what to say; they seemed queer and set apart, like poets, or homosexuals, so that it was hard to think of them as real people."

It is Judge Coates who has the last word. "Don't be cynical," he tells Abner. "A cynic is just a man who found out when he was about ten that there wasn't any Santa Claus, and he's still upset. . . . There'll be deaths and disappointments and failures," he continues. "When they come, you meet them. Nobody promises you a good time or an easy time." That civilization survives is a miracle, and that is where Abner comes in. "What do you want of me?" Abner asks. And now Judge Coates, man of reason, really does have the last word: "We just want you to do the impossible," he says.

From the beginning Cozzens has not tried to conceal his belief that the majority of people are stupid and incompetent, and he has written almost exclusively about men and women who are superior in one way or another to the masses. The only important exception is Mr. Lecky in *Castaway*, who may be regarded as a common man; but his incompetence is one of the major themes of the book. In his first two novels Cozzens portrayed European aristocrats, first of the present and then of the past; and in the Cuban novels the heroes are marked by their ability to dominate the masses of men. *S.S. San Pedro* shows what happens when a natural leader breaks down, losing the qualities on which his leadership has rested. Doctor Bull goes his own way, fortified by a good-natured contempt for most of his fellow townsmen. Ernest Cudlipp believes it his Christian duty to love "cheap people," but he knows they are "no good," and Francis Ellery, aware as he is of his shortcomings, never doubts that he is a superior person, nor does Cozzens question his assumption.

By the time he wrote *The Just and the Unjust*, Cozzens was clear as to what kind of superior man he most admired—the man of reason. Judge Coates, with his tolerance for human frailty, his realism, his distrust of emotion, his resistance to nonsense and folly, is a prime example of the man of reason. Abner, on the other hand, is only an apprentice, but

he is learning, and in the course of the novel he loses some of the illusions that have kept him from growing up. He will make a man of reason in due time.

Cozzens' next novel did not appear for six years, part of which he spent in the United States Air Force, rising to the rank of major. From this experience came *Guard of Honor* (1948), which is a novel not about combat but about the military under wartime tensions. The scene is an air force base in Florida, called Ocanara, and the action takes place in three days.

Although it is the most complicated of his novels, with a large cast of characters and a great number of subplots, *Guard of Honor* is beautifully constructed, with each part in its proper place. The first chapter introduces many of the principal characters on a plane bound for Ocanara. Cozzens describes the flight with his usual precision, but the plane is important because of its passengers, and what matters is the way they reveal themselves. General Beal, Colonel Ross, Lieutenant Colonel Carricker, Captain Hicks, Lieutenant Turck (WAC), and Master Sergeant Pellerino—these are some of the persons we are to follow through the book, and we know them reasonably well by the time they reach Ocanara. Events connected with their landing precipitate the first of the crises with which the book deals.

General Beal, the principal figure in the principal actions of the book, has to confront these crises. The first arises when, after the landing, Benny Carricker punches a Negro lieutenant. The next day the race problem becomes urgent, and on the last day several paratroopers are drowned in a celebration of Beal's birthday. As Cozzens shows him, Beal is a charming man, almost boyish in manner, a good leader of men, especially in battle, but likely to act on impulse. His closest friend is Colonel Carricker, a war hero, even more impulsive and reckless than the general.

Cozzens does not underestimate the importance in wartime of such men as Beal and Carricker, but he knows that there has to be somebody to pick up the pieces, and that is the part played by Colonel Ross, the character whom Cozzens most admires and with whom he identifies himself. Ross, a judge in civilian life, is a man of reason, and as such he strives to save Beal from the consequences of his follies.

Cozzens often tells us what is going on in Ross's mind, as, for instance, when he has been handling one of his many problems with a caution that he knows he would have scorned twenty years earlier: "Colonel Ross was not sure whether today's different attitude came from being twenty years wiser or just twenty years older. He had, of course, more knowledge of what happens in the long run, of complicated effects from simple causes, of one thing stubbornly leading to another. Experience had been busy that much longer rooting out the vestiges of youth's dear and heady hope that thistles can somehow be made to bear figs and that the end will at last justify any means that might have seemed dubious when the decision to resort to them was so wisely made. Unfortunately, when you got to your end, you found all the means to it inherent there. In short, the first exhilaration of hewing to the line waned when you had to clean up that mess of chips. The new prudence, the sagacious long-term views would save a man from many mistakes. It was a pity that the counsels of wisdom always and so obviously recommend the course to which an old man's lower spirits and failing forces inclined him anyway."

Ross reflects that most men at Ocanara,

and for that matter most people in the world, have not grown up and are engaged in a game of make-believe that they take seriously. "You found it funny or called it silly at your peril. Credulity had been renamed faith. Each childish adult determinedly bet his life and staked his sacred pride on, say, the Marxist's ludicrous substance of things only hoped for, or the Christian casuist's wishful evidence of things not so much as seen. Faiths like these were facts. They must be taken into account; you must do the best you could with them, or in spite of them." His awareness of human fallibility is the foundation of his philosophy: "There never could be a man so brave that he would not sometime, or in the end, turn part or all coward; or so wise that he was not, from beginning to end, part ass if you knew where to look; or so good that nothing at all about him was despicable." Thinking about General Nichols, Beal's superior, who by and large seems to him a wise man, Ross concludes: "To the valuable knowledge of how much could be done with other men, and how much could be done with circumstance, he might have to add the knowledge of how much could be done with himself. He was likely to find it less than he thought."

As he looks back on what he has done in the course of three days to prevent the bad from becoming worse, he thinks that it has been "a near thing, all precarious, all at hazard; no plan for it; and no theory better than anyone's good guess that the Nature of Things abhors a drawn line and loves a hodgepodge, resists consistency and despises drama; that the operation of man is habit, and the habit of habit is inertia. This weight is against every human endeavor; and always the best bet is, not that a man will, but that he won't."

If Ross is in some sense Cozzens' spokesman, there are many other characters in the book, each of them insistent on speaking for himself. Captain Hicks tries to be a man of reason and also tries to be a faithful husband, but he finds himself in bed with Amanda Turck—to the subsequent regret of both of them. Captain Duchemin, on the other hand, moves happily from bed to bed, with not a moment of remorse. And then there is Captain Andrews, a mathematical wizard, deeply and wholly in love with his wife and devastated when he thinks he must lose her.

If Cozzens is almost unique in having written sympathetically about clergymen, he is equally exceptional in treating military men of high rank with respect. Most of his characters are officers, and these officers are not seen through the eyes of a victimized private, as in so many novels of both world wars, but are taken at face value. Like all other groups Cozzens writes about, they are a mixed lot, but their being officers is not held against them.

Guard of Honor was more discussed than any of Cozzens' earlier novels had been, and in some quarters it was extravagantly praised, but there was nothing like the tumultuous reception given, nine years later, to *By Love Possessed* (1957). There were dissentient voices, the most strident being Dwight Macdonald's, but many critics called it a great novel, and within a few months more copies of it had been sold than of all Cozzens' other books put together.

Like Abner Coates and his father in *The Just and the Unjust* and Colonel Ross in *Guard of Honor*, the hero of *By Love Possessed*, Arthur Winner, is a lawyer. While Cozzens had made careful studies of several professions, it appears that the law was the most congenial to his mind, presumably because it seemed to him that the man of reason was given more scope by the law than by any other profession.

The term "Man of Reason," as used by Cozzens, appears for the first time in *By Love Possessed*, and it appears there almost on the first page, when Arthur Winner thinks of his father—"the nearly unique individual; the Man, if not perfectly, at least predominantly, of Reason." He continues: "By his fruits, you knew that man. They, the many accomplishments, were for his father a simple matter. Uncluttered by the irrelevant, uncolored by the emotional thinker's futile wishing and excesses of false feeling, the mere motion of his father's thought must usually prove synonymous with, the same thing as, perfect rightness. Any end being proposed, the Man of Reason considered means. At a glance, he separated what was to the purpose from what wasn't. Thus simply, he determined the one right way to do the thing. You did it that way; and there you were."

The counter-theme has already been stated: "Love conquers all," says the scroll on the gilt clock, and there is a little scene to illustrate the maxim. Winner meditates: "Love pushed aside the bitter findings of experience. Love knew for a fact what was not a fact; with ease, love believed the unbelievable; love wished and made it so. Moreover, here where love's weakness seemed to be, love's strength resided. Itself all unreality, love was assailed by reality in vain."

Thus the issue is stated at the outset: reason versus unreason, otherwise known as love, sometimes called "feeling." For Cozzens, as for everyone else, "love" is a word that has many meanings, and the exploration of some of the meanings is one of the purposes of the novel. Like most of Cozzens' heroes in his later work, Winner is a dispassionate man. More than most men, he has lived his life in the light of reason, and at fifty-four he can legitimately take satisfaction in this achievement. The novel follows him through a period of forty-nine hours, during which he is confronted with what must be, even for him, an unusual number of difficult problems, and we are forced to respect his self-discipline, integrity, generosity of spirit, and wisdom. But Cozzens makes us understand that the life of reason is a constant struggle and that reason can never be fully triumphant.

The victories of unreason multiply as the story proceeds. A girl is brought into court, charged with murdering her newborn, illegitimate child. Young Ralph Detweiler, charged with rape, appears to have been involved with two girls. His older sister, Helen, who brought him up and dotes on him, is the faithful secretary of Winner's senior partner, Noah Tuttle. Because of her irrational devotion to the boy, Helen is thrown off balance, with far-reaching consequences. There is a political conflict and an ecclesiastical row, the latter involving a homosexual.

The irrationality of others, however, does not disturb Winner so much as the failures of his own reason. He thinks of his failure with his son Warren, who savagely rejected his father and to all intents and purposes destroyed himself. Then there are his memories of the summer after his first wife died, when he was involved in a deeply physical affair with Marjorie Penrose, wife of his partner and closest friend. Even in its most controlled form, sanctified both by marriage and affection, the sexual relationship may have unfortunate consequences: having made passionate love, on the night of that first eventful day, to his present wife, he realizes that his daughter by his first wife, whom he is trying to guide rationally through the difficult years of adolescence, has reason to suspect what has been happening.

But the wisdom that Winner hopes he has acquired is put to an even more severe test. Winner discovers that Noah Tuttle, the man he has most admired next to his father as a model of integrity, has for several years been taking money from various funds of which he is trustee in order to protect the investors in a company that has gone bankrupt. Julius Penrose, Winner's pitifully crippled partner and the man he once cuckolded, has kept Tuttle's peculations secret for many years, and urges Winner to do the same. Otherwise, he points out, the aged Tuttle, they and their families, and many others will be injured, and for what good? Arthur, who had thought, less than forty-eight hours earlier, that it was simple for his father to decide what was the right thing to do, now realizes that issues are not so clear and decisions not so easy. He thinks of all the good advice he has given to other people in the past day or two and is now about to disregard, and he is humbled. But even at this moment, as he bitterly recognizes the limitations of reason, it is in reason that he puts his trust; fallible though it is, man has no better guide.

Even for Cozzens, *By Love Possessed* is a remarkably complicated novel, and he has handled the complications with fine craftsmanship, playing one theme against another in the most elaborate and effective kind of counterpoint. Winner's own sexual activities, for example, are compared to and contrasted with Ralph Detweiler's unfortunate experiments; the religiosity of a friend's friend and the mindlessness of a juvenile delinquent are juxtaposed; the reflections of an aged Negro with a heart condition illuminate for Winner experiences of his own and of his friends. Everything is made to count for as much as possible.

Even in the texture of the writing Cozzens goes beyond what he had done before. He has always written with complete clarity and with none of the sloppiness so often associated with what is called "the common style." Here he has developed a more elaborate prose, and, though he sometimes get tangled up in his extremely involved sentences, he often achieves poetic power. He has endowed his principal characters with great articulateness, and, though the dialogue is no more realistic than Henry James's, he persuades us to accept it. A richness of literary allusions widens the implications of the writing, and an unobtrusive, uninsistent use of symbols points to deeper meanings.

Seven years after the appearance of *By Love Possessed* Cozzens published a collection of short stories named *Children and Others* (1964), to which it is not necessary to devote much attention. Of the seventeen stories the volume contains, thirteen were published between 1930 and 1937, most of them in the *Saturday Evening Post*. They originate, then, in the period in which Cozzens was finding himself as a novelist. All of them are competently written, but some are as slick as the paper on which they were originally printed. In particular I am bothered by some of the stories about preparatory school life, which seem to me to affirm conventional prep school values. Much the best is a recent story, not published elsewhere, called "Eyes to See," a perceptive and unusually sympathetic account of the difficult emergence from adolescence.

In 1968 came *Morning Noon and Night*, which, Cozzens has suggested, may be his last novel. ("I feel I've said my say so my only present plan is to shut up," in a postcard to Hicks, April 8, 1972.) It is the first of his novels to be written in the first person, and if in outward events it is no more autobiographical than most of the other novels have been, it may be regarded as a summing up of his views. The man speaking is Henry Dodd Worthington, descendant of New England clergymen, professors, and merchants. At sixty-odd he looks back on his youth, his success as an industrial consultant, his two mar-

riages, his daughter's marital troubles, and so on. He does not present the incidents of his life in chronological order but takes them as they are suggested by the thoughts that move through his mind. The novel might almost be regarded as a meditation on life, death, love, sex, war, business, education, literature, and other matters of importance. Perhaps it is no wonder that the book had a relatively small sale; but, in addition to expounding a philosophy, it does tell a story and it does show us a person. If the person is something of an old curmudgeon, he manages to talk rather amusingly about his foibles.

During his writing career, which has now extended over more than forty years, Cozzens has always stood some distance apart from his famous contemporaries. At the time he began his career the three most influential American novelists were Dreiser, Anderson, and Lewis. Cozzens' work had nothing in common with either Dreiser's clumsy naturalism or Anderson's quasi-mystical preoccupation with the inarticulate, nor did he ever show concern for the kinds of social problems that from time to time they tried to deal with. He has sometimes been compared with Lewis because both wrote of men in the professions, but Cozzens' purpose and method were completely different from Lewis'.

Although he was only a few years younger than Fitzgerald, Dos Passos, Hemingway, Faulkner, and Wolfe, his interests were not like theirs. He was never a rebel, as all of them were in one way or another. Except in *Castaway* he did not experiment with the form of the novel. He almost always wrote about man in society, not the isolated individual, usually modeled after his creator, who played so important a part in the fiction of Hemingway and Wolfe. Of the five, he was closest to Fitzgerald, who, in *The Great Gatsby* and *Tender Is the Night*, did write about man in society, but the differences in temperament were so great that the men appeared to be living in different worlds.

Except for his early romantic novels and the experimental *Castaway,* Cozzens has stayed within the bounds of the traditional social novel. Like Jane Austen, George Eliot, Anthony Trollope, Henry James, and Edith Wharton, he takes the social structure for granted, neither attacking nor defending the status quo. As a true conservative, he does not believe that whatever is is right, but he is convinced that, people being what they are, any change is likely to be a change for the worse. In any case he is not much interested in society as such but as a frame within which individuals perform their roles. Recognizing that man is a gregarious animal, he believes that men reveal themselves most fully in society.

It is often said that the traditional social novel requires a compact, homogeneous society and that such a society does not exist in the United States. In a sociological sense the latter statement is probably true, but for literary purposes serviceable substitutes may be found, as Marquand, O'Hara, and Auchincloss have shown. Cozzens has not limited himself geographically, but he has made a particular segment of the American people, the upper middle class, his kingdom. His predilection became clear in the two novels about Cuba, but it was not until *The Last Adam* that he staked out a field for himself. His small Connecticut town gave Cozzens as wide a range as he needed. There are some members of the working class, not given much prominence but treated with respect, and there are the incompetents, the bums, the *Lumpenproletariat.* But the principal characters are Doctor Bull, who, in spite of his recalcitrancy is a member of the middle class by virtue of his profession, and Herbert Banning, who, whatever his wife might like to think, is still within the middle class, though in its highest bracket.

Men and Brethren is set in New York City, but both its geographical range and its social span are narrow. Childerstown in *The Just and the Unjust* and Brocton in *By Love Possessed* seem ideally suited to Cozzens' purposes. They are small cities rather than small towns, with a considerable upper middle class, made up of lawyers, doctors, clergymen, bankers and a few well-to-do persons engaged in unspecified businesses. Most of these men and women belong to the older families of the community, and there are ties of kinship as well as of long-established social intimacy. The existence of the respectable working class is recognized, but its members are not important in the development of the story. Even in *Morning Noon and Night,* whose hero-narrator is a successful industrial consultant, his operations are barely sketched, and nothing is done with his powerful clients. When he can afford to, moreover, he transfers his office from the city to the small town in which he grew up.

It is clear that Cozzens has no interest in farmers or factory workers, whatever the color of their collars. He has no interest in the very poor, as Dreiser and Anderson had, as Bellow and Malamud have. What is more surprising, he has no interest in the very rich and the very powerful. There are no big bankers or big industrialists in his novels, and the only politicians are on the county level. The great political crises of the past three decades are almost completely ignored, and in *Guard of Honor* the war itself plays little part. Indeed, Cozzens observes, with sardonic intent, that the conscientious Colonel Ross sometimes thinks about the purpose and progress of the war, which makes him almost unique on the base.

I am not complaining about Cozzens' limitations—even Balzac and Tolstoi were limited—but I am trying to define them. All his major characters and most of his minor ones are white Anglo-Saxon Protestants. I shall comment later on his treatment of Negroes, Jews, and Catholics, but for the moment it is enough to say that they are given minor roles. If Cozzens manages to create a more or less homogeneous society, such as he needs for the sake of the kind of novel he wants to write, he does so by thrusting away from him large segments of the American people.

Cozzens has to believe, as he does believe, that the people he writes about are the people who, in broad social and moral terms, most deserve his attention. He can believe this because he is a conservative. What the man of reason, the wise man, does, as we have seen again and again, is to accept the status quo, not because it is perfect but because it is what we have to work with. Cozzens has only contempt for radicals and reformers. Ernest Cudlipp ridicules the assistant who flirts with Communism. Judge Coates and District Attorney Bunting knock the idealistic nonsense out of Abner's temporarily muddled mind. Lieutenant Edsell, the self-styled "liberal" in *Guard of Honor,* is a fool and a hypocrite. The "liberals" who attend a writers' conference described in *Morning Noon and Night* are incompetent and silly.

In 1942, in one of his rare personal statements, Cozzens wrote in *Twentieth Century Authors*: "My social preference is to be left alone, and people have always seemed willing, even eager, to gratify my inclination. I am more or less illiberal, and strongly antipathetic to all political and artistic movements. I was brought up an Episcopalian, and where I live the landed gentry are Republican." One gets the impression, however, that he takes his Republicanism no more seriously than his Episcopalianism. As John Lydenberg has observed, it is difficult to imagine Cozzens as an enthusiast for either Eisenhower or Nixon, and it is even more difficult to believe that he was an admirer of Goldwater, though he may have voted for him.

Cozzens has sometimes been accused of anti-Semitism and segregationist sympathies. When, in *By Love Possessed*, a Jewish lawyer comes to Brocton, Noah Tuttle is outspokenly anti-Semitic, but his outburst is regarded by his associates as a diplay of bad manners. Arthur Winner's prejudice against Jews is milder and is courteously concealed from Mr. Woolf, but it does exist, and it may be that, in this as in other matters, Winner speaks for Cozzens. Whether that is true or not, it must be remembered that in the long run Woolf is seen in a favorable light.

In the same novel members of a Negro family, the Reveres, know their place, and Winner admires them for this. Critics have objected to a passage in which Cozzens tells, with approval, that Alfred Revere, who was sexton of the Episcopal Church, never took communion until the last, lest he offend white members of the congregation. But what Cozzens approves is Revere's tact, not the prejudices of the whites.

The race question is central in *Guard of Honor,* both because the base is a southern town and because a group of Negro flyers is being trained at Ocanara. Most of the white officers are full of prejudice, talking constantly of "niggers," "dinges," and "jigaboos," and one is an articulate white supremacist. The only spokesman for the other side is the obnoxious Lieutenant Edsell, who does nothing but discredit his cause. But, though the segregationists seem to have the better of the argument, Cozzens has said that he does not believe in segregation. On the other hand, he does believe that one must always face facts, however unpleasant, and in the South racial prejudice is a fact. "We are having a little trouble with some Negro officers," Colonel Ross tells his wife. "They feel they are unjustly treated. I think in many ways they are; but there are insurmountable difficulties to doing them justice." In an interview that appeared in *Time,* Cozzens is said to have said, "I like anybody if he's a nice guy, but I've never met many Negroes who were nice guys." For that matter, he seems not to have met many white men who were nice guys. The point is that he is guilty of snobbishness rather than discrimination against Negroes.

Cozzens has also offended many Catholics. It seems clear that, though he may accept the Episcopal Church as a useful social institution, he finds religion in general full of superstition and sentimentality, and in particular he dislikes the Roman Catholic Church. "Regard that overweening hierarchy," Winner thinks; "above those mostly poor-boy bishops, elated by their local power, those impudent princes of the church—this plump, canting pudge of an eminence here; this malapert, threatening ignoramus of an eminence there! Regard that state within a state . . ." and he goes on with his indictment. To be sure, these are Winner's thoughts, not necessarily Cozzens', but Arthur's opponent, Mrs. Pratt, is quite simply a fool.

Despite whatever lip service he may pay to Episcopalianism, Cozzens appears to be a secularist of a Stoic sort. Not merely in *By Love Possessed* but in every one of his novels the role of chance is emphasized: Cerise's death in *Confusion,* the exposure of incest in *The Son of Perdition,* the typhoid epidemic in *The Last Adam,* the capture of the gangsters in *The Just and the Unjust,* the death of the parachutists in *Guard of Honor.* Fate, he points out again and again, does not play fairly with us. But he does not repine, he does not protest; he

simply affirms that man must prepare himself for the worst that fate can bring. He can say with Hamlet, "The readiness is all." He might also say with Thomas Hardy, "These purblind Doomsters had as readily strown/Blisses about my pilgrimage as pain." And Henry Worthington in *Morning Noon and Night* goes out of his way to emphasize the fact that he has been the beneficiary of a series of lucky breaks.

If nothing else distinguished Cozzens from the majority of his contemporaries, his treatment of sex would do so. In a manner of speaking, sex was discovered, for literary purposes, in the period to which Cozzens belongs: Lawrence and Joyce and Proust and most of the people who have been writing novels since them have given the sexual act a central importance it had not had in literature since the Restoration and in a way had never had. That the sexual drives are powerful Cozzens recognizes, but he seems to deny what might be called the philosophical significance of sex. In *By Love Possessed,* Winner and his second wife have sexual intercourse very pleasantly, and Cozzens describes their physical sensations in some detail, as if to prove that he, too, knows what it's all about. But for most of the characters in the novels, including Winner at one time of his life, the sexual impulse leads to disaster. Janet Cardmaker and Doctor Bull have been carrying on illicitly and happily for many years, but Bull attributes the success of the affair to the fact that it is not "at all an emotional matter." Abner Coates in *The Just and the Unjust* triumphs over his sexual impulses, but it doesn't seem much of a battle. Captain Hicks and Amanda Turck finally go to bed together, but with no great pleasure on either side. Moreover, as Stanley Edgar Hyman has pointed out, homosexuality, sadism, incest, and a kind of necrophilia are scattered through the novels. Certainly Cozzens has a right to make all he can of the less pleasant aspects of sexual experience, which have often been overlooked by novelists intoxicated with the "new freedom," but the length to which he carries his antiromanticism may be significant.

It should also be noted that few of his characters are capable of strong emotions of any kind. To be sure, he does not approve of strong emotions, but they do exist, and Shakespeare, for instance, to whose writings Cozzens is constantly alluding, was much concerned with men and women who were overcome by them. One cannot imagine Cozzens creating a Lear, a Macbeth, an Othello, or an Antony—or, for that matter, a Captain Ahab or a Joe Christmas.

Cozzens is also surprisingly indifferent to artists and the arts. Cerise in *Confusion* is educated in all the arts, and several of the characters in *Michael Scarlett* are poets, but since then Cozzens' characters, except for the more or less autobiographical Francis Ellery, have had no interest in creating art and not much in exposing themselves to it in any form. Arthur Winner, it is true, has read more widely than one would expect of a busy lawyer, but most of the writers he refers to lived before or soon after 1800. (Cozzens himself says that his models are Shakespeare, Swift, Steele, Gibbon, Jane Austen, and Hazlitt.) In 1957 *Time* wrote of Cozzens: "It is seventeen years since he and his wife saw a movie, more than twenty since they went to a theater, to a concert or an art gallery." According to the same source, he has only contempt for Hemingway, Steinbeck, Lewis, and Faulkner.

Within his limitations, which, as we have seen, are considerable, Cozzens has built a formidable career. To the traditional social novel he has brought many attributes, in particular a concern with compactness and density. By the time he wrote *Cock Pit,* he was learning to tighten his structure for the sake of dramatic effect, and in *The Son of Perdition*

he skillfully managed the simultaneous development of two themes. In *S.S. San Pedro* he produced a sparse, rapid narrative but at the expense of depth of characterization. In *The Last Adam,* which covers exactly four weeks, he achieved depth, complexity, and compactness. In *Men and Brethren* the actions are quite as complicated and the span of time, less than two days, even shorter.

It is in the later novels, however, that Cozzens has brought his method close to perfection. *The Just and the Unjust* is limited to the few days required for the trial, but in those days many things happen that tell us much about the characters. The action of *Guard of Honor,* which, we have seen, is extremely complex, takes place in three days, and the action of *By Love Possessed* in forty-nine hours. Cozzens seems to be trying to do more and more in shorter and shorter periods of time. Each of the major characters in the later novels has a past as well as a present, and one is impressed by the way in which Cozzens, without much reliance on formal flashbacks, endows each man and woman with a history, at the same time that he explores the tangled relationships of both people and events.

According to Frederick Bracher's *The Novels of James Gould Cozzens,* Cozzens, in a letter to his English publisher about *Guard of Honor,* said: "What I wanted to write about here, the essence of the thing to be said, the point of it all, what I felt to be the important meaning of this particular human experience, was its immensity and its immense complexity. . . . I could see I faced a tough technical problem. I wanted to show . . . the peculiar effects of the inter-action of innumerable individuals functioning in ways at once determined by and determining the functioning of innumerable others—all in the common and in every case nearly helpless involvement in what had ceased to be just an 'organization' . . . and become if not an organism with life and purposes of its own, at least an entity, like a crowd." This was the kind of problem that by now he had learned to solve. The sense of complexity that John Dos Passos tried to render by a series of experimental devices in *U.S.A.* Cozzens came close to achieving within the form of a traditional novel.

Although he has never acknowledged a debt to Henry James, Cozzens has come to be as much concerned with the matter of point of view as the master himself. At first he wasn't, and he shifted his point of view without much plan. In *The Last Adam*, however, he relied chiefly on the point of view of Doctor Bull, but entered other minds as circumstances demanded. In *Guard of Honor* the consciousness of Colonel Ross is central, but the point of view moves about so that various themes can be developed simultaneously. In *By Love Possessed,* on the other hand, we enter no consciousness but Arthur Winner's, and Cozzens' success in telling so complicated a story from a single point of view might have won Henry James's admiration, and so might his successful handling in *Morning Noon and Night* of most of the problems inherent in first-person narrative.

Cozzens' style in his first two novels was lush and pretentious in a juvenile way, but by the time he wrote *Cock Pit* and *The Son of Perdition* he was capable of a competent, straightforward prose, and in *S.S. San Pedro* his style was disciplined and quite adequate to the demands put upon it. In *Castaway*, as Stanley Edgar Hyman pointed out almost twenty years ago, Cozzens made a great advance stylistically, achieving a distinction of which his earlier work had shown little promise. To prove his point, Hyman quotes from this novel part of "a dissertation on the types of mania": "Let the man you meet be, instead, a paretic. He has taken a secret departure from

your world. He swells amid the choicest, most dispendious superlatives. In his arm he has the strength to lift ten elephants. He is already two hundred years old. He is more than nine feet high; his chest is of iron, his right leg is silver, his incomparable head is one whole ruby. Husband of a thousand wives, he has begotten on them ten thousand children. Nothing is mean about him; his urine is white wine; his faeces are always soft gold. However, despite his splendor and his extraordinary attainments, he cannot successfully pronounce the words: electricity, Methodist Episcopal, organization, third cavalry brigade. Avoid them. Infuriated by your demonstration of any accomplishment not his, he may suddenly kill you."

Cozzens' writing has rarely been as imaginative as this, but there have been important developments as the years have gone by. His style in *Men and Brethren, Ask Me Tomorrow,* and *The Just and the Unjust* is unpretentious, sometimes slightly formal, always highly polished. He often says things neatly, and his figures of speech are sometimes effective, but on the whole his style is unobtrusive, almost transparent. All this begins to change in *Guard of Honor* and changes greatly in *By Love Possessed*. His sentence structure becomes more complicated, and his language more exotic—though he has always been fond of unusual words. His prose is no longer transparent, nor does he want it to be.

It was the style of *By Love Possessed* that Dwight Macdonald attacked most vehemently. He was not wrong all of the time, for a few of the sentences he quotes are awkwardly put together or unnecessarily involved, but much that he condemns is, in context, perfectly sound, and he ignores the many bold experiments in the use of language that prove successful. On the whole, I prefer the style of *Guard of Honor* to that of *By Love Possessed,* but the latter has virtues that should not be overlooked. In *Morning Noon and Night* the use of the first person sanctions a degree of eccentricity, but in general Cozzens avoids excesses and lets his man speak for himself in what can be felt as an appropriate voice.

Frederick Bracher has written: "The best of Cozzens' works are evidence that the traditional social novel, with its high seriousness and moral urgency, is still viable in a period of experiment and disorder." This much is surely true. Cozzens has made the traditional novel an effective medium for the expression of his vision of life. That other novelists, with other methods and other aims, have made revelations about the human condition that seem more valuable to some of us than anything we find in his work should not persuade us to underestimate the substance and validity of what he has done.

Selected Bibliography

WORKS OF JAMES GOULD COZZENS

Confusion. Boston: B. J. Brimmer, 1924.
Michael Scarlett. New York: Boni, 1925.
Cock Pit. New York: Morrow, 1928.
The Son of Perdition. New York: Morrow, 1929.
S.S. San Pedro. New York: Harcourt, Brace, 1931.
The Last Adam. New York: Harcourt, Brace, 1933.
Castaway. New York: Random House, 1934.
Men and Brethren. New York: Harcourt, Brace, 1936.
Ask Me Tomorrow. New York: Harcourt, Brace, 1940.
The Just and the Unjust. New York: Harcourt, Brace, 1942.
Guard of Honor. New York: Harcourt, Brace, 1948.
By Love Possessed. New York: Harcourt, Brace, 1957.
Children and Others. New York: Harcourt, Brace & World, 1964.
Morning Noon and Night. New York: Harcourt, Brace & World, 1968.

BIBLIOGRAPHY

James B. Meriwether. "A James Gould Cozzens Check List," *Critique,* 1:57–63 (Winter 1958).

CRITICAL AND BIOGRAPHICAL STUDIES

Bracher, Frederick. "James Gould Cozzens: Humanist," *Critique,* 1:10–29 (Winter 1958).
———. *The Novels of James Gould Cozzens.* New York: Harcourt, Brace, 1959.
———. "Of Youth and Age," *Pacific Spectator,* 5:48–62 (Winter 1951).
Hicks, Granville. "The Reputation of James Gould Cozzens," *College English,* 11:177–83 (January 1950).
Hyman, Stanley Edgar. "James Gould Cozzens and the Art of the Possible," *New Mexico Quarterly,* 19:476–98 (Winter 1949).
———. "My Favorite Forgotten Book [*Castaway*]," *Tomorrow,* 7:58–59 (May 1957).
Lydenberg, John. "Cozzens and the Conservatives," *Critique,* 1:3–9 (Winter 1958).
———. "Cozzens and the Critics," *College English,* 19:99–104 (December 1957).
Macdonald, Dwight. "By Cozzens Possessed," *Commentary,* 25:36–47 (January 1958). (Reprinted in *Against the American Grain.* New York: Vintage, 1965. Pp. 187–212.)
Ward, John W. "James Gould Cozzens and the Condition of Modern Man," *American Scholar,* 27:92–99 (Winter 1957–58).

—GRANVILLE HICKS

Hart Crane

1899-1932

IN "Words for Hart Crane" Robert Lowell called Crane *"Catullus redivivus"* and "the Shelley of my age"; in a *Paris Review* interview he said: "I think Crane is the great poet of that generation. . . . Not only is it the tremendous power there, but he somehow got New York City: he was at the center of things in the way that no other poet was. All the chaos of his life missed getting sidetracked the way other poets' did, and he was less limited than any other poet of his generation. There was a fullness of experience. . . ." As the major poet of a later generation, Lowell speaks with authority, and he expresses an opinion that seems to be increasingly prevalent.

In life and in poetry, Crane was intense, extreme, and uncompromising; he is as effective a flutterer of dovecotes as Catullus or Blake or Rimbaud. He challenges the imagination and compels judgment; no tepid response either to him or to what he stands for is possible. He was unquestionably a man of principle, whatever the merit of his principles. (His severest critic called him "a saint of the wrong religion.") Precisely what was wrong with these principles, aesthetic and religious, was defined early and very fully by several of our most brilliant critics. This was a necessary task, for certainly Crane was a dangerous model and an example variously instructive. Forty years

after his death, however, he has been so disinfected by the passage of time that he is hardly likely to spread any contagions, and it seems more profitable now to focus attention on his achievement than on the nature and significance of his failure. Allen Tate, the finest of the critics who defined Crane's errors, recognized this in adding to his essay "Hart Crane" an "Encomium Twenty Years Later" celebrating Crane as "a great lyric poet" and "our twentieth-century poet as hero."

Crane has been the hero of many cults, on grounds often both dubious and inconsistent. Homosexuals naturally canonized him and made him their patron, as St. Hart the Homintern Martyr (to adapt the title W. H. Auden once gave to Wilde). But Allen Tate, his close friend, calls him "an extreme example of the *unwilling* homosexual" and observes that he was never alienated in the sense of rejecting the full human condition, any more than his poetry rejects the central tradition of the past. Patriots and optimists have sometimes hailed him as the Pindar of machinery, the modern Whitman who celebrates America and proves that our civilization is no Waste Land but a triumphant Bridge. Crane did harbor such aspirations, intermittently, but he was not taken in by them. Social critics from Marxist to Beat have made Crane's "crackup," like that of F. Scott Fitzgerald, a type of the fate of the writer in modern America. Crane does indeed exhibit all the pressures of our civilization in their most extreme form, though he also furnishes an almost embarrassingly obvious case history for the psychological critic. Finally, Crane has been adulated by the followers of all kinds of poetic unreason; much fake poetry has been perpetrated in his name, and increasingly of late he has been used as a stalking-horse by the Neo-Romantics. It is true that Crane expounded and sometimes practiced a kind of irrationalism or mysticism, as we shall see; but it is also true that he was a meticulous craftsman, seeking not to break with but to follow the central tradition in poetry, and he strove to eliminate obscurity.

Crane's poetry has, then, provided the text for many sermons and the ground for many controversies. The essential fact is, however, that it is still alive as poetry, that it still speaks powerfully both to readers encountering it for the first time and to those who go back to it. Its influence on Allen Tate, Robert Lowell, Dylan Thomas, and many lesser figures is plain. Now, some forty years after his suicide, we can say that his work survives all the contemporary disputes and passions, and that in spite of its small bulk and its obvious limitations and defects, it will remain among the permanent treasures of American poetry in the twentieth century.

Because Crane's life was spectacular and portentous, it tends to distract attention from his poetry. The biographical approach to the poetry is misleading; it gives chief prominence to Crane's personal disintegration and his unsuccessful attempt to create a myth. But these are not the central issues in his work, which like all true poetry has a life of its own apart from the poet. I shall therefore confine myself to a short biographical summary before considering the poetry.

Harold Hart Crane was born in 1899 in Ohio, into the midwestern small-town cultural milieu satirized by Sinclair Lewis and so many others. He was an only child and the product of a broken home; his childhood was dominated by the tension between his parents, who first separated in 1909, when Hart was ten, sending him to live with his maternal grandmother. His father, a hard-headed businessman highly successful in the manufacture of candy and in other enterprises, was remote from his son and showed him small understanding or sympathy. The mother enveloped and dominated him, turning him bitterly against the father and dragging him through all their quarrels (he said later that his childhood had been a "bloody battleground" for his parents' sex lives). This classic Oedipal situation was no doubt the basis of his homosexuality and his other psychological peculiarities. After quarrels, separations, and temporary reconciliations spanning Hart's childhood and early adolescence, the parents were finally divorced, and both later remarried. Hart had, of course, taken his mother's side throughout the quarrels—he had traveled with her through the West and to the Isle of Pines, south of Cuba—and after the divorce he symbolically truncated his name, using the maternal surname "Hart" as his first name and thus rejecting the father who had rejected him. In 1916, at the age of seventeen, he abandoned high school and went alone to New York to live. In this year he had published his first poem and prose piece (he had begun to write three years before), and he now committed himself irrevocably to poetry as a vocation.

Crane emerged from this background emotionally crippled, morbidly overstimulated, rootless, and unable ever to adjust to a "normal" pattern of living. Like most Americans, he cherished the notion of making quick money by writing a movie scenario or a popular story or novel; but aside from brief periods working in bookstores, in his father's factories and candy stores, and as a salesman, his closest approaches to success in earning a living were as an advertising copy writer—a profession chiefly dedicated to the debasement of language and the deception of the public. New York, citadel and symbol of the pressures toward rootlessness and alienation, was inevitably the place he would live most of the time, and partly in the underground world of the homosexual.

When Crane went to New York in 1916, one of the books he took with him was Mary Baker Eddy's *Science and Health with Key to the Scriptures*. Both his mother and grandmother were fervent advocates of Christian Science, and although Hart did not remain a believer in it as a religion for long, he remained convinced of its psychological efficacy. He wrote in 1919: "What it says in regard to mental and nervous ailments is absolutely true. It is only the total denial of the animal and organic world which I cannot swallow." His training in this faith, with the influence and example of the two people to whom he was closest, had a lasting effect on him. Born out of the union of American transcendentalism and American hypochondria, Christian Science holds that states of consciousness are the only reality, that matter is unreal, that all causation is mental and apparent evil the result of erring belief. Crane's predisposition to optimism and irrationalism and his later pseudo-mystical strivings for the "higher consciousness" undoubtedly owe much to his early background.

A similar and perhaps even more powerful influence in the formation of his aesthetic and religious attitudes was his early study of Plato. According to Philip Horton, Crane's earliest biographer, he underscored doubly with red ink the passages on the necessity of madness in a true poet, and the Platonic concept of a progression upward from earthly beauties in a search for absolute beauty became fundamental to his thought. Nietzsche, about whom Crane wrote an article as early as 1918, also played an important part in his development. Nietzsche's antiphilistinism, his exaltation of the artist, and his celebration of Dionysian joy appealed strongly to Crane and merged with other powerful currents. One such was the *Tertium Organum* (first published in the United States in 1920) of P. D. Ouspensky, a rhapsodic and pseudo-mystical work from which Crane took the phrase "higher consciousness," and which advocated the Dionysian type of mystical experience and the artist as guide to spiritual truth. Other currents in the mystical and pantheistic stream were the Bengali poet Rabindranath Tagore, whom Crane met in Cleveland in 1916, and such visionary and antirational poets as Blake, who exerted a powerful and continuing influence on Crane, and Rimbaud, whose disciple and heir Crane early came to consider himself.

Counterbalancing these powerful tendencies toward irrationalism, mysticism, and occultism was Crane's relation to his American literary heritage. When he was fifteen he spent several weeks at the establishment of Elbert Hubbard, a highly successful purveyor of culture and homely philosophy to the American public; as one of Crane's biographers, Brom Weber, puts it, he "capitalized upon the contradictory and confused American temper at the turn of the century by clothing materialism with an atmosphere of romance and culture." But, if he contributed to Crane's decision to go into advertising and his belief that he could somehow make money out of literature, he also helped to acquaint Crane with the classic American poets. Crane recognized early, at a time when it was by no means the truism it is now, that the great American writers were

Whitman, Melville, Dickinson, and James, with Poe as progenitor and type. (He seems not to have been aware of Hawthorne.) Through Mrs. William Vaughn Moody, who befriended him, he became acquainted with some of the new writers and the "little magazines" that were their chief media of publication; and he also knew the older generation of writers such as Sherwood Anderson, Lindsay, Masters, and Sandburg.

Though Crane was from the beginning intensely aware of the new movements and the emerging writers, and though Pound and Eliot were soon to become his chief mentors, it is curious and interesting that the dominant influences on his early poetry (roughly 1916–20) were Swinburne, the early Yeats, and especially Wilde, Dowson, and the other "Decadents." *Bruno's Weekly* and *Bruno's Bohemia* frequently reprinted the works of Dowson and Wilde and praised Wilde's life and writings; Crane's first poem, called "C 33" (Wilde's designation in Reading Gaol), appeared in the former in 1916 and his "Carmen de Boheme" in the latter two years later; both are, as the titles suggest, *fin de siècle* in spirit and conventional in form. Crane's first published prose, a letter to *The Pagan* (1916), reveals the way ninetyish aestheticism and the "new" coexisted harmoniously in the literary awareness of the time. He said, "I am interested in your magazine as a new and distinctive chord in the present American Renaissance of literature and art. Let me praise your September cover; it has some suggestion of the exoticism and richness of Wilde's poems." New York in the winter of 1916–17 was especially exciting, not only because of the war, but because the literary "American Renaissance" of which Crane spoke was at its height. Since the founding of *Poetry* by Harriet Monroe in 1912 numerous "little magazines" had been established and many anthologies, as well as volumes by in-

dividual poets, had appeared. There had been much agitation about Imagism, with Amy Lowell taking over the movement from Ezra Pound. In 1917 Pound transferred his allegiance from *Poetry* to the *Little Review*, which had just moved from Chicago to New York; thenceforth the *Little Review* followed his cosmopolitan aim of bringing together the best English and French writers with the best of the Americans—a program cultivated by the *Dial* also after 1920. Other magazines, notably *The Seven Arts*, had a more nationalistic emphasis.

These magazines, and numerous others with such names as *The Egoist, Blast, The Modern School, The Modernist*, were the main agents of Crane's education. His chief teachers in the years during which he would have been attending a college or university, in the normal course of affairs, were Pound and Eliot, with Pound first dominating (as early as 1917) and then, a year or two later, Eliot most decisively. Both as critics and as poets, they form his taste, stimulate and provoke him, and teach him the craft of poetry. It is through them that he discovers the Elizabethans and Metaphysicals (special enthusiasms being Donne, Marlowe, and Webster), Dante (whom he did not, however, study intensively until 1930), and most overwhelmingly the French poets from Baudelaire on.

By 1921, Crane had achieved full poetic maturity, finding his own voice, style, and themes; and in the same year he broke decisively with his father. From his first departure for New York in 1916 until this time, he had felt the "curse of sundered parentage" with particular virulence. He had returned to Cleveland and had lived in Akron and Washington, D.C., for varying periods in response to pleas from his mother or offers of work in various capacities (all humble—clerk, salesman, supervisor) in his father's candy business. The year

1921 did not mark the achievement of any sort of stability, emotional or economic, but it may be said to signal the end of the process of education and definition of himself as poet and as person.

The external events of the rest of his life require little space to describe. In the single decade remaining to him, he tried with small success to find a satisfactory means of support in advertising or other hackwork. The increasing disorder of his personal life, dominated by alcoholism and homosexuality, made the various forms of temporary patronage he finally received of little use to him. The chief of these were a grant from the banker Otto Kahn in 1925 and a Guggenheim fellowship in 1931, though he also served briefly as traveling secretary to a wealthy stockbroker and enjoyed the extended hospitality of Harry and Caresse Crosby in Paris. His first volume, *White Buildings*, was published (after many delays and difficulties) in 1926. In the same year he made another stay on the Isle of Pines, writing there many of the poems collected as *Key West: An Island Sheaf* and published posthumously, and much of *The Bridge*. Late in 1928 he sailed for Europe, spending the first half of 1929 mostly in Paris, where he found society all too congenial to his vices. The Crosbys did, however, provide him with the stimulus to finish *The Bridge*—which Crane had begun in 1923 and worked on at intervals since— by undertaking to print it at their Black Sun Press in Paris; it was published both there and in New York in 1930. In 1931 he went to Mexico on his Guggenheim fellowship, projecting an epic on the conquest of Mexico; but in spite of devoted efforts by several people to help him—Hans Zinsser, the famous bacteriologist; Katherine Anne Porter, his neighbor in Mexico; and Peggy Baird, former wife of Malcolm Cowley, with whom he lived for a time in a last approach to heterosexual love—

he was able to do little writing. Quarrelsome, drunk much of the time, alternating between manic exhilaration and suicidal depression, he had little control of himself and was frequently on, and sometimes across, the border of insanity. He did produce one last poem as good as anything he ever wrote, "The Broken Tower," in February–March 1932. A month later he leaped from the stern of the ship taking him from Mexico to the United States, acting out the symbolism of many of his poems by drowning in the Caribbean. A final symbolic touch was added to the story when his mother died in 1947 and her ashes were scattered, according to her directions, from Brooklyn Bridge.

Crane's talent was astonishing indeed to survive the extreme disorder of his life and all the other forces inimical to it and enable him in spite of everything to produce poetry of lasting value. But Crane was by no means passive, a mere vessel; his attitude toward his poetry was much more conservative and shrewd and disciplined than the sensational outlines of his life would suggest. His constant effort was to educate himself poetically, to discipline his gifts, to establish a valid relation to tradition. He was rarely taken in by fads or extremists, and his critical comments show great penetration. His letters, collected in 1952, seem to me the most impressive since Keats's, and fully worthy of comparison to them; they are profoundly moving human documents, colorful, penetrating, often humorous, and rich in moral insight (unexpected as this quality might seem). The letters reveal much about the nature of our civilization in that crucial period 1916–32, and the symptomatic aspect of Crane's career; they also have the special human interest and pathos of portraying the artist who dies young and as victim. (He wrote in 1922, "I shall do my best work later on when I am about 35 or 40.")

The challenge of Crane's poetry called forth from several of our best critics essays that remain classics. Such are Allen Tate's crucial pieces, R. P. Blackmur's explorations of how Crane's language works, and Yvor Winters' definitions of how Crane was misled by the "American religion" of Whitman and Emerson. Full-length studies of Crane's poetry and his life have likewise been of high caliber. Philip Horton's biography of 1937 is exceptionally readable without sacrifice of thoroughness and accuracy. Brom Weber's study, a decade later, presented much further information; Weber also skillfully edited Crane's letters. L. S. Dembo's study (1960) of *The Bridge* is an impressive Neo-Romantic interpretation. The books (both 1963) by Samuel Hazo and Vincent Quinn are useful brief introductions. In the last few years there has been a resurgence of interest in Crane, manifested in a new edition of the poems, with selected letters and prose, edited by Brom Weber (1966), a reprint of the letters (1965), full-length critical studies of the poetry by R. W. B. Lewis (1967), H. A. Leibowitz (1968), and R. W. Butterfield (1969), and a massive critical biography by John Unterecker which won the National Book Award in 1969.

Turn now to specific discussion of the poetry. Of the twenty-eight poems in *White Buildings*, all but two were written in 1920–25, and most of them in the latter part of that period. (The two Crane chose to preserve from the large number he had produced before 1920 were "North Labrador" and "In Shadow.") They are all mature work, and an approach in terms of development and chronology is not very revealing. Perhaps the best way is to begin with some poems about the nature of poetry and the poet.

"Chaplinesque" is an early and relatively simple presentation of one aspect of the situation of the poet.

We make our meek adjustments,
Contented with such random consolations

As the wind deposits
In slithered and too ample pockets.

For we can still love the world, who find
A famished kitten on the step, and know
Recesses for it from the fury of the street,
Or warm torn elbow coverts.

It was inspired by Chaplin's *The Kid*, and Crane explained his intentions in several letters: "I am moved to put Chaplin with the poets [of today]; hence the 'we.' . . . Poetry, the human feelings, 'the kitten,' is so crowded out of the humdrum, rushing, mechanical scramble of today that the man who would preserve them must duck and camouflage for dear life to keep them or keep himself from annihilation. . . . I feel that I have captured the arrested climaxes and evasive victories of his gestures in words, somehow. . . . I have made that 'infinitely gentle, infinitely suffering thing' of Eliot's into the symbol of the kitten."

The Romantic irony of the clown-poet figure and the tone and language of this poem suggest the French Symbolists, whom Crane had been studying; he had recently translated three poems by Laforgue. But the poem also illustrates a more distinctive and lasting influence: that of the graphic arts. Fundamental to Crane's aesthetic was the similarity between poetry and painting (and such related graphic arts as photography). Painting was, from early adolescence, almost as important to him as poetry, and he surrounded himself with prints as well as books. When he went to New York in 1916, Carl Schmitt, a young painter, went over Crane's work, giving him the benefit of the painter's sensitive response to rhythm and movement. They agreed, according to Horton, that Crane ". . . should compose a certain number of poems a week simply as technical exercises with the purpose of breaking down formal patterns. These he would bring to his critic as he wrote them, and the two would read them over together, Schmitt illustrating with pencil on paper the rising and falling of cadences, the dramatic effect of caesural breaks, and the general movement of the poem as a whole. . . . Surprisingly enough, this conscious experimentation with verse forms did not lead him, as it might well have done during those flourishing days of *vers libre*, to abandon meter and rhyme." Both Schmitt and Crane also composed nonsense verses in which meaning played no part; the main purpose was to exploit the sounds of words and letters as if they were musical notes.

After his return to Cleveland, Crane became friendly with a group of painters who further stimulated his interest in the art and taught him much about it. His closest friend among them was William Sommers, whom he celebrated in "Sunday Morning Apples"; in this poem the "Beloved apples of seasonable madness" are transfigured by art in a Dionysiac metamorphosis, poised "full and ready for explosion." Specific paintings by El Greco and Joseph Stella provided part of the inspiration for *The Bridge*, and the analogy with painting seemed to be constantly in Crane's mind. As Horton puts it, his attitude toward his poems "was primarily plastic. . . . Crane intended these poems not as descriptions of experience that could be *read about*, but as immediate experiences that the reader could *have*. . . ."

In replying to a friend's request for an explanation of "Black Tambourine," Crane said, "The value of the poem is only, to me, in what a painter would call its 'tactile' quality,—an entirely aesthetic feature. A propagandist for either side of the Negro question could find anything he wanted to in it. My only declaration in it is that I find the Negro (in the popular mind) sentimentally or brutally 'placed' in this midkingdom, etc." This remark is especially interesting because Crane is denying any intentional concern with a social and moral value that is certainly in the poem. Crane is, of course, right when he says that it is a "bundle of insinuations, suggestions," remote from propaganda; but its imaginative apprehension of the Negro's plight is not a purely aesthetic phenomenon:

The interests of a black man in a cellar
Mark tardy judgment on the world's closed
    door.
Gnats toss in the shadow of a bottle,
And a roach spans a crevice in the floor.

Æsop, driven to pondering, found
Heaven with the tortoise and the hare . . .

In the light of later events, readers now can hardly avoid calling the poem prophetic, though its prophecy is not the vision of a seer but the best kind of social consciousness and moral perceptiveness. (It was written in 1921.) The Negro in the cellar (driven underground, pushed out of sight) regards the "world's closed door." His situation keeps him dirty and drives him to drink (at least this is one interpretation of the bottle and the roach). The second stanza considers Aesop, who perhaps would not have pondered had he not been a slave, and notes that he counseled patience in his fable of the tortoise and the hare; he "found Heaven" with them in the sense that he achieved literary immortality, but the "Fox brush and sow ear" on his grave suggest ironically that his solution was not complete. Aesop is appropriate here also because so many of the Uncle Remus stories derive from him, and the images of the ancient and the modern slaves fuse: both wise, both counseling resignation and patience ("Uncle Toms" in contemporary language), and both dead—i.e., the situation has changed. The "mingling incantations" suggests both the remains of primitive superstition and the singing of Negroes. The last stanza puts explicitly the dilemma of the Negro, wandering forlorn between his recent past in America, symbolized by the tambourine of the minstrel show, when he could be regarded merely as a clown, a stock figure of fun, and his savage and primitive origins in Africa, symbolized by the "carcass quick with flies." But the day of the minstrel show is past; the tambourine is stuck on the wall, and the Negro has been closed up in the cellar. The poem has a poise and taut restraint that are remarkable, and an intensity of perception not inferior to the more obviously emotional later poems.

"Praise for an Urn" is an elegy for Ernest Nelson, at whose funeral in December 1921 Crane, with Sommers, had been a pallbearer. Nelson was a Norwegian who had come to the United States at fifteen, gone to art school and done some good paintings and written some good poems, but then been forced to go into lithography to make a living. Crane called him "One of the best-read people I ever met, wonderful kindliness and tolerance and a true Nietzschean. He was one of many broken against the stupidity of American life. . . ." The funeral, Crane said, was "tremendous, especially the finale at the crematorium . . . That funeral was one of the few beautiful things that have happened to me in Cleveland." I have quoted these remarks from Crane's letters because they reveal the feelings that went into the poem and contrast with its poise and restraint; they also clarify some of its allusions.

> It was a kind and northern face
> That mingled in such exile guise
> The everlasting eyes of Pierrot
> And, of Gargantua, the laughter. . . .

In this first stanza, "exile" is richly ambiguous: the Mediterranean qualities of Pierrot and Gargantua lived, in exile, in Nelson's "northern" face, and Pierrot, the pathetic clown, and Gargantua, who laughed at the serious world, counterbalance each other nicely. Further, Nelson was himself in exile both from his original Norwegian home and from the world of art, as he worked in his Cleveland lithography factory. His thoughts (in the second stanza) passed on to Crane were "inheritances"—tradition in the literal sense—but in a world where traditions are increasingly precarious, "Delicate riders of the storm," and Crane hopes to pass them on in turn. The third stanza describes shared experiences in which they discussed such traditions (and perhaps more personal kinds of immortality also); but the clock of the fourth contradicts this, with its insistent comment reminding of death. Survival even in memory is dubious in the penultimate stanza, and the last bids an ironic and resigned farewell to the friend's ashes and to the elegy ("these well-meant idioms"); both will be scattered and lost in the smoky spring of the typical modern suburbs.

These two poems in quatrains exhibit a moral and aesthetic poise as well as a moral penetration and awareness that are not often found in Crane's later work. The major poems of the next few years follow a new line and method of composition. A letter to his good friend Gorham Munson points the direction. He had had a mystical experience in a dentist's chair—an anesthetic revelation: ". . . under the influence of aether and *amnesia* my mind spiraled to a kind of seventh heaven of consciousness and egoistic dance among the seven spheres—and something like an objective voice kept saying to me—'You have the higher consciousness—you have the higher consciousness. This is something that very few have. This is what is called genius.' . . . A happiness, ecstatic such as I have known only twice in 'inspirations' came over me. I felt the two worlds. And at once . . . O Gorham, I have known moments in eternity."

The essence of Crane's later poetic may be found in "The Wine Menagerie." The title indicates very precisely the whole theme of the poem. "Menagerie" suggests both a collection of wild animals and, etymologically, a household; hence it evokes immediately the central image of the contents of the mind as wild animals. (Yeats's "Circus Animals' Desertion" uses a very similar metaphor.) "Wine" suggests that the menagerie exists (or, perhaps, that the animals become wild) only through the stimulus and release of alcohol. When "wine redeems the sight," then a "leopard ranging always in the brow/Asserts a vision in the slumbering gaze." The lying reality of everyday ("glozening decanters that reflect the street" as the poet sits in a bar) is transcended; the poet sees "New thresholds, new anatomies! Wine talons/Build freedom up about me. . . ." But the whole experience is viewed with romantic irony: the wild animals are dangerous to the poet, and the world not really transcended: "Ruddy, the tooth implicit of the world/Has followed you." The poet is betrayed, his head separated from his body like those of Holofernes and John the Baptist; and he is as ineffectual as the puppet Petrushka's valentine. This is, of course, the notion of the poet as visionary and seer, capable of a higher consciousness, a divine madness, which Crane took primarily from Blake and Rimbaud (who provide the epigraphs for two of his three volumes) and ultimately from Plato and Nietzsche. Crane, notoriously, often strove to achieve this condition through the stimulus both of alcohol and of a phonograph playing loudly and repetitiously.

In "General Aims and Theories," he described his poetic theory at some length. The core of this essay is Crane's insistence that he is not an impressionist, but an "absolutist." The impressionist, he says, "is interesting as far as he goes—but his goal has been reached when he has succeeded in projecting certain selected factual details into his reader's consciousness. He is really not interested in the *causes* (metaphysical) of his materials, their emotional derivations or their utmost spiritual consequences. A kind of retinal registration is enough, along with a certain psychological stimulation. And this is also true of your realist . . . and to a certain extent of the classicist. . . . Blake means these differences when he wrote:

We are led to believe in a lie
When we see *with* not *through* the eye."

The absolutist, however—and the predecessors Crane cites are Donne, Blake, Baudelaire, and Rimbaud—hopes to "go *through* the combined materials of the poem, using our 'real' world somewhat as a spring-board, and to give the poem *as a whole* an orbit or predetermined direction of its own." Such a poem aims at freedom from the personalities of both poet and reader, and is "at least a stab at a truth"; hence it may be called "absolute." Crane then suggests the kind of truth such poetry attempts to embody: "Its evocation will not be toward decoration or amusement, but rather toward a state of consciousness, an 'innocence' (Blake) or absolute beauty. In this condition there may be discoverable under new forms certain spiritual illuminations, shining with a mortality essentialized from experience directly, and not from previous precepts or preconceptions. It is as though a poem gave the reader as he left it a single, new *word,* never before spoken and impossible to actually enunciate, but self-evident as an active principle in the reader's consciousness henceforward." As to technique,

Crane says that the "terms of expression" employed are often selected less for their logical or literal than for their associational meanings: "Via this and their metaphorical inter-relationships, the entire construction of the poem is raised on the organic principle of a 'logic of metaphor,' which antedates our so-called pure logic, and which is the genetic basis of all speech, hence consciousness and thought-extension."

He then goes on to explain and defend the difficulty of his poems in terms of these principles, speaking of the "implicit emotional dynamics of the materials used" and the "organic impact on the imagination" of the poem; the poet's business, he says, is the "conquest of consciousness." In a letter to Harriet Monroe, he put it more plainly: "as a poet I may very possibly be more interested in the so-called illogical impingements of the connotations of words on the consciousness (and their combinations and interplay in metaphor on this basis) than I am interested in the preservation of their logically rigid significations at the cost of limiting my subject matter and perceptions involved in the poem." And in the essay "Modern Poetry," he casts further light on his notion of poetic truth: "poetic prophecy in the case of the seer has nothing to do with factual prediction or with futurity. It is a peculiar type of perception, capable of apprehending some absolute and timeless concept of the imagination with astounding clarity and conviction."

We may now consider some of the poems in *White Buildings* that follow and exemplify this poetic. "Recitative" begins:

Regard the capture here, O Janus-faced,
As double as the hands that twist this glass.
Such eyes at search or rest you cannot see;
Reciting pain or glee, how can you bear!

It is so very difficult that even Allen Tate had trouble with it, and Crane wrote an apologetic explanation to him: "Imagine the poet, say, on a platform speaking it. The audience is one half of Humanity, Man (in the sense of Blake), and the poet the other. ALSO, the poet sees himself in the audience as in a mirror. ALSO, the audience sees itself, in part, in the poet. Against this paradoxical DUALITY is posed the UNITY . . . in the last verse. In another sense, the poet is *talking to himself* all the way through the poem, and there are, as too often in my poems, other reflexes and symbolisms in the poem, also, which it would be silly to write here. . . ." As usual in explaining his own poems, Crane begins here by describing the dramatic situation, and his comments, as always, are convincing and helpful; but they are far from resolving the difficulties of the poem. The situation itself is so ambiguous, with so many alternative interpretations (as Crane indicates), that visualizing is not much help. The fourth stanza is the source of the title of the volume:

Look steadily—how the wind feasts and spins
The brain's disk shivered against lust. Then
    watch
While darkness, like an ape's face, falls away,
And gradually white buildings answer day.

The white buildings, contrasted with darkness and the ape's face, are embodiments of the Ideal, testaments of the Word; they are, specifically, poems of the sort Crane is writing. They are also, of course, New York skyscrapers transfigured by the dawn light. It is worth noting that the redemption takes place although—or perhaps because—the brain is unable to control lust. The next two stanzas describe the magnificence and isolation of the skyscrapers, and urge: "leave the tower" for the bridge—abandon isolation for unity. The final stanza evokes unity in the image of "All hours clapped dense into a single stride" in the sound of "alternating bells." Crane called the poem "a confession," and certainly the contrast between the violent dualisms and the final vision of unity is characteristic; the images of the Bridge and the Tower also anticipate strikingly the use Crane was to make of them in later poems.

"Passage" is another difficult and visionary poem. Biographically, it probably derives from the feeling of refreshment Crane experienced in spending the summer of 1925 in the country. This is, however, very little help. The poem is about the experience of vision, of "higher consciousness," which is for Crane synonymous with the writing of poetry; it is in this respect like "The Wine Menagerie," though the perspective here is autobiographical, through time and distance, rather than a close-up as there of the physiological aids and the experience itself. The title suggests a voyage, as often in Crane, and perhaps also the anthropologist's *rite de passage,* a farewell to childhood. The first four stanzas describe the experience of the visionary voyage, promising "an improved infancy"—i.e., a rebirth, a return to innocence. Memory, described scornfully in the second stanza, is left behind. The feeling is of heightened life, of unity with nature, and the voyage almost reaches its goal (the valleys are in sight); but the wind dies, the vision fails, through time and smoke (the evil in man's heart? "chimney-sooted heart of man"), as so often ("a too well-known biography"). The speaker returns to the ravine where he left Memory, and finds a thief beneath the "opening laurel," holding the poet's book. (The laurel is opening because the poet is beginning to gain some reputation; the thief is presumably Memory, or perhaps the Intellect—those faculties, at any rate, that the poet as visionary has abandoned.) After a brief dialogue, Memory closes the book (perhaps in sign of reconciliation), and there is a further visionary experience: History (the sand from the Ptolemies) and Time (the serpent) bring

consciousness of past and future (unpaced beaches), and there are further incommunicable revelations ("What fountains . . . speeches?") which overstrain Memory. One meaning (and here, as in much of the preceding, I follow Dembo) would seem to be that Memory is accepted as part of the visionary experience, necessary to it in its mature form, as opposed to the simpler childish form described in the first four stanzas. The poem is evocative of Rimbaud, though very much Crane's own; it has a peculiar intensity, a haunting quality that is remarkable.

"Paraphrase" describes a different kind of vision. It had its inception, according to Horton, in Crane's experience of waking from a drunken sleep into the bright morning light and thinking himself dead. The first two stanzas evoke such an experience: "One rushing from the bed at night" finds, more or less reassuringly, the "record wedged in his soul" of the regular and dependable alternations of life in its various cycles of light and dark, sleeping and waking, expansion and contraction, and the like. The "steady winking beat between/ Systole, diastole" suggests such devices as the cardiograph which attest and observe the regularity of the life processes; the tone is clinical. The following phrase, "spokes-of-a-wheel," however, suggests the hysterical and terrifying quality of the experience, as these processes seem speeded up in panic until the alternations blur and seem to reverse, like the spokes of a rapidly revolving wheel. The second stanza represents the sleeper's nightmarish experience with ironic detachment: to the sleeper death has seemed a physical force or object trying to get in between the sheets and immobilize his fingers and toes ("integers of life" suggests also the integrity and unity of body and soul that constitutes life). The last two stanzas evoke that inevitable morning when the experience will be real and not illusory, when the sleeper will really (in the language of folk humor) wake up to find himself dead. However "desperate" the light, however systematically morning floods the pillow, until it is like an "antarctic blaze" of whiteness, it "shall not rouse" the sleeper, whose head will only post "a white paraphrase" among the "bruised roses" of the wallpaper. The word "paraphrase" suggests, together with the "record" of the first stanza, an analogy between the inadequacy as descriptions of natural processes of records such as the cardiogram and the inadequacy of the dead body as equivalent of the living man who was an "integer," a unity. In the simplest terms, the dead body is a paraphrase (with the connotations both of "translation" and of "explanation") and a poor one, of the living man.

Of course I should not insist on any exclusive validity for this reading, though I hope it is convincing enough to demonstrate, at least, that the poem is not centrally obscure. It is difficult, but with a tension and power inseparable from the difficulty. The comparatively regular four-stress lines arranged in quatrains with only an approximation to rhyme in each stanza until the last, when "paraphrase" emerges as a full rhyme to "blaze," produce an effect of climactic intensity.

"Possessions," which follows in *White Buildings,* returns to the visionary theme with its characteristic obscurity. The situation would seem to be that the poet is embarking on a new (homosexual) affair, driven by his lust, and almost sure that this affair will turn out like all the others, but going on nevertheless with his tormented seeking. The first stanza contrasts the rain, which has direction, and the key, which finds its proper lock and turns its bolts, with the poet's "undirected" condition and his phallic "fixed stone of lust" which is no key. The second stanza recites the total of such past experi-

ences. The third places the poet specifically in Greenwich Village, apprehensive beyond words, inspecting his lust, and "turning on smoked forking spires"—the image is apparently of being roasted as on a turnspit over the "city's stubborn lives, desires." The last stanza changes the metaphor to the poet as gored by the horns of lust (as bullfighter or simple victim?); he who "bleeding dies" after such goring achieves nothing but "piteous admissions" to make up a "record of rage and partial appetites." But in spite of all there is the final affirmation:

The pure possession, the inclusive cloud
Whose heart is fire shall come,—the white
    wind raze
All but bright stones wherein our smiling plays.

The word "possession" has, of course, the double sense of amorous consummation, with the pure one to wash away all the preceding impure (in the sense both of unchaste and of adulterated) experiences, and the supernatural or diabolical sense of being possessed by another spirit and personality; there is perhaps also the third sense of possessions as merely the physical things one owns. The pure possession, when it comes, will be a guiding force like the biblical pillar of fire by night and pillar of cloud by day, with the myth rationalized to mean that the heart of the cloud must be fire—or, to put it crudely, that passion is the only guide. When the state of possession, of ecstasy (in the etymological sense) is complete (for "partial appetites" are worthless), then the troublesome and archaic stone of lust will be transformed into "bright stone wherein our smiling plays." But one serious difficulty with the poem is that the logical and rhetorical relation of the last three lines to the rest of the poem is not clear. Perhaps the "pure possession" is death—its fiery and destructive force suggests this—and the "bright stones" of the last line are seen only after the purgation of death, as the kind of automatic resurrection or guaranteed paradise suggested in many other poems. But the primary suggestion would seem to be a contrast between those who die through failure to achieve complete appetites, pure possessions, and those who do achieve them and therefore do not die. The poem seems to me, however, far less effective than "Paraphrase," partly because of this central ambiguity.

I have thought it better to present reasonably detailed accounts of those poems in *White Buildings* that seem to me central to Crane's achievement than to attempt to mention all of them, though this has meant omitting, for instance, "Repose of Rivers," Crane's most magical example of incantation and control of sound. Something must be said briefly, however, of "At Melville's Tomb." Crane placed it immediately before the series of "Voyages" at the end of the volume, and it forms a kind of prelude to them, introducing the Voyage symbol which had been implicit in many of the preceding poems. Crane wrote a famous letter (reprinted in Horton's appendix) to Harriet Monroe, editor of *Poetry,* explaining the poem and defending it against her objections; the letter is too long to quote, but may be recommended as containing Crane's detailed explications of some of his most intricate images. The poem seems to me notable, however, as a tribute to Melville and an introduction to "Voyages" rather than as an achievement in its own right.

"Voyages" is, in my judgment, Crane's best long poem. The first section was written in 1921 and an early version of the sixth in 1923, all the rest in 1924–25. Some of the literary inspiration came from the poems of Samuel Greenberg, which Crane had read in manuscript (Greenberg had died in 1916 at the age of twenty-three); but the principal inspiration was Crane's affair with an imaginative and sensitive sailor-lover. As Horton says, "Possibly no other writer but Melville has ever been able to express the mysteries and terrors of the sea with such eloquence and imagination . . ." and this is probably part of the explanation of Eugene O'Neill's enthusiasm for Crane's poetry.

The first section, written much earlier than the others, is much less ambitious. Crane originally called it "The Bottom of the Sea Is Cruel" and, in a letter, "Poster" (saying deprecatingly, "There is nothing more profound in it than a 'stop, look and listen' sign"); the latter title is indicative of its attractive simplicity. The contrast of the children's innocence and gaiety and the mystery, the cruelty and terror, the lightning and thunder of the sea (in the depths beyond the "fresh ruffles" of the surf) is almost Wordsworthian. Its sense of the sea's fatal attraction, which will render the warning to the children futile, foreshadows the theme of the rest of the poem. Compared to the other sections, it is minor art; but it forms an effective introduction to the sequence.

Section II is the most widely anthologized and admired part of the poem; Winters called it "one of the most powerful and one of the most nearly perfect poems of the last two hundred years." Rhetorically, this section would seem to be a counterstatement to the first: the sea is cruel, "And yet" it exempts lovers from its cruelty, regarding them with special favor and sympathy. The sea is a "great wink of eternity"—the wink as sign of complicity and secrets shared only with lovers. (The image also suggests, perhaps, wink as lapse of attention, and hence the sea as escape from time.) Her vast belly bending moonward (and the connotation is not only of the tides but the moon as patron of lovers) is "Laughing the wrapt inflections of our love"—and on one level the image is of the sea as a fat old woman, a bawd or go-between for lovers (like Juliet's nurse), laughing at their raptures while encouraging them and participating in them. This connotation is qualified by the preceding image of the sea as "Samite sheeted and processioned"— the Lady of the Lake and other exalted or mysterious ladies in Arthurian legend wore white samite (often with gold thread)—and these qualities of remoteness, legendary and ritualistic and awesome, are attributed to the sea.

The dominant image of the second stanza is of the sea as Judge, terrible and severe to all but lovers: "The sceptred terror of whose sessions rends . . . All but the pieties of lovers' hands." The next stanza explores this partiality of the sea to lovers: as the undersea bells of the sunken cathedral answer and correspond to the stars reflected on the surface of the sea, so "Adagios of islands" complete the "dark confessions" spelled by her veins. Crane explained the former phrase in "General Aims and Theories": ". . . the reference is to the motion of a boat through islands clustered thickly, the rhythm of the motion, etc. And it seems a much more direct and creative statement than any more logical employment of words such as 'coasting slowly through the islands,' besides ushering in a whole world of music." Presumably the meaning is that the rhythm of the blood in the lover's veins (and "O my Prodigal" addresses Crane's lover directly for the first time) echoes and corresponds to the sea's rhythm (as the stars and bells have echoed each other above). The dark confession is, then, that the sea is like the lover's feelings; her veins are like his veins.

The next stanza draws a kind of conclusion: since the sea (or love) is in time ("her turning shoulders wind the hours"), the lovers should commit themselves to time and "Hasten, while they are true," for "sleep, death, desire" (and the equation of all three is highly significant) are all as much in time, as transient, as "one floating flower." The magnificent last stanza is a prayer (to vague and pantheistic deities of sky and sea—clear Seasons and minstrel galleons) that the lovers may be allowed enough time and committed fully enough to it, and granted enough sense of wonder ("Bind us in time . . . and awe"), to penetrate the secret— which will mean death. Being bequeathed to an "earthly shore" would mean, presumably, abandoning the life of passion and remaining alive. The grave is a "vortex" which will reveal the sea's depths and secrets and hence answer (provide the only fulfillment of) the "seal's wide spindrift gaze toward paradise." (The last image suggests the equation of sea and death once more: spindrift is windblown spray, hence sea united with air, as the seal is a sea creature which breathes air and has humanoid eyes.) Crane is not asking to live long enough to learn the secret, as some commentators have said, but to remain in the element of the sea—i.e., the passionate life, or love—until he learns the secret through dying.

The third section continues the exploration of the blood relation ("Infinite consanguinity") between the sea and time-bound love and death; in a sense it develops and explains the somewhat cryptic images of the last stanza of the preceding section. The first image is of the relation between sea and sky (the otherworldly, the paradisal), imagined as together supporting the lover's body as "tendered theme." But death is also present in the "reliquary hands" of the sea. The second stanza presents the dramatic climax or resolution: the poet therefore will commit himself, immerse himself in the destructive element (there is no echo of Conrad, but the theme is closely parallel), in the faith that death "Presumes no carnage, but this single change,— . . . The silken skilled transmemberment of song"—a sea change like that in *The Tempest,* which

Crane called the "crown of all the Western world," or like Eliot's "Death by Water," but without any of Eliot's dual possibilities of outcome or supernatural significance; this is a purely secular baptism into passion, with its closest parallel Wagner's *Liebestod*. The fusion is complete in the last line, where "love" is both the lover and the sea (the exaltation of poetry and the state of being in love): "Permit me voyage, love, into your hands."

Sections II and III seem to me the best parts of the poem. The chief point I shall hope to establish concerning the remaining parts is that the poem constitutes a genuine sequence and unity. In IV, the lovers are separated and the sea (which literally separates them) is imagined as the element that unites them (for love is a voyage upon this element, this passionate state of being) and conveys the poet's love through song; he has a vision of reunion after suffering (after being lost in "fatal tides" the "islands" will be found through the spiritual geography of the lover—"Blue latitudes and levels of your eyes") when the final mysteries ("secret oar and petals of all love") will be revealed.

The fifth section, however, presents a sad contrast. The lovers are now physically united once more, but the harmony is broken and love is dead. Waking past midnight, "lonely" though his lover is with him, the poet uses images of hardness, coldness, brittleness to suggest the broken relation. One image seems to be, proleptically, of a bridge with broken cables ("The cables of our sleep so swiftly filed,/ Already hang, shred ends from remembered stars"). Moonlight is "deaf," tyrannous, inexorable as the tide, in contrast to the sympathetic moon of II. (The suggestion is also, of course, that this outcome is as inevitable as the tides.) The sky, instead of being mysteriously consanguine with the sea, is a "godless cleft . . . Where nothing turns but dead sands

flashing" (the dead and meaningless moon). The lovers part, unable to communicate; as the sailor-lover leaves, the poet accepts the separation (even though he cannot understand it) and bids him farewell in a moving stanza.

The sixth and last section presents the poet's affirmation, in spite of everything, of his continued commitment to the sea (in all its meanings). Though he is "derelict and blinded," he continues to believe in the bond between sea and sky ("O rivers mingling toward the sky") and in the possibility of reaching the harbor which is as rare as the phoenix; though "thy waves rear/More savage than the death of kings" he still awaits "Some splintered garland for the seer." The second half of the poem describes the vision of reaching this harbor of resurrection and fulfillment. Belle Isle, "white echo of the oar" of love's mystery imagined at the end of IV, will contain the "lounged goddess" and will be found through the "imaged Word" (which will, presumably, correspond to "Creation's blithe and petalled word" once thundered to the "lounged goddess" of the island). It will transcend time, hold "Hushed willows anchored"; it will eliminate all betrayals and partings, making love perfect: "It is the unbetrayable reply/Whose accent no farewell can know." The amorous vision and the poetic vision, then, are one; the perfect Word (to which the perfect poem can be reduced) will also redeem love.

I have postponed discussion of "For the Marriage of Faustus and Helen," Crane's first long poem (written in 1922–23), because it seems best to consider it in relation to *The Bridge*, to which it is precursor and parallel. It is a very ambitious performance indeed, similar in intention to Joyce's *Ulysses* and Eliot's *Waste Land* in suggesting a fusion of present and past, a "bridge between so-called classic experience and . . . our seething, confused cosmos of today," in Crane's words. Of *The Waste Land,* Crane said, "After this perfection of death—nothing is possible in motion but a resurrection of some kind"; and this he hoped that his poem would provide. He described his plan thus in a letter: "Almost every symbol of current significance is matched by a correlative, suggested or actually stated, 'of ancient days.' Helen, the symbol of this abstract 'sense of beauty,' Faustus the symbol of myself, the poetic or imaginative man of all times. . . . Part II . . . begins with *catharsis,* the acceptance of tragedy through destruction. . . . It is Dionysian in its attitude, the creator and the eternal destroyer dance arm in arm. . . ." Actually, the Faustus-Helen symbolism is of very limited validity, not going far beyond the title (Crane seems not to have known Goethe's *Faust;* Marlowe was his only source), and the structural parallels between past and present are flimsy indeed. Though there are several fine passages, the poem seems to me of interest chiefly for the full embodiment of Crane's visionary theme in the last part: the fourth dimension, the mystical "lone eye," the Dionysian acceptance and transcendence of war, tragedy, and death. It was written not long after his mystical, or anesthetic, revelation in the dentist's chair and his commitment to the visionary poetic, with the Rimbaudian program of intoxication and derangement of the senses.

The Bridge was begun in 1923 as an attempt to carry further the kind of interpretation of modern life and its relation to the past that Crane had made in "For the Marriage of Faustus and Helen." The greater part of it was written during the visit to the Isle of Pines in 1926; but Crane was constantly occupied with the project, revising and adding to it, until its publication in 1930. Crane thought of it as his magnum opus, his poetic testament; he spoke

of it as an epic like the *Aeneid,* planned like the Sistine Chapel, embodying the Myth of America, and refuting Eliot's pessimistic *Waste Land* to provide an affirmative interpretation of modern civilization. These rash and grandiose claims were demolished promptly and definitively by Allen Tate and Yvor Winters when the poem appeared. We may begin, therefore, by granting that *The Bridge* is not the Great American Epic, or any kind of epic, and that it is not a mature or responsible interpretation of American history or of the modern world. What kind of poem is it, then, and what kind of interest does it have now, after several decades?

In his highly persuasive exegesis, Dembo calls it "a romantic lyric given epic implications" and defines its theme as "the exiled poet's quest for a logos in which the Absolute that he has known in his imagination will be made intelligible to the world. . . . Crane tried to find in the history of American society some evidence that this society was capable of a psychological experience essentially identical with the poet's ecstatic apprehension of the Ideal as Beauty. The narrator in *The Bridge* thus journeys to a mythic Indian past that represents 'the childhood of the continent,' becomes an Indian himself, and marries Pocahontas in a ritual fire dance. Having thus learned the Word, attained the guerdon of the goddess, he returns to his own time. . . . Although he now sees Pocahontas not as a fertile goddess, but as a sterile prostitute, the poet keeps his faith and concludes the poem with a hymn celebrating the Bridge as a modern embodiment of the Word."

The key Dembo finds in Nietzsche's theory of tragedy, which provided Crane "with a metaphysical argument with which to meet disillusion, whatever its source, and thus associated him not merely with Whitman, but with the whole tradition of optimism in nineteenth-century romantic literature." "Simply put, Crane accepted the proposition that resurrection always follows suffering and death. That is really the essence of what he took from Nietzsche." Except for the emphasis on Nietzsche, and the consistency and penetration of supporting analysis, Dembo's thesis is not new; Yvor Winters long ago observed that Emerson and Whitman taught a similar doctrine, and he argued that Crane merely put it into practice, following it to its logical end of suicide. For most of us, Dembo's association of the doctrine with Nietzsche and the Dionysiac tradition makes it more palatable; but I cannot see that it answers any of the objections of Winters and Tate. We are, however, concerned primarily not with the intrinsic merits of the doctrine, but with its effectiveness as theme of the poem. Conceding it all possible efficacy as a unifying force, the unity of the poem remains very loose indeed, and some parts remain very much better than others.

The "Proem" begins with the image of the seagull in its poise and freedom (its "inviolate curve," as in Hopkins' "Windhover," which Crane had certainly not yet read, suggesting a balance of the forces of control and release). This image is contrasted with that of the file clerk in his confined routine work, taken aloft only by elevators, dreaming of sails, and with that of the denizens of the cinema who hope for revelation there. The Bridge is then evoked as a parallel to the seagull, uniting motion and stillness, freedom and necessity; though, ironically, the madman commits suicide by leaping from it. It is a symbol of the Divine, but its rewards are mysterious: its accolade is anonymity, but it also shows "vibrant reprieve and pardon." It is both harp and altar, threshold of the future, prayer of the outcast, and cry of the lover; it condenses eternity and cradles

night. "Only in darkness is thy shadow clear" —and the poet, standing under it at night in winter and in the symbolic darkness of suffering, prays to it to take the place of his lost religious mythologies:

> Unto us lowliest sometime sweep, descend
> And of the curveship lend a myth to God.

The first section, "Ave Maria," is a monologue of Columbus as he is returning from his first voyage. Columbus is, of course, the poet-voyager, and Cathay is the terrestrial paradise, or the Absolute, or the Word. He praises God (and Crane notes that here the rhythm changes from the earlier "waterswell" to a suggestion of the "great *Te Deum* of the court, later held"), who "dost search/Cruelly with love thy parable of man" in experiences of which this voyage is a type, and testifies to awareness of His presence: "Elohim, still I hear thy sounding heel!"

The second section, "Powhatan's Daughter," has five subdivisions. The basic symbol is Pocahontas as the mythical body of America to be explored and known, the past, the Absolute. "The Harbor Dawn" presents very beautifully the protagonist's vision of her, between sleeping and waking, in the modern city. In "Van Winkle" he merges with the legendary character from an older New York and takes the subway, which, in "The River," becomes the symbolically named "20th Century Limited" train; there is then the associated picture of the hobos, who, with all their faults, "touch something like a key perhaps"; they remember the past and know the country: "They know a body under the wide rain." Both Tate and Winters consider "The River" the best part of *The Bridge,* with its description of the journey down the Mississippi as it appears both to the "Pullman breakfasters" on the modern train and to the hobos, who merge with the pioneers;

there is no strained philosophy or symbolism, but a loving evocation of the country and the people, past and present, in concrete terms. "The Dance" follows, and is the climax of the section: the protagonist consummates his union with Pocahontas; he becomes Maquokeeta, an Indian, and is the sacrificial victim burned at the stake in a ritual death dance; he is then resurrected and symbolically united with Pocahontas, now become America. The poetry is intense and beautiful; but it is hard to forget Winters' comment: "one does not deal adequately with the subject of death and immortality by calling the soil Pocahontas, and by then writing a love poem to an imaginary maiden who bears the name of Pocahontas." With regard to the pantheism of the whole section, Winters remarked, "I believe that nothing save confusion can result from our mistaking the Mississippi Valley for God." The last part of the section, "Indiana," is a sentimental portrait of the pioneer woman; by common consent it is one of Crane's worst lapses.

"Cutty Sark," the third section, begins the loosely connected and generally less effective group that deals with the protagonist's effort to preserve his faith while living in a world that seems to deny the Ideal; it is this part that corresponds to Crane's description of the poem as an "epic of the modern consciousness." "Cutty Sark" Crane described as a fantasy on the period of the whalers and clipper ships, built on the plan of a fugue with two voices, one that of the pianola, expressing the Atlantis or Eternity theme, and the other that of the derelict sailor encountered in the South Street dive. On the way home, the protagonist sees a phantom regatta of clipper ships from Brooklyn Bridge; Crane uses the historical names, and meant the arrangement on the page to be significant: he called it a cartogram, and said "The 'ships' should meet and pass in line and

type—as well as in wind and memory. . . ." (In this section particularly, Crane's description of his intentions is more elaborate and more interesting than the achieved result.) Some commentators who have puzzled about the significance of the title seem not to have been aware that the trademark of "Cutty Sark" whisky is a clipper ship.

"Cape Hatteras" Crane described as a "kind of ode to Whitman." It is also an ironic celebration of the airplane as embodiment of the modern, its speed and its conquest of space. Man is drunk with power and blind with pride —"the eagle dominates our days" with its "wings imperious"; he neglects the past (the recurrent symbols of the eagle for space and the serpent for time here receive new emphasis) and the imaginative meaning of infinity. His technological triumphs have led only to more destructive war, and Crane evokes the dogfights of World War I. But the Falcon-Ace has "a Sanskrit charge/To conjugate infinity's dim marge"—in Dembo's interpretation, "to plumb beneath death to resurrection and thereby . . . define the Word." War is justified in that beyond it lies resurrection and a new understanding of the Word; Whitman gives him a rebirth of faith through his vision of the rebirth of the slain.

"Three Songs" portrays three distortions of love in the modern world, perversions of the ideal Pocahontas. The most effective of them is "National Winter Garden," where the mythic dance is reduced to a burlesque show. "Quaker Hill" pictures the corruption of the countryside by commercialism and philistinism: the Quaker meeting house in Connecticut is now a weekend resort called the New Avalon Hotel.

"The Tunnel" describes, literally, the subway ride under the river to get to the bridge; figuratively, as the epigraph from Blake suggests, the final descent into the abyss before the ascent. Thus it is a kind of Inferno, a descent into hell, into the dark winter night before morning.

The phonographs of hades in the brain
Are tunnels that re-wind themselves, and love
A burnt match skating in a urinal . . .

The protagonist sees himself in Poe, the martyred poet. But he emerges, "like Lazarus," to stand by the East River and look at the harbor he has been under.

"Atlantis," the final section, Crane called "a sweeping dithyramb in which the Bridge becomes the symbol of consciousness spanning time and space." It is ironic that this, the most ecstatic section of the poem, was the first to be completed. "Atlantis" presents the imagined fulfillment of the quest and the end of tragedy: "Vision of the Voyage," Cathay, Belle Isle, as seen by the archetypal voyager and quester Jason; the vision is "Deity's glittering Pledge," "Answerer of all," and the "white, pervasive Paradigm" of Love; it is, of course, the Bridge apotheosized. Perhaps it is ultimately the poetic imagination. The poet prays, "Atlantis,—hold thy floating singer late!" The image is a pathetic one, since the singer is floating because Atlantis is not there, and the poem ends on an unanswered question.

Tate seems to me to put his finger on the trouble with the symbolism of *The Bridge*. He observes that the framework of symbol in "For the Marriage of Faustus and Helen" "is an abstraction empty of any knowable experience." Crane became dissatisfied both with its style and with the "literary" character of the symbolism, and so "set about the greater task of writing *The Bridge*." But the Bridge "differs from the Helen and Faust symbols only in its unliterary origin. I think Crane was deceived by this difference, and by the fact that Brooklyn Bridge is 'modern' and a fine piece of 'mechanics.' . . . The single symbolic image,

in which the whole poem centers, is at one moment the actual Brooklyn Bridge; at another, it is any bridge or 'connection'; at still another, it is a philosophical pun and becomes the basis of a series of analogies. . . . Because the idea is variously metaphor, symbol, and analogy, it tends to make the poem static. The poet takes it up, only to be forced to put it down again *when the poetic image of the moment is exhausted*. The idea does not, in short, fill the poet's mind; it is the starting point for a series of short flights, or inventions connected only in analogy—which explains the merely personal passages, which are obscure, and the lapses into sentimentality."

Crane had intended "For the Marriage of Faustus and Helen" to be an answer to the pessimism of the school of Eliot, and *The Bridge* was to be an even more complete answer. But, Tate comments, "There was a fundamental mistake in Crane's diagnosis of Eliot's problem. Eliot's 'pessimism' grows out of an awareness of the decay of the individual consciousness and its fixed relations to the world; but Crane thought that it was due to something like pure 'orneryness,' an unwillingness 'to share with us the breath released,' the breath being a new kind of freedom that he identified emotionally with the age of the machine." And, he observes, "I think he knew that the structure of *The Bridge* was finally incoherent, and for that reason . . . he could no longer believe even in his lyrical powers; he could not return to the early work and take it up where he had left off. Far from 'refuting' Eliot, his whole career is a vindication of Eliot's major premise —that the integrity of the individual consciousness has broken down."

Key West: An Island Sheaf is a small volume of twenty-two poems that Crane left ready for publication at his death. (It was not issued separately but forms one section of the *Complete Poems*.) Most of them were written during or soon after his stay on the Isle of Pines in 1926; Waldo Frank accompanied him, and they stayed on the plantation belonging to Crane's maternal grandmother until it was wrecked by a hurricane. Some of the poems, however, were plainly written later, the last being "The Broken Tower," begun in Mexico only two months before Crane's suicide. Aside from being presumably Crane's choice of the best poems he had produced during these years (apart from *The Bridge*), the poems are unified by tropical imagery and feeling, the juxtaposition of fecundity and waste, beauty and death. Most of them are lower keyed, more "representational," and therefore more accessible than the poems of *White Buildings*; they are also more objectively personal and more varied in themes and techniques. Most critics have regarded these poems as exhibiting a great falling-off from the earlier volume, perhaps largely because Crane himself took this view —and certainly a primary motive for his suicide was his belief that "The Broken Tower" testified to the failure of his powers. But Crane was emphatically wrong about this poem, and he may therefore have been wrong about the whole trend. At any rate, it is possible to judge these poems by standards other than Crane's own "visionary" one, and to avoid equating them too closely with his personal agony and disintegration. Looked at thus independently, the poems in *Key West* and many of those labeled "Uncollected Poems" in the *Complete Poems* show a resemblance to the recent trend sometimes called "poetry of experience"—the direct and open-textured poetry, similarly related to personal crises, of Robert Lowell's *Life Studies* and W. D. Snodgrass' *Heart's Needle*, for example.

The title poem, "Key West," is a kind of farewell to the U.S.A. and to the modern civilization of which it is the most advanced embodiment.

Because these millions reap a dead conclusion
Need I presume the same fruit of my bone
As draws them towards a doubly mocked confusion
Of apish nightmares into steel-strung stone?

The "apish nightmares into steel-strung stone" is a negative counterpart to the lines in "Recitative"; in that poem, skyscrapers could be redeemed, at least metaphorically, when "darkness, like an ape's face, falls away,/And gradually white buildings answer day." But now the apish nightmares remain, and are embodied in the skyscrapers. The poet's only recourse is to go to his tropical island, while knowing that he cannot escape the modern world.

"O Carib Isle!" is about death in the tropics. Nothing mourns the dead: neither the "tarantula rattling at the lily's foot" nor the other creatures. Against the pitiless violence of the scene the poet can invoke only the fecundity of vegetation; but the wind—the most violent force of all, as in tropical hurricanes—"that knots itself in one great death—/Coils and withdraws. So syllables want breath." With no confidence in gainsaying death, the poet therefore asks where and what the ruler of this kind of nature is—the metaphor suggesting that He must be as bloodthirsty as the legendary Captain Kidd. The last three stanzas show the poet envisioning his own death in terms that are a kind of tropical equivalent of those of the *Divine Comedy*. He hopes that he can die under the "fiery blossoms" of the poinciana so that his "ghost" can ascend until "it meets the blue's comedian host." What he fears is a slow and helpless death like those of the "huge terrapin" overturned and spiked "Each daybreak on the wharf" to await slow evisceration; and, as he congeals, in the "satin and vacant" afternoons, he fears that the tropics are making him like the turtles. The shell (presumably both the shell of the poet as turtle and the island itself) is a gift of Satan; a "carbonic amulet" created by cosmic violence, "the sun exploded in the sea."

Only a few of the other poems in the volume can be mentioned. "The Idiot" is a vivid, uncomplicated, and very powerful rendering of an idiot boy whom Crane also describes in a letter: "When I saw him next he was talking to a blue little kite high in the afternoon. He is rendingly beautiful at times: I have encountered him in the road, talking again tout seul and examining pebbles and cinders and marble chips through the telescope of a twice-opened tomato can." The poem describes the embarrassment and ridicule he produces, with "squint lanterns in his head, and it's likely/Fumbling his sex . . ."; it presents the kite and tin-can telescope scene, and finally his song "Above all reason lifting"; the poet's "trespass vision shrinks to face his wrong." Quinn is probably right in suggesting that Crane sees the idiot implicitly as a distorted parallel to himself, a parody of the visionary poet, similarly derided and rejected. It is not necessary to read the poem in this way, but it helps to explain the moving quality it undoubtedly possesses. "Royal Palm" and "The Air Plant"—both in regular quatrains, like most of the poems in the volume—may be regarded as tropical "bridges," as Hazo suggests: the palm ascends to heaven, and the air plant ("This tuft that thrives on saline nothingness") lives in air, welcoming hurricanes as well as breezes. Both poems are relatively simple, straightforward, and emblematic in technique; they are herbal equivalents of bestiaries like those of Marianne Moore, making the plants types of human qualities. "The Hurricane" evokes the power of an awesome divinity, its archaism suggesting the Old Testament god of the whirlwind. (There is an implicit parallel in several of these poems between the hurricane and the force of poetic inspiration.)

By common consent, the best poem in the volume, and one of Crane's greatest lyrics, is "The Broken Tower." Crane's letters give the background of the poem fully, and it is a very important and moving biographical document. Crane wrote it in February–March 1932, under the stimulus of his late and unexpected love affair with Peggy Baird. It was, of course, based on an actual experience of helping to ring the church bells at dawn in Taxco, Mexico. The poem testifies to his feeling of rebirth and integration both in what it says and in the fact of its existence, for it was the first poem Crane had been able to finish in two years. But the feeling of hope and confidence evaporated during the weeks of revision; the people to whom he sent the poem happened not to reply promptly; and Crane became convinced that the poem was a failure and that it proved his creative powers to be exhausted. This conviction was the basis of his despair in those fantastic final days in Mexico; with nowhere to go, feeling at a dead end, he alternated between drunken debauchery and paranoiac suspiciousness until the threats of suicide reached their inevitable conclusion. The poem can hardly be detached entirely from this biographical context—any more than can, say, the late sonnets of Keats or the "terrible sonnets" of Hopkins—or from the context of Crane's other poetry, and it derives added significance from the fact that it is a final triumphant affirmation of the visionary theme and a kind of poetic testament.

The basic image is the implicit identification of the utterance of the church bells and the utterance of the poet; both are expressions and embodiments of vision and of divine love. The poet himself is both the tower and the sexton within it, pulled up and down in exultation and despair as the sexton is by his work of pulling the bell ropes. (The images are inconsistent visually, but not thematically; the poet is in both cases the agent and vehicle of Poetry, which enslaves and destroys him.)

The bells, I say, the bells break down their
    tower;
And swing I know not where. Their tongues
    engrave
Membrane through marrow, my long-scattered
    score
Of broken intervals. . . . And I, their sexton
    slave!

The fifth stanza makes explicit the identification of the two kinds of music—or perhaps it would be better to say, the substitution of poetry for any other religion. The poet's dedication is religious: he has become a poet ("entered the broken world," become a broken tower) for no other purpose than to "trace the visionary company of love," however fleeting its voice. The next stanza, however, voices doubt of the validity of the identification. "My word I poured." But was it really divine, was it the Word? His blood supplies no answer; but "she/Whose sweet mortality stirs latent power" revives and reassures him, so that he is "healed, original now, and pure. . . ." Although the biographical reference is clear enough, in terms of the poem the "she" is also a psychic force, a feminine part of the personality (although there is no evidence that Crane ever read Jung, anyone who has can hardly avoid thinking of the Jungian *anima*) which brings about an integration of the personality (the new tower built within, not stone, for "Not stone can jacket heaven," but "slip of pebbles") and unites human and divine love. The tower in the last stanza becomes the brazen tower of Danaë which Zeus entered in a golden shower, thus uniting human and divine: "Unseals her earth, and lifts love in its shower." Whether this psychological resolution of the question of the status and origin of the vision

seems satisfactory will depend on the reader's convictions; in terms of imagery and tonal climax, at least, it works brilliantly.

Many of Crane's poems raise the question of belief in a peculiarly urgent form. Not only do they proclaim allegiance to a "higher consciousness," a transcendent Vision attained through sexual passion or alcohol or art, but they exalt this dedication to ecstatic passion and death (with automatic resurrection) into a substitute religion, transferring to it the language and feeling of Christian devotion. This is particularly clear in the long poems, "For the Marriage of Faustus and Helen" and *The Bridge*. One's final judgment in this matter cannot be separated from one's religious and aesthetic beliefs. A number of able critics have recently asserted the claims of Neo-Romanticism in its various forms—Dionysiac ecstasy, vision, occultism, and mysticism—as against Eliotian classicism. My own view is that the formulations of Tate and Winters are still accurate: Crane was the "archetype of the modern American poet whose fundamental mistake lay in thinking that an irrational surrender of the intellect to the will would be the basis of a new morality" (Tate); "a poet of great genius, who ruined his life and his talent by living and writing as the two greatest religious teachers of our nation recommended" (Winters). Whether Crane took the doctrine primarily from Whitman and Emerson, as Winters thought, or from Nietzsche, as Dembo argues, makes no fundamental difference, nor does Quinn's attempt to make it respectable by associating it with Maritain's "creative intuition." Dembo's emphasis on the primacy of aesthetic reference in the doctrine—the poet seeking the absolute—makes it less repugnant; but it was more than aesthetic, it was the only religion Crane had. If we take it seriously as such, it is hard to see how it can be called (to use Eliot's criteria) a mature or coherent or responsible interpretation of the meaning of life and death. Aside from the odor of spilt religion, there is a feeling of strain in those poems in which the doctrine is presented explicitly, rather than as embodied in specific experience. This feeling, together with the ultimate incommunicability and obscurity of the doctrine in itself, is, I think, responsible for many of Crane's failures. Sometimes his linguistic effects—such as "adagios of islands" —seem not to correspond to any experience of poet or reader; they can be explained (as Crane brilliantly explained this one), but they still appear contrived and therefore ultimately mere tricks. Similarly, the symbolic structure of Crane's two long poems is abstract and "willed," standing for no real experience. Crane's "doctrine," then, is both shoddier and more dangerous than Yeats's "system," and immensely less viable in poetry. Yeats's system enabled him to "hold reality and justice in a single thought"; Crane's allowed him too often to transcend, or to ignore, both.

Crane had no messianic ambitions, however, and it is unfair to him to overstress the "doctrine." In general, he seems to me most completely successful when he has a subject other than the pure visionary gospel, and that takes him outside himself and provides a dramatic situation. I have indicated by my choice of poems to discuss which I think are his best. After all possible reservations and subtractions have been made, there remains a substantial number of great lyrics, unique, splendid, and powerful; and these are enough. In the other poems—the minor successes and partial failures—there are unforgettable passages, images, phrases. Crane exploits the resources of the verbal medium to and sometimes beyond its limits; his language is always charged with meaning (to recall Pound's definition of poetry)

and it never lacks excitement and challenge. At his best, he has a directness and immediacy, a haunting intensity and candor that are unlike anything else in English poetry.

Selected Bibliography

WORKS OF HART CRANE

POETRY AND PROSE
White Buildings: Poems by Hart Crane, with a foreword by Allen Tate. New York: Boni and Liveright, 1926.
The Bridge. Paris: Black Sun Press; New York: Liveright, 1930.
The Collected Poems of Hart Crane, edited with an introduction by Waldo Frank. New York: Liveright, 1933. (Includes the essay "Modern Poetry.")
The Complete Poems and Selected Letters and Prose of Hart Crane, edited with an introduction and Notes by Brom Weber. New York: Liveright, 1966.

LETTERS
The Letters of Hart Crane, 1916–1932, edited by Brom Weber. New York: Hermitage House, 1952. (Reprinted, Berkeley and Los Angeles: University of California Press, 1965).

BIBLIOGRAPHIES
Rowe, H. D. *Hart Crane: A Bibliography.* Denver: Alan Swallow, 1955.
Schwartz, Joseph. *Hart Crane: An Annotated Critical Bibliography.* New York: D. Lewis, 1970.

BIOGRAPHIES
Brown, Susan Jenkins. *Robber Rocks: Letters and Memories of Hart Crane, 1923–1932.* Middletown, Conn.: Wesleyan University Press, 1969.

Horton, Philip. *Hart Crane: The Life of an American Poet*. New York: Norton, 1937. (Includes as appedixes an essay and several letters by Crane explaining his beliefs about poetry in general and his specific intentions in some of his own poems.)

Unterecker, John. *Voyager: A Life of Hart Crane*. New York: Farrar, Straus and Giroux, 1969.

Weber, Brom. *Hart Crane: A Biographical and Critical Study*. New York: Bodley Press, 1948. (Includes previously uncollected poetry and prose.)

CRITICAL STUDIES

Alvarez, Alfred. *Stewards of Excellence: Studies in Modern English and American Poets*. New York: Scribners, 1958. Pp. 107–23.

Blackmur, R. P. *Form and Value in Modern Poetry*. Garden City, N.Y.: Doubleday Anchor Books, 1957. Pp. 269–85.

Butterfield, R. W. *The Broken Arc: A Study of Hart Crane*. Edinburgh: Oliver and Boyd, 1969.

Cambon, Glauco. *The Inclusive Flame: Studies in American Poetry*. Bloomington: Indiana University Press, 1963. Pp. 120–82.

Cowley, Malcolm. *Exile's Return*. New York: Viking, 1951. Pp. 227–34.

Dembo, L. S. *Hart Crane's Sanskrit Charge: A Study of* The Bridge. Ithaca. N.Y.: Cornell University Press, 1960.

————. "Hart Crane's Early Poetry," *University of Kansas City Review*, 27:181–87 (1961).

Frank, Waldo. *In the American Jungle*. New York: Farrar and Rinehart, 1937. Pp. 96–108.

Friar, Kimon, and J. M. Brinnin, eds. *Modern Poetry: American and British*. New York: Appleton-Century-Crofts, 1951. Pp. 449–56.

Friedman, Paul. *"The Bridge: A Study in Symbolism,"* *Psychoanalytic Quarterly*, 21:49–80 (1952).

Gregory, Horace, and Marya Zaturenska. *A History of American Poetry 1900–1940*. New York: Harcourt, Brace, 1946. Pp. 468–81.

Hazo, Samuel. *Hart Crane: An Introduction and Interpretation*. New York: Barnes and Noble, 1963.

Koretz, Gene, "Crane's 'Passage,'" *Explicator*, Vol. 13, No. 8, Item 47 (1955).

Leibowitz, Herbert A. *Hart Crane: An Introduction to the Poetry*. New York: Columbia University Press, 1968.

Lewis, R. W. B. *The Poetry of Hart Crane: A Critical Study*. Princeton. N.J.: Princeton University Press, 1967.

Matthiessen, F. O. "American Poetry, 1920–1940," *Sewanee Review*, 55:24–55 (1947).

Miller, James E., Jr., Karl Shapiro, and Bernice Slote. *Start with the Sun: Studies in Cosmic Poetry*. Lincoln: University of Nebraska Press, 1960. Pp. 137–65.

Quinn, Vincent. *Hart Crane*. New York: Twayne, 1963.

Rosenthal, M. L. *The Modern Poets: A Critical Introduction*. New York: Oxford University Press, 1960. Pp. 168–82.

Tate, Allen. *Collected Essays*. Denver: Alan Swallow, 1959. Pp. 225–37, 528–32.

Trachtenberg, Alan. *Brooklyn Bridge: Fact and Symbol*. New York: Oxford University Press, 1965. Pp. 143–65.

Vogler, Thomas A. "A New View of Hart Crane's Bridge," *Sewanee Review*, 73:381–408 (1965).

Waggoner, Hyatt Howe. *The Heel of Elohim: Science and Values in Modern American Poetry*. Norman: University of Oklahoma Press, 1950. Pp. 155–92.

Winters, Yvor. *In Defense of Reason*. New York: Swallow Press and W. Morrow, 1947. Pp. 575–603. (Same essay in *On Modern Poets*. New York: Meridian Books, 1959. Pp. 120–43.)

—MONROE K. SPEARS

Stephen Crane

1871-1900

SOME writers work their way up to popularity in a long and difficult climb; others hit upon success almost overnight. Stephen Crane's early attempt at literary creation, his novel *The Red Badge of Courage*, met with triumphal acclaim in 1896, but he only lived long enough to enjoy a few years of controversial fame.

Experimenting in various media—journalism, fiction, poetry, playwriting—Crane was for his contemporaries above all a picturesque figure of the world of the press. His professional commitments kept him in close touch with the life of his country, and he explored slums and battlefields with unabating eagerness, seeing war in two brief conflicts in 1897 and 1898. The conjunction of highstrung temperament and obstinate neglect of his health brought Crane's life to an early close, when he was not yet twenty-nine.

During the two decades following his death, in 1900, he was to be almost forgotten. Then in 1923 Thomas Beer published an impressionistic biography which served to focus attention on Crane once more, and *The Work of Stephen Crane* (1925–27), edited by Wilson Follett, made most of his writings available to a scholarly audience. This limited edition contained laudatory prefaces by creative writers such as Amy Lowell, Sherwood Anderson, H. L. Mencken, and Willa Cather, a few assessments by professional critics, and reminiscences by fellow journalists. Crane's reputation was also enhanced by the faithful support of some of his friends, especially Edward Garnett, Joseph Conrad, H. G. Wells, and Ford Madox Hueffer, later known as Ford Madox Ford. The thirties saw in him a champion of the cause of the common man, and the forties continued to fit him into a realistic tradition; in the next two decades he has appeared to critics primarily as a symbolist, but a wide range of interpretations has confronted the student with a mass of conflicting scholarship. In 1950 John Berryman's *Stephen Crane* established him as an American classic. The Modern Library edition of *The Red Badge of Courage* came out the following year with a preface written by R. W. Stallman, whose extensive work on Crane, climaxed by his monumental biography in 1968, has aroused much enthusiasm and controversy. D. G. Hoffman's *The Poetry of Stephen Crane*, a very lively and perceptive study, appeared in 1957. Since 1951 there has also been a steady outpouring of articles, dissertations, monographs, and reprints. When, in the summer of 1966, a *Stephen Crane Newsletter* was founded and began to be issued regularly by Ohio State University, Stephen Crane had come into his own.

Stephen Crane had deep roots in the soil of New Jersey and was extremely proud of his American heritage. One of his ancestors bearing the same name had, according to Crane, "arrived in Massachusetts from England in 1635." The man who wrote *The Red Badge of Courage* was, on his father's side, descended from a long line of sheriffs, judges, and farmers, and another Stephen Crane had been one of the leading patriots of New Jersey during the Revolution; in his mother's family, as he humorously put it, "everybody, as soon as he could walk, became a Methodist clergyman— of the old, ambling-nag, saddle-bag, exhorting kind."

Born in a Methodist parsonage in Newark, New Jersey, on November 1, 1871, Stephen was the fourteenth child of Jonathan Townley Crane, D.D. He grew up in various parsonages in New Jersey and New York State, his father being, according to the custom of his church, shifted from one charge to another every two or three years. The death of Dr. Crane in Port Jervis, New York, in 1880 brought this itinerancy to a close. Still a child when his father died, Stephen always cherished his memory.

After the death of her husband Mrs. Crane returned to Newark for a while, but soon made a permanent home in Asbury Park, New Jersey, which was a new stronghold of American Methodism. There she settled in 1883 and, that same year, was elected president of the Woman's Christian Temperance Union of Asbury Park and Ocean Grove. Frequently lecturing in neighboring towns, she occasionally traveled to distant cities as a delegate of that organization. A well-educated woman, she also dabbled in journalism to eke out her meager resources and reported on the summer religious meetings on the New Jersey shore, contributing mostly to the *New York Tribune* and the *Philadelphia Press*. She suffered from mental illness for some months in 1886 and was to die in 1891. Her religious zeal did not inspire a similar response in Stephen and he left the fold of the church; but he remained dominated by fundamental religious precepts and patterns—charity, fraternity, redemption, and rescue—which he usually kept at an earthly level.

At the age of fourteen he left Asbury Park to go to the Pennington Seminary, a Methodist academy in New Jersey, and thus attended a school over which his father had ruled for ten years (1849–58). He did not complete the four-year course there but transferred in the middle of the third year to Claverack College and Hudson River Institute, a semi-military Methodist school near Hudson, New York. He stayed there from January 1888 to June 1890. His university education lasted only one year: it began at Lafayette College, a Presbyterian institution at Easton, Pennsylvania, where he spent the autumn term of 1890, and ended at Syracuse University the following June. All these schools stressed religious and classical studies, and at no time did the young man feel any sympathy for these two branches of knowledge. He was already a rebel resolutely hostile to formal education and preferred to study "humanity."

Crane suffered both from his mother's moral severity and from her physical neglect of him, but in Asbury Park he enjoyed a happy freedom near the "soft booming sound of surf." The deaths of his father, his sister Agnes, his brother Luther, and finally his mother must have made his childhood and adolescence a period of many severe trials. Three of his older brothers played the part of father-substitutes, offering either material assistance or a questionable but attractive model. William, who became a lawyer in Port Jervis in 1881, and Edmund, a man of limited education but of generous heart who, in 1894, settled at Hartwood, near Port Jervis, often helped the young man in his financial difficulties at the beginning of his literary career. Jonathan Townley Jr.'s bohemian tastes exerted a powerful influence on his younger brother; almost twenty years older than Stephen, he was in the late 1880's the coast correspondent of the *New York Sun*, the *New York Tribune*, and the Associated Press in Asbury Park and so a well-known regional journalist. Stephen, as early as 1888, began helping him in his reportorial work on the New Jersey shore. His oldest sister, Nellie, who then kept an art school in Asbury Park, may have introduced Stephen to the world of color and prepared him for an aesthetic exploration of his environment.

Stephen Crane's sensitivity was thus early aroused and developed through a gradual training of his faculty of observation: Methodism forced him to probe his own soul, journalism taught him how to note facts with accuracy, and art provided his craving for reality with chromatic patterns.

After publishing a few pieces in *Cosmopolitan* and the *New York Tribune*, a paper for which he wrote his "Sullivan County Sketches," boyish tales of the woods, in the early part of 1892, he was fired by the *Tribune* for an ironic article about a parade of workers in Asbury Park, and became a free-lance journalist in New York. (This brief report had expressed, in the tone of a sententious aesthete, his mild amusement at the sight of "an uncut and uncarved procession" of men with "principles" marching past a "decorous" throng of "summer gowns" and predatory Asbury Parkers.) Then began his apprenticeship in bohemianism in the metropolis, where he lived with struggling young artists. Occasional visits to his brothers Edmund and William helped him keep from starving; they provided him with handy refuges where he could escape from the hardships and turmoil of New York. His pride, however, prevented him from making frequent use of them. In 1893 he published his first book, *Maggie: A Girl of the Streets*, under a pseudonym and at his own expense. The audacity of the subject did not deter Hamlin Garland and W. D. Howells from praising that novel, but they were almost the only critics to notice it. They both encouraged him to write proletarian sketches, some of which appeared in the Boston *Arena* and others in the *New York Press*, enabling him to attain some financial security. His picture of the big city was centered around the life of the underprivileged in their ordinary setting, the southern tip of Manhattan.

Gradually acquiring self-reliance, experience, and ambition, he immersed himself in the most significant venture of his literary life, the writing of *The Red Badge of Courage*, an imaginative reconstruction of a Civil War battle; it was first printed in an abbreviated form as a newspaper serial distributed by the Bacheller Syndicate in December 1894. The success of the story led to an assignment as roving reporter in the West and Mexico at the beginning of 1895. When he came back in May, his first volume of verse, *The Black Riders*, had just appeared in print and proved that the young man was impelled by the spirit of religious and social rebellion. Appleton published *The Red Badge* as a book in New York in October 1895, and the London firm of Heinemann included it in its Pioneer Series at the end of November. Warmly received by English reviewers, it soon became a popular novel in the United States as well and its tenth American edition was issued in June 1896.

In that year Crane's celebrity reached a

peak. All at once praised, parodied, and harshly criticized, he found it difficult to cope with success. Going from one apartment to another in New York and probably from one girl to another, he ended up challenging the impregnable metropolitan police force on behalf of a prostitute who claimed she was being unjustly harassed. Then, rushing into escape, he accepted a commission to report the insurrection in Cuba against Spanish rule, but his ship sank off the coast of Florida on January 2, 1897, and he returned to Jacksonville, where before sailing he had met Cora Howorth (known there as Cora Taylor), the proprietress of the Hotel de Dream, a somewhat refined house of ill-fame. She had already been married twice and, at the time of her first meeting with Crane, was thirty-one years old. They were to live together for the rest of his life. His previous adventures with women had been inconclusive episodes. At the age of twenty he had fallen in love, at Avon-by-the-Sea, a resort near Asbury Park, with a certain Helen Trent, who was already engaged. In 1892 a love affair with a young married woman, Lily Brandon Munroe, enlivened his summer in Asbury Park and inspired some of his more moving love letters. Nellie Crouse, a provincial maiden whom he met at a social tea in New York, flirted with him by mail but finally rejected him. In 1896 he started sending money to Amy Leslie, a former actress now past her prime who had become a drama critic for the *Chicago Daily News*. He kept doing so until January 1898, when she succeeded in having a warrant of attachment issued against him to recover $550 of the $800 she had allegedly given him in 1896 to deposit for her. The details of their relationship remain somewhat obscure but, in November 1896, when he set out for Florida, he was probably fleeing from her as well as from the New York police.

The year 1896 was not marked by any really new work from his pen, except his "Tenderloin" sketches for the *New York Journal*: Crane was too busy with his public and private life. *Maggie*, made respectable by the success of *The Red Badge* and slightly revised, came out under his real name, accompanied by another tale of the slums, *George's Mother*, which had been completed in November 1894. A volume of war stories, *The Little Regiment*, appeared in New York late in 1896 and in London in February 1897.

Crane's longing for adventure had apparently been only whetted by the shipwreck off Florida, in which he nearly lost his life; periodically the urge to see violent action was aroused in him. The Greco-Turkish War, which he covered in a disappointing manner for the *New York Journal* and the *Westminster Gazette*, took him to Europe in the summer of 1897; his bad health interfered with his reportorial duties in Greece, but he saw enough fighting to conclude on his return to London that *"The Red Badge* [was] all right."

Obviously conscious of the impossibility of introducing his "wife"—there is no record of a marriage ceremony—to his family, and still afraid of retaliatory action by the New York police, he decided to stay on in England after the Greek war was over. His shipwreck had inspired him to write a brilliant short story, "The Open Boat," which *Scribners* printed in June 1897. About the same time he published *The Third Violet*, a novel based on his experiences in the highly contrasted worlds of Hartwood, New York, and New York City. Crane's stay in England did not provide the writer with a fresh batch of literary topics but it did enable him to see his own life in a new perspective. Many of his western adventures and several accounts of urban poverty went into a volume published in 1898 under the title *The Open Boat and Other Stories*. This volume, which contains seventeen tales, gives a sample of Crane's best talent. His meeting with Joseph Conrad brought him into contact with a writer whose aesthetics was very close to his own. In his "villa," situated on the borderline between Oxted and Limpsfield, Surrey, where he settled in the fall of 1897, Crane was not far from Ford Madox Hueffer and Harold Frederic. A few English Fabians, the Sydney Oliviers and the Edward Garnetts notably, lived in the vicinity.

In 1898 he was hired by Pulitzer to write for the *New York World* and, seeing war for the second time, reported the Spanish-American conflict, which left deep scars on his body and mind; the symptoms of the tuberculosis that was to prove fatal had already set in. In the fall he lingered in Havana, where he served as special correspondent for the *New York Journal* and wrote the first draft of a novel, *Active Service*, based on his Greek assignment.

Early in 1899 he was back in England and, because of harassing creditors in Oxted, decided to move from Surrey to Sussex, his new English residence being the medieval manor of Brede Place situated near Rye on the charming Sussex coast. There his literary production reached a peak, but his efforts to avoid bankruptcy proved vain in the face of a rising tide of debts and recurring signs of failing health. He kept writing doggedly, now coaxing, now threatening his literary agent, James B. Pinker, from whom he tried to obtain more and more advances, and even the best work of this period shows the effects of haste and worry. Drawing upon his recent experiences, he completed a series of eleven fictional and autobiographical accounts of the Cuban war, which were posthumously collected in *Wounds in the Rain* (1900). He also wrote thirteen children's stories which first appeared in *Harper's Magazine* and were assembled in book form after his death under the title *Whilomville Stories* (1900). In the course of 1899 three other books

saw print: a volume of verse, *War Is Kind*, containing a variety of poems whose composition embraced a period of seven years; *Active Service*, a novel which he himself regarded as second-rate; and the American edition of *The Monster and Other Stories*. Reminiscing about his family's role during the Revolutionary War, he composed three "Wyoming Valley Tales" and, creating an imaginary country, chose it as the setting for a series of archetypal battles, the "Spitzbergen Tales," which began to appear in English and American magazines in 1900.

Taking a mild interest in Cora's passion for entertaining, he watched streams of guests come to visit him in his dilapidated mansion, among whom were some distinguished writers (Conrad, Wells, Henry James) and many parasites. He decided or was persuaded by Cora to arrange a Christmas party for his literary friends, producing an original play for the occasion. The play was very aptly called *The Ghost* and, in spite of a widely advertised collaboration with famous English and American authors, most of it was written by Crane himself. During the festivities he almost died of a lung hemorrhage. He was to drag on for a few more months, his body and his brain gradually weakening, but he went on writing to his deathbed. With the help of Kate Lyon, Harold Frederic's mistress, he turned out a series of articles on nine great battles of the world for *Lippincott's Magazine*, outlined the plot and wrote the first twenty-five chapters of *The O'Ruddy*, a picaresque novel of the eighteenth century with an Irish hero and an English setting. But it was left uncompleted when Crane died on June 5, 1900, in Badenweiler, Germany, where Cora had seen fit to take him in the idle hope of a miraculous recovery from tuberculosis. Crane's friend Robert Barr agreed to write the final chapters of the novel which, after picaresque ups and downs, was eventually published in New York in October 1903.

The inescapable trait of Crane as a writer is his desire to express his own mind candidly, regardless of accepted opinion, conventions, and satirical attacks. The world first appeared to him with the colors, shapes, and sounds of the Psalms and of Wesleyan hymns, and he unconsciously made frequent use of the rhythms and imagery of Biblical stories. His parents' participation in charitable work encouraged his interest in slum life, and he soon discovered, through his own deep concern with the mainsprings of fear, a strange curiosity about war.

In Crane's generation "low life" was a subject of reportage, fiction, and melodrama. When he moved into this area of literature he did so with the seriousness, the intentness, and the acuteness of a minister's son who had received his training as a journalist. Even if he did not know New York well at the time he wrote *Maggie*, he must have caught by then a few glimpses of the poorer districts of the American metropolis, which was so close to Asbury Park where he lived between his stays at boarding school or college.

The approach to slum life of Crane's first novel was new in that it did not preach and did not encourage "slumming"; it simply aimed, he said, to "show people to people as they seem[ed] to [him]." Maggie is the daughter of the Johnsons, a family of poor tenement dwellers living on the lower East Side of Manhattan. A large part of the story is devoted to drinking bouts, and Maggie's home is the scene of a daily fight for survival. We thus attend the growth and brutal extinction of the heroine, who has "blossomed in a mud-puddle" to become a "pretty girl" strangely undefiled by her surroundings. She tries to escape the de-grading atmosphere of her home by working in a collar-and-cuff factory, but soon discovers the dull routine and corruption of the sweat-shop. Then Pete, a commonplace bartender, comes into her life, and to Maggie he seems to be "a supreme warrior," "a knight." He takes her to dime museums, beer gardens, and theaters, and thus satisfies her vague and romantic longings for culture and refinement. Seduced and abandoned by her lover, rejected by her drinking mother and callous brother on "moralistic" grounds, Maggie finally turns to prostitution. Shortly afterwards, "upon a wet evening," she abruptly ends her life in the East River while in the distance "street-car bells [jingle] with a sound of merriment."

The problem this story hinges on is not primarily a social one, and Crane is not merely content with studying the causes and consequences of prostitution. Mainly concerned with the "soul" of the young prostitute, he tries to challenge the beliefs of Sunday school religion. Can an "occasional street girl" be expected to end up in Heaven, irrespective of the indignant frowns of "many excellent people"? The answer is never made explicit in a narrative brimming over with irony, but it could not be other than positive. Maggie falls because "environment is a tremendous thing in the world," because she herself is romantic and weak, and also because nobody is interested in her fate. She, however, redeems herself by committing suicide, her only possible escape from a life of moral degradation. By doing so she undergoes an ironic purification in the foul waters of the East River while her brother Jimmie, who had "clad his soul in armour," and her mother, who belatedly "ferg[ave]" her, are allowed to continue their degenerate lives of vice and hypocrisy in the human jungle to which they are perfectly adapted.

As a first novel *Maggie* revealed on the part

STEPHEN CRANE / 411

of the author a deep seriousness and the powerful urge to gain an audience. It posited the imperative need for a new ethical code and, through a consistent use of irony, debunked the false values worshiped by society and exposed the part played by collective passivity in the destruction of innocence. "Indifference is a militant thing," Crane commented in a story of 1897; this idea is implied throughout *Maggie*. Much of this early Crane is reminiscent of the young Zola's passion for social rescue, which found its most moving expression in *La Confession de Claude* (1865). The critics who wonder whether *Maggie* should be called a tragedy or a melodrama raise a fruitless issue, because the book is undeniably filled with pity and fear, and Howells was right when he discovered in it "that quality of fatal necessity which dominates Greek tragedy."

George's Mother is a companion piece to the drama of the New York prostitute, and it takes up again the problem of the corruption of innocence, this time in the person of a young workingman, George, who has recently settled in New York and lives in a tenement with his widowed mother, a very religious woman. The path leading to George's physical and moral destruction opens early in the story when he meets a former acquaintance, a certain Jones, who introduces him into a circle of alcoholics. He thus misses work one day and invents a lie as an excuse for his absence. His mother, who tries to keep him from drifting, induces him to go with her to a prayer meeting which only "prov[es] to him again that he [is] damned." Plunging more resolutely into drink and dissipation, the young man inflicts great moral torture upon his mother, who finally dies, worn down by disappointed expectations. The last scene shows her in the grips of her death agony, while her son, hastily called to her bedside, suddenly feels "hideous crabs crawling upon his brain." This book shows more the interest in abstract ideas than in real people; it demonstrates the baneful effects of Sunday school religion upon George, who seeks refuge from it in drink, and the failure of this primitive faith to succor the mother in her sorest need. It also points to the impossibility of communication between human beings. The power corruptive influences and environment exert on immature minds is here again illustrated. This rather flimsy novel raises a number of issues but solves none, and throughout are heard distinct echoes of Crane's conflict with his own mother.

The confined world of *George's Mother* could easily be contrasted with the maelstrom of life in Crane's New York City sketches, which he ranked among his "best work." He started his field study in the poorer districts of southern Manhattan, observing the motley streams of passers-by on Broadway, breadlines, crowds gathering outside cheap lodging houses, jingling streetcars, fires, Italian fruit vendors, tramps, policemen, and here and there his camera eye stopped on a detail, a "tiny old lady" lost in "the tempest of Sixth Avenue," or two children fighting for a toy. His sympathy drew him instinctively to the cause of the common man, but he was more inclined to study the actual working of minds than the possible consequences of economic systems. In his study of the "Tenderloin," undertaken for the *New York Journal* in 1896, he calls up a picture of restaurants, dance halls, and opium dens where, beneath the superficial gaiety, slumbers the fire of an ever-present violence.

His technique in these city sketches follows three main patterns: that of the journey of initiation, exemplified by "An Experiment in Misery" and "An Ominous Baby"; that of canvas painting, in "The Men in the Storm," "An Eloquence of Grief," and "The Auction"; and that of the parody, in some of his "Tenderloin" stories. The reporter-errant selects a certain situation which becomes a pretext for a psychological study of urban conflicts. To him "the sense of city [was] battle."

How did Crane's war novel, *The Red Badge of Courage*, come into being against this background of urban literature? The book is not an ordinary Civil War novel. Although the theme is the baptism of fire of a Union private, Henry Fleming, during the battle of Chancellorsville, the tone is psychological rather than military. Its main characters are most of the time designated as figures in an allegory, "the tall soldier," "the loud soldier," "the tattered man," "the man of the cheery voice"; and the protagonist, usually referred to as "the youth" in the early chapters, only acquires his full identity in Chapter XI.

The author's observation of "the nervous system under fire" is conducted on the level of Henry's restless mind; before the battle we witness the premonitory misgivings of this farm boy in uniform; then comes his moment of reassurance after a first onslaught of the enemy has been repulsed. A second attack launched against his side causes his sudden panic and flight. Driven by shame to wander on the fringe of the battlefield, he seems to be helplessly floating in a nightmarish atmosphere; this, for our cowardly private, is the beginning of a journey of expiation. He meets a "tattered soldier" whose wounds and embarrassing questions increase his sense of guilt. The two men are caught up in the procession of wounded soldiers who make their way to the rear. Among them they see Henry's friend, Jim Conklin, the mortally wounded "tall soldier" who, after horrible sufferings climaxed by a gruesome "danse macabre," dies under their petrified gaze. After this shattering experience Henry abandons the "tattered man" whose very presence seems to him an accusation. Retreat-

ing Union soldiers fly past him, and one of them, whom the youth tries to question, knocks him down with the butt of his rifle, ironically giving him the "red badge of courage" he had been longing for. After regaining consciousness Henry meets a man with "a cheery voice" who takes him back to his regiment and, from then on, the protagonist's attitude is altogether changed. He feels full of aggressive but specious self-confidence and, because he does not reveal the real cause of his wound, derives much unmerited respect from his fellow soldiers for his ostensibly courageous conduct. The last chapters show him turning into a daredevil, fighting at the head of his unit during a victorious charge, but at the end of the story—which is no pamphlet for recruiting officers—Henry's regiment finds itself recrossing the river it had crossed a few days before and thus going back to its previous position on the other bank of the Rappahannock as if nothing had happened. Henry's first impression had been right after all: "It was all a trap."

A constant ironic counterpoint aims to debunk the traditional concept of glorious war. The whole thing seems absurd: generals shout, stammer, and behave childishly on the battlefield; Henry's wound confers upon him a spurious glory; Wilson, the "loud soldier," has become as meek as a lamb in the last chapters, and the whole tumult has resulted in no gain of ground for the Union forces and no loss for the Confederates. What remains in the mind of the reader is a series of confused movements with, from time to time, "men drop[ping] here and there like bundles" and, in the protagonist's "procession of memory," sad nerve-racking images suddenly blurred with a sense of relief when the "sultry nightmare [is] in the past."

Like all the great classics of literature *The Red Badge of Courage* speaks of different things to different minds. However, only an oversimplified interpretation could see in Henry's final charge the proof that he has become, as he himself thinks, "a man." The pattern of this book is that of a spiritual journey, but the final goal remains in doubt when we reach the conclusion: "Over the river a golden ray of sun came through the hosts of leaden rain clouds." The youth, in his baptism of fire, has acquired self-knowledge and experience, but a radical change has not taken place within him: he remains, in his heroic pose at the end, just as grotesque as the fearful "little man" he was at the beginning. The dialogue he has been carrying on with his own conscience often contains overtones of legalistic chicanery: it is a constant search for excuses to justify his cowardly conduct. Occasional flashes of inner sincerity are defeated by his attempts to demonstrate that what he did was logically and morally valid, but his arguments would fail to convince anyone and only add to his torment. Through a series of excruciating experiences which follow his shameful act he manages to keep his secret and even to rise in stature in the eyes of his regiment. But, instead of closing the book with a reassuring epiphany, the author preserves the ironic structure throughout. Henry's conscience is still disturbed when the book ends, and his concealed guilt spoils "the gilded images of memory."

The Red Badge of Courage contains the account of a half-completed conversion. It is only in a satellite story entitled "The Veteran" that Henry pays the full price for his "sin" and goes through the final stage of his itinerary of redemption. Then, by belatedly but unequivocally confessing his lack of courage on the battlefield, he purges himself of his former lie. In the last scene of "The Veteran," determined to save two colts trapped in his burning barn, he plunges into the flames never to come out, thus making a gesture of genuine and unconventional bravery. Rejecting his previous

irony, Crane presents here a real conversion, grounded on cool, selfless determination and not on spurious enthusiasm, as was Henry's sudden reversal of mood on the battlefield.

In Crane's war novel religious imagery prevails, centered on an itinerary of spiritual redemption which leads not to eternal salvation but to a blissful impasse. Alone in the middle of the forest the hero discovers the imaginary "chapel" with its "columnlike" trees where a "hymn of twilight" is heard. When the "tall soldier" dies, wildly gesturing in his final agony, he seems to resemble "a devotee of a mad religion"; most significant in the same creative process is Henry's illusion after his cowardly flight: he looks for "a means of escape from the consequences of his fall" and, unable to reach redemption through mere introspection, returns to "the creed of soldiers." But his final charge does not purge him of his guilt in spite of a temporary exultation due to the repression of his fear; "the ghost of his flight" and "a specter of reproach" born of the desertion of "the tattered man" in his sorest need keep haunting the youth at the close of the book. Some obvious similarities with the theme of concealment in Hawthorne's fiction can also be noted: "veil" metaphors and similes clustered around the character of Henry Fleming keep recurring in the narrative. In Chapter I the hero "wish[es] to be alone with some new thoughts that [have] lately come to him"; in Chapter VII he "cring[es] as if discovered in a crime" and, under the burden of his hidden guilt, soon feels that "his shame [can] be viewed." But an ironic glimmer of hope reappears in his consciousness when he imagines that "in the battle blur" his face will be hidden "like the face of a cowled man."

Beside this procession of religious images there appears here and there a scattering of scenes with animal characters which seem to be fables in miniature. The style abounds in symbolic rabbits, squirrels, horses, cows, and snakes which form a conventional bestiary by the side of a Christian demonology swarming with monsters directly borrowed from Biblical literature.

Another facet of this book is its consistent use of legalistic terminology. A dossier is being minutely, if inconclusively, revealed to us: the youth of this story approaches his problem of fear in a logical manner and determines to "accumulate information of himself"; at first he tries to "mathematically prove to himself that he [will] not run from a battle." Then, after experiencing his shameful flight, he acts as his own lawyer and attempts to present a convincing defense of his case: "He had done a good part in saving himself, who was a little part of the army. . . . His actions had been sagacious things. They had been full of strategy. They were the work of a master's legs." A strong ironic coloring, one of the main characteristics of Crane's style in the whole book, can easily be detected here. Henry is constantly trying to show his actions to advantage; when he returns to his regiment after his cowardly escape, he even considers using the "small weapon"—a packet of letters—which Wilson in a panic had left in his hands before the battle. This "exhibit" would, Henry thinks, "prostrate his comrade at the first signs of a cross-examination."

The mechanistic imagery of *The Red Badge of Courage* already adumbrates the development of Crane's war motif in his writings after the Cuban conflict of 1898, and serves to highlight the complexity and destructiveness of modern war: "The battle was like the grinding of an immense and terrible machine to him. Its complexities and powers, its grim processes, fascinated him. He must go close and see it produce corpses."

If military courage had been one of the values pitilessly probed in *The Red Badge of Courage*, it also furnished the central topic for a satellite story entitled "A Mystery of Heroism." Private Fred Collins ventures into no man's land under the pretext of procuring some water for his company; but in fact his action has been prompted by the desire to prove himself that he is not "afraid t' go." After being "blindly . . . led by quaint emotions" he returns unscathed to his lines, but the author wastes no sympathy on his "heroic" deed. "Death and the Child' deals with the same theme, the scene being now the Greco-Turkish war of 1897; the central character, a war correspondent, soon sees his battle fury die out and, instead of fighting by the side of the soldiers of his mother country, flees and encounters a child who asks him this embarrassing question: "Are you a man?"

In his reporting of the same war and of the Cuban conflict Crane fell in with the conventions of his time and did not aim at more than ordinary journalistic style. But when reworking his factual accounts of battles and recollecting his war experiences in tranquillity he achieved the spare and severe economy of *Wounds in the Rain* (1900), a moving and realistic adaptation in fiction of his own adventures with the American forces sent to Cuba in 1898. His protagonist then ceased to be a dreamy amateur like Henry Fleming in *The Red Badge* or Peza in "Death and the Child," and the figure of Private Nolan, the regular, as anonymous and unromantic as any true regular, stood out in the foreground. Crane was now dealing with war as a special trade, and his soldiers at work were shown to be "as deliberate and exact as so many watchmakers." In "The Price of the Harness" he went beyond the phantasmagoria of his early definition of war and made of "a great, grand steel loom . . . to weave a woof of thin red threads, the cloths of death," the essential metaphor of his battle symbolics. Henceforth, in the logbook of the war correspondent, what had been in *The Red Badge* a "monster," "a dragon," or a "blood-swollen god," gradually came down to the lowly estate of "death, and a plague of the lack of small things and toil." Crane could not have gone any further in deglamorizing that image of "vague and bloody conflicts" which had once "thrilled [Henry Fleming] with their sweep and fire."

A gradual reduction of the concept of war to the archetype can be found in Crane's later stories, if we leave aside as mere pot-boiling and unoriginal work his *Great Battles of the World* (1901). It is in the "Spitzbergen Tales" that the war metaphor is suddenly brought down to its essentials, the taking of a coveted hill, the storming of a redoubt, or a burial scene on the front line. The typical hero of most of these stories is no longer a private but a non-commissioned or low-ranking officer, the problem of conduct being then studied in an almost abstract context and the main issue being the duty of the responsible professional toward his command. Primarily concerned with war as a personal test, Crane avoided the approach of the historian, that of the strategist, and deliberately worked out that of the moralist.

To him war, in its various manifestations, was the alpha and omega of human life, essentially a testing ground, but adventure could be a fair substitute. Sent to the West and Mexico by the Bacheller Syndicate as a roving reporter early in 1895, he drew upon his tour for a few outstanding stories. His shipwreck off the coast of Florida in January 1897 furnished material for "The Open Boat," a tale which won immediate recognition and found in Conrad and H. G. Wells two faithful admirers. The latter even went so far as to say about it: "[It is], to my mind, beyond all question, the crown of all his work."

Stephen Crane depended on adventure, vicarious or real, as fodder for his imagination.

He had to *feel* intensely to *write* intensely. As soon as the pace of his life became relaxed because of illness and a general weakening of his spiritual energy, he was compelled to turn to his childhood reminiscences, also fraught with intense emotions, or to an archetypal war metaphor in order to write successfully.

The short stories "The Blue Hotel," "The Bride Comes to Yellow Sky," and "The Open Boat" outline his personal attitude toward the literary utilization of experience. Although fond of exotic settings and people, Crane is not a local colorist. The colors of his adventures are the colors of his soul. For example, the real fight that he saw in a saloon in Lincoln, Nebraska, which is supposed to have been the germ of "The Blue Hotel," was transmuted by him into a moral study on the theme of collective and individual responsibility. The narrative in this tale is conducted on two levels, straight storytelling and ironic counterpoint. A Swede who has lived for ten years in New York and is now traveling in the West experiences forebodings of violent death and is eventually justified in his fear, since he meets his doom at the hands of a professional gambler. Crane, however, succeeds in keeping up the suspense by leading his main character into ominous situations at the Palace Hotel which are ironically deflated and prove harmless to the frightened hero. Once the latter feels that all danger is over and is about to celebrate his escape from the hotel in a neighboring saloon, he is stabbed to death by a gambler whom he wanted too insistently to befriend. Crane here comes back again to an analysis of fear. In the Swede's mind this feeling follows a pattern similar to that of Henry's itinerary in *The Red Badge*: from timidity to unrestrained arrogance. Both Henry and the Swede are intoxicated, the former with a belatedly discovered battle fury, the latter with repeated drinking. Crane also explores the comic overtones of violence, and notes the grotesque fall of the Swede's body, "pierced as easily as if it had been a melon." The protagonist obviously brought about his own destruction, but the writer is not just censuring one man's attitude, and the easterner, Mr. Blanc, who acts as point-of-view character, declares: " 'We are all in it! . . . Every sin is the result of a collaboration.' " Once again the creator of *Maggie* stigmatized the unpardonable sin, indifference: no one had done anything to prevent the final denouement from taking place. The hotel-keeper and the bartender had provided drink; the other "collaborators," Johnnie excepted, since he had been most active in arousing the Swede's anger, had each exhibited a different form of passivity.

"One Dash—Horses" is another study of fear, this time in a Mexican setting. In its gaudy and alluring garb this tale reads like a direct transcript of experience, but the narrative is not limited to the account of a thrilling man-hunt; Crane is more interested in exploring the psychological springs of fear and the power of illusion. The young American and his guide are afraid of the Mexican bandits, and the latter are terrorized by the thought of the mounted police—the "rurales"—but it is an abstract stereotype of the traditional enemy which causes this feeling in both cases. The Mexican bandits prove to be playthings in the hands of the gods, and the arrival of a group of prostitutes scatters to the winds their plans of murder and plunder; later on, when their lust has been appeased and they have resumed the chase, a detachment of rurales frightens them away without firing a single shot. The real power of the story lies in its subtle use of irony and in its cascading evocations of fear in a western-style pursuit.

In "The Bride Comes to Yellow Sky" Crane reached a peak in his exploration of the humorous overtones of fear. A favorite of the author

himself and of many of his admirers, "The Bride" raises the western story to the level of the classic by consistently applying to a trite but dramatic situation the powerful lever of irony. It deals with a very unromantic event, the homecoming of a town marshal after his wedding with a plain-looking and timid bride. This town marshal is afraid of nothing except public opinion and, since his marriage was secretly arranged, he fears the hostile reaction of the inhabitants of Yellow Sky, an obvious projection of Crane's own predicament in his life with Cora. When, after walking through the deserted town, the couple reach the door of their home, they meet Scratchy Wilson, the local outlaw. A bloody encounter to come, we might think, but in fact nothing happens: the outlaw is defeated by the mere sight of the town marshal seen for the first time as a married man and walking home unarmed. "Defeated by a woman's mute presence" might have been the headline for such a story if it had been printed in a "yellow" newspaper. Crane thought that "The Bride" was "a daisy," and he was right. From beginning to end this charming tale proves that the whole mystique of the wild West was for him nothing but a game, and he enjoyed watching this game in its closing stages.

But no judgment of Crane's ability as a storyteller can be reached without a proper assessment of "a tale intended to be after the fact" entitled "The Open Boat," which relates the concluding phase of an almost fatal adventure. The newspaper report he sent to the *New York Press* in January 1897, immediately after his shipwreck, gave a detailed account of every episode excluding the "thirty hours" spent in an open boat. It took a few weeks for the definitive story to crystallize in his mind as a parable of human existence. We follow the ordeal of four survivors during their long wait in a lifeboat, their desperate attempts to reach the shore after their ship has sunk. Finally the captain decides to risk steering the frail dinghy through the breakers: the four men—the captain, the cook, the oiler, and the correspondent—have, each of them, felt the "subtle brotherhood" born of their shared distress and struggle. Once in the breakers the boat is overturned and the oiler is killed. The other three set foot safely ashore. Crane never wrote a more orderly tale: the correspondent, acting as point-of-view character—although he is also a participant—helps to bring the main facets of the story into focus. We learn much about the transformation of his mind in the crucible of experience. This shipwreck is for him a journey leading from cynicism to humility. But here again Crane retains the ironic approach, especially when he shows the correspondent's indignation leveled at the serene indifference of God. "Shipwrecks are *apropos* of nothing" puts into a nutshell the meaning of the whole story. There is the world of facts on one side and the world of ideas and literature on the other, but facts as such do not exist to *prove* anything. However, some lessons can be drawn from the chaos of experience if men manage to be "interpreters." Crane's message here is one of endurance, brotherhood, and stoic acceptance of man's fate; his vision of the universe is one in which man appears frail and insignificant when isolated but surprisingly strong in a united effort. Ruthlessly debunking all the conventional views about heroism, he seems to imply that the only courage worthy of esteem is unobtrusive, silent, and more self-denying than self-assertive.

The true power of this story comes from a style which, in descriptive passages, is almost that of a prose poem. The dialogue, spare and accurate, gives balance to the general tone. According to Edward Garnett, Crane's art at its best was "self-poising as is the art of the perfect dancer." Joined to the grace of the dancer we find in this tale of human frailty a superb control of emotion which makes it a masterpiece of classical art, the epic flow of the narrative being constantly tempered and toned down by gentle touches of irony.

There always remained in Crane, as Alfred Kazin has pointed out, "a local village boy." Essentially American in his stance, although a rebel against many things American, he willingly spoke about his experience of the small town. Far from idealizing his vision, he set it against the background of his urban and cosmopolitan environment and judged it unemotionally.

The Crane brothers loved the countryside of Sullivan County, New York, where they fished, hunted, rode horses, and camped during the summer months. The hills, mountains, and valleys of this still rather wild area form a recurrent image in many of Stephen Crane's stories, poems, and prose poems. Although he used this background indirectly in his fiction, he made of it the infrastructure of his vision of the world.

The Third Violet (1897) reflects a deep attachment to the colors and shapes of Sullivan County. It exploits both the popular theme of the "summer hotel" and Crane's own experience at the Art Students' League in New York. In this novel the author has captured some of the flavor of bohemianism, but his treatment of this subject lacks originality. *The Third Violet*, which won very little applause from critics except for Ford Madox Hueffer, is saved from mediocrity by contrasting vignettes of rural and urban life. This book hints at the difficult struggle of young artists with the commercial values of their age: Hawker, a young painter, goes to Sullivan County where his farmer parents live; he is merely in search of peace and inspiration but, in a neighboring hotel, the summer has brought adventure in the shape of a rich New York heiress, Miss Fanhall. It is love at first sight, and the novel abounds in meetings and vapid conversations between the two lovers and a few other characters, a "writing friend" of Hawker's called Hollanden, a rival in love, named Oglethorpe, who is the irresistible rich suitor, and a group of irresponsible young artists belonging to Hawker's circle in New York. Among the latter stands out a rather colorful young model in love with Hawker, Florinda. We close the book unconvinced by the plot which, with the gift of a final violet symbolizing the reconciliation of the two lovers, seems to be heading for a conventional epilogue. Crane did not want his novel to end tragically, as his real-life romance with Nellie Crouse had done.

"The Monster," a story set in a rural background, can be regarded as one of the most important of his short works. It is centered on the disastrous consequences of a generous action: a doctor's son has been rescued from his burning house by a Negro servant, Henry Johnson, whose face is "burned away." Out of gratitude the doctor decides to nurse his heroic servant and insists on keeping him in his reconstructed house, but the sight of the "monster" frightens everyone in the neighborhood; the doctor soon becomes an object of opprobrium and loses much of his practice. A deputation of influential citizens tries to persuade him to compromise with public opinion and asks him to turn Henry over to an institution, but the doctor remains adamant. The last scene shows him returning from his rounds and finding his wife crying over the teacups of guests who have not come. This brilliant exposition of village mores is enhanced by symbolic touches which, in the laboratory scene during the fire, reach a climax with the lurid vision of threatening and fantastically colored shapes. Besides the fear born of physical danger, the author probes the blind unreasoning panic generated by the sight of the harmless and horribly maimed Negro, and the many anxieties caused by public opinion. He has also, by the very choice of his protagonist, indicated that true heroism is not the privilege of the whites alone.

Crane began reminiscing about his early youth when he had used up the store of material born of his adult experience. Port Jervis, New York, was the nucleus around which the *Whilomville Stories* took shape. It is "any boy's town," but also a very specific one within reach of New York City, yet quite provincial and sleepy with its backdrop of fields, rivers, hills, and forests, a place where boys and girls can roam at peace except when under the ferule of their school or Sunday school teachers. The fields are close by and the farmers' slow and benevolent manner offers a sharp contrast with the "barbarous" habits of the villagers who give tea parties, launch into charitable campaigns, and, in the summertime, entertain relatives from the city.

The rural life depicted by Crane is more civilized than that Mark Twain had evoked before him; it is less sentimentally reconstructed than the *Boy's Town* of W. D. Howells. Abhorring as he did the "Little Lord Fauntleroy" craze which had swept his country in the 1880's, Crane did not hesitate to show us real children. He is aware of their tastes and distastes and conscious of their cruelty—at times they appear to him as "little blood-fanged wolves." In fact, more than a picture of childhood, he gives a picture of town life, since the children project an image of their parents' world stripped to its essentials. Although fond of the company of youngsters and a great favorite with his nieces, Crane was not holding a brief in favor of youth. To quote Robert Frost out of context, he "lov[ed] the things he love[d] for what they [were]"; his children were, like their adult counterparts, charmingly deluded in their vision of the world, and we can safely smile at their innocent pranks, for Crane did not allow them to give free rein to their worst instincts. At the critical moment something happened: a bully relented or an adult came into view, and none of these little dramas of the backyard turned into a real tragedy.

By profession a journalist and a writer of fiction, Crane had a higher regard for his poetic endeavors than for the rest of his literary work. He preferred his first volume of verse, *The Black Riders* (1895), to his *Red Badge of Courage* because "it was a more ambitious effort. My aim was to comprehend in it the thoughts I have had about life in general while 'The Red Badge' is a mere episode in life, an amplification."

But he did not observe the traditions and conventions of poetic expression respected by most of his contemporaries, except isolated rebels like Walt Whitman and Emily Dickinson. Alfred Kazin has called Crane "our first *poète maudit*," and such a label fits him to perfection, for he regarded poetry, more than prose, as a vehicle for ideals generally unconventional or iconoclastic.

It is easy to find models for the patterns if not for the tone of Crane's early verse. He had obviously read Biblical parables, and some of the work of Emily Dickinson, Whitman, Ambrose Bierce, and Olive Schreiner, but his poetry remained essentially the expression of his own vision.

The sharpness and brevity of the sixty-eight pieces forming his *Black Riders* remind many readers of Emily Dickinson's great verbal economy. Like that of the poetess of Amherst his voice was one of protest. His own rebellion went against the God of the Old Testament, and he strove to debunk a cluster of false values, especially ambition, conformity, worldly wisdom, military glory, and tradi-

tional religion. The universe pictured by Crane in his poetry has elements of pessimism which have caused some critics to regard it as naturalistic, but the poet also exalts the positive virtues of love, endurance, and self-reliance. Crane feels a great admiration for the "little man" who keeps facing the mountains fearlessly, for the lonely individualist who "sought a new road" and "died thus alone," for "they said he had courage." The first themes of his poetic vision radiate from a central concern, the problem of man's relation with God. Even earthly love can be poisoned by the idea of sin, and man must free himself from his obsessive fear of God and from the network of illusions woven by his imagination. Crane's rebellion was sound, but the occasionally crude phrasing of his protest and the printing of the volume in small capitals made it fair game for the parodists.

His second book of poetry, *War Is Kind* (1899), contained thirty-seven poems: fourteen of these had already been printed between 1895 and 1898; a group of ten love poems called "Intrigue" and some of the remaining pieces belonged to a second poetic output. The iconoclastic note had not died out and the author went on debunking the outward forms of religious ritual:

> You tell me this is God?
> I tell you this is a printed list,
> A burning candle and an ass.

But his poetry gradually became more concrete and more socially oriented. Instead of dealing with abstract imaginings, vague and remote parables, it drank deep from the fountain of experience. His bitter satire on the popular glorification of military courage in such a poem as "War Is Kind" (which, although the initial piece in the second volume, belongs to the first period) had been expressed along general lines. With the "The Blue Battalions" and the poems inspired by the Spanish-American War, Crane did not hesitate to present war as the utmost form of God's playful fancy and violently denounced the exploitation of "patriots" by "practical men" as well as the imperialistic overtones of America's help to the Cuban rebels.

Several poems stigmatized other forms of exploitation of man by man. The gaudy and showy splendor of the mansions of the new rich aroused his metaphoric ire with a vision of

. . . a crash of flunkeys
And yawning emblems of Persia
Cheeked against oak, France and a sabre,
The outcry of old beauty
Whored by pimping merchants
To submission before wine and chatter.

And he ironically rejected the basic injustice of laissez-faire economics:

Why should the strong—
—The beautiful strong—
Why should they not have the flowers?

If the theme of love had, in the poems of the first poetic manner, taken on few romantic dimensions except in the sheltering gesture of a woman's "white arms," the second volume of verse and some posthumous poems enable us to probe deeper into Crane's house of love. "On the desert" and "A naked woman and a dead dwarf" fly the banner of Baudelairean decadence most clearly and remind us of "La femme et le serpent" and, as has been recently pointed out, of a prose poem by the French symbolist entitled "Le fou et la Vénus." "Intrigue," the last section of *War Is Kind,* represents Crane's attempt to bring into focus the many components of his love poetry: sensuality, sin-consciousness, and jealousy form the dark side of man's central passion, but Crane's

bitter lyricism is spoiled by hackneyed romantic imagery, skulls "with ruby eyes," cracked bowls, castles, temples, daggers, and specters.

He discovered a better instrument for his highly sensitive nature in the prose poem. "The Judgment of the Sage" and "The Snake" are true fables, and the same ingredients are found in them as in his verse; but whereas the verse rejects all traditional rules (rhyme, regular meter, and very often stanzaic form), the prose poems retain a classical mode of expression. They remind us of Baudelaire's utilization of the same medium, but here again Crane's manner remains distinctly his own. He thus studied some archetypes, those of charity, material success, earthly conflict or cosmic battle. "The Judgment of the Sage," which raises the ghost of a Kantian dilemma, briefly tells us the story of a vain quest, that of worldly wisdom. Should we practice charity "because of God's word" or because the beggar is hungry? Crane does not solve this riddle; God seems to play with man his eternal game of hide-and-seek and keeps him on the run. "A Self-Made Man" parodies the Horatio Alger type of success story. " 'To succeed in life . . . the youth of America have only to see an old man seated upon a railing and smoking a clay pipe. Then go up and ask him for a match.' " "The Voice of the Mountain" and "The Victory of the Moon" are focused on the conflict between man and a mysterious cosmic power which can occasionally be defeated by "the little creature of the earth." With "The Snake" the inevitable fight for survival is brought to its emotional climax: the two most antagonistic creatures in the world, man and the snake, confront each other in a ruthless duel in which the principals fight with equal arms, the snake with its venom and man with his stick. If the snake is defeated it is not for lack of courage. Thanks to a clever manipulation of language

Crane combines in a unified whole the simplicity of the fable, the logical structure of the sermon, and the raciness of the tall tale.

His poetry at times foreshadows Imagism, as Carl Sandburg pointed out in his "Letters to Dead Imagists," but some pieces of the second volume of verse show a tendency to explode the small abstract capsule of the early poems. It is difficult to say where Crane's real poetic genius lies, whether in his spare, concise parables, in his longer symbolistic compositions, or in his prose poems. He worshiped brevity as the first tenet of his literary creed, but he was also touched by the wave of decadent aesthetics that Copeland and Day, his publishers, who were also the American publishers of the *Yellow Book,* had helped to introduce into the United States. There was, however, too much love of moral integrity in Crane for him to become a true decadent. In his verse he often displayed the pathetic agony of a fallen albatross, but the prose poem was perhaps the literary instrument whose scope and subtle rhythm best suited his genius.

Crane's style has a certain number of idiosyncrasies: it is primarily the language of a writer in transition betraying an inner conflict between a romantic tradition and realistic impulses. He began with what he called his "Rudyard-Kipling style" and the "Sullivan County Sketches" contain the germs of most of his future work, displaying as they do a love of abstraction and a systematic use of color, patterning the narrative with structural irony, and building up an oneiric atmosphere laden with threat. It is a gradual mastery of form that we witness in the passage from the style of the early years to that emerging between 1894 and 1898.

Impelled by a desire to control the deep stirrings of his soul, he soon declared that he wished "to write plainly and unmistakably, so that all men (and some women) might read and understand." Crane's literary aesthetics was close to that of the French master of the short story, Guy de Maupassant. According to the author of *Pierre et Jean,* "Les grands artistes sont ceux qui imposent à l'humanité leur illusion particulière." Such a position might very well have been defined by Stephen Crane, who wanted the writer to tell the world what "his own pair of eyes" enabled him to see and nothing else. Maupassant's universe, however, differed significantly from Crane's: whereas the French writer often indulged in an excess of sensual evocations, Crane preserved throughout his writing career the viewpoint of the moralist and usually conveyed his ethical comments by means of ironic counterpoint.

He was deeply conscious of man's littleness and of God's overbearing power. Man's wanderings on the earth were pictured by him as those of a lonely pilgrim in a pathless universe. Crane's phraseology comes directly from the Bible, the sermons, and the hymns which had shaped his language during his youth. The topography of his stories, where hills, mountains, rivers, and meadows appear under symbolic suns or moons, is, to a large extent, an abstraction fraught with religious or moral significance. With its "monsters" of various kinds and its "dragons," the demonology of *The Red Badge of Courage* evinces a truly apocalyptic quality. In Crane's best work the imagery of the journey of initiation occupies a central position and reaches a climactic stage with some experience of conversion. He did not accept, it is true, the traditional interpretation of the riddle of the universe offered by the Methodist church. Nevertheless he constantly used a Christian terminology, and the thought of "sin" inspired his characters with guilty fears and stirred up within them such frequent debates with a troubled conscience that it is impossible to study his achievement outside a religious tradition.

But he did not remain a prisoner of the stylistic patterns which he derived from his revivalist heritage. New York street life very early made an impact on his language, which thus acquired its liveliness and its ability to picture violence in colorful terms. Crane's dialogues abound in expletives, in stereotyped phrases, in phonetic transcriptions of common verbal corruptions and dialectal idiosyncrasies. Yet they never fall into the trap of overspecialization. His ear was good, whether he listened to Irish, German, Italian, or Cuban immigrants in New York, to farmers in Sullivan County, or to Negroes in Port Jervis, but he never tried to achieve a perfect rendering of local dialect. In *The Red Badge of Courage* he used dialogue to introduce some degree of differentiation between Henry Fleming and his comrades but, on the whole, Crane's characters all speak one language which is Crane's own, a youthful and casual version of the American vernacular of the 1890's often heard in artists' studios and among students.

Language is in the mouths of his central characters a stylized medium carrying universal overtones, and this trait reveals an essential aspect of his fictional techniques, namely the dramatic approach. He tried his hand several times at playwriting and, although his various attempts in this literary genre were of modest stature, he was naturally inclined to work out his tales and some of his verse in terms of stage stylistics. He completed three very slight plays. *At Clancy's Wake* (1893) is a one-act sketch which brings to life the hilarious moments of an Irish wake in New York; *The Blood of the Martyr* (1898) satirizes in three brief acts German imperialistic policies in China. Another attempt at playwriting was his "Spanish-American War Play," unpublished in Crane's lifetime but recently included in *The War Dispatches of Stephen Crane* (1964): this two-act drama gives a mildly amusing but superficial picture of stereotyped national traits against the background of a real conflict that the author had seen at first hand. Only a fragment of the text of "The Ghost"—his English play—has reached us so far and it is difficult to take seriously what was meant to be a mere Christmas entertainment. All his other attempts at playwriting were abortive.

What remains most striking in Crane's style considered as a whole is a concern for brevity and a constant use of irony which serves a twofold purpose: it provides his best work with tightly knit thematic structures and reveals his tacit belief in a rigid set of values which condemns indifference and conformism, and extols moral courage and integrity.

Seen in the perspective of the years which have elapsed since his death, Crane's work is surprisingly modern. His influence on the war literature of the twentieth century in England and America has been very significant. Many of Hemingway's novels and short stories disclose a similar preoccupation with "the moral problem of conduct" and obvious stylistic affinities; distinct echoes of *The Red Badge* can be heard in *A Farewell to Arms*. In England we could trace recurring correspondences in the work of Joseph Conrad and Ford Madox Ford. Ford, like Conrad, had been a good friend of Crane's during the last three years of his life, and both defended his literary and moral reputation in magazine articles or prefaces after his death. The plight of the isolated hero, which became a favorite theme of Conrad's, stemmed directly from *The Red Badge of Courage*. Obsession with the fear of showing a white feather haunted the soul of the author of *Lord Jim* as much as that of the creator of Henry Fleming. In his own fiction Ford Madox Ford used complex techniques and mixed many strands of life, but some of the most dramatic scenes in *A Man Could Stand Up,* which are mere vignettes of life at the front, remind us in their bare and rugged prose of deliberately unpoetic descriptions of war in *The Red Badge.* Like Crane, Ford emphasized "the eternal waiting that is War" and the crippling effects of noise on a battlefield. And, in order to describe the subtle change taking place in a soldier's mind, he used almost Cranean terms.

Among the pioneers of the "free-verse army" Crane is often neglected by anthologists or literary critics. Yet he gave to the poetry of his country the patterns and rhythms of an "exasperated prose" that foreshadows modern poetic expression.

Carl Van Doren wrote in 1924: "Modern American literature may be said, accurately enough, to have begun with Stephen Crane." This statement needs to be qualified, but Crane was one of the leading figures of protest of his generation and thus showed the way to American liberalism. His influence in the field of the novel has affected a mode of thought rather than literary techniques, if we leave aside his synesthetic use of imagery which survives almost intact in F. Scott Fitzgerald. Crane's impact has been felt mostly in the genre of the short story, for which he displayed a personal preference. "The Blue Hotel," "The Bride Comes to Yellow Sky," and, above all, "The Open Boat" are some of the finest models of American literary achievement in this genre, and the greatest successes of Faulkner, Sherwood Anderson, Hemingway, Fitzgerald, and other modern American short story writers hark back to these models. Accuracy in details, conciseness, and effective rendering, framed and supported by an ironic structure, are now frequently regarded as essential re-

quirements by American practitioners of the short story.

Most of Crane's work could be explained in terms of his religious background, and he always betrays, even in his most sportive mood, the serious preoccupations of the born moralist. However, his slum stories, instead of aiming to move the reader by exaggerated pathos and convert him to the cause of reform, wish to convert him to the cause of psychological truth; social implications are left for the reader to discover but are not explicitly stated. When dealing with his main theme, war, he gradually worked out a revolutionary stand, doing away with externals and reducing human conflict to a classic drama of internal forces struggling with elemental powers. From Henry Fleming in *The Red Badge* to Timothy Lean in the "Spitzbergen Tales" the itinerary of heroism evolves from a path sprinkled with doubtful victories to a road doggedly followed with a sturdy and silent acceptance of personal responsibility; diseased and action-hampering introspection eventually gives way to selfless and unassuming patterns of affirmation. "The Open Boat" contains a plea for human solidarity and *Wounds in the Rain,* in spite of a persistent and depressing background of military servitude, discreetly affirms the superiority of collective to individual prowess. A subtle feeling of warmth and brotherhood pervades the later studies of Crane on war; even "The Upturned Face," a macabre piece which describes a burial scene on the front line, places the reader in the midst of an ultimate manifestation of soldierly brotherhood.

It is in the novel of manners that Crane's achievement is at its lowest ebb. He did not try to study complex human relationships born of urban settings but dealt with a few basic themes, rivalries between lovers, or conflicts between generations and social classes. Often unable to provide his puppets with life, he proved his mastery in the art of reproducing informal dialogue. He experimented in the field of the picaresque novel—a medium he had already used in several short stories—but *The O'Ruddy* cannot be regarded as a genuine offspring of his mind since Robert Barr gave this novel its conclusion and ultimate form.

Crane's identity runs no risk of being drowned in a backflow of imitators, because his style remains his own. His unerring eye for color, his brilliant use of synesthetic effects, his love for the potent metaphor made him controversially famous in his lifetime and now stamp him as a truly original artist. His sometimes erratic grammar no longer shocks us, while his cinematic techniques have come into their own.

It was his aim to underline elements of absurdity in human life, and his work contains disquieting overtones for sedate minds. His was a voice of dissent which rejected the ostensibly impregnable soundness of historical Christianity, the conventional vision of a well-ordered society and that genteel tradition of culture which never left drawing rooms and libraries. Crane inherited the New England habit of individual assertion. He fits well into the American liberal tradition and can, in some respects, be regarded as a spiritual son of Emerson. Any form of dogmatism in any field of human life seemed to him both childish and harmful to what he valued above everything else, the integrity of the human soul. No problem could, according to him, ever find a definitive solution and he had certainly listened to Emerson's advice: "Congratulate yourself if you have done something strange and extravagant, and broken the monotony of a decorous age." This sentence adorned a beam in one of the studios of the old Arts Students' League building in New York where Crane lived sporadically in 1893 and 1894. Above and beyond this cult of nonconformism is another idea of Emerson's which involves the deeper regions of the soul: "Always do what you are afraid to do." Crane put this motto into practice so consistently that he wrecked his health and seriously endangered his moral reputation in his own country.

His recent popularity, essentially due to a revival of critical interest during the 1950's, should help prepare the ground for a clearer assessment of Crane's achievement. To our generation he can still teach moral integrity, a revised conception of courage, and psychological truth, all the more effectively because he did not resort to traditional didactic devices. He can also show modern prose writers the flexibility of the English language and encourage them to make linguistic experiments and create a language free from any excessive tyranny of the past, perfectly in tune with the spirit of the age and yet retaining the robust vitality which is the trademark of the classic.

Selected Bibliography

WORKS OF STEPHEN CRANE

NOVELS

Maggie: A Girl of the Streets (A Story of New York), by Johnston Smith (pseud.). N.p. [1893]. (Revised edition, *Maggie: A Girl of the Streets.* New York: Appleton, 1896.) There have been three recent reprints of note: one edited by Joseph Katz (Gainesville, Fla.: Scholars' Facsimiles and Reprints, 1966); another by Maurice Bassan (*Stephen Crane's Maggie, Text and Context,* Belmont, Calif.: Wadsworth Publication, 1966); and another by Donald Pizer (San Francisco: Chandler, 1968).

The Red Badge of Courage. New York: Appleton, 1895.

George's Mother. New York and London: Edward Arnold, 1896.

The Third Violet. New York: Appleton, 1897.

Active Service. New York: Frederick A. Stokes, 1899.

The O'Ruddy. New York: Frederick A. Stokes, 1903.

The Complete Novels of Stephen Crane, edited by Thomas A. Gullason. New York: Doubleday, 1967.

SHORT STORIES AND SKETCHES

The Little Regiment and Other Episodes of the American Civil War. New York: Appleton, 1896.

The Open Boat and Other Stories. New York: Doubleday and McClure, 1898.

The Monster and Other Stories. New York: Harper, 1899. (Contains only "The Monster," "The Blue Hotel," and "His New Mittens.")

Whilomville Stories. New York and London: Harper, 1900.

Wounds in the Rain. New York: Frederick A. Stokes, 1900.

Great Battles of the World. Philadelphia: Lippincott, 1901.

The Monster. London: Harper, 1901. (Contains "The Monster," "The Blue Hotel," "His New Mittens," "Twelve O'Clock," "Moonlight on the Snow," "Manacled," and "An Illusion in Red and White.")

Last Words. London: Digby, Long, 1902.

Men, Women and Boats, edited with an introduction by Vincent Starrett. New York: Boni and Liveright, 1917. (Contains seventeen stories and sketches.)

A Battle in Greece. Mount Vernon, N.Y.: Peter Pauper Press, 1936. (Contains a reprint of the battle sketch which appeared in the *New York Journal* of June 13, 1897.)

The Sullivan County Sketches, edited by Melvin Schoberlin. Syracuse, N.Y.: Syracuse University Press, 1949.

The Complete Short Stories and Sketches of Stephen Crane, edited by Thomas A. Gullason. New York: Doubleday, 1963.

The New York City Sketches of Stephen Crane and Related Pieces, edited by R. W. Stallman and E. R. Hagemann. New York: New York University Press, 1966.

Stephen Crane: Sullivan County Tales and Sketches, edited by R. W. Stallman. Ames: Iowa State University Press, 1968.

WAR DISPATCHES

The War Dispatches of Stephen Crane, edited by R. W. Stallman and E. R. Hagemann. New York: New York University Press, 1964.

POETRY AND PLAYS

The Black Riders and Other Lines. Boston: Copeland and Day, 1895.

A Souvenir and a Medley. East Aurora, N.Y.: Roycroft Printing Shop, 1896. (Contains seven poems, as well as a sketch entitled "A Great Mistake" and a fifteen-line piece printed in capitals, "A Prologue," which reads like stage directions.)

War Is Kind. New York: Frederick A. Stokes, 1899.

At Clancy's Wake, in *Last Words*. London: Digby, Long, 1902.

The Collected Poems of Stephen Crane, edited by Wilson Follett. New York: Knopf, 1930.

The Blood of the Martyr. Mount Vernon, N.Y.: Peter Pauper Press, [1940]. (A play originally printed in the Sunday magazine of the *New York Press* on April 3, 1898.)

Drama in Cuba, in *The War Dispatches of Stephen Crane,* edited by R. W. Stallman and E. R. Hagemann. New York: New York University Press, 1964.

The Poems of Stephen Crane, a critical edition by Joseph Katz. New York: Cooper Square Publishers, 1966.

COLLECTED EDITIONS

A new edition of the complete works of Stephen Crane is being prepared at the University of Virginia.

The Work of Stephen Crane, edited by Wilson Follett. 12 vols. New York: Knopf, 1925–27. (Reprinted in 6 vols., New York: Russell and Russell, 1963.)

Stephen Crane: An Omnibus, edited by R. W. Stallman. New York: Knopf, 1952.

Stephen Crane: Uncollected Writings, edited with

an introduction by Olov W. Fryckstedt. Uppsala: Almqvist and Wiksell, 1963.

LETTERS

Stephen Crane: Letters, edited by R. W. Stallman and Lillian Gilkes. New York: New York University Press, 1960.

BIBLIOGRAPHY

A new bibliography has been prepared by R. W. Stallman for Iowa State University Press. Since 1963 Syracuse University has issued an annual Crane bibliography in *Thoth*.

Williams, Ames W., and Vincent Starrett. *Stephen Crane: A Bibliography*. Glendale, Calif.: John Valentine, 1948.

BIOGRAPHIES

Beer, Thomas. *Stephen Crane*. New York: Knopf, 1923.

Berryman, John. *Stephen Crane*. New York: William Sloane Associates, 1950. (Reprinted in 1962 as a Meridian paperback with an additional preface.)

Gilkes, Lillian. *Cora Crane*. Bloomington: Indiana University Press, 1960. (Although centered on Cora, this contains much information on the life of the couple in England.)

Raymond, Thomas L. *Stephen Crane*. Newark, N.J.: Carteret Book Club, 1923.

Stallman, R. W. *Stephen Crane*. New York: Braziller, 1968.

CRITICAL STUDIES

Bassan, Maurice. "Crane, Townsend, and Realism of a Good Kind," *Proceedings of the New Jersey Historical Society*, 82:128–35 (April 1964).

Berryman, John. "The Red Badge of Courage," in *The American Novel*, edited by Wallace Stegner. New York: Basic Books, 1965.

Berthoff, Warner. *The Ferment of Realism: American Literature, 1884–1919*. New York: Fress Press, 1965.

Cady, Edwin H. *Stephen Crane*. New York: Twayne, 1962.

Cazemajou, Jean. *Stephen Crane, écrivain journaliste*. Paris: Didier, 1969.

Colvert, James B. "The Origins of Stephen Crane's Literary Creed," *University of Texas Studies in English*, 34:179–88 (1955).

Ellison, Ralph. Introduction to *The Red Badge of Courage*. New York: Dell, 1960. (Reprinted in *Shadow and Act*. New York: Random House, 1964).

Geismar, Maxwell. *Rebels and Ancestors*. Boston: Houghton Mifflin, 1953.

Gibson, Donald B. *The Fiction of Stephen Crane*. Carbondale: Southern Illinois University Press, 1968.

Gordan, John D. "*The Ghost* at Brede Place," *Bulletin of the New York Public Library*, 56:591–96 (December 1952).

Greenfield, Stanley B. "The Unmistakable Stephen Crane," *PMLA*, 73:562–72 (December 1958).

Gullason, Thomas. "Stephen Crane's Private War on Yellow Journalism," *Huntington Library Quarterly*, 22:200–08 (May 1959).

Hoffman, D. G. *The Poetry of Stephen Crane*. New York: Columbia University Press, 1957.

————. "Stephen Crane's Last Novel," *Bulletin of the New York Public Library*, 64:337–43 (June 1960).

Katz, Joseph. " 'The Blue Battalions' and the Uses of Experience," *Studia Neophilogica*, 38:107–16 (1966).

————., ed. *Stephen Crane Newsletter,* Fall 1966 to date.

Kazin, Alfred. "American Fin de Siècle," in *On Native Grounds*. New York: Reynal and Hitchcock, 1942.

La France, Marston. *A Reading of Stephen Crane*. London: Oxford University Press, 1971.

Lytle Andrew. " 'The Open Boat': A Pagan Tale," in *The Hero with the Private Parts*. Baton Rouge: Louisiana State University Press, 1966.

Martin, Jay. *Harvests of Change: American Literature, 1865–1914*. Englewood Cliffs, N.J.: Prentice-Hall, 1967.

Modern Fiction Studies, 5:199–291 (Autumn 1959). (Essays on Crane by Thomas A. Gullason, Robert F. Gleckner, Peter Buitenhuis, James B. Colvert, R. W. Stallman, Hugh Maclean, Eric Solomon, James T. Cox; also contains a good selective bibliography.)

Nelson, Harland S. "Stephen Crane's Achievement as a Poet," *University of Texas Studies in Literature and Language*, 4:564–82 (Winter 1963).

Ross, Lillian. *Picture*. London: Penguin Books, 1962. Reprinted from the *New Yorker*, May–June 1952. (An account of the filming of *The Red Badge of Courage* for MGM under the direction of John Huston.)

Schneider, Robert W. *Five Novelists of the Progressive Era*. New York: Columbia University Press, 1965.

Solomon, Eric. *Stephen Crane: From Parody to Realism*. Cambridge, Mass.: Harvard University Press, 1966.

Vasilievskaya, O. B. *The Work of Stephen Crane*. Moscow: Nayka Editions, 1967. (A critical study in Russian.)

Walcutt, Charles Child. *American Literary Naturalism, a Divided Stream*. Minneapolis: University of Minnesota Press, 1956.

Weisenberger, Bernard. "The Red Badge of Courage," in *Twelve Original Essays on Great American Novels,* edited by Charles Shapiro. Detroit: Wayne State University Press, 1958.

Weiss, Daniel. "The Red Badge of Courage," *Psychoanalytic Review*, 52:32–52 (Summer 1965), 52:130–54 (Fall 1965).

Westbrook, Max. "Stephen Crane's Poetry: Perspective and Arrogance," *Bucknell Review*, 11:23–34 (December 1963).

Ziff, Larzer. *The American 1890s*. New York: Viking Press, 1966.

—JEAN CAZEMAJOU

E. E. Cummings

1894-1962

OBEDIENT to the world spirit of change, in the early decades of the twentieth century a group of notable poets, by diverging from traditional practices, transformed American poetry. The most thorough "smasher of the logicalities" among them was a transcendentalist: one who views nature as a state of becoming rather than as a stasis and who believes that the imaginative faculty in man can perceive the natural world directly. He was also a troubadour who said: "enters give/whose lost is his found/leading love/whose heart is her mind." He was not only poet but novelist, playwright, and painter. In following his vision he roused hostility in academic critics and readers, apparently repelled by his idiosyncratic typographical and stylistic devices, but he was from the beginning admired by his fellow innovators, William Carlos Williams, Marianne Moore, Ezra Pound, and T. S. Eliot—and eventually he won the esteem of his critics.

"I am someone," remarked E. E. Cummings late in his career, "who proudly and humbly affirms that love is the mystery-of-mysteries . . . that 'an artist, a man, a failure' is . . . a naturally and miraculously whole human being . . . whose only happiness is to transcend himself, whose every agony is to grow." In a world oriented to dehumanized power, transcendentalism is a synonym for absurdity. Cummings recognized this early. In an address at his Harvard commencement in 1915, he had said, "we are concerned with the natural unfolding of sound tendencies. That the conclusion is, in a particular case, *absurdity,* does not in any way impair the value of the experiment, so long as we are dealing with sincere effort." The manifesto he issued then was that of one man to himself. He would experiment, and he would not fear being absurd; he would use the absurdity principle to the limit of its usefulness. As he worked at his trade of wordsmith, the implications of what he had said in 1915 were clarified in a remarkable stream of poems. From the start he used absurdity to leaven the commonplace, to startle readers into "listening" instead of merely hearing. In his later years he discovered a new significance in the concept: experimental living and the practice of his craft had redefined absurdity; it came to mean the truth of earthly living and a promise of eternity.

Edward Estlin Cummings, son of the Reverend Edward Cummings (lecturer at Harvard and Unitarian minister) and of Rebecca Haswell Clarke Cummings, was born at Cambridge, Massachusetts, on October 14, 1894.

His parents had been brought together by their mutual friend William James. Dr. Cummings was a woodsman, a photographer, an actor, a carpenter, an artist—and talented in all that he undertook. Mrs. Cummings was a shy woman who overcame conventional influences to respond joyously and effectively to life. The son was educated in public schools and at Harvard University where he received an A.B., *magna cum laude,* and an M.A. for English and classical studies.

While Cummings was in graduate school he helped to found the Harvard Poetry Society. He and some of his friends in the society put together *Eight Harvard Poets* (published in 1917). In it, by a printer's error, according to one story, Cummings' name and the "I's" as well were set in lowercase letters. He seized upon this as a device congenial to him and later had "e. e. cummings" legalized as the signature to his poems.

After Harvard, Cummings went to New York. In this city he held his first and only job, three months with P. F. Collier & Son, Inc., mail-order booksellers. He was twenty-one at the time. In mid-1917 he went to France to serve as a volunteer ambulance driver. There he was interned for a minor military offense—what happened was that he refused to say he hated Germans; instead, with typical Cummings care for precision, he repeated: "I like the French." From his experiences at La Ferté Macé (a detention camp) he accumulated material for his documentary "novel," *The Enormous Room* (1922), one of the best war books by an American.

Upon his release, he returned to the United States, but when the war ended he went back to Paris—this time to study art. He made the acquaintance of the poet Louis Aragon and of Picasso and their circle of poets and painters; he became friendly with many visiting writers such as Archibald MacLeish and Ezra Pound. On arriving back in New York in 1924 he found himself a celebrity—for his documentary novel and for *Tulips and Chimneys* (1923), his first book of poems. The next year he won the *Dial* Award for "distinguished service to American Letters." A roving assignment from *Vanity Fair* in 1926 permitted him to go abroad again, where he established a routine he was to follow most of his life: he painted in the afternoons and wrote at night.

From his experiences in the two cities he loved, New York and Paris, came the material for scintillating or extravagant essays on burlesque, the circus, modern art, and the foibles of the day, later collected into *A Miscellany* (1958) and *A Miscellany, Revised* (1965). He wrote forewords to books and brochures for art exhibits, and he sold sketches and paintings. Three volumes of poetry appeared in quick succession: *&* (*And*) and *XLI Poems* in 1925, *Is 5* in 1926. The play *Him,* a phantasmagoria in 21 scenes, which was a forerunner of what is now called the Theater of the Absurd, was published in 1927 and produced by the Provincetown Players in 1928 and was acclaimed by avant-garde critics. In 1931 he published a collection of drawings and paintings, *CIOPW,* which took its title from the initial letters of the materials used: charcoal, ink, oil, pencil, watercolor. In that same year came *W* (*ViVa*), a thick book of poems. A travel journal published in 1933, *Eimi* (*I Am*), recorded his revulsion against an even more "enormous room" than the military detention camp: the collectivized Soviet Union.

After 1930, although Cummings continued to travel abroad, he divided most of his time between a studio apartment in Greenwich Village, at 4 Patchin Place, and the family farm at Silver Lake, New Hampshire. This yearly contact with New England soil occasioned one of his finest poem-portraits: "rain or hail/sam done/the best he kin/till they digged his hole." A similar earthy wisdom is in a poem that may be a comment on himself: "my specialty is living said/a man(who could not earn his bread/because he would not sell his head)."

Because he had in common with T. S. Eliot not only a New England Unitarian background but also cosmopolitan traits, it is stimulating to observe the differences between them. Eliot became a British citizen. Cummings, responding to French art, always admiring the French civilization, nonetheless spent most of his life in the United States. He was a goldfinch needing a native tree to sing from. Through the years, from his perch, he continued to pour forth his songs: *No Thanks* (1935), *50 Poems* (1940), *1 x 1* (*One Times One*, 1944) *Xaipe* (1950). A *Collected Poems* appeared in 1938. The ballet *Tom* was published in 1935 and the plays *Anthropos* and *Santa Claus* were published in 1944 and 1946.

Honors and rewards came with frequency—now. In 1950, for "great achievement," he was given the Fellowship of the Academy of American Poets. In 1952 he was invited to give the Norton Lectures at Harvard (published as *I: Six Nonlectures* in 1953), an urbane but lively analysis of the Cummings quest to discover "Who as a writer am I?" These lectures could have been subtitled "And who as a person are you?" because—like Walt Whitman with his phrases addressed to future generations who would cross on Brooklyn Ferry—Cummings was always reaching out from the persona, the neutral "i," to the "you" out there. In 1955 he received a special citation from the National Book Awards for *Poems 1923–1954* (1954) and in 1957 he received both the Bollingen Prize for Poetry and the Boston Arts Festival Poetry Award. A year later the last of his poetry collections to appear during his lifetime

was published, *95 Poems*. Cummings the painter was also honored: he had one-man shows in 1944 and 1949 at the American-British Art Centre, and in 1945 and 1959 at the Rochester Memorial Gallery. His wide-ranging interest in the visual arts was reflected in *Adventures in Value* (1962), on which he collaborated with his third wife, photographer Marion Morehouse.

Cummings died on September 3, 1962, in New Hampshire. He left a manuscript of poetry published the following year as *73 Poems*.

"The artist's country is inside him," said Cummings. This was another way of saying that he would abide only by the laws of his own mind. His formalities—the literary devices he developed—were intended to show how the outer appearance reinforces the inner vision. His disordered syntax and typographical disarrangements were intended, not to bewilder, but to heighten the understanding. He described what he was trying to do in the 1926 Foreword to *Is 5*: "my theory of technique, if I have one, is very far from original; nor is it complicated. I can express it in fifteen words, by quoting The Eternal Question And Immortal Answer of burlesk, viz. 'Would you hit a woman with a child?—No, I'd hit her with a brick.' Like the burlesk comedian, I am abnormally fond of that precision which creates movement." One of his methods to achieve this was tmesis (the separation of parts of words by intervening words). It became almost like a signature for him. As Karl Shapiro put it in his *Essay on Rime,* Cummings was concerned with the "Integers of the word, the curve of 'e',/Rhythm of 'm', astonishment of 'o'/And their arranged derangement." By the analysis of words into their parts, both syllables and individual letters, and by considered use of space and punctuation marks, as well as by "arranged derangement," Cummings hoped to extend meaning beyond traditional limits.

Cummings used space in his typographical rhetoric to indicate tempo of reading: single words may have spaces within them to force the reader to weigh each syllable, as in "can dy lu/minous"; or words may be linked, as in "eddieandbill," to convey the act of boys running. A comma may be used where a period is expected, within a poem or at the end of it, to produce a pause for the reader to imagine what the next action might be. Or commas, colons, and semicolons may be used within a word to arouse new sensations and intuitions. In examining the poem beginning "as if as" (*No Thanks*) the reader disentangles from the typography the idea that it is a poem about sunrise. But it is not like other accounts of sunrise, nor, probably, does it reflect the reader's own experience. Toward the end of the poem the word "itself" is fractured into "it:s;elf." The "s" suggests the sun as well as the viewer. "Elf," relating to an earlier phrase, "moon's al-down," is a hint, in this instance, of the supernatural impact of dawn. The daily sun is no longer a habit but a miracle. In a later work (Number 48 in *73 Poems*), the word "thrushes" is divided into "t,h;r:u;s,h;e:s" so that the reader may perceive, with the poet, the individual sleepy birds gripping a branch at moonrise and, by implication, the transcendental relationship between all living things. Of the exclamation point beginning the first poem in *50 Poems*, "!blac," Cummings himself said that it might be called an emphatic "very"; the unpronounceable "?" and ")" are often similarly used. To focus the reader's attention a capital letter may be thrust into the middle of a word. In the opening poem of *No Thanks* capitals are used to imitate the roundness of the moon and to imply the eternity of the circle:

mOOn Over tOwns mOOn
whisper
less creature huge grO
pingness

In "i will be" (*And*) the word "SpRiN,k,LiNg" is manipulated to make a visual representation of sunlight filtering through wing feathers. In this poem, too, a parenthesis is used in the middle of the word "wheeling" to place simultaneously before the reader's mind the flutter of the pigeons and their effect on the sunlight:

whee(:are,SpRiN,k,LiNg   an   in-stant   with
    sunLight
t h e n)l -
ing . . .

Cummings made varied use of parentheses: for an interpolated comment or to split or combine words as a guide to his thought. Frequently they occur, in poem-parables, to clarify the relationship between two sentences that run simultaneously through the poem. In "go (perpe)go," published in *No Thanks,* we have a typical Cummings juxtaposition. The parenthetical sentence is a surrealist collection of "perpetual adventuring particles" describing the action of a disturbed ant heap and an anteater getting his dinner. The sentence outside the parenthesis, "go to the ant, thou anteater," is an allusion to Proverbs 6:6: "Go to the ant, thou sluggard." The poem is description and social comment, disguised as a joke. Critic Norman Friedman analyzed it succinctly: "Cummings is satirizing a certain kind of worldly and prudential wisdom. The ant's activity represents for Cummings merely busy work rather than a model of industry, and he who is advised to 'go to the ant' is the one creature who can possibly profit from such a visit—the anteater. In thus reducing the proverb to its simply 'realistic' aspects—by refusing to make the metaphorical transference intended—Cummings deflates the whole implied point of view."

Some of Cummings' poems utilize the "visual stanza" in which lines are arranged in reference, not to rhyme and meter, but to a shape reflecting the poet's thought. This kind of typographical design, with poems contrived in the form of roses, diamonds, and hourglass figures, was in fashion during the Elizabethan age and continued to be used in the seventeenth century. With changes in taste and technical practice in the last two centuries, this device fell into disuse, although it has been revived occasionally, as when Lewis Carroll used it for his mouse's "long and sad tale." More recently it appeared in the *Calligrammes* of Guillaume Apollinaire and in the "quaint" patterning of Dylan Thomas' poem "Vision and Prayer." However, the visual appearance of Cummings' poems can be largely accounted for by his interest in contemporary art forms, rather than by influence from other writers. From artists like Picasso who were bringing new vitality to painting, he learned the effectiveness of distorting lines and reshaping masses; and he juxtaposed words as they did the pigments (in John Peale Bishop's apt phrasing)—to bring perception of things into sharper focus. Cummings specifically disclaimed any stylistic influence from Apollinaire's mimetic typography, and as Gorham B. Munson observed very early, Cummings' typographical design, unlike that of the *Calligrammes,* reinforces the literary content of his poems. Some of Cummings' poems are designed to be read vertically; in others, stanzaic structures are balanced for mass, as are certain colors in painting. Effective examples of Cummings' use of the visual stanza are the poem "!blac" and the ironic dedication to *No Thanks,* which lists in the shape of a wineglass all the publishers who had rejected the manu-

script. In *XLI Poems* there is a poem, "little tree," that visually suggests a Christmas tree, and another that on the page resembles smoke puffing out of a locomotive:

the
   sky
      was
can dy lu
minous

Another important device by which Cummings intended to enlarge the reader's comprehension was word coinage. He kept already existing root words, joining to them new affixes. In such compounded words the prefixes are familiar enough, but his use of the suffixes *-ly, -ish, -est, -ful* and adverbs (such as *less*) in unexpected combinations, a dimension natural to classical and romance languages, produces in English an intensifying of perception. Introduce one or two of these words— *riverly, nowly, downwardishly, birdfully, whichful, girlest, skylessness, onlying, laughtering,* etc.—into a verse of recognizable words and the reader has to explore possibilities in a creative way. In reading creatively a phrase like "on stiffening greenly air" he will cross the threshold of transcendence. Articles and particles were rearranged by Cummings for the same purpose—"some or if where." One part of speech may be used for another, as in the first line of a much-anthologized poem from *And,* "Spring is like a perhaps hand." The charm of this line is due in large part to the use of an adverb when an adjective is expected, to emphasize the tentative nature of springtime. This is reinforced by an image of the window dresser who moves things and changes things "without breaking anything," in contrast to the destruction of winter.

In all of these ways Cummings broke language from its conventionalized mold; it became a nourishing soil through which "faces called flowers float out of the ground" (*Xaipe*). Cummings' virtuosity was directed to capture in words what the painter gets on canvas and what children, violently alive in response to objects and seasons, display in their street games. His poems are alive on the page, as he told the printer when he instructed him not to interfere with the "arrangement." Any change would be an injury to living tissue. In discontinuous poems he tried to pin down the "illuminated moment," to ransom from oblivion the fleeting present, in words seasonal, contemporary, and timeless—like a writer of haiku. To get at the realities, Cummings smashed the logicalities, an idea in harmony with Oriental art and philosophy, with which he had acquaintance, as shown by a quotation from the Tao that appears near the end of *Eimi*: "he who knoweth the eternal is comprehensive . . . therefore just; just, therefore a king; a king, therefore celestial; celestial, therefore in Tao; in Tao, therefore enduring." Cummings' perpetual concern with transcendental ideas led to the shining leaps on the page that make his work unique.

One needs to remember, however, that this innovating poet was practiced in conventional Western literary tradition. The young Cummings learned from Elizabethan song and eighteenth-century satire, as well as from the Pindaric ode. He was rooted in the same soil as Thoreau, Emerson, and Emily Dickinson. Intermittently he read Aeschylus, Homer, and the French troubadours—as evidenced by his quotations in the *Six Nonlectures*. He cut his literary teeth on the strict rules of villanelle, roundel, and ballade royale. Nonetheless his genius led him to quite different patterns: a poem in *ViVa*, for example, records phonetically not only a conversation but a revelation of the hearts of lost men: "oil tel duh woil doi sez/dooyah unnurs tanmih essez pullih nizmus tash,oi/dough un giv uh shid oi sez. Tom."

The emphasis is deliberate and made with care.

Cummings said that Josiah Royce (who appears in one of the poem-portraits) directed his attention to Dante Gabriel Rossetti, especially to Rossetti's sonnets, and that made him a sonneteer. Certainly Cummings wrote some of the finest sonnets of our century: celebrating love, savagely ridiculing human stupidity, and recording his pilgrimage to the transcendental. From the somewhat conventional, Cummings' sonnets developed, as Theodore Spencer has said, to achieve "specific gravity." Yet the only discernible influence of the Pre-Raphaelite school is in the early lyrics and might as easily have been been picked up direct from a reading of the sonnets of Dante. There is internal evidence that Shakespeare was the dynamic influence in his sonnet-making: sensory details, the absence of hypocrisy, even the rhythm of the snap at the end, as in a couplet from "being to timelessness as it's to time" in *95 Poems*: "—do lovers love?Why then to heaven with hell./Whatever sages say and fools,all's well." In an interview with Harvey Breit in 1950 Cummings said: "Today so-called writers are completely unaware of the thing which makes art what it is. You can call it nobility or spirituality, but I should call it intensity. Sordid is the opposite. . . . Shakespeare is never sordid . . . because his poetry was the most intense."

Cummings' experimentation was clearly within Western literary tradition, as was Eliot's, but, finally, whatever he did resulted in poems that could not have been written by anyone else. He has had no sucessful imitators. And because of its nature Cummings' work cannot be held within the bounds of conventional literary analysis. The critic must stretch his own powers to find the significant new insights waiting to be revealed by this poet's language in action. What is required is "intelligence functioning at intuitional velocity"—Cummings used the phrase to characterize a work of the sculptor Lachaise but it admirably describes the approach a perceptive critic-reader must take to Cummings' writing.

For a study of Cummings' philosophy and of his devices to achieve art in motion and at a peak of excitement, the play *Him*, called by the critic Edmund Wilson "the outpouring of an intelligence, a sensibility, and an imagination of the very first dimension," is especially useful.

The action is divided between "exterior" and "interior" happenings that develop the love story of a man and the predicament of an artist. The satirical exterior scenes are presented before a garish curtain like that used in carnival shows. The deliberate lack of a third dimension is one of the poet's "absurdities"; it symbolizes the "unworld." The curtain and the parodies of circus and burlesque in the play's action reflect his interest in folk amusements. The interior scenes explore the psyche of the creative temperament. Connecting the two phases is the chorus: the three Fates, Atropos, Clotho, Lachesis. They are disguised as the Misses Weird and are nicknamed "Stop," "Look," and "Listen." They sit with their backs to the audience, rocking and knitting, as they swap a nonsensical version of backfence talk and advertising slogans. The stage directions integrate the themes and devices of the play.

In the complex design of *Him*, described by one commentator as "a play of lucid madness and adventurous gaiety," Cummings sets up a confrontation: man, a social being, versus the artist. In the *Six Nonlectures* he repeats: "Nobody else can be alive for you; nor can you be alive for anybody else. . . . There's the artist's responsibility. . . ." Yeats knew this human instinct to fulfill strenuous conditions for the

sake of an ideal: writing of the Irish playwright J. M. Synge, he said, ". . . to come out from under the shadow of other men's minds . . . to be utterly oneself: that is all the Muses care for." At first glance Yeats's statement seems callous but when it is illustrated in the creative life it leads to service for the community. In the poems beginning "i sing of Olaf glad and big" (*ViVa*) and "a man who had fallen among thieves" (*Is 5*), Cummings is urging awake the sleeping conscience of his fellows. And in *Him* Cummings develops a metaphor, found with varying emphasis in his poetry, that strikingly illustrates his view. The artist is likened to a circus performer who sits astride three chairs stacked one on top of the other and balanced on a high wire. He explains to his lover, "Me," that the three chairs are three facts: "I am an Artist, I am a Man, I am a Failure."

The label on the top chair, "Failure," is disconcerting but acceptable when the reader becomes familiar with the paradoxes of Cummings' vocabulary. To distinguish true accomplishment from the disappointing successes of the salesman-politician-warmongering world, he uses words that for him state the ultimate emptiness of the prizes the crowd pursues and often captures. Throughout Cummings' poems occur the words *failure, nothing, nobody, zero* and the prefixes *non-* and *un-*. They are also scattered through the prose of *The Enormous Room* and *Eimi*. By these negatives he separated his ideals from the pleasures of a conformist world and showed his condemnation of "mobs" and "gangs" and his concern for the individual. The phrase "you and i" dominates his response to relationships: lovers, mother and child, a man and a city, a man and a tree.

The other two "chairs" of *Him* have a subordinate but vital function in the metaphor. The experiences of the man are limited to the senses until they are fused with the perceptions of the artist. It is from the artist and his transcendental realizations that the reader or viewer learns to distinguish the genuine from the pinchbeck. The artist is also dependent on the report from his five senses to actualize his ideas. So Cummings found spiritualities in "facts" and celebrated them in his poems of love and compassion. The significance that Cummings assigned to "failure" is further evident in a sonnet from *Is 5*, "if i have made, my lady, intricate/imperfect various things . . ." And a study of the Foreword to *Is 5* will reveal affirmations of the themes of *Him*: that the poet knows he is "competing" with reality and therefore "failure" is predestined. What is increasingly noticeable in the play and in the volumes of poems that follow it is the changing concept of love and the frank presentation of the artist's self-doubt. He insists on finding out who he is before he can be either artist or lover. Cummings' belief that the artist's total attentiveness to an object or subject should result in simultaneity for his audience—which was also the aim of the Imagist movement in poetry and of Cubism in painting—was not completely realizable. He therefore began to think of art as a series of mirrors reflecting the "object" in various lights and not as the thing-in-itself. So, with a sense of the "awful responsibility" of the poet, he regarded his extraordinary successes in putting on the page a flying bird, a grasshopper, a falling leaf as "failures" and called himself a nonhero.

The falling leaf poem is the first of the *95 Poems*. It is not a complete sentence and there are only four words. The form has the narrowness of a needle. In a time when novels tell no story and music is not melodic—relatively speaking—this pictogram brings new insights, which have been perceptively set forth by Norman Friedman and Barry A. Marks in their

critical studies of Cummings; their lead is followed here.

l(a

le

af

fa

ll

s)

one

l

iness

Each of the first four lines has but one consonant and one vowel: two *l*'s, three *a*'s, one *e*, and two *f*'s. This suggests the fluttering pattern of a falling leaf. The next line, treated as a stanza, is a double *l*, extending meaning as the reader waits for the necessary completion. The poem ends on a shifting note which accentuates the import of "alone," "one," and "oneliness" (defined as "own").

The mind of the reader seizes the two ideas: loneliness and the parenthetical interjection of the fall of a leaf. In splitting "loneliness" Cummings shows by variations on a word blurred by indiscriminate use that it is, as Marks noted, "quite a singular word." Cummings strips the sheath from the ordinary, and the extraordinary is revealed. The "le/af/fa/ll" involves both sound and visual values; the musical relation echoes the meaning emerging from "le" and "af."

The *l* in "leaf" repeats the first *l* in "loneliness" and helps the reader keep in mind simultaneously the material inside and outside the parentheses. His old typewriter played an important role here in Cummings' idea of form as it affects thought: in the first line *l* can be either the digit "one" or the letter "el." A parenthesis separating it from *a* suggests that while the idea of doubling up on "oneness" is attractive, it is not plausible. Following the trail of the parenthesis, the reader discovers a "verse" that reinforces the necessity that *l* be "el" in the fourth stanza. The word "one" and an apparent digit reflect back to the initial *l* and in their interplay the digit vanishes into the letter.

The reader is pleased with his success in working out the "puzzle"; casually he has participated in the dance of the poet's mind. Then he arrives at the last line, "iness." The isolation and the desolation of the individual, the I alone with the I, be it a leaf or a man, have been established. Forgotten are the secondary ideas of oneness with the universe or the intimations of autumn: the reader now knows he has misunderstood the form if he accepted it as a needle stitching together all created things. However, as Henry James asserted by implication in *The Wings of the Dove*, the tragic element is art and art is delight. Yet another idea is added to the possibles of interpretation: man's unhappy isolation comes from self-loving activities and trivial goals. Self-forgetfulness is the reward of the disciplined athlete and of the artist, with the result an unblemished performance. The ever-evolving devices of Cummings are a witness to his profoundly moral nature in conflict with an imperfect world, and to his vision that it *could* be perfected.

The "puzzle" of the following lines from *No Thanks* is similarly rewarding to the reader willing to work it out:

r-p-o-p-h-e-s-s-a-g-r
          who
a)s w(e loo)k
upnowgath
          PPEGORHRASS
                    eringint(o-

aThe):1
     eA
        !p:
S   a

The poet, through spacings of word and letter and the unorthodox use of capitals, presents a grasshopper living in his muscles. At first he is invisible, coming from the grass to us only in the sounds reverberating from earth or pebbles. But as Lloyd Frankenberg pointed out in his study of modern poetry, *Pleasure Dome*: "These sounds—some soft, some loud, some intermittent—are rearrangements of his name; just as he rearranges himself to rub forewing and hind leg together. Then he 'leaps!' clear so that we see him, 'arriving to become, rearrangingly, grasshopper.'" The reader has been, briefly, the grasshopper and that has extended his capacity for being alive. Note that in this poem Cummings used a device resembling Cubistic painting: "r-p-o-p-h-e-s-s-a-g-r" and "PPEGORHRASS" and ".gRrEaPsPhOs" (which appears after the lines quoted above) record the "realization" of experiences that he wished to share with his readers.

In other poems which demonstrate his delight in the natural world, Cummings often used mimicry. Cummings had a talent like that of the Greek comic playwright Aristophanes, who in his oft-quoted line "Brekekekéx koáx koáx" sought to reproduce the sound of frogs. A similar mimicry is found in such unlikely Cummings poems as the colloquial "buncha hardboil guys from duh A.C. fulla" (*ViVa*) and "joggle i think will do it although the glad" (*Tulips and Chimneys*). In a punning poem, "applaws)" (*One Times One*), the "paw" is a kind of mimicry and a reminder that fundamentally we are animals.

Another aspect of the "creaturely" life that interested Cummings is to be found in his poems about horses, those animals now vanishing from sight, except in parades or circuses. In the lines below from a poem in *No Thanks* the scene is set by "crazily seething of this/ raving city screamingly street." What opens the windows to be "sharp holes in dark places" is the light from flowers. And what do the "whichs" and "small its," the half-alive, half-asleep people see?

what a proud dreamhorse pulling(smoothloom-
    ingly)through
(stepp)this(ing)crazily seething of this
raving city screamingly street wonderful

flowers And o the Light thrown by Them opens

sharp holes in dark places paints eyes touches
    hands with new-
ness and these startled whats are a(piercing
    clothes thoughts kiss
-ing wishes bodies)squirm-of-frightened shy
    are whichs small
its hungry for Is for Love Spring thirsty for
    happens
only and beautiful

Through the raucous sounds of a city street a horse is pulling a load of flowers. In that setting his movements have a grace such as is found in dreams. The horse establishes his reality as we watch him "stepp . . . ing"—the poet has plowed with horses his family's fields; he has watched milk wagons in the city. However, as Lloyd Frankenberg has suggested, the horse, "whose feet almost walk air," brings to mind Pegasus. That wingèd steed of the Muses is associated in legend with Hippocrene, the fountain of inspiration, which supposedly sprang from the earth at a blow from his fore-hoof. In one legend the Greek hero Bellerophon, with the aid of Pegasus, slew the Chimaera, a ravaging beast. Then he tried to fly to heaven, thereby offending the gods, and

fell to earth. A poet is often trying to fly and often he fails. So we come back to the name that Cummings gave himself, "nonhero."

In another city sonnet, from *And* ("my sonnet is A light goes on in"), we meet the dray horses that sleep upstairs in a tenement stable. "Ears win-/k funny stable. In the morning they go out in pairs." Implied in the poet's words is the ancient horse sacrifice to the sun, to encourage the sun to rise again. So the sonnet comes to a climax on a line of life and beauty: "They pull the morning out of the night." There is the same fidelity to sensory perception in poems that include references to rain: "the rain's/pearls singly-whispering" (from "the moon is hiding in," *Tulips and Chimneys*) and "i have found what you are like/the rain" (*And*).

The opening lines of an early poem, from *Tulips and Chimneys*, show both Cummings' delight in the natural world and his ability to respond freshly to it:

    stinging
    gold swarms
    upon the spires
    silver

       chants the litanies the
    great bells are ringing with rose
    the lewd fat bells

The poet avoided the obvious ideas that cluster around the subject of sunset: the timeworn meanings of silver and gold are freshened by the adroit combination of "stinging" and "swarms"; sound and image suggest the flight of a young queen and the creation of a new hive. "Spires" is echoed later in the poem in the phrase "a tall wind," and the poem concludes with an image of a dreamy sea. In an experiment Laura Riding and Robert Graves converted the pattern of this poem, the last part of which imitates a retreating wave, into conventional stanzas and concluded, rightly, that in the process the significance as well as the poetry was lost.

Informed critics, among them Barry A. Marks and the poet William Carlos Williams, have directed attention to "nonsun blob a" as probably the most difficult of Cummings' poems and yet as one containing very useful clues for the reader. It has a regularity of stanza, an Elizabethan tone, and a simplicity that might place it among the poet's charming verses for children. However, it offers a severe challenge to the mind: to put away old habits of associative thinking and to examine each stanza, line by line and word by word, for the relationships the poet has evoked. It also sums up Cummings' innovations and ideas to a remarkable degree. The emphasis Cummings himself placed upon it is evident in its position as the opening poem of the volume *One Times One*.

> nonsun blob a
> cold to
> skylessness
> sticking fire
>
> my are your
> are birds our all
> and one gone
> away the they
>
> leaf of ghosts some
> few creep there
> here or on
> unearth

Here the senses become elements of thought and the emotions are objictified to an extreme degree. The first stanza has neither verb nor expected sequences nor is it broken up to be reassembled, like an anagram. Each word compresses experiences from years of winter days; it is demanded of the reader that he be alert at all points so he may follow the clues in this celebration of bare, daunting specifics of a northern winter. Look at a winter sky: sunlessness is its chief characteristic but there is a gray waver, a "blob," sending out an almost invisible shine. The closing line, "sticking fire" —in which some critics observe a sexual connotation—brings into focus a dumb fear of being lost in a glacial world and paradoxically suggests all the physical and moral efforts to bring life-giving warmth to man, from Prometheus to nuclear industrial activities.

As we move on to a consideration of the second stanza, an observation made by Marks in his *E. E. Cummings* is especially illuminating. He noted: "the words of the first two lines . . . form two mathematical equations. One says, 'my + your = our.' The other, based on the phonetic pun, 'our' and 'are,' says, 'my = your'; 'my + your = birds'; 'my + your + birds = all.'" Intimations of what concerned Cummings—that the nature of unity is love—occur in the merging of the possessive pronouns: "mine" into "yours" into "ours" into "all." This unity is felt on repeated readings of the poem. But a Cummings poem is always in motion; the second stanza ends with the unity destroyed, the bird flock scattered in quest of a vanished leader.

The "a" which ends the first line of the poem is significant for an understanding of the third stanza. In its isolation it is related to autumn leaves creeping like crippled birds on a cold earth as indifferent as the cold sky recorded in the third stanza. Unfriendliness deprives the earth of its nourishing function; therefore Cummings used the prefix *un-* to modify the word *earth*. What is to be made of a typical Cummings inversion: "leaf of ghosts"? A remnant of birds or leaves in the increasing cold is described in the first stanza; later, birds reduced to creeping are non-birds, and cold earth is heartless as cold sky; both environments when deprived of their function as givers and nourishers, and therefore of their reality, are also ghosts. What Henry James called "perception at the pitch of passion" is involved in this "circular" poem. The implication is that of Greek tragedy: the helplessness of the alive, be it leaf or bird or a man and a woman. Yet there is joy in the contemplation of the real: a sun so clouded it may have burned out centuries ago; the relationship between the afflicted birds, leaves, and lovers—and the reader of the poem. Cummings, keeping his agonies to himself, nearly always ends on a note of joy.

This poem in twelve lines anticipates the essence of the nine stanzas of a later poem, "rosetree,rosetree" (*95 Poems*). The last stanza of "rosetree,rosetree" tells us again what the poet believes and hopes for:

> lovetree!least the
> rose alive must three,must
> four and(to quite become
> nothing)five times,proclaim
> fate isn't fatal
> —a heart her each petal

The reader may wonder why this master of experimental form chose rhymed stanzas for this piece. It is another instance of Cummings' sensitivity to choice among the formalities—an Elizabethan song brimming with transcendental ideas although the rose is a literal rose in a sizzle of bees. Traditional form attracts simple ideas: tree-bird, mob-war, flower-death-love. In this poem it serves as a counterweight to the complex ideas of a mystic, the poet "dreaming-true." Norman Friedman in a reasoned study of 175 worksheets of "rosetree, rosetree," rescued by Marion Morehouse Cummings from the usual destruction of preliminary work, reveals Cummings as a craftsman perfecting his materials over a long period of time. Throughout the fifty-four lines of the

poem—in the adjustment of negative to positive, the victory in the final stanza over darkness and fatality—the cerebral element is always in play.

A poem that relates to this one—by melodic form and a transformation of abstracts so that they are vivid images—is the remarkable "what if a much of a which of a wind" (*One Times One*). Its rhythm perhaps reflects the influence of a ballad (attributed to Thomas Campion) which begins with "What if a day or a month or a year." But there the similarity ends. In the Cummings poem we have a deeply felt comment on the plight of universal life—nature and man—communicated by pairs of opposites: "gives the truth to summer's lie"; "when skies are hanged and oceans drowned,/ the single secret will be man." In this "song" there are combinations that are reminiscent of Cummings' intriguing phrase "the square root of minus one" which he employed in at least three different contexts, notably in the Introduction to his *Collected Poems* where he wrote: "Mostpeople have less in common with ourselves than the squarerootofminusone." When he says, "Blow soon to never and never to twice/(blow life to isn't:blow death to was)/ —all nothing's only our hugest home," he has made eloquent poetry of his abstract idea.

William Troy has commented that certain pages of Cummings' Russian travel journal, *Eimi*, are as good as all but the best of his poetry. Certainly there is a relation between the prose and poetry in theme and technique.

In *Eimi* Cummings' words are positioned logistically to establish the impact of viewing Lenin's tomb. Others had written, according to their political bias, of that tomb. Cummings presented what his senses reported: the smells and sounds of the never-ending line of humanity descending into the bowels of the earth to get a glimpse of the corpse of a small man with a small face, their Messiah—as secret in death as he was in life. Cummings had gone to Russia to find out what the socialistic experiment was doing to help man toward being more alive. He found men and women with "a willingness not to live, if only they were allowed not to die," in John Peale Bishop's words. In some circumstances apathy is a means of survival, but for the poet this was too little—or so it seemed to the young man of Harvard and New Hampshire. Vivid, even gay, portraits of Russians lighten the record but the following passage—illustrative of his firming style, that "specialization of sensibility"—is what he understood at Lenin's tomb:

facefacefaceface
   hand-
         fin-
             claw
   foot-
        hoof
   (tovarich)
             es to number of numberlessness (un
-smiling)
   with dirt's dirt dirty dirtier with others' dirt
      of themselves
dirtiest waitstand dirtily never smile shuffle-
      budge dirty pausehalt
   Smilingless.

Francis Fergusson has referred to this passage as the beginning of "a sleepwalking death-rite." Cummings' deliberate abandonment of conventional syntax, which is based on an arrangement of thoughts and sensations already completed, makes the "instantaneous alone . . . his concern," as Troy put it, and he takes the reader into "an unworld of unmen lying in unsleep on an unbed of preternatural nullity."

Sensory awareness has been a dominant theme of Cummings' work discussed so far. A second primary theme in his work, both poetry

and prose, is the integrity of the individual. The last lines of a sophisticated little poem about a Jewish tailor in Greenwich Village, "i say no world" (*50 Poems*), put his view succinctly: "unsellable not buyable alive/one i say human being)one/goldberger." Beginning with *The Enormous Room* and *Tulips and Chimneys*, Cummings celebrated individuals, perceiving the transcendental under the ephemeral disguise. Some of his poem-portraits focused on the famous: Buffalo Bill ("Buffalo Bill's/defunct," *Tulips and Chimneys*), the tragicomic dancer Jimmy Savo ("so little he is," in "New Poems" of *Collected Poems*), Picasso ("Picasso/you give us Things," *XLI Poems*). In others he turned a clear but sympathetic eye on burlesque queens, circus clowns, "niggers dancing," the Greenwich Village "Professor Seagull." He wrote too of bums —and caught the spirit of their search for a "self" even as they scoured the gutters for a cigarette butt.

It follows that anything threatening individuality would be the object of his hatred. War, for example:

    you know what i mean when
    the first guy drops you know
    everybody feels sick or
    when they throw in a few gas
    and the oh baby shrapnel
    or my feet getting dim freezing or
    up to your you know what in water or
    with the bugs crawling right all up
    all everywhere over you all . . .

In these lines from "lis/-ten" (*Is 5*) Cummings conveys—through the agonized, almost hysterical, words of a soldier who was there—his deep-felt indignation against the senseless destruction of individuals. And the poet's skill transforms the ephemeral statistic of a newspaper battle account into transcendental man.

   The threats to the integrity of the individual

posed by a mechanized society are many and pervasive. "Progress is a comfortable disease," commented Cummings in "pity this busy monster, manunkind" (*One Times One*), but a disease nonetheless. The attempts of man to identify with his inventions—to become the turbines and computers he developed—stir Cummings to remark: "A world of made/is not a world of born." And so "when man determined to destroy/himself he picked the was/of shall and finding only why/smashed it into because" ("when god decided to invent," *One Times One*).

In the morality *Santa Claus* Cummings speaks sharply against the blighting forces that keep a man from knowing his spontaneous self. "Knowledge has taken love out of the world/and all the world is empty empty empty . . . joyless joyless joyless." The Child in the morality, however, can "truly see," as in Hans Christian Andersen's story "The Emperor's New Clothes." And when the Woman calls for death and Santa dressed as Death enters, she sees through the disguise because she looks with the eyes of the heart. Ironies of belief and unbelief are frequent in *Santa Claus*; the interchange of mask and costume is reminiscent of Shakespeare, and even more of the melodramatics of tent shows that toured the hinterland of the United States, and these again are related to the commedia dell'arte which began as skits performed on a wooden cart pulled by a donkey—to amuse Italian peasants. Cummings, writing to Allen Tate in 1946, said that the whole aim of *Santa Claus* was to make man remove his death mask, thereby becoming what he truly is: a human being.

In his concern to remove the death mask Cummings often employed satire. The satirist, it has been said, needs both irreverence and moral conviction. Cummings had both. His satire is like that of Swift; it comes from con-

viction that something is awry, as when he declared that this world is all aleak and "i'd rather learn from one bird how to sing/than teach ten thousand stars how not to dance" ("New Poems," *Collected Poems*).

In the successful satires the penetration is trenchant, underlined by a cheerful ribaldry. At other times his intention is mislaid in a junk pile of name calling and irrelevant detail. Indignation sometimes results in an absence of poetic statement and a series of stereotypes. As Philip Horton has noted, Cummings is at times guilty of bad puns and satires that miss their mark ("a myth is as good as a smile" from "little joe gould"; "obey says toc,submit says tic,/Eternity's a Five Year Plan" from "Jehovah buried,Satan dead," both in *No Thanks*). However, in a notable example of the satiric, "A Foreword to Krazy" (1946; collected in *A Miscellany*), Cummings explained the symbolism of George Herriman's comic-strip characters and at the same time he defined his own position as a satirist. The cast is made up of Ignatz Mouse, a brick-throwing cynic, Offissa Pupp, a sentimental policeman-dog, and the heroine, "slightly resembling a child's drawing of a cat." On the political level Offissa Pupp represents the "will of socalled society" while Ignatz Mouse is the destructive element. The benevolent overdog and the malevolent undermouse, as Cummings saw it, misunderstood Krazy Kat. Not only is she a symbol of an ideal democracy but she is personal—she transforms the brick into a kiss; the senses aided by the spirit produce joy.

These ideas ran counter to those expressed in T. S. Eliot's essay "Tradition and the Individual Talent" which for so long after its publication made the personal in literature suspect. But the swing of the pendulum through the centuries from the formalized prosaic (classic) to the formalized romantic is always rectifying the errors of critics. Poets like John

Berryman and Robert Lowell have carried on experiments in the personal that Cummings would have found in his vein.

In two poems, "anyone lived in a pretty how town" and "my father moved through dooms of love" (both in *50 Poems*), Cummings very effectively worked the personal into a universal application. He used for one a contemplative narration of ideal lovers and for the other a portrait of the ideal man. The maturity of the poet's insights is displayed by his bold use of regular, rhymed stanzas to control a considered emotion and to weld it to his opinions, now sufficiently explored, of the social dilemma. The refrains are a charming blend of nursery rhyme ("sun moon stars rain" and "with up so floating many bells down") and sophisticated observation ("My father moved through theys of we").

Barry Marks has pointed out that as contemporary painters (like Juan Gris and Picasso) ambiguously employed a single curve for the neck of a vase and the edge of a guitar, so Cummings often deranged his syntax in order that a single word would both intensify a statement and question its validity; an example is the "how" in "anyone lived in a pretty how town." This word suggests, among other things, that the townspeople ask how and why about things from an emptiness of mind and an incapacity for simultaneity and the intuitive grasp. The direct vision of the painter-poet is similar to a child's delight in believing that a rain puddle is the ocean; it is a transcendental conception.

In the pretty how town "anyone" and "noone" are lovers; they live and love and die in a landscape of changing seasons, among children growing into adults and forgetting the realities and adults, "both little and small," without love or interest in life—from Cummings' penetrative view. The lively series of contrasts reinforces the ballad form; emotion and thought are strictly held to the development of the charade: "anyone" versus "someones," the individual opposed to the anxious status-seekers who "sowed their isn't" and "reaped their same." Children guessed the goodness of love between anyone and noone, because children are close to the intuitive life, but living things grow by imitation, so the children forgot as they imitated their "someones."

In the last line of the third stanza, "that noone loved him more by more," the word "noone" is emphasizing the public indifference as well as providing the identification of the "she" in the next stanza:

> when by now and tree by leaf
> she laughed his joy she cried his grief
> bird by snow and stir by still
> anyone's any was all to her

A compression of meanings is achieved in "when by now," "bird by snow," "tree by leaf," and they in turn are manipulated by repetitions suggested by later rhyme and alliteration: "all by all and deep by deep/and more by more . . ." The climax of the ballad is in the line "and noone stooped to kiss his face." In the second to the last stanza the poet states the triumph of the individual way of life, as the lovers go hand in hand into eternity:

> noone and anyone earth by april
> wish by spirit and if by yes

Cumming's testament for his father, "my father moved through dooms of love," is a ballad only by stanza and innerly varied refrain; intertwined are seasonal references, as in "septembering arms of year extend," which gives individuality to the general term "harvest." It is heroic by virtue of lines that paraphrase the Prophets: "his anger was as right as rain/his pity was as green as grain." The poem is distinguished by some fine couplets:

"and should some why completely weep/my father's fingers brought her sleep," and "if every friend became his foe/he'd laugh and build a world with snow," which describes pretty accurately the poet himself. There is no narrative as such, but the poem is held together by the feeling of compassion toward humble or unfortunate people.

In contrast to the abstract quality of "my father moved through dooms of love," a sequence of colorful details characterizes an early poem for Cummings' mother, "if there are any heavens" *(ViVa)*. The opening lines establish clearly the heroic light in which Cumming's viewed this woman who said of herself after a remarkable recovery from an automobile accident, "I'm tough":

if there are any heavens my mother will(all by
    herself)have
one. It will not be a pansy heaven nor
a fragile heaven of lilies-of-the-valley but
it will be a heaven of blackred roses

Cummings' virtuosity in the management of his mechanics may especially be noted in several poems revealing his intense concern with the individual. In one, the free-form poem beginning "5/derbies-with-men-in-them" *(XLI Poems)*, the reader is presented with a charade. With the poet he has entered a café that, like the Englishman's pub, seems more a social club than a restaurant: the customers play games such as backgammon and read and discuss the news while drinking coffee. Identity of place is established in the fourth stanza when one of the customers buys the Bawstina-mereekin from a paperboy. But Cummings builds up an un-Yankee atmosphere with carefully chosen details: the men smoke Helmar cigarettes, one of them uses the word "effendi" and "swears in persian," two speak in Turkish, an Armenian record is played on the phonograph. This is, then, a Near Eastern café in Boston. Far from the feuds of the Old Country, proprietor and customers are united by homesickness. The men are not named; instead Cummings identifies them by lowercase letters:

a has gold
teeth b pink
suspenders c
reads Atlantis

And x beats y at backgammon. This device permits Cummings both to control his flood of feeling for the men and to stress their brotherhood. When two of them—the man with the gold teeth and the winner at backgammon—leave, Cummings says "exeunt ax"; and the coupled "by" follow. Cummings' characteristic use of space and capitals to underscore meaning is also to be found in this poem: "the pho/nographisrunn/ingd o w, n" and then "stopS."

Capital letters (not meant to be pronounced) serve as an organizing and emphasizing device in "sonnet entitled how to run the world)" *(No Thanks)*, which begins:

A always don't there B being no such thing
for C can't casts no shadow D drink and

E eat of her voice in whose silence the music
    of spring
lives F feels opens but shuts understand
G gladly forget little having less

with every least most remembering
H highest fly only the flag that's furled

Here we have a commentary on the existence of "mostpeople." This satire on the "unworld" employs the comparatives "less" and "least" to emphasize the triviality and sterility of that world, while the clause "in whose silence the music of spring/lives" indicates what, for Cummings, is one of the symbols of the real world, the transcendental world. There is a flash of mocking humor in the repetition of the pedantic "entitled" in the ninth line of the poem, "(sestet entitled grass is flesh . . ." but even this line has a serious purpose: to reinforce the idea of a world where people merely exist. It is followed by a richly thought-provoking statement, "any dream/means more than sleep as more than know means guess)," which prepares the way for the masterly concluding line, "children building this rainman out of snow." In this poem Cummings uses for the most part simple words but combines them so that the repetitions and contrasts of sound add a fresh dimension to the theme and subtly contribute to the feeling of empathy evoked for the individuals trapped in the "unworld."

Where in these two poems Cummings used, variously, lowercase and capital letters as controlling devices, in "there are 6 doors" (*ViVa*), it is repetition of the phrase "next door" that governs the orderly sequence. "Next door(but four)" lives a whore with "a multitude of chins"; "next door/but three" a ghost "Who screams Faintly" is the tenant and "next/Door but two" a man and his wife who "throw silently things/Each at other." Then Cummings tells what happens to some men who have been jettisoned by society.

,next door but One
a on Dirty bed Mangy from person Porous
sits years its of self fee(bly
Perpetually coughing And thickly spi)tting

Finally, "next door nobody/seems to live at present . . . or,bedbugs." The reader is left to ponder several kinds of waste of human life. Emerson wrote in his essay "Self-Reliance," "This one fact the world hates, that the soul *becomes*"; Cummings recorded in poem after poem instances of the world preventing the action of the soul—but with the purpose of rousing the transcendental spirit latent in his readers.

The individuals pictured in "mortals)" (*50 Poems*) are very different from those in the rooms "next door" and so are the technical devices used. Cummings here turns to highly skilled acrobats and puts them into motion on the page:

mortals)

climbi
        ng i
        nto eachness begi
        n
dizzily
        swingthings
of speeds of
trapeze gush somersaults
open ing
        hes shes
&meet&
        swoop
                fully is are ex
                        quisite theys of re
turn
        a
        n
        d
fall which now drop who all dreamlike

(im

"Eachness" is a critical word in this poem: as George Haines IV has pointed out, the individuality of the performers is emphasized by the separation of "climbi" and "begi" from the end letters "ng" and "n"; the swinging of the trapeze is in the line repetition "of speeds of." The reader discovering a similar pattern in "&meet&" by this time is responding with a jump of his muscles, as occurs in watching ballet or circus. As the "fully" continues into "is are ex," movement has entered the area of the unknown; the symbol x ("ex") is equal to the mystery of the encounters of the "is" and "are," "the "hes" and "shes." The use of "a/n/d" permits visualization of the trapeze.

The fortunate climax of "who all dreamlike" brings together the specific skills and the hovering mystery of art, whose function is to redeem what otherwise would vanish from the earth like a dream. In another sense, the acrobats are a congruent image since even the most skilled is in peril at every performance (mortals, Cummings called them), yet they are completely and happily themselves in the exercise of their art. From the final line to the first one in this "circular" poem—"im" plus "mortal"—the poet justifies his contention that precision makes motion which makes life, and that the "dark beginnings are his luminous ends."

Why did Cummings choose the symbol of acrobats for a metaphysical statement? He may have been inspired, as was Rilke, by "Les Saltimbanques" of Picasso. More likely, his enjoyment of folk amusements dictated the vehicle for his fundamental belief: mortals, by devotion to a skill, an art, become immortal.

Before leaving this aspect of Cummings' work, we may appropriately turn back to his prose to find a revealing conjunction of theme and technique. In *The Enormous Room* Cummings had used a phrase of John Bunyan's, the "Delectable Mountains," to refer to certain individuals—physically mistreated, spiritually mutilated, and yet triumphantly overcoming their situations. Of one example, whom he christened The Zulu, he said, "His angular anatomy expended and collected itself with an effortless spontaneity. . . . But he was more. There are certain things in which one is unable to believe for the simple reason that he never ceases to feel them. Things of this sort—things which are always inside of us and in fact are us and which consequently will not be pushed off or away where we can begin thinking about them—are no longer things; they, and the us which they are, equals A Verb; an IS. The Zulu, then, I must perforce call an IS." Thus, using one of his typical devices, substitution

of one part of speech for another, Cummings converted one way of seeing and of thinking into another to emphasize a theme that would be meshed in all of his writings. Whenever *is*, the verb, is turned into a noun, it becomes even more of a verb; it is dramatized, it gains—as Lloyd Frankenberg put it—the force of the colloquial "He is somebody." In other words, the quality of being becomes an active principle, the individual becomes a whole person, responding to the totality of experience.

A third major theme in Cummings' work, already touched upon, is the revelation of what it means *truly* to love. In his experiments with the idea of love Cummings assigned to the word the multiple connotations inherent in it: sexual, romantic, platonic. The most intense love, paradoxically, must function with the greatest objectivity; subjective impressions must be corrected by intent observation of objects, human or otherwise. Dante could write of his ideal Lady; Cummings addressed to a platonic vision a bawdy valentine that is revelatory of his stance toward life and art ("on the Madam's best april the," *Is 5*).

In the era following World War I and acceleration of industrial growth, disregard of an earlier generation's restraints on sex became a means of protesting against the increased restrictions of the national life. In literature, Sherwood Anderson, Ernest Hemingway, Eugene O'Neill, and Henry Miller emphasized the necessity for sexual freedom. Cummings participated in this critique of the dehumanizing forces dominating the modern scene. Frankly rejoicing in sexuality as a nourishing element in an integrated life, a bond between man and the cosmos, or satirizing customs based on habit and fear of public opinion, he wrote "O sweet spontaneous" (*Tulips and Chimneys*) and "she being Brand" (*Is 5*) and "i will be/Moving in the Street of her" (*And*). A poem on Sally Rand, "out of a supermetamathical subpreincestures" (*No Thanks*), is not only a celebration of the fan dancer of the 1930's but also a transcendental view of the wonder of life. And it is a significant contrast to "raise the shade/will youse dearie?" (*And*), a realistic piece exposing the joylessness in the pursuit of "pleasure."

Cummings eventually went "beyond sex as a critique of society and . . . beyond self-indulgence to self-discipline based on a new understanding of love," as Barry Marks put it. Cummings believed that morality depends on whether there is genuine giving on both sides. Sexuality is an ingredient of any I-you relationship, in the impersonal way that there is a trace of sugar in all vegetable and animal tissues, even if they taste salty or bitter. He illustrated insights into giving in a philosophical poem, "(will you teach a/wretch to live/straighter than a needle)," and in a comment on poverty that moves in nursery-rhyme couplets from realistic deprivations to a more desperate psychological dilemma, "if you can't eat you got to/smoke and we ain't got/nothing to smoke" (both in *50 Poems*). And a poem (from *No Thanks*) with neat stanzas to control his vehemence tells the reader from what a distance the poet has come, smiling in a wry wisdom:

> be of love(a little)
> More careful
> Than of everything
> guard her perhaps only
>
> . . . .
>
> (Dare until a flower,
> understanding sizelessly sunlight
> Open what thousandth why and
> discover laughing)

Lloyd Frankenberg, in his introduction to a London reprint of *One Times One*, said that, in effect, all of Cummings' poems were love poems. A neat summation, but then an "anatomy" of love is also necessary. Conventional behavior in love is related to conventional punctuation in prosody. And for a poet who lived on the tips of not only his nerves but also his mind, love covers all of existence: in one aspect it is involved with spit on the sidewalk and in another with moonlight on the thighs of his lady; the value of a thing or an experience is its revelation of an involvement with life. Finally, in *95 Poems* and *73 Poems*, Cummings came to a position whose simplicity may have surprised him: a filial relation to the Divine So this was what it meant, the witty comment he made on his own struggles in *Is 5*:

> since feeling is first
> who pays any attention
> to the syntax of things
> will never wholly kiss you;
>
> . . . .
>
> for life's not a paragraph
>
> And death i think is no parenthesis

In his critical studies T. S. Eliot repeated his view that the entire output of certain writers constitutes a single work similar to an epic (*The Divine Comedy* or Williams' *Paterson*) and that individual pieces are endowed with meaning by other pieces and by the whole context of the work. This view may assist to an understanding of Cummings: fragmentation dissolves in the continuity of recurrent themes; interrelated images and symbols by their organizing force reflect and echo each other with cumulative effect. Cummings would have said it more specifically: in the here and now we can be happy and immortal if we use our wits and our will. Even if evil and death are the co-kings of this world, love is my king, and in serving him is my joy.

It is a leap into faith when a man casts off the customary motives of humanity and ventures to trust himself as taskmaster; he will need courage and vision "that a simple purpose may be to him as strong as iron necessity is to others"—so Emerson thought. From *Tulips and Chimneys* to *Poems 1923–1954*— a constellation of refracted and repeated images—to the posthumous *73 Poems*, Cummings led a succession of readers to accept his declaration: "I have no sentimentality at all. If you haven't got that, you're not afraid to write of love and death."

The metaphysical cord on which Cummings' sonnets are threaded was in evidence in the early "a connotation of infinity/sharpens the temporal splendor of this night" (*Tulips and Chimneys*), in "put off your faces,Death:for day is over" (*ViVa*), and in "Love/coins His most gradual gesture,/and whittles life to eternity" ("it is so long since my heart has been with yours," *Is 5*). The efficacy of love in its multiple aspects pervades the notions of death until death becomes a gate to life. Dying is a verb as opposed to a deathly noun: "forgive us the sin of death." In another early poem, "somewhere i have never travelled,gladly beyond/any experience" (*ViVa*), the abstraction "spring" is personified and its essential mystery is presented through the adverbs *skilfully, mysteriously, suddenly*, used as in the later poetry are *miraculous, illimitable, immeasurable*: adjectival aspects of natural phenomena capable of being perceived but incapable of being truly labeled or measured.

The concern of Cummings, even in his Sitwellian phase, with juxtaposed improbables— locomotives with roses—was an effort to get at the quintessence of an apparently trivial subject. Its mystery could be reached successfully only by the evolution of devices he had scrupulously crafted. In his war against formal "thinking" he was not against study or ideas; it was an opposition to the conformity which the accumulation of "knowledge" is inclined

to impose. To discover the true nature of the world—to know it; to act in it; for the artist, to depict it—is the Cummings metaphysic, his politics, and his aesthetic. The world of cyclical process is for him a timeless world. He does not deny either the past or the future; rather he denies that hope or regret should warp the living moment. In this way he is related to Coleridge and to Blake (related doubly to the latter by reason of his sensitive drawings, such as the celebrated sketch of Charlie Chaplin). His eyes are fixed on fulfillment, consenting to the perpetuation of life through death, as in "rosetree, rosetree." The individual rose dies that a hundred roses may be born; true lovers will be reborn into perfect love.

The antithesis between the false routine world and the true world is seen with icy clarity by a poet who feels mortality sitting on his shoulder. The result is a complexity of vision. That it should have cost so much to get there does not trouble the poet of transcendence; he is a compeer of all seekers, including a tramp on the highway. A poet's function is to embody in a poem the dynamics of nature (including his own response), which is primarily a mystery. Heightened awareness leads to a new dimension that leads into transcendentalism supported by specific detail: in "luminous tendril of celestial wish" (*Xaipe*), the cyclical moon is regarded as evidence of process leading to death and rebirth; the poet's humility is indicated by "teach disappearing also me the keen/illimitable secret of begin."

In *95 Poems* the poetic argument rises into an intense clarity. The affirmative transcending the negative as in "All lose,whole find" ("one's not half two," *One Times One*) and in "the most who die,the more we live" ("what if a much of a which of a wind," *One Times One*) has entered a final phase. The poet has now realized that the transcendental cannot abolish the "fact" of death but he proves the worth of the affirmative as the polarizing element of his philosophy. The former devices of making nouns into verbs and shifting the placement of antitheses are less in evidence; the reality of "appearances" is acknowledged: "now air is air and thing is thing:no bliss/of heavenly earth beguiles our spirits,whose/miraculously disenchanted eyes/live the magnificent honesty of space." This is a reminder of the early "let's live suddenly without thinking/under honest trees" (*And*). The poet, however, has come into the higher turn of the spiral of mystical development where the phenomenal world is transfigured and a tree is really understood.

In this volume Cummings has collected all of his phases: (1) look at what is happening around you; (2) the imagination is more real than reality; (3) the search for life and self brings you back to a transformed reality that is shared with a grasshopper on a flowering weed. As S. I. Hayakawa wrote in *Language in Thought and Action*, the only certainty and security is within the disciplined mind; so when Cummings says in "in time of daffodils(who know"

> and in a mystery to be
> (when time from time shall set us free)
> forgetting me,remember me

the troubadour is telling his lady to forget his life *in* time; to remember that his mortal love always looked toward lovers in immortality. Just so did his preoccupation with twilight reach beyond mist and the "dangerous first stars" to a world new to the senses.

Begin as you mean to go on. The English proverb may explain why the young Cummings was attracted to a statement of Keats: "I am certain of nothing but the holiness of the Heart's affections, and the truth of Imagination." The innovative devices that the young Cummings developed to implement this idea were a successful means of communication in the modern world. But the Cummings of *73 Poems* has traveled farther than that: into the realm of transcendence. The poet who said "—who'll solve the depths of horror to defend/a sunbeam's architecture with his life" ("no man, if men are gods," *One Times One*) has earned the right to explain time by timelessness. In total compassion he declares, in the last poem in *73 Poems*:

> (being forever born a foolishwise
> proudhumble citizen of ecstasies
> more steep than climb can time with all his
>   years)
>
> he's free into the beauty of the truth;
>
> and strolls the axis of the universe
> —love. Each believing world denies, whereas
> your lover(looking through both life and death)
> timelessly celebrates the merciful
>
> wonder no world deny may or believe.

Growing from poem to poem—shedding skin after skin—Cummings emerges as really himself, and therefore as everyone: that is the true definition of transcendence. The artist's formalities have become clear as a washed windowpane, or the purity of a flower upturned to receive a heavenly dew—the canticles of a mystic.

Selected Bibliography

WORKS OF E. E. CUMMINGS

For convenience of reference the capitalization of book titles in this essay follows conventional form rather than the typographical style of the title page in each book, which often reflected Cummings' own preference for lowercase letters.

Eight Harvard Poets: E. Estlin Cummings, S. Foster Damon, J. R. Dos Passos, Robert Hillyer, R. S. Mitchell, William A. Norris, Dudley Poore, Cuthbert Wright. New York: Laurence J. Gomme, 1917. (Contains eight poems by Cummings.)

The Enormous Room. New York: Boni and Liveright, 1922.

Tulips and Chimneys. New York: Seltzer, 1923.

& (And). New York: Privately printed, 1925.

XLI Poems. New York: Dial Press, 1925.

Is 5. New York: Boni and Liveright, 1926.

Him. New York: Boni and Liverright, 1927.

Christmas Tree. New York: American Book Bindery, 1928.

[No title] New York: Covici, Friede, 1930.

CIOPW. New York: Covici, Friede, 1931.

W (ViVa). New York: Horace Liveright, 1931.

Eimi. New York: Covici, Friede, 1933.

No Thanks. New York: Golden Eagle Press, 1935.

Tom. New York: Arrow Editions, 1935.

1/20 (One Over Twenty). London: Roger Roughton, 1936.

Collected Poems. New York: Harcourt, Brace, 1938.

50 Poems. New York: Duell, Sloan and Pearce, 1940.

1 x 1 (One Times One). New York: Henry Holt, 1944.

Anthropos: The Future of Art. Mount Vernon, N.Y.: Golden Eagle Press, 1944.

Santa Claus: A Morality. New York: Henry Holt, 1946.

Puella Mea. Mount Vernon, N.Y.: Golden Eagle Press, 1949.

Xaipe. New York: Oxford University Press, 1950.

I: Six Nonlectures. Cambridge, Mass.: Harvard University Press, 1953.

Poems 1923–1954. New York: Harcourt, Brace, 1954.

E. E. Cummings: A Miscellany, edited by George J. Firmage. New York: Argophile Press, 1958.

95 Poems. New York: Harcourt, Brace, 1958.

100 Selected Poems. New York: Grove Press, 1959.

Selected Poems 1923–1958. London: Faber and Faber, 1960.

Adventures in Value, with photographs by Marion Morehouse. New York: Harcourt, Brace and World, 1962:

73 Poems. New York: Harcourt, Brace and World, 1963.

E. E. Cummings: A Miscellany, Revised, edited by George J. Firmage. New York: October House, 1965.

LETTERS

Selected Letters of E. E. Cummings, edited by F. W. Dupee and George Stade. New York: Harcourt, Brace and World, 1969.

BIBLIOGRAPHIES

Firmage, George J. *E. E. Cummings: A Bibliography.* Middletown, Conn.: Wesleyan University Press, 1960.

Lauter, Paul. *E. E. Cummings: Index to First Lines and Bibliography of Works by and about the Poet.* Denver: Alan Swallow, 1955.

CRITICAL COMMENTS AND STUDIES

Abel, Lionel. "Clown or Comic Poet?" *Nation,* 140:749–50 (June 26, 1935).

Baum, S. V. "E. E. Cummings: The Technique of Immediacy," *South Atlantic Quarterly,* 53:70–88 (January 1954).

———, ed. *EΣTI: E. E. Cummings and the Critics.* East Lansing: Michigan State University Press, 1962. (Good bibliography.)

Blackmur, R. P. "Notes on E. E. Cummings' Language," in *Language as Gesture.* New York Harcourt, Brace, 1952. Pp. 317–40.

Bode, Carl. "E. E. Cummings and Exploded Verse," in *The Great Experiment in American Literature.* New York: Praeger, 1961. Pp. 79–100.

Breit, Harvey. "The Case for the Modern Poet," *New York Times Magazine,* November 3, 1946, pp. 20, 58, 60–61.

———. "Talk with E. E. Cummings," *New York Times Book Review,* December 31, 1950, p. 10.

Davis, William V. "Cummings' all in green went my love riding," *Concerning Poetry,* 3:65–67 (Fall 1970).

———. "Cummings' next to of course god america i," *Concerning Poetry,* 3:14–15 (Spring 1970).

Deutsch, Babette. *Poetry in Our Time*. New York: Henry Holt, 1952. Pp. 111-18.

Dickey, James. "E. E. Cummings," in *Babel to Byzantium: Poets and Poetry Now*. New York: Farrar, Straus and Giroux, 1968. Pp. 100–06.

Fergusson, Francis. "When We Were Very Young," *Kenyon Review*, 12:701–05 (Autumn 1950).

Frankenberg, Lloyd. *Pleasure Dome: On Reading Modern Poetry*. Boston: Houghton Mifflin, 1949. Pp. 157–94.

Friedman, Norman. *E. E. Cummings: The Art of His Poetry*. Baltimore: Johns Hopkins Press, 1960.

————. *E. E. Cummings: The Growth of a Writer*. Carbondale: Southern Illinois University Press, 1964.

Gunter, Richard. "Sentence & Poem," *Style*, 5:26–36 (Winter 1971).

Haines, George, IV. "::2:1—The World and E. E. Cummings," *Sewanee Review*, 59:206–27 (Spring 1951).

Hart, J. "Champion of Freedom and the Individual," *National Review*, 21:864 (August 26, 1969).

Harvard Wake, No. 5 (Spring 1946). (A special Cummings number.)

Hollander, John. "Poetry Chronicle," *Partisan Review*, 26:142–43 (Winter 1959).

Honig, Edwin. " 'Proud of His Scientific Attitude,' " *Kenyon Review*, 17:484–90 (Summer 1955).

Horton, Philip, and Sherry Mangan. "Two Views of Cummings," *Partisan Review*, 4:58–63 (May 1938).

Marks, Barry A. *E. E. Cummings*. New York: Twayne, 1963.

Metcalf, Allan A. "Dante and E. E. Cummings," *Comparative Literature Studies*, 7:374–86 (September 1970).

Moore, Marianne. "People Stare Carefully," *Dial*, 80:49–52 (January 1926).

————. "One Times One," in *Predilections*. New York: Viking Press, 1955. Pp. 140–43.

Munson, Gorham B. "Syrinx," *Secession*, 5:2–11 (July 1923).

Norman, Charles. *E. E. Cummings: The Magic-Maker*. New York: Macmillan, 1958.

Riding, Laura, and Robert Graves. *A Survey of Modernist Poetry*. London: Heinemann, 1927. Pp. 9–34.

Shapiro, Karl. *Essay on Rime*. New York: Reynal and Hitchcock, 1945. Pp. 20–21.

Sitwell, Edith, *Aspects of Modern Poetry*. London: Duckworth, 1934. Pp. 251–57.

Spencer, Theodore. "Technique as Joy," *Harvard Wake*, 5:25–29. (Spring 1946).

Tate, Allen. "E. E. Cummings," in *Reactionary Essays on Poetry and Ideas*. New York: Scribners, 1936. Pp. 228–33.

Time, September 14, 1962. (A full-page obituary.)

Troy, William. "Cummings's Non-land of Un-," *Nation*, 136:413 (April 12, 1933).

Untermeyer, Louis. "Quirky Communications from an Exuberant Hero," *Saturday Review*, 52:25–26 (July 5, 1969).

Voisin, Laurence. "Quelques poètes américains," *Europe: Revue Mensuelle*, 37:36–37 (February–March 1959).

Von Abele, Rudolph. " 'Only to Grow': Change in the Poetry of E. E. Cummings," *PMLA*, 70:913–33 (December 1955).

Wegner, Robert E. *The Poetry and Prose of E. E. Cummings*. New York: Harcourt, Brace and World, 1965.

Williams, William Carlos. "E. E. Cummings' Paintings and Poems," *Arts Digest*, 29:7–8 (December 1, 1954).

Wilson, Edmund. *"Him," New Republic*, 70:293–94 (November 2, 1927).

—*EVE TRIEM*

Emily Dickinson

1830-1886

On Tuesday, August 16, 1870, Thomas Wentworth Higginson visited Emily Dickinson at her home in Amherst, Massachusetts. It was their first meeting, although they had been in correspondence since April 1862 when the poet addressed herself to the well-known critic "to say if my Verse is alive." Higginson's account of this first meeting is given in a letter to his wife. "A step like a pattering child's in entry," he reported, "& in glided a little plain woman with two smooth bands of reddish hair & a face a little like Belle Dove's; not plainer— with no good feature—in a very plain & exquisitely clean white pique & a blue net worsted shawl. She came to me with two day lilies which she put in a sort of childlike way into my hand & said 'These are my introduction' in a soft frightened breathless childlike voice—& added under her breath Forgive me if I am frightened; I never see strangers & hardly know what I say. . . ." Perhaps Emily Dickinson protested her shyness too much. When she chose to speak, she had no difficulty in finding voice. On this occasion, indeed, "she talked soon & thenceforward continuously—& deferentially —sometimes stopping to ask me to talk instead of her—but readily recommencing." Higginson thought some parts of the conversation worth quoting. "If I read a book," Emily Dickinson said, and if "it makes my whole body so cold no fire ever can warm me I know *that* is poetry. If I feel physically as if the top of my head were taken off, I know *that* is poetry." She spoke of finding "ecstasy in living." When Higginson asked "if she never felt want of employment, never going off the place & never seeing any visitor," she answered, "I never thought of conceiving that I could ever have the slightest approach to such a want in all future time," adding, "I feel that I have not expressed myself strongly enough." In Emily Dickinson the tokens of frailty are genuine, but they do not deny a certain independence of spirit.

Emily Elizabeth Dickinson was born in Amherst on December 10, 1830, the second child of Edward and Emily Dickinson. Her brother William Austin Dickinson was born on April 16, 1829, her sister Lavinia Norcross Dickinson on February 28, 1833. The Dickinsons were an important family in Amherst. Emily's father was a prominent man in public life, treasurer of Amherst College from 1835, a member of the state legislature for several terms, a member of Congress for one term. He was a dedicated Whig, and a resolute defender of temperance. As a parent, he was somewhat harsh, or at best remote: "thin dry & speechless," he appeared to Higginson; "I saw what her life has been." Emily Dickinson told Higginson, "My father only reads on Sunday—he reads *lonely & rigorous* books." " 'I say unto you,' Father would read at Prayers, with a militant Accent that would startle one." "Could you tell me what home is," Emily Dickinson asked Higginson; "I never had a mother. I suppose a mother is one to whom you hurry when you are troubled." In 1862 she wrote, "I have a Brother and Sister—My Mother does not care for thought—and Father, too busy with his Briefs—to notice what we do—He buys me many Books—but begs me not to read them—because he fears they joggle the Mind." When her father died, however, in June 1874, Emily was deeply distressed: "Though it is many nights, my mind never comes home." A year later, her mother suffered paralysis and became an invalid for the rest of her life. During those years Emily attended her mother and came to love her. "We were never intimate Mother and Children while she was our Mother—but Mines in the same Ground meet by tunneling and when she became our Child, the Affection came." Mrs. Dickinson died in November 1882: "We hope that Our Sparrow has ceased to fall, though at first we believe nothing."

But "Childhood's citadel" was a somber place. The three children were devoted to one another, but their home did not provoke gaiety. When Austin Dickinson married Susan Gilbert in 1856 and set up house next door, gaiety began to find its natural home. One visitor, Kate Anthon, later recalled happy days to Susan. "Those happy visits at your house! Those celestial evenings in the Library—The blazing wood fire—*Emily—Austin,*—The music—The rampant fun—The inextinguishable laughter, The uproarious spirits of our chosen—our most congenial circle." But that was next door. Edward Dickinson's house was an upright place, indeed perpendicular, in some respects like Mr. Wentworth's house in Henry

James's *The Europeans*, where responsibilities are taken hard. "Where are our moral grounds?" Mr. Wentworth demands on an occasion of great stress in that novel, challenged by moral ambiguities painfully French. Emily Dickinson read the novel and quoted Mr. Wentworth's question in a letter to her friend Mrs. Holland. There is a certain propriety in the question, as Emily Dickinson recalled it, since she herself grew up in a place and time of such questions. To her, in that setting, conscience was "Childhood's nurse." Father might be remote, but he was an inescapable moral fact, God but more than God. "I see—New Englandly," Emily Dickinson said in a poem (numbered 285 in the Johnson edition; the numbers in parentheses hereafter refer to that edition.) She sees New Englandly for the same reason that, in the same poem, she takes the robin as her "Criterion for Tune," because "I grow—where Robins do."

She went to school at Amherst Academy, studying Latin, French, history, rhetoric, botany, geology, and mental philosophy. In 1847 she entered Mount Holyoke Female Seminary at South Hadley, a lively school where she confronted the large religious questions and engaged in the more tangible study of history, chemistry, Latin, physiology, and English grammar. But her official education was often interrupted by debility and poor health. With the exception of brief visits to Boston, Philadelphia, and Washington, her life was lived entirely in a small New England circle of which Amherst was the center. Even in Amherst her life was not omnivorous. In October 1856 she won the second prize and 75 cents for her rye and Indian bread at the local cattle show, and the following year she was a member of the committee in that category. But she did not roam the hills; she saw what could be seen from her window, from her garden, from next door, occasionally from the church. She chose to live in that way, as if to do so were then to live New Englandly. There is no reason to assume that her choice was morbid. Rather, it was conscientious.

In 1881 she wrote to Higginson. "We dwell as when you saw us—the mighty dying of my Father made no external change—Mother and Sister are with me, and my Brother and pseudo Sister, in the nearest House—When Father lived I remained with him because he would miss me—Now, Mother is helpless—a holier demand—I do not go away, but the Grounds are ample—almost travel—to me, and the few that I knew—came—since my Father died." As a young girl she took her seclusion more lightly. From Mount Holyoke she wrote to her brother, asking, "Has the Mexican war terminated yet & how? Are we beat? Do you know of any nation about to besiege South Hadley?" Years later, she told Mrs. Holland that her notion of politics was accurately represented by the sentence "George Washington was the Father of his Country," qualified by the rejoinder "George Who?" But in fact she kept up with current events, mainly because of her devotion to the *Springfield Daily Republican.* A letter to Susan in September 1882 makes a literary joke of the capture of Ahmed Arabi Pasha at Tel-el-Kebir. Gordon and the British garrison at Khartoum are fodder for a witty letter to Theodore Holland in 1884. True, she was not interested in "the stale inflation of the minor News." She was odd, reticent, private. In Amherst she was considered a mythological being. Children longed to see her, since the sight would constitute a vision. When the doorbell rang, she ran away, deeper into the house. "All men say 'What' to me," she told Higginson; so she restricted the number of questioners.

If she was a lonely girl, by common standards, loneliness was her choice. Company did not flee her. Some requirement of her sensibility was fulfilled by seclusion which could not have been fulfilled by company. It is clear in the poems that loneliness was one of the conditions she chose to know. Sometimes she thought of isolation as her fate, "circumstance of Lot" (1116), and in the love poems absence of the beloved constitutes a terrible kind of loneliness, "The Horror not to be surveyed" (777). But in one poem (1695) she speaks of "That polar privacy/ A soul admitted to itself,' calling it "Finite Infinity." This was the solitude she chose to know; it was like the solitudes of space, sea, and death, but greater than these, because deeper. It occupied a "profounder site" than any other solitude. It is evoked again in another poem (1116) as "another Loneliness/ That many die without." This loneliness is the consequence of "nature," sometimes, and sometimes of "thought," "And whoso it befall/ Is richer than could be revealed/ By mortal numeral." Emily Dickinson elected to be "rich" in this sense, at whatever common cost. Higginson said that the Dickinson home in Amherst was "a house where each member runs his or her own selves." This was especially true of Emily Dickinson's life; she ran her own life, she conducted her own "self." Her sufferings were of the common kind, abrasions of feeling, the pain of loss, partings, deaths; the experiences were not extraordinary, only the particular character of their reception. Loneliness was one of those experiences, remarkable only in the intensity of its reception. It might almost be said that Emily Dickinson did not suffer loneliness; she commanded it. She commanded everything she needed. When she needed a relationship, she commanded it.

The pattern of these relationships is exemplified in Emily Dickinson's friendship with

Benjamin Franklin Newton, a law student who spent two years in her father's office in Amherst. Newton was nine years older than Emily Dickinson; he "became to me," she said, "a gentle, yet grave Preceptor, teaching me what to read, what authors to admire, what was most grand or beautiful in nature, and that sublimer lesson, a faith in things unseen, and in a life again, nobler, and much more blessed." He died on March 24, 1853. "When a little Girl, I had a friend," Emily Dickinson later wrote to Higginson, "who taught me Immortality—but venturing too near, himself—he never returned." For the rest of her life, Emily Dickinson sought gentle yet grave preceptors, men older than herself, more accomplished in the ways of the world. It may be said that she sought a father, a more benign father than her own. But this does not say much. The men she found were diverse in character and temper; further differences were prescribed in the terms of each relationship. The Reverend Charles Wadsworth was Emily Dickinson's spiritual preceptor for several years. Samuel Bowles, editor of the *Springfield Daily Republican,* was important as an object of feeling: "We miss your vivid Face and the besetting Accents, you bring from your Numidian Haunts." Higginson was Emily Dickinson's literary guide, critic, surgeon. "And for this, Preceptor, I shall bring you—Obedience—the Blossom from my Garden, and every gratitude I know." Her most impassioned relationship was with Judge Otis P. Lord: it appears that Emily Dickinson was in love with him for the last six years of his life, from 1878 to 1884. And there is the unknown man, unless he is Bowles, addressed as "Master": "I want to see you more—Sir—than all I wish for in this world—and the wish—altered a little—will be my only one—for the skies."

These relationships were important to Emily Dickinson, in different ways and in different degrees. It is impossible to be precise; not enough is known. Where a friendship was crucial to her, she commanded it even beyond the grave, writing to Bowles's widow, for instance, as if to retain the affection by reciting it. Some of her greatest poems were provoked by moments in the drama of these relationships. "He fumbles at your Soul" (315) may be a poem about God, or about some less celestial power; whatever its ostensible subject, it is totally dependent upon the experience of one soul "mastering" another. That experience may be real, or imaginatively conceived; but that it came, however deviously, from Emily Dickinson's sense of master and pupil, there can be no doubt. The least that may be said of these relationships is that they tested, extended, and sometimes tormented her sensibility, with results good in the poems if hard in the life.

Some of the relationships were easy enough. Higginson never quite decided whether his Amherst correspondent was a genius or merely crazed, but it is clear that, within his limits, he helped her. He thought her poems wayward and disorderly, he protested that he could not understand. She promised to do better, next time. But there is no evidence that he damaged the work or disabled the genius. When he published, with Mabel Loomis Todd, Emily Dickinson's *Poems,* the second series, in 1891, one of the first readers was Alice James, sister of Henry James and William James. In her Diary for January 6, 1892, she wrote: "It is reassuring to hear the English pronouncement that Emily Dickinson is fifth-rate—they have such a capacity for missing quality; the robust evades them equally with the subtle." Then she continued: "Her being sicklied o'er with T. W. Higginson makes one quake lest there be a latent flaw which escapes one's vision." There were, indeed, latent flaws in Emily Dickinson: a tendency to play up problems as if they were mysteries, a disposition to cultivate the breathless note, a certain coyness disfiguring the charm. But there are no grounds for assuming that Higginson was responsible for these flaws; they were in Emily Dickinson long before she knew her mentor. He is blameless. If he had understood her more profoundly, he would have been, in addition, angelic.

So Emily Dickinson ran her life at Amherst, moving between the kitchen, the garden, her room. She baked bread, made puddings, attended to her knitting, sent messages next door, wrote hundreds of poems and hundreds of letters as pointed as poems. She played the piano. In the garden she had green fingers, succeeding where others failed with Daphne odora, violet, and the day lily. She walked with her dog Carlo, "large as myself, that my Father bought me." From her window, she saw the circus pass. "I saw the sunrise on the Alps since I saw you," she wrote to Mrs. Holland. "Travel why to Nature, when she dwells with us? Those who lift their hats shall see her, as devout do God." Her dreams were bountiful, as in a poem (646) she invoked "Certainties of Sun" and "Midsummer—in the Mind." In the same mood she identified Nature with "what we know," in her own case with the hill, the afternoon, the squirrel, the bumble bee, the bobolink, thunder, the cricket—the unquestionable things. "Nature—the Gentlest Mother is,/ Impatient of no Child" (790). But there were other moods; as Emerson wrote in the essay "Circles," our moods do not believe in each other. In one of those moods (364) nature seemed to Emily Dickinson rude, uttering jubilee the morning after woe; and in another (1624) "an Approving God" sets his minions to work, making pain, sorrow, and death. There is no contradiction. Emily Dickinson is a moody poet, giving herself to the moment.

Perhaps she trusted that, at some level, everything would cohere; one moment would not disown another. "All her life," R. P. Blackmur wrote of her, "she was looking for a subject, and the looking *was* her subject, in life as in poetry." Perhaps she knew this, or hoped against hope that it might be so. In a blunt paraphrase, many of her poems would contradict one another; but her answers are always provisional. Only her questions are definitive. She spent, but did not waste or consume, her life in looking for a subject. Looking for one thing, she nevertheless lived by taking whatever each occasion offered; if it was not the definitive thing, it would serve, for the present, instead of finality. "Forever—is composed of Nows" (624). So she trusted in the significance of Now, and in the search conducted under present auspices. Many poems speak of the "exultation" of search, the thrill of voyaging, "the going/ Of an inland soul to sea" (76). "Our lives are Swiss" (80), she says, except that the imagination discloses to us the Alps and Italy beyond. Let us say that her imagination was Alpine, ascribing to the poet a corresponding urge to scale the heights of experience. "I would go, to know!" (114). In a letter to Higginson she wrote, "Nature is a Haunted House —but art—a House that tries to be haunted." This does not demean art; rather, it gives the terms of its challenge. To Emily Dickinson, art is the place of experiment and risk, to write is to dare, the imagination sends up strange words as trial balloons. The greatest risks are taken by the inland soul. "To fight aloud, is very brave," she concedes. "But *gallanter,* I know/ Who charge within the bosom/ The Cavalry of Wo" (126). For ignorance, there is nothing to be said. "At least, to know the worst, is sweet!" (172). No wonder Emily Dickinson was content to stay in her room, her garden; with an imagination as challenging as hers, practical experience was bound to appear dull, predictable, banal. She was already far beyond anything life could give as event or experience, because she had already imagined it. She had haunted every house.

This was her way. She tested everything, whether it was given by experience or by imagination. Every house had to be searched for ghosts. Many of her poems apply to the great religious doctrines the same interrogative pressure. Of her own religious faith, virtually anything may be said, with some show of evidence. She may be represented as an agnostic, a heretic, a skeptic, a Christian. She grew up in a Christian family, but she was not devout. She did not possess a talent for conviction. In 1873 her father, his own faith recently renewed, arranged that the local Congregational minister, J. L. Jenkins, would offer Emily some spiritual guidance. The interview took place. The minister's son later wrote, "All that is really known is that my father reported to the perplexed parent that Miss Emily was 'sound,' and let it go at that." The report was generous. At about the same time as her spiritual interview, Emily Dickinson wrote to her cousins Louise and Frances Norcross: "There is that which is called an 'awakening' in the church, and I know of no choicer ecstasy than to see Mrs. [Sweetser] roll out in crape every morning, I suppose to intimidate antichrist; at least it would have that effect on me." But, in fact, Emily Dickinson's Christianity was never a firm conviction. As a schoolgirl, she resisted the religious stirrings of her circle; the Amherst revival in 1844 did not succeed with her. In January 1846 she reported to a former schoolmate, Abiah Root, "I was almost persuaded to be a christian," but the strongest word was "almost."

Throughout her life, there were moments in which she longed for faith. In a late poem she wrote:

Those—dying then,
Knew where they went—
They went to God's Right Hand—
That Hand is amputated now
And God cannot be found—

The abdication of Belief
Makes the Behavior small—
Better an ignis fatuus
Than no illume at all—   (1551)

But this was one moment among many different moments. Emily Dickinson seems to have thought of religious faith as an enforced choice: one must choose between God and man, between eternity and time. In 1846 she wrote: "I have perfect confidence in God & his promises & yet I know not why, I feel that the world holds a predominant place in my affections." The question of faith was the question of affection, and in the Calvinist idiom one affection canceled another. In 1848 she wrote: "There is a great deal of religious interest here and many are flocking to the ark of safety. I have not yet given up to the claims of Christ, but trust I am not entirely thoughtless on so important & serious a subject." But within a short time, she declared herself "standing alone in rebellion, and growing very careless." She quarreled with Susan about religion: "and though in that last day, the Jesus Christ you love, remark he does not know me—there is a darker spirit will not disown it's child." Again, it is momentary bravado, one rhetoric incited by another. A more urbane version appears some months later: "I went to church all day in second dress, and boots. We had such precious sermons from Mr. Dwight. One about unbelief, and another Esau. Sermons on unbelief ever did attract me." Sermons on Christian doctrine did not attract her. When Mr. Steele preached upon "predestination," she refused to listen; "I do not respect 'doctrines.' " She wrote to Higginson of her family: "They are religious—except me—and address an Eclipse, every morning—whom they call their 'Father.' "

While Emily Dickinson's early emotions often took a religious turn, she was never willing to have them curbed by the discipline of belief. Doctrine was discipline, and therefore alien to a sensibility always somewhat willful. She would have believed, if she had been allowed to believe anything she liked. In later years her emotions took several different turns, as if her will were the wind. Now, for the most part, she was content to think of the "Supernatural" as "the Natural, disclosed." Of course, many of her pronouncements upon first and last things are more occasional than definitive. She was sincere, but her idea of sincerity was to say whatever, on the given occasion, would help. One of her poems, "How brittle are the Piers" (1433), urges that we may still believe in God and His promises, the evidence being Christ's word. But the poem was enclosed in a letter to Higginson, consoling him after the death of his wife. Another occasion supplied another need, perhaps a different note of consolation; as she wrote, again to Higginson, "To be human is more than to be divine, for when Christ was divine, he was uncontented till he had been human." Reading *Middlemarch,* she was convinced that "the mysteries of human nature surpass the 'mysteries of redemption,' for the infinite we only suppose, while we see the finite." When a neighbor, Mrs. Stearns, called to inquire if the Dickinsons did not think it shocking for Benjamin Butler to "liken himself to his Redeemer," Emily's answer was "we thought Darwin had thrown 'the Redeemer' away." But in one of her most ardent letters to Judge Lord, Emily Dickinson, reciting a high ethic, ascribed it to God: "The 'Stile' is God's—My Sweet One—for your great sake—not mine—I will not let you cross—but it is all your's, and when it is right I will lift the

Bars." In the same letter: "It may surprise you I speak of God—I know him a little, but Cupid taught Jehovah to many an untutored Mind—Witchcraft is wiser than we."

Again it is fair to say that Emily Dickinson would have been a Christian if she had been permitted to ascribe to Christ the same status which she ascribed, in that ardent moment, to Cupid and Jehovah; the same, but no more. Clearly, that Christianity would have been merely a function of self, Emily Dickinson's aspiration in one of her many moods. Indeed, it is arguable that religion was never more to her than a book of metaphors. She did not believe in a Mosaic religion, though the figure of Moses was especially vivid to her. What she wanted, when she wanted anything in this way, was an Orphic religion, in which dogma and doctrines would penetrate her sensibility, like music. Truth would suggest itself as harmony, unassertive because unquestionable, audible to instinct. "Orpheus' Sermon captivated—/ It did not condemn" (1545). But to be entranced by Orpheus' song was one thing; to follow Christ, obeying his word, was another. Christianity offered itself as truth, embodied with whatever degree of divergence in doctrine, but it had to reckon with Emily Dickinson's sensibility. It was the mark of that sensibility either to discard what was offered or to translate it, imperiously, into her own terms.

So she took her Christianity not as she found it but as she altered it. She read her Bible as a rhetorical manual. Her poems and letters are full of references to Genesis, Revelation, the Psalms, and the Gospels, but the references are invariably rhetorical. Nothing is necessarily to be believed, only entertained as a trope. There are several poems in which Gabriel is invoked, but Emily Dickinson's Gabriel is merely an idealized version of Samuel Bowles or another wise preceptor, bringing glad tidings and praise. "Get Gabriel—to tell—the royal syllable" (195); but the syllable in question is part of the earthly lover's vocabulary. In "The face I carry with me—last" (336) Gabriel is again assimilated to an earthly function, endorsing the idiom of love and compliment. In "Where Thou art—that—is Home" (725) Emily Dickinson is featured as Mary in Gabriel's praise, but the purpose is hyperbole; the sacred moment is invoked only to be transcended by the earthly love declared. In a love letter to Judge Lord she writes, "Dont you know you have taken my will away and I 'know not where' you 'have laid' it?"; Mary Magdalene's words give the lover's complaint its appropriate style.

Emily Dickinson used her hymnbooks in the same way. They are metaphorical and tropical. She owned three hymnbooks: *The Psalms, Hymns, and Spiritual Songs of the Rev. Isaac Watts,* edited by Samuel Worcester; *Church Psalmody, Selected from Dr. Watts and Other Authors,* edited by Lowell Mason and David Greene; and *Village Hymns, a Supplement to Dr. Watts's Psalms and Hymns,* edited by Asahel Nettleton. The letters and poems often depend upon the recollection of a hymn or of phrases from a hymn. A letter of September 1877 to Mrs. Holland recalls, somewhat loosely, a phrase from Watts's hymn "Were the Whole Realm of Nature Mine." But again the hymn is recalled for the phrase. "How precious Thought and Speech are! 'A present so divine,' was in a Hymn they used to sing when I went to Church." For Emily Dickinson, the estate of the hymns is ablative; rhythms and phrases are retained, but not their endorsing faith. What she took from the hymns, beyond that need, was a prosody; like other English and American poets she wrote secular poems in the meters of the Psalms, particularly the common measure.

The pattern persists in her reading. She took what her sensibility needed, from whatever source. Her motive in reading other writers, great and small, was not to discover the variety and potentiality of the art she shared with them, but rather to find there a provocation of her own imagination. Sometimes a phrase was enough. She was deeply engaged by the Brontës, but on the other hand the abiding interest of Emily Brontë largely resolved itself in a magical line, "Every existence would exist in Thee," from "No Coward Soul Is Mine." The line is quoted three times in letters. A few writers were deeply pondered. "After long disuse of her eyes," Higginson said, "she read Shakespeare & thought why is any other book needed." But even with Shakespeare her needs were exclusive. Sometimes a line moved her because of its associations: " 'An envious Sliver broke' was a passage your Uncle peculiarly loved in the drowning Ophelia," she told Abbie Farley, niece of Judge Lord. The same phrase occurs in a letter, nearly five years earlier, to Mrs. Holland. The reading of Longfellow's *Kavanagh* caused a domestic flurry, so it lodged inordinately in her imagination. Reading novels, she often compared the relationships with her own, playing personal games with *David Copperfield* and *The Old Curiosity Shop.* She read the American writers, notably Bryant, Emerson, Hawthorne, and Lowell, when their current work appeared in the *Atlantic Monthly* or when it was announced in a current periodical, *Scribner's Monthly* or another. She was assiduous in reading Higginson. Often, as in that case, her interest in the work was primarily an interest in the writer. She was enchanted by the Brownings, Elizabeth "that Foreign Lady" and Robert "the consummate Browning." She read virtually everything by George Eliot, and admired her greatly, but she never chose to say anything of critical significance about the works, except that *Daniel Deronda* was a "wise and tender Book." But she was fascinated by the news of George Eliot's life, and pursued every biographical detail. When she read of the novelist's death, she wrote to the Norcrosses: "The look of the words as they lay in the print I shall never forget. Not their face in the casket could have had the eternity to me. Now, *my* George Eliot." Clearly, Emily Dickinson's interest in George Eliot as a romantic and heroic figure transcended her critical concern with the novels; she was moved by George Eliot's representative character, the aura surrounding her. The books merely provided evidence that the personal interest was not grossly misplaced.

This may help to explain the vagaries of Emily Dickinson's literary taste. Sometimes the explanation is simple; if a writer reached her under Higginson's auspices, he was sure of approval. There were exceptions. Higginson appears to have suggested that she read Joaquin Miller's *Songs of the Sierras,* but she declined. "I did not read Mr. Miller because I could not care about him—Transport is not urged." On the other hand she read Helen Hunt Jackson's poems, recommended by Higginson, and echoed his praise. "Mrs. Hunt's Poems are stronger than any written by Women since Mrs—Browning, with the exception of Mrs Lewes." Later, she went further. When Higginson's *Short Studies of American Authors* appeared in 1879, she wrote to him: "Mrs Jackson soars to your estimate lawfully as a Bird, but of Howells and James, one hesitates —Your relentless Music dooms as it redeems." But the real difference between Mrs. Jackson and her male competitors was that Emily Dickinson had already met and approved the authoress; she never met James or Howells. Her critical standards were largely determined by the local requirements of her sensibility. A multitude of poetic defects might readily be covered by her friendship and affection. In any case, her reading was casual. Books came to her, and she read them, but she never allowed

her mind to be intimidated by anything she read. Indeed, she was easily put off by a personal consideration. It is not certain that she ever read Poe: "Of Poe, I know too little to think." "You speak of Mr. Whitman," she wrote to Higginson; "I never read his Book— but was told that he was disgraceful."

That her sensibility was strange is clear enough. It often appears, in the relation between her imagination and reality, that very little reality was required, her imagination being what it was, exorbitantly acute. Reading her poems, one is surprised to find that they have any base in reality or fact, since a base in that element is what they seem least to need. Philosophers have sometimes wondered what would happen if our senses were to be, for some inordinate reason, acutely intensified, the first conclusion being that the victim would inhabit a different universe of relationships. There is a passage in *Middlemarch* (Chapter XX) where George Eliot considers how little reality the human frame can bear. "If we had a keen vision and feeling of all ordinary human life," she says, "it would be like hearing the grass grow and the squirrel's heart beat, and we should die of that roar which lies on the other side of silence." It often seems as if Emily Dickinson's senses were of this order. But there is a difference. The sensory power, as George Eliot conceives it, is still a power of response to reality, and it serves reality as its first and last object. It claims nothing for itself; it is willing to lose itself in the grass of ordinary human life. But the intensity of Emily Dickinson's imagination has a different object. She is not, after all, one of the great celebrants of life, the proof being how little of life, in the common sense, she chose to live. It is the peculiar nature of her sensibility that it deals with experience by exacerbating it, as if prompted by a conscience for which nothing less would do. No wonder she restricted the amount of life she was prepared to live, since the living had to be so intense, so relentlessly acute.

Santayana has written of the "Poetry of Barbarism," meaning in the given cases Browning and Whitman; in general, the barbarian "is the man who regards his passions as their own excuse for being." So far as this goes, Emily Dickinson is a barbarian, and her barbarism arises from the same source, the rejection of classic and Christian ideals of discipline. But there is a crucial distinction. To Emily Dickinson, the passions required no excuse because they were the life and form of her sensibility; and sensibility was one guise of her conscience. In this way and from this direction, the exercise of sensibility became the exercise of conscience and duty. She saw and heard the grass grow, but she saw and heard New Englandly; so she wore the rue of her barbarism with a difference. This is why she gives the impression, contrasted with Whitman and Browning, of living upon her nerves; in this contrast, Whitman and Browning appear even more nonchalant than they are.

Think, for instance, how she goes out of her way to cultivate what others go out of their way to avoid, the intensities of apprehension made possible by pain. "A *Wounded* Deer—leaps highest" (165), so wounds are sought. The "scant degree/ Of Life's penurious Round" (313) can only be raised by leaps of perception, magic, witchcraft. The leaps are facilitated by "Opposites," which therefore "entice" as "Water, is taught by thirst" (135). "I like a look of Agony," she says, "Because I know it's true" (241). In a later poem (963) "A nearness to Tremendousness—/ An Agony procures," and the agony is its own justification. This is, in other poems, the idiom of awe, an epic grandeur of spirit which shames the petty difference between happiness and misery. One of her most powerful poems (281) begins,

" 'Tis so appalling—it exhilirates." This is not a melodramatic indulgence, a self-regarding exercise in Gothic horror; it is, for this New England poet, the conscientious imagination at its sworn task. Emily Dickinson's special way of feeling is to drive apprehension to the pitch of awe; at that pitch, the discrimination of subject and object in the act of perception is dissolved, and a new state strains to be released. This is the moment at which "Perception of an object costs/ Precise the Object's loss" (1071). The object does not detach itself from the subject; rather, the dualism of subject and object is, in a flash, consumed. What occupies the scene then is a new state of consciousness. The given object, like experience itself in Emily Dickinson, must take the risk of losing itself to a new state, becoming something else which is not the sum of experience and sensibility but their product. Consciousness is X, an unknown quantity, unknown because its limits have never been reached. Free of limits, it can enter into majestic equations with other quantities, known by name if not yet measured. In a poem on the free soul (384) Emily Dickinson says, "Captivity is Consciousness—/ So's Liberty."

Her word for this unknown quantity, when she does not call it consciousness, is circumference. In one poem (1620) it is "Circumference thou Bride of Awe." In "Circles" Emerson says: "The life of man is a self-evolving circle, which, from a ring imperceptibly small, rushes on all sides outwards to new and larger circles, and that without end." These circles are always deemed to be known, because divinely allowed and consistent with the human mind. The circles, in another version, are concentric, with man at the center, so they can be verified at any moment. But circumference, as Emily Dickinson uses the word, marks an area, on all sides, where consciousness ranges beyond enclosure. It is her version of the sublime. Circles define what they enclose; since an expanding circle depends upon the force of soul, in Emerson's terms, it may be held at any point. But circumference marks the end of definition and the beginning of risk. As Emily Dickinson put it (633), "When Cogs—stop—that's Circumference—/ The Ultimate —of Wheels," using Emerson's words with her own inflection. Another kindred word is impossibility: in one poem (838), "Impossibility, like Wine/ Exhilirates the Man/ Who tastes it; Possibility/ Is flavorless." And there is, in forty poems, immortality; which, nearly enough, is the spiritual form of impossibility. They are all sublime terms, as Emily Dickinson uses them, outrunning nature. "I worried Nature with my Wheels/ When Her's had ceased to run" (786).

But the key word is consciousness. Sometimes it is equated with God. "The Brain—is wider than the Sky"; it is "deeper than the sea." Finally, it is "just the weight of God"; if it differs from God, it is only as "Syllable from Sound" (632). In another poem it is equated with life itself. "No Drug for Consciousness—can be" (786); this is the form of "Being's Malady," the only escape is to die. The justification of consciousness is the justification of will; given the power, one must use it. "What are the sinews of such cordage for/ Except to bear" (1113). But there is another justification. Samuel Beckett has ascribed to Proust some thoughts on habit. "If Habit is a second nature, it keeps us in ignorance of the first, and is free of its cruelties and its enchantments." To Emily Dickinson, it appears, the common part of experience was a habit. She seems to have thought of religious belief, for instance, as a habit, perhaps a good habit, but open to the same disability, that, congealed as second nature, it prevents us from seeing our first. Institutions were dedicated to the formation of habit. But the chief means of defeating or circumventing habit was the imagination, consciousness. The imagination insists upon penetrating to the cruelties and enchantments of our first nature; that is its particular glory, and from thence it acquires its heroic note. This perhaps explains why Emily Dickinson is constantly forcing her mind beyond or beneath the familiar marks of the senses, the easy gifts. If she sees something, she never rests content with sight or even with possession of what it sees; she always goes further, further back or further forward, in her own directions. Very often her mind, in a typical cadence, starts with the sense, or with the declared failure of sense, only to run from it, above or below:

Not seeing, still we know—
Not knowing, guess—
Not guessing, smile and hide
And half caress—

And quake—and turn away . . .   (1518)

Or, more urbanely: "To see is perhaps never quite the sorcery that it is to surmise, though the obligation to enchantment is always binding." It is as if the senses themselves, for all their merit, merely beguiled one into habit, and something else was needed, a sixth sense, critical and subversive, to correct the happy five. The sixth sense is the imagination.

There is another way of putting it. In the Preface to *The Portrait of a Lady* Henry James, explaining the special light in which he saw his heroine Isabel Archer, says that he conceived of the center of the subject as Isabel's consciousness, with one particular qualification. Shakespeare's heroines, George Eliot's heroines, are mainly revealed in their relations to other characters. Isabel Archer is mainly revealed in her relation to herself. This is, preeminently, the main direction of her consciousness. We think of Emily Dickinson in this character, without forcing the comparison. Emily's relations to other people were sufficiently numerous and sufficiently engrossing for her particular purposes, but they were all, in varying measure, as James says of Isabel's relations to other people, "contributive only to the greater one," her relation to herself. Some of Emily Dickinson's most daring poems turn the speaker into a haunted house, where she is at once the house, the ghost, and the haunted inhabitant:

> Ourself behind ourself, concealed—
> Should startle most—
> Assassin hid in our Apartment
> Be Horror's least.   (670)

In another poem, the mind's quarrel with itself is conducted in terms of banishment, monarchy, and abdication:

> But since Myself—assault Me—
> How have I peace
> Except by subjugating
> Consciousness?   (642)

Indeed, when we speak of Emily Dickinson's relation to herself, we should think of it rather as a relation to her many selves, the different ghosts haunting her house.

So the "charm of the actual," which James recites in his *Autobiography*, had to meet, in Emily Dickinson, the resistance of a demanding sensibility. There are several poems in which the charm, like Orpheus, overcomes the resistance, but the defeat of resistance was never final. Emily Dickinson seems to have a scrupulous objection, a qualm of conscience, whenever any charm comes too easily. To lie in Abraham's bosom seems a guilty indulgence. Certainly, her imagination is more often animated by the feeling which flows toward its object, and then flows away, than by the feeling which rests there. There are several poems on expectation, which qualify the common estimate of the relation between expec-

tation and fulfillment. "Expectation—is Contentment—/ Gain—Satiety" (807); the reason is that there must be "an Austere trait in Pleasure." "Danger—deepens Sum," partly because the sense of danger, like fear, may be exhilarating, and partly because, at such moments, the will is exercised. But the will is exercised even more dramatically in Emily Dickinson's afterwords. Indeed, there is a special rhythm in her sensibility which is heard when the chosen estate is ablative.

There is an extraordinary letter to the Norcrosses, August 1876, in which Emily Dickinson speaks of cats, and especially of her sister Vinnie's new cat, "the color of Branwell Brontë's hair." Then she says: "You remember my ideal cat has always a huge rat in its mouth, just going out of sight—though going out of sight in itself has a peculiar charm. It is true that the unknown is the largest need of the intellect, though for it, no one thinks to thank God." But if the unknown has this status among needs of the intellect, equal status must be given to that which has been known and is now gone. To Emily Dickinson, a peculiar charm resides in "going out of sight," when the object, lost or consumed, becomes a part of memory, loss, and need. "By a departing light/ We see acuter, quite,/ Than by a wick that stays" (1714). In Emily Dickinson generally, experiences are more intensely apprehended just after their loss. Wallace Stevens wrote of "credences of Summer," but Emily Dickinson believed in summer more profoundly when it was just gone. "Summer has two Beginnings—/ Beginning once in June—/ Beginning in October/ Affectingly again" (1422). Indeed, she owned an October imagination, with June for experience. To apprehend June in June is of course a joy, called "Riot," but the October sense of June is "graphicer for Grace," presumably because Grace is a mode of the imagination. For the same reason, "finer is a going/ Than a remaining Face"; a remaining face is merely entertained, the other is recovered by a strain of will. "That it will never come again/ Is what makes life so sweet" (1741). This is why Emily Dickinson's imagination so often moves along "a route of evanescence," as if on one side everything were premonition, and on the other the fatality of loss. In one of her most majestic poems, "As imperceptibly as Grief," when the summer has "lapsed away,"

The Dusk drew earlier in—
The Morning foreign shone—
A courteous, yet harrowing Grace,
As Guest, that would be gone—   (1540)

The morning sunshine is foreign because alien, intractable in its resistance to the rhythm of lapse and departure.

There are many variants in the rhythm of evanescence. Some are easy, like the "dear retrospect" (1742) in which the dead are recalled. When evanescence is positively sought, it is called renunciation, "The letting go/ A Presence—for an Expectation." A few lines later, "Renunciation—is the Choosing/ Against itself—/ Itself to justify/ Unto itself" (745). This is another version of Emily Dickinson's scruple, where evanescence is felt New Englandly. In the love poems, evanescence is absence of the lover, where absence recalls and enforces presence so vividly that both states are transformed to something else, for which the poem is the only name. The transformation is achieved by writing the poem. "To lose thee—sweeter than to gain/ All other hearts I knew" (1754). And there is a consolatory poem, sent to Higginson when Emily Dickinson read of his infant daughter's death: "The Face in evanescence lain/ Is more distinct than our's" (1490). Indeed, it almost appears that Emily Dickinson welcomed pain and loss for the intensity they provoked; or, if that is excessive, that she was extraordinarily resourceful in finding power where common eyes see only pain.

If this sounds somewhat Emersonian, the association may be allowed and pursued. In the fifth chapter of the long essay *Nature*, there is a beautiful passage of evanescence. "When much intercourse with a friend has supplied us with a standard of excellence, and has increased our respect for the resources of God who thus sends a real person to outgo our ideal; when he has, moreover, become an object of thought, and, whilst his character retains all its unconscious effect, is converted in the mind into solid and sweet wisdom, it is a sign to us that his office is closing, and he is commonly withdrawn from our sight in a short time." This goes beyond acceptance to a deep assent, an Emersonian "yea." The equivalent in Emily Dickinson is more resistant, less urbane; or the urbanity may be presumed to reach the words much later. Emerson's posture is one of assent, even before the circumstances arrive to request assent. Emily Dickinson takes up no position at all, makes no promises, until the occasion demands an answer. There is a passage in *The Spoils of Poynton* which is closer to her spirit. In Chapter XXI of James's novel Fleda Vetch goes to visit Mrs. Gereth at her house, Ricks. Fleda is enchanted with the place, and particularly with what Mrs. Gereth has made of it. The house declares a sense of loss, but this is part of its distinction—"the impression somehow of something dreamed and missed, something reduced, relinquished, resigned: the poetry, as it were, of something sensibly *gone*." She conceives of the house as haunted by its characteristic ghosts. Ricks has been owned by Mrs. Gereth's old maiden aunt, to whom Fleda now ascribes "a great accepted pain." This is something like the pain of Emily Dickinson's world, great and accepted but still pain. It is the note of tragedy where Emerson's is the note of romance or, finally, the note of comedy. We hear Emily Dickinson's note in a poem (910) about the incrimination of mind and experience; the discipline of man forces him to choose "His Preappointed Pain."

This is Emily Dickinson's special area of feeling: the preappointed pain, how we choose it, the consequences of the choice. If her poems had titles, the names would fix themselves upon the great abstractions, the large words which range the individual acts and sufferings of man in categories, as pain, love, self, will, desire, expectation, and death. From these grand categories the particular experience issues, moving toward the sensibility; there the drama begins, if it has not already begun in the mind's engagement with itself. For the poem, it does not matter; great poems have been written according to both prescriptions. With Emily Dickinson's poems in view it is only a minor extravagance to say that nearly everything is sensibility. "Tell me what the artist is," James said in the Preface to *The Portrait of a Lady*, "and I will tell you of what he has *been* conscious."

So we come, by a long way round, to the definitive poems; or to a sample, barely enough to suggest what the extraordinary enterprise of Emily Dickinson's vision came to.

After great pain, a formal feeling comes—
The Nerves sit ceremonious, like Tombs—
The stiff Heart questions was it He, that bore,
And Yesterday, or Centuries before?

The Feet, mechanical, go round—
Of Ground, or Air, or Ought—
A Wooden way
Regardless grown,
A Quartz contentment, like a stone—

This is the Hour of Lead—
Remembered, if outlived,

As Freezing persons, recollect the Snow—
First—Chill—then Stupor—then the letting
    go—   (341)

In a letter to Higginson, April 25, 1862, Emily Dickinson wrote: "I had a terror—since September—I could tell to none—and so I sing, as the Boy does by the Burying Ground—because I am afraid." It is agreed that this poem issued from the September terror, whatever other form that terror took, including "a funeral in my brain" (280). But the reverberation of the poem comes not from one historical crisis but from a classic situation, "felt in the blood" and exacerbated till it released itself in this form. The situation, as given in another poem (396), is "Pain's Successor—When the Soul/ Has suffered all it can." So the poem is a ritual, imaginatively conducted from the great accepted pain to the "letting go." But the ritual has been practiced in many other poems, which we may call afterpoems to indicate a characteristic figure already glossed. Indeed, it may have been necessary for Emily Dickinson to practice her ritual in twenty more or less preparatory poems, all devoted to the same figure, so that she might employ the ritual in this great poem once for all.

The poem allows the experience whatever latitude it needs to impose its own nature, as the nerves, the heart, and the feet maintain the disjunct semblance of life, everything but its animating principle—the formula, without the spiritual form. This is what experience brings to sensibility. What sensibility has done to the experience is exacerbation, but in a peculiar kind. The experience is all intensity, and in an exactly equal and opposite measure the sensibility is all resistance. Discipline is the enabling form of resistance, in this poem and for this occasion. What seems like numbness in the poem is ostensible; it is really the effect of resistance offered by sensibility to the experience. Set off against the terror and the pain there are the strict sentences, severe, formal, ascetic. That is to say, the sensibility is operative pre-eminently in the syntax. The wilder the experience, the more decorous the sentence. In another poem (735), giving the same principle, Emily Dickinson speaks of "Life's sweet Calculations" imposed upon "Concluded Lives"; music played at a funeral "Makes Lacerating Tune": "To Ears the Dying Side—/ 'Tis Coronal—and Funeral—/ Saluting—in the Road."

Of the demanding passions in Emily Dickinson, the first is love. "Till it has loved—no man or woman can become itself—Of our first Creation we are unconscious," she wrote to Higginson. Is there more than love and death, she asked Mrs. Holland. It often seems as if, for the good of her poems, nothing more was required. "I cannot live with You" (640) is one of her grand love poems, one to remind the reader of many; and "Unable are the Loved to die" (809) will serve to hold the two motifs together, as they so often come together in this poet. "Born—Bridalled—Shrouded—/ In a Day," she exclaims in a famous poem (1072). The love lyrics, naturally enough, are subject to exacerbation. If she writes of desire, there is the demand for fulfillment, but the demand is hardly spoken until it is almost retracted, "lest the Actual—/ Should disenthrall thy soul" (1430), a characteristic sequence. Do not, she says in another poem (1434), try to "climb the Bars of Ecstasy," since "In insecurity to lie/ Is Joy's insuring quality." Love, indeed, is one of the two great absolutes in Emily Dickinson's world, the other being death. Many of her poems enact certain moments on the way toward love, including desire, expectation, premonition, fear. But more poems still dispose certain moments on the other side of love, as loss, despair, terror, then death.

For despair, there are several poems, and those among her finest achievements. In "There's a certain Slant of light" (258) despair is absolute, beyond question or argument:

> There's a certain Slant of light,
> Winter Afternoons—
> That oppresses, like the Heft
> Of Cathedral Tunes—

Heft means weight, with a further note of heaving, strain, oppression. The cathedral tunes oppress because of the sullen weight of faith which they ask the listener to receive and to lift. These intimations course back through "oppresses" to the slant of light, which would be neutral and innocent, even with the addition of winter afternoons. This is one of Emily Dickinson's common procedures, to start a poem with a first line which is neutral, or as neutral as the barest narrative can be; and then to expose the line to alien associations, until it, too, is tainted and there is nothing but the alien. On the face of it, the slant of light is innocent, but its innocence cannot survive the accretion of oppressive effects. The sinister element is not visible, in the nature of the case cannot be visible, light being merely light; so the sinister element is within. By the beginning of the second stanza, the light brings "Heavenly Hurt," again invisible, making only an internal difference, "Where the Meanings, are." Now its absolute nature appears, alien like the cathedral tunes, an absolute music, malign and in that nature heavenly. Emily Dickinson now gathers these intimations together, calling them despair, "An imperial affliction/ Sent us of the air"; so the air, too, like the wintry light, is tainted, slave of Heaven:

> When it comes, the Landscape listens—
> Shadows—hold their breath—
> When it goes, 'tis like the Distance
> On the look of Death—

It is as if the landscape were on the poet's side, sharing the terror; there is enmity even between the light and nature, alien premonitions. But the poet does not call upon the landscape to receive her, hiding her feeling from the light. She merely notes a further enmity, another figure, oppressed in its own way. Perhaps the distance between the poet and her landscape is narrowed somewhat by the shadows; but again there is no kinship. When the despair goes, it leaves behind not its opposite but a memory of itself, looking now like the face of death. Distance and death are cousins in many of Emily Dickinson's poems, especially in the love poems, where the absence of the lover, his distance, is indeed like death. Here the despair has defined its "seal" or sign as the personification of death; when the seal is defined in this final sense, the poem is finished.

The same association of despair merging in death is made in another poem (305):

> The difference between Despair
> And Fear—is like the One
> Between the instant of a Wreck—
> And when the Wreck has been—

Fear is not further described, it is absolute in its way. But despair is given as an image in the second and last stanza; it is transformed to death:

> The Mind is smooth—no Motion—
> Contented as the Eye
> Upon the Forehead of a Bust
> That knows—it cannot see—

It is a quartz contentment. Emily Dickinson often uses words like "contented" and "content" in a special sense. When something is, once for all, what it is, when it is the "perfection" of itself, with all its possibilities embodied in one figure, it may be fancied to be content, whatever its nature or character. Good or bad is indifferent. If one is thinking of existence, merely, then all things which equally exist are equal. In another poem (756) she describes an inordinate blessing she had, "A perfect—paralyzing Bliss," definitive, ultimate. Then she says, "Contented as Despair," meaning that both the bliss and the despair were absolute. They may decorously be compared with each other, or with anything else similarly perfect. This is one of the marks of Emily Dickinson's sensibility, that it takes particular note of a thing's perfection, whatever its nature; takes note, and allows to the perfection of pain the same credence as to the perfection of joy. Both are definitive, therefore contented. In Emily Dickinson, everything is allowed to become itself, whatever the character of that self; it will not be deprived of its possibilities. This is why we think of her as preeminently associated not with pain, joy, or loneliness, but with accepted pain, accepted joy, accepted loneliness. Her ministry does not end with acceptance, but it never begins without acceptance. To accept that something is what it is, and that its character is its own, is the first act of her sensibility. What the later acts are, only the poems can say. "It might be lonelier/ Without the Loneliness" (405), because the loneliness has become a character, almost a person, in Emily Dickinson's life, a member of the house. Darkness and a room have been prepared for his reception; even such a person might be missed. "Not seeing, still we know" (1518), the statues may say; but if all they know is that they cannot see, that is despair, fear's afterword.

It is evident that there is an apocalyptic element in Emily Dickinson's imagination. We think of it when we advert to its rage for completeness, perfection; it insists upon conceiving what lesser imaginations, or more genial imaginations, are content to hint. It forces itself to the end of the line. Mostly, in Emily Dickinson's poems, the end of the line is death; so her imagination insists upon conceiving that, too. There is a passage in one of George Eliot's letters, July 1, 1874: "Your picture of Mr. and Mrs. Stirling, and what you say of the reasons why one may wish even for the anguish of being *left* for the sake of waiting on the beloved one to the end—all that goes to my heart of hearts. It is what I think of almost daily. For death seems to me now a close, real experience, like the approach of autumn or winter, and I am glad to find that advancing life brings this power of imagining the nearness of death I never had till of late years." This is very much in Emily Dickinson's spirit. Among perfections, death is hardly to be challenged. "To be alive—is Power" (677); true enough, and especially true in Emily Dickinson's poems, but if all absolutes are, in this respect, equal, an apocalyptic imagination attends most upon death. Or rather, upon dying, since this slight change in the character of the word makes the conceit more approachable.

A motto for these death poems is provided in a poem (412) in which Emily Dickinson says, "I made my soul familiar—with her extremity—/ That at the last, it should not be a novel Agony." As always, she exacerbates what is domestic, domesticates the apocalypse; either way, the imagination asserts itself. Death and the soul are to be "acquainted—/ Meet tranquilly, as friends," or if not as friends, then as neighbors, to whom courtesy is due. In "The last Night that She lived" (1100) Emily Dickinson notes that "It was a Common Night/ Except the Dying—this to Us/ Made Nature different." The tone is properly judicious; the mourners are, to an unusual degree, aware of things, but we are not to hear the grass grow. Ordinary things are "Italicized—as 'twere." The feelings are ordinary, too, the common resentment that the dead child has been chosen and others less worthy left:

We waited while She passed—
It was a narrow time—
Too jostled were Our Souls to speak . . .

The mourners merely wait while the dying one goes; because the waiting is oppressive, the time is narrow; even in the hours and minutes before the death, friends are already conceived as attending the funeral, sitting around the corpse, congested. The language of soul is taken from the language of body, as the language of eternity is derived from the language of time, because there is no other language. All language is, in this sense, domestic. Death poems are life poems. Emily Dickinson's death poems accept this condition; acceptance gives them their extraordinary resilience. It is as if she had only to assent to the temporal nature of language, cooperating with its domestic bias, to write death poems which are among the greatest short poems in the language. "Too jostled were Our Souls to speak": here the imagination is going about its proper business, not by trying to do the whole work but by cooperating with the language. "Jostled" is the product of a dramatic imagination in league with a domestically inclined language; knowing, too, that what is beyond experience must accept a finite language, or remain silent. At the end of the poem the mourners are released to their own lives: "And then an awful leisure was/ Belief to regulate." To regulate; to govern, direct, or control, a discipline domestic in its language, esoteric in its particular application. The strongest link in Emily Dickinson's chain is invariably the common word, taken from a domestic language and applied, with the force of courtesy, where ostensibly it does not belong. This is why her triumphs so often appear, on first reading, to be wrong; and then we know them to be incalculably right: "I died for Beauty—but was scarce/ Adjusted in the Tomb . . ." (449).

This is to say that Emily Dickinson uses a plebeian language with a patrician imagination; willingly, with the commitment of knowledge. That the words are plebeian has perhaps already appeared; that the imagination is patrician appears in its independence, its pride, its *sprezzatura*. Where both forces are fully engaged, the result is a classic poem, as near perfection as the association allows. "I heard a Fly buzz—when I died" (465) is such an occasion. The speaker is the dying one, the "post of observation" her deathbed. The mourners are given as eyes and breaths, the breaths "gathering firm/ For that last Onset—when the King/ Be witnessed—in the Room." Then the dying one sees a fly interposed "Between the light—and me"; "And then the Windows failed—and then/ I could not see to see." Death is imagined, in the last stanza, as the end of a sequence in which the first parts are played by things not yet to die. In the victim's failing life the buzzing fly is there, but "With Blue—uncertain stumbling Buzz," then the windows fail, two failures prefiguring a third, "I could not see to see." Allen Tate has recalled the last scene in Dostoevski's *The Idiot*, where Prince Myshkin and Rogozhin stand, in the dark, over the corpse of the murdered Nastasya. A fly appears, out of nowhere, and settles upon Nastasya's pillow. Mr. Tate says of the fly that it "comes to stand in its sinister and abundant life for the privation of life, the body of the young woman on the bed." In Emily Dickinson's poem the fly hovers to represent all the remaining things, alien because resistant, which detach themselves from the dying; privation, yes, but perhaps in greater measure, alienation. The imagination, when it is dramatic, seeks to establish relations between perceiver and the thing perceived, as here the dying speaker draws fly and window to herself, to her own lapse and failure. The effort fails when, with death, detachment is complete. There is a passage in Wordsworth's Preface to his *Poems* of 1815 where the poet describes this tendency of the imagination; he speaks of "images independent of each other, and immediately endowed by the mind with properties that do not inhere in them, upon an incitement from properties and qualities the existence of which is inherent and obvious." In Emily Dickinson's poem the imagination, conceiving of the mourners, the fly, the air in the room, and the windows, draws everything into the circle of lapse and failure until the last line, when the center fails, and there is nothing.

For the same reason, in "Because I could not stop for Death" (712) the imagination represents the grain as "Gazing." The gaze is transferred from the speaker; or rather, the speaker draws the grain toward herself, to share in the nature of her vision. Indeed, this imaginative principle is active in the structure of the poem. Grim death is domesticated, fitted to the common sequences of life, a gentleman of Amherst come to call upon a lady. Yeats speaks of "that discourtesy of death," Emily Dickinson enacts its civility. The gentleman caller arrives, and conveys his lady to the carriage. The poem has been compared with Browning's "The Last Ride Together," partly on the strength of Browning's lines—

> What if we still ride on, we two
> With life for ever old yet new,
> Changed not in kind but in degree,
> The instant made eternity . . .

It is a nice conjunction, especially when we recall that Emily Dickinson, reading Browning's poem several years later, was struck by the line. "So, one day more am I deified" in the second stanza. But Browning's poem has nothing of Emily Dickinson's civility. A comparison nearer home is feasible, a later poem by Emily Dickinson herself (1445) in which death is personified as "the supple Suitor/ That wins at last"; a comparison the more attractive because both poems stroke death with the melody of love. In the later poem death's "stealthy Wooing" is first conducted by "pallid innuendoes":

> But brave at last with Bugles
> And a bisected Coach
> It bears away in triumph
> To Troth unknown
> And Kinsmen as divulgeless
> As throngs of Down—

It is a different pageantry, of course. The pageantry of "Because I could not stop for Death" is a more equable courtship, featured in the slow drive into the country, the courtesy with which the gentleman pauses so that they may look at the old house. So the conclusion is quieter, there are no bugles:

> Since then—'tis Centuries—and yet
> Feels shorter than the Day
> I first surmised the Horses' Heads
> Were toward Eternity—

Surmise; meaning, to go somewhat beyond the evidence. Evidence gives the direction, but not the distance or the end. It is as if the whole enterprise, death's designs upon the soul, were conducted by "stealthy Wooing," without the bravery of bugles and triumph. In "surmised" one stealth is quietly answered by another.

What is remarkable in the poem is the power of an imagination which can live, apparently, upon so little. We feel that a poem which aspires to do so much might reasonably claim, for its essential materials, pretty nearly everything. But this poem does more with poverty than other poems with wealth; or so it is permissible to feel. A few common words, a simple plot, almost nothing in the way of description, no thoughts, no ideas; and the extraordinary work is done. There is some-

thing of this seeming ease in another poem about death (1078), or rather about the morning after a death:

> The Bustle in a House
> The Morning after Death
> Is solemnest of industries
> Enacted upon Earth—
>
> The Sweeping up the Heart
> And putting Love away
> We shall not want to use again
> Until Eternity.

William Dean Howells quoted the last lines in his review of *Poems of Emily Dickinson* in January 1891, and he recalled them, several years later, when he visited his daughter's grave in Boston. "What an indescribable experience!" he wrote to Mark Twain, October 23, 1898; "I thought I could tell you about it, but I can't. Do you know those awful lines of Emily Dickinson?" And he quoted them. Deaths were many in Amherst, as Emily Dickinson's poems and letters show; and, to her, the only really accredited rituals were domestic, the daily industries. It is typical of her imagination to see the solemnity of death yield, as a matter of domestic fact, to the sense of continuing life, while the accepted loss persists. So the domestic rituals are the serious endgames, played when one season yields to another, but there is no attempt to assuage the loss by invoking the rhythms of seasonal time to transcend it. Loss is absolute, too.

In October 1883, Emily Dickinson's nephew Gilbert died, the youngest child of Austin and Susan, eight years old, from typhoid fever. "Dawn and Meridian in one," she wrote to Susan, enclosing an elegy, "Pass to thy Rendezvous of Light,/ Pangless except for us" (1564). To Emily herself, sorrow was inexpressible. Within a few weeks she was ill. "The Physician says I have 'Nervous prostration.'

Possibly I have—I do not know the Names of Sickness. The Crisis of the sorrow of so many years is all that tires me." In March 1884, Judge Lord died. "I hardly dare to know that I have lost another friend, but anguish finds it out." In June, she herself suffered a nervous collapse. "I have not been strong for the last year," she told her friend Mrs. Mack; she was never to be strong again. The last letters tell the story, often in single lines. There are occasional spurts of energy, and the result is a longer letter, or a few lines of verse. In August 1885, Helen Jackson died. During the following months Emily Dickinson's letters are necessities of condolence, often picking up fragments of the dead lives and sharing them with friends. Her health improved a little in the spring of 1886: "The velocity of the ill, however, is like that of the snail," she told Charles Clark, Wadsworth's friend. In May, she became ill again. On the thirteenth she passed into a coma, paralysis as a consequence of Bright's disease. She died on Saturday evening, May 15, 1886.

Some time after her death, her sister Lavinia found a locked box containing about seven hundred short poems. The pages were bound together in fascicles of four or five sheets. Emily had been averse to publication. It was as foreign to her thought, she told Higginson, "as Firmament to Fin." Publication, she wrote in a poem (709), is "the Auction/Of the Mind of Man." In a letter to Higginson in 1862 she wrote: "If fame belonged to me, I could not escape her—if she did not, the longest day would pass me on the chase." But Lavinia determined to show that fame belonged to her sister. Susan Dickinson was approached, without success; then Higginson was asked to edit the material; finally Mabel Loomis Todd, wife of a professor at Amherst College, agreed to work on the manuscripts. Higginson had undertaken to look over the poems if they could be shown to him in fair copies; Mrs. Todd would do the heavy work first. Collaborating, they eventually published *Poems by Emily Dickinson* (1890), a selection of 116 poems. By herself, Mrs. Todd edited a selection of Emily Dickinson's letters in 1894. In 1896, however, a quarrel broke out between Lavinia and Mrs. Todd; the first result was that Emily Dickinson's manuscripts were divided. The papers in Lavinia's possession passed to Susan Dickinson, and subsequently to Martha Dickinson Bianchi, Emily's niece. From 1914 until her death in 1943, Mrs. Bianchi issued several volumes of Emily Dickinson's poems. But Mrs. Todd's share of the manuscripts remained under lock until her daughter, Millicent Todd Bingham, published about 650 unpublished poems as *Bolts of Melody* (1945). Finally, Thomas H. Johnson brought all the known poems together in *The Poems of Emily Dickinson* (1955), in three volumes, giving all the available poems and their variant readings. *The Letters of Emily Dickinson*, edited by Mr. Johnson and Theodora Ward, was published in three volumes in 1958. Mr. Johnson has also published *The Complete Poems of Emily Dickinson* in one volume (1960) and a rich sample called *Final Harvest: Emily Dickinson's Poems* (1961), a selection in paperback of her choice work, 576 poems from the 1775 of the variorum edition.

Appropriately, Mr. Johnson's work on the manuscripts has been greatly praised. Before 1955, it was impossible to know precisely what authority the printed volumes had. It was feared that the early editors had been more zealous than scrupulous; they had a difficult, angular poet on their hands, so perhaps they had smoothed the rough patches. In fact, they compromised, retaining the exact text when it was tolerably lucid and altering a word or two when the poet ran beyond that mark. Not very many poems are seriously affected. "Further in Summer than the Birds" (1068) was smoothed by Higginson's hand, the third stanza made to follow a more conventional grammar than that given in the original version. There are some readers, including Yvor Winters, who prefer the smooth version; they met Emily Dickinson's poems for the first time in the old editions, and they resent the modern scholar's insistence upon textual fidelity, if it means revising old affections. The same readers, long accustomed to the conventional punctuation of the old editions, cannot welcome the dashes, Emily Dickinson's favorite gesture, reproduced in the Johnson edition. It has been argued that the dashes are rhetorical rather than grammatical notes, hints to the reading voice rather than to the silent eye. There is also the problem of the capitals: not every noun in the manuscripts is awarded a capital, but a method is dimly visible. In most cases the capitalized words are those upon which the fate of the line largely depends, so it is natural that the poet should wish to give them a mark of special favor, "italicized, as 'twere." The words thus appraised begin to look and sound like moral universals; as if they were more than nouns. Again, many of the best poems exist in different versions; the poet often incorporated them in letters, and she felt inclined to tinker with them, perhaps in deference to their recipients. Mr. Johnson is reasonably sure, in the crucial poems, how the sequence of the manuscripts goes. In some instances the versions are sufficiently distinct to make separate poems. Where choice is obligatory, Mr. Johnson has nearly always chosen well. But the procedure is doubtful in one respect; as a general policy, later texts are preferred, but in some cases the later version

spoils the poem. There are two copies of "I Years had been from Home" (609) and it is possible to think the earlier version of 1862 the better poem, more powerful than the official version of 1872. Logically, Mr. Johnson's policy gives preference to the later poem, so this is the only one offered in *Final Harvest*. On the other hand, Mr. Johnson has chosen the earlier version of "The Moon upon her fluent Route" (1528) for sound poetic reasons. The result is a certain confusion between editorial principle in the selection of copy texts and a natural desire to see Emily Dickinson represented by her best poems. In some cases a satisfactory choice cannot be made. "Essential Oils—are wrung" (675) exists in two versions, their implications mutually incompatible, one hopeful, one despairing. Both were written about the same time. Mr. Johnson has given the hopeful one his preference, so it stands in *Final Harvest*; the despairing voice can only be heard in small print in the variorum edition.

But these are minor troubles, hardly to be counted at all in the great satisfaction: the extraordinary body of poetry is available. Readers make their own anthologies, the choice poems brought to memory. There are readers who love the comic poems, which I have not mentioned; Emily Dickinson's wit was not continuous, but it was strong when it appeared. There are other readers who care for the quirky poems, sardonic glances at eternal verities. Emily Dickinson was often irreverent; some readers are attracted by her boldness. In "God is a distant—stately Lover" (357) Christ's coming on earth in behalf of the Father is compared to John Alden's service in behalf of Miles Standish in Longfellow's poem. The Reverend Brooke Herford read the verses in the Boston *Christian Register* and thought them "one of the most offensive bits of contemptuous Unitarianism that I have met with." The editor of the *Register* disagreed, and wrote an editorial to defend the poet. But Emily Dickinson's transaction with God is a longer story.

If I admit a bias, it is in favor of those poems in which Emily Dickinson's sensibility encounters the great moral universals: love, pain, loss, doubt, death. What happens to the universals, what happens to the sensibility: the poems which give this double drama are among the greatest poems in the language. R. P. Blackmur said that in Emily Dickinson "direct experience (often invented, sometimes originally contingent) was always for the sake of something else which would replace the habit and the destructive gusto (but not the need) of experience in the world, and become an experience of its own on its own warrant and across a safe or forbidding gap." The gap is visible, or nearly visible, in the letters. The "something else" for which Eimly Dickinson lived is in the poems, unless we say, with no more ado, that it is the poems themselves, poetry. The something else may be fulfilled in the poetry, with no remainder; or the poetry may be an instrument, means to a further end on the other side of silence. Between such alternatives it is hardly necessary to make a choice.

Selected Bibliography

WORKS OF EMILY DICKINSON

Poems of Emily Dickinson, edited by Mabel Loomis Todd and T. W. Higginson. Boston: Roberts Brothers, 1890.
Poems by Emily Dickinson, Second Series, edited by Mabel Loomis Todd and T. W. Higginson. Boston: Roberts Brothers, 1891.
Poems by Emily Dickinson, Third Series, edited by Mabel Loomis Todd. Boston: Roberts Brothers, 1896.
The Single Hound, edited by Martha Dickinson Bianchi. Boston: Little, Brown, 1914.
The Complete Poems of Emily Dickinson, edited by Martha Dickinson Bianchi and Alfred Leete Hampson. Boston: Little, Brown, 1924.
Further Poems of Emily Dickinson, edited by Martha Dickinson Bianchi and Alfred Leete Hampson. Boston: Little, Brown, 1929.
The Poems of Emily Dickinson, edited by Martha Dickinson Bianchi and Alfred Leete Hampson. Boston: Little, Brown, 1930.
Unpublished Poems of Emily Dickinson, edited by Martha Dickinson Bianchi and Alfred Leete Hampson. Boston: Little, Brown, 1935.
Poems by Emily Dickinson, edited by Martha Dickinson Bianchi and Alfred Leete Hampson. Boston: Little, Brown, 1937.
Ancestors' Brocades: The Literary Debut of Emily Dickinson, by Millicent Todd Bingham. New York: Harper, 1945. (Contains some poems and letters published for the first time.)
Bolts of Melody: New Poems of Emily Dickinson, edited by Mabel Loomis Todd and Millicent Todd Bingham. New York: Harper, 1945.
The Poems of Emily Dickinson, edited by Thomas H. Johnson. 3 vols. Cambridge, Mass.: Harvard University Press, 1955.
The Complete Poems of Emily Dickinson, edited by Thomas H. Johnson. Boston: Little, Brown, 1960.
Final Harvest: Emily Dickinson's Poems, edited by Thomas H. Johnson. Boston: Little, Brown, 1961.

LETTERS
The Letters of Emily Dickinson, edited by Mabel Loomis Todd. 2 vols. Boston: Roberts Brothers, 1894.
The Life and Letters of Emily Dickinson, edited by Martha Dickinson Bianchi. Boston: Houghton Mifflin, 1924.
Letters of Emily Dickinson, edited by Mabel Loomis Todd. New York: Harper, 1931.
Emily Dickinson Face to Face: Unpublished Letters with Notes and Reminiscences, edited by Martha Dickinson Bianchi. Boston: Houghton Mifflin, 1932.

Emily Dickinson's Letters to Dr. and Mrs. Josiah Gilbert Holland, edited by Theodora Van Wagenen Ward. Cambridge, Mass.: Harvard University Press, 1951.

Emily Dickinson: A Revelation, by Millicent Todd Bingham. New York: Harper, 1954. (Contains letters published for the first time.)

The Letters of Emily Dickinson, edited by Thomas H. Johnson and Theodora Ward. 3 vols. Cambridge, Mass.: Harvard University Press, 1958.

The Years and Hours of Emily Dickinson, edited by Jay Leyda. 2 vols. New Haven, Conn.: Yale University Press, 1960.

CONCORDANCE

Rosenbaum, S. P., ed. *A Concordance to the Poems of Emily Dickinson.* Ithaca, N.Y.: Cornell University Press, 1964.

BIOGRAPHICAL STUDIES

Higgins, David. *Portrait of Emily Dickinson: The Poet and Her Prose.* New Brunswick, N.J.: Rutgers University Press, 1967.

Johnson, Thomas H. *Emily Dickinson: An Interpretive Biography.* Cambridge, Mass.: Harvard University Press, 1955.

Ward, Theodora. *The Capsule of the Mind: Chapters in the Life of Emily Dickinson.* Cambridge, Mass.: Harvard University Press, 1961.

Whicher, George F. *This Was a Poet: A Critical Biography of Emily Dickinson.* New York: Scribners, 1938.

CRITICAL STUDIES

Aiken, Conrad. "Emily Dickinson," *The Dial,* 76:301-08 (April 1924). (Reprinted in his *A Reviewer's ABC.* New York: Meridian Books, 1958. Pp. 156-63.)

Anderson, Charles R. *Emily Dickinson's Poetry: Stairway of Surprise.* New York: Holt, Rinehart and Winston, 1960.

Blackmur, R. P. *Language as Gesture.* New York: Harcourt, Brace, 1952.

———. "Emily Dickinson's Notation," *Kenyon Review,* 18:224–37 (Spring 1956).

Cambon, Glauco. "Emily Dickinson and the Crisis of Self-Reliance," in *Transcendentalism and Its Legacy,* edited by Myron Simon and Thornton H. Parsons. Ann Arbor: University of Michigan Press, 1966.

Capps, Jack L. *Emily Dickinson's Reading, 1836–1886.* Cambridge, Mass.: Harvard University Press, 1966.

Chase, Richard. *Emily Dickinson.* New York: William Sloane Associates, 1951.

Donoghue, Denis. *Connoisseurs of Chaos.* New York: Macmillan, 1965.

Franklin, R. W. *The Editing of Emily Dickinson: A Reconsideration.* Madison: University of Wisconsin Press, 1967.

Frye, Northrop. *Fables of Identity.* New York: Harcourt, Brace and World, 1963.

Gelpi, Albert J. *Emily Dickinson: The Mind of the Poet.* Cambridge, Mass.: Harvard University Press, 1965.

Griffith, Clark. *The Long Shadow: Emily Dickinson's Tragic Poetry.* Princeton, N.J.: Princeton University Press, 1964.

Pearce, Roy Harvey. *The Continuity of American Poetry.* Princeton, N.J.: Princeton University Press, 1961.

Poulet, Georges. *Studies in Human Time,* translated by Elliott Coleman. Baltimore: Johns Hopkins Press, 1956.

Ransom, John Crowe. "Emily Dickinson: A Poet Restored," *Perspectives USA,* 15:5–20 (Spring 1956).

Tate, Allen. *Collected Essays.* Denver: Alan Swallow, 1959.

Warren, Austin. "Emily Dickinson," *Sewanee Review,* 65:565–86 (Autumn 1957).

Wells, Henry W. *Introduction to Emily Dickinson.* Chicago: Packard, 1947.

Winters, Yvor. *Maule's Curse.* Norfolk, Conn.: New Directions, 1938.

———. *Forms of Discovery.* Denver: Alan Swallow, 1967.

—DENIS DONOGHUE

John Dos Passos

1896-1970

Over a period of forty years, in some thirty published volumes, John Dos Passos carried on a romantic, constantly disappointed love affair with the United States. His books, crowded with personal experiences and historic events, are at once celebrations, indictments, and pleas for reform. Yet though his passionate complaints seem always to be set in political terms, his own political attitudes swung in a large arc from left to right. Obviously something profounder than politics was at work.

Dos Passos was not the first to try to encompass in fiction the whole history of his time. In France Alfred de Musset, writing after the glory and defeat of Napoleon, discovered postwar generations—especially "lost" ones—as literary material. Balzac, conceiving a social generation as "a drama with five or six thousand leading characters," thought that the novelist, "by making a selection from the chief social events of the time and composing types made up of traits taken from several homogeneous characters," could go deeper into social reality than historians had. Emile Zola took the next step by treating social institutions—the church, the army, department stores, farms, and mines—as superhuman beings with lives of their own.

If what Balzac said is true, that a novelist is simply a secretary who writes down what society dictates to him, then much still depends on the secretary's training and temperament. For the ambitious task Dos Passos set himself, his background seems ideal.

His paternal grandfather was a Portuguese immigrant from Madeira who married a Quaker of early Colonial stock. Their son, John Randolph Dos Passos, fought in the Civil War when he was not much younger than his son would be in 1917. He was fifty-two in 1896 when this son was born; thus, by the time John Dos Passos produced *Midcentury*, his own and his parents' experience had spread over more than 110 years of American history.

Time was not the only spectacular span. The father rose from poverty to the highest levels of law, big business, and finance. After he had educated himself in Philadelphia, he became a criminal lawyer in New York, defending notorious murderers, including the one who killed Jim Fisk. Then he moved on to corporation law, and for organizing the American Sugar Refining Company received the largest fee ever paid a lawyer up to that time. He knew several Presidents while he was lobbying in Washington, and in the year of his son's birth was campaigning for his friend William McKinley.

John Randolph Dos Passos was even an author. Most of his books were legal or business texts, but one—*The Anglo-Saxon Century*

—was an appeal to the American people, with perspectives as bold as those beginning his son's *U.S.A.* The Boer War and the Spanish-American War, he said, marked the end of an era. By intervening in Cuba and the Philippines our country had become committed on a world scale. We would be the dominant power of the next hundred years if we worked closely with the British. From England we had received our language, our religion, the blood of our founding fathers, and—even more precious—our common-law tradition, respect for life, liberty, and property, and a government with sharply restricted powers. It was to preach exactly these principles that his son was to write *Midcentury* sixty years later.

This was clearly no coincidence. But the younger Dos Passos was not just an admiring disciple of his father. Theirs was a complex relationship, as any reader can see from the novels. The fathers are usually remote, often repellent figures, their strengths and weaknesses mingled in such a way as to make life very troubled for the sons. Toward the end of his own life, in the autobiography, *The Best Times (1966)*, Dos Passos gave a rather different impression. There the father, so affectionate toward his son and so adventurously interested in everything—food, fox hunts, yachts, the English gentry, financial speculation, politics, Greek, singing, legal reform—is a fascinating, appealing figure.

To Dos Passos the problem of identity was more than a popular literary theme. Because his own family circumstances were like those described in *Chosen Country*, he and his mother lived apart from his father, often in Europe, and he himself was not publicly acknowledged as a son until 1916. His mother was forty-eight when he was born, and after this Caesarean birth she was frail and dependent like the typical mother in his novels. His years with her on the Continent gave him vivid memories of places—his books are rich with them—but he always felt homeless, different from other boys, especially when he went to school in England. His return to America, repeating in a sense his grandfather's immigration, is reflected in the beginning of *Manhattan Transfer*, where Jimmy Herf is first seen as a boy debarking with his mother from an ocean liner in New York on the Fourth of July.

After Choate School, Dos Passos entered Harvard in 1912, a year of great cultural stir in America. *Poetry* was only one of the periodicals springing up to welcome new artistic impulses from Europe and to rediscover native folk strains at home. The Imagist movement, started in England by T. E. Hulme and Ezra Pound, was rapidly being Americanized by Amy Lowell, sister of the president of Harvard. Pound began referring to it as "Amygism." For the Harvard *Advocate* Dos Passos reviewed Edgar Lee Masters, T. S. Eliot, and Pound. Some of his own college verse was later collected in *Eight Harvard Poets* (1917) along with the poetry of Robert Hillyer and E. E. Cummings, his fellow ambulance drivers in France.

This early exposure to imagism and aestheticism kept out of his work the drabness that sometimes goes with naturalism. He would never write like Theodore Dreiser or James T. Farrell. In *Manhattan Transfer* passengers pour out of the ferry house "like apples fed down a chute into a press"; a newborn baby squirms "in the cottonwool feebly like a knot of earthworms." Sometimes he is too literally colorful, as if the names of pigments could actually create an impressionistic painting on the printed page.

Harvard gave Dos Passos more than aestheticism. He began reading Thorstein Veblen as well as James Joyce. Much of his fiction, with its language borrowed from *A Portrait of the Artist as a Young Man* and *Ulysses*, is an extended illustration of *The Theory of the Leisure Class* and *The Engineers and the Price System*. To a mind absorbing Veblen's ironic analyses of American capitalism, the news in the papers had a sharpened impact. It was the time of the textile workers' strike in Lawrence, Massachusetts, with the poet Giovannitti as its leader, and of another in Paterson, New Jersey, for which John Reed helped stage a pageant in Madison Square Garden.

Dos Passos reviewed Reed's *Insurgent Mexico* and heard him lecture at Harvard. Reed was a great romantic, an impressionist poet, who could throw himself passionately into social struggles. Then, too, there was the contemporary Belgian poet Verhaeren, an impassioned traveler, who described his intense inner life in images drawn from his fascination with factories, railroads, stock markets, and the "tentacular" industrial cities of Europe.

After he graduated from Harvard in 1916, Dos Passos was eager to join the Norton-Harjes volunteer ambulance service, not because he approved of the war but because he loved adventure and wanted to help his fellow men. Afraid that he would be killed, his father offered him a year of architectural study in Spain instead. Dos Passos yielded, but when his father died suddenly the next spring, he volunteered, serving in Italy as well as France.

Out of this war experience came his first brief novel, *One Man's Initiation—1917* (published in England in 1920). In it he seems perhaps less the man of action than the aesthete, the sensitive spectator. It is dedicated to "those with whom I saw rockets in the sky a certain evening at sunset on the road from Erize-la-Petite to Erize-la-Grande."

Like most of his later books it begins with a man traveling, this time to France. Snatches of war songs set the mood, and a pretty girl offers to chloroform all surviving Germans. It ends with a long discussion between the young hero, Martin Howe, and a group of French soldiers. He asks, as John Reed might have, whether they can carry through the social revolution they feel coming. They say No, they are only intellectuals. The ones who have the power and nerve are "the stupid average working-people." The intellectuals can only try to fight falsehood.

In "Hugh Selwyn Mauberley" Ezra Pound tells of young men dying for old men's lies, and in *A Farewell to Arms* Ernest Hemingway describes how soldiers at the front felt when they had to listen once again to the words "sacred, glorious and sacrifice and the expression in vain." Only the names of places retained their dignity. Martin Howe says of the propaganda that takes away our humanity, "We are slaves of bought intellect, willing slaves."

The writing in *One Man's Initiation* is young and self-conscious, still in the aesthetic mode of Walter Pater and the early Joyce. Unlike Hemingway, whose youthful work was blue-penciled by Ezra Pound and Gertrude Stein, Dos Passos had no master hand to cut out his excessive description and the parts of his dialogue that did not ring true. He never learned to "listen completely" when people talked, to discover the revealing phrase and then play on it wittily, as Hemingway and F. Scott Fitzgerald at their best could do. Even after Martin Howe reaches the front to take up ambulance duty, passages from Shelley and Blake run through his head, and he spends his off-hours contemplating a ruined abbey and dreaming of the Middle Ages. But when this poetic impressionism is used to describe the chaos of war in the French countryside, the results are brilliant.

The book is purely episodic, made up of unconnected scenes, but they take separate and satisfying shape as vignettes or short stories. There is not just one initiation but a whole series of them—encounters with death, fear,

Paris, women, theft, corruption, anarchism, Catholicism. In both style and construction the novel is clearly indebted to *The Red Badge of Courage* by Stephen Crane.

One Man's Initiation was a kind of preparatory exercise to the far maturer novel, *Three Soldiers*, written the following year, mostly in Spain, while Dos Passos was free-lancing as a journalist and essayist. The most vivid direct account of army life among our common soldiers during World War I, *Three Soldiers* helped create an antimilitaristic mood in readers of the twenties and thirties, and even left its mark on major novels written after World War II. *The Naked and the Dead* and *From Here to Eternity*, for instance, have leading characters chosen much as Dos Passos had chosen his. Mailer and Jones follow his pattern, too, in stressing the intensity of the conflicts within the army itself.

Dos Passos gives his three soldier parts to Andrews, a Harvard-educated pianist-composer from New York and Virginia; Fuselli, an optical worker from San Francisco eager to make good in the army; Chrisfield, a homesick farm boy from Indiana obsessed with hatred for a sergeant whom he finally kills with a hand grenade in the confusion after a battle.

All three men are broken by the army. Fuselli contracts a serious venereal disease. Chrisfield deserts and leads a precarious underground existence in Paris. Andrews, studying at the Sorbonne while still in the army, gets into trouble with some M.P.'s who dislike his manner, is beaten up and sent to a labor battalion. He escapes by plunging into the Seine, helped by a working-class soldier who drowns while trying to rescue him. Saved then by an anarchist bargeman, Andrews finds his way, after many adventures, to the French girl he loves. She lets him down badly when she learns of the trouble he is in. He is rearrested, with a long federal prison term ahead of him. The

music he has been working on, inspired by his reading of Flaubert, blows symbolically away.

Certainly Dos Passos was stacking the cards by having all three soldiers end badly, but this was the mood of the best postwar writers. Robert Graves called his war reminiscences *Goodbye to All That*. The hero of Hemingway's *Farewell to Arms* makes a "separate peace" by plunging into the Arno. *The Enormous Room* by E. E. Cummings is an account of his experiences in a French military prison after being arrested for something he wrote in a letter home. Dos Passos himself was threatened with disciplinary action because of his views.

Antagonism is evident enough in the titles he uses for the divisions of the book, "Making the Mould," "The Metal Cools," "Machines," "Rust," "The World Outside," and "Under the Wheels." In *Three Soldiers* there is no discussion of military tactics, the strategy of trying to defeat Germany, or even international politics. Compared with the French, its American characters have little interest in ideas, radical or otherwise. Andrews is an exception, but his mood is one of total rejection of the "system." And after his experience in the labor battalion, he says something to the French girl that suggests the persistent fear of organized society of any kind which underlies Dos Passos' frequent shifts in political position.

Andrews lands in prison because he has refused to give himself up passively to dehumanized power. But at times he fears that society will always be anti-individualist: "organizations growing and stifling individuals, and individuals revolting hopelessly against them, and at last forming new societies to crush the old societies and becoming slaves again in their turn. . . ."

Many readers were shocked by the spade-calling realism of *Three Soldiers*. Despite this and its attitude toward the army, it was enthusiastically received. Heywood Broun called it a book "with not an atom of pose," representing "deep convictions . . . eloquently expressed." Critics were amazed that in a book describing free souls crushed and deadened by an institution there could be "a sense of beauty on every page." Dos Passos was bitterly critical of army life, but he had a young and romantic appreciation of new experience of every kind. Both created intensity: at the same time they sufficiently balanced each other so that *Three Soldiers* remains one of the best novels of World War I as well as one of the most objective accounts of what war service in France was like.

Between the two major books of his early period, *Three Soldiers* (1921) and *Manhattan Transfer* (1925), Dos Passos not only wrote a play, *The Garbage Man*, and many articles for magazines, but published his volume of poems, *A Pushcart at the Curb*; his collection of essays on Spain called *Rosinante to the Road Again*; and a novel, *Streets of Night*. Much of this is apprentice work, but very revealing of the man who made himself secretary to American Society in *U.S.A.*, *District of Columbia*, and *Midcentury*.

Before Hemingway visited Spain to study death in the bull ring, Dos Passos, a friend of Hemingway, already had chosen it as the best place in which to get a clear perspective on his own values and those of his native country. He liked Spain and sympathized with Spanish reasons for being distrustful of America.

Rosinante to the Road Again (1922) describes this experiment. Essays on Spain and Spanish writers alternate with the dialogue of two travelers who represent different aspects of the author, or perhaps represent the author as he was and as he would have liked to be. Telemachus is thoughtful, inhibited, questing; his friend Lyaeus is relaxed, spontaneous, daring, enjoying life in a mildly Dionysian way.

It is remarkable that *Rosinante* was published in the same year as Joyce's *Ulysses*, in which Stephen Dedalus is Telemachus. But Dos Passos had stronger personal reasons than Joyce —or Thomas Wolfe, who also used the name —to identify himself with a classic hero whose whole youth was spent separated from his wandering warrior father. Moreover, in exploring Iberian life Dos Passos was returning to the sources of the immigrant strain which figures so largely in his sense of himself.

He read the Spanish social novelists, especially Pío Baroja, a kind of Spanish Gorki, who believed that everything of value in a country comes from the despised and neglected masses. "A profound sense of the evil of existing institutions," Dos Passos said, "lies behind every page he has written." Dos Passos spoke of Baroja as believing that a writer of the middle classes can serve the revolution only through his negations, his nay-saying, but found such negation perfectly compatible in Baroja with an intense feeling for immediate reality. His characters are "men of the day, people in love with the passing moment." Like Dos Passos, Baroja was fantastically productive. Among his scores of novels were three social trilogies. He changed his political position even more extremely than did Dos Passos. In 1937 he came out for fascism as the lesser of two evils. After exile in France during World War II, he returned to become a highly honored writer in Franco's Spain. Yet his individualism and skepticism about institutions persisted.

Many of the poems in *A Pushcart at the Curb* are set in Spain or Portugal. Though the poet and social critic in Dos Passos collaborate brilliantly in the novels, the poet, when alone, writes in a soft and outmoded vein. With none of the tough wit of Eliot or the later Yeats, these poems are mere traveler's sketches, imitating with words the brightly pigmented street scenes of a Pissarro or Sisley.

In one important respect, these poems are closer to *One Man's Initiation* than to the later fiction. Martin Howe's romanticism is still expressed by frequent references to medieval and ancient history, to Isis, Pan, spice cargoes entering Venice, nightingales strangled for Nero's supper, and a Bacchic rout of "ruddy boys with vineleaves in their hair." Praising *Ulysses* in 1925, T. S. Eliot proclaimed that the future of the novel depended on its moving toward myth. But this was just the time when the legendary and mythical elements vanished from Dos Passos' writings, never to return. If he had kept and nurtured them, perhaps his characters would not have been so completely the creatures of their social roles, and his criticism of American culture itself would have had more depth.

His play *The Garbage Man*—first produced at Harvard in 1925 under the title *The Moon Is a Gong*—is poetically far more vigorous than *A Pushcart at the Curb*. Like John Howard Lawson's *Processional* and Elmer Rice's *The Adding Machine*, it derives from the German Expressionist theater of Georg Kaiser and Ernst Toller.

Kaiser's play *Gas* dramatizes the dangers of uncontrollable industrial power; his *From Morn to Midnight* is about money madness. Toller wrote *Masses and Man* when he was in prison for his part in the Bavarian Communist *Putsch* of 1919. He shows how the common people and the capitalists are alike dehumanized by industrialization. It is Man who counts, and he can be saved only by love and individual responsibility. The themes are boldly stated, with striking mass effects and much use of rhythm and recurrence. Stockbrokers dance a foxtrot to the clink of coins, and chant higher and higher bids in musical crescendo as war reports pour in.

Tom, the musical-comedy-type hero of *The Garbage Man*, says: "We'd pick up raindrops for quarters. We'd skim greenbacks off the rollers out at sea. There's a lot of gold in your hair Jane." Jane is more realistic, and knows that money has to come from somebody's hard work. "Tom listen to the engine in the powerplant; that's all people. The engines are made out of people pounded into steel. The power's stretched on the muscles of people, the light's sucked out of people's eyes."

Jane seems to approach success, but it is in the false world of publicity and the theater. She wants "act, not dream" from Tom. After roaming romantically through the far places of the world, Tom actually does climb up to the moon, whereas Jane is in danger of being carried off by the mysterious figure of the garbage man. At the final curtain, Tom and Jane fly off up into space together.

Though romantically confused in its "message," *The Garbage Man* makes lively reading, offering train wrecks, jewel robberies, prosperity parades, and patriotic oratory. A Negro servant breaks out into an eloquent sermon. The telescope man sees the city in the same sort of total vision that *Manhattan Transfer* will create: "In all the offices . . . typewriters clucking an' chirruping like canarybirds . . . an' tickers roll out fours an' eights an' dollar signs an' ciphers, reeling out millions that don't exist. In all the houses, in apartments like shoeboxes, women in sacques and old pink kimonos . . ."

Streets of Night (1923), begun while Dos Passos was still an undergraduate, is very immature but it shows how personal relations looked to him before he began treating them socially and mixing them up with public events.

The "three soldiers" of *Streets of Night* are Fanshaw, an art instructor at Harvard, Wendell, a graduate student in anthropology, and Nancibel, a bachelor girl studying music. Fanshaw, very much a mother's boy, had been unable to make love to a chorus girl on an outing at Norumbega Park. He daydreams of marrying Nancibel, but realizes that he is "much too fond of Wenny, his dark skin, his extraordinary bright eyes." Nancibel is also drawn to Wendell, but is afraid of commitment and the act of sex. Tantalized by Nancibel's hesitations, Wendell picks up a prostitute, but flees when she confronts him naked. Convinced that his clergyman father has made life impossible for him, he shoots himself on a bridge parapet and drops into the Charles River. "Now in me," he thinks, "my father'll be dead." In Faulkner's *The Sound and the Fury*, Quentin Compson, another father-doomed Harvard man, dies in very much the same way.

Though *Streets of Night* is entirely non-political, the lower classes, especially the recent immigrants, are romantically endowed with superior freedom and vitality. Before his suicide Wenny has a long envious talk with a hungry vagabond. He dreams of being like him, "walking down roads, hopping freights: Tallahassee and South Bend and Havana and Paris and Helsingfors and Khiva and Budapest and Khorasan." After Wenny's death, Fanshaw gazes at the muscles of workers repairing tracks. "Wenny would have wanted to be one of them, redfaced spitting men with skillful ugly hands."

Finally in Italy, with the war over (only a page is devoted to it), Fanshaw gets drunk with an offensive Frenchman and goes with him—purely out of curiosity, he thinks—to a house of assignation, where he wakes up in a strange room beside a sleeping girl. It is not clear from Fanshaw's speedy retreat whether he is any surer of his sexual orientation than before.

The wasted lives in *Three Soldiers* are attributed to the crushing effects of the military machine. The characters in *Streets of Night* are under no such pressure, but end badly too.

They blame their parents and their parents' values. Dos Passos may have had an unusual personal reason for his sense of alienation and his inability to participate spontaneously in "real" life. But it was one that drove him to use even more intensely the theme that was popular with writers as varied as Van Wyck Brooks, Edwin Arlington Robinson, Sherwood Anderson, and Edgar Lee Masters. In Joyce's *Dubliners* the key word is "paralysis."

Though *Orient Express* did not appear until 1927, it describes a trip which Dos Passos had taken for the Near East Relief before he returned to New York to write *Manhattan Transfer*. Far more brilliant and evocative than his later travel books, it deserves to rank with the best in this genre by Graham Greene or Evelyn Waugh.

When only four years old he had gone aboard a fully equipped Trans-Siberian train in a dark shed at the Paris Exposition of 1900. Lighted scenes of exotic places rolled past the windows. "I've often wondered about the others who had tickets taken for them on that immovable train of the Trans-Siberian in the first year of the century," he wrote in *Orient Express*, "whose childhood was full of *Twenty Thousand Leagues* and Jules Verne's *sportsmen* and *globetrottairs* (if only the ice holds on Lake Baikal), and Chinese Gordon stuttering his last words over the telegraph at Khartoum, and Carlotta come back mad from Mexico setting fire to a palace at Terveuren. . . ."

Dos Passos goes where his romantic heroes had dreamed of going—to Trebizond, Ararat, Baghdad—but as an official trying to deal with famine, disease, revolution. He sees ways of life, unchanged since the time of Mahomet or Moses, about to be destroyed by Americanism, or at least by some of its exportable industrial techniques. "Henry Ford's gospel of multiple production and interchangeable parts will win hearts that stood firm against Thales and Democritus, against Galileo and Faraday. There is no god strong enough to withstand the Universal Suburb."

The exciting urban novel *Manhattan Transfer* was written by a man now mature, who had come back after seven years to look critically at his own country in a time of boom and changing mores. Though this is a long novel, it is as crowded as *The Garbage Man* with short, swift scenes full of crime, violence, and destruction, especially by fire. The book has the same conventional sort of heroine and hero, too. Ellen Thatcher, an actress, had grown up with a doting father who found her more fascinating than his sick, complaining wife. Jimmy Herf's early years were spent alone with his mother in Europe. Like Wenny and Fanshaw in *Streets of Night*, he looks wistfully at workingmen and wonders how it would feel "to be dirty and handle coal all day and have grease in your hair and up to your armpits." Later as a reporter he becomes the friend of a dark-skinned curly-haired former cook's helper from a French liner, who is dangerously and profitably involved in bootlegging.

Sex is no longer a fearful wonder. Jimmy and Ellen marry and have a baby, but the marriage does not last. Restless, unsure of herself, not really enjoying the life of the body, Ellen plunges into a series of love affairs. In the last pages of the novel, she marries an aging politician, chiefly because she needs security. Life in New York seemed full of possibilities, but because of her inner emptiness they come to nothing. It is the same mood that Sister Carrie reached in the end. And although Jimmy Herf, just turned thirty, is too young to be a Hurstwood, we see him penniless in the last scene, trudging out of the city past acres of smoldering dumps. When a truckdriver asks him how far he is going, he says, "I dunno. . . . Pretty far."

The life of the city is refracted through the minds of a dozen people nearly as important as Jimmy and Ellen: politicians, laborers, swindlers, chorus girls, housewives, down-and-outers, prissy vulgarians, high-class drunks. Many are mere types—Dos Passos always has this problem—but what they see and remember is vividly particular. With unfailing resourcefulness Dos Passos can create what seems like spontaneous memories appropriate to literally hundreds of variegated characters. And though the scenes often flash past two or three to the page, they have such consequence for the human beings in them—a girl going to an abortionist, a man discovering arson—that they never blur or seem perfunctory. Public moods are recalled with equal intensity. While Ellen Thatcher's father waits at the hospital for her birth, he reads about the legislation that is full of promise for the new century in New York.

Dos Passos sharpens even more the sense of moment and movement—to which the whole turbulent life of the city contributes—by shifting rapidly back and forth from one group of characters to another. A business, political, amatory, or criminal affair is treated for a few pages as if it were the center of the world—which it would be, of course, in real life, for the people concerned—and then cut off abruptly, to be picked up again without explanation, twenty or thirty pages later.

The division of chapters into as many as fifteen separate sections recalls the "Wandering Rocks" chapter of *Ulysses*, which describes eighteen incidents occurring in various parts of Dublin between three and four o'clock on one afternoon. Dos Passos was also influenced by the montage experiments of the film directors David Wark Griffith and Sergei Eisenstein. Griffith's fantastically ambitious *Intolerance* tries to tell four stories at once: the fall of Babylon, the crucifixion, the St. Bartholomew's Day massacre, and the suppression of a strike in a modern mill town. As the narratives approach a climax, the scenes become briefer, with quicker changes from story to story. Even more complex shifts without transition make Eliot's *The Waste Land* and Pound's *Cantos* such difficult reading.

Manhattan Transfer is clearly selective, as *Three Soldiers* had been. While responding imaginatively to the vigor and beauty of a great city, it concentrates on those characters most easily led astray by its temptations or least able to bear its pressures. It has very little more directly political implication than Dreiser's *Sister Carrie*, which had treated the same theme twenty-five years earlier.

What New York in the 1920's meant to Dos Passos is vividly described in the autobiography, *The Best Times*. It was the speakeasy period, a period of cynicism and disenchantment, but also of gaiety and wit. "Conversation in the early twenties had to be one wisecrack after another." Dos Passos knew intimately some of the most brilliant writers and talkers of his generation, E. E. Cummings, the Scott Fitzgeralds, Robert Benchley, Edmund Wilson, John Howard Lawson, Edna St. Vincent Millay. Too, there was romance at "a time in a man's life when every evening is a prelude. Toward five o'clock the air begins to tingle. It's tonight if you drink enough, talk enough, walk far enough, that the train of magical events will begin. Every part of town had its own peculiar glow."

What had happened to Dos Passos' political convictions since his Near East trip shows more clearly in the play *Airways, Inc.*, written in 1928. This was the year he visited Russia, the year after Lindbergh's flight and the execution of Sacco and Vanzetti. A drunken aviator, prototype of Charley Anderson in *U.S.A.*, breaks his back in a crash when he is sent to scatter leaflets over a strikers' meeting. The characters are crushed by a variety of disasters, all blamed on the social roles they choose or are forced to play.

Edmund Wilson reviewed the play admiringly, feeling that Dos Passos was superior to Hemingway, Fitzgerald, and Thornton Wilder in his ability to view society as a whole. But he doubted that American life then, or human life almost anywhere, was as unattractive as Dos Passos made it. Those on the right side suffer and are snuffed out; those on the wrong side are unattractive even when young, even in their pleasures. "We begin to guess some stubborn sentimentalism at the bottom of the whole thing . . . of which misapplied resentments represent the aggressive side. And from the moment we suspect the processes by which he has arrived at his political ideas, the ideas themselves become suspect."

These ideas were tested in action while Dos Passos was writing his great trilogy, *U.S.A.* The first volume, *The 42nd Parallel,* was published in 1930, the year after the stock market crash. In 1931, Dos Passos was indicted for criminal syndicalism when he and Theodore Dreiser tried to help the striking miners in Harlan County, Kentucky. The second volume, *1919*, came out in 1932, the year its author publicly supported the Communist candidate for President. Dos Passos was then treasurer of the National Committee for the Defense of Political Prisoners. But by 1936, when *The Big Money* concluded the trilogy, Dos Passos had attacked the Communists and backed Roosevelt's bid for a second term.

Though Dos Passos was never a Marxist he shared the belief current among intellectuals that history was heading toward some sort of final conflict. No writer could stand aloof. Whatever he said would add its thrust to one of the forces—progressive or destructive—that were coming into collision. The sense of social change, of released energy, which had given power to *Manhattan Transfer*, was expressed on a far vaster scale in *U.S.A.*

Like *Manhattan Transfer*, *U.S.A.* begins around 1900, at the time of the fighting in Cuba and the Philippines. The oratorical prophecies in the first Newsreel recall his father's expectations in *The Anglo-Saxon Century*. The trilogy is intended to be a total history of public moods and social changes through some twenty-five years, as experienced by twelve very different Americans. Public events are far more important than in *Manhattan Transfer*; the political analysis is more explicit and revolutionary. To cope with such tremendous matters, Dos Passos makes daring experiments in form. Never afterward did he use these techniques so fully.

In *U.S.A.* four distinctive modes of presentation have crystallized: the Newsreel; the Camera Eye; biographical sketches; and extended fictional narratives.

Dos Passos had always enlivened his narratives with newspaper quotations, political oratory, and popular songs. Now, in the Newsreels, he brings this material together as in a collage, juxtaposing verbal fragments in an artful pattern that has its own rhythms and recurrences. Not only does he evoke the events and moods of past years, but by mixing the trite and trivial ironically with the crucial he shows how fatuous and inconsistent America's public image of itself can be.

The Camera Eye sections are brief, impressionistic prose poems capturing poignant or decisive moments in the narrator's life. They are brilliantly done, and remind us that *U.S.A.* does not give us social reality as such, but social reality viewed by a particular man with a particular past—"I, John Dos Passos" succeeds the "I, Walt Whitman" of an equally formidable try at embracing the whole American experience of the century before.

The biographical portraits, vivid and compressed, describe as poetically but in expressionist style the lives of prominent Americans of the period. The inventor Steinmetz, for instance, "jotted a formula on his cuff and next morning a thousand new powerplants had sprung up and the dynamos sang dollars." For John Reed he uses a refrain, "Reed was a westerner and words meant what they said."

The choice of public figures in *U.S.A.* reflects the author's political mood and the limitations of his interests. In the first volume are two radical labor leaders, Eugene Debs and Bill Haywood; two defeated politicians, William Jennings Bryan and Robert La Follette; two capitalists, Andrew Carnegie and Minor C. Keith; and three experimenters, Thomas Edison, Luther Burbank, and Charles Proteus Steinmetz. The range is about the same in the second volume, but in *The Big Money* Isadora Duncan, Frank Lloyd Wright, Rudolph Valentino, and Thorstein Veblen provide more diversity. Only Veblen is strictly a man of ideas, and in all of *U.S.A.* there are no medical men, athletes, philosophers, creative writers, pure scientists, or religious leaders.

Most of *U.S.A.* lavishly reproduces the immediately felt experiences of its twelve chapters, in diction and rhythms and ways of thought appropriate to them. Dos Passos learned this mode from Joyce, but he uses it here with great authority and flexibility, especially when he enters the minds of women and children. The characters who dominate the trilogy toward the end are types already familiar from *Manhattan Transfer*—nervously ill wives and mothers, unmarried career women and dabblers in the arts, men of power corrupted by success, unsuccessful men who become mere drifters. Everybody is on the move, socially and geographically. Even more than *Manhattan Transfer, U.S.A.* dramatizes American mobility. Sex as a driving force, a nervous release, adds to the general restlessness. But profound and sustained love, like profound religious or creative excitement, is totally absent.

The individual lives tend to start and finish badly. We are introduced to Eleanor Stoddard by these sentences: "When she was small she hated everything. She hated her father, a stout redhaired man smelling of whiskers and stale pipetobacco." True to the odorous tradition of naturalism, the house where Fainy McCreary was born "was choking all day with the smell of whale-oil soap."

The ends are bad in more spectacular ways. Charley Anderson and Daughter die in plane and motor accidents, Eleanor Stoddard by suicide. Even more significant is the inner defeat, the degradation unsuccessfully narcotized by drunkenness. This is a society in which success—the success of power or money—is really failure. There are no sustaining values, except in rebellion. No one takes satisfaction in building or creating, whether it be a house, a family, an institution, a work of art.

Two leftists, Ben Compton and Mary French, are shown at the end still devoting their lives to unselfish purposes, but Ben has been thrown out of the Communist party for opposing its betrayal of the striking miners, and Mary has been deserted by the Communist functionary she has loved.

Even so, *U.S.A.* creates a positive effect because of the richness of the felt experience, the importance of the events, and the boldness of its challenge. And though the four separate modes of presentation might seem a confession of disunity, they are skillfully employed to bring diverse materials together according to certain dominant themes.

Toward the end of *The 42nd Parallel*, for instance, Eleanor Stoddard's frequent meetings with J. Ward Moorehouse cause his wife to threaten divorce. This is serious; Mrs. Moorehouse controls the fortune that can save him from bankruptcy. But then America declares war on Germany, and the resulting sudden shift in the business situation seems certain to benefit him. He is put on the President's Public Information Committee. He and Eleanor face his wife and persuade her that nothing is wrong. With everyone in a patriotic, excited mood, his personal crisis passes.

As Eleanor and Moorehouse cross Times Square "suddenly a grindorgan began to play *The Marseillaise* and it was too beautiful; she burst into tears and they talked about Sacrifice and Dedication and J.W. held her arm tight through the fur coat and gave the organ-grinder man a dollar." On the way to Long Island the drive over the Queensboro Bridge "was like flying above lights and blocks of houses and the purple bulk of Blackwell's Island and the steamboats and the tall chimneys and the blue light of powerplants." At the confrontation, Mrs. Moorehouse's "salmon-colored teagown stood out against the black. His light hair was ashgray in the light from the crystal chandelier against the tall ivorygray walls of the room." Eleanor finds the whole scene "like a play, like a Whistler, like Sarah Bernhardt." She decides to join the Red Cross and go to France.

The Newsreel immediately following echoes these themes in its snatches of the war song "Over There," its scraps of patriotic oratory, and its references to war profiteering.

The next Camera Eye describes the narrator's journey at this time to France on a ship containing Red Cross officials. He lands in Bordeaux to find profiteering there too: "up north they were dying in the mud and the trenches but business was good in Bordeaux and the winegrowers and the shipping agents and the munitionsmakers crowded into the Chapon Fin and ate ortolans and mushrooms and truffles. . . ." Some of the prose in this Camera Eye suggests Hemingway's "In Another Country." On the voyage, "the barman was brave and the stewards were brave they'd all been wounded and they were very glad that they were not in the trenches and the pastry was magnificent."

Then comes a sketch of Fighting Bob La Follette which also dramatizes the politics of the declaration of war. Dos Passos says that "we will remember" how in March 1917 La Follette, trying to block the drive toward war, held the vast governmental machine at deadlock for three days, though the "press pumped hatred into its readers" against him and "they burned him in effigy in Illinois." He died "an orator haranguing from the capitol of a lost republic."

All this is covered in just eighteen pages of the nearly fifteen hundred in the trilogy. The brief accounts of Joe Williams' many voyages as seaman and of Charley Anderson's financial involvements are equally packed. Dos Passos devotes ten pages to experiences which Henry James or Joseph Conrad would have analyzed in three hundred. Obviously he cannot equal them in depth of character or dramatic implication, but the narrative is more than mere synopsis. The authentic details seem remembered rather than invented. The result is to give history the grounding which Balzac thought only a novelist could give it, in the day-to-day lives of the people of a nation or a generation.

The history Dos Passos sees, though, is rather limited. He has not used what he knows of the world outside the United States to help us understand the unique character of the American experience. Even when he devoted himself after 1940 to an intensive study of the founding fathers, the books that came from it—such as the composite account of Hamilton and Jefferson, *The Men Who Made the Nation* (1957)—focus so sharply on the

immediate events that the larger issues are blurred.

Even in so massive an undertaking as *Mr. Wilson's War* (1962) his "Notes on Sources" shows how novelistic and personal his approach as a historian remained. "My method was to try to relate the experience of the assorted personalities and their assorted justifications to my own recollections of childhood and youth during those years; and to seek out, wherever possible, the private letter, the unguarded entry in the diary, the newsreport made on the spur of the moment." In his youth, under his father's direction, Dos Passos had been given a sound classical education, including the study of Greek, but with very little effect on his later thinking. It never seemed to occur to him to judge the American republic with Plato's *Republic* in mind, or Roosevelt's New Deal in reference to Machiavelli or Tacitus.

No one in *U.S.A.* thinks of the centuries before. It is as if history began with the sinking of the battleship *Maine* in Havana Harbor. In his sketch of La Follette, Dos Passos applies the term "lost" not only to his own generation but to the republic as well. Here again he speaks in the accents of his period, when the most talented writers, in exile and at home, tended to blame all that they disliked about America on the war of 1917–18, with the profiteering, propaganda, intolerance, and xenophobia that accompanied or followed it. But many charges Dos Passo makes in *U.S.A.* could as well have been made at the time of the suppression of the Philippine rebellion, or during the Reconstruction period after the Civil War, or even during the 1830's. Indeed, they were made, and just as emphatically, by Mark Twain, Whitman, and Emerson.

As a second-act curtain to the trilogy as a whole, *1919* concludes with a portrait of the unknown soldier—the most terrifying expression Dos Passos ever gave of his emotions about World War I and the men who made it. The bewildered lost soldier, hit by a chance shell as he tries to find his way back to his outfit, is a composite of all Dos Passos' heroes, with the working-class vagabond to the fore. There is an echo of Whitman's "Carol of Occupations" in the list of the soldier's jobs: "busboy harveststiff hogcaller boyscout champeen cornshucker of Western Kansas bellhop at the United States Hotel at Saratoga Springs office boy callboy fruiter telephone lineman longshoreman lumberjack plumber's helper." Yet he is a unique living being with all his stored experience blasted into nullity in an instant of time. "For twentyodd years intensely the nerves of the eyes the ears the palate the tongue the fingers the toes the armpits, the nerves warmfeeling under the skin charged the coiled brain with hurt sweet warm cold mine must dont saying print headlines."

What remains after the trench rats and bluebottle flies have done their work is taken to God's Country on a battleship and buried under the folds of Old Glory. For his montage Dos Passos makes a selection that contrasts with devastating irony the soldier's real life and the cynical, sentimental oratory of the official ceremonies led by President Harding.

The climax of the third volume, *The Big Money,* is a Camera Eye section on the electrocution of the anarchists Sacco and Vanzetti, found guilty six years earlier of murder during a payroll robbery. They had been arrested on the basis of rather questionable evidence during the wave of hysterical antiradicalism and fear of foreigners which was a direct consequence of the war and its propaganda. The fact that the passionate united effort of thousands of liberals had failed to save Sacco and Vanzetti convinced Dos Passos that reaction ruled the country. "All right we are two nations," the narrator concludes. "They"

have won; "we" are defeated. "They" control the politicians, newspaper editors, judges, college presidents. "America our nation has been beaten by strangers who have turned our language inside out who have taken the clean words our fathers spoke and made them slimy and foul."

In its context—coming after scenes outside the Charlestown jail in which the fictional characters Mary French and Don Stevens are beaten by the police—this Camera Eye is deeply moving. Of all Dos Passos ever wrote, it is the most eloquent statement of a militant personal commitment to a specific cause. In the light of the earlier works, we can see why the Sacco-Vanzetti case had such appeal. These were immigrants, anarchists, individualists crushed, like John Andrews, by an official juggernaut impervious to reason.

As objective political analysis, however, this Camera Eye is very confusing, especially in the terms it uses. It speaks of "the old words of the immigrants" that are "being renewed in blood and agony tonight," and of "the immigrant haters of oppression" who lie quiet in black suits in an undertaking parlor in the North End of Boston. The earlier immigrants were "our fathers," haters of oppression, creators of democracy and a language in which "words meant what they said." But at some point "our nation" was beaten by mysterious strangers who "cut down the woods for pulp and turned our pleasant cities into slums and sweated the wealth out of our people."

In the final Camera Eye, describing the visit of a delegation to terror-haunted mine country, he speaks in even more extreme language about being made to feel like a foreigner in his own country. "They" are a conquering army which has "filtered into the country unnoticed they have taken the hilltops by stealth." "They" have the "strut of the power of submachineguns sawed-offshotguns teargas and vomittinggas the power that can feed you or leave you to starve . . . we have only words against."

This conquest of the country by an identified "they," by strangers, is imaginatively exciting, but has a paranoiac quality, and is not a very precise picture of social fact. President A. Lawrence Lowell of Harvard, one of those most condemned by intellectuals for his part in the Sacco-Vanzetti case, came of an old and cultivated American family, as did Supreme Court Justice Oliver Wendell Holmes, whose refusal of a stay of execution is announced in one of the Newsreels. President Lowell, along with his sister Amy, derived his fortune from the exploitation of labor in the mills of Lawrence and Lowell, but these had sprung up before the Civil War. The great power of the House of Morgan, blamed in *1919* for the way America went to war and the way it made peace, grew from family speculations in Hartford, Connecticut, in the 1830's.

It is hard to say what Dos Passos means by "strangers." Most of his capitalists and wielders of power, both actual and fictional, have thoroughly American backgrounds. America and American standards of success have shaped them, as *U.S.A.* itself makes amply clear. The trilogy gives no adequate explanation of what went wrong and how it can be corrected, or which of the opposed elements in the American tradition are responsible for the good "we" and the bad "they." Things are amiss in the nation because the wrong "they" have taken over, and only a few brave individuals are trying to do something about it. This is why the later novels can continue to accuse in the same tone, whether the villains are capitalists, Communists, labor leaders, or New Dealers.

Dos Passos wrote social novels without sociology, without social institutions. He could show powerful individuals making secret deals, but not the corporate determination of policy within churches, universities, magazines, the Senate, or even the Communist party. Because of this inadequacy, when Dos Passos wrote introductory and concluding sketches for the 1937 one-volume *U.S.A.* he could not find a symbol that would really suggest either the country or his own vast and important work of imagination. At the beginning he lists a jumble of things or qualities, and then decides that "mostly U.S.A. is the speech of the people."

This is not borne out by the trilogy itself. Like other writers as different as Ezra Pound and Sherwood Anderson, Dos Passos speaks of the way language is being corrupted by the false commercial and political uses to which it is put. But reproducing the direct speech of common Americans is what he does least well. He gives it a very mechanical "dese-dem-dose" character with none of the delightful comedy discovered in it during the same period by Ring Lardner, Sinclair Lewis, and James Thurber, not to mention Hemingway and Fitzgerald, who could themselves be extremely witty.

The 1937 edition's final summarizing sketch, entitled "Vag," repeats exactly the situation at the end of *Manhattan Transfer*. A young man with no prospects stands at the side of a concrete road beckoning with his thumb as cars hiss past. Wants "crawl over his skin like ants." Romanticized in the earlier novels, now the vag travels hopelessly, uselessly, from nowhere to nowhere, hectored by bullying cops, his belly knotted with hunger. Overhead flies a silver transcontinental plane, occupied by men with bank accounts, thinking of "contracts, profits, vacationtrips." One of them, airsick, vomits into his carton container the steak and mushrooms he ate in New York. America is represented by two individuals with queasy stomachs. In between there is nothing but air and the names of places the plane has flown over, the vast geography of the continent.

Dos Passos expresses his most personal and nostalgic identification with the country in some of the early Camera Eye pieces. One of them poignantly re-creates the experience of hearing *The Man without a Country* read aloud. The young listener identifies the voices of the judge and naval officers with the voice of Mr. Garfield, who is reading, and feels that he himself is Philip Nolan. Tears come into his eyes when he finds himself rejected by his country and condemned to endless travel abroad. He doesn't remember whether after he dies he is brought home or buried at sea, but anyway, "I was wrapped in Old Glory." Here, in a mingling of alienation and patriotism, are the basic emotions of all Dos Passos' writing.

Though *Adventures of a Young Man* (1939) is politically symptomatic, it is a great letdown after *U.S.A.* Dos Passos had gone to Spain with Hemingway and Joris Ivens to help make a documentary film about the Civil War. His sympathies were as deeply engaged as theirs, but he withdrew because of Communist interference. Party functionaries directed by Russians had taken over in Spain, liquidating those they could not dominate. When he heard that a Spanish doctor friend had been killed by one of their firing squads, Dos Passos began to write his novel.

Only the last twenty pages of *Adventures of a Young Man* are devoted to Spain. Where Andrews in *Three Soldiers* was beaten up and imprisoned by military authority, Glenn Spotswood is shot. In both cases an isolated individual is destroyed by a machine, but in the second case the circumstances are more explicitly political. The killing is done by Communists.

Glenn Spotswood is a typical young American radical of the thirties who risks his life for striking miners and reacts violently when the Communists cold-bloodedly sacrifice the miners to other party interests. Here Dos Passos draws again on his experience in Harlan County, Kentucky, but the political arguments which were the breath of life to American intellectuals in the late thirties are treated in a very perfunctory fashion. Never much interested in leftist theory, Dos Passos is now too completely alienated to be able to re-create the highly involved quasi-theological debates that went on endlessly among and within the various factions of the left. But without these debates, in which the debaters thought they spoke for History itself, the intellectual fascination of Marxism cannot be understood.

Much of the novel, in a kind of reversion to *Streets of Night*, recounts Glenn's immature love affairs. As a student boarder he has awkward, rather amusing romances with two young married women, one Communist, one left-liberal. No matter how many love affairs Dos Passos describes—and there must be well over a hundred in his novels—the circumstances are always new, and the emotional perturbations convincing. But the *Adventures of a Young Man* holds little of the romantic joy in experience for its own sake that had countered the social negativism in *U.S.A.* Experimental techniques have been abandoned completely.

The elder Spotswood, a weak man who burdens Glenn and his older brother, Tyler, with moralistic advice, recalls in his inadequacy the father figures of earlier novels. And the talks Glenn has in Spain with anarchists are like the youthful discussion at the end of *One Man's Initiation*.

In his later book, *The Theme Is Freedom*, Dos Passos blames the defeat of the Spanish republic on a combination of communism and American neutralism. Since Russia was the only country supplying arms to the Loyalists, it could dictate policy, and it did so in an entirely divisive and self-interested way. Hemingway and George Orwell describe this death struggle directly; Dos Passos, in *Adventures of a Young Man,* devotes himself to the narrower topic of Communist factionalism in American labor defense cases. The subject had already been introduced in *The Big Money,* but as one strand in a richly woven fabric. Here it is the only social theme, and it is treated in the narrowly didactic fashion that makes us feel, in much of Dos Passos' later fiction, that we are not confronting life itself but incidents invented to illustrate a lecture.

Number One (1943), based on the career of Huey Long, is more forceful politically. Tyler Spotswood has the same relation to Chuck Crawford that Jack Burden has to Willie Stark in *All the King's Men* by Robert Penn Warren. Though Tyler is less philosophical and eloquent than Jack Burden, the vigor, unscrupulousness, and political agility of the Huey Long figure keep the action lively. But the end is disappointingly sentimental. After he has been trapped and ruined by corrupt politicians, as Glenn had been by the Communists, Tyler receives a letter which Glenn wrote before he was executed. It warns Americans not to let "them sell out too much of the for the people and by the people part of the oldtime United States way." Tyler, very drunk, has patriotic visions like those of the small boy in *U.S.A.*—"the little dome above the big dome and the clouds around and Old Glory nailed to the top of the mast . . ." He becomes obsessed with Custer's Last Stand. Custer had made a military mistake and he bravely took the consequences. Glenn made a political mistake and died bravely too. Tyler has made a moral mistake, and now he decides to take the consequences, take them on his own, beholden to nobody. In the last sentence

he walks alone "with fast strides up the windy avenue."

The Grand Design (1949) followed *Adventures of a Young Man* and *Number One* to complete a rather loose trilogy called *District of Columbia.* Though the books of *U.S.A.* had been bound together by techniques, themes, and characters, there is little of that unity here. Actually *The Grand Design* resembles the earlier trilogy more than it does its two companion novels, and can be read most satisfactorily as a separate work.

Dos Passos was clearly moved to try, as he had in writing *1919,* to capture the mood of a war in fiction. He had plenty of material from his wide travels at home and at the front during the forties. And since his two books of war reportage—*Tour of Duty* and *State of the Nation*—consisted chiefly of letting ordinary Americans speak for themselves, he had learned to listen. This improved the dialogue in *The Grand Design.* Its narrative moves swiftly, too, but the style is perfunctory, with little of the sensuous vividness of *U.S.A.*

Imperfect as the book is in execution, it has actually a rather grand design. It is one of the few novels bold enough to describe the later New Deal years in Washington. Henry Wallace, Felix Frankfurter, and other leaders appear in very transparent disguises, though in the formal disclaimer Dos Passos goes even further than is customary, declaring that each character is invented "through and through."

The novel is frankly didactic, showing the psychological and political dangers of giving great power to administrators and makers of opinion. (Glenn Spotswood's father, rather incredibly, has become a famous radio commentator.) The Communists successfully exploit this situation. Opposing them are the self-sacrificing officials Paul Graves and Millard Carroll. They try to protect local initiative, aid small farms and businesses, preserve popular control over the national administration, and, after the war breaks out, prevent aid to the U.S.S.R. from serving the Soviet drive toward world conquest. They fail, and have to leave government service.

Franklin Roosevelt in *The Grand Design* is strikingly like Woodrow Wilson in *U.S.A.* Both men are increasingly shut off from the people in their self-righteous use of the colossal power the people have handed over to them. "Wilson became the state (war is the health of the state), Washington his Versailles." Roosevelt, aging, ill, a cripple, "could play on a man like a violin. . . . We danced to his tune. Third Term. Fourth Term. Indispensable. War is a time of Caesars." In *The Theme Is Freedom* (1956) Dos Passos says, "The political act I have most regretted in my life was voting for Franklin D. Roosevelt for a third term."

In *1919*, three old men, Wilson, Clemenceau, and Lloyd George, sitting alone together, dealt out the destiny of peoples as they might have dealt out cards. Wilson was outplayed by the other two. At Teheran once again a triumvirate of old men—Roosevelt, Stalin, and Churchill—without consulting their peoples, "divided up the bloody globe and left the freedoms out. And the American People were supposed to say thank you for the century of the Common Man turned over for relocation behind barbed wire so help him God."

The endings of the three novels in *District of Columbia* show isolated individuals being bowled over by different kinds of political combinations. Their resistance to the abuse of power is a principled one, of the good old American sort, but deeply imbued with Dos Passos' sense of alienation. They are a remnant, fighting those who have taken over, seized control. There is no suggestion that they are, or could be, a saving remnant. The trilogy is quite undialectical politically. We are given no objective picture of the mixture of elements in the New Deal, the genuinely American character of the compromises it often made, and the renewal of spirit it brought to so many individuals on so many levels of society. Nowhere in this trilogy or the one which preceded it does Dos Passos offer dramatic evidence of the continuing sources of democratic strength which enabled him to feel—as his war reporting revealed—so much better about America in the Pacific in 1944 than he had in France in 1918.

To see what literary difference a fascination with religion can make—even when it is skeptical or ironic—one need only compare this purely political and moral treatment with Thomas Mann's rich mythologizing of the New Deal in the Joseph series. Dos Passos always showed remarkably little interest in theological or metaphysical questions. When he edited a selection of Tom Paine's writings, he omitted the notorious attack on Biblical Christianity in Paine's *Appeal to Reason.* He left it out not because he disagreed with Paine but because he did not feel that this was a live or relevant issue.

For the three novels published between *The Grand Design* and *Midcentury,* Dos Passos drew on autobiographical materials he had used before. Of the three, *Chosen Country* (1951) has most substance. In his parents, his war experience, his travels in the Middle East, his involvement in something like the Sacco-Vanzetti case, Jay Pignatelli is a composite of the earlier autobiographical heroes. When stirred by patriotic emotion, he is like Tyler Spotswood, or the small boy in *U.S.A.*: "the yearning of a man who might have been a man without a country (Damn the United States: I never want to hear her name again) for the country of his choice that made him feel so proud and humble when he saw the striped flag fly." The end is even more sentimental. This time no one walks off alone down a concrete road. Jay is honeymooning in a cottage by the sea. "The waves breathed in the cove. 'Husband,' she said. 'Wife,' he said. The words made them bashful. They clung together against their bashfulness. 'Today we begin,' he said, 'to make . . .' 'This wilderness our home,' she said. The risen sun over the ocean shone in their faces." The best parts of the novel, which have the same evocative magic as the high points of *U.S.A.*, are five biographies of Americans of an earlier generation.

During the writing of *Chosen Country*, Dos Passos had remarried and was living on a portion of the old family farm in Virginia. His daughter Lucy, his only child, was born in 1951. His first wife had been killed in 1947 in an automobile accident in which Dos Passos was badly injured.

In contrast to *Chosen Country, The Great Days* (1958) is thoroughly negative and bitter. Once again a book starts with its hero at the top of a gangway, but now he is a man of fifty-nine, in a belted raincoat like a Graham Greene adventurer, going to meet a much younger woman for a holiday in Cuba. A once-famous journalist, he is sick of seeing himself in print. "Every time he publishes anything the critics tear down his poor old name." All he believed important about America he had put into *Blueprint for the Future,* a title suggesting *The Prospect before Us,* in which Dos Passos had made his proposals for the future. "Nobody read it. What's the use of writing things nobody reads?"

The journalist's romance is a failure and he is robbed of three thousand dollars, his total resources. While life deteriorates in Havana, he thinks back over his past, his wife's death, his troubles with his sons, his long relationship with a government leader who—especially in the way he dies—suggests Secretary of the Navy James Forrestal. The journalist has worked with him as Tyler Spotswood had

worked with Chuck Crawford, but this official is an unselfish man who fears that the country will be outmaneuvered and destroyed by the Soviet Union. When he cannot convince others of the danger, he kills himself.

The journalist's reminiscences of the war and its aftermath are copied almost verbatim from the author's own previously published reportage. This is only one indication of Dos Passos' refusal to distance himself artistically from his material. In his uncomfortably personal tone, his emphasis on the hero's age and distinction and on the world's lack of appreciation, Dos Passos matches Hemingway's self-exposure in *Across the River and into the Trees.* He spares us one major embarrassment, though, in his realistic treatment of the love affair.

The preceding novel, *Most Likely to Succeed* (1954), is even less engaging. Many reviewers said it meant the final exhaustion of Dos Passos' talents. Its hero, a crude fellow named Jed Morris, has returned from adventures in Morocco to write proletarian dramas for the Craftsman's Theatre. After leftist politics and other troubles destroy the enterprise, the survivors move on from New York to fortune and power in Hollywood.

In both places Jed's dealings with the Communists are as confused and emotional as George F. Babbitt's with his fellow Rotarians. Though he is almost feeble-minded politically, Jed is chosen for important work by the Russian agent who directs the local party operations. When the Communists stop him in an act of human sympathy, he tries to resist, but his old comrades threaten to destroy him. He yields (lacking the courage of General Custer or Glenn Spotswood) in a scene of melodramatic humiliation.

The role of Communists in political and cultural affairs on the West Coast during this period has real historical interest because of the accusations made in later congressional inquiries. But Dos Passos is too impatient, just as he was in *Adventures of a Young Man,* to re-create the situation as it looked to some of the idealistic and extremely intelligent people involved in it. Once again, the love affairs are more convincing than the politics. Even the once popular television serial *I Led Three Lives* was a more serious study of Communist operations.

After these two minor novels, the scope and technique of *Midcentury* (1961) came as a surprise.

In style, selection, and explicitness, the biographical sketches are very like those in *U.S.A.* Labor leaders are most numerous, and Dos Passos shows his changed attitude toward military responsibility, if not toward war, by including two generals. There had been none in *1919.* The twenty-five Documentaries are soberer than the Newsreels of *U.S.A.,* with longer excerpts and more attention to science.

In the portraits, Dos Passos repeats what he had said in *District of Columbia* and *The Theme Is Freedom*: that America conducted the war and made the peace in a way that chiefly benefited the Communists. "People in America discovered that the war had been won," he writes, telling the story of Robert Oppenheimer, "not by their kind of democracy (where everybody tells everybody else what to do) but by 'people's democracy' where everybody does as he's told . . . can that be what the dogooding professors wanted?"

Robert La Follette, Jr., understood this while it was happening. "When secret agreements at Teheran, Yalta, Potsdam portended the loss of the peace young Bob tried to remind the Senate and the American people of the tragic results of the Peace of Versailles twenty-five years before." But he spoke to deaf ears, and ended his life a suicide.

Reporting the war in the Pacific, Dos Passos had felt a great life of spirit from living and talking with ordinary Americans who were tackling difficult jobs under strange circumstances and doing them well. He missed "the feeling of crazy adventure of the first world war," but he reports in *The Theme Is Freedom* that he came back with deep respect for the professionals of the army, navy, and marine corps.

His mood darkened as he reported the Nuremburg Trials. Though he spoke of the Nazi atrocities in *The Theme Is Freedom,* he gave more coverage to American misdeeds, the mass air bombings of civilians, the postwar mistreatment of the Germans, and our failure to check Russia's subjugation of many small nations formerly friendly to us. Dos Passos always had curiously little to say about naziism, perhaps because he feared communism so much more. During the war, when the Communists were busy entrenching themselves, "American liberals were too busy hating Hitler to see anything amiss." This bias makes him say in *Midcentury* that Senator Joseph McCarthy was "hounded to his grave by the same strange alliance, the same 'storm of smearing vilification and misrepresentation' that had caused the last La Follette to lose his seat in the Senate."

His mood darkened still further during the Korean war. In his *Midcentury* portrait of General Dean, the heroic prisoner, he is bitter about the younger Americans who surrendered in such numbers and behaved so shamefully while imprisoned. They were "the kids who'd been soaked in wartime prosperity while their elder brothers manned the amphibious landings and the desperate beachheads and the floating bases and the great air-strikes of World War II; raised on the gibblegabble of the radio between the family car and the corner drugstore and the Five and Ten. Nobody had ever told them anything except to get more and do less."

The very youngest generation comes off even worse. The last portrait, called "The Sinister Adolescents," sketches the short resentful life of James Dean and the commercially exploited cult his death started among teen-agers. "Kicks are big business: the sallow hucksters needle the nerves." In the final fiction narrative the disillusioned young nephew of a business leader, sounding like Holden Caulfield of *Catcher in the Rye,* tells how he started out on a spending spree with his uncle's credit card. Its title, "Tomorrow the Moon," recalls the fantastic flight which ended *The Garbage Man.*

Principally *Midcentury* is an attack on the kind of leadership given to labor unions by Harry Bridges, Dave Beck, Jimmy Hoffa, John L. Lewis, and even the Reuther brothers. Many of the incidents could have been drawn from evidence produced before Senator McClellan's Select Committee on Improper Activities in the Labor and Management Field.

Organized labor, with tough, shrewd, imperially ambitious leaders, gained power phenomenally in the favorable atmosphere of the New Deal and the war. At first, while business also prospered, no one seemed to care how this was done. Then complaints increased, and the Senate committee discovered "denial of the working man's most elementary rights, the underworld's encroachment on the world of daily bread, sluggings, shootings, embezzlement, thievery, gangups between employers and business agents, the shakedown, the syndicate, oppression, sabotage, terror." Seven sections of "Investigator's Notes" in *Midcentury* show such evidence being gathered, often from victims afraid to talk.

The longer stories are of men defeated while bucking the interests. Terry Bryant is forced out of union organizing because he won't let racketeers and politicians betray the workers. Col. Jasper Milliron is forced out of a huge milling company because he fights for a scientifically improved product. Terry Bryant finally gets his head bashed in, working for Jasper Milliron's son-in-law who is trying to save an independent taxicab company against an alliance of union gangsters, politicians, and financiers. Though the company has put up a glorious fight, it seems likely to slip into the hands of the same hissing Judge Lewin who was a party to Milliron's ouster. Lewin, who compares himself to Spinoza and Einstein, says that when his skills win him control of a corporation, "I have to consider it a problem in pure finance. I can't be bothered with what it takes or what it sells. I can't be distracted by worrying about administration, who gets fired from what job, all the grubby little lives involved. . . . I leave that sort of thing to my public relations men."

Quite separate is the life of Blackie Bowman told from a bed in a veterans' hospital. Blackie has been a Wobbly, a reader of Kropotkin, an admirer of Eugene Debs, a fighter in some of the great labor battles early in the century. By evoking Joe Hill, Centralia, and the McNamara case, Dos Passos recaptures the spirit of the Fainy McCreary and Ben Compton sequences in *U.S.A.* But the unnatural sentences in which Blackie tells his story make a far less flexible medium than the indirect discourse of *U.S.A.*

Presenting Blackie so sympathetically, Dos Passos means to show how consistent his own underlying principles have been. "It's mass organization that turns man into a louse," Blackie declares, echoing the sentiments which

John Andrews expressed at the end of *Three Soldiers.* The unions "opened up the Promised Land to dues paying members only, and then only so long as you keep your trap shut." The Communists took the hopes of mankind and shut them up in a concentration camp.

In *The Theme Is Freedom,* Dos Passos wrote that "If some of us who had seen the Abominable Snowmen, pointed out that the Communist Party was a greater danger to individual liberty than all the old power mad bankers and industrialists from hell to breakfast, we were promptly written down in the bad books as reactionaries." Radicals and liberals froze in their attitudes, and refused to see that the causes which had cost them so much could become vested interests too. The standards learned "trying to defend Sacco and Vanzetti and the Harlan miners, the Spanish republicans and a hundred other less publicized victims of oppression" must be applied impartially against threats to freedom from any quarter. The power of the bureaucrats and social engineers was far greater than that of J. P. Morgan, and equally liable to abuse.

Strangely mixing didacticism and despair, *Midcentury* attacks financiers and labor leaders with equal bitterness. Sounding at first like an illustrated editorial intended to provoke effective action against specific abuses, it shades off into old-fashioned pessimistic naturalism. Right-thinking individuals stand up for their principles, and without exception are defeated or destroyed. They have done the best they could, and the author—though he speaks out freely enough on all subjects including psychoanalysis—does not suggest how other people, perhaps working together, can do better. In the grimmest of postscripts he makes the situation seem hopeless.

Once more at the last a man trudges along a highway, though this time, his comfortable house nearby, he is walking a dog. He "drags beaten strides, drained of every thought but hatred." He declares his loathing for those who have risen to power by exploiting hatred, but his own disgust, which he permits to overwhelm all thought, goes unexamined.

The quarrel with others makes rhetoric, Yeats said; the quarrel with oneself makes art. The sole formal device which Dos Passos never revived after *U.S.A.* was the Camera Eye, with a uniquely sensitive and developing personality—his own—behind it. At the end of *Midcentury* he denounces men of power as passionately as he had cried out against the executors of Sacco and Vanzetti thirty years earlier. But there is no longer the positive passion for experience which once enabled him to live out so fully the lives of all his characters, good and bad. In *U.S.A.* he had understood the self-doomed, like Dick Savage and Charley Anderson, as well as those doomed from outside. With the weakening of this savoring of experience for its own sake came a deadening of his prose.

In his later work Dos Passos mentions good and evil frequently, and even speaks of God, but without the kind of thought which Berdiyaev and Niebuhr, Camus and Sartre, devoted during these same years to the problem of moral man in an immoral society. Dos Passos studied American history, but the character of the country eluded him because he had stopped trying to define himself as well.

Abuse of power and disrespect for the individual are not peculiar to America. The year after the war Dos Passos quoted in agreement this indignant statement from an army captain in Berlin: "With all our faults we have invented a social system by which the majority of men for the first time in human history get a break, and instead of being cocky about it we apologize."

The democratic strengths which made the captain proud are never dramatized in Dos

Passos' novels. His imagination seizes almost exclusively on lost causes, beaten men, sensitivity helpless before power. Clearly it is not America he is writing about, but the human condition. In the historical America, good as well as evil sometimes triumphs; civil liberties and democratic self-government somehow survive and grow.

Dos Passos as Quixote or Telemachus sets out on a search that could have no terminus in space. This is why his novels—thematically unresolved—so often conclude with the image of a man striding he knows not where. The inner needs of Dos Passos were mixed up with politics and patriotism in ways he never attempted fully to understand or to express. He kept blaming America for the fickleness of Dulcinea, for the many years Odysseus had to wander.

So long as his quest preserved its romantic spirit, the infusion of nostalgia and hope into politics made art possible. When romance faded, only bitter partisanship remained.

American writers have always been romantic, absorbed in experience, unwilling to master a difficult traditional wisdom. Growing old is a desperate business for them, and in the latter half of their careers they fail to find new sources of power and depth. This was notably true of the novelists of the twenties and thirties: Hemingway, Lewis, Fitzgerald, Wolfe, Anderson, Steinbeck, and O'Hara.

Dos Passos had been particularly at the mercy of changing historical moods, since he was at once their product, their chronicler, and their judge. When his own sense of alienation and historic commitment coincided—as during the writing of *U.S.A.*—with the profoundest feelings of the best minds of his generation, the result was one of the greatest works of the rich period between the wars.

Despite the weaknesses of the later novels, he gave us altogether—even more in what he implied than in what he stated—a challenging commentary on the quality of American experience. The idealism which made Dos Passos so critical of his nation is itself very American. So is the stubborn individualism and distrust of authority which led him to regard each new institutional development as a final threat to popular government. And yet the lost republic is always there to be lost again, and the leaders he attacks so bitterly are as traditionally American as his complaints against them. In ways that Dos Passos himself did not recognize, his fiction as a whole drew its strength from its subject, his chosen country.

Selected Bibliography

WORKS OF JOHN DOS PASSOS

One Man's Initiation—1917. London: Allen and Unwin, 1920.

Three Sodliers. New York: Doran, 1921.

A Pushcart at the Curb. New York: Doran, 1922.

Rosinante to the Road Again. New York: Doran, 1922.

Streets of Night. New York: Doran, 1923.

Manhattan Transfer. New York: Harper, 1925.

The Garbage Man. New York: Harper, 1926.

Orient Express. New York: Harper, 1927.

Facing the Chair: Story of the Americanization of Two Foreignborn Workmen. Boston: Sacco Vanzetti Defense Committee, 1927.

Airways, Inc. New York: Macaulay, 1928.

The 42nd Parallel. New York: Harper, 1930.

1919. New York: Harcourt, Brace, 1932.

In All Countries. New York: Harcourt, Brace, 1934.

Three Plays. New York: Harcourt, Brace, 1934. (Contains *The Garbage Man, Airways, Inc.,* and *Fortune Heights*.)

The Big Money. New York: Harcourt, Brace, 1936.

U.S.A. New York: Harcourt, Brace, 1937. (Comprises *The 42nd Parallel, 1919,* and *The Big Money,* together with the prologue "U.S.A." and the epilogue "Vag.")

Journeys between Wars. New York: Harcourt, Brace, 1938.

Adventures of a Young Man. New York: Harcourt, Brace, 1939.

The Living Thoughts of Tom Paine: Presented by John Dos Passos. New York: Longmans, Green, 1940.

The Ground We Stand On. New York: Harcourt, Brace, 1941.

Number One. Boston: Houghton Mifflin, 1943.

State of the Nation. Boston: Houghton Mifflin, 1944.

First Encounter. New York: Philosophical Library, 1945. (Reprint of *One Man's Initiation —1917,* with a new introduction by the author.)

Tour of Duty. Boston: Houghton Mifflin, 1946.

The Grand Design. Boston: Houghton Mifflin, 1949.

Life's Picture History of World War II. New York: Time, Inc., 1950.

The Prospect before Us. Boston: Houghton Mifflin, 1950.

Chosen Country. Boston: Houghton Mifflin, 1951.

District of Columbia. Boston: Houghton Mifflin, 1952. (Comprises *Adventures of a Young Man, Number One,* and *The Grand Design.*)

The Head and Heart of Thomas Jefferson. New York: Doubleday, 1954.

Most Likely to Succeed. Englewood Cliffs, N.J.: Prentice-Hall, 1954.

The Theme Is Freedom. New York: Dodd, Mead, 1956.

The Men Who Made the Nation. New York: Doubleday, 1957.

The Great Days. New York: Sagamore Press, 1958.

Prospects of a Golden Age. Englewood Cliffs, N.J.: Prentice-Hall, 1959.

Midcentury. Boston: Houghton Mifflin, 1961.

Mr. Wilson's War. New York: Doubleday, 1962.

Brazil on the Move. New York: Doubleday, 1963.

Occasions and Protests. New York: Regnery, 1964.

World in a Glass: A View of Our Century Selected from the Novels of John Dos Passos, with an introduction by Kenneth Lynn. Boston: Houghton Mifflin, 1966.

The Best Times: An Informal Memoir. New York: New American Library, 1966.

The Shackles of Power: Three Jeffersonian Decades. New York: Doubleday, 1966.

The Portugal Story. New York: Doubleday, 1969.

Easter Island. New York: Doubleday, 1971.

BIBLIOGRAPHY

Potter, Jack, *A Bibliography of John Dos Passos.* Chicago: Normandie House, 1950.

CRITICAL AND BIOGRAPHICAL STUDIES

Astre, Georges-Albert. *Thèmes et Structures dans l'oeuvre de John Dos Passos.* 2 vols. Paris: Lettres Modernes, 1956.

Belkind, Alan, ed. *Dos Passos, the Critics and the Writer's Intention.* Carbondale, Ill.: Southern Illinois University Press, 1972.

Brantley, J. D. *The Fiction of Dos Passos,* New York: Humanities Press, 1968.

Eastman, Max, and others. *John Dos Passos, An Appreciation.* New York: Prentice-Hall, 1954.

Gelfant, Blanche H. *The American City Novel.* Norman: University of Oklahoma Press, 1954. Pp. 133-74.

————. "The Search for Identity in the Novels of John Dos Passos," *PMLA,* 76:133–49 (March 1961).

Kazin, Alfred. *On Native Grounds.* New York: Reynal and Hitchcock, 1942. Pp. 341–59.

Sartre, Jean-Paul. "John Dos Passos and '1919,' " in *Literary and Philosophical Essays.* London: Rider, 1955. Pp. 88–96.

Wrenn, John H. *John Dos Passos.* New York: Twayne, 1961.

—ROBERT GORHAM DAVIS

Theodore Dreiser

1871-1945

IN ADDITION to his eight novels, Theodore Dreiser's work includes four books of short stories and sketches, four about travel, two of autobiography, one of poems, one of plays, and four, best described as miscellanies, in which he mixed science, more autobiography, politics, and social problems. But we read the rest of his writing mostly because it illumines the novels. They are his claim to greatness, and it is on them that any attempt to assess his achievement must fix attention. Current criticism tends to honor him most for *Sister Carrie* (1900) and *An American Tragedy* (1925), assigning second best either to *Jennie Gerhardt* (1911) or to the first two parts of his "Trilogy of Desire," *The Financier* (1912) and *The Titan* (1914); much less is said in praise of the third part of the trilogy, *The Stoic* (1947), or of *The Bulwark* (1946); and of *The "Genius"* (1915) more critical evil has been spoken, probably, than good. We have only recently begun to concede what the Europeans have told us for years, that the achievement these novels represent was truly a major one.

Current manuals credit Dreiser with "power" and "compassion," and they are right, just as they are right in adding that often the power is "crude" and the compassion "mawkishly sentimental." But such formulas label without explaining. The source of his originality was a trait of character: he was constitutionally unable to say he saw what he did not in fact see, what wasn't there to be seen. His drafts show him trying to restrain this gift—for example, in revising *Sister Carrie*, to avoid offending current taste he worked to make his heroine less promiscuous and less willing to be kept than he had originally conceived her—but such attempts failed because the gift was instinctive and visceral. This naive innocence of vision in his novels made a shambles of the public moral assumptions of his time.

People were supposed to be guided by conscience, but the lives he observed, including his own, were shaped by the blind, incomprehensible "forces" of nature. Everyone agreed that success came from grit, enterprise, honest industry, and clean living, but in his experience the successful were those who combined the most ruthless wheeling and dealing with great good luck. Happiness was supposed to reward deep love and devotion to one woman—with book, bell, and candle—but he learned for himself what his heroes confirm, that the woman we love today may become tomorrow's millstone. Unselfish devotion and kindness were recommended to all women, but he couldn't see that they had lightened his mother's burdens, and they bring little but grief to Jennie Gerhardt, whereas the girl who keeps her eyes open doesn't necessarily come to a bad end because she goes to bed with other women's husbands; witness Carrie Meeber. Such discoveries may strike us today as rudimentary, but the point is that in Dreiser's time no one was supposed to make them. Hence the impact of his novels.

American mores have changed so much that our cultural history seems unreal. It is hard for us to believe that the so-called Genteel Tradition was not a cynical conspiracy among an established elite to legitimize their fortunes and justify the society they headed. Thinkers like Max Weber and Thorstein Veblen have persuaded us so thoroughly that the ethic of the rising and expanding middle class was what the middle class needed to believe that we forget that millions of people did in fact believe in it as they believed in the gospel from which they thought it derived. For many readers, even so late as the Coolidge administration, Dreiser was denying the meaning of their lives.

The fairy tale doesn't report that the child who dared speak of the emperor's nakedness became a popular hero; and although the moral and religious issues that once made dispassionate discussion of Dreiser's work difficult have long since disappeared with the cant that surrounded them, our praise is too often limited to the niggardly admission that he "told the truth" about American life as he saw it. Yet a reader who believes that a characteristic function of the novel is to penetrate appearance and reveal the reality beneath is in no position to dismiss Dreiser so summarily. And if he also agrees that when the reality revealed is important ethically, socially, or culturally, the novelist who reveals it must be granted a kind of importance also, then he must concede a certain stature to Dreiser. The reality itself may be unpalatable—although this is less

likely today than when the novels were new. And we may have little taste for the ways and means Dreiser used in the revelation—as is more than likely since we have become so aware of fictional technique in the interim. The achievement isn't thereby explained away.

No one contests that Dreiser knew the kind of American life he wrote about at first hand. Few novelists have written their own experience into their novels with so little transposition, or made it so clear afterwards (see *Dawn*, 1931) that they have done so. (He had to abandon an early draft of *An American Tragedy* because he had poured so much of his youth into that of his hero as to knock the story out of proportion.) Life in America, as he knew it, was absorbing but also rough, harsh, and often nasty.

His father, John Paul, had immigrated from Mayen on the German Moselle, not far from Coblenz, and moved across the country from job to job, doing reasonably well at the weaver's trade until fire destroyed his woolen mill in Sullivan, Indiana, and he was injured by a falling beam during the rebuilding. Nothing he touched thereafter prospered long; he devoted the rest of his life to paying his debts, and retired into what the younger Dreiser considered a very superstitious and bigoted Catholicism. Responsibility for the family, which increased with dreary regularity, fell largely on Sara Maria Schänäb Dreiser, the Moravian farm girl John Paul had married on his way west. The children were Paul, the minstrel and hoofer, who changed the spelling of his last name to Dresser and wrote songs like "On the Banks of the Wabash" and "My Gal Sal"; Rome, who became an alcoholic bum; Emma; Sylvia; Mame, who like Emma got an early reputation for promiscuity and, later, ran a whorehouse; Theresa; Al; Theodore, who was born two years after the father's accident, in Terre Haute, on August 27, 1871; Ed; and Claire. With such help as she could get from the older ones as they left home, the mother dragged her brood from Sullivan, to Terre Haute, to Vincennes, back to Sullivan, to Evansville, to Warsaw (Indiana), and to Chicago, according to where chances looked best of keeping them fed, clothed, and alive. These wanderings assured Theodore an insecure childhood.

The family was never in one place long enough to establish itself, even had it had money to do so. The behavior of the older sisters rapidly earned it the kind of name that meant exclusion from the society of such rural, or semi-rural, communities. Schooling was erratic: Dreiser saw enough of parochial schools to leave him with a lifelong aversion to nuns and priests, and had one experience of a public school that was luminous by comparison. Later, one of his teachers paid his way through a year at Indiana University. He had few friends and few ways of making any. The first volume of his autobiography, *Dawn*, pictures an uncertain, rather unhappy little boy, and then a sensitive, awkward, and no happier adolescent, "on fire with sex."

His novels would be the richer for this life. His uninhibited sisters were material for *Sister Carrie* and *Jennie Gerhardt*. The weak failure of a father and the courageous, responsible, and drudging mother recur in *Jennie Gerhardt* and *An American Tragedy*. The uneasy, unhappy boy, ashamed of his parents and of the way the family lives, and deprived by birth of the pleasures other children seem born to, is embodied later in Clyde Griffiths, the hero of *An American Tragedy*. In addition to such easily recognizable patterns, the fear of poverty and failure that pervades the novels comes straight out of an underprivileged midwestern childhood.

Once he was old enough Dreiser was off to Chicago on his own, employed at first at such jobs as dishwashing in a greasy restaurant or driving a laundry wagon, but in time finding newspaper work on the *Daily Globe*, where he began what turned out to be a long and slow apprenticeship. Wherever he went more experienced hands taught him what they knew. From Chicago he moved to St. Louis and jobs on the *Republic* and the *Globe-Democrat*. Then he drifted slowly eastward, looking for a place to settle down, with stops in Grand Rapids, Toledo, Cleveland, Buffalo, and finally Pittsburgh, where he found a job on the *Dispatch*.

He was training his eye. His early pieces were not momentous journalism, but they show an alertness to the picturesque, especially as it emerges from a drab urban background. He was as fascinated by what goes on in back streets and alleys, away from the glare and glitter, as by the lives of the wealthy under the bright lights. He learned what a newspaper writer so rapidly learns: not to trust his reader's power of inference or his ability to understand what he isn't told explicitly. Less rapidly he learned the value of feeding his reader a diet of concrete facts.

In the Pittsburgh Public Library he read Balzac, who gave him an example of what the novel could be, and a model from which his own fictions would rarely depart. In *Dawn* he regrets that the discovery didn't come sooner, at Indiana University, but one wonders whether Balzac's great value for Dreiser would have been available except for the latter's own previous experience with writing. The Balzac he discovered was clearly not the visionary, "metaphysical" author of *Seraphita* and *Louis Lambert*, but rather the one most apt to teach a feature writer what to do with his material— whose long, factual, third-person narratives, told by a narrator who sees and knows everything, could be accounts of real lives in the jungle of contemporary society. Novels like *Lost Illusions* are built from accumulations of detail that sounds as if directly observed, with the flow interrupted only by essay passages in which the novelist impenitently breaks off the story to explain motives and comment on the action. Elaborate techniques are absent, or else hidden; and Balzac often appeals to contemporary scientific theory to illumine the ways of his characters. Years later, sophisticated critics like Joseph Warren Beach, mindful of the divergent ways of Balzac and James, would reproach Dreiser for being too like his master. They were entirely right in identifying the relationship: Dreiser owes far more to Balzac than to Zola or the other French naturalists, for example. But was Balzac such a bad master to adopt?

After Pittsburgh he joined his brother Paul in New York. In 1894 newspaper work was hard to find. He caught on as a "stringer" with the *World*, but found that the money paid per inch of space wouldn't keep him alive, and moved to a staff job on *Ev'ry Month*. Plainly he had become a hack, and as a hack he soon took to free-lancing articles for periodicals like *Success*—a curious publication dedicated to fostering the great American cult. His interviews with tycoons follow a required format such that one wonders why Dreiser, himself, wasn't embarrassed. The facts are that he wasn't, that material success would never cease fascinating him, and that what he learned at this time would be most useful when he came to write his novels about Frank Algernon Cowperwood.

In 1898, to his permanent chagrin, he married. Sara White was attractive, somewhat older than he, like him from the Midwest, but unlike him disposed to social conformity. Dreiser says that after his first ardor he cooled

rapidly but married her anyhow; the union was doomed from the start. They separated after a few years, but even after the separation became permanent, Sara White—"Jug," as he called her—would never consent to divorce and the marriage stayed on the books until her death. In his novels, Eugene Witla (the "genius"), Cowperwood, Clyde Griffiths, and —seen from another angle—Lester Kane in *Jennie Gerhardt*, all commit themselves to women and repent at leisure.

Meanwhile, early in 1900 he finished *Sister Carrie*. Frank Doubleday, the publisher, heeded the enthusiastic recommendation of his editorial reader, Frank Norris, to accept the manuscript. What happened next has been disputed. Dreiser's prefatory note in later editions says that Mrs. Doubleday was so shocked by the story that she urged her husband to withdraw from the contract and that when Dreiser held him to their agreement Doubleday honored it in the letter only, printing and binding the book indeed but making no effort to promote it.

Recent studies find Dreiser's account somewhat one-sided. Doubtless the Doubledays did discover that they had taken on a shocking book, and quite possibly Mrs. Doubleday was no woman to approve of Carrie Meeber, but they may also have had second thoughts about what the public would accept and buy and simply decided to cut losses. In any event, the record shows that they did publish the book and sold, in 1901–02, about 900 copies. It was, at the time, a failure.

Failure haunted, just then, this author of success stories. His marriage was going badly; he was restless and depressed; he worried about his health and even his sanity. In 1902 he got so low that his brother Paul stepped in and sent him to a rest camp operated by William Muldoon, a reconditioner of businessmen, trainer of boxers, and figure in the New York sporting world. Muldoon's rigorous discipline and some fresh air eventually got Dreiser back to a point where he could cope with life. But he left the camp only to find a job at hard, physical labor on a railroad crew, and not until late December 1903 did he return to his familiar setting—and then not as a writer but to fill a series of editorial jobs.

Successively he was on Frank Munsey's *Daily News, Smith's Magazine*, and the *Broadway Magazine*, of which he was briefly managing editor. Finding that he was better at editing than at managing, he moved in 1907 to the *Delineator*. There he was well paid, and apparently found work and surroundings congenial. When his hero, Witla, in *The "Genius"* reaches a similar point, Dreiser clearly thinks him a success. Some even feel that, if Dreiser had remained so comfortably situated, he might never have finished another novel.

But, in 1910, the mother of Miss Thelma Cudlipp objected so vehemently to Dreiser's attentions to her daughter that she packed the daughter off to Europe and got Dreiser fired from the *Delineator*. In the same year he and Sara White completed their separation. The year following he published *Jennie Gerhardt*. The next fifteen years were to be his period of incessant productivity.

After *Jennie Gerhardt* came *The Financier, The Titan, The "Genius,"* the short stories, plays, essays, one of the autobiographies, and finally in 1925, his fifty-fourth year, *An American Tragedy*. Dreiser didn't write easily, and his drafts show that he labored over the revisions. These must have been years of unremitting work. The reward wasn't, perhaps, the literary equivalent of the success he had admired, studied, speculated about, and doubted in other men, but he had reached material security, his books were read—perhaps more often read than admired—and he had become a visible public figure. He had also forced

the reading public to accept serious, grim realism.

Sister Carrie is undeniably a serious and grim story. Carrie Meeber finds life in Chicago as harsh as it was back in Wisconsin, and learns that no one cares much whether she starves on what she can earn in a factory. Money and commodities are what count, and the men she meets teach her that physical attractiveness is a commodity, fully negotiable. There is no moral conflict and she isn't bright enough to be cynical; she just exploits the one commodity she has.

She lets Charles Drouet, the salesman she meets on the train from home, set her up in an apartment. She quits him for Hurstwood, the manager of Fitzgerald and Moy's prosperous saloon, who steals his employer's funds, abandons his wife and family, and runs away with her to New York. While Hurstwood's fortunes decline, she parlays her small talent, and her good looks, into a career on the stage, and eventually cuts him loose. He goes downhill to a suicide that is literally a pauper's death, while Carrie, when last seen, is on her way to further fame and fortune.

If Dreiser had made her a calculating little vixen who stopped at nothing to get what she wanted, the story would not be half so effective. In the finished version she isn't even really promiscuous, and none of her moves toward secure ease is really planned. She moves in with Drouet because she doesn't want to go back to Wisconsin, and leaves him again because she suspects that he won't ever put through the "little deal" that would let them marry: Hurstwood has something more substantial to offer. Her conscience nags her, but never loudly enough. She drops Hurstwood, in turn, when she sees the luxuries other women enjoy. She is not even particularly shrewd.

Her men are almost as passive as she.

Drouet picks her up on the train because it isn't in him not to try to pick up a pretty girl. Having a pretty mistress, and being known to have one, flatters his vanity. But he is nowise disposed to entangle himself permanently, so that the same instinct that made her attractive to him in the first place now warns him off. Poor Hurstwood is also a creature of circumstances. His marriage has cooled, and his wife is dominating, grasping, and shrewish. Naturally—as Dreiser knew from experience—he is drawn to any girl who promises to renew his youth, and can be had. Yet he sees the attendant inconveniences, and blind luck makes his crucial decision for him: he is still not sure that he will abscond and take Carrie with him when, as he is closing his firm's safe for the night, he is tempted by the sight of so much money and takes out a sheaf of bills to fondle it; he is still listening to an inner voice telling him to put it back when the door of the safe snaps shut.

Chance plays a similar role in *An American Tragedy* when the accident the hero has planned to bring about takes place without his actually causing it. In both novels the protagonist's responsibility is incomplete; and in both what Dreiser thought of as natural "forces" push them into the situations where they are so vulnerable. Luck combines with nature to determine their fates.

One can see how Frank Doubleday may have despaired of selling *Sister Carrie* in a country where belief in moral responsibility was fundamental. Yet Dreiser was working from life. His sister Emma had come from the country to Chicago, and had formed a liaison with one L. A. Hopkins who, like Hurstwood, had stolen money so that they could run away to New York. Emma hadn't had Carrie's subsequent success, but in other respects Carrie is no more an invention than is his picture of the mean life of poverty she wants to avoid

at any cost. The life of the urban poor he knew at first hand; he had been jobless in Chicago himself and knew the skid rows of a half-dozen cities; some of the pages in *Sister Carrie* are lifted almost verbatim from Dreiser's early newspaper sketches of more or less picturesque misery. A strict moralist could condemn Carrie and Hurstwood, and also condemn Dreiser for not condemning them, but he could hardly deny the authenticity of their story.

His reading had convinced Dreiser that there must be "laws" by which the "forces" governing our lives may be seen to operate, and these laws must be open to scientific explanation. Hence a basic determinism in human affairs. Yet at the same time, we must have some degree of free will, at least a limited liberty of choice, or else life is meaningless. He pondered the dilemma for forty years without reconciling the opposites to his final satisfaction.

At this point the difference between his naturalism and that of Zola and the French is fundamental. Zola felt that he was demonstrating the applicability of established scientific law. As he had gotten it from Taine, heredity, environment, and the historical moment determine human behavior, so that he could write, case after case, the "natural history" of two interrelated families under the Second Empire. The formula was already in existence when he began writing, and was entirely familiar to his audience, so that however monumentally wrong Zola may have been in accepting it, he had the advantage of not having to explain it in his fictions. He could take it as a datum.

Dreiser is in exactly the opposite position. He is demonstrating nothing. From *Sister Carrie* to *The Stoic* he pictures life with all the faithfulness he can muster, but casts about gropingly for explanations. They are often inadequate, to a point that such notions as his theory of the "chemisms" that determine personality, or of the electricity that passes from one person in love to the other, are best taken as metaphor. And because he often seems unaware of the inadequacy, his disquisitions may strike an irritable reader as pompous ignorance.

If a naturalist is a writer who treats humans as products of nature, and nature in turn as the seat of the "forces" that shape life, and if in doing so he leaves the impression that nature means more to him than art, then Dreiser was indeed a naturalist. Taine had written that vice and virtue are chemical products like sulfuric acid and sugar; and Dreiser says in *Dawn* that with a slight change in the mixture of body chemicals his brother Paul would have been a great man. Such parallels are endless, and make the point irrefutably. But it is not from a theoretical naturalism that Dreiser's novels derive their power.

Once the reader of *Sister Carrie* has seen the characters and knows their situation, he knows what will happen. Even before Hurstwood's luck snaps shut the safe door, we are sure that he will steal the money and that from that point we shall be following the trajectories of two lives, one still climbing, the other always pointed downward. The inevitability of the outcome is in the characters themselves: Carrie will go on being Carrie, and Hurstwood has already made his own ruin. There is no tragic acceleration of events. Time, as measured by the clock and the calendar, will be inexorable.

Sister Carrie may be classified as objective realism, but beneath the surface one suspects a basic personal fantasy. In Hurstwood, but for luck, went Theodore Dreiser—and who knows how long luck will hold? Dreiser had not exorcised the memory of his unhappy, ineffectual father. Attentive students have de-

tected symptoms of fundamental insecurity even in his endless pursuit of women, believing that he was really looking for the warm protection against the consequences of failure that one woman, his mother, had once given him. The articles written for *Success* are implicit reminders that success does not exist unless its opposite exists also.

Carrie Meeber's success must be compensated by Hurstwood's decline. He must lose his investment in the saloon he has bought into in New York, must try only feebly to find other income, must sink to living on the twelve dollars a week Carrie earns as a chorus girl, must grow shabby and old before our eyes, must go from one mean job to another meaner one, and finally to wretched illness and suicide. One remembers that at that moment Dreiser was headed for a nervous breakdown of his own.

Thus his sympathy for Hurstwood—the first manifestation of his celebrated compassion—may be interpreted, and perhaps discounted, as indirect self-pity. In any event, it differentiates him at one more point from the European naturalists, whose dispassionate detachment was their hallmark. In *Sister Carrie* his pity is muted, but Dreiser is already the man who years later, when he saw the 1931 film of *An American Tragedy*, burst into tears.

Most of the perennial objections concerning technique apply as well to *Sister Carrie* as to any of Dreiser's later novels. His omniscient point of view permits him to tell us what kind of people his characters are instead of letting us see them in action and decide for ourselves. Too often he characterizes them by describing externals, as if all one needed to know about a person were revealed by his dress. Sometimes he puts a terrible strain on credibility: how, for example, can Carrie be so dumb as to want Hurstwood to marry her when she knows that he is already married? What the characters say reveals little that we do not know already; he reports the event and then what was said during the happening, so that the dialogue doesn't, as (say) Hemingway's dialogue does, advance the story.

Much of this kind of criticism boils down to saying that Dreiser was blissfully unaware, in 1900, of the prescriptions that Percy Lubbock would propose as precept, following the example of Henry James, in *The Craft of Fiction*, in 1921. Just how does it happen that a novel written without benefit of such wisdom can affect its reader so deeply? One possible answer could be that in the house of fiction there are several mansions.

Jennie Gerhardt again draws upon Dreiser's family. Jennie's father is a poor, disabled, aggressively religious (but Lutheran, not Catholic), unassimilated immigrant. A drudging mother courageously struggles to keep the family going. Jennie, as passive a character as Carrie Meeber, and not half so lucky, is modeled upon the sisters Mame and Emma.

Working with her mother in a hotel in Columbus, Jennie catches the eye of George Sylvester Brander, the junior senator from Ohio, who is moved by her sweetly simple ways and good looks. He helps her bedraggled family, overrides her father's surly objections, and says he intends to marry her. More out of gratitude than love Jennie goes to bed with him. Then, before he can make good his promise, the bad luck that besets Dreiser's protagonists intervenes: Brander dies suddenly. Jennie finds herself pregnant, has her baby secretly, and in time goes to work as a maid in an important Cleveland family.

A friend of her employers, Lester Kane, son of a rich Cincinnati manufacturer, finds her compellingly attractive, but has no intention of marriage. From love, this time, Jennie accepts a liaison and lives with Kane in Chi-

cago for a number of years. Even after he learns that the child she has been providing for is her own, Kane seems perfectly satisfied, but Jennie's peace is troubled by the disdain of neighbors who detect her status. Then Kane's father dies, and he learns that to inherit his share of the business he must end the liaison. In time Jennie persuades him that he should do so and he subsequently marries a widow of his own social status. One sorrow is heaped on another when her child dies of typhoid. And then Kane himself dies, and Jennie last appears, unrecognizable through heavy veils, following his funeral at a distance from the legitimate mourners.

This is what the poor may expect of life. In all senses but the technical, Jennie is a good woman—kind, loving, loyal: she has been helpful to an unresponsive family; she even takes in and cares for the old father who once wanted to put her out of the house; she is a good mother to her child, and devotedly faithful to Kane. The latter does not leave her in want, but otherwise her goodness has to be its own reward. Like the heroine of Flaubert's *Simple Heart*, she has loved without return.

Perhaps she is too good to be true. She learns little from experience, and, the complete opposite of Carrie Meeber, she lacks all instinct of self-protection. Her beauty and charm must be taken on faith. (They captivate Senator Brander, but thanks to Dreiser's preference for telling us about character instead of exhibiting it in action, we aren't prepared for his being swept so easily off his feet.) Poverty and bad luck don't embitter her as they do her brothers and sisters. Dreiser was probably combining certain traits of his sisters with some of his mother's in an idealized portrait. In any case, it is certain that Jennie, in his eyes, is an innocent victim of life's injustice.

Here another American myth is punctured: not only do girls like Carrie sometimes not have to atone, but sweet and kindly girls like Jennie can suffer just because they are too poor to protect themselves. Is it possible to be poor and moral, too? The question dogged Dreiser all his life. The impulses that in his later years involved him in such liberal causes as those of Tom Mooney, the Scottsboro boys, and the striking miners in Harlan, Kentucky, go back to his instinctive hatred of poverty. It seems clear that even his joining the Communist party, shortly before he died, was not based on conversion to a theory. He was not a systematic social thinker, and there is much to suggest that his espousals and allegiances were more emotional than rational. He simply disliked seeing strong people push weaker people around.

As Walter Allen insists in a famous study of English fiction, it is characteristic of the novel to protest against the abuse of power. For Dreiser as for Dickens, power and wealth are synonyms, and poverty exposes people to coercion. The poor man has fewer social and moral options: Jennie's brother Bass lands in jail for stealing coal from the railroad—but the alternative would be to let his family freeze. It is a measure of Hurstwood's degradation that he scabs in a motormen's strike because he has no other means of earning two dollars a day. Jennie has the looks and good nature to make Kane an attractive mistress, but not the culture and education to make her acceptable to him, and his family, as his wife. Very little, here or elsewhere in Dreiser's writing, is revolutionary. The word "equity," which he uses so frequently, means little more than that extremes of poverty and wealth are unfair, and that a society that tolerates them should be reformed.

Jennie Gerhardt is not, however, a social tract. Dreiser's aim is less to stir indignation than to evoke pity, and to do so simply by drawing the contours of a life. As in *Sister Carrie*, the structure of this novel is the simplest possible, following the lines of a biography. Time is again treated as rectilinear, the mere unwinding of the years. He feels no need of sophisticated craftsmanship.

He is relatively indifferent to writing in "scenes," and entirely capable of using an entire chapter to discuss what has happened earlier, without advancing the action a step. A more typical procedure starts a chapter with a discussion of a situation or the state of a character's mind; then may come the narration of a new event, perhaps followed by the dialogue that accompanied it; finally there may be summaries of the effect of the event on one or more characters. In terms hallowed by recent use, "report" often replaces "dramatization," and the "authorial voice" is persistently audible, while the "point of view" is entrusted to one character or another to suit the novelist's convenience.

It is in the discussions, where he speaks in his own voice, that Dreiser most clearly confirms the criticism that he writes "like a rhinoceros." The following, from the opening of Chapter 11 of *Jennie Gerhardt*, is not an unfair example: "It is curious that a feeling of this sort should spring up in a world whose very essence is generative, the vast process dual, and where wind, water, soil, and light alike minister to the fruition of that which is all that we are. Although the whole earth, not we alone, is moved by passions hymeneal, and everything terrestrial has come into being by the one common road, yet there is that ridiculous tendency to close the eyes and turn away the head as if there were something unclean in nature itself. 'Conceived in iniquity and born in sin,' is the unnatural interpretation put upon the process by the extreme religionist, and the world, by its silence, gives assent to a judgment so marvelously warped."

Such a mixture of circumlocution, inversion

of adjective and noun, uncertainty in vocabulary, and burdened syntax identifies the self-taught writer. Dreiser tells us that in childhood he had read whatever he could get his hands on, but the English and American romantics he goes on to mention, especially when not offset by generous amounts of the English Bible such as sustained Crane, Norris, and even Sherwood Anderson, could be bad models for a style. In addition, the son of an immigrant workman and a Moravian farm girl who learned to write from her children's copybooks can't have heard simple, idiomatic English at home. Dreiser writes an acquired language. So did Joseph Conrad, but it is one thing to write an acquired language, as Conrad did, after having mastered another in the natural way, and something quite different to write one starting as Dreiser did, so to speak, from zero.

The critical moaning over the defects in Dreiser's English can be overdone. His barbarisms are notorious, and it is quite true that he is at times embarrassed to find what Flaubert called the *mot juste*. But it will be noticed that the passages most often quoted to discredit him are those in which he speaks directly to the reader, in his own voice. At the worst they show him being overelaborate, wordy, perhaps pompous, sometimes even arch. In other words, he shared the difficulty with elevated style that characterized his generation. Even Stephen Crane was forced to fall back upon the treasury of pulpit oratory and Fourth-of-July cliché for the loftier passages of *The Red Badge of Courage*. Dreiser's style was formed in the climate of the "Cross of Gold" speech, as the least respect for historical contexts obliges us to remember. He was born too soon to belong to the generation who solved the problem of elevation by avoiding it and adopting the tones and rhythms of *Huckleberry Finn*. And even where his prose

offends he is never frivolous; his seriousness and sobriety are evident; however awkward, he means what he says.

Pity is the presiding emotion in *Jennie Gerhardt*, and the emotion is unmixed. The uncomplicated nature of his disposition toward his heroine may indeed explain why this novel should be so simple in outline and, except for the curiously blurred final chapter, so relatively rapid in the narration. On the twin patterns of success and failure, which he had adumbrated in *Sister Carrie*, his feelings were far more complex, and his subsequent novels dealing with them become correspondingly more deliberate in their pace.

Dreiser did not equate success with the mere jingling of millions. Even in his hack-writing days he had included among the specimens he interviewed for *Success* a few who, like John Burroughs, had reached the top without amassing money. In *Sister Carrie*, young Bob Ames, who speaks for Dreiser, explains to Carrie that some satisfactions are not for sale. In various novels Dreiser disdains a number of cautious, conservative, upward-bound types who devote their lives to making as much money as possible at the least possible risk. Lester Kane's brother who runs their family business, Clyde Griffiths' cousin waiting to inherit his father's factory, Orville Barnes in *The Bulwark*, with his fears that his sister's behavior will compromise his own career, are treated without sympathy. Dreiser's aversion to such fellow travelers of capitalism was total.

What interested him was the uninhibited, freewheeling paragon of unleashed energy, the "buccaneer" capable of taking whatever he wanted against any opposition. For such men success is a kind of game played as much for the mere winning as for any tangible prize. In that this figure obeys no rules but those he makes for his own convenience he has something vaguely Nietzschean about him; he also has some of the lineaments of a romantic hero, condemned to operate in the world of business.

Some critics argue that this ultimate descendant of the Romantic Outlaw appealed to Dreiser because the novelist could easily identify with him, as he had for opposite reasons with Hurstwood and as he needed to do with all his heroes. They point out that after *Jennie Gerhardt* Dreiser devoted his life to variations on the rags-to-riches formula, and view his tycoons as examples of wish fulfillment. The argument is plausible: day-dreaming has served many novelists well. But it is also true that Dreiser used the success-failure patterns for exploring character in a way that transcends the interest of success and failure in themselves.

Charles E. Yerkes had been a traction magnate who, after making and losing fortunes by manipulating the finances of street railways in Philadelphia and Chicago, had narrowly missed taking over, just before his death, the underground tube system of London. He had bounced back to relative respectability after a term in prison, had been as flamboyantly spectacular in love as in finance—he had retained a law firm to come to terms with his abandoned flames—and might also have gone down in history as a great philanthropist if death had not interrupted his public benefactions. Yet if Yerkes is remembered today it is because Dreiser took him for the model of Frank Algernon Cowperwood. He researched Yerkes' biography with great care, and the trilogy parallels it closely.

Cowperwood is not, surely, a human type found only in America, but just as surely he is one that flowered to fullest perfection in the favorable climate of the expanding American economy. He grows up around Philadelphia, exhibiting all the thrift and industry recommended by the Quaker tradition but un-

touched by the corresponding moral restraints. His eye for the main chance discovers an opening in street railway stocks, and before he is out of his twenties he is a man of substance, with wealth, a wife who is a cut above him socially, and a lovely home. But his acquisitiveness, which is the expression of his restless energy, is unsatisfied, and as his sophistication grows with his wealth he develops a knowing eye for art and women. He takes for his mistress a young and beautiful girl, Aileen Butler.

Trouble comes when a crash in the market following the Chicago fire catches him short and he is unable to cover his losses. He serves a prison term for embezzlement, and gets out, wiser and cannier but fundamentally unchanged, in time to pull together his fortunes by taking advantage of another crash—Jay Cooke's. He resolves to make himself a new life in the West.

At the beginning of *The Financier* the youthful Cowperwood stops to watch a lobster in the tank of a fish market window eat a live squid. This, he realizes as he meditates the revolting performance, must be the law of life: the lobster eats without compunction and will in turn be eaten by a creature farther up the scale. Cowperwood's subsequent career bears out the law. Dreiser does not make him a wittingly cruel man, but one whose instincts will not let him be bested in the struggle for survival. Latter-day readers may feel, more simply, that Cowperwood has the personal and social morals of a lobster, but in Dreiser's perspective he is only obeying the law of his own nature, which derives from the law of nature herself.

In *The Titan* Cowperwood has left Philadelphia for Chicago, where Aileen marries him as soon as his first wife agrees to the divorce foreshadowed at the end of *The Financier*. New operations in public utilities—first illuminating gas and then traction once again—multiply his wealth. He collects art and women, the latter recklessly: an unbroken succession of mistresses includes wives and daughters of close business associates. Aileen, whose social inadequacies have made her a liability anyhow, discovers Cowperwood's philandering, beats up one lady in a vulgar brawl, and eventually drifts into affairs of her own. Finally, knowing that they will never crack Chicago society, Cowperwood installs her in an ostentatious mansion in New York.

Meanwhile, Cowperwood's stock-watering, sharp dealing, keen foresight, and sheer nerve make him a national power. He squeezes adversaries, bribes politicians, and buys elections until he seems ready to get control of all the surface transport of Chicago. But at last he comes up against a man of principle who won't be bought, and who is the governor of Illinois. He vetoes the bill that would grant the long-term franchises Cowperwood needs to consolidate his holdings—and the legislature fails to override the veto. Although still enormously wealthy, Cowperwood has to give up Chicago as a bad job.

This "Trilogy of Desire," as Dreiser called it, was to be completed by *The Stoic*, but he delayed too long in reviving his hero, and the novel, published posthumously, can't be judged as one would judge a finished work. Cowperwood's last foray is his try to take over the London underground. Bright's disease interrupts it and he comes back to New York to die. The museum and hospital he had planned as his memorials are not realized, and a flock of legal vultures rapidly pick his fortune apart.

The Stoic further complicates the moral ambiguities of an already ambiguous story. The rapid crumbling of Cowperwood's fortune suggests that Dreiser may have come to feel that his tycoon's whole life illustrates the vanity of vanities. In addition, the concluding chapters increase the uncertainty by following Cowperwood's last mistress to India in search of a guru who can tell her the meaning of life. What the lesson is can be the object of disagreement, but this unworldly man surely does not tell her that the good way to live is identifiable with Cowperwood's.

James T. Farrell, an admirer of Dreiser and one of his literary executors, reports that Dreiser was so uncertain about *The Stoic* that he asked Farrell to read the manuscript and advise him. Farrell attributes the move to the old man's doubting the survival of his talent, and doubtless this was most likely. But one wonders also if Dreiser, in later years, hadn't lost some of his sympathy and admiration for his hero, and perhaps his taste for the values Cowperwood represents. Had he become aware of the moral ambivalence of the earlier sections of the trilogy?

For Cowperwood is, clearly, a malefactor of great wealth. In his private life he pulverizes the Decalogue—except that he does not commit murder—and gets away with doing so because he is rich. In the public sphere he is indefensible: ultimately his dividends could only come from the pockets of the little people who paid more than the ride was worth to get back and forth between home and work. But Dreiser's eye is resolutely turned away from the social damage a man like Cowperwood causes.

Dreiser sees him covered with glamour, richly dressed, handsome in a "leonine" way, and somewhat bigger than life. Cowperwood's great moment comes when, having brought a financial crisis on the other traction enterprises in Chicago, he confronts a meeting of the bankers who have supported them. Thinking that he is short of liquid funds, they tell him that they will call all his loans. But he has foreseen exactly this move, and his position is completely solid. He faces them down, saying that he is ready to pay every penny if they insist. But, he adds, if they do insist, he will "gut every bank from here to the river." Dreiser's admiration here seems complete.

One obvious explanation is that during the years after he left the *Delineator* to return to writing, Dreiser was privately trying the mantle of success for size. This is inescapable in the case of Witla, in the autobiographical *The "Genius." The Titan* and *The Financier* may be read as a portrait of the artist as a success of another kind. For Cowperwood forces his way over the "moralists and religionists" who exist to frustrate the superior individual.

Cowperwood wins through by doing what Nietzsche calls becoming what he is—as much a product of nature as the lobster in the tank. So much the worse if this makes him one of the strong who push about the little people whom Dreiser momentarily forgets. Cowperwood can't imagine failure, and doesn't know what insecurity means. When he wants a woman he takes her, and the women are happy to be taken. He refuses to let marriage become a trap, and summarily unloads women who go stale on him. Friends he doesn't need, so long as he can buy lieutenants who are faithful through self-interest or fear. What luxury he wants he simply buys. He even ends by finding the perfect mistress for an old man in beautiful, young, clever, charming, educated, and above all devoted Berenice Fleming. These are, one notes, rewards nature hadn't lavished on the novelist, but just as, but for luck, he might have been a Hurstwood, so also, with a slightly different mixture of chemicals in his body, he might have been a Cowperwood. Even a self-proclaimed realist may dream occasionally, especially if, as Dreiser does in *Dawn*, he proclaims in the same breath that he is a romanticist by temperament. Few of us feel responsible for the morality of what we dream.

A reader brought up on more recent fiction may feel the defect of the trilogy to be one of technique. As always, Dreiser is following the example of Balzac—but, in this instance, somewhat inattentively. Balzac is perfectly relentless about stopping his narrative to tell his reader in advance what the character on display is going to be like. But when Balzac arrests the narrative flow of, for example, *Le Curé de Tours* to give us the "physiology" of the Old Maid, and tell us what to expect of Sophie Gamard, Mlle Gamard goes on to do exactly what we have been made to expect. "Action is character," wrote Scott Fitzgerald in one of the notes found with the manuscript of "The Crack-Up." "A man is what he does," echo the existentialists, following André Malraux. The obligation a novelist incurs, when he discusses a character with his reader, is to remember that what the person does characterizes him also, and the two ways of characterization had better not contradict each other. Quite simply, what one sees of Cowperwood in action disagrees with Dreiser's estimate of the manner of man he is.

The fault is not completely Dreiser's, however. Cowperwood may be fascinating as a full development of the potentials of a certain human type, but culturally he is a museum piece. Little could be more foreign to us now than his world of unregulated business, and few or no inhibiting taxes, where the public conscience was less offended than overawed by the Robber Barons. The best part of the trilogy is set in the time of Dreiser's own youth; the streetcars Cowperwood modernizes are still drawn by horses and the big deals he brings off are of the gaslit, horse-car era. A time that prefers security to free enterprise must read these novels as historical fiction, or else out of interest in Dreiser.

Interest in Dreiser is necessarily the best reason for picking up *The "Genius."* Whereas the Cowperwood story is fictionalized biography—the kind of fleshing out of veritable fact with unverifiable, imagined detail that the French call *vie romancée*—the life The "Genius" puts on public display is his own. An element of self-justification, as in most such more-or-less veiled confessions, creeps in, along with a tendency to touch up and correct the details of his own destiny.

Eugene Witla grows up in a midwestern town, but in a family less desperately poor than Dreiser's and not driven to the grim expedients his own adopted. The boy is sensitive and shy, but not made to feel painfully excluded from the life around him. His sisters don't embarrass the family, and his father, though not an imposing figure, isn't a bigot or a walking ruin. In other words, Dreiser makes Eugene's a less special case than his own.

Young Witla drops out of school, where he has not done particularly well, works awhile for the town newspaper, and then moves on to Chicago. There his lessons at an art school bring out the wisp of talent he has suspected in himself, and determine his vocation. There also he has his first experiences with women, including an easygoing model at the school, and then Angela Blue, an attractive, farm-bred girl, somewhat older than he and of a deeply conventional nature. When he leaves Chicago for New York he and Angela are somewhat vaguely engaged to marry.

Marry her Eugene finally does, but after his work has begun to attract attention, and after he has come to know young women more cultivated and interesting as well as less conventional than Angela. His early success in painting continues, but he becomes weary of the conformity of his bride. Angela Blue is Sara White, of course, and the story continues to parallel Dreiser's own—though with certain adjustments—through breakdown, temporary loss of belief in his gift, increasing estrangement from his wife, a job on a magazine and dismissal from the job when he becomes too attentive to the daughter of an influential family.

The "Genius" isn't one of those novels in which the protagonist learns the difference between appearance and reality, and finally comes to some triumph of self-understanding. Witla seems no wiser about himself at the end than at the beginning. His feeling—clearly Dreiser's also—that an artistic temperament entitles him to exemption from the rules of normal decency and fairness that ordinarily govern conduct, not only in sexual behavior but in social and business activities also, is hard for the reader to share. There is something too self-centered and priggish in the callous way he terminates his liaison with the model, and not much less in his relations with Angela. One gets a feeling that where there is so much ego there should be more talent.

Dreiser wrote most of *The "Genius"* in 1911, while his mind was also occupied by Cowperwood. (His publisher of the moment advised delaying publication.) Cowperwood is as exempt from the rules as Witla, so far as actual behavior is concerned, but he asks for no special treatment beyond what he can force the world to give him. The closest he ever comes to self-righteousness is when, in *The Titan*, he tells Aileen, who has caught him red-handed, that he can't change what he is and that she had better put up with him. The quotation marks in the title of Witla's story may be ironic, but the irony isn't based on a perception that Witla's values are rather confused. As a self-portrait, *The "Genius"* is too self-indulgent.

For the satisfactions Witla wants from art are those that Cowperwood wanted from business: money, luxury, women, position, perhaps even power. On this scale, Witla's gift for painting comes perilously close to falling in the same category as Cowperwood's proficiency in watering stocks.

Outside the context of its moment, *The "Genius"* doesn't seem a particularly subversive book or one to endanger public morals. But on the eve of World War I disquieting reports were abroad that revolt against the reigning mores was sweeping such bohemias as Greenwich Village. Young-lady poets were writing poems about burning candles at both ends, and young artists, back from Paris, were full of new and alien ideas. Very naturally, Dreiser's novel came to the attention of John B. Sumner and the other custodians of virtue. Probably no novel in which sex played such an important role could have escaped, but *The "Genius"* was only the more challenging because it was so serious. Dreiser was no smart aieck to be dismissed as merely frivolous. Such a book had to be suppressed. The total effect of suppression was, of course, to advertise the novel and increase the notoriety of its author.

Thus *The "Genius"* is a modest part in the history of the conflict between Artist and Philistine, American style. Despite its defects it does reveal the awkward situation of the painter or writer—at a point in history when "alienation" had not yet become a cliché. Subtler minds than Dreiser's, from Veblen on, had made many of the same points and analyzed the causes more deeply, but no one else had made such an attempt to show what could be the consequences on an individual life.

Meanwhile the conception of art that emerges from Dreiser's discussion of Witla's work adumbrates the aesthetic of his own fictions. Witla's preferences attach him to the Ash Can school. He likes subjects suggestive of the color, roar, and rattle of the great city, such as earlier painters avoided as inherently ugly—streets on rainy nights, the clutter of crowded squares, freight yards with massive cars, glistening rails, and mighty locomotives. He goes in for strong, if not violent, color, broad and sweeping effects, and the feeling of motion and activity. In brief, as Dreiser puts it, he painted "Life." With due allowances for looseness of language, the identification of art with life is the basis for a realism from which the picturesque is not excluded. There is much talk about "the beauty of life," also, in his autobiographies, as well as the assumption that the power to feel this beauty marks the "poet." In Dreiser's literary practice this can be reduced to the statement that the observation of life as actually lived can be the source of strong emotions. The formula suggests that his realism, as he remarked himself, was romantic.

Only a romantic realist could have written *An American Tragedy*.

Critics agree generally that out of all Dreiser's novels this is the one with which we are most obliged to come to terms. It is either a literary monument or a monumental failure. Over the years readers have come to perceive that *An American Tragedy* is a shrewdly planned structure of calculated effects, that Dreiser knew what he was about, and that little if anything gets into it by chance. It is immaterial, for example, whether or not he borrowed the questions and answers of an actual courtroom dialogue for the trial of Clyde Griffiths; what is material is that the pages sound, and are meant to sound, like a transcription. They have the exact value of an account based on a stenographer's record. Either one grants the validity of the technique or one doesn't. Whichever the decision one's grounds will be ultimately aesthetic: what one wants of a novel is either life, in Dreiser's sense, or what art makes of life. Dreiser imposes the decision on us.

For years he had been collecting news

stories about young men who had tried to extricate themselves by violence from transient love affairs like his own with Sara White. He was particularly fascinated by the case of one Chester Gillette, who, back in 1906, had chosen to murder rather than marry his pregnant working-girl sweetheart. Current newspapers had followed Gillette's capture, trial, appeal, and execution industriously. A general outline of events and no little detail were there for Dreiser to appropriate.

World War I appears to have deferred the start of the writing. Like many Americans of German blood he was disturbed and uncertain of his sympathies; his participating in the debates between intellectuals that preceded the entry of the United States into the war suggests the extent of his preoccupation. He could, and did, bring together and publish collections of short stories, plays, and essays, but it is reasonable to assume that he had no stomach for undertaking a long piece of work. He waited until 1919.

The procedure could not be quite the one he had used for Yerkes-Cowperwood, since this time he needed some changes in the central character: the Gillette of the newspaprs had to be made more passive, less decisive and brutal; incident had to be manipulated so as to intensify the tragedy; the hero had to dream of success but be frustrated by nature, weakness of character, and sex.

Not that Clyde Griffiths' dream is at all complex. He is not bright enough to think out what he wants. In its elementary form, the dream consists of rising in business until you can have the money, luxuries, pleasures, and, especially, women you want—"a good time," as Clyde thinks of it; "the better things," according to Dreiser. Clyde would like to be like his uncle, who owns a factory in Lycurgus, New York, or like his cousin, who will one day inherit and meanwhile drives a car of his own.

He would like to sport about with a wealthy, glamorous girl like Sondra Finchley. For wanting nothing better than this he ends in the electric chair.

His parents are street preachers who run a "mission" in Kansas City, and who live a grubby and mean life; they are rigidly religious and dirt poor. He leaves school as soon as he can, and eventually gets a bellhop's job in a flashily luxurious hotel. The glamour he sees about him is everything home isn't. Dimly he wants something like it for himself, just as he wants to play about with the other bellhops and their girls. The fun ends abruptly when a group of them make off with a car for a joyride and manage to run down a small child. Clyde has to disappear.

The early version in which Dreiser drew so many details from his own youth had to be abandoned, but the finished text reveals all the familiar patterns of his family life. In addition to the parents, the pregnant sister, and the rest, there is especially the boy who wants something better than he has been born to. After Dreiser-Hurstwood, Dreiser-Cowperwood, and Dreiser-Witla, now comes Dreiser-Clyde—but for luck and a few chemicals.

Working in a club in Chicago, Clyde meets his father's successful brother, whom he persuades to try him in a job at the factory in Lycurgus, near Utica. In Lycurgus the Griffithses are people of standing; they do as little for this unimpressive relative as decency requires. Clyde lives in drab lodgings, works at a monotonous job, watches his young cousins and their friends from a distance, and learns how wide a gap money can create. He is desperately lonely, but determined to win acceptance.

Here the story falls into another familiar pattern. Loneliness prevails over ambition, and he begins what he intends to be a passing affair with Roberta Alden, a farm girl who has come to work in the factory. She is his reality; the dream remains one of sharing the life of the local smart set and having a girl like glittering Sondra Finchley. By the time he learns that the group is beginning to accept him because Sondra finds him interesting, he learns, also, that Roberta is pregnant.

When she insists on marriage, Clyde panics at the loss of his evaporated dream. Other expedients failing, he forms a half-baked plan of contriving an accident and lures her to a lonely lake in the Adirondacks. Actually the accident that occurs is genuine: Roberta rises in their rowboat and lurches toward Clyde; he hits her unintentionally with his camera; they overturn; a gunwale strikes her on the head and she drowns. Clyde leaves her in the water, wanders about the country awhile and then joins his rich friends at their summer resort.

His movements have been so inept that the law traces him easily to Lycurgus and back, turning up new evidence at every stop. Clyde is held for murder. An ambitious district attorney has done his work well: letters Clyde has forgotten to destroy, marked travel folders, his behavior where the couple stopped on their way to the lake, what he took with them in the rowboat, and the transparent falsehood of the story Clyde's lawyers cook up for him combine to hide the one fact that might save his life: that he had lost the will, or the nerve, to kill her before Roberta stood up in the boat. The jury finds guilt in the first degree. When both his appeal and a plea to the governor fail, Clyde is executed.

Many readers have complained that Part III of this novel, devoted to the events that follow the drowning, is too long and too painful. But given Dreiser's intention, what else was possible? As is entirely clear at the end, everything in the story is pointed, from the beginning, toward the electric chair. Clyde is caught by his family's circumstances, by his ignorance and inexperience, by his unintelligence, and

most of all by his dream of success. Roberta's pregnancy is almost an afterthought of fate. This trap is a machine, and it is of the essence that its movement should not accelerate: it needn't hurry for fear of losing its victim. It is in Part III that we realize fully how unaccidental the seeming accidents of Clyde's life have been.

Actually the trap is life itself. For some years Dreiser had been deeply interested in the work of Jacques Loeb, the physiologist whose studies of elementary forms had led him to the conclusion that any life is a simple matter of mechanics. Expose a flower to light, a chemical change takes place within the plant tissues, and the flower turns its head. Dreiser not only read Loeb's writings but also corresponded with him, and with passing time turned from the determinism of "laws" and "forces" he had learned from the nineteenth-century British toward a mechanistic position of his own. If life in a plant or a fruit fly can be explained as the functioning of a machine, then why not the more complex forms of life and ultimately the universe as a whole? Loeb himself had recommended to psychologists that they investigate the chemical bases of behavior. Years afterward Dreiser was still warmly interested in what Loeb had done. It would be hard to doubt that the theory of mechanism stirred his imagination when he was writing *An American Tragedy* and affected his basic, visceral feeling of life. Not only is Clyde Griffiths caught in a machine, he is a machine—or part of a universal one.

The paradox of *An American Tragedy* is, of course, that machines do not weep over their condition.

Henry James complains because Flaubert confided the role of "central moral consciousness" to such "mean" and uninteresting characters as Emma Bovary and Frédéric Moreau. Obviously the same criticism would apply to

Dreiser's novel—if it were indeed true that the only people with a story worth telling are those gifted with intelligence fine enough to understand the moral implications of what happens to, and around, them. Clyde Griffiths is just not morally conscious. Like most of the population of Dreiser's novels, he lives on a plane where moral alternatives aren't visible. He never perceives the tawdriness of his dream of success. In a sense, Dreiser manages to place the moral consciousness not in a character, and not in the omniscient narrator, but in the reader.

However repellent a free animal may be, in a trap it becomes an object of pity. Pity is the dominant emotion of *An American Tragedy*, not for Clyde alone, but for the mother who writes sob-sister reports of his trial so that she can earn the money to be there and goes on an improvised lecture tour to raise more money for the appeal; and for the poor, ignorant farmers who are the parents of Roberta Alden; and for Roberta herself; even for Clyde's weak, incompetent father; and for the poor, dumb victims of the American Dream, everywhere.

The nice critics who complain that to win us over Dreiser has to appeal to the morbid fascination that keeps us panting over the daily accounts of sensational murder trials may not be wholly wrong. But what has Clyde done worse than believe, however dumbly, what he has been taught to believe, and want what he was supposed to want: money, the kind of life one sees more fortunate people lead, love? His excuse is Eugene Witla's: if American life had proposed less sleazy satisfactions he would have aimed at them. In this sense only, the title of this novel is appropriate. Clyde may be cubits beneath the stature of a tragic hero, but America is big enough to have a tragic flaw.

Judged by standards much less stringent than we apply to James and Flaubert, *An American Tragedy* is not a well-made novel. Even H. L.

Mencken, for years Dreiser's stout supporter—and who had vigorously defended the earlier novels—found it too long and rambling. It puts many burdens on its reader; the dialogue is awkward; the pace is slow. In contrast, the other great American novel whose hero is killed by his dream of success is written in neatly constructed scenes, and has Nick Carraway in it to judge it for us and to tell Jay Gatsby that he is finer than the Buchanans. But one doesn't finish *The Great Gatsby* with sorrow in one's heart. Neatness may not be the ultimate criterion.

Actually, Dreiser's craftsmanship is of a higher order than his critics willingly admit. His basic procedure has to be situational irony, since so much of the effect depends on the reader's understanding better than the characters do what is happening to them. Hence the value of a structure of parallel incidents: the pregnancy of Clyde's sister in the early part and Roberta's pregnancy; the accidental death of the child the joyriders run down and the accident on the lake; the similar scenes with which the novel opens and closes, with the Griffiths family out evangelizing on the sidewalk. Such examples can be multiplied indefinitely. Other ironies are produced by Clyde's wrong estimates of people: his models among the bellhops in Kansas City, whom he takes for experienced men of the world, the reader recognizes as uncouth louts; the uncle he considers a tycoon is in truth a timid small-town businessman somewhat overawed by big-city surroundings; Sondra, his dream woman, actually expresses the full content of her mind in the most repulsive baby talk. For the sake of irony Dreiser is even willing to stretch credibility severely: the farmer from whom Clyde asks directions when he is out driving with his rich friends turns out to be the father of Roberta. With these he devises parallels of language and echoes, such that his reader is reminded of earlier incidents when he learns of later ones, which create something like a fabric of constant cross-reference. How carefully Dreiser planned his work must be obvious. A novel about confused characters, as one critic has said of this one, is not necessarily a confused novel.

At fifty-five, Dreiser had become a public figure. His attitude toward any matter of general interest became news. He had never been one to avoid exposure. The essays of *A Traveler at Forty* (1913), the miscellany called *Hey Rub-a-Dub-Dub* (1920) and *A Book about Myself* (1922) had exhibited his personality, directly or indirectly, from various angles. Now *Dawn* revealed the story of his youth, with great frankness and occasional charm, but also with perceptible self-indulgence. Over the years he had inclined increasingly toward socialism—which may be why society seems more clearly at fault in *An American Tragedy* than in the earlier novels—and he now became repeatedly involved in conspicuous liberal causes.

Few seem to have found his personality a winning one. He made heavy demands on his friends and was easily hurt by them, even when they had been as generous as Arthur Henry and H. L. Mencken. Dreiser and Henry had met in Toledo, where the latter was on the staff of the *Blade*, and the friendship had blossomed rapidly. Henry invited Dreiser and Sara to spend the summer of 1899 in Maumee, where, with Henry's encouragement, Dreiser began *Sister Carrie*. Henry helped revise the manuscript; scholars even believe that some of the holograph is in his hand. Later he aided Dreiser to find work in New York and advised him in his dealings with Doubleday. Relations remained warm until 1904, when Dreiser spent part of his vacation as Henry's guest on an island in Long Island Sound. Henry was between marriages, and Dreiser may not have

taken to the new lady. Whatever the cause, he became an awkward companion and put a grave strain on his welcome. Henry, doubtless annoyed, made him a character in a novel, *An Island Holiday*; Dreiser recognized the unflattering portrait and the friendship ended for all time.

With Mencken his relationship lasted longer—from 1907 until Mencken reviewed *An American Tragedy*—and the rift between them was later patched up, but the pattern is similar. The men corresponded cordially for years. Mencken was generous with advice and helpful with ideas. He praised Dreiser's books privately and in print, and stormed at the critics who neglected them. But one unfavorable review was enough to cancel everything. As still other friends, like the British publisher Grant Richards, had learned, the kinder one was to Dreiser the easier it was to wound him.

His stands on foreign affairs were timed as if he wanted them to be unpopular: he delayed condemning the Nazis until after his countrymen had done so almost unanimously; he persisted in trying to join the Communist party—which rejected his applications so long as Earl Browder had a say in its affairs—years after the Russo-German nonaggression pact of 1939 had disabused American liberals about the idealism of the Kremlin. Even favorable critics thought him wrongheaded.

Abstract thinking had never been his forte. His year at Indiana University had not taught him to read critically. He never learned to distinguish science from pseudo-science. Students detect echoes of Herbert Spencer, for example, in his novels, mixed with fragments of psychological theory according to which dwelling on pleasant or unpleasant thoughts induces the formation of corresponding "anastates" and "katastates" in the psyche. This he had culled from the writings of a certain Elmer Gates, who practiced "psychology and psychurgy" in

Chevy Chase, Maryland. As he grew older his respect for science seems only to have increased, but what he said about it only added to his reputation for confused thinking.

The truth was that he had grown old. His friends were dying off. His own health was failing. He was no longer sure of the quality of what he wrote. Yet, almost despite himself, he would finish *The Stoic* and *The Bulwark*.

The story of *The Bulwark* had been in his mind since 1912, when a Pennsylvania Quaker girl, Miss Anna Tatum, had told him about her father's grief over his children's departure from the strict Quaker faith. He had drafted occasional bits of it, but invariably put the drafts aside to work on more pressing subjects. Now in old age he took it up again, turning out a novel that may betray some loss of powers—it is briefer and less loaded with detail than his other stories—but is probably the neatest and sharpest of his novels, and humanly a very touching one.

Solon Barnes is a Quaker and follower of the Inner Light who comes from humble beginnings on a Maine farm to a place of power in a Philadelphia bank, acquiring without loss to his integrity the wife, home, family, and respect of his neighbors which are the fruits of success. A crisis comes when he sees that his colleagues in the bank are following practices which, while within the law, remind confirmed readers of Dreiser of Cowperwood. Guided by the Inner Light, and firm in his principles, he resigns from the bank and retires to his family. But the very principles that have sustained him have opened a gulf between him and his children. He has been rigid and authoritarian. One daughter, embittered by her physical homeliness, finds what satisfaction she can in being an assistant to a professor of psychology at Llewellyn College for Women. The other, like Miss Tatum, abandons the quiet Quaker life for the bohemia of Greenwich Village. His

son Orville turns into one of those cautiously conservative success seekers Dreiser could never abide. His second son, caught in an escapade that results in the death of a girl, commits suicide in jail. Then his beloved wife, who has stood by him through everything, dies. Seeing how old he is and in what wavering health, and how much he needs them, his daughters come home to be with him—and discover that he has become a man at peace. He has learned to accept his virtues and his faults in humility. When he dies the Quakers call him the Bulwark of their faith.

On one of his last walks through his rural property, Barnes comes on a small puff adder which, in its fright, rises up like a small cobra. He talks quietly to the tiny snake and it relaxes. Later it slithers fearlessly away across the toe of one of his shoes. The old man is deeply stirred, as his daughters see when he tells them of what happened. Barnes, and Dreiser, have moved out of the world of Frank Cowperwood and his lobster into one where the ultimate verity is not that each order of life preys on the one below it. Life does live on life, he muses as he watches an insect eat a leaf, but this must be part of a universal plan—an order in another sense, corresponding to the feeling of order within him.

That Dreiser's mind dwelt much on such ultimately religious questions in his last years would be clear in any case from the concluding pages of *The Stoic*, where Berenice listens to the teaching of the guru. But whereas in that novel the pages come as a puzzling intrusion, *The Bulwark* is something very rare, especially in American literature—a religious novel of impressive dignity and power.

Thematically, the materials of *The Bulwark* are not new: the family that becomes oppressive, the effect on the children of the father's religious inflexibility, the conflict of moral systems, the meaning of success and the values that constitute it. Three of the children also renew character types that are already familiar. But Dreiser has reversed or displaced his values. Material success is no longer a synonym for success in life. Peace of mind, internal harmony, and love are prime satisfactions. The role of the family is not necessarily to frustrate. Nothing can stop the changes brought by passing time, but time itself can bring the understanding that certain fundamental virtues survive.

On December 28, 1945, Dreiser himself died.

Published a year after his death, *The Bulwark* did little to change critical opinion. It was an old man's book, and perhaps a book for old men. And his voice came from a remote past.

Broad sectors of American criticism had resisted him for years. The "New Humanists" of the teens and twenties had deplored what they called his "determinist naturalism" and kept up a defense of established morality that frightened off several publishers besides Doubleday. The James revival of the thirties had attached supreme value to the kind of novel Dreiser was least able to write. His old-fashioned technique didn't lend itself to the vivisection of the "New Criticism." The metropolitan "Liberal Intellectuals" had small patience with a novelist who, they held, wrote poorly because he thought poorly. In the two decades between *An American Tragedy* and *The Bulwark*, a generation of technicians like Faulkner, Hemingway, and Fitzgerald had changed ideas about what could be done with the novel as a form. The increasing trend away from realism, beginning at the end of World War II, probably predisposed younger critics to see Dreiser's novels only as vast accumulations of detail, undigested and unformed by any controlling imagination.

The resistance had never been unanimous, of course. From early on there had been Mencken. V. L. Parrington had admired Dreiser, as is evident from an unfinished chapter in the last volume of his influential *Main Currents in American Thought*. Even when Dreiser's stock was at its lowest, the thoughtful and independent Alfred Kazin broke through the clichés of critical disapproval to do him justice in *On Native Grounds* and again in introductions to the reprints of several of the novels. F. O. Matthiessen, after writing luminously about the Jameses, undertook to write a monograph which would offer a balanced view of Dreiser and, indeed, does so, even though left incomplete by Matthiessen's death. And most recently, Robert Penn Warren, with the combined authority of an eminent novelist and a respected critic, marked Dreiser's centennial with his *Homage to Theodore Dreiser*. It should be added that practicing novelists, from Frank Norris to Scott Fitzgerald, James T. Farrell, John Dos Passos, Saul Bellow, and now Warren, have always been more generous in praise of Dreiser than have their critic contemporaries.

It would be gratifying to report that at long last Dreiser had had his due. But is this the truth? The case may be that, after the years that have elapsed, only those who value his work write about him, while the rest care too little to break silence. Even today the Dreiser monument in Terre Haute commemorates not the novelist but the brother who wrote "On the Banks of the Wabash" and "My Gal Sal." As one English student of America, Marcus Cunliffe, remarks in his brief history of American writing, Dreiser remains a special problem for American readers.

Yet he upset the dictum of Henry James, that American life is too thinly textured and culturally unvaried to support the novel, and showed, indirectly, that James was merely indicating the limits of the novel of manners. He shared with Edgar Lee Masters and Sherwood Anderson the somewhat elegiac feeling that even the anonymous, average—or perhaps sub-average—American had his own poignant and significant story. The everyday ordinariness of his people makes his so-called naturalism very different from that of Frank Norris. Norris' notion of naturalism emphasized the abnormal character—Vandover, McTeague—treated in realistic detail but seen through the sensibility of the romantic, and thus infallibly as material for melodrama. Dreiser's people have absolutely nothing of "the beast within," and are not monsters: no Dreiser character, for example, has the innate malevolence of S. Behrman, whose ominous shadow darkens the action of *The Octopus*. For Dreiser, human affairs are always of human size, even when they involve the "Titan," Frank Cowperwood. What happens to the people in his novels could happen to anyone.

Consequently he brought our naturalistic novel into closer similarity to European realism than to the theory-bound oeuvre of Zola. For all of Dreiser's interest in science, science has nothing directly to do with the interest of his stories. The physical environments of his characters aren't animal habitats in the biological sense so much as human situations. As he was deeply aware, himself, he looks back to Balzac.

Yet his achievement is different in nature from Balzac's. Dreiser's novels don't attempt to picture a society or account for the way it works. If he was aware of the broad variety of human types that constitute a world, he made no attempt to represent the variety in his books. Even the most indulgent of his adherents must admit that the secondary figures derive their interest less from what they are than from their relationships to the principals. Pushing the similarity with Balzac too far ob-

scures the basic fact that Dreiser was a master of case histories.

Failure to draw some such distinction has led European readers to assume not only that these cases are typically American, and fully representative of American life, but also that there is little more to American life than what they represent. Marxist critics in particular have used Dreiser's novels as a stick for beating their effigy of American capitalism, holding capitalism responsible for the monotonous cultural poverty to which the novels testify. In the eyes of no few serious students of American literature in the European universities, who forget that when Dreiser finally had some free money, after *An American Tragedy,* he found little better to do with it than play the stock market, he figures among "the artisans of revolt."

Granting that a constant concern with money is an identifying trait of realistic fiction everywhere, Dreiser's realism is set apart by the exclusiveness of the concern. His perspective on life is relentlessly economic: even the artist, Witla, struggles for economic status, and this is true of the rest of his characters whether they concentrate on amassing fortunes or on staying out of the almshouse. Apart from sex, they have few other occupations; they rarely play or indulge in any other gratuitous activity; leisure, to occupy or be bored with, seems foreign to their natures—as indeed does the notion of enjoyment.

The perspective could not but be conditioned by his own experience of life. By birth he belonged to the disadvantaged; in a family that had left an old culture behind without acquiring a new one, and in a rural area, his chances of getting a broader view were small. Nor could such education as he got help greatly. The point is often made that he was among the first American writers whose perspective wasn't that of the East Coast and whose blood wasn't that of the "old stock." This is partly true at best, and perhaps misleading to boot; what is surely relevant is that he grew up in cultural and financial poverty. He tells in *Dawn* of having been sent home from school because the weather was getting cold and he had no shoes.

On this point again he contrasts sharply with Norris, who looks poverty in the eye nowhere in his novels. Vandover loses some inherited wealth, but because of an advancing pathological condition; McTeague's rage for gold is again pathological; the people forced off their ranches are threatened by pauperdom, but we see only two of them suffer its effects, and only briefly, at the very end. At the age when he undertook serious writing, Norris had lived comfortably in London and Paris, and studied at Berkeley and Harvard; Dreiser, at the same age, had barely made it from Terre Haute and Chicago to New York.

By consensus, his most durable novels are those of which he knew the subjects most intimately: *Sister Carrie, Jennie Gerhardt, An American Tragedy.* Obviously he was just as familiar with the materials of *The "Genius,"* but in this instance the distance between author and subject is wrong. Few critics maintain that the Cowperwood trilogy is of the same quality; one sees so much of Cowperwood, over so many years, and in situations that can't help being repetitious, that unless one shares Dreiser's curiosity about the techniques of fast dealing his hero becomes somewhat too predictable and thus monotonous.

Taken together, these novels don't offer a picture *of* American life so much as pictures *from* American life. The most successful focus on people who start at a disadvantage in the universal competition of a society that substitutes a theoretical social mobility for class distinctions. In this matter of subject Dreiser was not innovating, of course: at least sporadi-

cally, the realists of the nineties, especially Crane and Norris, had recognized the interest of such lives as an area for fiction to explore. Dreiser's originality is that, as a native of the area, he could write about life in it without sounding as if he had gone on a slumming expedition. It was in this that he set the example to be followed by the realists of the years between the publication of *An American Tragedy* and World War II—Steinbeck, Farrell, Dos Passos, and the others.

What made him unpopular for a long time was also what made him the kind of novelist he was, that naive innocence of vision that made him report what he saw rather than what he was supposed to see. Good and bad were words; what counted in reality was strength or weakness. Free will was a word; people as he saw them were helpless against external "forces." Morality was a word; the observable reality was nature. He could not resolve such dilemmas, but he could, and did, refuse to sweep them away. Europeans have been trying to tell us that this kind of novelist should command more than perfunctory respect.

Selected Bibliography

WORKS OF THEODORE DREISER

Sister Carrie. New York: Doubleday, Page, 1900.
Jennie Gerhardt. New York: Harper, 1911.
The Financier. New York: Harper, 1912.
A Traveler at Forty. New York: Century, 1913.
The Titan. New York: John Lane, 1914.
The "Genius." New York: John Lane, 1915.
Plays of the Natural and Supernatural. New York: John Lane, 1916.
A Hoosier Holiday. New York: John Lane, 1916.

Free and Other Stories. New York: Boni and Liveright, 1918.

The Hand of the Potter. New York: Boni and Liveright, 1918.

Twelve Men. New York: Boni and Liveright, 1919.

Hey Rub-a-Dub-Dub. New York: Boni and Liveright, 1920.

A Book about Myself. New York: Boni and Liveright, 1922. (Republished as *Newspaper Days.* New York: Horace Liveright, 1931.)

The Color of a Great City. New York: Boni and Liveright, 1923.

An American Tragedy. 2 vols. New York: Horace Liveright, 1925.

Moods Cadenced and Declaimed. New York: Boni and Liveright, 1926.

Chains: Lesser Novels and Stories. New York: Boni and Liveright, 1927.

Dreiser Looks at Russia. New York: Horace Liveright, 1928.

A Gallery of Women. New York: Horace Liveright, 1929.

Dawn. New York: Horace Liveright, 1931.

Tragic America. New York: Horace Liveright, 1931.

America Is Worth Saving. New York: Modern Age Books, 1941.

The Bulwark. Garden City, N.Y.: Doubleday, 1946.

The Stoic. Garden City, N.Y.: Doubleday, 1947.

CRITICAL AND BIOGRAPHICAL STUDIES

Beach, Joseph Warren. *The Twentieth-Century Novel: Studies in Technique.* New York: Appleton-Century-Crofts, 1932. Pp. 321–31.

Campbell, Louise, ed. *Letters to Louise.* Philadelphia: University of Pennsylvania Press, 1959.

Cargill, Oscar. *Intellectual America: Ideas on the March.* New York: Macmillan, 1941. Pp. 107–128.

Elias, Robert H. *Theodore Dreiser: Apostle of Nature.* New York: Knopf, 1949. (Emended edition, Ithaca, N.Y.: Cornell University Press, 1970.)

————, ed. *Letters of Theodore Dreiser.* 3 vols. Philadelphia: University of Pennsylvania Press, 1959.

Geismar, Maxwell. *Rebels and Ancestors.* Boston: Houghton Mifflin, 1953. Pp. 287–379.

Hicks, Granville. *The Great Tradition.* New York: Macmillan, 1933. Pp. 226–37.

Kazin, Alfred. *On Native Grounds.* New York: Reynal and Hitchcock, 1942. Pp. 78–91.

————, and Charles Shapiro. *The Stature of Theodore Dreiser.* Bloomington: Indiana University Press, 1965.

Lehan, Richard. *Theodore Dreiser, His World and His Novels.* Carbondale: Southern Illinois University Press, 1969.

Matthiessen, F. O. *Theodore Dreiser.* New York: William Sloane Associates, 1951.

Moers, Ellen. *Two Dreisers.* New York: Viking Press, 1969.

Shapiro, Charles. *Theodore Dreiser: Our Bitter Patriot.* Carbondale: Southern Illinois University Press, 1962.

Spiller, Robert E., and others. *Literary History of the United States.* Revised edition, New York: Macmillan, 1953. Pp. 1197–1208.

Swanberg, W. A. *Dreiser.* New York: Scribners, 1965.

Walcutt, Charles C. *American Literary Naturalism, a Divided Stream.* Minneapolis: University of Minnesota Press, 1956. Pp. 180–221.

Warren, Robert Penn. *Homage to Theodore Dreiser, August 27, 1871–December 28, 1945, on the Centennial of His Birth.* New York: Random House, 1971.

—*W. M. FROHOCK*

Richard Eberhart

1904-

ANYONE surveying the developments in American poetry during the last four decades and noting the emergence of a new and powerfully equipped generation of poets in the period between the middle 1930's and the close of World War II must be attracted immediately by the figure of Richard Eberhart. Born in 1904 at Austin, Minnesota, he is the oldest of three senior poets (the other two are Stanley Kunitz and the late Theodore Roethke) who broke ground for that generation, which also includes Robert Lowell, the late John Berryman, and Karl Shapiro. But recognition has come to him, as it has to Kunitz and Roethke, slowly and belatedly. Together with them Eberhart explores the possibilities of a personal lyricism enclosing a broad spectrum of human experience and boldly testing the forms and language for articulating what imagination gives and intuition seizes. Dispensing for the most part with the device of the persona or fictional speaker so profitably employed by Eliot, Pound, and Stevens, and lacking any inclination to commit themselves to systematic frameworks of ideas or to build private mythologies to support the imaginative interpretation of experience, these three poets and the others of their generation openly engage the material of their work in fresh, dramatic, and often original ways.

While certain general affinities may be traced among these poets when they are viewed in the perspective of the literary historian, it is not the intention here to look for them. Indeed the individual achievement of a writer such as Eberhart can be seriously distorted if examined through the odd lenses of similarities and relationships, for he has found a prominent place in the generation of which I have been speaking only by traveling an independent route and appearing from a different direction than his contemporaries. In background and youthful experience, in many of the artistic and intellectual influences that contrived to shape his thought and poetry, Eberhart needs to be sharply distinguished from most other American poets of his approximate age. Not easily classifiable, he continues over the years to stand out as a highly individual, sometimes even slightly eccentric poet who is unswervingly dedicated to the life of the imagination and the craft of poetry.

Eberhart studied for a year at the University of Minnesota, then attended Dartmouth, where he received his B.A. in 1926. When he was only eighteen his mother contracted cancer of the lung and suffered a "nine-month birth of death through utmost pain" which he "witnessed intimately" and which became a turning point in his life. Subsequently he wrote that this terrible ordeal was the probable cause of his selection of a poet's career, and in fact his mother's illness and premature death appear several times in poems as well as in one of the verse plays.

Before resuming his studies in England, Eberhart journeyed to the Orient as a steamer hand. In 1929 he was awarded a B.A., in 1933 an M.A. from St. John's College, Cambridge. While at Cambridge he was exposed to the teaching of I. A. Richards and F. R. Leavis; two young poets, Kathleen Raine and William Empson, were students there at the same time. Eberhart read thoroughly the then excitingly new and radical poetry of Gerard Manley Hopkins (whose work did not become available until after World War I), T. S. Eliot, D. H. Lawrence, and other pioneer modernists, but he must have devoted himself equally to the writings of Shakespeare, Donne, Wordsworth, Coleridge, and Shelley. The influence of some of these poets shows, naturally enough, in his earliest verse.

From this milieu, rather than an American one, Eberhart launched himself as a poet. His first book, *A Bravery of Earth* (1930), was published in a year which the author spent tutoring the son of King Prajadhipok of Siam—an exotic beginning for a lifetime of service as a teacher of literature and of poetic accomplishment of a high order. From 1933 until 1941 he taught at St. Mark's School, Southboro, Massachusetts, where he met Robert Lowell, then a pupil. During the war Eberhart acted as a naval gunnery officer and instructor, a role which prompted several of his fiercest and most dramatic poems, and afterwards returned to teaching, with a six-year interlude in the business world. Since 1956 he has been a professor of English and Poet in Residence at Dartmouth College, and has spent a term as Consultant in Poetry at the Library of Congress. His *Collected Poems 1930–1960* was honored with the Bollingen Prize.

Eberhart's poems set themselves in a curiously singular relationship to established canons of modern poetic practice, which they seldom heed. These poems treat philosophical themes abstractly; their method is frequently deductive rather than inductive, as Philip Booth has persuasively argued; they rely much of the time on inspiration, in the poet's own words, "burst into life spontaneously," during a period in which critical opinion emphasizes careful craftsmanship, the poem as a discovered but also a *made* object; as a final impertinence they are apt to level undisguised moral judgments while still fighting shy of dogma and firmly insisting on the ultimate mysteriousness of existence, the impenetrable heart of reality. In his handling of words Eberhart may be playful and witty, as in this excerpt from a speech in "Triptych," a play for voices:

Shallow? Then air is shallow,
Through which we see to heaven.
Shallow? Then water is shallow,
Of which we are composed.
Shallow? Then morning's atmosphere,
Lakes, rivers, rills and streams
Are shallow. What is your jealous depth
But layers and layers of shallows?

Or to take one of many possible examples, this from "The Recapitulation," he can be austere and reflective:

Not through the rational mind,
But by elation coming to me
Sometimes, I am sure
Death is but a door.

Or he can express, with the impatience of anger and disgust, his judgment of the inhumane folly of men in conflict, as in "At the End of War":

For they cannot think straight, or remember
    what they said,
Cannot keep their word,
Or realize how soon they will be dead,
Nor distinguish between verities
Who lust over presences,
Nor be faithful
Who are wrathful,
Nor escape animal passion
With cross-bow, slit-trench, Napalm bomb,
    atom bomb.

Or at the opposite end of his emotional range he can become purely lyrical:

> Cover me over, clover;
> Cover me over, grass.
> The mellow day is over
> And there is night to pass.

These passages give a mere sampling of the variety of moods to be found in Eberhart's writing and the language he uses to evoke them. It ought also to be remarked in passing that sometimes emotional pressure or the love of wit exceeds the poet's control and discrimination with consequent faults in diction, tone, and rhythm; but that seems a small price to pay for many successes and for a recognizably original voice. Eberhart's notion of poetic creation, of the act of composition, and of the operations of the poet's mind, all of them so intimately connected with what he conceives to be his essential artistic task, makes him vulnerable to these dangers as well as leading him to an abundance of fine poems. In the following pages we will examine briefly this poetic theory and some of the work which is its concrete manifestation.

To start with, Eberhart thinks of the poem as being, at its highest level, inspirational in origin, an idea which, if not critically popular in our century, has managed to survive as a legacy of the Romantics and has received confirmation in varying degrees by modern poets as different as Rainer Maria Rilke, D. H. Lawrence, Herbert Read, and Robert Graves. Of course it is doubtful that any of these poets would say *each* of his poems arrived in its entirety, bursting upon the mind in a moment of trance-like vision or imaginative possession, nor would Eberhart himself make such a claim; yet all of them could point to some of their best work as originating in luminous instances of this sort. In a response to comments in a recent symposium on one of his own poems Eberhart refers to and quotes Plato's *Ion*. He designates several of his pieces "as coming under this [Platonic] theory of creation": namely " 'Now Is the Air Made of Chiming Balls,' " " 'If I Could Only Live at the Pitch That Is Near Madness,' " "1934," " 'Go to the Shine That's on a Tree,' " and "Only in the Dream." Several others, including "The Groundhog," "Maze," "For a Lamb," and " 'In a Hard Intellectual Light,' " are also cited but are "less purely" the result, in the words of Plato's dialogue, of "falling under the power of music and meter," of being "inspired and possessed." Eberhart does not, however, stop with these disclosures; he goes on to remark how he "grew up in the convictions of ambiguity, ambivalence, and irony as central to poetry and cannot rationally accept Plato's last words 'when [the poet] has not attained to this state, he is powerless and is unable to utter his oracles.' " Thus poems which are *given in their totality* are few and far between, the product of rare occasions of unalloyed inspiration.

Nonetheless the infrequency of poems dictated with no necessity for alteration does not preclude another kind of inspiration at work in the rest of Eberhart's poetry. This second type of inspiration likewise derives from moments of special perceptiveness and extraordinary sensitivity, in short, moments of revelation; but the difference from the first, or higher, inspirational experience lies in the fact that now the dictation is less complete and must be augmented by the poet's conscious efforts. In this case the poem does not come, as it were, gratuitously, and he tries to grasp in an order of language as much as he can of a fleeting intuition before it vanishes. Eberhart's "Notes on Poetry" offers further explanations: "A poet does what he can do. Poetry is dynamic, Protean. In the rigors of composition it seems to me that the poet's mind is a filament, informed with the irrational vitality of energy as it was discovered in our time in quantum mechanics. The quanta may shoot off any way. (You breathe in maybe God.) If you dislike the word inspiration, say then that the poet in a creative state of mind is in a state different from that of his ordinary or logical state. This leads on not to automatic writing, but to some mysterious power latent within him which illuminates his being so that his perceptions are more than ordinarily available for use, and that in such moments he has the ability to establish feelings, ideas and perceptions which are communicable in potential degree and with some pleasure."

Whatever may be felt about the applicability of the analogy with modern physics this passage holds up as one of the best of several statements Eberhart has written insisting upon the poet's unusual condition of attentiveness and receptivity immediately preceding a seizure of creative activity. The validity of his account rests on its experimental nature, for it is quite without theoretical pretensions and simply essays a description at first hand of what happens to Eberhart when he writes a poem. Yet the passage does more than tell us generally how many of his poems come about; we will find on reading through the body of Eberhart's

work that the observations here have an additional relevance both to its formal aspects and to its themes. A sense of the processes of his art is indispensable for a full understanding and appreciation of what it attempts.

In view of these procedures in poetic composition, sketched here rather hastily, it should not be surprising to the reader that the primary qualities he notices in Eberhart probably will be spontaneity and the immediate presence of, involvement with, a particular experience. Even *A Bravery of Earth,* which is a book-length autobiographical poem, achieves such effects, though as a whole it is not very satisfactory. Like many initial endeavors with a long poem this one is packed with everything that has seemed important in the writer's life thus far. The book divides into two parts, the first of which, opening with a lovely lyric section, forms a kind of allegory of the self from innocence to experience, from the natural life and the free enjoyment of the senses through the acquaintance with love to the discovery of reason and the shocking knowledge of death. Too often the poet loses himself and control over his material in the currents of his strong but conflicting emotions. Yet the movement of the poem, in spite of its awkwardness and confusion (interspersed with fine, compelling passages), and as Peter Thorslev has said, its obvious indebtedness to Wordsworth, carries the reader along at a rapid pace and impresses on him a sensation of the vital flow of living experience, even if that experience is not always adequately directed and defined. Of course this sort of sensation belongs to literature generally, but in Eberhart's case, as no doubt in others, it makes special claims on our consideration and endows his poetry with uncommon energy and drama.

Of his long poem Eberhart has retained only three rather brief portions for inclusion in his *Collected Poems,* and the best of these is a lyric prologue which I quote in part as evidence of already estimable gifts:

> This fevers me, this sun on green,
> On grass glowing, this young spring.
> The secret hallowing is come,
> Regenerate sudden incarnation,
> Mystery made visible
> In growth, yet subtly veiled in all,
> Ununderstandable in grass,
> In flowers, and in the human heart,
> This lyric mortal loveliness,
> This earth breathing, and the sun.

In the second half of the poem Eberhart continues his autobiographical narrative but now shifts from the lyrical account of his affective inner life to a detailed picture of the external world, of person and place as he meets them on his global voyage, working aboard a steamer. This transition from inner to outer focus at last brings about the completion of a pattern in the poet's existence:

> Into the first awareness trembling,
> Girded with mortality;
> Into the second awareness plunging,
> Impaled upon mentality;
> Into the third awareness coming
> To understand in men's action
> Mankind's desire and destiny,
> Youth lies buried and man stands up
> In a bravery of earth.

Looking back on these lines from the poem's conclusion with the advantage of time one is apt to think that while they round off nicely the author's formal intentions here, the three types of awareness he distinguishes are not, as it seems, easily succeeded in later poems by a point of view unhindered by their troubling presence. In fact "mortality," "mentality," and "men's actions" may be said to become Eberhart's chief themes throughout his career. For our purposes we might better read the end of *A Bravery of Earth* as an announcement of things to come, of thematic resources yet to be tapped. With the publication of *Reading the Spirit* (1937) these resources are opened and the long phase of this poet's genuine accomplishment, extending to his newest collection, *Shifts of Being* (1968), begins. With few exceptions he confines himself after his first book to the short or medium-length poem, kinds more suited to the alternatively meditative and intuitive character of his imagination. Poems of these proportions can more readily approximate to the flashes of perception which usually initiate them. As we know, for Eberhart the poet's primary obligation is to voice the truth disclosed by a specific experience with all the force of the revelation itself, and so it is a note of immediacy or urgency that his poetry most often, if not always, strikes.

Reading the Spirit still contains traces of its author's deep attachment to Wordsworth, coupled with some evidence of Hopkins' influence, in "Four Lakes' Days," and indeed Eberhart has a love for nature, for land- and seascape, that associates him with these two English poets, though he rapidly develops his own manner of treating it. Most apparent in this second book, however, is not a feeling for nature but a terrible intensity of vision, a radical, piercing insight into psychic and spiritual processes reminiscent of Blake, which was hardly to be predicted on the basis of *A Bravery of Earth.* Themes we noted in that poem are now embodied in the dramatic presentation of experiences at once peculiarly individual and clearly universal.

"Maze," for example, starts out as a pastoral poem in which we expect to find a fundamental harmony of man with nature elaborated:

I have a tree in my arm,
There are two hounds in my feet,
The earth can do me no harm
And the lake of my eyes is sweet.

The unity proclaimed in this stanza is, nonetheless, of short duration; not only has a fire destroyed the tree and a lack of blood starved the hounds but questions of "will" and "a human mind that has bounds" interrupt what was obviously a mode of existence from which intellectual calculation was quite absent. In the third stanza disruption is completed by a more pointed questioning which is answered in oracular fashion in the fourth:

It is man did it, man,
Who imagined imagination,
And he did what man can,
He uncreated creation.

This leads to a concluding stanza which is an ironic version of the poem's beginning:

There is no tree in my arm,
I have no hounds in my feet,
The earth can soothe me and harm,
And the lake of my eyes is a cheat.

Undoubtedly the reader will have several ways of interpreting various details in this poem, but puzzling as some things may seem we can be fairly certain of what has been taking place. In archetypal or symbolic terms the poem recounts a fall from innocence, wholeness, and a sort of grace into a state of experience, characterized by the intrusion of self-consciousness, inquisitiveness, and intellectual activity. The maze of the title is what reality becomes after the breakup of the original unity: there the individual, driven by will, relentlessly seeks knowledge.

This theme of "mentality," to use Eberhart's word from *A Bravery of Earth,* appears regularly in his poetry, often in connection with different experiences of knowing. One early poem, "Request for Offering," pursues the theme in a strictly allegorical manner through the figures of a "baleful lion" and "the virgin pap/ Of the white world." If seen as showing ferocious intellect poised to attack the beautiful mystery of the cosmos the poem makes sense; it also suggests a violation or rape, so that the intended assault takes on a more specific moral cast. But the poem's direction is halted abruptly in the fourth stanza, where the lion's attack meets a surprising resistance:

Amaze your eyes now, hard
Is the marble pap of the world
And the baleful lion regard
With the claws of the paw curled.

The next, and final, stanza merely repeats the first one, which utters the "request" for the sacrifice or "offering," the implication being that it will probably be made again and again but that the impenetrability of the world will remain secure.

Another poem, " 'If I Could Only Live at the Pitch That Is Near Madness,' " from Eberhart's third book, *Song and Idea* (1942), examines the same fall from innocence and the unified life into knowledge that we saw in "Maze," but here the emphasis on perception —the childish vision as the clearest and most discerning one—is pronounced. The first two stanzas belong to a tradition in modern poetry, reaching from Blake through Rimbaud to E. E. Cummings and Dylan Thomas, which equates the child's intensity of vision with a hallucinated perception liberated from routine habits of mind that impose a conventional method of looking at the world without ever seeing it:

If I could only live at the pitch that is near
    madness

When everything is as it was in my childhood
Violent, vivid, and of infinite possibility:
That the sun and the moon broke over my
     head.

Then I cast time out of the trees and fields,
Then I stood immaculate in the Ego;
Then I eyed the world with all delight,
Reality was the perfection of my sight.

In this instance of enlightenment the visible universe discloses its hidden energies, time is overcome, and selfhood is enjoyed in all of its pristine innocence and completeness. We know from the poem's beginning that this vision does not survive as a constant mode of seeing and experiencing reality; only at extraordinary moments, when the individual approaches the sheer unreason and heightened consciousness of madness, will that kind of perceiving be reawakened. Stanza three makes plain the fact that "the race of mankind" cannot countenance a world where "fields and trees" have "a way of being themselves," and so the child is required to supply "a moral answer" for his vision, to learn the adult's distinction between good and evil, to share the adult's burden of guilt, with disastrous results:

I gave the moral answer and I died
And into a realm of complexity came
Where nothing is possible but necessity
And the truth wailing there like a red babe.

The poem ends, then, in a confirmation of human misery and torment, in a divided, fateful state very much like the confused one with which "Maze" finishes. The "moral answer" brings evil into the child's universe, shattering his unified, positive view. The point should be stressed that the fall from simple harmony with creation and the loss of the vision which is so essential a part of it appears quite unavoidable. As it does for T. S. Eliot, Edwin

Muir, Kathleen Raine, and a number of other modern poets, the lapse from grace and wholeness in the child has for Eberhart metaphysical and religious implications prior to any merely psychological effects, though these are not always set forth in specifically Christian terms. Yet the English poet and critic Michael Roberts in his introduction to *Reading the Spirit* remarked that Eberhart's poetry "represents the Western, Christian, Aristotelian view of life against the Oriental and Plotinic view; its music is alert and energetic rather than mellifluous and drowsy; and the delight at which it aims is the delight of intense mental and physical activity, and not of passivity and disembodied ecstasy." This description is quite accurate; only in some of his later poems, of which more presently, does Eberhart contradict it.

Man's fallen condition, his inner disunity, as we have seen it represented in these poems certainly furnishes the poet with a basis for his ambivalent role with regard to his intuitions and for the tension which so often obtains between them. In an autobiographical sketch for *Twentieth Century Authors,* Eberhart calls himself a "dualist" and a "relativist" rather than a "dogmatist." The poet needs to adopt a "sitting on the fence attitude" which "allows him to escape whole decades of intellectual error, while it provides radical use of the deepest subjective states of mind toward vision felt as absolute when experienced." What he trusts is the intuition or perception which comes from the poetic imagination and the sudden unique truth it extends. Such intuitions occasionally conflict with one another, but that is because they emerge from the opposing forces operating in man's divided state. In "Notes on Poetry" Eberhart says: "Divisive man can know unity only at death (or so he can speculate), and he cannot know what kind of unity that is. He lives in continuous struggle with his imperfection and the imperfection of life. If one were only conscious of harmony, there would be no need to write." The relativism of Eberhart therefore consists in a submission to the dictates of each imaginative experience as it takes hold of him without concern for its close agreement with other experiences or with any pre-existing structure of ideas: in Wallace Stevens' words, "The poem is the cry of its occasion." Consequently, while poems might seem to challenge each other in attitude, such apparent inconsistencies should not obscure the poet's larger purpose, which is his endeavor through "vision felt as absolute when experienced" to attain to what deep if partial truths, what glimpses and approximations of a transcendent and, from a limited human position, unfathomable unity he can.

"The Skier and the Mountain," included in *Undercliff* (1953), is a poem about the difficulties of reaching any firm and final plane of reality, of opening up a clear route of access to the supernatural; it is only one of many poems in which Eberhart proceeds toward the extremes of his "mentality" theme, moving into regions of divinity on the "elusive" and tricky waves of the imagination. Though the visionary events of the poem occur in the midst of a day's skiing, the first line prepares us for them by introducing spiritual realities before physical ones:

The gods are too airy: feathery as the snow
When its consistency is just the imagination's,
I recognize, but also in an airy, gauzy way
That it will capture me, I will never capture it.
The imagination is too elusive, too like me.
The gods are the airiness of my spirit.
I have dreamed upon them tiptop dreams,
Yet they elude me, like the next step on the ski.
I pole along, push upward, I see the summit,
Yet the snow on which I glide is treachery.

The gods are too airy. It is their elusive nature
I in my intellectual pride have wished to know.

We begin with "the gods," and snow, summit, and skis may strike the reader as obvious metaphorical devices used to support Eberhart's speculations on the life and activity of the imagination rather than substantial things in their own right. Up to a point that interpretation is correct, but only so far as the first stanza is concerned; the second stanza incarnates the actual experience of vision, which took place sometime in the past during a skiing expedition. Thus Eberhart has reversed the temporal order in the poem, perhaps to underline its reflective character: stanza one, composed in the present tense (with hints of the past: "I have thought I knew what I was doing"), contains meditations prompted by the experience recounted in stanza two, which is written in the past tense. To get at the center of the poet's thought here we must also confront this experience:

I saw an old country god of the mountain,
Far up, leaning out of the summit mist,
Born beyond time, and wise beyond our
    wisdom.
He was beside an old, gnarled trunk of a tree
Blasted by the winds. Stones outcropped the
    snow,
There where the summit was bare, or would
    be bare.
I thought him a dream-like creature, a god
    beyond evil,
And thought to speak of the portent of my
    time,
To broach some ultimate question. No bird
Flew in this flying mist. As I raised my voice
To shape the matters of the intellect
And integrate the spirit, the old, wise god,
Natural to the place, positive and free,
Vanished as he had been supernatural dream.
I was astonished by his absence, deprived

Of the astonishment of his presence, standing
In a reverie of the deepest mist, cloud and
    snow,
Solitary on the mountain slope: the vision
    gone,
Even as the vision came. This was then the
    gods' meaning,
That they leave us in our true humanity,
Elusive, shadowy gods of our detachment,
Who lead us to the summits, and keep their
    secrets.

The first half of the poem is devoted to affirming the impossibility of coming into close contact with "the gods," who are not only independent beings but are also identified with the ethereal nature of the poet's own spirit. Eberhart recognizes how his "intellectual pride" wishes rationally to conquer and explain these puzzling deities, but the single means of approach is through the imagination, itself an elusive instrument. In fact the "soaring" of the imagination leads to the poet's realization that he is "the captured actor, the taken one" of the gods, and he knows finally that he is "their imagination, lost to self and to will." At the stanza's end pride has melted to "humility."

Stanza two, as we have seen, concentrates on the vision and pursuit of a god. The incident, haunting in the detail Eberhart has given it, provides matter for the more abstract thinking done in the previous stanza and demonstrates the ultimate failure to establish direct relations between man and the divine. Will and reason may be thwarted, but the last lines tell us something important all the same. The gods will not lift us from our "true humanity," Eberhart says there, and this notion serves to enforce his interpretation of the human estate as a fallen, disharmonious one. Yet the gods do compel us "to the summits," stirring our latent fascination for a higher plane of

reality while remaining forever mysterious. Whether we assume them to be projections of the poet's imagination or find them to be forms of the supernatural, these gods, by their enigmatic attractions, urge us toward "our detachment," by which I take Eberhart to mean the release and free exercise of the spirit in its quest for enduring truth.

But Eberhart never intends that a quest of this sort shall lose itself in regions where earthly, human nature is alien or forsaken: "the saving grace of a poem may light the reader likewise out of some darkness," he writes in "Notes on Poetry," "and art is essentially social." In "The Goal of Intellectual Man" from *Song and Idea*, one of his poems about the artist's responsibilities, he defines the object of the quest. The "intellectual man," by which term he certainly designates the poet in the broadest sense, seeks "To bring down out of uncreated light/Illumination to our night," that is, he can aim at a visionary knowledge through the imagination, a knowledge which reflects divinity. The "uncreated light" of the first stanza and the "fire" of the second are both used here and elsewhere as traditionally representative symbols for God or Ultimate Being (see also, for example, the poems "The Incomparable Light" and "A Meditation"). Quite clearly, however, the poet does not wish to possess this divine fire for himself, nor does he desire the annihilation of his own human identity in an absolute. Unlike Prometheus, he does not defy the deity. His "goal" is not, either, a deathly "imageless place,"

But it is human love, love
Concrete, specific, in a natural move
Gathering goodness, it is free
In the blood as in the mind's harmony,

It is love discoverable here
Difficult, dangerous, pure, clear,

The truth of the positive hour
Composing all of human power.

Love, as Eberhart employs the word here, includes compassion, understanding, a respect for the inviolability of the individual person, an awareness of the abundant beauty of the natural world and all its creatures, the relationship between man and woman, but this true center of feeling and value must encounter inevitably in his work as in his life the strongest opposition. The chief forces of that opposition manifest themselves in those poems which fall under the two other thematic headings mentioned earlier: "mortality" and "men's actions."

Death readily captures prominence as the most obvious opponent to Eberhart's values, and, not surprisingly, we shall see that it blends into the theme of human behavior. Mortality constantly occupies the poet's mind from *A Bravery of Earth* on. Some of this concern stems from the profoundly disturbing experience of his mother's untimely death and her long, agonizing battle against it. While the signs of that terrible initiation never disappear entirely from the poetry, the shocking confrontation with death puts Eberhart in the way of a variety of imaginative considerations of mortality, of the sundering of spirit from body, the separation of the dead from the living. Occasionally he uses a dead animal as an object to draw his mind into meditation on the fate of all creatures. In "For a Lamb" the analogies with man are not stated, but they hardly need suggesting. At the beginning the poet comes upon the carcass of "a putrid lamb,/Propped with daisies"; the juxtaposition of the mutilated physical body and the indifferent serenity of nature fixes the paradoxical mood of the poem. With the start of the second stanza Eberhart asks a pointed question, the answers to which, if we can call

them that, are provokingly ambiguous and end the piece:

Where's the lamb? whose tender plaint
Said all for the mute breezes.
Say he's in the wind somewhere,
Say, there's a lamb in the daisies.

The question is really that perennial one we ask when faced with the still, emptied body we once knew so full of life: where has that life, that vital being, gone? Eberhart gives us no certain or comforting reply. First he is boldly crude and spiritual at the same time, for in locating the lamb in the wind he is referring both to the offensive stench of the disemboweled carcass which hovers in the air and to the traditional identification of the life principle or spirit with the element of air or the wind. Yet in the final line he withdraws from these subtleties to the only sure answer: the lamb is *there*, he is *that* dead heap lying in the grass and flowers; beyond such facts we cannot go. We should not, however, accept this poem as proof of a settled conviction on the poet's part; we have to remember his avowed artistic method of expressing a subjective intuition as it occurs. Poems "become what one was at the moment of composition."

"The Groundhog," included in the same volume, *Reading the Spirit*, with the elegiac "For a Lamb," also focuses on a dead carcass, but here there is an intense visualization, an elaboration of physical detail and of the poet's response to it, that are missing from the other, much briefer poem. These qualities put it in a line of descent from Baudelaire's terrifying poem "Une Charogne." In the present piece Eberhart finds the groundhog's body lying "amid the golden fields" of June; his accidental discovery resembles that of "For a Lamb." From then on, however, the poem gathers its own very potent dramatic strengths. Drama springs from the tension generated between observing poet and observed object over a considerable period of time, a period marking the gradual disintegration and, at last, the total disappearance of the groundhog's carcass. Watching this process of decay with an extraordinary but very human fascination, the poet leaves us only faintly aware of the transitions in time from one visit to the field to the next; we seem almost to be witnessing the entire decomposition, so intently is the imagination brought to bear upon the actual details of change and their implications. Though the facts of violent death are presented bluntly in "For a Lamb," they are set forth in an objective, ironical manner which is in distinct contrast to the mode of presentation in "The Groundhog." The poet's reaction to the corpse now is instantaneous; he appears startled not merely by what he has unexpectedly found but also by a piercing realization of its significance for himself as a creature: "Dead lay he; my senses shook,/And mind outshot our naked frailty."

Aroused by what he sees, the poet obsessively decides to investigate further the relentless progress of destruction:

There lowly in the vigorous summer
His form began its senseless change,
And made my senses waver dim
Seeing nature ferocious in him.
Inspecting close his maggots' might
And seething cauldron of his being,
Half with loathing, half with a strange love,
I poked him with an angry stick.
The fever arose, became a flame
And Vigour circumscribed the skies,
Immense energy in the sun,
And through my frame a sunless trembling.
My stick had done nor good nor harm.

The aggressive gesture with the stick stirs the maggots to a fury of activity; but the poet is suddenly exposed to an awakening still more frightening, for the seething energy about the corpse releases in him an almost hallucinatory sensation of nature's all-consuming power which brings in its wake a fearful comprehension of the precariousness of his own personal existence. In spite of his terror Eberhart's fascination is hypnotic and complete; he stays rooted to the spot, "watching the object, as before." At length the efforts to calm himself, to master the curious "passion of the blood" aroused in him by the awful vision of decomposition, fail, and he kneels, "praying for joy in the sight of decay." The dark and fiery god of nature, the pantheistic "Vigour," has won his submission.

In the space of the next two lines several months pass; the season turns to autumn and the poet "strict of eye" revisits the groundhog, "the sap gone out" of it and only "the bony sodden hulk" remaining. His attitude has likewise altered, his passionate response becomes a slightly aloof thoughtfulness:

But the year had lost its meaning,
And in intellectual chains
I lost both love and loathing,
Mured up in the wall of wisdom.

Eberhart implies in this passage that the first jolting vision of disintegration has robbed the year and its seasons of their sense—that is, the rhythm and pattern of time in his perception of them dissolve into chaos—and has deprived him of his feelings: his whole being is now subordinate to the shattering knowledge of death and reabsorption by nature's thriving energies. "Wisdom," as Eberhart applies the word in this poem, consists in knowing death and guilt; it signifies the knowledge discussed earlier as integral to the descent from innocence to experience. On this occasion the same kind of knowledge is equally crippling because it traps the poet in his intellect, a life-denying bondage.

Two more returns to the scene of the

groundhog's death, one in the following summer, the other three years later, occur before the poem's climactic finish. The first of these summer days, "massive and burning, full of life," recalls the previous June, the time of the poet's discovery, but the atmosphere of the day contrasts noticeably with the barren appearance of the animal's remains when Eberhart has again "chanced upon the spot" (the word "chanced" suggests that while his original encounter with the dead groundhog imposed upon him a heavy burden of knowledge not readily disposed of, he may still have forgotten the object which was its cause until he found it once more during a walk):

> There was only a little hair left,
> And bones bleaching in the sunlight
> Beautiful as architecture;
> I watched them like a geometer,
> And cut a walking stick from a birch.

The bones retain hardly a semblance of the flesh and blood they once structured; Eberhart scrutinizes them dispassionately as he would something formally pleasing but nevertheless coldly abstract. Around him nature hums and blazes with renewed vitality and with an abundance whose price is death and anonymity.

Perhaps it is this dreadful combination, the loss of life and the loss of any indication that a particular life was ever lived, which hastens Eberhart to a resurgence of emotion at the end. After three years "there is no sign of the groundhog," though the poet stays standing in the midst of a "whirling summer," nature's eternal return. He cannot avoid feeling the life drying up in him as it has done in that animal carcass; the terrible human message of his experience breaks in waves upon his consciousness: how long is memory, how can civilization or individual achievement finally endure?

> I stood there in the whirling summer,
> My hand capped a withered heart,
> And thought of China and of Greece,
> Of Alexander in his tent;
> Of Montaigne in his tower,
> Of Saint Theresa in her wild lament.

To the emotional outburst of these last lines Eberhart has no counterbalance of reasoned explanation, nor can he satisfy himself as Yeats does in "Lapis Lazuli" and elsewhere with a pose of desperate Nietzschean gaiety at the spectacle of civilizations collapsing and being replaced: such theoretical apparatus is alien to his poetry. Death holds a central, unquestioned position in his imagination, and its relationship to the endless cycle of nature remains visible throughout his work. Even in a recent poem, "Sea Burial from the Cruiser *Reve*" included in *The Quarry*, dispersal into and assimilation by the elements seem quite appropriate for someone who originated with them. As Bernard Engel tells us, backed by a letter from the poet, "the poem refers . . . to the burial of a cousin . . . its details of cruising and flowers are literally true."

> She is now water and air,
> Who was earth and fire.
>
> *Reve* we throttled down
> Between Blake's Point and Western Isle,
>
> Then, oh, then, at the last hour,
> The first hour of her new inheritance,
>
> We strewed her ashes over the waters,
> We gave her the bright sinking
>
> Of unimaginable aftermaths,
> We followed her dispersed spirit
>
> As children with a careless flick of wrist
> Cast on the surface of the sea
>
> New-cut flowers. Deeper down,
> In the heavy blue of the water,

Slowly the white mass of her reduced bones
Waved, as a flag, from the enclosing depths.

She is now water and air,
Who was earth and fire.

Eberhart's artistic interest in this relationship of death and nature does not always show itself with the dramatic power of "The Groundhog" but can be lyrical and elegiac, as the lines above prove. So far each of the poems we have looked at keeps the treatment of death to the material and historical levels and refuses to venture beyond them. On such a basis death appears absolute, but that is merely a partial view, easily contradicted by our previous examination of poems directed toward experience of a visionary or mystical order.

Death never really loses its essential strangeness of appeal for Eberhart, and in a number of poems he does attempt imaginatively to trespass its shadowy, indefinite boundaries. In "Grave Piece" and " 'Imagining How It Would Be to Be Dead' " he tries, as Dylan Thomas does in certain of his early poems, to envisage his own dissolution. The concluding lines of both pieces leave the poet poised on the threshold of a spiritual reality, but before he arrives at that stage it is necessary for him to participate through a moment of vivid imaginative possession in the process of decay imposed by death. The earliest of the two poems, "Grave Piece," from *Song and Idea*, is somewhat encumbered by the influence of Hopkins, Blake, and Empson, though the authenticity of perception cannot be denied.

There in the vasy tomb of bone-green icicles,
And gelid grasses of cold bruise to touch;
Of looking roots, night agate eyed . . .

This excruciating process ends with a liberating and transcendent vision in which the poet sees growing "A crystal Tear/Whose centre is

spiritual love." The second poem, collected in *Burr Oaks* (1947), has that unabashed directness of speech that is so compelling a feature of Eberhart's work. In this poem the imagined death consists of an expansion and transformation of self dominated by one element, air, and from the outset it is presented as a desirable rather than a difficult or terrifying series of events. The weight of time, consciousness of which comes as a consequence of the fall from innocence and the disappearance of the child's vision, is thrown off as the body itself disperses into the air and the omnipresent nature of that element is enjoyed:

I lost my head, and could not hold
Either my hands together or my heart
But was so sentient a being
I seemed to break time apart
And thus became all things air can touch
Or could touch could it touch all things,
And this was an embrace most dear,
Final, complete, a flying without wings.

The concluding lines clarify the release into a further dimension of spiritual reality, but the poem halts at the frontiers, so to speak, of what is felt yet stays unseen and intangible. Eberhart must rest content to point the direction in which his experience has taken him, for language too has its limits and is attached to the world of things:

From being bound to one poor skull,
And that surrounded by one earth,
And the earth in one universe forced,
And that chained to some larger gear,
I was the air, I was the air,
And then I pressed on eye and cheek
The sightless hinges of eternity
That make the whole world creak.

The poem "A Meditation," published in *Song and Idea*, does, however, project itself daringly beyond the borders of mortal existence; in form it is the monologue of a dead man who addresses a living person through his skull, probably discovered by the latter in some ancient ruin or graveyard, though such details are irrelevant to the piece. While it is not stated, we understand that the individual who holds the skull wishes it could yield up its secrets to him. But true to what we have already remarked about Eberhart's attitudes the emphasis of the monologue falls on life, on what should be found there before it vanishes, rather than on any secrets which the dead can disclose:

I cannot get back, cannot reach or yearn back,
Nor summon love enough, nor the intellectual
      care—
Being dead, you talk as if I had spirit at all—
To come back to you and tell you who I am.

He places the responsibility for prophesying on his listener, who is still among the living, who is yet "full of imagination" and can create images beyond himself: oracular and speculative activities "can only be talked of by men," for those ideas belong exclusively to earthly existence. The speaker lightly chides the living man for his intellectual labors and their remoteness from the truth, then offers him a *memento mori* in the repeated line: "Life blows like the wind away."

   As the poem proceeds and the speaker stresses the perennial "wish" of man "to know /What it is all about, meaning and moral dimension," we are brought nearer to a glimpse of supernatural reality. This revelation is comprised mostly of warnings about the utter difference between the human estate and the pure life of the spirit existing in a region completely foreign to earthly experience. A total transformation apparently separates the two realms of being, and the mortal flesh shrinks from this frightening change, as the voice of the dead speaker declares:

You would withdraw in horror at my secret.
You would not want to know, your long-
      lashed eyes aglare,
Of the cold absolute blankness and fate of
      death,
Of the depths of being beyond all words to
      say,
Of your profound or of the world's destiny,
Of the mind of God, rising like a mighty fire
Pure and calm beyond all mortal instances
Magnificent, eternal, Everlasting, sweet and
      mild.

In this passage, with its visionary perception, we find once again the confirmation of Eberhart's fundamental religiousness. His convictions are often tested and shaken by tragic or brutal circumstances, by agonies of doubt and questioning; nevertheless they hold firm against these storms of experience, touchstones of belief to which the poet continues to return. The lasting riddle of death and of man's situation afterwards is no further unveiled than we have seen; the stanza below enunciates the obligation to live out the human span in human terms. The difficult but "simple truth" is

That you are to be man, that is, to be human,
You are imperfect, will never know perfection,
You must strive, but the goal will recede
      forever,
That you must do what the great poets and
      sages say,
Obeying scripture even in the rotten times . . .

Of course death will close out each life and let it "blow like the wind away." In the final stanza the speaker explains the value of his listener's "solemn meditation" on mortality as an enterprise that should lead him back to "seek among [his] fellow creatures whatever is good in life." As before, Eberhart directs the results of spiritual vision to the conditions of existence in *this* world.

The utilization of visionary or mystical experience to illuminate life here and now, and, more particularly, the emphatic sounding of moral imperatives in the concluding portions of "A Meditation" bring that poem near in spirit to the third category of Eberhart's work: "men's actions." I have indicated how he frequently and unashamedly adopts the role of moralist and critic, a role usually disowned in theory by modern poets but one very evident in their practice. Eberhart's best-known works as a moralist are, rightfully, his war poems, surely among the finest and most outspoken pieces of that variety in American literature, but his achievement in other areas should not be neglected: his judgments of contemporary society also merit our consideration.

If some authors of excellent poems about World War II—John Ciardi or James Dickey, for example—write from actual combat experience and from the point of view of the airman totally immersed in war or in the military life, Eberhart chooses the transcendent, objective role of the prophet or seer-poet who envisages the conflict in terms of moral absolutes and of all humanity. War looked at from this position is a cosmic event drawing into play the larger forces of good and evil in the universe and exhibiting to men—should they notice it—their basic imperfection, their underlying savage desire for complete destruction. The adoption of a vatic mask might seem to the skeptical reader an easy way to handle the problematic matter of warfare in poetry, but I think this interpretation would be wrong. No voice is more difficult to raise and to sustain authentically in a poem than the prophetic one, which requires great skill and imagination for its realization. Thus Eberhart's tech-

nique must function smoothly and effortlessly, as it were, within the period of inspirational seizure that is germane to his method of poetic production; if it does not the poem may develop rough or awkward spots, however pure the inspiration. Similarly an excess of emotion, of outrage at man's evil, or of abstract thinking can severely damage a poem of this sort—and does so in several instances.

We may take here the justly famous and moving poem "The Fury of Aerial Bombardment" in *Burr Oaks* to exhibit Eberhart's prophetic manner at its best. The poem starts off the first stanza exaltedly, on a cosmic plane boldly challenging God for His apparent refusal to intervene in the affairs of men and to put an end to the viciousness and slaughter of war:

You would think the fury of aerial
    bombardment
Would rouse God to relent; the infinite spaces
Are still silent. He looks on shock-pried faces.
History, even, does not know what is meant.

You would feel that after so many centuries
God would give man to repent; yet he can kill
As Cain could, but with multitudinous will,
No farther advanced than in his ancient furies.

The use of the "you" in these two stanzas is a brilliant stroke because it establishes contact between poet and reader at the same time that it serves as part of an opening passage of vigorous rhetorical appeal.

Having called upon "history" in general and the figure of Cain, the first murderer, to support the portrayal of man's age-old desire to kill rather than love his brother (the implied contrast between the single murder committed by Cain and the wholesale killing accomplished by the latest inventions of war is, of course, intentionally disturbing), Eberhart begins to wonder if God is after all simply "indifferent"; this third stanza closes with the somber thought that "the eternal truth" perhaps consists only of "man's fighting soul/Wherein the Beast ravens in its own avidity." Such a question really means to ask if God exists at all: should the answer be negative, the inner malice of mankind emerges as the ultimate, eternal reality. But if the poet poses this question he does not pretend to give a reply of any general sort; instead the last stanza of the poem moves suddenly into the realm of the particular, borrowing from Eberhart's personal acquaintance:

Of Van Wettering I speak, and Averill,
Names on a list, whose faces I do not recall
But they are gone to early death, who late in
    school
Distinguished the belt feed lever from the belt
    holding pawl.

Even the relatively specific character of these lines is not permitted to do more than modify a bit the aloofness and exaltation of the poet's speech, and then only to drive home his point in another way. The oddly formal construction of this one-sentence stanza strengthens the feeling of distance maintained in spite of the introduction of personal details and names. Various meanings may be attributed to the stanza: possibly most important is the shock which occurs in shifting from the universal, philosophical level of the three preceding stanzas to the frank, objective enumeration of facts—the deaths of certain named individuals. The ravening "Beast" abruptly takes on real and deadly proportions: its victims are listed.

The religious or metaphysical implications of the poem are not, as I have said, brought to any conclusive formulation, nor should we expect them to be when we remember Eberhart's avowed dedication to the truth of each poetic vision as he receives it. With that commitment in mind we should also observe that other poems than the present one ("New Hampshire, February" and "Reality! Reality! What Is It?" are two of them) assert with great forthrightness the moments of deepest doubt, of religious belief assaulted by seemingly chance fatefulness. Over against the poems of metaphysical anguish, which originate in the crushing pressure of events on the poet's reason and conscience, one has to set the larger bulk of poetry that surpasses suffering, injustice, and doubt to approach the zone of what Eberhart calls "Psyche." In one of several lectures he has delivered on Will and Psyche in poetry he defines the latter: "Psyche poetry pertains to the soul, to peace, quiet, tranquillity, serenity, harmony, stillness and silence. It provides psychic states of passive pleasure." We will recall how Michael Roberts indicated that the young Eberhart avoided this style, but in recent years he has produced with some frequency poems representative to one degree or another of the category. These poems coincide with their author's intellectual and artistic maturity, with an attitude of calm reflectiveness, and with the contemplation through a number of suggestive terms and images ("light," "love," "unity," "the unfound beyond," "height," or, taken altogether, "God") of a transcendent reality, a divine source.

By way of contrast, Eberhart's war poems belong to the class of "Will poetry," as do his other pieces which express a moral view of human behavior. "Will poetry exists because of the power in the cell beyond its energy to maintain itself. Will results in action, through wish, zeal, volition, passion, determination, choice and command. Will makes something happen in poetry." Not all Will poems, occupied with men's actions, employ the vatic manner of "The Fury of Aerial Bombardment." Eberhart takes the part both of intimate witness and of commentator in "Fragment of

New York, 1929" from *Undercliff*, which has as its chief metaphor for the cold, vicious character of modern society the slaughtering and butchering of animals. The poet begins with an early morning awakening and depicts himself as the city-dweller, whose movements are habitual and mechanical, whose awareness of his own identity is often shaky, who fears the direction in which his thought will lead him. As he goes out into the pre-dawn urban streets under "the one untormented integer," the "surprise moon, four-thirty moon," he feels as if he were going "into Hell again."

In subsequent stanzas Eberhart's graphic rendering of the routines of the slaughterhouse creates a highly charged symbolic vision of contemporary life, of those buried desires and antagonisms that seek their fulfillment in the act of killing. We can elicit for ourselves a variety of topical analogies with the actualities of twentieth-century history—with concentration camps, city gangs, or the sick fantasies of the mass media. The poet gives us a shockingly effective image of our sex and death obsessions in the figure of the beasts' executioner at his daily task:

> The killer's face! He is baffled now,
> Seems. Moment. He poises
> The tip of the knife at the throat.
> So little is life. He cannot make
> The one swift entry and up-jab.
> Curious copulation, death-impregnation.

As if indeed this nightmare experience were a journey into hell, Eberhart ends his poem with indications of emergence and rebirth:

> Death I saw,
> And wormed through it. And make fragment
> Of the end of a time, when seethed
> So thick the life, it knew not,
> In savage complexity, modernity,
> The harsh omnipotence of evil.

Obvious reference is made here to the time specified in the poem's title: the year of the stock market crash, the beginning of the Depression, the finish of a frenzied postwar era. But the substance of the poem has no more special relevance to that period than it does to the present day; rather, it fashions a general picture of inhumanity and spiritual vacuity.

If we want to see Eberhart's definite handling of the quality of life in American society at a certain level, then we must turn to the play *The Visionary Farms*, which is, in addition, his most ambitious and successful effort as a verse dramatist. Denis Donoghue, who has discussed the play shrewdly and at length, speaks of it as "expressionist" in style, "a *drame à thèse* . . . with a difference"; the difference lies in the fact that while Eberhart pictures the triumph and failure of a huge business empire and the three men who are its executives he does not attack his material in the spirit of naturalism or social realism but blends elements of fantasy and extravagant comedy with, as he has said himself, "a study of evil Will in a man" and the insidious temptations of money and success, the American dream ("Money is stronger than life, Adam, much stronger," the president of the company tells his vice-president, a man whom he is about to ruin and whose wife is dying). The conventions of realism are further avoided by the poet's use—common to almost all of his plays—a group of characters, including the Consulting Author, who gather on the stage as in a living room to joke, talk, pun, and finally to watch the play *The Visionary Farms*; but the Consulting Author puts the group under a spell so that they become more than an audience: they are metamorphosed into the actors of the drama they came to see.

Each thus becomes a part of Everyman. What is, is what might happen to him.

And each can share in the scenes of fabulous
   life
As if imagination were reality,
For reality is strange as imagination.

Considered from another angle, the portion of "reality" in the play is not negligible, for the plot is clearly grounded in the experience of Eberhart's father, a businessman who, his son wrote, "was betrayed by the notorious Cy Thompson, who embezzled over a million dollars" from George A. Hormel and Company, of which Eberhart senior was vice-president. Here he has been developed into the character of Adam Fahnstock, secretary and vice-president of the Parker Corporation, a soap manufacturer. During the course of the play his wife, Vine, is discovered to have an incurable cancer. The main figure is not Fahnstock, though, but "Hurricane" Ransome, the company treasurer, a man of extraordinary business daring whose wild ideas and enormous expenditures (marvelously and wittily caricatured by Eberhart) have brought the firm very high sales and have made him, Fahnstock, and the president, Roger Parker, rich men.

Yet things are not all they seem. The play opens with Ransome giving a Sunday School sermon to the children of the small mid-western town in which the company's employees and executives live. He shows them a silver dollar—"See how clean it is, hard and pure" —as "a symbol of the American dream," and then by thrusting the coin into hydrochloric acid, where it turns "black, fuming," demonstrates how "If you do evil, your soul will turn black/ Immediately, like this hideous dollar." A silver dollar makes an odd symbol for the soul and prepares us for what follows. As the play continues we learn that Ransome is, ironically enough, very like that blackened dollar

himself. Though a man prodigiously gifted, he has become inwardly warped; over a number of years he has embezzled increasingly large sums of money from the company and by clever maneuvering of the accounts has kept his thievery hidden. "Success," Ransome remarks at one point, "is a trick," and the trickery exacts a destructive price of the spirit and of human dignity. What started as a relatively harmless borrowing of five dollars from the company has expanded into a monumental swindle. The Visionary Farms, an extraordinary venture in chicken-farming, is invented by Ransome simply as another means of keeping money circulating, the books balanced, and his robbery concealed; thus the American dream of fantastic financial success appears to be a crippling delusion. As Ransome confesses to himself, echoing *King Lear* by the way:

It is the evil getting me from the inside.
The slightest, innocent-seeming insinuation
When it all began, back in 1914,
Has grown in my hand to my most monstrous
   sin.
I am bound upon a wheel of fire.
There is no end to the agony I am in.

Ransome's crime is uncovered by the president's son, and the calculating executive is imprisoned; with hilarious irony Eberhart has him at the play's finish ruling the prison and its warden with the same energetic business daring and hocus-pocus as he lavished on the Parker Company and his surrealist chicken farms. Ransome typifies an indefatigable American desire for success, fortune, manipulative powers; and while Eberhart shows us this embezzler reaching a tragic moment of self-recognition we still find that his knowledge does not in any fashion curb his basic impulses or cause him to change.

Differing noticeably from Ransome, the figure of Adam Fahnstock stands out as representative of innocence, good will, endurance, victimization, love, and loss. Not only is his wife dying but he is forced at last to relinquish his stock in the company to Parker, a move by which the latter betrays Fahnstock's friendship and ruins him financially. Success for Mr. Parker, or the next thing to it, the salvaging of his honor, is also a trick. Fahnstock remains the embodiment of genuine values in the play; in a scene in his apple orchard he is compelled to explain to his children the impending death of their mother and the collapse of his fortunes. Against the fateful circumstances that have overtaken them and the death which will intrude upon one of them prematurely Adam proposes the single worthy countermeasure:

> While there is love there can be no death
> For we carry love with us to our own end.
> Love we carry in our memories.

In an earlier poem, "Orchard," from *Song and Idea* Eberhart composed a somewhat different version of the disclosure of his mother's mortal illness. There the mother is herself present; she and her husband are cognizant of what must come, but the children can merely guess it from the extremely troubled atmosphere surrounding them. The two brothers are "placed in the first light/ Of brutal recognition," though their sister registers the disturbance without comprehending its source. The concluding stanza elevates the forces in conflict within this family group to a stage at which they exemplify, as they do in *The Visionary Farms*, the inescapable vicissitudes of life and the human will to meet them. These lines from the poem help us to perceive the role of Fahnstock and his family, as well as his sturdy opposition to cheating, greed, and misfortune, in the play:

> And in the evening, among the warm fruit trees
> All of life and all of death were there,
> Of pain unto death, of struggle to endure,
> And the strong right of human love was there.

Eberhart's experiments in the theater, all of them rather recent (with the exception of the brief "Triptych" they date from 1950 when he began to work in earnest on verse drama), have had some interesting effects on his poetry too. These are most evident in his collection *The Quarry*, where, besides poems of philosophical speculation, elegies, and visionary lyrics, one finds an assortment of pieces unusual in Eberhart's writing: letters in verse (to W. H. Auden and the late William Carlos Williams), dramatic monologues utilizing fictional speakers ("A New England Bachelor," "A Maine Roustabout," "The Lament of a New England Mother") or character sketches ("Ruby Daggett"), and dialogues which are indeed miniature dramas ("Father and Son," "Father and Daughter"). The high quality of these poems indicates yet another direction in which Eberhart's free and generous imagination may operate.

In spite of such influences deriving from his experiments with verse drama, however, the predominant trait of Eberhart's later poetry is of another kind. I am referring to the reflective or Psyche poems, in which the author contemplates sympathetically and dispassionately the nature of life, the function of his art, the full spectrum of experience discussed here under separate and partial thematic headings of perception, death, and human behavior. Not all of this poetry fits into the category of Psyche of course, but much of it does, to use Eberhart's own words, because it "works partially through a religious attitude." Progression away from the world of desire and act toward the lasting realities of spirit, toward contemplation entered upon for its own sake or for the sake of vision alone, without any wish to turn the experience to practical account, is characteristic of the purer types of Psyche poem. "Life as a Visionary Spirit," a recent piece from his *Collected Poems*, exhibits this mood of the imagination but also contains certain inherent qualifications of the mood, for Eberhart never produces the absolutely pure Psyche poem:

Nothing like the freedom of vision,
  To look from a hill to the sea,
Meditating one's bile and bible: free
  From action, to be.

The best moment is when
  Stillness holds the air motionless,
So that time can bless
  History, blood is a caress.

Neither in landwork nor in seawork
  Believe. Belief must be pure.
Let the soul softly idle,
  Beyond past, beyond future.

Let it be said, "A great effulgence
  Grows upon the sandspit rose.
A rare salt harrows the air.
  Your eyes show divine shows."

Though retaining some traces of place, of the physical cosmos, at the start, this poem departs in the third stanza for the world of spirit or psyche, for the regions outside time, for a reality beyond what is immediate to the senses, and advocates a passivity of the soul as the way of attaining such a superior state of being. The realm of appearances, though substantial in itself, becomes illusory if it is believed in as *all* that exists, yet Eberhart neither ignores nor tries to do away with it. The human and the particular, if we look, are stubbornly there, merging and exchanging themselves with the spiritual: while touched with unearthly radiance, the rose in the final stanza keeps its

natural identity; the air, element of the spirit, is cut by the salt of the sea; and the manifestations of the divine are seen mirrored in a pair of human eyes. These persistent attachments to earth, even in Psyche poems, put us in mind once again of Eberhart's feeling for location, for man's position in the middle kingdom of the natural world. He writes very accurately of his attitude in the last two stanzas of "Autumnal":

We have been living the full year,
  It is still full, it is here
  In the late recline of sun,
    A grand red one.

What is going on beyond
  I have not found, am bound
  To the love of the unfound
    Beyond, but here.

The first of these stanzas purposefully recalls the poetry of Wallace Stevens, not only in diction and tone but in attitude; the view expressed closely resembles Stevens' statements about the earthly paradise, about life lived to its completion within the precincts of the material universe and transfigured by the powers of the imagination. I think there can be no doubt that Eberhart also wishes to evoke feelings of fulfillment with regard to life in this world: earlier stanzas of the poem dwell on nature's richness, on the details of creation, praising both their multiplicity and their beauty. These feelings he communicates are ones which he obviously shares with Stevens. But the closing stanza of "Autumnal" marks an unequivocal return by Eberhart to his own voice and to the balance between earthly and visionary commitment which, as frequently noted in this essay, he never fails to hold. Eberhart, with the onset of his later years ("the late recline of the sun"), joins Stevens in approving the profusion of gifts extended by creation even as he travels toward death; however, where Stevens limits reality to the physical world and the work of imagination within it, Eberhart reaffirms his acquaintance with a transcendent and divine reality which he may be incapable of penetrating altogether but which is not less real to him for that.

Eberhart continues in a number of these more recent poems to test, by thought and meditation or in the sudden disclosure by an observed scene or event of a previously unrecognized significance, the extent and validity of that acquaintance. Some of the best pieces are, like "Life as a Visionary Spirit" and "Autumnal," representatives of the Psyche poem, though again they are perhaps less than pure examples of their type because they too hold firmly to images of the natural world. In "Light from Above" Eberhart stands alone on an October afternoon in the "vigor and majesty of the air," which is "empurpled" by rays of sunlight showing through wind-blown clouds onto the landscape he surveys. This light, first described as "the imperial power/ Greater than man's works," becomes as the poem proceeds the visible manifestation of a transcendental "unity" for the poet, who has already confessed himself to be delighted by "unsymbolic gestures of eternity." (I gather "unsymbolic" means here something natural as opposed to something designed or imagined by man.) At its conclusion this poem—and we could profitably read it along with "The Illusion of Eternity," from *Selected Poems 1936–1965*, which has similarities of season, setting in nature, and timelessness—rises toward an affirmation in which the natural and supernatural blend before the poet's eye in the actual scene witnessed:

> here, the great sky,
>
> Full of profound adventure beyond man's losses,
> Tosses the locks of a strong, abrasive radiance

From the beginning, and through the time of man,
And into the future beyond our love and wit,

And in the vigor and majesty of the air
I, empurpled, think on unity

Glimpsed in pure visual belief
When the sky expresses beyond our powers

The fiat of a great assurance.

Given his methods of composition and his understanding of what, in his own practice, the poem is, we can hardly expect him to claim for his work the coherent structure of a total aesthetic universe, and of course he does not do so. Yet much in his work compensates for its absence. Reading and rereading his poems one comes to recognize—and to appreciate more completely each time—the marvelous and fruitful vantage point he has secured for himself as an artist; this vantage point is actually a condition of the lyric poet's inner life or consciousness and its primary quality remains throughout his career an independent availability to experience which permits him to embrace with equal ardor and sympathy the events of existence in the world and the revelations of the spirit. This position, with all its risks and uncertainties, cannot have been an easy one to maintain over the years, but Eberhart has been amply rewarded in the poetry that has resulted from it. The end of "The Incomparable Light," the poem with which he concludes his *Collected Poems 1930–1960*, should keep us reminded of Eberhart's constant dedication:

The light beyond compare is my meaning,
It is the secret source of my beginning,
Issuance of uniqueness, signal upon suffering,
It is the wordless bond of all endings,
It is the subtle flash that tells our song,
Inescapable brotherhood of the living,
Our mystery of time, the only hopeful light.

Selected Bibliography

WORKS OF RICHARD EBERHART

POETRY

A Bravery of Earth. New York: Jonathan Cape and Harrison Smith, 1930.

Reading the Spirit. New York: Oxford University Press, 1937.

Song and Idea. New York: Oxford University Press, 1942.

Poems, New and Selected. Norfolk, Conn.: New Directions, 1944.

Burr Oaks. New York: Oxford University Press, 1947.

Brotherhood of Man. Pawlet, Vt.: Banyan Press, 1949.

An Herb Basket. Cummington, Mass.: Cummington Press, 1950.

Selected Poems. New York: Oxford University Press, 1951.

Undercliff: Poems 1946-1953. New York: Oxford University Press, 1953.

Great Praises. New York: Oxford University Press, 1957.

Collected Poems 1930-1960. New York: Oxford University Press, 1960.

The Quarry: New Poems. New York: Oxford University Press, 1964.

Thirty One Sonnets. New York: Eakins Press, 1967.

Shifts of Being. New York: Oxford University Press, 1968.

PLAYS

Collected Verse Plays. Chapel Hill: University of North Carolina Press, 1962.

PROSE

"Empson's Poetry," in *Accent Anthology,* edited by Kerker Quinn and Charles Shattuck. New York: Harcourt, Brace, 1946. Pp. 571-88.

"Notes on Poetry," in *Mid-Century American Poets,* edited by John Ciardi. New York: Twayne, 1950. Pp. 225-29.

"The Stevens Prose," *Accent,* 12:122-25 (Spring 1952).

"Will and Psyche in Poetry," in *The Moment of Poetry,* edited by Don Cameron Allen. Baltimore: Johns Hopkins Press, 1962. Pp. 48-72.

"Tragedy as Limitation: Comedy as Control and Resolution," *Tulane Drama Review,* 6:3-14 (Summer 1962).

"Emerson and Wallace Stevens," *Literary Review,* 7:51-71 (Autumn 1963).

"On Theodore Roethke's Poetry," *Southern Review,* 1:612-20 (Summer 1965).

"How I Write Poetry," in *Poets on Poetry,* edited by Howard Nemerov. New York: Basic Books, 1966. Pp. 17-39.

EDITED ANTHOLOGY OF POETRY

War and the Poet (with Selden Rodman). New York: Devin-Adair, 1945.

BIOGRAPHY

Roache, Joel. *Richard Eberhart: The Progress of an American Poet.* New York: Oxford University Press, 1971.

CRITICAL STUDIES

Booth, Philip. "The Varieties of Poetic Experience," *Shenandoah,* 15:62-69 (Summer 1964).

Dickey, James. "Richard Eberhart," in *The Suspect in Poetry.* Madison, Minn.: The Sixties Press, 1964. Pp. 95-96.

Donoghue, Denis. *The Third Voice.* Princeton, N.J.: Princeton University Press, 1959. Pp. 194-95, 223-35.

————. "An Interview with Richard Eberhart," *Shenandoah,* 15:7-29 (Summer 1964).

Engel, Bernard F. *The Achievement of Richard Eberhart.* Glenview, Ill.: Scott, Foresman, 1968.

Hall, Donald. "Method in Poetic Composition," *Paris Review,* 3:113-19 (Autumn 1953).

Hall, James. "Richard Eberhart: The Sociable Naturalist," *Western Review,* 18:315-21 (Summer 1954).

Hoffman, Daniel. "Hunting a Master Image: The Poetry of Richard Eberhart," *Hollins Critic,* 4:1-12 (October 1964).

Mills, Ralph J., Jr. "Richard Eberhart," in *Contemporary American Poetry.* New York: Random House, 1965. Pp. 9-31.

"On Richard Eberhart's 'Am I My Neighbor's

Keeper? ' " in *The Contemporary Poet as Artist and Critic*, edited by Anthony Ostroff. Boston: Little, Brown, 1964. Pp. 141–66. (This includes short essays by Louise Bogan, Philip Booth, and William Stafford, and Eberhart's reply.)

Rodman, Selden. "The Poetry of Richard Eberhart," *Perspectives U.S.A.,* 10:32–42 (Winter 1955).

Rosenthal, M. L. *The Modern Poets.* New York: Oxford University Press, 1960. Pp. 246–48.

Thorslev, Peter L., Jr. "The Poetry of Richard Eberhart," in *Poets in Progress,* edited by Edward B. Hungerford. Evanston, Ill.: Northwestern University Press, 1962. Pp. 73–91.

—*RALPH J. MILLS, JR.*

Jonathan Edwards

1703-1758

ROBERT LOWELL in his meditative poem "Jonathan Edwards in Western Massachusetts" remarks:

Ah paradise! Edwards,
I would be afraid
to meet you there as a shade.
We move in different circles.

We do move in different circles now, more than two hundred years after Edwards died from a faulty smallpox inoculation. Yet the shade of Jonathan Edwards still haunts poets and scholars. Of course he is important historically: one can hardly understand colonial America without him. The great nineteenth-century historian George Bancroft claimed that "He that would know the workings of the New England mind in the middle of the last century, and the throbbings of its heart, must give his days and nights to the study of Jonathan Edwards." Many modern historians would agree essentially with Bancroft's idea, if not entirely with his phrasing. But Edwards' historical importance as spokesman for many of the minds and hearts of eighteenth-century America does not sufficiently account for the fascination he still exercises upon men who move today in different circles. For beyond Edwards the spokesman, there is Edwards the man, who lived an intense and dramatic life

in difficult times, and Edwards the symbol, the figure Americans have chosen to represent, in our national mythology, as a powerful dimension of American life. I should like to focus this brief discussion upon these three aspects of Edwards: man, spokesman, and symbol.

The man Jonathan Edwards inspires Lowell's visits to Northampton, where, as a modern pilgrim in search of a relic of Edwards' life, he discovers only "the round slice of an oak/ you are said to have planted." And the recollection of that life informs Lowell's poem on the pilgrimage, a meditation in which the poet reviews the ironic story of the rise and fall of Jonathan Edwards. Lowell recognizes the importance of the man's ideas, to be sure: "Poor country Berkeley at Yale,/ you saw the world was soul. . . ." And in earlier poems on Edwards—"After the Surprising Conversions" and "Mr. Edwards and the Spider," both concerned with the Great Awakening—Lowell deals with Edwardsean doctrines, which he seems to find at once repellent and fascinating. But finally it is the human side of the Great Awakener that enables Lowell to pay him the homage withheld in the earlier poems:

I love you faded,
old, exiled and afraid
to leave your last flock, a dozen
Houssatonic Indian children . . .

When Lowell works his way behind the fearful stereotype of Edwards the fire-breathing evangelist and discovers the complex quality of the man, he finds something to admire and even to love.

The quality of that life was surely intense and dramatic—some would say tragic—for Edwards felt the burden of great expectations, knew the satisfactions of exceeding them, and eventually paid the heavy price they exacted. Born on October 5, 1703, to the Reverend Timothy Edwards and his wife, Esther, of East Windsor, Connecticut, Jonathan was the middle child and only boy in a family of eleven children. As his juvenilia indicate, he was a brilliant and precocious youngster. The only son of a minister and the grandson on his mother's side of Solomon Stoddard of Northampton, perhaps the most powerful New England clergyman of his time, he was conscious of a long-standing heritage of ministerial vocations. His family situation—surrounded by sisters, influenced by a highly intelligent, willful mother and a demanding father, and considered a likely heir to Stoddard—surely exerted great psychological pressure upon him. Historical circumstances also contributed a share of the burden. As the Puritan experiment in America neared its centennial anniversary in the early eighteenth century, great changes had taken place in the social, political, and religious climate since the founding of the colonies. The zealous commitment of the first generations of New Englanders to the Puritan way of life seemed to many to have diminished almost to the vanishing point. To counter this trend, loyal descendants of the Puritans strenuously insisted upon the need for a reawakening of that early religious life, and young Jonathan Edwards grew up aware of the importance of such a mission.

His father prepared him for college, and in 1716, just before his thirteenth birthday, he entered the recently founded Collegiate School at New Haven (now Yale University). Although he spent a couple of years at Wethersfield, while rival communities vied to gain the college permanently, he was graduated at New Haven in 1720. He stayed on for graduate study in theology from 1720 to 1722. While a graduate student, he underwent, after a long period of struggle, the religious conversion he was later to dramatize and analyze in his *Personal Narrative*.

Completing his graduate study, he was licensed in 1722 to preach as a candidate for the ministry and accepted an offer from a Presbyterian congregation in New York. He spent eight months there, but, unsatisfied with his prospects, he returned home in the spring of 1723. In September, Yale awarded him the Master of Arts degree; before the year was out, the college invited him to return as a tutor. He did so, and spent the next two years teaching at New Haven. In 1726, to the surprise of no one, Northampton invited him to join the church there as assistant to his aging grandfather, Solomon Stoddard. He accepted, and was ordained. The next year, at the age of twenty-three, he married Sarah Pierrepont, a beautiful, witty, and pious girl of seventeen. Two years after Edwards came to Northampton, Solomon Stoddard died, and Edwards was made the sole pastor.

He became famous at Northampton. Two of the most important religious revivals in American history took place during his pastorate there, and Edwards was a key figure in both of them. The first was the time of "surprising conversions" during 1734 and 1735, recounted in Edwards' *A Faithful Narrative* (1736) and in our day powerfully reconsidered in Lowell's "After the Surprising Conversions." The second revival was the Great Awakening itself, that extraordinary flood of religious excitement that surged across the colonies in the early 1740's. Generations of New England ministers had been praying earnestly for just such "outpourings of the Holy Spirit" to revitalize the land's diminishing piety; in 1734, God seemed to have answered their prayers by sending his Spirit to Jonathan Edwards' backyard. Under the influence of the young pastor's preaching and example, the youth of the town, notorious for their religious apathy, began to feel deep concern for their souls. Soon the change touched the entire community, and before long hundreds were crowding the church and asking the scriptural question "What must I do to be saved?" As the news spread to neighboring towns, many people traced the remarkable events to the work of Edwards, who had prepared the way for this extraordinary visitation of the Spirit. The Northampton awakening came to a shattering close in 1735, however, when Joseph Hawley, Edward's uncle by marriage, in despair over the unhappy state of his soul during a time of widespread conversions, committed suicide by cutting his throat. The death seemed to the town a signal that God had withdrawn his favor, and by 1736 the excitement had subsided.

But it did not subside for long. In 1738 and 1739, while New Englanders were still discussing Edwards' report of the events at Northampton, newspapers began to carry accounts of the extraordinary success in England, and then in American southern and middle colonies, of a young evangelist named George Whitefield. In 1740, Whitefield traveled to New England and was instrumental in launching the Great Awakening. Emphasizing direct, personal experience of God, insisting upon the sinner's thoroughgoing dependence upon divine mercy, Whitefield and such itinerant evangelistic disciples as Gilbert Tennent and James Davenport used powerful, persuasive oratory to move enormous numbers of the apathetic to a fresh consideration of their spiritual lives.

Hundreds became convinced that God, in his mercy, had touched them with saving grace. News spread quickly of great crowds reduced to remorseful tears and groans; of startling increases in church membership throughout the colonies; of an unprecedented surge of spirituality everywhere in the land. As the tally of conversions mounted, many New Englanders concluded that God had selected these very days for a special outpouring of his Spirit, perhaps as a last chance for mankind before the millennium. At any rate, something mysterious and exciting was taking place.

And, as the Awakening advanced in 1741 and 1742, other reports—of wild-eyed excesses, deliberate cultivation of emotionalism for its own sake, and the growth of bitterness and antagonism within the churches—began to create doubts about the authenticity of the phenomenon. The Awakening could hardly sustain such a peak of intensity indefinitely; when serious men began to question whether the past couple of years had truly been a work of God, the fervor began its decrescendo.

Edwards warned from the beginning against the dangerous excesses likely to appear during the Awakening. He welcomed Whitefield to Northampton, for example, but privately remonstrated with him for relying too much upon impulse in religion. Edwards also publicly recommended due caution. Nonetheless, he considered the errors and excesses mere accidental effects; the Awakening was essentially a work of the Holy Spirit, and he cooperated in that work with his powerful preaching (such sermons as *Sinners in the Hands of an Angry God* and *The Future Punishment of the Wicked* date from this period) and writing. "In the summer of 1741," Perry Miller observes, "Edwards was at the height of his career and influence." The Great Awakening was, Miller continues, "Edwards' greatest moment." When, during the next few years, such critics as Boston's Charles Chauncy began to attack the Awakening, its supporters looked to Edwards as their champion, and his writings in explanation and defense of the phenomenon established him in the public mind as the foremost spokesman of the pro-Awakening forces against the attacks of Chauncy and the anti-Awakening group.

Even after its power had been spent and the outbreak of King George's War in 1744 had captured the attention of most of New England, Edwards continued thinking and writing about the Awakening. His masterly *Treatise concerning Religious Affections* appeared in 1746, but for all its intellectual brilliance, it did not rekindle the revival.

Instead, some of the ideas in the treatise contributed to the collapse of Edwards' career in Northampton, a collapse which in 1750 resulted in his dismissal as pastor. When in 1744 the people of Northampton listened to the series of sermons upon which *Religious Affections* was to be based, they discovered not only that Edwards had produced, as they had expected, a penetrating analysis, from a psychological standpoint, of the converting effects wrought by the operation of the Spirit—wrought in such spectacular fashion during the recent Awakening—but also, surprisingly, that he had changed his mind about the town's long-standing liberal practice (begun by Stoddard in 1677) of admitting to church membership any person who desired it. Instead, Edwards now said, further study had convinced him that the rule of the early Puritan settlers had been correct: true Christian practice should restrict full church membership to those able to make a profession of faith and give evidence of their conversion. Northampton had long enjoyed a widespread reputation as the very seedbed of the liberal, "Stoddardean" approach to church polity; Stoddard was revered and memorialized there; and now Ed-

wards dared to repudiate the town's most cherished tradition. His rationale for such a drastic step will be discussed later in this essay. Suffice it to say at this point that although the move was consistent with his developing theology, it was inconsistent with the temper of the times, with Northampton's heritage, and with Edward's own previous practice. Had he searched the countryside, he could not have found a spot less likely to accept the doctrine he was advancing.

Between 1744 and 1748, although everyone knew Edwards' new thinking, the issue smoldered because not a single applicant presented himself for membership. Other controversies flared up, however, and by the time the issue of profession of faith finally exploded in late 1748, the people of Northampton needed only an excuse to turn them against Jonathan Edwards. Family jealousies, quarrels over money, political intrigues, chronic resentments over slights real and imaginary, and a classic American "dirty book" scare coalesced during those years to create a bitter, petty context for the theological dispute.

One can follow the complicated curls and twists of this chain of events in the biographies of Edwards by Sereno Dwight, Samuel Hopkins, Perry Miller, and Ola Winslow. It is enough here to suggest the various factors at work to create the inflammatory situation at Northampton. A running feud between Edwards and his cousins, the Williams family of Hatfield, came to a climax during this time. A series of disputes over Edwards' requests for salary increases, and the disgruntled suspicion of many that the pastor's family lived extravagantly, primed the town for trouble. Struggles for power in town politics between the clergy and gentry and the rising business interests crystallized around the theological issue. But the most damaging incident in this period occurred early. It developed from Edwards' clumsy handling of an episode in 1744 involving a handbook for midwives. A parishioner had informed Edwards that several youngsters in town were snickering over the book and circulating it among themselves. Over the years, New England had developed rather simple, effective procedures to deal with such misbehavior (and much more serious offenses): an inquiry, a confession of guilt, an admonishment. As pastor, Edwards routinely set this machinery in motion, keeping the congregation after service for a few minutes to state the issue, and asking the people to elect a committee of inquiry. For some reason, he then read publicly the names of the youngsters involved. Many came from the town's best families. Edwards' own list of names survives, and reveals that he himself discriminated between genuine suspects and mere witnesses. But his public recitation lumped them all together, and the indictment inflamed Northampton's most powerful factions against him. After this, the investigation became absurdly involved with intrigue. Out of it came this memorable evaluation of the investigating committee, voiced by Timothy Root, one of the prime suspects: "They are nothing but men moulded up of a little Dirt; I don't Care a Turd, or I don't Care a Fart for any of them." Timothy, along with Simeon Root and Oliver Warner, finally confessed, but in the meantime Edwards had done enormous damage to himself. For the next four years, his handling of the book incident provided an easy reference point for his enemies.

In December 1748, an application for admission brought the controversy over church membership to a boil. Edwards required a profession of faith and was refused. He then declared a state of controversy to exist between the pastor and the people, thus initiating the series of moves and counters that lasted a year and a half and resulted in his dismissal.

Throughout the proceedings, he tried to keep the focus sharply on the theological point, arguing his case in a treatise entitled *An Humble Inquiry into the Rules of the Word of God, concerning the Qualifications Requisite to a Compleat Standing and Full Communion in the Visible Christian Church*. This essay also rebutted charges that Edwards desired sole power to judge the worth of an applicant. He knew he would lose, but he felt that if he forced the theological issue, he would provide the people with an inescapable dilemma: either refute him theologically or admit that actually they opposed him out of spite and vindictiveness. He was confident that his theological position was irrefutable.

The people did not read his book. By the time it appeared in 1749, most had decided that they had seen enough of Mr. Edwards without consulting what they felt sure would be an attack on the venerable memory of Solomon Stoddard. When Edwards tried to argue his case in a series of five public lectures during March 1750, visitors from throughout the Connecticut Valley packed the meetinghouse, but his own people stayed away. The vote of a council of churches, called to advise Northampton, went against him, and on June 22, 1750, the church voted for dismissal. As Edwards recalled later, "nothing would quiet 'em till they could see the Town clear of Root & Branch, Name and Remnant."

After delivering his famous *Farewel-Sermon*, in which he left the issue between himself and his flock up to God (but seemed persuaded that divine judgment would vindicate him), Edwards, now the father of eleven children, remained in town with his family for nearly a year after his dismissal. While the town considered candidates to replace him, he considered a few offers from other communities —Canaan, Connecticut, and Lunenburg, Virginia, inquired about him and there was talk of a post in Scotland—but he gave little support to a proposal of his friends to gather a second church in Northampton. For all his fame and brilliance, he was clearly too controversial for most congregations.

He finally accepted the most unusual opportunity of all. Stockbridge, the frontier site of a mission to the Housatonic Indians and the home of a few white families, had lacked a missionary for two years. In September 1750, Edwards' friend Samuel Hopkins sponsored him for the position. The formal offer came in December 1750. Edwards, insisting to the end on the proprieties, sought the advice of a council in Northampton. After missing no chance to vilify their former pastor, the councilmen, on May 19, 1751, of course advised him to leave. Thus in the summer of 1751, ten years after he had carved out an international reputation, Jonathan Edwards became a backwoods preacher, making his way—to use Perry Miller's comparison—"as deep into America as though in 1851 a man had gone, let us say, from Albany to the Dakotas."

Edwards undertook the mission to Stockbridge fully aware that he might be courting another disaster. He knew that he lacked the temperament and training for this sort of missionary work; he knew he was leaving behind many opportunities for stimulating intellectual exchange; and he knew that the move, after all these years, would be hard on his family. But he also knew the wilderness, having grown up in the Connecticut hinterlands, and his stormy career had accustomed him to going it alone. Besides, Stockbridge was all he had.

It was no bower of bliss. Frontier life was as rugged as he had remembered. Beyond this, the town was not a harmonious commune of good country people, drawing benevolence and virtue from their proximity to untrammeled nature. Instead, Edwards' seven years there were alive with troubles. Difficulties with the

Williams clan (who exercised considerable power in Indian affairs), a community bristling with friction, the exasperations of dealing with poorly equipped schools and inept schoolmasters, and the outbreak of war in 1754, along with serious personal illness, combined to plague him during his stay.

He took pains, however, to save time for his studies. The last word had not been said about the Northampton controversy; the post-Awakening years had seen the rise of many erroneous doctrinal positions; and important speculative questions remained to be settled. There was clearly much to occupy his pen. While at Stockbridge, he wrote *Misrepresentations Corrected, and Truth Vindicated*, a testy reply to Solomon Williams' attack on his position regarding church membership; the great treatises on *Freedom of the Will, Original Sin, The Nature of True Virtue*, and *The End for Which God Created the World*; a treatise on grace; and notes toward his projected *History of the Work of Redemption*. Contrary to what some might have expected, he was a more productive writer at Stockbridge than at Northampton and did his most ambitious work in exile.

That work did not pass unnoticed, and in 1757, upon the death of the president of the College of New Jersey, Aaron Burr (Edwards' son-in-law and the father of the future vice-president of the United States), the trustees of the college (now Princeton University) offered the presidency to Edwards. He tried to turn them down. He and his family finally felt settled at Stockbridge. He had grown accustomed to his exile and was fearful of a return to public life. He believed himself too dull and stiff for a college presidency, worried that his health would fail him, and balked at interrupting the momentum he had achieved in his writing. Stockbridge had given him the chance to plunge into his studies, which, he told the trustees, "have long engaged, and swallowed up my mind, and been the chief entertainment and delight of my life." The many teaching duties of the president (in addition to running the school, Burr had taught every subject to one of the classes and all the languages to the entire college) would severely jeopardize his chance to complete the great projects he saw ahead of him.

He and the trustees struck a bargain: if he could have reduced instructional duties (he suggested merely instructing the senior class in the arts and sciences, doing "the whole work of a professor of divinity," and teaching Hebrew!) he would accept. It was settled, and, in February 1758, Edwards, then fifty-four years old, arrived at Princeton, once more to assume new duties. This time, however, the duties were scholarly, and he was greeted by an attitude of welcome respect. Prospects for Edwards and for the college looked bright.

There was, however, a shadow in the picture. An epidemic of smallpox had struck the town a few months before. A decade or so earlier, the townspeople would have lacked an effective defense against the disease, but by 1757 doctors had shown that inoculation could ward off its most serious effects. Although more and more people were choosing this procedure, it was still risky and far from foolproof. Since Edwards had never contracted the disease, inoculation, despite the risks, seemed to him and to the trustees the prudent step to take. All went well at first, but, as a contemporary account explains, "a secondary fever set in; and by reason of a number of pustules in his throat, the obstruction was such, that the medicines necessary to staunch the fever, could not be administered." After a month of painful illness, Edwards died, on March 22, 1758, having been president of Princeton for five weeks.

The death of Jonathan Edwards reverberates with ironies beyond the simple twist that the protective measure proved fatal. In fearing that coming to Princeton might ruin his health and abort his scholarship, Edwards proved himself a prophet in ways no one had anticipated. The paradoxical nature of his death is somehow apt, for odd turns constantly mark the story of his life: a rise that leads to a fall, which turns out to be a blessing, which leads to a further, but reluctantly accepted blessing, which proves instead a catastrophe in disguise. Surely these surprising conversions contribute to the quality of drama that makes Edwards the man so intriguing.

The drama, moreover, is heightened because its chief actor is so intensely and strongly drawn. He did little by halves. Walking through a meadow, he could burst into ecstatic song to express his delight in the glory of God he found revealed there. Yet he could also, with quiet ferocity, glorify God by assuring a terrified gathering of Massachusetts farmers that most of them were ticketed for the bottomless pit of hell. He was a man with sufficient courage to stand fast for what he saw as his duty, knowing full well that his stubbornness would cost him dearly, yet willing nonetheless to acknowledge his deficiencies and fears. Because he seemed to practice so rigorously his boyhood resolution "To live with all my might, while I do live," he can still attract the notice of men such as Robert Lowell and Perry Miller, who pointedly disavow, in Miller's phrase, any "partisanship for his creed" and still "eagerly take his part" because he was, finally, in his own strange and deep and narrow way, a great man.

Edwards spoke for the great American tradition of Puritan piety that recognizes the distinction between God and man. That piety sometimes deteriorates into mere dogmatism or legalism, but its true spirit acknowledges the awful fact that man is ungodly.

We prefer to ignore this fact. To acknowledge it would require us to admit our limitations and recognize a superior being. It would force us to see ourselves as we are. Such an insight can be unpleasant and humbling. We want to believe it doesn't matter. It did matter to Edwards. The keynote of his thought is the radical distinction between the human and the divine. Whatever the immediate occasion of his writing, he insists on the point that man, for all his accomplishments and abilities, is not God, nor can he make himself godly. This is the theme of the Awakening sermons; it is the thesis of his treatises on the psychology of conversion; it is the basis of his quarrels, during his last years, with the "liberals" who wished to limit God and exalt man.

Yet he insists upon this point in order to clear the way for another. Man can be made godly. The divine can exalt the human and make man a "new creature." While on the one hand Edwards constantly reminds man that he is weak and dependent, on the other he celebrates the majesty of God and the wonderful work of regeneration. The work is made more wonderful by the fact that man deserves punishment, not exaltation. Since the Fall of Adam and Eve, he has had no claim on God's favor, yet on occasion God has seen fit to bridge the chasm created by Original Sin.

Edwards dealt with these points in traditional theological terms. The "covenant theology" of New England, which he inherited, explains the familiar story of Original Sin and Redemption as a series of agreements, or covenants, between God and man. Since Edwards based much of his work upon this foundation, a brief outline of the main points may be helpful.

The all-powerful and all-wise Creator gave all creatures the same purpose: to serve and glorify God. Yet the creatures are different, one from the other, and unequal; the plan calls for harmonious subordination of inferior to superior with each creature fulfilling its role according to its own nature. Although man occupies the highest station in the visible creation, he is nonetheless a servant of God.

In the beginning, out of love for his creatures, God provided Adam with intelligence, strength, beauty—gifts superbly suited to his function—and a paradisiacal arena in which to realize his purpose. Moreover, God, as creator under no obligations to his own creatures, yet moved by love for men, deigned to oblige himself to offer the reward of happiness to Adam for the services which man was bound by nature to provide. This agreement the Puritans called the Covenant of Works.

As the story of the Fall makes abundantly clear, however, Adam broke his part of the agreement. He chose to serve himself instead of God. Thus he offended an infinite being, violated his true purpose, disturbed the entire order of creation (since subordinate creatures had been designed to help man serve his creator, not himself), and exchanged reward for punishment. Instead of enjoying the gifts of his original righteousness, Adam and his progeny were justly condemned to labor under the weakness and depravity of mere flesh.

But God embodies all attributes entirely, perfectly, simultaneously, and without contradiction. He is merciful as well as just. Once again he deigned to relieve the obligations of justice, offer his love to his unworthy creatures, and undertake a new agreement with man. To Abraham, mankind's representative, he promised to send a redeemer who would atone for Adam's offense, restore order in creation, provide a path from misery to happiness, and repair the relationship between man and God.

Since Adam had sinned against an infinite and all-just being, however, the debt owing to God was itself infinite and therefore beyond the capacity of finite man to satisfy. As an infinite obligation, it was repayable only by the infinite being—God himself. Still it was man's debt, incurred by mankind through its representative, and only another human representative could restore the shattered covenant. It was required, then, that a being at once fully God and fully man would redeem creation by offering himself as infinite atonement for Adam's sin; hence Christ, the second person of the trinity, was promised as the redeemer. The promise represented a new covenant between God and man. But this time God went even further than before: he no longer required performance, or works; he merely asked for belief, or faith, in the redeemer. And knowing man's post-lapsarian weakness, he took still greater measures: he even provided man with the *means* to believe. The Holy Spirit would grant certain men grace, the power to have faith. Through faith in Christ's sacrifice, man, incapable on his own of satisfying divine justice, could share in the benefits earned by Christ, the new Adam. This agreement the Puritans called the Covenant of Grace.

Saving faith, in the Calvinist-Puritan view, is not open to all. In his wisdom, God "elected" certain of his creatures to salvation. Those not among the chosen "saints" receive their just damnation; but the elect are not favored because of any merits on their part. Man can do nothing to "earn" his salvation through his good works; God freely and graciously gives it through Word and Spirit. For his regeneration man must depend entirely upon the will of the sovereign God. Those given the grace to believe, however, are converted from "natural" to "spiritual" men, from men of sin to men of faith—new creatures who enter into the Covenant of Grace in a personal way, binding themselves, for their part of the covenant, to sincere efforts toward personal sanctification, to seeking out God's will and keeping his commandments.

To Edwards, the Great Awakening signaled a fresh appreciation of the distinction between the divine and the human with which the covenant theology is concerned. Throughout the colonies, great numbers of people set aside their smug self-confidence, recognized the great gap between themselves and God, and admitted their utter dependence upon him for salvation. In short, they had been awakened, and the preachers had helped teach them these lessons. The focus of Edwards' most famous sermon, *Sinners in the Hands of an Angry God,* for example, is on awakening the unregenerate to a true sight of sin. He jolts his audience into a fresh appreciation of their insufficiency and the precariousness of their position. It is one of the many ironies of his life that *Sinners* was too successful. The force of its logic and language is so strong that even today Edwards is chiefly remembered as a terrifying Awakener. But *Sinners* has a limited aim and exemplifies only one dimension of Edwards' thought on the problem of the divine and the human, the natural and the spiritual.

How can this great gulf between God and man be closed? Edwards deals with this question frequently, but he sets forth his answer most brilliantly in his *Personal Narrative* and in the *Treatise concerning Religious Affections.* There he insists upon some fundamental points: God alone repairs the rift. A debt owing to infinite justice must be repaid; only God can provide the means. God deigns to enter the Covenant of Grace. Hence true conversion is an extraordinary experience, Edwards insists, for it means a new birth, a drastic, radical change in man's mind and heart. As *Sinners* demonstrates, natural, sinful man is far from God. But even if a man comes to understand

Christian doctrine, performs pious duties, becomes a useful, prosperous citizen and good neighbor, he is graceless and unconverted unless God works an interior change in his very manner of seeing, thinking, and feeling.

The *Personal Narrative* vividly conveys the emotional charge that accompanied Edwards' own conversion. As he tells us, he had not accepted his heritage unquestioningly; instead he wrestled strenuously with doctrines near the very heart of Puritan theology. "From my childhood up," he says, "my mind had been wont to be full of objections against the doctrine of God's sovereignty, in choosing whom he would to eternal life, and rejecting whom he pleased; leaving them eternally to perish, and be everlastingly tormented in hell. It used to appear like a horrible doctrine to me." Two "remarkable seasons of awakening," one as a boy and one after a serious illness at college, seemed to promise relief from his "great and violent inward struggles"; but these proved inconstant and illusory. True conversion came, instead, unexpectedly and surprisingly. He traces its beginning to a passage from I Timothy: "Now unto the King eternal, immortal, invisible, the only wise God, be honour and glory for ever and ever, Amen." While reading these words, he recalls, "there came into my soul, and was as it were diffused thro' it, a sense of the glory of the Divine Being; a new sense, quite different from any thing I ever experienced before." He found himself desiring to "enjoy that God, and be wrapt up to God in Heaven, and be as it were swallowed up in Him."

In like manner, his objections to the doctrine of sovereignty faded: "But I remember the time very well, when I seemed to be convinced, and fully satisfied, as to this sovereignty of God, and his justice in thus eternally disposing of men, according to his sovereign pleasure. But never could give an account, how, or by what means, I was thus convinced . . . but only that now I saw further, and my reason apprehended the justice and reasonableness of it. However, my mind rested in it; and it put an end to all those cavils and objections." This acquiescence gave way, moreover, to an even more significant experience. "I have often since," he recalls, "not only had a conviction, but a *delightful* conviction. The doctrine of God's sovereignty has very often appeared, an exceeding pleasant, bright and sweet doctrine to me."

At first, he did not attribute his experience to any spiritual source. But the feeling returned and grew into "a sweet burning in my heart; an ardour of soul, that I know not how to express." After discussing these stirrings with his father one day, Edwards, lost in contemplation, wandered alone into his father's fields. "And as I was walking there, and looking up on the sky and clouds; there came into my mind, a sweet sense of the glorious majesty and grace of God," a sense inexpressible in its power. As days passed, more delights poured in. Edwards found "God's excellency, his wisdom, his purity and love," in every natural object. He steeped himself in nature. Even his youthful fears of thunderstorms gave way to rejoicing in the "majestic and awful voice" of God he found there. He began to take long, solitary walks, chanting his prayers as he strode through the fields. These new delights "were of an exceeding different kind, from those . . . that I had when I was a boy . . . and what I then had no more notion or idea of, than one born blind has of pleasant and beautiful colours. . . ." His youthful awakenings seemed paltry when measured against the true conversion. "These former delights, never reached the heart; and did not arise from any sight of the divine excellency of the things of God; or any taste of the soul-satisfying, and life-giving good, there is in them."

After the climactic experience of conversion, the new dispositions continued, with occasional depressions, into Edwards' adulthood. But he discovered that they provided not only "delight and pleasure"; they also increased his sense of unworthiness. "I have had," he recalls, "a vastly greater sense of my own wickedness, and the badness of my heart, since my conversion, than ever I had before. . . . It is affecting to me to think, how ignorant I was, when I was a young Christian, of the bottomless, infinite depths of wickedness, pride, hypocrisy and deceit left in my heart."

Thus Edwards knew from personal experience that conversion produces an "inward, sweet delight in God and divine things," entirely different from natural feelings and infinitely more powerful. Surely God himself, through his Spirit, causes this remarkable effect, but how? The question intrigued Edwards, and he devoted great attention to it in his works of the 1740's, especially in *Religious Affections*. He had inherited a theory of the psychology of conversion from such seventeenth-century divines as Thomas Shepard, who had grappled with the problem in terms of the scholastic "faculty" psychology. Like Shepard, Edwards used the traditional terms "understanding," "will," and "affections" to refer to the faculties of the mind. Unlike the earlier psychologists, however, he resisted the tendency to consider these faculties distinct parts of the soul, each with its separate function, operating like a system of gears. Nor did he believe the faculties to be hierarchically arranged, ascending from the lower bodily powers to the intellectual, with the understanding claiming the highest position. Nor did he attach the traditional meanings to the traditional terms. Instead he relied heavily upon the thinking of John Locke, whose *Essay concerning Human Understanding* he had mastered while a boy at college.

In the first place, Edwards insisted with Locke that one cannot actually separate the faculties of the soul into distinct entities, each functioning independently. Knowledge is an act of the human person, the self, not merely an act of the understanding or the will. The head and heart act together. Secondly, as Locke had argued, the faculties themselves are not distinct "things" or agents. They are actually *powers* of the *unified* self. Thus Edwards retained the idea that the "intellect" and the "will" form the chief powers of the soul, and used the traditional terms, but he modified their definitions. The intellect is man's power to perceive and speculate; the will is his power to approve or disapprove what he considers. But the acting agent is the man.

Edwards also redefined another important term, the "affections." He used the word to signify not a separate—and inferior—agent of the soul, but the "vigorous exercise" of the will. Hence the affections are not properly distinct from the will or inferior to it; they are, instead, identical with the will, one of man's chief powers. Thus to emphasize the role of affections in "true religion" is not to denigrate religious experience, but to honor it.

Edwards agreed further with Locke that what a man knows, he knows by experience. For Locke, two "fountains of knowledge" provide man with "all the *materials* of thinking." These fountains he calls "sensation"—our experience of particular sensible objects—and "reflection"—the "notice the mind takes of its own operations." These operations furnish the mind with "simple ideas" (ideas such as "yellow, white, heat, cold, soft, hard, bitter, sweet" and "perception, thinking, doubting, believing, reasoning, knowing, willing"). The mind also has the power to combine, compare, or abstract these materials, or simple ideas, thus forming either "complex ideas," "ideas of relations," or "general ideas." Hence we form such ideas as "beauty, gratitude, a man, an army, the universe."

Edwards adapts Locke's concept of the simple idea to explain the kind of knowledge we gain in the spiritual order. The saint learns from experience. When he experiences grace, he has, in Edwards' words, "an entirely new kind of perception or sensation"—a spiritual sensation—which could not be produced by "exalting, varying, or compounding" the perceptions already existing in the mind, and which is "in its whole nature different from any former kinds of sensation of the mind, as tasting is diverse from any of the other senses." When the saint exercises this new idea in "spiritual and divine things," he perceives something "as entirely diverse from anything that is perceived in them, by natural men, as the sweet taste of honey is diverse from the ideas men get of honey by only looking on it, and feeling of it. So that the spiritual perceptions which a sanctified and spiritual person has, are not only diverse from all that natural men have, after the manner that the ideas and perceptions of the same sense may differ one from another, but rather as the ideas and sensations of different senses do differ."

As the natural man needs light to perceive, so the saint needs light for his "spiritual perceptions." Thus the Holy Spirit, as the source of the spiritual idea, casts a "divine and supernatural light" upon the mind of the saint. The Spirit does not provide merely a fleeting illumination; on the contrary, Edwards says, "The Spirit of God is given to the true saints to dwell in them, as his proper lasting abode; and to influence their hearts, as a principle of new nature, or as a divine supernatural spring of life and action." The light shines constantly upon the souls of the saints. Moreover, as an active, indwelling principle, it causes them to shine forth as well. In *Religious Affections*, Edwards clarifies this point by using his favorite image of emanation and re-emanation. The soul of the saint, he says, ". . . receives light from the Sun of Righteousness, in such a manner that its nature is changed, and it becomes properly a luminous thing: not only does the sun shine in the saints, but they also become little suns, partaking of the nature of the fountain of their light. In this respect, the manner of their derivation of light, is like that of the lamps in the tabernacle, rather than that of a reflecting glass; which though they were lit up by fire from heaven, yet thereby became, themselves burning shining things. The saints don't only drink of the water of life, that flows from the original fountain; but this water becomes a fountain of water in them, springing up there, and flowing out of them; cf. John 4:14 and ch. 7:38–39. Grace is compared to a seed implanted, that not only is in the ground, but has hold of it, has root there, and grows there, and is an abiding principle of life and nature there." Here Edwards uses three traditional metaphors for the operation of the Spirit—the shining of light, the flowing of water, and the implanting and growth of a seed—to indicate analogically an epistemological point. This new spiritual sense is "not a new faculty of understanding, but it is a new foundation laid in the nature of the soul, for a new kind of exercises of the same faculty of understanding." It enables the saint to exercise his powers in a new way. "So that the new holy disposition of heart that attends this new sense, is not a new faculty of will, but a foundation laid in the nature of the soul, for a new kind of exercises of the same faculty of will."

It follows from Edwards' argument, then, that only those affections (those "vigorous and sensible exercises of the inclination and will of the soul") arising from the new simple idea of grace are "holy" or "spiritual." Affections arising from impressions on the imagination, bodily sensations, merely human teaching, or any other source are vain. The chief holy affection, and the "fountain" of all the others, is love of God. From a "vigorous, affectionate, and fervent love to God," Edwards insists, "will necessarily arise other religious affections: hence will arise an intense hatred and abhorrence of sin, fear of sin, and a dread of God's displeasure, gratitude to God for his goodness, complacence and joy in God when God is graciously and sensibly present, and grief when he is absent, and a joyful hope when a future enjoyment of God is expected, and fervent zeal for the glory of God. And in like manner, from a fervent love to men, will arise all other virtuous affections towards men."

To sum up, if the Spirit casts the divine and supernatural light upon a man, providing him the new spiritual perception and abiding with him as a new principle of activity, then spiritual and gracious affections—based upon love for God—will attend this new idea. Edwards can hereby conclude that true religion consists not merely in good behavior, in pious practices, or even in intellectual assent to doctrine, but instead in "holy affections." One might understand divine truths passively—he might "speculate and behold" as Edwards himself had done at first with the doctrine of sovereignty. But true religion requires more. The emotions, or affections, of the truly converted person come into play: he *loves* truths and *desires* God; in short, he "relishes and feels."

Yet this is not to say that proper behavior is unnecessary. "Gracious and holy affections," Edwards says, "have their exercise and fruit in Christian practice." If the Holy Spirit truly abides as a new, ongoing principle, a man will direct his behavior by Christian rules, give the practice of religion the preeminent place in his life, and persevere in it all his days.

Edwards does not halt, however, with his admonition to be doers of the word. Practice alone does not suffice; what we say is also important. He insists that "when the Scripture speaks of Christian practice, as the best evidence to others, of sincerity and truth of grace, a profession of Christianity is not excluded." It is, in fact, "requisite and necessary." Not only does Edwards require profession as well as practice, he also implies that "others" have the right and duty to judge the professing Christian's sincerity. (His dogged insistence that this principle of covenant theology, long since abandoned by Northampton, was requisite and necessary and must therefore be resumed led, of course, to his dismissal.)

Edwards clearly set his standards impossibly high. What ordinary man has the resources to meet them? No ordinary man, and that is the point Edwards drives home. What is impossible for man is possible for God. These heights have been reached, and precisely because God's grace can make an ordinary man extraordinary. To recognize the difference between what man can do on his own and what God can help him do is to stand in awful respect of limitless divine power and to honor each conversion as a manifestation of God's glory.

But at mid-century, Edwards recognized with alarm a growing movement to reduce the requirements for salvation in order to place them within the reach of every natural man and to limit God's sovereignty by requiring him to act according to what man considers reasonable, just, and fittting. True religion, said the new thinking, depends not upon "holy affections" arising from a basic change in mind and heart, but upon mere compliance with moral law. And the concept of God as a mighty, absolute monarch should give way to the image of God as a benevolent father, or as a proper, kindly gentleman, or as a cosmic mechanic.

These arguments exalting man's own capabilities arose within and without the Protestant camp, partly in response to the discoveries of Locke and Newton and partly in reaction against the Awakening. Newton had shown that the universe is orderly indeed and apparently has always been so; in short, the world did not behave as if it were fallen. Man's reason, supposedly so dim in its natural state, had discovered the rules of the universe without recourse to scripture, grace, or providence; in short, all men in their natural condition seemed quite capable of rational activity and rational—that is to say, moral—behavior. To many, man hardly seemed in need of redemption from a Fall. Or if he did require grace, surely he could earn it by accepting Christian doctrine and keeping the commandments. For the other requirements seemed very hard to meet, and would hardly be demanded by God —the divine Architect of the intricate universe—who was nothing if not reasonable and well regulated and was not given to pique, irrational behavior, or fits of temper against his creatures.

, To Edwards, these ideas seemed to blink at a fundamental fact of existence. He had for years opposed any tendency within the Protestant camp toward "Arminianism"—a term derived from the teachings of the Dutch Calvinist Jacobus Arminius (1560–1609) and loosely applied to any theory making grace resistible and man capable of earning his salvation. Now, whether the danger came from the Arminians or the secular Deists, he took each challenge to the doctrine of sovereignty as an invitation to reach for his pen. He was kept very busy. Many of his most famous treatises of the 1750's, such as *The Great Christian Doctrine of Original Sin Defended, A Careful and Strict Enquiry into . . . Freedom of Will* (usually called simply *Freedom of the Will*), *The Nature of True Virtue,* and *Concerning the*

End for Which God Created the World (the latter two not published until 1765), were written as rebuttals to the arguments of the rationalists.

The best-known polemic, *Freedom of the Will,* is a frontal attack on the Arminian position that virtue and vice, reward and punishment, depend upon free will. Unwilling to limit God's sovereignty in this way, Edwards relentlessly applies the technique of *reductio ad absurdum,* driving the Arminians into self-contradictions and absurdities at every turn, and concluding that although man is free to *act* on his own choices, those choices are not self-determined. For self-determination supposes a series of choices leading back inevitably to a first choice. If that choice is to be free, it must depend upon another, prior, free choice: but this is contradictory, since an act cannot at once be free and subsequent. Sooner or later the chain of acts much reach an unchosen beginning point, and Edwards allows no escape from the dilemma this presents.

If the Arminian position leads to absurdity, how then can we speak of the will, and what is the nature of true virtue? In *Freedom of the Will* and *The Nature of True Virtue,* Edwards considers these questions by carrying over the ideas of *Religious Affections* into the realm of ethics. He reestablishes his claims that the unified self, not discrete faculties, knows and wills; that the "will" is actually the person's *power* to approve or disapprove what he considers; that, just as in the natural order a simple idea gives rise to vigorous exercises of the willing power, or affections, so in the spiritual order the simple idea involved is grace, which gives rise to holy affections, the chief of which is love of God. In *Freedom of the Will,* he goes beyond these basic points to explain in detail what motivates the soul to approve or disapprove an object. In *True Virtue,* he explores the relationship between the affections and virtue.

If willing always involves some choice (approving, disapproving, liking, disliking), toward what is that choice directed? Edwards' answer specifies the requisites for an object of volition and applies a technical vocabulary to them. First, he uses the term "motive" to mean "the whole of that which moves, excites, or invites the mind to volition, whether that be one thing singly, or many things conjunctly." Further, this "motive" must be something perceived. Finally, it must possess "some sort and degree of tendency, or advantage to move or excite the will, previous to the effect, or to the act of the will excited." Edwards calls this tendency of the motive its strength. Three forces determine the strength of a motive: the "nature and circumstances of the thing viewed, the nature and circumstances of the mind that views, and the degree and manner of its view." Between a weaker or stronger motive, the mind will naturally always choose the stronger. These distinctions are complicated, but they are necessary to Edwards' total argument. Bearing them in mind, Edwards concludes that "the will is always determined by the strongest motive." Now, he continues, we consider any motive having the tendency—whether stronger or weaker—to invite the volition of the soul, as a "good," using "good" to mean "something agreeable." (For what is disagreeable, or "evil," is by definition uninviting.) It follows that if "motive" means "a good," or "something agreeable," then "strongest motive" means "the greatest good" or "that which is most agreeable." Hence Edwards concludes not only that the will is in some sense "determined" by the strongest motive, but that "volition always has for its direct and immediate object the thing which appears most agreeable," or, in a famous phrase, "the will is as the greatest apparent good is."

Precisely what quality makes a "motive" inviting? What is the nature of this attractive "tendency" of the motive to "move or excite the will"? The scholar Roland Delattre has made a strong case that "beauty" is the crucial element in Edwards' thinking on the will. Edwards' own remarks in *Freedom of the Will* lend great weight to Delattre's contention that "beauty" is the attractive quality of the "motive."

For Edwards, the essence of beauty is "order" and "agreement" rather than discord. Just as he distinguishes, when discussing faith, between natural, merely speculative knowledge and saving, spiritual knowledge, so in this case he posits lower and higher kinds of beauty. Natural beauty is the harmonious arrangement of things. But spiritual beauty rises above mere proportionate arrangement; it signifies an emotional harmony of agreement between things, a desire of one being for another. It can exist, therefore, only between beings capable of thought and emotion.

A motive will be strong, then, according to the quality of its beauty; it will be strongest if it partakes of the highest kind of beauty. This is why Edwards insists upon all three ways of determining strength—the nature of the object viewed, the mind viewing, the degree and manner of viewing. In itself, the nature of the object cannot establish the quality of its beauty: the object might be proportionately arranged, but unless it is capable of thought, and the mind viewing is "cordially" engaged, it cannot participate in the highest kind of beauty or exercise the highest kind of strength, agreeability, or goodness. That order of being, obviously, occurs only in the heartfelt agreement or harmony between a being and Being, or God.

In discussing *Religious Affections,* we saw that for Edwards love of God is the paramount holy affection and the basis of true religion. We can now see why. Only the regenerate man, the spiritual man, under the enlightening influence of grace, has the spiritual capacities to give "cordial consent" of his being to Being-in-general, or God. In his "Notes on the Mind," Edwards explains that the consent of "minds towards minds" is love; the consent of minds toward other things is choice. The will of the graceless, or "natural," man also inclines toward the strongest motive apparent to it, but his motive can only reach a "natural" strength; his vision has only natural capacities for choice. Love of God is the chief holy affection, and God is lovable because he is all-Being and all-Beauty.

The Nature of True Virtue carries on this line of thought. It opens with strikingly similar language: true virtue "must chiefly consist in LOVE TO GOD; the Being of beings, infinitely the greatest and the best." Thus true religion and true virtue both depend upon the same essential ingredient—the paramount "holy affection." And that depends upon grace. In this book the lines of Edwards' thought come together to form a carefully balanced whole.

Although *True Virtue* provides a pleasing symmetry to the shape of Edwards' thought, it propounds a hard teaching. By tying true virtue to faith, he denies it to the ordinary man and restricts it to the saint. True virtue is not self-love; nor is it merely love for man, because placing creatures before God risks idolatry. The truly virtuous man seeks first the glory of God and loves creation the way God does, delighting in creatures not for their own sake, or for man's sake, but for God's sake because they show forth his glory. Man does have a conscience, he is moved to loving acts toward his fellow creatures, he exercises such benevolent natural instincts as filial and sexual affections. These acts of love are all very fine, and can support true virtue, but they are only natural. Ethical systems (such as those of Hutcheson and Shaftesbury, popular in Ed-

wards' time) which contend that these acts can be truly virtuous are mistaken.

It follows that they are also mistaken if they find man naturally disposed to true virtue. On the contrary, because it requires holy affections, natural man cannot attain true virtue. As Edwards argues in *Original Sin*, unredeemed man looks not to God but to himself; he acts not from benevolence to Being-in-general but from self-love. Even natural benevolence depends upon self-interest. When we treat others the way we would prefer to be treated, or object when we are mistreated, we judge these matters according to our own self-interest, not according to a disinterested love of God and a view of the grand general scheme of being which shows forth his glory.

The glory of God. The concept appears again and again in Edwards' work, even in the "terror" sermons such as *Sinners* and *The Justice of God in the Damnation of Sinners*. It is the theme of the dissertation *Concerning the End for Which God Created the World*, for in Edwards' view, God created the world in order "that there might be a glorious and abundant emanation of his infinite fulness of good *ad extra*, or without himself, and that the disposition to communicate himself, or diffuse his own FULNESS, was what moved him to create the world." To explain this emanation of goodness, Edwards returns to his favorite image of God as an infinite, inexhaustible fountain of light. It is the controlling metaphor of the dissertation and perhaps the controlling metaphor of all Edwards' work. It suggests a dynamic source of activity at once totally full, yet constantly streaming and flowing. Thus God, possessing all perfections in absolute fullness, still sends out unending streams of divine and supernatural light, knowledge, and holiness. When we speak of God's glory, we mean this emanation. Yet the process is not one-sided. God not only *sends forth* his glory, he *is glorified* by the emanation. In a passage reminiscent of the "Sun of Righteousness" figure noticed earlier, in *Religious Affections*, Edwards sums up the ruling principle of his thought: ". . . the knowledge communicated is the knowledge of God; and the love communicated, is the love of God: and the happiness communicated, is joy in God. In the creature's knowing, esteeming, loving, rejoicing in, and praising God, the glory of God is both *exhibited* and *acknowledged*; his fulness is *received* and *returned*. Here is both an *emanation* and *remanation*. The refulgence shines upon and into the creature and is reflected back to the luminary. The beams of glory come from God, are something of God, and are refunded back again to their original. So that the whole is *of* God, and *in* God, and *to* God; and he is the beginning, and the middle, and the end."

Sad experience had shown Edwards that most men, blind to the beams of divine light, do not glorify God by their actions, but reflect merely their own self-love. He also believed, however, that a time was coming when God would be glorified on earth in a magnificent manner. And such a day was not far off. Edwards' projected summa, the *History of the Work of Redemption*, along with his other writings on eschatology, demonstrates that he accepted the standard Protestant belief that human history since the Fall had passed through three great dramatic movements and was rapidly approaching its final stage. The first movement extended from the Fall to the Incarnation of Christ; the second, intense and pivotal, covered the life of Christ on earth; the third included the centuries between the Resurrection and the defeat of Anti-Christ. In the conventional view, the second coming, the general resurrection, the last judgment, and the consummation of the world would take place at this point. Here, as C. C. Goen has

shown, Edwards diverged from the standard theory, believing that he had found scriptural evidence that the church, after the fall of Anti-Christ (the papacy), would enter a golden age for a thousand years. Only after this millennial reign of love and piety would Satan emerge again and Christ return. He trusted that the glorious reign was at hand, hoped that the Great Awakening signaled its onset, and suspected that America would be its locale.

To turn to Edwards' *History*, writes the contemporary historian Peter Gay, "is to leave the familiar terrain of the modern world with its recognizable features and legible signposts for a fantastic landscape, alive with mysterious echoes from a distant past, and intelligible only—if it can be made intelligible at all—with the aid of outmoded, almost primitive maps." Other scholars, citing the literal acceptance of scripture that informs Edwards' work, the Calvinistic framework of his thought, and his defense of the Puritan mode of life, agree with Gay's conclusion that, among the intellectuals, Edwards was "the last medieval American."

They call him medieval to rebut Perry Miller's claim that he was the first modern American. Granted, says Miller in his 1949 biography, "he speaks from a primitive religious conception which often seems hopelessly out of touch with even his own day, yet at the same time he speaks from an insight into science and psychology so much ahead of his time that our own can hardly be said to have caught up with him." Following Miller's suggestion that the real life of Jonathan Edwards is the life of the mind, "the interior biography," Edwards scholars have bent their efforts at locating that mind, so swallowed up in its studies, in a tradition; and the choices seem to have narrowed down to medieval or modern.

The debate appears to turn on the point that Edwards was, and considered himself to be, a thoroughgoing, true-believing Christian. By and large, those who call him modern believe that he transcended his Christianity; those who call him medieval wish that he had transcended it but regret his failure to do so. Dealing with Edwards in this way seems to lead to stalemate. Perhaps a more fruitful approach to his symbolic value would be to accept his Christianity and try to locate him not as a medieval thinker or a modern intellectual but as an American artist.

For many American artists share his fascination with the idea that man must locate himself in relation to God. Ours is a tradition of cosmic explorers, whose field notes have become literary classics. Sometimes the adventurer goes no farther afield than Walden Pond; sometimes his investigation takes him to Mont-Saint-Michel and Chartres; in any case, the surveyors have the common goal of mapping the realms of the divine and the human. Their acounts of those vast territories, however, do not always tally one with the other.

Emerson, in the early nineteenth century, for instance, submitted the classic report of the transcendental party when he found no barriers between the divine and human save those temporary obstacles erected by society. He spoke for the party that proclaims man's innocence and good nature and envisions as its mythical hero the New American Adam, described by R. W. B. Lewis as "a radically new personality, the hero of the new adventure: an individual emancipated from history, happily bereft of ancestry, untouched and undefiled by the usual inheritances of family and race; an individual standing alone, self-reliant and self-propelling, ready to confront whatever awaited him with the aid of his own unique and inherent resources."

Some of Edwards' modern readers, noticing the important role of heightened sensitivity in his life and thought, regret that he stopped short of the party of hope. If only he had not been intellectually isolated in America (Stockbridge, yet), crippled by his Puritan heritage, and diverted by a series of nettling challenges to it, then he might have become, in Vernon Parrington's phrase, a "transcendental emancipator." But, alas, he merely wasted himself "re-imprisoning the mind of New England." Whether or not Edwards was a transcendentalist manqué or the jailer of the New England mind, he was certainly not a "transcendentalist emancipator." He found a boundary between the realms of the divine and the human and was unwilling to violate it. To him, man has no right to encroach uninvited upon his rightful Sovereign's territory. He was terribly aware that men are the sons of the Old Adam and carry crushing burdens of ancestry, history, and race. He recounted the old adventure. His hero was the pilgrim, and he knew that man could not struggle uphill to Zion by relying on his own unique and inherent resources. Yet, even as he recognized the imperfections of human nature and the terrors of living in a world controlled by forces beyond human understanding, he did not concede that the world is a perverse joke. He did not enlist in a party of despair. Man *could* become a "new creature," he could enjoy a ravishing experience of transcendence, and he could enter Zion— the *Personal Narrative* testifies to that promise —but he needs assistance at every step.

If Edwards has affinities with any party of classic American artists, it is with that of Hawthorne and Melville. They did not share his religious doctrines, of course; but they shared his cast of mind. They also tried to locate the proper relationship between man and God. (Melville once sent a "grand, ungodly, god-like man" on precisely such an errand, and Hawthorne devoted a masterpiece to a minister who agonized over the question of whether he could "ransom" his soul.) In an optimistic age, they had their doubts about rationalists and transcendental emancipators alike. In a country yearning for simplicity and unity, they valued complexity and alternative possibilities. Melville, reviewing Hawthorne's *Mosses from an Old Manse* in 1850, finds Hawthorne strong because his stories are a rich and complicated mixture of light and shadow; the emancipators had not quite freed him of his Puritan heritage. "Certain it is," Melville remarks, "that this great power of blackness in him derives its force from its appeals to that Calvinistic sense of Innate Depravity and Original Sin, from whose visitations, in some shape or other, no deeply thinking mind is always and wholly free. For, in certain moods, no man can weigh this world, without throwing in something, somehow like Original Sin, to strike the uneven balance." Edwards, Hawthorne, and Melville, when they "weigh this world," are always aware of the uneven balance.

Edwards told the Princeton trustees, "So far as I myself am able to judge of what talents I have, for benefiting my fellow creatures by word, I think I can write better than I can speak." He wrote constantly and voluminously. A charming tradition has it that while walking or riding he would jot his ideas on slips of paper and pin the notes to his coat, to be removed and reworked at journey's end. He wrote in a great variety of prose forms: treatises, sermons, histories, narrative reports, autobiography, biography, and letters. He did not try fiction as such, but his accounts in the *Faithful Narrative* of Phebe Bartlet and Abigail Hutchinson—prodigies of piety during the Northampton awakening—and his self-depiction in the *Personal Narrative* demonstrate his ability to create characters. He did not try

verse, but his treatises and sermons reveal a powerful grasp of rhetorical strategy and a fascination with the poetic image. He wanted to move his listeners and readers as well as instruct them, but he avoided rhetoric merely as decoration. He tried to write in a plain style that made use of figures for a purpose but not chiefly for their own sake. He drew many of his images, of course, from scripture; others he drew from natural objects, which he believed were "images and shadows" of divine things, manifestations in the natural world of God's supernatural glory. He had a good grasp of narrative strategy (witness his sense of the audience in *Sinners* and his *Farewell Sermon*) and a fine sense of timing. When his purpose was not narrative or hortatory, but expository, he displayed an extraordinary ability to manage a complicated argument in a sustained fashion. *Freedom of the Will* has long been regarded as his highest accomplishment in this vein, but for sheer expository skill in working with a complex, subtle subject, *Religious Affections* is surely a masterpiece.

For all this, a great deal of his work is unknown and much remains to be published. More than sixty of his works have seen print, but the Yale Library has over five hundred unpublished sermons and five hundred more outlines of sermons, along with nine enormous volumes of "miscellanies" and thousands of pages of notes for books and sermons. A major scholarly project, the Yale edition of his works, has been continuously under way since the 1950's.

Obviously, new discoveries about Edwards remain to be made. New books on his thought appear every year. Each new textbook of American literature finds room for a large selection of his writing. Publishers have begun to issue paperbound reprints and anthologies of his basic works. Clearly, Edwards has recaptured the interest of American scholars, artists, and students of American culture. We have learned that we can admire as well as condemn Edwards the man, for his integrity and toughness if for no other reason. We have even been forced to reconsider the piety for which he was the most eloquent spokesman. It had no patience with the lukewarm formalist, and affirmed a fact the twentieth century has made brutally clear: that man should not be overly optimistic about his godly propensities. Finally, the life and works of Jonathan Edwards redirect our attention to a powerful dramatization of one of the great symbolic figures in our literature—the pilgrim, struggling in his progress but hopeful, always hopeful, of a glorious reception in Zion.

Selected Bibliography

PRINCIPAL WORKS OF JONATHAN EDWARDS

God Glorified in the Work of Redemption, by the Greatness of Man's Dependence upon Him, in the Whole of It. Boston: S. Kneeland and T. Green, 1731.

A Divine and Supernatural Light, Immediately Imparted to the Soul by the Spirit of God, Shown to Be Both a Scriptural, and Rational Doctrine. Boston: S. Kneeland and T. Green, 1734.

A Faithful Narrative of the Surprising Works of God in the Conversion of Many Hundred Souls in Northampton, and the Neighboring Towns and Villages of New-Hampshire in New-England. Boston: S. Kneeland and T. Green, 1736.

The Justice of God in the Damnation of Sinners (1734). First published in *Discourses on Various Important Subjects.* Boston: S. Kneeland and T. Green, 1738. Collected in Vol. VII of the Austin edition of the *Works* and in Vol. VI of the Dwight *Works.*

The Distinguishing Marks of a Work of the Spirit of God. Boston: S. Kneeland and T. Green, 1741.

The Future Punishment of the Wicked Unavoidable and Intolerable (1741). First published in *Sermons on the Following Subjects.* Hartford, Conn.: Hudson and Goodwin, 1780. Collected in Vol. VII of the Austin edition of the *Works* and in Vol. VI of the Dwight *Works.*

Sinners in the Hands of an Angry God. Boston: S. Kneeland and T. Green, 1741.

Some Thoughts concerning the Present Revival of Religion in New-England. Boston: S. Kneeland and T. Green, 1742.

A Treatise concerning Religious Affections. Boston: S. Kneeland and T. Green, 1746.

An Humble Attempt to Promote Explicit Agreement and Visible Union of God's People in Extraordinary Prayer for the Revival of Religion and the Advancement of Christ's Kingdom on Earth, Pursuant to Scripture—Promises and Prophecies concerning the Last Time. Boston: D. Henchman, 1747.

An Account of the Life of the Late Reverend Mr. David Brainerd, Minister of the Gospel . . . Boston: D. Henchman, 1749.

An Humble Inquiry into the Rules of the Word of God, concerning the Qualifications Requisite to a Compleat Standing and Full Communion in the Visible Christian Church. Boston: S. Kneeland, 1749.

A Farewel-Sermon Preached at the First Precinct in Northampton, after the People's Publick Rejection of Their Minister . . . Boston: S. Kneeland, 1751.

Misrepresentations Corrected, and Truth Vindicated, in a Reply to the Rev. Mr. Solomon Williams's Book . . . Boston: S. Kneeland, 1752.

A Careful and Strict Enquiry into the Modern Prevailing Notions of That Freedom of Will, Which Is Supposed to Be Essential to Moral Agency, Vertue and Vice, Reward and Punishment, Praise and Blame. Boston: S. Kneeland, 1754.

The Great Christian Doctrine of Original Sin Defended . . . Boston: S. Kneeland, 1758.

Two Dissertations: I. Concerning the End for

Which God Created the World. II. The Nature of True Virtue. Boston: S. Kneeland, 1765.

Personal Narrative. First published in *The Life and Character of the Late Reverend Mr. Jonathan Edwards,* by Samuel Hopkins. Boston: S. Kneeland, 1765.

A History of the Work of Redemption. Edinburgh: W. Gray, and London: J. Buckland and G. Keith, 1774.

Images or Shadows of Divine Things, edited by Perry Miller. New Haven, Conn., and London: Yale University Press, 1948.

"The Mind" of Jonathan Edwards: A Reconstructed Text, edited by Leon Howard. Berkeley and Los Angeles: University of California Press, 1963.

Selections from the Unpublished Writings of Jonathan Edwards, edited by Alexander B. Grosart. Edinburgh: Ballantyne, 1865.

COLLECTED WORKS

The Works of President Edwards, edited by Edward Williams and Edward Parsons. 8 vols. Leeds: Edward Baines, 1806–11.

The Works of President Edwards, edited by Samuel Austin. 8 vols. Worcester, Mass.: Isaiah Thomas, 1808.

The Works of President Edwards, edited by Sereno E. Dwight. 10 vols. New York: S. Converse, 1829–30.

The Works of President Edwards. 4 vols. New York: Jonathan Leavitt and John F. Trow, 1843–44. (Reprint of Worcester Edition.)

The Works of Jonathan Edwards, Perry Miller, general editor. New Haven, Conn.: Yale University Press, 1957. Vol. I (edited by Paul Ramsey), *Freedom of the Will;* Vol. II (edited by John E. Smith), *Treatise on Religious Affections,* 1959. Vol. III (edited by Clyde Holbrook), *Original Sin,* 1970. Vol. IV (edited by C. C. Goen), *The Great Awakening,* 1972.

BIBLIOGRAPHIES

Faust, Clarence H., and Thomas H. Johnson. "Selected Bibliography," in *Jonathan Edwards: Representative Selections,* revised by Stephen S. Webb. New York: Hill and Wang, 1962.

Johnson, Thomas H. *The Printed Writings of Jonathan Edwards, 1703–1758: A Bibliography.* Princeton, N. J.: Princeton University Press, 1940.

BIOGRAPHIES

Allen, Alexander V. G. *Jonathan Edwards.* Boston: Houghton Mifflin, 1889.

Christie, Francis A. "Jonathan Edwards," in *Dictionary of American Biography,* VI, 30–37.

Dodds, Elisabeth D. *Marriage to a Difficult Man: The "Uncommon Union" of Jonathan and Sarah Edwards.* Philadelphia: Westminster Press, 1971.

Dwight, Sereno E. *The Life of President Edwards.* Vol. I of the *Works,* edited by Dwight. New York: S. Converse, 1829–30.

Hopkins, Samuel. *The Life and Character of the Late Reverend Mr. Jonathan Edwards, President of the College of New Jersey: Together with a Number of His Sermons on Various Important Subjects.* Boston: S. Kneeland, 1765. (Reprinted in David Levin, ed., *Jonathan Edwards: A Profile.* New York: Hill and Wang, 1969.)

McGiffert, Arthur Cushman. *Jonathan Edwards.* New York: Harper, 1932.

Miller, Perry. *Jonathan Edwards.* New York: William Sloane Associates, 1949.

Parkes, Henry Bamford. *Jonathan Edwards: The Fiery Puritan.* New York: Minton, Balch, 1930.

Winslow, Ola Elizabeth. *Jonathan Edwards, 1703–1758: A Biography.* New York: Macmillan, 1940.

CRITICAL STUDIES

Aldridge, Alfred Owen. *Jonathan Edwards.* New York: Washington Square Press, 1964.

Buckingham, Willis J. "Stylistic Artistry in the Sermons of Jonathan Edwards," *Papers on Language and Literature,* 6:136–51 (1970).

Bushman, Richard L. "Jonathan Edwards as Great Man: Identity, Conversion, and Leadership in the Great Awakening," *Soundings: An Interdisciplinary Journal,* 52:15–46 (1969).

Cady, Edwin H. "The Artistry of Jonathan Edwards," *New England Quarterly,* 22:61–72 (1949).

Carse, James. *Jonathan Edwards and the Visi-*

bility of God. New York: Scribners, 1967.

Cherry, Conrad. *The Theology of Jonathan Edwards: A Reappraisal.* Garden City, N.Y.: Doubleday, 1966.

Crabtree, Arthur B. *Jonathan Edwards' View of Man: A Study of Eighteenth Century Calvinism.* Wallington, Eng.: Religious Education Press, 1948.

Davidson, Edward H. "From Locke to Edwards," *Journal of the History of Ideas,* 24:355–72 (1963).

————. *Jonathan Edwards: The Narrative of a Puritan Mind.* Boston: Houghton Mifflin, 1966.

Delattre, Roland A. *Beauty and Sensibility in the Thought of Jonathan Edwards: An Essay in Aesthetics and Theological Ethics.* New Haven, Conn., and London: Yale University Press, 1968.

Elwood, Douglas J. *The Philosophical Theology of Jonathan Edwards.* New York: Columbia University Press, 1960.

Faust, Clarence H. "Jonathan Edwards as a Scientist," *American Literature,* 1:393–404 (1929–30).

Gay, Peter. *A Loss of Mastery: Puritan Historians in Colonial America.* Berkeley and Los Angeles: University of California Press, 1966.

Gerstner, John H. *Steps to Salvation: The Evangelistic Message of Jonathan Edwards.* Philadelphia: Westminster Press, 1960.

Goen, C. C. "Jonathan Edwards: A New Departure in Eschatology," *Church History,* 28:25–40 (1959).

Haroutunian, Joseph. "Jonathan Edwards: A Study in Godliness," *Journal of Religion,* 11:400–19 (1931).

Heimert, Alan. *Religion and the American Mind from the Great Awakening to the Revolution.* Cambridge, Mass.: Harvard University Press, 1966.

Hornberger, Theodore. "The Effect of the New Science upon the Thought of Jonathan Edwards," *American Literature,* 9:196–207 (1937).

Johnson, Thomas H. "Jonathan Edwards' Background of Reading," *Publications of the Colonial Society of Massachusetts,* 28:193–222 (1931).

Laskowsky, Henry J. "Jonathan Edwards: A Puritan Philosopher of Science," *Connecticut Review,* 4:33–41 (1970).

Levin, David, ed. *Jonathan Edwards: A Profile.* New York: Hill and Wang, 1969. (A collection of biographical and critical essays on Edwards.)

Lowance, Mason. "Images or Shadows of Divine Things: The Typology of Jonathan Edwards," *Early American Literature,* 5:141–77 (1970).

Opie, John, ed. *Jonathan Edwards and the Enlightenment.* Lexington, Mass.: Heath, 1969. (A collection of writings by and about Edwards.)

Parrington, Vernon Louis. *Main Currents in American Thought.* New York: Harcourt, Brace, 1927.

Pierce, David C. "Jonathan Edwards and the 'New Sense' of Glory," *New England Quarterly,* 41:82–95 (1968).

Shafer, Thomas A. "Manuscript Problems in the Yale Edition of Jonathan Edwards," *Early American Literature,* 3:158–71 (1968–69).

Shea, Daniel. "The Art and Instruction of Jonathan Edwards's *Personal Narrative,*" *American Literature,* 37:17–32 (1965).

Tomas, Vincent. "The Modernity of Jonathan Edwards," *New England Quarterly,* 25:60–84 (1952).

Townsend, Harvey G., ed. *The Philosophy of Jonathan Edwards from His Private Notebooks.* Eugene, Ore.: University of Oregon Press, 1955.

Turnbull, Ralph G. *Jonathan Edwards, the Preacher.* Grand Rapids, Mich.: Eerdmans, 1958.

Walker, Williston. *Ten New England Leaders.* New York: Silver, Burdett, 1901.

BACKGROUND READING

Chauncy, Charles. *Seasonable Thoughts on the State of Religion in New-England.* Boston: Rogers and Fowle, 1743.

Foster, Frank Hugh. *A Genetic History of the New England Theology.* Chicago: University of Chicago Press, 1907.

Gaustad, Edwin Scott. *The Great Awakening in New England.* New York: Harper, 1957.

Haroutunian, Joseph. *Piety versus Moralism: The Passing of the New England Theology.* New York: Henry Holt, 1932. (Reprinted, Hamden, Conn.: Archon Books, 1964.)

Heimert, Alan, and Perry Miller, eds. *The Great Awakening: Documents Illustrating the Crisis and Its Consequences.* Indianapolis and New York: Bobbs-Merrill, 1967.

Lewis, R. W. B. *The American Adam: Innocence, Tragedy, and Tradition in the Nineteenth Century.* Chicago: University of Chicago Press, 1955.

Locke, John. *An Essay concerning Human Understanding,* edited by Benjamin Rand. Cambridge, Mass.: Harvard University Press, 1931.

Miller, Perry. *Errand into the Wilderness.* Cambridge, Mass.: Belknap Press of Harvard University Press, 1956.

———. *The New England Mind: From Colony to Province.* Cambridge, Mass.: Harvard University Press, 1953.

———. *The New England Mind: The Seventeenth Century.* New York: Macmillan, 1939.

Morgan, Edmund S. *Visible Saints: The History of a Puritan Idea.* New York: New York University Press, 1963.

Niebuhr, H. Richard. *The Kingdom of God in America.* Chicago: Willet, Clark, 1937.

Schneider, Herbert W. *The Puritan Mind.* New York: Henry Holt, 1930.

Smith, James Ward, and A. Leland Jamison. *The Shaping of American Religion.* Princeton, N.J.: Princeton University Press, 1961.

Walker, Williston. *The Creeds and Platforms of Congregationalism.* New York: Scribners, 1893. (Reprinted, with an introduction by Douglas Horton, Boston: Pilgrim Press, 1960.)

Wright, Conrad. *The Beginnings of Unitarianism in America.* Boston: Starr King Press, 1955.

—*EDWARD M. GRIFFIN*

T. S. Eliot

1888-1965

*I*PERCEIVED that I myself had always been a New Englander in the South West [meaning St. Louis, Missouri], and a South Westerner in New England." This comment of T. S. Eliot's, referring to his childhood and youth in the United States, was published in 1928— a year after he had become an English subject and had entered the Church of England. About thirty years later, in an interview conducted in New York, he affirmed that his poetry belongs in the tradition of American literature: "I'd say that my poetry has obviously more in common with my distinguished contemporaries in America, than with anything written in my generation in England. That I'm sure of." To the question whether there was "a connection with the American past," he answered: "Yes, but I couldn't put it any more definitely than that, you see. It wouldn't be what it is, and I imagine it wouldn't be so good; putting it as modestly as I can, it wouldn't be what it is if I'd been born in England, and it wouldn't be what it is if I'd stayed in America. It's a combination of things. But in its sources, in its emotional springs, it comes from America." (The interview from which this and other statements are quoted was conducted by Mr. Donald Hall, and appears in the *Paris Review*, Number 21, Spring–Summer 1959.)

The poet's parents were both descended from old New England families. His paternal grandfather had come to St. Louis from Harvard Divinity School to establish the city's first Unitarian church and then to found and preside over Washington University. His father, Henry Ware Eliot, became president of a local industry, the Hydraulic Press Brick Company of St. Louis. His mother, Charlotte Champe Stearns, was the author of a long poem on the life of Savonarola and an extended biography of her father-in-law. Thomas Stearns Eliot, the youngest of seven children, was born September 26, 1888. In his own words, the family in St. Louis "guarded jealously its connexions with New England."

After attending the Smith Academy in St. Louis, Eliot completed his preparation for college at the Milton Academy in Massachusetts and then entered Harvard in the fall of 1906, where he pursued philosophy as his major field of study. As an undergraduate he edited and contributed poems to the *Harvard Advocate*. He completed the college course in three years and then continued to study philosophy in the Graduate School, with an interruption for one year's study (1910–11) at the Sorbonne. In 1914 he returned to Europe, studying first in Germany and then, after the outbreak of the war, at Oxford. Although he completed a doctoral dissertation on the philosophy of F. H. Bradley, he never returned to Harvard for formal acceptance of the degree. After marrying Miss Vivienne Haigh Haigh-Wood in 1915, Eliot was employed briefly as a teacher of various subjects at a boys' school near London, and after that at Lloyds Bank. A physical condition prevented him from entering the U.S. Navy in 1918. From 1917 to 1919 he was assistant editor of the *Egoist*, and for that period and the years immediately following, besides writing poetry, he supported himself by writing for magazines and periodicals reviews and essays, some of which have since become famous. Eliot's personal literary relations led him into the publishing business —eventually to become a director of Faber and Faber, a position which he held until his death in January of 1965. He became editor of the *Criterion* at its outset in 1922, a quarterly review which played an important part in literary developments for the period of its duration. (It ceased publication, by Eliot's decision, at the approach of World War II.) After an absence of eighteen years, he returned to the United States in order to give the Charles Eliot Norton lectures at Harvard in 1932–33. He made increasingly frequent visits to his native country, lecturing and giving readings at various institutions, and accepting official awards of honor. The British Order of Merit and the Nobel Prize for Literature were awarded to him in 1948, and other distinctions of international eminence followed. In 1947 his first wife died, after prolonged illness and residence in a nursing home. In January of 1957 he married Miss Valerie Fletcher, who had been his private secretary.

It would be too crudely simple to regard the divided regional identity of Eliot's youth as the cause of qualities which have characterized his thought and work. But this early dual identity does prefigure and illustrate a large and inclusive pattern. Eliot was both westerner and New Englander, but not wholly one or the other. So with his migration to England and Englishness. In his early literary criticism, the prose of the twenties and thirties, there are sometimes tones and gestures which out-English the English as only a foreigner, and perhaps only an American, could do. In religion he became a "Catholic" and an apologist for Catholicism, but he was not a Roman Catholic. His criticism urged a program of the classical, the traditional, and the impersonal, while he was producing a poetry which is poignantly romantic, strikingly modernist, and intensely personal. When others protested that there was a marked contradiction between his theory and his practice, Eliot explained: "In one's prose reflexions one may be legitimately occupied with ideals, whereas in the writing of verse one can only deal with actuality." And yet, in the later stages of his career Eliot frequently referred to the intimate relation between his prose—especially the discussions of specific poets—and his own poetry. Of that kind of criticism—which he called "workshop criticism"—he said that it was an attempt "to defend the kind of poetry he is writing, or to formulate the kind he wants to write," and again, that "its merits and its limitations can be fully appreciated only when it is considered in relation to the poetry I have written myself."

Eliot's boyhood enthusiasms for poetry were commonplace enough, and yet they also prefigure his own development. At the age of fourteen he was deeply impressed and excited by the *Rubáiyát*, and then by Byron and Swinburne—for all the differences, a body of poetry marked by melancholy, cynicism, and cleverness. But it was at about the age of nineteen, while he was a junior at Harvard University, that an event took place which was to be of the greatest importance to Eliot as a poet—

and to the course of English poetry in the twentieth century. The event was his discovery of *The Symbolist Movement in Literature*, a book on the French Symbolist writers of the nineteenth century by the English critic Arthur Symons. Eliot was eventually to be influenced, in a general way, by several of the French poets, from Baudelaire to Mallarmé, but it was Jules Laforgue, discovered through Symons' book, who was to have by far the greatest effect. Eliot's acknowledgment of this is well known: "The form in which I began to write, in 1908 or 1909, was directly drawn from the study of Laforgue together with the later Elizabethan drama; and I do not know anyone who started from exactly that point." Insofar as Eliot started from an *exact point*, it was exclusively and emphatically the poetry of Laforgue. The later Elizabethan dramatists had a less immediate and less intense effect, and their influence is not positively apparent until "Gerontion," which was written about ten years after the initial encounter with Laforgue. The early poems published in the *Harvard Advocate* during 1909–10 read like translations or adaptations from Laforgue. "Conversation Galante," included in *Prufrock and Other Observations*, still has a highly imitative quality and serves very well to illustrate the first stages of influence. The poem is obviously modeled on "Autre Complainte de Lord Pierrot," which is quoted entire by Symons. These two stanzas are enough to show the closeness between the two poems:

Et si ce cri lui part: "Dieu de Dieu que je t'aime!"
—"Dieu reconnaîtra les siens." Ou piquée au vif:
—"Mes claviers ont du cœur, tu sera mon seul thème."
Moi: "Tout est relatif."

And I then: "Someone frames upon the keys
That exquisite nocturne, with which we explain
The night and moonshine; music which we seize
To body forth our own vacuity."
She then: "Does this refer to me?"
"Oh no, it is I who am inane."

If we consider these two poems, Laforgue's and Eliot's, and then recall Eliot's "Portrait of a Lady," it is easy to see how that poem, too, is another *conversation galante*, a dialogue between a man and a woman in which at once too much and too little is being communicated. In like manner, the *Harvard Advocate* poem called "Spleen" may be seen as a rudimentary form of "The Love Song of J. Alfred Prufrock." This early poem records the distraction and dejection produced by the "procession . . . of Sunday faces," by the social routines of the day and the sordid aspects of an urban alley, and then ends with a personification of "Life" as a balding and graying man, fastidiously attired and mannered, waiting with self-conscious correctness as a social caller upon the "Absolute." But "Prufrock" is also related to the "Portrait" and "Conversation Galante." The poem opens with the promise "To lead you to an overwhelming question . . ." and this question is not so much an interrogation as a problem—the problem of communication between a man and a woman.

And would it have been worth it, after all,
After the cups, the marmalade, the tea,

.   .   .   .

To have squeezed the universe into a ball
To roll it toward some overwhelming question,
To say: "I am Lazarus, come from the dead,
Come back to tell you all, I shall tell you all"—
If one, settling a pillow by her head

Should say: "That is not what I meant at all.
That is not it, at all."

This theme of the failure of communication, of a positive relationship, between a man and a woman is found again in the other early poems "Hysteria" and "La Figlia che Piange," and it is indeed a major theme of the whole body of Eliot's work. It appears early in *The Waste Land* with the image of the "hyacinth girl."

—Yet when we came back, late, from the Hyacinth garden,
Your arms full, and your hair wet, I could not
Speak, and my eyes failed, I was neither
Living nor dead, and I knew nothing,
Looking into the heart of light, the silence.

This theme is developed by various means throughout Eliot's poetry and plays. It becomes related to other emerging themes, especially to religious meanings—for example, in the symbolic imagery of the "rose-garden" which appears in *Ash Wednesday, Four Quartets, The Family Reunion,* and *The Confidential Clerk.*

One of the most familiar aspects of Eliot's poetry is its complex echoing of multiple sources. In the early poems, those of the "Prufrock" period, this aspect is not yet very marked, but it is nonetheless already present in some degree. The title "Portrait of a Lady" immediately suggests Henry James, and there is indeed much about this poetry which is Jamesian. For one thing, the theme of the man-woman relationship frustrated or imperfectly realized is a common one in James's fiction. Commentators have noticed particularly a similarity of situations in Eliot's poem and the short novel called *The Beast in the Jungle*—in which the protagonist becomes poignantly and devastatingly aware of a woman's love for him only after she has died. Besides this specific similarity, there is a general Jamesian atmosphere which pervades the early poems. The man and woman of the "Portrait," Prufrock himself, "The readers of the *Boston Evening Transcript*," Aunt Helen, Cousin Nancy, the foreign Mr. Apollinax and his American hosts, all are Jamesian personae. Eliot, like James, presents a world of genteel society, as it is seen from within, but seen also with critical penetration, with a consciousness that is deliberately and intensely self-consciousness. Both writers, in their ultimate meanings, show a liberation from the genteel standard of decorum, while the style and manner which have familiarly attended the decorum not only remain, but have become more complicated and intense. After the period of the early poems, the Jamesian qualities, like the Laforguean, are not abandoned but are assimilated and survive in the later stages of development. The opening strophe of *The Waste Land,* with its vision of a cosmopolitan society, ends on a Jamesian note: "I read, much of the night, and go south in the winter." The Jamesian quality emerges with great clarity in all the plays on contemporary subjects. They are all set in James-like genteel worlds. Such dramatic intensity as they have resides, as in so much of James's fiction, in crises of sensibility and awareness. Significantly enough, a specific Jamesian note is strongly sounded at the opening of the earliest of these plays. In the very first minute of *The Family Reunion* Ivy echoes *The Waste Land* with rather heavy emphasis:

I have always told Amy she should go south in the winter.
Were I in Amy's position, I would go south in the winter.

. . . .

I would go south in the winter, if I could afford it. . . .

In the same scene, only a few minutes later, Agatha is commenting on Harry's return to his parental home, and she speaks the phrase "it will not be a very *jolly* corner," thus invoking Henry James, who had written a story called "The Jolly Corner," also about a man's homecoming and his search for an earlier identity.

While the theme of estrangement between man and woman is, so to speak, an ultimate subject throughout much of Eliot's work, it also signifies the larger theme of the individual's isolation, his estrangement from other people and from the world. There are intimations of this larger theme even in "Portrait of a Lady," where the young man's twice-mentioned "self-possession" means not only his poise but, in the Eliotic context, his isolation, his inability to give himself to or to possess others. In "Prufrock" the theme of isolation is pervasive and represented in various ways, from the "patient etherised upon a table," at the beginning, to the mermaids, at the end, who will not "sing to me"—but especially in the well-known lines

I should have been a pair of ragged claws
Scuttling across the floors of silent seas.

In a sense, all of Eliot's works in verse are variations on the theme of isolation. *The Waste Land* presents a procession of characters locked within themselves. The subject emerges into definition toward the end of the poem.

We think of the key, each in his prison
Thinking of the key, each confirms a prison. . . .

When we turn to the plays, we find characters either accepting isolation or struggling to escape from it. In *Murder in the Cathedral*, the saint, Thomas, is by definition set apart from ordinary humanity. Harry, toward the end of *The Family Reunion*, says, "Where does one go from a world of insanity?"—and the implication of his subsequent and final statement is that he goes the way of the saint and the martyr. This is the way, too, that Celia Coplestone goes in *The Cocktail Party*, while the estranged Edward and Lavinia Chamberlayne are reconciled, not to love, or even to understanding, but merely to mutual toleration, making "the best of a bad job." The theme of isolation is in focus throughout the play, and with especial clarity in such words as these of Celia to the psychiatrist, Sir Henry Harcourt-Reilly:

No . . . it isn't that I *want* to be alone,
But that everyone's alone—or so it seems to me.
They make noises, and think that they are talking to each other;
They make faces, and think they understand each other.
And I'm sure that they don't.

Unlike the earlier plays, *The Confidential Clerk* contains no suggestion of the martyred saint, but nonetheless the central character, Colby Simpkins, like Harry and Celia before him, goes his own way. Finally indifferent as to who are his earthly parents, he turns to religion, first to be a church organist, and probably in time an Anglican clergyman. *The Cocktail Party* and *The Confidential Clerk* are each in turn, and with increasing measure, departures from the extreme and intense isolation represented in *The Family Reunion*. In *The Cocktail Party* marriage is regarded as a way of life, though cheerless, yet necessary and acceptable, "the common routine." *The Confidential Clerk* offers a brighter perspective on marriage and on the possibilities of mutual sympathy and understanding among human beings.

Then, with *The Elder Statesman*, there is the most marked departure of all from the theme of isolation. Lord Claverton, invalided and retired statesman and business executive of hollow success, has been a failure as friend, lover, husband, and father. His frustrations and anxieties are dramatized by the return of the man and woman whom in his youth he had abused. But his daughter Monica and her fiancé Charles encourage him to explain his problems, and in explaining he confesses all the pretenses and deceptions of his life, while they listen with an understanding and sympathy which restore him to himself and thus release him from his isolation. He discovers not only the love which Monica and Charles have for him, but also the love which they have for each other. In *The Elder Statesman*, Eliot has for the first time depicted with ardency and exaltation real and normal relations between a man and a woman. Toward the very end of the play, Charles tells Monica that he loves her "to the limits of speech, and beyond." And she replies that she has loved him "from the beginning of the world," that this love which has brought them together "was always there," before either of them was born. As compared to Eliot's other plays, there is no apparent religious dimension in *The Elder Statesman*—except for the intimations of these words of Monica. The play is an affirmation of human relations, a drama of escape from isolation within the limits of those relations.

It has been said of some writers that they write as if no one has ever written before. Of Eliot it is the reverse which is true—and true with a special significance, so that one cannot speak of his *sources* in the usual scholarly fashion. The point is that Eliot was in a respect his own scholar, bringing to his work not only the influence of his sources but what might more aptly be called an awareness of his predecessors. This is true in a variety of ways. For example, the theme of isolation is so obviously universal and so readily available that a writer might very well pursue it without any awareness of particular antecedents or analogues. But for Eliot there is such an awareness. This is indicated by the footnote which Eliot fixed to the "key-prison" passage of *The Waste Land*. The footnote refers us to *Appearance and Reality*, a work by the British philosopher F. H. Bradley, and quotes as follows from that work: "My external sensations are no less private to myself than are my thoughts or my feelings. In either case my experience falls within my own circle, a circle closed on the outside; and, with all its elements alike, every sphere is opaque to the others which surround it. . . . In brief, regarded as an existence which appears in a soul, the whole world for each is peculiar and private to that soul." Eliot's deep interest in this idealist philosopher is indicated by his Harvard doctoral thesis (1916), "Experience and the Objects of Knowledge in the Philosophy of F. H. Bradley," and by a few other pieces, one of which is included in his *Selected Essays*. The Bradleyan element in Eliot's thought emerges as an echo of the circle image in one of the choruses of *The Family Reunion*.

> But the circle of our understanding
> Is a very restricted area.
> Except for a limited number
> Of strictly practical purposes
> We do not know what we are doing;
> And even, when you think of it,
> We do not know much about thinking.
> What is happening outside of the circle?
> And what is the meaning of happening?

To consider further the relationship between source and theme in Eliot, we can return to the writings of Jules Laforgue and to the chapter on him in Arthur Symons' book. Laforgue had written a number of prose tales which he called collectively *Moralités Légendaires*. Among the stories which Laforgue retold with witty and ironical modernization, there is one called "Hamlet"; and in his chapter Symons quotes, using his own translation, a passage from Laforgue's version of the graveyard monologue, part of which follows: "Ah! I would like to set out to-morrow, and search all through the world for the most adamantine processes of embalming. They, too, were, the little people of History, learning to read, trimming their nails, lighting the dirty lamp every evening, in love, gluttonous, vain, fond of compliments, hand-shakes, and kisses, living on bell-tower gossip, saying, 'What sort of weather shall we have to-morrow? Winter has really come. . . . We have had no plums this year.' "

Aside from the question of possible echoes in Eliot's work, one may find in this passage a quality of voice, of rhythm and tone, which is also a quality of Eliot's poetry, from "Prufrock" to *The Elder Statesman*. One way of testing the similarity, if it is not immediately obvious, would be to recite any section of "Preludes" and then turn to Laforgue—"They, too, were," etc.—and continue *reciting*. As for specific echoing, it comes at a point in Eliot's development when, according to several critics, the Laforguean influence was supposed to have been left far behind. In the second Chorus of *Murder in the Cathedral* the Women of Canterbury describe themselves as *les petites gens de l'Histoire*—in their own words, as "the small folk drawn into the pattern of fate, the small folk who live among small things." And these "small folk," like the *petites gens*, speak of weather, seasons, and the failure of the plums:

Sometimes the corn has failed us,
Sometimes the harvest is good,

One year is a year of rain,
Another a year of dryness,
One year the apples are abundant,
Another year the plums are lacking.
Yet we have gone on living,
Living and partly living.

Returning to the question of theme, we recall readily that Shakespeare's character Hamlet has been during and since the nineteenth century the symbol par excellence of isolation and alienation. Laforgue's modernization of the character has significantly the quality of parody, for in his Hamlet self-consciousness has been intensified to the point of self-irony and self-mockery, to the emphatically nonheroic—the seed of which already exists in Shakespeare's play. Prufrock is himself already a Laforguean Hamlet, an early Eliotic Hamlet, in making the analogy by negation: "No! I am not Prince Hamlet, nor was meant to be." But neither is Prufrock one of the "lonely men in shirt-sleeves, leaning out of windows." The "men in shirt-sleeves" residing in "narrow streets" are typical figures in that modern landscape, comprising both human and nonhuman elements, which stretches through so much of Eliot's work. And it is a landscape which is continuous with the vision Laforgue's Hamlet has of people "trimming their nails, lighting the dirty lamp every evening, in love, gluttonous, vain," etc. Eliot has defined his position by vividly portraying the world from which he is isolated and alienated. This practice is consistent with the Bradleyan philosophy. The individual mood, the quality of consciousness, the private feeling, is continuous with, in a sense identical with, the seemingly objective material that has provoked it. A person's identity is defined by his world, and to escape one is as difficult as to escape the other. This concept is implied in that early poem "Spleen," where a "waste land" is already beginning to emerge, where an environment of people and things is a "dull conspiracy" against which depression is "unable to rally." Prufrock's escape to the beautiful and the ideal from the ugly and the real, his reverie of the mermaids, is only momentarily sustained, "Till human voices wake us, and we drown."

Characteristically, the moments of beauty in Eliot's work are meager and brief and are obviously calculated to serve as a contrasting emphasis on the opposite, as in *The Waste Land*:

> . . . the nightingale
> Filled all the desert with inviolable voice
> And still she cried, and still the world pursues,
> "Jug Jug" to dirty ears.

Up through *The Waste Land* Eliot's poetry is richly furnished with images of the sordid, the disgusting, and the depressing, and with personalities of similar quality. In the poems of the "Prufrock" group (1917) there are the one-night cheap hotels and sawdust restaurants, the vacant lots, faint stale smells of beer, a thousand furnished rooms and the yellow soles of feet, the dead geraniums, the broken spring in a factory yard, all the old nocturnal smells, the basement kitchens, and the damp souls of housemaids. In the poems of the "Gerontion" group (1920), there are "Rocks, moss, stonecrop, iron, merds," and such obnoxious persons as Bleistein, Sweeney, and Grishkin. *The Waste Land* (1922) and *The Hollow Men* (1925) are titles indicating clearly enough the grounds of alienation. *The Waste Land* is a grand consummation of the themes, techniques, and styles that Eliot had been developing, and *The Hollow Men* is at once an epilogue to that development and a prologue to a new stage in the career.

The new stage is marked by the difference between the titles *The Hollow Men* and *Ash Wednesday* (1930), and by Eliot's entry into the Church of England in 1927. But the new stage is not, of course, a sudden and abrupt change. Its emergence may be seen, especially in retrospect, in the prose—even as early as 1917, the date of "Tradition and the Individual Talent," which is relevant by both its title and its general argument—and the emergence may be seen in the poetry as well. The continuity of Eliot's poetry is, indeed, most impressive, already indicated here in some measure, and will be further considered. For the moment, it is appropriate to observe that *The Waste Land* and *The Hollow Men* have in retrospect been considered more Christian than they originally appeared to be. The way in which theme and imagery of *The Waste Land* blend and merge into those of *Ash Wednesday* is illustrated by these passages from *The Hollow Men*:

> This is the dead land
> This is cactus land
> Here the stone images
> Are raised, here they receive
> The supplication of a dead man's hand
> Under the twinkle of a fading star.

> * * *

> Sightless, unless
> The eyes reappear
> As the perpetual star
> Multifoliate rose
> Of death's twilight kingdom
> The hope only
> Of empty men.

The rocks that are red in *The Waste Land* reappear in *Ash Wednesday* as cool and blue. In the one poem there is the lament "Amongst the rocks one cannot stop or think," while the other poem moves toward conclusion with the prayer

Teach us to care and not to care
Teach us to sit still
Even among these rocks.

Eliot's deliberate echoing of the earlier poem in the later one signifies that the difference in position is produced by a development rather than a departure or a break. While the position of isolation and alienation from the world is the foremost theme of the poetry up through *The Waste Land*, the same position, but with respect to God, is the theme of *Ash Wednesday*. Thus the first position, considered as a problem, has not been resolved. It has, rather, been incorporated into the second position and thus reinterpreted and re-evaluated. If one does not love the world, one is already well prepared for making an effort to love God. Isolation and alienation from the world become a stage in the discipline of religious purgation, an ideal to be further pursued. With Eliot's profession of Christian belief, this is the meaning which has been found in the lines concluding *The Waste Land*:

Shall I at least set my lands in order?
London Bridge is falling down falling down
   falling down
Poi s'ascose nel foco che gli affina . . .

A distinction can be made between the sources and the influences which lie behind Eliot's work. Many writers have been incidental sources without having been actual influences—while all influences are, in varying ways, also sources. Laforgue was, of course, both. And so, too, was the fiction of Joseph Conrad, especially the well-known story "Heart of Darkness." As in other cases, Eliot has provided cues to the relation between himself and Conrad. The original, but deleted, epigraph to *The Waste Land* was Kurtz's whispered cry "The horror! the horror!" and then another phrase, "Mr. Kurtz—he dead," was used as

epigraph to *The Hollow Men*. In *The Waste Land* there are verbal echoes of several of Conrad's works, such as the allusion to Conrad's title in the phrase "heart of light," which occurs still again in *Burnt Norton*. Such details are evidence of Eliot's use of Conrad as a source, and they may also be cues to that larger and more complex relation which is called influence, when and if it exists. The following passages from "Heart of Darkness," from Marlowe's comments on his experience after Kurtz's death and on his own return to the European city, may indicate some of the facets of the larger and more complex relation.

" 'I have wrestled with death. It is the most unexciting contest you can imagine. It takes place in an impalpable grayness, with nothing underfoot, with nothing around, without spectators, without clamour, without glory, without the great desire of victory, without the great fear of defeat, in a sickly atmosphere of tepid scepticism, without much belief in your own right, and still less in that of your adversary. . . .

" 'No, they did not bury me, though there is a period of time which I remember mistily, with a shuddering wonder, like a passage through some inconceivable world that had no hope in it and no desire. I found myself back in the sepulchral city resenting the sight of people hurrying through the streets to filch a little money from each other, to devour their infamous cookery, to gulp their unwholesome beer, to dream their insignificant and silly dreams. They trespassed upon my thoughts. They were intruders whose knowledge of life was to me an irritating pretence, because I felt so sure they could not possibly know the things I knew.' "

It takes only a slight effort of the "auditory imagination" to hear in these cadences of Conrad's prose the familiar rhythm and music, the voice, of Eliot's poetry. The remarkable thing is that while there are no specific and immediately recognizable borrowings by Eliot from these passages of Conrad's prose, they provoke associations along the whole range of Eliot's verse, from "Prufrock" and "Preludes" to *Four Quartets* and the plays. The effect is produced not only by the recurring rhythms of the grammatical elements, but by the combination of these with images and meanings: the distressed sensibility, the individual's isolation, the distasteful view of the external world, and the alienation from others—"they could not possibly know the things I knew." There is thus a striking similarity of tone and meaning between the passages of prose quoted here from Laforgue and Conrad. The curious fact is that we do not feel Eliot's style to be Laforguean or Conradian, but feel rather that in these passages the older writers are strangely Eliotic. Eliot has so clearly and firmly created and sustained his own style that it is his quality which we feel when we encounter some of the sources from which it derives. Because Eliot has repeated the accents of Laforgue and Conrad for his own controlled purposes, we discover that he has left something of his own accent on their language—he has tuned our ears to hear them in a special way. To hear Conrad in this way helps us understand what Eliot meant when he said (in "Swinburne as Poet," 1920) that "the language which is more important to us is that which is struggling to digest and express new objects, new groups of objects, new feelings, new aspects, as, for instance, the prose of Mr. James Joyce or the earlier Conrad."

The idea of isolation, of the impossibility of communication and understanding, has a direct bearing on Eliot's style, his mode of composition, and the structure of his poems, for the thematic problem is not only that of communication between one person and another but, finally, that of articulation itself. Prufrock, toward the end of his monologue, declares,

It is impossible to say just what I mean!
But as if a magic lantern threw the nerves in
    patterns on a screen . . .

This statement has a multiplicity of implications which are appropriate to Eliot's work, both the poetry and the criticism. The statement is Prufrock's, and it is also Eliot's spoken through the mask of Prufrock. We may consider first its relevance to the poem in which it occurs. A familiar complaint about Eliot's early poetry, including "Prufrock," was that it was difficult, obscure, and so on—that it did not clearly and directly say what it means. And indeed, it does not. Instead, like a magic lantern, it throws "the nerves in patterns on a screen." The poem "Prufrock" is like a series of slides. Each slide is an isolated, fragmentary image, producing its own effect, including suggestions of some larger action or situation of which it is but an arrested moment. For example, "Prufrock" proceeds from the half-deserted streets at evening, to the women coming and going, to the yellow fog, to Prufrock descending the stair, and so on, to the mermaids at the end of the poem. Each part of the poem, each fragment, remains fragmentary even within its given context—a series of larger wholes is suggested, and yet the series of suggestions is itself a kind of whole. It is the poem. It is Prufrock. He has gone nowhere and done nothing. He has conducted an "interior monologue," as the critics have said, and he is the monologue. All the scenery of the poem, indoor and outdoor, is finally the psychological landscape of Prufrock himself. The streets, rooms, people, and fancies of the poem all register on Prufrock's consciousness, and thus they are his consciousness, the man himself. Prufrock the man, his self-awareness, his state of feeling—each is equal to the other, and to his *meaning*. In order to say *just what* he means, he must render the essential man himself, he must throw, as it were ("But as if"), the nerves in patterns on a screen. But so to project the *real* nerves, the feelings in all their fullness which are the man himself, is impossible. It is the incommunicable secret of the mystics, and the ideal of romantic lovers. It is also the myth of romantic poets, from Byron and Shelley to Whitman, and since then. And it is distinctive of Eliot's modernness, of his modern romanticism, that he knows that it is a myth, while still recognizing the impulse (which is not the same as the desire) to pursue it.

Emerging from these considerations of "Prufrock" are generalizations which are applicable to all of Eliot's poetry. The characteristic poem, whether "Prufrock" or other, is analogous to the series of slides, highly selective and suggestive. And like "Prufrock," the poem contains a statement acknowledging this aspect of the poem and of its structure. (In this regard Eliot is more conservative than the French Symbolist poets who served him as model and authority for this mode of composition.) "Preludes" is a series of four sketches of urban scenes in winter, followed by an explicatory comment:

> I am moved by fancies that are curled
> Around these images, and cling:
> The notion of some infinitely gentle
> Infinitely suffering thing.

"These images" constitute the main body of the poem. The poet has tried to guide the reader toward the "meaning" of the poem by mentioning the "fancies" which attend the images, and then by illustrating with a particular "notion." There are still other fancies or notions in the conclusion to the poem.

> Wipe your hands across your mouth, and laugh;
> The worlds revolve like ancient women
> Gathering fuel in vacant lots.

The final image picks up thematically from the first scene the image of "newspapers from vacant lots." The poem thus ends on the note of the fragmentary, which is in various senses the subject of the poem.

In the earlier stages of Eliot's development "Prufrock," "Gerontion," and *The Waste Land* are obviously the major landmarks. Each of these poems in turn deepens, expands, and complicates features of the preceding poem, and among such features are the theme of alienation, the fragmentary quality of the parts, and finally the acknowledgment of these within the poem. While Prufrock exclaims that it is impossible to say just what he means, Gerontion announces that he has lost all the faculties of perception:

> I have lost my sight, smell, hearing, taste and
>   touch:
> How should I use them for your closer contact?

And Gerontion concludes with a statement which is a characterization of the monologue he has delivered:

> Tenants of the house,
> Thoughts of a dry brain in a dry season.

At the opening of the poem he calls himself "A dull head among windy spaces," and thus at the opening and close of the poem there are justifications, and hence admissions, of the nature of the poem—of its lack of conventional continuity and coherence. It is the critics who have described "Prufrock" as an "interior monologue," but it was Eliot himself who indicated the peculiarly private relevance of "Gerontion": "Thoughts of a dry brain."

As for *The Waste Land*, only a few reminders serve well to evoke the central themes and general qualities of that work. "A heap of broken images"; "I could not/ Speak"; "Is there nothing in your head?"; "I can connect/ Nothing with nothing"; "We think of the key, each in his prison." And then finally, at the end of the poem, among the collection of quoted fragments, there is the statement "These fragments I have shored against my ruins." The fragments are, of course, the amalgam of quotations in which the statement is imbedded. But the statement may also be taken as a reference to the entire poem, for the whole of *The Waste Land* is in a respect an amalgam of quotations, of fragments. At the opening there are the snatches of conversation, and then the poem is under way, with the addition of fragment to fragment, selected parts of a variety of sources mingled together and flowing into each other, the sources being life itself past and present as well as writings, until all the broken images are assembled into the heap which is the poem itself, the completed mixture of memory and desire. The series of fragments at the end compresses and intensifies the technique, the mode of expression, which has operated throughout the poem. In this respect, the very technique of the poem, especially as symbolized by the conclusion, is significant of the poet's meaning—or of part of his meaning—which is his despair of ever succeeding in fully articulating his meaning. If the poet's own voice finally fails him, he can at least intimate that much, confirm his prison, by withdrawing almost altogether, while the poem dies away with the echo of other voices, and thus reaches a termination which is, appropriately, not altogether a conclusion. It is impossible for the poet to say *just* what he means, and yet he manages to say that much. And to say that much, to say it effectively, to make the claim persuasively, is after all a kind of consumma-

tion. If he could have entirely articulated his meaning, then it would no longer have been the meaning with which he was concerned.

There are external facts related to these subjects of the fragmentary and the problem of articulation. It is well known, for example, that the form in which *The Waste Land* was published was the result of Ezra Pound's extensive editing of Eliot's manuscript. The story of the manuscript itself is famous, but too complex and obscure for detailed comment here. Because it seemed mysteriously and irretrievably lost, its discovery in 1968, complete with Pound's editorial markings and comments, was an item of international news and an event certain to produce extensive scholarly reverberations for years to come. A facsimile edition of the manuscript, edited by the poet's widow, appeared in 1971. Certain details were known, from published correspondence between Pound and Eliot and from Eliot's testimony, long before the reappearance of the manuscript. Pound had persuaded Eliot not to use as epigraph a quotation from Conrad's "Heart of Darkness," not to use "Gerontion" as a prelude to *The Waste Land*, to retain the section called "Death by Water" (which is Eliot's translation of his own French verses in "Dans le Restaurant"), and to accept excisions which reduced the poem to about half its original length. Eliot's decision to accept Pound's recommendations is, of course, part of his own creative responsibility and achievement, but it also forcibly illustrates the essential fragmentariness of Eliot's work. *The Waste Land* could survive, and with benefit, the amputation of fragments because it was and is essentially an arrangement of fragments. But it is no more so than the poetry that had been written earlier and the poetry that was to follow. Both *The Hollow Men* and *Ash Wednesday* began as short individual poems published independently in periodicals, and the pieces were later fitted together and other sections added to make the completed longer poems. This piecemeal mode of composition is emphasized by the fact that some of the short poems written during the same period and having similar themes, style, and imagery are excluded from *The Hollow Men* and in the collected editions preserved among the "Minor Poems." There is a nice implication here—that "minor" pieces, when assembled under an inclusive title and according to some thematic and cumulative principle, produce a "major" and more formidable whole. The relationship between whole and parts is again suggested by the "Ariel Poems," first published between 1927 and 1930 (except for "The Cultivation of Christmas Trees," 1954), the same period during which *Ash Wednesday* was taking shape. The earlier "Ariel Poems" are closely related in structure, style, and meaning to those poems which eventually became sections of *Ash Wednesday*. It is conceivable that some of the "Ariel Poems" might have been built into larger wholes and the earliest sections of *Ash Wednesday* left as separate poems. As it is, the "Ariel Poems" make a kind of series of appendixes to *Ash Wednesday*.

Turning from the external to the internal, we find in *The Hollow Men* and *Ash Wednesday* the same features already noted in earlier work. In *The Hollow Men* the themes of the fragmentary and the inarticulate are represented by both the form and the content of the statements. Throughout the poem the themes are symbolized by a wealth of images, and especially notable are "broken glass," "broken column," "broken stone," and "broken jaw." At the opening of the poem the voices of the hollow men "Are quiet and meaningless," and toward the end their speech is broken into stammered fragments of the Lord's Prayer.

The first and last passages of the final section are inane and sinister parodies of a children's game song. Similar elements are present in *Ash Wednesday*. The poem begins with the translated quotation from Cavalcanti, and this is immediately broken into fragments, thus suggesting, among other things, the speaker's struggle to find expression:

> Because I do not hope to turn again
> Because I do not hope
> Because I do not hope to turn . . .

Exactly the same passage, but with "Because" changed to "Although," opens the final section of the poem. Section II is centrally concerned with fragmentation as symbolized by the scattered bones which sing, "We are glad to be scattered, we did little good to each other." As for the problem of articulation, it is the "unspoken word" which is the central concern of Section V:

> Where shall the word be found, where will the
>   word
> Resound? Not here, there is not enough silence
> Not on the sea or on the islands, not
> On the mainland, in the desert or the rain
>   land . . .

The final words of the poem are "Suffer me not to be separated/And let my cry come unto Thee." These statements are fragments quoted from Catholic ritual—and they clearly convey both of the familiar related themes: isolation (which is also fragmentation) and spiritual communion (which is also articulation).

In the collected editions of Eliot's poetry, placed between "Ariel Poems" and "Minor Poems," there is a section called "Unfinished Poems." This is comprised of *Sweeney Agonistes* and "Coriolan." The two parts of *Sweeney Agonistes* are "Fragment of a Prologue" and "Fragment of an Agon," and they first appeared in 1926 and 1927 respectively. Arranged together, they are described by Eliot in a subtitle as "Fragments of Aristophanic Melodrama." But *Sweeney Agonistes* is not actually an "unfinished" work. Each part and the two parts together are deliberate ironical parodies of surviving fragments of classical texts, and thus the fragmentariness is a justifiable aspect of the finished product. The device of parodying (classical) fragments provided Eliot with an opportunity for experimental exercises in the use of dramatic verse and thus also in the use of rhythms borrowed from the conventions of the music hall and of colloquial speech. Another aspect of the fragmentariness is the deliberate continuity with, or reiteration of, elements from his earlier work—meaning, of course, that Sweeney had first appeared in the quatrains of *Poems* (1920) and then again briefly in *The Waste Land*. In the satirically trite and empty speech which makes up so much of the dialogue in these pieces, the subject of articulation, of communication, is plainly implicit, and it is finally explicit in the lines spoken by Sweeney toward the end of the second "Fragment":

I gotta use words when I talk to you
But if you understand or if you dont
That's nothing to me and nothing to you. . . .

The fragmentariness of *Sweeney Agonistes* is a structural device, but also, as in earlier works, it is related to subject and meaning. "Coriolan," on the other hand, is appropriately described as "unfinished." Its two sections, "Triumphal March" and "Difficulties of a Statesman," appeared respectively in 1931 and 1932. The work was apparently motivated by the political pressures of the time. Eliot's description of "Coriolan" as unfinished is meaningful in a number of ways. It obviously signifies that a suite of sections constituting a larger and self-contained work was intended.

Eliot clearly abandoned the project at an early date, for in *Collected Poems 1909–1935* the work is already classified as unfinished. And "Coriolan" does have a quality of incompleteness in greater measure than is characteristic of Eliot's work. There is, for example, more "completeness," more clarity of effect, a more decided achievement of tone, in any section of *The Waste Land* or *The Hollow Men* or *Ash Wednesday*. Perhaps Eliot was aware of this measure of failure in deciding to abandon the project and then to classify it as unfinished. It was, in fact, uncharacteristic of Eliot to have projected a poem on so large a scale, and the failure of the project is therefore significant. When questioned by an interviewer, Eliot clearly acknowledged what was otherwise implicit in his practice. To the question whether *Ash Wednesday* had begun as separate poems, he answered: "Yes, like *The Hollow Men*, it originated out of separate poems. . . . Then gradually I came to see it as a sequence. That's one way in which my mind does seem to have worked throughout the years poetically—doing things separately and then seeing the possibility of fusing them together, altering them, and making a kind of whole of them."

A *kind* of whole—that is an apt and significant description. That kind of whole is nowhere more obvious than in Eliot's final major performance in nondramatic verse, the *Four Quartets*. He has informed us that the first of these, *Burnt Norton*, grew out of passages deleted from his play *Murder in the Cathedral*. The *Four Quartets* was hardly conceived as "a kind of whole" at the time of the composition of *Burnt Norton*. That poem, eventually to be the first quartet, appeared in 1935, and the next quartet, *East Coker*, not until 1940. Thus the *Four Quartets* had an unpremeditated beginning in the salvaging of fragments removed from the play. *Burnt Norton* itself becomes a "kind of fragment" in retrospect from the other quartets. In the years immediately following its appearance it received relatively little attention, while the *Four Quartets* was soon, and then often, praised as Eliot's supreme achievement. By itself, *Burnt Norton* revealed themes and elements of structure familiar enough against the background of earlier work. Like *The Waste Land*, it is divided into five sections. It has affinities of meaning and style with *Ash Wednesday* and *Murder in the Cathedral*, and also with the play *The Family Reunion*, which came later (1939). But in serving as the model for the other three quartets, it derived a clarity of structure and patterning of themes which could not otherwise be claimed for it. To extend the musical metaphor of the inclusive title, it is the variations which locate and define the theme. And it is that title which announces most succinctly the quasi-wholeness and quasi-fragmentariness which are characteristic of Eliot's work. The title *Four Quartets* allows for the separate unity of each of the quartets, and at the same time makes each a part of the larger whole.

While this ambivalence of parts and wholes is a structural convenience of which Eliot had always availed himself, it operates with special purpose in *Four Quartets*. A central subject of the work is the relation of the individual consciousness and identity to the passage of time—and time is meaningful in the work not only as a consideration and a grounds of discourse, but also in respect to the history of the composition of *Four Quartets*, to its having been written over a period of time. During this period of time there were changes in the poet's attitudes. According to *Burnt Norton*, "To be conscious is not to be in time." Escape from time into consciousness is achieved in the transcendent ecstasy symbolized by "the moment in the rose-garden," so that all other time, unless it is a means to this end, is meaningless:

> Ridiculous the waste sad time
> Stretching before and after.

The later quartets, on the other hand, are less subjective and are increasingly concerned with reconciling the temporal and the timeless—as toward the end of *The Dry Salvages*:

> . . . And right action is freedom
> From past and future also
> For most of us, this is the aim
> Never here to be realised;
> Who are only undefeated
> Because we have gone on trying. . . .

Four Quartets is (or are) essentially meditative and reflective poetry, but the mode of composition over a period of time, the fresh attack in each quartet on the same themes, the willingness to acknowledge and define changes in attitude—these give a dramatic quality to the reflections. The changes wrought by time are thus not only a general subject of the work, they are a particularized and dramatized meaning, and in being such they are also a lineament of the form. The poet's awareness of this fact is among the reflections he makes in the poetry. In *East Coker* there is the plaintive observation that "every attempt/ Is a wholly new start," and in *The Dry Salvages* the problem is expressed again, this time as a broader, less subjectively personal preoccupation:

> . . . time is no healer: the patient is no longer
>   here.
> .   .   .   .
> You are not the same people who left that
>   station
> Or who will arrive at any terminus. . . .

Each of the quartets and then all of them together have a greater conventional unity than Eliot's previous nondramatic poetry. Whereas so much of the earlier work is a direct representation of the fragmentariness of experience,

Four Quartets is a deliberate and sustained discourse on that subject, and it ends with a serene vision of that wholeness which lies beyond the reach of time:

And all shall be well and
All manner of thing shall be well
When the tongues of flame are in-folded
Into the crowned knot of fire
And the fire and the rose are one.

As in earlier work, the problem of articulation is among the interrelated themes of *Four Quartets*. In *Ash Wednesday* blame was placed upon the external world for this problem:

. . . there is not enough silence

. . . .

The right time and the right place are not here. . . .

The same complaint is made in the early quartets, as in the final section of *Burnt Norton*:

. . . Words strain,
Crack and sometimes break, under the burden,
Under the tension, slip, slide, perish,
Decay with imprecision, will not stay in place,
Will not stay still. Shrieking voices
Scolding, mocking, or merely chattering,
Always assail them.

In *East Coker* the poet complains of "the intolerable wrestle/ With words and meanings." If it is impossible to say just what he means, this is because his meanings have changed with the passage of time,

Because one has only learnt to get the better
of words
For the thing one no longer has to say, or the
way in which
One is no longer disposed to say it.

Blame is still put upon the external world, for the struggle must be made, he says,

. . . now under conditions
That seem unpropitious.

In the final quartet, *Little Gidding*, there is greater candor, greater objectivity, an acknowledgment of his own achievement, but still a note of alienation, as the poet sees his work (so long a dominant and determining influence) recede with the passage of time into the perspective of literary history:

. . . Last season's fruit is eaten
And the fullfed beast shall kick the empty pail.
For last year's words belong to last year's
language
And next year's words await another voice.

In the last section of *Little Gidding* there is a final statement on the subject, a statement which combines a celebration of the possible with an acceptance of the inevitable.

. . . And every phrase
And sentence that is right (where every word
is at home,
Taking its place to support the others,
The word neither diffident nor ostentatious,
An easy commerce of the old and the new,
The common word exact without vulgarity,
The formal word precise but not pedantic,
The complete consort dancing together)
Every phrase and every sentence is an end and
a beginning,
Every poem an epitaph.

As already noted, the isolation of the individual is a theme of Eliot's plays, and closely related to it is the problem of articulation and mutual understanding. In *The Cocktail Party*, two ways of life are set in contrast, the way of the saint and the way of ordinary experience. While it is allowed that "Both ways are necessary," that a choice must be made of one or the other, and that the ordinary way is not inferior, it is nonetheless presented unattractively. Husband and wife, representing the ordinary way, are described as

Two people who know they do not understand
each other,
Breeding children whom they do not
understand
And who will never understand them.

If in *The Cocktail Party* there is an affirmation of the ordinary way, the affirmation includes the attitude of being resigned to isolation. With *The Confidential Clerk*, however, the polarities of absolute isolation and absolute understanding are resolved by the acceptance of intermediate possibilities, of partial understanding. Colby Simpkins, the young confidential clerk, speaks of the limitations of mutual understanding not as a negative aspect of human relations but as a ground for mutual respect:

I meant, there's no end to understanding a
person.
All one can is to understand them better,
To keep up with them; so that as the other
changes
You can understand the change as soon as it
happens,
Though you couldn't have predicted it.

The Confidential Clerk ends on the theme of understanding between husband and wife and between parents and children. The aging couple, Sir Claude and Lady Elizabeth, have finally achieved a measure of understanding with each other. When she says, "Claude, we've got to try to understand our children," her illegitimate son (who is engaged to his illegitimate daughter) says, "And we should like to understand *you*." *The Elder Statesman* simply finds dramatic resolution in the understanding achieved between the generations, between the father on the one hand and the daughter and her fiancé on the other. Toward the end of the play the familiar problem of articulation arises between the lovers, when Charles tells Monica that he loves her beyond "the limits of speech," and that the lover, despite the inadequacy of words, must still struggle for them as the asthmatic struggles for breath. Not the measure of communication achieved, but the will and effort to communicate receive the emphasis.

In the dedicatory verses to his wife at the opening of the published volume of *The Elder Statesman*, Eliot returned yet again to the matter of words and meanings. In this poem he spoke of himself and his wife as "lovers" who share each other's thoughts "without need of speech" and who "babble . . . without need of meaning." The dedication ends with the statement that some of the words of the play have a special meaning "For you and me only." These lines document the extreme change in attitude that had taken place since Eliot first recorded Prufrock's lament that he could linger among the sea-girls of his restrained erotic fantasies only "Till human voices wake us, and we drown." In these lines to his wife he celebrated a mutual understanding which requires no articulation and a speech which does not strain toward meaning. In the final lines there is again an isolation which is shared—"For you and me only"—and thus it is also communion—but still, in a sense, isolation. Eliot had changed his attitude without departing from his theme. "A Dedication to My Wife," with interesting revisions, is included in *Collected Poems 1909–1962*.

In his criticism Eliot said a number of times that the entire output of certain writers constitutes a single work, that there is a meaningful interrelationship of compositions, and that individual pieces are endowed with meaning by other pieces and by the whole context of a writer's work. Like so many of Eliot's generalizations, this is particularly applicable to his own poetry. If there is a fragmentary aspect to much of his work, there is also continuity and wholeness. As we have already seen, a frequent practice of Eliot's was "doing things separately" and then "making a kind of whole of them," so that the fragmentary quality of the work is finally operative in the unity of the whole. The recurrent themes of time, alienation, isolation, and articulation obviously contribute to the continuity. And so does a steadily developing pattern of interrelated images, symbols, and themes. There is, for example, the underwater imagery of the poems of the "Prufrock" group:

I should have been a pair of ragged claws
Scuttling across the floors of silent seas.

We have lingered in the chambers of the sea
By sea-girls wreathed with seaweed red and
    brown
Till human voices wake us, and we drown.

    The memory throws up high and dry
    A crowd of twisted things;
    A twisted branch upon the beach . . .

The brown waves of fog toss up to me
Twisted faces from the bottom of the street. . . .

His laughter was submarine and profound
Like the old man of the sea's
Hidden under coral islands
Where worried bodies of drowned men drift
    down in the green silence,
Dropping from fingers of surf.

Comparable images, of water and underwater, of rain and river and sea, continue to appear throughout the poetry, reflecting and echoing each other with cumulative effect. There is a similar development of flower and garden imagery, from beginning to end, and extending into the plays. The "hyacinth girl" of *The Waste Land* is related to the "smell of hyacinths" in "Portrait of a Lady," to the girl, "her arms full of flowers," in "La Figlia che Piange," and to the little girl ("Elle était toute mouillée, je lui ai donné des primevères") of "Dans le Restaurant." The rose-garden dialogue of Harry and Agatha in *The Family Reunion* remains enigmatic unless related to this garden imagery in Eliot's poetry, and especially to the symbolic rose-gardens of *Ash Wednesday* and *Burnt Norton*. Each garden passage, whether early or late, gains in clarity and scope of meaning when in relation to the others. At the outset of *The Confidential Clerk*, when Eggerson speaks of Colby—

He's expressed such an interest in my garden
That I think he ought to have window boxes.
Some day he'll want a garden of his own.

—the informed reader is alerted to the spiritual and religious intimations of the ecstatic childhood experience in the rose-garden, variously represented elsewhere in Eliot's poetry. In addition to such meaningful recurrence of symbolic imagery, there is at times a merging of one kind of imagery with another, as in these lines from "Marina":

Whispers and small laughter between leaves
    and hurrying feet
Under sleep, where all the waters meet.

Here the garden imagery and the water imagery are related to each other, and related also to that deeper realm of consciousness in which such associations occur. Two patterns of imagery, each already intricate and extensive, have been joined to produce a pattern that is still larger and more intricate.

In the continuity of Eliot's poetry, there is not only an accumulation of meaning but an alteration of meaning, a retroactive effect of later elements upon earlier. For example, the lines quoted from "Marina" have a relevance to the final lines of "Prufrock." Marina is the girl, the daughter, in Shakespeare's *Pericles,* and, as her name indicates, a "sea-girl." There are, thus, in both passages the details of underwater, of sleep, and of the sea-girls. Considered alone, the sexual fantasy of the earlier passage is expressive of Prufrock's isolation and alienation—"Till human voices wake us, and we drown." But when considered in relation to "Marina" and to the entire pattern of the rose-garden imagery, Prufrock's erotic daydream becomes an intimation of what is represented in later poems as spiritual vision. The mermaids of Prufrock's self-indulgent reverie are an antecedent type of the female figure who is later to represent spiritual guidance—such as the Lady in *Ash Wednesday,* who is "spirit of the fountain, spirit of the garden . . . spirit of the river, spirit of the sea."

Another example of retroactive effect is Eliot's use of ideas found in the mystical work of St. John of the Cross, *The Dark Night of the Soul.* The Spanish mystic outlines a course of spiritual discipline leading to purgation and spiritual rebirth. The initial condition requisite for entering this discipline is described by St. John as of a negative nature, a state of inertia of sense and of spirit, the purpose being ultimately to eliminate the sensual and to bring the spiritual under control. This condition is one of isolation, alienation, bleakness, emptiness, dryness. St. John's system is summarized in *Burnt Norton* and *East Coker,* in each case in the final passage of Section III—with particular clarity in *Burnt Norton*:

> Internal darkness, deprivation
> And destitution of all property,
> Desiccation of the world of sense,
> Evacuation of the world of fancy,
> Inoperancy of the world of spirit . . .

It is this system of spiritual discipline which provides the underlying scheme of *Ash Wednesday* and which is the clue to the meaning of that poem. The renunciation and impotency of Section I, the dry and scattered bones of Section II, seem to be a reiteration of the bleaker themes of *The Waste Land* and *The Hollow Men*—but with a difference. In *Ash Wednesday* there is an acceptance of the plight, and the bones sing, "We are glad to be scattered." The wasted and hollow condition, unrelieved in the earlier poems, is in *Ash Wednesday* a preparation for "strength beyond hope and despair" (Section III). Hence the ambiguous prayer, in the first and last sections, "Teach us to care and not to care." In *Ash Wednesday* Eliot maintains the themes of the earlier poetry, but in relating them to St. John's system of spiritual discipline the themes are reinterpreted and re-evaluated. Thus, from the perspective of *Ash Wednesday* and the *Four Quartets,* the earlier poetry takes on a meaning which it did not previously have. Once we have followed Eliot in relating his themes to St. John's system, the relevance extends to all expressions of the theme. The statement in "Gerontion," "I have lost my sight, smell, hearing, taste and touch," becomes an anticipation of "Desiccation of the world of sense." This is not to say that the earlier apparent meanings of "Gerontion," *The Waste Land,* and *The Hollow Men* are canceled out by the later poems, any more than one quartet cancels another, or the later plays the earlier plays and poems. While each work remains itself, it takes on an additional aspect, a qualification of meaning, in the larger context. Eliot's observation, in "Tradition and the Individual Talent," about literature in general, that "the past [is] altered by the present as much as the present is directed by the past," is precisely applicable to his own career as a poet.

In discussing Eliot's poetry, we have, inevitably, considered some of the ways in which the poetry and the criticism are related to each other. This intricate and extensive subject has received the attention of numerous critics, including Eliot himself in his later years. But a few more illustrations of the relation will be appropriate and will serve as a further documentation of the emphases here pursued. It is particularly some of the more famous essays which lend themselves to this purpose. For example, in "The Metaphysical Poets" (1921) we find ideas which are applicable to Eliot's poetry, such as the following familiar passage: "We can only say that it appears likely that poets in our civilization, as it exists at present, must be *difficult*. Our civilization comprehends great variety and complexity, and this variety and complexity, playing upon a refined sensibility, must produce various and complex results. The poet must become more and more comprehensive, more allusive, more indirect, in order to force, to dislocate if necessary, language into his meaning." This belongs to the period of *The Waste Land*, and it is clearly enough of an argument for such poetry. At the same time, one may see in this argument a recurring theme of Eliot's verse: the poet's struggle to state his meaning and the obstacles he faces in the contemporary world. Eliot offers the metaphysical poets as a precedent for this forcing and dislocating of language. But such deliberate struggle seems hardly to accord with the "direct sensuous apprehension of thought" and the ability to "feel their thought as immediately as the odour of a rose" which Eliot approvingly attributes to the metaphysical poets. These *direct* and *immediate* abilities of the metaphysical poets are, of course, functions of that "unified sensibility" which Eliot claimed for them. But when he speaks of them as being "engaged in the task of trying to find the verbal equivalent for states of mind and feeling," the poets would appear to be in pursuit of something rather than already in possession of it. Eliot's theory of the sensibilities—"unified" and "dissociated"—which has had such tremendous influence, crumbles into confusion with his later (1931) remark that a "deep fissure" was already evident in Donne's sensibility. Whatever inconsistencies and changes there may have been in the critic's theories, it is clear that the poet's sustained preoccupation has been with "the verbal equivalent for states of mind and feeling."

This idea is repeated in the criticism in various ways and at various times throughout Eliot's career. Even the famous "objective correlative" defined in "Hamlet and His Problems" (1919) has this meaning: "The only way of expressing emotion in the form of art is by finding an 'objective correlative'; in other words, a set of objects, a situation, a chain of events which shall be the formula of that *particular* emotion; such that when the external facts, which must terminate in sensory experience, are given, the emotion is immediately evoked." Although the statement is more involved, the essential meaning is the same—the poet seeks to say exactly what he means, to find "the verbal equivalent for states of mind and feeling." Eliot's purpose in defining the objective correlative was to indicate what he considered to be a failing in Shakespeare's play: "Hamlet (the man) is dominated by an emotion which is inexpressible, because it is in *excess* of the facts as they appear. . . . We must simply admit that here Shakespeare tackled a problem which proved too much for him." It is not necessary to agree with this view of *Hamlet* in order to find it impressive—indeed, fascinating. For here again Eliot is concerned with the poet's struggle to express and evoke his meaning in all its fullness. The comment on *Hamlet* is especially interesting when compared with remarks Eliot was to make, so many years later, in the *Paris Review* interview:

"I think that in the early poems it was a question of not being able to—of having more to say than one knew how to say, and having something one wanted to put into words and rhythm which one didn't have the command of words and rhythm to put in a way immediately apprehensible.

"That type of obscurity comes when the poet is still at the stage of learning how to use language. You have to say the thing the difficult way. The only alternative is not saying it at all, at that stage. By the time of *The Four Quartets,* I couldn't have written in the style of *The Waste Land.* In *The Waste Land,* I wasn't even bothering whether I understood what I was saying."

These remarks forcefully suggest that in the essay on *Hamlet* Eliot was characteristically preoccupied with his own problems as poet. Nor is it, again, necessary to agree with the remarks in order to find them valuable and meaningful. If Eliot's earlier meanings exceeded his ability to express them, then the inability was actually an essential part of the meaning—and the meanings were expressed, after all! For we have seen that so much of Eliot's meaning, so much of the "state of mind" evoked by his poetry, is the state of isolation, of the ineffable and inarticulate. It is impossible to conceive of Eliot's earlier meanings as having any measure of fullness without the intimations of the ineffable. We have seen how much of this theme contributes to the continuity and the larger meaning of his work. Although Eliot contrasted *The Four Quartets* with *The Waste Land,* it is well to recall that in *East Coker* he said

. . . one has only learnt to get the better of
    words

For the thing one no longer has to say, or the
    way in which
One is no longer disposed to say it.

Other comments made by the author of *The Waste Land* on his own poem serve to illustrate various aspects of his behavior as a critic. In "Thoughts after Lambeth" (1931) he said: ". . . when I wrote a poem called *The Waste Land* some of the more approving critics said that I had expressed the 'disillusionment of a generation,' which is nonsense. I may have expressed for them their own illusion of being disillusioned, but that did not form part of my intention." This passage has been a favorite target of Eliot's detractors, but it has also been cited justly enough by more objective critics in calling attention to the haughty posturing which at times marred his pronouncements. Eliot himself was eventually to acknowledge a distaste for the pontifical tone which occasionally appears in his earlier prose. But to return to *The Waste Land*—when the interviewer observed that "more recent critics, writing after your later poetry, found *The Waste Land* Christian," Eliot answered, "No, it wasn't part of my conscious intention." We may surmise that Eliot had his own poetry in mind when in 1951 he was discussing the poetry of Virgil. He said then that while a poet may think that he has given expression to a "private experience" but "without giving himself away," his readers may find his lines expressing "their own secret feelings . . . the exultation or despair of a generation."

Much of Eliot's later criticism and comment is concerned with readjusting his position, with recording an achieved capacity for tolerance and a catholicity of taste, and with diluting or eliminating the asperity with which he had treated various figures and issues. The essays on Tennyson, Milton, Goethe, and Kipling present such readjustments and reconsiderations. In both the prose and the poetry, Eliot showed an increasing tendency to talk candidly about himself, and with less fear of "giving himself away." It must have been as clear to Eliot as to his readers that Harry, the protagonist of *The Family Reunion*, in his complacent suffering and arrogant isolation, was a recognizable "objective correlative" for the author—since in "Poetry and Drama" (1950), Eliot said of Harry that "my hero now strikes me as an insufferable prig." It should not be necessary to quibble about what and how much the author intended to give away in these few words. But it is well worth pondering, along with the harsh judgment of Harry, Eliot's equally sound opinion (stated in the interview) that "*The Family Reunion* is still the best of my plays in the way of poetry."

Eliot was less concerned to publicize a readjustment of position on political and social questions than on matters of literary criticism. He was comparatively reticent on those political pronouncements which, in the light of later history, have appeared to be in accord with Fascist programs and practices. It may at least be said for him that he was not alone in failing to envisage the brutality to which the Nazis would extend the "corrective" doctrines of the reactionary position. Closely related to some of the quasi-Fascistic pronouncements made by Eliot is the question of anti-Semitism. The distasteful portrayal of Jews in "Gerontion" and in some of the quatrains of *Poems* (1920)—

But this or such was Bleistein's way:
  A saggy bending of the knees
And elbows with the palms turned out,
  Chicago Semite Viennese.

—may be considered as literary grotesqueries comparable to the portraits of Sweeney and Grishkin. But the evidence of the prose is another matter. In *After Strange Gods* (1934), discussing the virtues of a regional culture and homogeneous community, he said: ". . . reasons of race and religion combine to make any large number of free-thinking Jews undesirable. . . . And a spirit of excessive tolerance is to be deprecated." The contrived allusion to Karl Marx (in 1935) as a "Jewish economist" was again an amazing lapse in dignity. Merely to assert that he was not anti-Semitic is an insufficient reckoning with such indiscretions. But it is a well-established habit of Eliot's readers and critics to discover meanings by relating seemingly remote details from various parts of his writings. It may therefore be no excessive tolerance to apply to Eliot's earlier deprecations the splendid and moving lines, in *Little Gidding,* with which the "familiar compound ghost" describes "the gifts reserved for age":

. . . the conscious impotence of rage
  At human folly, and the laceration
  Of laughter at what ceases to amuse.
And last, the rending pain of re-enactment
  Of all that you have done, and been; the shame
  Of motives later revealed, and the awareness
Of things ill done and done to others' harm
  Which once you took for exercise of virtue.
  Then fools' approval stings, and honour stains.

In 1955 Eliot said of Wordsworth, "his name marks an epoch," and it is even more true of Eliot himself. But this has already been said in various ways by various writers with various intentions. Indeed, so much has been said about the poet, dramatist, critic of literature and culture, that any effort to add a further comment can hardly escape repetitions of the familiar. And so, to end briefly with an appropriate summation and illustration of his achievement as poet and critic, it may be most fitting to follow in the convention of quoting the man himself: ". . . the best contemporary poetry can give us a feeling of excitement and a sense of fulfilment different from any sentiment aroused by even very much greater poetry of a past age." If "next year's words await another voice," it is to be hoped that the voice will be not only different from Eliot's, but equal to it in giving us excitement and fulfillment.

Selected Bibliography

WORKS OF T. S. ELIOT

POETRY AND PLAYS

Prufrock and Other Observations. London: The Egoist, Ltd., 1917.

Poems. Richmond (England): L. and V. Woolf, 1919.

The Waste Land. New York: Boni and Liveright, 1922; Richmond (England): L. and V. Woolf, 1923.

Ash Wednesday. London: Faber and Faber, 1930; New York: Putnam, 1930.

Sweeney Agonistes. London: Faber and Faber, 1932.

The Rock. London: Faber and Faber, 1934.

Murder in the Cathedral. London: Faber and Faber, 1935; New York: Harcourt, Brace, 1935.

The Family Reunion. London: Faber and Faber, 1939; New York: Harcourt, Brace, 1939.

Old Possum's Book of Practical Cats. London: Faber and Faber, 1939; New York: Harcourt, Brace, 1939.

Four Quartets. New York: Harcourt, Brace, 1943; London: Faber and Faber, 1944.

The Cocktail Party. London: Faber and Faber, 1950; New York: Harcourt, Brace, 1950.

The Confidential Clerk. London: Faber and Faber, 1954; New York: Harcourt, Brace, 1954.

The Elder Statesman. London: Faber and Faber, 1959; New York: Farrar, Straus and Cudahy, 1959.

The Waste Land: A Facsimile and Transcript of the Original Drafts Including the Annotations of Ezra Pound, edited by Valerie Eliot. London: Faber and Faber, 1971; New York: Harcourt Brace Jovanovich, 1971.

SELECTED AND COLLECTED EDITIONS

Ara Vos Prec. London: Ovid Press, 1919.

Poems. New York: Knopf, 1920.

Poems 1909–1925. London: Faber and Gwyer, 1925; New York: Harcourt, Brace, 1932.

Collected Poems 1909–1935. London: Faber and Faber, 1936; New York: Harcourt, Brace, 1936.

The Complete Poems and Plays. New York: Harcourt, Brace, 1952.

Selected Poems. London: Faber and Faber, 1961; New York: Harcourt, Brace and World, 1967.

Collected Poems 1909–1962. New York: Harcourt, Brace, and World, 1963.

Poems Written in Early Youth. New York: Farrar, Straus, and Giroux, 1967.

PROSE

The Sacred Wood. London: Methuen, 1920.

Homage to John Dryden. London: L. and V. Woolf, 1924.

The Use of Poetry and the Use of Criticism. London: Faber and Faber, 1933; Cambridge, Mass.: Harvard University Press, 1933.

After Strange Gods. London: Faber and Faber, 1934; New York: Harcourt, Brace, 1934.

Elizabethan Essays. London: Faber and Faber, 1934.

The Idea of a Christian Society. London: Faber and Faber, 1939; New York: Harcourt, Brace, 1940.

Notes towards the Definition of Culture. London: Faber and Faber, 1948; New York: Harcourt, Brace, 1949.

SELECTED AND COLLECTED EDITIONS

Selected Essays 1917–1932. London: Faber and Faber, 1932; New York; Harcourt, Brace,

1932. (Enlarged editions, called *Selected Essays*, were published in New York in 1950 and in London in 1951.)

Essays Ancient and Modern. London: Faber and Faber, 1936; New York: Harcourt, Brace, 1936.

On Poetry and Poets. London: Faber and Faber, 1957; New York: Farrar, Straus, and Cudahy, 1957.

To Criticize the Critic and Other Writings. New York: Farrar, Straus, and Giroux, 1965.

BIBLIOGRAPHY

Gallup, Donald. *T. S. Eliot: A Bibliography*. London: Faber and Faber, 1952; New York: Harcourt, Brace, 1953. (Besides listing all editions of Eliot's books and pamphlets through 1951, this includes books and pamphlets edited or with contributions by Eliot, his contributions to periodicals, translations of his writings into foreign languages, and recordings of his readings.)

INTERPRETIVE AND CRITICAL STUDIES

Blamires, Harry. *Word Unheard: A Guide through Eliot's Four Quartets*. London: Methuen, 1969.

Browne, E. Martin. *The Making of T. S. Eliot's Plays*. New York: Cambridge University Press, 1969.

Drew, Elizabeth. *T. S. Eliot: The Design of His Poetry*. New York: Scribners, 1949.

Fabricius, Johannes. *The Unconscious and Mr. Eliot: A Study in Expressionism*. Copenhagen: Nyt Nordisk Forlag-Arnold Busck, 1967.

Frye, Northrup. *T. S. Eliot*. London: Oliver and Boyd, 1963; New York: Grove Press, 1963; reissued New York: Barnes and Noble, 1966.

Gardner, Helen. *The Art of T. S. Eliot*. London: Cresset Press, 1949; New York: Dutton, 1950.

Germer, Rudolf. *T. S. Eliots Anfänge als Lyriker (1905–1915)*. Heidelberg: Karl Winter, Universitätsverlag, 1966.

Greene, E. J. H. *T. S. Eliot et la France*. Paris: Boivin, 1951.

Headings, Philip R. *T. S. Eliot*. New York: Twayne, 1964.

Howarth, Herbert. *Some Figures behind T. S. Eliot*. Boston: Houghton Mifflin, 1964.

Jones, David E. *The Plays of T. S. Eliot*. London: Routledge and Kegan Paul, 1960.

Jones, Genesius, O.F.M. *Approach to the Purpose: A Study of the Poetry of T. S. Eliot*. New York: Barnes and Noble, 1965.

Kenner, Hugh. *The Invisible Poet: T. S. Eliot*. New York: McDowell, Obolensky, 1959.

———, ed. *T. S. Eliot: A Collection of Critical Essays*. Englewood Cliffs, N.J.: Prentice-Hall, 1962.

Kirk, Russell. *Eliot and His Age*. New York: Random House, 1972.

Knoll, Robert E., ed. *Storm over The Waste Land*. Chicago: Scott, Foresman, 1964.

Martin, Jay, ed. *A Collection of Critical Essays on The Waste Land*. Englewood Cliffs, N.J.: Prentice-Hall, 1968.

Matthiessen, F. O. *The Achievement of T. S. Eliot*. New York: Oxford, 1935. Second edition, enlarged, 1947. Third edition, with additional chapter by C. L. Barber, 1958.

Maxwell, D. E. S. *The Poetry of T. S. Eliot*. London: Routledge and Kegan Paul, 1952.

Montgomery, Marion. *T. S. Eliot: An Essay on the American Magus*. Athens, Ga.: University of Georgia Press, 1969.

Preston, Raymond. *Four Quartets Rehearsed*. New York: Sheed and Ward, 1946.

Rajan, B., ed. *T. S. Eliot: A Study of His Writings by Several Hands*. London: Dobson, 1947.

Robbins, R. H. *The T. S. Eliot Myth*. New York: Schuman, 1951.

Sencourt, Robert. *T. S. Eliot: A Memoir*. New York: Dodd, Mead, 1971.

Smidt, Kristian. *Poetry and Belief in the Work of T. S. Eliot*. Oslo: Jacob Dybwad, 1949; revised edition, New York: Humanities Press, 1961.

Smith, Carol H. *T. S. Eliot's Dramatic Theory and Practice*. Princeton, N.J.; Princeton University Press, 1963.

Smith, Grover. *T. S. Eliot's Poetry and Plays: A Study in Sources and Meaning*. Chicago: University of Chicago Press, 1956. (The third impression, 1960, is enlarged.)

Southan, B. C. *A Guide to the Selected Poems of T. S. Eliot*. London: Faber and Faber, 1968; New York: Harcourt, Brace and World, 1968.

Tate, Allen, ed. *T. S. Eliot: The Man and His Work.* New York: Delacorte, 1966.

Unger, Leonard, *T. S. Eliot: Moments and Patterns.* Minneapolis: University of Minnesota Press, 1966.

_____, ed. *T. S. Eliot: A Selected Critique.* New York: Rinehart, 1948; reissued New York: Russell & Russell, 1966.

Williamson, George. *A Reader's Guide to T. S. Eliot.* New York: Noonday Press, 1953.

—*LEONARD UNGER*